Journeys of Desire

Cary Grant's journey of desire led to triumph in Hollywood

Journeys of Desire

European Actors in Hollywood
A Critical Companion

edited by
Alastair Phillips and Ginette Vincendeau

bfi Publishing

First published in 2006 by the
BRITISH FILM INSTITUTE
21 Stephen Street, London W1T 1LN

The British Film Institute's purpose is to champion moving image culture
in all its richness and diversity across the UK, for the benefit of as wide an audience
as possible, and to create and encourage debate.

Set by Fakenham Photosetting Limited, Fakenham, Norfolk
Printed in the UK by The Cromwell Press, Trowbridge, Wiltshire

Cover design: Mark Swan
Cover images: Marlene Dietrich, Antonio Banderas, Maurice Chevalier, Greta Garbo, Daniel Day-Lewis, Hedy Lamarr
Stills courtesy of BFI Stills, Posters and Designs

British Library Cataloguing-in-Publication Data
A catalogue record for this book is available from the British Library

ISBN 1–84457–124–6 (pbk)
ISBN 1–84457–123–8 (hbk)

Contents

Acknowledgments   vi

Contributors (key to contributors and notes on contributors)   viii

PART I   **Film Trade, Global Culture and Transnational Cinema: An Introduction**   3

Alastair Phillips and Ginette Vincendeau

PART II   **European Actors and the Hollywood Film Industry**

1   The Long Fade: French Actors in Silent Hollywood   21
    Richard Abel

2   Russian Film Extras in 1920s Hollywood   31
    Rashit M. Yangirov

3   German Actors in Hollywood: The Long View   37
    Tim Bergfelder

4   Opera, Theatre and Film: Italians in 1920s and 1930s Hollywood   45
    Giuliana Muscio

5   The Studio, the Star and International Audiences: Paramount and Chevalier   53
    Martine Danan

6   'Star trading': The British in 1930s and 1940s Hollywood   61
    Sarah Street

7   In Search of Global Stardom: French Actors in 1990s Hollywood   71
    Irène Bessière

PART III   **Emigré Actors, Cultural Types and Stereotypes**

8   Small Victories and Grand Failures: Russian Actors in Hollywood   77
    Natalia Noussinova

9   Changing Bodies, Changing Voices: French Success and Failure in 1930s Hollywood   85
    Alastair Phillips

10   The 'Foreign Woman' in Classical Hollywood Cinema   95
    Christian Viviani

11   The Ultimate Irony: Jews Playing Nazis in Hollywood   103
    Joseph Garncarz

12   'Not for Export': Jean Gabin in Hollywood   115
    Ginette Vincendeau

13   Louis Jourdan – The 'Hyper-sexual' Frenchman   125
    Hilary Radner

14   The Latin Masquerade: The Spanish in Disguise in Hollywood   133
    Vicente Sánchez-Biosca

15   Acting Nasty?: British Male Actors in Contemporary Hollywood   141
    Andrew Spicer

PART IV   **A Dictionary of European Actors in Hollywood**

Aims and Conventions   151

A to Z of European Actors in Hollywood Cinema   153

Select Bibliography   473

Index   482

Acknowledgments

This project emerged out of the research network 'Les Européens dans le cinéma américain' at the Maison des Sciences de L'Homme, Paris. Our thanks go particularly to Irène Bessière, initiator and head of the project, and to Christine Grosse. Equally, we are extremely grateful to Andrew Lockett at the BFI for commissioning this book and supporting it during his time as head of BFI Publishing, and to Sophia Contento, also at BFI Publishing, for her help throughout. We also wish to thank Rebecca Barden (Head of BFI Publishing) for her support for this book.

We could not have completed the project without help from our respective universities and other institutions. At the University of Warwick, Ed Gallafent and Heather Hares provided both financial and practical assistance in compiling and typing the inventory; Tracey Bale helped with viewing material, Richard Perkins with library material and Elaine Lenton with many queries. At the University of Reading, Lib Taylor provided departmental assistance for the inventory and Chris Bacon helped with viewing material. We were also fortunate to obtain a Small Grant in the Creative and Performing Arts for translation costs from the AHRB and funding from the British Academy for the European Actors in Hollywood Symposium, which we held in Paris in June 2002.

Our contributors all worked extremely hard in conducting valuable original research, whether they were writing on major stars or obscure, uncredited players, and we recognise that they wrote their material to sometimes tight deadlines and for little financial reward! We are proud to include their work in this volume. We are particularly indebted to some of them, as well as other colleagues and friends for their editorial advice at various stages of this project. Particularly helpful were Jon Burrows, Sheldon Hall, Mike Lynch and Valerie Orpen. Special mention must also be made of Andrew Spicer for being so co-operative and efficient at very short notice.

Colleagues, contributors and friends also provided invaluable help with documentation, fact checking and translating material. Our thanks in this respect go especially to Renée Fenby, whose help went beyond the call of duty, as well as to Ann Wright, Constanza Burucúa, Sheldon Hall, Mats Björkin and Simon Caulkin.

In addition, we would like to thank the following individuals for various kinds of support and assistance over the years: José Arroyo; Caroline Beven; Noll Brinckmann; Erica Carter; John Caughie; Raymond Chirat; Jim Cook; Roland Cosandey; Natasa Durovicova; Richard Dyer; Karim Ghiyati; Julian Graffy; Sue Harris; Andrew Higson; Jim Hillier; Frank Kessler; Min Lee; Gabi Limon; Arne Lunde; Olga Matich; Jean-Pierre Mattei; Clare Monk; Teresa Murjas; Robert Murphy; Diane Negra; Mark Sandberg; Geneviève Sellier; Richard Taylor; Ebbe Villadsen; Christian Viviani; Chris Wagstaff; Leila Wimmer; Mike Witt.

Our research – and that of our contributors – was greatly helped by these individuals, but it was also facilitated by a number of institutions. In particular we wish to acknowledge: the BFI National Film Library in London; the Bodleian Library, Oxford; La Cinémathèque Corse, Porto-Vecchio; the Bifi, Bibliothèque Nationale de France and Forum des Images in Paris; La Cinémathèque Royale de Belgique, Brussels; Genossenschaft deutscher Bühnen-Angehörigen (German Stage Actors' Union); L'Institut Lumière, Lyon; and the Dutch Filmmuseum, Amsterdam.

Finally, in the years this project has taken to come to fruition, help has taken other forms – friendship, hospitality and moral support. In this respect, Irène Bessière and Peter Graham are gratefully acknowledged, but Mark Kurzem and Simon Caulkin deserve special gratitude for their patience, unfailing support and enthusiasm.

Acknowledgments

Alastair Phillips would like to thank, for help with his chapter 'Changing Bodies, Changing Voices: French Success and Failure in 1930s Hollywood': the British Academy for a Small Research Grant; Dana Polan and Janet Bergstrom for their assistance in Los Angeles; Ned Comstock (USC Special Collections); Julie Graham (UCLA Arts Special Collections); Barbara Hall (Margaret Herrick Library); Peter Graham for his hospitality and Ginette Vincendeau and Valerie Orpen for their comments. An earlier version of the chapter was published in *Screen* vol. 43 no. 2 (Summer 2002), when Jackie Stacey was especially helpful with the editorial process.

Ginette Vincendeau wishes to thank, for help with her chapter ' "Not for Export": Jean Gabin in Hollywood': Peter Graham and Yves Desrichard for supplying the rare and essential tapes of respectively *Moontide* and *The Impostor*; Yves Desrichard, Alastair Phillips and Nick Potamitis for help with archival documents; and Alastair Phillips, Richard Dyer, José Arroyo and V. F. Perkins for their comments.

Key to Dictionary Contributors

AM	Alex Marlow-Mann		MF	Martin Fradley
AP	Alastair Phillips		MH	Mike Hammond
AQ	Angel Quintana		MHu	Martin Hunt
AR	Antonio Rodrigues		MJ	Mats Jonsson
AS	Andrew Spicer		MK	Maaret Koskinen
BR	Bujor T. Rîpeanu		MP	Mona Pedersen
CB	Charles Barr		MW	Michael Williams
CBu	Constanza Burucúa		OB	Oksana Bulgakowa
CF	Claudia Fellmer		OR	Ohad Rosen
CH	Catherine Hellegouarc'h		RA	Richard Abel
CHo	Chris Holmlund		RB	Ruth Barton
CS	Chloe Stephenson		RBe	Roger Beebe
CV	Christian Viviani		RBu	Rob Burns
DI	Dina Iordanova		RJK	Robert J. Kiss
DN	Dominique Nasta		RM	Russell Merritt
EC	Erica Carter		RMo	Rachel Moseley
EE	Elizabeth Ezra		RY	Rashit Yangirov
EO	Elzbieta Ostrowska		SdL	Sonja de Leeuw
EU	Eva Urzaiz		SH	Sheldon Hall
FG	Frances Guerin		SHa	Susan Hayward
GM	Giuliana Muscio		SL	Sarah Leahy
GS	Geneviève Sellier		SLo	Simon Louvish
GV	Ginette Vincendeau		SS	Sarah Street
HJW	Hans J. Wollstein		TB	Tim Bergfelder
JA	José Arroyo		TH	Theodora Hadjiandreou
JB	Jon Burrows		TJ	Tamar Jeffers McDonald
JP	Jacques Polet		TR	Tom Ryall
JS	Jamie Sexton		TS	Tytti Soila
KV	Kathleen Vernon		US	Ulrike Sieglohr
LW	Louise Wallenberg		VH	Vinzenz Hediger
MB	Martin Barnier		VO	Valerie Orpen
MBj	Mats Björkin		YH	Ylva Habel

Notes on Contributors

THE EDITORS

Alastair Phillips is a Lecturer in Film Studies in the Department of Film, Theatre and Television at the University of Reading, UK. He is the author of *City of Darkness, City of Light. Émigré Filmmakers in Paris 1929–1939* (Amsterdam University Press, 2004), and the co-editor (with Julian Stringer) of *Japanese Cinema: Texts and Contexts* (Routledge, 2006). His articles have appeared in a number of journals and edited collections, including *Screen, Iris, Positif, The French Cinema Book* (BFI, 2004) and *Film Analysis: A Norton Reader* (W. W. Norton, 2005). He is currently completing a book on *Du Rififi chez les hommes* (I. B. Tauris, forthcoming).

Ginette Vincendeau is Professor of Film Studies at King's College London. She has written widely on popular French and European cinema. She is the editor of *The Encyclopedia of European Cinema* (BFI/Cassell, 1995) and co-editor, with Susan Hayward, of *French Film: Texts and Contexts* (Routledge, 1990 and 2000). Among her recent books are *Pépé le Moko* (BFI, 1998); *Stars and Stardom in French Cinema* (Continuum, 2000); *Jean-Pierre Melville: An American in Paris* (BFI, 2003); and *La Haine* (I. B. Tauris, 2005).

OTHER CONTRIBUTORS TO THE VOLUME

Richard Abel is a Collegiate Professor in Film and Video Studies at the University of Michigan, USA. His recent books include the *Routledge Encyclopedia of Early Cinema* (Routledge, 2005); *The Red Rooster Scare: Making Cinema American, 1900–1910* (University of California Press, 1999); and (co-edited with Rick Altman) *The Sounds of Early Cinema* (Indiana University Press, 2001). His *Imagining Community in US Cinema, 1910–1914* (University of California Press) is forthcoming.

José Arroyo is a Lecturer in the Department of Film and Television at the University of Warwick, UK. He is currently researching the effect of changing mediascapes on traditional questions in film aesthetics. He has widely published on issues of national and sexual representation, Spanish cinema and contemporary Hollywood cinema. He is currently writing on Antonio Banderas and Javier Bardem, and his next project is on 'Impact' Aesthetics. He is the editor of *Action/Spectacle. A Sight and Sound Reader* (BFI, 2000).

Martin Barnier is a Lecturer in Film Studies at Lumière-Lyon 2 University, France. He is the author of *En route vers le parlant. Histoire d'une évolution technologique, économique et esthétique du cinéma (1926–1934)* (Éditions du CÉFAL, 2002) and *Des Films français made in Hollywood. Les versions multiples (1929–1935)* (L'Harmattan, 2004) and co-editor (with Raphaëlle Moine) of *France/Hollywood. Échanges cinématographiques et identités nationales* (Éditions L'Harmattan, 2002).

Charles Barr is Professor of Film Studies at the University of East Anglia, UK, and a specialist in British cinema, Alfred Hitchcock and the history of television. His books include the edited collection *All Our Yesterdays: 90 Years of British Cinema* (BFI, 1986), *Ealing Studios* (3rd edn, Cameron and Hollis, 1999), *English Hitchcock* (Cameron and Hollis, 1999) and *Vertigo* (BFI, 2002).

Ruth Barton is OíKane Senior Research Fellow at the Centre for Film Studies, University College Dublin, Ireland. She is the author of *Jim Sheridan: Framing the Nation* (Liffey Press, 2002), *Irish National Cinema* (Routledge, 2004) and the co-editor of *Keeping It Real: Irish Film and Television* (Wallflower Press, 2004).

Roger Beebe is an Assistant Professor of Film and Media Studies in the Department of English at the University of Florida, USA. He has previously published on Arnold Schwarzenegger in *Meta-Morphing: Visual Transformation and the Culture of Quick-Change* (University of Minnesota Press, 2000). He is the co-editor of two collections of essays on popular music: *Rock over the Edge: Transformations of Popular Music Culture* (Duke University Press, 2002) and *Music Video / Music Television / MTV* (Duke University Press, forthcoming).

Tim Bergfelder is Head of Film Studies at the University of Southampton, UK. He has published on popular European cinema and its genres, international co-productions and questions of transnationalism in cinema. He is the author of *International Adventures. German Popular Cinema and European Co-Productions in the 1960s* (Berghahn, 2005), and has co-edited *The German Cinema Book* (BFI, 2002) and *The Titanic in Myth and Memory: Representations in Visual and Literary Culture* (I. B. Tauris, 2004).

Irène Bessière is the creator and head of the Research Programme 'Les Européens dans le cinéma américain' at the Maison des Sciences de L'Homme (MSH), Paris, France, and was recently involved in the setting up of the Institut National d'Histoire de l'Art (INHA), and its inclusion of film research. She is the author of 'Le Récit fantastique ou la poétique de l'incertain' (Larousse) and of numerous articles, including one on the relationship between cinema and literature and another on the future of *cinéma fantastique* in the light of new technologies and special effects.

Mats Björkin is Senior Lecturer in Film Studies in the Department of Culture, Aesthetics and Media at Göteborg University, Sweden. His doctoral thesis (Stockholm University, 1998) examined the debates on American films and film culture in Sweden during the 1920s. He is currently working on a project on industrial films and local media culture in Sweden during the 1950s.

Oksana Bulgakowa is Professor of Film Studies at the International Film School, Cologne, Germany, and a Visiting Professor in Slavic Literature and Film Studies at Stanford University, USA. She has published several books on Russian and German cinema: *Sergei Eisenstein: Three Utopias. Architectural Drafts for a Film Theory* (Potemkin Press, 1996); *FEKS – The Factory of Eccentric Actors* (Potemkin Press, 1997) and *The Adventures of Doctor Mabuse in the Country of Bolsheviks* (Freunde der Deutschen Kinemathek, 1998). Her biography of Sergei Eisenstein was published in 2001.

Rob Burns is Professor of German Studies at the University of Warwick, UK, where he has taught since 1974. He is the author of *Protest and Democracy in West Germany* (Macmillan Press, 1988), *German Cultural Studies* (Oxford University Press, 1995) and various articles on German cinema.

Jon Burrows is a Lecturer in the Department of Film and Television Studies at the University of Warwick, UK. He is the author of *Legitimate Cinema: Theatre Stars in Silent British Films, 1908–1918* (University of Exeter Press, 2003) and has published articles on different aspects of early British cinema in journals such as *Screen* and *Film History*. He is currently working on a study of film exhibition in Edwardian Britain.

Constanza Burucúa was awarded a PhD in the Department of Film and Television Studies at the University of Warwick, where she also worked as a teaching assistant. Her research focuses on questions of film and history in the Argentine cinema of the post-dictatorship years (1984–93). She has previously taught Film History at the University of Buenos Aires, Argentina.

Erica Carter is Professor of German Studies at the University of Warwick, UK. Her publications include *How German is She? Postwar West German Reconstruction and the Consuming Woman* (University of Michigan Press, 1997); *The German Cinema Book* (co-edited with Tim Bergfelder and Deniz Göktürk) (BFI, 2002); and *Dietrich's Ghosts: The Sublime and the Beautiful in Third Reich Film* (BFI, 2004).

Martine Danan is Assistant Dean at the Defense Language Institute in Monterey, California. She has written extensively on the socio-political context of cinema and national identity, especially in relation to the growing competition between Hollywood and French cinema. Her articles in this area have appeared in journals ranging from *Media, Culture and Society* to *Film History* and the *Journal of Popular Film and Television*. Additional recent essays investigating these themes are also part of the following edited collections: *La fiction éclatée, grands et petits écrans français et francophones*, edited by J.-P. Bertin-Maghit and G. Sellier (INA/L'Harmattan, forthcoming); and *The European Cinema Reader*, edited by Catherine Fowler (Routledge, 2002).

Sonja de Leeuw is Professor of Television in the Department of Theatre, Film and Television Studies at the University of Utrecht, Netherlands. She publishes regularly on Dutch television culture in an international context and diasporic media and cultural diversity. She is also chair of the board of the Stimuleringsfonds Nederlandse Culturele Omroepproducties (Dutch Cultural Broadcasting Promotion Fund), which subsidises most of the cultural productions shown on Dutch public television.

Elizabeth Ezra is Senior Lecturer in French at the University of Stirling, Scotland. She is the author of *The Colonial Unconscious: Race and Culture in Interwar France* (Cornell University Press, 2000) and *Georges Méliès: The Birth of the Auteur* (Manchester University Press, 2000). She is co-editor, with Sue Harris, of *France in Focus: Film and National Identity* (Berg, 2001) and editor of *European Cinema* (Oxford University Press, 2003).

Claudia H. L. Fellmer wrote her doctoral thesis on stars in East German cinema at the University of Southampton and contributed to *The German Cinema Book* (BFI, 2002) and *Millennial Essays on Film and Other German Studies* (Peter Lang, 2002) with articles on Armin Mueller-Stahl and Erwin Geschonneck.

Martin Fradley is a Lecturer in Film Studies at the University of Aberdeen, Scotland. His work has appeared in Yvonne Tasker's edited collections *Fifty Contemporary Filmmakers* (Routledge, 2002) and *Action and Adventure Cinema* (Routledge, 2004).

Joseph Garncarz is Lecturer at the Institut für Theatre-Film-und Fernsehwissenschaft at the University of Cologne, Germany. He specialises in German film history and has published in journals such as *Film History*, *Hitchcock Annual* and *KINtop* and contributed numerous articles to edited collections and reference books. He is the author of *Filmfassungen: Eine Theorie signifikanter Filmvariation* [*Film Versions: A Theory of Significant Film Variation*] (Lang, 1992) and *Populäres Kino in Deutschland: Internationalisierung einer Filmkultur 1925–1990* (forthcoming from WVT).

Frances Guerin is a Lecturer in the Department of Film Studies at the University of Kent, UK. She is the author of *A Culture of Light: Cinema and Technology in 1920s Germany* (University of Minnesota Press, 2004). Her articles on German and other European cinemas have appeared in a number of journals, including *Cinema Journal, Film and History* and *Cinema e Cie*. She is currently completing a book entitled *Through Amateur Eyes: Nazi Film and Photography*.

Ylva Habel is a Lecturer in the Department of Cinema Studies, Stockholm University, Sweden. She is the author of a PhD thesis entitled 'Modern Media, Modern Audiences: Mass Media and Social Engineering in the 1930s Swedish Welfare State' (2002) and has recently published on the Swedish reception of Josephine Baker.

Theodora Hadjiandreou is a research student in the Department of Film and Television Studies at the University of Warwick, UK, where she has also worked as a teaching assistant. She is presently completing her doctoral dissertation on the expatriate American director Jules Dassin.

Sheldon Hall is a Lecturer in Film Studies at Sheffield Hallam University, UK. He has contributed to *The Movie Book of the Western* (Studio Vista, 1996), *The British Cinema Book* (2nd edn, BFI, 2002), *British Historical Cinema* (Routledge, 2002) and *Genre and Contemporary Hollywood* (BFI, 2002), and is the author of *Zulu: With Some Guts Behind It* (Tomahawk Press, 2005) and (with Steve Neale) *Spectacles, Epics and Blockbusters* (Wayne State University Press, forthcoming).

Mike Hammond lectures in Film at the University of Southampton, UK. He has written extensively on the transnational reception of American cinema in Britain in the 1910s, on British cinema in the silent period and on contemporary Hollywood war films. He is author of *The Big Show: British Film Culture in The Great War* (University of Exeter Press, 2005).

Susan Hayward is the Established Chair of French at Exeter University, UK. She is the author of *French National Cinema* (Routledge 1993 and 2005), *Luc Besson* (Manchester University Press, 1998), *Cinema Studies: The Key Concepts* (3rd Routledge edn, 2006) and *Simone Signoret: The Star as Cultural Sign* (Continuum, 2004). She is the founder of the journal *Studies in French Cinema* (co-edited with Phil Powrie) and the co-editor (with Ginette Vincendeau) of *French Film: Texts and Contexts* (Routledge, 1990 and 2000).

Vinzenz Hediger is Alfried Krupp von Bohlen und Halbach Foundation Professor of Film and Media Studies at the Ruhr University, Bochum, Germany. He has published a book on movie trailers, *Verführung zum Film. Der amerikanische Kinotrailer seit 1912* (Schüren, 2001), as well as two anthologies on film and culture in Switzerland.

Catherine Hellegouarc'h currently works at the University of Caen, France. She is conducting PhD research into French émigrés in Hollywood in the 1930s and 1940s and has contributed to Bill Marshall (ed.), *France and the Americas: Culture, History, Politics* (ABC-Clio, 2005).

Chris Holmlund is Lindsay Young Professor of Cinema Studies, Women's Studies and French at the University of Tennessee, USA. She is the author of *Impossible Bodies* (Routledge, 2002) and co-editor (with Justin Wyatt) of *Contemporary American Independent Film: From the Margins to the Mainstream* (Routledge, 2005) and (with Cynthia Fuchs) of *Between the Sheets, in the Streets: Queer, Lesbian, Gay Documentary* (Minnesota University Press, 1997). Current book projects include *American Cinema of the 1990s: Themes and Variations* (Rutgers University Press) and *Stars in Action* (Routledge).

Martin Hunt lectures at Yeovil College, Somerset, UK. He has an MA in Film and Television Studies from the University of Westminster, and is currently undertaking doctoral research into genre theory at Birkbeck College, London. He has published on the films of Terence Davies, Ealing Studios, Powell and Pressburger and British film music. He is also a contributor to the *BFI Reference Guide to British Film Directors*.

Dina Iordanova is Chair in Film Studies at the University of St Andrews, Scotland. She is the author of *Cinema of Flames: Balkan Film, Culture and the Media* (BFI, 2001), *Emir Kusturica* (BFI, 2002) and *Cinema of the Other Europe: The Industry and Artistry of East Central European Film* (Wallflower Press, 2003).

Tamar Jeffers McDonald is Senior Lecturer in Film Studies at Buckinghamshire Chilterns University College, UK. Her research interests centre on the problematic representation of virginity in film, especially Hollywood film of the 1950s; costume; stardom; and romantic comedy. Forthcoming monographs include *Romantic Comedy: Boy Meets Girl Meets Genre* (Wallflower Press) and *Hollywood Catwalk* (I. B. Tauris).

Mats Jonsson is an Associate Professor in Film Studies at Örebro University, Sweden, where presently he is involved in an interdisciplinary research programme entitled 'The Language of Politics in the Media Public Sphere'. He is co-editor of an upcoming anthology studying films from the Archive of the Swedish Labour Movement. He writes regularly for the Swedish film journal *Filmhäftet*.

Robert J. Kiss is the author of *The Doppelgänger in Early German Cinema (1895–1914)* (Berghahn, 2006) and the co-editor (with Erica Carter) of *Béla Balázs: Visible Man* (Berghahn, 2006). His writings on queer cinema and early film comedy have appeared in a number of British and German essay collections, and he is currently working on a biography of Hollywood actor and radio presenter Dudley Manlove, entitled '*All You of Earth are Idiots!*'.

Maaret Koskinen is Docent Professor in the Department of Cinema Studies, University of Stockholm, Sweden, and film critic for the national daily *Dagens Nyheter*. She has published in various national and international film journals and is the author of two books on Ingmar Bergman, and the co-editor of *Swedish Film Today* (The Swedish Institute/AIACE, Rome, 1996).

Sarah Leahy is a Lecturer in Film and Television at Northumbria University, UK. Her doctoral thesis examined Simone Signoret and Brigitte Bardot as icons of French femininity in the 1950s. She has published various articles on stars in French cinema and has completed a study of Jacques Becker's *Casque d'or* (I. B. Tauris, 2006).

Simon Louvish is the author of twelve works of fiction and has written biographies of W. C. Fields, the Marx Brothers, Keystone's Mack Sennett, Mae West and Laurel and Hardy.

Alex Marlow-Mann graduated in Film Studies and Italian from the University of Kent, UK, and obtained an MA from the University of East Anglia, UK. He has worked for the British Film Institute and is currently researching a PhD on Neapolitan cinema at the University of Reading, UK. His publications include articles on the Italian historical epic and British silent serials.

Russell Merritt teaches Film History as a Visiting Professor at UC-Berkeley. He is the co-author (with J. B. Kaufman) of *Walt in Wonderland: The Silent Films of Walt Disney* (Gemona, 1993) and a forthcoming book on the Silly Symphonies. He has also published on D. W. Griffith, nickelodeons, animation, colour and Eisenstein.

Rachel Moseley is a Lecturer in Film and Television Studies at the University of Warwick, UK. She has published on a range of subjects in popular film and television, and is the author of *Growing Up with Audrey Hepburn: Text, Audience, Res-*

onance (Manchester University Press, 2000). She is the editor of *Fashioning Film Stars: Text, Culture, Identity* (BFI, 2005), and is currently working on a critical history of teen television.

Giuliana Muscio is Associate Professor of Cinema at the University of Palermo, Italy. She is the author of *Hollywood's New Deal* (Temple University Press, 1996) and of works both in Italian and English on screenwriting, cold war cinema, the 1930s, women screenwriters in silent American cinema, film and history, radio and cinema in Italy in the 1930s, USA/Italy film relations in the 1920s and in the 1950s. She is on the Editorial Board of *Cinema Journal*.

Dominique Nasta is Head of the Department of Film Studies at the Université Libre de Bruxelles, Belgium. Her publications include *Meaning in Film: Relevant Structures in Soundtrack and Narrative* (Peter Lang, 1991) and *New Perspectives in Sound Studies / Le Son en perspective: nouvelles recherches* (Bern, 2004). She is the editor of a new bilingual series published by Peter Lang entitled 'Rethinking Cinema/Repenser le cinéma'.

Natalia Noussinova is Director of Research at the Institute for Cinema Research in Moscow, Russia. She has published widely on the history of Russian cinema and French film history, and on Russian emigration to Europe and the USA. She is the editor of *Truffaut o Truffaut* [*Truffaut on Truffaut*] (Raduga, 1987); *La Jeunesse de Kozintsev et Trauberg* (*Les débuts de la FEKS, 1921–1925*) [*Kozintsev and Trauberg's Youth (The Beginnings of FEKS, 1921–1925)*] (STUC, 1992) and *Léonide Trauberg et l'excentrisme* [*Leonid Trauberg and Eccentricism*] (Yellow Now, 1993).

Valerie Orpen is a freelance writer and translator. She has published several articles on French cinema and *The Art of the Expressive: Film Editing* (Wallflower Press, 2003). She has completed a book on Agnès Varda's *Cléo de 5 à 7* (I. B. Tauris, 2006).

Elzbieta Ostrowska is an independent scholar currently based in Canada. Publications include *The Cinema of Andrzej Wajda. The Art of Irony and Defiance* (co-edited with John Orr) (Wallflower, 2003); *Gender-Film-Media* (co-edited with E. Oleksy) (Rabid, 2001); *Gender in Film and the Media. East–West Dialogues* (co-edited with E. Oleksy and M. Stevenson) (Lang, 2000) and various articles on film history and women in cinema.

Mona Pedersen is Assistant Professor in Film and Media Studies at Hedmark University College, Norway. Her publications include *Henie i Hollywood* [*Henie in Hollywood*] (Norsk Filminstitutts skriftserie no. 16/2002).

Jacques Polet teaches Film Theory and History at the Université Catholique in Louvain, Belgium. He has published widely on diverse aspects of Belgian cinema, including *Les premiers temps du cinéma Belgique*, *Revue belge du cinéma*, no. 38–9 (1995).

Angel Quintana is Professor of History and Theory of Cinema at the Universitat de Girona, Spain. He is the author of monographs on Roberto Rossellini, Jean Renoir and Olivier Assayas and is the Spanish translator of the work of James Agee and André Bazin's *Jean Renoir*. His book *Fabulas de lo visible: el cine como creador de realidades* [*Fables of the Visible: The Cinema as Creator of Realities*] (Acantilado, 2003) won the Spanish Association of Cinematographic Historians – Asociación Española de historiadores del cine – Best Cinema Book Prize in 2003.

Hilary Radner is Professor of Film and Media Studies at the University of Otago, New Zealand. She has published widely on topics such as consumer culture, fashion photography and contemporary Hollywood cinema. Her areas of research include film theory, cultural studies, feminist theory, consumer culture and film melodrama. She is the author of *Shopping Around: Feminine Culture and the Pursuit of Pleasure* (Routledge, 1995) and co-editor of *Film Theory Goes to the Movies* (Routledge, 1993), *Constructing the New Consumer Society* (Macmillan, 1997) and *Swinging Single: Representing Sexuality in the 1960s* (University of Minnesota Press, 1999). She is currently preparing a manuscript on the representation of agency in feminine consumer culture.

Bujor T. Rîpeanu has been a film critic since 1957 and worked for the National Film Archive in Bucharest, Romania, between 1966 and 2001. He is the author of the three-volume *Productia cinematografica din România* [*Film Production in Romania*] (1970–6) and *Filmat în România Vol. I: 1911–1969* [*Film in Romania Vol. 1: 1911–1969*] (Archiva Nationala de Filme, 2003).

Antonio Rodrigues has programmed the Cinemateca Portuguesa in Lisbon, Portugal, since 1994. He is the author of *Cinema e arquitectura* [*Cinema and Architecture*] (Cinemateca Portuguesa – Museu du Cinema, 1999) and has contributed to the *Dictionnaire des personnages de cinéma* [*Dictionary of Film Characters*] (Bordas, 1993), *900 Cinéastes français* **xiii**

d'aujourd'hui [*900 Contemporary French Film-makers*] (Éditions du Cerf, 1988) and the *Dictionnaire du cinéma mondial: mouvements, écoles, tendances et genres* [*Dictionary of World Cinema: Movements, Schools, Tendencies and Genres*] (Éditions du Rocher, 1994).

Ohad Rosen has published several articles in Israeli print and online journals on the subject of actors and classical Hollywood cinema. He is a member of the Education Committee in the city hall of his home town, Kiryat-Ono, where he also serves on the board of the College of Photography.

Tom Ryall is Professor of Film History at Sheffield Hallam University, UK. He is the author of *Anthony Asquith* (Manchester University Press, 2005), *Britain and the American Cinema* (Sage, 2001), *Alfred Hitchcock and the British Cinema* (2nd edn. Croom Helm, 1996) and *Blackmail* (BFI, 1993). He has also contributed to *The Encyclopedia of British Film* (Methuen/BFI, 2003), *The Oxford Guide to Film Studies* (Oxford University Press, 1998) and *The British Cinema Book* (BFI, 1997), among others, and had articles published in *Screen, Sight and Sound* and the *Journal of Popular British Cinema*.

Vicente Sánchez-Biosca is Lecturer in Film Studies at the University of Valencia, Spain, and editor of Archivos de la Filmoteca. He has worked on many areas of film history and aesthetics, including avant-garde, postmodernism, theories of editing and German Expressionism. Among his publications are *Teoría del montaje cinematografico* [*Theory of Film Editing*] (Filmoteca, Generalitat Valenciana/IVAECM/Generalitat Valenciana/Conselleria de Cultura, Educacio, Cultura, 1991); *NO-DO; El tiempo y la memoria* [*Time and Memory*] (with Raphael R. Tranche) (Catédra/Filmoteca Española, 2000) and *Cine y vanguardias artísticas* [*Cinema and the Artistic Avant-gardes*] (Paidos, 2004).

Geneviève Sellier is Professor of Film Studies at the University of Caen, France. She is the author of *La Nouvelle Vague, un cinéma au masculin singulier* [*The New Wave, a Cinema in the First Person Masculine*] (CNRS, 2005) and books on Jean Grémillon (Editions Méridiens Klincksieck, 1989) and *Les Enfants du paradis* (Nathan, 1992). She is also the co-author (with Noël Burch) of *La Drôle de guerre des sexes du cinéma français (1930–1956)* (Nathan, 1996). She has co-edited *L'Exclusion des femmes, masculinité et politique dans la culture au XXe siècle* (Éditions Complexe, 2001); *Femmes de pouvoir, mythes et fantasmes* (L'Harmattan, 2001) and *Culture d'élite, culture de masse et différence des sexes* (L'Harmattan, 2005).

Jamie Sexton is a Lecturer in Film and New Media at the University of Wales, Aberystwyth, UK. He is the co-editor (with Laura Mulvey) of *Experimental British Television* (Manchester University Press, forthcoming), and is currently working on a book on alternative British film culture in the interwar period.

Ulrike Sieglohr is Senior Lecturer in Media at Staffordshire University, UK. Her publications include *Focus on the Maternal: Female Subjectivity and Images of Motherhood* (Scarlet Press, 1998) and, as editor, *Heroines without Heroes: Reconstructing Female and National Identitities in European Cinema, 1945–51* (Cassell, 2000). She has also published essays on women filmmakers and various aspects of New German Cinema.

Tytti Soila is Docent Professor in Cinema Studies at Stockholm University, Sweden. She has published widely on Nordic cinema and feminist film theory. She is co-editor of *Nordic National Cinemas* (Routledge, 1998) and a forthcoming volume on Scandinavian cinema in the 24 Frames series for Wallflower Press.

Andrew Spicer is Reader in Cultural History at the Bristol School of Art, Media and Design, University of the West of England, UK. He has published widely on British cinema, including *Typical Men: The Representation of Masculinity in Popular British Cinema* (I. B. Tauris 2001), and is the author of *Film Noir* (Longman, 2002). He has recently completed a study of Sydney Box for the British Film Makers series (Manchester University Press), and is currently editing a collection of essays on European film noir, also for MUP.

Chloe Stephenson recently completed her PhD on 'Italian Cinema from the Late 1920s to the Early 1940s and the Soviet Model' at the University of Reading, UK. She is currently teaching Italian cinema at the University of Manchester.

Sarah Street is Professor of Film at the University of Bristol, UK. Her publications include, as co-author (with Margaret Dickinson), *Cinema and State* (BFI, 1985), and as author, *British National Cinema* (Routledge, 1997), *British Cinema in Documents* (Routledge, 2000), *Costume and Cinema* (Wallflower, 2001), *Transatlantic Crossings: British Feature Films in the USA* (Continuum, 2002) and *Black Narcissus* (I. B. Taurus, 2005). She has co-edited three books: *Moving Performance: British Stage* *and Screen* (with Linda Fitzsimmons) (Flicks Books, 2000), *European Cinema: An Introduction* (with Jill Forbes) (Palgrave, 2000) and *The Titanic in Myth and Memory: Representations in Visual and Literary Culture* (with Tim Bergfelder) (I. B. Tauris, 2004).

Eva Urzaiz has a BA in Hispanic Studies and holds a master's degree in European Culture and Modern Thought from Queen Mary, University of London, UK.

Kathleen Vernon is Associate Professor in the Department of Hispanic Languages and Literature at the State University of New York at Stony Brook, USA. She has published widely on various aspects of Spanish cinema. Her current projects include a book entitled *The Rhythms of History: Cinema, Music and Memory in Contemporary Spain.* She is also a member of an international research project supported by the AHRC devoted to producing an oral history of cinemagoing in 1940s and 1950s Spain.

Christian Viviani is Lecturer in Film Studies at the University of Paris I–Sorbonne, France. His research interest focuses on American cinema and actors. He has contributed to numerous publications on film and is the author of several books, including *Le Western* (Henri Veyrier, 1982), *Les Séducteurs du cinéma américain* (Henri Veyrier, 1984), *Ernst Lubitsch* (with N. T. Binh) (Rivages, 1992) and *Al Pacino, Robert De Niro, regards croisés* (with Michel Cieutat) (Dreamland, 2000). He is editor and co-ordinator at *Positif.*

Louise Wallenberg has a PhD in Cinema Studies from Stockholm University, Sweden, where she teaches film and television. She has published articles on film and gender in Swedish and in English, and is due to publish her thesis, 'Upsetting the Male: Feminist Interventions in The New Queer Wave', with Wesleyan University Press. She is working on a study of queer masculinities in popular Swedish cinema of the 1930s.

Michael Williams lectures in Film Studies at the University of Southampton, UK. He is the author of *Ivor Novello: Screen Idol* (BFI, 2003). He has also published on Noel Coward and has forthcoming articles on the heritage film in *Screen Method: Comparative Readings in Screen Studies* (Wallflower Press) and *Queer British Cinema* (Routledge); Belgian film-maker Bavo Defurne in *Queer Cinema in Europe* (Intellect Books) and film adaptations of *The Talented Mr Ripley* in the *Journal of Romance Studies.* He is currently co-editing a book on British cinema and the World War I.

Hans J. Wollstein is a former actor and the author of *Strangers in Hollywood* (Scarecrow Press 1994) and *Vixens, Floozies and Molls* (Filmmakers Series, 1999). He has written thousands of essays for the internet's *All-Movie Guide* and is a regular contributor to *Classic Images.*

Rashit M. Yangirov is a historian specialising in twentieth-century Russian culture and is one of the leading specialists of the 'Russia Abroad' Foundation. He is a member of the Russian Film-makers Union and a long-standing contributor to *Film Art.* He has contributed to books such as *Testimoni silenziosi. Film russi 1908–1919 / Silent Witnesses. Russian Films 1908–1919* (Biblioteca dell'unimagine, 1989) and *The Sounds of Early Cinema* (Indiana University Press, 2001) and his articles have appeared in the *Historical Journal of Film, Radio and Television, Film History* and *1895.*

Part I Film Trade, Global Culture and Transnational Cinema: An Introduction

Film Trade, Global Culture and Transnational Cinema: An Introduction

Alastair Phillips and Ginette Vincendeau

'Hollywood is a place that you can't geographically define. We don't really know where it is.' (John Ford[1])

Journeys of Desire documents, analyses and celebrates the long-standing presence of European actors in Hollywood cinema. Screen icons such as Greta Garbo, Marlene Dietrich, Cary Grant, Audrey Hepburn, Maurice Chevalier, Arnold Schwarzenegger and Antonio Banderas (to name just a few of the most famous), as well as scores of more modest players, have helped to shape the history of American cinema. Films like *Ninotchka* (1939), *Casablanca* (1942) and, more recently, *Green Card* (1990) have based their plots and appeal on the labour, screen presence and star personae of European actors. These émigrés have, in no small part, contributed to the propagation of images of Europe and of European national types and stereotypes to a worldwide audience.

The story of some of these émigrés is already familiar, thanks to various biographies and histories of their picturesque, and sometimes tragic, trajectories from the 'old continent' to the Californian 'paradise' – a metaphor reflected in the titles of several books on the topic, including Anthony Heilbut's *Exiled in Paradise* (1993) and John Russell Taylor's *Strangers in Paradise* (1983). Central to this phenomenon has been the dramatic tale of political (often Jewish) refugees from Nazi Germany. Film history, however, must also take account of the larger movements of personnel between Europe and America, from the very beginning of the film industry to the present day. In this respect, books such as Dominique Lebrun's *Paris-Hollywood: les Français dans le cinéma américain* (1987) and Hans Wollstein's *Strangers in Hollywood: The History of Scandinavian Actors in America* (1994) have widened the perspective away from purely political emigration and provided an invaluable inventory of the careers of various stars and lesser-known émigré actors. Concurrently, a growing amount of work on Hollywood and stardom, within the context of transnational studies, has focused on European stars and their specific role in screen representations of Europe. Particularly germane to our project have been recent books by Ruth Vasey (1997) and Diane Negra (2001) – for a complete list of works on the subject, see the bibliography at the end of this volume. Our aim has been to combine these various approaches, and also to redress the balance of studies of European émigrés in Hollywood, which tend to focus on directors rather than actors, by offering a truly pan-European perspective on the trajectories, personae and screen performances of the many European actors who have worked in Hollywood cinema.

For the first time in one volume, we have assembled a comprehensive guide[2] to European actors in Hollywood, which includes entries on individual actors as well as national overviews, and a set of fifteen critical essays. These chapters explore selected aspects of the topic: more in-depth case studies of prominent individuals or wider reflections that are either national, industry or genre-based. Drawing on a team of nearly seventy international experts, this book thus charts the varied experiences of about 900 European actors – from Victoria Abril to Mai Zetterling – who appeared in Hollywood films, experiences that range from global celebrity to outright failure with a kaleidoscope of happiness, frustration, disappointment, comic episodes and tragedy in between. The Californian paradise occasionally was mean and nasty and, as Bertolt Brecht put it, for some it could be 'unsuccessful as hell'.[3]

Émigré actors' rendez-vous: Paul Henreid (left), Ingrid Bergman (centre) and Claude Rains (right) in *Casablanca* (1942)

Hollywood stardom for Charles Boyer and Greta Garbo in *Conquest* (1937)

When we started this project, we had a relatively clear picture of the typical trajectories of European actors in Hollywood cinema. One type of performers were exiles (or refugees) who moved to Hollywood out of political or economic necessity. Another were émigrés who relocated to Los Angeles, motivated by a personal 'journey of desire' or the invitation of a Hollywood talent scout with the promise (or reality) of a studio contract. We also thought that to compile the Hollywood filmographies of these actors would be straightforward. In the course of writing and editing this book, however, many of these assumptions have been challenged, and our perception of the boundaries between European film production and Hollywood – and between 'Europeans' and 'Americans' – has altered considerably.

First, we encountered difficulties in determining who our 'émigré actors' were. Many of the actors mentioned in this book already had fluid European identities. For example, Lillian Harvey and Peter Lorre, who have typically been considered as 'German', were respectively British and Czechoslovak by birth. In the 1920s and 1930s, many émigrés from Russia transited through Paris and many 'Middle European' actors through Berlin and Paris. These people thus already had 'hyphenated' cultural lives that in turn became absorbed into a 'double emigration' on arrival in Los Angeles. Furthermore, some of these actors never settled permanently on the West Coast and found themselves moving backwards and forwards between the USA and Europe, forming a pattern of 'demi-emigration'. We also had to make difficult choices in relation to the *degree* to which actors of European parentage, but who were raised in the USA, could be considered 'émigré actors'.

Second, we encountered other difficulties in determining what constituted a Hollywood film, especially since the demise of the Hollywood studio system and the globalisation of film production, when it has become increasingly difficult to define what a 'Hollywood film' actually *is*. Although the great majority of films included in this book were indeed shot in the USA and wholly funded by Hollywood studios and corporations, we have also included (when the information has been available) majority US-financed co-productions, 'runaway productions' and 'quota films' shot outside the USA (sometimes in Europe), taking in those financed by subsidiaries of the Hollywood majors. 'Hollywood' has thus emerged as a term subject to the same fluid transnational currents and tensions as the careers of the actors who are the subject of this book. This points to some interesting discrepancies between *Journeys of Desire* and many standard accounts of the relations between European and American cinemas.

A film like *The Citadel* (1938), for example, which starred Robert Donat, Rex Harrison, Felix Aylmer, Ralph Richardson and Nora Swinburne, may be technically considered British since it was shot at Denham studios, but the project was actually financed by MGM's British subsidiary. It was budgeted and eventually marketed as a Hollywood 'A feature' film and therefore, as far as we are concerned, is part of these actors' American filmographies. Similarly, Visconti's *The Damned/La caduta degli dei* (1969), with Dirk Bogarde and Ingrid Thulin, was shot in Europe but significantly funded by Warner Bros. Therefore, although some sources would see these films as 'European', they have been included in the actors' respective Hollywood filmographies.[4]

Unsurprisingly, this issue is particularly complex when it comes to British cinema, where the common language further blurs the porous borders between 'national' film productions. With the fluctuating (part or whole) overseas ownership of European companies by North American corporations, it has become extremely difficult to locate genuinely nationally specific sources of funding and thus ascribe a national identity to a film. And yet, as the recent fracas over Jean-Pierre Jeunet's 2004 *Un long dimanche de fiançailles/A Very Long Engagement* (a film with a French topic, source book, director, actors and locations, but part-financed by Warner Bros. and thus deemed 'American') has revealed, national identity does continue to matter. If 'Hollywood' has come to define, in Miriam Hansen's words, 'the incarnation of *the modern* . . . up-to-date with Fordist-Taylorist methods of industrial production and mass consumption',[5] and if, as John Ford puts it, its location is hazy, it is nevertheless essential to assess the contribution of individual European émigré actors and the 'European' representations they projected, and to relate these to the overall political, institutional, economic and aesthetic history of Hollywood film production. This is what

Charlie Chaplin (centre), the most successful British actor in Hollywood of all time

Journeys of Desire sets out to do. (A complete listing of the book's aims and conventions regarding these matters can be found at the beginning of Part IV of this book.)

History of Emigration

The history of the migration of European actors to Hollywood is itself predicated on earlier waves of socio-political emigration from Europe during the nineteenth century and early years of the twentieth century. The presence of powerful German-speaking Middle European communities on the East Coast helped to establish a vital émigré entertainment culture from which Hollywood's founding fathers, such as Adolph Zukor, emerged. Pre-existing networks within the Russian and Italian communities similarly facilitated the assimilation of European performers as they moved from the migrant stage to the American studios. Touring stage celebrities such as Sarah Bernhardt, or visiting troupes such as Karno, which included the young Chaplin, also facilitated the transition between stage and film and helped the subsequent trail of European actors coming directly to Hollywood.

Once in Hollywood, from the 1920s onwards, the émigrés joined established communities of compatriots or like-minded Europeans – communities that were significant for a number of reasons. Many contributors note how Hollywood recruited European actors in order to facilitate the assimilation of ethnically specific audiences. Irish screen actors, for example, already in demand because of the growing influence of directors and producers from Irish backgrounds such as John Ford, Herbert Brenon and Raoul Walsh were able to address a vast migrant audience with a pre-existing network of local cinemas, social clubs and entertainment venues. The same is true of Italian actors, especially in terms of their already established relationship with migrant Italian (and Yiddish) theatrical

6   British actress Kate Winslet triumphs in the global hit *Titanic* (1992)

culture. But these performers were also recruited in the hope that they would help Hollywood target lucrative national audiences overseas. As Ruth Vasey has pointed out, Garbo's Hollywood films 'consistently depended on her immense following abroad', since she had been originally recruited in the knowledge that 'Sweden had one of the highest per capita expenditures on motion pictures in Europe'.[6]

Émigré actors also formed new parallel communities at once separate from and overlapping with existing migrant networks. Locations such as Miklosz Dora's restaurant 'Little Hungary' on Sunset Boulevard, the Russian-American Arts Club and the private homes of people such as Jacques Feyder and Françoise Rosay, Marlene Dietrich and Charles Laughton were vibrant centres of émigré life. While wishing to integrate in Hollywood life, Europeans were also keen to preserve their identity and customs. As Jon Burrows points out, 'many British settlers in California *behaved* like members of a colonial outpost [. . .] Tea was always served at four both at home and on the studio backlot for many of the Hollywood British.'[7] The formation of this 'archipelago of "little islands" '[8] – to use Max Ophuls' phrase – served more than just a social role. It also led to the constitution of mutually beneficial production networks, with many émigré actors being offered roles in each other's productions. These re-formed communities in exile illustrate the difficulties, but also potential rewards, faced by European actors in Hollywood, as well as the tension between assimilation and the conservation of cultural identity.

In some cases these communities also took a political colour. Although the majority of European actors who migrated to Hollywood were motivated by socio-economic rather than political reasons, a good number of émigré actors, such as Francis Lederer (from the former Czechoslovakia), were involved in the development of small radical theatre groups during the 1930s that trained both prominent screen actors and supporting players for the studios. As Joseph Garncarz shows in Chapter 11, Paul Kohner's European Film Fund – the focal point of Hollywood's European refugee community after the collapse of the Hollywood Anti-Nazi League – provided key financial support to émigré actors. It also lobbied studios to release temporary contracts for performers still in Europe. Many of these actors went on to appear in the numerous anti-Nazi films produced by Hollywood during the war, thus intensifying a link between the émigrés and the political goals of the USA. This included, for instance, the morale-boosting efforts of performers such as Marlene Dietrich and Charles Boyer, who regularly entertained troops and appeared in propaganda broadcasts.

The Industry

Hollywood's films 'were uniquely designed for "vertical" consumption across barriers of age, experience, and predilection in a single site of exhibition, and "horizontal" consumption across widely diverse geographic and cultural territories'.[9] European actors were a fundamental aspect of this process and their migrations clearly followed larger institutional and financial shifts within the international film industry. Interestingly, as Giuliana Muscio and Sarah Street demonstrate in Chapters 4 and 6 respectively, emigration often took place when European film industries were in a position of relative strength vis-à-vis Hollywood – and not as one might have expected when they were weak. This was especially true of leading UK actors who were 'star-traded' with their American counterparts in the 1930s and 1940s, with the dual aim of facilitating British studios' export strategies and shoring up Hollywood's domination of the British market.

Some performers arrived in Los Angeles as politically motivated exiles, such as the Russians in the 1920s and the Middle European diaspora – especially from Germany – during the 1930s. But during the first phase of structured travel and recruitment – up to the end of the 1940s – European performers would usually be contracted to a single studio, having been recruited either directly in entertainment venues in New York and Chicago or overseas. Hollywood kept a constant watch on successful stage and film actors in Europe and in the USA. Jon Burrows notes, for example, that throughout the 1930s 'up to fifty of the orchestra seats on a Broadway opening night would be filled with Hollywood scouts' looking for new British acting talent.[10] Local observers kept an eye on trends in European stage and film, and studio heads such as Darryl F. Zanuck and Irving Thalberg went on tours of important territories themselves; both Ilona Massey and Hedy Lamarr were signed to MGM, for instance, during Louis B. Mayer's prominent 1937 European talent-seeking tour. The recruitment of prominent stars was part of the intense competition between studios. Jesse Lasky hired Chevalier on the strength of a screen test initiated by Thalberg, and Paramount's hiring of Marlene Dietrich, for example, was a deliberate riposte to MGM, who could now promote Greta Garbo on the basis of domestic and international audiences hearing their favourite silent star speak. Similarly, the short-lived decision by MGM, Warners and Fox to shoot films in the USA in multiple European-language versions (which meant that European actors were brought to the USA to perform in their native tongue) was countered by Paramount, who went on to shoot similar multi-language versions in Paris.[11]

On arrival in the USA, leading European players would be greeted with the fanfare of intense domestic and foreign media publicity, usually in New York harbour as they stepped down from glamorous transatlantic liners, and on arrival in Los Angeles after a long transcontinental Pullman car journey. They would then be groomed for stardom by the studio's production management and publicity department, in a process that carefully tailored their 'foreignness' for American consumption (a process in which the stars participated more or less willingly). Some, like Maurice Chevalier and Marlene Dietrich, quickly achieved A-list status. In Chapter 5, Martine Danan recounts how Paramount's publicity staff worked to enhance Chevalier's international star status on both sides of the ocean with 'a hero's send-off from France' and 'a welcome ceremony in California in October 1928 to the sound of the French national anthem'. These events were accompanied by an essay-writing competition on 'why I love Chevalier', a French-language promotional documentary, and planned press stories about the star's various romantic intrigues. As well as intense recruitment strategies, Hollywood invested substantial sums into the grooming and salaries of European émigré actors. After her arrival in Los Angeles in 1925, for example, Greta Garbo spent several months having her appearance stylised by MGM experts before she made her film debut the following year. Similarly, as an indication of his enormous prestige for Paramount, Charles Laughton was already earning $2,500 a week by the end of his first year in Hollywood.

Despite this major investment, the success of Hollywood films featuring European actors was uneven, both at home and overseas — a potent running theme through this book. Tales of disappointment and frustration resound, since the high expectations of studios and actors were, in many cases, not met by subsequent roles and careers. Many performers found themselves working in (often uncredited) routine character roles or minor parts. Some of these actors' filmographies — especially British and German examples — were enormous: see, among others, entries for Olaf Hytten (268 Hollywood films) and Arno Frey (99 Hollywood films). As the classical studio era drew to a close, and Hollywood diversified and increased its overseas productions (especially in Europe), European actors started working on American productions on a more fluid and temporary basis. Actors today often move to the USA for one-off projects and keep parallel careers at home. They appear in English-language films largely financed by Hollywood but shot around the world. From luxury transatlantic crossings to rapid jet travel, the 'journeys of desire' to Hollywood have evolved significantly. Yet the mecca of cinema has not lost its appeal. As Irène Bessière puts it in Chapter 7, young French actors today are still drawn to it 'in search of global stardom', despite the evidence that extremely few of them make any impact outside domestic production.

Many reasons have been advanced by both the actors themselves and by commentators. The more paranoid notion is that Hollywood sometimes deliberately attracted European stars in order to ruin their reputation with ludicrously inadequate parts in mediocre films — thus weakening the European film industries while enhancing Hollywood films' export potential on the international market. A more 'Darwinian' scenario envisages Hollywood as a commercial jungle in which only those who adapt succeed. Indeed, especially at the height of emigration from Europe in the 1930s and 1940s, Hollywood certainly could not have accommodated the flow of émigrés. It is also the case, as discussed later in this introduction, that many other factors intervened: language, performance and the adequacy of star personae to Hollywood genres and narratives that determined or hindered the 'translation' of actors to American film.

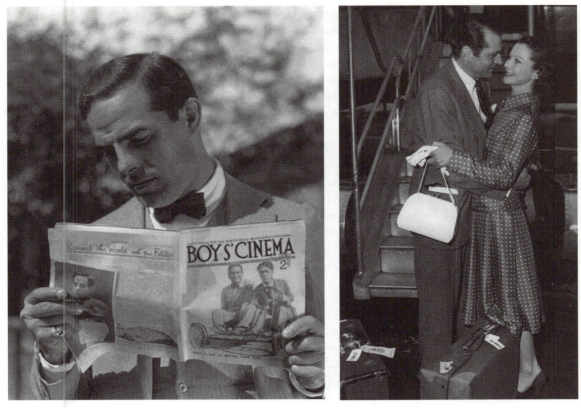

The dark, handsome Spanish actor Antonio Moreno was one of the most popular representations of the 'Latin Lover' in classical Hollywood cinema

The star British couple in Hollywood: Laurence Olivier and Vivien Leigh

While Hollywood in the 1930s and 1940s became a mini Tower of Babel, the postwar period saw the internationalisation of Hollywood film production outside the USA. First, the Paramount case of 1948, which forced studios to separate exhibition from production and distribution, encouraged organisations to seek profit in different ways. American studios therefore took advantage of the new legislation aimed at encouraging overseas investment within local industries. As Thomas Guback has noted, the Anglo-American Film Agreement of the same year allowed US companies to withdraw a percentage of their earnings in the UK, thus 'leaving more than $40 million each year to accumulate in blocked accounts . . . in exchange for access to the British market unhindered by import quotas'. These frozen profits led to the development of 'runaway productions' 'that met every legal requirement for being declared "British" '.[12] Furthermore, as long as these American-financed films employed a sufficient number of British personnel, they became entitled to subsidies from the Eady Levy production fund set up in 1950.[13] Thus the Anglo-American Bond franchise emerged, financed by the deal set up between Harry Saltzman and Albert R. 'Cubby' Broccoli and United Artists. The Bond films focused on Anglo-American relations and appealed to domestic European audiences with their attractive European locations and casts – while being technically 'American', hence their incorporation in this book. Similar schemes were set up by Spain and Italy, out of which came films such as Nicholas Ray's multinational epic *55 Days at Peking* (1963), which starred a host of actors featured in this book: David Niven, Harry Andrews, Flora Robson, Paul Lukas, Elizabeth Sellars, Jacques Sernas and José Nieto.

It would be misleading, however, to see this process as simply a pernicious symptom of American hegemony. As Tim Bergfelder has argued, European film industries in the postwar period benefited from the move away from an explicitly national film culture, and indeed 'many European producers of the 1960s [actually] preferred American co-operation over inter-European agreements where such co-operation was available'.[14] The careers of new mid-Atlantic stars such as Sean Connery, Michael Caine and Julie Christie – but also actors like Curt Jürgens – clearly gained from American investment in European film during the 1960s. The phenomenon has endured and between 1990 and 1998 Hollywood revenue from 'runaway' film and television production rose from $500 million to $2.8 billion per annum.[15]

Thus a growing percentage of European feature films are now co-productions, making it ever more difficult to locate the 'national identity' of a film, especially when it comes to English-language films. In this case, can Hollywood – certainly the kind of Hollywood that attracted the likes of Greta Garbo to California – be said to exist any more? With Hollywood's increasing dependence on subcontracted multinational companies, the proliferation of screen formats – and all that means in terms of marketing, distribution, spectatorship and representation – and the rampant globalisation of plant, location and personnel, the place of European actors in Hollywood has become increasingly transient. Nevertheless, Hollywood continues to be the most powerful disseminator of European identities and thus issues of representation remain, as they have always been, on the cultural agenda.

Language and Performance

If the studio system was set up and run by Jewish émigrés from Central Europe, these pioneers were keen to establish their American credentials rather than to promote heterogeneity in Hollywood. Their concrete aim was to make the new American film industry prosper – in particular to counter the French hegemony over pre-1914 world cinema – and their ideological project was to build up powerful representations of American lifestyle and values on screen. As Richard Abel points out in Chapter 1, 'once an indigenous industry arose to compete with and eclipse the French, its subjects and personnel (and especially actors) had to be defined clearly as "American"'.

This process of Americanisation had crucial consequences for the Europeans who flocked to Los Angeles. As several writers in this book show, even in the silent period, an actor's origins strongly affected his or her chances of success in Hollywood, since their cultural identity and professional background had an immediate impact on their performance. Directors and technicians behind the camera, by contrast, had a relatively easier time fitting in. American actors thus had a headstart in a star system designed, among other things, to promote core American values. Indicative in this respect was the fate of the great Russian star Ivan Mosjoukine. Despite being prepared to change his name and even his looks (his nose was shortened), in a desperate bid to blend in and make 'simple and wholesome' American movies, Mosjoukine returned defeated to Europe after barely completing two films (see Natalia Noussinova's discussion in Chapter 8). To be sure, silent Hollywood included European actors who forged prominent careers – whether spectacular successes like Charlie Chaplin, Stan Laurel and Garbo, or more modest stars such as Renée Adorée, Lars Hanson, Jetta Goudal, Charles de Rochefort, Alla Nazimova and Antonio Moreno. But apart from Chaplin and Garbo, none really rivalled the likes of Mary Pickford, Lillian Gish and Douglas Fairbanks.

If things were not easy for the European émigrés in the silent period, the coming of sound obviously created a further barrier in making their foreignness plainly audible. Yet paradoxically, the now hegemonic Hollywood studio system was hungrier for talent, thus opening the door to stardom for Maurice Chevalier, Marlene Dietrich, Charles Boyer and Laurence Olivier among others. This is a paradox that writers in this book repeatedly show to be emblematic of the fate of European actors in Hollywood. The émigrés were further cast into 'otherness' with their now conspicuous, or certainly perceptible, accents, yet when success beckoned, it was precisely because of their alterity.

There was, nevertheless, a basic obstacle to overcome, namely speaking decent English. Many new arrivals in Hollywood such as Dietrich and Chevalier had thick accents, while others like Vilma Bánky and Anna Sten were unable to speak English at all. The studios readily provided extra language lessons and private coaches to help their recruits improve their linguistic skills. The American press focused on this issue mercilessly, either by mocking actors' linguistic shortcomings or by praising their efforts and ingenuity in trying to overcome them. For instance, in 1941, Jean Gabin was reported as practising his English 'on grocery store clerks, studio works and his Filipino houseboy' (see Ginette Vincendeau, Chapter 12). The Hungarian-born opera singer Ilona Masey, briefly promoted as 'the singing Garbo', showed such reluctance to pursue English (and acting classes) that she soon found herself relegated to B-movies and nightclub appearances. Whether they tried hard or not, major European stars like Gabin, Annabella, Marcello Mastroianni, Isa Miranda and Alain Delon floundered in Hollywood partly on account of accents that were discordant, faintly ridiculous or simply difficult to understand. In this respect, several contributors show the essential role the stage played in helping the actors overcome language problems. Knowing how to project your voice in a foreign language was crucial, especially in the classical era when clarity was key. Although it is impossible to generalise, there is evidence that theatrically trained actors tended to do better than others (in Chapter 9, for instance, Alastair Phillips contrasts the success of Charles Boyer – who was an experienced theatre actor – to the failure of his compatriot Annabella, who was not).

To complicate matters, social and in some cases political factors intensified linguistic problems. Some accents emerged as more 'acceptable' than others, and in this respect Germanic-sounding people suffered most – in part

Three French stars in Hollywood: Louis Jourdan (left), Leslie Caron (centre) and Maurice Chevalier (right) in *Gigi* (1958)

because of the legacy of both world wars (see Tim Bergfelder's discussion in Chapter 3). For instance, the Hungarian actresses Vilma Bánky and Lya de Putti both fell from favour, since their voices were considered unsuitable for romance because of their guttural intonation. Even the most popular or critically acclaimed German-speaking actors such as Dietrich, Luise Rainer and Paul Henreid were not considered suitable for all roles. As Lotte Palfi – a respected German stage actress who failed to make her mark in Hollywood – bitterly commented: 'I said to myself that America was a melting pot. So many nationalities met there and spoke different varieties of English that my German accent would not be an obstacle. I never made a greater mistake.'[16]

Foreign accents became more acceptable in the more international postwar period, but the audibly foreign actors nevertheless tended to be confined to subaltern roles (see Vicente Sánchez-Biosca's discussion of Sara Montiel in Chapter 14). One major exception is Audrey Hepburn. Of Belgian and Dutch parentage, Hepburn spoke with almost no accent and this helped her blend of sophisticated European femininity to cross over to a wholly American image. In the more globalised context of the turn of the twenty-first century, younger actors such as Julie Delpy as well as Valeria Golino, Goran Visnjic and Connie Nielsen, among others, are linguistically much more skilled. As well as no longer having to change their names, they have been able to move more freely between Hollywood and their own national cinemas. These performers tend to duplicate their cultural distinctiveness, rather than subsume their original ones under American identities. The language barriers, however, have by no means come down, as the continuing small number of European stars who truly become part of the Hollywood 'A-list' shows.

The impact of language for the émigré actor is not only relevant to obtaining reasonable parts, or even the nature of these parts, it also affects the subtleties of performance style. Many émigré actors are reported to have complained that the speaking of a foreign language interfered with their body movements and the ability therefore to perform 'naturally' – an issue that must be taken into account when trying to understand why so many failed to reach the same level of stardom as in their native country. Jean Gabin complained that 'In English, I could *hear myself speak* [. . .] Nothing seemed to correspond to what I was saying, neither my gestures, my body, or anything I felt physically, or thought.' Similarly, the fact that Mastroianni, in his Hollywood films, had to recite his lines phonetically created a noticeable unease in his expression. The connection between language and performance could be a personal one, as for Gabin, Mastroianni and others, but it could also be the result of a clash between European and Hollywood acting traditions – despite the huge efforts deployed by the studios to smooth over these difficulties by, for example, providing acting coaches. This was felt by Russian actors from the Moscow Art Theatre (MKHaT) (or Stanislavsky) school, as Noussinova discusses in Chapter 8, and also by British actors from the London stage, despite the fact that they were speaking the same language (see Sarah Street's argument in Chapter 6).

And yet, in what has by now become a familiar paradox, having a foreign accent was not necessarily always a handicap, since there was an ongoing demand for foreigner roles, especially in European-themed films such as *Ninotchka*. Indeed, 'foreign'-speaking actors often made such characters believable. A particularly prominent case was *Casablanca* in which the vast majority of players were not American. As Pauline Kael put it, '[i]f you think of *Casablanca* and think of all those small roles being played by Hollywood actors faking the accents, the picture wouldn't have had anything like the color and tone it had'.[17] In other words, the European actors' accent was their major job asset and cultural capital – if only to provide 'color' and 'tone' – as well as their greatest handicap.

Stereotypes and Beyond

In its portrayal of French, British, Russian, Italian or other European identities, Hollywood relied on cultural typologies already established in literature, theatre and popular entertainment. In some cases, these traditions were literally taken across the Atlantic via migrant theatrical troupes from countries such as Ireland and Italy and from individual stage performers such as Maurice Chevalier, Charles Laughton, Laurence Olivier and Stewart Granger (see Martine Danan's discussion of Chevalier in Chapter 5 and Sarah Street's discussion of the British actors in Chapter 6). In other cases, the process took place via adaptations of European literary classics (e.g. the novels of Dickens, Zola

Respected Spanish actress Penelope Cruz became a worldwide celebrity in Hollywood when she co-starred with Tom Cruise in *Vanilla Sky* (2001)

Nastassja Kinski as the 'incestuous, innocent yet deadly' heroine of Paul Schrader's *Cat People* (1982)

or Dostoevsky) or biographies of eminent historical European personalities such as Napoleon and Beethoven or various Roman emperors and Russian tsars. There was also the less traceable and yet pervasive cultural currency of particular stereotypes such as 'excitable' Mediterraneans, 'gloomy' Nordic people, 'passionate' Russians, 'oh la la!' Parisians, and so on.

At a basic level, however limiting they may have seemed to the actors concerned, these stereotypes nonetheless proved a substantial source of employment for everyone from anonymous extras to fully fledged stars. For instance, retired tsarist military men for a while cornered the market in crowds of men doing risky stunts on horseback, as Rashit Yangirov reveals in Chapter 2. At a slightly higher level, there were, as already noted, scores of players in tiny, sometimes uncredited, parts. British actors specialised in interfering manservants and patrician aristocrats. Irish actors, drawn from the theatre, embodied a parade of 'drunken fathers, hapless maids, pious mothers and luckless labourers'.[18] Russian actors played terrorists, taxi drivers or balalaïka players. Italians – usually further reduced to Southern Italians see Giuliana Muscio's discussion in Chapter 4) – specialised in volatile waiters and mafiosi. French women played haughty couture house managers or 'naughty' maids. Hispanic actors, Vicente Sánchez-Biosca argues in Chapter 14, 'masqueraded' as fiery Latinos of all descriptions. Starring roles have also been no guarantee of escaping national stereotyping. Thus Ronald Colman, David Niven and Roger Moore are three, among several, notable British actors who have specialised in suave gentlemen, while Hugh Grant has often been associated with the handsome, bumbling middle-class fool. Italian leading men such as Rossano Brazzi and French stars like Maurice Chevalier, Charles Boyer and Louis Jourdan, offered variations on the 'Latin lover'. The force of such images has meant that actors who wished to escape 'their' national typecasting, or whose types did not 'export' to American genres, found it extremely hard to obtain significant roles – see, among others, the disappointing American careers of Alain Delon, Jean Gabin, Romy Schneider, Melina Mercouri, Emmanuelle Béart, Anna Magnani and Irene Papas compared to their high domestic standing.

Beyond these national variations, two pan-European stereotypes emerge: European men as villains and European women as exotic temptresses. The tradition of European actors playing villains is pervasive, though it affects some nations more than others. It originated with the equation of organised crime with the Mafia, and thus with Italians and Sicilians. For obvious historical reasons, German-speaking actors have played the ultimate villains: the Nazis. Conrad Veidt, Ludwig Stössel, Fritz Kortner, Reinhold Schünzel and many others – including those who occasionally played heroic roles, for instance Carl Esmond, Helmut Dantine and Paul Henreid – have repeatedly embodied these types. Martin Kosleck, for example, was Goebbels on five occasions. What Joseph Garncarz (Chapter 11) has discovered, however, is that for these actors ideology was secondary to professional status. These performers defined themselves as artists, not as political victims, and were therefore more interested in the prominence of the role and whether it was a speaking or just a walk-on part than in its political colour. More recently, the nationality consistently associated with villains in Hollywood has been British, as discussed by Andrew Spicer in Chapter 15. Jeremy Irons, Malcom McDowell, Ian McKellen, Alan Rickman, Michael Gambon, Tim Roth and Gary Oldman, among others, have embodied elegant, devilish and well-spoken villains, usually opposite the film's hero played by an American. Another recent development is that the previously Italian mafioso has shifted to the Balkans and Russia. As Dina Iordanova points out,[19] actors like (Croatian) Rade Serbedzija and (Bosnian) Sergej Trifunovic are repeatedly typecast as 'sleazy villains of unspecified East European/Russian origins' or 'wild and uncontrollable bullies'. In short, to quote the Dutch actor Rutger Hauer, who, despite speaking perfect English, has tended to play villains in the mould of his breakthrough Hollywood role as android Roy Batty in *Blade Runner* (1982): 'Hollywood's number one rule is: American actors play heroes, foreign actors play villains'.[20]

It could be argued that the casting of European women as femmes fatales has only added a twist of exoticism to the pervasive sexualisation of women on screen, designed to engage with and allay social anxieties about changes in women's status; yet as several of our contributors show, in doing so European women have brought an extra layer of difference. In the silent period, the success of many European actresses in Hollywood was predicated on their appeal as dark, exotic, often threatening figures who contrasted with the all-American (often blonde) heroines. The Polish actress Pola Negri and the Franco-Dutch Jetta Goudal (described as 'orchid-like' and 'the most exotic personality on the screen') projected exotic otherness, as did the Russian Alla Nazimova, who specialised in mythical, dangerous beauties such as Cleopatra, Sappho and Salomé. With the coming of sound and the implementation of the Production Code, this pattern diversified, but European actresses still played variations on the femme fatale. The glamorous Garbo and Dietrich were cast as spies, adulteresses and occasional prostitutes. Their identities were sometimes nationally specific, sometimes vaguely 'European'. But in a familiar gender divide, where male actors' identities were historically grounded, the actresses' screen identities were sexual first and cultural or political second. Even when Garbo and Dietrich played historical queens (respectively Christina of Sweden and Catherine of Russia), the emphasis was on their sexual rather than social power. Other stars, like Hedy Lamarr, Anna Sten and Isa Miranda, were put through the same mould, more or less successfully. As Christian Viviani argues in Chapter 10, Hollywood repeatedly used European actresses to project transgressive values deemed unacceptable in their American counterparts during the Production Code era. An extreme case was that of Simone Simon, who became the mythical embodiment of unhealthy and European female sexuality in the horror film *Cat People*. (In a perhaps unique case of reverse stereotyping, British actresses such as Deborah Kerr and Julie Andrews frequently embodied sexual repression.) When screen representations moved towards a more naturalistic style in the 1940s, Ingrid Bergman offered a new way of 'making the unacceptable accepted', as Viviani puts it, since like Alida Valli and Hildegard Knef she combined transgressive roles with a 'healthy' and innocent aura. For Romy Schneider, Senta Berger and others,

Hollywood failed again to extend its range of female roles beyond the femme fatale or the highly sexualised woman. Revealingly, when Julie Christie, Isabelle Huppert and Milla Jovovich appeared in Hollywood Westerns, it was as brother-keepers. Contemporary European actresses such as Penelope Cruz and Juliette Binoche, while benefiting from more diverse roles, continue to be confined to sexy 'exotic' figures.

Although, as noted above, male representations have generally been more historical, they have not escaped sexualisation. It is interesting in this respect that many European actors – especially those from Mediterranean countries – fit within this framework. The stereotype of the Italian male tended to emphasise his otherness from the WASP ideal, since he was both more 'primitive' and more sophisticated through an association with culture. And, as Hilary Radner shows in Chapter 13, the attraction and the limitation of Louis Jourdan's portrayal of a 'hyper-sexuality' was that it took its meaning as *excess* in relation to a more 'rugged', and normative, American masculinity. Before Jourdan, Boyer's persona as a romantic seducer also took feminised, and at times sinister, 'unnatural' undertones (as in *Gaslight* [1944]).

Conversely, the blonde and blue-eyed whiteness of Nordic actors, such as Lars Hanson, Ingrid Bergman, Garbo, Dietrich and the briefly (but hugely) successful Norwegian ice-skating star Sonja Henie, offered a different kind of otherness by emphasising an ideal of extreme Aryan whiteness. Recently, this has shifted to more exaggerated and 'unnatural' forms. The Swedish martial arts star Dolph Lundgren and action men Arnold Schwarzenegger (from Austria) and Jean-Claude Van Damme (from Belgium) have, with their robot-like, toned muscular bodies, arguably connoted a crypto-fascist version of whiteness.[21] In a clever way they – like Henie much earlier – have also, in their body-based performance style, bypassed the cultural and linguistic differences that have hindered so many other European émigrés. Over the last twenty years they have become the image of the successful European émigré star.

In Hollywood's galaxy of representations, European actors have thus conventionally figured as the 'other'. Moreover, their difference from their American counterparts has frequently been expressed in terms of an overtly 'theatrical' performance style. Hollywood's tendency to cast Europeans as villains, pumped-up muscle-men and femmes fatales has by contrast projected Americans on screen as normative and authentic, as opposed to these deviant and 'inauthentic' Europeans. Nonetheless, no matter how 'dark' and exotic, the representation of Europeans on screen has remained within the boundaries of whiteness. The stereotypes discussed above have clearly never shared the racist virulence of representations of African-Americans or Arabs. For example, as Jack G. Shaheen shows, Arabs have systematically been represented as 'brutal, heartless, uncivilized religious fanatics and money-mad cultural "others" bent on terrorizing civilized Westerners'.[22] Europeans have by contrast evinced a range of more subtle portrayals, both positive and negative, some derogatory or comic, and some glamorous and affectionate. Close cultural ties between Europe and America – in which the émigré actors have played a key part – and in some cases the lobbying power of particular communities (such as the Irish), have ensured more of a give-and-take approach. Conscious of the damaging consequences of gross stereotyping or racism for the box-office potential of its films abroad, Hollywood has used European actors to project a 'safe' ethnic difference. To borrow from the title of Diane Negra's ground-breaking study,[23] they have enabled 'off-white' representations that acted as a safety valve. The American film industry used European actors to shore up idealised American values. At the same time it used them to evoke, and defuse, the threat of more radically 'other' identities such as those of African-Americans, American-Indians, Arabs or Mexicans.

This may be small comfort to French, British, German, Italian, Spanish and Russian actors who found themselves in the stereotypical roles outlined above, but the reverse of the coin is a kind of 'stereotypical void', to use Dina Iordanova's phrase.[24] Actors from countries without ready-made cultural associations either find no roles at all, or are subject to an even greater degree of 'ethnic blurring' than those from more established nations. This is the case especially for actors from Balkan states such as Romania and Bulgaria; or from Switzerland, Belgium, Denmark and other 'small' countries, who tend to play unspecified Europeans. Even a respected Swedish actor such as Max von Sydow is often typecast as a brooding, vaguely spiritual Scandinavian when in Hollywood. It remains an interesting irony in this respect that when it came to the stereotype of the Southern Italian gangster, Paul Muni (an American actor of German origins) and the Romanian-born Edward G. Robinson both contributed more than Italian actors such as Eduardo Ciannelli, Paul Porcasi and Frank Puglia to the mafioso stereotype. Ethnic blurring, however, could also provide useful camouflage or even progressive counter-stereotyping, especially in the case of Jewish actors from Europe. Actresses such as Alla Nazimova and Lily Palmer had roles that made no reference to their Jewishness, and Marcel Dalio found that his Hollywood parts tended to emphasise his Frenchness rather than his Jewish ethnicity (contrary to what had been the case in France).

National or pan-European types and stereotypes, along with their cultural and linguistic identities, have thus had a highly ambivalent function for European actors and for the representation of Europe on screen. While actors could certainly use their European-ness as a selling point, they understandably did not want to be subordinated into 'otherness'. The most successful émigrés in this respect have been those – particularly British actors – who could move from initially foregrounding their national specificity to more American or international identities (Cary Grant, Claude Rains and Herbert Marshall come to mind). Even a highly successful star like Antonio Banderas – Hollywood's latest A-list star of European origins at the time of writing – is not allowed to be 'everyman' on screen in the way Tom Hanks or Tom Cruise are, or indeed in the way he was in his Spanish films. Multiculturalism has become the norm in a global film market, but the 'glass ceiling' of ethnicity still operates today.

The nine hundred or so players in this book (and the few who inevitably have escaped our attention) represent a kaleidoscope of nationalities, styles, ambitions and careers. Beyond the uniqueness of each case, affected by parameters of gender, age, ethnicity, looks, nationality, performance style, politics and so on, four broad categories have emerged. First, a minority of European actors have become major Hollywood stars – a list that includes the names of Chaplin, Garbo, Dietrich, Chevalier, Bergman, Schwarzenegger and Banderas and some now half-forgotten such as Henie. Second, a larger band of actors rose to stardom in highly specific genres – a select category best illustrated by Bela Lugosi and Boris Karloff in the horror film – or as high-profile leading men: people like Claude Rains, Louis Jourdan, Peter Ustinov, Hedy Lamarr, Rossano Brazzi and many more.

Our third category includes an even larger group of actors who played character parts of various sizes, from the medium to the tiny (and often uncredited), in roles that usually emphasised national stereotypes – from Peter Lorre, Sydney Greenstreet and Marcel Dalio to Eric Blore, Emile Chautard, S. Z. Sakall, Sig Arno and many others. These constitute a kind of army of 'unknown foot soldiers', some of whom became the object of a cult (e.g. Lorre) and some familiar by sight but not by name. The fourth category constitutes perhaps the most poignant set of émigrés in Hollywood: people who were major stars in their own countries but failed in Hollywood to gain a status anywhere near their domestic stardom – a roll-call that includes Ivan Mosjoukine, Isa Miranda, Jean Gabin, Marcello Mastroianni, Hildegarde Knef, Milena Dravic, Alain Delon and Emmanuelle Béart.

In reflecting on what determined the success of some and the failure of others, many factors have to be taken into account. We cannot dismiss questions of chance on the one hand, nor of individual talent and drive on the other. But there are also less speculative parameters, in addition to those of language and performance discussed above.

First of all, it has become apparent that the very successful European stars in Hollywood are those whose personae matched dominant genres. The success of Chevalier, for example, is clearly linked to the vogue for musicals and sophisticated, risqué comedies of the early 1930s; conversely, his American star waned with the genre, only to resurface briefly in postwar musicals and through television. Garbo and Dietrich similarly corresponded both to pre-Production Code mores and to the triumph of the 'woman's film' – thus their powerful sexual auras became a problem in New Deal America, when cute, unthreatening child stars such as Shirley Temple rose to prominence. Hence, at the time when both Garbo and Dietrich were branded 'box-office poison' (in 1938), Temple but also Sonja Henie became major stars. In this respect, as with the passing of silent stars such as Pola Negri, 'failure' can also be recast as resistance.[25] A similar case can be made for the link between the triumph of Schwarzenegger, Van

Damme, Lundgren and Hauer (and in a different register Banderas) in the last twenty years or so and the dominance of action movies. The fact that the most popular major European stars of the 1930s and 1940s were people like Garbo, Chevalier, Grant, Colman, Dietrich, Boyer and Olivier, while those of the 1980s onwards are the 'muscle-men', echoes the shift from 'soft' romantic comedies and melodramas to the testosterone-filled genres that form an important part of Hollywood production today. Although it would be dangerous to fall within a reflectionist approach, it may also be possible to read the fate of European stars in Hollywood in terms of larger geopolitical and cultural trends – hence the tendency to cast British actors as villains may be read in terms of the relationship between Britain and the USA, while the success of a star like Banderas relates to the prominence of 'Latino' culture (in music, for instance) and social shifts in the American population.

The actors in this book all in their own way helped American cinema create myths of European national identities and histories, which it then sold back to these countries (and the rest of the world), with more or less success. In the bargain, historical distortion may or may not have balanced the added glamour conferred by Hollywood, but for these actors the 'journey of desire' was always bound up with the myth of reinventing oneself and the desire for global exposure.

Notes

1. Quoted in Toby Miller, Nitin Govil, John McMurria and Richard Maxwell, *Global Hollywood* (London: BFI, 2001), p. 1.
2. We are aware that it would be utopian to hope for a truly exhaustive guide. For one thing, such a dictionary remains a living piece of work: as we write, new European actors appear in countless Hollywood productions. For another, many obscure players, who are often uncredited, are extremely difficult to trace and thus document.
3. Bertholt Brecht, 'Hollywood Elegies', quoted in Aljean Harmetz, 'The Refugee Trail', in *Round up the Usual Suspects: The Making of 'Casablanca' – Bogart, Bergman, and World War II* (London: Weidenfeld & Nicolson, 1993), p. 218.
4. A film like *Lara Croft Tomb Raider: The Cradle of Life* (2003), however, which starred Til Schweiger, was a co-production between five nations, with only 20 per cent US production funding, and so it has not been included in Schweiger's Hollywood filmography.
5. Miriam Hansen, 'The Mass Production of the Senses: Classical Cinema as Vernacular Modernism', in Christine Gledhill and Linda Williams (eds), *Reinventing Film Studies* (London: Arnold, 2000), p. 337.
6. Ruth Vasey, *The World According to Hollywood, 1918–1939* (Exeter University: Exeter Press, 1997), p. 164.
7. Jon Burrows, national entry for UK in this volume (author's italics).
8. Quoted in Saverio Giovacchini, *Hollywood Modernism. Film and Politics in the Age of the New Deal* (Philadelphia: Temple University Press, 2001), p. 9.
9. Vasey, *The World According to Hollywood*, p. 225.
10. Burrows, national entry for UK.
11. The list of European émigré actors who went to Hollywood but only appeared in non-English-speaking multi-language version films, or who participated in US-financed multi-language versions shot in Europe – for instance in the Paramount studios in Joinville near Paris – includes such names as Marcel André, Catalina Bárcena, André Berley, Luisa Caselotti, Ana María Custodio, Rosita Díaz Gimeno, Pierre Etchepare, Gustav Fröhlich, Karl Etlinger, Jeanne Helbling, Georges Mauloy, Danièle Parola, Julia Serda, Yvonne Vallée and Geymond Vital.
12. Thomas Guback, 'Hollywood's International Market', in Tino Balio (ed.), *The American Film Industry* (Madison: University of Wisconsin Press, 1976), p. 400.
13. See Sarah Street, *Transatlantic Crossings: British Feature Films in the USA* (London and New York: Continuum, 2002), p. 169.
14. Tim Bergfelder 'The Nation Vanishes: European Co-Productions and Popular Genre Formulae in the 1950s and

1960s', in Mette Hjort and Scott Mackenzie (eds), *Cinema & Nation* (London and New York: Routledge, 2000), p. 141.

15. Miller *et al.*, *Global Hollywood*, p. 59.

16. Lotte Palfi-Andor, 'Memoiren einer unbekannten Schauspielerin', in Erich Leyens and Lotte Palfi-Andor, *Die fremden Jahre: Erinnerungen an Deutschland* (Frankfurt am Main: Fischer, 1994), p. 90 (originally in German).

17. Quoted in Harmetz, 'The Refugee Trail', in *Round up the Usual Suspects*, p. 212.

18. Ruth Barton, national entry for Ireland in this volume.

19. Dina Iordanova, national entry for the former Yugoslavia in this volume.

20. Sonja de Leeuw, entry for Rutger Hauer in this volume.

21. As discussed by Richard Dyer in *White* (London and New York: Routledge, 1997).

22. Jack G. Shaheen, 'Reel Bad Arabs', in *How Hollywood Vilifies a People* (New York: Olive Branch Press, 2001), p. 2.

23. Diane Negra, *Off-White Hollywood: American Culture and Ethnic Female Stardom* (London and New York: Routledge, 2001).

24. Dina Iordanova, national entry for the former Yugoslavia.

25. See Diane Negra's discussion of Pola Negri in *Off-White Hollywood*, pp. 55-83.

Part II European Actors and the Hollywood Film Industry

1 The Long Fade

French Actors in Silent Hollywood

Richard Abel

'Bernhardt Now Partly American.' So read the headline in a small piece in *Moving Picture World*, on 25 December 1915.[1] Not that Sarah Bernhardt★ had come to the USA to act in an American film production or even taken up residence. No, she simply had added a new artificial leg, 'an American model of 1915', to her collection of two dozen; and, supposedly, she had worn it in Paris during the shooting of *Jeanne Doré* (1915), Louis Mercanton's adaptation of a Tristan Bernard stage play, which Universal was then releasing in the USA.[2] If the headline turned Bernhardt's new limb into a joke at French expense, a Christmas present little better than a stocking filler, that joke also suggests why, during the era of silent cinema, so few French actors did emigrate and assimilate, or at least become accepted as 'partly American', even during World War I. A handful were lured across the Atlantic, to be sure, including stars such as Max Linder★ and later Ivan Mosjoukine★ (a Russian actor who worked in the Parisian studios), but none was ever all that popular or successful, particularly in contrast to émigré film-makers such as Maurice Tourneur, Albert Capellani and Léonce Perret. The reconstruction Bernhardt underwent obviously was far too radical for others; besides, she already was 'partly American', having performed for years on American stages before briefly reigning as a movie star – and suffering involuntary dismemberment. Moreover, what other forms of reconstruction did succeed forced actors to fit themselves to one of several 'foreign' stereotypes acceptable to Americans.

In the late nineteenth century, the USA was a mecca for European stage artists, and not only the East Coast metropolises of New York, Boston and Philadelphia. Supported by an extensive transcontinental and regional railroad system, the westward progression of expanding settlements in the Midwest and West led to a boom in theatre construction and a flourishing circuit of touring theatrical performances – as it would lead later to the spread of nickelodeons.[3] The classics of European culture were especially in demand, including the historical dramas of French playwright Victorien Sardou, and who better to perform them than French stars such as Bernhardt and Gabrielle Réjane? Between 1880 and 1901, Bernhardt made five American tours of legitimate theatres, repeatedly playing the 'modern Magdalene', Marguerite Gautier, in *Camille* and a series of femmes fatales in Sardou's *Theodora*, *Cleopatra* and *La Tosca*.[4] Réjane visited in 1895 and then again in 1904, acting not only in *Camille* but performing her signature title role in *Madame Sans-Gêne*.[5] For her sixth tour (1905–6), Bernhardt gambled on reaching a much larger mass audience by presenting 'high points' of her famous stage roles in vaudeville houses and tent shows throughout the South, West and Midwest.[6] So profitable were these shows and so beneficial to her status as a celebrity that, despite her advancing age and infirmity, Bernhardt agreed to do three more tours of theatres and vaudeville houses throughout 1918. Foreign acts such as that of the French music-hall singer Yvette Guilbert already had been exploited by vaudeville promoters for their 'artistic' and/or 'exotic' appeal before Bernhardt appeared, but her ability

Terry Ramsaye thought that 'Max came across, but he did not go over'. Despite elusive success, Max Linder for a while lived up to his stylish standards in Hollywood

to draw crowds prompted them to engage other French performers such as the pantomime artists Séverin and Pilar-Morin★, who also proved popular.[7] All these invitations to 'foreign invasion' helped to set up favourable conditions for French film actors as well, but not for long.

The early review discourse on moving pictures in the US trade press generally admired the performers in French films that so dominated exhibition, at least up to 1909. In a survey of film manufacturers in late 1908, for instance, the *New York Dramatic Mirror* noted how French performers were much more adept than their American counterparts 'in talking with their hands, their shoulders, their bodies, and their facial expressions'; Pathé-Frères players in particular – who, although still unnamed, were 'readily recognized' and had 'become favorites with habitual patrons' – were said to excel in 'superior pantomime'.[8] Such praise was also lavished on the initial Film d'Art and SCAGL films distributed by Pathé, prompting the *Mirror* to claim that their performances achieved 'the same quality . . . that we see in Broadway theatres', and *Moving Picture World* to report this outburst from a spectator at the finish of *La Tosca* (1909): 'What acting!'[9] This attitude evidently led Edison to hire Pilar-Morin, in the autumn of 1909, according to Richard deCordova, as 'the star member of the Edison stock company'.[10] The *World* made much of this contract between an American firm and a celebrated French stage performer, publishing her article on pantomime in screen acting as an authoritative text and predicting that her appearances would help to establish a 'star system' in moving pictures.[11] At least one of the half-dozen special releases in which she starred, *Comedy and Tragedy*, was ranked by the *Mirror*, in late 1909, as 'one of the few film classics of the year'.[12] Yet six months later, the same trade weekly had decided that Pilar-Morin's pantomime in *The Piece of Lace* – however 'graceful . . . polished and expressive' – was too closely tied to the theatre – that is, expressed too often 'directly to the spectators (otherwise the camera)' – and had 'no place in picture playing'.[13] For the star system that did soon develop would accept only American actors and depend on a more 'naturalistic' kind of acting.[14]

This was only one of several complaints that became attached to French film actors and now began to compromise their success in the USA, but it was enough to end Pilar-Morin's American screen career. Another accusation, just as serious, was that French actors appeared in far too many films judged to be unsavoury or immoral according to American tastes, from gross comedies and farces to sensational crime thrillers – from Éclair's *The Auto Bandits of Paris* (1912) to Gaumont's *Fantômas* (1913), the latter of which tended either to be dismissed or condemned after widespread newspaper reports of the capture and execution of Bonnot and his gang of automobile thieves in early 1912.[15] Consequently, all three of the French companies (Pathé, Éclair, Gaumont/Solax) that organised production units and even built studios in the USA between 1910 and 1912 made sure that the subjects of their American films suited American tastes. Equally important, none of them imported French actors to perform in those films. Some studio heads (Louis Gasnier, Alice Guy Blaché), production managers (Emile Chautard), directors (Etienne Arnaud, Emile Cohl), cameramen (Lucien Andriot, René Guissart, Georges Benoit) and set designers (Henri Ménessier, Ben Carré) may have been French,[16] but *actors* had to be American – that is, as 'clean, good-looking' and youthful as the 'Anglo-Saxon models' in mass magazine ads.[17]

The one exception, if only 'part-ly' so, was Bernhardt's starring performance in *Les Amours de la Reine Elisabeth/Queen Elizabeth* (1912). Although shot in London with a French and British cast and crew (directed by Louis Mercanton and Henri Desfontaines), the film was released in the USA as the product of a new firm, Famous Players, which had purchased exclusive rights to its distribution.[18] Concealing its origins, but not its alleged 'historical accuracy', Famous Players implicitly promoted *Queen Elizabeth* as an American film, perhaps the first to run more than three reels in length.[19] Accentuated by 'superb' acting, according to most critics,[20] Bernhardt's celebrity status turned the film into a blockbuster that circulated widely, after opening in August 1912, with late or return engagements running into the winter of 1913 – which in turn promoted her eighth American tour that spring. *Queen Elizabeth*'s box-office success not only confirmed the new company's viability as a major player in the US industry but it helped to create a market, in legitimate theatres no less, for feature-length historical spectacle films.

Perhaps the best director of such films in France, before the outbreak of the Great War in 1914, was Albert Capellani, who headed SCAGL, where his younger brother Paul Capellani★ also worked as a leading actor, yet always in the shadow of Henry Krauss.[21] That several of his historical films, including *Les Mystères de Paris/ The Mysteries of Paris* (1911) and *Les Misérables* (1911), had been quite successful in the USA probably led Albert to accept an offer in early 1915 to work as a director for World Film, which, after assuming control of Éclair's East Coast studio earlier that year, was already releasing profitable and acclaimed films made by other French émigrés: directors Chautard and Tourneur and set designer Ménessier.[22] Paul soon joined his brother and continued acting, first at World Film and then at Lewis J. Selznick Productions, where Albert followed Clara Kimball Young to be her principal director. Paul's most notable appearances were as Kimball Young's co-star in *Camille* (1915) and then as Alice Brady's co-star in *La Vie de Bohème* (1916), both revised and expanded remakes of SCAGL productions that the two brothers had completed several years before.[23] Along with Ménessier, Albert would soon go on to join Metro and, at its West Coast studio, direct Alla Nazimova★ in a series of major productions, including *Out of the Fog* (1919) and, most memorably, *The Red Lantern* (1919).[24] Paul, by contrast, failed to get another leading role in Hollywood and, after the war, returned to France to resume his career as a character actor in such films as Marcel L'Herbier's *Le Carnaval des vérités* (1920) and Mercanton's *Phroso* (1922). The diverging paths taken by the brothers in the American film industry was emblematic of what kinds of French artists and artisans (from the prewar generation, at least) could be accepted and assimilated and what could not.

The experience of France's most celebrated comic star, Max Linder★, was even more disappointing. As early as 1910, the *New York Morning Telegraph* had called Linder 'the famous comedian who for years has made such a hit all over America', and titles in his *Max* series often received special attention on cinema programmes across the country throughout 1914.[25] A combination of severe illness (exacerbated by voluntary service during the war) and of restricted production conditions in France led Linder, in the autumn of 1916, to accept what seemed a generous offer from Essanay to come to the USA to resume his film-making career.[26] His contract called for one two-reel comedy per month, and Linder finished two – *Max Comes Across* and *Max Wants a Divorce* – in Chicago during several harsh winter months and completed a third – *Max in a Taxi* – in Los Angeles the following spring, before bronchial pneumonia forced him to abandon his plans for others and finally return to a sanatorium in Switzerland in order to recover his health.[27] Illness alone may have compromised Linder's Hollywood career, but there were plenty of other reasons for his lack of success. For one thing, Essanay had just lost Charlie Chaplin★ to Mutual, and the company promoted Linder not simply as a rival but as a successor (the two actually admired one another and became friends), setting up expectations that were impossible to fulfil.[28] For another, writes Jean Mitry, Linder found it difficult to adapt his improvisational methods, rooted in the relatively 'open' practices of prewar French film-making, to the strictly organised system of American production.[29] Perhaps most telling, however, was the public's lukewarm response to the films. The trade press certainly did its part in promoting all three titles,[30] but none matched the level of achievement that marked the earlier *Max* series; and they paled in comparison not only to Chaplin's Mutual comedies but to those starring Douglas Fairbanks, Mabel Normand, Harold Lloyd and Roscoe 'Fatty' Arbuckle (now joined by the young Buster Keaton).[31] In a sense, Linder's experience paralleled and even exceeded that of Pilar-Morin, prompting Terry Ramsaye's later infamous line, 'Max came across, but he did not go over.'[32]

The only other French actors to enjoy a modicum of success during or just after the war, interestingly, owed a partial debt to Bernhardt. Léon Bary★, for instance, had played Armand Duval to Bernhardt's Camille during her 1910–11 American tour, and that well-known role, along with his French acting experience with Pathé later in

France, won him a contract with Pathé-Exchange when he returned to the USA in 1915.[33] Bary became a familiar figure, always in secondary parts, in the company's popular serials (some starring Pearl White), most notably as the traitorous Ravengar in *The Shielding Shadow* (1916). His most important role, however, came after the war, as Athos in Fairbanks' *The Three Musketeers* (1921), which he was then asked to reprise in the actor's swashbuckling swansong, *The Iron Mask* (1929). Much like Capellani, Bary would eventually return to France and content himself with playing secondary film roles throughout the 1930s and 1940s. The Bernhardt connection also proved fortuitous for the much younger Gaston Glass★, who, after performing in the actress's last American tour in 1917–18, decided to take his chances in Hollywood.[34] Glass appeared in more than fifty films between 1920 and 1929, among them a version of *Monte Cristo* (1922) and Gasnier's adaptation of the patriotic *The Hero* (1923). Although his acting career extended into the 1930s, Glass would later find even greater success heading Fox's make-up department and finally serving as a television production manager.

Once the war ended in 1918, a dozen French producers and film-makers took advantage of the open seas to visit American studios in New York and Los Angeles in order to study the latest methods and techniques of film production.[35] Two of them, Marcel Vandal and Charles Delac, even came back with Fannie Ward (the star of Cecil B. DeMille's *The Cheat* [1915]), who agreed to appear in several Film d'Art productions that they hoped would make French films saleable once more on the US market (during the war they had been largely absent) – but their plans proved to be a pipe dream.[36] Despite his earlier disillusionment, even Linder could not escape Hollywood's lure. After a long convalescence in Switzerland, Linder had agreed to star in a feature-length comedy, *Le Petit café* (1919), adapted from Tristan Bernard's most popular boulevard play.[37] Although the film proved unexpectedly successful in Europe, the producer, Henri Diamant-Berger, was unable to export it to the USA, as planned, and Linder again found it difficult to secure financing for film projects. Counting on friends in Hollywood (including probably Chaplin), the French comic returned to the USA in 1920 and set up his own company in Los Angeles to produce, direct and star in feature-length comedies that would be distributed through, first, Robertson-Cole and, then, United Artists.[38] Although he risked much of his own money in this venture, the first two films, *Be My Wife* (1921) and *Seven Years Bad Luck* (1921), proved profitable enough that Linder could mount a more lavish production, using sets left over from *The Three Musketeers*.[39] Not only did Max finally 'go over' with *The Three Must-Get-Theres* (1922), at least with critics, but the film 'burlesqued' the Fairbanks spectacle and his persona in much the same way as the American star himself had mocked genre heroes earlier in his film career.[40] Unfortunately, however, the film fared poorly at the box office, and Linder returned to France once more, only to run into more difficulties – now with tragic consequences – in trying to resume his film career.[41]

As American companies consolidated their dominance of the market in Europe in the early 1920s, a number of aspiring French actors were attracted to Hollywood.[42] Most of these, revealingly, were young women whose success depended on their appeal as 'exotic', often threatening figures. A dancer on stages in Paris, London and New York, Renée Adorée★ (Renée de la Fonte) appeared in a range of films, from Buster Keaton's *Day Dreams* (1922) to *Monte Cristo* (opposite Glass), until she landed major roles, with MGM, in King Vidor's *The Big Parade* (1925) and *La Bohème* (1926).[43] Most typical perhaps was her Chinese 'vamp' in *Mr Wu* (1927). Unable to sustain a theatrical career in Paris, Paulette Duval★ also became a dancer in New York, before Sidney Olcott signed her, again with MGM, to play opposite Rudolph Valentino in *Monsieur Beaucaire* (1924).[44] Her best films included Victor Sjöström's *He Who Gets Slapped* (1924) and *The Divine Woman* (1928). Throughout her Hollywood career, studios typecast Duval as a 'pernicious creature who broke up couples, destroyed homes, ruined men, and made mothers and children weep'. Even Louise Lagrange★, one of the earliest arrivals in Hollywood in 1919, played minor roles (against her husband's wishes) before returning to France to star in several hit films directed by Léonce Perret in the late 1920s, winning the title 'Princess of the French cinema'.[45] Perhaps the most intriguing of these women was Jetta Goudal★, who briefly acted on Broadway before making several films with Olcott, most notably *Salome of the Ten-*

ements (1925).[46] Known principally for her cool femme fatale roles and promoted as 'the girl with the inscrutable face and the expressive hands', Goudal signed a contract with DeMille just as he was embarking on independent production. After appearing in *The Road to Yesterday* (1925) and several other films, she quarrelled with the film-maker and, at great risk, sued his company for violating a contractual clause – and won in court, establishing a precedent for screen actors. Although Goudal made several more films in the late 1920s, her interest turned to costuming, set design and home decoration, which became her profession in the 1930s.

Interestingly, besides Bary and Glass, few male French actors were lured to Hollywood during the 1920s. An exception was Charles de Rochefort★, who had starred in a number of major French films after the war, including André Antoine's *L'Arlésienne* (1921).[47] That his athletic physique surprised the American film industry, where he was called the 'French Adonis', suggests how strongly American notions of masculinity at the time worked to exclude the French as unfit. Yet he too was typecast in a half-dozen films either as a villain or an exotic 'other' – from a gypsy or Hindu prince to a pharaoh in DeMille's *The Ten Commandments* (1923). More acceptably masculine was former director Emile Chautard★, who revived his career as an actor in the late 1920s by fulfilling the stereotype of the distinguished elder Frenchman, with a distinctive moustache.[48] The actor who most suffered from American notions of what made a masculine hero was the Russian émigré actor, Ivan Mosjoukine, who had such a following among audiences and critics in his adopted country that he was 'partly French' by acclamation.[49] Several of his French films – for instance, *Michel Strogoff* (1926) – had been critically well received and moderately successful in the USA, and Universal tempted Mosjoukine to play a Russian officer in an adaptation of a Jewish stage play, *Lea Lyon*, long popular in Germany and Austria.[50] Years later, Edward Sloman reported that he found Mosjoukine 'quite pleasant to work with' on the resulting film, *Surrender* (1927), despite the latter's lack of English, and quick to follow his directorial instructions.[51] According to Juan Arroy, the Russian officer was intended to be a kind of Valentino figure; unfortunately, some critics found that Mosjoukine's 'pale romantic features' more closely resembled those of comic Larry Semon.[52] In a *New York Times* review, Mordaunt Hall simply dismissed him as 'by no means ingratiating, neither does he lend strength to the character'.[53] After this debacle, Mosjoukine worked briefly for Ufa in Germany, then returned to France, where his heavily accented French reduced his acting career to increasingly minor roles.

For nearly two decades prior to the advent of sound cinema, the USA and its film industry were rarely hospitable to French actors. From an American perspective, French films and performers briefly were welcomed, and even celebrated, during the period of the cinema's emergence; but once an indigenous industry arose to compete with and eclipse the French, its subjects and personnel (and especially actors) had to be defined clearly as 'American'. Even in the 1920s, when the US film industry had consolidated its worldwide dominance enough to begin 'buying' European talent, the demand was for directors and technicians more than actors. Moreover, those French actors who were lured to Hollywood, and were accepted, found they had to fit certain stereotypes of masculinity and femininity that usually made them less than American. From a French perspective, French actors thus experienced a kind of double bind – a strong attraction to the US industry, checked by an equally strong, and quite reasonable, hesitation and desire not to be subordinated into 'otherness'. It was a bind summed up rather neatly in the dual role that the French music-hall star Mistinguett plays in *Fleur de Paris* (1916).[54] There, as a music-hall actress, Mistinguett fulfils the dream of accepting, much like Bernhardt, an impresario's offer of a lucrative contract to tour the USA; but her decision amounts to an implicit 'betrayal' (heightened by the war) of her acting partner, who is left to fend for himself. In her second role as a poor dressmaker fascinated by the theatre, however, Mistinguett also eventually (after all, this is a melodrama) fulfils the dream of taking the actress's place on stage – winning her new partner's heart as well – and thus succeeds, in a double sense, 'at home'. From famous stars to those just aspiring to act in the movies, most French women and men would have to forgo the first dream, of becoming 'partly American' – even if not as physical as Bernhardt's, the reconstruc- **25** tion too often came at great cost — and settle for the latter, at least until the 1930s. Only then would the story of the small colony of French actors first established in the 1920s, freshly expanded with new recruits, have a happier ending.

Notes

1. 'Bernhardt Now Partly American', *Moving Picture World*, 25 December 1915, p. 2354.
2. See, for instance, the review of *Jeanne Doré* in the *New York Times*, 21 October 1915, p. 11.
3. See, for instance, the catalogue of the excellent exhibition organised at the New York Public Library, 6 April–7 July, 2001: Alice C. Hudson and Barbara Cohen-Stratyner, *Heading West / Touring West: Mapmakers, Performing Artists, and the American Frontier* (New York: New York Public Library, 2001).
4. Hamilton Mason, 'Introduction', in *French Theatre in New York: A List of Plays, 1899–1939* (New York: AMS Press, 1966 [1940]), pp. 21, 29–30; Susan A. Glenn, 'The Bernhardt Effect', in *Female Spectacle: The Theatrical Roots of Modern Feminism* (Cambridge, MA: Harvard University Press, 2000), pp. 10 and 17.
5. Mason, 'Introduction', pp. 21, 31.
6. Glenn, 'The Bernhardt Effect', pp. 17–18.
7. Douglas Gilbert, 'The Foreign Invasion', in *American Vaudeville: Its Life and Times* (New York: Dover, 1963), pp. 135–51. Richard Abel, *The Red Rooster Scare: Making Cinema American, 1900–1910* (Berkeley: University of California Press, 1999), pp. 129 and 147–8. See also the ads for Proctor's and Koster & Bial's in *New York Journal*, 1 April 1897, p. 7; 4 April 1897, p. 61; and 4 December 1898, p. 34.
8. 'Earmarks of Makers', *New York Dramatic Mirror*, 14 November 1908, p. 10.
9. 'Spectator's Comments', *New York Dramatic Mirror*, 22 May 1909, p. 17; 'Notable Film of the Week', *Moving Picture World*, 19 June 1909, p. 832.
10. Richard deCordova, *Picture Personalities: The Emergence of the Star System in America* (Urbana: University of Illinois Press, 1990), p. 43.
11. Mlle Pilar-Morin, 'The Value of Silent Drama; or, Pantomime in Acting', *Moving Picture World*, 13 November 1909, p. 682; Lux Graphicus, 'On the Screen', *Moving Picture World*, 5 February 1910, p. 167.
12. 'Licensed Reviews', *New York Dramatic Mirror*, 13 November 1909, p. 15.
13. 'Reviews of Licensed Films', *New York Dramatic Mirror*, 11 June 1910, p. 20. Other titles in which Pilar-Morin appeared included *The Cigarette Maker of Seville* (May 1910), *From Tyranny to Liberty* (August 1910) and *The Key to Life* (November 1910).
14. As deCordova points out, Pilar-Morin was also much older than the young actors at Edison and other companies who would become American stars: for instance, Mary Fuller (Edison), Florence Lawrence (Biograph/Imp/Victor), Florence Turner (Vitagraph), Mary Pickford (Biograph/ Majestic), Kathlyn Williams (Selig). DeCordova, *Picture Personalities*, pp. 51–2.
15. See, for instance, 'Auto Bandits Terrorize Paris, Rivaling the Exploits of Most Notorious Westerners', *Des Moines News*, 13 April 1912, p. 4; 'The Phantom Bandits: Paris, Ever the Home of the Unusual, Furnishes the World Its Very First Automobile Ghost Story', *San Francisco Sunday Chronicle*, 21 April 1912, Magazine Section 2; and Maurice LeBlanc, 'Bonnot, Tiger Bandit', *Cleveland Sunday Leader*, 12 May 1912, C1-2. For a more extensive analysis of this changing attitude towards French films, see Abel, *The Red Rooster Scare* and Abel, 'The "Culture War" of Sensational Melodrama, 1911–1914', in Yvonne Tasker (ed.), *Action and Adventure Cinema* (London and New York: Routledge, 2004).
16. For good synopses of these and several other French figures, see Dominique Lebrun, *Paris-Hollywood: les Français dans le cinéma américain* (Paris: Hazan, 1987), pp. 20–51.

17. See, for instance, 'What Is an American Subject?', *Moving Picture World*, 12 February 1910, p. 206. See also T. J. Jackson Lears, 'American Advertising and the Reconstruction of the Body, 1880–1930', in Kathryn Grover (ed.), *Fitness in American Culture: Images of Health, Sports, and the Body, 1830–1940* (Amherst: University of Massachusetts Press, 1989), pp. 47–66.

18. See, for instance, Richard Abel, *The Ciné Goes to Town: French Cinema, 1896–1914* (Berkeley: University of California Press, 1994), p. 315; and Michael Quinn, 'Distribution, the Transient Audience, and the Transition to the Feature Film', *Cinema Journal* vol. 40 no. 2 (2001), p. 48.

19. See the Famous Player ads in *Moving Picture World*, 27 July 1912, p. 311; 3 August 1911, p. 411; and 17 August 1912, p. 679. George Kleine promoted *Quo Vadis?* in much the same way in the summer and autumn of 1913.

20. See, for instance, 'Bernhardt as Queen Elizabeth', *New York Dramatic Mirror*, 17 July 1912, p. 31; and W. Stephen Bush, 'Queen Elizabeth', *Moving Picture World*, 3 August 1912, p. 428.

21. 'Les Collaborateurs de Pathé-Frères: M. Paul Capellani', from *Bulletin Hebdomadaire Pathé-Frères* (1912), reprinted in Henri Bousquet, *Catalogue Pathé des années 1896 à 1914: 1910–1911* (Bassac: Henri Bousquet, 1994), n. p.

22. *Les Misérables*, for instance, had a twelve-week exclusive run at the Tremont Temple Theatre in Boston, from early September to the middle of November in 1913. 'Emile Chautard', *Moving Picture World*, 6 March 1915, p. 1460; 'Albert Capellani', *Moving Picture World*, 24 April 1915, p. 541; 'World Offers Strong Program', *Moving Picture World*, 15 January 1916, p. 401; and 'Emile Chautard', *Moving Picture World*, 27 May 1916, p. 1500. See also, Léon Barsacq, *Caligari's Cabinet and Other Grand Illusions: A History of Film Design* [revised and edited by Elliott Stein] (Boston: New York Graphic Society, 1976), p. 227.

23. See, for instance, the World Film ad in *Moving Picture World*, 24 June 1916, p. 2185. See also *The American Film Institute Catalog: Feature Films, 1911–1920* (Berkeley: University of California Press, p. 1988).

24. See, for instance, 'Nazimova Will Lead Metro's Exodus', *Moving Picture World*, 19 October 1918, p. 390; '*The Red Lantern*', *Moving Picture World*, 10 May 1919, p. 933; and the reviews of each film in *The New York Times*, 10 February 1919, p. 11, and 5 May 1919, p. 11.

25. 'Interesting Notes from the Field', *New York Morning Telegraph*, 13 March 1910, 4.1, p. 4. See also 'Pathé Pointers', *Film Index*, 19 March 1910, p. 7; 'Reviews of Licensed Films', *New York Dramatic Mirror*, 14 May 1910, p. 20; and 'The Popular Max Linder', *New York Dramatic Mirror*, 30 July 1910, p. 25.

26. See, for instance, 'Max Linder, Celebrated Comedian, Is Due', *Moving Picture World*, 18 November 1916, p. 987; and 'Max Linder Now With Us', *Moving Picture World*, 25 November 1916, p. 1144.

27. Jean Mitry, 'Max Linder', *Anthologie du cinéma* II (Paris: L'Avant-Scène/CIB, 1967), pp. 306–8. See also 'Linder Finishing First Comedy', *Moving Picture World*, 13 January 1917, p. 211; and 'Linder Finishes First Comedy', *Moving Picture World*, 20 January 1917, p. 353.

28. In his account of the French comic's career, Jack Spears emphasises the disagreements between Linder and George Spoor, who headed Essanay. Spears, 'Max Linder', *Films in Review* vol. 16. no. 2 (May 1965), pp. 283–4.

29. Mitry, 'Max Linder', p. 308.

30. See, for instance, James McQuade, 'Max Comes Across', *Moving Picture World*, 24 February 1917, p. 1207; Edward Weitzel, 'Max Wants a Divorce', *Moving Picture World*, 7 April 1917, p. 115; and Hanford C. Judson, 'Max in a Taxi', *Moving Picture World*, 5 May 1917, p. 811.

31. Compare the reviews of *Max Comes Over* and of the first film produced by Fairbanks' own company, *In Again, Out Again*, respectively, in *The New York Times*, 19 February 1917, p. 9; and 23 April 1917, p. 7.

32. Terry Ramsaye, *A Million and One Nights: A History of the Motion Picture through 1925* (New York: Simon & Schuster, 1926), p. 738.

33. See Lebrun, *Paris-Hollywood*, pp. 54–5. Although not technically French, Lou Tellegen*, another actor who played

opposite Bernhardt in the early 1910s (most notably in *Queen Elizabeth*), could be mentioned here, since he gained some success, in the late 1910s and early 1920s, as co-star with Geraldine Ferrar, to whom he was married for a short time – see, for instance, Dominique Lebrun, *Trans Europe Hollywood: les Européens du cinéma américan* (Paris: Bordas, 1992), p. 46.

34. See Lebrun, *Paris-Hollywood*, pp. 56–7.

35. They included producers such as Henri Diamant-Berger, Marcel Vandal and Charles Delac, and film-makers such as Abel Gance, Germaine Dulac and Jacques de Baroncelli.

36. See, for instance, Richard Abel, *French Cinema: The First Wave, 1915–1929* (Princeton, NJ: Princeton University Press, 1984), p. 16.

37. Ibid., pp. 223–4.

38. Spears, 'Max Linder', pp. 285, 288; and Mitry, 'Max Linder', p. 309.

39. Mitry, 'Max Linder', pp. 309–10.

40. See, for instance, the review in *The New York Times*, 28 August 1922, p. 14.

41. Spears, 'Max Linder', p. 289. Linder would make only two more films in France – *Au Secours!* (1923), co-directed with Abel Gance, and *Le Roi du cirque* (1925), shot in Vienna – before committing suicide with his young wife, Hélène Peters, in Paris, on 31 October 1925.

42. As one sign of that dominance, in 1921, the new French trade journal *Cinémagazine* sent its own correspondent, Robert Florey (a former assistant to Louis Feuillade), to Hollywood to report directly on the American film industry. The majority of European talent co-opted by the American film industry, of course, came from northern Europe, and most were film-makers: from Germany, Ernst Lubitsch, F. W. Murnau, Paul Leni and, briefly, Erich Pommer; from Sweden, Victor Sjöström and Mauritz Stiller. French film-maker Jacques Feyder was an exception, hired by MGM late in the decade to direct Greta Garbo★ in *The Kiss* (1928). Feyder was not the only Frenchman involved in *The Kiss*, as Richard Becherer has discovered: in designing the sets for Garbo's house in the film, Cedric Gibbons drew heavily on architect Robert Mallet-Stevens' own house in Paris. See Becherer, 'Picturing Architecture Otherwise: The Voguing of the Maison Mallet-Stevens', *Art History* vol. 23 no. 4 (November 2000), pp. 559–98.

43. See Lebrun, *Paris-Hollywood*, pp. 84–5.

44. See Lebrun, *Paris-Hollywood*, pp. 76–7.

45. Lagrange's husband was the producer-director William Elliott, who demanded that she sacrifice her career to raise their children; she left him to return to France in 1926. See René Jeanne and Charles Ford, *Histoire encyclopédique du cinéma 1: le cinéma français, 1895–1929* (Paris: Robert Laffont, 1947), pp. 460–1; and Lebrun, *Paris-Hollywood*, pp. 82–3. Arlette Marchal★, who befriended Gloria Swanson on the set of Perret's *Madame Sans-Gêne* (1925) in France and was convinced to come to Hollywood, also sacrificed her brief acting career to her husband, director Marcel de Sano. See Lebrun, *Paris-Hollywood*, pp. 80–1.

46. See Lebrun, *Paris-Hollywood*, pp. 72–3.

47. See Jeanne and Ford, *Histoire encyclopédique du cinéma 1* pp. 564–5; and Lebrun, *Paris-Hollywood*, pp. 86–7.

48. See Lebrun, *Paris-Hollywood*, pp. 26–7.

49. For good studies of Mosjoukine's career in France, see Jean Mitry, 'Ivan Mosjoukine', *Anthologie du cinéma* no. 48 (October 1969); and François Albera, *Albatros: des Russes à Paris, 1919–1929* (Paris: La Cinémathèque française/Mazzoti, 1995), pp. 113–31.

50. Kevin Brownlow, 'The Lost Work of Edward Sloman', *The Parade's Gone By* (New York: Knopf, 1968), pp. 178, 185.

28 51. Ibid., p. 185. For further details on Mosjoukine, see Natalia Noussinova's chapter in this volume [editors' note].

52. Juan Arroy, *Ivan Mosjoukine* (Paris: Publications Jean Pascal, 1927), cited in Albera, *Albatros*, p. 114, fn. 10. See also David Robinson, *Hollywood in the Twenties* (New York: Paperback Library, 1970), p. 89.
53. Mordaunt Hall, 'The Screen', *The New York Times*, 11 October 1927, p. 27.
54. For an analysis of *Fleur de Paris*, see Richard Abel, 'Peak Practice', *Sight and Sound* vol. 11 no. 5 (May 2001), p. 26. Mistinguett herself did not tour the USA until after the war. Andrea Stuart, 'Mistinguett – Beginnings', *Showgirls* (London: Jonathan Cape, 1996), p. 42.

The Last Command (1928): von Sternberg 'turned a historical drama into a "film about film", in which former heroes and fighters on both sides of the Revolution clashed as extras on a film set'

2 Russian Film Extras in 1920s Hollywood

Rashit M. Yangirov

The Russian presence in Hollywood involved a few notable film stars, such as Alla Nazimova* and Ivan Mosjoukine*,[1] but also many other types of film personnel. Studio owners in the 1920s in particular came to acknowledge the importance of film extras, and associate them with Russian émigrés. This exotic business became a characteristic of 'Russia Abroad', alongside balalaïka players and taxi drivers. Fleeing the Soviet (Bolshevist) Revolution, Russians filled the studios of Berlin and Paris, working as extras, while some of them flocked to Hollywood.[2] This enduring trend was ignored by Western observers and later by most film historians, but it was frequently discussed in the contemporary Russian émigré press. Within a few years this phenomenon had produced its own curious legend concerning the Revolutionary leader Leon Trotsky, who, having emigrated to the USA in the years preceding the Revolution, reputedly earned money there as a film extra. In 1932, when he was expelled from the USSR, a Russian magazine even published a still from Emil Wester's spy melodrama *My Official Wife* (1914) featuring a performer who looked like Trotsky.[3] Later this 'fact' became part of film history, until it was disproved by Kevin Brownlow.[4]

As an ethnic group, Russians entered the American film industry around 1923–4. By 1927 their number reached the significant figure of 1,000.[5] Alongside professional technicians and performers were people from other walks of life, including cinema fans who were eager to try their luck in the movie business. Following international trends, Hollywood producers at the time took a great interest in Russia and Russian subjects and these appeared in dozens of films from a variety of angles. These films' artistic value and faithfulness to Russian realities were often in dispute.[6] The émigré community especially objected to the artificiality and lack of plausibility of these supposedly 'Russian' film plots and 'Russian' characters. On the other hand, the fashion for Russia was considered by some as a good business opportunity, one that created a demand for numerous technicians, experts and performers, including, of course, extras – the subject of this chapter.

At the beginning of the Russian 'invasion' of Hollywood, an observer reviewed the position of his compatriots who worked as extras. Generally, this 'army' was divided into several groups. The lowest one consisted of so-called 'atmospheres'. It is worth quoting at length St Kurtz, a Hollywood reporter for *Ekran* (a Russian film magazine published in Berlin), on the conditions operating at the time:

> For a day of filming which may take 24 hours, they earn from $5 to $7.50. Shooting starts at 8am. But when it finishes depends completely on the director's patience. [. . .] A film extra's monthly salary is not enough even if he works 15 or in the best cases 20 days, due to the high cost of living in California. They can't struggle for their rights or form trade unions. One attempt to do so was called bolshevism by 'democratic' America and suppressed without mercy, as is common in American business. Some of those film extras are involved in difficult and risky stunts but nobody cares about the frequent accidents among them, if they occur. If the elephants at Universal crush three people today, tomorrow they will be replaced by another 3,000.
>
> So called 'extra works', who are similar to 'dress-coat' extras in Europe, have a more privileged position. They earn $15–20 a day, although they are not free from numerous humiliations. These start from the very moment when they are hired. The film director orders the 'casting director' to assemble several hundreds of extras by a certain time. They are called to the studio and wait there, already dressed and with make-up. The director selects the necessary persons and all the rest may go away without any payment for this call. [. . .] Bribery is widespread. They bribe with money, tobacco or prohibited spirits. New female extras cannot avoid importunate courting from film assistants, as is also widespread in 'rotten' Europe.[7]

Throughout the 1920s, the number of Hollywood extras remained more or less stable and normally only 1,500 of them had jobs on a daily basis. We know that during those years several calculations were made by the local labour exchange. In 1929, unofficial research was undertaken in order to find out the average employment figures. These were based on the polling of the 17,541 officially registered extras, but observers estimated the real figure to be twice this amount. The calculations demonstrated that Russians made up no more than 10 per cent of the total number of film extras as was estimated in 1929.[8]

Who were these people and what was their background? In one Russian reviewer's opinion nearly all of them were

'Has-beens': former public and political men, former generals and senior officers, former journalists, writers, counts, barons, princes, doctors, judges, lawyers, businessmen, industrialists, actors [. . .]. And now they are only extras . . . that is to say 'rubbish', with whom the masters, the 'film directors' do not stand on ceremony . . . The directors boss them around, roughly and arrogantly shout at them, demonstrating their power and superiority [. . .]. One has to see this with one's own eyes to stay forever away from the film studios, where salaries are occasional, scant and are earned by hard work under burning projectors.[9]

The most notable Hollywood Russians were former military men, such as generals Alexander Ikonnikov (1884–1936), Michael Pleshkoff, Vyacheslav Savitsky (1880–1963) and Nickolas Konovaloff. There was also Fyodor Lodyzhensky, who later became famous when he appeared in James Flood's *Shanghai* (1935). After shooting one of the scenes, the director told him: 'General, You are an excellent actor. Your tears enrich the sincerity of the whole piece.' The extra answered: 'These were not stage tears, I was really crying as I remembered the distant past, which, like many other Russian émigrés, it upsets me to see on film once again.'[10] There was also the very popular group of fifty Cossacks from the Don. They were often used as 'atmospheres', but they also performed various riding stunts or were used as military experts and advisers.[11] Alexander Ikonnikov was the most successful in this category: by the end of the 1920s he became a staff adviser at the Paramount studio with a weekly salary of $150.

Contemporaries were fascinated by the film career of Serge Temoff (born Sergei Utemov; 1901–1995), who came from a small, remote Siberian village. At the age of seventeen he enlisted in the White Army of Admiral Kolchak. After the army was defeated, his detachment was evacuated to Harbin, China (originally a Russian city), where he trained as a ballet dancer. In 1923, the young Russian found himself in Seattle, where he tried various professions, but finally managed to get into Hollywood. Like other newcomers he started as a film extra, but in the course of filming *The Son of the Sheik* (1926), the producer discovered his unique likeness to Rudolph Valentino and made him the permanent stand-in for the star. Quite soon Temoff, as he renamed himself in the USA, established close and informal relationships with prominent figures in Hollywood. As a result, this former extra became a popular back-up performer in late silent and early sound productions by United Artists, including Fred Niblo's *The Devil Dancer* (1927), Robert De Lacey's *Tyrant of Red Gulch* (1928) and Rouben Mamoulian's *We Live Again* (1934).[12]

Obviously, most film extras were not as lucky as Temoff. A poignant case is that of former Odessa resident Matilda Ganschaft (stage name Mata Gan). In 1920, she married a Frenchman, Latty Floren (1895–1938), and emigrated with him to the West. They came to Hollywood around 1926, whereupon Floren tried to start a career as a film director, but as a first step the couple worked as film extras. Matilda wrote to her mother: 'Dearest Mummy, [. . .] at the moment we are in a film studio, where he [Floren] is working for the second day after getting a very good part. In general we hope that in the near future Latochka[13] will direct a film. And now we earn a living as actors.' Less than two months later another postcard was sent to Moscow: 'We are well and earning enough to make ends meet. We still hope that Latochka will soon sign a contract as a film director, while now he is working as an actor and gaining success [. . .]'[14]

This unpredictable, often humiliating, yet potentially promising milieu sometimes led to ironic situations. For instance, the star Ivan Mosjoukine★, while staying in Hollywood, undertook an experiment. One morning he visited several film studios incognito, introducing himself as a film extra; he was rejected by all the casting directors, who found him insufficiently photogenic.[15] Iosif Polonskii, a Russian who had come to Hollywood via the German studios and who later (in 1931) was appointed chief of the international department at MGM, witnessed the filming of *Love* (1927) (based on Tolstoy's *Anna Karenina*) with Greta Garbo★ and John Gilbert. The treatment of extras made him indignant:

> I recognized nearly all of them. Throughout the last five, six or even seven years they have formed the crowd of so-called 'atmospheres' in films. [. . .] Six to seven years! Is this not enough for them to understand the hopelessness of their hankering after glory and money? No, obviously, it is not enough. Up to the end of their lives, up to their old age every rank and file soldier of the Hollywood army is pretty sure that his promotion to 'general' is waiting around the corner.[16]

Naturally, Hollywood film extras were immortalised on celluloid: for example, in Robert Florey's short film *The Life and Death of 9413: A Hollywood Extra* (1928). Even more impressive in this respect was Josef von Sternberg's *The Last Command* (1928), which specifically dealt with a Russian topic. The plot – suggested to Sternberg by Ernst Lubitsch – turned a historical drama into a 'film about film', in which former heroes and fighters on both sides of the Revolution clash as extras on a film set. Attentive Russian observers pointed out that this film faithfully reconstructed real events, such as the tragic death of White Army Commander-in-Chief General Nikolai Dukhonin, who, in December 1917, died at the hands of a Revolutionary mob. Beyond these records on film, the émigré press regularly reported colourful scenes of everyday life in the studios that concerned Russian extras: 'The crush of 500–600 bearded men at the gates of the Paramount studios, the distribution of military coats, boots, rifles and hats. [. . .] One can see film extras crowded together, visiting make-up rooms and digging artificial trenches.'[17] Another item noted the record-breaking number – 900 – of Russian film extras used for Alan Crosland's *The Song of the Flame* (1930). In this case, to produce a strong Russian 'colour', studio make-up artists made 4,300 artificial beards.[18] Journalists also noted that there were several Hollywood film-makers – including Douglas Fairbanks and Adolphe Menjou – who were particularly fond of employing Russian staff in their films.[19]

By the end of the silent era, the reputation of the Russian film extras was widely recognised by film professionals, whose comments focused on the special virtues of the Russians as a group, virtues rarely found among other ethnic groups. On this subject, it is worth quoting at length Olga Blazhevich:

> Russian film extras are a first-class resource for any film. Many openly declare that a Russian contingent is necessary for assembling a lively, inspired and natural crowd on screen. Of course, this is true: only a Russian émigré [. . .] can produce a realistic image of a Russian, whether in court dress, banker's or well-bred gentleman's suit, or military uniform with a general's shoulder straps. Who, other than Russian émigrés, could embody such grand and proud individuals with natural, noble, pride among 'court ladies' and charm them with genuine good manners in reception rooms? Despite their hard struggle for life not one of them has lost his breeding, forgotten how to kiss a lady's hand or how to sit in a gilded chair [. . .] Nearly all of them, while preparing themselves for filming, feel some kind of holy trepidation while trying on a general's uniform and pinning their own medals on it [. . .] Thanks to the cinema they return, for an hour or a day, to their former lives.[20]

As well as attracting the attention of journalists, Russian film extras also, from early on, became an object of study for a number of scholars. In the late 1920s, the Slavist historian George Martin Day carried out research into the process of social adaptation by Russian émigrés in Hollywood. He surveyed 1,500 Russians who had settled in and around Hollywood[21] and described a number of individual cases from within the community; in particular, he pointed out the major role played in the cultural and social life of the Russian colony by the Russian-American Art Club founded by Michael Vavitch★ in the mid-1920s, and which ran until 1934:

> Acquaintance with the personnel of the club management and with the performing artists makes clear how prominent the motion picture industry is in the life of the club. Practically every Russian affiliated with it depends upon movies

for a living and the club in return depends largely upon the patronage of the motion picture industry. Hence the movie people are bound to influence to a large degree the type of performance presented on the club stage. Quite naturally attitudes and values centering about motion pictures have become the dominant ones at the club.[22]

The American scholar was astonished to find that, despite years of exile and hardship, the Russians in Hollywood had by and large preserved many of the daily patterns and spiritual values that they had brought with them from their native country. He emphasised their unusual conservatism, which they saw as a precondition for preserving their national identity: 'They still live in the past, idolize and idealize it, and are fearful lest their children grow up and forget the cultural traditions of old Russia.'[23]

A thorough study of the roots and meaning of this cultural phenomenon led Day to the following conclusion:

> Finally, the significance in value of this study of the culture conflict in the Hollywood colony lies in a timely under-standing of this conflict, which, so aggressive, so dramatic, is going on apace before our eyes, and which, when fully understood and appreciated, holds great potentialities of mutual cultural benefit to both the Russians of Hollywood and to the American community.[24]

Inevitably, the sound film era put an end to the popularity of the Russian film extras in Hollywood. The first and foremost reason was the end of the vogue for Russia in Western arts. But there was also a 'technical' problem: despite their good manners and real skills as performers, Russian film extras were never able to hide their unacceptably bad English accents.[25] Only a few converted their Russian persona to a 'Latin' or 'Eastern' type, while others had to find new kinds of employment, often as technicians or other support personnel. By the end of the 1930s, only the last and most persistent Russian film extras (about one hundred) remained in Hollywood.[26] As they dance in Clarence Brown's *Conquest* (1937) or trick-ride in Michael Curtis and William Keighley's *The Adventures of Robin Hood* (1938), we can thus glimpse the last, poignant, traces of them as a group on screen.

Notes

1. As well as other prominent actors, such as Fyodor Kozloff (Theodore Kosloff), Nickolai Dunajev (Nicholas Dunaew) and Daniil Makarenko (Daniel Makarenko). For further discussion of Mosjoukine and Nazimova, see also Natalia Noussinova's chapter in this volume.
2. I discuss this subject in a previous study: R. Yangirov, 'Kinostatist kak zerkalo russkoi revoliutsii' [The Film Extra as a Mirror of the Russian Revolution], *Minuvshee* [The Past] no. 16 (Moscow and St Petersburg: Atheneum-Feniks Publishers, 1994).
3. *Illiustrirovannaia Rossiia* [Russia Illustrated] (Paris), no. 35 (1932), p. 17.
4. Jay Leyda, *Kino. A History of the Russian and Soviet Film* (London, Boston and Sydney: Collier Books, 1973), p. 91; Yuri Tsivyan, 'Istoricheskii fil'm i dinamika vlasti: Trotskii i Stalin v sovetskom kino' [Historical Film and Dynamics of Power: Trotsky and Stalin in Soviet Film], *Daugava* (Riga), no. 4 (1988), pp. 98-9; Kevin Brownlow, *Behind the Mask of Innocence* (New York: Alfred A. Knopf, 1990), pp. 357–8.
5. Yugs, 'Russkie v Hollivude' [Russians in Hollywood], *Gun-Bao* (Harbin), 13 May 1928, p. 5; A. Svetlokamnev, 'Russkie v amerikanskom kino' [Russians in American Cinema], *Novoe russkoe slovo* [The New Russian Word] (New York), 15 April 1935, p. 3.
6. Nearly all the film directors who were involved in producing so-called 'Russian films' were sure that fable was a necessary requirement for box-office success. For example, Ernst Lubitsch sincerely believed that Russia had to be pictured in the 'Style Russe', otherwise it would be unconvincing: 'We are not historians or biographers, we have to impact on the audience's imagination and feelings'; quoted in Konstantin Arensky [Arensburger], *Pisma v Gollivud* [Letters to Hollywood] (Monterey and Munich, 1968), p. 15. On this question, see also Natalia Noussinova's chapter in this volume.

7. St Kurtz, 'Za kulisami amerikanskoi kinematografii' [Behind the Scenes of the American Cinematography], *Ekran* [The Screen] (Berlin), no. 4 (1924), p. 32. The film extras' salaries had been stable in the next decade. According to the autumn bulletin of 1936, published by the Central Bureau of the Film Extras in Hollywood, 'atmospheres' were paid $3.2, 'extra works' $15 and 'stand-ins' $25. Anon, 'V Gollivude' [In Hollywood], *Poslednie novosti* [The Latest News] (Paris), 2 October 1936, p. 4. See also Anon, 'Skol'ko dnei v godu rabotaiut "ekstra"' [How Many Days a Year 'Film Extras' are Employed], *Novaia zaria* [The New Dawn] (San Francisco), 22 November 1930, p. 2.

8. K-in, 'Gollivudskie ekstra. Issledovanie psikhologicheskoe' [Hollywood Extras. A Psychological Study], *Novaia zaria*, 29 March 1929, p. 3. See also: George Paris, 'Odin den' pered kameroi' [A Day in Front of a Film Camera], *Novaia zaria*, 23 April 1929, p. 3; *Novaia zaria*, 22 November 1930, p. 2.

9. B. Borskii, 'Raby "Velikogo Nemogo"' [Slaves of the 'Great Silent'], *Utro: Voskresnaia gazeta* [The Morning: a Sunday paper] (Paris), 23 December 1928, p. 2.

10. Fyodor Lodyzhensky, *Poslednie novosti*, 29 November 1935.

11. 'Kazaki v N'iu-Iorke' [Cossacks in New York], *Novoe russkoe slovo*, 20 May 1926, pp. 2–3; '"Dzhigity" v Amerike' ['Dzhigits' in America], *Zarnitsa* [The Summer Lightning] (New York), no. 13 (1926), p. 25; *Novoe russkoe slovo*, 30 October 1927, p. 5; 'Kazaki v Gollivude' [Cossacks in Hollywood], *Poslednie novosti*, 24 February 1928, p. 3; O. P[olonsky], 'Kazaki v "Kazakakh". Russkii otriad na Gollivudskom fronte' [Cossacks in the 'Cossacks'. A Russian Detachment on the Hollywood Front], *Ekho* [Echo] (Kaunas), 24 February 1928, p. 3. Among the Russian trick-riders, the most popular was the Kuban Cossack Gavrila Solodukhin, who once stood in for Lupe Vélez in Douglas Fairbanks' *The Gaucho* (1927). It was also said that Russian riders acted as stand-ins for nearly all the leading actors except Douglas Fairbanks Sr and Tom Mix, who did their own tricks. Anon, 'Russkie v Gollivude' [Russians in Hollywood], *Poslednie novosti*, 5 June 1931, p. 4.

12. Anon, 'Kinokar'era russkogo' [Film Career of the Russian], *Novaia zaria*, 24 May 1930, p. 6. See also: Yuri Sato [Satovsky], 'Rasskaz o tom, kak Rossiiskii muzhichok popal v artisty' [Story of How a Russian Peasant Managed to Become an Actor], *Russkaya zhizn* [Russian Life; the only Russian paper on the Pacific Coast, based in San Francisco], 1 July 1927, p. 7.

13. 'Latochka' was how Floren was known at home.

14. Postcards dated 18 August and 2 October 1926, from the author's collection. By the end of the decade, the couple had failed in their numerous efforts and left the USA for Paris, where they attempted to get into the film business, still without success. See *Poslednie novosti*, 29 August 1930, p. 3.

15. *Rul* [The Rudder] (Berlin), 6 November 1928, p. 4.

16. I[osif] P[olonskii], 'Armiya, v kotoroi kazhdyi soldat mechtayet stat' generalom' [An Army, in Which Every Rank and File Soldier Dreams of Becoming a General], *Novoe russkoe slovo*, 7 August 1927, p. 5.

17. V. Krymskii, 'Russkii Hollywood na ekrane' [Russian Hollywood on Screen], *Novoe russkoe slovo*, 24 January 1928, p. 3.

18. *Mir i iskusstvo* [World and Art] (Paris), no. 7 (1930), p. 13.

19. Anon, 'Russkie v Gollivude' [Russians in Hollywood], *Poslednie novosti*, 8 May 1931, p. 4.

20. Olga Blazhevich, 'Mimoletnye sny' [The Transient Dreams], *Mir i iskusstvo*, no. 5 (1930), p. 13.

21. In fact, only 950 Russians of all ages lived in Hollywood itself, with others in surrounding locations. Besides the Orthodox Church, the main Russian centres included the following restaurants: 'The Two-Headed Eagle', 'The Russian Bear', 'The Moscow Inn' and 'The Filmarte Theater', all of which were located close to Sunset Boulevard. George Martin Day, *The Russians in Hollywood: A Study in Culture Conflict*, Social Series No. 7 (Los Angeles: University of Southern California Press, 1934), pp. 2–3.

22. Day, *The Russians in Hollywood*, p. 40.

23. Ibid., pp. 2–3.

24. Ibid., p. 102.

25. Anon, 'Tragediia Russkikh Gollivudtsev' [The Tragedy of Russians in Hollywood], *Rupor* [The Megaphone] (Harbin), 8 September 1929, p. 2; Anon, 'Russkie v Gollivude' [Russians in Hollywood], *Poslednie novosti*, 8 May 1931, p. 4.

26. Tais'ia Bazhenova, 'Russkii Los Andzheles' [The Russian Los Angeles], *Novaia zaria*, 5 January 1940, p. 5.

3 German Actors in Hollywood

The Long View

Tim Bergfelder

The aim of this chapter is to provide socio-cultural and historical contexts to the patterns of, and motivations for, the migration of German-speaking actors to Hollywood.[1] My chapter will not consider American actors of German parentage or ancestry, which would include figures from Doris Day to Leonardo DiCaprio, Sandra Bullock and Kirsten Dunst. It is my contention that at least for the period up to World War II, the concept of 'German-ness' should most fruitfully be understood less in the contemporary sense as a national or ethnic signifier, but rather as an unstable cultural and linguistic identity, which shifts its meanings and functions not only according to historical circumstance but also according to where and by whom it is invoked. In this respect, the 'German' case differs significantly from other patterns of migration, where national, ethnic and cultural signifiers may be less ambiguously identified as being distinct. There is a historical and terminological indeterminacy to the notion of German-ness, which occasionally overlaps with other identities such as Jewish, Austrian, Swiss, Hungarian, Polish or Russian. Thus, my chapter will also cover German-speaking actors who may be defined by other categories as well. For the period up to World War II in particular, I suggest that it makes more sense to conceive (in a holistic and comparative way) of an older, more inclusive, identity, around the notion of *Mitteleuropa* or Central Europe. This notion encompasses today's Eastern Europe, the remnants of the multicultural Habsburg Empire and today's Germany. What complicates the issue of identity further is the fact that many of the Middle European émigrés of the first part of the twentieth century already were bi- or multicultural and bi- or multilingual long before they added an American identity, either permanently or temporarily, to their personal profile.

Although the popular image of the German émigré actor or film-maker invokes the period of the 1930s and 1940s, the plight of the Jewish refugees from Hitler and iconic stars such as Marlene Dietrich★ and Conrad Veidt★ (neither of whom, incidentally, were in the first instance political refugees or Jewish), the interaction between Germany and the American film industry goes back much further. In fact, it originates in a different context for migration and in the presence and shifting importance of German culture both in the USA and in Europe. I shall focus on this early period in more detail than the others, mainly because these origins are discussed far less frequently than the later periods, but also because the later developments are fundamentally shaped by contexts that go back to the nineteenth century. In this respect, the 1930s and 1940s constitute in many ways an anomaly in the migration patterns between Germany and Hollywood.

Phase 1: 1895–1918

The history of German-speaking actors' migration to Hollywood can be divided roughly into four phases. During the first phase (1895–1918), Hollywood emerged as a major industry, founded by Central European émigrés, who drew, as I will outline shortly, on a Middle European cultural symbiosis that at the turn of the century was centred

Conrad Veidt, one of the most successful German actors of his generation, here in his signature Hollywood role as Major Strasser in *Casablanca* (1942)

in American big cities on the East Coast. It is worth remembering in this context that throughout the nineteenth century, German-speaking immigrants constituted by far the biggest single contingent of new American citizens, and it is only at the beginning of the twentieth century that German immigration to the USA was outnumbered by an influx from Russia and Italy.[2] Between 1816 and 1914 it is estimated that 5.5 million Germans emigrated to the USA, most of them for socio-economic reasons, with a significant minority of political refugees after the failed nationalist revolutions of 1848. Excluded from the estimate are German-speaking Swiss and Austrians, as well as a vast number of ethnic German émigrés from Eastern Europe. Also excluded from the estimate of 5.5 million are countless bilingual émigrés from Central and Eastern Europe, many of whom were Jewish, for whom German was either the first or a natural second tongue – people who aspired to German cultural models, even where official German culture was institutionally anti-Semitic.[3] Throughout the nineteenth century, German was the official language of the Habsburg Empire (whose territory included Austria, today's Czech Republic and Slovakia, Hungary, most of the former Yugoslavia, parts of Romania and Poland), in Prussia (which extended well into what is now Russia and Poland) and other German provinces before the formation of the Reich in 1870. It was also an important trade language in other European countries, particularly in the East, as well as a marker of education, and consequently a sign of social aspiration and cultural prestige.

Thus, far from being the parochial, introspective and nationalistic identity it was turned into by the propagandists of the Wilhelmine Reich, and later on by the Nazis, the notion of German-ness before World War I provided a supra- or transnational identity that could be negotiated alongside other cultural, religious or linguistic affiliations. As such, it is perhaps not too much of a surprise that the community of German-Americans very early insisted on their new hyphenated identity – since for many of them a hyphenated existence was nothing new.[4] This, however, meant for the new Americans a curious and ambivalent pathway (a pathway that would eventually become impossible by the time of World War I) that embraced American citizenship while remaining attached to sometimes multiple former affiliations. These multiple identities were often given cohesion by the notion of German-ness.

In the latter half of the nineteenth century, German culture was extremely prominent in the USA, a fact that was repressed after World War I. Around the turn of the twentieth century, the biggest German city in terms of inhabitants after Berlin was New York. German immigrants concentrated in urban areas far more than other Americans, creating in the process distinctive metropolitan neighbourhoods that nevertheless avoided the self-ghettoisation of later immigrant groupings. New York alone boasted four daily German-language newspapers, as well as numerous German theatres, social clubs, restaurants and dance halls.[5] On the whole, these cultural institutions were socially and culturally far more inclusive than their counterparts in Europe. Thus, German-language theatres in New York's Lower East Side catered to high cultural and bourgeois tastes with adaptations of Goethe and Schiller, while also producing Yiddish plays for Jewish immigrants coming from the rural *shtetls* of Central Europe. Moreover, these theatres provided an important opportunity not just for permanently emigrated actors to establish themselves in the USA, but also for touring companies from Europe. In both cases, these ethnically defined theatres became springboards to a career in films, particularly in the early days of film-making when production was still centred in New York. Examples include father and son Rudolph Schildkraut★ and Joseph Schildkraut★, who came from Vienna via the Berlin stage and German films. At New York's Jewish Art Theatre, they appeared both in productions of Schnitzler and Wedekind and in Yiddish plays, before being discovered by American film producers.[6] Another actor who began his American career at the German-language and Yiddish Jewish Art Theatre was Lemberg-born Friedrich Meier Weisenfreund, who later became famous in Hollywood as Paul Muni.[7] There are also examples of a two-way traffic: Viennese-born Mady Christians★, for example, first became a child star under the direction of her father at New York's Irving Place Theater, before returning to German cinema and theatre in the 1920s, and then emigrating again after 1933 to pursue a stage and film career in the USA.[8]

It was from the cultural environment of this metropolitan and cosmopolitan Middle European melting pot that Hollywood's founding fathers also emerged, all of whom juggled multiple identities. According to Neal Gabler,

Paramount's founder Adolph Zukor, although born into a Jewish orthodox family in Hungary, rejected both his Hungarian and Jewish backgrounds, while simultaneously cultivating a sophisticated European sensibility (which translated mostly into a German high-culture paradigm), and what he understood to be American gentility.[9] Among the earliest prestige films Zukor initiated, however, was an adaptation of the Bavarian passion play of Oberammergau, which must have courted a principally German or German-oriented urban audience. Carl Laemmle of Universal, by contrast, remained all his life a quintessential hyphenated German-American, regularly visiting his home town of Laupheim in south-west Germany, establishing a nepotistic network of countless relatives, and equally balancing his affiliations to his country of origin and to the USA.[10] Far more assimilationist and eager to blend into an Anglo-Saxon-defined Americanism were fellow founding fathers William Fox (from Hungary) and Louis B. Mayer from Russia, although again both of them had been crucially shaped by the German-Jewish-Middle European symbiosis of New York's Lower East Side. Gabler's suggestion is that all of Hollywood's founding fathers' incomplete assimilation and divided loyalties provide the main answer as to why they were drawn in the first place to a medium and entertainment business that was initially too disreputable for more established Americans, and why cinema became their main tool in establishing and proving their American credentials.

Phase 2: 1918–33

During this second phase, Hollywood consolidated itself as a major industrial oligopoly and began to expand seriously into global markets and audiences. Germany becomes an important element in these ambitions for several reasons. In terms of population size, Germany provided a significant potential audience, while postwar restrictions on German trade gave American companies easy access to those markets.[11] Moreover, many of the major US studios had long-standing personal as well as professional ties to Germany. At the same time, Germany opposed Hollywood on two major fronts: despite US oversupply, German audiences remained largely lukewarm and unimpressed with American products compared to indigenous fare, and the German film industry re-established itself surprisingly quickly after World War I with a string of international hits.[12] The migration of German actors to Hollywood during this period thus needs to be seen against the background of the competition between the two film industries. The motivation of Hollywood producers for luring German talent to the West Coast was manifold: it was meant to weaken the German film industry simply through loss of exceptional personnel and also through the possibility of offering the German audiences films with familiar faces. At least in theory, it also brought advantages on the American domestic market, in that the use of an internationally renowned actor or director might raise the prestige of a studio or an individual production. In practice, this strategy proved reasonably successful with imports such as Conrad Veidt and Emil Jannings★ in the late 1920s (the latter winning the first ever Best Actor Academy Award). Similar prestige vehicles would in the late 1930s be made with immigrant actors such as Paul Muni and Edward G. Robinson, and the English import Charles Laughton★. As the German cultural paradigm gradually faded in American public estimation and as the German language disappeared too from US public life, it was frequently replaced by the rising prestige of British-ness – as shown by the shift in star status from Jannings and Veidt in the late 1920s to Laughton and Laurence Olivier★ in the late 1930s. The change from silent film to sound further accentuated the restrictions of German actors in leading parts, not just because of their heavy German accents (as in Jannings' case) but also in terms of their often highly theatrical acting style that was increasingly at odds with the naturalism and understatement associated with the majority of American actors then being recruited from the Broadway stage.

Jannings and Veidt's brief interludes in the 1920s initiated a tendency for fleeting visits by German actors to the USA, followed by a return to the indigenous film industry. Thus, set against Dietrich's success, one has to count the failure of renowned German actresses such as Lil Dagover★, Lillian Harvey★ and Camilla Horn★ to make an impact in their few Hollywood productions. It is during this period, too, that many German actors, but also directors (Ernst Lubitsch is a case in point), became principally assigned to a restricted selection of genres. German actors were frequently cast in costume films and historical epics, in which their acting histrionics and accents could be plausibly explained and where they even added to the genre's verisimilitude, as these were primarily films with a European (and often German, Austrian or fairytale) settings. Peter Krämer, Thomas Elsaesser and others have suggested that these films were made with a global, and specifically Middle European, audience in mind.[13] German actors were also typecast in a number of explicitly anti-German productions made during and immediately after World War I. The studios soon stopped making these films, as Hollywood renewed its courtship with, and did its best to avoid giving offence to, German audiences and, as Ruth Vasey has documented, German political opinion too.[14] Instead, in the 1920s, the figure of the decadent Prussian, as Janet Staiger has shown, became attractive through stars such as Erich von Stroheim.[15] Female German imports that began to make their mark during this period in Hollywood, from Pola Negri★ to Dietrich, on the other hand, were less clearly marked as German or, in Negri's case, Polish, than as vaguely exotic. This marked the beginning of a split between the typecasting of German actresses from that of their male counterparts. In the 1930s, glamorous Middle European imports included some temporarily successful stars such as Austrian-born Hedy Lamarr★ and the double Academy Award-winner Luise Rainer★, while others, such as the Hungarian Franciska Gaal★ and the Russian Anna Sten★, failed to make an impact. Most of these imports – like Greta Garbo★ earlier – arrived in Hollywood via a professional stopover in the German studios.

Phase 3: Political Exile

To a certain extent, what followed the exchanges of the 1920s and early 1930s was an intensification of the preceding decade. While the economic motivations of studio executives towards German immigrants initially underwent no significant change, as the decade moved closer towards war, the export motivation for employing foreign actors diminished as more and more European countries became off-limits to the Hollywood majors. By the early 1940s, the number of émigré actors and other personnel from Germany and German-speaking areas in Europe was staggering. But in the majority of cases, the threat to life replaced socio-economic reasons for migration.[16] Among the exiled German actors, the most prolific and consistently successful group were frequently not established stars from German stage and screen, but what in German is called a *Charge*, a term not fully covered by the roughly equivalent English term of 'character actor'. In Germany, *Charge* were minor players, often with an eccentric personal style of acting, occasionally also with pronounced physical idiosyncrasies bordering on the grotesque. Among such character actors working in Hollywood in the 1940s are Felix Bressart★ (who had been the best-loved German film comedian of the early 1930s and who later gave poignant performances in Lubitsch's *The Shop around the Corner* [1940] and *To Be or Not to Be* [1942]), Sig Arno★ (the quintessential servant and restaurant waiter in numerous Hollywood films) and Curt Bois★ (whose career began as a child actor in 1907 and ended, via his role as the pickpocket in *Casablanca* [1942], with Wim Wenders' *Der Himmel über Berlin/Wings of Desire* in 1987). On the other hand, it must have been more demeaning for prestigious German stage and film actors such as Albert Bassermann★, Ernst Deutsch★ and Fritz Kortner★ to be effectively reduced to a *Charge* in exile, even if it provided relatively continuous employment. Beyond often comical character parts (usually as a servant figure) or the role of the paternal or grandfatherly authority figure (Bassermann's domain throughout the 1940s), the cultural stereotype of the 'ugly German' intensified with the requirements of propagandistic and anti-Nazi productions during the war, as Joseph Garncarz's chapter in this volume outlines. Heroic or leading parts for any male actor with a remotely German accent were the exception; examples include Carl Esmond★, Helmut Dantine and most famously Paul Henreid★ (the romantic lead in *Now, Voyager* [1942] and *Casablanca*), all of whom, however, found themselves equally cast in villainous roles. Socially, despite the existence of Hollywood's famous expatriate communities, affiliations and loyalties were not necessarily tied to geographical, cultural or national backgrounds. Thus, throughout the 1930s, the Jewish film tycoon Harry Cohn expressed his admiration for Mussolini, while the quintessential Prussian officer's daughter Dietrich became closely involved in Hollywood's liberal and anti-Fascist response to Hitler. On screen, however, Dietrich was rarely cast during the war in roles that were identifiably German, playing Arabian harem dancers (*Kismet* [1944]), and gypsies (*Golden Earrings* [1946]) instead. Lamarr, too, camouflaged her Austrian origins in parts that required her to be enigmatically European or unidentifiably exotic.

To summarise the patterns of migration from the early years to the end of World War I, the legacy of what I have called the Middle European mindset emerges as one of the major factors of Central European and German migration well into the middle of the twentieth century. This mindset, originating in the uneven and fragile, but nevertheless fertile, multiculturalism of Middle Europe, became a strategy for survival in the face of eroding certainties in terms of belonging and home. These changes began in the late nineteenth century and gained an ever more unsettling force with the end of World War I, the demise of the Austro-Hungarian Empire, the rise of Fascism and World War II. The trajectory of the actress Lilli Palmer★ provides a good example of such disruptions.[17] Palmer was born in Posen, a city that throughout the nineteenth and early twentieth century sat precariously between Prussia (later the German Reich), Poland, the Austro-Hungarian Empire and Russia. Palmer's family was thoroughly assimilated Jewish-German, and she was born into a city that at the time was nominally politically independent. After 1945, when Palmer returned to Europe from an odyssey that had included being a nightclub singer in Paris, a film actress in Britain and then a studio star in Hollywood, Posen had become the Polish Poznan, but she continued her career as a 'German' actress in West German, French and multinational European productions. It is easy to see why simple national labels, or identity formations that are based on national parameters, may not suffice for diasporic trajectories typical of a lifestyle imposed on many people during the twentieth century. On the other hand, a mindset so crucially dependent on masquerade, on the camouflage of ethnic, national and psychological signifiers, and on the negotiation of multiple identities, serves as a metaphor not only for the acting profession, but more specifically for the dream factory and myth-making process of Hollywood itself – an institution that over the years has overhauled and transformed many identities.

Phase 4: 1945–present

Following World War II, the number of German actors in Hollywood declined as the postwar political settlement segued into settled national divisions in Europe. While many earlier immigrants remained in Hollywood, there were comparatively few German newcomers from the late 1940s. Again, as in the prewar period, the major motivation to launch German actors in Hollywood productions appears to have been, at least where the US studios were concerned, to gain access to German-speaking markets by employing performers successful with German audiences. Thus, one of the biggest new German stars of the late 1940s, Hildegard Knef★, was briefly brought over to the USA in order both to attract US audiences with a glamorous exoticism in the Dietrich mould, and to be sold back to the Germans with American production values. A similar strategy appears to have been behind a succession of temporary visits to the USA by German stars of the 1950s, 1960s and 1970s. In most cases, this strategy backfired, because German audiences tended to reject their stars in American guise. This was true of, among others, Maria Schell★, Romy Schneider★ and Hanna Schygulla★. Nevertheless, throughout the 1950s, 1960s and early 1970s, Hollywood courted German audiences and tried to win them over with film projects in which German actors were employed, a strategy that only receded by the mid-1970s, by which time the battle over German cinematic tastes had been won by Hollywood productions.[18] It is only since the 1990s, significantly since indigenous German productions have risen again at the German box office, that a reciprocal traffic has resumed. Recent German Hollywood 'tourists' include heart-throb Til Schweiger★, who, in his own words, has been 'testing the waters' with appearances in a number of Hollywood films (e.g. *The Replacement Killers* [1998]; *Driven* [2001]; *Investigating Sex* [2001]),[19] and Franka Potente★ of *Run Lola Run* (1998) fame, who recently made her entry into US productions with Todd Solondz's *Storytelling* (2001) and the action thriller *The Bourne Identity* (2002). Alongside these, a new generation of German film-makers have become resident in Hollywood, including the directors Roland Emmerich (*Independence Day* [1996]; *Godzilla* [1998]) and Wolfgang Petersen (*Air Force One* [1997]; *The Perfect Storm* [2000]), **41** cinematographers Michael Ballhaus (*Bram Stoker's Dracula* [1992]; *The Age of Innocence* [1993]), composer Hans Zimmer (*Gladiator* [2000]; *Black Hawk Down* [2001]) and transatlantic producer Bernd Eichinger (*Resident Evil* [2002]). There are also a number of German character actors, such as Armin Mueller-Stahl★, Udo Kier★ and more sporadically Jürgen Prochnow★, who work consistently in American productions.[20] Altogether, something like a new German wave seems to have emerged again in Hollywood.

Arguably the only German-speaking real Hollywood star since Dietrich has been Austrian-born Arnold Schwarzenegger★, whose career follows a trajectory closer to that of the earlier immigrants. It is open to debate whether his entry into film acting via bodybuilding, rather than a traditional acting career, could have happened anywhere else than Hollywood, particularly if one considers the professional hierarchies governing casting decisions and the prestigious cultural connotations still associated with a traditional actor's training in Europe. In any case, in his unique career trajectory as well as in his star status, Schwarzenegger remains an exception. Instead, many post-war German stars' trajectories suggest that since 1945 far fewer have been prepared to make the life-changing step of a permanent emigration, and prefer instead to come to Hollywood for occasional projects. In so doing, they eschew genuine Hollywood stardom, but gain greater personal independence and flexibility in the process. Such 'jet-set careers' include, from the 1950s onwards, those of Curt Jürgens★ (who, while never a Hollywood star, was perhaps the most successful of all postwar German actors on an international scale), Horst Buchholz★, Hardy Krüger★, Elke Sommer★ and Maximilian Schell★. Contemporary actors such as the aforementioned Schweiger, Kier, Mueller-Stahl and Prochnow balance transatlantic, sometimes truly global, multimedia careers. It appears therefore that the idea of journeys of desire made from German-speaking countries to Hollywood – with all its often severe existential and life-changing implications – has nowadays been firmly replaced by the more pragmatic practice of international business travel.

Notes

1. For different perspectives on this topic, see also Thomas Elsaesser, 'Ethnicity, Authenticity, and Exile: A Counterfeit Trade? German Filmmakers and Hollywood', in Hamid Naficy (ed.), *Home, Exile, Homeland. Film, Media, and the Politics of Place* (London and New York: Routledge, 1999), pp. 97–123; and Peter Krämer, 'Hollywood in Germany/Germany in Hollywood', in Tim Bergfelder, Erica Carter and Deniz Göktürk (eds), *The German Cinema Book* (London: BFI, 2002), pp. 227–37.
2. John A. Hagwood, *The Tragedy of German-America. The Germans in the United States of America During the Nineteenth Century and After* (New York and London: G. P. Putnam's & Sons, 1940), pp. 54–73. See also Günter Moltmann, 'The Pattern of German Emigration to the United States in the Nineteenth Century', in Frank Trommler and Joseph McVeigh, *America and the Germans. An Assessment of a Three-Hundred-Year History, Volume One* (Philadelphia: University of Pennsylvania Press, 1985), pp. 15–24.
3. Hagwood, *The Tragedy of German-America*, pp. 54–73.
4. Ibid., pp. 267–86.
5. See 'Einführung. Die deutsche Auswanderung in die USA', in Wolfgang Helbich, Walter D. Kamphoefner and Ulrike Sommer (eds), *Briefe aus Amerika. Deutsche Auswanderer schreiben aus der Neuen Welt, 1830–1930* (Munich: C. H. Beck, 1988), pp. 11–31.
6. See Andreas Ungerböck, 'Joseph Schildkraut: Porträt des Künstlers als schöner Mann', in Christian Cargnelli and Michael Omasta (eds), *Aufbruch ins Ungewisse. Österreichische Filmschaffende in der Emigration vor 1945, Volume One* (Vienna: Wespennest, 1993), pp. 143–55.
7. *Editors' note*: Paul Muni, like Helmut Dantine and Edward G. Robinson (discussed later in this chapter), do not feature in the dictionary part of this book because they did not have a film career in their own country before emigrating to Hollywood.
8. 'Mady Christians', in Christian Cargnelli and Michael Omasta (eds), *Aufbruch ins Ungewisse. Österreichische Filmschaffende*

in der Emigration vor 1945, Volume Two: Lexikon, Tributes, Selbstzeugnisse (Vienna: Wespennest, 1993), p. 24.

9. Neal Gabler, *An Empire of Their Own. How the Jews Invented Hollywood* (New York and London: Anchor Books, 1989), pp. 11–46.

10. Ibid., pp. 47–64. See also Clive Hirshhorn, *The Universal Story* (New York: Crown, 1983); and James Curtis, *James Whale: A New World of Gods and Monsters* (Boston and London: Faber & Faber, 1999), pp. 111–13.

11. See Kristin Thompson, *Exporting Entertainment: America in the World Film Market 1907–1934* (London: BFI, 1985); and Ruth Vasey, *The World According to Hollywood, 1918–1939* (Exeter: University of Exeter Press, 1997).

12. See Thomas J. Saunders, *Hollywood in Berlin: American Cinema and Weimar Germany* (Berkeley, Los Angeles and London: University of California Press, 1994); and Joseph Garncarz, *Populäres Kino in Deutschland: Internationalisierung einer Filmkultur 1925–1990* (unpublished *Habilitationsschrift*, University of Cologne, 1996).

13. Elsaesser, 'Ethnicity, Authenticity, and Exile'; Krämer, 'Hollywood in Germany/Germany in Hollywood'.

14. Vasey, *The World According to Hollywood*, p. 52.

15. Janet Staiger, 'The Handmaiden of Villainy: Foolish Wives, Politics, Gender Orientation, and the Other', in *Interpreting Films: Studies in the Historical Reception of American Cinema* (Princeton, NJ: Princeton University Press, 1992), pp. 124–38.

16. See Joseph Garncarz's chapter in this volume. See also Jan-Christopher Horak, *Fluchtpunkt Hollywood: Eine Dokumentation zur Filmemigration nach 1933* (Münster: MAkS, 1984); Ronny Loewy (ed.), *Von Babelsberg nach Hollywood: Filmemigranten aus Nazideutschland* (Frankfurt am Main: Deutsches Filmmuseum, 1987); Helmut G. Asper, *'Etwas Besseres als den Tod . . .'. Filmexil in Hollywood, Porträts, Filme, Dokumente* (Marburg: Schüren, 2002).

17. Michael O. Huebner, *Lilli Palmer. Ihre Filme. Ihr Leben* (Munich: Wilhelm Heyne, 1986); Lilli Palmer, *Change Lobsters and Dance: An Autobiography* (London: W. H. Allen, 1976).

18. Krämer, 'Hollywood in Germany/Germany in Hollywood'.

19. Malte Hagener, 'German Stars of the 1990s', in Bergfelder *et al.* (eds), *The German Cinema Book*, p. 102.

20. Claudia Fellmer, 'Armin Mueller-Stahl – From East Germany to the West Coast', in Bergfelder *et al.*, (eds), *The German Cinema Book*, pp. 90–7.

4 Opera, Theatre and Film

Italians in 1920s and 1930s Hollywood

Giuliana Muscio

Before the 1950s, Italian actors were not particularly prominent in Hollywood films. Yet, like an underground river, they were not easy to detect, but they were there. The movement of actors between Italy and the USA involved three areas: American productions in Italy, the development of immigrant theatre in the USA, and the emigration of Italian actors to Hollywood. From a cultural point of view, a key factor in the Italian–American relationship was the complex interplay between theatre, music and cinema. In addition to this interaction, the cultural influence of Italian cinema is detectable in the development of the American star system, following the pattern created by the diva, in the tradition of the theatrical and operatic prima donna and in its decadent connotation as the vamp.

Following World War I, after a peak in international prestige, Italian cinema fell into a sudden and long-lasting decline. We might suppose that this crisis in Italian film production, combined with the coming of Fascism, would have encouraged Italian actors to emigrate towards more flourishing film industries, such as Hollywood. But this did not happen, or at least not on the scale one would have anticipated. On the contrary, in the 1920s, important American film companies shot several films in Italy, including MGM's *Ben-Hur* (1925) and *Mare Nostrum* (1926).[1] Evidently Italy had maintained its cultural influence. Such American film productions made use of the beauty and artistic connotations of Italian settings, as well as the versatile local talent. The American publicity material for *The White Sister* (1923), shot in Naples and Rome with Lillian Gish and Ronald Colman★, was presented like a theatre programme, listing Italian actors as coming from Teatro Costanzi, a prestigious Roman theatre. While it emphasised the connection to the theatre, the programme, with its illustrations inspired by famous paintings, also stressed the Italian pictorial tradition.[2]

Among the first Italian actors to go to Hollywood during the silent period, both Sandro Salvini★ and Guido Trento★ had worked in American films shot in Italy (*Nero* [1922] and *The Shepherd King* [1925]). And yet this does not mean that there was an automatic link between this experience and going to Hollywood. Rather, the connections between Salvini and American cinema are a good example of the mediation performed by the theatre. Salvini was the nephew of famous Shakespearean actor Tommaso Salvini, and he himself had an impressive international stage experience. After working in Italian theatre and cinema with the diva Francesca Bertini and on the English stage, he met director Herbert Brenon in London. Back in Italy, Salvini was the protagonist of a number of American films, such as *Nero* and *Beatrice* (1922), the latter shot in Sicily by Brenon. He later worked in American films, both in Hollywood and at the Paramount studios in Joinville, near Paris.[3] But Trento and Salvini were exceptional cases, with a certain amount of continuity. Many of the Italian actors who appeared on the credits of American films made in Italy in the 1920s never made it to Hollywood, and those who did, rarely stayed for long.

After the coming of sound, multi-language versions of American films, shot both in the USA and in Joinville, contributed to another type of filmographic confusion: between 1930 and 1933, Italian actors appeared on the credits of 'American' films. Yet, as in the 1920s, this did not always signify their presence in Hollywood. To add further complications, Italian-sounding names did not necessarily belong to Italian actors: Pola Negri★ was a Polish actress, while Virginia Valli and Nita Naldi were American; Elissa Landi (real name Elizabeth Marie Christine Kuehnelt), though born in Venice, was educated in Canada and England, acted on the British stage and went to Hollywood after a successful career on Broadway. On the other hand, others changed their Italian names, such as Lido Manetti who became Arnold Kent★ in Hollywood.

I should stress here that the choice of an Italian surname in show business went against the common behaviour of Italian immigrants in the USA – during this period, one of the least accepted European communities in the USA. Immigrants from Italy often modified their last names to be less identifiable as Italians or were compelled to do so by immigration authorities. The contrary practice in music, theatre and later film is thus testimony to the prestige of Italian culture in relation to the arts. For instance, there was a long tradition of famous Italian stage actors, such as Eleonora Duse and Tommaso Salvini, who toured the USA, often performing Shakespeare and other classics in Italian. In this respect, William Uricchio and Roberta Pearson have emphasised the significant impact of Italian culture at a time when American cinema was fighting for cultural legitimation.[4] Thus, Italian families in the USA who were involved in music and film (such as the Coppolas) proudly kept their names and cultural traditions, staying in touch with the mother country and showing Italian films together with American ones in their theatres, where they also played opera and Neapolitan songs.[5]

Immigrant Theatre

The connections discussed above indicate the relevance and impact of the Italian theatrical and musical community within early American film history. As part of this, the rise of immigrant theatre deserves a special mention.

In their reports, the Italian emigration authorities noted the great number of theatre people moving to North America between 1890 and 1914. Important Italian actors often toured the USA, as well as Sicilian companies such as those led by Angelo Musco and Giovanni Grasso. Some actors from these troupes decided to remain in the new country and contributed to the setting up of the New York Italian immigrant theatre. The circuit included high and low cultural forms, both in terms of repertoire and venues. Shows ranged from *pupi* (puppets) to *sceneggiate* (a theatrical genre that included songs), from *café chantant* to opera, and vernacular plays alternated with Shakespeare, in a plurality of languages: standard Italian, Italian dialects and English. The Italian immigrant theatre also exchanged spaces and productions with the Yiddish theatre.[6] It was highly mixed and multicultural, though dominated by Southern Italian traditions and dialects (only Ferrando's Hall nightclub in New York put on shows in Piedmontese and Milanese). From this Southern Italian culture came the strong interplay between film and theatre, and idiosyncratic forms of spectatorial participation. Neapolitans saw their films in cafés and theatres, together with a variety of shows, and they reacted loudly or sang along with the performers.[7] This habit remained with the immigrants, who kept a heterogeneous diet of music, theatre and film, the mix including Italian, Neapolitan and American products.

Members of these Italian theatrical families went on to work in American cinema: for example, director Robert G. Vignola (originally a Shakespearean actor), as well as actresses such as Rosina Galli. Emelise Aleandri,[8] the historian of New York's Italian immigrant theatre, has confirmed that other performers from the immigrant theatre also worked in film. For instance, Mimi Aguglia★ travelled to the USA with Giovanni Grasso's Sicilian company and performed on the immigrant stage; she worked in film in the 1930s, on Spanish versions of Hollywood films, demonstrating the interchangeability between Southern Italians, Spanish and 'Latin' characters in Hollywood cinema.

An interesting case study of an actor commuting between the immigrant theatre stage and Hollywood was the versatile Gugliemo Ricciardi★ of the prestigious Compagnia Comico-Drammatica Italiana of Brooklyn. On stage he performed equally in *macchiette* (comic scenes) and the classics, and he sang Neapolitan duets with Enrico Caruso★. In the silent period, under the name William Ricciardi, he made eight films, often playing opera impresarios or performers of sorts, or a member of European high society; only in one film, *Puppets* (1926), was he an Italian-American. In the 1930s, after the introduction of sound, he made eleven films, cast in similar roles, though he was by then playing Italians more frequently. Interestingly enough, one of his more important roles was connected to his theatrical career: director George Fitzmaurice saw him on stage in London, performing *Mister Malatesta*, and hired him for the screen adaptation of Pirandello's *As You Desire Me* (1932) with Greta Garbo★ and Erich von Stroheim. Later, Ricciardi appeared in other prestigious films such as *Anthony Adverse* (1936) and *San Francisco* (1936), but altogether the parts he played in his Hollywood films were restricted to supporting roles. The type of characters Ricciardi played on stage, his Southern Italian origins and his musical talents all contributed to the roles he performed on film from the beginning, but his *Italianicity* was evident only in the 1930s. This had to do with language but also with the socio-cultural context of the New Deal, when Hollywood was building a stronger American identity, reinforced by the fixing of a variety of ethnic and national stereotypes and identities.[9]

In the late 1990s, Martin Scorsese's Film Foundation[10] restored a short film featuring the most famous *macchiettista* (comic sketch performer) in New York, Eduardo Migliaccio, known as Farfariello. The film, entitled *The Movie Actor* (1932), allows Farfariello to demonstrate his great talent, playing three different 'types': Pasquale Passaguai, the ignorant immigrant who has a hard time adapting to American language and behaviour; a gangster-*guappo* from Little Italy; and La Parigina, a vaudeville singer (with Farfariello in drag). Gestures and linguistic invention immediately evoke the popular Neapolitan theatre, that of Raffaele Viviani and Totò, and reveal how the traditions of Southern Italian theatre were adapted to the USA. Yet this adaptability is far from assimilation. As Giorgio Bertellini argues, '[Farfariello] played a major role in the development of immigrants' Southernist double (or plural) consciousness, centred on their stance as a Southern Italian "dissonant" colony within the American context.'[11]

Southern Italian culture seems indeed to have resisted assimilation: this generation of Italian performers spoke mostly Italian and/or dialect, they referred to theatrical conventions and formats that were typically Southern Italian and adapted peculiar types of shows, such as the *sceneggiata* (an archetypal Neapolitan musical melodramatic genre) to the American situation. One of the few existing films made within the immigrant community – and one of Scorsese's restorations – *Santa Lucia Luntana*, made in New Jersey in 1931, was an Americanised version of a *sceneggiata*, displaying its strong melodramatic elements and characters, which included the son as the family's 'black sheep', the sacrificial parent and a deep nostalgia for Naples expressed through song. The acting was also typical of the Southern Italian *koiné*[12] genre developed in New York: Raffaele Bongini, one of the stars of the Compagnia Drammatica Siciliana, played the father, while Orazio Cammi, one of the main directors and playwrights of popular New York Neapolitan theatre was the prodigal son. Bongini had also appeared in a few silent Hollywood films. In typical Southern Italian fashion, personal connections play a key role and Italian names often appear in groups on the credits, even when the story is not connected to Italy or Little Italy. Thus, in *The Humming Bird* (1924), we find Bongini together with, among others, Ricciardi and Cesare Gravina★. Bongini also appeared in *A Sainted Devil* (1925) with Rudolph Valentino and Nita Naldi. In 1932, he could be seen in *Amore e morte*, an American *Cavalleria rusticana* produced and directed by Sicilian actor and playwright Rosario Romeo. Thus, stars of the immigrant theatre not only acted in Hollywood cinema, they also produced their own films.

The coming of sound and the consequent crisis in ethnic spectatorship encouraged the production of films in Italian for the immigrant audience, because of the community's resistance to learning English. Most of these Italian-American films were made at Fort Lee, New Jersey, an important film production centre of the early silent period, although not much is known about them.[13] Only one film was made in Hollywood, *Sei tu l'amore* (1930), starring Alberto Rabagliati★ (the Italian winner of the Fox contest for a new Valentino) and the beautiful contralto Luisa Caselotti.[14]

Therefore, up to the mid-1930s, Italian immigrant film entertained a complex relation with American culture – of alterity and slow adaptation. The very existence of a separate film production (as for Yiddish cinema) indicates the persistence of a distinct market, which became more obvious with sound films. In the 1930s, with the dominance (and standardising force) of radio and film, the use of English eventually prevailed.[15] Italian immigrant theatre in New York endured, but the second generation privileged radio. The immigrant community opened up to the American media, while keeping a relative cultural autonomy. The link with radio also confirms the centrality of music in Italian émigré culture, and the persistence of a separate Italian-American audience, enjoying among other things special programmes sponsored by pasta manufacturers.

Among the theatrical families of this phase were the Barbatos. They had arrived in New York with Giovanni Grasso's tour, but while Attilio Barbato became a famous radio performer, Olga Barbato★ appeared on the immigrant stage, as well as working in radio and film – much later she would play Angelina in Woody Allen's *Broadway Danny Rose* (1984), while Mimi Cecchini★ (Aguglia's niece) would play Italian-American roles in *Dominick and Eugene* (1988), *Cadillac Man* (1990) and *Wise Guys* (1986), pointing to the continuity between these theatrical families and Hollywood up to the present day. The popularity of Italian-American culture in the wake of the Coppola–Scorsese–de Palma films clearly also facilitated the involvement of representatives of this earlier theatrical tradition in contemporary Hollywood.

Italian Actors in Hollywood

As mentioned at the beginning of this chapter, the crisis in Italian cinema after Word War I and the rise of Fascism did not prompt a wave of film personnel emigration to Hollywood. Perhaps provincial Italians did not travel because of the language barrier, but in silent cinema, this would not present a problem. Among the few Italian silent actors to migrate to the USA were Luciano Albertini★, Tullio Carminati★, Rina De Liguoro★, Agostino Borgato★ and the already mentioned Lido Manetti, Sandro Salvini, Cesare Gravina and Guido Trento. As we shall see, their experiences varied.

Albertini was one of the muscular heroes of Italian silent cinema, but he had an unsuccessful experience with the Universal serial *The Iron Man* (1924) and moved to Germany. Manetti went to Hollywood in 1925 and, changing his name to Arnold Kent, played the romantic lead opposite the likes of Pola Negri and Clara Bow. Unfortunately, after this promising start, he died in a mysterious car accident in 1928. In Italy Borgato had been lead player in Duse's stage company and then in the cinema. Like many others, he left for Hollywood in 1925 but ended up playing mostly bit parts, including roles in a number of Spanish-American titles. Gravina was a musician as well as the head of a successful theatre company in Italy. Between 1915 and 1929, he enjoyed an impressively long and successful career in Hollywood, featuring as one of Erich von Stroheim's favourite actors. The coming of sound, however, saw him return home: indeed, he is the only one in the group who did not make the transition to sound.

Having married into an aristocratic family, Rina De Liguoro made a few films in Hollywood; together with Francesca Braggiotti★ and Tullio Carminati, she represented the – then substantial – aristocratic section of the Italian film world, a group who experienced diverse fortunes in Hollywood. Born in Italy, Braggiotti was a beautiful dancer who emigrated to the USA with her cultivated musical family and married the American actor John Lodge. Her Hollywood career, however, was confined to a small part in *Rasputin and the Empress* (1933) before she went back to Italy and appeared as Queen Sophonisba in Carmine Gallone's famous epic *Scipione l'africano* (1937). Count Tullio Carminati, on the other hand, was a leading man in Italian silent cinema; in 1925 he moved to the USA, where he 'enjoyed popularity as a suave matinee idol on Broadway and in films'.[16] His most popular role was as Giulio Monteverdi, an Italian music teacher, in *One Night of Love* (1934), co-starring Grace Moore. During the war, however, he had to return to Italy when he was suspected of Fascist sympathies. Carminati (as well as Rabagliati) replicated on a smaller scale the image of Valentino as the handsome 'Latin lover'. Later they both acted in postwar American films shot in Italy, Carminati making a notable appearance in *Roman Holiday* (1953).

The journey from Italy to Hollywood intensified in the 1930s, when personalities such as Vittorio Mussolini went to the USA to study Hollywood's working methods (Mussolini was one of the sons of the Fascist leader

Benito Mussolini, and a film producer and critic). The remake of Vittorio De Sica's* hit comedy *Darò un milione* (1936), directed by Walter Lang as *I'll Give a Million* (1938), brought the popular star to the attention of Twentieth Century-Fox. Although De Sica does not appear in the remake, he was asked to do a singing screen test.[17] However, his rendering of 'Blue Moon' and improbable English dissuaded the studio from hiring him.

The only Italian star of international status from that era to go to Hollywood was the glamorous blonde diva Isa Miranda*, who was promoted as a cross between Marlene Dietrich's seductive beauty and Greta Garbo's spiritual tension. In the event, however, she only made *Hotel Imperial* (1939) and *Adventure in Diamonds* (1940). She was considered too intense and 'European' by Hollywood standards and her fiery temper caused her to be fired from George Cukor's *Zaza* (Claudette Colbert took her place in this 1936 production, although Miranda later starred in the 1944 Italian version, *Zazà*). The problem was reciprocal: if at the beginning Miranda enjoyed being away from provincial Fascist Italy, she never learned to like the 'movie factory'. The neurotic, intense diva may be a stereotype, but clearly some European actors found it difficult to accept the rule of the studios and corresponding loss of control over their own image. Miranda would much later appear in small parts in *The Shoes of the Fisherman* (1968) and in the British-American production *Summertime* (1955).

Unlike Miranda and some of the actors discussed so far in this section, other Italian émigrés in the 1930s had no previous film experience in Italy. They had, however, worked in theatre and vaudeville as well as, most significantly, in music: thus Eduardo Ciannelli*, Paul Porcasi*, Frank Puglia* and Franco Corsaro* all began their careers as singers. Ciannelli made his American debut as a baritone, and enjoyed a successful career on Broadway.[18] On screen he often played tough guys (both Italian and Latin); particularly memorable is his gangster modelled on Lucky Luciano in *Marked Woman* (1937). Porcasi was a tenor who started his career in American silents, but most of his film roles belong to the 1930s and 1940s, when he played in major and minor productions, often cast as an Italian or a 'Latin' character. Puglia was a singer and an actor who was discovered on stage by D.W. Griffith. After his debut in *Orphans of the Storm* (1921), he enjoyed a very long Hollywood career playing priests and waiters and several music conductors in a phenomenal number of films, including *Maytime* (1937), *Balalaika* (1939) and *The Phantom of the Opera* (1943). Corsaro, too, emigrated as a tenor, invited by Italian-American director Robert Vignola in the early 1930s. As a character actor, he appeared in an impressive number of Hollywood films – albeit of uneven quality – that included *Goin' to Town* (1935), *Jezebel* (1938), *The Mark of Zorro* (1940) and *Casablanca* (1942), playing a waiter in no fewer than seven films; he also worked in dubbing at Fox, as well as on the radio and on the stage.

Finally, I should also mention here Monty Banks (Mario Bianchi), who went to the USA as a dancer, worked with Fatty Arbuckle and later directed and acted in comic films of exquisite rhythm, and Fred Malatesta*, who had a brilliant international career on the stage – including on Broadway – before making more than a hundred films in Hollywood.

The Southern Italian as Stereotype

As we have seen, Italian actors in Hollywood in the 1920s and 1930s came from a variety of backgrounds, but most were connected to show business and had artistic backgrounds, notably the theatre and music. On screen, they evolved a very specific set of stereotypes of 'Italianicity', a concept with which I want to conclude this chapter. I will focus on the case study of Henry Armetta, who, despite emigrating to the USA as a boy with no prior training as a performer in Italy, perfectly embodied the Hollywood version of 'the Italian'. He started his career on the immigrant stage and in vaudeville, and became a very popular character actor in Hollywood. His filmography includes more than 150 titles from 1915 to 1946, including *The Silent Command* (1923), *Street Angel* (1928), *Lady of the Pavements* (1929), *Scarface* (1932) and *The Merry Widow* (1934). In these films he played moustachioed waiters, restaurant owners, music players, barbers and taxi drivers. In sound films, in particular, Armetta was cast very specifically as the 'Italian', to the extent that critic Frank Nugent wrote:

He generally appears as an explosive Italian with an ample waistline, a list to starboard when he walks, a ferocious grin, an amazing scowl, a habit of thwacking himself on the forehead with open hand and of biting his moustache in moments of stress and strain – which are almost constant.

This description of Armetta is very revealing of critics and audiences' expectations of 'Italian gestures'. Armetta was also appreciated for being 'inimitable, comical and yet pathetic',[19] a peculiar combination of tones that is not uncommon in the discourse about Italian actors. Indeed, Italian performers used a rich variety of tones and acting styles in both comedy and drama, which contributed to the establishment of the Italian stereotype in Hollywood cinema. Actors who were dark-haired and had a moustache frequently represented 'Latin' characters and more generally Europeans. In most cases, they played bit parts, but Armetta and Ciannelli stand out for some memorable roles: Armetta as an amusing innkeeper, in *The Devil's Brother* (1933, with Laurel and Hardy), associated with drinking and eating; Ciannelli as a menacing mobster of impeccable manners, for example as the (uncredited) cartel member in *Gilda* (1946) Each character represented the two poles of the Italian stereotype.

In any cast, Italian actors tended to come in packs. In addition to recalling Southern Italian solidarity, this grouping itself became a kind of national typecasting, connected to specific genres – films set in Mexico, in Europe, costume films, metropolitan dramas and musicals – where they constituted an interchangeable gallery of background characters. The fact that on-screen Italians were so strongly associated with Southern Italians is due to the fact that they were the most numerous subgroup among the community of immigrants, but also that there were so many actors from Southern Italy available in Hollywood. This also explains the marked musical component of the Italian stereotype.

Italian character actors came to represent a recognisable national identity in American cinema, especially in the 1930s, creating (or confirming) national stereotypes. On American screens, 'Italianicity' was presented as 'difference'. Italians were passionate, romantic but also violent and irrational; they belonged to a primitive nature. At the same time, they were associated with a cultured past, with theatre, art and music. In silent melodramas, they represented the opposite of WASP culture, as mafiosi, but also as loving parents. Rudolph Valentino tilted the balance in favour of Latin sentimentality and seductiveness, which has lasted through to Leonardo DiCaprio; but the Mafia stereotype is persistent, too, pervasive across American media from the *The Black Hand* (1906), one of the first crime films, to the television series *The Sopranos* (1999–).

Notes

1. Other silent American productions shot in Italy include three films directed by Herbert Brenon for the Italian company UCI: *La principessa misteriosa* (1920), *Il colchico e la rosa/Sisters* (1921) and *Beatrice* (1919). Henry King directed *Romola* (1925) with Lillian Gish and Ronald Colman★; George Fitzmaurice shot *A Society Exile* (1919), *The Man from Home* (1922), *Bella Donna* (1923) and the pro-Fascist *Eternal City* (1923).

2. Publicity booklet for *The White Sister* preserved at the MOMA Library. On King in Italy, see Kevin Brownlow, *The Parade's Gone By* (New York: Knopf, 1968), and *Behind the Mask of Innocence* (New York : Alfred A. Knopf, 1990).

3. When Brenon returned to the USA, he told the press of his intention to make a screen adaptation of *La cena delle beffe* (*The Jest*) by Italian playwright Sam Benelli, which was then John and Lionel Barrymore's greatest Broadway hit. On the Italian stage, Sandro Salvini played the role of Giannetto in the Italian version of the play. This episode confirms the complex interplay between Italian theatre, cinema and Hollywood at the time. According to Mario Quargnolo in *La parola ripudiata* (Gemona: La Cineteca del Friuli, 1986), p. 53, Salvini followed the Fox crew to Hollywood, working as an assistant director. This is not confirmed by other sources, but *La parola ripudiata* is the most reliable source on the interaction of American and Italian cinemas during this period.

4. William Uricchio and Roberta Pearson also discuss the role of Italian historical films and of performances of Shakespeare in Italian in the USA, in *Reframing Culture: The Case of Vitagraph Quality Films* (Princeton, NJ: Princeton University Press, 1993).

5. Francesco Pennino, grandfather of Francis Ford Coppola, was a musician. He also ran a theatre that put on shows in Italian, Southern dialects and American English, and included films, variety sketches and music in the intermissions. He evidently communicated pride in Italian culture to his family, as seen in the incorporation of Italian theatrical and musical traditions in Coppola's films.

6. The same building in East Harlem, the Grand Eden Theatre, also called Ricciardi's Grand Eden Caffè and Vega's Music Hall, became Mrs Marino's Nickelodeon. The star of Italian-American dramatic theatre Antonio Maiori and Yiddish actor Jacob Adler often shared the Grand Theatre in the Bowery, alternating in the same shows and using the same sets and costumes.

7. On early Southern Italian film culture, see Giuliana Bruno, *Streetwalking on a Ruined Map: Cultural Theory and the City Films of Elvira Notari* (Princeton, NJ: Princeton University Press, 1993). Speaking about the continuity of the immigrant theatre with national and regional traditions, Giorgio Bertellini writes in his authoritative research on Southern Italian culture and film: 'The resulting cultural stance thus turned out to be a productive reaction, articulated through mimesis, nostalgia, and identifications. These were the typical traits of their diasporic identity, made of novel elaborations of past cultural traits rather than simple continuations [. . .] Southern popular culture, in fact, did not emerge as the surviving constituency of an archaic tradition, dramatically challenged by the demands of modernity – as a common anthropological interpretation has long suggested. On the contrary, Southernist *koiné* emerged as a dynamic new cultural configuration, symptomatic of, and enriched by, strategic operations of self-repositioning.' Giorgio Bertellini, *Southern Crossings: Italians, Cinema and Modernity (Italy, 1861–New York, 1920)*, PhD dissertation (New York University, 2001).

8. Emelise Aleandri, *The Italian-American Immigrant Theatre in New York City* (Charleston, SC: Arcadia, 1999).

9. See Giuliana Muscio, *Hollywood's New Deal* (Philadelphia: Temple University Press, 1996).

10. The Foundation was created by Martin Scorsese, with Woody Allen, Francis Ford Coppola, Stanley Kubrick, George Lucas, Sydney Pollack, Robert Redford and Steven Spielberg, who were later joined by Robert Altman and Clint Eastwood. Scorsese also expresses his deep love for Italian cinema in his documentary *Il mio viaggio in Italia* (1999).

11. 'Ultimately, Farfariello popularized a poetics of "colonial" self-knowledge and of ethnic mimesis that praised regional origins and a moderate adaptation, but that also expressed anxiety over the hypothesis of complete assimilation.' Bertellini, *Southern Crossings*, p. 536.

12. *Koiné* refers to the ancient Greek language under Alexander's Empire.

13. These Italian-American productions included *Così è la vita* (1931), with Eduardo Ciannelli, and *Tormento* (1932), directed by Bruno Valletti (sometimes credited as Valetty, an attempt at Americanising his name).

14. Luisa Caselotti was the sister of Adriana Caselotti, who later dubbed the voice of Snow White in *Snow White and the Seven Dwarfs* (1937); she grew up in a typical Italian-American musical family.

15. The same phenomenon took place in Italian-American literature, where immigrant writers abandoned their native language.

16. Journalist Arnaldo Fraccaroli described his meeting with Carminati and the small Italian community making American films in *Hollywood paese d'avventura* (Milan: Treves, 1929, pp. 131–4).

17. In the screen test, De Sica appears with Milly Vitale★, who worked in Hollywood in the post–World War II period.

18. Ciannelli acted in *The Front Page, Reunion in Vienna* and *Winterset*, which was loosely based on the Sacco and Vanzetti affair. He also wrote a play, *Foolscap*, in which 'Pirandello' and 'George Bernard Shaw' wander in a madhouse; on the stage Ciannelli himself played Pirandello.

19. Undated items from a clipping file at the Rose Library, New York. The number of obituaries testifies to Armetta's wide popularity, which was not limited to the Italian community.

5 The Studio, the Star and International Audiences

Paramount and Chevalier

Martine Danan

With remarkable resilience, Hollywood has always managed to emerge stronger from challenges to its global hegemony. The first major threat to Hollywood's dominance over the international market came from the advent of sound in the late 1920s, which suddenly erected language barriers. Each major studio evolved a different strategy to cope with this technological revolution, with regard in particular to the manufacture and marketing of international stars, the symbols of Hollywood glamour at home and abroad. The simultaneous development of radio networks in the 1930s also played a key role in promoting the stars. A quarter of a century later, television appeared, once again, to endanger Hollywood's empire. The film industry, however, quickly realised the importance of forming an alliance with this new medium, especially in light of the profound economic shift linked to the demise of the studio system. In order to assess how these economic changes and technological innovations affected the choice and marketing of foreign actors in Hollywood as well as the selection of stories suitable for an international audience, I will focus on the case of Maurice Chevalier★.

Chevalier is unique because his American film career evolved in two distinct stages precisely at the critical moments in Hollywood history discussed above – from 1929 to 1934 and 1957 to 1967. During the first phase of his career in the early years of sound films, the famous French music-hall artist became the leading male star at Paramount, the most powerful studio at the time. Paramount found in this bilingual star a powerful ally in its struggle to regain dominance over foreign markets, and consequently mounted extensive international publicity campaigns around him. An examination of Paramount's strategies also reveals the studio's propensity to develop a symbiotic relationship with other entertainment forms and media such as live performances, the music industry and radio. In contrast to the first phase, the resurgence of Chevalier's American career in the mid-1950s took place against the demise of the studio system and the rise of television. Having emerged as a new television celebrity and a 'recycled' film star, Chevalier was cast in a number of 1950s and 1960s productions shot in Europe and geared to the world market. The following analysis of this international superstar's longevity, adaptability and timeliness will demonstrate how Hollywood was able constantly to devise new strategies and capitalise on all profitable media to maintain its global dominance.

In an effort to preserve their international empires threatened by the advent of sound in the late 1920s, MGM and Paramount, Hollywood's two most powerful majors, were intent upon recruiting throngs of foreign artists, especially for their multilingual versions that flourished between the autumn of 1929 and 1931 (when several versions were shot with different languages and casts). For their prestige pictures, however, they needed to identify and bring to

Relaxing at home Hollywood style: Maurice Chevalier enjoys the fruits of his triumphant career in the early 1930s

Hollywood a handful of film stars truly able to enthral both domestic and foreign audiences, as in the silent era, and ideally able to act in more than one language.[1]

Maurice Chevalier, who in the early 1920s was one of the most internationally successful music-hall performers, was predictably of great interest to the two leading studios. By 1927, Chevalier was billed in London as 'the world's highest paid star', and his Parisian shows, which incorporated some numbers in English (learned from a fellow prisoner during World War I), had an enthusiastic cosmopolitan following.[2] In addition, he was regularly making records for Columbia, an American firm recently established in France.[3] Chevalier's talent as a singer was particularly attractive to Hollywood in the early days of sound when musicals prevailed, in part because they seemed to transcend language barriers with minimal translation and have general appeal with international audiences.[4]

MGM's Irving Thalberg first offered Chevalier a contract for $5,000 per week in late 1927 after a favourable screen test, but the performer turned the proposal down on the grounds that he was earning twice as much as a Parisian music-hall star.[5] A few months later, Jesse Lasky, head of production at Paramount, granted Chevalier a trial contract meeting the artist's financial expectations. Beyond the rivalry between these two competing film executives, the story is revealing of each studio's strategic priorities. MGM continued to promote its most famous silent foreign film stars, among them Greta Garbo★. Paramount, on the other hand, was willing to pay handsomely to attract known artists from the legitimate theatre and the music hall, or to sign up rising foreign actors, such as Marlene Dietrich★.[6]

Paramount was quick to extend Chevalier a lucrative long-term contract after the instant world success of *Innocents of Paris* (1929), his first American feature and the start of his meteoric rise, making him Hollywood's number-one male film star by 1931. Since Paramount owned the most extensive theatre network in film history (thanks to its Publix theatres subsidiary) and had set up an efficient international network of distribution exchanges, Chevalier quickly became popular across the USA and all over the world.[7] *Variety*, in its yearly rating of the leading stars based on film grosses from American and foreign markets, noted that after his first two features, Chevalier had, in 1929, already climbed to third place in the roster of Paramount players because 'the foreign strength of his drawing power proved unusually heavy'.[8] By the end of 1931, *Variety* went on to remark that with sound film and the tendency in foreign markets to favour domestic stars, there were 'less than half a dozen names left in the film industry that can command box office returns in every corner of the world', with Maurice Chevalier 'undoubtedly the biggest money grabber in theatres spread around the globe'.[9]

Lasky was pleased to note that the public liked the 'happy-go-lucky ne'er-do-well' character played by Chevalier in the 'sentimental flimsey whimsey' *Innocents of Paris*, but he also remarked that 'a hundred actors could have played his part', except for 'his intriguing accent'. Lasky sensed that 'in a musical comedy of Continental sophistication [Chevalier] would have no peer' and decided to entrust him to German director Ernst Lubitsch, who had 'an unequalled instinct for Continental sophistication and wit'.[10] Thus Paramount, which had been touted as the most European studio, achieved through the Chevalier–Lubitsch partnership and their many international collaborators (from screenplay writers to lyricists and featured players) one of the aims of film-making in the studio system: differentiation from other studios' products. In Lubitsch's most witty and somewhat risqué musicals inspired by nineteenth-century operettas – such as *The Love Parade* (1929) and *The Smiling Lieutenant* (1931) – Chevalier starred as a jaunty, irresistible nobleman or charismatic officer with 'Gallic charm' in an imaginary kingdom (whose depiction, as with other mythical locations, was unlikely to offend the sensibilities of any foreign nationals).[11]

With *The Love Parade* and its world box-office records (according to *Variety*'s list of top-grossing films), the archetypal Chevalier image had been created.[12] He ended up playing European charmers in the sixteen musical comedies (including five French-language versions) that he made at Paramount between 1929 and 1933. Thus, a Paramount–Chevalier film, primarily conceived as a star vehicle around a formulaic plot, relied on a strong element of standardisation, the second keystone principle of studio film-making. Once a successful formula had been found, repeating it would normally draw the public back for more and instil confidence in exhibitors, who would be willing to pay a higher rental fee.[13] Although many, including Chevalier, resented being typecast, the studios had complete control over the roles and image of the stars they had under contract. However, to prevent saturation with typecasting and give the audience the impression of constant innovation, Chevalier's roles also included variations. For example, he was cast in a rags-to-riches story in *The Big Pond* (1930) and *The Playboy of Paris* (1930), while *A Bedtime Story* and *The Way to Love* (both 1933) also took place in a modest contemporary Parisian setting. He even made a guest appearance as himself in *Make Me a Star* (1932).

In spite of its apparent complexity and ever-changing character, Chevalier's predictable 'French' star image thus gave rise to definite audience expectations, further heightened by the studio's centralised publicity campaigns and aggressive advertising machines, which skilfully blended an artist's screen persona and private life.[14] As soon as Paramount 'acquired' Chevalier, its publicity department endeavoured to boost his international star status on both sides of the ocean, commencing with a 'whirlwind flurry of press releases', gala receptions and special engagement performances.[15] It organised a hero's send-off from France in the autumn of 1928 and featured a ceaselessly smiling Chevalier discovering American attractions in *Bonjour New York!*, a short French-language 'newsreel-travelog-documentary' intended as a promotional novelty item for European audiences.[16] This was followed by a welcome ceremony in California in October 1928 to the sound of the French national anthem, while an official biography/press kit transformed the star into a war hero, chronicled his former relationship with French music-hall queen Mistinguett and highlighted his fame in France.[17]

By April 1929, *Variety* was noting that the 'quickest, most expensive and most extensive nationwide ballyhoo ever accorded a new favourite' was surrounding the new sex symbol, the '"It" man for women on the screen'.[18] Building on Chevalier's screen persona as an object of desire, the Paramount publicity staff encouraged female fans' worship of the 'Idol of Paris'.[19] For instance, after the success of *The Big Pond* among female audiences, Paramount sponsored an essay competition on the theme 'why I love Chevalier'.[20] Chevalier's image as a sex symbol was bolstered by well-publicised affairs with starlets (detailed in studio 'copy' relayed by fan magazines and gossip columnists), and rumours of an affair with Marlene Dietrich, who by the early 1930s had become Paramount's other foreign superstar. The American mystique was also played up for French and other foreign fans as hundreds of publications around the world were regularly provided with translated stories about Chevalier's glamorous life in Hollywood, which echoed the high production values of his American films.[21]

Paramount executives also recognised the value of drawing upon older, more established forms of entertainment, which imparted a sense of immediacy and community to screen representations.[22] Chevalier's magnetic presence as a music-hall artist was recaptured when, breaking from established cinematic rules, the singer was allowed to address the audience directly in his films, as on a stage. For example, in *The Smiling Lieutenant*, Chevalier makes his standard 'singing-his-libido-directly-to-the-camera entry'.[23] In *One Hour with You* (1932), his confidential asides about marital difficulties periodically interrupt the narrative.[24] And in *The Love Parade*, Chevalier even puts on his famous straw hat before singing his farewell song directly to the camera.[25]

Paramount also encouraged Chevalier to remain in touch with his fans through live performances in the USA and Europe, and it contractually agreed to pay for two annual trips to France. Live performances did not simply help maintain a star's contact with audiences; they also encouraged tie-ins between various branches of the music business. Theme songs popularised by successful films became standards in the live vaudeville performances that usually preceded feature films in the deluxe movie theatres until 1934.[26] Hundreds of Chevalier impersonators performed Chevalier hits such as 'Valentine', 'Louise' (from *Innocents of Paris*) and 'Mimi' (from *The Love Parade*). In addition, movie companies invested heavily in the sheet-music industry that had been dominated by the small Tin Pan Alley companies set up in Lower Manhattan at the turn of the twentieth century. A major success meant the sale of up to half a million sheets for a song (and a similar number of records) within a month of a musical's release.[27]

Not only did Paramount executives believe in the benefits of a symbiotic relationship between live performances, the music industry and cinema, but the studio also actively pursued a partnership with radio, which by 1927 **55** had become part of everyday life in the USA. That year, NBC, the first national, advertising-based radio network was founded by RCA (Radio Corporation of America), and in 1928 a second network, CBS, had begun to operate.[28] Viewing radio as a source of new talent and free advertising, Paramount was the only studio, with the exception of RKO (founded by RCA in 1928), to embark upon a rapid large-scale alliance with radio – a strategy facilitated by Paramount's acquisition of 49 per cent of CBS stocks in 1929.[29] New releases could be hyped in the weekly 'Paramount-Publix Hour', popular songs like 'Louise' were played daily and stars like Chevalier were offered highly lucrative contracts to sing in a series of radio shows.[30]

Paramount took advantage of another 1929 radio technological breakthrough – the first satellite transmission – to heighten 'global' awareness of its productions and increase its stars' international visibility.[31] More specifically, in 1929 and 1930 Paramount produced several radio programmes incorporating *The Love Parade*'s soundtrack and featuring Chevalier singing. These programmes were broadcast simultaneously in the USA, Paris and London in order to bolster the studio's huge international publicity campaign for this film. The March 1930, two-hour broadcast was for the first time extended to the entire French territory by means of relays and pickups.[32] But all these experiments were short-lived. Declining theatre attendance in the wake of the Great Depression, accusations of unfair radio competition and growing financial difficulties due to huge mortgage payments forced Paramount to sell its stock back to CBS in 1932 and rely on less innovative marketing techniques.[33]

By 1933, the studio was on the verge of receivership, and a number of its stars had started to move to MGM, the most profitable film company at the time. Chevalier was no exception – this time Paramount was unable to match an offer made by Irving Thalberg.[34] At MGM, Chevalier starred in *The Merry Widow* (1934), then was loaned to Twentieth Century-Fox for *Folies Bergère de Paris*[35] (1935) for a part Charles Boyer⋆ had declined.[36] Although by 1932 Hollywood had recognised the failure of most multilingual versions, these two films were made in two languages (English and French), both versions starring Chevalier, which attests to the studios' sustained belief in the power of attraction of some of their international superstars.

The Merry Widow was critically acclaimed but made little profit given its record $1.6 million production cost.[37] Chevalier's popularity was also waning fast with both domestic and foreign markets.[38] Foreign audiences were getting increasingly intolerant of non-translated English songs, and the public in general was growing tired of musicals, which had over-saturated the market. Many Chevalier films, whose European sophistication and risqué nature had irritated middle America, became the target of censors enforcing the Hays Code by 1934.[39] As the novelty of sound was wearing off, movies could no longer simply be star vehicles and nostalgic recreations of live entertainment. More than anything else, the public expected strong plots. According to *Variety*, 'The day of the star drawing over the picture seems to be going or has already gone. [. . .] The element during 1933 was story first and cast afterwards.'[40]

No longer a sure box-office draw, Chevalier failed to negotiate top billing for his next scheduled film, *The Chocolate Soldier*, with Grace Moore as co-star. The project collapsed[41] and a disillusioned Chevalier returned to France. He was not to make another American film until *Love in the Afternoon* for Allied Artists in 1957.

It was another technological innovation and a very different business environment that brought Chevalier back to the USA in the 1950s. By that time, the studio system had disintegrated and television had become commonplace, with 85 per cent of American homes equipped with television sets by 1956–7.[42] The demise of the studio system had been triggered in 1948 by the famous Paramount anti-trust case decision forcing the majors to break up their vertically integrated operations and give up their control of exhibition. The breakdown was accelerated by the changing lifestyles of the American public, then in the process of migrating to the suburbs, spending more on consumer goods and turning to television for entertainment.[43] As in the early days of radio, television was first perceived by studio executives as a dangerous competitor taking away a shrinking audience from movie theatres. But as with radio, it soon appeared that co-operation between television and cinema was far more fruitful than an adversarial relationship. Co-operation became particularly beneficial in the recruitment of talent. The need for countless hours of programming created an artist shortage, which forced television executives to import numerous foreign actors and bring back former celebrities. *Collier's* magazine emphasised this trend in a 1955 article: 'Burning up stars and material faster than it can find replacements, TV has now reached across the sea for top attractions – snaring both exciting new faces and some of the greatest names of other years.'[44] Among the highest-rated television programmes of the mid-1950s were musical variety shows, which incorporated earlier entertainment traditions such as vaudeville, and relied on the aura of former Hollywood stars, whose glamour, popularity and box-office draw suddenly appeared hard to match. Soon, not only television stations but studios too started 'competing energetically' for rediscovered 1930s stars, and Hollywood strove to recycle their personae in new narratives.[45]

And so, an ageing Chevalier was able to re-enter American show business through television. His debut took place in December 1954, as the guest of Bob Hope, who was actively recruiting European performers for his show, and he received an invitation to participate in the 1955 Academy Awards ceremony soon after.[46] In December 1955, he was featured in his first ninety-minute NBC live spectacular, *The Maurice Chevalier Show*, reviving in older moviegoers recollections of 'the tilt of the straw, the jut of the jaw and the glib Gallic nuances of the man who sang Louise'.[47] Impressed by his performance, movie executives invited him to sing 'Louise' at the 1956 Academy Awards ceremony (accompanied in the background by a clip from *Innocents of Paris*). This latest television appearance allegedly brought him to the attention of Billy Wilder, who directed Chevalier in the star's first postwar American film, *Love in the Afternoon*.[48] He was subsequently invited to appear in numerous one-man shows and television variety shows such as CBS's top-rated *Ed Sullivan Show*, which between 1948 and 1971 showcased the best-known international performers. In 1959, ninety million spectators watched Chevalier receive an honorary Academy Award for his 'contribution to the world of entertainment for more than half a century'. Through television, younger generations discovered Chevalier, while older spectators were reminded of the dashing Frenchman of their youth. At a time of dwindling cinema attendance, the ability to attract a variety of constituencies was soon perceived as a key to box-office success.[49]

It was even more important to attract foreign audiences, since the American box-office potential was severely reduced, while overseas rentals, especially from Western Europe, surpassed domestic grosses by the late 1950s.[50] To differentiate itself from television and attract a cosmopolitan audience, Hollywood deliberately aimed at creating a 'global product'. This strategy concentrated on a smaller number of high production value blockbusters (benefiting from technological improvements such as CinemaScope and VistaVision), which were based on wide-appeal, action-oriented stories situated in a striking foreign locale. Such productions generally embodied exoticism and lavish expenditure in the eyes of the domestic public, but they also seemed to cater to the interests of an international audience.[51]

Another reason for the choice of foreign settings in the 1950s and 1960s was purely economic, with the reliance on the so-called 'runaway productions', which were shot abroad with the assistance of foreign artists and technicians. This postwar production trend resulted from foreign legislative restrictions, which forced American film companies to reinvest frozen assets into local production. However, the majors soon observed that films made abroad could be less expensive and that under the guise of their own overseas subsidiaries, they could also qualify for multiple financial aid schemes set up by other countries to boost their own film industries.[52] Consequently, a great many films were shot in Europe, especially in Italy, England and France, the countries with the most extensive film subsidies and the largest potential audience for American movies.[53] It is estimated that films financed by American funds abroad represented 60 per cent of the total American film production in the 1960s.[54]

Chevalier's American career in the late 1950s and early 1960s perfectly illustrates this runaway production trend. Both *Love in the Afternoon* and MGM's hit *Gigi* (1958) – for which a part specially written for Chevalier was added to Colette's original story – were filmed in France. In the wake of *Gigi*'s success, Chevalier continued playing other avuncular, debonair versions of his 1930s screen persona with his age-old boating hat and appreciating eye for young ladies: in *Count Your Blessings* (1959), another MGM film shot in England and France; in Twentieth Century-Fox's *Can-Can* (1960), shot in Hollywood but based on a stage musical about the famous dance in turn-of-the-century Montmartre; in Paramount's *A Breath of Scandal* (1960), filmed in Italy but set in Austria; and in his last major film, Warner Bros.' *Fanny* (1961), a condensed version of the famous 1930s trilogy of films by Marcel Pagnol, which had already been turned into a Broadway musical.

Several of these films were musicals attempting to capitalise on the Broadway shows' popularity, perhaps paralleling the escapism of the Depression era. *Gigi*, which (as a musical) was inspired by *My Fair Lady* and endowed with a score by the same Lerner–Loewe team, met with tremendous success in the USA. Yet, in spite of an impressive publicity campaign, replete with the reconstitution of a late-nineteenth-century Paris on opening night, *Gigi* met with a lukewarm reception in France. Musicals were becoming increasingly unpopular outside the USA, perhaps because they alienated foreign audiences with their reliance on stereotypical images of Europe and their English-language songs.[55] By 1960 Hollywood dropped its musical productions to an all-time low, largely because it could not afford to alienate over half its market.[56] Chevalier's film career waned after this last burst of musicals, and he was relegated to secondary roles or cameo appearances in minor films.

Towards the end of his career, Chevalier had become less a film star with a mystique than a touring celebrity. He became an unofficial French ambassador invited to public events with heads of state, and was featured in numerous magazine articles. Chevalier's fame was strengthened by his own uncanny ability for self-promotion, as he told the story of his life in twelve autobiographical books and managed to turn each new birthday into a media event. In his '81st year', Chevalier placed a full-page advertisement in *Variety* to remind American film producers that he was still seeking employment in the movie business:

> Dear Variety,
> I am in my 81st year and have decided to quit doing 'One man Shows' while everybody is still asking from everywhere
> – That's that – But I still feel I could do a fine job on international television – also on the big screen – So – wish me
> luck with the same kind of heart that I wish the very best of luck – in 1969 – to the great U-S-A-
> Maurice Chevalier[57]

Unfortunately, he had by then become more valuable as an enduring icon of Hollywood prestige than as a performer.

A quintessential showman who evolved from international sex symbol to nostalgic grandfatherly image, Maurice Chevalier 'made in America' turned out to be Hollywood's ideal emissary at key points in the history of the film industry. By the early 1930s, at the apex of the studio system with its elaborate marketing techniques, Paramount had turned the music-hall artist into the number-one international male star. When in the 1950s the studio system disintegrated and domestic revenues declined, Hollywood bounced back with the reintroduction of early sound stars like Chevalier, coupled with the search for fresh global formulas. Chevalier's lasting success is a telling example of Hollywood's ability to accommodate technological innovations and changing economic structures, while adapting its narratives to international tastes.

Notes

1. Ginette Vincendeau, 'Hollywood Babel: The Coming of Sound and the Multiple-Language Version', in Andrew Higson and Richard Maltby (eds), *'Film Europe' and 'Film America': Cinema, Commerce and Cultural Exchange 1920–1939* (Exeter: Exeter University Press, 1999), pp. 220–1; Martine Danan, 'Hollywood's Hegemonic Strategies: Overcoming French Nationalism at the Advent of Sound', in Higson and Maltby, *'Film Europe'*, pp. 234–7.

2. Michael Freeland, *Maurice Chevalier* (New York: William Morrow & Co., 1981), p. 95; Edward Behr, *The Good Frenchman: The True Story of the Life and Time of Maurice Chevalier* (New York: Villard Books, 1993), p. 117.

3. Claudine Kirgenec, *Maurice Chevalier: itinéraire d'un inconnu célèbre* (Paris: Vernal/Philippe Lebaud, 1988), p. 99.

4. Kristin Thompson, *Exporting Entertainment: America in the World Film Market 1907–1934* (London: BFI, 1985), p. 159.

5. Freeland, *Maurice Chevalier*, p. 99.

6. Douglas Gomery, *The Hollywood Studio System* (New York: St Martin's Press, 1986), pp. 40, 45.

7. Ibid., pp. 26–9, 34.

8. Arthur Ungar, 'Leading Film Stars, 1929', *Variety*, 8 January 1930, p. 80.

9. Wolfe Kaufman, 'Few International Stars', *Variety*, 29 December 1931, p. 13.

10. Jesse Lasky, *I Blow My Own Horn* (Garden City, New York: Doubleday & Co., 1957), p. 226.

11. James M. Collins, 'The Musical', in Wes Gehrings (ed.), *Handbook of American Film Genres* (New York: Greenwood Press, 1988), p. 271; 'Mythical Sylvania Great for Versions', *Variety*, 19 November 1930, p. 6; Ruth Vasey, 'Foreign Parts: Hollywood's Global Distribution and the Representation of Ethnicity', *American Quarterly* vol. 44 no. 4 (1992), pp. 621, 635.

12. Tino Balio, *Grand Design: Hollywood as a Modern Business Enterprise, 1930–39* (New York: Scribner's Sons, 1993), p. 405.

13. Ibid., pp. 144, 168.

14. Janet Staiger, 'Announcing Wares, Winning Patrons, Voicing Ideals', *Cinema Journal* vol. 29 no. 3 (1990), pp. 13–14; Gomery, *The Hollywood Studio System*, p. 29; Balio, *Grand Design*, p. 169.

15. Lasky, *I Blow My Own Horn*, p. 225.

16. Gene Ringgold and Bodeen DeWitt, *Chevalier: The Films and Career of Maurice Chevalier* (Secaucus, NJ: Citadel Press, 1993), p. 70.

17. Behr, *The Good Frenchman*, pp. 137, 139, 141.

18. 'Showing "It" on to the French Star and Paramount's Ballyhoo', *Variety*, 24 April 1929, p. 1.

19. 'Innocents of Paris', *Variety*, 1 May 1929, p. 26.

20. Freeland, *Maurice Chevalier*, p. 113.

21. O. R. Geyer, 'Putting over Foreign Publicity', *Variety*, 7 August 1929, p. 24.

22. Jane Feuer, *The Hollywood Musical*, 2nd edn. (Bloomington: Indiana University Press, 1993), p. 2.

23. Richard Barrios, *A Song in the Dark: The Birth of the Musical Film* (Oxford: Oxford University Press, 1995), p. 345.

24. 'One Hour with You', *Variety*, 29 March 1932, p. 24.

25. Feuer, *The Hollywood Musical*, p. 38.

26. Balio, *Grand Design*, p. 27.

27. Alexander Walker, *The Shattered Silents: How the Talkies Came to Stay* (New York: William Morrow, 1979), p. 179.

28. Michele Hilmes, *Hollywood and Broadcasting: From Radio to Cable* (Urbana and Chicago: University of Illinois Press, 1990), pp. 37–8.

29. Richard Jewell, 'Hollywood and Radio: Competition and Partnership in the 1930s', *Historical Journal of Film, Radio and Television* vol. 4 no. 2 (1984), p. 126.

30. Ibid., p. 127; Freeland, *Maurice Chevalier*, pp. 110, 125.

31. Behr, *The Good Frenchman*, pp. 162, 163.

32. 'Par. and Tiffany Plan Ballyhoos', *Variety*, 25 December 1929, p. 1; 'Broadcasts Smash Hit all over France', *Variety*, 19 March 1930, p. 7.

33. Jewell, 'Hollywood and Radio', p. 128; Gomery, *The Hollywood Studio System*, p. 31.

34. Ringgold and De Witt, *Chevalier*, p. 119.

35. The French version of the film was entitled *Folies-Bergère* (1936).

36. James Harding, *Maurice Chevalier: His Life 1888–1972* (London: Secker and Warburg, 1982), p. 125.

37. Barrios, *A Song in the Dark*, p. 424.

38. Arthur Ungar, 'Leading Names of '34', *Variety,* 1 January 1935, pp. 1, 36; Wolfe Kaufman, 'Film Stars' World Draw', *Variety*, 1 January 1935, p. 28.

39. Barrios, *A Song in the Dark*, p. 346.

40. Arthur Ungar, 'Leading Film Names of '33', *Variety*, 2 January 1934, p. 1.

41. A version of *The Chocolate Soldier* was made in 1941 with Nelson Eddy and Risë Stevens.

42. Erik Barnouw, *Tube of Plenty: The Evolution of American Television*, 2nd edn. (Oxford: Oxford University Press, 1990), p. 198.

43. Thomas Guback, 'Hollywood's International Market', in Tino Balio (ed.), *The American Film Industry* (Madison: University of Wisconsin Press, 1976) p. 398.

44. Evelyn Harvey, 'TV Imports', *Collier's*, 14 October 1955, p. 54.

45. Denise Mann, 'Spectacularization of Everyday Life', in Jeremy Butler (ed.), *Star Texts: Image and Performance in Film and Television* (Detroit, MI: Wayne State University Press, 1991), pp. 336, 339–40; Fred Hift, 'Old Film Stars Never Die – Just Keep B.O. Rolling Along', *Variety*, 7 September 1955, p. 7.

46. 'Old Hands across the Seas: Hope Goes Abroad to Get Chevalier and Lillie for His TV Show', *Life*, 6 December 1954, p. 121; Ringgold and DeWitt, *Chevalier*, p.49.

47. Harding, *Maurice Chevalier*, p. 179; Harvey, 'TV Imports', p. 55.

48. 'Special Movies Report', *Newsweek*, 2 March 1959, p. 54.

49. John Izod, *Hollywood and the Box-Office 1895–1986* (New York: Columbia University Press, 1988), p. 158.

50. Mitchel Gordon, 'Film for Foreigners', *Wall Street Journal*, 25 February 1959, p. 1; Guback, 'Hollywood's International Market', p. 403; Izod, *Hollywood and the Box-Office*, p. 159.

51. Gordon, 'Film for Foreigners', pp. 1, 6.

52. Guback, 'Hollywood's International Market', pp. 400–1.

53. Thomas Guback, 'Film as International Business', *Journal of Communication* vol. 25 no. 1 (1974), p. 92.

54. Ibid., p. 97.

55. 'O'Seas Chill Reducing U.S. Musicals', *Variety*, 20 January 1960, p. 3; Herm Schoenfeld, 'Filmusical Dip Cues the Blues', *Variety*, 28 January 1959, p. 43; Gordon, 'Film for Foreigners', p. 1.

56. 'O'Seas Chill', p. 3.

57. Maurice Chevalier, handwritten letter, *Variety*, 8 January 1969, p. 63.

6 'Star trading'

The British in 1930s and 1940s Hollywood

Sarah Street

During the 1930s and 1940s many British film stars travelled to Hollywood, some for short periods of time, while others managed to establish careers on a longer-term basis. Those who appeared in a considerable number of films over many years tended to adjust well to the Hollywood system, their path facilitated by the common language and vogue for British literature and history. Although British actors did travel to Hollywood in the 1920s, it was the arrival of sound that encouraged a more sustained wave of emigration. Many were invited over by American companies after demonstrating success in British films, for example Robert Donat★, Deborah Kerr★ and James Mason★, whose work for Alexander Korda and the Rank Organisation advertised their suitability for export. For others, including Charles Laughton★, Laurence Olivier★ and Stewart Granger★, a theatrical background was of key importance. Success on Broadway was an established path whereby actors' performances would be studied by Hollywood executives. The best actors would be singled out as interesting prospects for the screen and offered film contracts, in some cases after a screen test, though the latter was not always necessary if the actor was particularly famous. The extent of theatrical experience was a crucial indicator of screen potential. On the other hand, as John Baxter has argued, too much allegiance to 'the theatre' encouraged in some actors a snobbish attitude towards screen acting, and actors who thought of themselves as 'belonging' to the theatre tended not to stay in Hollywood.[1] Laurence Olivier and John Gielgud★ were therefore first and foremost stage actors, bringing to their intermittent screen performances a thespian sensibility that Hollywood found attractive. Yet neither actor ever considered abandoning their stage careers for glittering Hollywood offers, as was the case for lesser-known stage performers who became established screen actors, such as Ronald Colman★ or Leslie Howard★. For older actors, including Herbert Marshall★, C. Aubrey Smith★ and Cedric Hardwicke★, who had enjoyed distinguished stage careers, Hollywood provided the security of well-paid supporting roles that saved them from financial anxiety and fading glory. As Mark Glancy has put it: 'Being British was their livelihood.'[2]

'At home and not at home': Hollywood Britishness

Hollywood's eagerness to sign up British actors and writers in the early 1930s relates to a fascination with 'Britishness' that highlighted the class system, British history and institutions. As Glancy observes, this suggests an ambivalent attitude towards Britain, on the one hand rejecting its traditions as distinct from American democratic ideals, while on the other relishing stereotypical representations of country house life, public schools, Oxbridge and the British Empire.[3] Hollywood had an insatiable appetite for British culture, buying the rights to novels and plays and having no qualms about producing films with largely British casts, set in British locations created on Hollywood lots. For some actors, this created an unreal feeling, of being at home but not at home. Robert Donat likened Hollywood to an Ideal Homes exhibition, a giant film set where no one actually lives.[4] This fascination extended to the way the so-called British community in Hollywood was reported in fan magazines. As John Russell-Taylor has suggested, there was a large element of Hollywood fantasy about the British colony that belied the actual complexity of living there, working on a day-to-day basis with other Europeans and Americans.[5] If anything, the persistence of the stereotype indicates the extent to which complex nationality was subsumed, adapted and processed by Hollywood into a one-dimensional yet potent representation. Rather than acknowledge that various actors expressed different 'versions' of Britishness, and did not all live the same way, Hollywood preferred to suggest that British actors behaved much as expatriates in the British Empire, serving tea at four o'clock, buying *The Times* and organising cricket matches. While there is a certain amount of truth in this image as represented by actors such as C. Aubrey Smith, there is a world of difference between his 'Britishness' and that of, say, Charles Laughton, who mixed very much with other European émigrés and did not fit into the stereotype of a refined English gentleman as conveyed by Ronald Colman. When Michael Redgrave★ first went to Hollywood in 1947, he was promoted by Universal as 'the clean-limbed, all-weather type of Englishman', only to be re-presented to audiences by RKO months later as an 'English classical actor, pipe-smoking, reclusive, deeply philosophical'.[6] Significant degrees of variation therefore existed beneath the dominant image.

An intriguing aspect of the absorption of British actors into the classical Hollywood studio system is the way in which British accents, considered to be incomprehensible in British films, were adapted to suit American ears. While the arrival of sound cinema promised a wider audience for British films based on the common language, this was not unproblematic. Reviewers frequently complained that the accent was difficult to understand. In one extreme case, *White Face* (1932), an adaptation of an Edgar Wallace play produced by Michael Balcon, was dubbed with American accents. By the 1950s, British producers were learning that it was not so much the accent itself but how it was presented that was the key to solving the problem. In its use of the British accent, Hollywood had made it more acceptable by giving actors diction coaching for clearer enunciation, sharper delivery and a sense of even pacing. When Michael Truman, Ealing's chief editor, went to the USA in the late 1940s to edit Ealing's films for the American market, he studied the differences between accents in British and American films. He concluded that in British films words were 'drawled out', indistinct and difficult to follow, commenting that by contrast Americans 'probably speak more rapidly than we do, they enunciate each syllable separately, keep air between the words and balance their weight in the sentences to form colour and emphasis'.[7] This general observation could be extended to the way American producers and directors approached British accents. As British director Ronald Neame observed on a visit to Hollywood in 1945: 'All new actors out here receive instruction on voice production . . . Perfect screen voices are those of Robert Donat, Ronald Colman, Herbert Marshall, Greer Garson and Vivien Leigh.'[8] As well as voice training, extensive post-synchronisation was common Hollywood practice, giving quick and clear results.

Star Trading

As well as the natural advantages provided by the common language, moving to Hollywood was an attractive proposition for many British actors during this period, largely because of the assumed economic benefits. Many saw the move as a logical step forward from a successful career in British films. They also hoped that they could pursue careers in both countries, even if at times this could be problematic. By the 1930s, the British film industry had recovered from the severe recession it had experienced in the 1920s. Larger companies, such as Gaumont-British and London Film Productions, forged links with American film companies in the hope that British films would be distributed effectively in the USA. It was hoped that once British actors became better known in the USA there would be a greater demand for British films and actors. 'Star trading' operated as part of film industry economics in a decade when Hollywood was concerned about maintaining its domination of the British market, and when British film producers were keen to develop export strategies. It also symbolised the Anglo-American 'special relationship' in commercial and political terms, as announcements of the various transatlantic crossings made by British stars and directors were reported on a regular basis by the trade press. By dint of the common language, British films occupied a particular place in the American market and were distributed by United Artists, Universal and a host of small independent distribution companies.[9] The international success of Korda's *The Private Life of Henry VIII* (1933), for example, introduced Merle Oberon★ and Robert Donat to American audiences. Both

Like many of his compatriots, Robert Donat embodied a class-based vision of Britishness, while he compared Hollywood to a giant film set where no-one actually lived

received offers to star in Hollywood films on the strength of their performances in this key film. The success of *Henry VIII* tapped into the American fascination with British history and institutions, as well as influencing Hollywood's later 'history' films such as *The Private Lives of Elizabeth and Essex* (1939). Contacts between British and American companies were often instrumental in facilitating an actor's initial entrée to Hollywood, as in the case of Stewart Granger (Rank's link with Universal), Merle Oberon (Korda's partnership in United Artists) and Madeleine Carroll★ (Michael Balcon's active pursuit of an export policy in the 1930s).

Both countries were able to acknowledge and exploit each other's economic priorities. Several reciprocal schemes were envisioned in recognition of the mutual benefits to be gained from 'star trading'. Michael Balcon visited the USA many times during the 1930s, planning to exchange actors contracted to Gaumont-British with American actors who he hoped would agree to appear in British films. This strategy was not applied indiscriminately, since not all the actors contracted to Gaumont-British were suitable for offering to American studios. Although Jessie Matthews★ demonstrated an appeal to American audiences in her 'art deco' musicals, her insistence on co-starring with her husband Sonnie Hale was strongly disapproved of by Balcon, who felt that Hale would be 'difficult' for the American market.[10] Balcon facilitated potentially productive partnerships with care. On his return after one visit to the USA in 1935, he announced contracts with American stars including Robert Young, Constance Bennett, Sylvia Sidney and Richard Arlen.[11] Other stars Balcon imported included Paul Robeson, Esther Ralston, Richard Dix, Edmund Lowe and Noah Beery. Notwithstanding the casting of Sonnie Hale, the pairing of Jessie Matthews and Robert Young in *It's Love Again* (1936) proved a box-office attraction in both Britain and the USA.

Despite these efforts, 'star trading' did not really work as a coherent policy, and the stakes were certainly not equal. Only a few American actors, such as those signed by Balcon, could be enticed to work in Britain, although this situation changed after 1938 when more American companies produced films on location in the UK in order to qualify for quota status as 'British' films.[12] On the other hand, it was not always the case that British stars were able simply to leave for Hollywood or, indeed, that they wished to do so. Once a British star was becoming well known on both sides of the Atlantic, as in the case of Madeleine Carroll after *The Thirty-Nine Steps* (1935), his or her value as exchange property increased. At the same time, Balcon's dependence on key stars such as Carroll made him reluctant to sanction their transfer to Hollywood for fear that they would never return. As the major vertically integrated British companies, Gaumont-British and the Associated British Picture Corporation, became more dominant, stars' contracts were more binding and longer-term than in the 1920s, when actors might work for several different companies in succession. While the will for reciprocity was therefore present, in practice it was frustrated by contractual complications and the fear of many British actors that once in Hollywood they could lose a considerable amount of freedom or be unable to return to Britain when opportunities arose for film or theatre work. As Clive Brook★, a British actor who left Hollywood in 1934 warned: 'Hollywood is a chain-gang, and we movie actors never escape'.[13]

Binding Contracts

While British contracts were becoming more stringent, they were nevertheless not so restrictive as those conventionally offered by Hollywood studios. This is revealed by the case of Warner Bros. vs. Robert Donat, an actor who was courted by Hollywood throughout the 1930s and 1940s but who refused to lose his independence to work where he liked and on which projects.[14] In November 1934, Irving Asher, a Warner Bros.' representative who had the reputation of being able to negotiate contracts with major stars and 'almost to hypnotise people into signing them', was anxious to sign Donat.[15] At the time, Donat was discussing his stage career and the possibility of appearing in the film *Anthony Adverse* (eventually produced in 1936 starring Fredric March and Olivia de Havilland). Asher cabled Warner Bros. in Hollywood, claiming that Donat was ready to sign for three films, one of which he wanted to be *Anthony Adverse*, but would have to receive a higher salary because Paramount had just offered him $5,000 a week. Warners' head office replied that it was impossible to guarantee Donat the lead part in *Anthony Adverse*, but agreed to three films at $25,000 each and other fairly generous financial provisions. Asher embellished this offer in a cable to Donat, implying that in addition to the financial provisions suggested by Warners, the company assured him that he was in a strong running position for *Anthony Adverse*, as well as guaranteeing him parts in *Captain Blood* (1935, eventually played by Errol Flynn) and *Don Juan* (an unrealised project). Most importantly, Asher erroneously implied that Warners would guarantee Donat agreement over story material. This more generous 'translation' of Warners' offer kept Donat interested but concealed a crucial element known as the 'Hunter contract'. This included clauses that gave the producer ultimate say as to how a part should be played. The arrangement was confirmed in a brief telephone conversation between Donat and Jack Warner, when neither of them knew that Asher had fabricated key aspects of the deal. They only discussed money, so Asher was able to produce a contract in December 1934, with Donat still under the impression that in essence it was identical to the terms of his original cable. Once Donat found out about the 'Hunter contract' clauses he regretted signing the document, claiming that Asher's cable constituted a more accurate pre-agreement. In May 1935, Warner Bros. served Donat with a writ that claimed that they had a binding and exclusive contract with him.[16] In the subsequent legal action, the Judge decided that since Asher had misrepresented Warners' view, the final contract was invalid. Donat was therefore freed from a contract he found restrictive and objectionable, and he never made a film for Warner Bros.

The case illustrates the inherent tensions within Hollywood's trawl for British talent. On the one hand, it shows the lengths to which a zealous employee would go in order to sign up a popular star, but on the other, it reveals the producer-oriented nature of Hollywood contracts that was intensifying at this time. The standard Hollywood contract was for seven years, giving a studio the option every six months either to continue with or to drop a star's services. The actor or actress had no legal right to break a contract, nor were they allowed to contradict a studio's decision about how to 'act, sing, pose, speak or perform' a particular role. Only the top stars, such as James Cagney and Bette Davis, could challenge the domination of the studios, while the majority of players were forced to conform to restrictive terms until well into the 1950s.[17] As a stage actor, Donat was used to having considerable say in the parts he played, and his work with Alexander Korda gave him flexibility as a screen actor. While the sums paid by British producers could not compete with the higher amounts offered by Hollywood, British actors were often reluctant to commit themselves to what they saw as unreasonably binding conditions. On the other hand, studios would often take advantage of foreign stars who were anxious to make a name for themselves in Hollywood. In 1950, Stewart Granger found himself committed to a seven-year contract with MGM when the company refused to pay the expenses he had incurred on his first arrival in Hollywood. He had mistaken the lavish reception he had been given as an indication of his worth as a star, assuming that MGM would foot the bill as part of their 'hospitality' to visiting stars presenting him with a bill for debts he could not pay, MGM manoeuvred Granger into signing a contract he resented in exchange for them bailing him out of his financial embarrassment.[18]

Different Concepts of Stardom

As mentioned earlier, some British actors maintained a fierce allegiance to the theatre despite inducements to move to Hollywood. Robert Donat found himself in dispute with MGM (the British unit) over a contract he had signed in 1938 to make six films. When war broke out, he wanted to stay in Britain even though the company was pressurising him to work for their main studio in Hollywood. Donat's contract gave him time in between films to do stage work, but in 1943 MGM issued him with an injunction restraining him from acting on stage in Shaw's *Heartbreak House* (1916–17, performed 1920), because it might conflict with the start of shooting a new film. In the event, Donat had to leave the play because of ill health but the incident is typical of the tension he always felt between theatre and film work. Like many British actors he considered his stage work to be a vital element of his career and resented it bitterly when the studios were not sympathetic. As he explained:

> It was not for nothing that I had fought with all my might and main against the strictures of the MGM set-up, which continually frustrated my desire to act on the stage. This desire is not merely a whim of mine. It is a dire creative need, and having

shaken off the shackles of Hollywood and resisted their oft repeated blandishments for some considerable time the theatre must come first and foremost in my life or I must forever suppress my artistic conscience and sell myself entirely to films.[19]

Consequently, Donat was one of the most sought-after British stars, who nevertheless remained aloof from Hollywood's repeated offers. These examples underline some of the fundamental differences between British and American conceptions of stardom. Whereas in Britain, actors such as Donat and Margaret Lockwood* equated 'good acting' primarily with theatrical experience and rejected the lures of Hollywood stardom, American and some British actors responded well to the demands the studio system made of them. A few, such as Charles Laughton, managed to diversify their careers so that theatrical and educational outlets were not inconsistent with their film work. Laughton's reading tours are an example of this, during which he perpetuated an image of intellectualism and independence from Hollywood.[20]

For other actors, problems with Hollywood extended beyond the contract. When British music-hall and film comedienne Cicely Courtneidge* went to Hollywood in 1935 for the first time to star in MGM's *The Perfect Gentleman* (1935), she experienced severe difficulties with the studio over their understanding of her performance skills. She was known for her light-hearted, musical-comedy/burlesque style that was very popular with British audiences, particularly in her sparring screen pairings with her husband Jack Hulbert. Care was taken in trying to make this very British star 'exportable'. Michael Balcon eased her path by alerting his contacts to her arrival. She was directed by Tim Whelan, an American who had worked in Britain in the early 1930s and had already directed Courtneidge in *Aunt Sally* (1933). She wrote home to Michael Balcon, complaining that the studio disagreed with the style she had developed with Whelan. Under threat of Whelan being replaced, Courtneidge and her favourite director were forced to comply with MGM's conception of the performance style and direction. In her deepest period of frustration, she wrote: 'I have done all they told me in this film but it is not good material and any of their people out here could do what I have been asked to do in the film.'[21] In this instance, the actress feared that the studio was seeking to stifle her individuality by favouring an approach that appeared to disregard the comic techniques she had developed in Britain. It is likely that once in the USA it soon became apparent that the 'indigenous' nature of Courtneidge's comedy was inappropriate for American audiences. Courtneidge soon returned to work for Gaumont-British.

Another actress who was 'misunderstood' was Mrs Patrick Campbell, the acclaimed stage actress who went to Hollywood in 1930 and was welcomed for her reputation, clear diction and friendship with George Bernard Shaw. Her unconventional behaviour, caustic tongue and general unsuitability for film acting consigned her screen career to only five years. While at first her theatrical background had been an advantage, she was unable to adapt her acting for the screen. Once under contract, the studios tried to be diplomatic about offering her fewer and fewer parts. She repeated their explanation to Shaw: 'The studios say I am too celebrated for small parts and too English to star – that Kalamazoo and Butte, Montana and Seattle would not understand my English style and speech.'[22] Nearer the truth was that the studios were concerned about her overt theatricality, failing memory and fading looks. Also, she failed to do what many of her male counterparts had done, to integrate themselves with Hollywood, its economic, political and social mores. Clearly, in cases such as these, 'Britishness' was purchased by Hollywood on its own terms and those who did not subscribe to them soon felt pressure to leave.

Maintaining Their Britishness: Kerr and Mason

In the 1940s, a new wave of actors with established reputations in Britain moved to Hollywood. Collaboration between film companies during and after World War II facilitated these developments, and loan agreements made it possible for stars to act in one or two films before committing themselves to longer-term contracts with American studios. These actors included Deborah Kerr, Stewart Granger, Michael Redgrave and James Mason, stars who went on to have relatively long Hollywood careers. In all of these cases, their previous image built in British films was adapted and extended by the American companies they worked for. Deborah Kerr's image as a polite, genteel and well-bred Englishwoman predominated in her first roles, and she had to be assertive in order to break the mould to play a sexualised American woman in *From Here to Eternity* (1953). In *The Hucksters* (1947), Kerr's first American film, in which she co-starred with Clark Gable, the *Variety* reviewer described her as 'a shade prissy for her volatile romantic role'.[23] In *The Prisoner of Zenda* (1952), on the other hand, she was more appropriately cast as 'the lovely princess . . . her looks and ability to wear period gowns are just what the part requires'.[24] A rather different verdict, recognising her versatility, was given for her performance in *From Here to Eternity*: 'Additional performance surprises are in the work turned in by Deborah Kerr, the nymphomaniac wife of the faithless c.o.'. The film was praised for maintaining the best-selling source novel's shocking reputation: 'The bawdy vulgarity and the outhouse vocabulary, the pros and non-pros among its easy ladies, and the slambang indictment of army brass have not been emasculated in the transfer to the screen.'[25] Yet despite the film's risqué content, Kerr seemed unable to shed completely her previous image as the genteel Englishwoman, and she was perceived as not altogether convincing as a seductive siren. This is reminiscent of an earlier role as Sally in the British film *Love On the Dole* (1941), which also demonstrated her ability to flout sexual conventions while retaining an overall demeanour of decorum. Arguably, therefore, it was not so much that Hollywood 'created' a star but enhanced an evolving persona that had been evident in films such as *Black Narcissus* (1947).

James Mason, advertised as 'that mean Mason man' in US promotional material for his British Gainsborough films, also took much from his British performances into his American roles.[26] The combination of sadism, sexual attractiveness, cool intellectualism and bravado, so evident in the British melodramas, provided a core image that was developed in Hollywood. *The Seventh Veil* (1946), a British melodrama, was very successful in the USA. *Variety* described Mason's role as a 'grim bachelor guardian' who subjects his concert pianist charge (Ann Todd) to 'merciless discipline'.[27] When he arrived in Hollywood, Mason was cast in roles such as the 'likeable heavy' Rupert of Hentzau in *The Prisoner of Zenda*.[28] Even though by the time he left for the USA he had broken with the Rank Organisation after having publicly criticised the company, there is no doubt that his reception in the USA would have been far more difficult without the Rank connection. The corporate interconnections between the Rank Organisation and Universal were significant in promoting stars such as Kerr and Mason as having transatlantic appeal. Maintaining an air of Britishness was still a valuable asset, far more valuable than developing a performance style that was imitative of an American star. When Diana Dors★ went to Hollywood in 1956, her promotion as 'the British Marilyn Monroe' failed to impress as a poor imitation of the real thing. Maintaining cultural specificity was therefore a key element in the Hollywood careers of many British stars, even though, as noted above, Hollywood circulated a series of 'preferred' images of Britishness.

Conclusion: What Difference Did They Make?

John Russell-Taylor has argued that British actors 'had little creative contribution to make to Hollywood or the American cinema'.[29] His contention is that the large number of British actors who crossed the pond did not significantly raise the intellectual and cultural value of the American films in which they starred. The dubious assumption that American mass culture is automatically inferior to that of Europe is, of course, lurking behind this argument, as is a negation of the high degree of cross-fertilisation between nationalities in Hollywood. It thus creates an artificial distinction between Europeans and Americans, underestimating the impact of the high number of European film personnel who worked in Hollywood. Taylor nevertheless raises important questions about the impact of the British émigré actors. How rigid was 'the system'? Were actors in a position to influence films at the level of story development or of performance? Clearly, actors such as Robert Donat thought not, but there are examples of actors who were able to chart a more independent course in an economic and creative system that is usually characterised as extremely controlling. In their different ways, Deborah Kerr, Madeleine Carroll and Charles Laughton, for example, exceeded the demands of the studios and at key points in their careers fought for a particular project or even, as in the case of Carroll, strayed from the predictable path of her career. In the early 1940s, she was one of Paramount's most popular stars, earning $100,000 a film, but she cancelled her contract during World War II to train as a nurse in New York, en route to Europe, where she assisted with the war effort.[30]

In spite of the existence of the 'Hunter contract' clauses that privileged producers over actors, it is clear that the most successful stars were not excluded from debates about treatments, dialogue and realisation. When Charles Laughton played Nero in *The Sign of the Cross* (1932), his vision for the role departed significantly from that originally envisaged by the director, Cecil B. DeMille.[31] Success gave actors bargaining power and even the financial security to break contracts that were becoming burdensome. On the other hand, for the many actors who were less successful, conditions could be binding and unforgiving, as with Diana Dors when both the box office and the Hollywood press delivered an unfavourable verdict.

It is therefore erroneous to say that British actors and actresses were mere players in a larger Hollywood story. Although they shared the same language, there were nevertheless issues of adaptation in terms of accent, delivery and performance. As well as grooming themselves for Hollywood cinema, the most successful were able to draw on the images they had established in Britain. This resulted in performances that often betrayed a debt to British cinema while also becoming integrated with Hollywood conventions. Rather than stifling their national identity, many were able to use their American experience in an active way, taking advantage of the demand for varieties of Britishness, on occasion extending the range beyond that of the stereotype or, like Deborah Kerr, branching out into roles that required them to play Americans. The British therefore did make a difference, shaping the world according to Hollywood in a particularly Anglophilic way.

Notes

1. John Baxter, *The Hollywood Exiles* (London: Macdonald and Jane's, 1976), p. 105.
2. H. Mark Glancy, *When Hollywood Loved Britain: The Hollywood 'British' Film, 1939–45* (Manchester: Manchester University Press, 1999), p. 166.
3. Ibid., p. 130.
4. Kenneth Barrow, *Mr Chips: The Life of Robert Donat* (London: Methuen, 1985), p. 69.
5. John Russell-Taylor, *Strangers in Paradise: The Hollywood Émigrés, 1933–1950* (London: Faber and Faber, 1983), p. 96.
6. Michael Redgrave, *In My Mind's Eye* (London: Coronet Books, Hodder & Stoughton, 1983), pp. 215–16.
7. Michael Truman in *Film Industry* vol. 7 no. 61 (17 November 1948), p. 8.
8. Ronald Neame in *Film Industry* vol. 1 no. 6 (December 1946), p. 9.
9. See Sarah Street, *Transatlantic Crossings: British Feature Films in the USA* (London and New York: Continuum, 2002).
10. Cable from Balcon to Maurice Ostrer, 22 March 1935, C/696. Michael Balcon Special Collection, BFI.
11. *Gaumont British News*, 13 December 1935.
12. Since 1927, the British film market had been protected by obligating distributors and exhibitors to handle and show a rising percentage of British films. In 1938, the legislation was extended, including inducements for American renters to produce films in Britain that could be classed as 'British'. See Sarah Street, 'British Film and the National Interest', in Robert Murphy (ed.), *The British Cinema Book* (London: BFI, 1997), pp. 17–26.
13. Clive Brook, quoted in Russell-Taylor, *Strangers in Paradise*, p. 95.
14. Donat made one film in Hollywood in the 1930s, *The Count of Monte Cristo* (1934).
15. Justice Goddard in Warner Bros.' writ and judgment, May 1935; RD 1/9/1/1–2, Robert Donat collection, John Rylands Library, University of Manchester.
16. RD 1/9/1/1–2, Robert Donat Collection.
17. Tino Balio, *Grand Design: Hollywood as a Modern Business Enterprise, 1930–39* (New York: Scribner's Sons, 1993), pp. 145–6.
18. Stewart Granger, *Sparks Fly Upward* (London: Granada, 1981), p. 167.
19. RD 1/1/350, Robert Donat to J. Arthur Rank, letter not sent, 28 March 1946, in Robert Donat Collection.
20. The texts Laughton read included Shaw's 'Don Juan in Hell', Stephen Benét's 'John Brown's Body' and selections from the Bible.

21. Cicely Courtneidge to Michael Balcon, 20 November 1935; Michael Balcon Special Collection, BFI.

22. Letter from Campbell to Shaw in 1934, quoted in Baxter, *The Hollywood Exiles*, pp. 109–10.

23. Derek Elley (ed.), *Variety Movie Guide '96* (London: Hamlyn, 1995), p. 452.

24. Ibid., p. 770.

25. Ibid., p. 351.

26. Similarly, the popularity of Ealing comedies in the USA made Alec Guinness★ a top star before he ever went to Hollywood.

27. Elley, *Variety Movie Guide*, p. 864.

28. Ibid., p. 770.

29. Russell–Taylor, *Strangers in Paradise*, p. 105.

30. Article on Madeleine Carroll in *Classic Images*, no. 245 (November 1946), pp. 14–18, 48.

31. Simon Callow, *Charles Laughton: A Difficult Actor* (London: Vintage, 1995), p. 52.

Virginie Ledoyen 'smoulders' but Leonardo DiCaprio gets all the attention in *The Beach* (2000)

7 In Search of Global Stardom

French Actors in 1990s Hollywood

Irène Bessière

Film historians have long noted the 'great' emigrations: the Italians for economic and/or political reasons; the Germans as a direct consequence of Nazism; and the continual toings and froings of the British. By contrast, French actors who moved to Hollywood, with the exception of the World War II years, did so for purely cinematic reasons. Their presence in Hollywood, as in the case of many other Europeans, however, also derives from the American strategy of laying claim to anything that brings success. Hence, a proven actor will almost certainly get a call from Hollywood, and the French are no exception in this respect, even if the results often leave something to be desired. In this article, after a brief examination of their standing in France, I propose to look at the generation of French actors who have attempted to carve out a career for themselves in the USA in the 1980s and 1990s, the advantages this has given them and the questions that arise from their dual French and American trajectory.

It is often said that French cinema is the bulwark of resistance to American hegemony. The vitality of French cinema is self-evident when we consider the number of films made, the new film-makers and the remarkable young actors currently on the scene. Yet, most of them, from Emmanuelle Béart★ and Sophie Marceau★ to Guillaume Canet★, Julie Delpy★ and Virginie Ledoyen★, try their luck in Hollywood, either because they have been summoned to the USA or of their own accord. Most talented young French actors try to forge a dual career, national and American (or should we say international). Clearly, they feel that going to Hollywood is an obligatory stepping-stone to an international audience. For reasons of space, I will confine myself to a limited number of cases: Juliette Binoche★, Emmanuelle Béart, Sophie Marceau, Vincent Perez★ and Jean Reno★, to represent the 'older' branch of the young actors, and Guillaume Canet, Virginie Ledoyen, Géraldine Pailhas★ and Julie Delpy, for the younger generation.

Unlike Hollywood, films in France nowadays are rarely made around a single actor, as a vehicle for a star to ensure the film's success at the box office. In France, this used to be the case until the late 1970s and early 1980s, with stars like Alain Delon★, Jean-Paul Belmondo, Gérard Depardieu★ and Catherine Deneuve★. Now films are more readily created around a group of actors, often the same 'clans' or 'packs' surrounding particular directors, especially in auteur cinema. Arnaud Desplechin, for example, launched Mathieu Amalric, Jeanne Balibar and Marianne Denicourt, while Benoît Jacquot and Virginie Ledoyen made three films together. We could almost call them 'troupes', in the theatrical sense of the word. Many of these actors began their careers in young directors' first low-budget films, or in original films by more established auteurs: for example, Jean Reno in *Le Dernier combat* (1983); Juliette Binoche in *Rendez-vous* (1985) and *Mauvais sang* (1986); Guillaume Canet – after work in television – in *En plein cœur* (1998); Virginie Ledoyen in *Le Voleur d'enfants* (1991); Julie Delpy in *Détective* (1985).

Sophie Marceau, on the other hand, began her career in mainstream cinema (*La Boum* [1980]), when she was fourteen years old, and Emmanuelle Béart came to international attention in the heritage film *Manon des sources* (1986). As is often the case in France, however, many actors combined off-beat films by young auteurs with mainstream movies: Jean Reno rose to stardom in the hit comedy *Les Visiteurs* (1993); Béart mixed films by Jacques Rivette and Claude Sautet with mainstream comedies such as *La Bûche* (1999); and Guillaume Canet combined work with an auteur such as Patrice Chéreau with co-starring in the digital historical fantasy *Vidocq* (2001). However, it is fair to say that the generation of French actors who appear in Hollywood films in the 1980s and 1990s on the whole come from French auteur cinema, and that they tend to work in 'clans' and creative teams, two of the main factors that give French cinema its diversity and dynamism.

While the French careers of these actors are roughly comparable, the same cannot be said for their international work: their experience of Hollywood has widely differed, they have not enjoyed the same success and their French careers have not benefited to the same extent. Few French actors have, in fact, attracted much attention from the US film industry or succeeded in forging the truly international career they hoped for.

The two French actors with the most successful Hollywood and international careers are, without a doubt, Binoche and Reno. Then come Marceau and Delpy, the latter a special case, since she has practically settled in Los Angeles. As a result, she has made more films in the USA than the others. Binoche and Reno expertly manage a dual French and international career. Binoche's good command of English has made it easier for American audiences to accept her, and her choice of international films in the 1990s may have been wiser than her French choices, with the exception of the critically derided *Chocolat* (2000). She is also one of the very few French actresses to have won an Academy Award in Hollywood – for Best Supporting Actress in *The English Patient* (1996). This international dimension makes her career more complete and rounded, giving it that something 'extra'. Likewise, Reno enjoys a dual French/American career, without losing his head or forgetting just how difficult it is for a French actor to make an authentic mark on Hollywood. As he himself said in an interview to *Le Journal du dimanche*, 'You work your way into Hollywood, bit by bit',[1] a strategy that has proved successful, since Reno is one of the few contemporary French actors Americans recognise. This has been, however, at the price of being confined to action movies and, by extension, to playing the same type of character, for example in *Mission: Impossible* (1996), *Ronin* (1998) and *Rollerball* (2002) – a typecasting that was no doubt encouraged by his part as a hit man in Luc Besson's highly successful New York set thriller *Léon* (1994).

Sophie Marceau has also achieved something of a dual career, appearing in a number of films outside France: among them *Pacific Palisades* (1990), the story of a young Frenchwoman staying in Los Angeles; *Braveheart* (1995), a big-budget costume film set in Scotland directed by and starring Mel Gibson, in which her role was, however, marginal; *Anna Karenina* (1997), a poor adaptation of the eponymous novel; and the Bond film *The World is Not Enough*, directed by Michael Apted in 1999. In this latter film, in contrast to the all-American Denise Richards who plays the 'good girl', Marceau is luscious as the exotic, sexy and wicked 'bad girl' Elektra King. Otherwise, her American films have offered neither rich nor complex characters, and *Anna Karenina* is her only real starring role apart from *Pacific Palisades*. Her American films, apart from expanding her international audience, seem primarily designed to show off her beauty rather than offer original or creative opportunities.

Julie Delpy's career is, unusually, more American than French. After an interesting start in France in such films as Bertrand Tavernier's *La Passion Béatrice* (1987) and the female lead in Krzysztof Kieslowski's *Three Colours: White* (1994), Delpy decided to embark on an American career. A resident of Los Angeles, she has become familiar to American independent film-makers and appeared in off-beat films such as Richard Linklater's *Before Sunrise* (1995) and *Before Sunset* (2004), Christopher Menaul's *The Passion of Ayn Rand* (1999) and Jamie Babbit's lesbian comedy *But I'm a Cheerleader* (1999). Delpy has also directed three films in Los Angeles, including *Tell Me* (2000) and *Looking for Jimmy* (2002). She still acts in films in France and Germany, and her career is thus poised between Europe and the USA.

Vincent Perez has made five films in the USA in the last five years, while his French career has continued apace. Unlike Reno, he has not been pigeon-holed and his American career straddles different genres: the fantasy-horror *The Crow: City of Angels*, directed by Tim Pope in 1996 (a sequel to the very successful *The Crow* by Alex Proyas in 1994), offered him a role that was very different from anything he had previously done in France. By contrast, *I Dreamed of Africa* (2000), with Kim Basinger, is a typical big-budget Hollywood adventure romance, in which Perez clearly finds it hard to breathe life into the character of an 'Italian'.

Emmanuelle Béart, for her part, has only ventured into American cinema twice: in Tom McLoughlin's *Date with an Angel* (1987) and, more prominently, in Brian De Palma's *Mission: Impossible* with Tom Cruise. Working with De Palma and Cruise was obviously an attractive proposition, especially in a film adapted from a cult television series that was bound to be a box-office hit. The film, accompanied by a barrage of publicity, was indeed an enormous commercial success. Unfortunately, Béart's character in this glossy action blockbuster is marginal and insipid, and

Mission: Impossible turned out to be an interlude in a career that has remained basically French and European.

The youngest French actors in Hollywood, Guillaume Canet, Virginie Ledoyen and Géraldine Pailhas, were picked by casting directors (Ledoyen and Pailhas from photographs, in other words, purely for their looks) and they went to the USA because they were asked to go. Pailhas appeared in only one American film, albeit one that has had a cult following: *Don Juan DeMarco*, directed by Jeremy Leven in 1995. Canet acted in two American films: Jerry Schatzberg's *The Day the Ponies Come Back* and Danny Boyle's *The Beach* (both 2000), in which he co-starred with Ledoyen, who had previously appeared in James Ivory's *A Soldier's Daughter Never Cries* (1998).

The most famous, and eagerly awaited, international film to feature young French actors was, of course, *The Beach*, because of the presence of Leonardo DiCaprio, who had become a superstar thanks to James Cameron's *Titanic* (1997). Canet and Ledoyen play a young French couple on a voyage of discovery, in search of the eponymous beach. In the event, however, they seem to be merely part of the furniture around DiCaprio rather than flesh and blood characters, and are frequently relegated to the background or edges of the frame. The huge publicity and gossip surrounding the film brought the two French actors a certain notoriety and projected them into the limelight – especially in France – for reasons, however, that had little to do with the quality of the film or of their acting. Adapted from Alex Garland's eponymous cult novel, the film was above all a vehicle for DiCaprio, targeted at an audience of teenagers and young adults. A comparison between the French and Anglo-American press reception of the film is illuminating in relation to the fate of French émigré actors in Hollywood.

The Anglo-American press hardly mentions the two French actors, except to say that they are a beautiful couple – 'a photogenic pair of lovebirds',[2] 'an attractive French couple (as if there were another kind)',[3] who bring sexual tension to the film. Virginie Ledoyen is 'ravishing', 'a smouldering French actress',[4] sensual and attractive, and 'exotically beautiful'.[5] However, the on-screen romance between DiCaprio and Ledoyen was deemed 'flat and uninviting',[6] and no romantic triangle develops in the film. The Anglo-American press was basically only interested in DiCaprio and in this respect duplicated Danny Boyle's *mise en scène*: 'The picture is a cocoon around DiCaprio', said *The New York Times*,[7] while *The Irish Times* stressed the impressive number of DiCaprio close-ups. Indeed, a typical shot in the film would have DiCaprio in the foreground, most of the time stripped to the waist; behind him to the right, Guillaume Canet, in the male supporting role, shows off the hero in a flattering light; and in the middle ground to the left, parading her beauty, stands Virginie Ledoyen.

By contrast, the French press naturally made a big fuss of Ledoyen and Canet, who gave a lot of interviews, though none of them were particularly in-depth. They too were, ironically, obsessed with DiCaprio: 'What is he like?', 'Arrogant, unaffected, the big star?'; 'Were he and Ledoyen linked romantically?'; 'Did Canet and DiCaprio become friends?'[8] and so on. There is little discussion of the film itself or the roles the young French actors played. Worth a mention, however, is the fact that the French critics were relatively kind to the film. The papers even went so far as talking about 'a fairy tale',[9] to which Ledoyen astutely replied that the film for her was, more than anything, a fantastic 'business card'. She kept a commendably clear head in the midst of such media hype, where the only thing that counted was having played opposite DiCaprio. As the film was, in the end, far from well received critically, it did Ledoyen and Canet only a limited amount of good on the international scene, and the whole episode was a bit of a damp squib, although it did bring them added publicity at home. Canet's role in *The Day the Ponies Come Back* was more prominent and more human, if cliché-ridden (he plays a young man in search of his father), but the film only had limited impact and thus did not much help his career.

Géraldine Pailhas, for her part, embodies the 'ideal woman' in *Don Juan DeMarco*, a romantic comedy in which Johnny Depp believes that he is the greatest lover in the world (while psychiatrist Marlon Brando and his wife, Faye Dunaway, try to cure him). Pailhas' beauty and graceful presence illuminate the film and contribute to its magical charm. Why was a French actress chosen for this role? Perhaps to create a distance between her and the other characters played by American actors, who, even if they live in an imaginary universe, belong to the 'real' world, while this gorgeous woman's exoticism and otherworldliness reinforce the unreality and enchantment of the film. Despite this extraordinary chance to work with three great American actors, *Don Juan DeMarco* did not lead on to an international career for Pailhas, neither does it seem to have significantly helped her French career. Despite the plethora of stars, the film's subject matter restricted it to a limited audience.

The experiences of young French actors in Hollywood in the 1980s and 1990s are, as we have seen, very different and yet they share certain features. A few, such as Reno, Delpy and Binoche, and to a lesser extent, Marceau, seem relatively comfortable with, and accepted by, American cinema. In the main, however, French actors were offered few starring roles and, even more irritatingly, those they were offered tended to be schematic and cliché-ridden.

Why then do French actors readily agree to make films in the USA, and even seek out the opportunity? The first reason is the oldest: the spell cast by Hollywood and American cinema. Then there is the chance to experience different working methods, encounter another world, to reach a wider public and open new horizons. There is also the difficult but attractive challenge to act in a language other than your mother tongue — an attraction that can, however, backfire. Nor can financial considerations be dismissed: an international career means not only fame but also higher pay packets. And finally, there is the idea of the 'business card' mooted by Ledoyen — illustrating the lucid and realistic approach some young French actors take to the Hollywood venture.

But perhaps the question one should ask is, rather, why Hollywood summons these French actors to give them, on the whole, such uninspiring parts and why so few contemporary French actors have succeeded in Hollywood. The first obvious explanation was mentioned at the start of this article: the fact that Hollywood lays claim to anything that smacks of success. The actors discussed here had all been successful in France, and a number of them were already established stars (Reno, Binoche, Marceau, Perez, Béart). Once transplanted into Hollywood, they seem to serve several purposes. They bring a touch of novelty, spontaneity and exoticism to the familiar patterns of Hollywood film-making. But by the same token, they become ciphers for the Americans' image of French people. As is clear from the roles offered to them, French actors in Hollywood films tend to be required to convey traditional stereotypes of Frenchness, such as arrogance and seduction. One major exception is Jean Reno, because he works in action films. Hollywood is attracted to French actresses because, while they are beautiful, their beauty is more idiosyncratic than that of their American counterparts (see Marceau, Pailhas and Ledoyen, the latter of whom is sometimes perceived as a new Brigitte Bardot). However, in order to make them more readily acceptable to American audiences, especially in mainstream films, the studio may ask these actresses to modify their appearance. For instance, Béart had her lips injected to make them fleshier. And French actors sometimes simply act as a foil to bolster the qualities of the American star of the film, as happened in *The Beach*.

In the end, we may ask ourselves if using foreign actors, in this case French, is just another — albeit subtle — attempt by Hollywood to make both Western culture and cinema more uniform. Frenchness then simply transfers from one stereotype to another, from the European to the American. Yet, although their Hollywood career rarely matches their French one, French actors no doubt will continue to go in search of global stardom.

Translated from the French by Renée Fenby and Ann Wright.

Notes

1. *Le Journal du dimanche*, 24 May 2000.
2. Kenneth Turan, *Los Angeles Times*, 11 February 2000.
3. *The Star* (Toronto), February 2000.
4. *San Francisco Gate*, February 2000.
5. Paul Clinton, CNN, 11 February 2000.
6. Jamey Hughton, *Movie Thing*; <www.moviething.com/cgi-bac/ecom9990057318319.cgi.>
7. Elvis Mitchell, *The New York Times*, 11 February 2000.
8. *Libération*, 16 February 2000.
9. *France Soir*, 16 February 2000.

Part III Emigré Actors, Cultural Types and Stereotypes

8 Small Victories and Grand Failures

Russian Actors in Hollywood

Natalia Noussinova

The story of Russian actors in Hollywood forms part of a wider spectrum of Russian emigration that has already given rise to significant work.[1] The Russian émigré writer Nina Berbérova perceptively pointed out that the moment of arrival in the USA was crucial for the Russian émigrés' careers and personal lives throughout their stay in the New World. According to her, in Europe émigrés were distinguished by their 'Russian past', that is to say their social class, political affiliation and/or geographical origins. In the USA, there was only one factor determining the émigrés's social position vis-à-vis their compatriots: 'When did they leave Russia: 1920? 1943? When did they arrive in America: 1925, 1939, 1950?'[2]

My own research, as well as Jan-Christopher Horak's analysis of 'Russian Hollywood',[3] enables us to see the accuracy of Berbérova's insight. The moment of the émigrés' arrival determined their American hosts' attitude, making their integration into their new life – and into the Hollywood production system – more or less difficult. Moreover, as Berbérova also notes, they were unable to integrate gradually, as was generally the case in Europe, but had to choose between remaining within their own community, isolated from professional activities, or 'making the jump' – as if going straight from the first generation to the third. Accordingly, this chapter on 'Russian Hollywood' will be organised along chronological lines and will highlight themes and key topics for each 'wave' or even 'wavelet' that carried Russian actors to the Pacific coast.

Chronology of Arrivals

When the 'first wave' of Russian émigrés – the White Russians who left the mother country in the wake of the 1917 Revolution – disembarked in the USA, they found individuals such as Alla Nazimova★ (who arrived in 1905) and Theodore Kosloff (1914), who were already perfectly integrated into Hollywood. Compared to the Russian émigrés in Western Europe, this first wave was quite small: in 1919–1920, among the few in the USA were Ivan Linow, Michael Visaroff★, Olga Baclanova★, Nicholas Soussanin★, as well as Maria Ouspenskaya★ and Akim Tamiroff★ (although it would be ten years before the last two began working in film).

Most Russian actors turned up in the USA as part of a 'second wave' of arrivals during the second half of the 1920s – individuals like Mischa Auer★, Alex Melesh, Alex Voloshin and Leonid Snegoff. In many cases, they were émigrés twice over, having, like Michael Vavitch★, transited via Western Europe. For some – among them Ivan Mosjoukine★ and Feodor Chaliapin Jr – this second emigration would be short-lived and disappointing.

Those who emigrated to the USA at the beginning of the 1930s, such as Leonid Kinskey★ and Anna Sten★, already belonged to a different school. They were émigrés from Soviet Russia, with new experiences and a new mentality. The difference was even greater for those who arrived in Hollywood at the end of the 1930s or the beginning of the 1940s. In most cases, they were also double émigrés , this time fleeing also the Fascist menace – among them, Mikhail Chekhov★, Eugenie Leontovich, Vladimir Sokoloff★, Tamara Toumanova★, Leonid Mostovoy and Zoia Karabanova.

'A rare exotic bird': former ballerina and Russian stage star Alla Nazimova in 1920s Hollywood

Before the Revolution: the Ballets Russes and Silent American Cinema

How should we understand the rapid success of the very first, pre-Revolution, Russian émigrés in Hollywood? For actors such as Nazimova and Kosloff, part of their seduction for Americans was that of the 'rare exotic bird'. But there were other reasons too. Theodore Kosloff was a star of the Ballets Russes, as well as painter and violinist, who had worked in Petrograd with Pavlova, Mordkine and Nijinsky. He came to the New York Winter Gardens in 1908 as a dancer, worked in England before moving to the cinema, settling in Hollywood for good in 1914. Kosloff had not planned to emigrate – he left considerable personal property in Russia, which he lost during the Revolution. Nazimova, for her part, arrived in New York with Pavel Orleneff's theatre troupe in 1905 and, after signing a contract with famous theatrical producers the Shubert brothers, never returned to Europe. She worked extensively in vaudeville and theatre, and, from 1916, the cinema (having learned English at an early age, she was also able to work in sound film). But the main asset of these two actors appears to have been their training in the reputed Russian ballet and vaudeville. This connection was striking enough to be noticed by the Soviet press of the 1920s:

> The impact of ballet is very marked in Theodore Kosloff, our compatriot who is an American resident. In all his films that we have seen, he never fails to use his dancing talent. [. . .] Such dynamism, and such a physique can only be found at the Bolshoï. [. . .] Kosloff does not act, he dances.

The same article observes, 'We have just seen "La Salomé" with Alla Nazimova. One can tell that she trained with Golejzovsky. Her way of holding her back, her arms, her head, her technique, her movements and gestures, all come from the contemporary ballet style.'[4]

These actors were accepted because their Ballets Russes and Russian vaudeville training could be successfully incorporated in the American film style: they brought a touch of local colour but did not stand out too much. A telling case is Kosloff's performance in *The Volga Boatman* (1926), directed by Cecil B. DeMille, a Hollywood melodrama that is also a good example of the mythical treatment of the Russian Revolution in American cinema. It fits in a series (or even genre), whose typical narrative line, according to Horak, is as follows: 'A peasant woman and a nobleman, or an aristocratic woman and a peasant, are caught up in the Revolution which hinders their marriage, but in the end they are united.'[5] In *The Volga Boatman*, Kosloff plays the (small) part of Stefan, a mute who expresses himself through pantomime. With only gestures and dance, he attempts to save Mariusha (Julia Faye), explaining to Red Army soldiers that she is a girl of modest origins, despite her aristocratic garb. It is no accident that the role of a mute in a silent film – in which by definition no one speaks – was given to a dancer. Interestingly, Kosloff was the only actual Russian actor in this 'Russian' film. The Revolutionary tribunal in the film pardons its enemies if they agree to join the new cause, a point that must have seemed particularly ironic to Russians who had lived through the Revolution and knew how bloody it was. Indeed, Kosloff could play this role and in all innocence help build up the Hollywood myth of the Russian Revolution because the Russia he knew predated the Revolution. He was already an 'ex-Russian', and he would never fully understand those who arrived in the USA after the Revolution.

The 'First Wave': The 1920s Émigrés
Russian actors vs. Hollywood commercialism

The fate of the generation that followed the early precursors discussed above was less fortunate. Apart from Olga Baclanova, who became an American star (albeit for a short while), no Russian actor of this 'first wave' exactly made a brilliant career in the USA. Their story is that of small victories and grand failures.

In his assessment of his friend Ivan Mosjoukine's career in Hollywood, Alexandre Vertinsky, a well-known cabaret performer, roundly condemned Hollywood's imperialistic practices vis-à-vis European stars:

After Paris, Mosjoukine went to the USA. But Hollywood neglected him – there they buy famous people like merchandise. What matters for the Americans is to remove a star from the film market in order to export Hollywood movies. This is why they get all the best actors in Europe: to ruin them on purpose, to make them fail in the eye of the public. The arrival of these actors in Hollywood quietly ends their careers. The market is filled with American stars.[6]

Obviously, Vertinsky's representation of Hollywood practice as an anti-European plot is an exaggeration. It is hard to believe that Hollywood consciously 'ruined' Russian actors. Something else was at stake. Hollywood hired European actors who possessed an exceptional personality. Yet as soon as they arrived in the USA, they were no longer allowed to be exceptional. They had to become American, adapt to Hollywood norms and please the American audience. The problem was not chauvinism, since the USA by definition was a country of émigrés; yet the newly arrived had to fall into line in order to be accepted. Hollywood took what it needed and rejected the rest without too many scruples. The sensitive and sentimental Russians took it very badly.

Maria Wrangel, mother of Piotr Nikolaevitch Wrangel, a famous White Army general, collected émigré actors' testimonies as part of a history of Russian emigration that she was planning to write. Ivan Lebedeff*, who worked in Hollywood from 1925, told her:

I can't say we're badly treated here because we are foreigners. It would be more accurate to say that sympathy has little to do with it. If they *need* you and hope you will make them earn a lot of money, then they are interested in you and they 'treat you well'. Otherwise it's a blank wall. In my opinion, cinema is the most ruthless business after the stock exchange [. . .]; Right now the majority of Russians have left the cinema (because of the talkies), and they are having a hard time surviving. I am currently the only Russian (in Hollywood) with a long-term contract.[7]

According to Lebedeff, the success of an actor in Hollywood was openly measured in terms of his salary, and he provides precious information on the going rate at the time:

Mosjoukine, our film star [. . .] has gone back to Europe after making two completely botched films for Universal. He never managed to get more than $750 a week, which is poor in relation to his status in Europe. It was also the time when Olga Vladim[irovna] Baclanova started to rise to fame. She was very successful, signed a contract with Paramount and was expected to replace Pola Negri* – and yet at the beginning of the talkies she failed because of her poor and strongly accented English. Apparently she got up to $600–750 a week, which is *very good* in her case, considering that up to that point she hadn't worked in film and that her name meant nothing at the box-office (she became famous just before sound cinema). Another one who did well was Michael[o] [Ivanovich] Vavitch (an operetta actor) who went up to $600 but did not manage the passage to sound cinema, although he is apparently beginning to resurface in character roles which allow his accent to be used.[8]

Even if the 'record-breaking' salaries for Russian émigrés in Hollywood were fairly modest compared to those of major American stars, financial issues were not alone in determining the relationship between Russian actors and Hollywood. Let us look more closely at a few case studies.

Ivan Mosjoukine, or Lost Illusions

The greatest star of tsarist cinema, Mosjoukine has come to symbolise that era for subsequent generations. He emigrated to France with a group of Russians who settled in Paris around the figure of Joseph Ermolieff, and became a pillar of this colony. Mosjoukine left Paris at the peak of his fame, having collaborated with the cream of Russian and French directors. He arrived in the USA hopeful, with the desire to make 'simple and wholesome films [. . .] American films, dammit, simple and unpretentious'.[9] Two years in Hollywood completely changed his mind. Yet he was ready **79** to make concessions and compromises in order to be accepted in the country of 'Charlie [Chaplin*] and Douglas [Fairbanks]'. Alexandre Volkoff, who was sorry to see this transformation in the great actor, accurately reflected that American films 'impressed him too much, they contaminated him because of their remarkable novelty'.[10]

At the beginning of his stay in the USA, Mosjoukine proved extraordinarily adaptable, giving in to Hollywood's requirements, going as far as accepting a kind of rebirth: 'Because the name Mosjoukine is allegedly too hard to pronounce, they call him Ivan Moskine.'[11] The Americans also forced Mosjoukine to have plastic surgery to shorten his nose. Yet in another sense, Volkoff's worries proved unfounded: he was certainly not allowed to become a new Chaplin or a new Fairbanks. He was cast in Hollywood melodramas, far removed from the dark, psychological Russian melodramas in which he had worked. *Surrender* (1927) proved too simplistic for his refined technique. In the end, Mosjoukine broke his contract and went back to Europe, commenting:

> It is a major disappointment . . . From a technical point of view American films are superior to all others. But . . . this is not enough! There is nothing spiritual. Psychology is strictly and ruthlessly banned from films . . . the actor has nothing to do.[12]

Mosjoukine's harsh verdict on Hollywood could also serve as a commentary on the fate of the actors from the famous Moscow Art Theatre, the MKHaT (created in 1898 by Stanislavsky and Nemirovich-Danchenko), who remained in Hollywood after touring the USA.

Russian theatre vs. Hollywood cinema

MKHaT provided Hollywood with a remarkable cast of actors: Michael Archansky, Ogla Baclanova, Feodor Chaliapin Jr, Mikhail Chekhov, Ivan Lebedeff, Alex Melesh, Maria Oupenskaya, Vladimir Sokoloff, Nicholas Soussanin, among others. Horak is right in saying that Stanislavsky's and Nemirovich-Danchenko's pupils often used their teachers' names as a visiting card in Hollywood, in the same way as German émigrés boasted of their experience with Max Reinhardt.[13] MKHaT may have been prestigious, but the performance style it taught was very different from the Hollywood acting tradition. The latter preferred the dynamism of action to the depth of complex feelings. Hollywood had little time for the representation of interiority, or the notion of the 'reincarnation' of the actor – a form of emotional realism derived from Chekhov, MKHaT's favourite playwright. Thus, although actors who emerged from this tradition were welcome in Hollywood, they generally had no future there.

Olga Baclanova – a change of school

Olga Baclanova had been one of the most famous MKHaT actresses, the adored pupil of Nemirovich-Danchenko. Her success in Hollywood provoked huge resentment in the Soviet press: 'Our "Lady of the steppes" is climbing the golden staircase – she is making films and is successful. [. . .] By turning her back on the USSR, she openly becomes a mouthpiece for the bourgeois ideology of American capitalism.'[14] At the same time, she provoked the ire of American newspapers, which commented on her appearing in Otto Brower's *Avalanche* (1928): 'Why do we have to give a foreigner a 100% American role?'[15] One may ponder whether she owed this success to her great theatrical mentor. In his article on *The Docks of New York* (1928), in which she plays Lou, a prostitute, Yuri Tsivian cites Baclanova as saying,

> I wanted to plunge into the human aspect of the role. That's how I wanted to act. Whereas [von] Sternberg wanted me to play it his way and this I could not accept. So I asked him, 'Why do you want me do to it this way?' And he replied 'Do as I say. And don't think that because you are from MKHaT, this means you know everything.' So I started playing it his way. He began shouting 'But this is horrible! It's terrifying!' We had a row, he insulted me, and I started to cry like a baby. And of course that's exactly what he wanted. The scene was a great success.[16]

Clearly, Sternberg used Baclanova's sensitivity and beauty against the grain of her training. He did not need an actress able to penetrate deeply into the spirit of her character. He put her to work as a 'model', using her remarkable looks and extracting from her the gestures and reactions he needed with 'below the belt' tactics. Baclanova's other important part, in Tod Browning's 1932 *Freaks*, was, according to her biographer Aleksandre Vassiliev,[17] both the apex and the swansong of her Hollywood career. It follows roughly the same pattern – there is nothing in it from the 'Stanislavsky method', nothing to do with the 'reincarnation' of the actor under the skin of the character – Baclanova simply appears as 'Cleopatra', a beautiful stranger.

Michael Vavitch – Hollywood's favourite crook

Another important personality in 'Russian Hollywood' was Michael Vavitch. In one critic's opinion,

> The characters he created were so remarkable and full of life, that even when sound cinema blew away silent films and foreigners were handicapped by language and forced to give way to Americans, Vavitch was still working. Even his limited English and strong accent were not obstacles [. . .]. Directors often said that Vavitch's bad diction was easier on the ear than American actors' good pronunciation.[18]

Such a testimony, almost a contradiction in terms, is easy to understand: Vavitch was Russian Hollywood's favourite personality. His role in his community (comparable to Mosjoukine's in Paris) clearly outstripped his artistic contribution, and his death was a trajedy for his compatriots. As Michael Visaroff put it:

> An enormous loss for the Russian colony was the death of Michael Ivanovich Vavitch which took place on Sunday 5 October 1930, at 10pm, following a heart attack. This occurred in a car, while he was driving along Sunset Boulevard, accompanied by Dimitri Tiomkine. [. . .] Vavitch was very popular not only among Russians but also in the highest artistic circles in American cinema. [. . .] His funeral was the grandest in the history of Hollywood. [. . .] Nobody can replace him.[19]

Vavitch was also a well-known benefactor, helping the poor and investing more than anyone else in the construction of the Los Angeles Russian church, buying icons for it out of his own pocket and installing crosses on its cupolas. He sang in its choir, attracting those who had loved his light-hearted operettas back in St Petersburg. Vavitch founded the Russian-American Arts Club, known as the 'Vavitch club', which thanks to 'Uncle Micha'' hospitality and charm, and his gypsy songs, trumped the rival 'Yurenev Varginsky club' – the latter became simply one of the many Russian restaurants in Hollywood (among others were Lodygevsky's in which Chaplin was an investor, and the restaurant of Russian producer Drankov; these venues incidentally ensured the livelihood of a number of former White Army generals who worked as waiters).

Paradoxically, although Vavitch thus basked in general adoration, he mostly played negative roles on screen. This puzzled the émigré press: 'Curiously, Vavitch is condemned to playing crooks, contrary to his great benevolence, well known in artistic milieux.'[20] It was also the case that he continued working in sound cinema, despite his bad English. The interesting question thus raised by Vavitch is whether poor English and a strong accent are insuperable obstacles in Hollywood, as is often believed. Was Vavitch the exception, a unique example? In order to explore this issue, I will look at three case studies: Anna Sten, Leonid Kinskey and Akim Tamiroff.

The Coming of Sound and Russian Accents: Obstacle or Asset?

Anna Sten arrived in Hollywood in 1933, on Samuel Goldwyn's invitation. She was then at the height of her Soviet fame with films like *Devushka s korobkoj/ Girl with the Hat Box* (1927), *Dom na Trubnoj/ The House on Trubnaya* (1928), both directed by Boris Barnet, and *Zemlya v plenu/ The Yellow Ticket* (1927), directed by Fyodor Otsep. Goldwyn invested heavily in Sten, whom he hoped would become 'the second Garbo★'. The Hollywood press, however, focused on her linguistic abilities:

> When she arrived in Hollywood to begin her American career, Miss Sten could not speak one word of English. 'This was my original reason for not permitting her to go about publicly', Goldwyn said. Expert instructors have spent two hours each morning and two hours each afternoon teaching Miss Sten English – not the American street speech, but the carefully modulated, fluid speech of the international theater. 'She still has a slight accent, however', Goldwyn said, 'and perhaps, always will. But it is delightful.'[21]

Yet later, 'Goldwyn conceded that he had made one of the few mistakes in his career – a costly one that led to Miss Sten's sobriquet in the industry as "Goldwyn's folly". He terminated her contract.'[22] Would this be because of her 'delightful accent'? Sten actually worked in Hollywood until the early 1960s, appearing in, among others, *Nana* (1934), *Three Russian Girls* (1944) and *The Nun and the Sergeant* (1962). Yet she never matched the level of her Soviet stardom.

The same Russian accent, however, did not prevent Leonid Kinskey from achieving a much more brilliant career in Hollywood. He tried to get rid of it, but was reported as saying, 'Each time when I seemed to be making the most progress, I would be called for work in a picture and handed a role that required an accent, if not Russian, then Greek or Swedish. So, I've just about given up in despair.'[23] It is likely, instead, that Kinskey's accent, as well as his prominent nose – which he did not have remodelled – in the end, became his trump cards: 'Kinskey's pinched face, Pinocchio nose and Russian accent were familiar to movie audiences from 1932 to about 1956. Today he lives in his North Hollywood home surrounded by mementos of the 100 or 150 films in which he featured.'[24]

As for Tamiroff, his entire career was underpinned by his accent, which was part and parcel of his charm and the type of roles he played, as attested to by the titles of a few articles devoted to him by the American press: 'Tamiroff – International Actor but the Accent Is Russian';[25] 'Tamiroff Calls Accent Key to His Success'.[26] He himself confessed to the press, 'Everybody says my accent is worth a million dollars.'[27] And perhaps even more, as revealed by the following anecdote about his 'thick, juicy Russian accent': 'He almost blasted his career when he started, however, when he said to the producer who signed him for his first job: "Now I learn to speak the good English". The astounded executive screamed: "If you do, you are fired!"'.[28]

Thus we have to conclude that a foreign accent in a literal as well as a metaphoric sense was not necessarily a handicap for a Russian actor in Hollywood. The very thing that could torpedo their careers could also save them, especially in the case of character actors. Success depended on the actors' ability to transform a weakness into an asset that would please the audience. But there were more general issues of adaptation. Mosjoukine tried to compromise, until he rebelled against a form of humiliation that did not even bring success. Others succeeded in becoming 'true' American stars while keeping, at least on the surface, their personality and European identity. Hollywood wanted the compliance of the newcomer, but preferably in a less obvious way than Mosjoukine. It was nevertheless essential to adapt to, and understand, the taste of the American audience. When Mikhail Chekhov tried to explain to an American producer that the Russia they were creating in Hollywood was completely false, the producer replied, 'We are not doing it for the Russians but for the Americans.'[29] Here is the key formula for understanding 'Russian Hollywood'.

Translated from the French by Ginette Vincendeau and Simon Caulkin.

Notes

1. See my 'I russi in America. Il cinema della prima emigrazione', in Gian-Piero Brunetta (ed.), *Storia del cinema mondiale II, Gli Stati Uniti* (Turin: Einaudi, 1999), pp. 959–80. See also Olga Matich, *Russians in Hollywood/ Hollywood about Russia* [Russkie v Hollywoode/Hollywood o Rossii], NLO.2002.N54.

2. Nina Berbérova, *Kursiv moj. Avtobiografia* (Moscow: Soglasie, 1996), pp. 575–6.

3. My research draws on sources in the Margaret Herrick Library, American Academy for Motion Picture Arts and Sciences, Los Angeles, California; the Hoover Institute Library, Stanford, California; the Moscow RGALI archives. See also Jan-Christopher Horak, 'Russi bianchi a Hollywood', *Cinemazzero*, special issue, October 1989, and Jan-Christopher Horak, 'White Russian Emigrés in Hollywood' (an unpublished filmography that the author was kind enough to let me see).

4. A. Abramov, 'Tanets v kino' [Dance in the Cinema], *Sovietskij ekran*, no. 28 (1925).

5. Horak, 'Russi bianchi a Hollywood', p. 15.

6. Alexander Vertinsky, 'Dorogoj dlinnoiu . . .' [The Road is Long] Moscow Pravda), 1991, p. 218.

7. Letter from Ivan Lebedeff to Maria Wrangel, 18 August 1930, Hoover Institute Archive, Maria Wrangel Collection, Box No. 30/4.

8. Ibid.

9. Michel G., 'Un quart d'heure avec Mosjoukine', *Cinéa-Ciné*, no. 74 (1926), p. 15.

10. RGALI Archives, Moscow, no. 2733/1/496, p. 1.

11. Edouard Roches, 'Ivan Mosjoukine est mort, vive Ivan Moskine', *Mon Ciné*, 24 February 1927.

12. Ivan Mosjoukine, *Novaia zaria*, no. 366 (7 December 1930).

13. Horak, 'Russi bianchi a Hollywood', p. 15.

14. P. A. 'MKHaT Stuff. O. Baklanova na zolotyh stupeniah' [O. Baklanova on the Golden Stairs], *Sovietskij ekran*, no. 38 (1928).

15. 1929 press dossier, Hoover Institution Archives, Maria Wrangel Collection, Box No. 30/11.

16. Quoted in Yuri Tsivian, '*The Docks of New York*', *Iskousstvo kino*, no, 1 (1998), p. 120.

17. Alexandre Vassiliev, 'Krasavitsa Baclanova' [Baclanova, a Beauty], *Kinovedcheskie zapiski*, no. 29 (1996,) pp. 170–1.

18. S. Lvov, 'Pamiati Vavitcha' [in Vavitch's Memory], *Novaia zaria*, 14 October 1930, p. 3.

19. Letter from Michael Visaroff to Maria Wrangel, 18 October 1930, p. 3. Hoover Institution Archives, Maria Wrangel Collection, Box No. 30/1. (New reference: Box No. 34. Folder ID:23.)

20. M. I. Vavitch and O. Baclanova, Hoover Institution Archives, Maria Wrangel Collection, Box No. 30/11.

21. 1933 press dossier, Anna Sten Collection, Special Collections, Margaret Herrick Library.

22. *Los Angeles Times*, 16 December 1993.

23. 18 April, 1941 press dossier, Leonid Kinskey Collection, Special Collections, Margaret Herrick Library.

24. *Los Angeles Times*, 15 February 1990.

25. Ibid., 3 September 1965.

26. *Patterson Call*, NJ. 21 December 1965.

27. Ibid.

28. John L. Scott, 'Tamiroff's Accent Pays Off', *Los Angeles Times*, 7 September 1958.

29. Liisa Byckling, 'Michael Tchekov v amerikanskom kino' [Michael Tchekov in American Cinema], *Kinovedheskie zapiski*, no. 33 (1997), p. 121.

9 Changing Bodies, Changing Voices

French Success and Failure in 1930s Hollywood

Alastair Phillips

In an interview with the American journalist Gladys Hall, Annabella★, one of France's most successful female film stars of the 1930s, vividly articulated her passion for cultural transformation. 'I always wanted to change, change all the time, never to stay in one place for so long.' she said. 'Very early on I decided that only in the cinema could I have this changing life, these changing bodies. In the cinema, I could shed the bodies, like dresses, one after the other.'[1] Like her French compatriot Charles Boyer★, Annabella's fascination with transition led her to Hollywood to pursue a new kind of acting role. This performance meant a complex and suggestive conflation between the notion of acting in relation to a fictional on-screen identity and the notion of acting in relation to an extra-textual persona marked as much by where it had come from as what it was in the process of becoming. This chapter will explore the economic and aesthetic tensions inherent in the various journeys that Boyer and Annabella made as actors to the USA in the early sound era. By choosing two different case studies, and ones with radically varying degrees of commercial success, I will shed light on some of the critical issues that must inform a historical understanding of the phenomenon of European actors' emigration to Hollywood in the early years of sound cinema.

Journeys and Trajectories

'It was the golden age of Hollywood and we lived as if in a dream. At one reception hosted by Warners, there were several gigantic dining rooms with walls covered in gardenias and carpets of the most immaculate whiteness sprinkled with brightly coloured orchids.'[2] Annabella's recollections vividly capture the perceived splendour of difference encountered by many of the European actors who arrived in Los Angeles during the early 1930s. As Ruth Vasey has argued, these performers had been recruited for a dual purpose. Their role was to create exotic aural and visual appeal for domestic North American filmgoers, but, equally importantly, they were also hired as part of a global industrial strategy to develop international audiences in the new economy of sound cinema.[3] Their journeys had often been long and symbolic. In the case of notable French performers such as Charles Boyer, who left St Lazare train station in Paris in a haze of national publicity, they sailed from the port of Le Havre in liners like the *Île-de-France*, the *Europa* or the *Paris*. During this six-day transatlantic crossing, the performers were fêted in luxury and largely protected from the bodies of the poorer classes of exiles and emigrants in the lower decks. After completing the necessary papers on arrival in New York, they then boarded trains like the *The Chief* and travelled for three days and four nights across the country before arriving on the West Coast.[4] Despite loaded expectations, however, success was not always instantaneous.

Charles Boyer, France's most successful émigré star next to his adopted friend Maurice Chevalier★, actually made this extended journey several times before finally settling in the USA. Boyer originally had no intention of solely pursuing a film career. His first journey as an actor had been to move from the provinces to Paris in the1920s. In the early years of his professional stage development, following training at the Sorbonne and the Conservatoire, he worked hard to develop a consistent reputation as a serious and adept performer in both the classical repertoire and contemporary boulevard productions such as Francis Carco's *Paname*.[5] By the turn of the decade, he could count among his circle of professional friends such people as the actress Françoise Rosay★ and her husband, the film director Jacques Feyder. It was due to Boyer's association with Rosay and Feyder, both now being lured to the USA, and the growing professional esteem in which his mellow and romantic voice was held, that he was initially recruited to Hollywood by MGM's Paul Bern in the spring of 1929. The studio wanted him to appear opposite Greta Garbo★ in what was to be a multi-language version of *The Kiss* (1929).[6] The project was never realised as a sound film though, and Boyer was hired instead to act in the multi-language *Le Procès de Mary Dugan* (1929).[7] Receiving no further firm offers of work, he eventually decided to return to Europe, where he signed a film contract with the Ufa studios in Berlin to appear in various multi-language versions.[8]

Boyer was asked a second time to Los Angeles in December 1930 to appear in another multi-language version, *Révolte dans la prison* (1930)[9], and he was subsequently offered his first English speaking role in *The Magnificent Lie* (1931). He recalled leaving the mists of a damp Parisian winter that year and feeling as if he had entered 'a bath of light'. 'Living for months in the theatre playing tormented roles in an anguished atmosphere, I suddenly seemed to have been taken to a marvellous country in which there was only youth, freshness and enthusiasm,' he commented.[10] In an indication of Boyer's still lowly status within the Hollywood hierarchy, however, his voice was not actually used for dubbing purposes when the film was released within French-language territories. The actor left the USA in a fury, but was tempted back again a year later by his friend Claudette Colbert to play opposite her in *The Man from Yesterday* (1932). As Matthew Bernstein has pointed out, Boyer's role, this time, was significantly tailored to suit his language ability. In a sign of Paramount's commitment to Boyer's potential attraction as a foreigner, the character was deliberately made to appear multilingual, and his accent was even explicitly referred to in the script as being 'thick as mud'.[11]

Boyer's fourth visit to Hollywood came in 1934 after the relative international success of his performance in Fritz Lang's only French film, *Liliom* (1934).[12] The actor starred in both the English and French versions of Erik Charell's European-based gypsy musical *Caravan/Caravane* (1934), which was an extravagant and costly attempt by Fox to emulate recent European musical successes such as Charell's own *Der Kongress tanzt/Congress Dances* (1931). Annabella was Boyer's co-star in the French-language version, but Loretta Young played her part in the English-speaking film.[13] *Caravan* failed dismally at the box office, though, and Boyer's English-speaking career only began to take off with his appearance as the principled, but also romantically inclined, doctor in *Private Worlds* (1935). This was the feature that established his commercially successful profile with American and international audiences as 'the French lover', and it introduced that key conflation of emotion, romance, Frenchness and authenticity that became the defining traits of his star persona in many succeeding Hollywood roles.

Annabella's relationship with Hollywood was equally complex, although rather more predicated on opportunity and plain desire. The daughter of the publisher of the aptly named *Le Journal des Voyages*, she derived her name from a piece of verse by the American writer Edgar Allen Poe. Unlike Boyer, she had no serious background in the Parisian theatre. Instead, she flowered as one of France's leading screen actresses of the early sound era, appearing in such films as René Clair's *Le Million* (1931) and *Quatorze juillet* (1933), as well as *La Bataille* (1933)[14] and the award-winning *Veille d'armes* (1935). Her attractive and photogenic face registered both an exterior shyness and a certain inner spirit of determination and quick-wittedness, and it was this winning combination with critics and audiences that also led to commercially successful leading roles in multi-language productions in both Germany and Hungary.[15] After the failure of her appearance in the English-speaking version of *Caravan*, and because of the fact that she could at this stage speak no English, Annabella returned immediately by plane to Europe and she was not called to Hollywood again until 1937. The internationalisation of her career gathered pace in the intervening years, however, and she appeared in three American-British productions shot in England, including the first European Technicolor feature *Wings of the Morning* (1937). It was her crucial contact with Fox's European-based producer Robert Kane that led to a second contract with the American studio. Having now acquired some rudimentary English language, she started work on *The Baroness and the Butler* (1938), but it was during the shooting of her second film for Fox, *Suez* (1938) that she came to the prominent attention of the American public for her adulterous affair with her co-star Tyrone Power.[16] The fictionalised account of Ferdinand de Lesseps' construction of the Suez Canal did not do well at the box office and after her next film, *Bridal Suite* (1939), made for MGM, Annabella did not act in Hollywood again until 1943.

French Tongues in an American Context

Why was it then that one French star succeeded and another failed when relocated in Hollywood? Tino Balio has demonstrated that by the end of the 1930s the star system in Hollywood had become 'the prime means of stabilising the motion-picture business'.[17] In this sense, the commercial potential of an individual performer was a leading factor in the vertically integrated management of the industry: it influenced both the financing of a project and its overall execution in terms of production and the final methods of distribution and exhibition. Boyer's encounter with Hollywood in the early sound era reveals a fascinating insight into the mechanics of this process and into how, with the requisite amount of good chance and skilful handling that Annabella seemed to miss, the system could work to enhance one individual's career.

Boyer's initial appearances in the USA were done on a short-term contract basis and, as we have seen, he was disappointed by the way the studios treated him. This is despite the fact that he had clearly been hired for his possibilities as a leading romantic male. He had originally been recruited for the potential of his (French) speaking voice, as much as his looks, and it was this aspect of his acting persona that was to be the key to the economic clout he would wield by the end of the decade. The voice had dual appeal, in the sense that it was, of course, conversant in two languages. Irving G. Thalberg (MGM's production chief) had arranged personal English-language tuition for Boyer in order to improve his spoken English, but all the studios were careful that the star never lost the significant 'Frenchness' of his accent. It could be foreign enough to be exotic, but, crucially, it should also be sufficiently understood and admired by English-language audiences. In an industry ruthlessly mindful of the international potential of its representations of 'otherness', this is an important point.

There is clear evidence that Boyer understood the benefits of this position in the way that he also managed his financial affairs. Indeed, he seems to have been particularly adept at playing the system from a relatively early stage in his Hollywood career. By the time of his contract with Fox to appear in the French-language *Caravane*, for example, Boyer was anxious not to abandon the appeal of his voice to his native audience, and he clearly stipulated that he must always dub his own performances when distributed in France.[18] One of his first actions on arriving back in Los Angeles in 1934 was to hire a successful agent, Charles Feldman, who went on to play a crucial role in initiating a set of one-picture contracts for the actor. Although typical of French working practices regarding the recruitment of stars, this arrangement would have been unusual in the Hollywood context. By 1936, Boyer had assembled an individualised administrative team that comprised of an accountant and financial adviser as well as personal secretary. The actor thus always made sure his 'voice' was heard in other ways.

One of the most important people who listened to Boyer in Hollywood was the independent producer Walter Wanger, who secured roles for the French star in films made for a variety of studios, such as the previously mentioned *Private Worlds*, as well as *Shanghai* (1935), *History is Made at Night* (1937) and *Algiers* (1938) – a remake of Julien Duvivier's *Pépé le Moko* (1937) – for which Boyer was asked to re-enact Jean Gabin's* leading role in the original film, something he disliked intensely.[19] Wanger was bilingual and had worked as an attaché to President

Wilson at the Versailles Peace Conference in 1919; by the mid-1930s, he had accumulated a range of valuable contacts through work experience with many of the major studios. He saw the potential for Boyer to become a speaking Valentino for the American public. 'I had seen him in Europe. I knew what he could do, and I knew that he had something no one else had on the American screen,' he argued.[20] The producer's significance lay in a winning combination of his financial status and acumen within the Hollywood system, and his key skill in placing the French star next to so many leading female actresses of the period. If we look, for example, at the details surrounding Boyer's appearance in *Tovarich* (1937), we can gain an insight into how rapid the French actor's promotion in Hollywood was. Only two years after his first real American success, Wanger leased the star to Warner Bros. for eight weeks for the sum of $100,000.[21] Boyer's co-star in the extravagant costume spectacular set in Paris was the top box-office draw Claudette Colbert, and it was arranged that the two would share billing above the titles.[22] Only the name of Colbert was to appear before Boyer in any print or screened advertising and publicity, and in all cases their names were to appear in equal type size.

The publicity surrounding *Tovarich* gives a further indication of the way Boyer was marketed within Hollywood. The promotional material for the film relied heavily on the conjugation of romance, emotion, authenticity, Frenchness and Paris identified earlier. Much, for example, was made of the detailed work that had gone into Anton Grot's set recreations of the French capital. The pressbook promised that 'the most elaborate preparations in history went into the filming of the kissing scene between Miss Colbert and Boyer'.[23] One poster image projected Colbert and Boyer's faces in front of the Eiffel Tower with the caption: 'Colbert in Paris! Boyer in Love! Together in the Year's Swellest Comedy'. The question of authenticity is an interesting one, in another aspect, for the narrative of the film actually concerns the mishaps of a Russian prince and princess who have fled the Revolution and are living in disguise as a maid and butler in a wealthy Parisian household. It suggests, then, that the fascination of Boyer's persona partly rested on a generalised notion of European sophistication that was truly non-American rather than specifically French. Coupled with the idea of foreignness came a different reading of masculinity that was romantically attractive for both its alterity and its corresponding qualities of suaveness, intelligence and truthfulness. We see this conjugation again in the marketing for Boyer's role as Napoleon in *Conquest* (1937). Here Boyer was teamed with Garbo, and their apparent shared otherness was thus presented in an advantageous way to appeal to the American moviegoing public. 'The uniforms that Charles Boyer wears in "Conquest" are authentic copies of those worn by Napoleon', the publicity went. In the hyperbole of the pressbook, a pre-prepared radio script, presented by Clarence Brown, even confidently equated the national prestige of Boyer with the national greatness of Bonaparte himself.[24]

Another key aspect of Boyer's successful persona rested in a certain combination of fidelity and intellectual concentration. Early on in his Hollywood career, the star had married a British actress – Pat Robertson – and he could not therefore be promoted as a footloose, romantically inclined French bachelor. Boyer's academic training, stable home life and apparent fine taste in his native food and wine therefore became the lynchpins in many press stories. In 1936, for instance, it was reported that he would be importing his own champagne.[25] The star was frequently pictured with his books in his personal library. As this type of coverage increased, so Boyer gradually became thought of by many people as an unofficial ambassador for a particular version of French high culture. This role had two intersecting dimensions. First, the Boyer household became a conduit for many other French professionals arriving in Los Angeles; second, Boyer would later develop his interest in Franco-American cultural relations by establishing the French Research Foundation. Boyer's Foundation would play an important role during the war years. As well as promoting and documenting France's engagement in the conflict, it also assisted in relocating such people as the director Julien Duvivier to Los Angeles. This deliberate positioning between the embracing of the new and the simultaneous guarding of the traditions of the old was perhaps one of the most durable secrets of the star's long-term appeal. It certainly accounts for the telling, but typical, anonymous press remark made about both Boyer and *Tovarich*: 'For once the continental touch has been brought within the field of ordinary American understanding.'[26]

Annabella's own encounter with Hollywood's production system similarly reveals an insight into how the studios dealt with the phenomenon of European emigration during these years. By the time of her second visit, it is clear from company records that Fox expected to make a major investment in the French actress. On 23 March 1937, she signed a contract with them for two films with an option on two subsequent features. After filming *The Baroness and the Butler*, a sophisticated comedy vehicle co-starring William Powell, she completed a new two-film contract with a significant fee of $75,000 per feature.[27] Annabella was taken under the personal wing of Darryl F. Zanuck, Fox's head of production, and offered a limited amount of tuition in her diction by a certain Miss Constance Collier. As in the case of Boyer, she was keen to protect the commercial potential of her voice and she insisted that her contracts always retained the right for her to dub her own words in subsequent French releases. The quality of her voice was also an important part of Fox's overall investment in Annabella's potential American popularity. Despite the efforts of the star to develop her spoken English, it is obvious that Zanuck and Fox went to great lengths to maintain her perceived 'European-ness.' She revealed to Gladys Hall, in an interview revealingly entitled 'Don't Let Hollywood Change You, Annabella', that she had been told by Fox that 'we keep experts away from Annabella. We have ask [sic] Annabella to come here because she *is* Annabella and we keep her Annabella'.[28] Zanuck revealed in one pressbook that the essence of Annabella's popularity would thus rest in her cultural difference. 'We have too many persons in Hollywood now who resemble one another', he argued. 'The public demands new faces, new personalities and we certainly can't fulfil that demand if we destroy freshness, vitality and originality by fitting each newcomer into one mould.'[29]

Despite the fact that the French star was rather mysteriously cast as the flirtatious daughter of the Prime Minister of Hungary in *The Baroness and the Butler*, Annabella was nonetheless promoted extra-textually as the studio's leading face of French sophistication. Press tie-ins prominently featured her sense of fashion and her elegant cosmopolitanism. 'Simplicity is the keynote of Annabella's chic', noted one typical piece of pre-prepared press advertising. This note of Parisian savoir-faire accounts for the title of her proposed, and then abandoned, second feature: the somewhat ironically named *Let's Go to Paris*. It also points to one of the possible reasons for Annabella's relative lack of success. Simply put, the studio failed to match Annabella's well-established French (and European) screen type with the right vehicles once she arrived in the USA. In Europe, she had been known for her rather humble and sentimental roles; whereas it appears that Fox seemed unable to position her successfully beyond a certain tamed and broad-based vision of Continental glamour. There is also the question of language – the critics universally noted her poor command of spoken English. Perhaps most astute was the *Variety* critic who wrote of her American speaking debut that

> Annabella's faltering delivery of the English language is too great a handicap to be overcome even by a flattering camera. [. . .] She is miscast. The story selected for her [. . .] is a light, frothy, continental comedy which calls for delicate shadings in speech and performance.[30]

Fox got the fit wrong again in *Suez*, Annabella's next feature. In a role originally conceived with her compatriot Simone Simon* in mind, Annabella was asked to be the humorous, zestful and boyish romantic foil to Ferdinand de Lesseps (Tyrone Power). Perhaps in a concession to her still limited linguistic abilities, it was proposed at a relatively early script conference to render her unable to read or write.[31] As the project evolved, it becomes clear looking through the Fox archives that the studio wanted a historical, not a romantic, drama and the film that was finally released offered little real potential to develop the marketing concerns initiated previously by the publicity department. With the clandestine affair and subsequent marriage between Annabella and Tyrone Power, Fox seemed willing to relinquish their ambitions for the French actress. Many years later, Annabella revealed in an interview that she had discovered that the disapproving Zanuck had placed her on an unofficial blacklist following the 'scandal' of her affair with Power – a revealing example of the degree of paternalistic patronage that a non-native female star in particular may have had to live with in the studio system. Zanuck's moralism can also be seen as part of the broader cultural shift in feminine representation on the part of Hollywood in the latter 1930s, as bold and dangerous screen behaviour on the part of female stars became curtailed. From this point on, Annabella's film career waned, but it did not stop MGM tartly changing the title of her final film of the decade, when it was released, from *Maiden Voyage* to the more headline-grabbing and apposite *Bridal Suite* (1939).

Performing Bodies and Mobile Voices

We have seen, so far, how Charles Boyer and Annabella were both partly brought to Hollywood on the basis of their voices, in that they were recruited as much for their potential to be heard as to be seen. If we now turn to the question of their performances, in particular Boyer's, we may see how further evidence for their varying levels of success during the early sound era also reveals crucially different levels of interaction between the performer, the camera and the new sound-recording technology.

By the mid-1930s, American sound cinema had already evolved to the extent that, with the aid of new lighter and more compact microphones, there had been a shift from the initial spatially variable levels of sound quality to what Rick Altman has termed 'a continuous sound track of nearly level volume and unbroken close-up characteristics'.[32] Altman argues that with this development, 'the criterion of intelligibility of dialogue [still] retained its primary importance'.[33] In addition to this concentration on audition and characterisation, one may note a renewed contiguous interest in the skilled integration of the script, actor's voice and actor's body – a concern that had not been so important in silent cinema. As Cynthia Baron has shown, the Hollywood studio system, during these years, was both fascinated and tested by the new demands of the body's role in audiovisual storytelling.[34] If we must see the actor's body as an integral part of the way each film project was conceived, developed, marketed and received, we must also therefore acknowledge the role acting itself played in terms of narration and spectatorial pleasure. The studios set about hiring dialogue coaches, for example, and dialogue directors were employed to assist performers with specific aspects of scenes involving heavy amounts of the spoken word. Crucially, for the basis of this paper, professional acting experts, such as Lilian Burns at MGM, were recruited to initiate acting training programmes in the belief that the trained performer would best serve a mode of production predicated on the centrality of the interpretation of the written script. Seen in this light then, someone like Boyer therefore became a different kind of professional investment than Annabella. While Boyer came from a long-established trained background in live stage performance, and had also toured widely outside France before coming to the USA, Annabella was a recent and less experienced acting phenomenon, whose stardom emerged purely from her roles in her own national cinema.

Baron quotes an acting teacher of the time who remarked that 'the fundamental difference between acting on the stage and the screen [was] the size of the actor from the viewpoint of the audience'.[35] There is clear evidence that Boyer learned this lesson early on in his American film career, as the publicity for *Caravan* suggests in the way it details the expressive potential of his physiognomy. It noted, for example, that 'with the soulful, romantic eyes of a poet, but the physique of a prizefighter, Charles Boyer is an anomaly. [He is] courteous, soft-spoken and retiring, [yet his face possesses] a remarkable mobility.'[36] If we look at *History is Made at Night*, one of Boyer's later Hollywood films of the 1930s, we can see again how adept the actor was at using both his voice and eyes to captivate the moviegoing audience. The film is fascinating for the way in which Boyer's vocal and gestural qualities become absorbed into a narrative that fictionalises the same destabilising process of cultural migration experienced on a personal level by the star and promoted on an extra-textual level by the industry. Boyer plays the role of a French gentleman burglar in Paris who interrupts the marital sting arranged by an American shipping magnate (Colin Clive★). The businessman wishes to put his wife Irène (Jean Arthur) in a compromising position with the couple's chauffeur, but he is foiled when Boyer and Arthur themselves end up spending a romantic evening together. Irène returns to the USA, but Boyer follows her and gets a job as the head waiter in an exclusive society restaurant. His attempt to lure the object of his desire succeeds and the couple both become temporary exiles as they plan to set off to Haiti. In Boyer's early scenes in the film, the actor's features are masked, but the lighting is carefully organised to accentuate the mercurial whiteness of his eyes. Subsequent set-pieces also make good use, in close-up, of the expressive potential of his eyebrows. It is as if a constant ironic register is being maintained by the interplay between Boyer's hinting eyes and the suave appeal of his accented voice. This sense of a focus on performance and a certain tamed exoticism, heavily dependent on coded notions of cultural authority about such things as fine food and wine, is crucial to the way the film articulates Boyer's role. For instance, in an early scene set in the back of a taxi while Boyer's character is still unidentified to the wealthy American, he charmingly suggests a little drink. 'But where?', she asks. 'Leave it to me. I know the best champagne in Paris,' comes the forceful reply.

The mobility of the character Boyer plays is also conveyed through the theme of ventriloquism. In one sense, this works as a means to foreground the actor's technique, but in another it seals the crucial theme of changed bodies that the film describes and Boyer's life entailed. Boyer's seduction of Arthur at the dining table revolves around the act of performing with his hands and with his eyes the pretend identity of a distinguished Frenchwoman. The camera is constantly alert to the range of the actor's gestures as he makes his partner laugh at his ability to assume the identity of another compatriot. For the spectator, however, there is a possible doubling of pleasure available in this sequence, for we witness here the extraordinary conflation of a well-known French actor in the USA embodying a Frenchman acting a Frenchwoman while supposedly in France. The film, as a whole, progresses with this theme 'of finding a voice', in that it revolves around Irène's romantic search to locate a role for her emotional longings and her choice between two differently coded vocalised versions of masculine appeal. Colin Clive, another – British – émigré actor, is therefore clearly cast for his long angular jaw, veiled eyes and hard, sharp voice, while his French counterpart, in contrast, appears with round features, open, alert and clear eyes and a distinctive softness of timbre in speech.

Boyer's narrative journey from disguise to something authentically Parisian in *History is Made at Night* in fact mirrors the history of his own career trajectory in Hollywood. If he started the decade often playing the 'foreigner', he ended it as the archetypal 'French lover'. Wanger's perception of Boyer's potential as the sound era's Valentino had thus been accurate. This was a 'fit' that Annabella never succeeded in completely finding. In one sense, her timing had been wrong: she did not benefit in the same way that Boyer did from his stage training and more extensive business contacts, and she did not receive the same successful roles that related to a pre-established European persona. Furthermore, only Boyer was cast in emblematic historical roles, such as Napoleon, which related back to governing notions of French cultural patrimony. In another sense, there was clearly also the question of gender and agency. In *Suez*, for instance, the camera sometimes seems more interested in observing her legs than her eyes and mind. Her role is essentially decorative and, while humourous, it is subsequently relegated in terms of narrative significance. The French actress is characteristically adept as a foil to the decorum and stature of her rival in love, the Empress Eugenie (Loretta Young), but the film evidently does not know what to do with her impetuous character. Her somewhat awkward persona – her English is still quite poor – is inserted in an unsuitable vehicle and the character inevitably dies. In more than one sense, her voice is simply not heard and she thus does not join in.

This question of 'joining in' or integration is then clearly central to any understanding of the place of the European actor in the Hollywood studio system. In conclusion, the industry wanted to tread a fine balance between assimilation and the preservation of a cultural difference that would have a distinctive national and international commercial appeal. This equivocal and problematic process, less characteristic when considering the wider terrain of Hollywood's strategy of overseas recruitment of directors and technicians, reveals a complex set of questions regarding cultural expectation, financial management and on-screen performance. At a time when Hollywood aimed to recuperate the heterogeneity of the European accent and create something obviously global in potential, the tension between the promise of reinvention and the seal of authenticity was always going to be managed differently according to the individual actor. This process depended upon the inevitable conflation of the cultural baggage and acting skills the actor carried, but it also depended on the crucial question of articulation: how the actors spoke as stars, how they were spoken to by agents and producers, and how they were spoken about by publicity directors, critics and audiences. In considering the cases of Annabella and Charles Boyer, we may thus surmise that although these two French stars shared a common tongue, they also simply possessed different voices.

Notes

1. *Motion Picture*, 13 November 1937.
2. Annabella interview in Christian Gilles (ed.), *Le Cinéma des années trente par ceux qui l'ont fait. Tome I* (Paris: L'Harmattan, 2000), p. 28.
3. See Ruth Vasey, *The World According to Hollywood, 1918–1939* (Exeter: University of Exeter Press, 1997), pp. 163–4.
4. See Alain Servel, *Frenchie Goes to Hollywood: la France et les Français dans le cinéma américain de 1929 à nos jours* (Paris: Éditions Henri Veyrier, 1987).
5. For further biographical information see Larry Swindell, *Charles Boyer – The Reluctant Lover* (London: Weidenfeld & Nicolson, 1983), and Guy Chassagnard, *Charles Boyer Acteur* (Figeac: Segnat Éditions, 1999).
6. Other associates of Charles Boyer in the transient French acting community in Hollywood at the time included, among others, Maurice Chevalier, Marcel Dalio★, André Luguet★ and Arlette Marchal★.
7. The very successful English-language version, *The Trial of Mary Dugan* (1929), starring Norma Shearer, had been shot several months previously. On the phenomenon of the multi-language versions, see Ginette Vincendeau, 'Hollywood Babel: The Coming of Sound and the Multiple-Language Version', in Andrew Higson and Richard Maltby (eds), *'Film Europe' and 'Film America': Cinema, Commerce and Cultural Exchange 1920–1939* (Exeter: University of Exeter Press, 1999), pp. 207–24, and Natasa Durovicova, 'Translating America: The Hollywood Multilinguals 1929–1933', in Rick Altman (ed.), *Sound Theory Sound Practice* (New York: Routledge, 1992), pp. 138–53. On the specific question of Hollywood's relationship with France at this time, see, for instance, Martine Danan, 'Hollywood's Hegemonic Strategies: Overcoming French Nationalism with the Advent of Sound', in Higson and Maltby (eds), *'Film Europe' and 'Film America'*, pp. 225–48.
8. Boyer had previously shot the multi-language *La Barcarolle d'amour* (1929), co-starring Annabella, in Germany. His Ufa multi-language films were *Tumultes* (1932), *I.F. 1 ne répond plus* (1933) and *Moi et l'impératrice* (1933). He also appeared in *The Empress and I* (1933), the English-language version of the latter.
9. The English-language version, *The Big House* (1930), was a major success in the USA, and it was perhaps because of this that Boyer's role attracted a lot of favourable press coverage when the French-language version of the film was released in his home country. Paul Féjos, originally known as Pál Fejös, also shot the film in Spanish and German.
10. Chassagnard, *Charles Boyer Acteur*, p. 44.
11. See Matthew Bernstein, *Walter Wanger, Hollywood Independent* (Berkeley: University of California Press, 1994), p. 104.
12. For more on Boyer and *Liliom*, see Alastair Phillips, 'Fritz Lang's *Liliom*. A Fateful Divide', in Douglas Pye (ed.), *Fritz Lang* (Cameron and Hollis, forthcoming).
13. André Berley, Pierre Brasseur★, Conchita Monténégro and Marcel Vallée also starred in the French version of the film.
14. Co-starring Charles Boyer.
15. Annabella also appeared in the following multi-language films: *La Barcarolle d'amour* (C1929), shot in Germany; *Son altesse d'amour* (Robert Péguy, 1931), shot in Germany; *Autour d'une enquête* (Henri Chomette and Robert Siodmak, 1931), shot in Germany; *Tavaszi zapor* and its French version *Marie, légende hongroise* (Paul Féjos/Pál Fejös, 1932), shot in Hungary; *Sonnenstrahl* and its French version *Gardez le sourire* (Paul Féjos/Pál Fejös, 1933), shot in Austria; and *Varieté* and its French version *Variétés* (Nicolas Farkas, 1935), shot in Germany.

16. She later married him after divorcing her former co-star, the French actor Jean Murat. A number of other French actors played secondary roles in the film. They included Jean de Briac, Marcelle Corday, Jacques Lory★, Odette Myrtil★ and Jacques Vanaire, and the Italian Fred Malatesta★.

17. Tino Balio, *Grand Design: Hollywood as a Modern Business Enterprise, 1930–1939* (New York: Scribner's Sons, 1993), p. 144.

18. See memo from George Wasson to G. S. Yorke (19 June 1934), Fox Legal Files, Box LR 30, File 2358 (UCLA Arts Special Collections).

19. Cromwell 'would run a scene from the original and insist we do it the same way', Boyer recalled. 'An actor never likes to copy another's style, and here I was copying Jean Gabin, one of the greatest. Terrible, a perfectly terrible way to work.' See 'Boyer and Some Thoughts about the Casbah', in *Woman's Day* (April 1950).

20. Quoted in 'Hollywood's Biggest Gambler' by Clarke Wales in Walter Wanger clippings file, Margaret Herrick Library, American Academy for Motion Picture Arts and Sciences.

21. This sum compares to the amount of $1,000 per week Boyer was paid by Paramount in *The Magnificent Lie* in 1931. See Paramount Pictures Corporation Collection File 853, Margaret Herrick Library, American Academy for Motion Picture Arts and Sciences.

22. See Charles Boyer Folder (Box 2824) in Warner Bros. Archive (Arts Special Collections, Doheney Library, University of Southern California).

23. Pressbook for *Tovarich* (BFI National Film Library, London).

24. Pressbook for *Conquest* (BFI National Film Library, London).

25. *Los Angeles Examiner*, 1 November 1936.

26. *Motion Picture Daily*, 2 December 1937.

27. Fox Legal Files, Box 751, File 2401 (UCLA Arts Library Special Collections).

28. *Motion Picture*, 13 November 1937.

29. Pressbook for *The Baroness and the Butler* (BFI National Film Library, London).

30. *Variety*, 16 February 1938.

31. Notes from the script conference for the first draft continuity script (1 March 1938), p. 8, in Darryl F. Zanuck File (Arts Special Collections, Doheney Library, University of Southern California).

32. Rick Altman, 'Sound Space', in Altman (ed.), *Sound Theory Sound Practice*, p. 54.

33. Ibid., p. 58.

34. Cynthia Baron, 'Crafting Film Performances: Acting in the Hollywood Studio Era', in Alan Lovell and Peter Krämer (eds), *Screen Acting* (London: Routledge, 1999), pp. 31–45.

35. Ibid., p. 37.

36. Pressbook for *Caravan* (BFI National Film Library, London).

10 The 'Foreign Woman' in Classical Hollywood Cinema

Christian Viviani

In Hollywood cinema, the presence of foreign actors, in particular European ones, is not solely a matter of economics. 'Foreigners' were often allowed to push to the limit – and even transgress – what the Production Code forbade and applied more strictly to characters that were wholly American. As a result, from the beginning, 'foreign women' were given particularly rich and contrasting roles. When the Production Code was implemented in 1934, the foreigner – and, in particular, the European woman – could, more than any other female characters, maintain the ambivalence that is such an essential characteristic of the Hollywood discourse.[1] The exceptional charisma of a Greta Garbo★ or a Marlene Dietrich★ permitted all that Hollywood did not dare – or only timidly dared – with more wholly American heroines like Janet Gaynor or Norma Shearer. For a time, Garbo, Dietrich and their peers could surround with an aura of romanticism and mystery behaviour that Bette Davis, Barbara Stanwyck or Joan Crawford had to atone for. The status of foreigner was metaphorical, independent of any precise geography or ethnicity: the Swedish Garbo played Italian, French and Spanish women; the Viennese Luise Rainer★ took the role of a Chinese; the Czech Hedy Lamarr★ became a Creole. Later, with neo-realist influence and the mutations of the Hollywood system, foreign actresses became more precisely situated, exhibiting a better fit between the character and the actress (Leslie Caron★, Pier Angeli★). Although American cinema continued to use European actresses (Sophia Loren★, Gina Lollobrigida★, Hildegard Knef★, Anna Magnani★), it gradually denied them a metaphorical dimension; thus, the otherness of the character and its sometimes transgressive role finally seems to be on the wane, as if a form of 'globalisation' had been visited on stereotypes (Emmanuelle Béart★, Sophie Marceau★ and Penelope Cruz★ in their most recent performances).

I Greta Garbo: The Sanctified Sinner

When the Swedish Garbo arrived in Hollywood in 1925, MGM had her film in succession two adaptations of works by Spanish writer Vicente Blasco Ibañez – *Torrent*, directed by Monta Bell, and *The Temptress*, completed by Fred Niblo after Mauritz Stiller had been sacked. With first a bogus Latino as a partner (Ricardo Cortez was Austrian), then a real one (Antonio Moreno★ from Madrid), Garbo made the impression we know on the American public with two incarnations of an exotic femme fatale. The pattern was set. In the clearly Nordic atmosphere of Clarence Brown's *Flesh and the Devil* (1926), Garbo plays a temptress of unspecified nationality, with a Latin name, Felicitas. Subsequently, she was Russian in five films (the two versions of *Anna Karenina*: Edmund Goulding's *Love* [1927] and Clarence Brown's *Anna Karenina*, [1935]; Fred Niblo's *The Mysterious Lady*, [1927]; Goulding's *Grand Hotel* [1932]; Ernst Lubitsch's *Ninotchka* [1939]), French in four (Victor Sjöström's *The Divine Woman* [1928]; Jacques Feyder's *The Kiss* [1929]; Clarence Brown's *Inspiration* [1931]; George Cukor's *Camille* [1936]), Italian in two (Clarence Brown's *Romance* [1930]; George Fitzmaurice's *As You Desire Me* [1932][2]), Dutch once (Fitzmaurice's *Mata Hari* [1931]) and a Pole in one (Clarence Brown's *Conquest* [1937]). Her Scandinavian origin was used only four times (Clarence Brown's *Anna Christie* [1930]; Robert Z. Leonard's *Susan Lenox, Her Fall and Rise* [1931]; Rouben Mamoulian's *Queen Christina* [1933]; Cukor's *Two-Faced Woman* [1941]). In two films, her origin was left unspecified (Sidney Franklin's *Wild Orchids* [1929]; Richard Boleslawski's *The Painted Veil* [1934]). In the silent cinema, she played two American roles, in Clarence Brown's *A Woman of Affairs* (1928) and John Stuart Robertson's *The Single Standard* (1929).

Of course, there had been other foreign actresses in Hollywood: for example, the Polish Pola Negri★, as well as Vilma Bánky★ and Lya de Putti★, two actresses born in Hungary who enjoyed international careers. But in their symbolism, Greta Garbo's early roles perfectly synthesised the screen experience of other actresses. Her first three American characters slipped effortlessly into the role of exotic temptress, the femme fatale, generally playing opposite a less interesting, plainer American counterpart. In this compensatory relationship, the virtues and rhetoric of the significantly less glamorous Gertrude Olmstead (*The Torrent*), Virginia Brown Faire (*The Temptress*) and Barbara Kent (*Flesh and the Devil*) serve as a sharp contrast to the woman who was to become 'The Divine' Garbo. In fact, Garbo's impact is such that she practically obliterates any female character opposite her. Thus, from *Love* on, the femme fatale turns into the 'great lover', exotic and irresistible. Other actresses promptly sought to duplicate the persona: in the same year, Negri shone in *Hotel Imperial*, also produced by Stiller, and Bánky began a string of films in which she starred opposite the British actor Ronald Colman★ in a generally Latin context – Fitzmaurice's *The Night of Love* (1927); Henry King's *The Magic Flame* (1927); Niblo's *Two Lovers* (1928); Victor Fleming's *The Awakening* (1928). Although very popular, Bánky did not survive the advent of sound because of her strong accent, the failure of *This is Heaven* (Alfred Santell, 1929) putting an end to the series. The same fate befell Negri, but for other reasons: her dark and emphatic persona, carried over wholesale from nineteenth-century popular tradition, looked totally obsolete overnight.

So we are left with the exemplary case of Garbo. In conversation, Henri Agel[3] opened my eyes to an unusual characteristic of Garbo's persona: he pointed out that her on-screen persona had a rare quality, almost unique among stars – namely, goodness, in a saintly, 'Franciscan' sense of the word. Interestingly, among the many eccentric projects initiated by the star, but never produced, were two roles in which she would have appeared as a man – Oscar Wilde's *The Picture of Dorian Gray* and a life of *Saint Francis of Assisi*. Before Garbo, foreignness in a woman represented evil. Her character could be blackened with impunity, sometimes to the point of caricature, and her origin was often unspecified, so that audiences from any country could project their disapproval on her. Garbo's charisma turned the status quo upside down. Felicitas in *Flesh and the Devil* marks this u-turn. Here is an archetypal femme fatale, already married, who comes between two men, wrecking their friendship to the point of setting the former blood brothers face to face in a duel. Secretive, cunning, insincere, she is struck by immanent justice when a frozen lake opens under her and engulfs her for ever. But this is the persona on paper. Her interpretation gives it quite another dimension: Felicitas' white and smooth, marble-like features that seem to bear no earthly trace place her straightaway in a different register. Garbo's Felicitas is no longer femme fatale – she is Woman in Love, such as American cinema had never known before. However, her consuming love has one victim, herself. Her sensuality touches on both blasphemy and mystical exaltation when, to kiss one of her lovers, she recreates a profane *pietà* (henceforth Garbo's signature in her roles as a woman in love): her lover's body lies across her lap as she leans over his face, taking it between her hands, to bring it closer to her lips. In another famous scene, also poised between blasphemy and mysticism, Felicitas turns the celebrant's chalice so that she can press her lips to the spot where her lover had drunk the consecrated wine. What ordinary femme fatale before Garbo could have made such gestures? The American actresses who played women in love were too matter-of-fact (like Gloria Swanson) or too stereotyped (like Theda Bara) to render them acceptable – in fact, such gestures did not even occur to them. But the 'otherness' of Garbo-the-foreigner liberates the imaginary, both in the film-makers and the audience, and joyfully blurs the frontier that separates the femme fatale from the woman in love.

Henceforth, the adulteress (*Love*, *Wild Orchids*), the collector (*A Woman of Affairs*, *The Single Standard*) and, indeed, the murderess (*The Kiss*) are represented in such a way as to elicit compassion, beginning a cycle that redeems the fallen woman. This moral ambiguity will finally lead to the strict implementation of the Production Code. Almost all Garbo's films during the run-up to strict application of the code ran into trouble with the Breen Office. This is not surprising in view of the almost saintly aura she confers on the archetypes of the adulteress (Anna Karenina), the courtesan (Camille), the unmarried mother (Marie Walewska). The controversy over *Two-Faced Woman* became a cause célèbre, following which she quit the cinema for good.

II Marlene Dietrich: The Ambiguities of Assimilation

Dietrich and Garbo – the contrast is clichéd but inescapable. Indeed, although she was slightly older and her first American screen appearance came five years after Garbo's,[4] Dietrich was launched as Paramount's answer to the MGM star. Her American career began with a series of six films directed by Josef von Sternberg, even more of a Pygmalion to her than Stiller had been to Garbo during her Scandinavian debuts. These six films attest to the freedom a movie-maker with a strong personality could enjoy in the Hollywood system. Three of them were hits (*Morocco* [1930]; *Dishonored* [1931]; and above all *Shanghai Express* [1932]). The others – *Blonde Venus* (1932); *The Scarlet Empress* (1934); and *The Devil is a Woman* (1935) – failed at the box office, but none can be reduced to mere commercial arithmetic. Some of the Dietrich–Garbo coincidences seem suspiciously like Hollywood scheming: in the year Garbo played Mata Hari, Marlene had a similar role in *Dishonored*; when Garbo was *Queen Christina*, Marlene matched her as Catherine the Great in *The Scarlet Empress*; while *Blonde Venus* is a real compilation of the misfortunes inflicted at the time on a fallen woman. But through Sternberg's freedom of tone and inspiration, we can see the six episodes as a reflection on the role of the foreigner, starting from the sanctification brought about with Garbo, then correcting and developing it. Marlene is, in turn, French (*Morocco*), Viennese (*Dishonored*, in which she also plays a fake Russian peasant), of vague nationality (Shanghai Lily in *Shanghai Express*) and finally an improbable Spaniard (*The Devil is a Woman*). The nationalities are, in any case, token gestures, since the symbolic persona of the foreign woman is underlined by a multitude of details that muddle the 'real' origin of the character. In *Morocco*, Amy is first seen in the neutral surroundings of an ocean liner – it is only when she sings the French song 'Quand l'amour meurt' ('When Love Dies') that we can guess her origin. At the end of the film, she renounces everything, including a confirmed, precise nationality offered by the archetypal 'Frenchman', Adolphe Menjou,[5] and follows her lover to join the 'foreign legion of stateless women' in the desert. In *Dishonored*, the Viennese Magda is a spy who is obliged to adopt several identities and dies deprived of her nationality. Shanghai Lily, in *Shanghai Express*, is also part of the 'women's foreign legion': was she British when she was the mistress of the officer played by Clive Brook*? In any case, she is now relegated to the rank of the Chinese prostitute played by Anna May Wong, with whom she shares her compartment. In *Blonde Venus*, Helen was German, married to an American. But, to earn her living, she goes back to her job as a singer in a number set in an African decor, and it is in the American Deep South that she falls into prostitution, before a miraculous trip to Paris turns her into a music-hall star. As if sanctified by celebrity and its tangible manifestations of furs and jewels, she returns to family life in the USA to sing to her child the German lullaby that was brutally interrupted at the beginning of the film. In *The Scarlet Empress*, Sophie Caroline is a German princess who will become Catherine, Empress of Russia. Finally, Concha Perez, in *The Devil is a Woman*, is, without doubt, the least Hispanic Spaniard the silver screen has ever seen. The only film of this period that she made without Sternberg, *The Song of Songs* (1933), directed by the Armenian Rouben Mamoulian, has a less blurred context: she is well and truly German. In her post-Sternberg manifestation, Hollywood cast Dietrich as French twice (in Frank Borzage's *Desire* [1936], and in Richard Boleslawski's *The Garden of Allah* [1936]), and once British (or Russian: the mystery of her origin is an important factor in Ernst Lubitsch's *Angel*, 1937). If Garbo was the mythical foreigner, Marlene is the stateless woman par excellence.

The next phase in the evolution of Dietrich's persona is unique. After *Angel* in 1937, she touched the nadir of her popularity in the USA. This decline might initially be explained as the result of abandoning the appealing exoticism exploited by her first three films. But, if Garbo and Dietrich both benefited from the most mythical imagery Hollywood ever created for female stars, their personality and acting style pushed this imagery in diametrically opposite directions: Garbo was sanctified, whereas Marlene was eroticised. The radicalisation of the foreign woman's image, perceptible in Dietrich, together with a refusal to adopt any specifically American identity,[6] eventually wearied or disturbed an American audience revitalised and reunited around national identity by the advent of Roosevelt.[7] *Blonde Venus*, *The Scarlet Empress* and *The Devil is a Woman* showcased an arrogant and triumphant foreigner in a foreign land. Helen, the heroine of *Blonde Venus*, is revived by going back to Europe, and, as a European, returns to reclaim the family position she has been deprived of – a kind of émigré triumphalism that we can now perceive as ironic. Catherine, in *The Scarlet Empress*, becomes aware of her erotic power, links it to political power and accedes to the throne in hussar uniform. In the end, Concha Perez is, together with Lola Lola in *Der Blaue Engel / The Blue Angel* (1930 shot in Germany), the only real femme fatale Marlene played: she makes men suffer, makes them die, and never atones for her sins. To be accepted anew by the American public, Marlene had to erase any visible sign of her 'otherness'.

Dietrich's greatest popular success came as saloon 'gal' Frenchy in the typical American genre, the George Marshall Western *Destry Rides Again* (1939), in which she dies of a stray bullet as if expiating her hitherto unpunished crimes. In full flow, she carried on with Tay Garnett's *Seven Sinners* (1940), Ray Enright's *The Spoilers* (1942) and Lewis Seiler's *Pittsburgh* (1942). In these three films, she plays more or less the same character – a saloon entertainer of foreign origins – and, moreover, acts opposite the very emblematically American John Wayne (as she had co-starred with James Stewart in *Destry Rides Again*). Towards the end of the war, her tour of the Allied troops in North Africa and Europe confirmed the revival of her popularity and her new image as a 'good girl'.

Does this signify successful integration for Dietrich – or a radical softening of the jarring qualities of the foreign woman? Difficult to say. But the postwar years brought a new shift, in which she gradually moved from the screen to the music hall. She was a gypsy in Mitchell Leisen's *Golden Earrings* (1947) and, strikingly, a former Nazi who survives on the black market in the ruins of Berlin in Billy Wilder's *A Foreign Affair* (1948), a role she only accepted after understandable hesitation. This latter performance was arguably Dietrich's best but, unsurprisingly, not a popular success. As a result, she was reduced to repeating herself in pretty much guest-star parts, such as in Alfred Hitchcock's *Stage Fright* (1950) and Henry Koster's *No Highway*, (1951), or reprising the Frenchy of *Destry Rides Again* in Fritz Lang's 1952 *Rancho Notorious*. To simplify, despite a spectacular, nearly successful integration, Dietrich's version of the 'foreigner' is more aggressive and ironic than Garbo's. Her parody performance in William Dieterle's *Kismet* (1944) is revealing in this respect: her skin is painted gold, she wears the most over-decorated dresses one can imagine, and her blonde hair is fashioned in an outrageously elaborate style that in a Hollywood film can only signify 'guilty woman'. Her character is a courtesan in a harem, a delirious and symbolic synthesis of her synchretic conception of the foreign woman.

III Ingrid Bergman: The Foreign Woman Beyond Guilt

In the middle of the period dominated by the Garbo/Dietrich dichotomy, roughly between 1925 and 1945, Hollywood tried out several other foreign actresses. Most of them were modelled either on Garbo (the German Luise Rainer for her sweetness, and the Austrian Hedy Lamarr for glamour) or on Dietrich: for instance, the Italian Isa Miranda★. Interestingly, the latter took over *Hotel Imperial* (a remake of a Pola Negri film), directed by Robert Florey in 1939, a project Dietrich had abandoned. Or they went for a skilful mix of the two, as in the case of the beautiful and talented half Ukrainian, Anna Sten★, whom even the efforts of producer Samuel Goldwyn failed to establish as a star. In her first Hollywood film, Dorothy Arzner's *Nana* (1934), Sten evoked Dietrich with half-closed eyes, a risqué song and a consummate way with a cigarette. In her second, Rouben Mamoulian's *We Live Again* (1934), she was a Garboesque fallen but still saintly woman. Finally King Vidor's *The Wedding Night* (1935) resolved the personality conflict by giving her the moving and tragic role of a Polish émigré. All to no avail. Other imports – for example from France – were even more ephemeral, like Danielle Darrieux★ in Henry Koster's *The Rage of Paris* (1938), or very disappointing, like Michèle Morgan★ in her wartime films. Two interesting cases remain. The first, in the Darrieux line, was Simone Simon★, Darryl F. Zanuck's first French import (followed later by the Franco-Polish Bella Darvi★, the singer-actress Juliette Gréco★, Irina Demick★ and Geneviève Gilles★, who became his last wife). Simon's roles were mostly of the insipid ingénue type, and her prestige declined after she signed a contract with RKO that condemned her to B-movies. There, however, she found her most memorable role as the Serbian-born Irena in Jacques Tourneur's *Cat People* (1942). This film can be read, among other things, as a metaphor for female sexuality. Irena, prisoner of a tradition/malediction, fettered by her origins (she is recognised in a restaurant by a mysterious woman who speaks to her in her mother tongue), incarnates a repressed and unhealthy sexuality, which could not have been embodied by the American Jane Randolph. Here we encounter again the notion of a compensatory relationship between the American and the 'foreign' woman, discussed above.

The other remarkable case is Ingrid Bergman. By eschewing artifice and classic glamour, she represented a decisive step towards the more naturalistic vision of the foreign woman that would dominate American cinema in the 1950s. In this respect, it is no surprise that it fell to her to forge the link between Hollywood and neo-realism. Her refusal to let herself be 'glamourised' according to the established rules was cleverly turned into a publicity line by David O. Selznick, who had brought her to the USA in the first place. Her first Hollywood film (Gregory Ratoff's *Intermezzo* [1939]) was a remake of her greatest European success, Gustav Molander's 1935 film of the same name. On paper, the public might have been expected to have difficulty accepting the role of the young musician who wrecks the home of the mature Leslie Howard★. But there is no doubt that Bergman's naturalness, her spontaneity and her limpid eyes offered a new way of making the unacceptable accepted. Where Garbo and Dietrich succeeded in imposing themselves through subtle cultural reference (literary and pictorial in Garbo) and artifice (Dietrich), Bergman radiantly triumphed through the lack of any sense of sin and the refusal of hypocrisy. In the stern elegance of her outfit in *Rage in Heaven* (1940), and in her mythical white suit topped by a wide-brimmed hat in *Casablanca* (1942), she gracefully embodies the acceptable face of adultery at a time when the (compensating) moral values of the Production Code were giving less fortunate actresses a much harder time.[8] In *Casablanca*, a chivalrous lover (Humphrey Bogart) and an understanding husband (Paul Henreid★) absolve her from any feelings of guilt: could it be that her serene example helped lift a weight of blame from the shoulders of more than a few war wives? American actresses such as Bette Davis, Joan Crawford and Barbara Stanwyck rarely escaped retribution for their faults – while the British Greer Garson★ was required to embody flawless conjugal and familial devotion. Within the same studio as Garson, Bergman succeeded in making the sensual crudity of a London prostitute touching in Victor Fleming's *Dr Jekyll and Mr Hyde* (1941), whereas in Rouben Mamoulian's previous version (1931), Miriam Hopkins, in the same role, was merely strident. Sam Wood's *For Whom the Bell Tolls* (1943) heavily toned down the love story of Hemingway's novel (not to mention its political aspect); but it is still a guilt-free sexuality that the Spanish-Scandinavian Bergman – a symbolic, free-floating foreigner, like Garbo earlier – implies in the nonetheless transgressive sleeping-bag episode.

After losing her glasses, Bergman's psychiatrist in Hitchcock's *Spellbound* (1945) guides Gregory Peck through the labyrinths of his memory like an angel – a redemptive role that forged another facet of the actress's image, as did her good-natured incarnation of a nun in *The Bells of St Mary's*, directed by Leo McCarey in 1945. These two performances strongly impressed the American audience – and undoubtedly fuelled the outrage felt by its most conservative element at her European adventure with Roberto Rossellini a few years later. In Hitchcock's *Notorious* (1946), Bergman plays the daughter of a Nazi traitor who accepts (possibly out of love) the role of semi-prostitute for the American secret service – a part more in keeping with her earlier persona than the saintly heroines of *Spellbound* and *The Bell of St Mary's*. For Bergman as actress and icon, *Notorious* is a culminating moment: her

Alicia, a loose woman and adulteress who kisses Cary Grant in a scene judged torrid at the time, sheds her make-up and reaches a near-mystical intensity in becoming the victim of her husband, Claude Rains★. She carries off a similar inversion of values in the same arousing manner in Hitchcock's *Under Capricorn* (1949), a film in which, under an icily controlled *mise en scène*, there simmers a burning affair à la D. H. Lawrence: in long *plans-séquences*, we see her consumed by passion, drawn to the abyss, then triumphing over them and regaining her unblemished surface free of any artifice. All these roles verged on the forbidden; we owe their existence and the truth drawn from them to the sweetness of Bergman's features, her naturalness and her proudly proclaimed otherness.

It was Bergman's precedent that made possible the less stereotypical representation of foreign women in the cinema of the immediate postwar period – for instance, the enigmatic Alida Valli★ in Hitchcock's *The Paradine Case* (1947, a role initially planned for Garbo), Irving Pichel's *The Miracle of the Bells* (1948) and Ted Tetzlaff's *The White Tower* (1950). Closer to the duplicitous model of Bergman's Alicia in *Notorious* was the Lithuanian Cornell Borchers★ in George Seaton's *Big Lift* (1950), the German Hildegard Knef in Henry Hathaway's *Diplomatic Courier* (1952), the Italian Pier Angeli in Andrew Marton's *The Devil Makes Three* (1952) and the Swedish Anita Björk★ in Nunnally Johnson's *Night People* (1954).

　　More recently, the use of foreign actresses has parallels with the increasing assertion of ethnicity by male actors (whether American, such as Dustin Hoffman, Robert De Niro, Al Pacino and Andy García, or European, like Antonio Banderas★). As much as their male counterparts, they make palpable the bubbling of a 'melting pot'. In the context of the Western genre, it is striking that in Robert Altman's *McCabe & Mrs Miller* (1971), Michael Cimino's *Heaven's Gate* (1980) and Michael Winterbottom's *The Claim* (2001), European actresses – Julie Christie★ (British), Isabelle Huppert★ (French) and Milla Jovovich (Ukrainian) – all play brothel-keepers with an eye for the business, thus embodying the dubious origins of capitalism. The Italian Valeria Golino★ (Jim Abrahams' *Hot Shots!*, 1991; Sean Penn's *The Indian Runner*, 1991), the British Catherine Zeta-Jones★ (Martin Campbell's *The Mask of Zorro*, 1998; Steven Soderbergh's *Traffic*, 2001), the Italo-Spanish Aitana Sánchez-Gijón★ (Alfonso Arau's *A Walk in the Clouds*, 1995) and the Spanish Penelope Cruz★ (Stephen Frears' *The Hi-Lo Country*, 1998) increasingly merge into the deep American landscape – and not even their accents seem to be a problem. What matters more now is to reflect the ethnic and cultural mosaic of the USA. Using foreign actresses fits the process of redefining (American) national identity, to the point where the 'foreigner', as a part, seems to be on the verge of disappearing.

　　Yet, that part played a crucial role at a time when Hollywood was relentlessly determined to give American identity a black-and-white idealised and coded image. Since no drama is viable without a few areas of shadow in its characters, foreign actors, and particularly the 'foreign woman', were better fitted to personify those shadows. The American cinema was able gradually to absorb these – sometimes increasingly darker – areas without having to resort to geographical labels. According to one's perspective, this may be seen as either a desire for hegemony or a greater open-mindedness.

Translated from the French by Renée Fenby and Ann Wright.

Notes

1.　See Lea Jacobs' superb book on the topic, *The Wages of Sin: Censorship and the Fallen Woman Film, 1928–1942* (Madison: University of Wisconsin Press, 1991).

2.　This relatively free adaptation of Luigi Pirandello's play is interesting as regards Garbo and her symbolic role as a foreigner. Her character, Zara, is a cabaret singer who has been found in Budapest; she has lost her memory and may be an Italian aristocrat. Clearly, Pirandello and Garbo shared, among other things, an interest in the issue of identity.

100　3.　Henri Agel: a well-known postwar French film critic noted for his work on film aesthetics and religion in the cinema. Agel also wrote a biography of Garbo: *Greta Garbo* (Paris: Librairie Séguier, 1990). 'Franciscan' refers to the extreme saintliness of Saint Francis of Assisi. [Editors' note]

4. Dietrich started in Germany in 1923, a year before Garbo was made famous by Stiller in *Gösta Berlings saga/The Legend of Gosta Berling* (1924). *Der Blaue Engel/The Blue Angel*, filmed in Germany by Josef von Sternberg in 1930, was far from being her first film (contrary to what Marlene and her discoverer claimed).

5. Despite his name (from his French father) and his specialising in debonair French men on screen, Menjou was an American actor, born in the USA. He spoke French, though, and appeared in some French versions of multi-language films at the coming of sound. [Editors' note]

6. In *Blonde Venus*, the most specific reference to the USA is also the most provocative: the fall of the heroine is linked with a 'going down' towards the South that has her rubbing shoulders with the black population.

7. Dietrich and Garbo were cited as 'box-office poison' – along with other actors such as Katharine Hepburn, Fred Astaire and Joan Crawford – in an infamous survey of film exhibitors published in 1938. The two actresses reacted differently to the affront. Dietrich changed, and even made fun of, her screen image and agreed to star in *Destry Rides Again* for a much lower salary than usual. There followed other successful films and great popularity among GIs. Garbo tried, more awkwardly, to change her image, but *Two-Faced Woman* failed, prompting her legendary retirement at the age of thirty-six.

8. Exemplary in this respect is the treatment inflicted on Joan Crawford in Michael Curtiz's *Mildred Pierce* (1944): returning home in the heavy rain after a romantic escapade, she finds her ex-husband waiting to tell her that her younger daughter is at death's door.

11 The Ultimate Irony

Jews Playing Nazis in Hollywood

Joseph Garncarz

At a major charity event during World War II, the exiled film writer Robert Thoeren joked:

> In two hundred years a clever child will raise its hand in class and ask the teacher, 'What did the Nazis look like?' When they go to the archives and show contemporary motion pictures, they will find that the Nazis were a purely Semitic tribe, because they were portrayed in Hollywood films by Fritz Kortner★, Sig Arno★, Curt Bois★, Alexander Granach★, Felix Basch★, Kurt Katch★ etc.[1]

During the Third Reich, German-speaking Jewish actors who were forced to leave Germany or Austria by the Nazis ended up playing Nazis in Hollywood films. As Alfred Polgar put it in 1942, they became 'portrayers of the bestiality of which [they themselves] were victims'.[2] In this chapter, I want to investigate how and why so many German actors went to Hollywood, what problems and opportunities they encountered in the labour market, how things changed with the production of anti-Nazi films and how the refugees from Nazi Germany reacted to playing Nazis. Was it a case of humiliation, revenge or political opposition for them, or was it simply a way of making a living?

The Kohner Files as Primary Source

To answer these questions, I have used the correspondence between a selected group of German-speaking actors who played Nazis in Hollywood and their agent, Paul Kohner.[3] In addition, I have used interviews with actors conducted by different researchers in later years. Since these interviews are reflective judgments and therefore less involved in day-to-day concerns, they show, more thoroughly than most of the Kohner files, how the actors reacted to playing Nazi roles.

Paul Kohner was the main agent in the USA for German and Austrian exiles. He was born in the former Austro-Hungarian Empire and came to the USA in 1921, following an invitation by Carl Laemmle, head of Universal. Kohner was put in charge of the then new foreign publicity department, and a few years later he became the director of German Universal, which produced films in Berlin from 1928 to 1934.[4] After working for MGM and Columbia for a short period of time, he finally set himself up as a Hollywood agent in 1938, selling his clients to the major companies.

On the initiative of Gero Gandert, the Berlin Film Museum bought all extant files after Kohner died in 1988. The so-called 'Sammlung Paul Kohner' contains about 155,000 pages of correspondence, contracts and the like.[5] The correspondence is bilingual: most of it is in English, but there are letters in German, too. When working with this collection, one should keep in mind that not all Kohner's documents have been preserved. Some were lost due

Anti-Nazi pictures ironically provided German-Jewish actors in exile with regular work in Nazi parts: Kurt Katch appeared, among many such films, in *Berlin Correspondent* (1942), *Counter-Espionage* (1942) and *The Strange Death of Adolf Hitler* (1943)

to water damage, some had already been sold before the Berlin Film Museum bought the archive. In addition, communications were not always conducted in writing. Although the telephone was very important for Kohner, unfortunately no records of these phone calls are extant. Nonetheless, the Kohner files – which have not yet been used systematically in relation to the history of film exile – are a unique source for studying the German-speaking actors in the USA.

Based on my own viewing and a variety of written sources,[6] I have selected an unbiased, random sample of male actors who are representative of the range of German-speaking actors who played Nazis in anti-Nazi films. They are: Rudoph Anders* (aka Rudolf Amendt, Rudolph Amendt, Rudolf Anders, Robert O. Davies, Robert O. Davis, Robert Davis), Ludwig Donath* (aka Louis Donath), Carl Esmond* (aka Willy Eichberger, Charles Esmond), Arno Frey*, Frederick Giermann* (aka Fred Gehrmann, Fred Giermann, Frederick Gierman), Oscar Homolka* (aka Oscar Homolka), Hans von Morhart*, Otto Reichow*, Sig Ruman* (aka Siegfried Rumann, Sig Rumann), Hans Schumm*, Reinhold Schünzel*, Tonio Selwart*, Walter Slezak*, Ludwig Stössel* and Wolfgang Zilzer* (aka John Voight, Paul Andor). Since nearly every German-speaking actor who worked in Hollywood during World War II played Nazis, the sample should even be typical of all German-speaking actors who worked in Hollywood at the time.

The 'Sammlung Paul Kohner' contains files on all of the selected actors except Anders, Frey, Giermann and Reichow. Only two of the remaining eleven actors, Sig Ruman and Walter Slezak, were not under contract to Kohner. Thus, nine out of fifteen, or 60 per cent of these actors had a contract with Paul Kohner, which clearly demonstrates his high status as an agent for German-speaking film personnel.

There are further difficulties in categorising my sample. Although all the actors in it spoke German, not all were Jewish, nor were they all political exiles or even Germans. In his autobiography, Slezak did not define himself as Jewish; furthermore, he was Austrian and he was not a political exile (he went to the USA in 1930 because he had been contracted by J. J. Shubert for a Broadway show). In the case of von Morhart, we have no information. Of the remaining fourteen actors, eight were born in Germany (Anders, Frey, Giermann, Reichow, Ruman, Schumm, Schünzel, Selwart), five in Austria (Donath, Esmond, Homolka, Slezak, Stössel), and one in the USA (Zilzer was born in the USA, the child of German parents who later returned to Germany). Apart from Slezak, Anders, Frey, Ruman and Schumm also went to the USA before the Nazis took power. However, this does not mean that these actors would not have been forced to leave their country after the Nazis seized power had they stayed in Germany. For example, Slezak would definitely have been persecuted as a Jew, since the Nazis defined his mother as Jewish.[7]

A list of German-speaking exiles from the film industry compiled by Günther Peter Stracheck[8] identifies nine actors from my sample as political exiles: Donath, Esmond, Giermann, Homolka, Reichow, Schünzel, Selwart, Stössel and Zilzer. However, this list is not wholly reliable: for example, Esmond claimed that he left Austria voluntarily after 1933, because he preferred to work in Britain and later in Hollywood.[9] As a rule, though, most of the Germans and Austrians who were forced to leave their countries had to do so because they were persecuted as Jews by the Nazis. Nazi anti-Semitic policies defined a Jew as a person with at least one Jewish grandparent, regardless of whether such a person defined him- or herself as a Jew.[10] In addition, many Jews' relatives left their country when, for example, their husband or wife was unable to get work because they were persecuted as a Jew. The files of the former Berlin Document Center, now part of the Bundesarchiv, show that out of my sample only Ludwig Stössel was persecuted as a Jew by the Nazis, which does not necessarily mean that the others would not have been, had circumstances been different. Those who hid from the Nazis or left the country even before the Nazis took power do not appear in the Nazi files.[11] However, according to Stracheck's analysis, 95 per cent of the exiled film personnel left the country because they were persecuted as Jews (the percentage of political persecution in other occupational groups, such as writers or academics, was even higher).[12] Thus, when I classify an actor as 'Jewish' in this chapter, I am primarily referring to the fact that the Nazis persecuted, or would have persecuted, him as a Jew according to their ideology; in other words, Jewishness would have been the relevant motive for exile. Furthermore, many of those who had not defined themselves as Jews in Germany began to do so after they had been forced into exile through Nazi persecution.

Going to Hollywood

In addition to the question of Jewishness discussed above, there were a variety of reasons why German-speaking actors went to Hollywood. Many went voluntarily, because they harboured expectations of economic and professional advantage; in our sample, this can be said of Anders, Esmond, Frey, Ruman, Schumm and Slezak. But when the Nazis took power in January 1933, within a couple of weeks, they enforced policies de facto prohibiting Jews from working in the film business. As a result, about 2,000 film workers fled to neighbouring countries and to the USA.

Most of the exiles first sought refuge in the neighbouring countries of Austria, Hungary, France and the UK before trying to flee to the USA. This is true for five of seven actors of my sample: Donath went first to Austria, then to Switzerland in 1938, then to the UK in 1939, before finally reaching the USA in 1940; Homolka went to the UK in 1935, before going to Hollywood in 1937; Reichow went to France in 1936, before emigrating to the USA in 1937; Stössel went to Austria in 1933, to Britain in 1938 and one year later to the USA; Zilzer left Germany for France in 1933, returned to Germany in 1935 and ultimately emigrated to the USA in 1937. Only two actors in my sample emigrated directly to the USA: Selwart in 1933 and Schünzel in 1937.

Austria could only be a transitional stage, not only because it was annexed by Nazi Germany in 1938 but because its film industry was always completely dependent on the German market. France and the UK were the two most important European asylum countries for German-speaking exiled film personnel, because their film industries were experiencing a period of dramatic growth at that time and because they had a substantial distribution market.[13] However, Continental European countries proved to be only an intermediate station for most German-speaking film personnel, partly because these countries' domestic film industries were in the end too small to absorb large numbers of new workers, and partly because the Nazis' influence steadily increased in these territories. In 1940, Germany occupied wide areas of France. Those who were captured by the Nazis died in concentration camps. The popular character actors Kurt Gerron and Otto Wallburg, for example, both died at Auschwitz.[14]

The USA was, for various reasons, the most popular place of refuge for German-speaking exiles. Hollywood, which at that time was a cartel controlled by eight companies, constituted the largest film industry in the Western world and produced a great number of films for the international market. To make American films more successful on other national markets and to address specific segments of the multicultural American market itself, Hollywood was always on the lookout for foreign creative talent. Paul Kohner's agency could fulfil this demand by offering European film personnel. As a rule, German and Austrian exiles had no problems receiving a visa in the USA as long as they had a job offer from an American film company. Therefore, it was easier to work in the USA than in Europe, where an exile had to get a work permit from the state before being able to work. In addition, the standardised Hollywood production methods were not unfamiliar to the German-speaking exiles, since the principal German production company, Ufa, had adopted similar methods in 1927 and, in any case, many Germans were already working in the USA, from directors such as Ernst Lubitsch to moguls like Carl Laemmle. Last but not least, the USA was also the safest place geographically to escape capture by the Nazis.[15]

Before World War II, only about 15 per cent of the total number of German-speaking exiled film personnel went to Hollywood. Many of them came to the USA with contracts from American film companies, especially directors, producers, cameramen and musicians such as Joe May, Erik Charell, Erich Pommer, Theodor Sparkuhl and Werner Richard Heymann. For actors, however, it was nearly impossible to get a contract in advance. In August **105**

1938, Kohner's collaborator Fritz Keller described the problem to Ludwig Stössel, who was staying in Switzerland at the time:

> Dr Otto Preminger forwarded to me your letter of July 23rd, and although I know the situation in Europe very well, and am most anxious to do everything possible for my old friends in Europe, I have to tell you it is utterly impossible to do anything for you here in Hollywood as long as you are not here personally.
>
> Please don't tell me that all the big studios here in Hollywood would be able to judge your capabilities, by screening one of your pictures which you made in Europe. These gentlemen here simply don't listen. They want to see the person; they want to talk to him and want to have the impression from the living personality. They will not judge from – what they consider beforehand as being – a bad picture and badly directed, because it was made in Europe.
>
> You know that I estimate your qualities as a fine actor, very highly, and I would like very much to do something for you, but unfortunately as explained above, I am not in a position to do anything as long as you are not here.[16]

After 1938–9, the stream of refugees to the USA increased dramatically. As a consequence, it became 'much more difficult . . . to place [an actor] who is not here, even if we have some very good photographs'.[17] Without a contract in advance, refugees needed a guarantor to give an affidavit that they would support the refugee financially if he or she was unable to earn enough money. Kohner founded the European Film Fund to get film personnel out of Nazi Germany and to support exiles financially.[18] In addition, he negotiated contracts with American film companies for well-known German writers, such as Alfred Döblin, Heinrich Mann and Alfred Polgar. Such initiatives allowed about 450 Germans and Austrians to move to Hollywood.

The Labour Market for Exiled German-speaking Actors in Hollywood

Unlike exiled writers, who continued to address a German-speaking public even though they had no chance of getting their work published in Germany or Austria, German-speaking exiles in the film industry did not make films for a German-speaking audience. On the contrary, they aimed their films at the audience of the country in which they were working and at the audiences of those countries that were not collaborating with, or occupied by, the Nazis.

Since they did not work in their mother tongue, language was therefore a problem. Lotte Palfi★-Andor explained in retrospect:

> I was under the illusion that I would be able to work as an actress again there. I said to myself that America was a melting pot. So many nationalities met there and spoke different varieties of English that my German accent would not be an obstacle. I never made a greater mistake.[19]

Indeed, in contrast to other occupational groups such as producers, directors or cameramen, exiled actors needed the ability to speak English on a level that was acceptable for English-speaking audiences. However, most of the German-speaking actors spoke English with a heavy accent, if at all. Albert Bassermann★, for example, spoke no English and refused to learn it. For his first film, *Dr Ehrlich's Magic Bullet* (1940), he had to learn 'his lines by rote, rehearsing phonetically'.[20] Thus, compared to other occupational groups of German-speaking exiles, actors had the greatest problems in adapting to the American film market, due to the importance of language.

Because of their accent, German-speaking actors were not considered suitable for all roles. Even the most popular or critically acclaimed actors and actresses, such as Marlene Dietrich★, Luise Rainer★ and Paul Henreid★, usually played foreigners, not necessarily from their own native country but any European country, or even 'exotic' locations such as China. However, having a foreign accent was not necessarily always a handicap, since there was some demand for foreigner roles, especially in European-themed films – for example *Ninotchka* (1939)

– and German-speaking actors made such characters believable. Thus, the actors' German accent was their major 'cultural capital' as well as their greatest handicap, thereby limiting the range of possible roles and their chance to become stars. When Wolfgang Zilzer was asked, 'Would it be an exaggeration to say that in this country you were only offered roles that justified the accent?' he answered, 'Yes, that was almost always true for film roles. And when I didn't do the accent enough, I was promptly asked: "Where's the accent?" so I had to put a little effort into it.'[21]

After 1938, when German-speaking actors began to flood the market in Hollywood, there were not enough of these roles around. Kohner certainly wanted to help his countrymen, but this became increasingly difficult, because the supply of actors far exceeded the demand. As a rule, actors eagerly sought contracts with Kohner, but among the actors in my sample, only in the case of Sig Ruman did Kohner take the initiative to offer a contract.[22] Since there were many more German-speaking actors than Hollywood needed, the studios usually signed contracts only on a film-by-film basis (Walter Slezak, who received a long-term contract, was an exception). In economic terms, it did not make sense to contract these actors on a one-year basis, as Sidney Buchman of Columbia Pictures explained to Ludwig Donath:

> There is a company policy against carrying character people on contract. They feel, with very few exceptions, that they cannot write off such charges in the year easily and that they would prefer paying even more to such a man when they need him. [Harry] Cohn made this explanation to me and after a certain point I could not urge him to change his company policy. This was true in the face of the fact that he has an extremely high regard for your work.[23]

German-speaking actors who were well known and formerly highly esteemed in Germany or Austria, but unknown to American audiences, expected to get leading roles in Hollywood or at least roles that were more than a walk-on part, but they were often disappointed.[24] For the exiled actors, this situation was frustrating, as evidenced by a variety of letters to Kohner:

> The point I want to make is that I feel the above mentioned assignment must be a first class job with a substantial part and not a 'fill in' job such as the one in *Panama Hattie* [1942] which I would accept (providing it is offered to me) because I want to keep going and keep in work as I feel it is better to be working than to be idle.[25]

Kohner was not always able to fulfil the hopes placed in him. Confronted with this situation, he sometimes resorted to making his clients believe that they were going to play more substantial roles than they actually would. This occasionally upset the actors, as Ludwig Donath complained to Kohner:

> You as my representative should instead fight for what we have to ask for like a lion. A full week I am now waiting for an answer from you. . . . Last week, when I got the call from Paramount about Dr Wassel, I saw you. You told me that they asked for Bassermann for this part and that you told them, he couldn't do it, but you have 'another very good actor . . . (me) etc.' It will be at least a two weeks job. It is a three days bit part and nobody at Paramount had ever the idea to ask for Bassermann. When I asked them about it, I was laughed at and told, 'Somebody made a fool of you'. Why do you do that to me?[26]

Anti-Nazi Films as a Solution

When anti-Nazi films started to be produced in Hollywood in great numbers during World War II, more than 130, or about 65 per cent, of all German-speaking exiled actors finally got a chance to work – including Jewish actors. Paul Kohner's brother and biographer, Frederick Kohner, described the new situation thus:

Paul knew that their time would come. And it did come, sooner than he had anticipated, with the flood of anti-Nazi pictures . . . Suddenly the industry needed Prussian generals, bullnecked SS officers, Fuehrers, Stuka fliers, Austrian zither players, Jewish scientists, U-boat captains, revolutionaries, spies and counterspies. Paul supplied them all. Actor Fritz Kortner went to work, as did Ernst Deutsch★, Alexander Granach, Carl Esmond, Felix Bressart★, Curt Bois, Sig Arno, Ludwig Stössel.[27]

The anti-Nazi films conveyed an anti-Fascist message via traditional genre films such as spy thrillers: *Confessions of a Nazi Spy* (1939), *Man Hunt* (1941); melodramas: *The Mortal Storm* (1940); and comedies: *To Be or Not to Be* (1942). American companies did not produce anti-Nazi films immediately the Nazis took power, since the industry did not want to hurt the feelings of any nation in the world, regardless of its politics,[28] and since America's public opinion initially followed a policy of isolationism. In addition, most of the American studios wanted to avoid offending the Nazis in order to keep a foothold in the German film market. In 1934, Warner Bros. was the first company to close its German branch, and in 1938, it became the first major company to produce an anti-Nazi film, *Confessions of a Nazi Spy*.[29] When Jewish shops were destroyed, synagogues burned down and Jews were humiliated, terrorised and killed in Germany during the night of 9–10 November 1938 (what the Nazis called *Reichskristallnacht*), the USA's public opinion began to change from isolationism to interventionism. Furthermore, by the end of 1939, the share of the German market held by those US companies that were still distributing their films in Germany, MGM, Fox and Paramount, was dwindling. Consequently, more and more Hollywood studios began producing anti-Nazi films. In reaction to this, the Nazis prohibited American companies from distributing their films in Germany. If a studio produced a single anti-Nazi film in the USA, it was forced to close its foreign branch in Germany (Paramount was the last to leave in October 1940). After the USA entered World War II in December 1941, the production of anti-Nazi films became a patriotic duty and the number of such films increased.[30]

Anti-Nazi films were therefore the big break for German-speaking exiled film personnel, in that they created a large number of jobs. According to Jan-Christopher Horak, about 180 such films were produced in the USA between 1939 and 1946. German-speaking actors participated in 90 per cent of these films and German-speaking producers, directors and screenwriters in 30 per cent.[31] The number of supporting and even leading roles for German actors thus grew significantly: only 45 per cent of these roles were still walk-on parts (16 per cent of roles were not credited). For German actors, therefore, anti-Nazi films offered the best opportunity, since they regularly included roles for which they were an exact fit – Germans with heavy German accents. Given their military slant, these films of course offered hardly any roles for women. For example, while Wolfgang Zilzer regularly found work, his wife, Lotte Palfi-Andor, only got bit parts from time to time, such as a nurse in *Confessions of a Nazi Spy* and the wife of a Resistance fighter in *Underground* (1941). She had to wait several months, sometimes years, between films.[32]

Actors in exile occasionally played refugees on screen: for example, Ludwig Stössel as Mr Leuchtag and Wolfgang Zilzer as the man with expired papers (both uncredited) in *Casablanca* (1942). They also played resistance fighters, such as Paul Henreid in the same film. But more often than not they had to play Nazis. The Nazi characters of the anti-Nazi films are portrayed, as a rule, as stereotypical anti-democrats: SS or Gestapo men subordinate to the totalitarian control of the 'Führer'. They are often characterised as brutal and stupid, ridiculous figures who do not argue: they obey if they are subordinates and never speak without shouting if they are officers. Last but not least, all these Nazi characters have a heavy German accent, even more exaggerated than in other roles; some of them, such as Hans Heinrich von Twardowski★, who played Reinhard Heydrich in *Hangmen Also Die* (1943), even spoke only German.

There are too many anti-Nazi films with actors from my sample to mention them all, so one role for each actor must suffice as an example: Rudolph Anders played a Gestapo agent in *To Be or Not to Be* (uncredited); Ludwig

Donath portrayed Hitler and his double in *The Strange Death of Adolf Hitler* (1943); Carl Esmond played the Nazi commander Major Paul Dichter in *First Comes Courage* (1943), avoiding the typical Nazi clichés; Arno Frey played a concentration camp commandant in *Escape* (1940) (uncredited); Frederick Giermann played Heinrich Himmler, one of the political leaders responsible for organising the concentration camps, in *The Strange Death of Adolf Hitler*; Oscar Homolka was the opportunist Lev Pressinger in *Hostages* (1943); Hans von Morhart and Otto Reichow played Gestapo men in *The Man I Married* (1940) and *Invisible Agent* (1942), respectively (both uncredited); Sig Ruman appeared as Colonel Erhardt in *To Be or Not to Be*; Hans Schumm was a Gestapo officer in *Escape*; Reinhold Schünzel played Gestapo inspector Ritter in *Hangmen Also Die* and Tonio Selwart the Gestapo commander Kurt Haas in the same picture; Walter Slezak played the ship commandant Willy in *Lifeboat* (1944); Ludwig Stössel was the opportunistic town mayor Herman Bauer in *Hitler's Madman* (1943); Wolfgang Zilzer played Joseph Goebbels, the Nazi's propaganda minister, who was responsible for organising the film industry, in *Enemy of Women* (1944).

Exiled Actors' Reactions to Playing Nazis

In studying the relevant sources, it became clear that the main hypothesis I started with in this research – that the actors hated or resented playing Nazis – was not supported by the evidence. Surprisingly enough, there are no complaints at all from the actors in Kohner's files about playing Nazis. On the contrary, Schünzel, who had been one of Germany's critically acclaimed directors, as well as an actor, even asked Kohner whether he could get him the role of prominent Nazi Himmler in *The Hitler Gang* (1944) (Luis Van Rooten got the part, his first).[33] Thus, for the refugees, playing Nazis does not seem to have been humiliating.

Playing Nazis may have been a moral and political undertaking for some actors, but, as far as I can see, this was not the case for those in my sample. There is no hint that these actors felt that playing Nazis was a form of revenge or an act of political resistance. When Zilzer was asked, 'Did you feel that with this role [Goebbels in *Enemy of Women*] you could get even with the Nazis?' he answered, 'Revenge? No, I never felt that way about it. When I play a role I have to try to make it as believable as possible.'[34]

Certainly, actors were often resentful of the limitations of the parts and were forced to accept the roles offered to them because they needed the money, as Carl Esmond complained to Kohner:

> My present role – which I had to accept only because of the money – and which is completely insignificant in artistic or professional terms, only confirmed my prior experience that I am only offered roles which have as their most important requirement the knowledge of the German language. I do not see how I will ever get a leading role or at least an artistically valuable one that way.[35]

However, the most interesting point revealed by the archival material is that the exiled actors' reaction to a Nazi role depended mainly on their professional self-definition. During this period, a connection with the theatre was an essential aspect of a German-speaking actor's identity. A study of actors' biographies shows that in 1926, 86.1 per cent of the German-speaking actors claimed to have an artistic background, with 77.9 per cent of the actors stating that they had started out in the theatre (in other words they had either theatrical training or they had begun their career in the theatre), and 8.2 per cent in ballet or opera.[36] Only 13.9 per cent said that they had begun work directly in film. In the 1930s, a theatrical background had become even more important due to the transition to sound. In a 1936 survey, 94.9 per cent of the actors refer to an artistic background, with 87 per cent stating that they had started in the theatre, and only 5.1 per cent directly in film.[37]

The German-speaking actors' professional self-definition was thus firmly based in the theatrical tradition and its concepts of 'good roles' and 'good acting'. These actors had been professionally trained, and in their work they defined themselves solely as artists, not as political victims. As individuals, however, many did take political action **109** against the Nazis, for example by joining the Hollywood Anti-Nazi League. Since Hollywood also needed more theatrically trained actors after the transition to sound, and was working to similar standards of professionalism, German-speaking actors had no problems in adapting to Hollywood conventions in this respect.

Since art was autonomous in the German-speaking actors' view, it was irrelevant for character actors whether the character they were to play was good or evil. As Carl Esmond put it, 'I played a very good part [in *First Comes Courage*] although I was a Nazi.'[38] Wolfgang Zilzer, when asked whether he had hesitated to accept the role of Nazi propaganda minister Joseph Goebbels in *Enemy of Women*, answered, 'No, I love to play any good role. Otherwise, who would want to play a character like Franz Moor?'[39] To Zilzer, it was of primary importance that the role was a leading one, and not a supporting or a walk-on part, as most Nazi roles usually were.

But the exiled actors' idea of a 'good role' was not only its importance in terms of narrative or screen time but also whether it offered the chance to portray an interesting and complex character. As a result, and since the actors defined themselves as character players, they strongly disliked being typecast. Zilzer told Hans Heinrich von Twardowski:

> Finally, each time I appeared in a film everyone knew right away that I would either be the Anti-Nazi or the opposite. . . . And when I wanted to play something else, it was doomed to failure from the start, because people thought that's the Nazi, or the Anti-Nazi, but what does he want, now he's something completely different – nobody would buy it.[40]

In addition, 'good acting' meant a chance to immerse oneself in a part completely, to act in a psychologically convincing manner so that the audience would forget about both the actor and the acting. If the illusion was not complete for the audience, the actor had failed to reach his goal. Zilzer felt very bad about Ernst Deutsch playing a Nazi, since in his opinion everybody could see that Deutsch was Jewish: 'He never looked as Jewish as he did in that Nazi-costume, it was terribly embarrassing.'[41]

There were a few German-speaking exiled actors who refused to accept Nazi roles, despite the fact that they needed the money and would even have liked to play these roles. One of these, Carl Esmond, said: 'There was a wonderful part in a very anti-German film, *Nurse Edith Cavell* (1939), and I turned it down. Then there was an anti-Nazi-picture, *Escape*, and I said I can't do it.'[42] Esmond rejected these roles because he wanted to protect his family, who were still in annexed Austria. Therefore, Kohner was glad that Esmond already had a job when 'Warner Brothers called me about you for *All Through The Night* (1942) – the Nazi part.'[43] Others did accept Nazi parts and changed their names to protect their families. Wolfgang Zilzer, for example, changed his name to John Voight to be able to appear in *Confessions of a Nazi Spy* without endangering his father, who was still in Germany. But it was in vain: Zilzer was recognised and his father died at the hands of the Gestapo.

Conclusion

During the Third Reich, German-speaking Jewish actors, who had been forced by the Nazis to leave their countries, flocked to Hollywood. They preferred the USA to other European states, since Hollywood was not only the largest film industry in the Western world but also the only one that was always on the lookout for foreign talent due to the multicultural nature of its home audience as well as its international markets. Compared to other occupational groups such as directors, foreign actors had the greatest problems finding work, since the potential range of roles was restricted to foreign characters because of language. As long as the number of exiles did not exceed the number of suitable (foreign) roles, which were a cornerstone of European-themed productions, the actors' German accent was their major 'cultural capital'. But when the number of exiled actors exceeded the demand, their 'cultural capital' became their greatest 'cultural handicap', excluding them from screen acting. However, when anti-Nazi films were produced in great numbers during World War II, increasing significantly the need for performers with German accents, male actors finally got a chance to act. Despite the fact that these new roles were mainly Nazi characters, the exiled actors' professional self-definition ensured that their identity as political victims did not interfere with their role as actors. Thus, for the refugees, apart from making a living, playing Nazis was neither an act of humiliation nor of political resistance. How the actors reacted to these roles depended mainly on their professional self-definition, which was based in the theatrical tradition and its concepts of 'good roles' and 'good acting'. A Nazi role was a 'good' one, if it was a major part, one that portrayed an individuated and complex character. The acting was 'good' if the actor managed to embody the character in such a manner that the audience could entertain the illusion of being confronted with a real Nazi and not with an actor. As contemporary documents and retrospective interviews show, there is no difference in terms of the actors' reactions to playing Nazi roles, whether they were political exiles or whether they came to Hollywood voluntarily, because both groups shared the same concept of professional and artistic identity. However, as individuals, the refugees indeed defined themselves as political victims who were fortunate to have survived the Holocaust in a free country, as the actor Hans von Morhart remembered after the war in a letter to Paul Kohner:

> Even if I didn't achieve professionally what I had once hoped for, I did manage to adapt to the new situation, and I was satisfied to be able to earn my living, albeit with varying success, in pleasant surroundings far away from the Nazi-terror, which would surely have cost me my life. I have learned very much here and am grateful to have lived in freedom in a democratic country.[44]

Translated from the German by Annemone Ligensa.

I would like to thank Anna Sarah Vielhaber, who did research for this chapter in Berlin, and Gerrit Thies, who is in charge of the Sammlung Paul Kohner.

Notes

1. Walter Slezak, *Wann geht der nächste Schwan?* (Munich: Piper, 1964), p. 324. This is an enlarged edition of Walter Slezak, *What Time's the Next Swan?* (Garden City, NY: Doubleday, 1962). As far as I can see, the quotation is not included in the English edition of Slezak's autobiography.
2. Alfred Polgar, 'Leben am Pazifik', in *Aufbau* vol. 8 no. 36, September 1942, p. 21, reprinted in Marcel Reich-Ranicki (ed.), *Alfred Polgar: Kleine Schriften, Band 1* (Reinbek bei Hamburg: Rowohlt, 1982), pp. 463–6 (originally in German).
3. On Kohner, see: Frederick Kohner, *The Magician of Sunset Boulevard: The Improbable Life of Paul Kohner, Hollywood Agent* (Palos Verdes, CA: Morgan Press, 1977); Frederick Kohner, *Der Zauberer vom Sunset Boulevard: Ein Leben zwischen Film und Wirklichkeit* (Munich: Droemer Knaur, 1974). Originally written in English, the book was first published in German and translated by Karl Otto von Czernicki, who cut references to the Nazis. See also: Stiftung Deutsche Kinemathek (ed.), *Film Exil, #1/1992* (Berlin: Edition Hentrich, 1992); see also the ZDF/arte-feature television documentary, *Der agent vom Sunset Boulevard: Paul Kohner und das amerikanische Filmexil/L'agent de Sunset Boulevard: Paul Kohner et l'exil américain du film allemand*, written by Heike Klapdor, broadcast in 1996.
4. See Erika Wottrich (ed.), *Deutsche Universal: Transatlantische Verleih- und Produktionsstrategien eines Hollywood-Studios in den 20er und 30er Jahren* (Munich: edition text + kritik, 2001).
5. Stiftung Deutsche Kinemathek (ed.), *Sammlung Paul Kohner Agency: Inventarverzeichnis.* (Berlin: Eigendruck, 1994).
6. Jan-Christopher Horak, *Anti-Nazi-Filme der deutschsprachigen Emigration von Hollywood 1939–1945* (Münster: MAkS, 1985); Christian Cargnelli and Michael Omasta (eds), *Aufbruch ins Ungewisse, Bd. 2: Lexikon, Tributes, Selbstzeugnisse* (Vienna: Wespennest, 1993).

7. Gerd Albrecht, *Nationalsozialistische Filmpolitik: Eine soziologische Untersuchung über die Spielfilme des Dritten Reichs* (Stuttgart: Ferdinand Enke, 1969), p. 208.

8. Deutsches Filmmuseum (ed.), *Von Babelsberg nach Hollywood: Filmemigranten aus Nazideutschland* (Frankfurt am Main: Deutsches Filmmuseum, 1987), pp. 7–22.

9. Carl Esmond: 'Ich war nicht keen, nach Amerika zu gehen', in Christian Cargnelli and Michael Omasta (ed.), *Aufbruch ins Ungewisse Bd. 1: Österreichische Filmschaffende in der Emigration vor 1945* (Vienna: Wespennest, 1993).

10. First supplementary decree of the Nürnberg Laws from 14 November 1935.

11. Letter from the Bundesarchiv, Berlin, to the author, 18 January 2002.

12. Jan-Christopher Horak, *Fluchtpunkt Hollywood: Eine Dokumentation zur Filmemigration nach 1933* (Münster: MAkS, 1984), p. 38, n. 2.

13. On German exiles in the film industry in Britain, see: Günter Berghaus (ed.), *Theatre and Film in Exile: German Artists in Britain, 1933–1945* (Oxford, New York and Munich: Berg, 1989); Kevin Gough-Yates, *Somewhere in England: British Cinema and Exile* (London: I. B. Tauris, 2000).

14. Ulrich Liebe, *Verehrt, verfolgt, vergessen: Schauspieler als Naziopfer* (Weinheim and Berlin: Quadriga, 1995).

15. Horak, *Fluchtpunkt Hollywood*, pp. 2–37; John Russell-Taylor, *Strangers in Paradise: The Hollywood Emigres, 1933–1950* (London: Faber and Faber, 1983).

16. Sammlung Paul Kohner, Keller to Ludwig Stössel, 4 August 1938.

17. Sammlung Paul Kohner, Keller to Ludwig Stössel, 11 October 1939.

18. Kohner, *The Magician of Sunset Boulevard*, pp. 109–12.

19. Lotte Palfi-Andor: 'Memoiren einer unbekannten Schauspielerin', in Erich Leyens and Lotte Palfi-Andor, *Die fremden Jahre: Erinnerungen an Deutschland* (Frankfurt am Main: Fischer, 1994), p. 90 (originally in German).

20. Kohner, *The Magician of Sunset Boulevard*, p. 118.

21. Wolfgang Zilzer: 'Ich habe ja meistens die Opfer gespielt', in Stiftung Deutsche Kinemathek (ed.), *Wolfgang Zilzer (Paul Andor)* (Berlin: 33. Internationale Filmfestspiele Berlin, 1983), p. 17 (originally in German).

22. Sammlung Paul Kohner, Kohner to Sig Rumann, 9 October 1939.

23. Sammlung Paul Kohner, Sidney Buchman (Columbia Pictures) to Ludwig Donath, 7 May 1946.

24. For example, Albert Bassermann; see Kohner, *The Magician of Sunset Boulevard*, p. 117.

25. Sammlung Paul Kohner, Carl Esmond to Kohner, 14 July 1941.

26. Sammlung Paul Kohner, Ludwig Donath to Kohner, 6 August 1943.

27. Kohner, *The Magician of Sunset Boulevard*, p. 121. Please note, spelling is as in the original quote in English.

28. Ruth Vasey, *The World According to Hollywood, 1918–1939* (Madison: University of Wisconsin Press, 1997).

29. Michael E. Birdwell, *Celluloid Soldiers – Warner Bros.'s Campaign against Nazism* (New York: New York University Press, 1999).

30. Markus Spieker, *Hollywood unterm Hakenkreuz: Der amerikanische Spielfilm im Dritten Reich* (Trier: Wissenschaftlicher Verlag, 1999), pp. 247–318.

31. Horak, *Fluchtpunkt Hollywood*, p. 28.

32. Lotte Palfi-Andor, in Zilzer, 'Ich habe ja meistens die Opfer gespielt', p. 2; Palfi-Andor, 'Memoiren einer unbekannten Schauspielerin', pp. 90, 102–4.

33. Sammlung Paul Kohner, Reinhold Schünzel to Kohner, 30 March 1943.

34. Zilzer, 'Ich habe ja meistens die Opfer gespielt', p. 17.

35. Sammlung Paul Kohner, Carl Esmond to Kohner, 8 June 1939 (originally in German)

36. Calculated on the basis of the 300 biographical entries in Kurt Mühsam and Egon Jacobson, *Lexikon des Films* (Berlin: Verlag der Lichtbildbühne, 1926).

37. Walther Freisburger, *Theater im Film: Eine Untersuchung über die Grundzüge und Wandlungen in den Beziehungen*

zwischen Theater und Film (Emsdetten: Lechte, 1936), p. 69.

38. Esmond: 'Ich war nicht keen, nach Amerika zu gehen', p. 220.

39. Zilzer: 'Ich habe ja meistens die Opfer gespielt', p. 18. Franz Moor is the villain in Friedrich von Schiller's play *Die Räuber* (1782).

40 Ibid., p. 19.

41 Ibid., p. 17.

42 Esmond: 'Ich war nicht keen, nach Amerika zu gehen', p. 219.

43 Sammlung Paul Kohner, Kohner to Carl Esmond, 13 June 1941.

44 Sammlung Paul Kohner, Von Morhart to Kohner, 23 May 1946 (originally in German).

12 'Not for Export'

Jean Gabin in Hollywood

Ginette Vincendeau

Reflecting on his acting in his two Hollywood films, Jean Gabin – remarked: 'I could hear myself say my lines [. . .] I felt I was no longer what I wished to remain, that is to say a Frenchman.'[1] By fusing anxieties over his performance in an unfamiliar language with the essence of his national identity, Gabin got to the heart of an issue affecting all émigré actors in Hollywood. Not only do they portray 'foreign' types more or less tightly connected to their original nationality, but in acting in a different language, their own relationship to this identity changes. When he moved to Hollywood, Gabin was the leading French male star of the 1930s, his star persona of 'proletarian hero' merged looks, language, class and national identity to an exceptional degree. By contrast, his two Hollywood films, *Moontide* (1942) and *The Impostor* (1943),[2] are usually written off as dull and uninspired. But if indeed they do not compare with his greatest French films, such as *La Grande illusion/The Grand Illusion* (1937), *Pépé le Moko* (1937) and *Le Jour se lève/Daybreak* (1939), they certainly deserve a second look. Gabin's two American movies throw into sharp relief the contingent difficulties experienced by the great majority of French actors in Hollywood, who, with the exception of Maurice Chevalier★ and Charles Boyer★, never really made it in the USA. But Gabin's experience also helps us understand the tight bond that exists between language, gestures and national identity.

Gabin goes to Hollywood

Rather than deliberately seeking stardom in Hollywood, Gabin was one of the many unwilling émigrés whose journey was dictated by the war. At the declaration of hostilities in September 1939, Gabin had to interrupt the shooting of Jean Grémillon's *Remorques* (1941) and join the French navy in Cherbourg. Following the debacle, armistice and chaotic *exode* of June 1940, he moved to the Côte d'Azur in the unoccupied zone for a few months. From there, he left for America via Spain and Portugal, arriving in New York in mid-February 1941, his baggage including his accordion and racing bike.[3] Gabin's exile was both an escape and a political statement. He refused to work for the German-controlled production house Continental Films and left the country without official authorisation.[4] In peacetime, he had declined invitations to work in the USA, insisting on his 'inexportable' Frenchness: one anecdote (among many) has Gabin turning down Walter Wanger's offer to remake *Pépé le Moko* at three times his French salary because 'his favorite wine didn't travel well'.[5] Now he was bound for Hollywood, but although Fox was offering a contract, he was no longer in such a strong position. *Pépé le Moko* had been remade with Boyer, and Hollywood was awash with European actors.

Indeed, in Hollywood Gabin joined French actors such as Michèle Morgan★, Annabella★, Marcel Dalio★, Jean-Pierre Aumont★ and of course Boyer, the central figure in the French community (although he was no friend of the latter, because of both prewar rivalry and disapproval of Boyer's adoption of American nationality). He met up

French critics thought Hollywood transformed Jean Gabin 'into a curious puppet, halfway between a gigolo with permed hair and a sentimental bandit' with directors he had worked with in France, in particular Duvivier and Jean Renoir. The latter sent him a welcoming letter: 'You have no idea how happy I am at the idea of seeing you [in Hollywood] soon.'[6] Gabin also enjoyed well-publicised romantic relationships beyond the French community, first with Ginger Rogers and then, more lastingly, with Marlene Dietrich★. Part of the prewar Gabin 'myth', which portrayed him on and off screen as a rugged man-of-the-people, lived on in Hollywood, for instance in his reported dislike of glamorous social occasions, which he eschewed, and his preference for intimate dinner parties at his and Dietrich's house — an attitude that may have been detrimental to his Hollywood career,[7] although Dietrich in other ways did her best to help him.[8]

Gabin's fame was substantial enough for the Fox publicity department to feed newspapers with descriptions such as 'the Number One dramatic actor of the French screen'.[9] However, like so many others, he ended up spending more time by the poolside than on the set. In two years he made only two films, spending most of the first year learning English, for which Fox provided dialogue coaches and advertised his efforts: 'He studied the language eight hours a day for 10 months, under three coaches, practiced it on grocery store clerks, studio works and his Filipino houseboy, studied President Roosevelt's diction.'[10] Some, like Morgan, praised his linguistic endeavour;[11] others, such as Renoir[12] and Gabin himself, were less complimentary, the latter assessment unfortunately borne out by his performances.

Gabin's two Hollywood films were very different projects. The first, *Moontide*, was produced by Mark Hellinger at Fox, with two solid co-stars, Ida Lupino and Claude Rains★. Fritz Lang, on contract to Ford, was assigned to direct, and legend has it that he left after four days (although Lang's biographer Patrick McGilligan reveals Lang worked for several weeks on the project[13]). He was replaced by the less prestigious Archie Mayo. Other changes took place – the press reported plans for a nightmare sequence by Salvador Dali, which does not appear to have been filmed.[14] *Moontide* was shot between 27 November 1941 and 9 February 1942, opening in New York on 29 April 1942. Reviews were on the whole positive, if lukewarm. *Variety*[15] found it 'a drama of rare beauty and potency' and *The New York Herald Tribune* approved '[Gabin's] triumphant initiation into Hollywood film-making'.[16] Even negative reviews, for instance Bosley Crowther's in *The New York Times*, were generous towards Gabin: 'Mr Gabin is an old favourite of this department for his memorable French films [. . .]. [He] is much better than "Moontide" and that still isn't giving him his dues.'[17] Despite an Academy Award for cinematographer Charles G. Clarke, box office was mediocre.

Gabin's second film, *The Impostor*, produced and directed by Duvivier for Universal, was a propaganda film for the war effort. Duvivier's script reprised his earlier *La Bandera*,[18] which had turned Gabin into a star in 1935, replacing North Africa and the Foreign Legion with French Equatorial Africa and the Free French army respectively, and incorporating real war events such as the victory of General Leclerc's troops at Koufra in March 1941. As part of a thriving subgenre of Resistance films, which included *Paris Calling* (1941), *The Cross of Lorraine*, *Hangmen Also Die*, *First Comes Courage*, *Edge of Darkness*, *This Land is Mine* (all 1943), *Passage to Marseille* (1944) and, most famous of all, *Casablanca* (1942), its aim was to swing public opinion and the press away from the dominant view that most of the French were collaborators.[19] At the end of 1942, Gabin had tried to enlist in the Free French army, only to be told by the Gaullist propaganda office in New York that he could help the cause better by making a film.[20] *The Impostor* was shot between August and November 1943 and opened in Washington on 27 January 1944, by which time Gabin had succeeded in joining up and left the USA. This enabled the press to cash in on his status as 'soldier on and off the screen', whose 'whereabouts [. . .] used to be an international news item. Now it is a military secret.'[21] Reviews of the film were mixed. The *New Yorker* disliked it, finding the dialogue, story and direction 'lame'.[22] Most frequent criticisms were that the film was too slow and too wordy. *Variety* was more indulgent, thinking the film 'a strong dramatically impelled story of the Free French in Africa' that 'offers Gabin a forceful opportunity for a top characterization'.[23] For *Hollywood Reporter*, it was a 'stirring war melodrama so ideally suited to the rugged characterizations associated with Jean Gabin that it is impossible to imagine any other star in the title role'.[24] As in the case of *Moontide*, Gabin's status was high with critics but not sufficient for audiences: *The Impostor* was not a box-office success, even though it was considered a good war effort movie.[25] The wishful headline published at the time of *Moontide* that 'Hollywood hopes it will make him as popular on Main St. as he was in his native France'[26] clearly had not come true.

For early 1940s American audiences, French screen masculinity meant Chevalier and Boyer. Indeed, promotion material and articles repeatedly emphasised Gabin's difference: 'He's the first rugged French star Hollywood has known. The others – Maurice Chevalier, Charles Boyer – have all been the suave, sophisticated type';[27] 'He is the first French actor to come here who isn't the dapper, debonair type';[28] 'He's a relief from the pretty boys'.[29] *The New York Times* brilliantly summed Gabin up as 'Charles Boyer from the other side of the railroad tracks'.[30] A variation on the Latin lover, Boyer and Chevalier's masculinity was defined by romance, eroticism and luxury in fantasy or historical contexts. Chevalier inflected the type comically, while Boyer offered a dramatic, at times sinister, version.[31] By contrast, Gabin was identified with realism and the working class, and this is what Fox and Universal tried hard to translate into 'ruggedness', insisting on his modest background, asserting that he would never play 'a wealthy man, such as a banker or manufacturer',[32] and dubbing him 'the French Spencer Tracy' – a comparison that would endure.[33] At the same time, Gabin was also profiled as a romantic lead 'whom the studio thinks will set millions of feminine hearts to palpitating'.[34] But whereas the prewar (French) Gabin myth had been based on the fusion of romanticism and working-class identity, this proved problematic in the American context.

Americanising the Gabin Myth

Moontide is the story of Bobo (Gabin), a 'Frenchie' who lives on a barge on the Californian coast. After a brawl in a bar, he believes – as his friend Tiny (Thomas Mitchell) suggests – that he killed a man while he was drunk. Having rescued Anna (Ida Lupino) from suicide by drowning, he falls in love and marries her, despite the jealousy of Tiny, who wants Bobo to accompany him to San Francisco. When Tiny tries to blackmail and rape Anna on the night of the wedding, she realises he is the real killer. Badly beaten up, she is saved just in time. Bobo chases Tiny to his death in the ocean and is happily reunited with Anna on the barge.

The project of *Moontide* is clearly to import Gabin's rebellious individuality and working-class authenticity into an acceptably Americanised version, as confirmed by reports that Gabin, Lang and Lupino went 'slumming' in the lower-class areas of Los Angeles to improve characterisation.[35] Rebellious individuality is expressed in setting the story among waterside down-and-outs (an obvious reference to *Le Quai des brumes/Port of Shadows* [1938]), in Bobo's barge home and in his readiness to stick up for himself. Authenticity is underlined by his innocence of the crime he is accused of, and ruggedness by his manners and cowboy-style outfit. Yet in many ways the film undercuts the Gabin persona. His individuality is caricatured into otherness. His statement 'I am a gypsy, not a *paysan*' suppresses his roots, something his French parts always insisted on. He plays a 'Frenchie' whose Frenchness is paradoxically denied, except in his accent. Where his French films promoted working-class male bonding and amplified his antagonism to bourgeois figures, *Moontide* devalues proletarian friendship (his mate Tiny turns out to be a blackmailer and traitor), while playing up his kinship with the more intellectual Nutsy, the philosopher-tramp played by Claude Rains. Where the core of Gabin's prewar persona was tragic self-awareness, here his character does not even know – because of his drunkenness – whether he committed the murder he is accused of or not. Finally, and very much in contrast to Gabin's prewar films, *Moontide* marries and domesticates Gabin: he helps Anna choose fabric for curtains, something comically inconceivable in his French films. In contrast to his late 1930s French films, which ended tragically, in *Moontide* he pulls through and forms a couple with Lupino in the film's happy end.

In *The Impostor*, Clément (Gabin) is a convicted murderer whose jail is bombed on the day he is to be guillotined. He escapes and is picked up by a truck of soldiers, which in turn is bombed, killing most of the soldiers. **117**

Clément steals the clothes, papers and identity of Sergeant Maurice Lafarge, ending up in south-west France, where he shows a cynical lack of interest in the war and the collapse of his country. He boards a ship bound for Africa, on which he meets a group of patriotic soldiers, and reluctantly joins the Free French army. The troop ends up in French Equatorial Africa, where they build an airfield named De Gaulle-ville. Gradually, Clément/Lafarge bonds with his fellow soldiers, loses his cynicism and wins their esteem, demonstrating leadership and courage. He is decorated, but finds it is for the real Lafarge's bravery in Champagne, not for his own at Koufra. This prompts him to confess to a friend. He also tells the truth to Lafarge's girlfriend Yvonne (Ellen Drew), but she keeps his secret. Later, a friend of Lafarge finds him out and denounces him to the military authorities. He is court-martialled, demoted and sent to the front, where he dies in an act of heroism. Having refused to divulge his real name, he is buried in an unmarked grave.

The Impostor visually quotes several 1930s Gabin films: as a soldier in the early scenes he strongly evokes *La Grande illusion* and *Le Quai des brumes*, while scenes in Africa recall *La Bandera* and *Pépé le Moko*. But the narrative of *The Impostor*, as already mentioned, is especially close to *La Bandera*. In that film, Gabin played Gilieth, a Parisian worker who commits a murder and joins the Foreign Legion to avoid arrest, but eventually dies a hero. In *The Impostor*, Duvivier uses the Gabin myth to turn *La Bandera*'s colonialist tale into an anti-Fascist story, while not totally removing the racist content of the first film. Black people are unnamed servants and when Yvonne visits the camp, two soldiers marvel at her presence and joke that they would not even remark on a black woman. *The Impostor* also simplifies the war through omissions and anachronisms.[36] But the same could be said of Renoir's *This Land is Mine*. Duvivier and Renoir were both operating without first-hand knowledge of the war and the German occupation of France, and they were working within the constraints of making films understandable to an American audience even less knowledgeable about the situation.

The Impostor, like *Moontide*, strips Gabin of his class identity. At the beginning of *La Bandera*, iconography, voice, accents, all build a strong picture of Gabin as a Parisian worker. By contrast, *The Impostor*, quite apart from a vague representation of France familiar in Hollywood films, starts in anonymous spaces: a jail and on the road. But the film has other difficulties in Americanising the Gabin myth. Superficially, Gabin's trajectory in *The Impostor* echoes that of Bogart in *Casablanca*, from 'I stick my neck out for no one' to patriotic commitment and friendship. But unlike Bogart, Gabin is denied redemption. The ending satisfied Hollywood censorship (which insisted that Gabin's death should not look like suicide), but still shocked American reviewers used to more upbeat denouements, even in war films. *Hollywood Reporter* noted that 'The ceremony of stripping his rank from him, although quite doubtless factual, is the one not quite acceptable note.'[37] Here is a clear indication of cultural difference between the USA and France, where tragic denouements were more acceptable, as witnessed by the success of Poetic Realist films. There is also an interesting difference between the ending of *La Bandera* and that of *The Impostor*. In *La Bandera*, Gabin's heroism moved him from the oblivion of the Foreign Legion to a clear French identity. In *The Impostor*, in a reverse trajectory, he moves from multiple identities to the status of the Unknown Soldier: the last shot is of his anonymous grave.

The Impostor uses Gabin's masculinity in a particularly complex way. He appears as a tough guy whose authority 'naturally' asserts itself over the other men. When a fellow soldier goes berserk with fever, it is Gabin who knocks him over the head. When another is wounded, Gabin knows how to cure him. Yet he is throughout a strangely powerless, nebulous figure who no longer is the absolute centre of the story. Unlike in *La Bandera*, where he formed a romantic couple with Annabella, in *The Impostor* he remains alone; Yvonne's quest is for the 'real' Lafarge. Yet in one respect, Duvivier subtly redresses the balance, in terms of ideology, through the contrast between Gabin and the other performers.

In *The Impostor*, the characters are all meant to be French, but Gabin is the only French actor. A few critics at the time did find this odd and more recently Yves Desrichard has argued that this 'reveals the folly of the film, which echoes that of the director, lost and confused among political and patriotic struggles'.[38] If indeed the isolation of the character can be read as a metaphor for Gabin and Duvivier in Hollywood, *The Impostor* makes a more interesting use of story and star than critics have credited it with. While Gabin's character, in narrative terms, adopts a series of incorrect positions (cynicism, lack of patriotism), the *mise en scène* reveals him to embody the *correct* — that is to say *Resistant* — stance. At several key moments, the framing emphasises his difference from the rest of the group. Early in the film, soldiers listen to Marshall Pétain's armistice declaration in a café. All are turned towards the radio, except Gabin left of frame, seemingly unconcerned, eating and drinking. In other words, in contrast to narrative events, the *mise en scène* shows us that the only 'true' Frenchman in the room turns his back on Pétain and, it is implied, collaboration. Similarly, when his colleagues extol the virtues of the Marseillaise, Gabin is the only one not joining in, thus rejecting pompous patriotism. By repeatedly stressing Gabin's 'truer' Frenchness, Duvivier offers an internal critique of a patriotic genre imposed by circumstances (which may indeed partly account for the film's failure), but he also subtly indicates, from the start of the film, Gabin's implicit Resistant position.

Out of Sync: Gabin in English

To the viewer familiar with Gabin's French films, his appearance in *Moontide* and *The Impostor* is startling. In both films Gabin's hair looks blond. In fact, it was turning grey. As *The New York Herald Tribune* put it, 'His hair is white now. There was no need to dye it however, because it screens blond.'[39] Following Fox's publicity hints, Gabin's refusal to dye his greying hair, as well as its bushy aspect, were picked up by reviewers as a sign of authenticity. They repeatedly pinpoint Gabin's 'unruly' and 'tousled' hair as an indication that he is a 'man of the people'.

But Gabin's hair is also longer, wavier and more set than in his French films. Different codes of authenticity are at work here, for in his prewar French films, on the contrary, Gabin always insisted that his light hair be made *not* to look blond, and he wore it shorter and straighter.[40] Hence the shock felt by French writer Georges Magnane, who saw *Moontide* in the USA and wrote in *L'Écran français* of Gabin, 'excellent at home playing men of the people, transformed here into a curious puppet, halfway between a gigolo with permed hair and a sentimental bandit'.[41] The (apparently) blond and wavy shock of hair both stressed Gabin's resemblance to Spencer Tracy and distinguished him further from the dark, slicked-back styles of Chevalier and Boyer. Showcased in close-ups, Gabin's hair was styled to pick up the light, and the mascara on his eyelashes sets off the lightness of his eyes. Yet something was not quite right. Some reviewers judged Gabin 'feminised' in *Moontide*.[42] Interestingly, Fox had thought of changing his first name to John to avoid the confusion with 'Jean', a woman's name. It is perhaps for this reason that, by contrast to his hair and make-up, Gabin's clothes in *Moontide* are particularly butch: he wears the cowboy outfit of bandana scarf, check shirt and corduroy trousers. In its attempt to translate Gabin's working-class ruggedness and underline his virility, the film paradoxically reaches for the iconography of the most American genre, the Western (by contrast, Chevalier and Boyer appeared in clothes that either emphasised European history — embodying Napoleon or Russian princes — or in upper-class tuxedo). What *Moontide* reveals sartorially is the inexportability of French working-class identity, when not recycled in self-conscious caricature (Chevalier in *Love Me Tonight* [1932]). *The Impostor* is less problematic in this respect, since Gabin wears military uniforms, though again these level down his class identity.

But ultimately, speaking English is the most conspicuous and problematic mark of difference, creating an oral exoticism that, for Gabin as for others, was both cultural capital and handicap.[43] Even in *The Impostor*, where Gabin is the only real Frenchman, his accented English paradoxically makes him stranger than the others. If all émigrés went through the experience of learning English, it seems to have been a particularly alienating one for Gabin:

In English, I could *hear myself speak* and I felt that someone else was speaking in my place. It was like an echo and I felt completely *out of sync*. Nothing seemed to correspond to what I was saying, neither my gestures, my body, or anything I felt physically, or thought. It was a very painful feeling.[44] (Italics in the original)

As mentioned earlier, there are conflicting views about how seriously Gabin applied himself to learning English. Certainly, the two films show an uneven grasp. There are moments, such as at the beginning of *The Impostor*, where what he says is incomprehensible, and he appears to speak through clenched teeth. At other times, he makes classic French mistakes, such as dropping 'h's.

The issue is also one of performance. Chevalier and Boyer had considerable stage training and experience and were supremely adept at projecting their voices. By contrast, Gabin was untrained and his experience of the stage was brief. His distinctiveness as a film star was indeed that he, more quickly than others, adopted the understated 'radio style'[45] of acting for the camera, connoted as more authentic. Thus, his better moments in the Hollywood films are the ones when he is speaking softly: for example, in close-up with Yvonne in *The Impostor*, and while seducing Ida Lupino in *Moontide* (where he even briefly reverts to French to say 'je t'aime' [I love you]). Correspondingly, his worst are when he speaks emphatically: he seems to lack confidence in his ability to be understood and compensates with histrionic gestures. 'He has a temper', says one character in *Moontide*, pinpointing a lack of control, far from the cool authority of the French films. In the same way that the narrative of both films destabilised his class identity, speaking English de-virilises him. During World War II, a French accent may have had more positive connotations than a German one, but it also had associations with luxury and romance – Chevalier and Boyer again – that clashed with Gabin's image. Maria Riva (Dietrich's daughter) is unkind but perceptive when she says that his 'French accent did not have the lilt of Chevalier's, nor the sexy softness of Boyer. Gabin growled; in French his voice could give a dead fish goose pimples, but in English, he sounded like an angry headwaiter.'[46] We may also recall at this point that in *La Grande illusion*, the English spoken as a lingua franca by the French and German aristocrats served to highlight Gabin's proletarian identity by contrast.

By joining the Free French, Gabin cut his Hollywood career short, though nobody was begging him to stay. It is in any case unlikely that he would have attained the status of a Chevalier or a Boyer. In David O. Selznick's words, 'There are very few great movies, and therefore very few great parts. And even fewer great parts with an accent!'[47] Discussing Chevalier in *The Merry Widow* (1934), Ruth Vasey rightly said, 'foreign civilians were typically either peasants or members of an aristocratic elite'.[48] Gabin could not be either of these and there was as a result a fundamental mismatch between his French screen persona and its American adaptation. His parts as 'gypsy' (*Moontide*) and Unknown Soldier (*The Impostor*) undermined the authority and historical anchorage of his French star persona, diluting the force of his myth. Out of its French context, Gabin's image no longer signified.[49]

Back into the Fold

Moontide and *The Impostor* both came out in France after the war, and met with a mixture of indifference and hostility. Gabin's second French career was going through a rough passage, but the release of his Hollywood films also suffered from a merciless historical conjuncture. Returning émigrés found themselves the target of opprobrium for having spent the war years 'sheltered' in Hollywood. This was part personal retaliation from those who were being punished for having stayed in France and collaborated, and part unwillingness to confront the still recent defeat. One reviewer of *The Impostor* put it thus: 'Duvivier probably succeeded in creating excellent propaganda for us in America. But for us French, with six years distance, it is not possible to swallow this exodus, this defeat without revolting against it.'[50] Unfairly, Gabin was branded as one of those actors 'made in USA'.[51] It may not have helped that he was then associated with Dietrich, with whom he made the mediocre *Martin Roumagnac* (1946) after they had jointly pulled out of the Marcel Carné-Jacques Prévert project *Les Portes de la nuit/Gates of the Night* (1946).

The tense climate was also due to the French film industry's fight to re-establish itself in the face of the vast number of American films banned during the war years, which were now flooding French screens. American films with French stars were adding insult to injury.

Hostility towards Gabin, however, quickly ceased once the bitter settling of scores of the Liberation was over. He was decorated in 1945 and Renoir, who himself suffered adverse French reviews for *This Land is Mine*, praised Gabin's military bravery thus: 'This great chap, so "French" – is a role model.'[52] Later still, Gabin's Resistance commitment retrospectively enhanced his glorious prewar myth, added to his renewed success from the early 1950s onwards, and in the process obliterated both the traumatic divisions of the war and his disappointing Hollywood episode. On the cover of a book on French artists during the German occupation,[53] styled like a French flag, Gabin in his Free French uniform occupies the central block, with Fascist writer Louis-Ferdinand Céline and actress Arletty, who had had an affair with a German officer, on either side of him. No longer an 'impostor', Gabin had come home – back at the core of both French cinema and the French idealisation of its national identity.

Notes

1. Jean Gabin, in André Brunelin, 'Une Vie d'acteur', *Cinéma 57*, September–October 1957, pp. 86–7.
2. *The Impostor* was initially called *Passport to Dakar*. The title was changed to avoid confusion with *Passage to Marseille*, the 1944 film with Humphrey Bogart and Michèle Morgan. It was later re-released in the USA as *Strange Confession* (1995).
3. André Brunelin, *Gabin* (Paris: Éditions Robert Laffont, 1988), p. 292.
4. See Brunelin (Gabin's biographer), for the difficulties surrounding the star's departure from France: Brunelin, *Gabin*, pp. 286–92.
5. *The New York Herald Tribune*, 26 March 1944.
6. Jean Renoir, letter to Jean Gabin, 7 March 1941; in Jean Renoir, *Lettres d'Amérique* (Paris: Presses de la Renaissance, 1984), p. 23.
7. According to Dietrich's daughter Maria Riva, 'This French cocoon my mother enveloped Gabin in was not constructive. He had to earn his living in America, work with American actors and crews; making no effort to meet them halfway did not help him. Jean Gabin, the man of the people, through Dietrich's influence became the aloof foreigner, and this affected his work and popularity.' Maria Riva, *Marlene Dietrich: By Her Daughter, Maria Riva* (London: Bloomsbury, 1992), p. 509.
8. Brunelin suggests that Dietrich was instrumental in Zanuck offering a contract to Gabin even before his arrival in the USA, and before she had met him (Brunelin, *Gabin*, p. 297).
9. Biography of Jean Gabin, Fox publicity department document (Academy of Motion Picture Arts and Sciences Library); Louise Levitas, *P.M.*, 12 April 1942.
10. 'Vital Statistics on *Moon Tide* [sic]', Fox publicity department document (Academy of Motion Picture Arts and Sciences Library).
11. Michèle Morgan, *With Those Eyes, An Autobiography* (London: W. H. Allen, 1978), p. 146.
12. Renoir, letter to Claude Renoir S, 11 May 1946; Renoir, *Lettres d'Amérique*, p. 225.
13. Patrick McGilligan, *Fritz Lang: The Nature of the Beast* (New York: St Martin's Press, 1997), pp. 282–4.
14. *Hollywood Reporter*, 18 November 1941.
15. *Variety*, 17 April 1942.
16. *The New York Herald Tribune*, 3 May 1942.
17. *The New York Times*, 3 May 1942.
18. Originally based on the novel by Pierre Mac Orlan, *La Bandera* (Paris: Gallimard, 1931).
19. According to Duvivier's son Christian Duvivier, the Hearst group was virulently anti-French. Interview with

Christian Duvivier by Aldo Tassone, in Pierre Billard and Hubert Niogret (eds), *Julien Duvivier* (Milan: Editrice Il Castoro, n. d.).

20. Brunelin, *Gabin*, p. 309.
21. *The New York Herald Tribune*, 26 March 1944.
22. *The New Yorker*, 4 February 1944.
23. *Variety*, 4 February 1944.
24. *Hollywood Reporter*, 4 February 1944.
25. Brunelin, *Gabin*, p. 310.
26. *P.M.*, 12 April 1942.
27. Harry Brand, Publicity Director, Fox publicity material, 1942 (Academy of Motion Picture Arts and Sciences Library, ref. Ca. 1942).
28. 'Hedda Hopper's Hollywood', *Los Angeles Times*, 2 March 1942.
29. James Francis Crow, 'Jean Gabin, Hollywood's New Heart Throb', *Look*, 16 June 1942.
30. *The New York Times*, 30 April 1942.
31. As in George Cukor's *Gaslight* (1944).
32. Fox publicity material, 1942 (Academy of Motion Picture Arts and Sciences Library, ref. Ca. 1942).
33. Review *Variety*, of *Moontide*, 22 April 1942. One of Ida Lupino's biographers reported that she was cast in *Moontide* 'opposite Jean Gabin, "the French Spencer Tracy"'. Jerry Vermilye, *Ida Lupino* (New York: Pyramid, 1977), p. 66.
34. Fox publicity material, 1942 (Academy of Motion Picture Arts and Sciences Library, ref. Ca. 1942).
35. 'Director Fritz Lang and Jean Gabin made a weekend tour of San Diego waterfront and hang-outs to gather color for 20th's "Moon Tide". The pair went shabby so they could mingle with the local boys.' *Hollywood Reporter*, 12 November 1941.
36. Yves Desrichard, *Julien Duvivier* (Paris: BiFi/Durante, 1999), p. 201.
37. *Hollywood Reporter*, 4 February 1944.
38. Desrichard, *Julien Duvivier*, p. 201.
39. *The New York Herald Tribune*, 26 March 1944.
40. I discuss Gabin's hair in his 1930s films in Claude Gauteur and Ginette Vincendeau, *Jean Gabin: anatomie d'un mythe* (Paris: Nathan, 1993), pp. 128–30.
41. Georges Magnane, *L'Écran français*, no. 18, 29 October 1945; article reproduced in Olivier Barrot, *L'Écran français 1943–1953, Histoire d'un journal et d'une époque* (Paris: Les Editeurs Français Réunis, 1977), p. 66.
42. For instance, Bosley Crowther thought that 'You might almost think the lights and camera were working on a glamorous female star from the way they are concentrated on Mr Gabin's roughly handsome phiz.' *The New York Times*, 30 April 1942.
43. For wider-ranging discussion of these issues, see Diane Negra, *Off-White Hollywood: American Culture and Ethnic Female Stardom* (London and New York: Routledge, 2001); and Ruth Vasey, *The World According to Hollywood, 1918–1939* (Madison: University of Wisconsin Press, 1997).
44. Brunelin, *Gabin*, p. 303.
45. Vincendeau, in Gauteur and Vincendeau, *Jean Gabin*, p. 126.
46. Riva, *Marlene Dietrich*, p. 510.
47. Quoted by Jean-Charles Tacchella, *L'Écran français*, no. 261 (3 July 1950) (reproduced in Barrot, *L'Écran français*, p. 318.
48. Vasey, *The World According to Hollywood*, p. 217.
49. There is a parallel in Gérard Depardieu's career outside France. While Depardieu has been relatively successful in international costume films (such as *1492: The Conquest of Paradise* [1992]), he has been unable to translate his earlier class-based French star persona, except in caricatural form (*Green Card* [1990]).

50. Monique Berger, *Le Populaire*, 30 July 1946, quoted in Janet Bergstrom, 'Émigrés or Exiles The French Directors' Return from Hollywood', in Geoffrey Nowell-Smith and Steven Ricci (eds), *Hollywood and Europe: Economics, Culture, National Identity 1945–95* (London: BFI, 1998), p. 97.

51. Among those accusing Gabin was Arletty, who had been jailed for her relationship with a German officer. Brunelin, *Gabin*, p. 326.

52. Renoir, letter to Jean Benoit-Lévy; Renoir, *Lettres d'Amérique*, p. 138.

53. Gilles Ragache and Jean-Robert Ragache, *La Vie quotidienne des écrivain et des artistes sous l'occupation, 1940–44* (Paris: Hachette, 1988).

13 Louis Jourdan – The 'Hyper-sexual' Frenchman

Hilary Radner

In 1947, the French actor Louis Jourdan, born Louis Gendre, arrived in Hollywood, where he began his new career as 'one of David O. Selznick's prized minions'.[1] In 1949, Bosley Crowther, critic for *The New York Times*, declared him 'electric' in his role as Madame Bovary's 'elegant lover'.[2] With his darkly handsome looks, chiselled profile, long graceful hands and melodic, cultivated accent, the young actor appeared poised for success. His career was certainly long and profitable. His Hollywood credits include such high-profile titles as: *The Paradine Case* (1947), *Letter from an Unknown Woman* (1948), *Madame Bovary* (1949), *Anne of the Indies* (1951), *Three Coins in the Fountain* (1954) and *Gigi* (1958); much later he also appeared in *Octopussy* (1983), *Swamp Thing* (1982) and *Year of the Comet* (1992). The list of his European credits is equally long if not as illustrious. Yet, though he worked with some of the most important directors and actors in Hollywood, stardom eluded him. Jourdan himself both confirms and denies this negative assessment of his career. He has commented: 'If I was not a great success in American films, neither was I a failure. I've been working for years without setting the world on fire, but managing to keep Quique, my wife, in caviar and champagne.'[3] He may not have reached the status of his male compatriots Maurice Chevalier★ and Charles Boyer★, but he certainly fared better than their female counterparts. Despite the visibility of French actresses such as Simone Simon★, Michèle Morgan★ and Simone Signoret★ (who won an Academy Award for Best Actress in 1959), there was no French equivalent in Hollywood to Marlene Dietrich★ or Greta Garbo★ (Brigitte Bardot★, perhaps the most visible of French female stars in the USA, systematically refused to make a film in Hollywood).

The career of Louis Jourdan offers us a particular instance of a French actor transplanted to Hollywood for whom nationality as an attribute of his screen persona both supported his career and undermined his reputation as a star. Ginette Vincendeau has remarked, in one of the first star studies to consider nationality, that 'The star's "myth" helps reconcile contradictions that exist in the social roles expected of men and women at key historical moments and "naturalises", thereby validating historical constructions.' Vincendeau emphasises that this 'mythic role' is played out in terms of national identity as well as gender.[4] A study of the contradictions implied in a career that was successful and yet never fulfilled its potential may serve to underline the relations between the representation of gender and nationality in determining the identity of a star and his or her spectators. The way in which nationality is incorporated into a star persona is not self-evident, though. Audrey Hepburn★ may have been of Dutch/Irish parentage (and born in Belgium), but this fact was not relevant to her star persona. By contrast, Jourdan's French identity was, as we shall see, a crucial element in the construction of his masculinity.

Alastair Phillips has remarked that the foreign actor's career in the USA depends on 'a fine balance between assimilation and the preservation of a cultural difference that would have a distinctive national and international appeal'.[5] Jourdan certainly exploited his 'Frenchness'; however, his nationality also limited the roles that he could play. He remained throughout his career in Hollywood 'the glamourous Gaul' who 'vows he'd rather use his brain than his handsome head', in spite of the fact that his good looks were his most marketable attribute.[6] Jourdan's

Forever 'the glamourous Gaul' in Hollywood, Louis Jourdan benefitted and suffered from his 'hyper-sexual' image

career, in other words, sheds new light on the ways in which stereotypes work for and against the émigré actor who seeks to pursue his or her profession in the USA.

During Hollywood cinema's classical era, French culture evoked notions of sensual laissez-faire in opposition to the ideological dominance of the US's Protestant work ethic. We may therefore ask whether American audiences were more forgiving of this quality in French male actors such as Chevalier, Boyer and Jourdan than in, say, American stars like Henry Fonda. In her best-known Hollywood film, *Cat People* (1942), Simone Simon is endowed with a preternatural sexual aura that is countered by her apparent frigidity. The contradiction between 'hyper-sexuality' and frigidity created a problematic screen persona that did not transfer to other roles. In contrast, the overt erotomania exhibited by Jourdan in his role as Stefan in *Letter from an Unknown Woman* is an explicit aspect of his screen persona that he carried from role to role in his Hollywood films. Scholars such as Robin Wood argue that this 'hyper-sexuality' prevented Jourdan from reaching his full potential as a star.[7] He appeared too attractive, too 'foreign', given the ideals of masculinity during this period in Hollywood. *Coronet Magazine*, attempting to explain Jourdan's initial failure to make an 'impression' in Hollywood, commented in 1960: 'After the struggle to save humanity, Americans seemed to prefer, in the late '40s and early '50s, the guntotin', hardridin' westerner − not the charming Frenchman.'[8] At the same time, however, this same attribute, or set of attributes, contributed to the longevity of Jourdan's career.

Jourdan's screen persona suggests a vexed position for the French actor and his relationship to masculinity, in which he is seen to be both too sexual and not sufficiently 'gendered'. As Susan White points out in her analysis of *Letter from an Unknown Woman*, the excessive sexuality of his character inevitably placed Jourdan in a 'feminised' position, which challenged a rigid masculine/feminine dichotomy in much the same manner as Rudolph Valentino's characters did.[9] Jourdan's screen persona was such that his masculinity became heightened and contaminated by a nationality that was 'Un-American' rather than specifically French (compared to Chevalier, for example). 'Jourdan travelled widely as a youth',[10] and appeared naturally to have the voice and accent that Charles Boyer deliberately cultivated a generation earlier for his Hollywood films. Boyer's (and Jourdan's) voice evokes, in the words of Phillips, 'a generalized notion of European sophistication that was truly non-American, rather than something that was specifically French'.[11] To this day, Jourdan is described as a weak 'copy' of Boyer in the popular press.[12]

The ambiguity of Jourdan's voice is illustrated by his performance in *Letter from an Unknown Woman*. Stefan resides in Vienna, yet his nationality is never defined. He has a 'foreign' accent in contrast with that of the heroine, played by Joan Fontaine, who appears to be a native speaker of English. Her accent is also without national specificity − it is British but softened by the demands of Hollywood. However, her character, Lisa, unlike Stefan, is a native of Vienna, the location of the film's story. The play of native speaker vs. non-native speaker contributes to the construction of character within this film and to that of the screen persona that actor and actress will transfer from film to film. Through his accent, Jourdan is marked as 'other' in a manner that Fontaine is not.

The methodological challenge in considering Jourdan is to avoid a facile equation between the role that he played in an individual film and the position that he more generally occupied as a 'star', if indeed he might be said to have acquired this status. At the same time, it seems imperative to consider the figure that he represented within a narrative or set of narratives, especially given that he did not generate an enduring extra-filmic narrative in the form of a significant biography or continued attention from the press, perhaps in part by choice. He positioned himself as someone above Hollywood intrigue who was searching for 'a measure of anonymity in the environs of Beverly Hills'.[13] Similarly, he was often described as 'a very private person'.[14]

Indeed, some of the films in which Jourdan appeared proved to be more resilient than his star persona. In its review of *The Paradine Case*, in which Selznick introduced the actor to Anglophone audiences, *Variety* noted somewhat ironically that 'Louis Jourdan, French actor, is a handsome, talented young man who will click with the femmes'.[15] In fact, *The Paradine Case* was a box-office failure.[16] *Letter from an Unknown Woman* was also a failure, incurring a net loss of $804,00.[17] Yet, of special significance in this context is the fact that *Letter from an Unknown Woman* has come to occupy such a privileged position in film studies and, in particular, Anglo–American feminist film theory. The screenwriter Gavin Lambert and film-maker Karel Reisz were the first to rescue the film from critical obscurity in their avant-garde journal *Sequence* during its first UK run.[18] The film was thus kept alive by scholars as part of Ophuls' auteur corpus until the 1980s, when it also became seen as a 'woman's picture'. Thanks, in large part, to the critical attention paid to the role of Stefan, *Letter from an Unknown Woman* achieved 'a central place in the current cannon of feminist film criticism'.[19] Feminist literature therefore added another extra-textual dimension to Jourdan's screen persona. To an extent, then, it was not until the 1980s that the actor would find the 'femme' audience predicted earlier by *Variety*. The longevity of this film as a key text in feminist theory indicates, from another perspective, the continued manner in which certain 'national' attributes come to inflect articulations of masculinity and femininity.

The fact that Jourdan as Stefan occupies a 'feminised' position, or, rather, that his persona is associated with such a position by these scholars, is fundamental to the interest that *Letter from an Unknown Woman* has inspired among feminist critics. Typically, White comments that the notion that the film depicts Stefan 'as an object of desire is irrefutable. The active aspect of his performance has been eliminated; he is now "emasculated", merely an image to be admired.'[20] Influential feminist readings, most notably that of Tania Modleski, see this construction of a passive masculinity as offering a resistant position to the female spectator.[21] Not coincidentally, Gaylyn Studlar points out that this type of 'feminised' masculinity is associated with 'only three actors, two of whom are European (Boyer and Jourdan)'.[22] According to the logic of Modleski and other feminist critics, this passivity permitted and even demanded the articulation of an active feminine desire in films such as *Letter from an Unknown Woman*.

The Paradine Case and *Madame Bovary* also place Jourdan in a role in which he inspires the active desire of a central female figure. In the same vein, commenting on his role in *Anne of the Indies*, Claire Johnson describes Jourdan as playing 'the castrated male in the position traditionally occupied by the female'.[23] Within the narrative, this masculine passivity proves fatal to both female and male characters. The fatality that is attached to Jourdan's 'nationalised' masculinity is understood here in terms of the fact that the assumption of an active desire is fatal for the female character. The fact remains, though, that the implications of this feminist reading for national stereotyping continue to be hidden by concerns about gender. Because the feminist treatment of Jourdan's character sets him apart from his more 'American' and more masculine contemporaries, it does little to disrupt the marginal position that he also occupied as a Frenchman within the context of Hollywood production.

Robin Wood's assessment of Jourdan's career defines the ambiguous position that he occupies in mainstream film criticism. Wood characterises Jourdan as 'among the most wasted stars of the Hollywood cinema'.[24] From him, Jourdan represents Hollywood's inability to 'import European performers and build them into major stars',[25] in contrast with actresses such as Garbo, Ingrid Bergman★ and Dietrich. As the object of the gaze, the European male, especially in his guise as the 'Latin lover', troubled a notion of masculinity in which the masculine is exclusively equated with active desire, of which the feminine is the passive object:

> Their [the Latin lovers'] exotic appeal is postulated on notions of sophistication, allure, beauty, rather than a ruggedly masculine handsomeness [. . .] they are to be looked at, constructing the spectator as feminine and evoking, for the male, all the dangers of repressed homosexual desire.[26]

In opposition, we might look to the status enjoyed by actors such as Humphrey Bogart, William Holden and Charlton Heston who typified the 'ruggedness' described by Wood.[27] Significant here might be Jourdan's role in *Madame Bovary*, in which he played a 'femme' Rodolphe (Emma's lover) opposite Van Heflin's 'butch' Charles Bovary (her husband). Wood goes so far as to describe Jourdan's character in *The Paradine Case* as 'gay'.[28] In this film, Jourdan as the valet is totally devoted to his master, rejects the advances of the beautiful Alida Valli★ and commits suicide when it appears that he might be responsible for his master's death.

Jourdan was indeed associated with homosexual roles even though he was also described as being devoted to his wife, whom he married in 1944.[29] *Coronet Magazine* depicted Jourdan fleeing Hollywood in his eagerness to play 'a homosexual archeologist' on Broadway in André Gide's play *L'Immoraliste/The Immoralist*. His success in this role 'made Jourdan the target of a thousand cranks, who write him abusive letters to this day'.[30] Furthermore, Jourdan's tastes were suspiciously un-American. He liked 'Bach, Debussy and Shostakovich'. When he cooked, his speciality was 'chicken cacciatore'. He also enjoyed conversation: 'Dinner over, Jourdan likes to huddle in a corner with the male guests for serious discussion of everything from Jean-Paul Sartre to Pirandello.'[31] The same article underlined Jourdan's appeal to women, an element that Wood's analysis does not illuminate. When Jourdan picks up his son from school, 'he is pursued by shrieking young ladies, who rate him the most exciting man in Beverly Hills'. Lest we suspect that Jourdan attracts only adolescent girls (an idea reiterated in the film with which he is perhaps most identified, *Gigi*), the article also reports that he was voted 'The Most Exciting Man in the World' by 'the Models' League of America' and that 'women fans gush over him' at 'roisterous Hollywood parties'.[32]

The fact that Jourdan's persona was characterised as exclusively directed towards women might very well have been another factor that obstructed his ascension as a 'star'. In post anti-trust Hollywood, the American film industry sought to acquire cultural status by also specifically attracting a male audience. Although it continued to make films for women (such as those of Douglas Sirk and Jean Negulesco), Hollywood could not afford to alienate male spectators. In the studio era, as Steven Cohan notes, 'one recurring strategy to prevent the male body from appearing too desirable [. . .] was to make the lover foreign (or if not foreign, then ethnic)'. In contrast, stars such as Rock Hudson, who were developed for a female audience in the 1950s, could also 'pass' as manly men and were able to incarnate 'the myth of the silent, rugged, and sexually innocent American male'.[33] Yul Brynner, for example, catered to this requirement by displaying his body in a manner that conformed to the codes of 'body building subculture', fitting the norms of 'the age of the chest', in Steven Cohan's terms.[34] The observance of these codes undercut Brynner's exoticism, while paradoxically the very presence of this exoticism also permitted a more overt display of the body than would normally be allowed with the 'manly man'. Though Jourdan was exotic, he failed as a 'manly man'. His sexuality became translated as weak or possibly even 'feminine'.

Jourdan's fashion-plate elegance also lacked these 'manly' elements. In *Anne of the Indies*, when he attempted a 'beef-cake' role, Crowther described him as 'a floorwalker in deshabillé'.[35] In this sense, Jourdan's reception echoes that of Valentino, who, as Miriam Hansen recalls, inspired hostility among male spectators.[36] There is also evidence that Jourdan himself was uncomfortable in his role as Latin lover – the elegant, cultivated 'feminised' male who appealed to women. For instance, he was suspended four times by Selznick because he 'balked' when offered another 'romantic role'. Jourdan is also claimed to have said: 'I didn't want to be perpetually cooing in a lady's ear. There's not much satisfaction in it.' Despite these concerns, he continued to be cast as the romantic 'European' lover when Darryl F. Zanuck bought Jourdan's contract from Selznick in 1948.[37]

Much later in his career, Jourdan offered various parodies of the cultivated foreign 'lover' when he was relegated to the category of character actor. In his performances as a camp Dracula in the television film *Count Dracula* (1977), Dr Anton Arcane in *Swamp Thing* and, most notably, Kamal Khan in the James Bond film *Octopussy* the actor suggested a certain disdain for the persona while still continuing to emphasise the persistence of certain stereotypes, especially in terms of nationality and ethnicity. His role as Kamal Kahn, a rich exiled 'Indian' prince, indicates the manner in which the changing category of 'otherness' easily becomes displaced from one ethnic group to another according to the political imperatives of a given period. However, the younger generation (for whom James Bond is often a cult figure, much as the woman's film is for the feminist theorist) knows Jourdan (if at all) as Kamal Khan, Bond's arch-enemy of the moment in *Octopussy*.[38] It is a part that highlights the differences between Jourdan and perhaps the most high-profile European male star of the post-World War II era, Sean Connery★. Just as Bond came to

define Connery, Connery *was* Bond, even though he delegated the role to other actors (Roger Moore★ plays Bond, in fact, in *Octopussy*). Connery may have only been eleven years Jourdan's junior, but this difference was crucial in terms of the evolution of Hollywood masculinity and stardom. Connery/Bond emerged in the 1960s as a lover *and* a man of action who could – unlike Jourdan's heroes of the 1940s and 1950s – appeal to both a male and female audience.

It is also the case that Connery is not an actor, but a star, for whom authenticity is a defining attribute. By contrast, Jourdan's inability to represent authenticity is highlighted by his performance opposite Brigitte Bardot in one of his French films, *La Mariée est trop belle* (1956). Here, Jourdan plays the same role he would take up two years later in *Gigi*. He may be only fifteen years older than Bardot, but she plays the part of a vital, young girl – a precursor of the new international youth culture – against his weakened, ineffective masculinity. Jourdan's character, the women's magazine editor Michel, is clearly Bardot's social, economic and cultural superior, but in spite of this authority, he remains overwhelmed by her. Crowther describes Jourdan in this film as Bardot's 'bland employer, an elegant magazine editor who can't see beyond the end of his nose'.[39] He plays an urbane sophisticated professional, his gestures and voice coded in terms of class and emasculated by the new culture of consumption. His character is fundamentally passive, his function is to be exchanged between two women. Jourdan assumes a persona that lacks authenticity – a quality that only Bardot, whose youth ensures a 'naturalness' uncontaminated by culture, can give him. Within the narrative, this authenticity enables Bardot to triumph over her rival, an older, glamorous and better-educated woman (Micheline Presle★). As in *Gigi*, Jourdan is identified with a role in which, his sophistication notwithstanding, he is the dupe of a young girl, and an object haggled over by women.

Although *Gigi* was described retrospectively as 'a personal triumph' for Jourdan,[40] Crowther, in *The New York Times*, failed to single him out as he had in previous, less successful films. He commented: 'Minnelli has marshaled a cast to give a set of performances that, for quality and harmony, are superb.' As the 'hero', Jourdan is qualified as merely 'suave'. Superlatives were reserved for Jourdan's fellow stars: Leslie Caron★ and Chevalier.[41] In terms of Jourdan's career, *Gigi* testified to the fact that 'French charm [. . .] had made a comeback'. Jourdan, by contrast, dismissed himself in *Gigi* as a 'bathroom baritone' and 'deplores this musical success'.[42] To go back to the comparison with Sean Connery, it is, in fact, impossible to imagine Connery playing such a role – or even Richard Burton★, to whom Jourdan's character loses Elizabeth Taylor in *The V.I.P.s* (1963). Much like *La Mariée est trop belle* and *Gigi*, *The V.I.P.s* explicitly developed Jourdan's persona by making it appear both 'unmanly' and attractive to women. Jourdan was lauded for his capacities as an actor, as well as for his ability to portray a certain type. In Crowther's words, he played

(O)ne of those wastrels, one of those sleek but pathetic men that Terrence Rattigan [. . .] always seems to draw so well. He is suave, self-possessed, complacent, charming, sweet and deferential [. . .] But underneath his smooth exterior, beneath his urbanity, is a troubled, uncertain, frightened and even lonely and empty man.[43]

Similarly, within French culture, in his role opposite Bardot, Jourdan was associated with the characteristics of the new middle-class businessman – the *cadre* – who was defined in terms of 'passivity', 'serviceability', 'a pleasant nature' and 'a distinct loss in virility'.[44] This persona perhaps, in part, explains his failure to achieve the same domestic status enjoyed by French stars such as Jean Gabin★, and more recently Gérard Depardieu★, who have typically been cast as 'working-class' characters with 'manly' personas. From an international perspective, this 'manly' persona, exemplified by Burton and Connery and the expression of an active, even violent virility, corresponds to changing definitions of masculinity and culture. Burton's and Connery's careers testify to the rise of 'the new European man' within the arena of international screen culture. It was the expression of a masculinity that echoed from the rugged, 'butch' image favoured by Hollywood in the 1950s. According to Tony Bennett and Janet Woollacott in their definitive study of the Bond phenomenon, Connery represented 'a young talent-based, classless, untraditional, anti-Establishment cultural elite'.[45] Connery was specifically not aristocratic. His status was his by right of innate authenticity, rather than by inherited culture. He was, in this sense, a working-class hero in an era suspicious of privilege, who was precisely what he appeared to be. This 'authenticity' is best understood as a construction – a per- **129** formance – that must be seen as working against a pre-existing idea of performance that stressed virtuosity, craft or 'artistry'. The play of artifice and authenticity was then a stylistic, rather than a substantive, opposition.[46]

Jourdan's persona was indeed one of cultivated artifice. It was expressed through fashion, gesture and, perhaps most notably, voice, although his voice was also one that masked his origins. While Connery retained vestiges of his Scottish accent as a sign of authenticity and Burton revealed his 'Welshness' in certain roles as evidence of his core 'self', Jourdan's ethnicity oscillated, not unlike that of Valentino. He was French, Viennese and finally 'Oriental' as Kamal Khan. Continuity was signalled through his voice as foreign without a distinct and recognisable origin and as, paradoxically, cultivated rather than authentic. When playing a villain, this worked in his favour. He was 'the most elegant and adroit star yet recruited to portray a villain' in the Bond series, demonstrating his virtuosity through his 'blithe phonetic command of a ridiculous-sounding name', 'Octopussy'.[47] His persona was 'cultivated' but lacked, then, a clearly defined national self, even when he was stereotyped as 'the Gaul'. It represented 'otherness' as an aspect of sexual fascination or its parody (as in the case of *Octopussy*). The position of 'national' other is the premise, the 'cover story', that permitted Jourdan to incarnate an 'un-American' sexuality at a time when sexual deviance was equated with political corruption and seditious activity within US culture. Jourdan's status as 'un-American' gave him currency as an actor, but it may have ultimately prevented his evolution as a star.

To return to Vincendeau's characterisation, if the star's role is to resolve certain contradictions, Jourdan's failure to achieve stardom might be the result of the fact that he incarnated a set of contradictions that could not be resolved at the moment in history in which he emerged as an actor. In particular, his persona, marked by artistry, spoke to a female audience who was portrayed as passive by the media, even as women as a demographic group were increasingly gaining economic and political autonomy within the USA.[48] The terrain of these contradictions, which defined masculinity, femininity and nationality in the late 1940s and 1950s – the most productive period of Jourdan's career – was completely rewritten in the 1960s with the explosion of youth culture, the consequences of which would not be felt in Hollywood until the late 1960s and early 1970s. In Hollywood cinema, Jourdan was too 'femme' for a 'butch' generation fascinated by 'beefcake' in the 'age of the chest'. The actor's sexual ambiguity – similar to the ambiguity that contributed to David Bowie's★ status as a multimedia star during the 1970s – worked against Jourdan, as did his nationality. Finally, he was too young for Hollywood and too old for youth culture.

Notes
1. Bosley Crowther, 'La Vie de Bohème', *The New York Times*, 27 November 1947, p. 18: 2.
2. Crowther, 'Madame Bovary', *The New York Times*, 26 August 1949, p. 15: 2.
3. Quoted in Ronald Bowers, *The Selznick Players* (South Brunswick, NJ and London: A. S. Barnes, 1976), p. 236.
4. Ginette Vincendeau, *Stars and Stardom in French Cinema* (London and New York: Continuum, 2000), p. 35.
5. See Alastair Phillips, 'Changing Bodies/Changing Voices. Success and Failure in Hollywood in the Early Sound Era', *Screen* vol. 43 (summer 2002), pp. 187–200, and Chapter 9 in this volume.
6. Rex Lardner, 'Jourdan, the Glamourous Gaul', *Coronet Magazine*, May 1960, p. 89.
7. Robin Wood, 'Louis Jourdan', in *International Dictionary of Films and Filmmakers – 3, Actors and Actresses* (Detroit: St James Press, 1992), pp. 612–13.
8. Lardner, 'Jourdan, the Glamourous Gaul', p. 91.
9. See Susan White, *The Cinema of Max Ophuls: Magisterial Vision and the Figure of Woman* (New York: Columbia University Press, 1995). See also Miriam Hansen, *Babel and Babylon: Spectatorship in American Silent Film* (Cambridge, MA: Harvard University Press, 1991).
10. Lardner, 'Jourdan, the Glamourous Gaul', p. 90.
11. See Phillips, 'Changing Bodies/Changing Voices'.
12. See, for example, Alison Kerr, 'The Face of the Day', *The Glasgow Herald*, 21 August 2000, p. 28.

13. Lardner, 'Jourdan, the Glamourous Gaul', p. 89.

14. See, for example, *People Weekly*, 14 January 1985, pp. 43–4.

15. *Variety*, 31 December 1947, p. 10.

16. Bowers, *The Selznick Players*, p. 38.

17. Gaylyn Studlar, 'Masochistic Performance and Female Subjectivity in *Letter from an Unknown Woman*', *Cinema Journal* vol. 33 no. 3 (1994), p. 51, fn1.

18. See Richard Roud, *Max Ophuls: An Index* (London: BFI, 1958); Paul Willemen (ed.), *Ophuls* (London: BFI, 1978); V. F. Perkins '*Letter from an Unknown Woman*', *Movie*, no. 29/30 summer 1982. For a discussion of film scholarship on Max Ophuls, with particular reference to the woman's film, see Hilary Radner, 'Lectures du mélodrame: Max Ophuls et le film de femme', *1895: Revue de l'association française de recherche sur l'histoire du cinéma*, vol. 34–5 (October 2001), pp. 121–36.

19. Charles L. P. Silet, '*Letter from an Unknown Woman*', in *The International Dictionary of Films and Filmmakers – 1: Films* (Detroit: St James Press, 1992), pp. 568–9.

20. White, *The Cinema of Max Ophuls*, p. 183. See White generally for an overview of feminist scholarship on Max Ophuls.

21. See Tania Modleski, 'Time and Desire in the Woman's Film', in Christine Gledhill (ed.), *Home Is Where the Heart Is: Studies in Melodrama and the Woman's Film* (London: BFI, 1987), pp. 326–38. See also Lucy Fischer, *Shot/Countershot: Film Tradition and Women's Cinema* (Princeton, NJ: Princeton University Press, 1989).

22. See Studlar, 'Masochistic Performance and Female Subjectivity in *Letter from an Unknown Woman*', p. 55, fn. 72.

23. Claire Johnson, 'Femininity and the Masquerade: *Anne of the Indies*', in E. Ann Kaplan (ed.), *Psychoanalysis and Cinema* (New York and London: Routledge, 1990), p. 67.

24. Wood, 'Louis Jourdan', p. 613.

25. Ibid.

26. Ibid.

27. See Steven Cohan, *Masked Men: Masculinity and the Movies in the Fifties* (Bloomington and Indianapolis: Indiana University Press, 1997), for an elaboration of this issue and its inherent contradictions.

28. Wood, 'Louis Jourdan', p. 613.

29. See Lardner, 'Jourdan, the Glamourous Gaul'; and Bowers, *The Selznick Players*.

30. Ibid., p. 89.

31. Ibid., p. 90.

32. Ibid., pp. 89–90.

33. Cohan, *Masked Men*, p. 182.

34. Ibid., p. 153.

35. Bosley Crowther, 'Anne of the Indies', *The New York Times*, 25 October 1951, p. 36: 3.

36. Miriam Hansen, 'Pleasure, Ambivalence, Identification: Valentino and Female Spectatorship', in Leo Braudy and Marshall Cohen (eds), *Film Theory and Criticism: Introductory Readings* (New York and Oxford: Oxford University Press, 1999), p. 594.

37. Bowers, *The Selznick Players*, p. 235.

38. I am indebted to my students Megan Eulberg and Chelsea Dodson for this insight about the persistence of James Bond.

39. Bosley Crowther, 'The Bride is Much Too Beautiful', *The New York Times*, 21 January 1958, p. 35: 1.

40. Lardner, 'Jourdan, the Glamourous Gaul', p. 91.

41. Bosley Crowther, '*Gigi*', *The New York Times*, 17 May 1958, p. 12: 1.

42. Lardner, 'Jourdan, the Glamourous Gaul', p 91.

43. Bosley Crowther, '*The V.I.P.s*', *The New York Times*, 20 September 1963, p. 29: 1.

44. Kristin Ross, *Fast Cars, Clean Bodies: Decolonization and the Reordering of French Culture* (Cambridge, MA and London: MIT Press, 1995), p. 175. Ross draws on the popular French novelist of the 1960s, Christine Rochefort,

for this definition.

45. Tony Bennett and Janet Woollacott, *Bond and Beyond: The Political Career of a Popular Hero* (New York: Methuen, 1987), p. 238.

46. For a discussion of stardom and authenticity, see Richard Dyer, *Heavenly Bodies: Film Stars and Society* (New York: St Martin's Press, 1986).

47. *The Washington Post*, 10 June 1983, p. B: 1.

48. Lynn Spigel, 'The Domestic Economy of Television Viewing in Postwar America', *Critical Studies in Mass Communication* vol. 6 no. 4 (1 December 1989), p. 34.

14 The Latin Masquerade

The Spanish in Disguise in Hollywood[1]

Vicente Sánchez-Biosca

In 2000, a new Spanish star secured her place within Hollywood stardom. Her name was Penélope Cruz★. Her career had begun when she was a teenager, hosting a music television programme targeted at youngsters (*La quinta marcha* [The Fifth March], 1990), and her first success in the cinema came with *Belle époque*, Fernando Trueba's 1992 Academy Award-winning feature as Best Foreign Language Film. For a decade, her film career was astounding, as shown by her emblematic collaboration with three different, yet all fashionable Spanish directors: Bigas Luna (*Jamón, Jamón,* [1992]), Pedro Almodóvar (*Carne trémula/Live Flesh* [1997]; *Todo sobre mi madre/All about My Mother* [1999]) and, finally, *enfant terrible* Alejandro Amenábar (*Abre los ojos/Open Your Eyes* [1997]; Cruz also starred in the Hollywood remake of this film, directed by Cameron Crowe as *Vanilla Sky* in 2001). In her transition to Hollywood, one could argue that Cruz simply followed in the footsteps of other Spanish figures, such as Assumpta Serna★, Victoria Abril★ and Javier Bardem★. But it is especially in Antonio Banderas★ that one finds a mirror image of the Cruz phenomenon, because of the level of their success and because of her relationship with actor and producer Tom Cruise (which echoes the marriage of Banderas and Melanie Griffith).

What is striking about Cruz's entrance into the American pantheon is that her first lead role, in the banal *Woman on Top* (2000), introduced a new stereotype and brought in a new set of questions about the way in which national identities are negotiated today in American culture. Cruz plays a Brazilian woman from the region of [San Salvador de] Bahia who, after finding out about her husband's infidelities, emigrates to Los Angeles and triumphs on television as the exotic hostess of a programme dedicated to her country's cuisine. A foreigner in California, the Spanish actress embodied a Brazilian woman from the most tropical and 'Africanised' region of Brazil, enabling her to develop her persona into an emblem of 'Latin-ness'. This 'Latin' persona was a composite of diverse features: a strong temperament, overwhelming sensuality, fondness for home traditions, the ability to express musical rhythm through her body and primitive religious beliefs. These aspects of the character were incorporated into the production design and the plot of the film, resulting in a wealth of colour, vivacity, fashionable music and exoticism.[2]

Cruz's 'tropical' identity, reminiscent of Carmen Miranda, fitted neatly into the history of American cinema. Miranda was the first 'Bahiana' who, thanks to the 'Good Neighbour Policy' between the USA and Latin America, triumphed in Hollywood in 1939 by showing off hyperbolic signs of 'the tropical', taking them to the limits of camp. Cruz's case, however, is different in the way the whole operation seems forced: unlike Miranda, Cruz neither carried on her shoulders a musical tradition nor had striking, easily recognisable Caribbean or tropical features. Moreover, unlike Miranda, who was brought up in Brazil, Cruz hailed from Spain, and her native tongue did not even coincide with the language of her character in the film. This symptomatic deviation of her identity in Hollywood therefore cannot be explained by either her career or her origins. The explanation has to be sought in Hollywood, and in particular the production of the 'Latino' stereotype and how it relates to American identity, because there is no doubt about it: today 'Latino' is fashionable, and not just in the movies.

The stereotype of the 'Latin', the most durable codification of which was the 'Latin lover', could be seen as a successful, simplified version of the tragic figure of Don Juan. This stereotype has been decisive in the destiny of many Spanish actors, such as Antonio Moreno★, Valentín Parera, José Crespo★, Julio Peña★ and José Nieto★, but also in that of actors from Italy, Mexico and other Latin American countries. Nevertheless, the stereotype has evolved **133**

134 Ethnic smoothness: Antonio Banderas embodies a 'softer' Latino identity in *Desperado* (1995)

through time in relation to changing social, ethnic and sexual contexts, which the American cinema, always in touch with other areas of culture (art, music, dance, fashion), was trying to shape. The term 'Latin' thus has significantly mutated. To its original, Mediterranean origins, Latin American elements have been added. Now, not only is its meaning exclusively Latin American but, through a further reduction, it has come to refer to the Caribbean or tropical. Such a transformation, however, is impossible to analyse exclusively in terms of film representations.

The Latin lover, the main gateway for Spanish actors in Hollywood, was associated during the classical era with men from the South – dark-skinned, seductive, hot-blooded lovers, but also ruthless with women who succumbed to their charms (the ultimate example being the Italian Rudolph Valentino, although the Mexican Ramón Novarro was another good exponent). Today, however, this seems anachronistic, since Latin-ness, while still encompassing the idea of sensuality and seduction, is more readily associated with what the music industry labels 'Latino music': Caribbean rhythms, whose African rhythmic origins have been simplified in order to reach a mass audience. This is a step forward in a process of hybridisation that, in the 1960s, produced salsa and had its epicentre in New York, through Cuban exiles, Puerto Rican musicians and emigrants from Panama, etc.[3] Nowadays, women have also assumed an important place in this new Latin-ness, as the film careers of singer Jennifer Lopez and actress Salma Hayek demonstrate.

My aim here is to examine how Spanish actors are inscribed in this process and the reasons why they have found themselves obliged to hide their European origins under a stereotype that was historically considered subordinate in relation to colonial history. The reasons are not to be found, of course, in the actual relationship between Spain and Latin America, or between Spain and the USA, but rather in cultural dialectics between the 'WASP' and the 'Other'. The Latino, the Chicano, the African-American or the Oriental are all incarnations of 'otherness' that have replaced the old dialectics between Latin American and European identities. Manifestly, the Latino image, into which the Spanish actor or actress has to be subsumed, is not that of the aboriginal people from Peru, Bolivia, Mexico or Central America, in which American cinema has shown zero interest, but the Caribbean type. And it is worth pointing out the hot spots of this imaginary topography: Castro's Cuba, the Colombia of drug-dealers, the Central America of the Revolution and the Contras, a Mexico of a still primitive and savage gusto. These topoi generate highly spectacular – if not openly exotic – narratives, which hinge as much around the present as the (recent) past. The best incarnation of this new Latino personality is Antonio Banderas, but one could also mention other Latin American actors from the music industry, such as Rubén Blades and even Chayanne, although they have represented the type in a less systematic manner.

In other words, while Hollywood has shown interest in the stereotype of the Austro-Hungarian, the French, the German and the Russian, often reflected in the choice of actors and actresses, as well as locations, the Spanish have not elicited much interest in American popular culture, with the exception perhaps of the myth of Carmen. The arsenal of bullfighters and popular songs, gypsies and seductresses, which constituted myths and stereotypes originally suitable for export, had a minor impact in Hollywood, unlike its great success in Europe.

My aim here is to study two different representations of Latin-ness through Spanish actors from two very different periods. First, I will examine Sara Montiel*, a Spanish actress who arrived in Hollywood from Mexico in the 1950s and worked in three films, in which she displayed a range of notions of Mexican-ness. Second, I will look at Antonio Banderas, who, in the 1990s, forged a fashionable stereotype, and whose success reached its zenith in 1999 when he directed *Crazy in Alabama*.

Sara Montiel is an unusual case in the Spanish star system. She is probably the only Spanish female sex symbol to arise during the Franco era, in a film industry characterised by a religious and sexual censorship that was more intransigent, long lasting and paranoid than its political censorship. As a cult actress (with the camp nickname of Sarítisima), Montiel was one of the few female stars (and the only successful one) to offer an alternative to the Andalusian stereotype. This folkloric type derived from several sources, ranging from the exoticism of Mérimée's *Carmen*[4] to the popularity of Andalusian music – a smoother, strictly speaking 'corrupted', version of flamenco. The Andalusian female stereotype – *la andaluza* – was in fact promoted by the Franco regime, no doubt because of her prover-   **135** bial chastity, within the dominant Catholic repressive morality. Moreover, *la andaluza* was related to the facile and chauvinistic populism of Spanish music, thereby minimising the gypsy origins of both music and female type, at a time when the gypsy ethnic group was itself perceived with suspicion by the regime.

A comparison between Montiel's trajectory and that of her Andalusian contemporary, Carmen Sevilla, clarifies matters: although Sevilla worked in 1950s multi-language versions in France, Mexico, Britain and the USA (for instance, in *Babes in Baghdad/Muchachas de Bagdad* [1952]; *Spanish Affair/Aventura para dos* [1958]), she never provoked much interest in the USA and was never offered a contract in Hollywood, with the exception of *King of Kings* (1961), produced and shot in Spain.

It was not Montiel's Spanish origin or career that took her to Hollywood. If she became known, it was mainly because of her solid career in Mexican cinema that included fourteen films, many of which co-starred the popular singer Pedro Infante.[5] In addition, she had the support of prestigious Mexican directors such as Emilio 'Indio' Fernández, Juan José Ortega and Miguel M. Delgado. Her American contract followed the success of the Mexican thriller *Piel Canela* (1953), in which she played the role of a singer whose beautiful face is marred by an awful scar (carefully concealed by her hair) caused by rat bites during a childhood spent in misery. Montiel's presence in Hollywood should also be seen in the context of the policy of good relations between the USA and Latin America, at a time when the dominant American image of the Latino had a lot to do with people from the other side of the Rio Grande, that is to say, the aboriginal.

Montiel's career in Hollywood is limited to three films, all of which draw on the Latino imagery of the 1950s, distanced from both the camp tropicalism of Carmen Miranda and the severe beauty of Dolores del Río.[6] Montiel's Hollywood films were *Vera Cruz* (1954), *Serenade*, directed in 1956 by the man who became her husband, Anthony Mann, and *Run of the Arrow* (1957). They constitute an interlude between her earlier Mexican successes and her later, very popular Spanish persona – that of a woman from the music hall, the honourable and proud victim of male seducers' hypocrisy, an image crystallised in *El ultimo cuplé/The Last Torch Song* (1957).

What roles did this Spanish woman play in Hollywood, and what do they reveal about the status of Latin-ness in American cinema? In *Vera Cruz*, Montiel embodies a Revolutionary Juarista aboriginal, presented as the purest expression of Mexican-ness; in *Serenade*, she is the Mexican daughter of a bullfighter, whose love is played by the Italian tenor Mario Lanza; in *Run of the Arrow*, she appears as 'Yellow Moccasin', a Sioux woman, a characterisation that required abundant make-up and her hair to be dyed black with bluish highlights. In each case, Montiel embodies a range of visions of 'otherness' within American cinema. In each of these roles, she is dignified and beautiful, never a femme fatale.

It is worth focusing for a while on *Vera Cruz*, since this was the film that launched the Montiel personality described above. Credited as 'Sarita' (to avoid her assimilation to a Jewish character or a black servant, allegedly on the advice of Burt Lancaster), Montiel plays Nina, a member of the Revolutionary Juaristas (followers of leader Benito Juarez). Her aboriginal features are enhanced by make-up and the spectacular production values of the film. The second of five films produced by the Ben Hecht–Burt Lancaster duo, entirely shot in Mexico and distributed by United Artists, *Vera Cruz* deploys luxurious Technicolor and was the first film to use the short-lived Superscope anamorphic process. It became a real blockbuster, one of the very few at United Artists.[7] Two male stars from different generations (Gary Cooper and Lancaster) play American mercenaries who intervene in the so-called 'War of the Mexican Reformation' (1858–61). Each represents a different attitude and a different background: Ben Trane (Cooper) is an elegant former landowner from Louisiana, imbued with the spirit of the land; Joe Erin (Lancaster) is a shameless rustler from Pittsburgh. The national divide between the two men is solved on the Mexican territory, where the liberal Juaristas are rebelling against the French colonialists led by Emperor Maximilian. The fact that Trane, already honourably defeated in the American Civil War, embraces the Juarista ideals demonstrates the importance of the Mexican stereotype, explicitly associated with the Juaristas. At the same time, it suggests that the spirit of the Old South is more in tune with the essence of the USA than the Northern ethos.

Montiel, as Nina, represents a mythical 'national body', emerging from the arid soil. Although Denise Darcel★ is privileged on the credits as the French Countess Marie Duvarre, whom Trane and Erin escort to the city of Veracruz, and she appears on screen longer than Montiel, it is the Spanish actress who symbolises both the earth and a heroic ideal. The national body and the feminine body symptomatically converge in a spectacular space, set within the exotic locations of the film. And that body is part of a production design that includes costumes, make-up and accessories, through which nature and the aboriginal ethnicity the actress represents (her smooth features contrasting with those of the other Mexican characters) are inscribed in the film. The way in which the voyeuristic displays of Montiel's body and outfits are inserted in the narrative is strategic and builds up the semantic coding of her exotic beauty.

Montiel first appears during the ambush sequence. The rustlers, led by the two male protagonists, thwart the attacking Juaristas thanks to their lack of scruples: they threaten to kill some innocent children whom they have taken as hostages. Nina is hardly able to speak English, and her scene is brief, yet, together with the fact that she is a Juarista, her appearance is very significant: she is wearing a white, low-necked shirt that generously reveals her shoulders, her long, straight black hair spread over her back. A pair of wide silver earrings completes the outfit, setting off her intensely red lips, while strong make-up darkens her skin, contrasting with the white wall behind her. This image of Montiel works as a catalyst to the events that threaten her people, since her outfit visually matches the simple white clothes of the Juaristas. Moreover, these graphic matches confirm, without any doubt, the conflation of the Mexican with the aboriginal. Mexican, Revolutionary and aboriginal are synonymous terms within the film, and the distance from the Americans is clear: there is no hybridisation. But the beauty of Montiel's indigenous body is contrived, since, as pointed out earlier, her features are smooth, unlike those of the other actors who play Mexican characters or, indeed, unlike real indigenous – even half-caste – women, as anyone with minimal knowledge of these ethnicities would know.

The next spectacular sequence in the film also coincides with Montiel's second appearance. During an ambush of the Emperor's forces by the Juaristas, Montiel appears in a reaction shot: her hair is untied and the earrings are the same as before, as are her red lips and make-up. But this time she is wearing a blue outfit, finished with white lace at the top. A restless journey through the plains, leading the caravan, creates a kinetic image for which this new outfit seems to have been designed: her hair in the wind, her white petticoat blowing and her figure silhouetted against a limpid blue sky anchor the Juarista woman into the Mexican landscape. It is precisely during this sequence that Nina is the victim of an attempted rape by American bandits, a scene that the trailer retained for the promotion of the film, accompanied by the following words: 'Introducing an exciting new screen discovery, Sarita Montiel, temptress . . .'.

A third outfit crowns the cluster of meanings around Nina, emphasising a folkloric-popular vein. On its way to Veracruz, the retinue stops in the city of Las Palmas, where the villagers are celebrating some local festivities: we are treated to some tap-dancing with an ambiguous Spanish flavour, and some typical Mexican dances. In the darkness of the night, Nina slips away between the carriages to find the hidden load of gold carried by the Countess, pretending that her only motivation is to find a beautiful, low-cut red dress that stands out in the dark, matching her lips, now made up with intense crimson lipstick. Feminine coquettry serves to conceal her Revolutionary belief, yet what the public gets to see is the spectacle of that false vanity. While on the soundtrack we can hear the musical theme of the film – the song 'Veracruz', sung in Spanish with guitar accompaniment – Trane and Nina reunite under a cascade with sparkly foam, in a sequence that seals a pact between them.

Montiel's three costumes, if considered in relation to the settings, the other characters and the narrative, suggest a series of meanings channelled through the beautiful body of the actress: the people (represented by the Revolutionaries and the children); the spectacle of nature and of a 'primitive' temperament that reacts with energy when sexually threatened; and the folkloric, exotic tone of the lovers' meeting.

The climate was very different when, in the early 1990s, Antonio Banderas assaulted the mecca of cinema. The stabilisation of his 'Latin' persona was caught in a series of identity problems relating to both Latino fashion (Latino in the narrow sense of Caribbean and tropical) and the powerful mediation of the music industry that transformed the 'Latin music' genre into a worldwide success. The process of Banderas' implantation was fast.

In March 1990, Banderas presented Almodóvar's film ¡Átame!/Tie Me Up! Tie Me Down! in the USA; at around the same period, he established himself in Los Angeles and appeared in a clothes commercial with actress Laura Harris. He heard about Arne Glimcher's intention to direct The Mambo Kings, based on the book by Oscar Hijuelos (Los reyes del mambo tocan canciones de amor [The Mambo Kings Play Love Songs]), which had won the Pulitzer prize. The Cuban-American Andy García had been first choice, but he had other commitments, leaving the door open for Banderas.

Symptomatically, The Mambo Kings (1992) reconstructs a 1950s nostalgic, pre-Revolutionary Cuban paradise – a hyperbolic Tropicana, with choreography in the style made popular in Hollywood by another Spaniard, the musician and caricaturist Xavier Cugat.[8] The story begins in a Havana nightclub in 1952. After a fight and a death threat, trumpeter Nestor (Banderas) is forced to migrate to New York with his brother Cesar (Armand Assante), where they eventually make it big in the world of music. Far from exploring the 'erotic animal' side of Banderas introduced by ¡Átame!, or asking him to play the Latin lover, The Mambo Kings makes Banderas' role (subordinate to Assante's) that of a shy young man who, significantly, is a 'one woman's man'. It is his brother who embodies the Latino stereotype: always looking for a fight, a womaniser, irresponsible, as capable of seducing any woman as of rivalling the famous 'Puerto Rican drummer' Tito Puente. Music and dance hybrids are plentiful: for example, the secret passion between Dolores (Maruschka Detmers) – the woman Nestor will marry – and Cesar is expressed through their dancing together, shortly after their first encounter, in a bizarre blend of Caribbean dance styles and Argentine tango.

The setting from which The Mambo Kings derives its Latino image is a musical hybridisation that already possessed a long history in North America, especially in New York during the 1950s. It is precisely this atmosphere that the film recreates, much helped by the soundtrack, which mixes different types of music and a variety of performers, such as Tito Puente, the Cuban singer Celia Cruz and Antonio Sandoval, while the repertoire draws on the better-known standards of Latino music (numbers such as 'Perfidia', 'Quiéreme mucho' and 'Guantanamera'). The mixing of bolero music with the theme song, 'Bella María de mi amor', also seems symptomatic. While it is sung in English by Assante in the film, Banderas also performs a Spanish version on the soundtrack CD, perhaps in an attempt to launch the actor as a music star.[9]

To sum up, the Banderas persona in Hollywood emerges at a transitional moment in the definition of the Latino stereotype, at the crossroads of different national identities (Cuban, Puerto Rican, Mexican) and of complex musical models.[10] But the most revealing and decisive film in the construction of this persona was Robert Rodríguez's Desperado (1995), the spin-off of El Mariachi, directed in 1992 by the same film-maker. The plot of the earlier film is based on a misunderstanding between a young and attractive Mexican and a bouncer: the former is a mariachi guitarist and the latter hides his deadly weapons in a guitar case. The opposition between the two actors who embody the lead characters could not be more striking: the unattractive bitterness of the assassin contrasts with the somewhat bland beauty of his opponent. In Desperado, by contrast, the features of both actors/characters have become an aggressive type of beauty, with strong features, dark skin and long hair flowing in the wind. This is the mark of a – discreetly attractive – Latino ethnicity (not a Chicano one, as in El Mariachi), Banderas' features smoothing over the disparate aspects of El Mariachi. As a guitarist and a dancer in the film, Banderas mobilises part of the Latino arsenal. His ethnic smoothness, attractive yet aggressively masculine, contains traces of a Latino identity that no longer has any real referent. It is a persona that would characterise Banderas' subsequent roles.

Many of the actors and actresses who migrated to Hollywood did it to embody roles (that is to say, stereotypes) that were representative of their respective countries of origin. Unlike some stars, such as Maurice Chevalier★ or Greta Garbo★, who portrayed national characters, the more exotic Spanish types – bullfighters, folk singers, gypsies – that had been common in world literature since the nineteenth century were not so prominent in Hollywood. Arguably, the only exception were the numerous Carmen adaptations. However, even though the actresses who played the role had to have 'different' ethnic features (Theda Bara, Edna Purviance, Dolores del Río), or suggest, in a spectacular manner, Hispanic antecedents (Rita Hayworth among others), a Spanish actress was not considered necessary.

By contrast, Latin-ness is pervasive in Hollywood, and many Spanish actors and actresses have had to camouflage their origin and endorse this image. Yet the American imaginary (and as a consequence its film representations) is not stable by any means. Sara Montiel and Antonio Banderas reveal two different, highly illustrative, clusters of discourses about Latin-ness in the American cinema.[11] While Montiel projected a feminine image of the exotic Latino beauty, related to the wild, spectacular nature of the Western, Banderas brings forth a musical scene and merges the image of the Latino with a new type of Caribbean Latin lover, which the American fan magazines refer to – in Spanish – as *caliente, caliente, caliente* (hot, hot, hot).

Translated from the Spanish by Constanza Burucúa.

Notes

1. This chapter has been written as part of the research project 'Presencias españolas en el cine norteamericano' (Spanish Presences in the American Cinema) (CYJT504G), financed by the Spanish Ministerio de Ciencia y Tecnología (2003–5). The author would like to acknowledge Josep-Lluis Fecé's collaboration during the early stages of the work and Marina Díaz for her opportune comments on the Mexican career of Sara Montiel.

2. It is curious that such a stereotyped commercial product should be offered to the Venezuelan director Fina Torres, recognised in Europe as an auteur.

3. The so-called 'Latin jazz' actually dates from the 1950s, when New York big bands began to include Afro-Cuban rhythms in their repertoires.

4. Prosper Mérimée's novella was published in 1845, and was made into an opera by Bizet in 1875.

5. This part of Montiel's career took place during the 'golden age' of Mexican cinema, which showed a huge capacity to create and export its own star system. See Julia Tuñón, *Mujeres de luz y sombra en el cine mexicano. La construcción de una imagen 1939–1953* [Women of Light and Darkness in Mexican Cinema: The Construction of an Image 1939–1953] (Mexico: Colegio de México/Instituto Mexicano de Cinematografía, 1998), for an in-depth study of female stars.

6. Dolores del Río was already a symbol of Latin-ness, a feminine version of Rudolph Valentino in Hollywood. However, as Ana López points out, even if Del Río played the role of the foreign woman (Russians, gypsies, dancers, mestizo women) several times, only exceptionally, and very late in her career, was she identified with Latin American characters and, even then, never with Mexicans. See Ana M. López, 'Hollywood-México: Dolores del Río, una estrella transnacional' [Dolores del Río, a Transnational Star], in Paulo Paranaguá and Alberto Elena, *Mitologías latinoamericanas* [Latin American Mythologies] (Archivos de la Filmoteca, no. 31, 1999), p. 20.

7. Tino Balio, *United Artists. The Company that Changed the Film Industry* (Madison: University of Wisconsin Press, 1987), p. 79.

8. Oscar Hijuelos' notes for the CD of the film's soundtrack confirm this nostalgic evocation of a mythical Latin and musical New York of the 1950s, which, symptomatically, Hijuelos never knew.

9. Significantly, the CD contains a third version of the musical theme, performed by the group Los Lobos, whose international fame partly followed the release of the soundtrack of another film, *La Bamba* (1986). Later, Los Lobos were in charge of the music for *Desperado*.

10. A very interesting case is that of *Dance with Me* (1998), starring Chayanne, a Cuban singer and dancer who emigrated to the USA and who offers a new style of more sophisticated dancing, called 'sport dancing'.

11. A significant detail demonstrates that this is perceived in a different way, as a continuity rather than as a rupture, by the Latin-American community: in February 2001, Sara Montiel received the Rita Moreno prize, awarded by HOLA (Hispanic Organisation of Latino Actors) to the actors and actresses who contributed to portrayals of non-stereotyped Hispanic peoples and cultures.

15 Acting Nasty?

British Male Actors in Contemporary Hollywood

Andrew Spicer

With their rigorous training in drama schools and on stage, British actors continue to represent high cultural capital ('class') for American producers and studio executives; as *Variety* recently phrased it: 'Hollywood is slave to the snob appeal of the British theatrical tradition'.[1] British actors are often first to be considered for a particularly demanding role, even if, as was the case with Oliver Stone's *Nixon* (1995), Anthony Hopkins★ had to play an American president.[2] But perhaps it was no surprise that a British actor should play such a crooked figure, as it confirms what has become a media cliché: British male actors always play villains in contemporary Hollywood films. One characteristic magazine article about the 'Brit Villain' mentions four striking instances: Christopher Lee's★ Saruman in *The Lord of the Rings* (2001/2), Alan Rickman★ as the Sheriff of Nottingham in *Robin Hood – Prince of Thieves* (1991), Ralph Fiennes'★ Amon Goeth in *Schindler's List* (1993) and Ian McKellen's★ Magneto in the *X-Men* films (2000/3).[3] The other example that immediately springs to mind is Anthony Hopkins' Hannibal 'The Cannibal' Lecter in *The Silence of the Lambs* (1991). Richard E. Grant★, who has played the villain in several American films, attributes this tendency to the particular resonance of the upper-class English voice: 'there is something in the way that the English speak which can sound terribly sinister to an American ear . . . I find that I have a kind of authority because I can sound so arrogant.'[4]

This arrogance has a deep cultural significance, as it activates the American folk memory of the imperial British as the 'original oppressors' lording it over their colonial subjects.[5] As Siegfried Kracauer noted, Americans regard the English as snobs, the product of a class-ridden and anachronistic society, and, as Hollywood always seeks to confirm popular prejudices, American films portray the English in this way.[6] One can go further and argue that not only do Americans see the English as snobbish, but also effete, over-educated, emotionally repressed and deviant. Hence, in addition to playing various types of villain, English actors also tend to play troubled or damaged men with deep-seated emotional and psychological problems, and also fools who display these undesirable qualities in order to be laughed at. Here, however, there is often a sense of wry self-mockery, which acknowledges, as Hugh Grant★, the chief exemplar of the diffident, repressed middle-class Englishman, puts it, 'how embarrassing and funny it is to be English'.[7]

However, there is a reverse side to this practice, which means that British actors do not only get paid for acting nasty.[8] The Englishman's patrician intonations can connote not ruthless arrogance, but authority and gravitas. Patrick Stewart's★ 'deliciously plumy [sic] tones' as Captain Picard in the *Star Trek* films were thought to lend even the dullest remark significance.[9] Ian McKellen's suavely sinister Magneto in *X-Men* was matched by his equally impressive performance as the benign Gandalf in *The Lord of the Rings*. Both Gandalf and Picard are examples of an additional important cultural type that is the preserve of the British actor: the tribal elder, an older man who acts as the wise mentor of a younger male. This type radiates authority, intelligence and wisdom born of long experience, usually softened by an ironic humour.

Hugh Grant, the comic version of the diffident, repressed middle-class Englishman, here in *Mickey Blue Eyes* (1999)

This division into broad cultural types is fundamental to the representational economy of Hollywood cinema (as it is to popular culture generally), which works by constructing very general images of masculinity that are instantly recognisable for audiences through repetition.[10] The types are not, with the partial exception of Hugh Grant's fool, specific national stereotypes, but broader and more dynamic entities. They are the product of complex, transnational and uneven cultural histories, and are constantly changing in subtle ways. However, the ability of British actors to play these particular types – villain, damaged man, fool, tribal elder – derives, as I have suggested, from their Britishness. And, in repeatedly playing a type, British actors deepen and refine its lineaments, as well as developing coherent personae that can be marketed and promoted with confidence to audiences. Exploring the complexities of these types drawn from a wide range of American films – including, where appropriate, some US/UK co-productions – can therefore help to make sense of the selective use of British actors in contemporary Hollywood, defined as from 1990 onwards.[11]

Villains

The current proliferation of British villains started in the summer of 1991, which saw not only Alan Rickman's arrogantly sarcastic Sheriff of Nottingham and Anthony Hopkins' Hannibal Lecter but also Timothy Dalton★ as the scheming thespian in *The Rocketeer* and Richard E. Grant's monomaniacal robber-baron in *Hudson Hawk*. As casting director Howard Feuer explained: 'British actors can do a bravura performance and yet still fit into an ensemble. There is also the intelligence necessary to be a true villain which British culture lends to a project.'[12] British actors were considered to be sexy in these roles, unlike Americans, who were judged merely frightening.[13] American actors were understandably reluctant to take such roles. As Mary Harron, director of *American Psycho* (2000), in which Welsh-born Christian Bale plays the psychopathic yuppie, observed: 'a mainstream actor with an eye on a Tom Cruise-like career wasn't going to touch it'.[14] (There is no space to deal with Jude Law★ who has emerged as a Hollywood leading man at the turn of the twenty-first century. I suggest that it is precisely Law's *lack* of conventional British thespian qualities that allows him to play a conventional hero.) Gary Oldman's★ Hollywood career has been made through playing a succession of maverick outsiders and criminals – from a psychotic criminal in *State of Grace* (1990) through to an orphaned, inbred small-time crook in *Nobody's Baby* (2001) – that American actors might baulk at. Oldman brings 'a visceral and intelligent radicalism to his roles in a way that would be likely to be crass and foolish in an American'.[15] Tim Roth★, indebted to Oldman in setting the precedent for English actors playing Americans, has essayed an even more varied assortment of hooligans and killers, though his commitment to American independent cinema has meant that he does not usually play in major films, the exception being *Planet of the Apes* (2001).[16]

However, within the range of villains that British actors play, two types are dominant: the sinister psychopath and the evil overlord. The evil overlord, the diabolical villain of the old-fashioned melodrama that lies at the heart of the special effects-driven fantasy genres that are such a feature of contemporary Hollywood, is especially suited to bravura playing and the resonance of the upper-class English accent. Examples include Jeremy Irons'★ wicked tyrant, Profion, in *Dungeons & Dragons* (2000) and Ian McKellen's malevolent super-mutant, Magneto, in *X-Men*, but above all Christopher Lee's characters in both *The Lord of the Rings* and the *Star Wars* series that have proved to be so successful for the 'boomers with kids' audience. Lee's height, sonorous 'operatic' voice (which even in his eighties has lost little of its potency), aristocratic looks and demeanour have made him an obvious choice for such roles since he played the eponymous villain in Terence Fischer's *Dracula* in 1958. Without overplaying, or attempting to be ironic or camp, Lee gives an effectively broad performance, the sweeping gestures and regal presence incarnating evil, as the corrupted Jedi, Count Dooku or the dark wizard, Saruman.

The other dominant figure of villainy, the psychopathic serial killer, appears to be sharply contemporary. However, as Philip Simpson argues, it is a mythical figure composed of Gothic elements (the 'fatal man' and the vampire), as well as aspects of the deviant criminal and the film noir psychopath. These elements combine to create the current image of the ultimate transgressor, the centre of a widespread interest in amoral, disturbed personalities and a fascination with terrifying evil.[17] Hopkins' Lecter, the most celebrated of these figures, is also a more extreme version of the hyper-intelligent crooked mastermind beloved of crime fiction. *Silence*'s director Jonathan Demme chose Hopkins on the basis of his combination of 'intense humanity and intense intelligence' as Dr Treves in *The Elephant Man* (1980). He thought that Hopkins invested Lecter, 'who we *know* has committed horrific crimes', with great humanity and compassion, making him both complex and unpredictable, therefore fascinating rather than repulsive or diabolical.[18] Hopkins plays Lecter with an urbane insouciance and debonair sexual charm, creating a distinctive, and strangely disturbing, way of speaking that the actor himself described as 'the disembodied voice at the end of a long dream'.[19] Particularly effective was the 'little breathy grace note' Hopkins added to the most diabolical lines that hovered between the exquisite taste of the connoisseur's civilised refinement and the madman's fathomless evil.[20] This subtle inflection was consistent with Hopkins' deliberately low-key performance. As he commented, because the films were 'packed with images of fear and terror and horror and all that, I don't have to do anything much at all, just be still and quiet and let the audience scare themselves'.[21] Although the later films in the trilogy – *Hannibal* (2001) and *Red Dragon* (2002) – have, inevitably, not quite matched the shock and intensity of Hopkins' Academy Award-winning performance in *Silence*, Lecter is now part of contemporary mythology, voted 'number one all-time screen villain' by the American Film Institute.[22]

The Damaged Man

The disturbing fascination of Lecter's distorted humanity grades into another type, the damaged man. Whereas an audience's interest lies in the villain's actions, here interest shifts to motivation and the instabilities of identity. The damaged man is psychologically scarred either by his past or his failure to live up to expectations. British actors' perceived ability to project depth and complexity makes them likely choices for such roles. The most conspicuous has been the aristocratic, RADA-trained Ralph Fiennes, who became a Hollywood star on the basis of his striking performance as SS-Hauptsturmführer Amon Goeth, the Commandant of the Plaszow labour camp in *Schindler's List*. Goeth is a monstrous sadist, but Fiennes brings to the part an intensity of self-loathing and grief, an angst-ridden conviction that all is irretrievably lost, which gives him a certain pathos. Director Steven Spielberg, who gave Fiennes considerable latitude in his interpretation of the part, admired his creation of 'sexual evil. It is all about subtlety; there were moments of kindness that would move across his eyes and then instantly run cold.'[23] Robert Redford, the director of *Quiz Show* (1994), also detected 'this wonderfully interesting interior – this dark, haunted quality beneath the perfect shell', which made him choose Fiennes as the Ivy Leaguer Charles Van Doren, the privileged scion of a self-appointed American cultural aristocracy – Paul Scofield★ plays his father Mark, a professor of literature – who is corrupted by the chance of money and celebrity on a rigged quiz show.[24] This 'haunted quality' of a man in search of unattainable grace was instrumental in Fiennes' creation of his most successful role, the enigmatic, tormented Hungarian Count Laszló Almásy in *The English Patient* (1996), where his patrician good looks and piercing blue eyes were used to great effect as the tragic lover. Hideously burned and dying in a decaying Tuscan monastery as the war draws to a close, Almásy is more deeply scarred by the memories of his adulterous affair with Katherine Clifton (Kristin Scott Thomas★), the woman he failed to rescue. Fiennes' creations were subtle and thoughtful, but he drew upon deep cultural roots: the European archetype of the Byronic anti-hero who embodies contradictory qualities and whose nobility is fatally flawed. This archetype is the domain of British actors: Gary Oldman's Count Dracula in *Bram Stoker's Dracula* (1992) and Kenneth Branagh's★ Baron Frankenstein in *Mary Shelley's Frankenstein* (1994).

An interesting alternative to this aristocratic figure, the troubled man of action, has become the property of Sean Bean★, also RADA-trained but without surrendering his northern working-class origins, accent and personality. Bean has the powerful muscularity and strong, hard handsomeness associated with the American action hero, but while he plays a hero on British television – in the five series of *Sharpe* (1993–7) – Hollywood producers use him **143** as a villain, the adversary of the American star. Thus he appears opposite Harrison Ford in *Patriot Games* (1992), Steve Guttenberg in *Airborne* (1998) and Michael Douglas in *Don't Say a Word* (2001), and as the volatile Spence, part of the motley gang of criminals led by Sam (Robert De Niro) in *Ronin* (1998), whose boast that he is ex-SAS is bogus. *Airborne*'s director, Julian Grant, commented that he chose Bean for the role of the mercenary Toombs because 'I had particularly wanted to expand outside of the typical North American actor and Sean had the refinement I was looking for . . . [he] brought class and panache to the role'.[25] Bean's distinction is to invest these desperate men with a vulnerability that gives the characterisation some complexity. Bean also made a deep impression as Alec Trevelyan, 006, Bond's dark self in *GoldenEye* (1995), who turns from trusted comrade to nemesis. Pierce Brosnan★, who played Bond, admired Bean's ability to project 'a deep-seated pain and anger, but also a sensitive vulnerability. There is a special longing to his countenance that was so effective.'[26] This 'special longing' was the basis of his excellent performance as the flawed hero Boromir in *The Fellowship of the Ring* (2001), whose inability to fulfil the expectations placed upon him lends a tragic humanity to the fantasy.

Fools: the Repressed Englishman

Hugh Grant's Hollywood stardom has been based entirely on the character of the flustered, tongue-tied, bewildered upper-class 'noodle' he played in his breakthrough film, the hugely successful *Four Weddings and a Funeral* (1994).[27] The popularity of the diffident, emotionally repressed, well-bred Englishman for contemporary American audiences is unsurprising, as it embodies deeply ingrained perceptions of English society as class-ridden and backward. Gael Sweeney argues that American viewers in particular take 'pleasure in Grant's masochistic display: to see the disgrace of a handsome, intelligent male, marked with all the class and cultural privileges of a British identity'.[28] For American women, it has been contended, Grant's classically English good looks represent the quintessence of reserved, Old World charm. Unlike his American counterparts, Grant was considered rather fey (but not effeminate), his sexual charisma built upon wit and irony not homespun sincerity. This made his seduction by an uninhibited American woman all the more satisfying.[29]

In interviews, Grant has tirelessly played up to the image of the affable and self-deprecating English gent while reprising his 'Brit twit' in *Nine Months* (1995) – whose box office was actually boosted by the scandal of his arrest with prostitute Divine Brown – and *Mickey Blue Eyes* (1999). Grant developed some well-honed performance traits, his 'repertoire of befuddled reactions, including much rapid eyelid fluttering, slight stammering and panicked expressions camouflaged by polite smiles', which were an essential part of his debonair charm.[30] Grant has extended his range in his 'British' films – in *Notting Hill* (1999), where he played an empathetic Everyman, as a predatory cad in *Bridget Jones's Diary* (2001) and its sequel *Bridget Jones: The Edge of Reason* (2004), and his immature thirty-something in *About a Boy* (2002) – but for American audiences this could be accommodated into an overarching conception of the well-bred, charming, sexy but emotionally inadequate toff. In *Two Weeks Notice* (2002), he is again the befuddled, blundering upper-class charmer in need of a strong woman (Sandra Bullock) to run his life for him. Although his character is not marked as specifically English, Grant plays him as if he were, another indication that class privilege and Englishness are synonymous in American eyes. His ruthless brother Howard is also played by a British actor, David Haig★, as if to transfer the unacceptable qualities of corporate greed from the Americans themselves to the 'original oppressors'.

Several other British actors have played the type, notably Colin Firth★ in the *Bridget Jones* films and in two recent romantic comedies that also exploit the Englishman's clash with a spirited American: *Hope Springs* (2003), in which Firth plays an artist (therefore cultured, sensitive) who washes up in a small Vermont town, and the critically trounced *What a Girl Wants* (2003), a modern-day version of the 1958 comedy *The Reluctant Debutante*, in which Firth, at his most clenched and constipated, plays the straight-laced father of a vivacious daughter who has been brought up in New York. Ralph Fiennes similarly plays a well-connected senatorial candidate who is smitten by a

working-class single mother (Jennifer Lopez) in *Maid in Manhattan* (2002), which explores (only to efface) class and ethnic divides and confirms Hollywood's preference for English actors as upper-class Americans. Fiennes, as in *The Avengers* (1998), looks uncomfortable in light comedy.[31] An interesting counterpoint, in which the latent homosexuality of the type is made overt, is Rupert Everett★, who has become the first openly gay A-list star, largely on the strength of his role as Julia Roberts' homosexual confidant in the highly successful *My Best Friend's Wedding* (1997). His role was considerably enhanced after enthusiastic responses from preview audiences.[32] He played a similar role in *The Next Best Thing* (2000) as Madonna's acerbic but witty companion, and was an obvious choice for the two Wilde revivals – *An Ideal Husband* (1999), in which he played the cynical but droll Lord Goring, and as Algy (opposite Firth's Jack) in *The Importance of Being Earnest* (2002).[33]

The Tribal Elder

As I have argued elsewhere, Sean Connery★ was instrumental in creating the current version of the ancient archetype of the tribal elder, in a series of roles beginning with his Academy Award-winning performance in *The Untouchables* (1987) through to *Finding Forrester* (2000).[34] Connery's Celtic Britishness – his characters' Irish or Scottish ancestry is often emphasised – allows him to play the figure as an outsider, both sage and dissident, who has been marginalised by a society where democratic values are under threat. This would be more difficult for an American actor, who would inevitably project conventional American values. It is his alternative perspective, a wisdom borne of long and often bitter experience, that gives substance to his role as the mentor of a younger man, always played by an American. The other actor who has also repeatedly played this role is Anthony Hopkins, his gentler, more cerebral performances contrasting with Connery's still-insistent physicality. Hopkins' best performances include a testy but incorruptible John Quincy Adams in *Amistad* (1997), the original Zorro in *The Mask of Zorro* (1998), the mysterious older man who fills a boy's fatherless void in *Hearts in Atlantis* (2001) and a jaded CIA agent in *Bad Company* (2002). But Hopkins' cultured voice and Old World refinement effortlessly project wisdom, intelligence and depth of character, as they did with Lecter, who may be regarded as the tribal elder's dark self. He thus has no interest in insisting on his Welsh origins and has in fact become an American citizen, averring that he has 'reinvented my own life. I didn't want to be bound up by patriotism or nationality.'[35]

Despite these differences, both actors have the capacity to imbue each utterance with an apparent profundity, nicely underscored with a wry humour. This quality is shared by Michael Caine★, whose career has undergone a significant revival in the late 1990s, shifting from supporting roles to starring ones as tribal elders in *The Cider House Rules* (1999) and *The Quiet American* (2002). In the former, Caine's caring Dr Larch, head of an orphanage, encourages his surrogate son (Tobey Maguire) to assume responsibility for others and continue his practice; in the latter, he plays British journalist Thomas Fowler, whose attempts to educate the doctrinaire young American (Brendan Fraser) about the realities of Indo-China fail. Fowler is less cynical than in Graham Greene's source novel and Caine, often acting solely through his eyes, creates both the pain and the frustration of the mentor who is ignored.

This association of Britishness with wisdom and authority explains Patrick Stewart's casting as Captain Jean-Luc Picard in the *Star Trek* series, both on television (178 episodes) and in the four film spin-offs. Stewart has commented that over the seven-year period in which he has played the role, he has been able to round out Picard's character, emphasising his patience, generosity and empathy.[36] Thus the cerebral Picard, the mentor of his crew, is an altogether different figure from his predecessor, the American William Shatner's instinctive man of action, James T. Kirk. In *Star Trek: Generations* (1994), which contrasts the two men, Picard cries when he reflects on the loneliness of his life, the family he longs for but has had to forgo in bending to the exacting demands of his duties as a Star Ship Commander. In *Star Trek: Nemesis* (2002), the villain is a dark incarnation of his young self, embodying all the anarchic desires that Picard has, with difficulty, kept in check. Stewart plays a similar role in the two *X-Men* films as the noble Professor Charles Xavier, the leader of the good mutants. When the decision to make a film from the best-selling comic books was announced, Stewart was the fans' overwhelming choice for the part, and the first of the cast to be signed up.

It may also be argued that Ewan McGregor★ has attained American stardom on the basis of being a tribal elder in embryo, playing the Jedi Obi-Wan Kenobi in the *Star Wars* prequels, the role taken by Alec Guinness★ in the original trilogy. George Lucas wanted a physical, but also reflective British actor who could gradually grow in stature over the course of the three films, changing from the impetuous warrior of *The Phantom Menace* (1999) into the more mature and wise mentor of Anakin Skywalker (Hayden Christensen) in *Attack of the Clones* (2002) who holds his own emotions in check, always the *métier* of the British actor.[37] American audiences may not be so alive to the irony of the star of *Trainspotting* (1996) stiffening his pronounced Edinburgh burr into a refined, slightly inflected English accent, which insinuates rather than impersonates Guinness' vocal inflections.

British Actors in Hollywood: a Paradoxical Situation?

Ian McKellen, apropos his celebrity status as Gandalf in *The Lord of the Rings* and its associated memorabilia, has reflected on the irony of the British actor in contemporary Hollywood: 'Who would have thought that after all those years in the classics, Anthony Hopkins would be best known for eating people's faces and they'd make me into a toy!'[38] Indeed, their roles may not always reflect their pedigree and training, and the days when the British actor could forge a career simply by being British in a succession of historical dramas or adaptations of literary classics are gone. Nevertheless, a number of British actors have carved out highly lucrative and successful careers in today's Hollywood, and have had the opportunity to appear in blockbusters whose scale dwarfs anything that the British film industry can produce. This has often been very satisfying and stimulating. Ewan McGregor has commented frequently on the thrill of appearing in the *Star Wars* prequels, starring in the successors of the films he revelled in as a child;[39] while Hopkins and others have found their roles as villains or damaged men challenging, rewarding and enjoyable. British actors are no longer exclusively bound to a punitive studio contract and can work freely on both sides of the Atlantic; Fiennes, McKellen and Stewart all return frequently to their theatrical roots. Both Oldman and Roth have used some of their Hollywood revenues to part fund dark and difficult British films – *Nil by Mouth* (1997) and *The War Zone* (1999) respectively – even as McGregor made *Nora* (2000) through Natural Nylon, a production company formed along the lines of United Artists, designed to give actors more influence in the production process.[40] This struggle for creative control is a reminder that actors, if well paid, remain essentially commodities, with little, if any, institutional power. However, if British actors have been used for a restricted range of types not of their own choosing, they have often created some of the most memorable performances in present-day American films and their extensive contribution to contemporary Hollywood deserves to be more widely recognised than it is.

Notes

1. John Dempsey, 'Inside Move: The British are Coming Again . . . as Yanks', *Variety*, 11 August 2002.
2. Ibid. Michael Gambon★ (actually born in Dublin) played Lyndon Johnson in *The Path to War* (2002). Mention should be made of Kenneth Branagh, who has almost single-handedly recreated the Shakespearean adaptation with considerable success on both sides of the Atlantic, making himself a star and creating numerous roles for other British actors; see Samuel Crowl, *Shakespeare at the Cineplex* (Athens: Ohio University Press, 2003).
3. Anon. 'Mad, Bad and British', *Sky the Magazine*, November 2003, p. 53.
4. Quoted in Steve Goldman, 'Best of British Villainy', <www.geocities.com/Hollywood/Film/7518/Villany/Villany.htm>, accessed 1 July 2003.
5. John Patterson, 'Vile Britannia', *Guardian*, 7 August 2003.
6. See Siegfried Kracauer, 'National Types as Hollywood Presents Them', in Roger Manvell (ed.), *The Cinema 1950* (Harmondsworth: Penguin Books, 1950), pp. 140–69.
7. Quoted in Anita Chaudhuri, 'Upper Class Treat', *Time Out*, 4–11 May 1994, p. 22.
8. For previous generations, the situation was very different – see H. Mark Glancy, *When Hollywood Loved Britain: The Hollywood 'British' Film, 1939–45* (Manchester: Manchester University Press, 1999); see also Sarah Street's

contribution to this volume. For a historical overview through to the early 1980s, see Sheridan Morley, *Tales from the Hollywood Raj* (London: Weidenfeld & Nicolson, 1983).

9. Joe Leydon, '*Star Trek: Insurrection*', *Variety*, 11 December 1998.

10. For a more extended discussion of cultural types, see Andrew Spicer, *Typical Men: The Representation of Masculinity in Popular British Cinema* (London: I. B. Tauris, 2001), pp. 1–5.

11. Regrettably, there is no space to consider a number of distinguished British actors who play supporting roles in American films: Alan Bates★, Brian Cox★, Albert Finney★, Ian Holm★, Bob Hoskins★, John Hurt★ and Malcolm McDowell★. I am, of course, excluding the Irish actors who have made such an impact on modern Hollywood; see Áine O'Connor, *Leading Hollywood* (Dublin: Wolfhound Press, 1996).

12. Quoted in Goldman, 'Best of British Villainy'.

13. Timothy M. Gray, 'This Brit No Fit for Archetype Villain', *Variety*, 3 September 2002.

14. Quoted in Jeff Snipe, 'Blood Symbol', *Sight and Sound* vol. 9 no. 7 (NS) (July 1999), p. 8. Leonardo DiCaprio declined the role after much speculation. Bale is hovering on the verge of American stardom as a leading man.

15. William Cash, 'Odd Man Out', *The Times Saturday Review*, 12 December 1992, p. 4.

16. See the interview with David Cavanagh, 'I Believe in America', *Empire* no. 72 (June 1995), pp. 70–3.

17. Philip L. Simpson, *Psycho Paths: Tracking the Serial Killer through Contemporary American Film and Fiction* (Carbondale and Edwardsville: Southern Illinois University Press, 2000).

18. Quoted in Quentin Falk, *Anthony Hopkins: The Authorised Biography* (London: Virgin, 2000), p. 214; original emphasis.

19. Ibid., p. 215.

20. Thomas Sutcliffe, 'The Iceman Cometh', *Independent*, Review, 18 February 2001, p. 5.

21. Quoted in Martyn Palmer, 'Empathy with the Devil', *The Times*, section 2, 16 February 2001, p. 16.

22. Reported in *Variety*, 3 June 2003.

23. Quoted in Thomas Sutcliffe, 'The Heart of Darkness', *Independent*, Review, 12 February 2000, p. 5.

24. Quoted in York Membery, *Ralph Fiennes: The Unauthorised Biography* (London: Chameleon Books, 1997), p. 124.

25. Quoted in Laura Jackson, *Sean Bean: The Biography* (London: Piatkus, 2000), p. 183.

26. Ibid., p. 158.

27. For a fuller account, see Andrew Spicer, 'The Reluctance to Commit: Hugh Grant and New British Romantic Comedy', in Phil Powrie, Ann Davies and Bruce Babington (eds), *The Trouble with Men: Masculinities in European and Hollywood Cinema* (London: Wallflower Press, 2004), pp. 77–87.

28. Gael Sweeney, 'The Man in the Pink Shirt: Hugh Grant and the Dilemma of British Masculinity', *CineAction!* no. 55, July 2001 pp. 58–67.

29. Katherine Muir, 'Hugh Grant', *The Times*, 26 April 1994.

30. Todd McCarthy, '*Nine Months*', *Variety*, 10 July 1995.

31. Fiennes commented: 'It was a great challenge – I had to find a level where there was no distress, frustration or despair – and I'd find myself thinking, "Is this it? Do I just smile, say hello and look like I love her?"' Quoted in *Switched On*, 19 August–5 October 2003, p. 19.

32. Lynn Barber, 'Top Fop', *Observer Life Magazine*, 14 September 1997, pp. 8, 10, 13.

33. Rowan Atkinson provided a much broader take on the 'Brit Twit' in *Johnny English* (2002).

34. Andrew Spicer, 'Sean Connery: Loosening His Bonds', in Bruce Babington (ed.), *British Stars and Stardom* (Manchester: Manchester University Press, 2001), pp. 218–30.

35. Quoted in Barbara Kantrowitz, '"I Don't See Enough Movies"', *Guardian*, 1 September 2003, p. 15.

36. See the interview with Tom Doyle, *Empire* no. 116 (February 1999), pp. 96–100.

37. Ian Nathan, 'To Infinity and Beyond', *Empire* no. 122 (August 1999), pp. 122–8.

38. Interview on the DVD version of *The Lord of the Rings: The Two Towers* (2003).

39. See, for instance, McGregor's National Film Theatre interview with Adrian Wootton, a transcript of which appeared in the *Guardian*, 23 October 2002.

40. Natural Nylon, founded in 1996, was the combined talents of the 'Brit-pack': McGregor, Jude Law, Sean Pertwee*, Sadie Frost, Jonny Lee Miller* and producer Damon Bryant. But the company is now in disarray; see 'Jude Law Drops Brit-Pack Production Company', *Guardian*, 9 January 2003.

Part IV A Dictionary of European Actors in Hollywood

Aims and Conventions

This dictionary section of the book provides two types of entries:

1. *Professional biographies* of individual European actors who have worked in English-language Hollywood cinema.
2. *National essays* that provide survey information about the broad trends behind nationally specific patterns of migration to Hollywood, including issues of recruitment, finance, politics, performance, representation and reception.

We have broadly divided the biographical entries on individual actors and their respective Hollywood careers into four categories according to the scale of their contribution to Hollywood cinema:

1. Actors who have had a substantial career in major mainstream Hollywood star-vehicle films as well as, normally, a European performance career or identity of significance.
2. Actors who have had a prominent presence in Hollywood through leading roles for a relatively short period – while, often, being a major star at home – *or* who have had a long career of either supporting roles or lead roles in middle-ranking Hollywood films.
3. Actors who have had a noticeable presence in Hollywood through lead roles for a very short period – while a major star or well-known actor at home – *or* who have had either some supporting roles in mainstream Hollywood productions or a presence in independent, marginal or minor Hollywood films.
4. Actors who have had relatively minor roles in their home country and in Hollywood (though they may have very long filmographies) or a very sporadic presence in Hollywood cinema.

Each biographical entry provides the following information:

- The stage name of the actor followed by their real name in brackets. If relevant, any significant variation in the way the actor's name was spelled during their Hollywood career has also been noted.
- The dates of birth and death of the actor.
- Details about the national origin of the actor.
- Relevant details about the actor's professional biography in Europe, including information about significant non-Hollywood films.
- A discussion of the contribution made by the actor to Hollywood cinema, taking into account, when necessary, issues of recruitment, finance, performance, representation and reception.
- The complete English-language Hollywood filmography of the actor up to the end of 2004 (when appropriate), including, where the information is available, various kinds of majority US-financed co-productions, 'runaway productions' and 'quota films' shot outside the USA either in Canada or Europe, taking in those financed by subsidiaries of the Hollywood majors.

Each entry observes the following conventions:

- In order to qualify as a Hollywood film, the majority of its finance must have been provided by an American company.
- The date of release, rather than the date of production or copyright, is included for all films.
- The filmographies include all identifiable uncredited performances and when there is a significant pattern to this, it is mentioned in the entry.

- The filmographies incorporate all the short films the individual actor appeared in and when there is a significant pattern to this, it is mentioned in the entry.
- Each European film mentioned presents the European-language film title first, followed by the English-language translation of the title, followed by the date of release: e.g. *Abwege/Crisis* (1928).
- The filmographies include all films featuring only the actor's voice: e.g. in the cases of animated features or voiceover narration. The following credit has been used: '*The Jungle Book* [voice]'.
- The filmographies include all serial films. The following credit has been used: '*The Return of Chandu* [serial]'.
- There is an internal system of cross-referencing within entries, where an asterisk at the end of an actor's name denotes a separate entry: for instance, 'as in the case of Charles Boyer★ . . .'. This has been used throughout the book, with the exception of the introduction (in order not to overload the text).
- Non-English-language multi-language version films have been excluded from the filmographies, but they have, when significant, been included in the main text of entry.
- Hollywood actors who were either born in Europe but did not have a prior performing career in Europe *or* who arrived in the USA at a very young age have been excluded from the book: e.g. Rudolph Valentino, Paul Muni, Edward G. Robinson, Claudette Colbert, Erich von Stroheim and Elizabeth Taylor.
- The book only lists the titles of Hollywood films consistent with existing main reference sources. Other variants have not been included.
- Other exclusions include: Canadian shorts and features, documentaries including those containing interview and archive material from previous Hollywood films and television films that were not given cinematic distribution.

A to Z of European Actors in Hollywood Cinema

ABRIL, Victoria (Victoria Mérida Rojas) (1959–)
Prolific, award-winning Spanish actress who is especially known for her numerous erotically charged and sexually ambiguous roles in films such as Vicente Aranda's *Cambio de sexo/Change of Sex* (1977) and Pedro Almodóvar's *Tacones lejanos/High Heels* (1991). A resident of France since 1982, Abril has maintained her strong standing in Spanish cinema while carving out an international career across a range of European productions. Her US career has been limited, perhaps due to the versatility and resistance to typecasting shown in her European performances. Apart from a role in José Luis Borau's US–Mexican border drama *On the Line*, which saw limited theatrical release in the USA, Abril has one major American film to her credit: Barry Levinson's less than successful shaggy dog story of Hollywood dreams and disappointments, *Jimmy Hollywood*. Abril was cast as Lorraine de la Peña, a wannabe actor's loving but level-headed girlfriend who harbours her own Hollywood dream of becoming the first woman hairdresser to the stars. The role complicated the Latina stereotype inevitably assigned to Spanish-language actresses, irrespective of national origin, by specifically acknowledging Abril's Spanish ethnicity. The character prepares and serves the signature national dishes of paella and Spanish omelette to Joe Pesci and Christian Slater. KV
FILMS: *On the Line* (1984); *Jimmy Hollywood* (1994).

ACKLAND, Joss (1928–)
Although a relative failure as a would-be romantic lead, Ackland worked steadily as an accomplished character actor in British theatre and television. The combination of a slightly disproportioned face, a pale, sweaty complexion and a deep velvety voice have latterly helped him carve out a prolific and lucrative sideline in villainous or unsympathetic Hollywood roles. JB

FILMS: *In Search of the Castaways* (1962); *The Happiness Cage* (1972); *S★P★Y★S*, *The Little Prince* (1974); *The Greek Tycoon*, *Who is Killing the Great Chefs of Europe?* (1978); *Saint Jack* (1979); *Rough Cut*, *The Apple* (1980); *The Sicilian* (1987); *Lethal Weapon 2* (1989); *The Hunt for Red October* (1990); *Bill and Ted's Bogus Journey* (1991); *Once Upon a Crime*, *The Mighty Ducks* (1992); *Nowhere to Run* (1993); *Mother's Boys*, *Miracle on 34th Street* (1994); *A Kid in King Arthur's Court* (1995); *Surviving Picasso*, *D3: The Mighty Ducks* (1996); *My Giant* (1998); *Passion of Mind* (2000); *The House on Turk Street*, *K-19: The Widowmaker* (2002); *I'll Be There* (2003).

ADJANI, Isabelle (1955–)
Adjani is internationally renowned for her portrayal of tragic heroines in films such as *L'Histoire d'Adèle H./The Story of Adele H* (1975), *Camille Claudel* (1988) and *La Reine Margot/Queen Margot* (1994). Despite many offers after her New York film critics' best actress award for *L'Histoire d'Adèle H.*, and given that she was voted 'one of the 50 most beautiful people in the world' by *People* magazine in 1990, her Hollywood career has been surprisingly sporadic and unsuccessful.

Her first American film, Walter Hill's *The Driver*, is a sparse thriller à la Jean-Pierre Melville that achieved cult status, although in this male genre her role is inevitably minor (some of her scenes were also allegedly cut). Adjani's blackmailing femme fatale role is not without glamour, but heavy make-up and a dubbed voice coarsen her image. Her second Hollywood venture, the comic epic *Ishtar*, in which she plays a 'sexy rebel' opposite Dustin Hoffman and Warren Beatty, was a legendary aesthetic and box-office disaster. Finally, the 1996 *Diabolique* attracted vitriolic comments for failing to match up to Clouzot's 1955 original *Les Diaboliques*. Adjani, who plays the victimised wife, goes **153** through the movie like a terrified spectre and is eclipsed by a flamboyant Sharon Stone. Maybe Adjani was unlucky in her choice of films. But resistance to working practices that she negatively contrasted to European ones may also have played a part: '[in Hollywood] the crew is really a proletariat subordinated to the star-system, a system which functions like a true dictatorship that nobody seems to contest'. GV

FILMS: *The Driver* (1978); *Ishtar* (1987); *Diabolique* (1996).

ADORÉE, Renée (Renée de la Fonte) (1898–1933)

Born in Lille into a circus family, the dark-haired Adorée trained in ballet and pantomime, acted and danced in plays and revues as a teenager. After touring with World War I troops in France, she moved to the USA in 1919, working on stage and then in film. Under contract with Fox from December 1921, she was lured away by L. B. Mayer to MGM in 1922. *The Big Parade* (1925), in which she played a 'typical Frenchwoman' in wartime France opposite John Gilbert, promoted her to stardom (and tripled her salary). For a couple of years, the sensual and 'effusive' beauty was a major Hollywood star, of whom gossip columnist Louella

154 Renée Adorée in her Los Angeles garden in the 1920s

Parsons said, 'Almost any picture in which she is cast has box-office value before it is made.' She appeared in a number of prominent pictures with Gilbert, and later Ramon Novarro. She also had the tempestuous private life to match her stardom. Twice married, she was briefly engaged to French émigré Gaston Glass★, and director Lynn Reynolds killed himself in 1927, allegedly over accusations by his wife of 'impropriety' with her. Adorée's career went into rapid decline, followed by her untimely death from tuberculosis at the age of thirty-five. GV

FILMS: *The Strongest* (1920); *Made in Heaven* (1921); *Honor First, Mixed Faces, A Self-Made Man, West of Chicago, Monte Cristo, Day Dreams* (1922); *The Eternal Struggle, The Six-Fifty* (1923); *The Bandolero, Defying the Law, A Man's Mate, Women Who Give* (1924); *Exchange of Wives, Excuse Me, Man and Maid, Parisian Nights, The Big Parade* (1925); *Blarney, La Bohème, The Flaming Forest, Tin Gods, The Exquisite Sinner, The Blackbird* (1926); *Back to God's Country, Heaven on Earth, Mr Wu, On Ze Boulevard, The Show* (1927); *A Certain Young Man, The Cossacks, Forbidden Hours, The Mating Call, The Michigan Kid, The Spieler, Tide of Empire, Show People* (1928); *The Pagan* (1929); *Redemption, Call of the Flesh* (1930).

AGUGLIA, Mimi (1884–1970)

Aguglia was a member of Giovanni Grasso's leading Southern Italian realist theatre company that toured Europe and the Americas during the 1910s and 1920s. She remained in the USA and formed a long-running Italian-American acting dynasty with her brother and sisters. During the 1930s, she worked on a number of Spanish-language version films shot in Hollywood. She also founded the Teatro Italiano in San Francisco. Aguglia went on to specialise in playing maternal roles in films set in the Italian-American community, such as Robert Siodmak's *Cry of the City* and Phil Karlson's *The Brothers Rico*. GM/AP

FILMS: *The Last Man on Earth* (1924); *The Lady Escapes* (1937); *The Adventures of Martin Eden* (1942); *The Outlaw* (1943); *Anchors Aweigh, A Bell for Adano* (1945); *The Time, the Place and the Girl* (1946); *Carnival in Costa Rica* (1947); *Captain from Castile, Cry of the City, Unconquered* (1948); *The Doctor and the Girl, That Midnight Kiss, We Were Strangers* (1949); *Black Hand, Deported, East Side, West Side, Right Cross, The Man Who Cheated Himself* (1950); *Cuban Fireball, Kim* (1951); *When in Rome* (1952); *The Rose Tattoo* (1955); *The Brothers Rico* (1957).

AGUTTER, Jenny (1952–)

Jenny Agutter developed a persona of a cool, yet sensual Englishness from her best-known roles in *The Railway Children* (1970) and *Walkabout* that was exploited in a series of leading parts, and then cameo roles, in Britain and the USA. MW

FILMS: *East of Sudan* (1964); *A Man Could Get Killed* (1966); *Star!* (1968); *Walkabout* (1970); *Logan's Run* (1976); *Equus* (1977); *An American Werewolf in London, Amy* (1981); *La donna giusta* (1982); *Amazon Women on the Moon, Dark Tower* (1987); *Child's Play 2, Darkman* (1990).

AHERNE, Brian (William Brian de Lacy Aherne) (1902–1986)

Aherne first appeared on the stage as a child, but only really took up his acting career in the mid-1920s in a number of British silent films. He had starring roles in prestige productions such as *Shooting Stars* and *Underground* (both 1928). The handsome star then crossed the Atlantic to appear on Broadway in *The Barretts of Wimpole Street*. While taking the production on tour, Aherne took time out to star opposite Marlene Dietrich★ in *The Song of Songs* and this precipitated his move to Hollywood. Aherne proved a reliable and appealing romantic lead. His frequent casting as the tweedy English gent perfectly suited the Hollywood ideal of the charming and sometimes villainous Englishman of the 1930s and 1940s. His status was given a boost by his Academy Award nomination for his performance as Emperor Maximilian von Habsburg opposite Bette Davis and Paul Muni in *Juarez* (1939). MW

FILMS: *The Song of Songs* (1933); *The Fountain, What Every Woman Knows* (1934); *I Live My Life* (1935); *Beloved Enemy, Sylvia Scarlett* (1936); *The Great Garrick* (1937); *Merrily We Live* (1938); *Captain Fury, Juarez* (1939); *Vigil in the Night, The Lady in Question, Hired Wife, My Son, My Son* (1940); *Smilin' Through, Skylark, The Man Who Lost Himself* (1941); *My Sister Eileen* (1942); *First Comes Courage, What a Woman!, A Night to Remember, Forever and a Day* (1943); *The Locket* (1946); *Smart Woman, Angel on the Amazon* (1948); *Titanic, I Confess* (1953); *A Bullet is Waiting, Prince Valiant* (1954); *The Swan* (1956); *The Best of Everything* (1959); *Susan Slade* (1961); *Rosie!* (1968).

AHO, Betty (Betty Alexandra Tuominen) (1897–unknown)

Finnish actress who moved to the USA after a 1923 theatrical tour. Aho signed to Paramount in 1926 and appeared in Josef von Sternberg's now lost thriller, *The Case of Lena Smith*. AP

FILM: *The Case of Lena Smith* (1929).

AIMÉE, Anouk (Françoise Sorya Dreyfus) (1932–)

Cosmopolitan French actress who also speaks fluent English. Aimée's first role of note was in *Les Amants de Vérone/TheLovers of Verona* in 1949 at the age of seventeen. She was offered a contract in Hollywood but wisely decided to wait until her European career had taken off. It was only in 1959 that she accepted a small part as Eva, a Hungarian freedom fighter, in Anatole Litvak's *The Journey*. Her multilingual European career included many roles in Italian, some in German and, of course, the majority in French in films such as *Lola* (1961) and *Un Homme et une femme/A Man and a Woman* (1966). It was the latter's international success that made the USA sit up and take notice of this sophisticated brunette. In 1969, she played similar leading parts in three American films. She was a jilted model in *Model Shop*, a beautiful model whom the male protagonist suspects is Rome's highest- paid prostitute in *The Appointment* and an ambiguous and evil seductress in *Justine*. Aimée was never taken with the USA and seemed more comfortable with more eclectic roles in Europe. She was married to Albert Finney★ between 1970 and 1978. Her last Hollywood film to date was Robert Altman's fashion world satire *Prêt-à-Porter*. VO

FILMS: *The Journey* (1959); *Model Shop, The Appointment, Justine* (1969); *Prêt-à-Porter* (1994).

ALBA, Maria (Maria Casajuana) (1910–1999)

Spanish actress who, after a few late silent features in Hollywood, specialised in Spanish-language multi-language versions such as *Los que danzan/Those Who Dance* (1930). Alba also played exotic foreigners like the Egyptian princess in the Boris Karloff★ serial *The Return of Chandu*. She left the USA in 1935, and subsequently made only sporadic appearances in Mexican and Brazilian films, before retiring from the screen. AM

FILMS: *Road House, Blindfold* (1928); *Joy Street* (1929); *Hell's Heroes* (1930); *Just a Gigolo, Goldie* (1931); *Mr Robinson Crusoe, Hypnotized, Almost Married* (1932); *Kiss of Araby* (1933); *The Return of Chandu, Flirting with Danger, Chandu on the Magic Isle* (1934); *West of the Pecos, Great God Gold* (1935).

ALBERGHETTI, Anna Maria (1936–)
Italian singer who was spotted by a Paramount talent scout while performing at Carnegie Hall and made her screen debut at fifteen. She played musical and dramatic roles for a decade, before retiring to concentrate on her singing and family. She made an unexpected return to the cinema in 2001. AM

FILMS: *The Medium, Here Comes the Groom* (1951); *The Stars are Singing* (1953); *The Last Command* (1955); *Duel at Apache Wells, Ten Thousand Bedrooms* (1957); *Cinderfella* (1960); *The Whole Shebang, Friends and Family* (2001).

ALBERNI, Luis (1887–1962)
Alberni left the Spanish stage for Broadway in 1921 and soon moved to Los Angeles, where he became a prolific character actor in Hollywood. He was short, slim and wide-eyed and was often cast as perplexed or excitable Europeans, especially Italians. He also appeared in a few Spanish-language Hollywood films such as *La Buenaventura* (1934). Alberni's most celebrated performances were opposite John Barrymore in *The Mad Genius* and *Svengali* (both 1931). EU

FILMS: *Little Italy* (1921); *The Man from Beyond* (1922); *The Bright Shawl, The Valley of Lost Souls* (1923); *The Santa Fe Trail* (1930); *Svengali, Side Show, The Mad Genius, Men in Her Life, Manhattan Parade, I Surrender Dear* (1931); *Cock of the Air, The Cohens and Kellys in Hollywood, Rule 'Em and Weep, The Woman in Room 13, Week-end Marriage, Crooner, A Parisian Romance, The Big Stampede, Guilty or Not Guilty, Hypnotized* (1932); *Artist's Muddles, Topaze, Child of Manhattan, Men Must Fight, The California Trail, When Ladies Meet, I Love That Man, The Man from Monterey, Goodbye Love, Above the Clouds, California Weather, The Sphinx* (1933); *Glamour, I Believed in You, La Buenaventura, One Night of Love, The Count of Monte Cristo, The Captain Hates the Sea, When Strangers Meet, Caravane* (1934); *The Gilded Lily, The Good Fairy, Roberta, Public Opinion, Let's Live Tonight, Goin' to Town, In Caliente, Love Me Forever, Manhattan Moon, The Gay Deception, Metropolitan, Bad Boy, Music is Magic* (1935); *Colleen, Ticket to Paradise, Anthony Adverse, Follow Your Heart, Hats Off, Dancing Pirate* (1936); *When You're in Love, Two Wise Maids, The King and the Chorus Girl, Sing and Be Happy, Easy Living, Madame X, Manhattan Merry-Go-Round, Under Suspicion, Hitting a New High, The Great Garrick* (1937); *I'll Give a Million, Love on Toast* (1938); *The Great Man Votes, Naughty but Nice, The Housekeeper's Daughter* (1939); *Enemy Agent, Scatterbrain, Public Deb No. 1* (1940); *That Hamilton Woman, Road to Zanzibar, San Antonio Rose, They Met in Bombay, World Premier, She Knew All the Answers, Obliging Young Lady, The Lady Eve, Babes on Broadway* (1941); *Mexican Spitfire's Elephant* (1942); *Two Weeks to Live, My Son, the Hero, Submarine Base, Here Comes Elmer, Harvest Melody, You're a Lucky Fellow, Mr Smith* (1943); *Machine Gun Mama, Men on Her Mind* (1944); *I Was a Criminal, A Bell for Adano* (1945); *In Fast Company, The Road to Hollywood, Hit the Hay* (1946); *Captain Carey, U.S.A.* (1950); *What Price Glory* (1952).

ALBERTINI, Luciano (1882–1945)
Italian actor whose performances combined intelligence with exceptional strength due to his training as a circus acrobat. Albertini was forced to emigrate during the 1920s by the crisis in the Italian film industry and was the protagonist of the now presumed lost Universal Pictures' serial *The Iron Man*. CBu

FILM: *The Iron Man* (1924).

ALCAÑIZ, Luana (Lucrecia Ana Ubeda Pubillones) (1904–1991)
Successful Spanish stage actress whose exotic, darkly attractive looks won her a 1930 contract with Fox to play a prominent role with Victor McLaglen★ in *A Devil with Women*. She went on to play leading or major roles in fourteen Spanish-language Hollywood films. EU

FILMS: *A Devil with Women* (1930); *Frontiers '49* (1939); *Doctor Zhivago* (1965).

ALLAN, Elizabeth (1908–1990)
Elegant English actress who moved to the USA in the early 1930s and became a contract player for MGM alongside her husband, Robert Montgomery. She returned to the UK in 1938 and was blacklisted in Hollywood by her studio after she sued them for replacing her in a lead role. MW

FILMS: *The Solitaire Man, No Marriage Ties, The Shadow, Looking Forward, Ace of Aces* (1933); *The Mystery of Mr X, Outcast Lady, Men in White* (1934); *A Tale of Two Cities, David Copperfield, Mark of the Vampire* (1935); *A Woman Rebels* (1936); *Camille, Slave Ship, The Soldier and the Lady* (1937); *Hollywood Goes to Town* (1938).

ALLGOOD, Sara (1883–1950)

Sara Allgood is largely remembered for playing the Irish mother on the American screen. Having taken memorable parts in the early Synge and O'Casey plays at Dublin's Abbey Theatre and appearing in several UK films, including Fox British's *The Londonderry Air*, she moved to Hollywood in 1940. She was the nurse in Robert Siodmak's *The Spiral Staircase*. RB

FILMS: *The Londonderry Air* (1938); *Dr Jekyll and Mr Hyde, Lydia, How Green Was My Valley* (1941); *Roxie Hart, This Above All, It Happened in Flatbush, The War against Mrs Hadley, Life Begins at Eight-Thirty* (1942); *Forever and A Day, City without Men* (1943); *The Lodger, Jane Eyre, Between Two Worlds, The Keys of the Kingdom* (1944); *The Strange Affair of Uncle Harry, Kitty* (1945); *The Spiral Staircase, Cluny Brown* (1946); *Mother Wore Tights, Mourning Becomes Electra, My Wild Irish Rose, Ivy, The Fabulous Dorseys* (1947); *The Man from Texas, One Touch of Venus, The Girl from Manhattan, The Accused* (1948); *Challenge to Lassie* (1949); *Cheaper by the Dozen, Sierra* (1950).

ANDERS, Rudolph (1895–1987)

German character actor (also credited as Robert O. Davis and Rudolph Amendt) who had a prolific American screen career, during which he often played German Nazis, spies and agents in such films as *Confessions of a Nazi Spy* and *To Be or Not to Be*. AP

FILMS: *When Strangers Marry* (1933); *The Fountain, Hell in the Heavens, Stamboul Quest* (1934); *Here's to Romance, I Live My Life, Rendezvous, Last of the Pagans* (1935); *Girl's Dormitory, The Golden Arrow, The Rest Cure* (1936); *Champagne Waltz, I Met Him in Paris, Thin Ice* (1937); *The Big Broadcast of 1938* (1938); *Confessions of a Nazi Spy, Escape to Paradise, Espionage Agent, The Mad Empress, Pack up Your Troubles* (1939); *Arise, My Love, Four Sons, Knute Rockne All American, The Man I Married, Meet the Wildcat, The Mortal Storm* (1940); *The Great Dictator, King of the Texas Rangers, A Dangerous Game, Down in San Diego, Mr Dynamite, Shining Vic-* tory, *Underground* (1941); *Berlin Correspondent, Billy the Kid's Smoking Guns, Desperate Journey, Spy Smasher, The Secret Code* [serial], *Eagle Squadron, The Great Impersonation, Junior Army, Nazi Agent, The Phantom Plainsman, The Pied Piper, Riders of the Northland, Sherlock Holmes and the Voice of Terror, To Be or Not to Be* (1942); *Assignment in Brittany, Chetniks, Sherlock Holmes and the Secret Weapon, The Strange Death of Adolf Hitler, They Got Me Covered, Tonight We Raid Calais, Watch on the Rhine* (1943); *The Hitler Gang, The Story of Dr Wassell* (1944); *Counter-Attack, Escape in the Desert* (1945); *Dangerous Millions, Her Sister's Secret, Under Nevada Skies* (1946); *The Beginning or the End* (1947); *Act of Violence* (1949); *Kill or Be Killed, No Way Out* (1950); *Target Unknown* (1951); *Actor's and Sin* (1952); *Phantom from Space, South Sea Woman, Captain Scarface* (1953); *Magnificent Obsession, King Richard and the Crusaders, Jungle Gents, A Star is Born, Superman in Scotland Yard, The Snow Creature* (1954); *She Demons, Frankenstein – 1970* (1958); *A Private's Affair* (1959); *On the Double* (1961); *The Pigeon that Took Rome* (1962); *The Prize* (1963); *36 Hours* (1965).

ANDERSON, Robert (1890–1963)

Danish comedian who played the comic-relief character of Monsieur Cuckoo in D. W. Griffith's World War I drama *Hearts of the World* (1918). Many critics felt he stole the film outright, but his only other noteworthy role was as the sadistic trader in W. S. Van Dyke's drama-travelogue *White Shadows in the South Seas* (1928). HJW

FILMS: *Intolerance* (1916); *Draft 258* (1917); *The Hun Within, Hearts of the World* (1918); *The Right to Happiness, The Heart of Humanity, Fires of Faith, Common Property, The Petal on the Current, Tempest Cody* (1919); *Below the Deadline, Under Sentence, Loose Lions, My Lady's Ankle, Once to Every Woman* (1920); *Uneasy Money, Dr Jim* (1921); *The Girl in His Room, Tillie, Up in the Air about Mary* (1922); *The Social Buccaneer, The Eternal Struggle, Slander the Woman* (1923); *The Lullaby* (1924); *The Beautiful Cheat, The Temptress* (1926); *The Wrong Mr Right* (1927); *Love Me and the World is Mine, White Shadows in the South Seas* (1928); *Clear the Decks* (1929); *Rasputin and the Empress* (1933); *Treasure Island, The Mighty Barnum* (1934); *It Could Happen to You* (1937).

ANDERSSON, Bibi (1935–)

As with Max von Sydow* and Ingrid Thulin*, Swedish actress Bibi Andersson's international career can be attrib- **157** uted to her collaboration with Ingmar Bergman. In the 1950s, she played the Madonna-like, travelling actress M(ar)ia in *Det sjunde inseglet/The Seventh Seal* (1957) and the pregnant, unmarried teenager in *Nära livet/Brink of Life/So Close to Life* (1958) for which she shared the Best Actress award at Cannes. In both films, she represented a certain girlish hope and positive femininity. After her tour de force performance in *Persona* (1966), Andersson received disappointing offers in Europe and the USA. She was the wife raped by Apaches in the Western *Duel at Diablo* and the German woman with a dark past in John Huston's thriller *The Kremlin Letter*. In *I Never Promised You a Rose Garden*, Andersson added her trademark underplayed realism to the role of Dr Fried, a vaguely Continental-accented psychiatrist. In the Swedish/US co-production *Beröringen/The Touch* (1971), perhaps her most demanding English-language role, she played a housewife torn between her family and her passion for a passing stranger (Elliot Gould). Here, directed again by Bergman, she was finally allowed to portray a warm, complex, deceiving and, at times, even funny woman. On the whole, it is this trait of normalcy that Hollywood has found most attractive, and Andersson could be best described as the European counterpart to the all-American girl next door. With her blonde, short hair and serious, open face, she has tended to remain – in her American films – wholesome, trustworthy and wise rather than a sexually enticing vamp. MK

FILMS: *Square of Violence* (1964); *Duel at Diablo* (1966); *The Kremlin Letter* (1970); *I Never Promised You a Rose Garden* (1977); *An Enemy of the People* (1978); *Quintet* (1979); *The Concorde – Airport '79, Exposed* (1983).

ANDOR, Paul (Wolfgang Zilzer) (1901–1991)

Born to German parents in the USA, but raised in Germany, Andor fled Germany in the late 1930s. Following an uncredited Hollywood debut in Ernst Lubitsch's *Bluebeard's Eighth Wife*, he was relegated to mainly minor Nazi roles in American anti-Nazi films. This included the brief but dramatic role of the man who is shot at the beginning of *Casablanca*. Andor married Lotte Palfi★ in 1943 and the couple settled in New York after the war and undertook further low-key stage and screen appearances. FG

FILMS: *Bluebeard's Eighth Wife, I'll Give a Million* (1938); *Confessions of a Nazi Spy, Hotel Imperial, Espionage Agent, Ninotchka, Hitler – Beast of Berlin, Television Spy, Everything*

Happens at Night (1939); *A Dispatch from Reuters, Three Faces West, Dr Ehrlich's Magic Bullet, Escape, Four Sons* (1940); *World Premiere, Underground, So Ends Our Night, Shining Victory* (1941); *Joan of Orzark, The Invisible Agent, The Lady has Plans, All through the Night, To Be or Not to Be, Casablanca* (1942); *Behind the Rising Sun, Hitler's Madman, Paris after Dark, Bomber's Moon, They Came to Blow up America, They Got Me Covered, Margin for Error, The Strange Death of Adolf Hitler, Appointment in Berlin, Behind the Rising Sun* (1943); *In Our Time, Enemy of Women, They Live in Fear* (1944); *Hotel Berlin, Counter-Attack* (1945); *Claudia: The Story of a Marriage, Walk East on Beacon!* (1952); *Singing in the Dark* (1956); *Mister Buddwing* (1965); *Union City* (1980); *Lovesick* (1983).

ANDRE, Gwili (Gurli Andresen) (1908–1959)

More ornamental than talented, Danish Gwili Andre became known as 'America's Most Beautiful Model' before embarking on a brief Hollywood career thanks to David O. Selznick. She proved wholly inadequate in her screen debut, however, and hardly lived up to Selznick's ambition of launching a 'new' Marlene Dietrich★. HJW

FILMS: *Roar of the Dragon, Secrets of the French Police* (1932); *No Other Woman* (1933); *Meet the Boyfriend, The Girl Said No* (1937); *A Woman's Face* (1941); *The Falcon's Brother* (1942).

ANDRESS, Ursula (1936–)

Swiss actress who made three Italian movies before her breakthrough role as the first Bond Girl, Honey Ryder, in the American financed, but British-made, *Dr No*. Her first appearance in the film, emerging from the ocean in a white bikini, earned her the title of 'the most beautiful woman in the world' and brought her to international attention. She was invited to Hollywood and made her US debut the following year in a spoof Western directed by Robert Aldrich that also co-starred Frank Sinatra and Dean Martin. She followed this with the Elvis Presley vehicle *Fun in Acapulco*, which reiterated the subtext of her role in the Bond film as just one more shapely love-interest in a line of women devoted to the male hero. Her subsequent European films similarly utilised the star's glamour and willingness to do nude scenes, but little else. TJ

FILMS: *Dr No* (1962); *4 for Texas, Fun in Acapulco* (1963); *What's New Pussycat, Once before I Die* (1965); *The Blue Max* (1966); *Casino Royale* (1967).

ANDREU, Gaby (Gabrielle Andreu) (1920–1972)

Considered a mere 'starlette' in France, this heady brunette made her screen debut in *Entrée des artistes/The Curtain Rises* (1938) and then went on to a successful European film career. She made a few American films in the 1950s after signing a contract with Warner Bros. in 1949 (where she was credited as Gaby André or Gabe André), while also pursuing a career in Italy. VO

FILMS: *Please Believe Me, Highway 301* (1950); *The Green Glove* (1952); *Pussycat, Pussycat, I Love You* (1970).

ANDREWS, Harry (Harry Fleetwood Andrews) (1911–1989)

British character actor most closely associated with 'salt of the earth' sergeant-major roles that embodied reliability and doggedness. In a 33-year film career, he worked sporadically in Hollywood films, mainly in supporting roles in period and historical dramas. Andrews also starred in numerous US-backed productions shot in Europe. MHu

FILMS: *The Red Beret* (1953); *The Black Knight* (1954); *Moby Dick, Helen of Troy, Alexander the Great* (1956); *Saint Joan* (1957); *I Accuse!* (1958); *The Devil's Disciple, Solomon and Sheba* (1959); *A Circle of Deception, In the Nick* (1960); *The Best of Enemies* (1961); *Barabbas, Lisa* (1962); *Nine Hours to Rama, 55 Days at Peking* (1963); *633 Squadron, The Truth about Spring* (1964); *The Hill, The Agony and the Ecstasy* (1965); *Modesty Blaise, The Deadly Affair* (1966); *The Night of the Generals, I'll Never Forget What's'isname* (1967); *Danger Route, The Charge of the Light Brigade, The Night They Raided Minksy's, The Sea Gull, A Dandy in Aspic* (1968); *Battle of Britain* (1969); *Wuthering Heights, Too Late the Hero, Country Dance* (1970); *Man of La Mancha, The Ruling Class* (1972); *The MacKintosh Man* (1973); *The Blue Bird, The Sky Riders* (1976); *Equus* (1977); *Superman, Crossed Swords* (1978).

ANDREWS, Julie (Julia Elizabeth Wells) (1935–)

In 1965, the year that Andrews first came to prominence among film audiences, David Shipman characterised her brand of Britishness as that of 'The All-Conquering Governess', and to a very large extent, despite the star's many efforts to the contrary, this 'jolly hockeysticks' type of Englishness remains the dominant connotation of her star image.

Julie Andrews was born on 14 October 1935 in Surrey, England. Her father was a schoolmaster and her mother a piano teacher with stage ambitions who secured a job in 1939 playing the piano in a music hall. There, she met and formed a professional and personal relationship with Ted Andrews, 'The Canadian Troubador'. Ted Andrews taught the young Julie to sing, and the couple sometimes incorporated her into their act. Aged seven, Julie auditioned for Lillian Stiles-Allen, a famous singing teacher, who was impressed but worried about working with her in case of damage to the child's vocal chords. A medical examination showed that Andrews had already developed an adult larynx, which accounted for her very wide vocal range of four octaves. Accepted as a pupil by Stiles-Allen, 'Little Julie Andrews' soon became a popular performer as she toured music halls around the country. At the age of twelve, she became exempt from the regulation barring children from appearing on the London stage, and was immediately cast in a revue called *Starlight Roof* (1947). She had also by this point performed on radio: her debut was in a duet with Ted Andrews on the BBC variety show, *Monday Night at Eight*. In 1950, she began appearing in the BBC radio show *Educating Archie*. Andrews continued performing under her 'Little' title well into her late teens, even though the maturation to adult roles and image was by then overdue.

At last, aged eighteen, she was signed to tour the USA for a year as Polly, the heroine in the American stage version of Sandy Wilson's *The Boy Friend*. Following this, Andrews entered discussions with Rodgers and Hammerstein for a role in their Broadway musical *Pipe Dream*, but Lerner and Loewe then offered her the chance to create the part of Eliza in *My Fair Lady*. She played Eliza for two years in New York and for eighteen months in London. Afterwards, she took the role of Guinevere in the duo's *Camelot*.

Despite success on the stage, film stardom eluded her at first. In December 1947, Andrews had taken a screen test for MGM, but they decided not to sign her. Later, when Warner Bros. were making the film version of *My Fair Lady*, Jack Warner also rejected her for Eliza, despite her success in creating the stage role. He wanted a bigger name. During the run of *Camelot*, though, Walt Disney saw Andrews and offered her the title role in *Mary Poppins*. Her performance as the calm, unflappable and somewhat antiseptic nanny won her an Academy Award and instantly **159**

160 Pier Angeli: Italian actress American style

crystallised a particular image of her in the public's eye. Her following success as Maria in *The Sound of Music* – another governess part – did nothing to dispel it. In between the two films, she had made *The Americanization of Emily*, but critics and audiences alike found her portrayal of a young woman's sexual skirmishes unconvincing. *Torn Curtain* fared similarly, despite the fact that it opened with the star in bed with Paul Newman.

Andrews' subsequent film roles attempted to extend her image, or guy it, as in the case of *Thoroughly Modern Millie*, but audiences seemed to prefer their musicals free of irony, and none of them matched the success of her earlier two performances as a governess. Since 1970, most of Andrews' films have been made in conjunction with her second husband, the director Blake Edwards; a first marriage to set designer Tony Walton lasted from 1959 to 1967. Andrews and Edwards worked together to reshape her star image to include more mature elements, and this explains the iconoclastic moment in *S.O.B.* where Andrews bares her breasts on camera. Besides the film roles, Andrews returned to the stage in a version of her film *Victor/Victoria* in 1985. She made a series of regular television specials during the 1980s. After an operation on her throat in 1997, the star lost her singing voice and subsequently sued the surgeons involved. She has now returned to straight, non-singing roles in films such as *The Princess Diaries* that popularly acknowledge her now somewhat regal persona. Andrews was made a Dame of the British Empire in 1999.

The dominant elements of Andrews' no-nonsense star persona are niceness, cleanliness, practicality and a lack of sensuality. Appropriately, she played Joyce Grenfell's★ daughter in *The Americanization of Emily*, where she exhibited the English actress's same bony, sexually awkward type of Englishness. The sex scene with Newman in *Torn Curtain* is uncomfortable for audiences exactly because of who Andrews is. Newman is reported as saying, 'there goes your Mary Poppins, Julie baby'. The sex, however, does not besmirch the nanny roles. In fact, the nanny roles sanitise the sex, with Andrews appearing too soapy clean to be sensuous. As perhaps with all stars, Andrews has found that her off-screen life is judged by the same standards as those set by her major roles, and life deviations from this antiseptic star image (such as her divorce) have been met with as much criticism as her divergent screen parts. Just as her parents were reluctant to let 'Little Julie Andrews' grow up into

a mature stage performer, her audiences have similarly seemed unwilling to countenance screen roles or 'real life' gossip that incorporate any element of adult sexuality. TJ

FILMS: *Mary Poppins, The Americanization of Emily* (1964); *The Sound of Music* (1965); *Torn Curtain, Hawaii* (1966); *Thoroughly Modern Millie* (1967); *Star!* (1968); *Darling Lili* (1970); *The Tamarind Seed* (1974); *10* (1979); *Little Miss Marker* (1980); *S.O.B.* (1981); *Victor/Victoria* (1982); *The Man Who Loved Women* (1983); *That's Life!, Duet for One* (1986); *Relative Values* (2000); *The Princess Diaries* (2001); *Shrek 2* [voice], *The Princess Diaries 2: Royal Engagement* (2004).

ANGEL, Heather (1909–1986)

English stage and screen actress whose promising talent drew her to the USA in the early 1930s, where she played several high-profile leads for Twentieth Century-Fox before Hollywood began to lose interest in the second half of the decade. Hereafter, Angel appeared mainly in B-pictures, which she supplemented by minor roles in films such as Hitchcock's *Lifeboat* (1944). MF

FILMS: *Pilgrimage, Charlie Chan's Greatest Case, Berkeley Square* (1933); *Romance in the Rain, Springtime for Henry, Orient Express, Murder in Trinidad* (1934); *The Mystery of Edwin Drood, The Informer, The Headline Woman, The Three Musketeers, The Perfect Gentleman, It Happened in New York* (1935); *The Bold Caballero, The Last of the Mohicans, Daniel Boone* (1936); *Bulldog Drummond Escapes, Western Gold, Portia on Trial, The Duke Comes Back* (1937); *Army Girl, Bulldog Drummond in Africa* (1938); *Arrest Bulldog Drummond, Bulldog Drummond's Secret Police, Bulldog Drummond's Bride, Undercover Doctor* (1939); *Kitty Foyle, Pride and Prejudice, Half a Sinner* (1940); *That Hamilton Woman, Singapore Woman, Suspicion, Shadows on the Stairs* (1941); *The Undying Monster, Time to Kill* (1942); *Cry Havoc* (1943); *Lifeboat, In the Meantime, Darling* (1944); *The Saxon Charm* (1948); *Alice in Wonderland* [voice] (1951); *Peter Pan* [voice] (1953); *The Premature Burial* (1962).

ANGELI, Pier (Anna Maria Pierangeli) (1932–1971)

Italian actress who had a promising but eventually tragic affair with Hollywood. Her delicate and beautiful, dark Mediterranean looks earned her numerous magazine covers in the 1950s and 1960s. After a triumphant screen test, she signed a seven-year contract with MGM and **161** starred in *Teresa*, for which she won a Golden Globe Award in 1952 for Most Promising Female Newcomer. She played various lead roles in the ten films she made with the studio and co-starred with the likes of Kirk Douglas, Paul Newman and Gene Kelly. More often than not, Angeli found herself playing the role of the innocent bride or the seemingly delicate but strong-willed faithful girl. Although she executed such roles to perfection, they also proved detrimental to her subsequent career. Angeli famously dated James Dean while he was starring in *East of Eden*, but her mother allegedly opposed the match on the grounds that Dean was not a Catholic. Following various illnesses and injuries and the break-up of her marriage to the actor-singer Vic Damone, Angeli returned to Europe in 1960. She made a brief comeback in Hollywood productions and co-productions in the late 1960s. She died of a barbiturate overdose in her Beverly Hills home. She was only thirty-nine years old. CS

FILMS: *The Light Touch, Teresa* (1951); *The Devil Makes Three, The Million Dollar Nickel* (1952); *The Story of Three Loves, Sombrero* (1953); *The Flame and the Flesh, The Silver Chalice* (1954); *Port Afrique, Meet Me in Las Vegas, Somebody up There Likes Me* (1956); *The Vintage* (1957); *Merry Andrew* (1958); *Sodom and Gomorrah* (1962); *Battle of the Bulge* (1965); *Octaman* (1971).

ANNABELLA (Suzanne Charpentier) (1907–1996)
Suzanne Charpentier was named Annabella by Abel Gance after a poem by the American writer Edgar Allan Poe. Her international career embodied this dialectic between the Old and the New World. One of France's most successful female film stars of the 1930s, she had made her name as the delicate and sentimental female star of two of René Clair's early sound features, but she also appeared in French multi-language film productions made in Hungary, Austria and Germany. Annabella also starred with Charles Boyer★ in the French-language version of *Caravan, Caravane* (Erik Charrel), shot in Hollywood in 1934.

Following her English-language work opposite Henry Fonda in the early British Technicolor film *Wings of the Morning* (1937), and her subsequent contact with producer Robert Kane, Annabella was offered a contract with Twentieth Century-Fox in the USA. Once in Los Angeles, Annabella was personally supervised by Darryl F. Zanuck and was groomed as the studio's leading face of Continen-

Annabella at home in Los Angeles

tal glamour and sophistication. Despite initially attracting negative comment for the awkwardness of her foreign accent, she was promoted in the William Powell comedy vehicle *The Baroness and the Butler* as a French fashion icon. 'Simplicity is the keynote of Annabella's chic', noted the pre-prepared press material. Simplicity in American terms evidently connoted a different mode of European-ness. At no point in the star's subsequent roles was there a reprise of the humble *midinette* type seen in her French screen persona. Instead, in the high-budget historical spectacular *Suez*, she was the boyish partner of Ferdinand de Lesseps (Tyrone Power), and in MGM's *Bridal Suite*, she was the classy, but mistaken, bride in a society marital comedy set in a luxury Swiss ski resort. Both films were relative failures. She had made *Bridal Suite* for MGM, as her clandestine affair with Power, which led to divorce with her husband Jean Murat★, had allegedly so incurred Zanuck's wrath that she was apparently placed on a blacklist. This split reveals the degree of paternalistic patronage that a non-native female star, in particular, had to live with in the studio system. From then on, Annabella's film career waned. She did, nonetheless, become an American citizen and she was a sterling figure in morale-boosting events across the USA during the war years. In 1943, she returned to the screen in two propaganda features, and a year after World War II, she made her last American film appearance as a French Resistance worker in *13 Rue Madeleine*. AP

FILMS: *The Baroness and the Butler, Suez* (1938); *Bridal Suite* (1939); *Tonight We Raid Calais, Bomber's Moon* (1943); *13 Rue Madeleine* (1946).

ANNIS, Francesca (1944–)

Former child actress and established star of British stage, television and film who has made occasional Hollywood appearances that include work with fellow juvenile starlet Pamela Franklin*. MF

FILMS: *Cleopatra* (1963); *Murder Most Foul, Flipper's New Adventure, The Eyes of Annie Jones* (1964); *The Walking Stick, Sky Pirate* (1970); *Dune* (1984); *Under the Cherry Moon* (1986); *Onegin* (1999).

ANWAR, Gabrielle (1970–)

English actress whose Hollywood profile was marked by a series of significant parts in the early 1990s in films such as *Scent of a Woman*. Subsequent roles suggest the likelihood of an uneven career history. MF

FILMS: *Manifesto* (1988); *Wild Hearts Can't Be Broken, If Looks Could Kill* (1991); *Scent of a Woman* (1992); *Body Snatchers, The Three Musketeers, For Love or Money* (1993); *Things to Do in Denver When You're Dead* (1995); *The Grave* (1996); *Sub Down, Whitechapel, Nevada* (1997); *Kimberley, The Guilty* (1999); *If You Only Knew, North Beach, Without Malice* (2000); *Flying Virus* (2001); *Save it for Later, Beach Movie* (2003).

ANYS, Georgette (Georgette Dubois) (1909–1993)

Plump French actress of the 1950s and 1960s who specialised in supporting working-class roles in films such as *La Traversée de Paris/Four Bags Full* (1956). She also had a respectable career in the USA, where she played similar parts. Given her lack of prior knowledge of English, her contract with Paramount stipulated daily English lessons and she was assisted by an interpreter on the set. VO

FILMS: *Little Boy Lost* (1953); *To Catch a Thief* (1955); *The Vintage* (1957); *Fanny* (1961); *Bon Voyage!, Jessica* (1962); *Love is a Ball* (1963); *Moment to Moment* (1965); *Cheech & Chong's The Corsican Brothers* (1984).

ARCO, Louis V. (Lutz Altschul) (1899–1975)

Austrian-Jewish Berlin stage regular who fled to Switzerland in 1933, and to Hollywood when war broke out in 1939. Adopting the pseudonym Louis V. (for 'Victor') Arco, he received only bit parts playing enemy officers in anti-Nazi pictures, although his non-speaking refugee in *Casablanca* (1942) constituted a fleeting exception. Arco

returned to Germany and his real name after the war, and appeared briefly in *Question 7* (1961), an American co-production shot in Berlin. RJK

FILMS: *Nurse Edith Cavell, Nick Carter, Master Detective* (1939); *Dr Ehrlich's Magic Bullet* (1940); *Underground* (1941); *All through the Night, Pacific Rendezvous, Berlin Correspondent, Desperate Journey, Casablanca* (1942); *Adventures of the Flying Cadets* [serial], *Chetniks – The Fighting Guerrillas, The Moon is Down, This Land is Mine, Edge of Darkness, Hangmen Also Die, Mission to Moscow, Action in the North Atlantic, Hitler's Madman, Bomber's Moon, Hostages, The Strange Death of Adolf Hitler, Appointment in Berlin, Gangway for Tomorrow, The Cross of Lorraine, The Song of Bernadette* (1943); *Address Unknown, The Hitler Gang, The Story of Dr Wassell, The Black Parachute, Secrets of Scotland Yard, Wilson, The Big Noise* (1944); *Son of Lassie, Counter-Attack* (1945); *Question 7* (1961).

ARLISS, George (George Augustus Andrews) (1868–1946)

George Arliss, Britain's first Academy Award winner, first appeared on the London stage in the 1880s, though he achieved much of his theatrical fame in exile in the USA. He first toured there in 1903 and remained permanently after 1905. As was customary for stage players of a certain eminence, he transferred a few of his most famous roles, such as *Disraeli*, to the silent screen in the early 1920s. This might have been the end of the matter had not Warner Bros. decided to make a new sound biopic of *Disraeli* in 1929. They logically turned to the actor most associated with the part in American popular culture, and after the film's enormous success, Arliss, at the age of sixty-one, won an Academy Award, an exceptional $10,000 a week salary and a secure status as one of the biggest stars of early sound cinema. Henceforth uniquely billed as 'Mr George Arliss' on screen, he capitalised on this abrupt good fortune with a succession of similar biographical portraits of great men of history, along with reworkings of his some of his favourite old stage melodramas. Unusually for a theatrical trouper of his generation, Arliss seems to have been genuinely fascinated by the medium of cinema and profoundly grateful for the new lease of life it gave his career. He devoted an entire volume of memoirs to the subject of his film experiences in 1940. Several British critics poked fun at American producers and audiences for lionising an actor they characterised as having been a relative nobody among the **163** glitterati of the West End, but Gainsborough Studios had no hesitation in breaking their salary scale to entice Arliss back to Britain for a series of films in 1935. JB

FILMS: *The Devil, Disraeli* (1921); *The Ruling Passion, The Man Who Played God* (1922); *The Green Goddess* (1923); *Twenty Dollars a Week* (1924); *Disraeli* (1929); *The Green Goddess, Old English* (1930); *The Millionaire, Alexander Hamilton* (1931); *The Man Who Played God, A Successful Calamity* (1932); *The King's Vacation, The Working Man, Voltaire* (1933); *The House of Rothschild, The Last Gentleman* (1934); *Cardinal Richelieu* (1935).

ARNA, Lissy (Elisabeth Arndt) (1904–1964)

Seen as an exotic beauty in German films of the 1920s, Arna followed Wilhelm Dieterle to Hollywood in 1930, where she made mainly German-speaking versions of American features. She returned to Germany the same year, but her star charisma did not survive the transition to sound. After 1931, she only played minor European screen roles while continuing her stage career. FG

FILM: *Beyond Victory* (1931).

ARNO, Sig (Siegfried Aron) (1895–1975)

Immensely popular German-Jewish character actor who, after fleeing Nazi Germany, arrived in Hollywood in 1939. Despite heavy promotion, he received only bit parts, often as mid-European waiters and doctors. They were frequently unbilled. Arno remained in California after the war – he stood out briefly as the parochial Louisiana mayor in the Mario Lanza vehicle *The Toast of New Orleans* – but undertook regular stage tours of Germany, where he received a lifetime achievement award in 1966. RJK

FILMS: *The Hunchback of Notre Dame, The Star Maker, Bridal Suite* (1939); *The Mummy's Hand, Diamond Frontier, The Great Dictator, This Thing Called Love, A Little Bit of Heaven* (1940); *Gambling Daughters, Dark Streets of Cairo, Raiders of the Desert, New Wine, Sing for Your Supper, Hellzapoppin, Two Latins from Manhattan, It Started with Eve, They Dare Not Love, The Chocolate Soldier* (1941); *I Married an Angel, Pardon My Sarong, Tales of Manhattan, The Mummy's Tomb* [in footage from *The Mummy's Hand* (1940)], *Two Yanks in Trinidad, The Palm Beach Story, Jukebox Jenny, The Devil with Hitler* (1942); *Let's Have Fun, Taxi, Mister, Du Barry was a Lady, Larceny with Music, Thousands Cheer, The Crystal Ball, Passport to Suez, His Butler's Sister, Over My Dead Body* (1943); *Standing Room Only, Up in Arms, Showboat Serenade, Song of the Open Road, The Great Moment, And the Angels Sing* (1944); *A Song to Remember, Bring on the Girls, I Was a Criminal, Roughly Speaking* (1945); *One More Tomorrow* (1946); *The Great Lover, Two Knights from Brooklyn* [in footage from *Taxi, Mister* (1943)], *Holiday in Havana* (1949); *Nancy Goes to Rio, Duchess of Idaho, The Toast of New Orleans* (1950); *On Moonlight Bay* (1951); *Diplomatic Courier* (1952); *The Great Diamond Robbery, Fast Company* (1953).

ARTHUR, George K. (Arthur George Brest) (1899–1985)

Upon seeing Arthur's debut film performance in the British film *Kipps* (1921), Charlie Chaplin★ predicted a glittering international career for the dapper young light comedian. Arthur travelled to the USA in December 1922 – making the crossing with Ivor Novello★. He gained full US citizenship shortly thereafter and enjoyed considerable success for the remainder of the silent era. JB

FILMS: *Madness of Youth, Paddy the Next Best Thing, Hollywood, The Cause of All the Trouble* (1923); *Flames of Desire* (1924); *The Salvation Hunters, Lady of the Night, Her Sister from Paris, Pretty Ladies, Sun-Up, Lights of Old Broadway*

G. K. Arthur, successful light comedian of the silent era

(1925); *Irene, Exquisite Sinner, Kiki, The Boob, Sunny Side Up, The Boy Friend, The Waning Sex, Almost a Lady, Bardelys the Magnificent, When the Wife's Away* (1926); *Rookies, Lovers?, Tillie the Toiler, The Gingham Girl, The Student Prince in Old Heidelberg, Spring Fever* (1927); *Baby Mine, Wickedness Preferred, Circus Rookies, Detectives, Show People, Brotherly Love* (1928); *All at Sea, China Bound, The Last of Mrs Cheyney, The Hollywood Revue of 1929* (1929); *Chasing Rainbows, The Rounder* (1930); *Where is the Lady?* (1932); *Oliver Twist, Looking Forward, Blind Adventure, Pleasure Cruise* (1933); *Riptide, Stand up and Cheer!* (1934); *Vanessa: Her Love Story* (1935).

ASLAN, Grégoire (Krikor Aslanian) (1908–1982)

Armenian actor born in Switzerland (or Istanbul). Aslan arrived in Paris at a young age. After a successful career in comic supporting roles in France, he appeared in a variety of Hollywood films, mainly as a nondescript 'foreigner'. TH
FILMS: *Act of Love* (1954); *Joe Macbeth* (1955); *The Roots of Heaven* (1958); *Our Man in Havana, Killers of Kilimanjaro* (1959); *The Devil at 4 O'Clock, King of Kings* (1961); *The Happy Thieves* (1962); *Cleopatra, Charade* [voice] (1963); *Paris – When it Sizzles* (1964); *The Yellow Rolls Royce, Moment to Moment* (1965); *Our Man in Marrakesh, A Man Could Get Killed, Lost Command* (1966); *A Flea in her Ear* (1968); *You Can't Win 'Em All* (1970); *The Girl from Petrovka* (1974).

ASTHER, Nils (1897–1981)

Danish stage actor who made his film debut in Sweden in 1916 and continued to work in Denmark and Germany before going to the USA in 1927. Asther often played handsome young men, while he really longed to play character roles, something he succeeded in doing with the part of the Chinese warlord in *The Bitter Tea of General Yen*. He was also the Javanese nobleman alongside Greta Garbo★ in *Wild Orchids*. The obvious comparison here is with the Swedish-American actor Warner Oland, who became famous for his many orientalist 'Chinese' characterisations. Both Asther and Oland represented a kind of Northern European exoticism that paradoxically became easily transformed into androgynous (Asther) or gentle (Oland) 'Asian' identities.

Asther went to the UK in the 1930s, but returned to Hollywood with the outbreak of World War II. During this time, both his professional and private life were troubled with rumours of homosexuality. During the 1950s, he turned to television and even tried to produce industrial films. He wrote plays and scripts, but without any success. In the early 1960s, Asther returned to Europe to make several screen appearances in Sweden and Denmark before his retirement in 1963. MBj
FILMS: *Topsy and Eva, Sorrell and Son* (1927); *The Blue Danube, Laugh, Clown, Laugh, The Cossacks, Loves of an Actress, The Cardboard Lover, Our Dancing Daughters, Dream of Love* (1928); *Wild Orchids, The Single Standard, The Hollywood Revue of 1929* (1929); *The King of Jazz, The Sea Bat* (1930); *But the Flesh is Weak, Letty Lynton, Washington Masquerade* (1932); *The Bitter Tea of General Yen, Storm at Daybreak, The Right to Romance, If I were Free, By Candlelight* (1933); *Madame Spy, Crime Doctor, The Love Captive, Love Time* (1934); *The Man Who Lost Himself, Forced Landing, Dr Kildare's Wedding Day, Flying Blind, The Night of January 16th* (1941); *The Night before the Divorce, Sweater Girl, Night Monster* (1942); *Submarine Alert, Mystery Broadcast* (1943); *The Hour before the Dawn, Alaska, The Man in Half Moon Street, Bluebeard* (1944); *Son of Lassie, Jealousy, Love, Honour and Goodbye* (1945); *The Feathered Serpent* (1949); *Samson and Delilah* (1950).

ATTENBOROUGH, Richard (1923–)

Richard Attenborough is best known today as a director, producer and leading figure and spokesman of the British film industry, but he has also appeared as an actor in over sixty films. He made his British film debut in 1942 in Noel Coward and David Lean's *In Which We Serve*. His performance as the nervous young sailor who leaves his post under fire set the tone for the sort of gauche juvenile roles that were to dominate his early career. Attenborough's break in a leading role came with the part of the vicious, small-town gangster Pinkie Brown in *Brighton Rock* (1947), and he subsequently appeared in various leading and supporting roles in British films of the 1950s and 1960s. Several of the actor's American films made during the 1960s further demonstrated his ability to blend an apparent confidence and authority with an underlying fragility of character. He made a successful transition to directing in 1969 with *Oh! What a Lovely War* and achieved his greatest success and a Best Director Academy Award for *Gandhi* (1982). Attenborough has continued to combine directing with acting. In the 1990s, he appeared most often in kindly, authorita-   **165** tive roles such as those in *Jurassic Park* and *Miracle on 34th Street*, where his voice and bearing epitomise an avuncular kind of Englishness. He was knighted in 1976 and received a life peerage in 1994. MHu

FILMS: *The Dock Brief* (1962); *The Great Escape* (1963); *Guns at Batasi* (1964); *The Flight of the Phoenix* (1965); *The Sand Pebbles* (1966); *Doctor Dolittle* (1967); *Only When I Larf, The Bliss of Mrs Blossom* (1968); *The Magic Christian* (1969); *10 Rillington Place* (1971); *Rosebud* (1975); *A Bridge Too Far* (1977); *Jurassic Park* (1993); *Miracle on 34th Street* (1994); *Jurassic Park – The Lost World* (1997).

ATWILL, Lionel (1885–1946)

Few stage and screen careers shared by a single actor have been quite so markedly different as those of Lionel Atwill. When Atwill arrived on Broadway in 1915 he was already a distinguished leading man on the London West End stage and he went on to headline many prestigious New York stage productions alongside actresses of the calibre of Alla Nazimova★ and Helen Hayes. Like many revered theatrical stars of the time, he made a few silent films in New York in the late 1910s and early 1920s, but his Hollywood career did not properly begin until the sound era. In 1932, Atwill went to California to make a film adaptation of his latest stage success, the courtroom drama *Silent Witness*. He subsequently appeared in the eponymous leading role of the Warners horror movie *Dr X* and quickly became a devotee of the medium and the genre, playing a long succession of charmingly urbane yet pathologically deranged mad scientists over the next fifteen years. Despite thus laying down of a lucrative typecasting blueprint for moonlighting British stage actors, Atwill was shunned socially by the British émigré colony in Hollywood. This may have had something to do with his casual abandonment of the stage – Atwill proclaimed in 1932 that 'I am one of those few stage actors who really like the films, and admit it!' – but it was probably more down to the disreputable publicity he attracted. Long-standing rumours of seasonal wild orgies at his Pacific Palisades mansion became a matter of public record in a series of much-publicised trials in the early 1940s, at which Atwill was charged with possession of illicit pornography and contributing to the delinquency of a minor. JB

FILMS: *Eve's Daughter, For Sale* (1918); *The Marriage Price* (1919); *The Eternal Mother* (1920); *The Highest Bidder* (1921); *Silent Witness, Dr X* (1932); *The Vampire Bat, The Secret of Madame Blanche, The Mystery of the Wax Museum, Murders in the Zoo, The Sphinx, The Song of Songs, Secret of the Blue Room, The Solitaire Man* (1933); *Nana, Beggars in Ermine, Stamboul Quest, One More River, The Age of Innocence, The Firebird, The Man Who Reclaimed His Head* (1934); *The Devil is a Woman, Mark of the Vampire, The Murder Man, Rendezvous, Captain Blood* (1935); *Lady of Secrets, Till We Meet Again, Absolute Quiet, The High Command* (1936); *The Road Back, The Last Train from Madrid, Lancer Spy, The Wrong Road, The Great Garrick* (1937); *Three Comrades, The Great Waltz* (1938); *Son of Frankenstein, The Three Musketeers, The Hound of the Baskervilles, The Gorilla, The Sun Never Sets, Mr Moto Takes a Vacation, The Secret of Dr Kildare, Balalaika* (1939); *The Mad Empress, Charlie Chan in Panama, Johnny Apollo, Girl in 313, Charlie Chan's Murder Cruise, The Great Profile, Boom Town* (1940); *Man Made Monster* (1941); *The Mad Doctor of Market Street, To Be or Not to Be, The Strange Case of Dr Rx, Junior G-Men of the Air, Pardon My Sarong, Cairo, Night Monster, The Ghost of Frankenstein, Secret Weapon* (1942); *Frankenstein Meets the Wolf Man* (1943); *Captain America, Lady in the Death House, Raiders of Ghost City, Secrets of Scotland Yard, House of Frankenstein* (1944); *Fog Island, Crime Inc., House of Dracula* (1945); *Lost City of the Jungle, Genius at Work* (1946).

AUBRY, Cécile (Anne-Marie-José Bénard) (1928–)

Youthful, blonde French actress who was recruited by Fox's Darryl F. Zanuck following her success in H. G. Clouzot's *Manon* (1949) as an amoral, pleasure-seeking woman escaping retribution at the Liberation. Her one American production was a historical adventure film with Orson Welles, Jack Hawkins★ and Tyrone Power. SL

FILM: *The Black Rose* (1950).

AUDRAN, Stéphane (Colette Suzanne Dacheville) (1932–)

French actress, renowned for her work with Claude Chabrol, whose distinctively feminine and glamorous appearance contrasts with a powerful, almost masculine voice. Audran has played various European characters (for instance, she was the Russian Anna Kemidov in *The Black Bird*, the 1975 comic sequel to the 1941 *The Maltese Falcon*) in the course of her small US filmography, which in no way matches her long and distinguished French and European career. SL/AP

FILMS: *The Black Bird* (1975); *The Big Red One* (1980); *Sons* (1989); *Maximum Risk* (1996); *Madeline* (1998).

AUER, Mischa (Mikhail Unkovsky) (1905–1967)

Russian actor whose distinctive accent led to a long-running Hollywood career either playing Russian noblemen in films such as *You Can't Take it with You* (1938) or Arabian or Mexican types in films like *The Gay Desperado* (1936). Auer was brought to the USA by his grandfather, the famous violinist Leopold Auer. After working as a film extra, his career flourished with the arrival of sound and by 1939, he had signed a seven-year contract with Universal on a salary of $15 an hour. Auer returned to Europe in the late 1940s to work mainly in Italian and French cinema. RY

FILMS: *Something Always Happens* (1928); *Marquis Preferred, The Studio Murder Mystery, The Mighty* (1929); *Guilty?, The Benson Murder Case, Paramount on Parade, Inside the Lines, Shooting Straight, Just Imagine* (1930); *The Royal Bed, No Limit, Command Performance, Women of All Nations, Always Goodbye, King of the Wild, Drums of Jeopardy, The Yellow Ticket, Working Girls, Women Love Once, The Unholy Garden, Mata Hari, The Lady from Nowhere, Delicious* (1931); *The Monster Walks, Murder at Dawn, The Midnight Patrol, Sinister Hands, Arsène Lupin, The Last of the Mohicans, The Western Code, Scarlet Dawn, Call Her Savage, The Unwritten Law, Rasputin and the Empress, The Intruder, No Greater Love, Beauty Parlor, The Sign of the Cross, Drifting* (1932); *Clear All Wires!, The Intruder, Gabriel over the White House, Corruption, Storm at Daybreak, Tarzan the Fearless, After Tonight, Cradle Song, Sucker Money, The Infernal Machine, Girl without a Room, The Flaming Signal, Dangerously Yours, I Loved You Wednesday* (1933); *Moulin Rouge* [scenes deleted], *The Crosby Case, Wharf Angel, A Woman Condemned, Viva Villa!, The Trumpet Blows, Change of Heart, Stamboul Quest, Beyond the Law, Bulldog Drummond Strikes Back, Student Tour, My Grandfather's Clock* (1934); *Biography of a Bachelor Girl, The Lives of a Bengal Lancer, The Adventures of Rex and Rinty, Clive of India, I Dream Too Much, We're Only Human, Mystery Woman, Murder in the Fleet, The Crusades, Condemned to Live, Anna Karenina* (1935); *My Man Godfrey, The Gay Desperado, Winterset, Tough Guy, Three Smart Girls, That Girl from Paris, Sons o' Guns, The Princess Comes Across, One Rainy Afternoon, The House of a Thousand Candles, Here Comes Trouble* (1936); *Vogues of 1938, Top of the Town, Pick a Star, Marry the Girl, The Merry-Go-Round of 1938, We Have Our Moments, Prescription for Romance, One Hundred Men and a Girl, It's All Yours* (1937); *The Rage of Paris, You Can't Take it with You, Little Tough Guys in Society, Sweethearts, Service de Luxe* (1938); *East Side of Heaven, Unexpected Father, Destry Rides Again* (1939); *Alias the Deacon, Seven Sinners, Trail of the Vigilantes, Spring Parade, Sandy is a Lady, Public Deb No. 1, Margie* (1940); *The Flame of New Orleans, Sing Another Chorus, Moonlight in Hawaii, Hold That Ghost, Helzapoppin, Don't Get Personal, Cracked Nuts* (1941); *Twin Beds* (1942); *Around the World, Dr Terror's House of Horrors* (1943); *Lady in the Dark, Up in Mabel's Room* (1944); *And Then There Were None, A Royal Scandal, Brewster's Millions* (1945); *She Wrote the Book, Sentimental Journey* (1946); *For You I Die* (1947); *Sofia* (1948); *Mr Arkadin* (1955); *The Christmas that Almost Wasn't* (1966).

AUGER, Claudine (Claudine Oger) (1942–)

Beautiful French actress who won the Miss France contest in 1958. Her most famous role in an English-language film was as Domino Derval, the 'James Bond girl' in the British co-produced *Thunderball* in 1965. Otherwise, her English-speaking work did not amount to much, but she pursued an extensive career in European exploitation films and television dramas. VO

FILMS: *In the French Style* (1963); *Thunderball* (1965); *The Eiger Sanction* [scenes deleted] (1975).

AUMONT, Jean-Pierre (Jean-Pierre Salomons) (1909–2001)

Although never a major star like Charles Boyer★, the French actor Jean-Pierre Aumont had a long and fairly successful career in Hollywood. Aumont combined stage appearances with minor parts on screen before getting the lead as the athletic swimming instructor in Marc Allégret's *Lac aux dames/Ladies Lake* (1934), co-starring Simone Simon★, and becoming an overnight sensation. The handsome young heart-throb became France's juvenile lead par excellence, appearing in films by Maurice Tourneur, Julien Duvivier and Marcel Carné.

When war broke out, Aumont's Jewish origins forced him to seek refuge and he went to Hollywood with his brother, the director François Villiers, in 1942. MGM, immediately interested in the tall, svelte, blond, blue-eyed actor, signed him for seven years. Desperate to play an active part in the war effort, Aumont only accepted two propaganda films, *Assignment in Brittany* and *The Cross of Lorraine* (the latter alongside Gene Kelly), before joining the **167**

Jean-Pierre Aumont, French heart-throb in Hollywood

Free French forces in 1943. Despite having just married his second wife Maria Montez, the Dominican 'Queen of Technicolor', with Jeanine Crispin★ and Boyer as witnesses, Aumont left for North Africa. His bravery and several wounds sustained during the campaign for the liberation of France won him a Croix de Guerre and the Légion d'honneur.

Aumont returned to his wife and home in Beverly Hills at the end of the war, and resumed his career on stage and screen in a variety of romantic lead roles that showcased his European charm and elegance. Throughout the early years of his Hollywood career, Aumont's private life was a regular feature in gossip columns, which linked him romantically to Grace Kelly, Hedy Lamarr★, Joan Crawford and Vivien Leigh★. The studios cast Aumont opposite Ginger Rogers, Yvonne de Carlo, Leslie Caron★ and Paulette Goddard, and cashed in on the Aumont–Montez couple in *Siren of Atlantis*. The Aumonts had a daughter in 1946, the actress Tina Aumont, and they divided their time between France and the USA until Montez's untimely death in 1953. After a two-year break, the ageing yet stylish actor pursued a long and highly diversified international career on screen, stage and television. Aumont married his third wife, Italian actress

Marisa Pavan★, twin sister of actress Pier Angeli★, in 1956. Also a writer and playwright, he was awarded a prize by the Académie Française in 1991 and an honorary César in 1992. His last two small parts in Hollywood movies in the mid-1990s show both his durable enthusiasm and respect from the profession. CH

FILMS: *Assignment in Brittany, The Cross of Lorraine* (1943); *Heartbeat* (1946); *Song of Scheherazade* (1947); *Siren of Atlantis* (1948); *Lili* (1953); *Charge of the Lancers* (1954); *Hilda Crane* (1956); *The Seventh Sin* (1957); *John Paul Jones* (1959); *The Enemy General* (1960); *The Devil at 4 O'Clock* (1961); *Castle Keep* (1969); *La Nuit américaine* (1973); *Mahogany, The Happy Hooker* (1975); *Something Short of Paradise* (1979); *Jefferson in Paris* (1995); *The Proprietor* (1996).

AUSTRIA

The history of Austrian emigration, like that of Austrian cinema in general, has most frequently been subsumed within German film history. Yet Austria represents both a crucial station in European cinema (e)migration and the source – through its émigrés – of an enduring paradigm for representing 'Austrianness' in Hollywood and other extra-territorial cinemas. It was in 1919, following the overthrow of the Béla Kun regime in Hungary, that Austria – and in particular Vienna – first assumed the mantle of a haven for fleeing cinema refugees, with figures including director Sándor (later Alexander) Korda and his star-actress wife Antónia Ferkas (Maria Korda) now adding a series of D. W. Griffith-inspired monumental epics to the landscape of 1920s Austrian feature production. After 1933, Austria again became a key destination for film personnel fleeing Nazi Germany, and such notables as Albert Bassermann★ and Curt Bois★ now sought to pursue careers there. However, although stage work proved forthcoming for these émigrés, the same could not be said of film roles, since producers swiftly observed that works featuring 'non-Aryan' or 'politically undesirable' actors could no longer be distributed in Germany, the largest single market for Austrian releases. Hence numerous émigrés, together with native Austrian actors including Paul Henreid★ and Rudolf Forster★, faced industry-supported attempts at exclusion well before Austria's annexation to the Third Reich in 1938. Most, therefore, emigrated onwards to Paris, London and the USA during these years, with a significant proportion of those berated in the American press as 'the German invasion of Hollywood' in fact being Austrians, or else Germans who had journeyed to North America only after an extended stay in Austria.

Once in Hollywood, Austrian, German and Hungarian émigrés often remained colleagues. They worked on the same productions, were offered similar roles (in particular, Middle European gentlemen and Nazis) and frequented the same clubs and restaurants. Composer Kurt Weill famously referred to the 'execrable German' of Hollywood's émigré community as an 'awful mixture of Hungarian and Viennese'. Émigrés from all three nations helped to foster a distinct cinematic representation of Austria in Hollywood – one which had originally risen to prominence in early German and Austrian talkies such as *Der Kongreß tanzt/Congress Dances* (1931). These so-called *Wienfilme* ('Vienna films') were romantic musical comedies focusing on dashing noblemen's adventures with wine, women and song in the 'good old days' of the Habsburg Empire. Examples of the genre's seamless continuation in Hollywood include Julien Duvivier's *The Great Waltz* (1938) and Curtis Bernhardt's *My Love Came Back* (1940). Ironically, the *Wienfilm* remained a mainstay of Nazi entertainment cinema also, even though its divergent accents, settings and monarchical nostalgia were clearly at odds with National Socialist notions of 'Greater German' unity.

In the postwar period, a number of Austrians have enjoyed prodigious careers in Hollywood, including action stars Arnold Schwarzenegger★ and Sybil Danning★ or stage actors Oskar Werner★ and Klaus-Maria Brandauer★. Significantly, though, little has ever been made in the USA of these stars' prior Austrian careers and – like their 1930s and 1940s forebears – they have consistently been portrayed and perceived as 'Germanic' or 'Teutonic', rather than specifically Austrian types. On screen, meanwhile, Austria has continued to be represented in Hollywood primarily as a Ruritanian musical setting, even when updated to include Nazi antagonists, as exemplified by *The Sound of Music* (1965). RJK

AYLMER, Felix (Felix Edward Aylmer-Jones) (1889–1979)

British character actor best remembered for a variety of gentle, avuncular roles as clerics, doctors, schoolmasters and aristocrats. Aylmer worked intermittently in Hollywood

during a thirty-eight-year film career, mainly in supporting roles in historical dramas such as Chamberlain in Anatole Litvak's *Anastasia* (1956). He also appeared in numerous US-funded films shot in Europe. MHu

FILMS: *The Shadow, Home, Sweet Home* (1933); *Doctor's Orders* (1934); *Hello, Sweetheart, The Price of a Song, Old Roses* (1935); *As You Like It, The Frog* (1936); *The Citadel* (1938); *A People Eternal* (1939); *Dr O' Dowd* (1940); *The Saint's Vacation, Once a Crook, Girl in the News, Atlantic Ferry, South American George* (1941); *The Young Mr Pitt* (1942); *Prince of Foxes* (1949); *No Highway, The House in the Square, Quo Vadis* (1951); *Ivanhoe* (1952); *The Master of Ballantrae, Knights of the Round Table, The Man Who Watched Trains Go By* (1953); *Anastasia* (1956); *Saint Joan* (1957); *The Doctor's Dilemma, The Two-Headed Spy, I Accuse!, Separate Tables* (1958); *From the Terrace, Exodus* (1960); *The Road to Hong Kong* (1962); *Becket, The Chalk Garden* (1964).

AZNAVOUR, Charles (Shahnour Varenagh Aznavurjian) (1924–)

French romantic singer and European screen actor whose American roles have included a hunchback in the sex comedy *Candy* and a Greek policeman in the thriller *Sky Riders*. SL

FILMS: *Candy* (1968); *The Games, The Adventurers* (1970); *Sky Riders* (1976).

BACLANOVA, Olga (Olga Vladimirovna Baklanova) (1896–1974)

After training at Moscow's prestigious Cherniovsky Institute, Baclanova joined the Moscow Art Theatre (MKHaT) and made her Russian film debut in 1914. Her celebrity as an actress and ballet star carried her name across Europe and beyond, and it was during a 1923 tour of the USA with a Soviet theatre company that Baclanova decided to stay on, initially to appear in the Broadway production of *The Miracle*, and then permanently. Following further successes on Broadway, Baclanova started her Hollywood career in 1927. Specialising in vamps and femme fatales, the naturally raven-haired Baclanova – who just as often appeared blonde – gained particular attention starring opposite Emil Jannings★ in *Street of Sin*, and went on to similarly lascivious roles in Josef von Sternberg's *The Docks of New York* and Paul Leni's *The Man Who Laughs*. Sound **169** hampered Baclanova's movie career. Her accent contributed to the very freakishness of her best-remembered role as the murderous trapeze artist Cleopatra in Tod Browning's *Freaks*. Thereafter, Baclanova primarily undertook stage revues and accent-exploiting radio work, before retiring to Switzerland after World War II. RJK

FILMS: *The Dove* (1927); *Three Sinners, Street of Sin, The Man Who Laughs, Avalanche, Forgotten Faces, The Docks of New York* (1928); *The Wolf of Wall Street, A Dangerous Woman, The Man I Love* (1929); *Cheer Up and Smile, Are You There?* (1930); *The Great Lover* (1931); *Downstairs, Freaks* (1932); *Billion Dollar Scandal* (1933); *The Telephone Blues* (1935); *The Double Crossky* (1936); *Claudia* (1943).

BADDELEY, Hermione (Hermione Clinton-Baddeley) (1906–1986)

Although she is perhaps more fondly remembered by American audiences for her charismatic television roles, this popular English stage and screen actress made regular minor appearances in Hollywood films during the 1960s. MF

FILMS: *Kipps* (1941); *Women without Men, Blonde Bait* (1956); *Midnight Lace, The Unsinkable Molly Brown* (1960); *Information Received* (1962); *Mary Poppins* (1964); *Harlow, Marriage on the Rocks, Do Not Disturb* (1965); *The Adventures of Bullwhip Griffin, The Happiest Millionaire* (1967); *The Aristocats* [voice] (1970); *C.H.O.M.P.S.* (1979); *The Secret of NIMH* [voice] (1982).

BAKER, Stanley (1928–1976)

Vigorous British character actor who often specialised in glowering villains and tough leading men. Baker generally refused to suppress his native Welsh accent or smooth the rough edges left by his working-class background. These factors, combined with his somewhat craggy features, made him stand out from other contemporary British stars who were more limited by their good manners, received pronunciation and parochial Englishness. Baker consequently attracted the interest of American and European filmmakers, who seemed to appreciate and exploit his rugged Celtic masculinity more successfully than domestic British directors and studios, who rarely seemed to know what to do with him.

Baker played a number of key supporting parts in 'runaway' Hollywood epics and action films made in Britain and Europe in the 1950s and early 1960s, including

Modred in *Knights of the Round Table* and Achilles in *Helen of Troy*. These, along with *Alexander the Great* and *The Guns of Navarone*, were big-budget, high-profile overseas productions financed by major Hollywood studios (and in the case of *Sodom and Gomorrah*, co-produced with a large European company) and they gave Baker valuable international exposure, if little opportunity to develop sustained characterisations. However, Baker's most distinguished work for the cinema was done on relatively low-cost British and European productions made in collaboration with two expatriate American directors, both fugitives from the HUAC Communist blacklist. He made four films with Joseph Losey – *Blind Date* (1959), *The Criminal* (1960), *Eva* (1962) and *Accident* (1967), the last containing perhaps his best performance, as a competitive, amoral academic – and six with Cy Endfield, including *Child in the House* (1956), *Hell Drivers* (1957), *Sea Fury* (1958) and *Jet Storm* (1959). For his fifth film with Endfield, Baker set his ambitions higher. He co-produced and starred in the imperial epic *Zulu*; the film's worldwide success (except in the USA) was rewarded by American impresario Joseph E. Levine and his backer, Paramount, with a contract to supply four more pictures. *Robbery* and *The Italian Job* (which was produced by Baker's company, Oakhurst, but in which he did not appear) were both successful in the UK, but none of the four (*Sands of the Kalahari*, his last with Endfield, and *Where's Jack?* were the others) made any significant impact in the US market.

Baker's subsequent films were mostly polyglot European co-productions, but he remained resident in Britain and resisted offers of long-term Hollywood contracts. His premature death at forty-eight (he always looked a decade older than his real age) came shortly after he had received a knighthood in Harold Wilson's resignation honours. He had been preparing to scout locations for *Zulu Dawn* (1979), a 'prequel' to *Zulu* subsequently completed by others. Had he lived, he would have played the part eventually taken by Burt Lancaster. SH

FILMS: *Captain Horatio Hornblower R.N.* (1950); *The Red Beret* [voice dubbed], *Knights of the Round Table, Hell Below Zero* (1953); *Helen of Troy, Alexander the Great* (1955); *The Angry Hills* (1959); *The Guns of Navarone* (1961); *Sodom and Gomorrah, In the French Style* (1962); *Zulu* (1963); *Dingaka, Sands of the Kalahari* (1965); *Robbery* (1967); *Where's Jack?, The Games* (1969).

BALFOUR, Eve (dates unknown)

This New Zealand-born actress was Britain's (proto-feminist) answer to the archetypal screen 'vamp' Theda Bara in the 1910s, but just as Bara's screen career declined after the war, so Balfour made little impact at Fox in the early 1920s. JB

FILMS: *Fantomas* [serial] (1920).

BANDERAS, Antonio (José Antonio Domínguez Banderas) (1960–)

Banderas is Spain's most successful export to Hollywood since Antonio Moreno★ in the silent era. He made his film debut in *Laberinto de pasiones/Labyrinth of Passion* (1982) and was a successful star of stage and screen in Spain before embarking on a Hollywood career. His path into American cinema was helped considerably by his work with Pedro Almodóvar: *La ley del deseo/Law of Desire* (1987) enshrined Banderas as a gay icon in the USA; *Mujeres al borde de un ataque de nervios/Women on the Verge of a Nervous Breakdown* (1988) was nominated for an Academy Award and became the most successful foreign film of its year Stateside; and the MPAA's attempt to land an X rating on *¡Atame!/Tie Me Up! Tie Me Down!* turned that film into a scandalous art-house success. He also became the only man in Madrid Madonna wanted to meet: her unsuccessful flirtations with him are obvious in the documentary *Madonna: Truth or Dare*. Being the man Madonna cannot get was undoubtedly a factor in his being cast in *The Mambo Kings*, his first starring role in an American film. Banderas did not yet speak English and had to learn the role phonetically, yet, though the film was not a success, Banderas and Armand Assante, playing Cuban brothers forced out of their country to try their luck in the show-business world of 1950s America, were both very well received. Banderas' Nestor – Latin, handsome, accomplished, emotionally volatile – set a firm foundation for his star persona in the USA. Over the next few years, the actor was to alternate showy supporting roles, as gay or sexually ambivalent characters, in big-budget successes (as Tom Hanks' boyfriend in *Philadelphia* and Armand, the vampire who longs for Brad Pitt's Louis in *Interview with the Vampire*), with straightforward romantic leads in international co-productions (opposite Jennifer Connelly in *Of Love and Shadows* and as Winona Ryder's love interest in the all-star cast of *The House of the Spirits*).

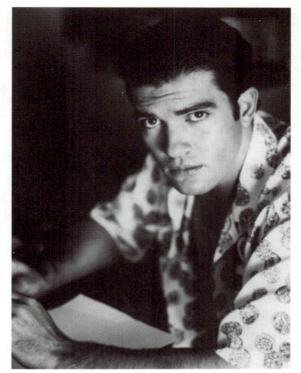

Antonio Banderas: Spain's most successful acting export to Hollywood since Antonio Moreno

It was a series of vivid performances in a remarkable range of films in 1995 that finally transformed Banderas into bona fide Hollywood star. First and most importantly, *Desperado*, Robert Rodriguez's low-budget remake of his even lower-budget Spanish-language *El Mariachi* (1992), was tailor-made to Banderas' talents. As the ads promised: 'He came to settle the score with someone. Anyone. Everyone.' *Desperado* showcased not only his beauty, but also the athletic grace, power and agility of his movements. Banderas helped make the film a box-office hit that appealed to both men and women and, in turn, the film helped make the actor a box-office star. Banderas continued in the action genre the same year as the young hitman hired to bump off Sylvester Stallone in *Assassins*. The film was only a minor hit but it solidified his stardom by implying, as it did, that Banderas was a worthy successor to Stallone's previous domination of the action genre. His Latin-hunk persona was not, however, neglected: *Rolling Stone* rated him a world-class charmer as the bongo-playing man with tattoos in strange places that Sarah-Jessica Parker falls for in *Miami* **171**

Rhapsody. In the little-seen *Never Talk to Strangers* opposite Rebecca de Mornay, he did meanwhile expand on the Latin Lover cliché, by highlighting the latent danger and duplicity inherent in the type.

If Banderas was not already a household name in the USA, he became one in 1996. His reunion with Madonna in *Evita* was heavily publicised. They were both critically acclaimed; Banderas brought panache to his acting and singing role as Che Guevara, and the film did solidly at the box office. The publicity Banderas received with Madonna was only a hint of what was to come when he started an affair with Melanie Griffith on the set of *Two Much*. Divorce from his wife Ana Leza, subsequent marriage to Griffith, the birth of their daughter, their marital problems, even their home, were to provide tabloid fodder for years to come.

Banderas has been listed by *People* magazine as one of the fifty most beautiful people in the world and *Empire* magazine voted him one of the hundred Sexiest Film Stars in history. Yet, his considerable rise as a Hollywood star has been somewhat blocked by the glass ceiling of his ethnicity. His national and cultural identity helped his career, in that there are many roles for Latinos, Chicanos, Cubans, Mexicans and Puerto Ricans in American films. But while it has proved easy for American cinema to elide the differences between Spanish and Hispanic, the move from Hispanic to average American has been harder to make. Banderas can never enjoy Tom Cruise's type of success at the Hollywood box office because he is not allowed to be 'everyman' on screen the way Cruise is or, indeed, the way Banderas was in his Spanish films. In Hollywood, whether as a Hispanic or otherwise (e.g. an Arab in *The 13th Warrior*), Banderas remains a de facto representative of otherness, subalternity, the subcultural, and is thus prevented from achieving the mixture of ordinary and extraordinary that is needed to have the semiotic and social signifying power enjoyed by the biggest stars.

Nothing illustrates this dilemma better than Banderas' greatest success to date: *The Mask of Zorro*. Banderas is a convincing everyman, because the film is set at a time when Mexico is fighting from its independence, a historical preamble to California becoming part of the USA. Even so, in order to make Banderas' Zorro an indigenous historic Californian, Anthony Hopkins★ and Catherine Zeta-Jones★ had to be cast as Spanish, while the villain of the piece,

Captain Harrison Love, is the blond, fair-skinned and blue-eyed Matt Letscher: not exactly the normal practice in Hollywood. Clearly such narrative and visual gyrations cannot always be accommodated and it is perhaps significant that Banderas' greatest success since *Zorro* has been in a top-billed but de facto supporting role as the Hispanic father married to the 'American' mother of *Spy Kids* and its sequels. The accentless, all-American kids are the real stars of that top-grossing series of films. JA

FILMS: *The Mambo Kings* (1992); *The House of the Spirits, Philadelphia* (1993); *Of Love and Shadows, Interview with the Vampire* (1994); *Desperado, Assassins, Four Rooms, Miami Rhapsody, Never Talk to Strangers* (1995); *Two Much, Evita* (1996); *The Mask of Zorro* (1998); *The 13th Warrior, Play it to the Bone, The White River Kid* (1999); *The Body* (2000); *Spy Kids, Original Sin* (2001); *Femme Fatale, Ballistic: Ecks. vs. Sever, Spy Kids 2: Island of Lost Dreams, Frida* (2002); *Spy Kids 3-D: Game Over, Desperado II: Once Upon a Time in Mexico, Imagining Argentina* (2003); *Shrek 2* [voice] (2004).

BANKS, Leslie (1890–1952)

Prominent British stage actor who specialised in debonair, upper-class leading men, officers and policemen. After the second of his brief spells in Hollywood, he returned to Britain in 1933, where he continued a successful career on stage and screen. His films included the MGM-backed *Busman's Honeymoon*. MHu

FILMS: *Experience* (1921); *The Most Dangerous Game* (1932); *I Am Suzanne* (1933); *Busman's Honeymoon* (1940).

BÁNKY, Vilma (Vilma Lonchit) (1898–1991)

After entering films as an extra, Bánky had gained moderate celebrity in her native Hungary through appearances in Austrian, German and Hungarian productions by the time Samuel Goldwyn 'discovered' her during his 1924 European vacation. Goldwyn supposedly spotted Bánky's image on a postcard and immediately decided to secure her for the American screen. Whether apocryphal or not, this story already bears testimony to Hollywood's purely scopophilic interest in the fair-haired, ochre-skinned Bánky as an embodiment of exotic beauty. Unable to speak English, Bánky arrived in the USA in March 1925. Five years were deducted from her age and a voluminous publicity campaign introduced her as 'The Hungarian Rhapsody'. As this epithet implies, her silent roles combined romance and

Vilma Bánky: 'The Hungarian Rhapsody'

exoticism, with Bánky playing everything from European princesses to an Arabian dancing-girl. Her American debut in *The Dark Angel* paired her with Ronald Colman★, whose character's blindness ironically robbed him of the very vision of beauty that audiences were intended to admire. A phenomenal critical and popular success, the film catapulted Bánky into two starring roles opposite Hollywood's foremost leading man, Rudolph Valentino, in *The Eagle* and *The Son of the Sheik*. After Valentino's death, Bánky was again paired with Ronald Colman in a series of lavish love-epics that rendered them the late 1920s' favourite screen couple, and Goldwyn's greatest money-makers. Bánky's salary, meanwhile, had risen from $100 to $5,000 per week. In June 1927, Goldwyn also paid for Bánky's wedding to fellow actor Rod La Rocque – an all-star Beverly Hills spectacle at which Goldwyn gave the bride away, while Louella Parsons served as matron of honour and Harold Lloyd was best man. Bánky became an American citizen in 1929.

The coming of sound put the brakes on her success, as her English remained extremely limited and her guttural intonation was not considered capable of connoting 'romance'. Goldwyn tailored the part-talkie *This is Heaven* to showcase the actress in a new light, as she played a Hungarian immigrant short-order cook who is gradually 'Americanised'. Despite acceptable reviews, Goldwyn dissolved Bánky's contract, in particular on account of the fact that she had charged all her English lessons to him. She attempted a second talkie, *A Lady to Love*, at MGM and starred opposite Edward G. Robinson, whose character's thick Italian accent was intended to offset hers. She travelled to Berlin to appear in one final film, *Der Rebell/ The Rebel* (1932), before retiring from show business and making millions alongside husband La Rocque selling Californian real estate. Dismayed at Hollywood's disinterest after she grew ill in the late 1980s, Bánky decreed that her death should not be made public. It remained unannounced for some eighteen months. RJK

FILMS: *The Dark Angel, The Eagle* (1925); *The Son of the Sheik, The Winning of Barbara Worth* (1926); *The Night of Love, The Magic Flame* (1927); *Two Lovers, The Awakening* (1928); *This is Heaven* (1929); *A Lady to Love* (1930).

BARBATO, Olga (1914–2003)
Member of a prominent Italian theatrical family who arrived in New York with Giovanni Grasso's touring company during the 1920s. Barbato largely appeared on the immigrant stage and radio and was president of the Italian Actors Union during the 1990s. She had a supporting role in Woody Allen's *Broadway Danny Rose*. GM
FILM: *Broadway Danny Rose* (1984).

BARDEM, Javier (Javier Encinas Bardem) (1969–)
The first Spanish actor ever to be nominated for an Academy Award is a member of one of the nation's great film dynasties. He is the grandson of stars Rafael Bardem and Matilde Muñoz Sampedro, son of distinguished actress Pilar Bardem and nephew of one of Spain's greatest film directors, Juan Antonio Bardem. Javier Bardem's status in Spanish cinema is unique and comparable only to that of Jean Gabin★ and Gérard Depardieu★ in France: the embodiment of the national 'everyman', an unparalleled box-office attraction and an actor capable of conveying an apparently limitless range of emotion while always seeming to be himself.

Bardem's first performance in an English-language film was in Alex de la Iglesia's *Perdita Durango*, a Spanish-Mexican-American co-production. Despite a relatively high **173** budget and the presence of Rosie Perez, *Perdita Durango* was badly reviewed and little seen, though viewers were offered another opportunity to catch Bardem's bold performance as the brutishly sexual Romeo Dolorosa when the film was re-released in the USA on video in 1999 as *Dance with the Devil*. It is perhaps because American critics' exposure to Bardem had been largely limited to the Iberian machos he had played, for instance in *Jamón, Jamón* (1992) and *Carne tremula/Live Flesh* (1997), that his performance as gay Cuban poet Reinaldo Arenas in *Before Night Falls* seemed so surprising. Bardem had in fact played gay characters before, including in his film debut as a hardened gay hustler in *Las edades de Lulú/The Ages of Lulu* (1990). The role of Arenas, from young, voraciously fun-loving poet persecuted in his home land of Cuba to the middle-aged exile shivering to his death from AIDS in New York, is undoubtedly a great one; and Bardem's performance was rightly hailed as a tour de force. He was nominated for every acting award going that year; and though he lost the Academy Award, he did win the Los Angeles Film Critics Award for Best Actor as well as a role in John Malkovich's *The Dancer Upstairs*. JA

FILMS: *Dance with the Devil* (1997); *Before Night Falls* (2000); *The Dancer Upstairs* (2002); *Collateral* (2004).

BARDOT, Brigitte (1934–)

The most famous French film star internationally, a sensational beauty and much imitated fashion icon, Brigitte Bardot notoriously and repeatedly said 'non!' to Hollywood. This was not for lack of enticing offers after the success of her breakthrough film *Et Dieu . . . créa la femme/And God Created Woman* (1956) was sealed by the scandal it provoked in the USA. But BB – who had earlier appeared in an American film shot in Italy, *Helen of Troy* – was not keen to leave husband(s)/partner(s)/pets/St Tropez. Reportedly, too, potential A-list US partners, including Gary Cooper, Frank Sinatra, Marlon Brando and Steve McQueen, were reluctant to get involved, for fear of being eclipsed by her aura.

In the event, Hollywood (Twentieth Century-Fox) came to Brigitte for her episode in *Dear Brigitte*, a comedy directed by Henry Koster and starring James Stewart – whose gravitas could evidently withstand the Bardot dazzle – as the father of a young maths prodigy obsessed with her. The boy keeps writing to Brigitte, who finally invites him **174** to Paris. In a city populated by Bardot clones, a taxi driver takes father and son swiftly from Orly airport to 'Brigitte Bardot's house', where – characteristically – she gives the boy a puppy.

Bardot did visit the USA. She married her third husband Gunther Sachs, for instance, in Las Vegas in 1966. Her most high-profile visit, however, which took place in Hollywood, was in December 1965, to promote *Viva Maria!*, co-starring Jeanne Moreau★. Her status as national treasure was such that the French press warned: 'We send America the most beautiful Christmas present imaginable. But, beware, this present is labelled "return to sender!"'. GV

FILMS: *Helen of Troy* (1956); *Dear Brigitte* (1965).

BARNES, Binnie (Gertrude Maude Barnes) (1903–1998)

Lively English actress who gained Hollywood popularity with a series of voluptuous, wisecracking and sometimes fantastically bitchy second leads. Often glamorous, scheming and caustic as the predatory 'other woman', Barnes enjoyed her Hollywood heyday in the 1930s and 1940s before effectively retiring to Europe with her producer husband. MF

FILMS: *One Exciting Adventure, Gift of Gab, There's Always Tomorrow, Forbidden Territory* (1934); *Rendezvous, Diamond Jim* (1935); *Sutter's Gold, Small Town Girl, The Last of the Mohicans, Magnificent Brute, Three Smart Girls* (1936); *Breezing Home, Broadway Melody of 1938* (1937); *The Adventures of Marco Polo, The First Hundred Years, Three Blind Mice, Always Goodbye, Tropic Holiday, Thanks for Everything, Holiday, Gateway* (1938); *The Three Musketeers, Wife, Husband and Friend, Man about Town, Frontier Marshal* (1939); *Day-Time Wife, 'Til We Meet Again, This Thing Called Love* (1940); *Angels with Broken Wings, New Wine, Tight Shoes, Three Girls about Town, Skylark* (1941); *Call Out the Marines, In Old California, I Married an Angel* (1942); *The Man from Down Under* (1943); *Up in Mabel's Room, The Hour before Dawn, Barbary Coast Gent* (1944); *The Spanish Main, It's in the Bag!, Getting Gertie's Garter* (1945); *The Time of Their Lives* (1946); *If Winter Comes* (1947); *My Own True Love, Dude Goes West* (1948); *The Trouble with Angels* (1966); *Where Angels Go, Trouble Follows* (1968); *40 Carats* (1973).

BARRAULT, Marie-Christine (1944–)

Blonde, romantic-looking French actress who was nominated for an Academy Award for her role in Jean-Charles

Tacchella's *Cousin, Cousine* (1975). Her American debut was as the object of Woody Allen's affections in *Stardust Memories*, but she subsequently has remained mostly a domestic star. VO

FILMS: *Stardust Memories* (1980); *Table for Five* (1983).

BARRIE, Wendy (Marguerite Wendy Jenkins) (1912–1978)

In the wake of her attention-grabbing performance as Jane Seymour in *The Private Life of Henry VIII* (1933), this English actress moved to Hollywood, where she spent a decade working tirelessly, and ultimately unsuccessfully, for the film stardom she craved, before eventually conceding defeat and moving into American television. MF

FILMS: *Without You* (1934); *It's a Small World, Millions in the Air, A Feather in Her Hat, College Scandal* (1935); *Speed, Ticket to Paradise, The Big Broadcast of 1936, Under Your Spell, Love on a Bet* (1936); *Breezing Home, Dead End, A Girl with Ideas, Wings over Honolulu, What Price Vengeance?, Prescription for Romance* (1937); *Pacific Liner, I Am the Law* (1938); *The Saint Strikes Back, The Hound of the Baskervilles, Five Came Back, The Witness Vanishes, Newsboys' Home* (1939); *Day-Time Wife, Cross Country Romance, Men against the Sky, Women in War, Who Killed Aunt Maggie?, The Saint Takes Over* (1940); *The Saint in Palm Springs, A Date with the Falcon, Repent at Leisure, Public Enemies, The Gay Falcon* (1941); *Eyes of the Underworld, Forever and a Day, Submarine Alert, Follies Girl* (1943); *It Should Happen to You* (1954); *The Moving Finger* (1963).

BARTHOLOMEW, Freddie (Frederick Llewellyn) (1924–1992)

Almost androgynous-looking English child actor who achieved overnight stardom with the title role in *David Copperfield* in 1935. He became enormously successful in a number of 1930s MGM classic adventure adaptations but his popularity eventually faded as he grew older. Bartholomew's substantial earnings were largely absorbed by multiple lawsuits competing for 'ownership' of the young performer. MF

FILMS: *David Copperfield, Anna Karenina* (1935); *Little Lord Fauntleroy, The Devil is a Sissy, Professional Soldier, Lloyds of London* (1936); *Captains Courageous* (1937); *Lord Jeff, Listen Darling, Kidnapped* (1938); *Two Bright Boys, The Spirit of Culver* (1939); *Swiss Family Robinson, Tom Brown's School Days* (1940); *Naval Academy* (1941); *Cadets on Parade, A Yank*

at Eton, Junior Army* (1942); *The Town Went Wild* (1944); *Sepia Cinderella* (1947); *St Benny the Dip* (1951).

BARY, Léon (1880–1954)

Bary (sometimes credited as Barry) had a successful career in silent films in Hollywood from 1916 to 1929, when he appeared with Douglas Fairbanks in *The Iron Mask* (he also directed a few films). With the advent of sound, he returned to France and started a long career in supporting roles. TH

FILMS: *The Shielding Shadow* (1916); *The Seven Pearls, Mystery of the Double Cross* (1917); *The Yellow Ticket* (1918); *Kismet* (1920); *The Three Musketeers, The Lure of Jade* (1921); *The Call of Home, The Galloping Kid, June Madness* (1922); *Suzanna, The White Flower, Bucking the Barrier, The Grail, The Temple of Venus* (1923); *George Washington, Jr, The King of the Wild Horses, The Lightning Rider, The Wise Virgin* (1924); *Midnight Molly* (1925); *The Iron Mask* (1929).

BASCH, Felix (1882–1944)

Former matinée idol and Austrian-Jewish film and theatre director Felix Basch left Nazi Germany for New York in 1933. Unable to find work, he spent time in London and Paris before returning to the USA when war broke out. A scheme to open a Viennese restaurant in Hollywood fell through, and he made his screen comeback after a twenty-year absence, taking small parts as Teutonic villains in anti-Nazi films until his sudden death. His son – whom he urged to avoid work in which an accent could become a hindrance – was the American celebrity photographer Peter Basch. RJK

FILMS: *Pacific Rendezvous, Enemy Agents Meet Ellery Queen, Desperate Journey, Destination Unknown, Once Upon a Honeymoon, Hitler – Dead or Alive, Reunion in France* (1942); *Chetniks – The Fighting Guerrillas, Mission to Moscow, The Boy from Stalingrad, The Falcon in Danger, Bomber's Moon, Above Suspicion, Hostages, Appointment in Berlin, The Cross of Lorraine, Women in Bondage, The Desert Song* (1943); *None Shall Escape, Uncertain Glory, The Hitler Gang, The Mask of Dimitrios, Wilson* (1944).

BASSERMANN, Albert (1867–1952)

Germany's foremost classical actor who helped establish German silent cinema's artistic reputation. Despite accolades from Goebbels after the Nazis' rise to power, the Jewish Bassermann sagely moved to Austria in 1934, **175** together with actress-wife Else Schiff-Bassermann and their mentally handicapped daughter. Upon Austria's annexation, the three fled to the USA. Bassermann arrived in Hollywood in 1939 as a seventy-two-year-old, gutturally accented unknown and was bolstered by strong support from émigré circles. Initial success in Hitchcock's *Foreign Correspondent* – for which Bassermann learned his part phonetically – brought an Academy Award nomination as Best Supporting Actor but few significant follow-up offers. This was because Bassermann refused to work on productions on which his wife was not also employed and because he also turned down anti-Nazi vehicles out of fear for relations left in Europe. When the war ended, the Bassermanns staged a triumphant comeback tour of fifty German towns. In 1948, Bassermann suddenly returned to international attention as Ratov in Powell and Pressburger's *The Red Shoes*. New offers came from Hollywood but Bassermann died, while finalising these, on an aeroplane between New York and Zurich. RJK

FILMS: *Dr Ehrlich's Magic Bullet, Foreign Correspondent, Knute Rockne – All American, Escape, Moon over Burma, A Dispatch from Reuters* (1940); *A Woman's Face, New Wine, The Shanghai Gesture* (1941); *Invisible Agent, Once upon a Honeymoon, Reunion in France, The Moon and Sixpence, Fly-by-Night, Desperate Journey* (1942); *Good Luck, Mr Yates, Madame Curie* (1943); *Since You Went Away* (1944); *I Was a Criminal, Rhapsody in Blue* (1945); *The Searching Wind, Strange Holiday* (1946); *The Private Affairs of Bel Ami, Escape Me Never* (1947).

BATES, Alan (1934–2003)

Alan Bates was one of the key stars of the British 'New Wave' and achieved equal iconic weight in the public consciousness as Albert Finney★ and Richard Harris★. Bates has never had the same kind of high profile in the USA, though, and it seems extraordinary that for the duration of the 1960s, a decade when Hollywood repeatedly looked to Britain for new talent, Bates did not set foot in an American studio – MGM's *The Fixer*, for example, for which Bates won his only Academy Award nomination was shot in Hungary. The explanation for this is partly to do with Bates' professed distaste for stardom and glamour and his stated preference for stage work. It seems telling that in an émigré-packed film adaptation of *Far from the Madding Crowd* (1967), Bates played the phlegmatic provincial

farmer from whom Julie Christie★ escapes to seek romance in the arms of the dashing Terence Stamp★. Nonetheless, Bates' award-winning Broadway appearances kept him in the radar of American film-makers and he landed the principal male roles in two big American studio productions at the end of the 1970s: *An Unmarried Woman* and *The Rose*. Not coincidentally, both films were directed by alumni of the Actor's Studio with strong professional connections to the stage (Paul Mazursky and Mark Rydell, respectively). JB

FILMS: *The Running Man* (1963); *Georgy Girl* (1966); *Far from the Madding Crowd* (1967); *The Fixer* (1968); *Women in Love* (1969); *Royal Flash* (1975); *An Unmarried Woman* (1978); *The Rose* (1979); *Nijinsky* (1980); *Duet for One, A Prayer for the Dying* (1987); *Gosford Park* (2001); *The Mothman Prophecies, The Sum of All Fears* (2002).

BAUCHAU, Patrick (Patrick Nicolas Jean Sixte Ghislain Bauchau) (1938–)

Belgian-born actor whose film career spans over forty years. He is one of the few contemporary actors to be an authentic international star, since he is fluent in French, English, German and Italian. His film debut was in Eric Rohmer's *La Carrière de Suzanne / Suzanne's Career* (1963) and *La Collectionneuse / The Collector* (1967), and he has subsequently appeared in a number of French, German and Belgian art films. His first American screen appearance was as a French gangster in Alan Rudolph's *Choose Me* in 1984. Bauchau moved to Los Angeles in 1989 – where he lives in Louise Brooks' former villa – largely thanks to his Academy Award-nominated role as Prince Scotti in *Le Maître de Musique / The Music Teacher*. He has since been relatively prolific both in Hollywood film and television and in European art productions. DN/VO

FILMS: *Choose Me* (1984); *A View to a Kill* (1985); *The Rapture* (1991); *From Time to Time, Chain of Desire* (1992); *Every Breath* (1993); *The New Age, Clear and Present Danger, The Dark Side of Genius* (1994); *Serpent's Lair* (1995); *Twin Falls Idaho* (1999); *The Cell, The Sculptress, The Beat Nicks* (2000); *Jackpot* (2001); *Panic Room, Secretary* (2002); *Shade* (2003); *Ray* (2004).

BEAN, Sean (1959–)

Handsome, sexy, virile British leading man who, although RADA trained, has retained his Yorkshire accent and direct-

ness. Bean achieved stardom through the television series *Sharpe* (1993–7) and is able to play action heroes and villains with equal conviction, investing his characters with vulnerability as well as strength and aggression. AS
FILMS: *Patriot Games* (1992); *Golden Eye* (1995); *Airborne, Ronin* (1998); *Don't Say a Word, The Lord of the Rings: The Fellowship of the Ring* (2001); *Equilibrium, The Lord of the Rings: The Two Towers* (2002); *The Big Empty, The Lord of the Rings: The Return of the King* (2003); *Troy, National Treasure* (2004).

BÉART, Emmanuelle (1965–)

Popular French actress with exceptional good looks whose Hollywood career is noteworthy for its discrepancy with the considerable status she enjoys at home. In her Hollywood debut, Béart starred as an angel in the romantic comedy *Date with an Angel*. Except for the end of the film, when her unmistakably French accent is explained by her angelic 'otherness', her part is dialogue-free. Her accent became more audible in her surprisingly marginal role in Brian De Palma's *Mission: Impossible*, which cast Béart as a secret agent opposite Tom Cruise. Here, her elegant allure stood for European sophistication. Despite courting international roles, Béart has continued to flourish in France, where she is also known for her political involvement in controversial social issues. Like Audrey Hepburn★, she has become an ambassador for Unicef. TH
FILMS: *Date with an Angel* (1987); *Mission: Impossible* (1996).

BELGIUM

There has been little discussion of Belgian-born Hollywood émigré actors inside Belgium. Yet over the years, some of the most prominent Belgian acting talents have developed professional links with the American film industry beneficial to their native country. For instance, in the 1920s, following his successful encounter with Hollywood, Jules Raucourt★ returned briefly to Belgium in order to help develop an industrial structure based on the American model. In the early 1950s, Warner Bros.' stock player Victor Francen★ similarly tried to set up a biopic of the Flemish painter Rubens. Nowadays, Patrick Bauchau★, an international character actor based in Los Angeles for more than a decade, regularly agrees also to appear in Belgian auteur films.

The fact is that despite several attempts, the Belgian film industry only became industrialised in the mid-1950s,

even though documentaries and a few isolated feature films had been produced and distributed much earlier. This explains why, as early as the 1910s, promising Belgian stage actors who desired a career in film had to tour Europe as members of theatrical companies and work in France before trying their luck in the USA or being recruited by Hollywood. Such was the case with Raucourt, Francen and Fernand Gravey★, whose journeys to Hollywood were, at different epochs, a success thanks to their diverse range of acting techniques acquired in European productions. Their typically Belgian adaptability also enabled them to avoid being systematically typecast as 'French', but rather as distinguished, sophisticated and often ambiguous, generically 'European' characters.

An important moment in the history of Belgians in Hollywood was the era of the multi-language film. During the early 1930s, Belgian-born émigré director Jacques Feyder played an important part in the integration of French-speaking actors in the multiple-language film industry in Hollywood. After a brief but convincing appearance as the police inspector in Feyder's last silent MGM Greta Garbo★ vehicle, *The Kiss* (1929), Raucourt, for instance, acted in half a dozen multiple-language versions, the most notable being Feyder's first French film in Hollywood, *Le Spectre vert / The Unholy Night* (1930). Fred Cavens★ (1880–1962), famous for having served as a fencing master for half a century in cloak-and-dagger films, also appeared in minor parts next to Raucourt and Maurice Chevalier★ in three multiple-language versions of the period.

No significant Belgian-born actor worked in Hollywood between the 1950s and the 1980s, with the exception of Monique van Vooren★ and Patrick Bauchau. After a wide-ranging career in European art cinema, the latter now enjoys the privilege of choosing his own Hollywood scripts. He shares with his compatriot predecessors an adaptability to a range of artistic situations and an excellent command of several languages. These factors may not have been so evident in the professional trajectory of Belgium's latest acting export, Jean-Claude Van Damme★, but there is no mistaking his commercial success in an era of global film culture that has seen his specific marketability with the Asian market leading to collaborations with the likes of John Woo and Tsui Hark.
DN

BELL, Tom (1932–)

Bell came to prominence as part of the British 'New Wave' in the early 1960s. His promising career as a brooding leading man was stymied by repercussions from a drunken insult he delivered to the Duke of Edinburgh and he briefly tried (unsuccessfully) to relaunch himself in American films. JB

FILMS: *H.M.S. Defiant* (1962); *Sands of Beersheba* (1965); *In Enemy Country* (1968); *Royal Flash* (1975); *Feast of July* (1995); *The Boxer* (1997).

BELLUCCI, Monica (1968–)

Glamorous, sultry Italian actress and former fashion model who has moved from the still to the moving image with a languid ease of expression. 'There are two different ways of being,' she says. 'In a photograph you look static, protected. But when you see yourself in a film . . . it is the first time you see yourself as you are in life.' Bellucci now combines a successful career in contemporary European cinema (e.g. *Le Pacte des loups / The Brotherhood of the Wolf* [2002]) with leading parts in prestige Hollywood productions. Following widespread international exposure as Persephone in the last two films of *The Matrix* trilogy, she was cast as Mary Magdalene in Mel Gibson's controversial *The Passion of the Christ*. AP

FILMS: *Bram Stoker's Dracula* (1992); *Under Suspicion* (2000); *Tears of the Sun, The Matrix Reloaded, The Matrix Revolutions* (2003); *The Passion of the Christ, She Hates Me* (2004).

BENIGNI, Roberto (1952–)

As an Italian comic actor, director and screenwriter, Benigni had already reached stardom in his native country when he met American independent director Jim Jarmusch in 1986. In Jarmusch's *Down by Law*, Benigni's performance as an Italian tourist who ends up in a New Orleans jail derived its humour from the misunderstandings that result from his character's poor spoken English. In his second appearance for Jarmusch, in a hilarious sequence in *Night on Earth*, Benigni performed in Italian as a Roman taxi driver who confesses his sex life to a priest. His debut in a Hollywood feature was in Blake Edwards' *Son of the Pink Panther*, where he played Inspector Clouseau's illegitimate son. Benigni's mastery of physical comedy made him well **178** suited for the role, but although his performance was praised by critics, it did not save a weakly scripted film from box-office failure. Benigni's *La vita é bella / Life is beautiful* (1997) was nominated for seven Academy Awards and awarded three: Best Music, Best Foreign Language Film and Best Actor in a Leading Role, making the Italian, together with Laurence Olivier★, one of only two actors to have directed themselves in Academy Award-winning performances. CBu

FILMS: *Coffee and Cigarettes, Down by Law* (1986); *Night on Earth* (1991); *Son of the Pink Panther* (1993); *Coffee and Cigarettes* (2003).

BERGER, Helmut (Helmut Steinberger) (1944–)

Blond Austrian Adonis whose notoriety in the USA stems primarily from his European films and widely reported extra-cinematic sexual exploits rather than his scant work in Hollywood. Berger was introduced to the screen by his long-term lover, Luchino Visconti, and swiftly became a regular in all-star European co-productions. A promotional tour of the USA for Visconti's *La caduta degli dei / The Damned* (1969), in which Berger famously 'dragged up' as Marlene Dietrich's★ Lola, attracted immense attention. It also established his American public persona as an embodiment of supposed European sexual decadence. Nude art photographs of Berger, along with stories about his hedonistic bisexual lifestyle, compounded this reputation and may have scared off the heterocentric Hollywood majors. Aside from two Hollywood productions shot in Europe, the television movie *Victory at Entebbe* (1976) and an ironic supporting role as chief accountant of the Vatican Bank in *The Godfather Part III*, Berger's longest stint in Hollywood came in 1993–4 when he appeared as the drug-addicted European playboy Peter De Vilbis in television's *Dynasty*. RJK

FILMS: *Ash Wednesday* (1973); *Code Name: Emerald* (1985); *The Godfather Part III* (1990).

BERGER, Senta (1941–)

Glamorous Austrian-born actress who was a regular in West German, Austrian and Italian films. After appearing in several American-financed productions in Europe, she made a brief unsuccessful stab at a Hollywood career during the mid-1960s, and swiftly returned to Europe. RJK

FILMS: *The Journey* (1959); *The Secret Ways* (1961); *The Waltz King, The Victors* (1963); *Major Dundee, The Glory Guys, The Spy with My Face* (1965); *Cast a Giant Shadow,*

Poppies are Also Flowers (1966); *The Ambushers* (1967); *Vienna* (1968); *If it's Tuesday, This Must Be Belgium, De Sade* (1969); *The Swiss Conspiracy* (1975).

BERGIN, Patrick (1951–)

Irish actor, once touted as the next Sean Connery★, who is best known for his tough guy roles such as Julia Roberts' obsessive and abusive husband in *Sleeping with the Enemy*. As is the case with other native contemporaries, Bergin currently moves between acting roles in Hollywood and Ireland. RB

FILMS: *Mountains of the Moon* (1990); *Sleeping with the Enemy, Robin Hood, Love Crimes* (1991); *Highway to Hell, Patriot Games* (1992); *Double Cross* (1994); *Lawnmower Man 2: Beyond Cyberspace* (1996); *Press Run* (1999); *When the Sky Falls* (2000); *Devil's Prey, Beneath Loch Ness, The Invisible Circus* (2001); *Ella Enchanted, Gas Station Jesus* (2004).

BERGMAN, Ingrid (1915–1982)

Ingrid Bergman was already at the zenith of her Swedish film career when David O. Selznick saw her play Anna in Gustaf Molander's *Intermezzo* (1936). The American producer immediately bought the rights to the script and when the beautiful young actress starred again in Gregory Ratoff's★ 1939 remake of the film, *Intermezzo: A Love Story*, it marked the beginning of one of classical Hollywood's greatest real-life stories.

Despite Bergman's youth, she successfully negotiated her own working conditions within the American studio system. Very soon she occupied a dressing room of her own. She was also allowed to keep the clothes specially made for each film role – a privilege only reserved for the leading stars of the time. The studio's investment swiftly paid off. After *Intermezzo*, she appeared in a couple of minor films, but her fourth Hollywood film, *Doctor Jekyll and Mr Hyde*, became an indisputable success. Selznick had originally planned the title role for Spencer Tracy and the part of the young and innocent Beatrix for Bergman. The actress thought otherwise. She did not want to play another colourless girl next door, so she persuaded Victor Fleming, the film's director, that she would make a suitable Ivy – the seductive barmaid in the story.

From then on, she worked with Hollywood's most famous directors such as George Cukor (*Gaslight*) and Alfred Hitchcock (*Spellbound, Under Capricorn* and *Notori-*

ous). Everyone wanted her, including Ernest Hemingway, who suggested Bergman for the role of Maria in *For Whom the Bell Tolls*. Bergman's performance as Paula in *Gaslight* led to her first Academy Award, but perhaps the Swedish actress's most unforgettable film was *Casablanca*. The film's original conception was confused and it was not anticipated to be a success. The script was written while the scenes were being shot and Bergman had no real clear idea about the motivations of the character she was playing. Many critics now believe that it was this element of uncertainty that made her so apt for the role of a woman torn between love and duty. The star herself later wrote that she never really understood the success of the film.

From the beginning, Bergman's professional career was marked by controversy. In Europe, the director of Stockholm's Royal Dramatic Theatre – where she had been a student – had criticised her for forsaking art in favour of mass entertainment when she signed to Sweden's largest film company, Svensk Filmindustri. Bergman also went her own way in Hollywood and repeatedly ignored the advice of various studio bosses. As a star, she refused to change her name, pluck her eyebrows or even stuff her bra. As an actress deeply devoted to her profession, Bergman resented the stereotypical casting patterns of the American film

Ingrid Bergman: Sweden's greatest émigré actress achieved lasting fame and success in Hollywood

industry. She also became a famous proponent of the Kuleshovian idea of a blank face and would advise her daughter Isabella Rossellini: 'Keep it simple. Make a blank face and the music and story will fill it in!' Bergman's distinctive 'blank face' certainly enabled audiences to project their feelings back to the screen image of the actress. It also contributed to the melodramatic quality of excess often found in her American pictures.

At the same time, somewhat paradoxically, Bergman was a great admirer of realism and she wanted to appear as 'real' and 'true' as possible on screen. It is unsurprising, therefore, that she was profoundly impressed by Italian neo-realism's leading director, Roberto Rossellini. After offering to work with him, she starred in Rossellini's *Stromboli* (1949) – a film that would mark a turning point in her life, and a disaster for her career. Before the shoot had come to an end, she was pregnant with Rossellini's first child, Isabella. The Catholic Church would not approve the director's divorce and Bergman left her own family to live with him in Italy. The public reaction was merciless towards the actress, who, in spite of her bold lifestyle, was a decent and conventional middle-class Swede. She suffered from the fact that she had hurt people important to her.

The films that Bergman made with Rossellini were not commercially successful and she later wrote that being a Hollywood star in a 'documentary' film just did not work. Bergman's return to American cinema was perhaps inevitable, but it also turned out to be triumphant. Her performance in the title role of *Anastasia* won her her second Academy Award. She later received a third Academy Award as Greta Ohlsson in *Murder on the Orient Express*.

In her youth, Bergman had made a number of successful comedies and her later films allowed a touch of her earlier rogueishness to be sensed beneath her surface serenity. One of the most important roles during the latter part of her career was in Ingmar Bergman's *Höstsonaten/Autumn Sonata* (1978). By the time of her last great performance, as the former Israeli Prime Minister Golda Meir in the 1982 television drama *A Woman Called Golda*, she was already marked by the cancer from which she died on her birthday that same year. TS

FILMS: *Intermezzo: A Love Story* (1939); *Rage in Heaven, Dr Jekyll and Mr Hyde, Adam Had Four Sons* (1941); *Casablanca* (1942); *For Whom the Bell Tolls* (1943); *Gaslight* (1944); *Spellbound, The Bells of St Mary's, Saratoga Trunk* (1945); *Notorious*

(1946); *Arch of Triumph, Joan of Arc* (1948); *Under Capricorn* (1949); *Anastasia* (1956); *The Inn of Sixth Happiness* (1958); *Goodbye Again* (1961); *The Yellow Rolls-Royce* (1965); *Cactus Flower* (1969); *Walk in the Spring Rain* (1970); *Murder on the Orient Express* (1974); *A Matter of Time* (1976).

BERGNER, Elisabeth (Elisabeth Ettel) (1897–1986)
Acclaimed German stage actress who entered German film in 1923. The erotic ambiguity of Bergner's silent film persona resurfaced after UK emigration in such films as *Catherine the Great* (1934). Bergner was prominent in the German exile community before starring in the anti-Nazi war drama *Paris Calling*. She continued a UK and German stage, film and television career after 1945. EC
FILM: *Paris Calling* (1941).

BERKOFF, Steven (Leslie Steven Berks) (1937–)
English actor whose serious theatrical career has been offset (and presumably part-funded) by an idiosyncratic choice of villainous Hollywood roles, often played with a variety of quasi-European accents. MF
FILMS: *The Sheriff of Fractured Jaw* (1958); *The Devil's Disciple* (1959); *A Clockwork Orange, Nicholas and Alexandra* (1971); *Barry Lyndon* (1975); *Outland* (1981); *Octopussy* (1983); *Beverly Hills Cop* (1984); *Rambo: First Blood Part II, Revolution* (1985); *Under the Cherry Moon* (1986); *Fair Game* (1995); *Love in Paris* (1997); *Legionnaire* (1998); *Head in the Clouds* (2004).

BERNHARDT, Sarah (Henriette Rosine Bernardt) (1844–1923)
Technically, Bernhardt never appeared in an American film produced in the USA. However, between 1880 and 1918, she made nine theatrical tours of the country. For the 1905–6, 1910–11 and 1912–13 tours, she shifted from acting in legitimate theatres to performing highlights of her famous roles to ever larger audiences in vaudeville houses and tent shows. These last two tours were especially significant in relation to the emergence of feature-length films in the USA. Film d'Art's *La Dame aux camélias/Camille* (1911), in which she reprised her role as Marguerite Gautier, functioned like a mini-tour (of the condensed play), usually booked for three-day or one-week runs in legitimate theatres throughout 1912 – often in conjunction with Film d'Art's *Madame Sans-Gêne* (with

Gabrielle Réjane). Although not shot in the USA, the next film in which Bernhardt starred, a four-reel adaptation of a failed stage play, *Queen Elizabeth*, was financed in large part by Adolph Zukor's new company, Famous Players, in exchange for distribution rights. Famous Players advertised *Queen Elizabeth* implicitly as an American feature, the first of more than three reels in length, and it enjoyed a smashing success for more than six months, beginning in August 1912. The film helped make the company a new force to be reckoned with in the industry, and it served as excellent promotion for the penultimate of Bernhardt's American tours. RA

FILM: *Queen Elizabeth* (1912).

BERTI, Marina (Elena Maureen Bertolini) (1924–2002)

Italian actress, sometimes credited as Maureen Melrose, whose first American role was alongside Orson Welles in *Prince of Foxes*. Although her career was firmly rooted in Italy, she appeared as a supporting actress in several Hollywood films. CS

FILMS: *Prince of Foxes* (1949); *Deported* (1950); *Up Front, Quo Vadis* (1951); *Ben-Hur* (1959); *Damon and Pythias, Jessica* (1962); *Face in the Rain, Cleopatra* (1963); *If it's Tuesday, This Must Be Belgium* (1969).

BEST, Edna (Edna Hove) (1900–1974)

British actress who was generally cast in gentle, soft-spoken, maternal roles in Hollywood productions. She took a leading role opposite husband Herbert Marshall★ in *Swiss Family Robinson* and is fondly remembered as Martha, housekeeper to Gene Tierney, in *The Ghost and Mrs Muir*. MHu

FILMS: *The Key* (1934); *Intermezzo: A Love Story* (1939); *Swiss Family Robinson, A Dispatch from Reuters* (1940); *The Late George Apley, The Ghost and Mrs Muir* (1947); *The Iron Curtain* (1948).

BINOCHE, Juliette (1964–)

'Bravo Juliette!' cried an ecstatic French press (temporarily forgetting its anti-American feelings) when Binoche won an Academy Award as Best Supporting Actress in *The English Patient*. This remains the crowning achievement of her select but successful international career, which has ensured that at the turn of the twenty-first century she was probably the best-known French actress of her generation.

Binoche made her name as one of France's leading auteur cinema stars in Leos Carax's *Mauvais sang/Bad Blood* (1986) and *Les Amants du Pont-Neuf/The Lovers on the Bridge* (1991). The latter was a cause célèbre for its long, difficult shoot, for which Binoche put her career on hold, and the fact that she was unwashed and wore an eyepatch for most of the film. Other European dramas and costume films – by Kieslowski, Malle, Akerman and Kurys, among others – exploited her glowing, delicate beauty more conventionally, but retained the same qualities of romantic passion, intellectual aura and classy eroticism. It is the latter that her international films brought forward, trading on the stereotype of the sexy Frenchwoman, and pairing her with the cream of brooding, handsome British stars: Daniel Day-Lewis★ in *The Unbearable Lightness of Being*, Ralph Fiennes★ in *Wuthering Heights* and – disfigured – in *The English Patient*, as well as Jeremy Irons★ in the Franco-British, English-language *Damage* (1992).

A departure from this pattern was *Chocolat* (2000), a romantic comedy in which Binoche set a French village and Johnny Depp alight with her mouth-watering chocolates and tight sweaters. The fact that neither her role nor the village resembled anything seen in France bothered critics but did not stop the success of the film . . . except in France. Time will tell whether *Chocolat* was an exception or a significant departure from Binoche's accustomed dramatic roles. However, her credentials and discernment (she turned down the 'bimbo' part in *Mission: Impossible* that went to Emmanuelle Béart★), and her good English – honed on the London and New York stage – set her in good stead for that rarity: a proper international career for a French female star. GV

FILMS: *The Unbearable Lightness of Being* (1988); *Wuthering Heights* (1992); *The English Patient* (1996); *Chocolat* (2000).

BIRELL, Tala (Natlie Bierl) (1908–1959)

Blonde, blue-eyed star of the European stage in the 1920s who was hailed by Hollywood as another Greta Garbo★, but soon settled into routine leading roles in B-pictures. In the 1940s, Birell retreated to supporting roles and by the end of the decade she had retired from the screen. FG

FILMS: *The Doomed Battalion* (1932); *Nagana, Let's Fall in Love* (1933); *The Captain Hates the Sea* (1934); *Air Hawks, Spring Tonic, The Lone Wolf Returns, Crime and Punishment,* **181**

Let's Live Tonight (1935); *The White Legion* (1936); *As Good as Married, She's Dangerous* (1937); *Bringing up Baby, The Invisible Enemy, Josette* (1938); *Seven Miles from Alcatraz, One Dangerous Night, China, Isle of Forgotten Sins* (1943); *Women in Bondage, Mrs Parkington, Till We Meet Again, The Purple Heart, The Monster Maker, Make Your Own Bed* (1944); *The Song of Bernadette, The Frozen Ghost, Girls of the Big House, The Power of the Whistler, Jungle Woman* (1945); *Dangerous Millions* (1946); *Philo Vance's Gamble, Philo Vance's Secret Mission, Song of Love* (1947); *Women in the Night, Homicide for Three* (1948).

BISSET, Jacqueline (Winnifred Jacqueline Fraser-Bisset) (1944–)

Former English model who made her screen debut alongside Charlotte Rampling★ in the US-backed *The Knack – and how to get it . . .*, before playing a minor role in Roman Polanski's *Cul-de-Sac* (1965). Bisset's extraordinary good looks earned her a contract with Twentieth Century-Fox and in the late 1960s and early 1970s she featured in undemanding high-profile roles opposite Frank Sinatra in *The Detective*, as Steve McQueen's love interest in *Bullit* and as Dean Martin's pregnant girlfriend in *Airport*. Back in Europe, Bisset earned praise for her leading role in François Truffaut's★ film about film-making, *La Nuit américaine / Day for Night* (1973). On her return to Hollywood later in the 1970s, she starred in an adaptation of Peter Benchley's *The Deep* and was notoriously promoted clad solely in a conveniently wet T-shirt. This dichotomy between European actress and Hollywood nymphette was gradually eroded when Bisset received Golden Globe nominations for *Who is Killing the Great Chefs of Europe?* and John Huston's *Under the Volcano*. Although her film appearances have been limited since the early 1980s, Bisset has continued to work regularly in a number of American television films and high-profile mini-series. MF

FILMS: *The Knack – and how to get it . . .* (1965); *The Cape Town Affair* (1967); *The Detective, The Sweet Ride, Bullit* (1968); *The First Time* (1969); *Airport, The Grasshopper* (1970); *The Mephisto Waltz, Believe in Me* (1971); *Stand up and Be Counted, The Life and Times of Judge Roy Bean* (1972); *The Thief Who Came to Dinner* (1973); *St Ives* (1976); *The Deep* (1977); *The Greek Tycoon, Who is Killing the Great Chefs of Europe?* (1978); *When Time Ran Out* (1980); *Rich and Famous* (1981); *Inchon* (1982); *Class* (1983); *Under the Volcano*

(1984); *Scenes from the Class Struggle in Beverly Hills* (1989); *Wild Orchid* (1990); *The Maid* (1991); *Once You Meet a Stranger* (1996); *Dangerous Beauty* (1998); *Let the Devil Wear Black* (1999); *Sleepy Time Gal* (2001); *Latter Days* (2003); *Swing* (2004).

BJÖRK, Anita (1923–)

Talented Swedish film and theatre actress who thanks, in part, to her fluent English was contracted by Warners to appear in Hitchcock's *I Confess* (1953). Björk arrived in Hollywood with her partner, the screenwriter Stig Dagerman, but relations with the studio broke down following the discovery that the couple's child was born out of wedlock and that Dagerman was still married to another woman. Björk starred opposite Gregory Peck in an unsuccessful cold war thriller shot in Europe the following year. AP

FILMS: *Night People* (1954); *Square of Violence* (1964).

BLAIN, Gérard (1930–2000)

Blain was closely associated with the French New Wave and cited by some as the era's equivalent to James Dean. His only Hollywood project, *Hatari!*, was with one of the New Wave's critical idols, Howard Hawks. He found the experience disappointing and returned to France after the lengthy shoot, despite the offer of a five-year contract with Paramount. AP

FILM: *Hatari!* (1962).

BLANC, Anne-Marie (1919–)

Blanc became Switzerland's most popular female film star with her role as a soldier's girl in the wartime melodrama *Gilberte de Courgenay* (1941). Unsuccessful postwar attempts at translating her domestic stardom into an international career included her only Hollywood film *White Cradle Inn*. VH

FILM: *White Cradle Inn* (1946).

BLESSED, Brian (1937–)

Blessed's bluff, hale and hearty presence first came to prominence in the long-running British television series, *Z Cars*. His commanding personality, weighty figure, booming voice and hirsute appearance have featured in various US-funded productions over the years – exemplified by the role of Lord Lockley in *Robin Hood: Prince of Thieves* – but his career has remained largely based in UK film and television. AP

FILMS: *Country Dance* (1970); *The Last Valley, The Trojan Women* (1971); *Man of La Mancha* (1972); *Flash Gordon* (1980); *High Road to China* (1983); *Robin Hood: Prince of Thieves* (1991); *Back in the U.S.S.R.* (1992); *Much Ado about Nothing* (1993); *Hamlet* (1996); *Star Wars Episode I: The Phantom Menace, Tarzan* [voice] (1999); *Alexander* (2004).

BLOOM, Claire (Claire Blume) (1931–)

Successful British Shakespearean stage actress who projected a combination of class, vulnerability and eroticism in *Limelight*, her first Hollywood film, which also co-starred Charlie Chaplin★. She has continued to display these qualities, both on stage and screen, especially in her two films made with Woody Allen. TJ

FILMS: *Limelight* (1952); *The Brothers Karamazov* (1958); *The Chapman Report* (1962); *Charly* (1968); *The Illustrated Man* (1969); *Crimes and Misdemeanors* (1989); *Mighty Aphrodite* (1995); *Daylight* (1996); *Wrestling with Alligators* (1998); *Imagining Argentina* (2003).

BLORE, Eric (1887–1959)

On British soil Blore's screen career was restricted to a solitary 1920 short, but Broadway musical comedy provided the launch pad for a prolific career as Hollywood's favourite interfering and judgmental manservant, most memorably in several Fred Astaire–Ginger Rogers musicals. With his unctuous lisp and habit of mastering and manipulating his masters' various predicaments, he laid down a blueprint for the Hollywood British butler that was still being closely followed by Terry-Thomas★ in the 1960s. JB

FILMS: *The Great Gatsby* (1926); *Laughter* (1930); *Tarnished Lady, My Sin* (1931); *Flying Down to Rio* (1933); *Folies-Bergère, The Gay Divorcee, Limehouse Blues* (1934); *Behold My Wife, The Good Fairy, The Casino Murder Case, Old Man Rhythm, Top Hat, I Live My Life, I Dream Too Much, Seven Keys to Baldpate, To Beat the Band, Diamond Jim* (1935); *The Ex-Mrs Bradford, Piccadilly Jim, Swing Time, Smartest Girl in Town, Two in the Dark, Sons o' Guns* (1936); *The Soldier and the Lady, Shall We Dance?, Sunday Night at the Trocadero, It's Love I'm After, Breakfast for Two, Hitting a New High, Quality Street* (1937); *Joy of Living, Swiss Miss, A Desperate Adventure* (1938); *Island of Lost Men, A Gentleman's Gentleman, $1,000 a Touchdown* (1939); *The Man Who Wouldn't Talk, 'Til We Meet Again, Music in My Heart, The Boys from Syracuse, Earl of Puddlestone, The Lone Wolf Strikes, South of Suez, The Lone*

Wolf Meets a Lady (1940); *Road to Zanzibar, Lady Scarface, New York Town, Confirm or Deny, Three Girls about Town, The Shanghai Gesture, Secrets of the Lone Wolf, Red Head, The Lone Wolf Takes a Chance, The Lone Wolf Keeps a Date, The Lady Eve* (1941); *Counter-Espionage, Sullivan's Travels, The Moon and Sixpence* (1942); *Forever and a Day, One Dangerous Night, Submarine Base, The Sky's the Limit, Passport to Suez, Holy Matrimony, Heavenly Music, Happy Go Lucky, Caribbean Romance* (1943); *San Diego I Love You* (1944); *I Was a Criminal, Penthouse Rhythm, Easy to Look At, Men in Her Diary* (1945); *Kitty, Abie's Irish Rose, The Notorious Lone Wolf* (1946); *Winter Wonderland, The Lone Wolf in London, The Lone Wolf in Mexico* (1947); *Romance on the High Seas* (1948); *The Adventures of Ichabod and Mr Toad* [voice] (1949); *Love Happy, Fancy Pants* (1950); *Bowery to Bagdad* (1954).

BOEHM, Karl (Karlheinz Böhm) (1928–)

Hugely popular Austrian-born blond and blue-eyed romantic lead in postwar West German films. Overnight, he became regarded as box-office poison after starring in Britain as the psychopathic killer in Michael Powell's universally condemned, but later revered, *Peeping Tom* (1960). Between 1961 and 1963, parts as archetypal 'German' figures in Hollywood productions shot in Europe offered Boehm a lifeline, but he never settled permanently in the USA. RJK

FILMS: *Four Horsemen of the Apocalypse* (1961); *The Wonderful World of the Brothers Grimm* (1962); *Come Fly with Me* (1963); *The Venetian Affair* (1967).

BOGARDE, Dirk (Derek Jules Gaspard Ulric Niven van den Bogaerde) (1921–1999)

Handsome and debonair English actor who graduated from being a matinée idol to an actor capable of great nuance and insight. Compared to his distinguished European career, Bogarde's work in Hollywood was disappointing, since he was clearly cast for his dashing looks, rather than his acting prowess. His work on the classical music epic, *Song without End*, which co-starred Capucine★, may at least have provided material for his satirical Hollywood novel *West of Sunset*. TJ

FILMS: *The Doctor's Dilemma* (1958); *Libel* (1959); *Song without End, The Angel Wore Red* (1960); *H.M.S. Defiant, The Password is Courage* (1962); *I Could Go on Singing* (1963); *Modesty Blaise* (1966); *Our Mother's House* (1967); *Sebastian,* **183**

The Fixer (1968); *Oh! What a Lovely War, Justine* (1969); *Permission to Kill* (1975); *A Bridge Too Far* (1977).

BOIS, Curt (1901–1991)

Popular German-Jewish comedian who entered films as a child actor in 1907. Fleeing Nazi Germany, he emigrated via Austria to New York in 1934. After three unsuccessful years on Broadway, the dark-haired, gaunt-looking actor resettled in Hollywood and established himself as a diverse and dependable character player, admirably free from typecasting and earning between $750 and $1,250 per week. In Germany, meanwhile, his screen image was vilified – like that of Peter Lorre★ – as 'evidence of Jewish depravity' in the propaganda film *Der ewige Jude/ The Eternal Jew* (1940). In 1950, dissatisfied with Hollywood corporatism and his own lack of stardom, Bois moved to East Germany, and became a familiar face in East and West German film and television comedy until his death. RJK

FILMS: *Tovarich* (1937); *Hollywood Hotel, Romance in the Dark, Gold Diggers in Paris, The Amazing Dr Clitterhouse, Boy Meets Girl, Garden of the Moon, The Great Waltz* (1938); *Hotel Imperial, The Hunchback of Notre Dame* (1939); *The Lady in Question, Boom Town, Bitter Sweet, Hullabaloo, He Stayed for Breakfast* (1940); *That Night in Rio, Hold Back the Dawn, Blue, White and Perfect* (1941); *My Gal Sal, Casablanca, The Tuttles of Tahiti, Pacific Rendezvous* (1942); *Destroyer, Paris after Dark, Princess O'Rourke, Swing Fever, The Desert Song* (1943); *Cover Girl, Gypsy Wildcat, Blonde Fever* (1944); *The Spanish Main* (1945); *Saratoga Trunk* (1946); *Jungle Flight* (1947); *French Leave, Arch of Triumph, The Woman in White, The Woman from Tangier, Up in Central Park, Let's Live a Little* (1948); *Caught, The Lovable Cheat, The Great Sinner, A Kiss in the Dark, Oh, You Beautiful Doll* (1949); *Joe Palooka Meets Humphrey, Fortunes of Captain Blood* (1950).

BONANOVA, Fortunio (Josep Lluis Moll) (1895–1969)

Successful Spanish actor and opera singer who made his Spanish film debut in the title role of *Don Juan Tenorio* (1921). Bonanova went to the USA in 1930 to co-star with Katherine Cornell on Broadway. He soon moved to Hollywood, where he began appearing in numerous Spanish- and English-language films. Bonanova made a lasting impression portraying likeable, big-hearted Latin characters such as the feverish singing teacher Signor

Matisti in *Citizen Kane*. In *Kiss Me Deadly*, he gave a heart-breaking performance as the pitiful opera singer bullied by the ruthless detective Mike Hammer. Bonanova continued playing small film roles throughout the 1950s and 1960s, as well as appearing in various American television series. EU

FILMS: *A Successful Calamity, Careless Lady* (1932); *The Devil on Horseback, Captain Calamity* (1937); *Bulldog Drummond in Africa, Tropic Holiday, Romance in the Dark* (1938); *The Mark of Zorro, Down Argentine Way, I Was an Adventuress* (1940); *Mr and Mrs North, Obliging Your Lady, They Met in Argentina, Two Latins from Manhattan, A Yank in the RAF, Unfinished Business, Moon over Miami, Blood and Sand, Citizen Kane, That Night in Rio* (1941); *The Black Swan, Sing Your Worries Away, Girl Trouble, Larceny, Inc., Four Jacks and a Jill* (1942); *Five Graves to Cairo, For Whom the Bell Tolls, Dixie, Hello Frisco, Hello* (1943); *The Falcon in Mexico, The Sultan's Daughter, Brazil, Mrs Parkington, Double Indemnity, Going My Way, My Best Gal, Ali Baba and the Forty Thieves* (1944); *A Bell for Adano, Men Alive, The Red Dragon, Where Do We Go from Here?* (1945); *Hit the Hay, Monsieur Beaucaire* (1946); *Rose of Santa Rosa, The Fugitive, Fiesta* (1947); *Angel on the Amazon, Adventures of Don Juan, Romance on the High Seas* (1948); *Whirlpool, Bad Men of Tombstone* (1949); *September Affair, Nancy Goes to Rio* (1950); *Havana Rose* (1951); *Conquest of Cochise, Second Chance, So This is Love, The Moon is Blue, Thunder Bay* (1953); *New York Confidential; Kiss Me Deadly* (1955); *Jaguar* (1956); *An Affair to Remember* (1957); *The Saga of Hemp Brown* (1958); *Thunder in the Sun* (1959); *The Running Man* (1963).

BONHAM CARTER, Helena (1966–)

Bonham Carter's choice of American roles might indicate a certain desire to free herself of both the genteel period trappings that first launched her onto the international screen, and an appearance typically described as 'pale and porcelain-pretty with a heart-shaped face'. Her roles in Merchant-Ivory's *A Room with a View* (1986) and *Howards End* (1992) did, however, bring her undeniable prestige in Hollywood, and so it was that her first truly international role – Ophelia in Zefferelli's *Hamlet* – became the perfect next step for her fragile form of beauty.

Nonetheless, those Edwardian (or are they Pre-Raphaelite?) locks and pale English rosiness seem a world apart from the chain-smoking, deathly pale Marla in David

Fincher's *Fight Club* and the addled drug addict who gets Steve Martin into trouble in *Novocaine*. And on top of this, almost as if to protest against her trademark countenance, Bonham Carter has even donned latex to appear as a half-human chimpanzee in Tim Burton's remake of *Planet of the Apes*. MW

FILMS: *Lady Jane* (1986); *Hamlet* (1990); *Mary Shelley's Frankenstein* (1994); *Mighty Aphrodite* (1995); *Twelfth Night: Or What You Will* (1996); *The Wings of the Dove* (1997); *Fight Club* (1999); *Novocaine, Planet of the Apes* (2001); *Big Fish* (2003).

BORCHERS, Cornell (Cornelia Bruch) (1925–)

Tall, blonde and slender Lithuanian-born German actress whose debut US film role in *The Big Lift* highlighted the fragile but telling cultural and political gulf between Germans and Americans in the immediate postwar period. Borchers played a beautiful *Trümmerfrau* (rubble woman) who becomes indebted to the generosity of an American serviceman (Montgomery Clift). Although compared by some to Ingrid Bergman★, Borchers in her ensuing Hollywood career never lived up to the promise signalled by *The Big Lift*'s utopian reconciliation between European and American interests. AP

FILMS: *The Big Lift* (1950); *Never Say Goodbye* (1956); *Istanbul* (1957); *Flood Tide* (1958).

BORDONI, Irène (1895–1953)

Born in Corsica, Bordoni was initially a child actress and vaudeville singer before making films for Pathé. After her Broadway debut in 1912, she became a major star of music-hall revues in Paris, London and the USA, where she remained after 1918, described as 'petite, chic, coquettish and the epitome of French oh-la-la'. Her US films were mostly filmed versions of her stage shows. MB/GV

FILMS: *The Show of Shows, Paris* (1929); *Just a Gigolo* (1932); *Du Barry Did All Right* (1937); *Louisiana Purchase* (1941).

BORGATO, Agostino (1869–1939)

Italian actor and director, sometimes known as Agostino, Augustino or Al Borgato, who moved from Italy to the USA in 1925 under contract to Pathé. He was often cast as a tough guy but also appeared in a number of uncredited minor parts as a foreign character. CS

FILMS: *The Street of Forgotten Men* (1925); *The Love Thief* (1926); *The Private Life of Helen of Troy, The Magic Flame, Hula, Horse Shoes, Fashions for Women, A Kiss in a Taxi* (1927); *A Woman of Affairs, A Perfect Gentleman* (1928); *Hot for Paris, Romance of the Rio Grande, Madame X, She Goes to War* (1929); *Behind the Make-Up, A Lady's Morals, Redemption* (1930); *Transgression* [scenes deleted], *The Maltese Falcon* (1931); *A Farewell to Arms, Bird of Paradise, Murders in the Rue Morgue* (1932); *Christopher Strong, The White Sister* (1933); *Marie Galante, All Men are Enemies, Now and Forever* (1934); *Mad Love, The Gay Deception, In Caliente* (1935); *Till We Meet Again, Wives Never Know, Ellis Island, Lloyds of London, Love on the Run, Suzy, Rose-Marie* (1936); *Love under Fire, Man of the People, Daughter of Shanghai, Internes Can't Take Money, The Firefly, The Bride Wore Red, The Emperor's Candlesticks, Maytime* (1937); *A Trip to Paris, Swiss Miss* (1938); *Hotel Imperial* (1939).

BOWIE, David (David Robert Jones) (1947–)

British pop legend whose early work self-consciously foregrounding issues of performance and stardom led to roles in European films such as Nic Roeg's *The Man Who Fell to Earth* (1976). Since his relocation to the USA in the 1980s, a number of leading American directors with a preference for foregrounding contemporary pop songs in their soundtracks have added Bowie to the visual mix. JB

FILMS: *Into the Night* (1985); *Labyrinth* (1986); *The Last Temptation of Christ* (1988); *The Linguini Incident* (1991); *Twin Peaks: Fire Walk with Me* (1992); *Basquiat* (1996); *Zoolander* (2001).

BOYD, Stephen (William Millar) (1931–1977)

Born in Northern Ireland, Boyd worked on the outskirts of British film and television before being cast as an Irishman spying for the Nazis in the British wartime thriller, *The Man Who Never Was* (1956). He was contracted to Twentieth Century-Fox and moved to Hollywood to take a role in *The Bravados*. Blessed with sculptural good looks, Boyd became associated with the epic films of the period and made his breakthrough opposite Charlton Heston as the villain Messala in William Wyler's *Ben-Hur*, a role for which he won a Golden Globe award. He was the first choice to play James Bond in *Dr No* (1962) and in 1963 was originally cast as Marc Antony opposite Elizabeth Taylor in *Cleopatra* – the part eventually went to Richard

Burton★. In the late 1960s and 1970s, Boyd principally appeared in a string of European co-productions such as *Shalako* (1968) with Sean Connery★ and Brigitte Bardot★.

RB

FILMS: *The Man Who Never Was* (1956); *Seven Waves Away, Island in the Sun* (1957); *The Bravados* (1958); *The Best of Everything, Woman Obsessed, Ben-Hur* (1959); *The Big Gamble* (1961); *Jumbo, Lisa* (1962); *The Fall of the Roman Empire* (1964); *Genghis Khan* (1965); *The Oscar, Fantastic Voyage, The Poppy is Also a Flower, The Bible – in the Beginning . . .* (1966); *The Caper of the Golden Bulls* (1967); *Slaves* (1969); *Evil in the Deep* (1976); *The Squeeze* (1977).

BOYER, Charles (1899–1978)

Charles Boyer is arguably the most successful French émigré actor to have worked in Hollywood. With his trademark dark heavy eyebrows, deep and resonant accented voice and mellow but profoundly romantic manner, he appeared in numerous leading roles during the 1930s and 1940s as the epitome of cultured, Continental sophistication. In terms of the frequent representation of Europe in his films, his flair for political effort on the part of French interests and his adeptness in choosing projects that often reworked existing French films, he bridged the divide between the Old World and the New for American and international audiences alike.

By the time that Boyer was first recruited by MGM's Paul Bern in 1929, he was already a highly successful *boulevard* stage *jeune premier* with experience in French cinema, but his early American film career may be read as a series of false starts, despite the encouragement of the studio's production supervisor, Irving Thalberg. It had originally been intended that Boyer should work with Greta Garbo★, but he made his US screen debut instead in the multi-language film, *Le Procès de Mary Dugan* (1929). *Révolte dans la prison* (1930) – another French multi-language version – followed during a second visit, during which Boyer finally made his English-language debut as a duplicitous French actor in Paramount's *The Magnificent Lie*. Subsequent roles in *The Man from Yesterday* (with Claudette Colbert) and *Red-Headed Woman* (with Jean Harlow) nonetheless had to be deliberately tailored to suit Boyer's prominent early linguistic difficulties. In the latter, as a romantically inclined French chauffeur, for example, he found Harlow preferred the words 'my darling!' to be spoken in his native tongue.

Charles Boyer: France's most successful Hollywood émigré actor

Boyer's involvement in both versions of fellow émigré Erik Charell's gypsy musical *Caravan/Caravane* was another disappointment, but it did lead to an influential association with the Hollywood agent Charles Feldman, who established a lucrative series of one-picture contracts. By now, Hollywood was becoming mindful of Boyer's true star potential and with *Private Worlds*, in the second of various doctor roles throughout his career, Boyer's persona was based on the assured embodiment of mature, European romantic savoir-faire. The actor's image as the 'French lover' still remained unstable, though. In part, this was due to Hollywood's general tendency to exoticise when it came to the projection of ethnically marked stardom, but it was also because of Boyer's own previous international success as a multi-ethnic Japanese Frenchman in *Thunder in the East* (1934) – the English-language version of his hit French film (and play), *La Bataille*. The independent producer Walter Wanger devised Boyer's unlikely half-Chinese character role in *Shanghai* as a temporary continuation of this trend, and the actor was later cast as a Russian in Paris in *Tovarich*, while stalwart British émigrés such as Basil Rathbone* were left to play the French. As Boyer said, 'I have only one accent, but as long as the accent sounds foreign, that is enough.'

Hollywood began to reconcile these disparate elements extra-textually by creating a star identity for the Frenchman that combined true romantic feeling with intellectual authenticity. In publicity photos for *Break of Hearts*, in which Boyer played a famous orchestral leader, he was specifically lit to accentuate the sensuality of his contemplative eyes. In contrast to more rugged native male performers of the time like Clark Gable, he was regularly pictured indoors (often reading). This would have three significant repercussions. First, it dealt with the question of sexual integrity, which mattered, since Boyer was no longer an eligible bachelor and disliked the glare of the limelight. Second, it pointed to an abiding association with the authority of traditional French history and culture – Boyer read widely in the French classics and received the first of three Academy Award nominations for his psychologically acute portrayal of Napoleon in *Conquest*. Third, it helped seal Boyer's political commitment to the role of his influential French Research Foundation (FRF) when it was established in autumn 1940 to counteract erroneous depictions of French culture.

World War II saw a turning point in terms of Boyer's relationship with the USA. On screen, he was increasingly being cast in women's films with stars such as Bette Davis and Margaret Sullavan, but off screen the actor also functioned as an important conduit for Franco-American cultural relations. His specially written part in *Love Affair* (with Irene Dunne) had already been rewritten when the French embassy showed concern that an affair between an American wife and a French ambassador might alienate the American public at a time of impending conflict. In a move emblematic of Boyer's distinctive transcontinental status, the film was relocated to a mid-Atlantic liner, with Boyer playing an eligible French bachelor painter instead.

Although Boyer briefly joined the French army and worked to gain security for French refugees, including Jean Renoir and Jean Gabin*, he was urged to play his part for the war effort by returning to the USA. There, he organised Red Cross fund-raising galas, welcomed fellow French émigrés such as Michèle Morgan* and Simone Simon*, founded the French War Relief Committee, narrated seven propaganda films for the American War Ministry and spoke regularly in French for Voice of America radio. By 1942 – the year Boyer finally took American nationality – the FRF and its three full-time archivists were principally documenting France's wartime activities. He won a special Academy Award in 1943 for his many artistic, cultural and political efforts to counteract isolationism.

Boyer's persona shifted away from the matinée idol after World War II. He won a third Best Actor Academy Award nomination for his performance as the suave but murderous husband in *Gaslight*. By 1945, he was becoming too old to be partnered opposite the rising generation of younger actresses and the studios sensed he was over-priced – he was Warners' highest-paid employee that year. His role as the lecherous clinic executive in *The Cobweb* ten years later may be read as a final deconstruction of his popular French lover identity.

Boyer worked instead on resurrecting his stage career. He became disillusioned with Hollywood after the HUAC investigations, wound down the FRF and purchased properties back in Europe. The new age of jet travel did, however, enable a transformation in Boyer's cosmopolitan profile. He returned to French cinema and became involved in the trend towards international co-productions; he also flew regularly between France and Los Angeles in conjunction with his hugely successful Four Star Television production company.

By the time of his son's suicide in California in 1965, Boyer's position within Hollywood had become permanently altered. On and off screen, he had been a vital lynchpin in the industry's international economic strategy during the formative years of the sound era. Now, just as his adopted home had always been seen by him as 'a geographical myth', so too was his version of exportable European identity ultimately renounced as an illusory ideal. AP

FILMS: *The Magnificent Lie* (1931); *The Man from Yesterday*, *Red-Headed Woman* (1932); *Caravan* (1934); *Private Worlds*, *Break of Hearts*, *Shanghai* (1935); *The Garden of Allah*, *Hotel Imperial* (1936); *History is Made at Night*, *Conquest*, *Tovarich* (1937); *Algiers* (1938); *Love Affair*, *When Tomorrow Comes* (1939); *All This, and Heaven Too* (1940); *Back Street*, *Hold Back the Dawn*, *Appointment for Love* (1941); *Tales of Manhattan* (1942); *The Constant Nymph*, *Flesh and Fantasy* (1943); *Gaslight*, *Together Again* (1944); *Confidential Agent* (1945); *Cluny Brown* (1946); *A Woman's Vengeance*, *Arch of Triumph* (1948); *The Thirteenth Letter*, *The First Legion* **187**

(1951); *The Happy Time, Thunder in the East* (1952); *The Cobweb* (1955); *Around the World in Eighty Days* (1956); *The Buccaneer* (1958); *Fanny* (1961); *Four Horsemen of the Apocalypse* (1962); *Love is a Ball* (1963); *A Very Special Favor* (1965); *How to Steal a Million* (1966); *Casino Royale, Barefoot in the Park* (1967); *The April Fools, The Madwoman of Chaillot* (1969); *Lost Horizon* (1973); *A Matter of Time* (1976).

BOZZUFFI, Marcel (1928–1988)

French character actor specialising in tough guy roles who made a few American films during the 1970s and early 1980s, following the success of *The French Connection*, in which he played a French hitman pursued by Gene Hackman in the New York subway. VO

FILMS: *The French Connection* (1971); *The Destructors* (1974); *March or Die* (1977); *Bloodline* (1979).

BRADNA, Olympe (1920–)

Olympe Bradna travelled to the USA as part of a Folies Bergère tour of the USA in 1934. The attractive young French brunette stayed in Hollywood, where she caught the attention of Paramount. Bradna embarked on a short career as a minor leading lady, mainly in adventure B-pictures, before marrying her Californian husband and retiring. CH

FILMS: *Three Cheers for Love, College Holiday* (1936); *Last Train from Madrid, Souls at Sea, High, Wide, and Handsome, Heaven on a Shoestring* (1937); *Stolen Heaven, Say it in French* (1938); *The Nights of Nights* (1939); *South of Pago Pago* (1940); *Highway West, International Squadron, Knockout* (1941).

BRAGGIOTTI, Francesca (1902–1998)

Italian-born dancer whose ballet company appeared in *Anna Karenina* (1935). She began working in the cinema dubbing Greta Garbo★ into Italian for MGM and played just one minor role in a Hollywood film before returning to Europe. AM

FILM: *Rasputin and the Empress* (1933).

BRAINVILLE, Yves (Yves de la Chevardière de la Grandville) (1914–1993)

French actor whose first credited American role was alongside compatriot Daniel Gélin★ as the Marrakech police

inspector in Hitchcock's *The Man Who Knew Too Much*. He continued to specialise mainly in law and order roles. VO

FILMS: *The Man Who Knew Too Much, The Mountain* (1956); *Paris Holiday* (1958); *Crack in the Mirror* (1960); *The Night of the Generals* (1967); *Love and Death* (1975).

BRANAGH, Kenneth (1960–)

Gifted Shakespearean stage actor whose central role in British film and theatre was assured following a triumphant leading role in *Henry V* (1987). For a while, Branagh was the new Laurence Olivier★, but his gentle irreverence and subsequent postmodern literary adaptations prompted critical accusations of unthinking populism. It is tempting to see the career in Hollywood of the self-described 'short-assed, fat-faced Irishman' as a deliberate provocation to dissenters back home, although that is not to say that his American films have been an unqualified success. While the convoluted neo-noir thriller *Dead Again* and the star-filled comedy *Much Ado about Nothing* (both also directed by Branagh) did well, the hyper-Gothic *Mary Shelley's Frankenstein* (directed by Branagh and produced by Francis Ford Coppola) met with severe criticism. Branagh's eagerness to test new waters has also led to a number of largely unconvincing performances: as a priest in *The Proposition*, a Deep South lawyer in Robert Altman's noirish *The Gingerbread Man* and a sub-Woody Allen neurotic in *Celebrity*. On the other hand, his suitably absurd take on moustachioed villainy was the highlight of the poorly received blockbuster *Wild Wild West*. Branagh's well-spoken persona lent him to consideration for the reprisal of Alec Guinness'★ role in the second *Star Wars* trilogy, though this was eventually given to the younger, and distinctly less 'English', Ewan McGregor★. MF

FILMS: *Dead Again* (1991); *Much Ado about Nothing, Swing Kids* (1993); *Mary Shelley's Frankenstein* (1994); *Looking for Richard, Hamlet* (1996); *The Gingerbread Man, The Proposition, Celebrity* (1998); *Wild Wild West* (1999); *Love's Labours Lost, The Road to El Dorado* [voice], *How to Kill Your Neighbor's Dog* (2000); *Harry Potter and the Chamber of Secrets* (2002).

BRANDAUER, Klaus-Maria (Klaus Georg Steng) (1943–)

Leading Austrian stage actor whose occasional forays into film have earned him numerous awards and an esteemed

position in international cinema comparable to that occupied by fellow countryman Oskar Werner★ during the
1960s. With his lived-in looks and a harsh, penetrating gaze,
the blond-haired Brandauer has brought psychological
depth and solid characterisation to his supporting roles as
generally villainous Germans and Russians in Hollywood
pictures. Already well established in German-language
theatre when he made his movie debut in the thriller *The
Salzburg Connection*, Brandauer was so disappointed with his
performance as neo-Nazi hoodlum Johann Kronsteiner
that he did not return to the screen for seven years. He first
rose to international acclaim playing actor Hendrik Hoef-
gen, who makes a Faustian pact with Nazism in István
Szabó's Academy Award-winning *Mephisto* (1981). This was
followed by his breakthrough role for American audiences
as James Bond's arch-nemesis Maximillian Largo in *Never
Say Never Again*. Brandauer's greatest success in the USA
came playing the Baron Blixen-Finecke, Meryl Streep's
uncaring, philandering husband, in *Out of Africa*. He earned
Academy Award and BAFTA nominations, a Golden
Globe, the National Board of Review Award and the New
York Film Critics Award. Follow-up roles in two undistinguished pictures, in which Brandauer's performance was
generally acknowledged as the only outstanding element,
failed to establish the actor's long-term presence in Hollywood. Brandauer returned to American attention portraying Otto Preminger in the HBO mini-series *Introducing
Dorothy Dandridge* (1999), for which he was Emmy- and
Golden Globe-nominated. The actor now lives between
Austria and New York. RJK

FILMS: *The Salzburg Connection* (1972); *Never Say Never
Again* (1983); *Out of Africa, The Lightship* (1985); *Streets of
Gold* (1986); *The Russia House* (1990); *White Fang* (1991).

**BRASSEUR, Pierre (Pierre-Albert Espinasse)
(1905–1972)**

Eminent French stage and screen actor who began his pro-
lific European screen career with a small part in Léonce
Perret's American-funded feature film shot in France about
Napoleon. SL

FILM: *Madame Sans-Gêne* (1925).

BRAZZI, Rossano (1916–1994)

Italian actor, singer and director whose Hollywood persona
of the Latin lover closely shadowed him in real life. Before

Rossano Brazzi: the personification of the 'Latin Lover'

breaking into the American film world, Brazzi had been a
popular face in Italian cinema of the Fascist era, while simultaneously being actively involved in the anti-Fascist
movement. He was a strikingly handsome man who at the
height of his fame attracted an average of 65,000 letters a
month in six languages from female fans. His good looks
were not successfully exploited in his first American role,
though, where he played the ageing Professor Behr in *Little
Women*, a film made under contract to David O. Selznick.
International acclaim came in 1954 when he appeared in
both *The Barefoot Contessa* and *Three Coins in the Fountain*.

By the time that Brazzi came to play the suave Renato
Rossi in David Lean's British-American *Summertime*,
Katharine Hepburn, the star of the film, suggested that he
have his name appear alongside hers above the titles
because she was so impressed by his acting. After working
with him on *Legend of the Lost*, Sophia Loren★ described
Brazzi as 'the personification of the bigger-than-life Latin
lover. Perfectly coiffed, impeccably dressed, he was a welcome relief, always performing, mimicking, prancing about,
throwing seductive looks in every direction, and always,
always singing, "Some Enchanted Evening".' Conversely,
despite his powerful voice, which did indeed earn him **189**

many musical roles, Brazzi's singing in *South Pacific* was not always up to scratch and he had to be dubbed by the voice of Giorgio Tozzi.

In the 1960s, Brazzi began writing, producing and directing films under the pseudonym Edward Ross. Although Brazzi often complained of being typecast as a romantic lead, the Baron or the 'Latin lover', in the first film he produced, *L'intrigo / Dark Purpose*, he willingly took on the role of a Count. He was finally given the chance to 'retaliate' in an episode of *Woman Times Seven*, when he played, as he put it, 'a satire of a Latin lover' opposite Shirley MacLaine. Brazzi continued to star in films and television shows in various countries from the 1960s to the 1980s. He maintained his status both at home and abroad, but also expanded his repertoire. He played Beckerman, the mastermind behind the robbery in the 1969 British classic, *The Italian Job*, and was Father DeCarlo, the nemesis of Damien and saviour of the world, in *Omen III: The Final Conflict*. CS

FILMS: *Little Women* (1949); *The Barefoot Contessa, Three Coins in the Fountain* (1954); *Angela, Summertime* (1955); *Legend of the Lost, Interlude* (1957); *South Pacific, A Certain Smile* (1958); *Count Your Blessings* (1959); *Light in the Piazza, Rome Adventure* (1962); *Dark Purpose* (1964); *The Battle of the Villa Fiorita, The Christmas that Almost Wasn't* (1965); *The Bobo, One Step to Hell, Woman Times Seven* (1967); *The Italian Job, Krakatoa, East of Java* (1969); *The Adventurers* (1970); *The Great Waltz* (1972); *Mr Kingstreet's War* (1973); *Mr Too Little* (1978); *Omen III: The Final Conflict* (1981); *Fear City, Final Justice* (1984).

BRENT, George (George Brendan Nolan) (1904–1979)

Irish matinée idol who became a minor star as a suave romantic lead during the studio era. Brent initially enjoyed a brief career with the Abbey Theatre actors before joining Michael Collins' guerrilla army as a despatch rider in the War of Independence. Following Collins' death, he fled the country for the USA. During the 1920s, Brent toured the country with a theatre group – his most successful appearance was as the lead in the Jewish-Irish hit, *Abie's Irish Rose* – and he used the proceeds from this to open his own theatre. In 1930, he appeared on Broadway, and on the strength of this landed a minor job at Fox. Following a screen test, Brent moved to Warners, where he was repeat-

Former Irish matinée idol George Brent became a dependable leading man in 1930s and 1940s Hollywood

edly cast opposite leading female studio stars such as Barbara Stanwyck and Bette Davis. Some of his most successful films were with the notoriously difficult Davis, notably *Jezebel* and *Dark Victory*. Brent's best-known role, though, remains Professor Warren in Siodmak's *The Spiral Staircase*. Brent's age militated against subsequent lead roles and he embarked on a brief and unsuccessful television career. As a contract actor, his chief function was to show Warners' leading ladies in their best light and consequently few of his roles, outside of *The Fighting 69th*, had any Irish content. RB

FILMS: *Under Suspicion* (1930); *Once a Sinner, Fair Warning, Charlie Chan Carries On, Ex-Bad Boy, Homicide Squad, The Lightning Warrior* (1931); *So Big!, The Rich are Always with Us, Weekend Marriage, Miss Pinkerton, The Purchase Price, The Crash, They Call it Sin* (1932); *42nd Street, Luxury Liner, The Keyhole, Lilly Turner, Private Detective 62, Baby Face, Female, From Headquarters* (1933); *Stamboul Quest, Housewife, Desirable, The Painted Veil* (1934); *The Right to Live, Living on Velvet, Stranded, Front Page Woman, Special Agent, The Goose and the Gander, In Person* (1935); *The Golden Arrow, Give Me Your Heart, The Case against Mrs Ames, More* than a Secretary, Snowed Under (1936); God's Country and the Woman, Mountain Justice, Go Getter, Submarine D-1 (1937); Lover Come Back, Gold is Where You Find it, Jezebel, Racket Busters, Secrets of an Actress (1938); Wings of the Navy, Dark Victory, The Old Maid, The Rains Came (1939); 'Til We Meet Again, The Man Who Talked Too Much, South of Suez (1940); Honeymoon for Three, The Great Lie, They Dare Not Love, International Lady (1941); Twin Beds, In this Our Life, Silver Queen, You Can't Escape Forever, The Gay Sisters (1942); Experiment Perilous (1944); The Affairs of Susan (1945); Tomorrow is Forever, My Reputation, The Spiral Staircase, Temptation (1946); Out of the Blue, The Fighting 69th, Adventure in Diamonds, The Corpse Came C.O.D., Christmas Eve, Slave Girl (1947); Angel on the Amazon, Luxury Liner (1948); Red Canyon, Illegal Entry, The Kid from Cleveland, Bride for Sale (1949); FBI Girl (1951); Montana Belle (1952); Tangier Incident, Mexican Manhunt (1953); Born Again (1978).

BRESSART, Felix (1890–1949)

Gaunt, serious-looking character actor who found fame in early German talkies essaying the screen persona for which he would also become known in Hollywood – that of a Middle European authority figure whose gruff exterior humorously gives way to reveal a heart of gold. The Jewish Bressart fled Germany the instant the Nazis came to power and made films in France, Switzerland and Austria before spending a year in London perfecting his English for Hollywood. Consequently immediately employable upon his arrival in 1938, Bressart received a long-term MGM contract and first stood out playing Deanna Durbin's music teacher in Three Smart Girls Grow Up and the hyper-materialistic Russian émigré Buljanoff in Ninotchka. He remained a familiar face, if never a household name, in the USA until his death. Bressart also held two doctorates, and may have been born as early as 1880. RJK

FILMS: Three Smart Girls Grow Up, Ninotchka, Swanee River, Bridal Suite (1939); The Shop around the Corner, It All Came True, Edison, the Man, Escape, Bitter Sweet, Comrade X, Third Finger, Left Hand (1940); Blossoms in the Dust, Married Bachelor, Ziegfeld Girl, Mr and Mrs North, Kathleen (1941); To Be or Not to Be, Iceland, Crossroads (1942); Don't Be a Sucker, Above Suspicion, Three Hearts for Julia, Song of Russia (1943); The Seventh Cross, Blonde Fever, Secrets in the Dark, Greenwich Village (1944); Dangerous Partners, Without Love (1945); The Thrill of Brazil, Her Sister's Secret, I've Always Loved You, Ding Dong Williams (1946); A Song is Born, Portrait of Jennie (1948); Take One False Step, My Friend Irma (1949).

BRISSON, Carl (Carl Brisson Pedersen) (1893–1958)

'One of the four biggest male draws in England', as an internal Paramount memo described him, Brisson had been a Danish welterweight boxing champion prior to becoming one of Europe's foremost operetta stars. He was a generously dimpled performer whose Count Danilo in the stage version of The Merry Widow was much admired. Brisson starred in the Hitchcock thrillers The Ring (1927) and The Manxman (1929), but it was his reputation as a matinée idol that attracted Hollywood's attention. MGM wanted him for the screen version of The Merry Widow (1934), but Maurice Chevalier★ was awarded the plum assignment instead because of conflicting schedules.

Paramount bought Murder at the Vanities especially for Brisson, but although he launched Sam Coslow's popular song 'Cocktails for Two', the musical flopped. All the King's Horses, co-starring the former opera diva Mary Ellis, followed, but this musical version of The Prisoner of Zenda fared even worse and Brisson ended his contract with the mediocre Ship Café.

Despite a European popularity so delirious at times that a popular set of dishes was named in his honour, Hollywood did not do right by Carl Brisson. Paramount obviously attempted to turn him and Mary Ellis into another Jeanette MacDonald and Nelson Eddy team, but the vehicles were clearly ill-chosen. Like Ellis, however, Brisson continued to thrill operetta and cabaret audiences in Europe. He remained best known in the USA as the father of the film producer Frederick Brisson and the father-in-law of Rosalind Russell. HJW

FILMS: Murder at the Vanities (1934); All the King's Horses, Ship Café (1935).

BROOK, Clive (Clifford Hardman Brook) (1887–1974)

With the end of World War I, Major Brook left military ranks to launch his acting career on the London stage. Within two years, this son of an opera singer and goldmining magnate had become a British film star at Gainsborough Pictures. In 1924, at the request of Thomas Ince, Brook left Britain for the USA and became contracted to **191**

Paramount, where his precise diction and upright poise soon earned him the nickname of 'the rock of Gibraltar'.

Brook's persona was fully realised in his debut talkie role as Sherlock Holmes in *The Return of Sherlock Holmes*. It was the first of two appearances as the great detective. During the 1930s, the actor's straight-laced appeal made him the perfect romantic foil to the more complex charms of co-stars such as Claudette Colbert and, particularly, Marlene Dietrich★, for whom he provided an unlikely love interest in von Sternberg's *Shanghai Express*. There was a leading role in the quadruple Academy Award-winning *Cavalcade* – a film that exploited his national credentials with its all-British cast. Brook later returned to the UK reporting that he was suffering from 'celluloid sickness'. He went back to the stage, but later appeared regularly on British film and television. MW

FILMS: *This Freedom* (1923); *Christine of the Hungry Heart, The Mirage, The Recoil* (1924); *Compromise, Declassée, Enticement, The Home Maker, If Marriage Fails, Playing with Souls, Pleasure Buyers, Seven Sinners, When Love Grows Cold, Three Faces East, The Woman Hater* (1925); *For Alimony Only, The Popular Sin, Why Girls Go Back Home, You Never Know Women* (1926); *The Devil Dancer, Afraid to Love, Barbed Wire, French Dressing, Hula, Underworld* (1927); *Forgotten Faces, Interference, Midnight Madness, Perfect Crime, Yellow Lily* (1928); *Charming Sinners, A Dangerous Woman, The Four Feathers, The Laughing Lady, The Return of Sherlock Holmes* (1929); *Anybody's Woman, Paramount on Parade, Slightly Scarlet, Sweethearts and Wives* (1930); *24 Hours, East Lynne, Husband's Holiday, The Lawyer's Secret, Scandal Sheet, Silence, Tarnished Lady* (1931); *Make Me a Star, The Man from Yesterday, The Night of June 13th, Shanghai Express, Sherlock Holmes* (1932); *Cavalcade, Gallant Lady, If I were Free, The Midnight Club* (1933); *Let's Try Again, Where Sinners Meet* (1934); *Dressed to Thrill* (1935); *The List of Adrian Messenger* (1963).

BROSNAN, Pierce (1953–)

Best known today as the Irish James Bond, Pierce Brosnan spent his early childhood in Ireland before moving to London, where he recalls adopting a cockney accent to protect himself from the ridicule of being Irish. He later claimed that early acting experiences gave 'a voice to express all the pain [and] angst of my childhood'. Brosnan's first screen role came with the television film *Murphy's Stroke*, which was followed by a part in the mini-series *The*

192

Mannions of America. When the series appeared on American television, Brosnan and his wife Cassandra, a former 'Bond girl', took a second mortgage on their home in London and bought tickets to the USA to cash in on his exposure. Brosnan auditioned for *Remington Steele* and eventually spent five years with the hit television show. He was initially offered the Bond role in *The Living Daylights* in 1986, but was unable to take the part because of contractual problems over *Remington Steele*.

Brosnan's first film role was as the IRA rent-boy in *The Long Good Friday* (1980). He made his first Hollywood appearance in John McTiernan's debut film, the psychological thriller *Nomads*, in which he played a French anthropologist haunted by the Inuit. He continued to be offered roles as hit men and played the killer in *The Fourth Protocol* (1987) and the violent debt collector in the minor Irish thriller *Taffin* (1988), where his dark good looks were used, as in so many later films, to suggest both danger and sexuality. Brosnan's first major role came with *The Lawnmower Man*, where he played the mad scientist who tampers with the possibilities opened up by virtual reality. By the time of the making of *Dante's Peak*, it seemed that Brosnan was destined to portray either hit men or scientists. In the same year, though, he played Bond for the first time in *Tomorrow Never Dies*, thus prolonging a tradition of having Celtic actors play the quintessential English gentleman hero. Brosnan has invested Bond with considerable postmodern irony and his performance in the successful remake of the 1968 film, *The Thomas Crown Affair*, clearly referenced his success as 007. Brosnan has used his American success to set up his own Irish production company, Irish Dreamtime, which makes films such as *Evelyn*, in which he also starred. RB

FILMS: *Nomads* (1986); *Mister Johnson* (1990); *The Lawnmower Man, Live Wire* (1992); *Mrs Doubtfire* (1993); *Don't Talk to Strangers, Love Affair* (1994); *GoldenEye* (1995); *Mirror Has Two Faces, Mars Attacks!, The Disappearance of Kevin Johnson* (1996); *Dante's Peak, Tomorrow Never Dies* (1997); *Quest for Camelot* [voice] (1998); *The Thomas Crown Affair, The World is Not Enough* (1999); *The Tailor of Panama* (2001); *Die Another Day, Evelyn* (2002); *After the Sunset* (2004).

BRUCE, Nigel (William Nigel Bruce) (1895–1953)

The numerous Hollywood characters Bruce played typecast him as a bumbling, but well-intentioned English gentleman of portly and slightly baronial appearance. Nonetheless, it is a testament to the talent of the Mexican-born actor that his performance as Dr Watson in the Sherlock Holmes films of the 1930s and 1940s remoulded the character from a sharp-witted companion into a comedic sidekick for many years to come. MW

FILMS: *Stand Up and Cheer!*, *Springtime for Henry*, *Treasure Island*, *Murder in Trinidad*, *Coming-Out Party* (1934); *Becky Sharp*, *The Man Who Broke the Bank at Monte Carlo*, *Jalna*, *She* (1935); *The White Angel*, *The Man I Marry*, *Follow Your Heart*, *The Charge of the Light Brigade*, *The Trail of the Lonesome Pine*, *Under Two Flags* (1936); *Thunder in the City*, *The Last of Mrs Cheyney* (1937); *Kidnapped*, *The Baroness and the Butler*, *Suez* (1938); *The Rains Came*, *The Hound of the Baskervilles*, *The Adventures of Sherlock Holmes* (1939); *Susan and God*, *Adventure in Diamonds*, *The Blue Bird*, *Lillian Russell*, *A Dispatch from Reuters*, *Hudson's Bay*, *Rebecca* (1940); *This Woman is Mine*, *Play Girl*, *Free and Easy*, *Suspicion*, *Eagle Squadron*, *The Chocolate Soldier* (1941); *Sherlock Holmes and the Secret Weapon*, *Roxie Hart*, *Journey for Margaret*, *This Above All*, *Sherlock Holmes and the Voice of Terror* (1942); *Sherlock Holmes Faces Death*, *Crazy House*, *Sherlock Holmes in Washington*, *Lassie Come Home*, *Forever and a Day* (1943); *The Pearl of Death*, *Sherlock Holmes and the Spider Woman*, *Follow the Boys*, *Frenchman's Creek*, *Sherlock Holmes and the Scarlet Claw*, *Gypsy Wildcat* (1944); *The Corn is Green*, *Son of Lassie*, *The House of Fear*, *Screen Snapshots Series 25, No. 4: Hollywood Celebrations*, *Pursuit to Algiers*, *The Woman in Green* (1945); *Terror by Night*, *Dressed to Kill* (1946); *The Two Mrs Carrolls*, *The Exile* (1947); *Julia Misbehaves* (1948); *Vendetta* (1950); *Hong Kong* (1951); *Bwana Devil*, *Limelight* (1952); *World for Ransom* (1954).

BUCHANAN, Jack (Walter John Buchanan) (1891–1957)

Scottish-born Jack Buchanan's slender American filmography does not quite capture the enormous popularity of this musical-comedy star on both sides of the Atlantic. His trademark 'white tie and tails' and his dancing ability marked him as a British Fred Astaire, though critics also compared him to Maurice Chevalier★, with whom he appeared in 1938 in the British film, *Breaking the News*. Despite the small number of Hollywood films, however, America did loom large in Buchanan's career. In the 1920s,

he established a considerable reputation in musical comedy on Broadway and worked in Britain for the American company First National, and during the 1930s he made various though largely unsuccessful attempts with producer Herbert Wilcox to make British films for the US market.

He appeared in three Hollywood films in the early sound period. *The Show of Shows* was an early revue-style picture and *Paris* was based on a Broadway hit. More important, however, was the Ernst Lubitsch film *Monte Carlo*, which paired Buchanan with another musical star of the period, Jeannette MacDonald. In the 1950s, he finally appeared with Fred Astaire in *The Band Wagon* and his work was subsequently included in the MGM compilation film, *That's Entertainment* (1974). TR

FILMS: *The Show of Shows*, *Paris* (1929); *Monte Carlo* (1930); *Penny Serenade* (1941); *Jack Armstrong* (1947); *Cody of the Pony Express* (1950); *The Band Wagon* (1953).

BUCHHOLZ, Horst (1933–2003)

German stage and screen actor with a prominent international career. Dubbed 'the German James Dean', handsome Buchholz was a star of German teenager movies in the 1950s before emerging on the international scene as 'Chico', the young 'Mexican' in John Sturges' influential Western *The Magnificent Seven*. There was some muttering on set about Europeans muscling in on this all-American genre – Yul Brynner, the philosophical leader of the Seven, was Russian by birth – but in fact this may be a truer reflection of the mongrel make-up of the Old West. At any rate, here Buchholz's naturalness (he laughs, cries, fools around, gets drunk) pleasingly sets off the stereotypical granite machismo of the others; he and Brynner are among the three survivors. The following year, he appeared in two other prominent American movies, Billy Wilder's *One, Two Three* (where he plays an East German Communist), and Joshua Logan's *Fanny*, a condensed version of Marcel Pagnol's trilogy, in which he embodies the romantic young Marius opposite veteran émigré stars Maurice Chevalier★ and Charles Boyer★. His Hollywood career subsequently dipped, despite high-profile parts, such as Gandhi's assassin in *Nine Hours to Rama*. Thanks to his excellent linguistic skills, Buchholz was able to work in the USA and Europe, though he was, to his chagrin, bypassed by the Young Turks of the New German Cinema. A dapper and distinguished figure in later life, Buchholz did stage and television work. **193**

Like many German actors before him, one of his last important roles was, ironically, that of a Nazi. He played Dr Lessing in Roberto Benigni's★ highly successful comedy about the concentration camps, *La vita è bella/Life is Beautiful* (1997). GV

FILMS: *The Magnificent Seven* (1960); *Fanny, One, Two, Three* (1961); *Nine Hours to Rama* (1963); *The Great Waltz* (1972); *Dead of Night* (1977); *Avalanche Express* (1979); *Code Name: Emerald* (1985).

BURTON, Richard (Richard Walter Jenkins Jr) (1925–1984)

Richard Burton's Hollywood career is typically portrayed as a tragically Faustian narrative. John Gielgud★, one of his most influential mentors and sponsors in the early part of his stage career in Britain, regularly voiced his regret at seeing potentially the greatest postwar classical actor swap his humble Welsh roots, his theatrical calling and, according to this viewpoint, his talent for an easier route to fame, riches and idle pleasures in California.

The full facts about Burton's Hollywood sojourn(s) reveal a somewhat more complicated process of negotiation between his multiple career commitments. Burton's handsome, if prematurely wizened, features and his extraordinary basso voice catapulted him to considerable fame and acclaim on the stage in London in 1949, with peers and seniors venturing awestruck assessments of the scale of his natural talent. Even at this early juncture, though, his first theatrical triumphs were accompanied by an instantaneous screen career: he made his first film in 1948 (the Warners' financed *Now Barabbas*) and signed a seven-film contract with Alexander Korda the following year. After two intervening and eye-catching Broadway engagements, Twentieth Century-Fox negotiated a loan of Burton's services from Korda in 1952 and he was contracted to make three films with them. Burton's automatic affinity with the riotous social life in Hollywood in the early 1950s, his instant rapport with older screen legends like Humphrey Bogart and his serial womanising have become well known.

This retrospectively celebrated off-screen notoriety has tended to obscure the equivocal success and relative brevity of Burton's first brushes with Hollywood. His initial progress was encouraging. He earned a Best Supporting Actor Academy Award nomination for the first of two relatively low-key films, and then appeared in Fox's biggest box-office success in 1953, *The Robe*, the first ever CinemaScope film. A further Academy Award nomination followed, along with the reputed offer of a $1 million, seven-year contract with Fox. He turned it down, however, to further enhance his stage reputation with a season of Shakespeare at the Old Vic in London. Intermittent returns to Hollywood were still accommodated. His early association with historical costume extravaganzas was extended into a consistent casting pattern, as Korda negotiated further loan-outs to Fox for *The Rains of Ranchipur*, *Prince of Players* and (for United Artists) *Alexander the Great*. *Prince of Players* straightforwardly traded off Burton's eminent theatrical credentials by casting him as the legendary eighteenth-century actor Edwin Booth, but sustaining his successful leap from stage to screen was proving difficult. All three films flopped badly and, much like Laurence Olivier★ in the 1930s, Burton retreated from a Hollywood that was coming to regard him as box-office poison in order to return to the Old Vic.

Further success on Broadway and in quality American television dramas kept Burton within the purview of American producers and although Warners' attempt in 1960 to relaunch him as a credible romantic lead had little discernible impact, a new cinematic breakthrough of sorts was around the corner. In September 1961, Burton was reacquainted with both Fox and his by now familiar toga when he joined the troubled Italian shoot of *Cleopatra* to play Marc Antony opposite Rex Harrison's★ Caesar and Elizabeth Taylor's eponymous heroine. The film's unprecedented budget ($44 million, or close to $300 million in modern dollars) fatally crippled its chances of reaping any substantial profit and caused it to be written off as an unsalvageable box-office disaster at the time. But when Burton began an illicit affair with Taylor behind the scenes early in 1962, he became the focus of the same obsessive media interest that had helped to make her the highest paid actress in the world at that time. American newspaper coverage of their liaison regularly dwarfed the column inches devoted to the Mercury-Atlas space missions and the build-up to the Cuban missile crisis. The ensuing scandal (both parties being married at the time) even provoked calls in Congress for Burton to be banned from American shores. In the event, Burton made a triumphant return to Broadway in a 1964 production of *Hamlet*, which was simultaneously filmed for the benefit of the crowds turned away nightly and as a perceived obligation to posterity. While he commanded a huge salary for various American-financed films in the remainder of the decade, public fascination tended to remain squarely focused upon reports surrounding the alcohol-fuelled divorce of Burton and Taylor and their brief alcohol-fuelled remarriage, rather than any of the eight subsequent pictures they made together.

Burton predominantly worked in Europe from the 1970s onwards. He received five further Academy Award nominations between 1964 and 1977, but the image of a talent wrecked and wasted by a suspect choice of women and recreational habits had become perhaps the dominant element of his star persona by the mid-1960s. It was memorably foregrounded in two of his better American films. *The Night of the Iguana* and *Who's Afraid of Virginia Woolf?* are both – in common with many other Burton vehicles in this period – adapted from celebrated stage plays. In the former, he plays a defrocked priest whose sexual indiscretions have destroyed his career, and in the latter, he essays the part of a burnt-out, alcoholic college professor locked into an abusive and destructive relationship with his spouse (Taylor, of course). In each role, Burton's remarkably powerful voice, hitherto most commonly employed to command armies into battle on screen, is fashioned into an incisive tool of bitter (self-)recrimination and regret. JB

FILMS: *Now Barabbas* (1949); *My Cousin Rachel* (1952); *The Desert Rats, The Robe* (1953); *Demetrius and the Gladiators* (1954); *The Rains of Ranchipur, Prince of Players* (1955); *Alexander the Great* (1956); *Bitter Victory, Sea Wife* (1957); *The Bramble Bush, Ice Palace* (1960); *The Longest Day* (1962); *Cleopatra, The V.I.P.s* (1963); *Zulu* [voice]; *Becket, Hamlet, The Night of the Iguana* (1964); *What's New Pussycat, The Sandpiper, The Spy Who Came in from the Cold* (1965); *Who's Afraid of Virginia Woolf?* (1966); *The Taming of the Shrew, The Comedians* (1967); *Boom!, Candy* (1968); *Where Eagles Dare, Staircase, Anne of the Thousand Days* (1969); *Raid on Rommel* (1971); *Hammersmith is Out* (1972); *The Klansman* (1974); *Exorcist II: The Heretic, Equus* (1977); *Lovespell* (1979).

BUSHELL, Anthony (1904–1997)

English actor who, after working on Broadway, had a number of roles in early American sound films such as James Whale's *Journey's End* (opposite Colin Clive★). He returned to Britain in 1932 and turned to mainly production and direction from the late 1940s onwards. TJ

FILMS: *Disraeli, The Show of Shows* (1929); *Lovin' the Ladies, Three Faces East, Journey's End, The Flirting Widow* (1930); *The Royal Bed, Born to Love, Five Star Final, Chances, Expensive Women* (1931); *A Woman Commands, Vanity Fair, Shop Angel, Escapade* (1932); *The Miniver Story* (1950); *The Red Beret* (1953); *The Black Knight* (1954); *Bitter Victory* (1957).

BUSSIÈRES, Raymond (1907–1982)

Small, wiry French character actor with an expressive face, much loved in France for his frequent supporting roles as faithful servants or gang members. Bussières was strongly identified with a working-class, Parisian persona and played similar parts in his American films – many of which were also set in the French capital. SL

FILMS: *Bedevilled* (1955); *Fanny* (1961); *Paris – When it Sizzles* (1964); *Up from the Beach* (1965).

BYRNE, Gabriel (1950–)

Born in Dublin, Byrne left teaching in 1977 to become an actor in the experimental Project Theatre, where he worked alongside Neil Jordan, Jim and Peter Sheridan and Liam Neeson★. His screen career started in the Irish soap, *Bracken*, where he was spotted by John Boorman and invited to cast for *Excalibur*. Byrne subsequently moved to Britain, where he played the investigative journalist in the thriller *Defence of the Realm* (1985). He was drawn to Hollywood, he says, because of its openness to outsiders and played a series of roles that drew on his dark looks and ability to suggest latent threat, notably in *Miller's Crossing* and *The Usual Suspects*. Byrne has also been cast in a number of 'religious' roles, in films such as *End of Days* and *Stigmata*. He has commented that Hollywood does not know what to do with European actors and has also been supportive of the Irish film industry by lending his name to a number of domestic productions. RB

FILMS: *Excalibur* (1981); *The Keep* (1983); *Gothic* (1986); *Siesta, Lionheart, Hello Again* (1987); *Miller's Crossing* (1990); *Cool World* (1992); *Point of No Return, A Dangerous Woman* (1993); *A Simple Twist of Fate, Trial by Jury, Little Women* (1994); *Dead Man, Frankie Starlight, The Usual Suspects* (1995); *Mad Dog Time, Somebody is Waiting* (1996); *This is the Sea* (1997); *Polish Wedding, The Man in the Iron Mask, Quest for Camelot* [voice], *Enemy of the State* (1998); *Stigmata, End of Days* (1999); *Emmett's Mark, Ghost Ship* (2002); *Shade* (2003); *P.S.* (2004).

CABOT, Sebastian (1918–1977)

Portly British radio, film and theatre actor who played various bearded Hollywood villains after making his US stage debut in 1947. His genial, but slightly pompous manner also lent itself to a number of voice-only character parts for Disney's animated features. AP

FILMS: *Midnight Episode* (1950); *Babes in Bagdad, Ivanhoe* (1952); *Kismet* (1954); *Westward Ho the Wagons!* (1956); *Dragoon Wells Massacre, Johnny Tremain, Omar Khayyam, Black Patch* (1957); *Terror in a Texas Town, In Love and War* (1958); *Say One for Me, The Angry Hills* (1959); *Seven Thieves, The Time Machine* (1960); *Twice-Told Tales, The Sword in the Stone* [voice] (1963); *The Family Jewels* (1965); *Winnie the Pooh and the Honey Tree* [voice] (1966); *The Jungle Book* [voice] (1967); *Winnie the Pooh and the Blustery Day* [voice] (1968); *Man, Monsters and Mysteries* (1973); *Winnie the Pooh and Tigger Too!* [voice] (1974); *The Many Adventures of Winnie the Pooh* [voice] (1977).

CAINE, Michael (Maurice Joseph Micklewhite) (1933–)

As a native south Londoner whose distinctive voice and mannerisms have inspired a host of affectionate impressions, Caine is universally recognisable as the cockney's cockney, but he has rarely been allowed to show the full extent of his abilities. He took his professional name from a cinema marquee advertising the 1954 film of *The Caine Mutiny* and after bit parts in more than a dozen British films, beginning with *A Hill in Korea* opposite Stanley Baker★ in 1956, he was given his first substantial screen role as a blue-blooded Victorian army officer in Baker's US production of *Zulu*. It won him favourable notices, but his contract with the film's American backer, Joseph E. Levine, was dropped and picked up by the British-based Canadian producer Harry Saltzman, who cast him as the bespectacled, domesticated spy of *The Ipcress File* (1965) and its Hollywood-financed sequels. Caine's success as Harry Palmer was followed by a charismatic performance as the lovable misogynist *Alfie* that, along with The Beatles, clearly established that a working-class British accent was no barrier to international stardom in the socially mobile 1960s. An enormous commercial hit, the film brought him the first of

several Academy Award nominations and made him bankable in the USA and Britain.

Caine subsequently became one of the leading lights of mid-Atlantic cinema in films made by the Hollywood studios and/or by Europeans resident in the USA for the international market, though few of these productions matched his individual fame with either commercial success or critical acclaim. Nonetheless, of his late 1960s and early 1970s films, *Play Dirty* and *Too Late the Hero* are excellent, underrated war pictures, *The Italian Job* and the original version of *Get Carter* are seminal crime thrillers, and his stardom survived numerous flops. Most of his 'British' pictures were Hollywood-financed, but in 1977 he eventually left the UK to live and work in the USA. He did not always choose his vehicles wisely and he became too frequently involved with inept disaster movies, embarrassing action films and feeble comedies. He returned to Britain after a decade away and remains as prolific as ever on both sides of the Atlantic.

Despite his public complaints that he has never been taken seriously in his homeland, few of Caine's US-based pictures have been as well received as the domestic productions *Educating Rita* (1983), *Mona Lisa* (1986), *Little Voice* (1998) or *Last Orders* (2001). It has often seemed that he prefers continuous employment to consistent quality, but there have been more memorable parts and more worthwhile films than might at first be recalled: standing up to Laurence Olivier★ in *Sleuth*; partnering Sean Connery★ in *The Man Who Would Be King*; mocking Hollywood manners in *California Suite* and *Sweet Liberty*; playing the transvestite psychiatrist in *Dressed to Kill* and the bisexual playwright of *Deathtrap*; and giving a memorable, Academy Award-winning performance under Woody Allen's direction in *Hannah and Her Sisters*. Pauline Kael, who scarcely ever gave a film of his an unfavourable review, described Caine as 'the least pyrotechnical, the least show-offy of actors . . . You don't observe his acting; you just experience the character's emotions. He may be in acting terms something like what Jean Renoir was in directing terms.'

Caine has in recent years been assured of iconic status as the epitome of heterosexual cool, especially among a younger male audience. In addition to numerous industry honours, he won a second Best Supporting Actor Academy Award for *The Cider House Rules*. But perhaps Caine's finest work, and his most complex character, remains his role as

Michael Caine en route

the German mercenary captain in James Clavell's little-seen 1970 medieval epic *The Last Valley*, which showed a rare philosophic side to his persona and displayed a dramatic range that has not often been demanded of him since. SH

FILMS: *How to Murder a Rich Uncle* (1957); *The Key* (1958); *Zulu* (1963); *Alfie* (1965); *Gambit, Funeral in Berlin, Hurry Sundown* (1966); *Woman Times Seven, Billion Dollar Brain* (1967); *Deadfall, The Magus, Play Dirty* (1968); *The Italian Job, Battle of Britain, Too Late the Hero* (1969); *The Last Valley* (1970); *Get Carter, Zee & Co.* (1971); *Pulp, Sleuth* (1972); *The Black Windmill, The Destructors, The Wilby Conspiracy* (1974); *Peeper, The Man Who Would Be King* (1975); *Harry and Walter Go to New York* (1976); *A Bridge Too Far* (1977); *The Swarm, California Suite* (1978); *Ashanti, Beyond the Poseidon Adventure* (1979); *The Island, Dressed to Kill* (1980); *The Hand, Victory* (1981); *Deathtrap* (1982); *Blame it on Rio* (1983); *Terror in the Aisles* (1984); *Sweet Liberty* (1985); *Hannah and Her Sisters, Half Moon Street* (1986); *Jaws: The Revenge* (1987); *Dirty Rotten Scoundrels* (1988); *A Shock to the System, Mr Destiny, Bullseye!* (1990); *Noises Off, Blue Ice, The Muppet Christmas Carol* (1992); *On Deadly Ground* (1994); *Blood and Wine* (1997); *Curtain Call, The Debtors, The Cider House Rules* (1999); *Quills, Get Carter, Miss Congeniality* (2000); *Austin Powers in Goldmember, The Quiet American* (2002); *The Actors, Secondhand Lions* (2003); *Around the Bend* (2004).

CALLOW, Simon (1949–)

The ostentatious talent and fruity vowels of the avuncular Simon Callow have led to numerous prestige stage and screen roles, such as his turn as Mr Beebe in Merchant-Ivory's *A Room with a View* (1986). He has now become a popular, often arch, presence in Hollywood productions. MW

FILMS: *Amadeus* (1984); *Manifesto* (1988); *Mr & Mrs Bridge, Postcards from the Edge* (1990); *Street Fighter* (1994); *Ace Ventura: When Nature Calls, Jefferson in Paris* (1995); *James and the Giant Peach* [voice] (1996); *Shakespeare in Love* (1998); *Notting Hill* (1999); *Thunderpants, Sex & Violence* (2002); *The Civilization of Maxwell Bright* (2003).

CALVERT, Phyllis (Phyllis Hannah Bickle) (1915–2002)

Like other British actors such as James Mason★, Margaret Lockwood★ and Patricia Roc★, Calvert was courted by a Hollywood determined to accommodate postwar British audiences' unprecedented, strong attachment to their native stars. However, with her strong received Home Counties pronunciation, Calvert was aurally much less at home than several of her peers. Calvert had appeared in a small number of US-financed films before her American debut in Robert Siodmak's *Time Out of Mind*. Unusually for a British actress, she was the leading lady in an authentic film noir – *Appointment with Danger* – although it is entirely in keeping with her past reputation and established range that she played a nun rather than a hard-boiled femme fatale. JB

FILMS: *They Came by Night* (1940); *Inspector Hornleigh Goes to it, Kipps* (1941); *The Young Mr Pitt* (1942); *Time Out of Mind* (1947); *My Own True Love* (1948); *Appointment with Danger* (1951); *The Battle of the Villa Fiorita* (1965); *Oh! What a Lovely War* (1969); *The Walking Stick* (1970).

CALVET, Corinne (Corinne Dibos) (1925–2001)

Beautiful French actress often compared to Rita Hayworth, who was generally cast as the sultry French femme fatale in Hollywood. After appearing in a few French films, Calvet was spotted by Paramount producer Hal B. Wallis in 1947. As her knowledge of English was non-existent, she had to learn English in the USA with a coach. Her first Hollywood film was William Dieterle's *Rope of Sand*, in which she appeared opposite Burt Lancaster and met her first husband, the actor John Bromfield. There was trouble, however, as Wallis cancelled Bromfield's contract when Calvet refused to succumb to his advances. When Wallis also punished Calvet by casting her in a role that clearly undermined her talent, in the comedy *My Friend Irma Goes West*, the actress moved to Twentieth Century-Fox. There she made a series of films for Darryl F. Zanuck before going to Universal in 1955, where she appeared in *So This is Paris* and *The Far Country*. Although she achieved a degree of success, Calvet remained ambivalent about Hollywood. She espoused its glamorous lifestyle but she also despised its superficiality. She particularly resented the stereotypical notions American men had about her as a French woman. VO

FILMS: *Rope of Sand* (1949); *When Willie Comes Marching Home, My Friend Irma Goes West* (1950); *Quebec, On the Riviera, Peking Express* (1951); *Sailor Beware, Thunder in the East, What Price Glory* (1952); *Flight to Tangier, Powder River* (1953); *The Far Country* (1954); *So This is Paris* (1955); *Plunderers of Painted Flats* (1959); *Hemingway's Adventures of a Young Man* (1962); *Apache Uprising* (1966); *Pound* (1970); *Too Hot to Handle* (1977); *Dr Heckyl and Mr Hype* (1980); *The Sword and the Sorcerer* (1982).

CAMPBELL, Eric (1870–1917)

Burly Scottish performer who, thanks to his propensity for playing villainous types, served as an exemplary adversary to Charlie Chaplin★ during his formative career at Mutual. Campbell was a fellow member of Fred Karno's troupe and was invited by Chaplin to work with him in the USA. AP

FILMS: *The Floorwalker, The Fireman, The Vagabond, The Count, The Pawnshop, Behind the Screen, The Rink* (1916); *Easy Street, The Cure, The Immigrant, The Adventurer* (1917).

CAMPBELL, Mrs Patrick (Beatrice Stella Tanner) (1865–1940)

A *grande dame* of the London stage and friend of the playwright George Bernard Shaw, for whom she was the first Eliza Dolittle in his *Pygmalion*, 'Mrs Patrick Campbell' moved to Hollywood in 1930 (she had appeared in one British film, *The Money Moon*, in 1920). Her American career, however, failed to match her British reputation, partly as a result of her overly theatrical performance style. Her advancing years also confined her to playing aristocratic ladies, with the exception of *Crime and Punishment*, where she was a pawnbroker. GV

FILMS: *The Dancers* (1930); *Riptide, One More River, Outcast Lady* (1934); *Crime and Punishment* (1935).

CANALE, Gianna-Maria (1927–)

Italian actress who, after reaching the finals of the 1946 Miss Italia contest, starred in a number of films directed by her future husband Riccardo Freda. She had two relatively minor roles in Hollywood. CS

FILMS: *Go for Broke!* (1951); *The Whole Truth* (1958).

CANET, Guillaume (1973–)

Canet's French screen profile has matured rapidly since his leading role in Pierre Jolivet's *En plein coeur / In All Innocence* (1998), and despite two US films that convey different points of contact between American culture and his youthful national identity, he has preferred to remain working in Europe. In *The Beach*, Canet's rivalry with leading Hollywood star Leonardo DiCaprio for the affections of Virginie Ledoyen★ is set among the international young travellers'

community in Thailand. In his second American film, he again played a young French traveller who, this time, journeys to New York in search of his lost father's identity. AP

FILMS: *The Beach, The Day the Ponies Came Back* (2000).

CANNON, Maurice (Maurice de Canonge) (1894–1979)

Stage actor who went to Hollywood in 1923 along with fellow French film-makers Henri de la Falaise, Henri d'Abbadie d'Arrast, Charles de Rochefort★ and Jean de Limur. Cannon was unable to obtain work beyond minor parts and he returned to France, where he had a long and successful career as a film director under his original name. CH

FILMS: *Fifty-Fifty, Trilby* (1923); *The Side Show of Life, Love's Wilderness, Peter Pan, Shadows of Paris, The Alaskan* (1924); *The Roots of Heaven* (1958).

CAPELLANI, Paul (1873–1960)

When Albert Capellani was hired as a director by World Films in early 1915, his younger brother Paul joined him to play romantic leads or romantic rivals, opposite Clara Kimball Young (usually) and Alice Brady (once), in a half-dozen films. After secondary roles in three more American films, Paul returned to France, performing as a character actor throughout the 1920s. RA

FILMS: *Camille* (1915); *The Common Law, The Dark Silence, The Feast of Life, The Foolish Virgin, La Vie de Bohême* (1916); *Babbling Tongues, One Law for Both* (1917); *The Richest Girl* (1918).

CAPUCINE (Germaine Lefebvre) (1931–1990)

Successful French fashion model who, when she arrived in Hollywood, was hailed as 'the new Garbo'. She first appeared on screen aged eighteen in Jacques Becker's *Rendez-vous de juillet / Rendezvous in July* (1949) with Daniel Gélin★. It was when she was modelling in New York in the 1950s that she met Charles Feldman, a Hollywood producer, who encouraged her to study acting under Gregory Ratoff★. She was put under contract by Columbia Studios and her first leading role was in George Cukor and Charles Vidor's *Song without End*, for which she received some very poor notices. Cukor considered her acting 'wooden' and her co-star Dirk Bogarde★ had to concede that although she was 'a patrician beauty, remote, elegant, imported, [. . .] she couldn't act'. Nonetheless, a spate of further roles fol- **199** lowed in the early 1960s. Her widest exposure was as Inspector Clouseau's wife in *The Pink Panther* series, a role originally intended for Ava Gardner. In 1965, she starred in Clive Donner's comedy *What's New Pussycat*. By then, however, her Hollywood star was on the wane and she returned to European productions. Her American swan-songs were in Joseph L. Mankiewicz's *The Honey Pot* and Ernest Pintoff's *Jaguar Lives!* Because of her Nefertiti-like features, Capucine was twice cast as a princess. She was certainly glamorous and intriguing, to the extent that she was rumoured to be a transsexual for many years. Her career finally trailed off into television work. She committed suicide in 1990. VO

FILMS: *Song without End, North to Alaska* (1960); *Walk on the Wild Side* (1962); *The Pink Panther* (1963); *What's New Pussycat, The Honey Pot* (1967); *Fraulein Doktor* (1969); *Jaguar Lives!* (1979); *Trail of the Pink Panther* (1982); *Curse of the Pink Panther* (1983).

CARAMITRU, Ion (1942–)

Stern-looking, black-haired Romanian stage and screen legend who led the storming of Ceausescu's Bucharest television station in December 1989. As a key figure in the provisional government, and later as Romanian Culture Minister (1996–2000) and vice-president of the European Council of Arts, Caramitru has been instrumental in opening up former Warsaw Pact states to international cinema ventures. Indeed, it has been ventures of this type that have facilitated his own participation in two Hollywood movies shot partly in the Czech Republic and a number of British television dramas, in which he has played a succession of sophisticated Middle European oddballs. RJK

FILMS: *Kafka* (1991); *Mission: Impossible* (1996).

CARDINALE, Claudia (1939–)

Cardinale's debut in Italian film revolved around the fact that she had been named the 'most beautiful Italian girl in Tunisia' in a beauty contest. In what became her adopted country, she was perceived as the successor to Gina Lollobrigida★ and Sophia Loren★ and her career in Hollywood was expected to follow the path taken by these Italian stars during the 1950s. By the time she arrived in Hollywood in the 1960s, she had established a solid international reputation for her acting abilities thanks to an association with Italian auteurs such as Luchino Visconti

and Federico Fellini. This early promise, however, was not matched by her American career and she never enjoyed a comparable level of popularity with American audiences. She was largely used to add glamour and exoticism to the Hollywood films she appeared in, playing an Indian princess in *The Pink Panther*, the mysterious Vicky Vincenti in *Blindfold* and an Algerian woman in *Lost Command*. Perhaps her two best 'American' performances were in Westerns – first in *The Professionals*, and then in Sergio Leone's *Once Upon a Time in the West*, where she played Jill McBain, a beautiful widow and former prostitute desired by both Charles Bronson and Henry Fonda.

In the 1980s and 1990s, European cinema continued to provide far better parts for her than Hollywood; she was Roberto Benigni's★ mother in *Son of the Pink Panther*, thirty years after her American debut in the original. CBu

FILMS: *The Pink Panther* (1963); *Circus World* (1964); *Blindfold* (1965); *Lost Command, The Professionals* (1966); *Don't Make Waves* (1967); *The Hell with Heroes, Once Upon a Time in the West* (1968); *The Salamander* (1980); *Sniper* (1987); *Son of the Pink Panther* (1993).

CARÈRE, Christine (Christiane Elisabeth Jeanne Marie Pelleterat de Borde) (1930–)

Vivacious actress who appeared in numerous French comedies of the 1950s. In the USA, she played French characters in a few comedies and musicals. VO

FILMS: *A Certain Smile, Mardi Gras* (1958); *A Private's Affair* (1959); *I Deal in Danger* (1966).

CARLYLE, Robert (1961–)

Versatile Scottish actor who came to international attention with his leading role in the surprise hit *The Full Monty* (1997). His Hollywood films with British directors Antonia Bird (*Ravenous*) and Danny Boyle (*The Beach*) both used his distinctive Scottish accent along with the more psychotic elements of his screen persona. JS

FILMS: *Angela's Ashes, Ravenous, The World is Not Enough* (1999); *The Beach* (2000); *The 51st State, To End All Wars* (2001).

CARMINATI, Tullio (Count Tullio Carminati de Brambilla) (1895–1971)

Italian stage and screen actor who went to the USA in 1925. After a successful stint on Broadway as a matinée idol, he appeared in American films from 1926 onwards. Carminati was frequently cast as a foreign nobleman. He returned to Italy during the 1940s on the basis of his reputed support of the Fascists, and later appeared in a number of American-funded films shot in Italy. He was Audrey Hepburn's★ aide, General Provno, in *Roman Holiday*. CS

FILMS: *The Bat, The Duchess of Buffalo* (1926); *Honeymoon Hate, Stage Madness* (1927); *The Patriot, Three Sinners* (1928); *Gallant Lady* (1933); *Moulin Rouge, One Night of Love* (1934); *Paris in Spring, Let's Live Tonight* (1935); *Safari* (1940); *Roman Holiday* (1953); *War and Peace* (1956); *A Breath of Scandal* (1960); *El Cid* (1961); *Hemingway's Adventures of a Young Man* (1962); *The Cardinal* (1963).

CAROL, Martine (1920–1967)

'France's number one sex goddess' turned briefly to English-language film production in the latter part of her career after her domestic star had waned in the mid-1950s. Hollywood kept Carol 'at home' in her only American appearance, in which she played 'a pretty tourist in Paris'. AP

FILM: *Around the World in Eighty Days* (1956).

CARON, Leslie (1931–)

A very pretty blue-eyed brunette and talented classical ballet dancer, Leslie Caron is undoubtedly the most successful French female star in Hollywood to date. She was born to an American mother and has always possessed good English. She was spotted by Gene Kelly when performing in the Ballet des Champs-Élysées. He immediately cast her as the lead female and his co-star in Vincente Minnelli's musical *An American in Paris*, where she replaced a pregnant Cyd Charisse. This high-profile introduction meant that Caron quickly gained world recognition and she subsequently appeared in several other musical extravaganzas including *Glory Alley, The Glass Slipper, Daddy Long Legs* (with Fred Astaire) and *Gaby*. She had the starring role in *Lili*, often regarded as her best film, and was nominated for a Best Actress Academy Award. As the lead in Minnelli's *Gigi*, she played opposite Maurice Chevalier★ and Louis Jourdan★.

Caron's spectacular American start gained her a contract with MGM and she appeared in various light dramas, comedies and musicals for the studio that showcased her natural charm, gamine personality and grace. Caron, however, took issue with this stereotypical foregrounding of French girlishness, and she entered into a rift with MGM regarding a

The ultimate *gamine*: Leslie Caron in *Gigi* (1958)

role in George Cukor's *Les Girls* (1957). She eventually turned the part down. Caron wanted to be taken seriously as an actress, and in 1963, she earned a Golden Globe and a second Academy Award nomination, but this time for her role in the British drama *The L-Shaped Room*. This part propelled her forward as a serious actress. Unfortunately, Hollywood was never really interested in Caron's genuine acting talents. Her career reached its peak early on, with her most successful work in the 1950s and early 1960s. Her ten-year second marriage to the British director Peter Hall saw her return to Europe and this also cut short her American success. She has nevertheless continued to make movies, both in Europe and in Hollywood, including the box-office hit *Chocolat* (starring Juliette Binoche★). In the 1960s, Caron expressed a wish to work with French directors such as those of the New Wave, but by then she was deemed too 'Americanised' in her native country. VO

FILMS: *An American in Paris, The Man with a Cloak* (1951); *Glory Alley* (1952); *Lili, The Story of Three Loves* (1953); *The Glass Slipper, Daddy Long Legs* (1955); *Gaby* (1956); *The Doctor's Dilemma, Gigi* (1958); *The Man Who Understood Women* (1959); *The Subterraneans,* (1960); *Fanny* (1961); *Father Goose* (1964); *A Very Special Favour* (1965); *Chandler* **201**

(1971); *Nicole* (1978); *Goldengirl* (1979); *Change Partners and Dance* (1980); *Reel Horror* (1985); *Courage Mountain* (1990); *Funny Bones* (1995); *Chocolat* (2000); *Le Divorce* (2003).

CARPENTIER, Georges (1894–1975)

French middleweight boxing champion, as well as a singer and dancer, whose cinematic career almost entirely revolved around his physique and boxing skills. His debut film was the American *The Wonder Man.* Warner Bros. later offered him a part in *The Show of Shows*, where he essentially played himself. VO

FILMS: *The Wonder Man* (1920); *The Show of Shows* (1929); *Hold Everything* (1930); *Legendary Champions* (1968).

CARROLL, Madeleine (Marie-Madeleine Bernadette O'Carroll) (1906–1987)

Blonde and 'ladylike' English actress who pursued a successful stage and film career despite the objections of her French mother and Irish father. Carroll's cool and dignified looks matched an acting style that was characterised by subtlety and understatement. She was contracted to Gaumont-British when she was loaned to Fox to appear in John Ford's *The World Moves On*. Her reputation as the cool, English blonde was enhanced by her appearance with Robert Donat★ in Hitchcock's *The Thirty-Nine Steps* (1935), and thereafter she attracted further offers from Hollywood studios.

Carroll signed an exclusive contract with producer Walter Wanger, and her first film, *The Case against Mrs Ames*, a courtroom drama, was released by Paramount. Wanger loaned her out to various studios, including Columbia and Paramount. In 1936, she replaced Merle Oberon★ to co-star with Gary Cooper in *The General Died at Dawn*. She was also loaned to David O. Selznick to play Princess Flavia in *The Prisoner of Zenda*, which co-starred Ronald Colman★, Douglas Fairbanks and Mary Astor. Her final film for Wanger was *Blockade*, an anti-war film set in Spain.

In 1940, Carroll began a long-term contract with Paramount and was widely publicised as 'Hollywood's Most Beautiful Blonde'. She made several films in quick succession but then requested a one-year suspension of her contract so that she could return to Europe to assist with the war effort. At first, Paramount was reluctant because she was by then a top star, earning $100,000 a film, but the studio eventually agreed and in 1943, she obtained American cit-izenship. Once released from film work, she went to New York and trained as a nurse. She then travelled to Europe, where she worked under a fictitious identity. Immediately after the war, Carroll and her third husband, the stage producer and former member of the French Resistance Henri Loverol, used her castle in France as a refuge for orphans and concentration camp survivors. She was awarded the Medal of Freedom by the US Government and the French Légion d'honneur for her war work. She did not return to Hollywood until 1948, when she starred in *An Innocent Affair*. A year later, she retired from film-making and devoted her time to stage, radio and television, as well as working for UNESCO. SS

FILMS: *The World Moves On* (1934); *The Case against Mrs Ames, The General Died at Dawn, Lloyds of London* (1936); *On the Avenue, The Prisoner of Zenda, It's All Yours* (1937); *Blockade* (1938); *Honeymoon in Bali, Café Society* (1939); *My Son, My Son, Safari, Virginia, North West Mounted Police* (1940); *One Night in Lisbon* (1941); *My Favorite Blonde, Bahama Passage* (1942); *An Innocent Affair* (1948); *The Fan* (1949).

CARUSO, Enrico (1873–1921)

The most famous Italian tenor of his time embraced the gramophone but disliked the cinema. He reluctantly appeared in two films shot back to back for Famous Players-Lasky. Neither film was based on an operatic subject and they were commercial failures. AM

FILMS: *My Cousin* (1918); *A Splendid Romance* (1919).

CASSEL, Vincent (1966–)

The angular-faced Cassel is best known for his violent, charismatic roles in French films such as Mathieu Kassovitz's acclaimed *La Haine/Hate* (1995) and Gaspar Noé's *Irréversible* (2002). He is clearly aiming for an international career, appearing in English-language European co-productions such as *Elizabeth* (1998) and *Birthday Girl* (2001). He supplied the voice of the oddly French-sounding Robin Hood, 'Monsieur Hood', in the animation hit, *Shrek*. VO

FILMS: *Shrek* [voice] (2001); *Ocean's Twelve* (2004).

CAVALIERI, Lina (1874–1944)

Opera singer famed as one of the most beautiful Italians of her time who had a brief film career in both Italy and Hollywood, principally in melodrama. She made two American films alongside her third husband, Lucien Muratore★. Gina Lollobrigida★ played her in the biopic *La donna più bella del mondo* (1955). AM

FILMS: *Manon Lescaut* (1914); *The Eternal Temptress* (1917); *Love's Conquest, A Woman of Impulse* (1918); *The Two Brides* (1919).

CAVANAGH, Paul (1888–1964)

Following his move to Los Angeles in 1930, this English actor of stage and screen enjoyed a prolific Hollywood career encompassing minor character parts, handsome romantic leads and dastardly villains. MF

FILMS: *Strictly Unconventional, Grumpy, The Storm, Virtuous Sin, The Devil to Pay!* (1930); *Unfaithful, Born to Love, Always Goodbye, Transgression, The Squaw Man, Heartbreak* (1931); *Devil's Lottery, A Bill of Divorcement, The Crash* (1932); *Tonight is Ours, The Sin of Nora Moran, The Kennel Murder Case* (1933); *Tarzan and His Mate, One Exciting Adventure, Uncertain Lady, Shoot the Works, Notorious Sophie Lang, Menace, Curtain at Eight* (1934); *Wings in the Dark, Goin' to Town, Without Regret, Thunder in the Night, Splendor, Escapade* (1935); *Champagne Charlie* (1936); *I Take this Woman, Within the Law, Reno, The Under-Pup* (1939); *Shadows on the Stairs, Passage from Hong Kong, Maisie Was a Lady, The Case of the Black Parrot* (1941); *Captain of the Clouds, The Strange Case of Doctor Rx, Pacific Rendezvous, The Hard Way, Gorilla Man, Eagle Squadron* (1942); *Adventure in Iraq* (1943); *The Secret Claw, Marriage is a Private Affair, The Man in Half Moon Street, Maisie Goes to Reno* (1944); *Club Havana, The Woman in Green, This Man's Navy, The House of Fear* (1945); *Night and Day, Humouresque, Wife Wanted, The Verdict, A Night in Paradise* (1946); *Banjo, Ivy, Dishonoured Lady* (1947); *Secret Beyond the Door, The Babe Ruth Story, The Black Arrow, You Gotta Stay Happy* (1948); *Madame Bovary* (1949); *The Iroquois Trail, Rogues of Sherwood Forest, Hit Parade of 1951, Hi-Jacked* (1950); *Tales of Robin Hood, The Sword of D'Artagnan, The Strange Door, The Son of Dr Jekyll, The Highwayman, Desert Fox: The Story of Rommel, Bride of the Gorilla, All that I Have* (1951); *Plymouth Adventure, The Golden Hawk* (1952); *The Bandits of Corsica, Port Sinister, House of Wax, The Mississippi Gambler, Flame of Calcutta, Charade, The All American* (1953); *Casanova's Big Night, The Law vs. Billy the Kid, The Raid, The Iron Glove, Magnificent Obsession, Khyber Patrol* (1954); *The Purple Mask, The Prodigal, The Scarlet Coat, The King's Thief* (1955); *Francis in the Haunted House, Diane,*

Blonde Bait (1956); *She Devil, The Man Who Turned to Stone, God is My Partner* (1957); *In the Money* (1958); *The Beat Generation, The Four Skulls of Jonathon Drake* (1959).

CAVENS, Fred (1882–1962)

Belgian performer and fencing master who was one of Hollywood's leading swordfight co-ordinators during the classical period. In addition to handling the choreography for films like *The Adventures of Robin Hood*, Cavens had a long-running career playing minor character roles such as French waiters, infantrymen and officials. AP

FILMS: *The Three Must-Get-Theres* (1922); *The Sword of Valor* (1924); *The King of Kings* (1927); *The Iron Mask* (1929); *Breed of the Border* (1933); *The Count of Monte Cristo, Marie Galante, Paris Interlude, Queen Christina, The World Moves On* (1934); *Kid Courageous, Cardinal Richelieu, Folies Bergère, Lottery Lover, The Three Musketeers* (1935); *Love on the Run* (1936); *Café Metropole, Romeo and Juliet* (1937); *The Adventures of Robin Hood, Kidnapped, Artists and Models Abroad* (1938); *The Man in the Iron Mask, Pack up Your Troubles, Tower of London* (1939); *The Black Swan, Eagle Squadron* (1942); *Ali Baba and the Forty Thieves, Around the World, Till We Meet Again* (1944); *Don Ricardo Returns, The Exile, Forever Amber* (1947); *The Black Arrow* (1948); *Adventures of Don Juan, Bagdad* (1949); *Buccaneer's Girl, Fortunes of Captain Blood* (1950); *Cyrano de Bergerac* (1951); *Lydia Bailey* (1952); *The Mississippi Gambler* (1953); *Around the World in Eighty Days* (1956).

CAZENOVE, Christopher (1945–)

Blond British actor who personifies a romantic, yet slightly caddish, form of Englishness. He remains chiefly known for his television rather than film work in the USA. He was the suave Ben Carrington in *Dynasty* during the 1980s. MW

FILMS: *There's a Girl in My Soup, Julius Caesar* (1970); *Royal Flash* (1975); *Zulu Dawn* (1979); *Until September* (1984); *Mata Hari* (1985); *Three Men and a Little Lady* (1990); *Aces: Iron Eagle III* (1992); *The Proprietor* (1996); *Shadow Run* (1998); *The Contaminated Man* (2000); *A Knight's Tale* (2001).

CECCHINI, Mimi (1923–1992)

Italian-born actress active on the New York immigrant stage. She turned to cinema only late in life, playing a number of small roles such as the grandmother in *Wise Guys*. AM

FILMS: *Slow Dancing in the Big City* (1978); *Broadway Danny Rose* (1984); *Wise Guys, Eat and Run* (1986); *Moonstruck* (1987); *Dominick and Eugene* (1988); *Cadillac Man* (1990).

___

CHAPLIN, Charles Spencer (1889–1977)

Chaplin was already a well-known music-hall star in 1912 when he embarked on his second US tour with the Fred Karno Company responsible for successfully exporting English music hall's style of sketch comedy to American vaudeville theatres since 1900. Although Mack Sennett claims to have discovered Chaplin when he appeared as the 'Inebriate Swell' in the sketch *Mumming Birds* (renamed *A Night in an English Music Hall* for American audiences), it was probably the New York Film Company executive Harry Aitken who first noticed him. In September 1913, Chaplin was signed to make comedies with their subsidiary company Keystone for $150 a week. Within two years, he had become, alongside Mary Pickford, the most popular film personality of his time and undoubtedly the most successful British actor in Hollywood ever.

This unparalleled rise can be seen as the result of three broad elements: the combination of Karno's pantomime slapstick techniques and the Keystone studios' fast-paced comedy style, the development of the tramp character 'Charlie' and the international influence of the burgeoning Hollywood film industry. Chaplin's gestural and nuanced performance style was well suited to silent film comedy, although not without adjustment due to the contrast between Keystone's frenetic style and Karno's emphasis on pace and the alteration of tempo. The fledgling film industry required a performer's identification with one particular character, and thus the tramp first appeared in *Kid Auto Races at Venice*, a uniquely reflexive film that documents the troubles a film director has in filming the day's proceedings when a tramp consistently muggs for the camera and blocks its view. As well as illustrating the altered pace and longer takes of the Karno style and presaging the improvisational technique that Chaplin utilised for most of his career, it provided the basis for the character of an outsider that Chaplin would elaborate on to create an international 'everyman'. By combining a clown/tramp type recognisable to American audiences with the staple tramp figure of English music hall and theatre, Chaplin astutely shaped his persona to fit European and American audience

expectations. None of this would have been possible had the American film industry not been developing an increasingly sophisticated international film distribution system. By 1914, along with the development of trade and fan magazines, the infrastructure for an international star system was now in place.

Chaplin gained popularity and by early 1914, Sennett allowed him to direct. After moving to Essanay studios in 1915, with an increase in salary to $1,250 per week (including a $10,000 bonus), he now wrote and directed all of his films, a status that lasted his entire career. Along with a set of stock players – many of whom also had English music hall backgrounds – Chaplin continued to develop his tramp figure and own cinematic style. Thanks also to Edna Purviance, a talented female lead who stayed with him for the next ten years, Chaplin began to incorporate more sophisticated character motivation through the introduction of pathos and romance. Chaplin left Essanay in 1916 and was contracted to Mutual for the unprecedented sum of $670,000. In films like *The Immigrant*, he refined his comic invention by also working with Eric Campbell★, another British émigré performer, who acted as the heavyweight often menacing foil to the tramp. Chaplin now took more time with his projects and developed ideas sparked by specific sets and props.

In June 1917, Chaplin left Mutual and formed his own studio with a $1 million deal to produce eight films for First National Exhibitor's Circuit. Chaplin produced some of his best work there in films such as *Shoulder Arms* and *The Kid*. In 1919, Chaplin, Mary Pickford, Douglas Fairbanks and D. W. Griffith formed United Artists. Chaplin was still under obligation to First National and his first United Artists film, *A Woman of Paris*, was not released until 1923. Chaplin continued to work for the studio until his exile from the USA in 1952.

As well as serious critical attention from people such as Gilbert Seldes in the USA and George Bernard Shaw in the UK, Chaplin had his detractors, such as the London newspaper magnate Lord Northcliffe, who attacked his failure to enlist in the British army for service at the front. It is possible to see a link between Chaplin's productive combination of humour and pathos and the political suspicion that he increasingly attracted. From the production of the war satire *Shoulder Arms* in 1918 to *The Great Dictator* in 1940, he did not shy from controversial subjects. Throughout the 1920s and 1930s, Chaplin's films increasingly focused on the outsider's relationship to society. Films such as *City Lights* and *Modern Times* revealed the condition of the dispossessed, the brutality of bureaucracies, the alienation of modern urban existence and the violence of new technologies. Such themes, combined with an unwavering popularity, provoked the anxiety and then the ire of reactionary forces in the USA, and the FBI opened a file on him in 1922. During (and after) the McCarthy era, Chaplin's films were scrutinised for veiled socialist messages and his private life monitored for Communist sympathies.

Chaplin's portrayal of the outsider was mirrored by his own émigré status in the USA. His tacit refusal to become an American citizen was criticised by the right and this overlapped with suspicion of internationalism, as Chaplin regularly kept the company of left-leaning artists and intellectuals. Chaplin consistently maintained his status as apolitical, but his work to raise support for the Russian war effort in World War II provoked further comment. *Monsieur Verdoux*, the story of a man who loses his job as a bank clerk and embarks on a career of marrying and murdering rich widows in order to keep his invalid wife and child was met with hostility in conservative postwar America.

Chaplin's re-entry visa was finally revoked by the American Attorney General while he and his family were en route to England, and he subsequently moved to Switzerland. He made two 'British' productions distributed by Universal and only returned once to the USA in 1972 to accept the Handel Medallion in New York and a Special Academy Award in Los Angeles. MH

FILMS: *Making a Living, Kid Auto Races at Venice, Mabel's Strange Predicament, Between the Showers, A Film Johnnie, Tango Tangles, His Favorite Pastime, Cruel, Cruel Love, The Star Boarder, Mabel at the Wheel, Twenty Minutes of Love, Caught in a Cabaret, Caught in the Rain, A Busy Day, The Fatal Mallet, Her Friend the Bandit, The Knockout, Mabel's Busy Day, Mabel's Married Life, Laughing Gas, The Property Man, The Face on the Bar Room Floor, Recreation, The Masquerader, His New Profession, The Rounders, The New Janitor, Those Love Pangs, Dough and Dynamite, Gentlemen of Nerve, His Musical Career, His Trysting Place, Tillie's Punctured Romance, Getting Acquainted, His Prehistoric Past* (1914); *His New Job, A Night Out, The Champion, In the Park, A Jitney Elopement, The Tramp, By the Sea, Work, A Woman, The Bank, Shanghaied, A Night in the Show* (1915); *Charlie Chaplin's Burlesque on Carmen, Police, Triple Trouble, The Floorwalker, The Fireman, The Vagabond, One A.M., The Count, The Pawnshop, Behind the Screen, The Rink* (1916); *Easy Street, The Cure, The Immigrant, The Adventurer* (1917); *A Dog's Life, The Bond, Shoulder Arms* (1918); *Sunnyside, A Day's Pleasure* (1919); *The Kid, The Idle Class* (1921); *Pay Day, The Pilgrim* (1922); *A Woman of Paris* (1923); *The Gold Rush* (1925); *The Circus* (1928); *City Lights* (1931); *Modern Times* (1936); *The Great Dictator* (1940); *Monsieur Verdoux* (1947); *Limelight* (1952); *A King in New York* (1957); *A Countess from Hong Kong* (1967).

CHAUTARD, Emile (1864–1934)

Emile Chautard was a successful French stage actor, as well as film and theatre director, who first came to the USA as a production representative for Éclair during the 1910s. He directed his first American film in 1915. Two years later, he appeared as himself in his US performing debut – Maurice Tourneur's self-reflexive comedy drama about the American film industry, *A Girl's Folly*. Chautard specialised in older character parts from the mid-1920s – he was Father Chevillon, for example, in Borzage's *Seventh Heaven* – and after the coming of sound, he combined French-language version film roles with work as English-speaking French ambassadors, concierges etc. He was the distinguished-looking French nightclub manager in *Blonde Venus*. AP

FILMS: *A Girl's Folly* [as himself] (1917); *Paris at Midnight, Broken Hearts of Hollywood, My Official Wife, Upstage, The Flaming Forest, Bardelys the Magnificent* (1926); *Blonde or Brunette, Upstream, Whispering Sage, Seventh Heaven, Now We're in the Air, The Love Mart* (1927); *The Noose, His Tiger Wife, The Olympic Hero, Lilac Time, Out of the Ruins, Caught in the Fog, Adoration* (1928); *House of Horror, Marianne, Times Square, South Sea Rose, Tiger Rose* (1929); *Just Like Heaven, Morocco, Sweeping against the Winds, Free and Easy, A Man from Wyoming* (1930); *The Common Law, The Road to Reno* (1931); *Cock of the Air, Shanghai Express, The Man from Yesterday, Blonde Venus, Rasputin and the Empress* (1932); *The California Trail, The Three Musketeers, The Devil's in Love, Design for Living* (1933); *Gallant Lady, Man of Two Worlds, Wonder Bar, Come on Marines, Riptide, Viva Villa!* (1934).

CHEIREL, Micheline (Micheline Leriche) (1917–)

Pretty French brunette whose fame in French cinema rests on her role as 'the good woman' in Julien Duvivier's *La Belle équipe/They Were Five* (1936). Cheirel followed her **205** husband, British leading man John Loder★, to Hollywood in 1939, where she played a few minor roles before being contracted by RKO in 1944. She was given the female lead in Edward Dmytryk's film noir *Cornered* but returned to France not long afterwards. CH

FILMS: *Hold Back the Dawn* (1941); *A Close Call for Ellery Queen, I Married an Angel* (1942); *Cornered* (1945); *Devotion, Flight to Nowhere, So Dark the Night* (1946); *Jewels of Brandenburg, Crime Doctor's Gamble* (1947).

CHEKHOV, Michael (1891–1955)

Nephew to Anton Chekhov and a leading tragic actor at the Moscow Art Theatre, Mikhail Chekhov came to Hollywood in 1943 to work among the community of European artists that were held as reserves for the production of war propaganda movies. Chekhov remained in California until the end of his life playing small roles as Russians, Poles or Jews. He also ran an acting school, developing new acting methods. Yul Brynner, Anthony Quinn, Marilyn Monroe and Gregory Peck were among his students. He was nominated for an Academy Award for his portrayal of the psychoanalyst in Alfred Hitchcock's *Spellbound*. OB

FILMS: *Song of Russia* (1943); *In Our Time* (1944); *Spellbound* (1945); *Specter of the Rose, Abie's Irish Rose, Cross My Heart* (1946); *Texas, Brooklyn and Heaven* (1948); *The Price of Freedom* (1949); *Holiday for Sinners, Invitation* (1952); *Rhapsody* (1954).

CHEVALIER, Maurice (1888–1972)

When MGM executive Irving Thalberg and his wife, the star Norma Shearer, visited Maurice Chevalier in his dressing room at the Casino de Paris in late 1927 to offer him a screen test, Chevalier was the biggest star on the Parisian music-hall stage and an international celebrity (who had already appeared in French silent films and turned down Hollywood offers). He did the test, but negotiations broke down. Paramount's Jesse Lasky saw it and offered Chevalier a six-week, all-expenses-paid contract that met with the star's approval. Chevalier sailed to New York on the *Île de France* in October 1928 with his wife Yvonne Vallée★, where he was met by fellow French émigré, director Robert Florey, who shot a promotional documentary on Chevalier entitled *Bonjour New York!*. In Hollywood, the rushes for Chevalier's first American feature, *Innocents of Paris*, were so conclusive that his contract was extended to

one year at a fabulous $500,000. *Innocents of Paris*, made in French and English versions, was a hit and Chevalier negotiated a new contract worth $20,000 a week (later $25,000).

Thus, at forty, Chevalier became one of the first sound cinema stars and the second French star to attain true world celebrity after Max Linder★. His next feature, *The Love Parade*, directed by Ernst Lubitsch in 1929, confirmed his success. As Lubitsch said, 'You are sitting on top of the world, Maurice!' *Innocents of Paris* and *The Love Parade* encompass the Chevalier screen persona that was to endure. It was a dual image: part street-wise working-class Parisian (usually with cloth cap), and part sophisticated *boulevardier* brimming with *joie de vivre*, wearing his stage ensemble of tuxedo, bow-tie and straw hat – or the fancy uniform of imaginary countries such as 'Sylvania'. The films reconfigured Chevalier's stage persona evolved from his early working-class cabaret act and the extravagant Paris and London music-hall revues. Indeed, between bouts of filming in Hollywood he continued a triumphant music-hall career in New York and Paris. Over the next few years, Chevalier starred in several Lubitsch films with Claudette Colbert and Jeanette MacDonald – *The Smiling Lieutenant, One Hour with You, The Merry Widow* (for which he moved to MGM) – and other hits, including Mamoulian's *Love Me Tonight*. Though plagued with personal problems (the death of his beloved mother, the breakdown of his marriage), he was at home in Hollywood, socialising with the likes of Douglas Fairbanks. He gravitated towards Charles Boyer's★

Maurice Chevalier, the most famous French music-hall artist of his time, arrives in Hollywood with his wife, Yvonne Vallée

circle and enjoyed a close friendship with Marlene Dietrich★. For a few years, his popularity and salary put him in the Hollywood top ten.

How can we understand Chevalier's spectacular success? There was of course his considerable talent and charisma, the genius and clout of Lubitsch and Mamoulian and the might of Paramount in world distribution. There was also a happy historical conjuncture. Chevalier arrived in Hollywood in the early days of sound cinema and of the popularity of the musical, perfect for his singing talent, and of the multi-language versions that needed his bilingual fluency. Chevalier's Frenchman epitomised the myth of Paris as spectacle, capitalising on the success of his stage revues with American tourists. He also embodied that other Parisian myth of sexual sophistication. Lubitsch's comedies showcased Chevalier's persona as risqué sex symbol. He was in this sense a pre-Hays Code star. Chevalier enacted Frenchness with emphatic gestures, protruding lower lip and strong accent – yet while stories circulated that he was not allowed to take English lessons, his elocution was always crystal-clear. He thus presented a pleasing, already mythologised and easily consumable 'touristic' view of France. No wonder commentators repeatedly linked him to other French icons: 'He bubbles like Champagne', said one journalist, while Mamoulian observed, 'He was born the year the Eiffel tower was built, and like it he became the symbol of Paris.'

Back in France in 1935, Chevalier's film career was disappointing, his Hollywood glamour clashing with French populism in Julien Duvivier's *L'Homme du jour/The Man of the Hour* (1936), Maurice Tourneur's *Avec le sourire/With a Smile* (1936) and Robert Siodmak's *Pièges/Personal Column* (1939). He also starred in Kurt Bernhardt's *The Beloved Vagabond* (1936) and René Clair's *Break the News* (1938), both made in London. He did, however, pursue a triumphant stage career towards the end of his life. A performing tour for French prisoners of war in Germany caused Chevalier problems at the Liberation, though he went on singing and acting, notably in Clair's *Le Silence est d'or/Man about Town* (1947).

The postwar period brought new problems. The tide temporarily turned against Europe, and Chevalier was denied a visa to visit the USA in 1951 for alleged Communism, having signed the Stockholm peace appeal. Allowed to re-enter the USA in 1955, he experienced a modest revival of his American career, especially with Billy Wilder's *Love in the Afternoon* and Vincente Minnelli's *Gigi*, and a number of successful television appearances. In both, he incarnated an older, wiser version of his earlier self, as, respectively, ingenious Parisian and ageing beau. *Gigi* crowned his career in another way. Having failed to gain an Academy Award earlier on (though he had been nominated for *The Love Parade* and *The Big Pond*), he was awarded an honorary Academy Award in 1959 for his whole career but also, one feels, for his ability to be, as *The New York Times* put it, 'The symbol and personification of all that is meant by the phrase "Gay Paree"'. GV

FILMS: *Innocents of Paris, The Love Parade* (1929); *Paramount on Parade, The Big Pond, The Playboy of Paris* (1930); *The Smiling Lieutenant* (1931); *One Hour with You, Make Me a Star, Love Me Tonight* (1932); *A Bedtime Story, The Way to Love* (1933); *The Merry Widow* (1934); *Folies Bergère de Paris* (1935); *Love in the Afternoon* (1957); *Gigi* (1958); *Count Your Blessings* (1959); *Can-Can, A Breath of Scandal, Pepe* (1960); *Fanny* (1961); *In Search of the Castaways* (1962); *A New Kind of Love* (1963); *Panic Button, I'd Rather Be Rich* (1964); *Monkeys, Go Home!* (1967); *That's Entertainment, Part II* (1976).

CHOUREAU, Etchika (Françoise Choureau) (1923–)
French actress whose screen debut was in the lead role of Antonioni's *I vinti/The Vanquished* (1953). She was spotted by a Warner Bros.' talent scout and cast by William Wellman as an untamed blonde beauty in two war dramas. VO
FILMS: *Lafayette Escadrille, Darby's Rangers* (1958).

CHRISTIANS, Mady (1900–1951)
Viennese-born Christians first came to the USA as a child in 1912, appeared in one film, and then on the New York stage alongside her father, Rudolph Christians★. Following her return to Europe in 1917, and training under Max Reinhardt, Christians became a celebrated actress of German stage and screen in the 1920s. Equally adept at dramatic roles, light comedy and operetta, Christians appeared in films by Ernst Lubitsch, F. W. Murnau, Carl T. Dreyer and Ludwig Berger. Forced into exile in 1933, she continued parallel stage and screen careers in the USA. She became particularly successful on Broadway, with leading parts in *Watch on the Rhine* and *I Remember Mama*, while her Hollywood career was mainly restricted to supporting roles. Her most memorable film appearances included the **207**

part of Joan Fontaine's mother in *Letter from an Unknown Woman*, and Paul Lukas's★ wife in the anti-Nazi thriller *Address Unknown*. Christians died of a cerebral haemorrhage shortly after being blacklisted and called to testify in front of the House Un-American Activities Committee during the McCarthy witch-hunts. TB

FILMS: *Audrey* (1916); *A Wicked Woman* (1934); *Ship Cafe*, *Escapade* (1935); *Come and Get it* (1936); *Seventh Heaven*, *The Woman I Love*, *Heidi* (1937); *Tender Comrade* (1943); *Address Unknown* (1944); *Letter from an Unknown Woman*, *All My Sons* (1948).

CHRISTIANS, Rudolph (Broekern Rudolf Christians) (1869–1921)

Classical stage actor who served as the director of New York's German-speaking Irving Place Theater from 1912 until its closure when the USA entered World War I in 1917. While opera singer wife Bertha Klein and actress daughter Margarete (later Mady) Christians★ returned to Germany, he remained in the USA and took major roles in five features at Universal and Paramount, before being cast as Special Envoy Mr Hughes in Erich von Stroheim's *Foolish Wives*. Christians succumbed to pneumonia during shooting and his scenes were completed by Robert Edeson. RJK

FILMS: *Burnt Wings*, *Her Five-Foot Highness*, *Human Stuff*, *The Secret Gift*, *Deep Waters* (1920); *Foolish Wives* (1922).

CHRISTIE, Julie (1941–)

Julie Christie, often referred to as the 'British Brigitte Bardot★', was born in Assam, India, and rose to fame in the 1960s through a series of roles perceived to embody the spirit of that decade. She first attracted attention as Liz in John Schlesinger's *Billy Liar* (1963), where she brought 1960s 'Swinging London' to a northern town by tripping jauntily through the streets and swinging her handbag. It was, however, through her Academy Award-winning performance as Diana Scott in Schlesinger's *Darling* (1965), which looked beneath the glamour of Swinging London, that she rose to international fame. These roles established Christie as the icon of a new, more liberated 1960s British femininity and her move towards Hollywood was secured when, on the strength of early footage of *Darling*, David Lean cast Christie as Lara, opposite Omar Sharif, in his epic *Doctor Zhivago*. *Darling*'s producer Joseph Janni, to whom

Christie was contracted for four years, only negotiated this release in order to secure funds to finish the film.

Christie's first film shot in Hollywood was British director Richard Lester's *Petulia*. It was on set that she met Warren Beatty, with whom she became romantically linked and co-starred in her major Hollywood films of the 1970s: *McCabe and Mrs Miller*, *Shampoo* and *Heaven Can Wait*. Christie continued to work on European productions such as Nicolas Roeg's thriller *Don't Look Now* (1973) and, since *Heaven Can Wait*, has mainly worked in British and European film and television productions, including short films, documentaries and voice work. Christie's liberated, middle-class British femininity has found her suited to a significant number of roles in period films and literary adaptations since *Doctor Zhivago*, including *Far from the Madding Crowd*, *The Go-Between* (1970), Maria Luisa Bemberg's *Miss Mary* and *Hamlet*, but she has also worked on a number of less mainstream productions, including François Truffaut's★ *Fahrenheit 451* and Sally Potter's *The Gold Diggers* (1983). Christie has been a committed political campaigner on issues including nuclear power, animal rights and feminism, and indeed many of her roles have engaged with feminist issues and the figure of the 'independent woman'. RMO

FILMS: *Young Cassidy*, *Doctor Zhivago* (1965); *Fahrenheit 451* (1966); *Far from the Madding Crowd* (1967); *Petulia* (1968); *McCabe and Mrs Miller* (1971); *Nashville*, *Shampoo* (1975); *Demon Seed* (1977); *Heaven Can Wait* (1978); *Power*, *Miss Mary* (1986); *DragonHeart*, *Hamlet* (1996); *Afterglow* (1997); *No Such Thing* (2001), *Snapshots*, *I'm with Lucy* (2002); *Troy*, *Harry Potter and the Prisoner of Azkaban* (2004).

CHRISTY, Ivan (Ivan Vöhlk Christensen) (1887–1949)

Danish stage and screen actor who emigrated to the USA in the early 1900s. Christy played numerous Hollywood villains such as the homicidal trader in *Island Wives*. He later worked as a studio security guard. HJW

FILMS: *The Wife's Stratagem*, *All for Business*, *The Fleur-de-Lis Ring*, *A Mother's Way*, *On the Heights*, *Peg O' the Wild Wood* (1914); *Coincidence*, *The Lady of Dreams*, *And by these Deeds*, *When the Tide Turns*, *The Beautiful Lady*, *Blow for Blow*, *Celeste*, *The Weaver of Claybank*, *The Sheriff's Story*, *Serge Panine*, *A Romance of Old California*, *Packer Jim's Guardianship*, *A Mystery of the Mountains*, *Money*, *Count*

Twenty, The Cowboy's Conquest, The Masterful Hireling, Luxurious Lou, Gratitude, The Ebbing Tide, The First Piano in Camp, Fool's Gold, Mister Paganini, His Fatal Shot (1915); *The Man Who Called after Dark, The Iron Will, The Guilt of Stephen Eldridge, The Angel of Piety Flat, The Chain of Evidence, The Battle of Truth, Fit for Burning, A Grip of Gold* (1916); *In Love's Laboratory, Luck of the Roaring Camp, Salt of the Earth* (1917); *The Glorious Adventure* (1918); *Coax Me* (1919); *Rainbow* (1921); *Island Wives, The Madness of Love* (1922); *Man of the Forest* (1926); *The Mysterious Rider, Nevada* (1927); *Seven Footprints to Satan* (1929); *Son of the Gods* (1930); *Men of the Night* (1934); *The Whole Town's Talking, Escape from Devil's Island, A Feather in Her Hat, Love Me Forever, The Lone Wolf Returns, Let's Live Tonight* (1935); *Rose of the Rancho* (1936).

CHURCHILL, Sarah (1914–1982)

British actress and daughter of wartime Prime Minister Sir Winston Churchill. She generally played in light romantic comedies and made her sole Hollywood film appearance in the role of Anne Ashmond alongside Fred Astaire, Jane Powell and Peter Lawford★ in *Royal Wedding*. Thereafter, she worked on American television hosting *The Sarah Churchill Show* (1951) and *Hallmark Hall of Fame* (1952–5). MHu
FILM: *Royal Wedding* (1951).

CIANNELLI, Eduardo (1889–1969)

After an operatic and theatrical career in Italy and the USA, Ciannelli became one of Hollywood's most important character actors. Although he won an Academy Award as the speakeasy owner in the 1940 comedy *Kitty Foyle*, his distinctive features and voice perfectly suited the villainous roles with which he became mainly associated. These included the gangster based on Lucky Luciano in *Marked Woman*. From 1948, he divided his time between a European and American career. AM
FILMS: *The Food Gamblers* (1917); *Reunion in Vienna* (1933); *The Scoundrel* (1935); *Winterset* (1936); *Criminal Lawyer, Marked Woman, Night of Mystery, Super Sleuth, The Girl from Scotland Yard, Hitting a New High, On Such a Night, The League of Frightened Men* (1937); *Blind Alibi, The Saint in New York* [scenes deleted], *Law of the Underworld* (1938); *Risky Business, Gunga Din, Society Lawyer, Bulldog Drummond's Bride, The Angels Wash Their Faces* (1939); *Strange Cargo, Outside the Three-Mile Limit, Forgotten Girls, Zanzibar,*

Eduardo Ciannelli's distinctive features and voice were suited to various villainous Hollywood roles

Foreign Correspondent, The Mummy's Hand, Mysterious Doctor Satan, Kitty Foyle (1940); *Ellery Queen's Penthouse Mystery, Sky Raiders, They Met in Bombay, Paris Calling, I Was a Prisoner on Devil's Island* (1941); *Dr Broadway, Cairo, You Can't Escape Forever* (1942); *Adventures of the Flying Cadets, They Got Me Covered, Flight for Freedom, For Whom the Bell Tolls, The Constant Nymph* (1943); *The Mask of Dimitrios, Storm over Lisbon, The Conspirators, Passage to Marseille* (1944); *Dillinger, Incendiary Blonde, The Crime Doctor's Warning, A Bell for Adano* (1945); *Gilda, Perilous Holiday, The Wife of Monte Cristo, Heartbeat, Joe Palooka, Champ, California* (1946); *Seven Keys to Baldpate, Rose of Santa Rosa, The Lost Moment, The Crime Doctor's Gamble* (1947); *I Love Trouble, A Miracle Can Happen, The Creeper, To the Victor, The Prince of Foxes* (1948); *The People against O'Hara* (1951); *Mambo* (1954); *Helen of Troy* (1955); *Love Slaves of the Amazon, Monster from Green Hell* (1957); *Houseboat* (1958); *Forty Pounds of Trouble* (1963); *The Visit* (1964); *The Chase, The Spy in the Green Hat* (1966); *The Brotherhood, Mission Impossible Versus the Mob* (1968); *Mackenna's Gold, Stiletto, The Secret of Santa Vittoria* (1969).

CLARK, Petula (1931–)

British entertainer who had music-hall and radio success as a child singer during World War II. She continued a career in popular song and appeared in many UK films before a brief stint in American cinema. TJ

FILMS: *Finian's Rainbow* (1968); *Goodbye, Mr Chips* (1969).

CLAVIER, Christian (1952–)

Well-known French comic character actor who has starred in big box-office French comedies such as France's greatest hit of the 1990s, *Les Visiteurs* (1993). Clavier's performance style on screen is often camp and excessive. His only English-speaking role so far has been alongside Jean Reno★ in *Just Visiting*, Jean-Marie Poiré's commercially unsuccessful American remake of *Les Visiteurs*. VO

FILM: *Just Visiting* (2001).

CLEESE, John (1939–)

Cleese's trademark gangly physical presence and slightly unhinged persona were a substantial feature of the renowned British television comedy shows *Monty Python's Flying Circus* and *Fawlty Towers*. They also contributed to the success of the Python films such as *Monty Python and the Holy Grail* (1975) and *Life of Brian* (1979). Cleese largely played against this type in the Western *Silverado* – his first film shot in the USA – but his cameo still contained an anomalous moment of Fawlty-esque slapstick. In the highly successful *A Fish Called Wanda*, he subsequently played a more subtle, repressed version of his earlier self who begins to break through existing emotional barriers. Cleese's success with *Wanda* has led to other Hollywood films such as the zany Bette Middler vehicle, *Isn't She Great*. Along with a regular role as the current Q in the Bond films, Cleese has also proved adept at providing voices for children's animated features such as *George of the Jungle*. His clear and authoritative voice, always capable of slipping into lunacy, seems perfectly suited to the genre. JS/AP

FILMS: *The Magic Christian, The Best House in London* (1969); *The Statue* (1971); *The Great Muppet Caper* (1981); *Silverado* (1985); *A Fish Called Wanda, The Big Picture* (1988); *Bullseye!* (1990); *An American Tail: Fievel Goes West* [voice] (1991); *Mary Shelley's Frankenstein, The Jungle Book, The Swan Princess* (1994); *Fierce Creatures, George of the Jungle* [voice] (1997); *The World is Not Enough, The Out-of-Towners*

(1999); *Isn't She Great, Quantum Project* (2000); *Harry Potter and the Sorcerer's Stone, Rat Race* (2001); *The Adventures of Pluto Nash, Harry Potter and the Chamber of Secrets, Die Another Day* (2002); *Charlie's Angels: Full Throttle, George of the Jungle 2* [voice], *Scorched* (2003); *Around the World in 80 Days, Shrek 2* [voice] (2004).

CLÉMENT, Aurore (1945–)

After she made her debut in Louis Malle's *Lacombe Lucien* (1974), the delicate, blonde-haired Clément became a staple of the European screen, working with French, Italian, German, Swiss and Belgian directors. Her only real experience of American cinema was in Francis Ford Coppola's Vietnam drama *Apocalypse Now*, where she played Christian Marquand's★ wife. Her mainly French-speaking scene was edited out of the final cut, but it has now been restored in the extended director's cut, *Apocalypse Now Redux*. VO

FILM: *Apocalypse Now* (1979 – in redux version only, 2001).

CLIVE, Colin (1900–1937)

The sensational success of the war play *Journey's End* in London in January 1929 transformed the lives of its three main creators, none of whom had any previous film experience. The subsequent film career of its star, Colin Clive, was less substantial than those of its writer, R. C. Sherriff or its director, James Whale, but his contribution to Whale's rapid Hollywood success should not be underestimated. Seeing him as no less indispensable than Whale himself to the filming of *Journey's End*, the producers went to great lengths to transport Clive by sea and rail to Hollywood for a few hectic weeks, before returning him to the play in London, after which he rejoined Whale at Universal for *Frankenstein*. His casting as Henry Frankenstein underlines the continuity between the horrors of the war and those of this multi-layered version of the Mary Shelley story – among other things, Clive is, as it were, reconstructing and reanimating the mutilated bodies of his lost comrades of the trenches – and his two performances convey a comparably vivid suppressed hysteria, with homoerotic undertones. Already suffering from the alcoholism that would cause his premature death, Clive went on to bring his trademark febrile intensity, and what Sherriff called his 'whisky voice', to a variety of tormented husbands, including the wife-beating aristocrat of *One More*

River, adapted from Galsworthy by the Whale–Sherriff partnership. His fourth and last film for Whale was *Bride of Frankenstein*, a triumphant sequel that confirms the equal status of his and Karloff's memorably interdependent roles and performances. CB

FILMS: *Journey's End* (1930); *Frankenstein* (1931); *Looking Forward, Christopher Strong* (1933); *The Key, Jane Eyre, One More River* (1934); *Clive of India, Bride of Frankenstein, The Gift From 10th Avenue, The Man Who Broke the Bank at Monte Carlo, The Widow from Monte Carlo, The Right to Live, Mad Love* (1935); *History is Made at Night, The Woman I Love* (1937).

CLIVE, E. E. (Edward E. Clive) (1879–1940)

Clive was a trained Welsh medical doctor who only started acting in his twenties. He moved to the USA in 1912, where he set up his own acting company in Boston. By the 1920s, it was operating in Los Angeles. Clive was the Burgermeister in *Bride of Frankenstein* and had a regular role as the butler 'Tenny' Tennison in Paramount's 'Bulldog Drummond' films. JS/AP

FILMS: *Cheaters at Play* (1932); *The Invisible Man* (1933); *The Poor Rich, Riptide, One More River, Bulldog Drummond Strikes Back, Charlie Chan in London, The Gay Divorcee, The Little Minister, Tin Pants, Service, Long Lost Father* (1934); *Father Brown, Detective, Mystery of Edwin Drood, Gold Diggers of 1935, Bride of Frankenstein, We're in the Money, Atlantic Adventure, Page Miss Glory, Three Kids and a Queen, A Feather in Her Hat, Stars over Broadway, The Man Who Broke the Bank at Monte Carlo, Remember Last Night?, Kind Lady, Sylvia Scarlet, The Widow from Monte Carlo, A Tale of Two Cities, David Copperfield, Captain Blood* (1935); *The Dark Hour, Love before Breakfast, Little Lord Fauntleroy, The Unguarded Hour, Dracula's Daughter, Show Boat, The Golden Arrow, Palm Springs, The White Angel, Ticket to Paradise, Piccadilly Jim, All American Chump, Cain and Mabel, Libeled Lady, Isle of Fury, The Charge of the Light Brigade, Tarzan Escapes, Lloyd's of London, Trouble for Two, Camille* (1936); *They Wanted to Marry, On the Avenue, Maid of Salem, Ready, Willing and Able, Personal Property, Bulldog Drummond Escapes, Night Must Fall, The Road Back, The Emperor's Candlesticks, Love under Fire, Danger – Love at Work, It's Love I'm After, Live, Love and Learn, The Great Garrick, Beg, Borrow or Steal, Bulldog Drummond's Revenge, Bulldog Drummond Comes Back* (1937); *Arsène Lupin Returns, The First Hundred Years,*

Bulldog Drummond's Peril, Kidnapped, Gateway, Bulldog Drummond in Africa, Submarine Patrol, The Last Warning, Arrest Bulldog Drummond, Mr Moto's Last Warning, The Little Princess, Bulldog Drummond's Secret Police, The Hound of the Baskervilles, I'm from Missouri, Rose of Washington Square, Man about Town, Bachelor Mother, Bulldog Drummond's Bride, The Adventures of Sherlock Holmes, The Honeymoon's Over (1939); *The Earl of Chicago, Raffles, Congo Maisie, Adventure in Diamonds, Pride and Prejudice, Foreign Correspondent* (1940); *Tales of Manhattan* (1942).

CLOSE, Ivy (1890–1968)

English actress who was once judged 'the most beautiful woman in the world'. Close was first a Hepworth player and then she ran her own studio. In 1916, she sailed to the USA to take up a lucrative one-year contract making comedy shorts for the Kalem company. MW

FILMS: *He Wrote Poetry, Meter in the Kitchen, The Stolen Jail, Tangled by Telephone* (1916); *The Battered Bridegroom, The Mysterious Double, Rival Artists, The Stolen Plumage, That Pesky Parrot* (1917).

COLLIER, Constance (Laura Constance Hardie) (1878–1955)

Collier made her screen debut in D. W. Griffith's *Intolerance* in 1916 after an impressive career on the British and American stage. Later, she frequently sailed into Hollywood roles as charming but rather grand ladies such as Mrs Atwater in Hitchcock's *Rope*. MW

FILMS: *Intolerance, Macbeth, The Code of Marcia Gray, The Tongues of Men* (1916); *Forever* (1921); *The Taming of the Shrew* (1929); *Shadow of Doubt, Peter Ibbetson, Anna Karenina, Professional Soldier* (1935); *Girls' Dormitory, Little Lord Fauntleroy* (1936); *Thunder in the City, A Damsel in Distress, Stage Door, Wee Willie Winkie* (1937); *The Baroness and the Butler* (1938); *Zaza* (1939); *Half a Sinner, Susan and God* (1940); *Week-End at the Waldorf, Kitty* (1945); *Monsieur Beaucaire, The Dark Corner* (1946); *The Perils of Pauline* (1947); *The Girl from Manhattan, Rope* (1948); *Whirlpool* (1949).

COLLINS, Joan (1933–)

Collins' early film roles in the UK with Rank did little to build the star image of venomous dialogue, big hair, plunging necklines, shoulder pads and LA ostentation with which she later became associated. Her move to Holly- 211 wood in 1955 saw her become an international star, though, and she was initially loaned to Warner Bros. to star in *Land of the Pharaohs* and then to Twentieth Century-Fox, where Darryl F. Zanuck bought her out of her contract with Rank. Collins explanation of her move the following year said it all: 'I went to Hollywood because I saw no future in playing juvenile delinquents – slopping about in dreary old clothes scraped together from second-hand shops.'

She did return to the UK in the mid-1960s, but was soon back in the USA, where she made a series of film and television appearances. In the 1970s, Collins returned to the UK again for a spell of clothes-shedding adventures in horror films of variable quality, before her vampish glamour was fully exploited, in every sense, in her legendary roles in *The Stud* (1978) and *The Bitch* (1979), both of which were based on her sister Jackie's best-selling novels. These parts formed the launch pad for her new persona as the impossibly wealthy 'super-bitch' of 1980s television: Alexis Carrington in *Dynasty*. With a capacity for wit, excellent comic timing and an agreeable willingness to play with her own screen image, Collins has shown increasing versatility and cult popularity in recent years on American and British film and television. She received an OBE in 1997. MW

FILMS: *The Girl in the Red Velvet Swing, Land of the Pharaohs, The Virgin Queen* (1955); *The Opposite Sex* (1956); *The Wayward Bus, Island in the Sun, Stopover Tokyo, Sea Wife* (1957); *Rally 'Round the Flag, Boys!, The Bravados* (1958); *Esther and the King, Seven Thieves* (1960); *The Road to Hong Kong* (1962); *Warning Shot* (1967); *If It's Tuesday, This Must Be Belgium, Can Hieronymous Merkin Ever Forget Mercy Humppe and Find True Happiness?* (1969); *Up in the Cellar, The Executioner* (1970); *Tales from the Crypt* (1972); *Empire of the Ants* (1977); *Zero to Sixty* (1978); *Sunburn* (1979); *Homework* (1982); *In the Bleak Midwinter* (1995); *The Line King: Al Hirschfeld* (1996); *The Flintstones in Viva Rock Vegas* (2000).

COLMAN, Ronald (1891–1958)

If one considers his front-rank matinée-idol status and box-office cachet, then Ronald Colman can stake a claim to being the most successful British émigré actor of all. After abandoning the British stage and screen, Colman came to enjoy a popular international appeal that remained undiminished for twenty years from the mid-1920s to the aftermath of World War II. His 'Englishness', signified by accent,

role and star persona, remained steadfastly undiluted throughout most of that run and established a blueprint of suave, gentlemanly (and nearly always moustachioed) elegance for the British male lead in Hollywood, of which David Niven★ was only the most obvious replica.

Colman's rigidly maintained Anglicisms are all the more significant given that he brought very little in the way of an established reputation or image with him when he first crossed the Atlantic in October 1920. After being invalided out of World War I early on, he achieved a degree of success on the London stage. His appearance in 1917 as the juvenile lead of the headline-grabbing play *Damaged Goods* – a cautionary tale of the spread of venereal disease – helped bring him to the attention of British film producers. By the beginning of the next decade, he had made eight films. Reputedly hindered by a conspicuous limp he retained from his war wounds, Colman never rose beyond the supporting ranks and with his West End career progressively also proving a disappointment, he made a speculative relocation to Broadway.

After two years of gradual progress and one tiny role in a New York-shot film, Colman was 'spotted' on stage by director Henry King and hired as Lillian Gish's leading man in *The White Sister*, which was shot largely on location in Italy. At this early stage in his Hollywood career, Colman was cast on more than one occasion as an exotic Latin lover in the Valentino mould. In 1924, he signed a contract with mogul Samuel Goldwyn. Goldwyn must take a lot of the credit for establishing Colman as a bankable leading man – a process that began with five films co-starring Vilma Bánky★ he chose to showcase him in. Goldwyn also helped to forge a star image that happily foregrounded Colman's English origins even before the advent of sound made this more or less unavoidable. The actor's association with Goldwyn lasted until 1933, when the latter's persistent association of Colman with stereotypical English qualities for publicity purposes was deemed by the actor to have reached ridiculous limits. In promoting *The Masquerader*, Goldwyn recycled an old Colman press story that suggested that he was so proper and reserved off camera that it required copious supplies of alcohol to soften his stiff upper lip in the film's love scenes. Seeing this as a considerable affront to his dignity and talent, Colman sued for $2 million libel damages. Although an out-of-court settlement was reached, Colman walked out on his contract. For the

Ronald Colman achieved front-rank matinee-idol status and box-office cachet over two decades

remainder of his career, he selectively made films for various studios at a relatively leisurely pace (usually one a year), before gradually winding down his commitments after winning an Academy Award, following three previous nominations, for *A Double Life*.

Colman's screen incarnations encompassed a number of different variations upon a basic genteel template. He was a dashing 'Boys' Own' soldier in the title role of *Beau Geste*, an Empire-builder in *Clive of India*, and he proved that he also possessed a dexterous light comedian's touch in his definitive interpretations of the gentleman-detective *Bulldog Drummond* and the gentleman-thief *Raffles*. Even in such nominally playful parts, though, there is an air of gravitas and a quizzical rather than playful detachment. This is more obviously exploited in a number of films that draw upon Colman's facility at suggesting a deep-seated sadness or trauma behind the outward courteous nobility of his heroes. The pattern would seem to have been established by his early (lost) performance as a British war veteran who conceals his blindness from his sweetheart to prevent her staying with him out of pity in *The Dark Angel*. He would

also be subject to bouts of tragic blindness in *The Light that Failed*. The gravitation towards wounded, incomplete protagonists similarly resulted in a strikingly common incidence of amnesiac episodes. In the first film version of James Hilton's novel *Lost Horizon*, Colman loses his memory and cannot define or articulate his longing to be back in the paradise of Shangri-La. In *Random Harvest*, another Hilton adaptation, he is struck with amnesia (twice!) and cannot remember where he belongs or even recognise his wife. In *A Double Life*, his Shakespearean actor cannot recall a secret existence in which he has been deliriously re-enacting the tragedy of *Othello* for real. In one sense, Colman's transplanted Englishness actively reinforced this productive undercurrent of dislocation, loss and exile in his star persona. In *The Late George Apley*, he is quite literally a man out of his time, a hostage to tradition and adrift from contemporary values. One might even argue that the flagrant air of Old World nostalgia associated with Colman from the beginnings of his time in Hollywood insured him against a loss of fashionability and helped to sustain a top-flight career of unusual longevity for the period. JB

FILMS: *Handcuffs or Kisses* (1921); *The White Sister, The Eternal City* (1923); *$20 a Week, Romola, Tarnish, Her Night of Romance* (1924); *A Thief in Paradise, The Sporting Venus, His Supreme Moment, Her Sister from Paris, The Dark Angel, Stella Dallas, Lady Windermere's Fan* (1925); *Kiki, Beau Geste, The Winning of Barbara Worth* (1926); *The Night of Love, The Magic Flame* (1927); *Two Lovers* (1928); *The Rescue, Bulldog Drummond, Condemned* (1929); *Raffles, The Devil to Pay!* (1930); *The Unholy Garden, Arrowsmith* (1931); *Cynara* (1932); *The Masquerader* (1933); *Bulldog Drummond Strikes Back* (1934); *Clive of India, The Man Who Broke the Bank at Monte Carlo, A Tale of Two Cities* (1935); *Under Two Flags* (1936); *Lost Horizon, The Prisoner of Zenda* (1937); *If I Were King* (1938); *The Light that Failed* (1939); *Lucky Partners* (1940); *My Life with Caroline* (1941); *Talk of the Town, Random Harvest* (1942); *Kismet* (1944); *The Late George Apley, A Double Life* (1947); *Champagne for Caesar* (1950); *Around the World in Eighty Days* (1956); *The Story of Mankind* (1957).

COMONT, Mathilde (1886–1938)

Blonde and plump French actress who played a variety of small supporting roles in Hollywood in the 1920s and early **213**

1930s. Comont's career started in silent films and she survived the coming of sound. She also appeared in a few French versions of multi-language films. CH

FILMS: *A Rogue's Romance* (1919); *Rosita* (1923); *The Thief of Bagdad, Mademoiselle Midnight, His Hour* (1924); *If Marriage Fails* (1925); *The Sea Beast, The Enchanted Hill, The Girl from Montmartre, The Far Cry, La Bohème, The Gilded Highway, Paris at Midnight, Puppets, The Passionate Quest, What Price Glory?, Rose of the Tenements, The Whole Town's Talking, Volcano* (1926); *The Loves of Carmen, Love, Streets of Shanghai, The Wrong Mr Wright* (1927); *The Charge of the Gaucho, A Woman's Way, Ramona* (1928); *Along Came Youth, Call of the Flesh, Romance, Just Like Heaven, The Lash, The Sea Bat* (1930); *The Lady Who Dared, Hard Hombre, The Cuban Love Song* (1931); *Lady with a Past, Careless Lady* (1932); *Laughing at Life, Design for Living* (1933); *A Wicked Woman, A Torch Tango, All Men are Enemies* (1934); *Here's to Romance, Waterfront Lady, Escapade, Ceiling Zero* (1935); *The Robin Hood of El Dorado, Poor Little Rich Girl, Anthony Adverse, The Longest Night, God's Country and the Woman, The Go Getter* (1937).

COMPTON, Fay (Virginia Lilian Emmeline Compton) (1894–1978)

English stage actress who starred in British films from 1914 onwards, including a number of US-financed productions. Compton played Emilia in Orson Welles' production of *Othello*. MF

FILMS: *This Freedom* (1923); *Fashions in Love* (1929); *Wedding Group* (1936); *So This is London* (1940); *The Prime Minister* (1941); *Britannia Mews* (1949); *Lady Possessed, Othello* (1952); *The Haunting* (1963).

CONNERY, Sean (Thomas Connery) (1930–)

Scottish actor with a significant Hollywood career who often retains a distinctive British accent while playing characters of diverse national identities. In a film such as *The Untouchables*, this extra-textual indicator actually serves to emphasise the immigrant status of the character he plays. After early careers in the Royal Navy and as a bodybuilder and model, Connery moved on to work in theatre and television in the 1950s. He rose to fame and remains best known for, and to an extent limited by, his performances as Ian Fleming's secret agent James Bond in the 1960s and early 1970s. The tag-line 'Sean Connery IS James Bond' has

proved prophetic, as he has struggled at times to escape both the invasion of privacy and the potential typecasting that has accompanied his international critical and commercial success in the role. He returned to the part in *Never Say Never Again* in 1983.

Connery had links with and worked briefly in Hollywood before his part as Bond catapulted him to international stardom. In 1957, he was cast in the lead role as a battered prize-fighter in the BBC television play *Requiem for a Heavyweight* (1957), after Jack Palance, who had played the part in the American production, proved unavailable. The play was seen by Bob Goldstein of Twentieth Century-Fox and Connery subsequently signed a seven-year deal with the studio. While he was groomed in Hollywood and given a star build-up, this arrangement yielded only *The Longest Day* and a few non-Fox productions such as *Another Time, Another Place* with Lana Turner, who chose him as her co-star. Connery returned to theatre and television work in Britain, before he was cast as Bond, a popular choice not just with critics but also with a public increasingly familiar with his television work. Connery's Bond transformed Fleming's upper-class Englishman into a class-less British hero partly through the retention of his deep voice and Scottish accent. The actor represented a new kind of British masculinity and indeed British stardom, bringing to the role a finely tuned combination of menacing hardness, sophistication and sarcasm as well as a charged and energetic physical presence. Produced by Harry Saltzman and Albert R. 'Cubby' Broccoli, *Dr No, From Russia with Love, Goldfinger, Thunderball, You Only Live Twice* and *Diamonds are Forever* were made in Britain but were actually financed by United Artists as part of a six-film deal. Connery, although contracted to the production company Eon for six Bond films, refused to make another film after *You Only Live Twice* and only returned for *Diamonds are Forever* on his own terms indicating that, by then, he was a star powerful enough to determine his own terms and conditions. In this case, the terms' involved a fee of $1 million and financial backing from United Artists for two subsequent projects of his choosing.

Connery returned to Hollywood in a break from Bond to play Mark Rutland in Hitchcock's *Marnie*, a role that was, nevertheless, successfully informed by the same kind of suave yet brutal sexual energy that marked the character of the British spy. While Connery broke the mould in his role as a Beat poet in *A Fine Madness*, British critics, unlike their American counterparts, found him impossible to accept; the film also did poorly at the box office. Through the 1970s, Connery worked in both British and American productions and in a range of genres: from science fiction to political thrillers like *Cuba* and more straightforward action adventures. The three films that perhaps enabled him to move beyond the grasp of the Bond cycle and demonstrate the breadth of his acting ability were *The Wind and the Lion*, John Huston's *The Man Who Would Be King*, with Michael Caine★, and *Robin and Marian*, with Audrey Hepburn★. In all of these films, he gave more gestural, naturalistic performances playing idealist characters in some way out of step with or distanced from the modern world. This is a strand that has continued in his later work in films like *Medicine Man* and *Indiana Jones and the Last Crusade*.

While there were significant exceptions (e.g. the French, Italian and Dutch co-production *The Name of the Rose* [1986]), Connery's work in the 1980s and 1990s was dominated by Hollywood action-adventure and thriller genres. He won a Best Supporting Actor Academy Award for his role in *The Untouchables*. Connery has retained strong links with Europe, making his home in Spain and remaining committed to the Scottish Nationalist cause. His stardom has remained linked to his role as Bond, though, and his most successful later work has been that which has combined this with roles as an outdated hero in films like *The Rock* and *Entrapment*. RMo

FILMS: *Another Time, Another Place* (1958); *Darby O'Gill and the Little People*, *Tarzan's Greatest Adventure* (1959); *The Longest Day*, *Dr No* (1962); *From Russia with Love* (1963); *Woman of Straw*, *Goldfinger*, *Marnie* (1964); *The Hill*, *Thunderball* (1965); *A Fine Madness* (1966); *You Only Live Twice* (1967); *The Molly Maguires* (1969); *Diamonds are Forever*, *The Anderson Tapes* (1971); *The Offence* (1973); *Zardoz* (1974); *Ransom*, *The Man Who Would Be King*, *The Wind and the Lion* (1975); *The Next Man*, *Robin and Marian* (1976); *A Bridge Too Far* (1977); *Cuba*, *Meteor* (1979); *Outland* (1981); *Five Days One Summer*, *Wrong is Right* (1982); *Never Say Never Again* (1983); *Highlander* (1986); *The Untouchables* (1987); *Memories of Me*, *The Presidio* (1988); *Family Business*, *Indiana Jones and the Last Crusade* (1989); *The Russia House*, *The Hunt for Red October* (1990); *Robin Hood: Prince of Thieves* (1991); *Medicine*

Man (1992); *Rising Sun* (1993); *A Good Man in Africa* (1994); *First Knight*, *Just Cause* (1995); *DragonHeart* [voice], *The Rock* (1996); *The Avengers*, *Playing by Heart* (1998); *Entrapment* (1999); *Finding Forrester* (2000); *The League of Extraordinary Gentlemen* (2003).

CONTI, Tom (1941–)

Renowned Scottish character actor who has worked mainly on stage and television. In an intermittent screen career, he has worked occasionally in Hollywood, most notably as the drunken, womanising poet Gowan McGland in *Reuben, Reuben*, for which he received a Best Actor Academy Award nomination. MHu

FILMS: *Reuben, Reuben* (1983); *American Dreamer* (1984); *Saving Grace* (1985); *Beyond Therapy* (1987); *Out of Control* (1998).

COOGAN, Steve (1965–)

Coogan has been a versatile and perceptive comic presence on British television screens since the early 1990s, with an uncanny grasp for revealing social pretension through his verbal mimicry. He came to international attention playing the leading role of Phileas Fogg in the high-tech, majority US-funded remake of *Around the World in 80 Days*. AP

FILMS: *The Indian in the Cupboard* (1995); *Coffee and Cigarettes* (2003); *Ella Enchanted* [voice], *Around the World in 80 Days* (2004).

COOPER, Gladys (1888–1971)

Cooper progressed from being a British pin-up chorus girl to a pioneering actress-manager in the theatre and frequent collaborator with Noel Coward★. She was also an occasional female lead in British cinema in the 1910s and 1920s. In 1940, she moved to Hollywood, via Broadway, and became a regular supporting player in dignified matron roles, three of which, in *Now, Voyager*, *The Song of Bernadette* and *My Fair Lady*, earned her Academy Award nominations. JB

FILMS: *Rebecca*, *Kitty Foyle* (1940); *That Hamilton Woman*, *The Gay Falcon*, *The Black Cat* (1941); *Now, Voyager*, *This above All*, *Eagle Squadron* (1942); *Forever and a Day*, *The Song of Bernadette*, *Princess O'Rourke*, *Mr Lucky* (1943); *The White Cliffs of Dover*, *Mrs Parkington* (1944); *Love Letters*, *The Valley of Decision* (1945); *The Green Years*, *The Cockeyed Miracle*, **215**

British stage star Gladys Cooper became a regular supporting player in dignified matron roles in 1940s Hollywood

Beware of Pity (1946); *Green Dolphin Street, The Bishop's Wife* (1947); *Homecoming, The Pirate* (1948); *The Secret Garden, Madame Bovary* (1949); *At Sword's Point* (1952); *Separate Tables* (1958); *The List of Adrian Messenger* (1963); *My Fair Lady* (1964); *The Happiest Millionaire* (1967).

COOPER, Melville (1896–1973)

Versatile British actor who appeared in a few US-funded films shot in Britain before moving permanently to Hollywood following his success with a supporting part in Korda's *The Private Life of Don Juan* (1934). Cooper specialised in butlers, military officers and aristocrats with a slightly effete and pompous air, although he also had a line in supercilious criminal types such as one of the card sharp trio in *The Lady Eve*. He is best remembered as the Sheriff of Nottingham in *The Adventures of Robin Hood* and for his unlikely amorous role as Mr Collins, opposite Greer Garson★, in *Pride and Prejudice*. AP

FILMS: *Two White Arms* (1932); *Forging Ahead* (1933); *The Bishop Misbehaves, Rendezvous* (1935); *The Gorgeous Hussy* (1936); *The Last of Mrs Cheyney, Personal Property* [scenes deleted]; *Thin Ice, The Great Garrick, Tovarich* (1937); *Women*

are *Like That, The Adventures of Robin Hood, Gold Diggers in Paris, Four's a Crowd, Garden of the Moon, Hard to Get, Comet over Broadway, Dramatic School, The Dawn Patrol* (1938); *I'm from Missouri, Blind Alley, The Sun Never Sets, Two Bright Boys* (1939); *Too Many Husbands, Rebecca, Escape to Glory, Pride and Prejudice, Murder over New York* (1940); *The Lady Eve, The Flame of New Orleans, You Belong to Me, Scotland Yard* (1941); *This Above All, The Affairs of Martha, Random Harvest, Life Begins at 8:30* (1942); *Immortal Sergeant, Hit Parade of 1943, Holy Matrimony, My Kingdom for a Cook* (1943); *Heartbeat* (1946); *13 Rue Madeleine, The Imperfect Lady* (1947); *Enchantment* (1948); *The Red Danube, Love Happy, And Baby Makes Three* (1949); *Father of the Bride, The Underworld Story, The Petty Girl, Let's Dance, The Return of Gilbert and Sullivan* (1950); *It Should Happen to You* (1954); *Moonfleet, The King's Thief* (1955); *Diane, Around the World in Eighty Days, Bundle of Joy* (1956); *The Story of Mankind* (1957); *From the Earth to the Moon* (1958).

COOTE, Robert (1909–1982)

British supporting actor who enjoyed a long film career in both the UK and Hollywood by almost cornering the market in silly-ass army officers and aristocrats. He played the amiable buffoon sidekick to such leading players as Gene Kelly, Cary Grant and David Niven★. MHu

FILMS: *Rangle River* (1936); *The Sheik Steps Out, The Thirteenth Chair* (1937); *Blonde Cheat, The Girl Downstairs, A Yank at Oxford* (1938); *Gunga Din, The House of Fear, Bad Lands, Mr Moto's Last Warning, Nurse Edith Cavell* (1939); *Vigil in the Night, You Can't Fool Your Wife* (1940); *Commandos Strike at Dawn* (1942); *Forever and a Day* (1943); *Cloak and Dagger* [scenes deleted] (1946); *The Ghost and Mrs Muir, The Exile, Lured, Forever Amber* (1947); *Berlin Express, The Three Musketeers* (1948); *The Red Danube* (1949); *Soldiers Three* (1951); *Scaramouche, The Merry Widow, The Prisoner of Zenda* (1952); *The Swan* (1956); *Merry Andrew* (1958); *A Man Could Get Killed, The Swinger* (1966); *The Cool Ones* (1967); *Kenner* (1969).

CORRI, Adrienne (Adrienne Riccoboni) (1930–)

Voluptuous, red-haired British actress who had an aura of dreamy eroticism that was perfectly exemplified in her first major US film, *The River*. Hollywood failed to find Corri sufficient roles and, along with subsequent roles in various US-financed films and co-productions shot in Europe, she became a familiar face in British horror and science-fiction film and television. TJ

FILMS: *Quo Vadis, The River* (1951); *Doctor Zhivago, Bunny Lake is Missing* (1965); *Africa – Texas Style!, Woman Times Seven* (1967); *A Clockwork Orange* (1971); *Rosebud* (1975); *The Revenge of the Pink Panther* (1978).

CORSARO, Franco (1900–1982)

Italian actor who emigrated to Philadelphia as a tenor after having travelled Europe in a theatrical troupe. In the early 1930s, he was the main Italian dubber at Fox. He then spent two decades as a prolific character actor appearing in a wide variety of roles, including a conspirator in *Casablanca* and a Spaniard in Billy Wilder's *The Emperor Waltz*. AM

FILMS: *The Captain Hates the Sea* (1934); *Let's Live Tonight, Love Me Forever, Goin' to Town* (1935); *The Bride Wore Red, Love under Fire, Prescription for Romance* (1937); *Western Trails, Jezebel, Personal Secretary, Secrets of a Nurse, Nurse from Brooklyn* (1938); *Rio* (1939); *Black Friday, I Was an Adventuress, Green Hell, My Favourite Wife, Down Argentine Way, The Mark*

of Zorro, *Phantom Raiders* (1940); *Week-End in Havana, Down in San Diego* (1941); *A Tragedy at Midnight, Spy Smasher, Casablanca* (1942); *For Whom the Bell Tolls, We've Never Been Licked, The Heavenly Body, The Desert Song* (1943); *Mrs Parkington, Marriage is a Private Affair, Three Men in White* (1944); *Without Love, Yolanda and the Thief, The Crime Doctor's Warning, A Bell for Adano* (1945); *Decoy, The Razor's Edge, Adventure, Dangerous Millions, Two Sisters from Boston* (1946); *Green Dolphin Street, The Beast with Five Fingers, Carnival in Costa Rica* (1947); *Arch of Triumph, The Emperor Waltz* (1948); *Prince of Foxes, Black Magic* (1949); *Four Girls in Town* (1956); *Istanbul, Top Secret Affair* (1957); *Pay or Die* (1960); *Two Weeks in Another Town* (1962); *Rachel, Rachel* (1968); *Master Gunfighter* (1975).

CORTESE, Valentina (1925–)

Italian star with dark hair and slightly sharp Mediterranean features who had been among the most popular actresses in 1940s Italy. Cortese's break in Hollywood came after her role in the British–Italian co-production *The Glass Moun-*

Valentina Cortese: the 'prostitute with a golden heart' in Jules Dassin's film noir *Thieves' Highway* (1949)

tain (1949). The same year, she appeared alongside Spencer Tracy and James Stewart in *Malaya* and starred as the sensual mistress of a truck driver in Jules Dassin's noir thriller *Thieves' Highway*.

After *Black Magic*, co-starring Orson Welles, Cortese signed a contract with Darryl F. Zanuck, who emphasised her Mediterranean background by changing the spelling of her name to Cortesa. In 1951, she starred opposite her future husband Richard Basehart as a girl pursued by a killer in Robert Wise's thriller *The House on Telegraph Hill*. After nine years of marriage, the couple divorced and Cortese returned to Italy, working with directors such as Antonioni, Fellini and Zeffirelli, continuing to produce some fine work in her later years. For example, she was the wife in a likeable retired show-biz couple on their second honeymoon in *When Time Ran Out* and she excelled as Queen Ariadne alongside Robin Williams in Terry Gilliam's *The Adventures of Baron Munchausen*. However, her best-known American role probably remains that of Countess Eleanora Torlato-Favrini in *The Barefoot Contessa*. CS

FILMS: *Malaya, Thieves' Highway, Black Magic* (1949); *The House on Telegraph Hill* (1951); *The Barefoot Contessa* (1954); *Magic Fire* (1956); *Square of Violence* (1961); *Barabbas* (1962); *The Visit* (1964); *The Legend of Lylah Clare* (1968); *The Secret of Santa Vittoria* (1969); *La Nuit américaine* (1973); *When Time Ran Out* (1980); *The Adventures of Baron Munchausen* (1988).

COSTER-WALDAU, Nikolaj (1970–)

The young stage actor Nikolaj Coster-Waldau enjoyed almost immediate cult status in Denmark as the mortuary attendant in Ole Bornedal's *Nattevagten/Nightwatch* (1994), but was replaced by Ewan MacGregor★ in the 1998 Hollywood remake. He rebounded with a strong performance in Ridley Scott's *Black Hawk Down*. HJW

FILMS: *Enigma, Black Hawk Down* (2001); *My Name is Modesty: A Modesty Blaise Adventure* (2003).

COTILLARD, Marion (1975–)

French actress who came to international attention with the success of the comic action film *Taxi* (1998) and its two sequels *Taxi 2* (2000) and *Taxi 3* (2003). The dark beauty has made a name for herself in a number of more demanding French films, and in Hollywood, where she played

Albert Finney's★ daughter-in-law in the Tim Burton fantasy, *Big Fish*. GV

FILM: *Big Fish* (2003).

COULOURIS, George (1903–1989)

Accomplished British stage, film and radio actor who arrived in Hollywood via Broadway in 1933. Although he generally played heavies and villains, he is best remembered for his performance as Walter Parks Thatcher, the stern guardian to the young Charles Foster Kane in *Citizen Kane*. Coulouris also worked in British cinema from the early 1950s onwards and appeared in a number of US-financed productions shot in Europe. MHu/AP

FILMS: *Christopher Bean* (1933); *All This, and Heaven Too, The Lady in Question* (1940); *Citizen Kane* (1941); *This Land is Mine, Watch on the Rhine, Assignment in Brittany* (1943); *Mr Skeffington, The Master Race, Between Two Worlds, None but the Lonely Heart* (1944); *Lady on a Train, Hotel Berlin, Confidential Agent, A Song to Remember* (1945); *California, The Verdict, Nobody Lives Forever* (1946); *Mr District Attorney, Where There's Life* (1947); *A Southern Yankee, Joan of Arc, Beyond Glory, Sleep My Love* (1948); *Kill or Be Killed* (1950); *Tarzan and the Lost Safari* (1957); *Spy in the Sky!, I Accuse!, No Time to Die* (1958); *Surprise Package* (1960); *King of Kings* (1961); *In the Cool of the Day* [scenes deleted], *Come Fly with Me* (1963); *Too Many Thieves, Arabesque* (1966); *The Assassination Bureau, Land Raiders* (1969); *Papillon* (1973).

COURTNEIDGE, Cicely (1893–1980)

This musical comedienne formed part of a popular comedy team with her husband Jack Hulbert in British films of the 1930s. She made only one film actually in Hollywood, which was apparently such a mismanaged disaster that Hulbert promptly turned back while en route to California rather than risk a similar experience. *Under Your Hat* and *Those Magnificent Men . . .* were both US-backed films shot in Europe. JB

FILMS: *The Perfect Gentleman* (1935); *Under Your Hat* (1940); *Those Magnificent Men in Their Flying Machines, or How I Flew from London to Paris in 25 Hours, 11 Minutes* (1965).

COWARD, Noel (1898–1973)

Celebrated British playwright, songwriter and author of West End musical comedies whose work as a writer was much sought after for adaptation. Coward's film debut was a small part in D. W. Griffith's *Hearts of the World*, filmed on location in Gloucestershire. Although he appeared in a few American films, he did not want to act in Hollywood, believing that he would not get paid enough: 'I'd rather have a nice cup of cocoa really,' he argued. SS

FILMS: *Hearts of the World* (1918); *The Scoundrel* (1935); *Around the World in Eighty Days* (1956); *Our Man in Havana* (1959); *Surprise Package* (1960); *Paris – When it Sizzles* (1964); *Bunny Lake is Missing* (1965); *The Italian Job* (1969).

COX, Brian (1946–)

LAMDA trained, Brian Cox had a successful career on stage and television in Britain, before his starring role as the first Hannibal Lecter in *Manhunter*. This was not a box-office success, but over the past decade the craggy, gravel-voiced Scot has become a prolific character actor in American films, often playing unsympathetic characters. AS

FILMS: *Manhunter* (1986); *Iron Will* (1994); *Rob Roy, Braveheart* (1995); *Chain Reaction, The Glimmer Man, The Long Kiss Goodnight* (1996); *Kiss the Girls, The Boxer* (1997); *Desperate Measures, Rushmore, Merchants of Venus* (1998); *The Minus Man, The Corruptor, For Love of the Game* (1999); *A Shot at Glory* (2000); *Super Troopers, L.I.E., The Affair of the Necklace* (2001); *Bug, The Rookie, The Bourne Identity, The 25th Hour* (2002); *X2, The Reckoning, Sin* (2003); *Troy, The Bourne Supremacy* (2004).

CRAWFORD, Michael (Michael Patrick Dumble-Smith) (1942–)

British actor and performer who has combined film and television work with a hugely successful stage career in international musicals. He played Cornelius Hackl in the Hollywood version of *Hello Dolly!*. JS

FILMS: *The War Lover* (1962); *The Knack – and How to Get it . . .* (1965); *A Funny Thing Happened on the Way to the Forum* (1966); *How I Won the War* (1967); *Hello, Dolly!* (1969); *The Games, Hello-Goodbye* (1970); *Condorman* (1981).

CREMER, Bruno (Jean Drillon) (1929–)

French actor whose long career includes his memorable television portrayal of Inspector Maigret. Cremer's sole American film was a remake of H. G. Clouzot's *Le Salaire de la peur/The Wages of Fear* (1953). SL

FILM: *The Sorcerer* (1977).

CRESPO, José (José Crespo Ferraz) (1900–1997)

Good-looking Spanish actor with slicked-back dark hair, expressive eyes and a neat moustache. Crespo was often cast as military officers and upper-class types in historical dramas. He became one of the most popular romantic leads in Hollywood Spanish-language films, but his strong accent limited his appearances in English-language productions. He became the director of New York's Spanish Theatre in the early 1950s. EU

FILMS: *Joy Street* (1929); *Revenge at Monte Carlo* (1933); *Hollywood Hoodlum* (1934); *Storm over the Andes* (1935); *Rascals* (1938).

CRISP, Donald (George William Crisp) (1880–1974)

Prolific Scottish actor-director who arrived in New York in 1906 and performed and directed on Broadway for several years before joining Biograph in 1908. He acted regularly for D. W. Griffith, alongside directing numerous silent movies such as *Don Q, Son of Zorro* and *The Navigator* (with Buster Keaton). Crisp also frequently worked as Griffith's assistant. Notable roles from this period include performances as General Grant in *Birth of a Nation* and Battling Burrows in *Broken Blossoms*; the latter, in particular, is a gloriously melodramatic performance of silent-era villainy. After directing his last film, *The Runaway Bride* (1930), Crisp moved exclusively into acting and worked with such notable Hollywood filmmakers as Howard Hawks, Michael Curtiz and Anthony Mann. A forceful actor with an imposing screen presence, Crisp won an Academy Award for Best Supporting Actor as Roddy McDowall's★ benevolent father in John Ford's sentimental paean to a Welsh mining community *How Green Was My Valley*. Crisp is most memorable in the variety of often stern patriarchal roles he played in films such as *National Velvet* and *The Man from Laramie*. As one critic suggested, '[e]xuding a mixture of obstreperousness and high moral rectitude, he made life very difficult for little girls and big dogs; the disapproval of a Crisp was indeed a terrifying prospect!' In addition to the Skye church-keeper in *Greyfriars Bobby*, Crisp's Scottish heritage was also obliquely acknowledged in *The Bonnie Brier Bush* (which he also directed), *The Little Minister* and *Mary of Scotland*. MF

FILMS: *The French Maid* (1908); *Sunshine Sue, Winning Back His Love* (1910); *The Two Paths, Fate's Turning, The Poor Sick*   **219**

Men, *A Wreath of Orange Blossoms*, *What Shall We Do with Our Old?*, *Lily of the Tenements*, *In the Days of '49*, *The White Rose of the Wilds*, *The Primal Call*, *Out from the Shadow*, *The Diving Girl*, *The Squaw's Love*, *Her Awakening*, *The Making of a Man*, *The Adventures of Billy*, *The Battle*, *The Miser's Heart*, *The Failure* (1911); *The Eternal Mother*, *The Inner Circle*, *The Musketeers of Pig Alley*, *When Kings Were the Law* (1912); *The Best Man Wins*, *Drink's Lure*, *The Daylight Burglar*, *Black and White*, *In the Elemental World*, *Pirate Gold*, *Near to Earth*, *The Sheriff's Baby*, *The Mothering Heart*, *Two Men of the Desert*, *By Man's Law* (1913); *The Battle of the Sexes*, *Home, Sweet Home*, *The Escape*, *The Avenging Conscience*, *Over the Ledge*, *Their First Acquaintance*, *The Tavern of Tragedy*, *The Warning*, *The Niggard*, *The Newer Woman*, *The Mysterious Shot*, *The Different Man*, *The Sisters*, *A Question of Courage*, *The Mountain Rat*, *The Great Leap*, *Another Chance* (1914); *The Birth of a Nation*, *The Love Route*, *The Commanding Officer*, *May Blossom*, *A Girl of Yesterday*, *The Foundling*, *The Blue or the Gray*, *Bred in the Bone*, *Such a Little Queen* (1915); *Ramona*, *Intolerance*, *Joan the Woman* (1916); *The Countess Charming* (1917); *One More American* (1918); *Broken Blossoms* (1919); *The Bonnie Brier Brush* (1921); *Don Q, Son of Zorro* (1925); *The Black Pirate*, *Stand and Deliver* (1926); *The River Pirate* (1928); *Trent's Last Case*, *The Viking*, *The Return of Sherlock Holmes*, *The Pagan* (1929); *Scotland Yard* (1930); *Svengali*, *Kick In* (1931); *Red Dust*, *A Passport to Hell* (1932); *Broadway Bad* (1933); *The Key*, *What Every Woman Knows*, *The Little Minister*, *The Life of Vergie Winters*, *The Crime Doctor* (1934); *Vanessa: Her Love Story*, *Oil for the Lamps of China*, *Mutiny on the Bounty*, *Laddie* (1935); *Mary of Scotland*, *The Charge of the Light Brigade*, *The White Angel*, *A Woman Rebels*, *Beloved Enemy* (1936); *Parnell*, *The Great O'Malley*, *That Certain Woman*, *The Life of Emile Zola*, *Confession* (1937); *Jezebel*, *Beloved Brat*, *The Amazing Mr Clitterhouse*, *The Sisters*, *Valley of the Giants*, *Comet over Broadway*, *The Dawn Patrol*, *Sergeant Murphy* (1938); *The Oklahoma Kid*, *Wuthering Heights*, *Juarez*, *Daughters Courageous*, *The Old Maid*, *The Private Lives of Elizabeth and Essex*, *Sons of Liberty* (1939); *Brother Orchid*, *City for Conquest*, *Dr Ehrlich's Magic Bullet*, *The Sea Hawk*, *Knute Rockne All American* (1940); *Dr Jekyll and Mr Hyde*, *How Green Was My Valley*, *Shining Victory* (1941); *The Battle of Midway* [voice], *The Gay Sisters* (1942); *Forever and a Day*, *Lassie Come Home* (1943); *The Adventures of Mark Twain*, *The Uninvited*, *National Velvet* (1944); *The Valley of Decision*, *Son of Lassie* (1945); *Ramrod* (1947); *Whispering Smith*, *Hills of Home* (1948); *Challenge to Lassie* (1949); *Bright*

Leaf (1950); *Hometown Story* (1951); *Prince Valiant* (1954); *The Long Gray Line*, *The Man from Laramie* (1955); *Drango* (1957); *Saddle the Wind*, *The Last Hurrah* (1958); *A Dog of Flanders* (1959); *Pollyanna* (1960); *Greyfriars Bobby* (1961); *Spencer's Mountain* (1963).

CRISPIN, Jeanine (Jeanine Crépin) (1911–2001)
Prominent young French stage and screen actress who appeared in fourteen French films between 1932 and 1938, before seeking refuge in Hollywood with her Jewish husband Georges Kessel and his brother, the writer Joseph Kessel, during the war years. The blonde actress featured only in a couple of supporting roles. CH
FILMS: *My Life with Caroline* (1941); *The Constant Nymph* (1943).

CROWE, Eileen (1899–1978)
Irish actress, best known for her work with the Abbey Players, who was introduced to Hollywood film-making through John Ford. She was married to F. J. McCormick★. RB
FILMS: *The Plough and the Stars* (1936); *Top o' the Morning* (1949); *The Quiet Man* (1952); *The Rising of the Moon* (1957); *Shake Hands with the Devil* (1959); *A Terrible Beauty* (1960).

CRUZ, Penélope (Penélope Cruz Sánchez) (1974–)
A top-ranked star in Spain throughout the 1990s as well as a critically acclaimed actress and winner of her country's top acting prize for *La niña de tus ojos/The Girl of Your Dreams* (1998). Cruz already had an international career before Hollywood and was in demand throughout Europe, working in Italy, Denmark, France and the UK, and she appeared in several of the few Spanish films to garner international art-house distribution: *Jámon, jámon* (1992), *Carne tremula/Live Flesh* and *Abre los ojos/Open Your Eyes* (1997), as well as the two Spanish films of that decade to win the Best Foreign Film Academy Award, *Belle epoque* (1992) and *Todo sobre mi madre/All about My Mother* (1999).

Her first foray into American film-making in 1998 consisted of modest supporting roles in *Talk of Angels* and *The Hi-Lo Country*. Both films failed to register at the box office but her outstanding beauty and charisma made a big impression within the industry and she was quickly cast opposite top box-office stars in a succession of high-profile projects: Matt Damon in *All the Pretty Horses*, Johnny Depp in *Blow*, Nicholas Cage in *Captain Corelli's Mandolin* (2001) and Tom Cruise in *Vanilla Sky*. Unsubstantiated but widely reported rumours of on-set affairs led to her being dubbed 'The Spanish Enchantress' and accused of breaking up the relationships of several of her co-stars. A contract with Ralph Lauren resulted in photos of an impossibly elegant Cruz plastered through the media across the USA and offered further visual proof of irresistible allure. When Cruz did in fact turn out to have a relationship with Cruise, her celebrity status went stratospheric. Yet her notoriety did not seem to help the box office of her films, as all except *Vanilla Sky* flopped and even that did not perform to the standards expected of a Tom Cruise feature. This is not necessarily her fault. As in many cases before, Hollywood has imported Cruz as a 'Leading Lady' rather than a star and her twofold function in Hollywood can be summed up as narrative catalyst and exotic beauty. It is fair to say that Cruz has done both very well. Yet, it is also true to say that while she has sometimes not been well used, she has not always been as good as she can be: her Sofia was better in the original *Abre los ojos* than in the *Vanilla Sky* remake. Of the American films, only the low-budget *Woman on Top*, a proper star vehicle, has demonstrated what Cruz is capable of. Her Isabella, the Brazilian chef who entrances all the men in San Francisco, is not only, as expected, irresistibly alluring, but also warm, touching and funny – the latter being a particular quality only fans of her Spanish films could possibly have expected. JA

FILMS: *Twice upon Yesterday, Talk of Angels, The Hi-Lo Country* (1998); *All the Pretty Horses, Woman on Top* (2000); *Blow, Vanilla Sky* (2001); *Waking up in Reno* (2002); *Masked and Anonymous* (2003); *Noel* (2004).

CUGAT, Xavier (Xavier Cugat Mingall) (1900–1990)

Popular Spanish musician and orchestra director who, as well as providing music and songs for numerous American films, appeared as himself in brief supporting roles in several Hollywood musicals during the 1940s. These included a number of Esther Williams' aquatic features. AQ

FILMS: *The Merry Widow* (1925); *Go West Young Man* (1936); *Let's Go Latin* (1937); *You Were Never Lovelier* (1942); *Stage Door Canteen, The Heat's On* (1943); *Two Girls and a Sailor, Bathing Beauty* (1944); *Week-End at the Waldorf, The Thrill of Romance* (1945); *No Leave, No Love, Holiday in Mexico* (1946); *This Time for Keeps* (1947); *A Date with Judy,* *Luxury Liner, On an Island with You* (1948); *Neptune's Daughter* (1949); *Chicago Syndicate* (1955); *The Eddy Duchin Story* (1956); *The Monitors* (1969); *The Phynx* (1970).

CULVER, Roland (1900–1984)

A typical English gentleman in British films, Culver appeared in several US-financed UK productions during the 1930s and then worked periodically in Hollywood from 1946, when he starred as Lord Desham, the lover of an Academy Award-winning Olivia de Havilland in *To Each His Own*. Culver also appeared in a number of American-funded productions shot in Europe. MW

FILMS: *A Voice Said Goodnight* (1932); *Her Imaginary Lover, Mayfair Girl* (1933); *Borrow a Million, Father and Son* (1934); *Fingers* (1941); *Perfect Strangers* (1945); *To Each His Own, Wanted for Murder* (1946); *Down to Earth, Singapore* (1947); *The Emperor Waltz, Isn't it Romantic?* (1948); *The Great Lover* (1949); *The Hour of 13* (1952); *Betrayed* (1954); *Safari* (1956); *Bonjour Tristesse* (1958); *The Yellow Rolls-Royce* (1964); *Thunderball* (1965); *A Man Could Get Killed* (1966); *The Magic Christian* (1969); *The Rise and Rise of Michael Rimmer, Fragment of Fear* (1970); *The MacKintosh Man, A Bequest to the Nation* (1973); *The Greek Tycoon* (1978); *No Longer Alone* (1979); *Rough Cut* (1980).

CUMMINS, Peggy (1925–)

British actress whose debut film, *Dr O' Dowd*, was funded by First National Pictures. As the least-established of the raft of UK actresses fêted by Hollywood in the immediate postwar years, she was also subjected to the greatest ignominy. After several juvenile supporting roles, her employers, Fox, cast her as the leading lady in *Forever Amber* (1947), only very publicly to sack her from the film during pre-production. But once relegated to B-movie work at poverty-row studio Monogram for her final made-in-Hollywood production, Cummins ultimately left a far more enduring impression than most of her peers as the amoral, gun-toting femme fatale in the cult film noir *Gun Crazy*. Retrospective testimony has it that Laurie's English identity in the film simply compensated for Cummins' inability to master an American accent, but this inversion of a genre trope also relates to the contemporaneous international success of *The Wicked Lady* (1945), which had established a minor vogue for the representation of heartless English women who got their sexual gratification from crime. JB   **221**

FILMS: *Dr O' Dowd* (1940); *The Late George Apley, Moss Rose* (1947); *Green Grass of Wyoming* (1948); *Gun Crazy* (1949); *Night of the Demon* (1957).

CURRIE, Finlay (Finlay Jefferson) (1878–1968)

Scottish character actor with an imposing figure, voice and manner whose UK screen appearances included Fox British's *Catch as Catch Can* (1937). His Hollywood appearances – which included several productions shot in Europe – principally involved playing noblemen and senators in biblical and historical epics such as Anthony Mann's *The Fall of the Roman Empire*. MHu

FILMS: *Catch as Catch Can* (1937); *So Evil My Love* (1948); *Edward, My Son* (1949); *The Black Rose, Treasure Island, The Mudlark* (1950); *Quo Vadis, People Will Talk* (1951); *Ivanhoe, Kangaroo, Stars and Stripes Forever, Walk East on Beacon!* (1952); *Treasure of the Golden Condor* (1953); *Beau Brummell, Rob Roy, The Highland Rogue* (1954); *Footsteps in the Fog, Captain Lightfoot* (1955); *Zarak, Around the World in Eighty Days* (1956); *The Little Hut, Seven Waves Away, Saint Joan* (1957); *The Naked Earth* (1958); *Ben-Hur, Solomon and Sheba* (1959); *Kidnapped, The Angel Wore Red, The Adventures of Huckleberry Finn* (1960); *Francis of Assisi* (1961); *Lisa* (1962); *Cleopatra, Murder at the Gallop* (1963); *The Three Lives of Thomasina, The Fall of the Roman Empire* (1964); *Bunny Lake is Missing, The Battle of the Villa Fiorita* (1965).

CURRY, Tim (1946–)

Theatre-trained Curry's show-stopping turn as the transvestite scientist Frank-N-Furter in the British stage and film versions of *The Rocky Horror Picture Show* (1975) has been etched firmly enough in popular cultural consciousness to sustain a career sideline in (predominantly) camp Hollywood villainy. JB

FILMS: *Times Square* (1980); *Annie* (1982); *Clue* (1985); *Pass the Ammo* (1988); *The Little Mermaid* [voice] (1989); *The Hunt for Red October* (1990); *Oscar* (1991); *Home Alone 2: Lost in New York, Passed Away, FernGully: The Last Rainforest* [voice] (1992); *Loaded Weapon 1, The Three Musketeers* (1993); *The Shadow* (1994); *The Pebble and the Penguin* [voice], *Congo* (1995); *Muppet's Treasure Island* (1996); *McHale's Navy, A Christmas Carol* [voice] (1997); *The Rugrats Movie* [voice] (1998); *Pirates of the Plain, Four Dogs Playing Poker* (1999); *Charlie's Angels, Rugrats in Paris: The Movie* [voice] (2000); *Scary Movie 2, Ritual* (2001); *The Scoundrel's Wife, The Wild Thornberrys Movie* [voice], *I, Crocodile* [voice] (2002); *Rugrats Go Wild!* [voice] (2003); *Kinsey* (2004).

CUSACK, Cyril (1910–1993)

Born in South Africa, Cusack moved to Ireland at an early age and appeared in his first film, *Knocknagow* (1918), aged seven. He often played the wily rogue in subsequent film appearances, including several US-funded pictures shot in the UK. Cusack acted in various US and European co-productions during the 1960s – he was Control in *The Spy Who Came in from the Cold* – and, by his death, was considered the grand old man of Irish film and stage. RB

FILMS: *Late Extra* (1935); *Once a Crook, Inspector Hornleigh Goes to it* (1941); *Escape* (1948); *The Secret of Convict Lake, Soldiers Three, The Blue Veil* (1951); *Saadia* (1953); *The Man Who Never Was* (1956); *The Rising of the Moon* (1957); *Gideon's Day* (1958); *Shake Hands with the Devil* (1959); *A Terrible Beauty* (1960); *The Spy Who Came in from the Cold, Where the Spies Are* (1965); *Fahrenheit 451* (1966); *The Taming of the Shrew* (1967); *Country Dance* (1970); *Harold and Maude* (1971); *The Homecoming* (1973); *The Abdication, Juggernaut* (1974); *Lovespell* (1979); *True Confessions* (1981); *Far and Away* (1992).

CUSHING, Peter (1913–1994)

Peter Cushing's experiences in Hollywood divide into a tale of two very distinct halves. As an apprentice actor who had mostly worked in British provincial repertory theatre, Cushing took the bold step of sailing to California to try his luck in the movies. His modest success after arriving essentially penniless at the Hollywood YMCA at the beginning of 1939 is a testament to the vogue for English actors and English subjects and the influence of the English exile community in Los Angeles. English director James Whale hired Cushing as an eyeline double and then an extra in *The Man in the Iron Mask*, before he walked into a role in Laurel and Hardy's *A Chump at Oxford* when Hal Roach went looking for actors with plummy English accents to populate the college scenes. Membership of C. Aubrey Smith's★ Hollywood cricket team led to a successful screen test for a more substantial role in RKO's *Vigil in the Night* – all arranged by his new batting partner Robert Coote★.

Cushing returned to Britain soon after to join the war effort and built a new career as a classical actor of substance in the West End and early television. His role as Baron Frankenstein in Hammer's *The Curse of Frankenstein* (1957) led to a prolific career throughout the 1960s and 1970s as an icon of British horror cinema. The impact of these films upon a rising generation of American film-makers is visible in the latter half of Cushing's Hollywood filmography. Paving the way for his Hammer stablemate Christopher Lee★, Cushing played one of the principal villains in the very first *Star Wars* movie. JB

FILMS: *The Man in the Iron Mask* (1939); *Laddie, Vigil in the Night, A Chump at Oxford, Women in War, The Howards of Virginia* (1940); *They Dare Not Love* (1941); *Moulin Rouge* (1952); *The Black Knight* (1954); *The End of the Affair* (1955); *Alexander the Great, Magic Fire* (1956); *John Paul Jones* (1959); *The Naked Edge* (1961); *Star Wars, Shock Waves* (1977); *Top Secret!* (1984).

(FORMER) CZECHOSLOVAKIA

First brought into being as a nation at the end of World War I, Czechoslovakia established an organised cinema industry significantly later than other European nations – really gaining momentum only in the late 1920s – and consequently lacked the power to make an impact in the USA through exports of either films or talent. Although several prominent émigrés – including Peter Lorre★ and Francis Lederer★ – were born in areas of the Hungarian Empire that subsequently became Czechoslovak territory, they were perceived (and regarded themselves) as German émigrés, whose journeys to the USA came about through involvement in internationally prestigious German productions.

The only substantial exodus of Czechoslovak cinema personnel followed the nation's invasion by Germany in 1939, but it was aimed primarily towards Britain, with actor Herbert Lom★ and directors Kurt Goldmeyer and Jiří Weissall continuing their careers at London studios (the latter pair returned to Czechoslovakia after the war). Even the one major name who made it to Hollywood, actor-director Hugo Haas★, settled in France and Portugal before finally crossing the Atlantic. Once in the USA, he remained an outsider both to the studio system and to other émigré communities, and was forced to spend his first months in cramped conditions with relations in Chicago's Czech quarter. Eventually securing character roles playing 'ethnic' heavies, Haas was able to buy Charlie Chaplin's★ old stu-

dios after the war, where, racked with homesickness, he produced 'B' melodramas.

Another Czechoslovak émigré from Nazism who secured only an outsider career in B-movies was former national ice-skating champion Vera Hruba Ralston, whom Republic Studios initially employed in the wake of the short-lived craze for ice-skating champion Sonja Henie★. Ralston was perpetually disdained for her bland, untrained acting and heavy accent, and there is little doubt that her career endured into the 1950s only because she was the mistress, and later wife, of Republic studio head Herbert J. Yates.

During World War II, the occupying Nazis had appropriated and built up the film studios in Prague, after those in Berlin were bombed. Ironically, this meant that Czechoslovakia was in a solid position to re-establish postwar production. As with other Eastern bloc nations, however, exposure to Hollywood influence remained negligible, and only during the 1968 uprising was there one significant defector to Hollywood: Miloš Forman, who went on to direct Academy Award-winning titles including *One Flew over the Cuckoo's Nest* (1975) and *Amadeus* (1984), while occasionally taking (largely ignored) acting roles, such as the immigrant janitor in Henry Jaglom's *New Year's Day* (1989). During the post-Communist era, actorly emigration from the Czech and Slovak film industries has remained negligible. RJK

DAGOVER, Lil (Maria Antonia Siegelinde Martha Lilitt Seubert) (1887–1980)

Grande dame of German cinema who starred in over a hundred German productions during a career spanning sixty years. Classic silent roles included *Das Cabinet des Dr Caligari / The Cabinet of Dr Caligari* (1919) and Fritz Lang's *Der müde Tod / Destiny* (1921). Dagover also enjoyed 1920s and early 1930s successes in French, Swedish and Czech co-productions, but flopped in her only Hollywood title, a romantic melodrama under the director Michael Curtiz. EC

FILM: *The Woman from Monte Carlo* (1931).

DAHLBECK, Eva (1920–)

Swedish actress who is best known for personifying a certain ideal of womanhood in Ingmar Bergman's comedies. The director called her his 'Battleship Femininity'. It was most likely for her blonde, statuesque looks that she **223** obtained a role in the mediocre spy thriller *The Counterfeit Traitor*. MK

FILM: *The Counterfeit Traitor* (1962).

D'ALGY, Helena (Helena Guedes Infante) (1906–) and D'ALGY, Tony (António Guedes Infante) (1905–1978)

Portuguese siblings who travelled to Hollywood to play a few minor roles for MGM. Helena had a supporting role opposite Rudolph Valentino in *A Sainted Devil* and also worked with Sjöström (*Confessions of a Queen*) and Carlos Gardel (in *Melodía de Arrabal* [1933], shot in New York). She retired from the cinema in 1933, whereas Tony continued to work in France and Spain until 1948. AR

FILMS: Helena D'Algy: *A Sainted Devil, It is the Law, Lend Me Your Husband, Let Not Man Put Asunder* (1924); *The Fool, Pretty Ladies, Confessions of a Queen, Daddy's Gone A-Hunting* (1925); *The Cowboy and the Countess, Siberia, Exquisite Sinner, The Silver Treasure* (1926). Tony D'Algy: *The Rejected Woman, Monsieur Beaucaire, Meddling Women, A Sainted Devil* (1924); *Soul Mates* (1925); *The Boob, Monte Carlo, The Gay Deceiver* (1926).

DALIO, Marcel (Israel Moshe Blauschild) (1900–1983)

Dalio began his career in French theatre and music hall, from where, like many of his contemporaries, he moved into film in the 1930s. Throughout the decade, he played supporting – though often memorable – roles in a large number of films, a pattern that changed little over the course of his long career. His larger and more interesting parts during this period include L'Arbi in Duvivier's *Pépé le Moko* (1937) and the Marquis de la Chesnaye in Renoir's *La Règle du jeu* (1939). The cultural stereotyping that confined Dalio, who was Jewish, largely to 'Semitic' roles perhaps reached its logical conclusion when the Nazis used a photograph of the actor labelled 'The Typical Jew' in their anti-Semitic propaganda.

Dalio and his wife, the actress Madeleine LeBeau★, fled to the USA at the outbreak of war. His English was poor and his beginnings inauspicious. Nevertheless, having been introduced to the agent Charles Feldman, Dalio carved out a persistent, if often under-recognised, presence in Hollywood films. His American roles traded greatly on his Frenchness, rather than his Jewishness, often to the point of caricature, as epitomised in the 1944 *To Have and Have Not*, in which his character is simply called 'Frenchy'. The short, dapper Dalio sometimes played aristocrats or important French figures such as Clémenceau in *Wilson*, but aided by his gentle and slightly obsequious performance style, he also appeared in many ancillary roles such as croupiers (*Casablanca*) and head waiters (*Pin-Up Girl* and *Can-Can*). After the war, Dalio resumed his French film career while simultaneously keeping his hand in American projects, with character parts in *The Merry Widow* and *Gentlemen Prefer Blondes*. In the late 1950s and early 1960s, Dalio made guest appearances on American television, but he ended his career in France, where he continued to appear on film and television throughout the 1970s. EE/VO

FILMS: *The Shanghai Gesture, One Night in Lisbon, Unholy Partners* (1941); *Tales of Manhattan, The Pied Piper, Flight Lieutenant, Casablanca* (1942); *The Song of Bernadette, Paris after Dark, Flesh and Fantasy, Tonight We Raid Calais, The Constant Nymph* (1943); *The Conspirators, Pin-Up Girl, To Have and Have Not, Action in Arabia, The Desert Song, Passage to Marseille, Wilson* (1944); *A Bell for Adano* (1945); *On the Riviera, Rich, Young and Pretty* (1951); *The Happy Time, The Merry Widow, The Snows of Kilimanjaro, Lovely to Look At* (1952); *Gentlemen Prefer Blondes, Flight to Tangier* (1953); *Sabrina, Lucky Me* (1954); *Jump into Hell,* (1955); *Miracle in the Rain, Anything Goes* (1956); *Istanbul, Ten Thousand Bedrooms, The Sun Also Rises, Tip on a Dead Jockey, Hell Bent for Glory, China Gate* (1957); *The Perfect Furlough, The Man Who Understood Women, Pillow Talk* (1959); *Can-Can, Song without End* (1960); *The Devil at Four O'Clock* (1961); *Jessica* (1962); *Donovan's Reef, The List of Adrian Messenger* (1963); *Wild and Wonderful* (1964); *Lady L, Made in Paris* (1965); *How to Steal a Million* (1966); *How Sweet it is!* (1968); *Justine* (1969); *Catch-22, The Great White Hope* (1970).

DALTON, Audrey (1934–)

Dalton enjoyed a successful American film career, though mainly in supporting roles, after being discovered on the London stage by a Hollywood talent scout. Her father, Emmet Dalton, was one of the co-founders of Ireland's Ardmore Studios and Abbey Films. She returned to Ireland to star in one of his productions, *This Other Eden* (1958). RB

FILMS: *My Cousin Rachel* (1952); *The Girls of Pleasure Island, Titanic* (1953); *Casanova's Big Night, Drum Beat*

(1954); *The Prodigal* (1955); *Hold Back the Night* (1956); *The Monster that Challenged the World* (1957); *Separate Tables, Thundering Jets* (1958); *Lone Texan* (1959); *Mr Sardonicus* (1961); *Kitten with a Whip* (1964); *The Bounty Killer* (1965).

DALTON, Timothy (1946–)

Tall, dark actor with sharp, slightly feline features who is best known for his hard-edged performance as the fourth James Bond and romantic action roles as a dashing and sometimes cruel Englishman. MW

FILMS: *The Lion in Winter* (1968); *Wuthering Heights, Cromwell* (1970); *Mary, Queen of Scots* (1971); *Permission to Kill* (1975); *Sextette* (1978); *Agatha* (1979); *Flash Gordon* (1980); *The Doctor and the Devils* (1985); *The Living Daylights* (1987); *Licence to Kill, Brenda Starr* (1989); *The Rocketeer* (1991); *Naked in New York* (1994); *Salt Water Moose* (1996); *The Informant, The Beautician and the Beast, The Reef* (1997); *Made Men* (1999); *Time Share* (2000); *American Outlaws* (2001); *Looney Tunes: Back in Action* (2003).

DAMITA, Lili (Liliane Marie-Madeleine Carré) (1904–1994)

French actress who married Errol Flynn in 1935. After success on the music-hall stage in Paris, she made films in several European countries before leaving for Hollywood, where she was put under contract by Samuel Goldwyn. In her American films (which included multi-language versions), she typically played petulant young women. MB

FILMS: *The Bridge of San Luis Rey, The Cock-Eyed World, The Rescue* (1929); *Fighting Caravans, Friends and Lovers, The Woman Between* (1931); *The Match King, This Is the Night* (1932); *Goldie Gets Along* (1933); *The Frisco Kid, Pirate Party on Catalina Isle* (1935); *The Devil on Horseback* (1936).

DANE, Karl (Rasmus Karl Therkildsen Gottlieb) (1886–1934)

Danish actor who emigrated to the USA in 1916 following to the decline of the entertainment industry during World War I. He made his Hollywood debut in the propaganda melodrama *To Hell with the Kaiser* in 1918. With prospects of an acting career quickly fading, he took any job he could find and while being employed as a carpenter at MGM, he was successfully taken on as the lead hero's sidekick in King Vidor's *The Big Parade*. Producer Harry Rapf subsequently joined the tall Dane with the much

shorter British actor George K. Arthur★ in a comedy team he called 'The Brawn and the Brain'. Dane enjoyed a successful and prolific American career in the late 1920s and early 1930s, but he never succeeded in making the transition to sound and in 1934 he shot himself in his Los Angeles apartment. MBj

FILMS: *To Hell with the Kaiser, My Four Years in Germany* (1918); *The Big Parade, His Secretary, The Everlasting Whisper, Lights of Old Broadway* (1925); *Bardelys the Magnificent, La Bohème, Monte Carlo, The Scarlet Letter, Son of the Sheik, War Paint* (1926); *The Enemy, The Red Mill, Rookies, Slide, Kelly, Slide* (1927); *Baby Mine, Brotherly Love, Circus Rookies, Detectives, Show People* (1928); *Alias Jimmy Valentine, All at Sea, China Bound, The Duke Steps Out, The Mysterious Island, Speedway, The Trail of '98, The Voice of the Storm, The Hollywood Revue of 1929, Navy Blues* (1929); *The Big House, Billy the Kid, Broken Wedding Bells, Free and Easy, Knights Before Xmas, Men Without Skirts, Montana Moon* (1930); *The Lease Breakers, A Put-up Job, Shove Off* (1930); *Summer Daze, Fast Life* (1931).

DANN, Roger (unknown)

After a few appearances in French films such as *La Vie Parisienne* (1935), this French singer was contracted in 1946 by Paramount, who hoped to use him in remakes of Maurice Chevalier★ vehicles. Dann remained typecast as the 'Frenchie' in a few minor films spanning four decades, though he played opposite Anne Baxter in Hitchcock's *I Confess*. CH

FILMS: *Variety Girl, Crime Doctor's Gamble* (1947); *I, Jane Doe* (1948); *I Confess* (1953); *Two for the Road* (1967); *The Tamarind Seed* (1974).

DANNING, Sybil (Sybille Johanna Danninger) (1949–)

Austrian-born player in German soft-core features who appeared in several American-financed productions in Europe before moving to Hollywood, where she ruled as 'Queen of the B's' during the 1980s. Her characters combined presumed European sexual decadence with Schwarzenegger★-like monosyllabic heroics and self-irony. Since 1989, she has worked chiefly in production. RJK

FILMS: *Sam's Song* (1969); *The Three Musketeers* (1973); *The Four Musketeers* (1974); *Crossed Swords, Cat in the Cage* (1978); *Meteor* (1979); *Nightkill, Battle beyond the Stars, The Man with*

Bogart's Face, How to Beat the High Co$t of Living, Cuba Cross-ing (1980); *Separate Ways, The Salamander* (1981); *Famous T&A* (1982); *Sam's Song, Chained Heat* (1983); *They're Playing with Fire* (1984); *Howling II, Young Lady Chatterley II, The Tomb, Malibu Express* (1985); *Reform School Girls, The Phantom Empire* (1986); *Warrior Queen, Talking Walls, Amazon Women on the Moon* (1987); *L.A. Bounty* (1989).

DANOVA, Cesare (Cesare Deitinger) (1926–1992)

Italian actor who, after starring in several Italian films in the 1940s and 1950s, signed with MGM in 1956. He appeared in numerous American film and television pro-ductions and was often typecast as a stereotypical hot-blooded Mediterranean. He died suddenly during a 1992 meeting of the Motion Picture Academy's Foreign Film Committee. CS

FILMS: *The Man Who Understood Women, Tarzan, the Ape Man* (1959); *Valley of the Dragons* (1961); *Tender is the Night* (1962); *Cleopatra, Gidget Goes to Rome* (1963); *Viva Las Vegas* (1964); *Boy! Did I Get a Wrong Number, Chamber of Horrors* (1966); *Che!* (1969); *Mean Streets* (1973); *Scorchy, Invisible Strangler* (1976); *Tentacles* (1977); *National Lampoon's Animal House* (1978).

DANTE THE MAGICIAN (Harry A. Jansen) (1883–1955)

Danish performer who followed in the wake of Harry Houdini's success in the USA. He appeared in *A-Haunting We Will Go* – arguably the worst of Laurel and Hardy's Twentieth Century-Fox vehicles. HJW

FILMS: *A-Haunting We Will Go* (1943); *Bunco Squad* (1952).

DARCEL, Denise (Denise Billecard) (1925–)

Denise Darcel (also known as Denise D'Arcel) had a che-quered career and a limited range. In Hollywood, her char-acters were either beautiful women (the Frenchwoman in *Battleground*; the voluntary émigrée and former prostitute in *Westward the Women*) or unimaginative stereotypes, where she merely had to 'look French' and roll her 'rs' mischie-vously (*Young Man with Ideas, Dangerous When Wet*). Her most memorable role was the (probably apocryphal) sensual aristocrat and spy in *Vera Cruz* who darts furious glances at Burt Lancaster. CV

FILMS: *To the Victor, Thunder in the Pines* (1948); *Battle-ground* (1949); *Tarzan and the Slave Girl, Westward the Women*

(1950); *Young Man with Ideas* (1952); *Dangerous When Wet, Flame of Calcutta* (1953); *Vera Cruz* (1954); *Seven Women from Hell* (1961).

D'ARCY, Alexander (Alexander Sarruf) (1908–1996)

After a few forgettable roles in the UK and in France (including Hitchcock's *Champagne* [1928] and Feyder's *La Kermesse héroïque/Carnival in Flanders* [1935]), D'Arcy's static bearing found its place in Hollywood. He was elegant and wore a moustache and so embodied the cliché of the Con-tinental lover in both the golden era of American comedy (*The Awful Truth*) and the kitsch and decadent narratives of Russ Meyer (*The Seven Minutes*). What luxury: in *How to Marry a Millionaire*, his eyepatch was encrusted with dia-monds! CV

FILMS: *Stolen Holiday, The Prisoner of Zenda, The Awful Truth, She Married an Artist* (1937); *Women are Like That, Flight to Fame* (1938); *Topper Takes a Trip, 5th Avenue Girl, Good Girls Go to Paris, Another Thin Man, Three Sons* (1939); *Irene, City of Chance* (1940); *The Blonde from Singapore* (1941); *Marriage is a Private Affair* (1944); *Man on a Tightrope, Vicki, How to Marry a Millionaire* (1953); *Soldier of Fortune* (1955); *The Festival Girls* (1962); *Fanny Hill* (1964); *The Incredible Sex Revolution* (1965); *Way . . Way Out* (1966); *The St Valentine's Day Massacre* (1967); *Blood of Dracula's Castle* (1969); *The Seven Minutes* (1971).

DARRIEUX, Danielle (1917–)

With twenty-four films in her native France to her credit already, the young Danielle Darrieux signed a five-year contract with Universal in 1937 (when she was only twenty), pledging to make two films per year. She left for Hollywood in September that year accompanied by her husband and manager Henri Decoin. In March 1938, she starred in Henry Koster's *The Rage of Paris*, opposite Dou-glas Fairbanks Jr, the story of a young Frenchwoman in New York determined to marry an American millionaire, whom she finally marries for love. The film was reasonably successful, though it did not further Darrieux's career and she returned to France with her husband in May 1938. It was Darrieux's refusal to give up her French career, rather than the war, that destroyed her American future.

After the war, she briefly went back to Hollywood, appearing in three supporting roles. In the romantic musical *Rich, Young and Pretty*, she played a Parisian singer who encounters the daughter she had left in the care of her American husband twenty years earlier. In the spy thriller *5 Fingers*, based on the true story of a double agent during World War II, her character – a deposed Polish countess who has an affair with her former valet-turned-spy – was added to liven up the plot. In the blockbuster *Alexander the Great* (directed in Spain by Robert Rossen), she played Alexander's criminal mother. The film was a failure. Her remaining English-speaking role was in the US-backed *The Greengage Summer*, in which she co-starred with Kenneth More★.

Altogether, Darrieux's American episode was thus very disappointing, since Hollywood failed to exploit her pert beauty and charm and considerable acting talent. However, it clearly did not harm her reputation in France, where she has enjoyed an extraordinarily prolific and successful career since *Le Bal* in 1931. She can be seen acting and singing in François Ozon's *8 femmes* (2002), aged eighty-five and still going strong. GS

FILMS: *The Rage of Paris* (1938); *Rich, Young and Pretty* (1951); *5 Fingers* (1952); *Alexander the Great* (1956); *The Greengage Summer* (1961).

DARVI, Bella (Bayla Wegier) (1928-1971)

French actress of Polish origin whose looks were reminiscent of Gene Tierney and Leslie Caron★. Darvi's experience of Hollywood was short-lived after being discovered by Darryl F. Zanuck in Paris in 1951. Her first film was *Hell and High Water*, in which she starred opposite Richard Widmark and Victor Francen★. After three unsuccessful films and personal trouble following her affair with Zanuck, she returned to Paris. VO

FILMS: *Hell and High Water, The Egyptian* (1954); *The Racers* (1955).

DAUPHIN, Claude (Claude Legrand) (1903–1978)

French actor who started as a set designer for the Parisian stage before taking up acting. Dauphin obtained his first screen role in 1930 and built up an impressive filmography of about thirty-five films, mostly light comedies, before going to the USA. He met the American director John Huston while on war duty and they both took part in the liberation of Paris in August 1944. Huston cast him in a Broadway play the same year. Dauphin's first Hollywood role was in Jean Renoir's war propaganda film *Salute to France*, followed by a number of American and inter-

national film and theatre productions in the 1950s. Dauphin's range ensured that he was cast in a variety of genres, though in Hollywood and British films he tended to be the archetypal elegant and debonair Frenchman. He was also occasionally a police detective, including in the 1953 European-filmed American television series *Paris-Precinct*, co-starring fellow French actor Jean-Pierre Aumont★. Dauphin returned to France in 1957, but continued to have a substantial international career on stage, film and television. CH

FILMS: *Salute to France* (1944); *Deported* (1950); *April in Paris, Little Boy Lost* (1952); *Phantom of the Rue Morgue* (1954); *The Quiet American* (1957); *The Visit* (1964); *Lady L* (1965); *Grand Prix* (1966); *Two for the Road* (1967); *Hard Contract, The Madwoman of Chaillot* (1968); *Rosebud* (1974).

DAVEN, André (1904–1981)

French film critic, producer and occasional actor. On a visit to Paris, Rudolph Valentino met the dark and handsome Daven and brought him to Hollywood to appear (uncredited) with him in a couple of films. Exiled in Hollywood during the war years, Daven produced a few films that included work for the war effort. CH

FILMS: *Stolen Moments* (1920); *Monsieur Beaucaire* (1924).

D'AVRIL, Yola (1907–1984)

Born in Lille, the stage actress and dancer D'Avril toured Europe before going to Canada. She moved to Hollywood, where she made a large number of films between the late 1920s and mid-1930s, specialising in saucy French girls. MB

FILMS: *Yes, Yes, Babette* (1925); *American Beauty, Hard-Boiled Hoggerty, Orchids and Ermine, Smile Brother Smile, The Tender Hour, The Valley of the Giants, The War Horse* (1927); *Lady Be Good, The Noose, Three-Ring Marriage, Vamping Venus* (1928); *Hot for Paris, The Love Parade, Shanghai Lady, She Goes to War* (1929); *All Quiet on the Western Front, The Bad One, Born Reckless, New Movietone Follies of 1930, Just Like Heaven, Those Three French Girls, Hollywood Theme Song, So This is Paris Green, The Truth about Youth* (1930); *The Common Law, God's Gift to Women, Just a Gigolo, The Last Flight, Suicide Fleet, College Vamp, The Right of Way, Svengali, Women Go on Forever* (1931); *Beauty and the Boss, Cock of the Air, The Man from Yesterday, A Parisian Romance, Scarlet Dawn, Finishing Touch, Strange Interlude, Passport to Hell, Sky Devils* (1932); **227**

part in *Gandhi* (1982). This was followed by a supporting role in *The Bounty*. His success in two widely differing roles in 1986 – as a homosexual punk in *My Beautiful Laundrette* and as Helena Bonham Carter's★ stuffy, upper-class fiancé in *A Room with a View* – brought him to the attention of American critics and audiences, and he subsequently received the New York Film Critics Award for Best Supporting Actor.

Offers from Hollywood followed and Day-Lewis was given a leading role in *Stars and Bars* in 1988. This comedy of an Englishman abroad in America's Deep South was an inauspicious start to his American career, in that it played neither to his strengths nor to audience expectations generated by earlier performances. *The Unbearable Lightness of Being* went some way to re-establishing his reputation, but it was Day-Lewis' performance as Christy Brown in *My Left Foot* (1989) that firmly established his place as one of the most accomplished and ambitious film actors of his generation. He received a Best Actor Academy Award. His next mainstream American

French actress Yola d'Avril specialised in 'saucy' roles

The Cat and the Fiddle, Glamour, Monte Carlo Nights, Kansas City Princess, Tarzan and His Mate (1934); *Captain Blood, Straight from the Heart* (1935); *The Unguarded Hour* (1936); *I Met Him in Paris* (1937); *Green Hell* (1940); *The Lady has Plans, Night in New Orleans, Now, Voyager* (1942); *Cloak and Dagger, Monsieur Beaucaire* (1946); *Sorry, Wrong Number* (1947); *Little Boy Lost* (1953).

DAY-LEWIS, Daniel (1957–)

Daniel Day-Lewis' career pattern suggests a concentration on demanding roles in quality dramas on both sides of the Atlantic. He is an actor of considerable range and power who combines a strong physical presence and arresting good looks with an absolute commitment to inhabiting the character he is portraying. The son of British Poet Laureate Cecil Day-Lewis and grandson of Sir Michael Balcon, legendary head of Ealing Studios, Day-Lewis appeared on the UK stage before making his adult screen debut in a minor

Daniel Day-Lewis in *The Age of Innocence* (1993)

film, Michael Mann's *The Last of the Mohicans*, was also a considerable box-office success.

From this point on, Day-Lewis seems to have been able to choose the type of film role to which he is best suited and which he finds sufficiently challenging and demanding. His controlled but passionate Newland Archer in Martin Scorsese's highly praised adaptation of Edith Wharton's *The Age of Innocence* was crucial to the film's success. His outstanding performance in the politically sensitive drama *In the Name of the Father* as Gerry Conlon, the man falsely accused and wrongly convicted of the IRA Guildford pub bombing, earned him an Academy Award nomination. Day-Lewis followed this with a well-received performance as John Proctor in Nicholas Hytner's version of Arthur Miller's *The Crucible*. He was reunited with Martin Scorsese on the violent epic *Gangs of New York*, for which he received another Academy Award nomination for his complex leading role as William 'Bill the Butcher' Cutting. MHu

FILMS: *Sunday, Bloody Sunday* (1971); *The Bounty* (1984); *The Unbearable Lightness of Being, Stars and Bars* (1988); *The Last of the Mohicans* (1992); *In the Name of the Father, The Age of Innocence* (1993); *The Crucible* (1996); *The Boxer* (1997); *Gangs of New York* (2002).

DE ALMEIDA, Joaquim (1958–)

Contemporary Portuguese actor who has combined a career in American-style Portuguese films with appearances as a Latino character in Hollywood movies. Because of Portuguese cinema's strongly auteur-led identity, de Almeida began his career abroad before becoming famous in his native country. After playing Fragonard in *Les Deux Fragonard* (1986), he appeared in the Taviani brothers' *Good Morning Babylon*, a Euro-American co-production whose theme – the journey to the mirage that is Hollywood – is the subject of this book. De Almeida's star image has never been very clear-cut. He could have been a very successful supporting actor in classical Hollywood cinema, but he has remained restricted to limited ethnic roles in films such as *Desperado*, in which, following the death of Raul Julia, he appeared with Hollywood's only real contemporary male Latino star: Antonio Banderas★. AR

FILMS: *Good Morning, Babylon* (1986); *Only You* (1992); *Clear and Present Danger* (1994); *Desperado* (1995); *On the*

Run (1998); *No Vacancy, One Man's Hero* (1999); *Behind Enemy Lines* (2001); *Demon Island* (2002).

DE FRANCE, Cécile (1976–)

Belgian-born actress, based in France, who was designated one of the most promising newcomers by *Screen International* in 2003. Versatile enough to act in comedies – such as *L'Auberge espagnole/Pot Luck* (2002) – and in horror (*Haute tension/High Tension* [2003]), the good-looking brunette made her Hollywood debut in a comic/action version of Jules Verne's classic, *Around the World in 80 Days*, as Monique, the love interest of hero Phileas Fogg (Steve Coogan★). GV

FILM: *Around the World in 80 Days* (2004).

DE LIGUORO, Rina (Elena Caterina Cataldi) (1892–1966)

Italian screen femme fatale considered by many to be the last diva of the silent period. De Liguoro became famous after her role as the protagonist in Enrico Guazzoni's *Messalina* (1923) and left the country during the crisis in the Italian film industry during the 1920s. After a short stay in Germany and France, she arrived in Hollywood in 1930 and made her American debut in *Romance* (co-starring Greta Garbo★), where she portrayed Nina, an Italian opera star. Her role, the same year, in Cecil B. DeMille's *Madam Satan* was a very minor one, but it marked the first occasion she was credited as Countess Rina De Liguoro. Like many other Italian divas, De Liguoro had married an aristocrat, Count Wladimiro De Liguoro, from where her stage name was derived. Whereas in Italy she had been a star, in the USA, with the exception of her appearance as Countess Slavotski in *Behold My Wife*, her minor roles rarely carried anything like the importance implied by her frequently credited aristocratic title. De Liguoro's most important films shot in Hollywood were actually two Spanish-language comedies: *Politiquerías* (1931) and *Angelina o el honor de un brigadier/Angelina or the Honour of a Brigadier* (1935). She returned to Italian cinema after 1935, and her only subsequent appearance in an American film was in a minor role in the Mexican–American co-production *The Mad Empress*. CBu

FILMS: *Madam Satan, Romance* (1930); *The Bachelor Father* (1931); *Behold My Wife* (1935); *The Mad Empress* (1940).

DE LINT, Derek (1950–)

Derek de Lint starred with Rutger Hauer★ and Jeroen Krabbé★ in the successful *Soldaat van Oranje/Soldier of Orange* (1977). The presence of a thoughtful character behind his dark romantic looks subsequently led to him playing a number of troubled men. De Lint has starred in many Dutch and international film and television productions, including a leading part in the American series *Poltergeist:The Legacy* (1996–9). SDL

FILMS: *Three Men and a Baby* (1987); *The Unbearable Lightness of Being* (1988); *Deep Impact* (1998).

DELON, Alain (1935–)

One of France's most prominent stars who has featured in some ninety-odd French films, as well as several Italian auteur films. Delon was noticed by one of David O. Selznick's talent scouts as early as 1956 and was offered an American contract that he turned down in favour of a part in Yves Allégret's *Quand la femme s'en mêle/When a Woman Meddles* (1957). In 1960, his stardom was firmly established thanks to René Clément's *Plein soleil/Purple Noon*, an adaptation of Patricia Highsmith's thriller *The Talented Mr Ripley*, and Visconti's *Rocco e i suoi fratelli/Rocco and His Brothers*. On the back of these two films alone, and thanks to his breathtaking good looks, Delon became sought after by Hollywood, where he was marketed as the 'French James Dean' and the most romantic actor since Charles Boyer★. This time, Delon did not resist the call.

In 1964, *The New York Herald Tribune* published an interview with Delon in which he expressed his desire to work in American cinema. He also allegedly dismissed French cinema for being amateurish and declared that he wanted to be 'a Cooper or a Grant'. Although Delon claims that these statements were apocryphal, they were nevertheless well received by Hollywood and boosted his chances of success. His first American film, *Once a Thief*, was a tough thriller in which he played the lead role. Delon's performance was applauded by American critics, though the film itself received poor notices and was a commercial failure in both the USA and France. Undeterred, Delon starred in *Lost Command* as a French captain and *Texas across the River*. Both films suffered a similar fate.

Delon never did become 'a Cooper or a Grant' nor did he fulfil his dream of working with Sam Peckinpah. Amer-

ican reviewers praised his acting skills, but deemed him to be 'too French', and Delon's famed rebelliousness angered MGM. Claiming that he missed French life, its bistros and its baguettes, he returned to France, where he pursued his highly successful career. VO

FILMS: *The Yellow Rolls-Royce* (1964); *Once a Thief* (1965); *Lost Command, Texas across the River* (1966); *Scorpio* (1973); *The Concorde:Airport '79* (1979).

DELPY, Julie (Julie Pilet) (1969–)

French actress who made her cinematic debut at the age of fourteen in Jean-Luc Godard's *Détective* (1985). She subsequently established a successful career in quality French and European films, gaining international recognition in Agnieszka Holland's *Europa, Europa* (1991). Her Hollywood debut came with a supporting role in the romantic costume drama *The Three Musketeers*. Her excellent command of English ensured that her American career took off. She was the eccentric Melodie in the German/American black comedy *Younger and Younger* (1993) and, a year later, she was the prostitute with a 'golden heart' in the French/American thriller *Killing Zoe*. She then co-starred in Richard Linklater's now cult romantic drama *Before Sunrise*, this time as the French student who meets the young American traveller Jesse (Ethan Hawke) in Vienna. Delpy also studied film-making at New York University and in 1995 made her own directorial debut with the short *Blah, Blah, Blah*. Since then she has continued to direct and appear in American productions, including a voice-only reprise of her *Before Sunrise* role in Linklater's animated film *Waking Life*. A Los Angeles resident, Delpy has continued to consolidate her reputation as one of France's most promising young exports. TH

FILMS: *The Three Musketeers* (1993); *Killing Zoe* (1994); *Before Sunrise* (1995); *The Treat* (1998); *But I'm a Cheerleader, The Passion of Ayn Rand* (1999); *Sand, Tell Me* (2000); *Investigating Sex, Waking Life* [voice], *MacArthur Park* (2001); *Cinemagique* (2002); *Before Sunset* (2004).

DEL VAL, Jean (Jean Jacques Gautier) (1891–1975)

French actor who specialised in playing minor French character parts such as waiters, hotel managers, customs officials, croupiers and military officers during an extensive US career. Del Val's voice has particular historical significance: he worked as a vocal coach during the era of Hollywood's multi-language film production, and he may be heard as the radio announcer at the beginning of *Casablanca*. AP

FILMS: *The Fortunes of Fifi, Heart's Desire* (1917); *Atonement, The Mystery of the Yellow Room* (1919); *A Sainted Devil* (1924); *A Man of Iron, Fifty-Fifty* (1925); *Back to Liberty* (1927); *Sea Legs* (1930); *Women Men Marry, The Magnificent Lie, Friends and Lovers, Possessed* (1931); *The Passionate Plumber, Rasputin and the Empress* (1932); *Block-Heads* (1938); *Pack up Your Troubles, The Flying Deuces, Everything Happens at Night* (1939); *The Man Who Wouldn't Talk, Broadway Melody of 1940, The House across the Bay, Brother Orchid, Mystery Sea Raider, Triple Justice, Drums of the Desert, Down Argentine Way, Arise My Love, The Mark of Zorro* (1940); *Hudson's Bay, Rage in Heaven, That Night in Rio, Sergeant York, Outlaws of the Desert, Paris Calling* (1941); *The Lady Has Plans, Secret Agent of Japan, Take a Letter Darling, The Pied Piper, Crossroads, Just Off Broadway, Dr Renault's Secret, Gentleman Jim, Casablanca* [voice], *Reunion in France* (1942); *Adventures of the Flying Cadets, Mission to Moscow, Action in the North Atlantic, Background to Danger, For Whom the Bell Tolls, Wintertime, Paris after Dark, The Song of Bernadette* (1943); *Passage to Marseille, Tampico, Uncertain Glory, Irish Eyes are Smiling* (1944); *Cornered, The Spider, Molly and Me* (1945); *Gilda, O.S.S., Monsieur Beaucaire, So Dark the Night, The Razor's Edge, The Count of Monte Cristo* (1946); *13 Rue Madeleine, Undercover Maisie, Buck Privates Come Home, The Private Affairs of Bel Ami, Repeat Performance, Life with Father, Down to Earth, The Foxes of Harrow, The Crime Doctor's Gamble* (1947); *I Walk Alone, Julia Misbehaves* (1948); *Siren of Atlantis, The Great Sinner, The Secret of St Ives* (1949); *Under My Skin, Last of the Buccaneers* (1950); *Rich, Young and Pretty* (1951); *Lovely to Look At, Park Row, The Iron Mistress* (1952); *The Hitch-Hiker, The 49th Man, Gentlemen Prefer Blondes, Little Boy Lost* (1953); *Living it Up, The Gambler from Natchez* (1954); *Pirates of Tripoli, Duel on the Mississippi* (1955); *Anything Goes* (1956); *Funny Face, The Sad Sack* (1957); *The Wreck of the Mary Deare* (1959); *Can-Can* (1960); *The Devil at 4 O'Clock* (1961); *Fantastic Voyage* (1966); *Wait Until Dark* (1967).

DE MEDEIROS, Maria (1965–)

Cosmopolitan and versatile Portuguese actress with a small stature but large eyes who is best known for her role in Quentin Tarentino's *Pulp Fiction*. De Medeiros was brought

up in Vienna, to where her parents had emigrated to escape Salazar's regime. Her first film role, at the age of fifteen in Portugal, was in João César Monteiro's *Silvestre* (1982), and this was followed by success on the French stage in the 1980s. She was warmly recommended to Philip Kaufman for the part of Anaïs Nin in *Henry and June* by the legendary Parisian agent Margot Capelier. De Medeiros then met Tarantino, who decided to cast the two *Henry and June* actresses, herself and Uma Thurman, in *Pulp Fiction*. Given her ability to act in several European languages, De Medeiros has preferred to develop her subsequent career outside the USA. AR

FILMS: *Henry and June* (1990); *Pulp Fiction* (1994); *The Woman in the Moon* (1995).

DEMICK, Irina (Irina Dziemiach) (1936–2004)

Another Darryl F. Zanuck discovery and 'protégée', along with Bella Darvi★, Demick first appeared in a Hollywood film as a Resistance fighter in *The Longest Day*. Her career with Fox failed to prosper and she returned permanently to European productions after 1968. VO

FILMS: *The Longest Day* (1962); *The Visit* (1964); *Up from the Beach, Those Magnificent Men in Their Flying Machines, or How I Flew from London to Paris in 25 Hours, 11 Minutes* (1965); *Prudence and the Pill* (1968).

DEMONGEOT, Mylène (Marie-Hélène Demongeot) (1936–)

Promoted as 'The Champagne Bubble' or 'The French Ball of Fire' by Columbia in Britain and the USA, Demongeot appeared in two American films: Otto Preminger's adaptation of the Françoise Sagan novel *Bonjour Tristesse* and *The Private Navy of Sgt O'Farrell*, a war comedy starring Bob Hope, in which she played Gina Lollobrigida's★ niece. VO

FILMS: *Bonjour Tristesse* (1958); *The Private Navy of Sgt O'Farrell* (1968).

DENEUBOURG, Georges (unknown)

Deneubourg had a prolific film and stage career in France before arriving in the USA in 1917, accompanying the stage star Sarah Bernhardt★, whom he would play opposite on the New York stage. He decided to stay on and his first part was as the German Emperor in *The Fall of the Romanoffs*. In *The Right to Lie*, he played another foreigner, an Italian gentleman. His final American film, *Tarnished* **231**

Reputations, was co-directed by Alice Guy and her husband Herbert Blaché. VO

FILMS: *The Fall of the Romanoffs* (1917); *The Thirteenth Chair, The Right to Lie* (1919); *Tarnished Reputations* (1920).

DENEUVE, Catherine (Catherine Dorléac) (1943–)

A demanding French actress in Europe, sought after by auteurs (Luis Buñuel, Jacques Demy, Roman Polanski, Lars von Trier, Marco Ferreri, Raul Ruiz, Manoel de Oliveira . . . the list is impressive), Catherine Deneuve is very famous abroad, particularly in the USA, but why should this be the case? Apart from the *succès de scandale* of Buñuel's *Belle de jour* (1967), it is unlikely that her French films could have promoted her more widely than her adverts for Chanel and Saint Laurent, which revealed the image of a super-model, a blonde ice-queen and the immaculate embodiment of French luxury. It is certainly this polished image that has been unimaginatively plundered in films such as *The April Fools* (where she lured Jack Lemmon away from his quiet American middle-class existence) and *The Hunger* (she was a bisexual vampire who wore veiled hats and seduced David Bowie and Susan Sarandon) – the latter nevertheless giving Deneuve a cult lesbian following. From this rather disappointing American filmography (one can imagine what Alfred Hitchcock, George Cukor or Vincente Minnelli would have drawn from her), one may, however, retain a little-known but beautiful noir film by Robert Aldrich, *Hustle*, where she accurately played a melancholic French call-girl offering a little tenderness to Burt Reynolds to the theme tune of 'Un Homme et une femme'. CV

FILMS: *The April Fools* (1969); *Hustle* (1975); *The Hunger* (1983).

DENNY, Reginald (Reginald Leigh Daymore) (1891–1967)

English stage and screen actor whose American stardom reached its zenith in a series of energetic action-oriented comedies of the 1920s, most notably as boxer 'Kid' Roberts in Universal's successful *Leather Pushers* series. Denny's fame waned as the coming of the sound era revealed this handsome all-American hero to be an impeccably accented Englishman. Denny was, however, frequently typecast hereafter as comically English buffons, and is fondly remembered for supporting roles typified by his recurrent turn as

sidekick Algy Longworth in the popular *Bulldog Drummond* series. MF

FILMS: *The Melting Pot* (1912); *Bringing up Betty, The Oakdale Affair* (1919); *A Dark Lantern, Experience, 39 East* (1920); *The Price of Possession, Disraeli, Footlights, The Beggar Maid, Tropical Love, The Iron Trail, Paying the Piper* (1921); *Never Let Go, Jenny Lind, Romeo in Pajamas, Sherlock Holmes, The Leather Pushers* [series of shorts comprising *Let's Go, Round Two, Payment through the Nose, A Fool and His Money, The Taming of the Shrew, Whipsawed*], *The New Leather Pushers* [series of shorts comprising *Young King Cole, He Raised Kane, Chickasha Bone Crusher, When Kane Met Abel*], *The Kentucky Derby* (1922); *Abysmal Brute, The Thrill Chaser, Madame Butterfly, The New Leather Pushers* [series of shorts comprising *Strike Father, Strike Son, Joan of Newark, The Wandering Two, The Widower's Mite, Don Coyote, Something for Nothing, Columbia the Gem and the Ocean, Barnaby's Grudge, That Kid from Madrid, He Loops to Conquer*] (1923); *Sporting Youth, The Reckless Age, The Fast Worker, Captain Fearless, The New Leather Pushers* [series of shorts comprising *Girls Will Be Girls, A Tough Tenderfoot, Swing Bad the Sailor, Big Boy Blue*] (1924); *Oh, Doctor!, I'll Show You the Town, California Straight Ahead, Where Was I?* (1925); *Skinner's Dress Suit, What Happened to Jones?, Take it from Me, Rolling Home, The Cheerful Fraud* (1926); *Fast and Furious, Out All Night, On Your Toes, Jaws of Steel* (1927); *The Night Bird, That's My Daddy, Good Morning, Judge* (1928); *Red Hot Speed, Clear the Decks, His Lucky Day, One Hysterical Night* (1929); *What a Man!, Madam Satan, A Lady's Morals, Those Three French Girls, Oh, for a Man* (1930); *Parlor, Bedroom and Bath, Kiki, Private Lives, Stepping Out, The Christmas Party* (1931); *Lovers Courageous, Strange Justice* (1932); *The Barbarian, Only Yesterday, The Big Bluff, The Iron Master* (1933); *The Lost Patrol, The World Moves On, Of Human Bondage, We're Rich Again, The Richest Girl in the World, One More River, The Little Minister, Fog, Dancing Man* (1934); *Without Children, Vagabond Lady, On More Ladies, Here's to Romance, The Lady in Scarlet, Remember Last Night?, Midnight Phantom, The Lottery Lover, Anna Karenina* (1935); *Preview Murder Mystery, Romeo and Juliet, Two in a Crowd, More than a Secretary, The Rest Cure, It Couldn't Have Happened – But it Did, Penthouse Party* (1936); *Bulldog Drummond Escapes, The Great Gambini, Women of Glamour, Let's Get Married, Jungle Menace, Join the Marines, Bulldog Drummond's Revenge, Bulldog Drummond Comes Back, Beg, Borrow or Steal, We're in the Legion Now* (1937); *Four Men and a Prayer, Blockade, Bulldog Drummond's*

Peril, Bulldog Drummond in Africa (1938); *Arrest Bulldog Drummond, Bulldog Drummond's Secret Police, Bulldog Drummond's Bride* (1939); *Rebecca, Seven Sinners, Spring Parade* (1940); *One Night in Lisbon, International Squadron, Appointment for Love* (1941); *Captains of the Clouds, Thunder Birds, Sherlock Holmes and the Voice of Terror, Over My Dead Body, Eyes in the Night* (1942); *The Crime Doctor's Strangest Case* (1943); *Song of the Open Road* (1944); *Love Letters* (1945); *Tangier, The Locket* (1946); *My Favourite Brunette, The Secret Life of Walter Mitty, Christmas Eve, The Macomber Affair, Escape Me Never* (1947); *Mr Blandings Builds His Dream House* (1948); *The Iroquois Trail* (1950); *The Hindu, Fort Vengeance, Abbott and Costello Meet Dr Jekyll and Mr Hyde* (1953); *Escape to Burma* (1955); *Around the World in Eighty Days* (1956); *Street of Sinners* (1957); *Advance to the Rear* (1964); *Cat Ballou* (1965); *Assault on a Queen, Batman* (1966).

DEPARDIEU, Gérard (1948–)

Or 'Dipardiou' as Rosanna Arquette called him. The most famous and prolific French male star since Jean Gabin⋆, Depardieu has succeeded in squeezing several Hollywood blockbusters into an already packed European career. Early on, he tackled films in languages other than French, and flirted with the USA. He played opposite Robert de Niro and Donald Sutherland, for instance, in the Italian-language production of Bertolucci's *1900/Novecento* (1976). In 1984, he was already gracing the cover of *Time* thanks to the transatlantic success of Bertrand Blier's *Préparez vos mouchoirs/Get Out Your Handkerchiefs* (1978) and *Le Retour de Martin Guerre/The Return of Martin Guerre* (1982).

Depardieu has been an avowed admirer of auteur cinema and he willingly accepted the lead role in Australian director Peter Weir's Hollywood film *Green Card*. Weir wrote the lead role specifically for Depardieu and worked some of the actor's traits and biographical past into the part. His rough-hewn features, ample frame and Gallic hedonism complemented the Andie MacDowell character's New York prissiness extremely well. Depardieu was not pressured into speaking English perfectly. He learned some of his lines phonetically, not always knowing what they meant. *Green Card* was hugely successful, grossing $30 million in the USA alone.

Depardieu had had the hunch that his departure to the USA would be 'either a great adventure or a tragic mistake'. After the initial hype over *Green Card*, it seemed to turn into the latter. In February 1991, *Time* published an interview in which the actor apparently confessed to a number of pre-teen rapes. His name was never officially cleared, although the tapes of the interview, conducted in French, bear evidence that his words were not only grossly mistranslated but also partly apocryphal. Depardieu's American career and morale were nonetheless severely tested for a couple of years and the scandal probably cost him an Academy Award for his leading role in *Cyrano de Bergerac* (1990).

In order to regain some approval in the USA, the French actor bravely took on the lead role of Christopher Columbus in Ridley Scott's epic *1492: Conquest of Paradise*. This time linguistic skills were of the essence and helped by a language coach he met the challenge. Unfortunately, *1492* was a relative failure. It made only $7 million in its commercial run.

Depardieu subsequently reprised his role as the short-tempered but loving father in *Mon père ce héros* (1991) for *My Father the Hero* – a rare instance of an actor playing the same role in both versions. Depardieu has never felt comfortable with blockbusters, though. He has certainly not accepted American roles for their salaries, which have been negligible compared to those of major Hollywood stars. In 1993, he thus returned to his old love – American independent cinema – by playing a small part in Nick Cassavetes' *Unhook the Stars*. Depardieu greatly admired Nick's father John, whose films he had distributed in France in 1992. Since then, Depardieu has made several appearances in Hollywood, including *Bogus*, opposite Whoopi Goldberg, *The Man in the Iron Mask* and *102 Dalmatians*. VO

FILMS: *Green Card* (1990); *From Time to Time, 1492: Conquest of Paradise* (1992); *My Father the Hero* (1994); *Unhook the Stars, Bogus, The Secret Agent* (1996); *The Man in the Iron Mask* (1998); *102 Dalmatians* (2000); *CQ* (2001); *City of Ghosts* (2002).

DE PUTTI, Lya (Amália de Szepesy) (1896–1931)

Swarthy, enigmatic silent star who played a succession of exotic femme fatales on both sides of the Atlantic. Born in Vecse, Austro-Hungary (now Slovakia), de Putti deserted her husband and two daughters in 1918. They thereupon erected a grave to her. After bit parts in Hungarian and Romanian films, she found enormous success in 1920s Berlin and, despite critical disfavour, was voted 'most popu- **233** lar screen actress' by readers of *Neue Illustrierte Filmwoche* in 1924. De Putti now claimed to have been born the daughter of an Italian count in 1899 and gossip columns overflowed with tales of her heavy drinking, suicide attempts and romantic intrigues. She gained Hollywood's attention playing the seductress Bertha in *Varieté/ Variety* (1925) – the film that also brought director E. A. Dupont and co-star Emil Jannings★ to the USA – and signed a contract with Famous Players-Lasky. Still portraying distinctly pre-Hays Code temptresses, she failed to secure a following, perhaps due to a lack of public interest in her now sanitised off-screen persona. Studio head Adolph Zukor, for example, wary after the 1921 Fatty Arbuckle scandal, preferred to play up her apparent aristocratic descent and (wildly exaggerated) career as a ballerina, while revising her year of birth to 1901. De Putti's career dissipated entirely after 1928 due to producers' reluctance to try her staccato accent in a talkie, although she did travel to Britain to make *The Informer* (1929). A Broadway comeback failed, and de Putti died in mysterious, headline-grabbing circumstances in New York in 1931. She supposedly contracted pneumonia after an operation to remove a chicken bone from her throat. RJK

FILMS: *The Sorrows of Satan, Prince of Tempters, God Gave Me Twenty Cents* (1926); *The Heart Thief* (1927); *Midnight Rose, Buck Privates, The Scarlet Lady* (1928).

DE SEGUROLA, Andrés (Andrés Perelló de Segurola) (1874–1953)

Spanish opera singer who first came to prominence at The Metropolitan in New York. De Segurola retired from the stage in 1923 and was encouraged by his friend Gloria Swanson to move to Hollywood. He made his 1927 screen debut as an opera impresario in *The Love of Sunya*. His elegant and distinguished looks won him other supporting parts in both Spanish- and English-language Hollywood films, where he became a frequent choice for minor opera singer roles in titles like *One Night of Love*. De Segurola was also a vocal instructor for such celebrities as Deanna Durbin. EU

FILMS: *The Love of Sunya* (1927); *Bringing Up Father, Glorious Betsy, The Cardboard Lover, The Red Dance, My Man* (1928); *Behind Closed Doors, Careers* (1929); *General Crack, Mamba, Song o' My Heart* (1930); *One Night of Love, We Are Rich Again* (1934); *Public Opinions, Goin' to Town* (1935).

234

DE SICA, Vittorio (1901–1974)

Italian actor-turned-acclaimed neo-realist director whose first approach to Hollywood was in the 1930s when, as one of Italian cinema's most popular male stars, he did a singing screen test for Fox, although this was unsuccessful. It was not until the late 1950s, when his directing career appeared to be in decline, that De Sica made his American screen debut. While his Italian screen persona had established him as the 'petit bourgeois hero', in Hollywood he played a range of comic and dramatic roles that consistently drew on his Italianness (the exception being *The Angel Wore Red*, where he portrayed a Spanish patriot during the Civil War). He appeared as Count Dino della Fiaba, a penniless aristocrat, in *Montecarlo Story*, as a suave attorney in *It Started in Naples*, and as a caricature of a Mafia boss in *The Biggest Bundle of Them All*. De Sica won an Academy Award nomination for Best Actor in a Supporting Role for his part as Major Alessandro Rinaldi in *A Farewell to Arms*. CBu

FILMS: *Montecarlo Story* (1956); *A Farewell to Arms* (1957); *The Millionairess, It Started in Naples, The Angel Wore Red* (1960); *After the Fox* (1966); *The Biggest Bundle of Them All, The Shoes of the Fisherman* (1968); *If it's Tuesday, This Must Be Belgium* (1969); *Snow Job* (1972).

DESNY, Ivan (1922– 2002)

Character actor, born to Russian parents in China, who appeared in West German, French and Italian films from 1950. Despite memorable roles in American productions shot in Europe, he never became a Hollywood name. RJK

FILMS: *Song without End* (1960); *Bon Voyage!, Escapade in Florence* (1962); *Blood Queen* (1973).

DEUTSCH, Ernst (1890–1969)

Prague-born Jewish luminary of German theatre and silent film who fled Berlin in 1933 and arrived in the USA in 1938. As an unknown middle-aged German – billed after 1941 as Ernst Dorian – he received few parts, usually playing Nazis. In 1947, he staged a triumphant return to Germany. RJK

FILMS: *Nurse Edith Cavell* (1939); *Escape, The Man I Married* (1940); *So Ends Our Night* (1941); *Island of Forgotten Sins, Prisoner of Japan, Enemy Agents Meet Ellery Queen, Reunion in France, Night Plane from Chungking* (1942); *The Moon is Down* (1943); *The Hitler Gang* (1944); *Isle of the Dead* (1945).

DIETRICH, Marlene (Maria Magdalene Dietrich) (1901–1992)

It is emblematic of the paradoxes surrounding Marlene Dietrich that she is claimed both in the USA and Germany as the quintessence of each country's cinematic golden age. Though Dietrich never returned to live in Germany after emigration in 1931, she was posthumously celebrated in a permanent exhibition at the Berlin Film Museum, as well as in the dedication to her memory of a central Berlin square, Marlene-Dietrich-Platz. Simultaneously, the Berlin-born Dietrich has been fêted as the 'genuine essence' of a Hollywood star. In her declining years, Dietrich's status as Hollywood legend was amplified by numerous television, film and print tributes, including: Billy Wilder's *Fedora* (1978), a portrait, thinly veiled as fiction, of the by now reclusive star; *Marlene Dietrich by Her Daughter* (1992), Maria Riva's often unflattering biographical account; grandson David Riva's television documentary *Dietrich: Shadow and Light* (1996); and Dietrich's voice-only farewell to the film medium, *Marlene*, directed by Maxi-milian Schell★ in 1984.

Schell's documentary – a montage of film extracts, with voiceover commentary from the camera-shy octogenarian star – is a moving tribute to an actress whose Hollywood career already reached back over fifty years. By 1930, when Dietrich, under contract to Paramount, set sail for the first time to the USA, she was already a minor Berlin stage star, and had played (largely in supporting roles) in seventeen German-language films. A child of the Prussian officer class, Dietrich's early aspirations for a career as a concert violinist were dashed by a wrist injury, and she embarked instead on theatre training, studying eventually in Reinhardt's

Berlin-born Marlene Dietrich became one of the greatest Hollywood screen legends – here with Clive Brook in *Shanghai Express* (1931)

drama school, and playing small theatre roles until her discovery for stage revue. A risqué duet with the singer Margo Lion in the revue *Es liegt in der Luft / It's in the Air* (1928) gained what was to be a lifetime gay and lesbian following. Among the theatre audience for the subsequent *Zwei Krawatten / Two Neckties* (1929) was the Austrian émigré director Josef von Sternberg, who instantly engaged Dietrich as the female lead in his dual-language *Der blaue Engel / The Blue Angel* (1930). As the vamp Lola Lola, Dietrich eclipsed *The Blue Angel*'s intended premier attraction, Emil Jannings★, and, on the very evening of *The Blue Angel*'s German premiere, she embarked for Hollywood to seek to duplicate her German success.

Dietrich's six subsequent collaborations with Sternberg have acquired the status of legend. In most accounts (including Dietrich's own), Sternberg figures as the Svengali who transformed Germany's darling 'Marlene' into Dietrich, the very essence of Hollywood myth. The director's studied use of light and shade fashioned from the raw and raunchy Dietrich of *Blue Angel* an altogether more sophisticated, slimmer, erotic yet coolly distant femme fatale. The sculpted forehead, high cheekbones and statuesque allure of Sternberg's Hollywood Dietrich are a far cry from Lola Lola's robust sexuality; yet her characters retain the ambiguities that were a source of Dietrich's mystery from early on. *Morocco* recalled the star's earlier lesbian associations when she donned tuxedo and top hat, and kissed a woman full on the lips on screen. Her exoticism was heightened by her films' foreign locations: China (*Shanghai Express*), Russia (*The Scarlet Empress*), Spain (*The Devil is a Woman*). At times, indeed, the coherence of Dietrich's star persona seemed threatened by its extreme ambivalences. Despite public avowals of fidelity to her husband, Rudolph Sieber, and daughter Maria (later Maria Riva), Dietrich's extramarital adventures were legion, and included liaisons with fellow émigrés Maurice Chevalier★, the screenwriter Mercedes de Acosta, Erich Maria Remarque and Jean Gabin★.

In *Blonde Venus*, Dietrich reproduced the paradoxes of her off-screen sexual history, playing a devoted wife and mother whose invalid husband ultimately (and rather implausibly) forgives her a temporary metamorphosis into an adulterous variety star. Negative reviews of *Blonde Venus* were the first signs of a critical hostility that was to culminate in Dietrich's 1938 damnation by *Variety* magazine as

'box-office poison'. Following a break with Sternberg, in part as a result of disappointing box-office returns, Dietrich began the first of a series of reinventions of her star persona. A comedy role in Lubitsch's *Desire* secured accolades for her recapturing of the 'freshness and gaiety of spirit that was hers in *Blue Angel*' (*The New York Times*). There followed – despite further box-office flops – high-level overtures from industry and Nazi state representatives seeking her return to German film; but Dietrich took US citizenship in 1939, and went on to star as the bar-room queen 'Frenchie' in a title from that most emblematic of US genres, the Western *Destry Rides Again*.

After her 1942 participation in state-sponsored advertising for US war bonds, Dietrich joined the United Service Organisation, set off in 1944 to entertain US front-line troops, and gained new prominence both as an Allied propaganda icon and as an object of enduring hostility from pro-Nazi and conservative quarters in Germany. Paradoxically again, Dietrich's 'Prussian' self-discipline is often cited as the source of her capacity to emerge as a heroine from front-line entertainment for Allied troops. In 1947, she became the first woman to be awarded the highest US civil honour, the 'Medal of Freedom'. The French state followed in 1950 with the award of Chevalier de la Légion d'honneur. Though never similarly honoured for her film roles (she won no Academy Awards in her career), Dietrich did gain occasional postwar critical acclaim, including for finely drawn portrayals of Nazi fellow travellers (*A Foreign Affair*, *Judgment at Nuremberg*), and cameo roles in Orson Welles' *Touch of Evil* and the David Bowie vehicle *Just a Gigolo* (1978). Her major postwar triumphs, however, began after Dietrich's final relaunching of her career, this time as a recording star and cabaret artiste. Her opening Las Vegas season began twenty years of international touring, including to South America, Western and Eastern Europe, the Far East, Israel and Australia. Following a mixed reception on a 1960 German tour – she was welcomed by many, including West Germany's future Chancellor and fellow émigré Willy Brandt, but vilified by sections of the press, and barracked by audiences for supposed World War II 'treachery' – Dietrich thereafter shunned her homeland, and retreated instead to secluded Paris retirement after the 1975 fall that ended her concert career. EC

FILMS: *Morocco* (1930); *Dishonored* (1931); *Shanghai Express*, *Blonde Venus* (1932); *The Song of Songs* (1933); *The Scarlet*

Empress (1934); *The Devil is a Woman* (1935); *Desire, I Loved a Soldier, The Garden of Allah* (1936); *Angel* (1937); *Destry Rides Again* (1939); *Seven Sinners, The Flame of New Orleans* (1940); *Manpower, The Lady is Willing* (1941); *The Spoilers, Pittsburgh* (1942); *Kismet, Follow the Boys* (1944); *Golden Earrings* (1947); *A Foreign Affair* (1948); *Jigsaw* (1949); *Stage Fright* (1950); *No Highway, Rancho Notorious* (1951); *Around the World in Eighty Days, The Monte Carlo Story* (1956); *Witness for the Prosecution* (1957); *Touch of Evil* (1958); *Judgment at Nuremberg* (1961); *Black Fox* (1962); *Paris When it Sizzles* (1963).

DIFFRING, Anton (Alfred Pollack) (1918–1989)

Britain's foremost Nazi screen villain of the 1950s who returned to his native Germany in the mid-1960s. A player in dozens of international co-productions – including eleven Hollywood pictures shot in Europe – Diffring showed little professional discrimination. He appeared, for example, in two unreleased American 'concentration camp comedies'. RJK

FILMS: *Never Let Me Go* (1953); *Betrayed* (1954); *The Blue Max* (1966); *Where Eagles Dare, Counterpoint* (1968); *The Day the Clown Cried* [unreleased] (1972); *Blood Queen* (1973); *The Swiss Conspiracy* (1975); *Operation Daybreak* (1976); *Valentino* (1977); *Hitler's Son* [unreleased] (1978); *Escape to Victory* (1981).

DIONE, Rose (1875–1936)

Born in Paris, Dione worked in theatre and made a few films for Pathé. The bulk of her film career, however, was in Hollywood, where she appeared in over fifty-five films. She tended to play middle-aged Parisian women in supporting roles. One of her last roles was as the circus owner Madame Tetrallini in Tod Browning's *Freaks*. MB/GV

FILMS: *The Secret Garden, The Tiger's Trail, The World and its Woman, It Happened in Paris* (1919); *Suds, The Woman and the Puppet, Silk Hosiery, The Luck of the Irish, The Land of Jazz, The Great Lover* (1920); *The Blushing Bride, Cheated Love, Little Lord Fauntleroy, Silent Years, A Parisian Scandal, Be My Wife* (1921); *Golden Dreams, Omar the Tentmaker* (1922); *Salome, Trilby, Drifting, Scaramouche, The French Doll* (1923); *Try and Get It, Beau Brummel, The Rose of Paris, The Lover of Camille, Inez from Hollywood, Shadows of Paris* (1924); *One Year to Live, Fifth Avenue Models* (1925); *Mademoiselle Modiste, Paris, The Duchess of Buffalo, Fools of Fashion, Love's Blindness, Camille* (1926); *When a Man Loves, The Beloved*

Rogue, Old San Francisco, Ragtime, Polly of the Movies (1927); *Mad Hour, Bringing up Father, Out of the Ruins, The Red Mark, Naughty Baby, His Tiger Wife* (1928); *One Stolen Night, Hearts in Exile* (1929); *Isle of Escape, Women Everywhere, On Your Back* (1930); *Salvation Nell* (1931); *Freaks, The King Murder, Back Street* (1932).

DOLENZ, George (1908–1963)

Italian actor and restaurateur who worked on the Riviera before moving to the USA. On arrival, Dolenz studied at Max Reinhardt's dramatic school in Hollywood. He was contracted by Howard Hughes, later RKO and then Universal. He also worked in television, starring in *The Count of Monte Cristo* for two years while simultaneously running the Marquis restaurant in Los Angeles. FG

FILMS: *Take a Letter, Darling, Unexpected Uncle* (1942); *Fired Wife, Young Ideas, Moonlight in Vermont, She's for Me, The Strange Death of Adolf Hitler, No Time for Love* (1943); *Enter Arsene Lupin, In Society, Bowery to Broadway, The Climax* (1944); *Resisting Enemy Interrogation, The Royal Mounted Rides Again, Easy to Look At, Song of the Sarong* (1945); *A Night in Paradise, Idea Girl, Girl on the Spot* (1946); *Song of Scheherazade* (1947); *Vendetta* (1950); *Scared Stiff, My Cousin Rachel, The Wings of the Hawk* (1953); *Sign of the Pagan, The Last Time I Saw Paris* (1954); *A Bullet for Joey, The Purple Mask, The Racers* (1955); *Timbuktu, The Sad Sack* (1959); *Look in Any Window, Four Horsemen of the Apocalypse* (1961).

DOLL, Dora (Dorothée Hermina Feinberg) (1922–)

French actress (born in Berlin) who made her name by playing blowsy screen vamps in the 1950s. Her first two American films were co-productions shot in Europe. She later appeared in a small part as a woman travelling through German-occupied Europe on a train in *Julia*. SL/AP

FILMS: *Pardon My French* (1952); *Act of Love* (1953); *Dictionary of Sex* (1964); *Julia* (1977).

DOMINGUIN, Luis Miguel (1927–1996)

Spanish bullfighting legend whose fame as a Hollywood playboy was cemented with a highly publicised romance with Ava Gardner. Dominguin had a cameo role in *Around the World in Eighty Days* and appeared as himself in *The Picasso Summer*. EU

FILMS: *Around the World in Eighty Days* (1956); *The Picasso Summer* (1969).

DONALDSSON, Arthur (1869–1955)

Swedish performer who first came to the USA in 1890 and subsequently enjoyed a successful career as a singer and actor for almost twenty years. Donaldsson made his screen debut in 1908 for the Lubin company and remained there until he went to Ireland with Kalem in 1911. When Kalem returned to the USA, Donaldsson went back to Sweden to appear in local film and theatre. He returned to the USA in 1913 to work with Kalem again, but soon moved on to other companies. Donaldsson was noted as a gifted character actor and regularly alternated small, but recognised, film parts with theatre projects. He produced and directed a short sound film experiment, *Retribution*, in 1925 but with the advent of sound his Hollywood career was over. MBj

FILMS: *Rory O'More, Arrah-na-Pogue, Colleen Bawn* (1911); *The Mystery of Pine Tree Creek* (1913); *The Day of Days, The Land of the Lost, Over Niagara Falls, Tricking the Government, Wolfe or the Conquest of Quebec* (1914); *Three Weeks, The Ghost of Twisted Oaks, Hearts of Men, The Moth and the Flame* (1915); *The Faded Flower, Her American Prince, Should a Baby Die?, A Woman's Honor, Who's Guilty* [serial] (1916); *Babbling Tongues, The Danger Trail, Enlighten Thy Daughter, For France, I Will Repay, Who Goes There?* (1917); *Find the Woman, The Golden Goal, The Green God, His Own People, Over the Top* (1918); *The ABC of Love, The Captain's Captain, Coax Me, Daring Hearts, Fighting Destiny, Me and Captain Kid, Mind the Paint Girl, Miss Dulcie from Dixie, The Undercurrent* (1919); *Atonement, Greater than Fame, The Hidden Light, A Modern Salome, Mothers of Men* (1920); *Gilded Lies, Is Life Worth Living?, The Passionate Pilgrim, Rider of the King Log, The Silver Lining* [also director and producer], *Wise Husbands* (1921); *Find the Woman, Orphans of the Ghetto, When Knighthood was in Flower* (1922); *America, The Bandolero, For Woman's Favor, Yolanda* (1924); *Down upon the Suwannee River, Fifty-Fifty, The Swan, School for Wives* (1925); *Love 'em or Leave 'em* (1926); *Broadway Drifter, The Winning Oar* (1927).

DONAT, Robert (Friedrich Robert Donath) (1905–1958)

Donat was a dark and handsome British actor with pale skin and a charming and cheerful smile. His performance style was understated and well suited to gentle comedy, but his versatility could also be stretched to play volatile char-

acters. He made his screen debut in Paramount British's *That Night in London* and became the most sought-after British actor of the 1930s, yet during that decade he only made one film in the USA. Like many British performers, Donat had first been drawn to the attention of Hollywood producers by his reputation as a stage actor, but he rejected an offer from MGM because it would have meant working in Los Angeles for several years. After appearing in *The Private Life of Henry VIII* (1933), Donat, however, accepted an offer to star in *The Count of Monte Cristo* for the high sum of £250 a week. In Hollywood, he was befriended by other British actors working there, particularly Charles Laughton★ and Elsa Lanchester★. The film was a great success and Donat received further offers from Reliance and Warner Bros. He did not accept them, because he preferred to work in Britain and did not want to become typecast in swashbuckling roles.

Warner Bros. took Donat to court, on the basis of a document they insisted constituted a contract, but the action was decided in Donat's favour. He thereafter continued to prioritise his theatrical opportunities over film work. When MGM offered him the part of Romeo for an enormous sum of £30,000 in a film version of *Romeo and Juliet*, for example, he turned it down because of a pre-existing stage commitment. MGM did not give up and managed to persuade Donat to sign an exclusive contract in 1938 to make films for their production unit in Britain. The £150,000 contract was for six films, five of which would be filmed in Britain. Under this contract, he made two of his most successful films, *The Citadel* and *Goodbye, Mr Chips*, but still insisted that he could pursue stage work in between pairs of films for MGM. The studio took Donat to court when he refused to travel to Hollywood, but in any case the actor was refused an exit permit in 1940. The matter had to be settled out of court and the experience confirmed Donat's reservations about Hollywood practice. During the war, he made films for American production companies based in Britain and his last film for MGM was *Perfect Strangers*. Donat's final film, *The Inn of the Sixth Happiness*, was made for Fox but actually registered as British. SS

FILMS: *That Night in London* (1932); *The Count of Monte Cristo* (1934); *The Citadel* (1938); *Goodbye, Mr Chips* (1939); *The Young Mr Pitt* (1942); *The Adventures of Tartu* (1943); *Perfect Strangers* (1945); *The Inn of the Sixth Happiness* (1958).

DONATH, Ludwig (1900–1967)

Prominent Berlin stage actor from 1928 to 1933, when he fled the Nazis for Hollywood. Donath was originally cast in a succession of World War II anti-Nazi films and later played a variety of character roles, the most memorable being Papa in *The Jolson Story* and *Jolson Sings Again*. FG

FILMS: *Reunion in France, The Secret Code, Falcon's Brother, Enemy Agents Meet Ellery Queen* (1942); *Hangmen Also Die, This Land is Mine, The Moon is Down, Margin for Error, Gangway for Tomorrow, Hostages, Lady from Chungking, The Strange Death of Adolf Hitler, Above Suspicion, Tonight We Raid Calais* (1943); *The Master Race, The Seventh Cross, The Hitler Gang, The Story of Dr Wassell, Tampico* (1944); *Counter-Attack, Prison Ship* (1945); *Blondie Knows Best, The Devil's Mask, The Return of Monte Cristo, Renegades, Gilda* (1946); *The Jolson Story, Cigarette Girl* (1947); *Sealed Verdict, To the Ends of the Earth* (1948); *Jolson Sings Again, The Great Sinner, The Loveable Cheat, The Fighting O'Flynn* (1949); *There's a Girl in My Heart, The Killer that Stalked New York, Mystery Submarine* (1950); *Journey into Light, Sirocco, The Great Caruso* (1951); *My Pal Gus* (1952); *Sins of Jezebel, The Veils of Bagdad* (1953); *Torn Curtain, The Spy in the Green Hat, Too Many Thieves* (1966).

DONNELLY, Donal (1931–)

Donnelly made his screen debut in John Ford's *The Rising of the Moon* set in rural Ireland. He has since appeared in a few Hollywood supporting roles, but has mainly moved between British and Irish theatre and television. RB

FILMS: *The Rising of the Moon* (1957); *Gideon's Day* (1958); *Shake Hands with the Devil* (1959); *Young Cassidy, The Knack – and How to Get it . . .* (1965); *Twister, The Godfather, Part III* (1990); *Squanto: A Warrior's Tale* (1994).

DONOHOE, Amanda (1962–)

British film actress whose limited Hollywood roles have tended to exploit her glamorous and seductive appearance. Donohoe, however, achieved long-running success on US television with a leading role in *L.A. Law* (1986–94). JS

FILMS: *Liar Liar* (1997); *One Night Stand* (1997); *I'm Losing You, Stardust* (1998).

DOODY, Alison (1966–)

Beautiful blonde Irish actress who made her screen debut in the James Bond film *A View to a Kill* (1985). Her first major Hollywood role was Dr Elsa Schneider in *Indiana Jones and the Last Crusade*. RB

FILMS: *A Prayer for the Dying* (1987); *Indiana Jones and the Last Crusade* (1989); *Major League II, Temptation* (1994).

DORN, Philip (Hein van der Niet) (1899–1975)

Dutch leading man who found stardom as Frits van Dongen in Third Reich Germany. When war broke out, he left for Hollywood and 'Americanised' his name. Despite coming second in a US exhibitors' poll to find the 'Stars of Tomorrow' in 1943, parts outside anti-Nazi films were seldom forthcoming. He returned to Germany in 1952. RJK

FILMS: *Ski Patrol, Enemy Agent, Diamond Frontier, Escape* (1940); *Ziegfeld Girl, Tarzan's Secret Treasure, Underground* (1941); *Calling Dr Gillespie, Random Harvest, Reunion in France* (1942); *Paris after Dark, Chetniks – The Fighting Guerrillas* (1943); *Passage to Marseille, Blonde Fever* (1944); *Escape in the Desert* (1945); *I've Always Loved You* (1946); *I Remember Mama* (1948); *The Fighting Kentuckian* (1949); *Spy Hunt* (1950); *Sealed Cargo* (1951).

DORS, Diana (Diana Mary Fluck) (1931–1984)

Britain's 'blonde bombshell' with an hourglass figure, pouting lips and a sultry, sexual expression went to Hollywood in 1956 on contract to RKO. She made two films there, *I Married a Woman* and *The Unholy Wife*, but left when the press turned against her and her husband, because of various alleged 'scandalous' affairs. She returned to the UK in 1960, and made three further films, but never realised her ambition to become a fully fledged Hollywood star. She later appeared in a number of US-funded productions shot in Europe. SS

FILMS: *The Unholy Wife* (1957); *I Married a Woman* (1958); *Scent of Mystery* (1960); *On the Double, King of the Roaring Twenties* (1961); *Berserk!, Danger Route, Hammerhead, Baby Love* (1968); *There's a Girl in My Soup, Deep End* (1970).

DOUGLAS, Robert (Robert Douglas Finlayson) (1909–1999)

British actor who was frequently cast in Hollywood films as a swashbuckling villain. He also became an American television director in the 1960s. TJ

FILMS: *The Decision of Christopher Blake, Adventures of Don Juan* (1948); *Homicide, The Lady Takes a Sailor, The Fountain-* **239** head (1949); *Buccaneer's Girl, Barricade, Spy Hunt, This Side of the Law, Kim, Mystery Submarine, The Flame and the Arrow* (1950); *Target Unknown, Thunder on the Hill* (1951); *At Sword's Point, Ivanhoe, The Prisoner of Zenda* (1952); *Fair Wind to Java, Flight to Tangier, The Desert Rats* (1953); *Saskatchewan, King Richard and the Crusaders* (1954); *The Scarlet Coat, The Virgin Queen, Good Morning, Miss Dove* (1955); *Helen of Troy* (1956); *The Young Philadelphians, Tarzan, the Ape Man* (1959); *The Lawbreakers* (1960).

DOWN, Lesley-Anne (1954–)

Former English model who came to fame in the British television series *Upstairs Downstairs*. She had a romantic leading role in *The Pink Panther Strikes Again* opposite Peter Sellers★ and Herbert Lom★. JS

FILMS: *The Pink Panther Strikes Again* (1976); *The Betsy* (1978); *The First Great Train Robbery* (1979); *Rough Cut* (1980); *Sphinx* (1981); *Nomads* (1986); *Out of Control* (1992); *Night Trap* (1993); *In the Heat of Passion II: Unfaithful, Munchie Strikes Back* (1994); *The Secret Agent Club, Saving Grace* (1996); *Meet Wally Sparks* (1997); *The King's Guard* (2000); *The Meeksville Ghost* (2001); *13th Child* (2002).

DRAVIĆ, Milena (1940–)

Leading Yugoslav (Serbian) actress with more than one hundred Yugoslavian roles to her credit. Internationally, she remains best known for her performances in Dušan Makavejev's films such as *WR – misterije organizma / WR: Mysteries of the Organism* (1971). Her only Hollywood appearance has been in the science-fiction film *The Return.* DI

FILM: *The Return* (1980).

DRIVER, Minnie (Amelia Driver) (1970–)

London-born actress who first came to prominence on British television, notably in the mini-series *Mr Wroe's Virgins* (1993) and *The Politician's Wife* (1995), and received rave reviews in the USA for her cinematic debut as Benny, the chunky heroine of the Irish-American period romance *Circle of Friends*. She has since established herself in Hollywood as a lively and versatile female lead, able to adapt to a wide range of characters and accents with equal facility. This includes the ability to easily pass for an American.

Driver displayed an especially light comic touch in *Grosse Pointe Blank* as the small-town radio phone-in host who quizzes hit man and old flame John Cusack on air about his desertion of her on prom night; and she redeemed her Academy Award–nominated role in *Good Will Hunting* from the ignominy of a simple love interest. Despite her unusual button-eyed, round-faced but square-jawed features, and the fact that she projects an intelligence and wit rare among contemporary Hollywood actresses, most of Driver's films have been undistinguished, and the popular press has preferred to concentrate on her off-screen love life rather than her clear acting talent. SH

FILMS: *Circle of Friends, GoldenEye* (1995); *Big Night, Sleepers, Baggage* (1996); *Grosse Pointe Blank, Princess Mononoke* [voice], *Good Will Hunting* (1997); *Hard Rain, At Sachem Farm* (1998); *An Ideal Husband, Tarzan* [voice], *South Park: Bigger, Longer and Uncut* [voice] (1999); *Return to Me, Beautiful, Slow Burn, The Upgrade* (2000); *High Heels and Lowlifes, D.C. Smalls* (2001); *Owning Mahowny, Hope Springs* (2003); *Ella Enchanted, The Phantom of the Opera* (2004).

DUNA, Steffi (Stefanie Berindey) (1910–1992)

Formerly an operetta singer and dancer on the European stage, Hungarian-born Duna portrayed temperamental Latinas and other exotic characters in British and Hollywood films of the 1930s, often in low-budget serials and B-Westerns. Married to Hollywood actor Dennis O'Keefe, Duna retired from films in 1940. TB

FILMS: *Man of Two Worlds, Let's Try Again* [scenes deleted], *La Cucaracha* (1934); *Red Morning, One New York Night* (1935); *I Conquer the Sea!, Anthony Adverse, Hi Gaucho, Dancing Pirate* (1936); *Escape by Night* (1937); *Rascals, Flirting with Fate* (1938); *Way Down South, Hitler – Beast of Berlin, Law of the Pampas, Panama Lady, The Magnificent Fraud, The Girl and the Gambler* (1939); *The Marines Fly High, River's End, The Girl from Havana, Waterloo Bridge, The Great McGinty, Phantom Raiders* (1940).

DUPEREY, Anny (Anny Legras) (1947–)

A well-known stage and film actress in France, Duperey was revealed in the cinema by her role as a prostitute in Godard's *Deux ou trois choses que je sais d'elle / Two or Three Things I Know about Her* (1967). She appeared in only one American film, as Al Pacino's mistress in Sydney Pollack's *Bobby Deerfield*. VO

FILM: *Bobby Deerfield* (1977).

DUPREZ, June (1918–1984)

Brunette English leading lady who was often cast in exotic or aristocratic roles. A memorable exception to this was her performance as a blonde 'piece of pastry' alongside a cockney Cary Grant in *None but the Lonely Heart*. TJ

FILMS: *The Thief of Bagdad* (1940); *They Raid by Night, Little Tokyo, U.S.A.* (1942); *Forever and a Day, Tiger Fangs* (1943); *None but the Lonely Heart* (1944); *And Then There Were None, The Brighton Strangler* (1945); *Calcutta* (1947).

DUVAL, Paulette (unknown)

Duval had a small stage and screen career in France before arriving in Hollywood, where she was an active supporting player in the mid-1920s. She often played aristocrats. VO

FILMS: *Nero* (1922); *Monsieur Beaucaire, He Who Gets Slapped, My Husband's Wives* (1924); *The Lady, Cheaper to Marry, Man and Maid, Time, the Comedian, Sporting Life* (1925); *The Skyrocket, Exquisite Sinner, Beverly of Graustark, Blarney* (1926); *Beware of Widows, The Magic Garden, Twelve Miles Out, Alias the Lone Wolf, Breakfast at Sunrise* (1927); *The Divine Woman, No Other Woman* (1928).

EGGAR, Samantha (Victoria Samantha Eggar) (1939–)

Soon after being spotted by the British producer Betty Box, Eggar was cast opposite Terence Stamp★ in William Wyler's *The Collector*. Although she was nominated for an Academy Award for her performance, her career largely failed to live up to its earlier promise. Eggar became a frequent face on American television from the 1970s. MW

FILMS: *The Collector* (1965); *Return from the Ashes, Walk Don't Run* (1966); *Doctor Dolittle* (1967); *The Walking Stick, The Lady in the Car with Glasses and a Gun, The Molly Maguires* (1970); *The Light at the Edge of the World* (1971); *A Name for Evil* (1973); *The Seven-Per-Cent Solution* (1976); *Unknown Powers* (1978); *The Exterminator* (1980); *The Hot Touch, Demonoid, Messenger of Death* (1981); *Ragin' Cajun* (1991); *Dark Horse, Round Numbers* (1992); *Inevitable Grace* (1994); *The Phantom* (1996); *Hercules* [voice] (1997); *The Astronaut's Wife* (1999).

EKBERG, Anita (1931–)

Anita Ekberg became one of the icons of European cinema as the beautiful and generously built woman with overflowing blonde hair, pictured bathing in the Trevi fountain dressed in a revealing black evening gown in Federico Fellini's *La dolce vita* (1960). Her particular 'journey of desire' went in the reverse direction, however, since her film career actually began in the USA and ended in Europe.

Ekberg had originally performed as a beauty queen – she was Miss Sweden in 1950 – and her participation in a Miss Universe contest led to a role in an Abbott and Costello vehicle and other minor Hollywood parts during the 1950s. After a role in King Vidor's US/Italian co-production *War and Peace*, Ekberg more or less stayed in Europe, where she continued to appear in several American-funded films. As a woman with magnificent looks, she was constantly positioned by Hollywood as an object of male desire, but if there ever was any acting talent within her, nobody ever bothered to find out. TS

FILMS: *The Mississippi Gambler, Abbott and Costello Go to Mars, The Golden Blade, Take Me to the Town* (1953); *Blood Alley, Artists and Models* (1955); *Zarak, War and Peace, Hollywood or Bust, Man in the Vault, Back from Eternity* (1956); *Valerie, Interpol* (1957); *Paris Holiday, Screaming Mimi, The Man Inside* (1958); *4 for Texas, Call Me Bwana* (1963); *The Alphabet Murders* (1965); *Way . . . Way Out* (1966); *Woman Times Seven* (1967); *If it's Tuesday, This Must Be Belgium* (1969); *Northeast of Seoul* (1972).

ELG, Taina (1931–)

Elg only appeared in minor film roles in her native Finland and was better known as a ballet dancer. She was brought to Hollywood by MGM in the wake of Anita Ekberg★ and became the winner of a Golden Globe Award as New Foreign Star of the Year in 1956. *Les Girls* gave Elg a chance to show off her dancing talents, but although she became a US citizen, her American film and television career failed to flourish. TS/AP

FILMS: *The Prodigal* (1955); *Gaby, Diane* (1956); *Les Girls* (1957); *Imitation General* (1958); *The 39 Steps* (1959); *Watusi, Mission of Danger* (1959); *Hercules in New York* (1970); *Liebestraum* (1991); *The Mirror Has Two Faces* (1996).

ELLIOTT, Denholm (1922–1992)

Respected English character actor who often specialised in gently seedy roles. Elliott became a familiar face to international audiences as the kind of slightly bewildered British gentlemen abroad epitomised by his part as Marcus Brody in the Indiana Jones films. MW

FILMS: *Scent of Mystery* (1960); *You Must Be Joking!*, *King Rat* (1965); *Alfie* (1966); *The Sea Gull*, *The Night They Raided Minsky's* (1968); *The Rise and Rise of Michael Rimmer*, *Too Late the Hero* (1970); *The Vault of Horror* (1973); *Robin and Marian* (1976); *A Bridge Too Far* (1977); *The Boys from Brazil* (1978); *Zulu Dawn*, *Saint Jack*, *Cuba* (1979); *Sunday Lovers* (1980); *Raiders of the Lost Ark* (1981); *Trading Places* (1983); *The Razor's Edge* (1984); *The Whoopee Boys* (1986); *September* (1987); *Keys to Freedom* (1988); *Indiana Jones and the Last Crusade* (1989); *Scorchers*, *Toy Soldiers* (1991); *Noises Off . . .* (1992).

ELSOM, Isobel (1893–1981)

In a similar pattern to Gladys Cooper★, Elsom rose from the ranks of a West End chorus line to become a popular young ingénue on stage and in British films of the 1910s and early 1920s. She appeared in several US-financed UK productions and, following Broadway success in the 1930s, worked regularly in Hollywood after 1941, where she specialised in playing posh matriarchs, as in *Love is a Many-Splendored Thing* and (alongside Cooper) *My Fair Lady*. JB

FILMS: *The Tower of London*, *Glamis Castle* (1926); *Dance Magic* (1927); *Stranglehold* (1930); *The Other Woman* (1931); *Illegal* (1932); *The Thirteenth Candle* (1933); *Ladies in Retirement* (1941); *The War against Mrs Hadley*, *You Were Never Lovelier*, *Seven Sweethearts*, *Eagle Squadron* (1942); *Forever and a Day*, *My Kingdom for a Cook*, *Laugh Your Blues Away*, *First Comes Courage* (1943); *Between Two Worlds*, *The White Cliffs of Dover*, *Casanova Brown* (1944); *The Unseen*, *The Horn Blows at Midnight* (1945); *Two Sisters from Boston*, *Of Human Bondage* (1946); *The Two Mrs Carrolls*, *The Ghost and Mrs Muir*, *Monsieur Verdoux*, *The Paradine Case*, *Love from a Stranger*, *Ivy*, *Escape Me Never*, *Addio Mimi!* (1947); *Smart Woman* (1948); *The Secret Garden* (1949); *Deep in My Heart*, *Desirée* (1954); *Love is a Many-Splendored Thing*, *The King's Thief* (1955); *23 Paces to Baker Street*, *Over-Exposed*, *Lust for Life* (1956); *The Guns of Fort Petticoat* (1957); *Rock-a-Bye Baby* (1958); *The Miracle* (1959); *The Bellboy* (1960); *The Errand Boy*, *Second Time Around* (1961); *Who's Minding the Store?* (1963); *My Fair Lady*, *The Pleasure Seekers* (1964).

ELWES, Cary (1962–)

After his British debut as Rupert Everett's beau in *Another Country* (1984), Elwes has cut a dash on the American

screen either as the wholesome hero seen in *The Princess Bride*, or the kind of vaguely suspect supporting player that might attempt to thwart him, as in *Twister*. MW

FILMS: *The Bride* (1985); *Lady Jane* (1986); *The Princess Bride* (1987); *Never on Tuesday* (1988); *Glory* (1989); *Days of Thunder* (1990); *Hot Shots!* (1991); *Bram Stoker's Dracula*, *Leather Jackets* (1992); *The Crush*, *Robin Hood: Men in Tights* (1993); *The Jungle Book*, *The Chase* (1994); *Twister* (1996); *Hercules* [voice], *The Informant*, *Kiss the Girls*, *Liar, Liar* (1997); *Quest for Camelot* (1998); *Cradle Will Rock* (1999); *Joan of Arc: The Virgin Warrior*, *Shadow of the Vampire*, *Wish You Were Dead* (2000); *Comic Book Villains* (2002); *Neo Ned*, *Ella Enchanted*, *Saw* (2004).

ENGELS, Wera (1909–1988)

Sultry German starlet, signed as a 'Dietrich clone' by RKO in 1933. Poorly promoted and paired with leading men whose star had waned, she returned to Germany in 1936 and retired from the screen altogether the following year. RJK

FILMS: *The Great Jasper* (1933); *Fugitive Road* (1934); *Together We Live*, *The Great Impersonation*, *Hong Kong Nights*, *Sweepstakes Annie* (1935).

ESMOND, Carl (Willy Simon) (1902–2004)

A dashing Viennese *charmeur* in Austrian (e.g. *Liebelei* [1933]) and British films of the 1930s under the name of Willy Eichberger, Esmond played mostly sinister parts in Hollywood from 1937, including suave Nazi villains. He appeared in European films after the war, such as Max Ophuls' *Lola Montès* (1955), billed under his real name. TB

FILMS: *The Prisoner of Zenda* (1937); *The Dawn Patrol* (1938); *Thunder Afloat* (1939); *Little Men* (1940); *Sundown*, *Sergeant York* (1941); *The Navy Comes Through*, *Seven Sweethearts*, *Panama Hattie*, *Pacific Rendezvous* (1942); *First Comes Courage*, *Margin for Error* (1943); *The Story of Dr Wassell*, *Address Unknown*, *Ministry of Fear*, *Experiment Perilous*, *The Master Race* (1944); *Her Highness and the Bellboy*, *Without Love*, *This Love of Ours* (1945); *Lover Come Back*, *The Catman of Paris* (1946); *Smash-Up: The Story of a Woman*, *Slave Girl* (1947); *Walk a Crooked Mile* (1948); *The Desert Hawk*, *Mystery Submarine* (1950); *The World in His Arms* (1952); *From the Earth to the Moon* (1958); *Thunder in the Sun* (1959); *Brushfire*, *Hitler* (1962); *Morituri* (1965), *Agent for H.A.R.M.* (1966).

ESMOND, Jill (Jill Esmond-Moore) (1908–1990)

English actress who played a number of Hollywood leads in the early 1930s before returning to the UK with her husband Laurence Olivier★. Esmond moved back to the USA following their divorce in 1940 and continued to play character parts until the mid-1950s. MF

FILMS: *Once a Lady* (1931); *Ladies of the Jury, State's Attorney, Is My Face Red?, Thirteen Women* (1932); *Random Harvest, Journey for Margaret, This Above All, The Pied Piper, On the Sunny Side, Eagle Squadron* (1942); *White Cliffs of Dover, Casanova Brown, My Pal, Wolf* (1944); *The Bandit of Sherwood Forest* (1946); *Escape* (1948); *Night People* (1954); *A Man Called Peter* (1955).

EVANS, Maurice (1901–1989)

Distinguished stage actor who travelled to Broadway in 1935. Evans' genial air of British gentility was immortalised in the character of Maurice in US television's *Bewitched* during the 1960s. MW

FILMS: *The Only Girl* (1933); *Kind Lady* (1951); *Androcles and the Lion* (1952); *The War Lord* (1965); *One of Our Spies is Missing* (1966); *Jack of Diamonds* (1967); *Planet of the Apes, Tarzan and the Four O'Clock Army, Rosemary's Baby* (1968); *Beneath the Planet of the Apes* (1970); *Terror in the Wax Museum* (1973); *The Jerk* (1979).

EVERETT, Rupert (1959–)

Everett first came to prominence as the James Dean of British Heritage cinema. Having been expelled from the Central School of Speech and Drama for insubordination, he typically played characters in conflict with the values of the establishment they were born into and whose confused rage boiled up and exploded from behind an immaculate upper-class veneer. His breakthrough period films *Another Country* (1984) and *Dance with a Stranger* (1985) attracted early Hollywood attention, but Everett took the part of the unstable pop star in his first American film *Hearts of Fire* seriously enough to announce retirement from acting in favour of a failed attempt to launch a career as a rock musician. His return to American film has been accompanied by a striking change of image: less James Dean and more Clifton Webb. Everett's ability to combine debonair light comedy with a penchant for the cutting remark was heralded by his considerable popular success as Julia Roberts'

gay confidant in *My Best Friend's Wedding*, a role considerably expanded in post-production when test audiences demanded more of him. This new star persona has been consolidated on several fronts: subsequent Hollywood pictures, Everett's public 'outing' of himself and the substantial success in the USA of two British film adaptations of Oscar Wilde plays in which he took leading roles: *An Ideal Husband* (1999) and *The Importance of Being Earnest* (2002). JB

FILMS: *Hearts of Fire, Duet for One* (1987); *Inside Monkey Zetterland* (1992); *Prêt-à-Porter* (1994); *Dunston Checks In* (1996); *My Best Friend's Wedding* (1997); *Shakespeare in Love* (1998); *A Midsummer Night's Dream, Inspector Gadget* (1999); *The Next Best Thing* (2000); *Unconditional Love, The Wild Thornberrys Movie* [voice] (2002); *Shrek 2* [voice] (2004).

FARRAR, David (1908–1995)

Tall and handsome British actor who enjoyed a successful UK film career during the 1940s that included three features financed by Warner Bros. His subsequent experience in Hollywood, where he was often cast as the villain (e.g. Gilbert Blunt, Earl of Alban, in *The Black Shield of Falworth*), was less rewarding. He made his final screen appearance as Xerxes in *The 300 Spartans*. MHu

FILMS: *The Dark Tower, The Night Invader* (1943); *The Hundred Pound Window* (1944); *The Golden Horde* (1951); *The Black Shield of Falworth* (1954); *The Sea Chase, Escape to Burma, Pearl of the South Pacific* (1955); *The Woman and the Hunter* (1957); *I Accuse!* (1958); *Solomon and Sheba, John Paul Jones, Watusi* (1959); *The 300 Spartans* (1962).

FARRELL, Colin (1972–)

Leading Irish screen actor who, like Pierce Brosnan★ and Gabriel Byrne★, has made the most of his dark good looks in order to take action roles that require a blend of menace and sexuality. Born in Dublin, Colin Farrell made his stage debut in Australia before returning to Ireland to attend the Gaiety School of Drama. He first made his name in the British-Irish soap opera *Ballykissangel*, in which he played a traveller. When performing as a semi-autistic character at the Donmar Warehouse in London, Farrell was noticed by Kevin Spacey and, as a result, landed a role as a gangster in Thaddeus O'Sullivan's *Ordinary Decent Criminal*, in which Spacey also co-starred. Farrell went to Los Angeles in 1998 and after acquiring an agent was cast as one of the lead actors in Joel Schumacher's *Tigerland*. Playing the rebel **243** recruit allowed Farrell to develop his 'bad boy' persona and in interviews at the time he also delighted in expletive-laden responses. After his role as the eponymous Lt Hart, alongside Bruce Willis, in *Hart's War*, Farrell extended his screen persona as the conventionally good detective in Steven Spielberg's *Minority Report*. Since then, he has moved into star billing in films such as *The Recruit* and Oliver Stone's *Alexander*. RB

FILMS: *Ordinary Decent Criminal, Tigerland* (2000); *American Outlaws* (2001); *Hart's War, Minority Report, Phone Booth* (2002); *S.W.A.T., The Recruit, Daredevil, Veronica Guerin* (2003); *A Home at the End of the World, Alexander* (2004).

FEHMIU, Bekim (1936–)

Noted Yugoslav actor often seen as a more romantic Jean-Paul Belmondo lookalike. He came to fame in Yugoslavia with the lead role in Aleksandar Petrović's Cannes-winner *Skupljaci perja/I Even Met Happy Gypsies* (1967). After playing Ulysses in the film and television mini-series *L'Odissea* (1968), he was cast in a number of Italian films throughout the 1970s. During that period, he came to the attention of Hollywood and subsequently appeared in supporting roles in a couple of routine action films. DI

FILMS: *Permission to Kill* (1975); *Black Sunday* (1977).

FELD, Fritz (1900–1993)

Versatile German film and television actor who played a succession of spies, chefs, butlers and gendarmes, but was probably best known for a gimmick in which he slapped his mouth with the palm of his hand, making a popping noise. Feld was an active member of various professional organisations, including the Academy of Motion Picture Arts and Sciences. FG

FILMS: *A Ship Comes In, Blindfold, The Last Command* (1928); *Broadway, Black Magic, One Hysterical Night* (1929); *The Wizard's Apprentice* (1930); *I Met Him in Paris, Expensive Husbands, Tovarich, True Confession, Lancer Spy* (1937); *Bringing up Baby, Out Where the Stars Begin, Romance in the Dark, Gold Diggers in Paris, The Affairs of Annabel, Campus Confessions, Artists and Models Abroad, I'll Give a Million, Swingtime in the Movies, Go Chase Yourself* (1938); *Idiot's Delight, When Tomorrow Comes, At the Circus, Quiet, Please, Little Accident, Everything Happens at Night* (1939); *Little Old New York, Millionaire Playboy, Ma, He's Making Eyes at Me, It's a Date, I Was an Adventuress, Sandy is a Lady* (1940); *Victory, You Belong to Me, Mexican Spitfire's Baby, World Permiere, Skylark* (1941); *Four Jacks and a Jill, Shut My Big Mouth, Sleepytime Gal, Iceland, Maisie Gets Her Man* (1942); *The Phantom of the Opera, Holy Matrimony, Henry Aldrich Swings It* (1943); *Passport to Destiny, Take it Big, Ever Since Venus, Knickerbocker Holiday* (1944); *The Great John L., George White's Scandals, Captain Tugboat Annie* (1945); *Catman of Paris, The Wife of Monte Cristo, Her Sister's Secret, Gentleman Joe Palooka, I've Always Loved You* (1946); *Cupid Goes Nuts, Fun on a Weekend, The Secret Life of Walter Mitty, Carnival in Costa Rica* (1947); *My Girl Tisa, The Noose Hangs High, Julia Misbehaves, Mexican Hayride, If You Knew Susie* (1948); *Trouble Makers, You Gotta Stay Happy, The Lovable Cheat* (1949); *Belle of Old Mexico, The Jackpot* (1950); *Rhythm Inn, Missing Women, Appointment with Danger, Kentucky Jubilee, My Favorite Spy, Sky High, Little Egypt, Journey into Light* (1951); *So You Want to Enjoy Life, Aaron Slick from Punkin Crick, O. Henry's Full House, Has Anybody Seen My Gal?* (1952); *So You Want to Be a Musician, Call Me Madam* (1953); *Crime Wave, The French Line, Paris Playboys, Casanova's Big Night, Riding Shotgun, Living it Up* (1954); *Jail Busters* (1955); *So You Want to Be Pretty* (1956); *Up in Smoke* (1957); *Juke Box Rhythm* (1959); *The Errand Boy, Pocketful of Miracles, The Ladies' Man* (1961); *Who's Minding the Store?, 4 for Texas, Promises! Promises!* (1963); *The Patsy* (1964); *Harlow* (1965); *Three on a Couch* (1966); *Caprice, Barefoot in the Park* (1967); *The Wicked Dreams of Paula Schultz* (1968); *Hello Dolly!* (1969); *The Computer Wore Tennis Shoes* (1970); *History of the World, Pt. 1* (1981).

FERNANDEL (Fernand Joseph Désiré Contandin) (1903–1971)

Fernandel began his entertainment career singing in music-hall revues, vaudeville and operettas in Marseilles. Trading on his distinctive horsey face and rubbery, wide-mouthed grin, he made his film debut playing a bell-hop in Robert Florey's *Le Blanc et le noir* (1930). He went on to become one of France's most famous and prolific actors of the era, starring in some 150 films over the next two decades.

Despite being a well-known figure abroad – his face was used by *Life* magazine to epitomise France – his American film career was limited. In 1956, he appeared in the Hollywood film *Around the World in Eighty Days* as David Niven's* French coachman. The producer, Mike Todd, badly wanted him to play Phileas Fogg's valet Passepartout, but Fernandel insisted that his English was not sufficiently good and that he would prefer a cameo part. However, Fernandel promised Todd that he would learn English for Todd's projected *Don Quixote*, although this was never made. In 1958, Fernandel appeared in *Paris Holiday*, a comedy produced by and starring Bob Hope about an American comedian who goes to Paris to purchase a film script. Fernandel's role consisted mainly of miming to Hope's wisecracking. Fernandel was never enthusiastic about working in the USA and he simply resumed his successful career in France. EE/VO

FILMS: *Around the World in Eighty Days* (1956); *Paris Holiday* (1958).

FIELD, Shirley Anne (Shirley Anne Broomfield) (1938–)

British actress who came to prominence opposite Albert Finney★ in *Saturday Night and Sunday Morning* (1960). Field worked briefly in Hollywood when she played the role of Ixchel, opposite Yul Brynner, in *Kings of the Sun*. MHu

FILMS: *Kings of the Sun* (1963); *The Good Doctor* (2000).

FIELDS, Gracie (Grace Stansfield) (1898–1979)

In 1935, Gracie Fields was rejected by MGM on the grounds that her appeal was 'too national'. As the singing star from Lancashire who had built up her singing and acting career in British films from music-hall performances, she was indeed an unlikely prospect for the USA, although she did have a minor uncredited part as a socialite in Gregory La Cava's *My Man Godfrey*. Two years later, Darryl F. Zanuck of Twentieth Century-Fox, was so impressed with her first international film, *We're Going to Be Rich*, that he signed her to a four-picture contract for a reported high sum of £200,000, which was equivalent to or more than the salary earned by the highest-paid actors in Hollywood. She travelled to the USA, attended receptions in New York and bought a house in Los Angeles.

During World War II, Fields toured in both Britain and the USA, singing in charity concerts. Her American commitments caused criticism in 1943 when she quit an ENSA fund-raising tour in Britain to honour a contractual agreement for a nationwide radio series and to make *Molly and Me* in the USA. Despite what might be regarded as an appeal that was indigenous to Britain, her *Variety Show* broadcasts and cabarets were a great success in the USA. She also completed a short for Fox in Hollywood to advertise war bonds. Her last film, *Paris – Underground*, about two women in the French Resistance, co-starred Constance Bennett. Although it was a success, she announced that she did not want to work in Hollywood any more and moved to her home in Capri, where she spent most of the rest of her life. SS

FILMS: *My Man Godfrey* (1936); *We're Going to be Rich, Keep Smiling* (1938); *Shipyard Sally* (1939); *Stage Door Canteen, Holy Matrimony* (1943); *Molly and Me, Paris – Underground* (1945).

FIENNES, Joseph (1970–)

Fiennes' lithe performance style and brooding, dark features received international acclaim following his leading role in the highly successful heritage drama, *Shakespeare in Love*. His intense and charismatic charm bears comparison with his older brother, Ralph Fiennes★, as does a decision to intersperse prominent Hollywood roles with other work in international co-productions. AP

FILMS: *Shakespeare in Love* (1998); *Enemy at the Gates* (2001); *Killing Me Softly* (2002); *Sinbad: Legend of the Seven Seas* [voice] (2003).

FIENNES, Ralph (Ralph Nathaniel Twisleton-Wykeham-Fiennes) (1962–)

Sardonic and aristocratic-looking British actor who is the elder brother of Joseph Fiennes★. After work for the RSC and National Theatre, Fiennes came to public attention with a television performance as Lawrence of Arabia. The blend of complex psychology and doomed heroism he brought to the part was incorporated in his first film role as Heathcliff in *Wuthering Heights*. The film was neither a critical nor a box-office success, but it did evoke a distinctly European and aristocratic screen image that was later developed in films by directors such as Steven Spielberg and Anthony Minghella. It also highlighted Fiennes' evident passionate romanticism, a trait that resonated off screen following his highly publicised break-up with his wife Alex Kingston★ and affair with Francesca Annis★, a woman seventeen-years his senior.

Fiennes' star persona seems brooding and introverted and his acting style attempts an intense interiority. His

Academy Award-nominated performance as the Nazi Amon Goeth in *Schindler's List* extended this range into overt depravity. Spielberg famously said that he had cast Fiennes because of his perceived aura of sexual evil. The part of Goeth was followed by three high-profile roles: in Robert Redford's *Quiz Show*, Kathryn Bigelow's *Strange Days* and, especially, as the wounded hero in Minghella's *The English Patient*. Fiennes' performance as John Steed in *The Avengers* was an opportunity to add dramatic comedy to this palette, but the film was unsuccessful and critics found Fiennes unconvincing. One called him 'a block of ice in Saville Row tailoring'. He followed this career-trough with another routine aristocrat role in *Onegin*. Fiennes also showcased his acting versatility by playing three separate roles in *Sunshine* (1999). His success in rehabilitating his credibility was marked by a leading part in *The End of the Affair* that allowed him to revisit his established persona of the doomed lover.

Fiennes dislikes the intrusiveness of fame and publicity and this accords well with his moody screen image. He continues to combine non-Hollywood productions, such as his leading role in David Cronenberg's *Spider* (2002), with mainstream projects like *Red Dragon*. He finally broke with conventional typecasting in *Maid in Manhattan* by successfully showing that he could handle romantic comedy, even though the part of the prim and proper scion of a wealthy New York family (opposite Jennifer Lopez's feisty blue-collar Cinderella) still retained many of the British upper-class connotations of his established star persona. TJ

FILMS: *Wuthering Heights* (1992); *Schindler's List* (1993); *Quiz Show* (1994); *Strange Days* (1995); *The English Patient* (1996); *Oscar and Lucinda* (1997); *The Avengers, The Prince of Egypt* [voice] (1998); *Onegin, The End of the Affair* (1999); *Red Dragon, Maid in Manhattan* (2002).

FINCH, Flora (1869–1940)

British actress who was one of the early stars of American silent cinema. Finch made her first film for D. W. Griffith and Biograph in 1908 and appeared in over 180 films until her retirement in 1939. She was best known for the series of shorts she made alongside John Bunny (aka 'Bunnygraphs') for Vitagraph between 1910 and 1915. MHu

FILMS: *The Helping Hand, Mrs Jones Entertains* (1908); *The Way of Man, Her First Biscuits, What Drink Did, Jones and the Lady Book Agent, A Sound Sleeper, Schneider's Anti-Noise Cru-*

Flora Finch: one of the most successful early stars of American silent cinema

sade, Jones and His New Neighbors, His Wife's Mother, Those Awful Hats, Mr Jones Has a Card Party (1909); *The Troublesome Baby, Uncle Tom's Cabin, Muggsy's First Sweetheart, All on Account of the Milk* (1910); *The Gossip, The Midnight Marauder, The Ventriloquist's Trunk, The Politician's Dream, Selecting His Heiress, Her Hero, Her Crowning Glory, Intrepid Davy, The Subduing of Mrs Nag, The Woes of a Wealthy Widow, Two Overcoats, The Derelict Reporter, The Wooing of Winnifred, Captain Barnacle's Courtship, The New Stenographer, The Misses Finch and Their Nephew Billy* (1911); *The Browns Have Visitors, Martha's Rebellion, Suing Susan, Freckles, Doctor Bridget, In the Flat Above, Lord Browning and Cinderella, Bunny All at Sea, Bachelor Buttons, A Vitagraph Romance, Bunny's Suicide, The Awakening of Jones, A Persistent Lover, The Foster Child, Her Old Sweetheart, The Troublesome Step-Daughters, The Church across the Way, Pseudo Sultan, Pandora's Box, Diamond Cut Diamond, Leap Year Proposals, Red Ink Tragedy, How He Papered the Room, The Jocular Winds of Fate, The Suit of Armor, The Old Silver Watch, The First Woman Jury in America, Irene's Infatuation, A Cure for Pokeritis, Bunny and the Twins, Umbrel-*

las to Mend, The First Violin, Stenographers Wanted (1912); *And His Wife Came Back, The Brown's Study Astrology, Bunny's Birthday Surprise, Bunny's Dilemma, The Classmates Frolic, Cupid's Hired Man, Fatty's Affair of Honor, The Feudists, The Fortune, A Gentleman of Fashion, The Girl at the Lunch Counter, The Golf Game and the Bonnet, He Answered an Ad, His Honor, the Mayor, Hubby Buys a Baby, Hubby's Toothache, The Locket, Love Laughs at Blacksmiths or Love Finds a Way, Love's Quarantine, A Millinery Bomb, One Good Joke Deserves Another, The Pickpocket, The Schemers, Stenographer Troubles, There's Music in the Hair, Those Troublesome Tresses, Three Black Bags, When Mary Grew Up, Which Way Did He Go?, The Wonderful Statue, Father's Hatband, The Autocrat of Flapjack Junction, John Tobin's Sweetheart, When Women Go on the Warpath, When the Press Speaks, No Sweets, Horatio Sparkins, Mr Bolter's Niece* (1913); *Bunny Backslides, Bunny Buys a Harem, Bunny Buys a Hat for His Bride, Bunny's Mistake, Bunny's Scheme, Bunny's Swell Affair, A Change in Baggage Checks, Father's Flirtation, Fixing Their Dads, Hearts and Diamonds, The Locked House, Mr Bunny in Disguise, The New Secretary, The Old Firehouse and the New Fire Chief, The Old Maid's Baby, Private Bunny, The Rocky Road to Love, Such a Hunter, Sweeney's Christmas Bird, Tangled Tangoists, The Vases of Hymen, How Cissy Made Good, Bunny's Little Brother, A Train of Incidents, Bunny's Birthday, Polishing Up, Love's Old Dream* (1914); *The Lady of Shalott, A Mistake in Typesetting, Two and Two, A Night Out, The Starring of Flora Finchurch* (1915); *The Brown Derby, Prudence the Pirate* (1916); *Flora in the Movies, Flora Joins the Chorus, Flora the Dressmaker, Flora the International Spy, Flora the Life-Saver, Flora the Manicure Girl, Flora the School Teacher, War Prides* (1917); *Boodle and Bandits, The Great Adventure* (1918); *Dawn, Oh Boy!* (1919); *Birthright, The She-Male Sleuth* (1920); *Lessons in Love, Orphans of the Storm* (1921); *Orphan Sally, Man Wanted, When Knighthood Was in Flower* (1922); *Luck* (1923); *Monsieur Beaucaire, Roulette* (1924); *Lover's Island, A Kiss for Cinderella, His Buddy's Wife, The Live Wire, The Wrongdoers, The Adventurous Sex, Men and Women, The Midnight Girl, The Early Bird* (1925); *Morning Judge, Oh, Baby!, The Brown Derby, Fifth Avenue* (1926); *Quality Street, Rose of the Golden West, The Cat and the Canary, Captain Salvation* (1927); *The Haunted House, Five and Ten Cent Annie, The Wife's Relations* (1928); *Come Across, The Faker* (1929); *Sweet Kitty Bellairs* (1930); *I Take this Woman* (1931); *The Scarlet Letter* (1934); *Way Out West* (1937); *The Women* (1939).

FINLAY, Frank (1926–)

British stage and television character actor who has only made occasional forays into cinema. Finlay had relatively minor roles in two films shot in the USA in the late 1960s: *The Shoes of the Fisherman* and *The Molly Maguires*. He also appeared in a number of US-backed productions shot in Europe. MHu

FILMS: *Private Potter, The Longest Day* (1962); *I'll Never Forget What's 'isname* (1967); *Inspector Clouseau, The Shoes of the Fisherman* (1968); *The Molly Maguires, Cromwell* (1970); *Gumshoe* (1971); *Sitting Target* (1972).

FINNEY, Albert (1936–)

British stage actor who rose to prominence in the leading role of *Saturday Night and Sunday Morning* (1960). Finney's well-built, roguish good looks were well suited to the part of the headstrong factory worker Arthur Seaton and his vigourous performance earned him a British Academy Award for Most Promising Newcomer. Finney was initially accepted for the title role in David Lean's *Lawrence of Arabia* (1962), but quit the film after only four days due to the extremely long shooting schedule. He concentrated instead on British theatre and film work and set up a stage and screen production company – Memorial Enterprises – with Michael Medwin in 1967, the same year he directed his only film to date, *Charlie Bubbles*.

Finney began to secure major Hollywood roles in the 1980s. He was a famous writer whose marriage is on the edge of a breakdown in Alan Parker's *Shoot the Moon* and a guilt-ridden, alcoholic ex-consul in John Huston's adaptation of Malcolm Lowry's *Under the Volcano*. His reluctance to take on big roles has been seen by some as a sign of discrimination, while others (such as Alan Parker) believe that Finney is a lazy actor, unwilling to stretch himself to the full.

Finney has certainly been reluctant to abandon the British stage and screen for Hollywood glamour, and while his choice of roles has not always been propitious, it has often been interesting. He has tended to specialise in characters whose repressed tensions are on the verge of bubbling up, but he has varied his parts and appeared in a number of different genres, such as John Huston's musical, *Annie*, and the Coen brothers' noir pastiche, *Miller's Crossing*. In Steven Soderbergh's acclaimed *Erin Brockovich*, Finney's role of the **247** grouchy attorney opposite Julia Roberts earned him an Academy Award nomination as Best Supporting Actor. JS

FILMS: *Tom Jones, The Victors* (1963); *Night Must Fall* (1964); *Two for the Road* (1967); *Charlie Bubbles* (1968); *The Picasso Summer* (1969); *Scrooge* (1970); *Gumshoe* (1971); *The Adventure of Sherlock Holmes' Smarter Brother* (1975); *Looker, Wolfen* (1981); *Shoot the Moon, Annie* (1982); *Under the Volcano* (1984); *Orphans* (1987); *Miller's Crossing* (1990); *The Playboys, Rich in Love* (1993); *The Browning Version* (1994); *The Run of the Country* (1995); *Washington Square* (1997); *Breakfast of Champions, Simpatico* (1999); *Erin Brockovich, Traffic* (2000); *Hemingway, the Hunter of Death, Delivering Milo* (2002); *Big Fish* (2003); *Ocean's Twelve* (2004).

FIRTH, Colin (1960–)

Tall, good-looking romantic lead who can also appear in comedy. Firth trained with the RSC and appeared in numerous theatre and television productions before attracting attention as Mr Darcy in the BBC's *Pride and Prejudice* in 1995. Firth has achieved success through variations on the type of the repressed Englishman, unable to show his true feelings, including – against Hugh Grant★ – in the *Bridget Jones* films. AS

FILMS: *Femme Fatale* (1991); *The English Patient* (1996); *A Thousand Acres* (1997); *Shakespeare in Love* (1998); *Bridget Jones's Diary* (2001); *Hope Springs, What a Girl Wants* (2003); *Bridget Jones: The Edge of Reason* (2004).

FIRTH, Peter (1953–)

British actor who came to notice in the stage production of *Equus* and received an Academy Award nomination for Best Supporting Actor when he reprised his role as Alan Strang in the 1977 film version opposite Richard Burton★. Firth principally works in television but makes the occasional film appearance in roles such as Captain Mervyn Bennion in *Pearl Harbor*. MHu

FILMS: *Equus* (1977); *When You Comin' Back, Red Ryder?* (1979); *A State of Emergency* (1986); *The Hunt for Red October, The Rescuers Down Under* [voice] (1990); *Amistad* (1997); *Mighty Joe Young* (1998); *Chill Factor* (1999); *Pearl Harbor* (2001).

FITZGERALD, Barry (William Joseph Shields) (1888–1966)

Irish supporting actor with a long and successful career in American cinema. Fitzgerald came to the USA with the

Barry Fitzgerald, a leading figure in Hollywood's Irish colony

Abbey Theatre and frequently worked on Broadway before moving to Los Angeles, where his small stature and roguish features ruled out a career as a romantic lead in Hollywood. He concentrated instead on playing Irish-Catholic priests and wily rogues – the latter being a staple of the Irish theatrical and filmic repertoire. He starred as such with his brother Arthur Shields★ in John Ford's *The Quiet Man*. Fitzgerald was a leading figure in Hollywood's Irish colony during the classical period. He won a Best Supporting Actor Academy Award in 1944 for *Going My Way*. In an Academy first, he was also nominated for the Best Actor title for the same role. RB

FILMS: *The Plough and the Stars* (1936); *Ebb Tide* (1937); *Bringing up Baby, Four Men and a Prayer, Marie Antoinette, The Dawn Patrol* (1938); *Full Confession, Pacific Liner, The Saint Strikes Back* (1939); *The Long Voyage Home* (1940); *The Sea Wolf, San Francisco Docks, How Green Was My Valley, Tarzan's Secret Treasure* (1941); *Two Tickets to London, The Amazing Mrs Holliday, Corvettte K-225* (1943); *Going My Way, None but the Lonely Heart, I Love a Soldier* (1944); *And Then There Were None, Incendiary Blonde, Stork Club, Duffy's Tavern* (1945); *Two Years before the Mast* (1946); *California, Welcome Stranger, Variety Girl, Easy Come, Easy Go* (1947); *The Naked*

City, Miss Tatlock's Millions, The Sainted Sisters (1948); *Top o' the Morning, The Story of Seabiscuit* (1949); *Union Station* (1950); *Silver City* (1951); *The Quiet Man* (1952); *The Catered Affair* (1956).

FITZGERALD, Geraldine (1914–)

Irish actress who made her Hollywood name in a series of strong female roles, notably as Isabella Linton in *Wuthering Heights* and as Bette Davis' devoted friend in *Dark Victory*. Her parts diminished after losing a fight with Warner Bros. over the contract system. RB

FILMS: *Wuthering Heights, Dark Victory* (1939); *A Child is Born, 'Til We Meet Again, Flight from Destiny* (1940); *Shining Victory* (1941); *The Gay Sisters* (1942); *Watch on the Rhine* (1943); *Ladies Courageous, Wilson* (1944); *The Strange Affair of Uncle Harry* (1945); *Three Strangers, O.S.S., Nobody Lives Forever* (1946); *So Evil My Love, Ten North Frederick* (1948); *The Fiercest Heart* (1961); *The Pawnbroker* (1964); *Rachel, Rachel* (1968); *The Last American Hero* (1973); *Harry and Tonto* (1974); *Echoes of a Summer* (1976); *Lovespell* (1979); *Diary of the Dead* (1980); *Arthur* (1981); *Blood Link* (1982); *Easy Money* (1983); *Poltergeist II: The Other Side, Arthur 2: On the Rocks* (1988).

FLETCHER, Bramwell (1904–1988)

Blond, second lead English actor who, after making his last film in 1943, worked in American television and theatre. TJ

FILMS: *So This is London, Raffles* (1930); *The Millionaire, Daughter of the Dragon, Once a Lady, Svengali* (1931); *Silent Witness, A Bill of Divorcement, The Face on the Barroom Floor, The Mummy, The Monkey's Paw* (1932); *Only Yesterday, The Right to Romance* (1933); *Nana* (1934); *Random Harvest, White Cargo, The Undying Monster* (1942); *Immortal Sergeant* (1943).

FORBES, Bryan (John Theobald Clarke) (1926–)

Forbes has become better known as a screenwriter, director and producer, but he enjoyed a fruitful career as a supporting actor in British films of the 1950s. His American screen appearances, in roles such as William Cleggett in *The World in His Arms*, have been rare. He is best remembered as the director of *The Stepford Wives* (1975). MHu

FILMS: *Flesh and Fury, The World in His Arms* (1952); *Sea Devils* (1953); *The Key* (1958); *The Guns of Navarone* (1961); *A Shot in the Dark, Of Human Bondage* (1964); *International Velvet* (1978).

FORBES, Mary (1883–1974)

English stage actress whose screen career only began in her thirties with a small number of UK film appearances. During a long Hollywood career, in generally minor roles, Forbes played a variety of maternal characters and aristocratic dowagers. She was James Stewart's mother, for example, in the Academy Award-winning *You Can't Take it with You*. JS/AP

FILMS: *Sunny Side Up, The Trespasser, The Thirteenth Chair, Her Private Life* (1929); *So this is London, Holiday, Abraham Lincoln, East is West, Devil to Pay!, Strictly Unconventional* (1930); *The Man Who Came Back, Born to Love, Chances, The Brat, Working Girls* (1931); *Stepping Sisters, Silent Witness, Vanity Fair, A Farewell to Arms* (1932); *Cavalcade, Bombshell* (1933); *You Can't Buy Everything, Carolina, Sadie McKee, Born to Be Bad, The Most Precious Thing in Life, Now I'll Tell You, Shock, Blind Date, British Agent, A Lost Lady, Two Heads on a Pillow, Happiness Ahead, We Live Again, Transatlantic Merry-Go-Round, The Painted Veil* (1934); *Roberta, McFadden's Flats, Laddie, Les Misérables, Dizzy Dames, Stranded, Anna Karenina, Rendezvous, The Widow from Monte Carlo, The Perfect Gentleman, Captain Blood* (1935); *The White Angel, Theodora Goes Wild* (1936); *Women of Glamour, Another Dawn, Wee Willie Winkie, The Life of the Party, One Hundred Men and a Girl, Stage Door, The Awful Truth* (1937); *Everybody Sing, Outside of Paradise, The Rage of Paris, Always Goodbye, Three Loves Has Nancy, Just around the Corner, You Can't Take it with You* (1938); *Risky Business, You Can't Cheat an Honest Man, Fast and Loose, Three Smart Girls Grow Up, Outside These Walls, The Sun Never Sets, Should Husbands Work?, I Stole a Million, These Glamour Girls, Espionage Agent, Hollywood Cavalcade, Ninotchka, The Adventures of Sherlock Holmes* (1939); *Laddie, All This and Heaven Too, Private Affairs, A Girl from Avenue A, Florian, South of Suez* (1940); *Back Street, When Ladies Meet, Nothing but the Truth, Paris Calling* (1941); *Klondike Fury, We Were Dancing, Twin Beds, This Above All, Almost Married, The Great Impersonation* (1942); *Sherlock Holmes in Washington, Two Tickets to London, Mr Lucky, Dangerous Blondes, Flesh and Fantasy, Women in Bondage, What a Woman!, Tender Comrade* (1943); *Ladies Courageous, Jane Eyre* (1944); *A Guy, a Gal and a Pal, I'll Remember April, Earl Carroll Vanities, That's the Spirit, Guest Wife, Lady on a Train, That Night with You, The Picture of Dorian Gray* (1945); *One Way to Love, Terror by Night, The* **249**

Kid from Brooklyn, A Stolen Life (1946); *Cigarette Girl, Ivy, The Secret Life of Walter Mitty, Down to Earth, The Exile, It Had to Be You, Song of Love, The Other Love* (1947); *The Black Arrow, You Gotta Stay Happy* (1948); *The Judge Steps Out* (1949); *Les Misérables* (1952); *Houseboat* (1958).

FORBES, Ralph (Ralph Taylor) (1902–1951)

London-born actor who became a ubiquitous face in American films from 1926 when he played one of the Geste brothers in *Beau Geste*. He continued as a supporting actor until the early 1940s, often in upper-class or royal roles such as Sir Hugo Baskerville in *The Hound of the Baskervilles* and Henry Tudor in *Tower of London*. MW

FILMS: *Blackboard and Blackmail* (1917); *Beau Geste* (1926); *Mr Wu, The Enemy* (1927); *The Trail of '98, The Latest from Paris, The Masks of the Devil, Under the Black Eagle, Restless Youth, The Whip, The Actress* (1928); *Inside the Lines, The Green Goddess, Lilies of the Field, The Lady of Scandal, Mamba, Her Wedding Night* (1930); *The Bachelor Father, Beau Ideal* (1931); *Smilin' Through, Thunder Below* (1932); *Christopher Strong, Pleasure Cruise, The Solitaire Man, The Phantom Broadcast, The Avenger* (1933); *The Fountain, Bombay Mail, Twentieth Century, Shock, The Barretts of Wimpole Street, Outcast Lady, Riptide, The Mystery of Mr X* (1934); *Streamline Express, Age of Indiscretion, Strange Wives, Enchanted April, The Goose and the Gander, Rescue Squad, La Fiesta de Santa Barbara, The Three Musketeers* (1935); *Piccadilly Jim, Daniel Boone, Love Letters of a Star, Mary of Scotland, Romeo and Juliet, I'll Name the Murderer* (1936); *Stage Door, Woman against the World, The Legion of Missing Men, Rich Relations, Make a Wish, The Thirteenth Chair, The Last of Mrs Cheyney* (1937); *Convicts at Large, If I Were King, Kidnapped, Women are Like That, Annabel Takes a Tour* (1938); *Tower of London, The Private Lives of Elizabeth and Essex, The Magnificent Fraud, The Hound of the Baskervilles* (1939); *Calling Philo Vance, Curtain Call, Adventure in Diamonds* (1940); *Frenchman's Creek* (1944).

FORBES-ROBERTSON, Johnston (1853–1937)

The most celebrated Hamlet of his generation made a silent version of his legendary performance in Britain in 1913. He subsequently reprised his second most popular role, the saintly stranger in Jerome K. Jerome's *The Passing of the Third Floor Back*, for First National. JB

250 FILM: *The Passing of the Third Floor Back* (1918).

FORQUET, Philippe (1940–)

French actor mainly cast in supporting parts in French and European co-productions. He is best remembered for his role as the eccentric artist Henri Bonnet in Henry Koster's comedy *Take Her, She's Mine*. Despite being nominated for a Golden Laurel Award for Best Male Newcomer in 1964, further success in Hollywood eluded him. TH

FILMS: *In the French Style* (1962); *Take Her, She's Mine* (1963).

FORSTER, Rudolf (1884–1968)

Tall, slim Austrian player of complex criminals and sneering aristocrats who enjoyed a fifty-year career in German film. Politically left-leaning, Forster came to the USA in 1937 and then disgusted the émigré community by returning to Nazi Germany in 1940 after work on Broadway dried up and just a single Hollywood B-movie role – playing an Oriental baron – proved forthcoming. Forster's only subsequent Hollywood movie appearance came in 1963 when he received a bit part in Otto Preminger's *The Cardinal*, filmed in Austria. RJK

FILMS: *Island of Lost Men* (1939); *The Cardinal* (1963).

FOSSEY, Brigitte (1946–)

Former child star who was one of the young protagonists in René Clément's war classic *Jeux interdits/Forbidden Games* (1952). On the back of this, with good English from having spent her formative years in England, Fossey starred in Gene Kelly's *The Happy Road* in 1957. A break followed while she grew up and after studying at the Actor's Studio in 1966, she pursued a long career in European film and television. VO

FILMS: *The Happy Road* (1957); *Quintet* (1979).

FOX, James (1939–)

James Fox began his career as a child actor and became well known for playing refined characters prone to weakness or decadence. His role as the aristocrat who becomes prey to the whims of his butler in Joseph Losey's *The Servant* (1963) typifies this screen persona. He had similar roles in Hollywood films like *King Rat* and Arthur Penn's *The Chase*, as well as the musical comedy *Thoroughly Modern Millie*, alongside Julie Andrews★.

Fox reached a crisis after playing a gangster in Nic Roeg's psychedelic underworld film, *Performance*.

Rumoured to have been greatly disturbed by the film, he deserted the profession in 1973 and joined a Christian missionary group. He returned to acting in the 1980s and has since maintained a prolific career. Fox's latter roles have tended to exploit his earlier screen image, whether this has meant appearances in big-budget thrillers such as *Patriot Games* or historical dramas such as *Anna Karenina*. JS

FILMS: *Timbuktu* (1959); *Those Magnificent Men in Their Flying Machines, or How I Flew from London to Paris in 25 Hours, 11 Minutes, King Rat* (1965); *The Chase* (1966); *Thoroughly Modern Millie* (1967); *Duffy, Isadora* (1968); *Performance* (1970); *No Longer Alone* (1978); *Greystoke: The Legend of Tarzan, Lord of the Apes, A Passage to India* (1984); *The Mighty Quinn* (1988); *Farewell to the King* (1989); *The Russia House* (1990); *Patriot Games* (1992); *The Remains of the Day* (1993); *Anna Karenina* (1997); *Shadow Run* (1998); *Mickey Blue Eyes* (1999); *Up at the Villa, The Golden Bowl* (2000); *The Mystic Masseur* (2001); *The Prince and Me* (2004).

FRANCE

The history of migration by French actors to Hollywood may be characterised in terms of a steady flux, rather than a succession of dense and significant waves. Since France, unlike Italy for example, has never been a great source of migrants to the USA, a set of oppositional myths has endured between the two countries ensuring that most transatlantic journeys undertaken by French actors have been seen in terms of an ongoing struggle between cultural adaptation and the necessary recognition of irreconcilable difference. With the rare exception of names such as Charles Boyer★, few performers have stayed for unlimited periods of time.

There are numerous reasons for this. First, there are the obvious and marked limitations of the spoken language, ensuring that French actors with a French accent could rarely become 'American' in the full sense of the world. Many arrived in Los Angeles to find their contracts stipulated daily English lessons and the assistance of an on-set interpreter. Language difference mattered when it came to the tone, pitch and rhythm of the spoken word, but it also concerned gesture, to the extent that body language and differentials in eye contact could also become coded as foreign and thus prone to the limitations of cultural stereotyping. The majority of French actors who have achieved some degree of success within the Hollywood system have largely done so by maintaining their cultural identities, albeit with some distinctive curtailing of their expressive personas.

For keen commercial reasons, Hollywood has sought to control French representation within English-language cinema, with numerous repercussions for the employment of French actors. The specificities of the spoken French language (frequently incorporated within scripts to limited degrees) repeatedly signified, for example, a telling blend of naughty sexual feeling, spectacular élan, luxurious sophistication and dangerous cosmopolitanism. This uneasy relationship between internationalised American mass pleasure and traditional elite European culture also became played out in the studios' representation of Paris, with hosts of French actors such as Maurice Marsac★, Louis Mercier★, Jacques Lory★ and Georges Renavent★ being employed to play a standardised repertoire of character roles as croupiers, stage performers, waiters, gendarmes, taxi drivers and such like. People such as Maurice Cannon★, Alphonse Martell and Robert Florey (who published several books on Hollywood in France) were appointed as 'technical advisers' on productions with a French theme, while the French writer Valentin Mandelstamm was carefully used by several studios to vet properties that might offend French sensitivities. The Séeburger brothers were famously employed by the International Kinema Research agency in Los Angeles between 1923 and 1931 to provide the documentary evidence necessary to mythologise the French capital à la Hollywood.

Central to French discourse about the American film industry has been the trepidation about the different modus operandi of the vertically integrated studio system and all that entails concerning differentiated working practices and sensitivities when it comes to the employment of overseas actors used to a more artisanal and communal model of production, with a higher degree of individual agency. French actors had to accustom themselves to altered norms concerning the relationship between script, *mise en scène* (especially framing) and editing (especially shot duration). Françoise Rosay★, among others, complained bitterly about the dependency on multi-layered personnel, the alienating factory-like approach to filming and the reliance on preview screenings to the success or failure of particular actors within Americanised narratives.

This, and the absence of large French émigré communities in other spheres of American life, points to per- **251**

Gérard Depardieu and Andie MacDowell in *Green Card* (1990)

companies such as Pathé, Éclair and Gaumont/Solax established production facilities in New York and Fort Lee between 1910 and 1912, but a growing preference for more naturalistic, native performance styles meant few émigré French performers were actually employed. French actors who did enjoy some American success during the 1910s were frequently indebted to the enormous success of Bernhardt's imported films and theatrical tours. Léon Bary★, for example, became contracted to Pathé-Exchange when he returned to the USA in 1915 and appeared in several of the company's serials. Gaston Glass★ worked on dozens of Hollywood features during the 1920s after appearing in the actress's final American tour between 1917 and 1918.

Morality and economics also provided limitations for the French émigré actor. Performers were often associated with an unwelcome licentiousness by American audiences due to their part in perceived vulgar comedies and sensational crime dramas. With political factors playing a weakened motivational role, it was only when there was a slowdown in the French film industry that actors such as Max Linder★ took their chances in the USA. Linder's first visit was initiated by the depletion of financial and material resources within France during World War I, but unlike that of his friend Charlie Chaplin★, his career in Chicago (with Essanay) and in Los Angeles was relatively short and unsuccessful.

The 1920s saw American film companies consolidate their dominant position in European territories and a number of French actors moved to Los Angeles with varying degrees of success. This was usually determined by gender. Actresses such as Paulette Duval★, Jetta Goudal★ and Louise Lagrange★ were required to play roles that emphasised their exoticism and dangerously 'other' sexuality. For a brief spell, Renée Adorée★ was a major star, appearing opposite John Gilbert and Ramon Novarro. With the exception of the athletic Charles de Rochefort★ – known to American audiences as the 'French Adonis' – few French male actors were recruited, since their presence appeared to trouble emerging emphatically North American norms of screen masculinity.

Having said this, American studios never lost sight of the revenue potential of screening representations of the French back to themselves, and, in turn, the rest of Europe. In March 1928, the MPPDA established an office in Paris

haps the central reason for the short duration of so many French actors' visits: the cultural and economic strength of native performance traditions, especially concerning the sophisticated dialogue between live, broadcast and recorded performing arts in France. The centralisation of venues and critical organs within Paris has led to a sense in which French audiences treasure the patrimonial value of their leading acting talents to an unusual degree. Simply put, since many French actors play such a prominent role in everyday national life, there has often been as much of an incentive to stay (or return) as leave.

Ironically, it was the temporary presence of touring French theatre and vaudeville players such as Sarah Bernhardt★, Pilar-Morin★ and Séverin – rather than the significant French dominance over the early international film industry – that established a short-lived appetite among American audiences for French screen actors in the
early years of the twentieth century. French production

against the backdrop of French government unease about the hegemonic position of Hollywood. With the advent of sound and the sudden erection of language barriers, compounded by the demand from European audiences for films in their native tongue, Hollywood was forced to construct new strategies with regard to the manufacture and marketing of international stars – now the key symbol of Hollywood's glamour both at home and abroad. Central to the new but still limited integration of French actors within the American production system was the evolution of the multi-language film version, in which numerous, linguistically different but otherwise usually near-identical versions of the same film were shot on the same set, usually one after the other. French performers such as Marcel André, André Berley, André Burgère, Huguette Duflos, Pierre Etchepare, Mona Goya, Jeanne Helbling, Georges Mauloy, Danièle Perola, Yvonne Valée and Geymond Vital worked solely on French-language multi-language versions shot in Hollywood between 1930 and 1932. These films were blocked identically, but censorship restrictions were sometimes eased regarding sexual content for non-English-language audiences. The actors made the six-day transatlantic crossing and arrived on the West Coast, where they swiftly became integrated within Hollywood's French colony nominally headed by Françoise Rosay and her Belgian husband, the director Jacques Feyder, who regularly held Sunday parties in their Beverly Hills mansion.

The success of Maurice Chevalier★ was a vital component of Paramount's international strategy during this time, not least for his ability to temporarily transcend any language problems with the vocal appeal of his musical talents. The studio initiated a highly successful dual publicity strategy that simultaneously guarded his contact with European audiences and promoted an exportable model of 'Frenchness' to the American public. Although it took longer to develop, this notion of dual audience appeal also mattered with the cultivation of Charles Boyer's hugely profitable French-lover persona. In a reversal of the previous decade's picture, few French actresses were able to match the global acclaim of these two actors. Some, like Mireille Balin★, who signed a seven-year contract with MGM after the international success of *Pépé le Moko* (1937), never even made the trip, because of the paucity of strong roles, while others such as Annabella★ were recruited to play a disappointing succession of typecast French female parts.

Hollywood's relationship with France altered with the onset of World War II; both in terms of the recruitment of French actors and the corresponding provision of French image on American screens. Although it took some time for a break in representation to occur, with the US government initially maintaining diplomatic relations with the new Vichy government, by 1941 Hollywood was engaged in the production of a series of melodramatic propaganda features such as *Tonight We Raid Calais* (1943), produced by the émigré producer André Daven★, which served to mythologise the heroism of the French against the German occupation and diminish the stigma of collaboration. Michèle Morgan★, one of several leading French émigré film actors who signed with the American studios, moved to Los Angeles in 1940 and appeared in films such as *Joan of Paris* (1941), where she played an ordinary French waitress protecting an RAF pilot in occupied France. For several actors like Marcel Dalio★ and Jean-Pierre Aumont★, emigration was a forced necessity due to their Jewish origins. Like all French exiles, they were forced to engage in the construction of an image of a conflict they had no first-hand knowledge of, though after appearing in *Assignment in Brittany* and *The Cross of Lorraine* (both 1943), Aumont did in fact leave the USA to join the Free French forces the same year.

A central element of Hollywood wartime effort was the co-ordinating role played by Charles Boyer's French Research Foundation (FRF), which had originally been constituted to inform Americans about France's glorious cultural patrimony, but now worked assiduously to provide positive and accurate information about the nation's contemporary plight. It also assisted in the migration of several French film personnel such as Jean Renoir and Jean Gabin★. Boyer and his French compatriots met frequently at Preston Sturges' restaurant on Sunset Boulevard – aptly named 'The Players'.

The end of the war saw a turn away from the USA on the part of many French actors, with French cultural discourse emphasising the recuperation of authentic national values after the equivocal experiences of occupation and exile. The French film press was now less keen to exaggerate the prestigious allure of a Hollywood contract and some harshly criticised the decisions made during wartime on the part of the French acting community. Nonetheless, the American studios continued their practice of employing European talent scouts, and new faces such as Cécile **253**

Aubry★ and Corinne Calvet★ were recruited by Darryl F. Zanuck for Twentieth Century-Fox and Hal B. Wallis for Paramount respectively, albeit with conventionally limiting results (David O. Selznick's recruitment of Louis Jourdan★ in 1947 was more successful).

The recovery of the European film industry and enhanced investment on the part of American studios in European co-productions or 'runaway productions' shot in Europe coincided with the emergence of powerful new French stars such as Alain Delon★, who was regularly courted from the late 1950s onwards by a Hollywood anxious to find the European equivalent to emerging box-office draws like James Dean. The now staid image of the French lover or the exotic French seductress was beginning to fade. This shift in representation was consolidated by the international appeal of the French New Wave. The vibrant portrayal of a modern and youthful French identity, spearheaded by names such as Jeanne Moreau★ and Gérard Blain★, created a sense that Hollywood was lagging behind in the ways that it employed French actors. To illustrate this crucial separateness in perception, one only has to compare the caricatural tone of Louis Jourdan's romantically warmhearted narration in Hollywood's comedy about Parisian prostitution, *Irma La Douce* (1963), with the complex articulation of Franco-American cinematic identities provided by Jean-Luc Godard's *Le Mépris* (starring Brigitte Bardot★), released the same year.

This appearance of France's leading popular female star in an auteur production points to the divergent but also overlapping directions that Hollywood's recruitment of French actors has moved in since the 1960s. Contemporary French cinema is marked by its diversity, with several performers such as Isabelle Huppert★ and Gérard Depardieu★ appearing regularly in both mainstream and auteur-led projects at home. This has had the ensuing result that work in American-funded English-language productions – be they shot in the USA or in Europe – has often appeared to be a secondary, temporary opportunity. Juliette Binoche★ and Julie Delpy★ have proved to be the exceptions, their international careers being maintained by a combination of excellent spoken English and a determination to resist cultural stereotyping.

The matter of stereotyping relates to a peculiar combination of genre and gender, and the generally limited opportunities for French actors to project an appeal equivalent to the way their domestic star personae have been harnessed by the French film industry. While successful French émigrés such as Boyer, Chevalier and to a lesser extent Jourdan were able to rework their European-ness into new configurations through melodrama, sophisticated light comedy and the musical, Hollywood tended to 'feminise' their star personae in relation to the dominant virility of the conventional American male. Thus, Hollywood never found a suitable way of transposing Gabin's taciturn proletarian identity or Delon's combination of startling handsomeness and minimalist performance style. But American cinema has had a particular problem in accommodating strong French female performers. Many 'failed' French actresses such as Micheline Presle★ were defeated on two fronts: they were expected to be the same as before and they were also not given enough opportunities to be different. They were cast in a succession of stereotypical female roles, such as actresses, dancers, singers and prostitutes – roles that echoed the unstable nature of their off-screen identities as Europeans in an American setting. Hollywood never gave French actresses the more complex roles they occupied in their national cinema, especially in auteur films (and we will never know what Hollywood would have made of the one truly major popular female star, Brigitte Bardot, since she refused to make the journey to LA).

The strength of French national mythologies has also played a role in curtailing assimilation. American cinema has frequently used France – especially Paris – as the paradigmatic site for the depiction of Continental otherness. Images of fine cuisine, sophisticated fashion as well as the convivial decadence of metropolitan bohemia have been employed to represent a world apart from the virtuous ideology of democratic egalitarianism projected by Hollywood. This has, inevitably, had repercussions in the treatment of class, with French performers being required to become associated with the antithesis of authentically American hard work and naturalness – a divide epitomised by Gérard Depardieu's role in *Green Card* (1990). Hollywood has thus chosen French actors to project back to its domestic audiences the success of American cultural and social assimilation, through a simultaneous emphasis on cultural difference. While this pattern echoes other European trajectories examined in this book, the employment of French actors is particularly ironic because of the privileged place France – and Paris – have occupied within Hollywood representations. AP

FRANCEN, Victor (Victor Franssen) (1888–1977)

The most successful Belgian actor in classical Hollywood, Victor Francen began his acting career on the Brussels stage before leaving for Paris. Although he altered his surname slightly (from Franssen) to make it look more French, Francen never disowned his origins and he often toured his native country. In his French filmography, he remained loyal to directors such as Marcel L'Herbier and Abel Gance – his most remarkable performance was in Gance's *J'accuse/ That They May Live* (1937), which was also shot in English – but he also successfully collaborated with Julien Duvivier, notably as the memorable ageing actor in *La Fin du jour/ The End of a Day* (1939). In both his French and American films, the blond, blue-eyed Francen typically embodied bearded characters who were dignified, gentle and soft-spoken. His performance style was glacially tortured and distant, and he often played distinguished cuckolded husbands opposite younger rivals.

In the USA, Francen began a second career that was both critically well received and extremely varied. This new departure was facilitated by his third wife, the American Elisabeth Kreutzer. Before being put under contract, Francen was a member of the 'stock company' at Warner Bros. and he also worked for Paramount, RKO and Twentieth Century-Fox. His Hollywood debut was *Hold Back the Dawn*, in which he briefly appeared opposite Charles Boyer★. The latter introduced Francen to the French expatriate community in Hollywood to thank him for once helping him in Paris. In Duvivier's American episode film, *Tales of Manhattan*, Francen's enthusiastic parody of Toscanini anticipated one of his most famous parts, as pianist Ingram in *The Beast with Five Fingers*. *The Mask of Dimitrios*, directed by another émigré, Jean Negulesco, epitomised the diversity of Francen's performance style. In it, he played an elderly music-lover who dazzles Peter Lorre★ with his verbal wit and aura of French high culture but later, in flashback, is revealed to be an accomplished crook.

Francen's later films were impressively eclectic. They included war propaganda, spy thrillers, melodramas and musicals. Using various accents, he often played ambiguous characters emblematic of Hollywood's idea of *Mittel Europa*. He played a Belgian character only once, as a boarding-house landlord in *Devotion*. In *Hollywood Canteen*, an entertainment vehicle in which stars played themselves, Francen

Victor Francen: Belgium's star émigré actor

obtained the same billing as Bette Davis and John Garfield, demonstrating his successful integration into the Hollywood star system of the day.

When Francen sought work with other studios, in Europe or the USA, he discovered that his Warner Bros. typecasting was hard to shake off. After his return to Europe, he remained an active presence in American productions with a strong European slant, demonstrating a remarkable longevity. Examples include *To the Victor* (shot in France) and *Fanny*, a remake of the Marcel Pagnol French classic also starring Boyer and Maurice Chevalier★. DN

FILMS: *Hold Back the Dawn* (1941); *The Tuttles of Tahiti, Ten Gentlemen from West Point, Tales of Manhattan* (1942); *The Desert Song, Madame Curie, Mission to Moscow* (1943); *Hollywood Canteen, The Conspirators, The Mask of Dimitrios, Passage to Marseille, In Our Time* (1944); *Confidential Agent, San Antonio* (1945); *The Beast with Five Fingers, The Beginning or the End, Devotion, Night and Day* (1946); *To the Victor* (1948); *Adventures of Captain Fabian* (1951); *Hell and High Water* (1954); *Bedevilled* (1955); *A Farewell to Arms* (1957); *Fanny* (1961).

FRANÇOIS, Jacques (1920–)

François made his debut in the USA, where he was put under contract with MGM. He played a French playwright in the musical *The Barkleys of Broadway* opposite Ginger Rogers and Fred Astaire. He subsequently became a popular romantic lead on stage and in film in France. VO

FILMS: *The Barkleys of Broadway* (1949); *Sorcerer* (1977); *Man, Woman and Child* (1983); *Until September* (1984).

FRANKLIN, Pamela (1950–)

English actress who can perhaps uniquely count tigers, dolphins, Marlon Brando and Orson Welles among her eclectic American co-stars. Franklin's sporadic Hollywood appearances map a rare transition from juvenile leads to adult roles. MF

FILMS: *The Innocents* (1961); *A Tiger Walks, Flipper's New Adventure* (1964); *The Night of the Following Day* (1968); *Sinful Davey, The Prime of Miss Jean Brodie* (1969); *Necromancy* (1972); *Ace Eli and Rodger of the Skies* (1973); *The Food of the Gods* (1976).

FRASER, Richard (1913–1971)

Scottish actor who moved to Hollywood in 1941. As well as leading roles in various B-films, he played supporting parts in a number of 1940s films such as Davy Morgan in *How Green Was My Valley* and James Vane in *The Picture of Dorian Gray*. MHu

FILMS: *How Green Was My Valley, A Yank in the RAF, Man Hunt* (1941); *Desperate Journey, Eagle Squadron, Edge of Darkness, The Gorilla Man, Busses Roar, Joan of Paris* (1942); *Truck Busters, Thumbs Up* (1943); *Ladies Courageous* (1944); *The Tiger Woman, Shadow of Terror, Scotland Yard Investigator, The Fatal Witness, White Pongo, The Picture of Dorian Gray* (1945); *Bedlam, Blonde for a Day, The Undercover Woman* (1946); *The Lone Wolf in London, Blackmail, The Private Affairs of Bel Ami* (1947); *Rogues' Regiment, The Cobra Strikes* (1948); *Alaska Patrol* (1949).

FREY, Arno (1900-1961)

Ambitious Munich-born actor who journeyed to late 1920s Hollywood under his own steam. Frey's heavy accent and severe looks led him to be cast exclusively in uncredited bit parts as leering Teutonic henchmen or supercilious waiters. He was only given more substantial roles as lip-smacking Nazi villains in budget-conscious wartime serials and in the poverty-row production company PRC titles **256** such as *Tiger Fangs*. RJK

FILMS: *The Awakening* (1928); *Best of Enemies* (1933); *Hell in the Heavens* (1934); *Mystery Woman, Rendezvous* (1935); *Human Cargo, Fifteen Maiden Lane* (1936); *Charlie Chan at the Olympics, Thin Ice, Lancer Spy* (1937); *The Great Waltz* (1938); *Midnight, Boy Friend, Espionage Agent, Hollywood Cavalcade, Pack up Your Troubles* (1939); *The Fighting 69th, British Intelligence, Escape to Glory, Earthbound, Four Sons, The Man I Married, Arizona Gangbusters, Yesterday's Heroes, Escape* (1940); *The Great American Broadcast, Man Hunt, Underground, Moon over Miami, Sergeant York, We Go Fast, Two-Faced Woman, H.M. Pulham, Esq., Paris Calling* (1941); *Texas Man Hunt, Right to the Heart, My Favorite Blonde, The Wife Takes a Flyer, Pacific Rendezvous, Spy Ship, Jungle Siren, Berlin Correspondent, Just Off Broadway, Desperate Journey, Girl Trouble, Once upon a Honeymoon, Valley of Hunted Men, The Valley of Vanishing Men* [serial], *Reunion in France* (1942); *Adventures of Smilin' Jack* [serial], *Adventures of the Flying Cadets* [serial], *Chetniks – The Fighting Guerrillas, Hangmen Also Die, Tonight We Raid Calais, They Came to Blow up America, Action in the North Atlantic, Bomber's Moon, First Comes Courage, Tiger Fangs, Appointment in Berlin, Paris after Dark, Northern Pursuit, The Cross of Lorraine, Around the World* (1943); *Broadway Rhythm, None Shall Escape, Tampico, Address Unknown, U-Boat Prisoner, Wilson, The Conspirators* (1944); *Jungle Queen* [serial], *Hotel Berlin, A Royal Scandal, Son of Lassie, Counter-Attack, Where Do We Go from Here?, Thrill of a Romance, Secret Agent X-9* [serial], *The Adventures of Rusty, Week-End at the Waldorf, Abbott and Costello in Hollywood, Paris Underground* (1945); *Rendezvous 24, The Searching Wind, Cloak and Dagger* (1946); *13 Rue Madeleine, The Beginning or the End, Golden Earrings, This Time for Keeps, Cass Timberlane* (1947); *Women in the Night, The Noose Hangs High* (1948); *In a Lonely Place, For Heaven's Sake* (1950); *Invitation, What Price Glory* (1952); *Call Me Madam, The Desert Rats* (1953).

FREY, Sami (Samuel Frey) (1937–)

Frey is known for playing handsome, but usually angst-ridden characters in French popular and auteur cinema. He briefly worked in the USA in the mid-1980s, appearing as a Palestinian terrorist in *The Little Drummer Girl* and the victim of the female serial killer in *Black Widow*. SL

FILMS: *The Little Drummer Girl* (1984); *Black Widow* (1987).

FRICKER, Brenda (1945–)

Irish actress commonly typecast in maternal roles in her American film work. Fricker initially became widely known for her role as Nurse Megan Roache in the long-running BBC hospital drama *Casualty*. Although she had already appeared in films, her breakthrough came with an Academy Award-winning performance as the mother – opposite Daniel Day-Lewis★ – in Jim Sheridan's *My Left Foot* (1989), a role strongly redolent of the fictional 'Irish mammy'. Sheridan cast her in a similar role in *The Field* (1990) and she reprised this performance for comic effect when she played Mike Myers' Scottish mother in *So I Married an Axe Murderer*. Fricker is dismissive of Hollywood in interview and makes little effort to secure parts that require relocation. She prefers appearing in films shot in Ireland – such as *Moll Flanders* – and continues to live there and work in television. RB

FILMS: *Of Human Bondage* (1964); *Sinful Davey* (1969); *Home Alone 2: Lost in New York* (1992); *So I Married an Axe Murderer* (1993); *Angels in the Outfield* (1994); *Moll Flanders, A Time to Kill* (1996); *Masterminds* (1997); *Veronica Guerin* (2003).

FRIEND, Philip (1915–1987)

British leading actor who had a three-year period in Hollywood, where he mostly appeared in swashbuckling roles without any major success. TJ

FILMS: *My Own True Love* (1948); *Buccaneer's Girl, Spy Hunt* (1950); *The Highwayman, Thunder on the Hill, Smuggler's Island* (1951).

FRÖBE, Gert (Karl-Gerhard Froeber) (1913–1988)

German character actor in numerous European co-productions who gained international attention as James Bond's eponymous nemesis in *Goldfinger*. Despite promotional tours to the USA, all his Hollywood films were shot in Europe. RJK

FILMS: *Man on a Tightrope* (1953); *The Longest Day* (1962); *Goldfinger* (1964); *A High Wind in Jamaica, Those Magnificent Men in Their Flying Machines, or How I Flew from London to Paris in 25 Hours, 11 Minutes* (1965); *Monte Carlo or Bust!* (1969); *Dollar$* (1972); *The Serpent's Egg* (1977); *Bloodline* (1979).

GAAL, Franciska (Franziska Zilverstrich) (1901–1972)

Budapest-born Gaal became a major star of Hungarian and Austrian films of the mid-1930s as a temperamental ingénue in comedies such as *Csibi der Fratz/Csibi the Brat* (1934) and *Frühjahrsparade/Spring Parade* (1935), frequently conceived by the team of director Henry Koster (Gaal's then husband), the writer Felix Joachimson (later Jackson) and producer Joe Pasternak. Following the Nazi takeover of Austria, Gaal arrived in Hollywood with much advance publicity on account of her European popularity, but found herself miscast in her American debut, the swashbuckling epic *The Buccaneer*. Dropped by the industry for her allegedly difficult behaviour, her life took a tragic turn. During the war, she returned to, and became trapped in, Nazi-occupied Hungary. After the war she went back to the USA, but unable to resume her career, she died forgotten after decades of hardship. Meanwhile, in the late 1930s and 1940s Koster, Pasternak and Jackson remade many of their collaborative European successes with Gaal as vehicles for the all-American Deanna Durbin. TB

FILMS: *The Buccaneer* (1938); *Paris Honeymoon, The Girl Downstairs* (1939).

GABIN, Jean (1904–1976)

When he went to Hollywood, Gabin was French cinema's greatest star, but he made only two films there. His brief and disappointing US career is, however, instructive about the difficulties in translating a particular kind of Frenchness into American cinema.

Gabin moved to Hollywood in early 1941, fleeing occupied France and an offer to work for the German-controlled Continental. Soon Fox offered him a contract. After a year spent learning English, he made *Moontide*, directed by Archie Mayo (but started by Fritz Lang), co-starring Ida Lupino. In this romantic melodrama, he plays a gypsy called 'Frenchie'. His second film, *The Impostor* (Universal), is a war effort drama directed by fellow émigré Julien Duvivier. The plot, which reprises the 1935 Gabin–Duvivier collaboration *La Bandera/Escape from Yesterday*, has Gabin play a ex-convict freed from jail by bombs and reluctantly thrown into the war, but who dies a patriotic hero. Neither film was successful. Gabin did not master English well, he disliked his permed hair and felt constrained in his acting ('I could hear myself say the lines'). **257**

Neither film could accommodate his French working-class rebel persona developed in films like Jean Renoir's *La Bête humaine/The Human Beast* (1938). Nor did his Hollywood roles fit the image of 'sophisticated' Frenchness perfected by Maurice Chevalier★ and Charles Boyer★. Gabin left Hollywood to join the Free French army and later enjoyed a hugely successful second career in France. GV

FILMS: *Moontide* (1942); *The Impostor* [re-released as *Strange Confession*] (1943).

GABOR, Zsa Zsa (Sari Gábor) (1917–)

Glamorous blonde pop-culture icon with a 'dahlink' Hungarian accent. Together with sisters Magda (1914–1997) and Eva (1919–1995), Zsa Zsa was groomed for stardom by matriarch and redoubtable Budapest diamond merchant Jolie Tilleman-Gábor. Zsa Zsa began her stage career in 1933 and was crowned Miss Hungary in 1936, while Eva found success on stage and as an ice-skater and Magda made her film debut in *Mai lányok/Today's Girls* (1937). Eva emigrated to the USA first after marrying Greta Garbo's★ osteopath Dr Erik Drimmer. The rest of the family followed after the outbreak of World War II. While Eva began her long career as an exotic supporting actress in Hollywood and on Broadway, Zsa Zsa's initial notoriety in the USA came through high-profile marriages to hotelier Conrad Hilton (1942–7) and actor George Sanders★ (1949–54). After entering films in 1952, Zsa Zsa's early roles were variations on her extravagant public persona. She appeared, for example, in diaphanous evening wear throughout the 1958 camp classic *Queen of Outer Space*. The Golden Globe she received the same year was tellingly not for any particular performance, but a special award for 'Most Glamorous Actress'.

During the 1950s, Zsa Zsa also inaugurated her career as a professional television guest star, where she recounted gossip-laden anecdotes and tongue-in-cheek aphorisms on men, wealth and marriage. Her subsequent film appearances have primarily been cameos playing this version of herself, alongside occasional accent-exploiting voice-work for animated features – something at which Eva, who voiced Duchess in *The Aristocats* (1970) and Miss Bianca in *The Rescuers* (1977), also excelled. After nine marriages (eight of them legal) and a lifetime of being famous for being famous, Zsa Zsa again grabbed the headlines in 1989 for slapping a Beverly Hills traffic cop. Footage from her trial and three-day imprisonment was presented in the grotesquely self-publicising *The People vs. Zsa Zsa Gabor*, a work made bearable only by the celebrity's keen sense of self-irony, a trait displayed also in her unlikely exercise video – made at age seventy-six – *It's Simple, Darling!* (1993). Increasingly reclusive since the deaths of her mother and sisters, Zsa Zsa has prolonged her celebrity through her 'actress' daughter Francesca Hilton, a prominent face at Hollywood functions and in American tabloids, whose major movie credit remains *Pterodactyl Woman from Beverly Hills* (1994). RJK

FILMS: *Lovely to Look At, Moulin Rouge, We're Not Married!, The Million Dollar Nickel* (1952); *Lili, The Story of Three Loves* (1953); *Three Ring Circus* (1954); *Death of a Scoundrel* (1956); *The Girl in the Kremlin* (1957); *Touch of Evil, Queen of Outer Space, Country Music Holiday* (1958); *For the First Time* (1959); *Pepe* (1960); *The Road to Hong Kong, Boys' Night Out* (1962); *Picture Mommy Dead* (1966); *Jack of Diamonds* (1967); *Drop Dead Darling* (1968); *Mooch Goes to Hollywood* [voice] (1971); *Won Ton Ton, the Dog Who Saved Hollywood* (1976); *Every Girl Should Have One* (1978); *Smart Alec, Charlie Barnett's Terms of Enrolment* (1986); *A Nightmare on Elm Street 3: Dream Warriors* (1987); *The Naked Gun 2 and a Half, The Smell of Fear, The People vs. Zsa Zsa Gabor* (1991); *The Naked Truth* (1992); *Happily Ever After* [voice], *The Beverly Hillbillies* (1993); *That's Entertainment! III* (1994); *A Very Brady Sequel* (1996).

GALLAGHER, Bronagh (1975–)

Irish actress who made her mark as a back-up singer in Alan Parker's adaptation of Roddy Doyle's *The Commitments* (1991). Gallagher has had occasional parts in Hollywood, but works more often on the stage. RB

FILMS: *Pulp Fiction* (1994); *Mary Reilly* (1996); *Star Wars: Episode I – The Phantom Menace* (1999); *Thunderpants* (2002).

GALLIAN, Ketti (1912–1972)

Pretty blonde French former chorus girl who appeared in a few important roles in 1930s Hollywood films such as the Astaire–Rogers musical *Shall We Dance?* However, her looks, reminiscent of contemporaries like Jean Harlow and Ginger Rogers, meant that competition was rife and she returned to France in 1938. CH

FILMS: *Marie Galante* (1934); *Under the Pampas Moon* (1935); *Espionage, Shall We Dance?* (1937).

GAMBON, Michael (1940–)

Respected British stage actor whose breakthrough television role as a hospitalised author leading a fantasy life as a hard-boiled American gumshoe in *The Singing Detective* (1986) won considerable transatlantic recognition. Like many British actors, Gambon has been typecast as a scene-stealing villain, though roles vary from mad generals (*Toys*) to more poker-faced sinister corporate crooks (*The Insider*). Gambon's aptitude for broad, parochial American accents – first demonstrated on television – has been also amply exploited. JB

FILMS: *Missing Link* [voice] (1988); *A Dry White Season* (1989); *Mobsters* (1991); *Toys* (1992); *The Browning Version, Clean Slate, Squanto: A Warrior's Tale* (1994); *Mary Reilly* (1996); *The Insider, Sleepy Hollow* (1999); *Gosford Park* (2001); *Open Range* (2003); *Harry Potter and the Prisoner of Azkaban, Sky Captain and the World of Tomorrow, The Life Aquatic with Steve Zissou* (2004).

GANZ, Bruno (1941–)

Swiss actor, generally considered the foremost living actor of the German stage, who was also a signature presence in the New German Cinema. Ganz's Hollywood career has been limited to a brief appearance as the scientist explaining human cloning to Laurence Olivier's★ Nazi-hunter in *The Boys from Brazil*. VH

FILM: *The Boys from Brazil* (1978).

GARAT, Henri (Émile Henri Camille Garassu) (1902–1959)

A variety dancer and singer, often playing Florelle's or Mistinguett's boyish partner, Henri Garat became a hugely successful matinée idol in early 1930s France. Opposite Lillian Harvey★, he was the ubiquitous star of operettas filmed in several languages in Berlin. But whereas Harvey also played in the German and English versions, Garat spoke only French and therefore was confined to the French versions. He also appeared in a few French versions of Paramount multi-language films shot in Paris such as *Rive Gauche* (1930). There were high hopes when he left for Hollywood: would he supplant Maurice Chevalier★, who was so successful in both languages? However, his only American film, *Adorable* (for Twentieth Century-Fox) – in which he reprised an earlier role as a dancing and singing lieutenant who seduces the princess of an operetta kingdom – failed, leading to his return to France. His career never really recovered; he gradually lost favour with audiences and by 1939 he was forgotten. MB

FILM: *Adorable* (1933).

GARBO, Greta (Greta Louisa Gustafsson) (1905–1990)

As the third child in a typical Swedish working-class family, seventeen-year-old Greta Louisa Gustafsson attended Stockholm's Royal Dramatic School somewhat unexpectedly. She soon became the protégée of the famous film director and Russian émigré Mauritz Stiller. In 1924, he cast her in *Gosta Berlings saga/The Legend of Gösta Berling*, the film that introduced Gustafsson to European audiences as 'Greta Garbo'. After a failed film project in Constantinople, Stiller took Garbo to Germany, where she co-starred with one of Europe's leading screen tragediennes, the Danish star Asta Nielsen, in G. W. Pabst's *Die Freudlose Gasse/Joyless Street* (1925). Stiller was visited in Berlin by MGM's vice-president, Louis B. Mayer. He was highly impressed by Stiller's work and offered the director a chance to come and work for him in Hollywood. Stiller insisted on a corresponding contract for his young protégée, and Mayer reluctantly agreed.

Garbo arrived in the USA in 1925 on a three-year contract at a starting salary of $350 a week. MGM had no film roles to offer her though and so, already homesick, she was kept out of work for several months. The actress had her teeth fixed and appearance stylised and began to find herself promoted as 'exotic' due to her prominent European identity. She was launched as an erotic and passionate temptress in *Torrent*, which co-starred Ricardo Cortez as the male lead. It was both a critical and box-office success.

The American critics found Garbo both attractive and enigmatic. Her seductive appeal on screen instantly made her one of MGM's leading stars – a status that she retained during her fifteen-year Hollywood career. She was soon labelled 'the Divine Garbo' by the cinematographers she worked with because of her perfectly photogenic face. Garbo not only had perfect features. Clarence Brown, who directed her in seven of his films, once said: 'She was not only a great star with a rare power to charm. She had an intuition that no one else in films has possessed.' The majority of people who worked with her would agree. **259**

One single take was often all that was needed. Garbo's romance with screen lover John Gilbert, which started in 1927 during the shooting of *Flesh and the Devil*, only contributed further to the dramatic sensual appeal of her initial stardom.

After only two years at the studio, Garbo tired of playing the tempting, yet cordial vamp and she went on strike to demand a more generous contract. Seven months later, Mayer was willing to meet her demands and the Swedish actress signed a new five-year contract with MGM. She was now to be paid $5,000 a week – a salary that would increase gradually to the sum of $6,000. This contract was different from the standard studio contract of the time. Instead of getting paid forty weeks a year – the standard procedure – Garbo was to be paid her $5,000 for every single week of the year. The new contract was not only economically satisfactory for Garbo, it also represented a significant professional advance. She now went from playing rather static, seductive vamps to portraying more subtle and complex characters. After *Love*, the adaptation of Tolstoy's classic novel *Anna Karenina*, Garbo's position as Hollywood's leading female star became unquestioned. Again, this was with the help of John Gilbert as her screen lover. This was also her first American film to appeal to Swedish audiences and critics, since the figure of 'Garbo the vamp' had never been a real success in her home country.

Anna Christie – Garbo's first sound film – went smoothly, even though MGM had their reasons to worry. The star's voice was deep, with an almost male timbre, and her foreign pronunciation was still rather distinct. A Swedish accent was therefore deliberately required for the part of Anna and her entry line 'Gimme me a whisky!' proved highly successful with both American and overseas audiences. Unlike Gilbert, whose voice was deemed unsuitable for sound pictures, Garbo continued to sparkle.

Garbo's melancholy on screen, as well as her much-publicised desire to be left alone in private, began to colour her public image. She became known as 'the loner' and 'the Swedish sphinx'. She was also seen as an inaccessible goddess due to her facial perfection. Her refusal to marry nurtured this image even further and to some audiences, her independence was read in terms of lesbianism or bisexuality. More recently, Garbo's real-life lesbian relationships have been uncovered by film historians and her true bisexuality has come to be accepted. Her main long-term lesbian affair

Greta Garbo: the 'divine "Sphinx"'

seems to have been with the Spanish scriptwriter Mercedes de Acosta during the 1930s. *Queen Christina*, filmed in 1933, had distinctly queer connotations and one can now see this film as the feature that captured Garbo's genuine persona most clearly. The overt playing with gender roles, transvestism, implicit lesbian romance, as well as the solitude and strength of the eponymous Swedish queen, especially in the final scene, makes this film distinctly 'Garbo-esque'.

Garbo disliked Hollywood and the process of filming and she would constantly long for Sweden, where she had her family and friends. While in Sweden in 1931, she more or less extorted a further production deal from Mayer, saying that she would only return to Hollywood on condition that she was to be provided with exactly what she wanted. Once again, Mayer could not refuse and the ensuing arrangement meant that Garbo was placed in charge of the number and type of films she made. She started to make fewer films after 1932. Of these worth mentioning are *Anna Karenina* and *Camille*, both romantic tragedies with Garbo cast as the tragic diva. In 1938, Garbo was one of five stars (another was Marlene Dietrich★) deemed 'box-office poison' and some change in her image took place. In 1939, she appeared in her first and only comedy, *Ninotchka*, directed by Ernst Lubitsch, which portrayed Garbo as a humorous and happy character. Not surprisingly, the film was marketed with the slogan 'Garbo laughs!'

Despite the success of *Ninotchka*, Garbo continued to be unhappy with film-making and she starred in her final film, *Two-Faced Woman*, in 1941 at the age of thirty-six. It received poor reviews – mainly because of the supposed immorality of the narrative – and Garbo decided to retire from her position as the queen of Hollywood. She withdrew to her New York flat, from where she could not be reached. Garbo never won an Academy Award, despite being nominated three times (for *Anna Christie*, *Camille* and *Ninotchka*). Nevertheless, she received an Honorary Award in 1955 and continued to enchant and puzzle her worldwide fans as the lonesome, yet divine, 'Sphinx' until her death and beyond. LW

FILMS: *Torrent*, *The Temptress* (1926), *Flesh and the Devil*, *Love* (1927); *The Divine Woman*, *The Mysterious Lady*, *A Woman of Affairs* (1928); *Wild Orchids*, *The Single Standard*, *The Kiss* (1929); *Anna Christie*, *Romance* (1930); *Inspiration*, *Susan Lenox, Her Rise and Fall*, *Mata Hari* (1931); *Grand Hotel*, *As You Desire Me* (1932); *Queen Christina* (1933); *The Painted Veil* (1934); *Anna Karenina* (1935); *Camille* (1936); *Conquest* (1937); *Ninotchka* (1939); *Two-Faced Woman* (1941).

GARDINER, Reginald (William Reginald Gardiner) (1903–1980)

Suave and cultured English stage and screen actor with a dapper manner and distinctive clipped accent and moustache. Gardiner appeared in a couple of Fox British features and following his 1935 Broadway debut, moved to Hollywood, where he was seen as a handsome and personable leading-man type. He often played urbane and eccentric British supporting characters. JS/AP

FILMS: *Virginia's Husband*, *Borrow a Million* (1934); *Born to Dance* (1936); *A Damsel in Distress* (1937); *Everybody Sings*, *Marie Antoinette*, *Sweethearts*, *The Girl Downstairs* (1938); *The Night of Nights*, *The Flying Deuces* (1939); *The Doctor Takes a Wife*, *Dulcy*, *The Great Dictator* (1940); *My Life with Caroline*,

A Yank in the R.A.F., *Sundown* (1941); *Captains of the Clouds*, *The Man Who Came to Dinner* (1942); *Immortal Sergeant*, *Forever and a Day*, *Sweet Rosie O' Grady*, *Claudia* (1943); *The Horn Blows at Midnight*, *Christmas in Connecticut*, *The Dolly Sisters*, *Molly and Me* (1945); *Do You Love Me*, *One More Tomorrow*, *Cluny Brown* (1946); *I Wonder Who's Kissing Her Now* (1947); *Fury at Furnace Creek*, *That Lady in Ermine*, *That Wonderful Urge* (1948); *Wabash Avenue*, *I'll Get By* (1950); *Halls of Montezuma*, *Elopement* (1951); *Androcles and the Lion* (1952); *Black Widow* (1954); *Ain't Misbehavin'* (1955); *The Birds and the Bees* (1956); *The Story of Mankind* (1957); *Rock-a Bye-Baby* (1958); *Back Street* (1961); *Mr Hobbs Takes a Vacation* (1962); *What a Way to Go* (1964); *Sergeant Dead Head*, *Do Not Disturb* (1965).

GARSON, Greer (1908–1996)

Born in County Down, Northern Ireland, Garson came to personify the understated virtues of the British middle class on the American screen, notably through her performance in the title role of William Wyler's wartime classic, *Mrs Miniver*. With her sculpted features and statuesque figure, she played many other strong, matronly roles throughout her long film career.

Greer Garson: Cowgirl

After working for a London advertising agency, Garson joined a theatre group in Birmingham and made her London stage debut in 1934. She was spotted by Louis B. Mayer and signed to MGM. Garson's first role for the studio was in the British-produced hymn to old England, *Goodbye, Mr Chips*. Her performance as Robert Donat's★ wife led to her first Academy Award nomination. She subsequently won an Award for her part as the exquisite, unflappable matriarch in *Mrs Miniver*, who seemingly deals with the intrigues of the local flower show and a German parachutist who appears in her kitchen with equal ease.

Throughout the 1940s, Garson played in a number of melodramas, including the equally sentimental *Random Harvest*, in which she was cast against type as a music-hall dancer but whose character displayed the same qualities of endurance and inventiveness that had so endeared her to audiences in *Mrs Miniver*. A similar role was that of Mrs Forsyte in *That Forsyte Woman* (aka *The Forsyte Saga*). Garson was nominated for six Academy Awards in the 1940s – for the aforementioned titles as well as *Blossoms in the Dust*, *Madame Curie*, *Mrs Parkington* and *The Valley of Decision*.

By the end of the war, Garson was one of MGM's most valued stars. Her position could be signalled by the famed tagline of her first postwar production, *Adventure*: 'Gable's Back and Garson's Got Him!' However, in the new social climate of the late 1940s, audiences showed less enthusiasm for the type of roles that Garson personified. Fortitude and discreet sexuality were no longer the order of the day. The patriotic embrace of British values had similarly waned. MGM found it increasingly difficult to match their star to the new women that popular taste demanded on screen and an attempt to recreate her winning performance in the follow-up, *The Miniver Story*, was less than successful. Garson's contract with MGM ended in 1954 and despite having settled in the USA and become a citizen, she played in fewer and fewer films. She did, however, gain another Academy Award nomination for her unglamorous role as Eleanor Roosevelt in *Sunrise at Campobello*. She also made a number of subsequent appearances on American television. RB

FILMS: *Goodbye, Mr Chips, Remember?* (1939); *Pride and Prejudice* (1940); *Blossoms in the Dust, When Ladies Meet* (1941); *Mrs Miniver, Random Harvest* (1942); *The Youngest Profession* (1943); *Madame Curie, Mrs Parkington* (1944); *The Valley of Decision* (1945); *Adventure* (1946); *Desire Me* (1947);

Julia Misbehaves (1948); *That Forsyte Woman* (1949); *The Miniver Story* (1950); *The Law and the Lady* (1951); *Scandal at Scourie, Julius Caesar* (1953); *Her Twelve Men* (1954); *Strange Lady in Town* (1955); *Sunrise at Campobello, Pepe* (1960); *The Singing Nun* (1966); *The Happiest Millionaire* (1967).

GASSMAN, Vittorio (1922–2000)

Although one of Italy's leading actors during the early 1950s, Gassman was largely unknown to American audiences when he signed his contract with MGM in 1952, just after marrying American actress Shelley Winters. He acted in four films during the next two years, portraying an outlaw in both *The Glass Wall* and *Cry of the Hunted*, a Mexican in the melodramatic musical *Sombrero* and a violinist who wins Elizabeth Taylor's heart in *Rhapsody*. After working with Silvana Mangano and his wife in the Italian-American co-production *Mambo*, Gassman divorced Winters and returned to Italy, resuming work in Italian cinema and theatre. He continued to make sporadic Hollywood appearances throughout his career, such as his portrayal of Anatole in King Vidor's epic *War and Peace* and his partici-

Vittorio Gassman signed his contract with MGM in 1952, just after marrying American actress Shelley Winters

pation, in the late 1970s, in two Robert Altman films. In *A Wedding* and *Quintet*, he was accompanied by fellow European art-cinema icons, Bibi Andersson★ and Fernando Rey★. Despite their differences of genre, quality and subject matter, Gassman's final Hollywood appearances saw him consistently cast as a villain or criminal leader. CBu

FILMS: *The Glass Wall, Sombrero, Cry of the Hunted* (1953); *Rhapsody, Mambo* (1954); *War and Peace* (1956); *The Miracle* (1959); *Barabbas* (1962); *Woman Times Seven* (1967); *A Wedding* (1978); *Quintet* (1979); *The Nude Bomb* (1980); *Sharky's Machine* (1981); *Tempest* (1982); *Sleepers* (1996).

GAUBERT, Danièle (1943–1987)

When Gaubert was a fifteen-year-old ballerina at the Paris Opera, she was noticed by Claude Autant-Lara, who gave her a part in *Les Régates de San Francisco* (1960). Her varied career included several films abroad such as *Flight from Ashiya*, where she played an Algerian girl opposite Yul Brynner. VO

FILMS: *Flight from Ashiya* (1963); *Underground* (1970); *Snow Job* (1971).

GAYE, Gregory (Grigory Grigoryevich Ge) (1900–1993)

Son of a prominent Russian actor and dramatist who played various multi-ethnic characters, primarily of noble origin, during his long Hollywood career. Gaye joined the legion of West Coast film extras in 1925 and by 1929, he had signed with Fox to be a supporting actor on a salary of $500 a week. He played a Russian writer in Robert Florey's *Hollywood Boulevard* and, like many émigré actors, had an uncredited part in *Casablanca*. RY

FILMS: *Tempest* (1928); *The Case of Lena Smith, The Black Watch, They Had to See Paris* (1929); *The Song of the Flame, What a Widow!, Renegades, High Society Blues* (1930); *Young as You Feel, Kept Husbands* (1931); *A Mail Bride, Once in a Lifetime* (1932); *Affairs of a Gentleman, Handy Andy, British Agent* (1934); *Hollywood Boulevard, Under Your Spell, Charlie Chan at the Opera, That Girl from Paris, Dodsworth* (1936); *Mama Steps Out, Wise Girl, Prescription for Romance, Lancer Spy, First Lady, Tovarich* (1937); *Straight, Place and Show, Too Hot to Handle, Thanks for Everything, Bulldog Drummond's Peril, Test Pilot, Love, Honor and Behave* (1938); *Ninotchka, Hotel for Women, The Man from Dakota, On Your Toes, The Three Musketeers, Paris Honeymoon* (1939); *Down Argentine*

Way (1940); *They Dare Not Love, I Wake up Screaming* (1941); *Flight Lieutenant, The Secret Code, Casablanca, Fall In, My Gal Sal* (1942); *Song of Russia, One Dangerous Night* (1943); *The Conspirators, Seven Doors to Death, The Purple Heart* (1944); *The Tiger Woman, Cornered, I Love a Mystery, Paris Underground, Pursuit to Algiers, Blood on the Sun, A Song to Remember* (1945); *Passkey to Danger, So Dark the Night* (1946); *Blackmail, The Trespasser, The Unfinished Dance, The Corpse Came C.O.D., The Bachelor and the Bobby-Soxer* (1947); *Black Magic, Dancing in the Dark* (1949); *Cargo to Capetown, Flying Disc Man from Mars, Counterspy Meets Scotland Yard, Big Momma's House, Harbor of Missing Men* (1950); *Ten Tall Men, When the Redskins Rode, The Magic Carpet, Mask of the Avenger, The Whip Hand, Peking Express* (1951); *Last Train from Bombay, Bal Tabarin, The World in His Arms* (1952); *The Juggler, South Sea Woman, Remains to Be Seen, Flame of Calcutta, Savage Mutiny* (1953); *Jungle Man-Eaters, Charge of the Lancers* (1954); *Creature with the Atom Brain, King of the Carnival* (1955); *The Eddie Duchin Story* (1956); *Bailout at 43,000, Silk Stockings, Kelly and Me* (1957); *Auntie Mame, Missile Monsters* (1958); *Cash McCall, Ocean's Eleven* (1960); *Blue Hawaii* (1961); *Four Horsemen of the Apocalypse, Hitler* (1962); *The Prize* (1963); *Batman* (1966); *Topaz* (1969); *Meteor* (1979).

GÉLIN, Daniel (1921–)

Charming, good-looking French matinée idol whose undisputed acting talents have contributed to enduring stardom in his native country. In the 1950s, Gélin's career was already well established. After formal training at the Cours Simon – he was in the same year as Louis Jourdan★ – and the Conservatoire, he acted in a number of plays and films, including Jacques Becker's *Rendez-vous de juillet/Rendezvous in July* (1949) and Max Ophuls's *La Ronde* (1950). In 1951, he was awarded the Victoire du Cinéma Français. Gélin was then approached by Alfred Hitchcock for the role of the mysterious Frenchman Louis Bernard in *The Man Who Knew Too Much* with James Stewart and Doris Day. In his autobiography, Gélin claims that this time was one of the high points of his career and qualifies working in Hollywood as a 'joy' and a 'dream'. Linguistic difficulties were ironed out with the help of a language coach. Despite subsequent offers to remain in Hollywood, however, Gélin could not afford to neglect his French career nor his family. Some nineteen French films later, he played a small part in **263**

The Longest Day. His scenes were sadly deleted from the final cut. In 1971, he played the lead in Jack O'Connell's *Christa: Swedish Fly Girls.* That was to be his last American film role, but in 1991, he accepted a part in *Iran: Days of Crisis* for American television. VO

FILMS: *The Man Who Knew Too Much* (1956); *The Longest Day* [scenes deleted] (1962); *Christa: Swedish Fly Girls* (1971).

GENN, Leo (1905–1978)

Prolific British character actor who was also a practising barrister. He played intelligent, understated roles on both sides of the Atlantic and was nominated for an Academy Award for his role as Petronius in *Quo Vadis.* MW

FILMS: *Mourning Becomes Electra* (1947); *The Velvet Touch, The Snake Pit* (1948); *The Miniver Story* (1950); *Quo Vadis?* (1951); *Plymouth Adventure* (1952); *The Red Beret, The Girls of Pleasure Island* (1953); *Beyond Mombasa, Moby Dick* (1956); *I Accuse!* (1958); *Invitation to Monte Carlo* (1959); *The Longest Day* (1962); *55 Days at Peking* (1963); *The Delhi Way* [voice] (1964); *Khartoum* (1966); *The Mackintosh Man* (1973).

GEORGE, Susan (1950–)

This sultry British sex-kitten was able to forge a modest Hollywood career in glamour roles on the back of her international success in *Straw Dogs.* JB

FILMS: *Come Fly with Me* (1963); *Billion Dollar Brain* (1967); *Up the Junction, The Strange Affair* (1968); *The Looking Glass War* (1970); *Straw Dogs* (1971); *Dirty Mary Crazy Larry* (1974); *Mandingo, Out of Season* (1975); *A Small Town in Texas* (1976); *Enter the Ninja* (1981); *The House Where Evil Dwells, Kiss My Grits* (1982); *Lightning, the White Stallion* (1986).

GERAY, Steven (Istvan Gyergyay) (1904–1973)

Prolific Hungarian-born character actor in European, then Hollywood, films, best remembered as the philosophical cloakroom attendant in *Gilda,* and, in a rare starring role, as a Parisian detective in *So Dark the Night.* TB

FILMS: *Inspector Hornleigh* (1939); *Dark Streets of Cairo, Man at Large, The Shanghai Gesture, Blue, White and Perfect* (1941); *Castle in the Desert, Secret Agent of Japan, The Mad Martindales, For the Common Defense!, Night Plane from Chungking, The Moon and Sixpence, A Gentleman at Heart, Eyes in the Night, The Wife Takes a Flyer,* (1942); *Above Suspicion, Henry*

264

Aldrich Swings It, Hostages, To My Unborn Son, Whistling in Brooklyn, Pilot #5, Assignment in Brittany, Heavenly Music, Background to Danger, Appointment in Berlin, The Phantom of the Opera (1943); *Easy Life, The Conspirators, Meet the People, In Society, The Mask of Dimitrios, The Seventh Cross* (1944); *Tarzan and the Amazons, Mexicana, Spellbound, Hotel Berlin, The Crimson Canary, Cornered* (1945); *Gilda, Deadline at Dawn, So Dark the Night, The Return of Monte Cristo, Blondie Knows Best* (1946); *When a Girl's Beautiful, The Unfaithful, Mr District Attorney, Gunfighters, Crime Doctor's Gamble, Blind Spot* (1947); *I Love Trouble, Ladies of the Chorus, Port Said, The Woman from Tangier, The Dark Past* (1948); *El Paso, Tell it to the Judge, Sky Liner, Once More, My Darling, The Lone Wolf and His Lady, Holiday in Havana* (1949); *In a Lonely Place, Under My Skin, All about Eve, Woman on the Run, Jungle Jim in Pygmy Island, A Lady without Passport, Harbor of Missing Men, Beware of Blondie* (1950); *The Second Woman, I Can Get it for You Wholesale, Target Unknown, The House on Telegraph Hill, My Favourite Spy, Savage Drums, Little Egypt* (1951); *Affair in Trinidad, The Big Sky, Lady Possessed, O. Henry's Full House, Bar Tabarin, Night without Sleep* (1952); *Gentlemen Prefer Blondes, Tonight We Sing, Call Me Madam, The Story of Three Loves, The Royal African Rifles, The Great Diamond Robbery, The Golden Blade* (1953); *The French Line, Paris Playboys, Knock on Wood, Tobor the Great* (1954); *To Catch a Thief, Artists and Models, Kiss of Fire, New York Confidential, A Bullet for Joey, Daddy Long Legs* (1955); *Attack, Stagecoach to Fury, The Birds and the Bees* (1956); *The Gift of Love, A Certain Smile, Verboten!* (1958); *Count Your Blessings* (1959); *Dime with a Halo* (1963), *Wild and Wonderful* (1964); *Ship of Fools* (1965); *The Swinger, Our Man Flint, Jesse James Meets Frankenstein's Daughter* (1966).

GERMANY

In the history of cinema, German emigration to Hollywood has found representation not predominantly as a 'journey of desire', but as a tale of compulsion dominated by Third Reich exile narratives of flight from political and/or existential threat. The reasons for that emphasis are compelling. In his first speech to film industry representatives in March 1933, the new Reich Minister for Propaganda and Popular Enlightenment, Joseph Goebbels, named as his goal the 'root and branch' eradication of 'ideas' unrooted in 'National Socialist soil'. There ensued a rash of anti-Semitic and anti-leftist film initiatives by or on behalf of the Nazi state, including the founding of the Reich Film Chamber in July 1933; compulsory licensing for all film personnel, and hence the de facto exclusion from the industry of Jews and other undesirable figures; the reclassification as non-German of films made with Jewish participation (thus 'Jewish' films produced in Germany became subject to quota restrictions on 'foreign' films); the massive extension of censorship, including films that offended against 'National Socialist . . . feeling'; and the organisation by Nazi activists of 'spontaneous' protests against 'Jewish' films.[1] The results are well known. The years immediately following the Nazi seizure of power in 1933 saw an unprecedented exodus of creative personnel from Germany. It has been estimated that around two thousand film practitioners, the majority of Jewish origin, emigrated or were exiled during the twelve years of the 'Third Reich'. Many headed first for European destinations – Vienna, Paris, London, Prague, Amsterdam, Budapest. Later, as Nazi annexation or conquest became a palpable threat, some sailed for the USA, joining an exile community in Hollywood that is estimated to have numbered, at its highest point, around eight hundred, including directors, producers, screenwriters, editors, composers, cinematographers, sound engineers, agents, cinema entrepreneurs – and an estimated two hundred or so actors and actresses.[2]

This is the period, then, that history remembers as the zenith of Hollywood's importation of German talent to its screens. To his 1944 article on 'What Our Immigration Did for Hollywood', published in the New York-based German-Jewish weekly *Aufbau*, the émigré journalist Hans Kafka, for instance, appended a roll-call of exile artistes that included such star names as Albert Bassermann★, Luise Rainer★, Peter Lorre★, Paul Henreid★ and Hedy Lamarr★, as well as a host of figures reduced after exile to (often uncredited) bit parts.[3]

Kafka's conclusion that the 'trickle' of German émigrés grew to an unprecedented 'flood' after 1933 is empirically accurate; yet it suggests a unidirectional movement and a unified logic that are rarely evident in processes of migration and international film-cultural exchange. Even during the early years of the 'Third Reich', trading relations between Hollywood studios and German-based distributors remained to an extent intact, if hampered by quota restrictions, and there were at least a handful of film practitioners (Lillian Harvey★, Pola Negri★, Rudolf Forster★) whose non-Jewish ethnicity permitted temporary or per-

manent re-emigration to Germany, where they helped sustain the illusion of internationalism for an increasingly creatively impoverished national industry.

The pattern of migration as a two-way traffic between Hollywood and Germany was, of course, set at a time when the German industry could more plausibly claim international status. German economic misery in the wake of World War I defeat gave a paradoxical boost to a film industry previously dominated by foreign product. The weakness of the postwar Reichsmark both protected the domestic market from foreign imports and improved the film industry's prospects of foreign sales. German studios responded with a cluster of artistically ambitious titles designed to launch the national industry as a significant player on the international stage. Decla-Bioscop's *Das Cabinet des Dr Caligari/The Cabinet of Dr Caligari* (1920), or Ufa's period dramas, most notably Ernst Lubitsch's *Madame DuBarry/Passion* (1919) and *Anna Boleyn/Deception* (1920), were but the most renowned among the imported titles that awakened postwar US studios, critics and audiences to the German challenge to Hollywood hegemony. In one study of *Caligari*'s US reception, Mike Budd has observed how *Caligari* was lauded as 'an example to Hollywood producers'.[4] Enthusiastic reception of Lubitsch's historical dramas confirmed German films' capacity for US market success. On one US list of 1921 box-office successes, *Passion* beat D. W. Griffith's *Way Down East* (1920) to the number-one slot, with *Caligari*, *Deception* and Lubitsch's *Carmen* (1918) close behind in positions four, five and eight.[5]

Hollywood's subsequent bid to recapture both domestic audiences and Continental European markets prompted a campaign of German talent recruitment that began in the early 1920s, peaked in mid-decade, then slumped when the advent of sound reduced the attraction to US producers of non-Anglophone stars. The emblematic figure of the first recruitment wave was the Polish-born Pola Negri, who attracted the competing attention of Fox, First National and Famous Players with her leading roles in two German titles, Ernst Lubitsch's *Carmen* and *Passion*. Arriving in New York just weeks behind the newly emigrated Lubitsch, in January 1922, Negri danced and rippled her way through a succession of Hollywood lead, supporting and bit parts as vamps, mildly degenerate aristocrats and exotic dancers. In those roles, she not only helped shape the enduring Hollywood stereotype of exotic seductress that would provide the framework (or straitjacket) for successive generations of émigré female stars. In commercial terms, too, she embodied the enduring Hollywood desire to secure European market supremacy through the strategic deployment of European directors, genres and stars.

That the strategy flopped in Negri's case, at least in respect of the German market, is illustrated by polls registering a recalcitrant German audience devotion to such home-grown (and internationally unsuccessful) talent as Henny Porten, Lil Dagover★ and Harry Piel.[6] More successful from a US perspective was the actor who rode on the crest of Hollywood's second German recruitment wave in mid-decade. Like his compatriot Conrad Veidt★, Emil Jannings★ remained popular at home throughout his four-year Hollywood sojourn. Jannings' Hollywood success – he won the first ever Academy Award for Best Actor for his role in Sternberg's *The Last Command* (1928) – served only to enhance the reputation as an artist of international standing that he had gained for virtuoso performances in such German productions as F. W. Murnau's *The Last Laugh* (1924) and E. A. Dupont's *Varieté* (1925).

Jannings' position is emblematic of a whole interwar generation of German émigrés – directors Lubitsch and Murnau, or later, Jannings' co-star in *The Blue Angel* (1930), Marlene Dietrich★ – who were fêted at home as overseas ambassadors for German cultural excellence, and simultaneously lauded in the USA as the 'foremost dramatic artist(s)' of world cinema *tout court*.[7] In other words, the paradoxical benefit derived by German actors from Hollywood's poaching in the silent period of their country's major talents was an increase in their cultural and market value both at home and abroad. Thus, for example, Jannings' Hollywood appearances can be credited with reviving what had threatened to become a flagging European acting career; it was in the wake of his Hollywood stay that Jannings became, by his own account at least, the first German actor since World War I to be offered theatre appearances across Continental Europe when he embarked in 1929 on a post-Hollywood European stage tour.[8]

The cross-fertilisation between the Hollywood and German star systems that Jannings' case exemplifies was abruptly interrupted by the coming of sound. Casualties of the language barrier included Jannings himself, who was **266** joined in his 1929 retreat to Europe by Pola Negri and

Peter Lorre at home in Hollywood

Conrad Veidt. Camilla Horn★ and Vilma Bánky★ were among a number of German and Austrian actors employed by Metro and Warner Bros. during those studios' foray into multi-language film between 1930 and 1931. When that short-lived experiment foundered, Horn joined in their return to Germany such recently US-recruited compatriots as Gustav Fröhlich, Lissy Arna★ and Theo Shall. The Weimar star Vilma Bánky stayed on, but shared the fate of other post-sound émigrés when her Hollywood career foundered.

Bánky bowed out of film altogether after a brief German reappearance in Luis Trenker's *Der Rebell/The Rebel* (1932). By that date, alongside Negri and Horn, she had in any case already been superseded by the one star who would sustain over several decades the cross-national appeal German actors enjoyed before the coming of sound. Marlene Dietrich's 1931 signing to Paramount was, in the first instance, a response to the commercial challenge posed by the rival MGM diva, Greta Garbo★. Though mildly mistrusted by US audiences, Garbo was by the early 1930s MGM's most lucrative audience magnet abroad, registering in twenty-six countries outside the USA as the national audience's most popular US star.[9] Dietrich's early Paramount films replicated the Garbo pattern in their ambivalent US reception. Despite enthusiastic reviews, *Morocco* (1930) yielded only mediocre box-office returns. *Shanghai Express* (1931) opened to 'rave reviews and crowded theatres', but press response to *Blonde Venus* (1932) was lukewarm, and the film fell short of box-office expectations.[10]

In Germany, by contrast, Dietrich replicated her *Blue Angel* success with a series of hits that continued even after the Nazi takeover in 1933. The Hollywood Dietrich's German popularity peaked in 1936 when Paramount premiered the Ernst Lubitsch title *Desire*, not in New York, but in 'Marlene's' native Berlin. The success of that event has been described as 'an indication of the unbroken popularity Dietrich enjoyed at home'.[11] But Paramount's emphatic foregrounding of Dietrich as the jewel in its émigré crown was a response also to the difficulty of sustaining a German audience for other émigré stars. Of the German-speaking actors who fled directly to Hollywood after the Nazi seizure of power, a handful – including Albert Bassermann, Paul Henreid, Luise Rainer, Hedy Lamarr – were, by the end of the 1930s, building a US star following. Bassermann won a 1940 Academy Award nomination for his role in Hitchcock's *Foreign Correspondent*; Henreid spent the prewar decade of UK exile building the persona as Continental lover in which he was to excel in the US titles *Now, Voyager* and *Casablanca* (both 1942); and Luise Rainer became the first actress ever to win two Best Actress Academy Awards consecutively for her roles in *The Great Ziegfeld* (1936) and *The Good Earth* (1937). But the fate of Rainer's two films in Germany exemplifies the difficulties faced by actors and actresses exiled (unlike Dietrich) on grounds of 'race' or political conviction. Both films fell foul of Nazi anti-Jewish boycotts, and were never shown in the 'Third Reich'. The Austrian-Jewish Rainer found herself in a situation that had become the norm among compatriots exiled after 1933. Deprived by Nazi boycotts of their potential Hollywood function as crowd-pullers for audiences back home, even the most successful artistes endured a career instability that compounded the experiential traumas of their exile condition. Thus, despite her Academy Award successes, Rainer herself fell into US obscurity after 1937, while such legendary figures of the Weimar stage and screen as Elisabeth Bergner★ and Fritz Kortner★ chased walk-on parts in a studio environment

described by Kortner in 1937 as reducing him to the status of 'domestic slave'.[12] Hampered also by visa constraints and quotas for émigré personnel, the first post-1933 exiles found their employment horizons further restricted by the limited typology of roles on offer in 'European' comedy (directors Wilder and Lubitsch were significant here), in horror (see, for instance Peter Lorre's early US roles) or in dramas with European characters and themes (for example, Sig Arno's★ bit parts as mid-European waiter, doctor etc. in successive 1930s and 1940s titles).

Perversely, the exiles' prospects improved in direct parallel with the worsening conditions of wartime persecution for their counterparts at home. As the likes of Kurt Gerron and Joachim Gottschalk were driven to their deaths in Nazi Germany – to joint suicide with his Jewish wife in Gottschalk's case, to the death camps in Gerron's – Hollywood's German-speaking exiles rode the crest of the wave of anti-Nazi films that followed the outbreak of war. By 1939, the émigré presence had already provided the seedbed for a nascent Hollywood anti-Fascism. The Hollywood Anti-Nazi League was active between 1936 and 1938 in anti-Fascist boycotts, demonstrations and press and public relations campaigns, including through its own newspaper, *Hollywood Now*. The European Film Fund, established by the agent Paul Kohner, alongside directors Ernst Lubitsch and (with his wife Charlotte) William Dieterle, had raised funds among existing émigré residents to provide financial aid to incoming exiles, and to fund and organise transatlantic transport for refugees fleeing the Nazi threat. Warner Bros. had been alone among US studios when, in 1934, it resisted Nazi pressures to dismiss Jewish personnel from its offices in the 'Reich': but Warners' early anti-Nazi titles – *The Life of Émile Zola* (1937), *Blockade* (1938), *Juarez* (1939) and *Confessions of a Nazi Spy* (1939) – were only the precursors of a genre that was to become entrenched in Hollywood after 1939. Between 1939 and 1946, Hollywood produced an estimated hundred anti-Nazi titles, over half of which featured German émigrés in leading or important supporting roles.[13]

Hollywood's wartime politicisation did not, however, function entirely to German émigrés' benefit. It was a paradox of the US state's peculiar blend of pragmatic anti-Nazism with a visceral anti-Communism that those émigré figures most prominent in their support for the US war effort became the target of FBI investigations against sus- **267** pected Communists, subversives and spies. Marlene Dietrich, legendary in her time for her anti-Fascist efforts as US troop entertainer, was for several years the object of FBI scrutiny over her alleged participation in such 'anti-American activities' as espionage (the latter never proven) and (apparently equally suspect) 'affairs . . . with notorious lesbians'.[14] The FBI's Dietrich file was closed in 1944; not so those of Henreid, Lorre, Francis Lederer★ and numerous others black- or grey-listed in the McCarthy era on the basis of investigations begun as early as 1940 into alleged 'Communist' agitation.

Despite the waning popularity of anti-Nazi titles after 1944, the genre and the political activities that had surrounded its emergence continued long after that date to define both the political climate for, and the career pathways of, German émigrés in their adopted Los Angeles home. Even such versatile talents as the Austrian Carl Esmond★ found themselves trapped after 1945 in what Esmond once lamented was the 'cul-de-sac' of often crudely stereotyped Nazi roles.[15] Successive actor generations have since seen their Hollywood horizons constricted within a limited 'Nazi' role spectrum that ranges from dastardly party functionary (Esmond in Fritz Lang's 1944 Ministry of Fear) to embattled war commander (Curt Jürgens★ in The Enemy Below [1957], Jürgen Prochnow★ in various roles recalling the troubled captain in the memorable Das Boot/The Boat [1981]). The stereotype of the 'enemy German' is mirrored on the female side by the Hollywood type of the European woman of mystery and dubious sexual intent. Postwar émigré actresses from Romy Schneider★ to Hildegard Knef★ and Senta Berger★ might have sought refuge in Hollywood from the constraints of their German typecasting as virgin-whore (Schneider on the virginal side, Berger and Knef in the camp of licentiousness and sexual subversion). Hollywood has regularly failed, however, to extend its range of female roles beyond the silent cinema stereotype of the European femme fatale: a situation summed up in one 1954 US press depiction of Knef that describes her as the actress who 'steps into Garbo's shoes and walks away with them'.[16]

Like her younger contemporary Schneider, Knef looked increasingly to European productions for an outlet for her larger artistic ambitions, realised in her case in such titles as Fedora (1978) and Flügel und Fesseln/ The Future of Emily (1984). One of the rare émigrés from the cinema of

the German Democratic Republic, Armin Mueller-Stahl★, found his East German background working in his favour when he was cast in Hollywood in successive roles as Hungarian, Pole, Russian, Eastern European Jew – characters that 'carry associations with victimisation, rather than German aggression'.[17] But it took a new generation of popular stars in the revived German genre cinema of the 1990s to pose a significant challenge to the Hollywood cliché of the evil (male)/mysterious but deadly (female) German. Franka Potente★ spent the latter half of the 1990s making a name for herself as action-movie heroine. Germany's foremost 1990s male star, Til Schweiger★, meanwhile, claims to have refused Nazi roles in such titles as Saving Private Ryan (1998) and Jakob the Liar (1999). His explanation: 'I have no desire to play a Nazi murderer. . . . They had a real existence, and they murdered millions – but that doesn't mean I want to play them.'[18] Schweiger's comment suggests that, in a globalised Hollywood, the parameters of German national stereotypes are finally changing – and that it is his generation who may become the emblems of a broader contemporary shift in German émigrés' place in international markets for star images. EC

GIANNINI, Giancarlo (1941–)

Versatile popular Italian actor whose Hollywood supporting roles have yielded uneven results. He was applauded as a classical flautist in Francis Ford Coppola's 'Life without Zoe' (in the portmanteau film New York Stories). His performance as a Mexican patriarch in A Walk in the Clouds was badly received, but he won praise as the corrupt police inspector in Hannibal, and this has prompted several appearances in Hollywood productions or co-productions. CBu
FILMS: The Secret of Santa Vittoria (1969); American Dreamer (1984); Saving Grace, Fever Pitch (1985); Blood Red (1988); New York Stories (1989); Once upon a Crime (1992); A Walk in the Clouds (1995); Mimic (1997); Hannibal, The Whole She-bang (2001); Joshua (2002); My House in Umbria (2003); Man on Fire (2004).

GIELGUD, John (Arthur John Gielgud) (1904–2000)

Gielgud was a quintessentially 'English' actor whose film work was overshadowed by his distinguished stage career, particularly in Shakespearean roles. His Englishness was founded on these theatrical connections and associated with the dominant 'high' cultural ethos of Britain's West

End theatrical and literary traditions. He made over a hundred film and television appearances from the 1920s, but did not strictly appear in a Hollywood film until 1953, when he played Cassius in *Julius Caesar* – *The Insult* and *The Prime Minister* were both US-financed UK productions. He was nominated for an Academy Award as Best Actor in a Supporting Role for his portrayal of King Louis VII in *Becket* and he later won an Academy Award for his performance as the butler in *Arthur*. SS

FILMS: *The Insult* (1932); *The Prime Minister* (1941); *Julius Caesar* (1953); *Around the World in Eighty Days* (1956); *Saint Joan, The Barretts of Wimpole Street* (1957); *H.M.S. Defiant* (1962); *Becket, Hamlet* (1964); *The Loved One* (1965); *Assignment to Kill, Sebastian, The Charge of the Light Brigade, The Shoes of the Fisherman* (1968); *Oh! What a Lovely War* (1969); *Julius Caesar* (1970); *Eagle in a Cage, Lost Horizon* (1972); *11 Harrowhouse* (1974); *Joseph Andrews* (1977); *The Elephant Man, The Formula* (1980); *Sphinx, Arthur* (1981); *The Wicked Lady* (1983); *Plenty* (1985); *Arthur 2: On the Rocks, Appointment with Death* (1988); *Shining Through* (1992); *Haunted, First Knight* (1995); *Dragonheart* [voice], *Looking for Richard, The Portrait of a Lady, Hamlet* (1996); *Quest for Camelot* [voice] (1998).

GIERMANN, Frederick (1902–1985)

German-Jewish stage and radio performer who received only minor parts as enemy soldiers and spies, principally in anti-Nazi films, after emigrating to Hollywood in 1936. His role as Father Pommer battling the regime in *Hitler* – *Beast of Berlin* proved a sympathetic exception. Giermann settled in Oregon after the war and gained local celebrity starring opposite his actress wife Gail Gardner in the hit KPTV children's show, *The Toymaker* (1953–4). RJK

FILMS: *One in a Million* (1936); *Lancer Spy, Prescription for Romance* (1937); *Confessions of a Nazi Spy, Espionage Agent, Hitler* – *Beast of Berlin, The Monroe Doctrine* (1939); *Calling Philo Vance, British Intelligence, Escape* (1940); *So Ends Our Night, Underground, Sergeant York, The Deadly Game, International Squadron, A Yank in the RAF* (1941); *Unseen Enemy, Danger in the Pacific, Berlin Correspondent, Desperate Journey, Destination Unknown, Once upon a Honeymoon, Hitler* – *Dead or Alive, Lucky Jordan, The Great Impersonation* (1942); *Adventures of Smilin' Jack* [serial], *Immortal Sergeant, Assignment in Brittany, The Moon is Down, Edge of Darkness, Tonight We Raid Calais, Five Graves to Cairo, They Came to*

Blow up America, Action in the North Atlantic, Background to Danger, Bomber's Moon, Let's Face It, Above Suspicion, Hostages, The Strange Death of Adolf Hitler, The Cross of Lorraine, Calling Doctor Death, Plan for Destruction (1943); *Meet the People, Address Unknown, The Hitler Gang, The Story of Dr Wassell, The Seventh Cross, U-Boat Prisoner, Secrets of Scotland Yard, They Live in Fear, The Unwritten Code* (1944); *Hotel Berlin, Son of Lassie, Counter-Attack, Paris Underground* (1945); *A Night in Casablanca, The Searching Wind, Cloak and Dagger* (1946); *The Beginning or the End, Calcutta, Golden Earrings* (1947); *Women in the Night* (1948).

GILLES, Geneviève (Geneviève Gillaizeau) (1951–)

Former Yves Saint Laurent model who became the protégée and long-term lover of Darryl F. Zanuck. Gilles appeared (as herself) in his short film, *The World of Fashion* (1968), after being recruited by Fox as 'a fashion consultant'. Zanuck persuaded the studio that the film was a great success and Gilles was contracted on $1,250 per week and given intensive English and acting lessons. She was cast as a French society hostess (opposite Michael Crawford★ and Curt Jürgens★) in her only Hollywood fiction film: the aptly titled, *Hello-Goodbye*. Relations with the Zanuck family deteriorated afterwards and she became embroiled in a damaging lawsuit after her mentor's death in 1979. AP

FILM: *Hello-Goodbye* (1970).

GINGOLD, Hermione (1897–1987)

Endearingly boisterous English actress and comedienne who made occasional British and American film appearances after a successful stage career on both sides of the Atlantic. Gingold is best remembered for her wonderfully grotesque performance as Madame Alvarez in Vincente Minnelli's *Gigi* (1958). MF

FILMS: *Merry Comes to Town* (1937); *Around the World in Eighty Days* (1956); *Gigi, Bell, Book and Candle* (1958); *The Naked Edge* (1961); *The Music Man, Gay Purr-ee* [voice] (1962); *I'd Rather Be Rich* (1964); *Harvey Middleman, Fireman* (1965); *Munster, Go Home* (1966); *Tubby the Tuba* [voice] (1976); *Garbo Talks* (1984).

GIRARDON, Michèle (1938–1975)

A supporting actress in New Wave films such as Eric Rohmer's *Le Signe du lion/The Sign of Leo* (1959), Girardon acted alongside John Wayne and fellow New Wave actor, **269**

Gérard Blain* in her only American movie, Howard Hawks' *Hatari!* Both Girardon and Blain had been sought by Paramount for their 'wholesome and sexy' personae, but whereas Blain played a Frenchman, Girardon succeeded in eschewing French typecasting. VO

FILM: *Hatari!* (1962).

GIRARDOT, Annie (Annie Suzanne Girardot) (1931–)

Major French stage and film star who rose to international fame in Visconti's *Rocco e i suoi fratelli/Rocco and His Brothers* (1960) and was top box-office attraction in France in the late 1960s and 1970s. She appeared in the French episode of *The Dirty Game* (1965), an international portmanteau film about spying, and played a French teacher in her only US movie. SL/GV

FILM: *All Night Long* (1981).

GIRARDOT, Etienne (1856–1939)

Born in London, this Anglo-French stage and screen comic actor had a well-established career before he appeared in American silent films in 1911. He went on to play bit parts in numerous films until his death. CH

FILMS: *Intrepid Davy, Her Hero, A Slight Mistake, One Touch of Nature* (1911); *Nicholas Nickelby* (1912); *Beau Brummel, Betty in the Lions' Den, Up in a Balloon* (1913); *Bunny's Birthday, Pigs is Pigs, Bread upon the Waters, David Garrick, The Violin of Monsieur, Too Many Husbands, The Hall-Room Rivals, Cherry, The Barrel Organ* (1914); *Uncle John, The Treason of Anatole, Mary's Duke, Circus Mary, The Blank Page* (1915); *Artie, the Millionaire Kid* (1916); *The Belle of New York, The Witness for the Defence* (1919); *A Stage Romance* (1922); *Advice to the Lovelorn, The Kennel Murder Case, Blood Money* (1933); *Fashions of 1934, Mandalay, Little Man, What Now?, Twentieth Century, Born to Be Bad, Return of the Terror, The Firebird, The Dragon Murder Case* (1934); *Clive of India, The Whole Town's Talking, I Live My Life, In Old Kentucky, Metropolitan, Hooray for Love, Grand Old Girl, Curly Top, Chasing Yesterday, The Bishop Misbehaves* (1935); *Half Angel, Hearts Divided, The Garden Murder Case, The Devil is a Sissy, The Longest Night, Go West Young Man, College Holiday, The Music Goes Round* (1936); *The Road Back, Wake up and Live, Breakfast for Two, The Great Garrick, Danger-Love at Work* (1937); *Professor Beware, There Goes My Heart, Port of Seven Seas, The Arizona Wildcat* (1938); *Fast and Loose, The Story of Vernon and Irene Castle, For Love or Money, Exile Express, The*

Hunchback of Notre-Dame, Hawaiian Nights, Little Accident (1939); *Isle of Destiny* (1940).

GLASS, Gaston (1898–1965)

Born in Paris, Glass started in show business at the age of seventeen at the Théâtre des Variétés. After touring North and South America with Sarah Bernhardt, he settled in the USA, playing supporting roles in a huge number of films, including some French versions of multi-language films such as *La Piste de géants* (US: *The Big Trail* [1931]). He also worked as assistant director on eighteen films from 1944 to 1955, for instance Joseph L. Mankiewicz's *All About Eve* (1950). MB

FILMS: *Let's Elope, The Lost Battalion, Oh, You Women, Open Your Eyes, The Women of Lies* (1919); *The Branded Woman, Humoresque, Mothers of Men, The World and His Wife* (1920); *Her Winning Way, The Lost Battalion, There are No Villains* (1921); *Glass Houses, I Am the Law, The Kingdom Within, Little Miss Smiles, Monte Cristo, Rich Men's Wives, The Song of Life* (1922); *Daughters of the Rich, Gimme, The Girl Who Came Back, The Hero, The Midnight Flower, Mothers-in-Law, The Spider and the Rose* (1923); *After the Ball, I Am the Man, Trouping with Ellen* (1924); *The Bad Lands, The Danger Signal, Fair Play, Flying Fool, The Mad Marriage, Parisian Nights, The Price of Success, Pursued, The Scarlet West, Three*

Gaston Glass

Keys, *The Verdict* (1925); *Broken Homes, The Call of the Klondike, Exclusive Rights, Her Sacrifice, The Jazz Girl, Midnight Limited, The Road to Broadway, The Romance of a Million Dollars, Subway Sadie, Sweet Daddies, Tentacles of the North, Wives at Auction* (1926); *Better Days, Compassion, False Morals, The Gorilla, The Love Wager, The Show Girl, Sinews of Steel* (1927); *Broken Barriers, A Gentleman Preferred, Innocent Love, My Home Town, Name the Woman, Obey Your Husband, The Red Mark, The Wife's Relations* (1928); *Behind Closed Doors, The Faker, Geraldine, Tiger Rose, Untamed Justice* (1929); *Just Like Heaven, She Got What She Wanted* (1930); *Becky Sharp, Lottery Lover, The Man Who Broke the Bank at Monte Carlo* (1935); *The Amazing Exploits of the Clutching Hand* [serial], *Desire, Fatal Lady, Gambling with Souls, Give Us this Night, Hearts Divided, Mary of Scotland, Princess Comes Across, Sutter's Gold, Sylvia Scarlett, Two in the Dark, Under Two Flags* (1936); *Death in the Air, Espionage, The King and the Chorus Girl* (1937); *Paris after Dark* (1943).

GLEESON, Brendan (1954–)

A former schoolteacher, Gleeson came to international attention playing alongside Mel Gibson in *Braveheart*. Now considered one of Ireland's most versatile actors, he moves between low-budget Irish productions and major Hollywood films such as *Gangs of New York*, in which he played the Irish migrant Walter 'Monk' McGinn. RB

FILMS: *Far and Away* (1992); *Braveheart* (1995); *Michael Collins* (1996); *Turbulence, The Butcher Boy* (1997); *Lake Placid, My Life So Far* (1999); *Mission: Impossible II* (2000); *The Tailor of Panama, Artificial Intelligence: AI* (2001); *28 Days Later, Dark Blue, Gangs of New York* (2002); *Cold Mountain* (2003); *Troy, The Village* (2004).

GOLINO, Valeria (1966–)

Italian-born actress of Italian-Greek parentage who has divided her time equally between the Italian and American industry. While she has played leading Italian roles and won awards for films like *Storia d'amore* (1986), her Hollywood career has either been in less demanding roles or as the romantic interest for actors like Tom Cruise in *Rain Man*. AM

FILMS: *Blind Date* (1984); *Dumb Dicks* (1985); *Big Top Pee-Wee, Rain Man* (1988); *Hot Shots!, The Indian Runner, Year of the Gun* (1991); *Hot Shots! Part Deux* (1993); *Immortal Beloved, Clean Slate* (1994); *Leaving Las Vegas, Four Rooms* (1995); *Escape from L.A., An Occasional Hell* (1996); *Side Streets* (1997); *Things You Can Tell Just by Looking at Her, Ivans xtc.* (2000); *Frida* (2002).

GORDON, Mary (Mary Gilmour) (1882–1963)

Scottish actress who enjoyed a twenty-five-year Hollywood career in supporting roles as nursemaids cleaning ladies, and housekeepers. She is best remembered as Mrs Hudson, housekeeper to Basil Rathbone's★ Sherlock Holmes in eight films made between 1939 and 1946. MHu

FILMS: *The Home Maker, The People vs. Nancy Preston, Tessie* (1925); *Black Paradise* (1926); *Clancy's Kosher Wedding, Naughty Nanette* (1927); *The Old Code, Old Gray Hoss* (1928); *One of the Bravest, The Saturday Night Kid* (1929); *His Honor the Mayor, Oh, for a Man, When the Wind Blows* (1930); *Subway Express, The Black Camel* (1931); *Almost Married, Call Her Savage, Dancers in the Dark, Texas Cyclone* (1932); *My Woman, Whirlwind, Nature in the Wrong* (1933); *The Little Minister, The Defense Rests, Beloved* (1934); *The Pace that Kills, Waterfront Lady, Bonnie Scotland, The Irish in Us, Bride of Frankenstein, Vanessa: Her Love Story, I'm a Father* (1935); *Great Guy, The Plough and the Stars, Forgotten Faces, Stage Struck, Yellowstone, Mary of Scotland, Share the Wealth, Laughing Irish Eyes* (1936); *The Man in Blue, Lady Behave, Double Wedding, Meet the Boyfriend, One Man Justice, Way Out West, The Great O'Malley* (1937); *City Streets, Angels with Dirty Faces, Kidnapped* (1938); *The Jones Family in Hollywood, The Marshal of Mesa City, Day-Time Wife, The Adventures of Sherlock Holmes, Captain Fury, She Married a Cop, Parents on Trial, Racketeers of the Range, Code of the Streets, The Hound of the Baskervilles, Tail Spin* (1939); *No, No, Nanette, Nobody's Children, The Invisible Woman, Flight from Destiny, My Son, My Son, When the Daltons Rode, The Last Alarm, I Take this Oath, Tear Gas Squad, Saps at Sea* (1940); *Appointment for Love, It Started with Eve, Sealed Lips, Riot Squad, Borrowed Hero, Double Cross, Pot o' Gold* (1941); *Fly-By-Night, Meet the Stewarts, Sarong Girl, Secret Weapon, Boss of Big Town, Half Way to Shanghai, The Mummy's Tomb, Sherlock Holmes and the Voice of Terror, Powder Town, It Happened in Flatbush, Dr Broadway, The Strange Case of Doctor Rx, Bombay Clipper* (1942); *Keep 'Em Slugging, Whispering Footsteps, Smart Guy, Sherlock Holmes Faces Death, Here Comes Kelly, Two Tickets to London, Sherlock Holmes in Washington* (1943); *The Last Ride, The Pearl of Death, Secrets of Scotland Yard, Follow the Leader, Hat Check Honey, Million Dollar Kid, Sherlock Holmes and the Spider Woman* (1944); *Captain* **271**

Eddie, See My Lawyer, Kitty, Strange Confession, Divorce, The Woman in Green (1945); *The Hoodlum Saint, Sentimental Journey, Sing While You Dance, Singin' in the Corn, Shadows over Chinatown, In Fast Company, Dressed to Kill, Little Giant* (1946); *The Invisible Wall, Exposed* (1947); *Highway 13, The Strange Mrs Crane, Fort Apache, Angels' Alley* (1948); *Shamrock Hill, Deputy Marshal, Haunted Trails* (1949); *West of Wyoming* (1950).

GOUDAL, Jetta (Julie Henriette Goudeket) (1891–1985)

A French-speaking stage actress born in the Netherlands (or France; birthdate possibly 1901), Goudal began touring Europe before moving to Broadway in 1918. She started making films in 1923. Thanks to *The Coming of Amos* (a film produced by Cecil B. DeMille), the dark-haired beauty became a sensation. For a few years, the 'beguiling' Goudal had her name above the credits, praised as 'the orchid-like Jetta Goudal, the most exotic personality on the screen'. Her stardom reached its peak in *White Gold* and she appeared in D. W. Griffith's *Lady of the Pavements*. Goudal also became known for her forceful personality on the set. Her successful lawsuit against DeMille over a contract and her involvement in the actors' trade unions were instrumental in enforcing actors' rights but detrimental to her career. After a few films, including the French multi-language *Le Spectre vert* (US: *The Unholy Night* [1929]), she married and retired from the cinema in 1933. GV

FILMS: *The Bright Shawl, The Green Goddess* (1923); *Open All Night* (1924); *The Coming of Amos, The Road to Yesterday, Salome of the Tenements, The Spaniard* (1925); *Her Man o' War, Paris at Midnight, Three Faces East* (1926); *Fighting Love, The Forbidden Woman, White Gold* (1927); *The Cardboard Lover* (1928); *Lady of the Pavements* (1929); *Business and Pleasure* (1932).

GOUGH, Michael (1917–)

Malayan-born actor whose gaunt looks led to appearances in a string of British horror films in the 1950s and 1960s. He is now mostly recognised as Bruce Wayne's devoted manservant, Alfred, in the 1990s Batman films. MW

FILMS: *The Sword and the Rose, Rob Roy, the Highland Rogue* (1953); *Konga* (1961); *What a Carve Up* (1962); *Black Zoo* (1963); *Beserk!* (1968); *Women in Love, A Walk with Love and Death* (1969); *Julius Caesar, Trog* (1970); *The Boys from Brazil*

(1978); *Top Secret!* (1984); *Out of Africa* (1985); *The Serpent and the Rainbow* (1988); *Batman* (1989); *Batman Returns* (1992); *The Age of Innocence* (1993); *Batman Forever* (1995); *Batman & Robin* (1997); *Sleepy Hollow* (1999).

GOWLAND, Gibson (1877–1951)

British actor with distinctive heavy-set features who was variously credited as T. H. Gibson Gowland, G. H. Gowland or T. H. Gowland, if at all, during his extensive career in Hollywood. He played the role of McTeague in Erich von Stroheim's *Greed*. TJ

FILMS: *Birth of a Nation, Jewel, Pennington's Choice* (1915); *Macbeth* (1916); *The Promise, Under Handicap, The Phantom Shotgun, The Climber, The Secret of Black Mountain, Molly Entangled* (1917); *Breakers Ahead* (1918); *The White Heather, Blind Husbands, Behind the Door* (1919); *The Right of Way, The Fighting Shepherdess* (1920); *Ladies Must Live* (1921); *With Father's Help* (1922); *Shifting Sands, Hutch Stirs 'Em Up, The Harbour Lights* (1923); *The Red Lily, The Border Legion, Love and Glory* (1924); *Greed, The Prairie Wife, The Phantom of the Opera* (1925); *The Outsider, Don Juan, College Days* (1926); *The Night of Love, The Broken Gate, The Land beyond the Law, The First Auto, The Tired Business Man, Sunrise, Topsy and Eva, The Isle of Forgotten Women* (1927); *Rose-Marie* (1928); *The Mysterious Island* (1929); *Hell Harbor, The Sea Bat, Cleaning Up* (1930); *Land of Wanted Men, A House Divided* (1931); *Without Honor, The Doomed Battalion* (1932); *S.O.S. Iceberg* (1933); *The Private Life of Don Juan, The Secret of the Loch* (1934); *The Mystery of the Marie Celeste, The Stoker, King of the Damned* (1935); *Highland Fling* (1936); *The Wife of General Ling, Cotton Queen* (1937); *The Storm, Tea Leaves in the Wind* (1938); *Raffles, Northwest Passage, Doomed to Die, The Ape* (1940); *Mutiny in the Arctic, Broadway Limited, Tanks a Million, How Green Was My Valley, The Wolf Man* (1941); *The Vanishing Virginian, The Remarkable Andrew, Crossroads, Isle of Missing Men* (1942); *The Moon is Down, The Man from Down Under, A Guy Named Joe, The Human Comedy* (1943); *Going My Way, Gaslight, Wilson* (1944); *The Picture of Dorian Gray, Kitty* (1945); *Gun Cargo* (1949).

GOZZI, Patricia (1950–)

Gozzi had a short but high-profile acting career as a child star in France, culminating in the Academy Award-winning *Les Dimanches de Ville d'Avray/Sundays and Cybele* (1962).

At the age of fifteen, she appeared in the US/French co-production *Rapture* as the confused daughter of a retired judge. TH

FILM: *Rapture* (1965).

GRAHAME, Margot (1911–1982)

Promoted as Britain's answer to Jean Harlow because of her striking blonde appearance, Grahame appeared in several US-backed films shot in the UK, before going to Hollywood in 1935 after signing a short contract with RKO. Her first role (opposite Victor McLaglen★) was as the prostitute Katie Madden in John Ford's *The Informer*. She returned to Britain in 1937. JS

FILMS: *Stamboul* (1931); *Postal Orders, A Letter of Warning, Illegal* (1932); *I Adore You, Forging Ahead* (1933); *Without You* (1934); *The Informer, The Arizonian, The Three Musketeers* (1935); *Two in the Dark, Counterfeit, Make Way for a Lady, Night Waitress, Crime over London* (1936); *The Soldier and the Lady, Criminal Lawyer, Fight for Your Lady* (1937); *The Buccaneer* (1938); *The Hal Roach Comedy Festival, The Fabulous Joe* (1947); *Black Magic* (1949); *The Crimson Pirate* (1952); *Saint Joan* (1957).

GRANACH, Alexander (Jessaja Granach) (1890–1945)

Born to Jewish parents in Werbowitz (now Werbkovice, Poland), Granach was one of Weimar Germany's foremost stage and screen actors whose Communist beliefs led him to appear in several anti-war and socialist pictures. Upon the Nazis' rise to power, Granach began touring Czechoslovakia and Poland when colleague Gustav von Wangenheim enticed him to Moscow, where the exiled German Communist Party was establishing an alternative German theatre and cinema. Granach's non-realist style met with Stalin's personal disapproval, however, and the actor was charged with spying and incarcerated in 1937. Receiving an exit visa in mysterious circumstances, Granach sped via Switzerland to the USA in 1938, where fellow Broadway and Hollywood émigrés furnished him with a succession of roles that exploited his guttural accent and swarthy Slavic features. Although he played supporting roles, Granach frequently stole the show. He garnered popular and critical attention for his portrayal of Kopalski – one of the three 'Karl Marx brothers' (together with Felix Bressart★ and Sig Rumann★) in *Ninotchka* – and the sinister Gestapo officers in *Joan of Paris* and *Hangmen Also Die*. Granach remained a familiar face in Hollywood until his sudden death. RJK

FILMS: *Ninotchka, The Hunchback of Notre Dame* (1939); *Foreign Correspondent, Comrade X* (1940); *So Ends Our Night, It Started with Eve, Marry the Boss's Daughter, A Man Betrayed* (1941); *Joan of Paris, Wrecking Crew, Half Way to Shanghai, Northwest Rangers, Joan of Ozark* (1942); *Hangmen Also Die, For Whom the Bell Tolls, Three Russian Girls, Mission to Moscow* (1943); *The Hitler Gang, The Seventh Cross, A Voice in the Wind, My Buddy* (1944).

GRANGER, Stewart (James Lablanche Stewart) (1913–1993)

Granger was a major star in postwar British cinema who consistently proved a box-office draw in Gainsborough melodramas as a smouldering, virile and swashbuckling romantic lead. He was tall, handsome and debonair with a charming, flirtatious smile. His performance style communicated a physicality, athleticism and bravado that was perfectly suited to the many adventurous heroes he played. Granger impressed Irene Selznick (ex-wife of David O. Selznick and daughter of Louis B. Mayer) in 1949, when he appeared in his London stage production of Tolstoy's *The Power of Darkness*, a venture that otherwise proved to be a critical and financial failure. She invited him to play opposite Vivien Leigh★ in Olivier's stage production of *A Streetcar Named Desire*, but he declined, preferring instead to direct his attentions to Hollywood. His former agent arranged a contract with MGM in Hollywood, where he moved with his wife, the actress Jean Simmons★.

Granger's film made in Hollywood, *King Solomon's Mines*, co-starring Deborah Kerr★, was a major success and it led to other roles that presented him as a rugged adventurer. Granger enjoyed the Hollywood lifestyle, and was befriended on arrival by Cary Grant, James Mason★ and George Sanders★. He was soon in dispute with MGM over expenses and found himself cornered when the studio agreed to pay his debts on condition that he signed a seven-year contract. Granger was reluctant to commit himself to Hollywood for so long but had no choice, since he could not pay the expenses himself. His next roles continued in the swashbuckling vein, particularly *Scaramouche* and *The Prisoner of Zenda*, films that placed him in the romantic, adventurous tradition of Douglas Fairbanks and Errol Flynn. This version of Englishness was clearly differ- **273** ent from other British actors who went to Hollywood, who were typified by a gentler, more subtle and intellectual sensibility.

Granger's attitude towards the USA was ambivalent. He became an American citizen in 1956, only to revert to British nationality in 1962. After enjoying the novelty of being in Hollywood, he soon became frustrated at what he considered to be a lack of perfectionism and an exploitative attitude towards stars. His outspoken attitude and reputation for being difficult with directors and studio bosses did not help to smooth his path, particularly when his financial problems became acute. He made some bad decisions, turning down lead parts in several films that would have made a decisive impact on his career, including the role played by Burt Lancaster in *From Here to Eternity* (1953) and that played by James Mason in *A Star is Born* (1954). In the 1960s, he appeared in German, Italian and British films, as well as on American television, most notably in the Western series *The Virginian*. In 1990, he returned to the British theatre and finally made his Broadway debut in a production of Somerset Maugham's *The Circle*, also featuring Rex Harrison★ and Glynis Johns. ss

FILMS: *So This is London* (1940); *King Solomon's Mines* (1950); *Soldiers Three, The Light Touch, The Wild North* (1951); *Scaramouche, The Prisoner of Zenda* (1952); *Salome, Young Bess, All the Brothers Were Valiant* (1953); *Beau Brummell, Green Fire* (1954); *Moonfleet, Footsteps in the Fog, Bhowani Junction, The Last Hunt* (1955); *The Little Hut, Gun Glory* (1957); *North to Alaska* (1960); *Sodom and Gomorrah* (1962); *The Secret Invasion* (1964); *The Last Safari* (1967); *The Wild Geese* (1978); *Hell Hunters* (1988).

GRANT, Cary (Archibald Alexander Leach) (1904–1986)

Cary Grant, the quintessential Hollywood leading man and one of the most popular and enduring stars of American cinema, was English, born Archibald Leach in a working-class area of Bristol. The entity Cary Grant did not emerge until 31 December 1931, the day he signed a long-term contract with Paramount. By that date, he had been working in the USA for twelve years, having travelled to New York in 1920 as an acrobat with the Pender troupe, where he worked on the vaudeville circuit, remaining in New York to pursue his own career, eventually securing Broad-

way roles from 1927 onwards. His new name was chosen by Paramount executives, who had hired Leach as a potential rival to Gary Cooper.

Paramount marketed their new leading man as 'suave and sophisticated . . . polished', and his early roles were usually continuations of the character he had played on Broadway: the elegantly attired man-about-town. But although he played opposite some remarkable female stars – including Marlene Dietrich in *Blonde Venus* and Mae West in *She Done Him Wrong* and *I'm No Angel* – Grant felt that he was poorly served by Paramount, where he was always second fiddle to Cooper. In an unprecedented and courageous move in an era of long-term studio contracts, Grant went freelance in 1936, even though he had to resign from the Motion Picture Academy. Grant controlled his career very closely from this point onwards and drove hard bargains, becoming the first star to get 10 per cent of a film's gross. He also became involved in the contract negotiations of other stars.

After an uncertain first few months, he made *The Awful Truth* for Columbia, the film that turned Grant from leading man into star. This romantic comedy had a witty script, played at a fast tempo and with a pronounced element of slapstick, which allowed Grant to develop a distinctive version of the debonair romantic hero. He was, as C. L. R. James recognised, 'a new type of Englishman on whom the influence of American civilisation has been very strong'. In essence, he embodied the contradictions of American society: the aspiration towards Old World gentility and style united with a New World self-assurance and democratic directness. Grant became the stereotypical Englishman who had embraced American values and attitudes: the modern gentleman, freed from class snobbery who was both intelligent and quick-witted.

Grant's incarnation of this new type drew on his complex cultural heritage, combining the casual elegance of his English models, Jack Buchanan★ and Noel Coward★, with the physical exuberance of the American star he most admired, Douglas Fairbanks. Thus, although Grant often poses nonchalantly, hands in pockets, shoulders slightly hunched and with a quizzical expression, he always exudes strength and athleticism, the product of his early training and his lifelong fitness. In the most refined of drawing rooms, he can execute a pratfall as deftly as Chaplin★, another seminal influence. Grant's performance style is

Cary Grant relaxes in style on the steps of his Hollywood home

based on specific gestures – the cocked head, eyepopping stare, the forward lunge – and the precise execution of particular actions. It was an 'external', mannered style that required exquisite control and timing, not reaching for pathos or the expression of intense emotion. Grant worked at this style with great dedication: his own copies of scripts were full of small notes concerning minute details of the *mise-en-scène*, how he was to be lit and dressed.

The other key element was his voice, that unplaceable (and much imitated) accent and speech cadences that are cultivated but classless, precise and clipped but without the patrician intonations of the British actors, such as Ronald Colman★, who traded on their Englishness. Grant did not mix socially with this set, the 'Hollywood Raj', nor did he share their public-school upbringing. Except for *The Amazing Quest of Ernest Bliss*, made in 1936 before his Hollywood stardom was secure, he never worked in British films. He resisted pressure to return to Britain during World War II, becoming an American citizen in 1942, when he legally changed his name to Cary Grant.

Although Grant played other types: the action hero in *Gunga Din* and a working-class cockney in *None but the*

Lonely Heart, his persona became fixed with a succession of variations on the American gentleman, including three robust comedies with Howard Hawks: *Bringing up Baby*, *His Girl Friday* and *Monkey Business*, and two more romantic ones directed by George Cukor: *Holiday* and *The Philadelphia Story*. His strength was to combine vulnerability with his self-assurance and hint at depth beneath the charming and handsome exterior. Grant was at his best when self-mocking, discomfited by events and needing reassurance. This combination gave him a strong romantic appeal, without alienating males, who felt reassured by his essential ordinariness.

However, Alfred Hitchcock deepened and developed the Grant persona, beginning with *Suspicion*, in which Grant plays a rakish character whom his wife (Joan Fontaine) suspects of wanting to murder her. Grant is disturbing in the part, even if the studio insisted on his ultimate innocence. In *Notorious*, he plays a saturnine secret agent, prepared to prostitute the woman he loves but cannot forgive (Ingrid Bergman★) in order to achieve his mission. If these roles suggested a dark, repressed self beneath Grant's polished exterior and famous smile, *North by Northwest* probes further. It strips away the shallow satisfaction of Grant's character Roger O. Thornhill, and through its 'wrong man' plot – Thornhill is mistakenly believed to be George Kaplan, a man who does not exist, having been fabricated by the CIA – plays very knowingly with the whole notion of a constructed identity, the essence of Cary Grant.

Grant had a remarkably long career as a star, with occasional breaks when he claimed to have retired. He retained his trim figure and good looks right through to *Charade*, when he decided that, at fifty-nine, he was too old to play the romantic lead; he had no desire to play character roles. Long ostracised by the Academy, he received a 'lifetime achievement' award in 1970. Grant always understood that his talent lay in perfecting a modern fantasy of worldly grace, the 'man from dream city' as Pauline Kael phrased it, whom women desired and men admired, the idealised self of Archie Leach. AS

FILMS: *This is the Night, Sinners in the Sun, Merrily We Go to Hell, Devil and the Deep, Blonde Venus, Hot Saturday, Madame Butterfly* (1932); *She Done Him Wrong, Woman Accused, The Eagle and the Hawk, Gambling Ship, I'm No Angel, Alice in Wonderland* (1933); *Thirty Day Princess, Born to Be Bad, Kiss and Make Up, Ladies Should Listen* (1934); *Enter*

Madame, Wings in the Dark, The Last Outpost (1935); *Sylvia Scarlett, Big Brown Eyes, Suzy, Wedding Present* (1936); *When You're in Love, Topper, The Toast of New York, The Awful Truth* (1937); *Bringing up Baby, Holiday* (1938); *Gunga Din, Only Angels Have Wings, In Name Only* (1939); *His Girl Friday, My Favorite Wife, The Howards of Virginia, The Philadelphia Story* (1940); *Penny Serenade, Suspicion* (1941); *The Talk of the Town, Once upon a Honeymoon* (1942); *Mr Lucky, Destination Tokyo* (1943); *Once upon a Time, None but the Lonely Heart, Arsenic and Old Lace* (1944); *Night and Day, Notorious* (1946); *The Bachelor and the Bobby-Soxer, The Bishop's Wife* (1947); *Mr Blandings Builds His Dream House, Every Girl Should Be Married* (1948); *I Was a Male War Bride* (1949); *Crisis* (1950); *People Will Talk* (1951); *Room for One More, Monkey Business* (1952); *Dream Wife* (1953); *To Catch a Thief* (1955); *The Pride and the Passion, An Affair to Remember, Kiss Them for Me* (1957); *Indiscreet, Houseboat* (1958); *North by Northwest, Operation Petticoat* (1959); *The Grass is Greener* (1960); *That Touch of Mink* (1962); *Charade* (1963); *Father Goose* (1964); *Walk, Don't Run* (1966).

GRANT, Hugh (Hugh John Mungo Grant) (1960–)

The figure of the handsome but flustered, bumbling bourgeois Englishman Hugh Grant tends to embody has proved especially attractive as a national stereotype in the USA. The narrow choice of parts Grant has had to date should not, however, prevent recognition of his genuine comedic skills and the ambition he has demonstrated to venture beyond the limits of his allotted image.

The son of middle-class English parents, Grant made his film debut as 'Hughie Grant' while still at Oxford University, in *Privileged* (1982), along with fellow heritage film alumnus James Wilby. In the 1980s and 1990s, he became identified with prissy upper-class roles in British period dramas, notably in the Merchant-Ivory productions *Maurice* (1987) and *The Remains of the Day*. He also played Lord Byron opposite his future partner Elizabeth Hurley in *Rowing in the Wind* (1983), and Lord D'Ampton for Ken Russell in *The Lair of the White Worm* (1988). He appeared twice as the composer Frederic Chopin, in *Nocturnes* (1988) and *Impromptu*, the latter also featuring Emma Thompson★, alongside whom he later acted in *Sense and Sensibility*.

Grant was subsequently cast as the tousled, lovelorn romantic hero of Mike Newell's *Four Weddings and a Funeral*

(1994), whose international success brought him a more contemporary, if no less privileged, persona and resulted in his first purpose-built Hollywood vehicle. The success of *Nine Months* may partly have been due to a real-life faux pas shortly before its release, in which Grant was arrested for soliciting sexual favours from Divine Brown, a Los Angeles prostitute. This resulted in one of the decade's great show business scandals. The publicity gave his stardom an additional boost and his image an interesting edge that suggested a darker side to a hitherto likeable but bland personality.

Brave attempts to extend his range – giving one of his best performances as a nicotine-stained seducer in Newell's mordant theatrical drama *An Awfully Big Adventure* (1994); appearing as a harassed courtier in the expensive period pageant *Restoration*; as the doctor hero of the New York-set medical thriller *Extreme Measures* and the son-in-law to a gangster in the Mafia comedy *Mickey Blue Eyes*, both co-produced with Hurley for their British joint production company, Simian Films – failed to find wide acceptance. It was left to *Four Weddings*' writer Richard Curtis to provide him with a follow-up hit, *Notting Hill*. The presence of co-star Julia Roberts, the mixture of romance, farce and sentimentality, and the somewhat whitewashed, visitor's-eye view of London ensured another enormous commercial success. Both that film and *Bridget Jones's Diary* enjoyed substantial American financial support and reward, the latter allowing Grant to revel in his role as an absolute cad. This twist on his smooth charm had been anticipated by Woody Allen when he cast him as a gold-digging style guru in *Small Time Crooks*. Similarly, the lure of forbidden sexuality had already been explored by Grant on screen in Roman Polanski's French film *Bitter Moon* (1992) and John Duigan's Australian film *Sirens* (1994). Both these underrated features arguably provided him with more incisive vehicles for his talents than the boyish upper-class protagonists of *Four Weddings* and *Notting Hill*.

Grant gave one of his most engaging performances to date in the Anglo-American adaptation of Nick Hornby's *About a Boy* (like *Bridget Jones's Diary* and *Notting Hill*, a Working Title production financed and released by Universal). In a further bid – this time successful – to widen his appeal, Grant's hair was designer cropped and his accent 'proletarianised' to that of a trendy layabout whose inherited wealth is due to the success of a popular song

rather than a landed title. The film preserved Hornby's sharp observation of male thirty-something anxieties and managed to present Grant convincingly as the representative, not of a privileged class stratum, but of an age-and-gender group neurosis. SH

FILMS: *Impromptu* (1989); *The Big Man* (1990); *The Remains of the Day* (1993); *Nine Months, Sense and Sensibility, Restoration* (1995); *Extreme Measures* (1996); *Notting Hill, Mickey Blue Eyes* (1999); *Small Time Crooks* (2000); *Bridget Jones's Diary* (2001); *About a Boy, Two Weeks Notice* (2002); *Love Actually* (2003); *Bridget Jones: The Edge of Reason* (2004).

GRANT, Richard E. (Richard Grant Esterhuysen) (1957–)

Swaziland-born British actor whose exuberant breakthrough performance as a frustrated, dipsomaniac would-be thespian in *Withnail and I* (1987) still looms over a Holly-

Richard E. Grant as a monomaniacal robber-baron in *Hudson Hawk* (1991)

wood career that has involved regular comic typecasting as neurotic eccentrics in films like *Gosford Park*. MF

FILMS: *Warlock* (1989); *Mountains of the Moon, Henry & June* (1990); *L.A. Story, Hudson Hawk* (1991); *The Player, Bram Stoker's Dracula* (1992); *The Age of Innocence* (1993); *Ready to Wear* (1994); *Twelfth Night: Or What You Will, The Portrait of a Lady* (1996); *Spice World* (1997); *The Little Vampire* (2000); *Gosford Park* (2001).

GRAVEY, Fernand (Fernand Mertens) (1905–1970)

Gravey's main American career lasted only two years, during which he played leading roles in just three films. However, he left his mark on Hollywood thanks to his natural ease and acting talent, trained on the Belgian stage. He had learned English in Britain during World War I and this enabled him to shoot the French and English versions of *A moi le jour, à toi la nuit/Early to Bed* (1932) and *La Guerre des valses* (1933) in Berlin, as well as play the role of a Viennese violinist in the British film *Bitter Sweet* (1934). He would later confess that he could speak 'American slang as well as Parisian *argot*'.

In *The King and the Chorus Girl*, Gravey played a dethroned king who meets a film extra (Joan Blondell) and decides to leave the trappings of royalty for her. In *Fools for Scandal*, he portrayed a French marquis pretending to be a chef's assistant who meets an American film star (Carole Lombard) in Montmartre. Finally, in Julien Duvivier's lavish *The Great Waltz*, he was a rebellious Johann Strauss in Austria. We can draw two conclusions from this trilogy: first, these films reveal young, Republican America's amused fascination with monarchies reductively associated with the 'Old Continent'. Second, Gravey – who became Gravet in the USA to avoid unfortunate puns – always embodied the charming and refined, but sometimes cocky, romantic male lead. His dark-haired characters were both likeable and ironic, but their nuanced teasing never extended to satirical attacks and, as a result, he was often dubbed the 'French Clark Gable'. Gravey's repertoire remained quite limited but it allowed him to blend in perfectly with the Hollywood generic conventions of the time. His wife, Jeanne Renouart, was at the core of the Hollywood French-speaking colony and a teacher of English there. JP

FILMS: *The King and the Chorus Girl* (1937); *Fools for Scandal, The Great Waltz* (1938); *How to Steal a Million* (1966); **278** *The Madwoman of Chaillot* (1969).

GRAVINA, Cesare (1858–1954)

Director of a highly successful touring Italian theatre company who emigrated to Hollywood when his actors were enlisted. Gravina worked as a character actor and played numerous dramatic roles in films, including several features by Erich von Stroheim. He returned to Italy and abandoned film before the conversion to sound. AM/CS

FILMS: *The White Pearl, Madame Butterfly* (1915); *Poor Little Peppina, Less than the Dust* (1916); *The Siren, The Fatal Ring, Miss Nobody, The Price She Paid* (1917); *Let's Get a Divorce, The Mysterious Client, The Street of Seven Stars* (1918); *Marriage for Convenience* (1919); *Mothers of Men, Scratch My Back, Madame X, From Now On, The Penalty* (1920); *Beach of Dreams, God's Country and the Law* (1921); *Foolish Wives, Merry-Go-Round* (1922); *Daddy, Circus Days, The Hunchback of Notre Dame* (1923); *The Humming Bird, The Family Secret, Butterfly, The Rose of Paris, Those Who Dare* (1924); *Greed* [scenes deleted], *Contraband, The Charmer, Fifth Avenue Models, The Man in Blue, Don Dare Devil, A Woman's Faith, The Phantom of the Opera, The Circus Cyclone, Flower of Night, Starvation Blues* (1925); *Monte Carlo, The Midnight Sun, The Blonde Saint, An Enemy of Men* (1926); *The Magic Garden, The Road to Romance, Cheating Cheaters, The Man Who Laughs* (1927); *The Divine Woman, The Trail of '98, The Wedding March, How to Handle Women* (1928); *Burning the Wind* (1929).

GRÉCO, Juliette (1927–)

Famous for being the black-clad singing muse of postwar France's Left Bank nightclubs, Gréco had worked with such film luminaries as Jean Renoir and Jean-Pierre Melville before being introduced to Fox's Darryl F. Zanuck by Mel Ferrer while in New York on an American musical tour. She was offered an optional contract with the studio and became Zanuck's protégée and eventual lover. Given the affection for American popular cultural forms in 1950s France and the reciprocal admiration by many leading American performers for the Parisian scene in Saint-Germain-des-Prés, it was perhaps inevitable that Gréco would make the journey to Hollywood. After appearing in the Hemingway adaptation *The Sun Also Rises*, she provided the music for, and starred as herself, in the film adaptation of Françoise Sagan's *Bonjour Tristesse*. Her international breakthrough came in John Huston's *The Roots of Heaven*, set in tropical Africa, where she starred as Minna, a golden-hearted Corsican prostitute. In France, Gréco had performed material developed by the likes of Jacques Prévert, Jean-Paul Sartre and Jean Cocteau. She subsequently complained bitterly about the quality of the written scripts she was presented with in the USA, and she also apparently resented Zanuck's paternalistic controlling tendencies. She returned to Europe after two further features. AP

FILMS: *The Green Glove* [scenes deleted] (1952); *The Sun Also Rises* (1957); *Bonjour Tristesse* (1958); *Naked Earth, The Roots of Heaven* (1959); *Crack in the Mirror, The Big Gamble* (1960); *The Night of the Generals* (1967).

GREECE

Greek cinema has long suffered from lack of funding and education and from amateurism in production and marketing. It is thus not surprising that many Greek films have aimed to appeal solely to the domestic audience. However, through their collaboration with well-established international directors, a few actors and actresses managed to break into the American market, albeit with differing degrees of success. Charismatic female stars such as Melina Mercouri★, Irene Papas★ and Katina Paxinou★ have been cast in leading roles in large-scale international productions such as *Never on Sunday* (1960), *Zorba the Greek* (1964) and *For Whom the Bell Tolls* (1943), though despite their artistic merits, they have failed to take the USA by storm. Because of linguistic difficulties (often strong accents) and dark looks, they have mostly been typecast in supporting roles as 'foreigners'. This casting pattern also reflects their overall social standing in the USA, where Greek actors have tended to resist assimilation and maintained their national identity outside the studio. Most of them – with the exception of Mercouri, Papas and Paxinou – have thus failed to achieve box-office hits or make the front page in the USA or at home. This is not to say that the Greeks lack national pride when it comes to the success of their compatriots abroad. It is rather the case that geographical and psychological distance makes American-made success seem detached from the geographical and cultural realities of Greek life. Many Greek stars abroad have felt this cultural alienation. Furthermore, the concept, as well as the phenomenon of stardom, still remains unusual practice in Greek society. In this small, almost compact domestic film industry, 'stars' and audiences have always successfully inter-mingled with each other on a regular and casual basis. This tends to highlight their humanity at the expense of the God-like quality of their Hollywood counterparts. TH

GREEN, Nigel (1924–1972)

Muscular six-foot-four South African-born actor who had a prolific British film career that alternated between brutish ruffians and imposing authority figures. Green appeared as such in a number of UK-shot American productions, but a meatier part as Michael Caine's★ duplicitous, steely-eyed MI5 paymaster in *The Ipcress File* (1965) brought him better international recognition and Hollywood agency representation. In the clutch of American films Green made before his accidental death, he continued to play soldiers and mercenaries, but his iconic association with the cold war thriller genre also saw him cast as shadowy string-pullers in *The Wrecking Crew* and *The Kremlin Letter*. JB

FILMS: *Bitter Victory* (1957); *Mysterious Island* (1961); *Zulu, Jason and the Argonauts* (1963); *The Masque of the Red Death* (1964); *Khartoum* (1966); *Africa – Texas Style!, Tobruk* (1967); *The Pink Jungle* (1968); *Fraulein Doktor, The Wrecking Crew* (1969); *The Kremlin Letter* (1970); *The Ruling Class* (1972).

GREENE, Richard (1918–1985)

Handsome and athletic British actor renowned for his leading role in British television's *The Adventures of Robin Hood* (1955–60). Greene made his film debut in John Ford's *Four Men and a Prayer* and subsequently played a leading role as Perry Townsend in Ford's *Submarine Patrol*. Until the late 1960s, he alternated between Britain and Hollywood, where he frequently appeared in historical adventures and swashbucklers. MHu

FILMS: *Four Men and a Prayer, Submarine Patrol, My Lucky Star, Kentucky* (1938); *The Little Princess, The Hound of the Baskervilles, Stanley and Livingstone, Here I Am a Stranger* (1939); *Little Old New York, I Was an Adventuress* (1940); *Forever Amber* (1947); *The Fighting O'Flynn, The Fan* (1949); *The Desert Hawk* (1950); *Lorna Doone* (1951); *Rogue's March, The Black Castle* (1952); *The Bandits of Corsica, Captain Scarlett* (1953); *Island of the Lost* (1967).

GREENSTREET, Sydney (1879–1954)

Kent-born Sydney Greenstreet was by no means the first theatrically trained British actor to carve out a successful Hollywood career playing urbane villains. But his iconic **279**

British actor, Sydney Greenstreet, was classical Hollywood's quintessential urbane villain

It seems fair to say that never before or since has a character actor of advanced years made such a revelatory impact on their screen debut. Greenstreet earned an Academy Award nomination for Best Supporting Actor, a long-term contract with Warner Bros. and effectively created a distinctively new variety of smooth-tongued English villainy in Hollywood cinema. A peculiarly unsettling menace lies in the disparity between his cheerful outward appearance and inscrutable inner resolve: the sheer lack of physical threat signified by his 357-pound weight and his impeccable manners and civil joviality ('By gad, sir!') make his callous disregard for human life seem infinitely more chilling. The sight of evil masked by a polite epicurean façade was still being exploited as a novelty right up to the end of Greenstreet's career: in the 1948 *The Woman in White*, his character disingenuously asks 'How can I be villainous? I'm too fat!'. Greenstreet did not always play the villain in the twenty-four films he made before retiring through ill-health at the end of the 1940s, but these were his most popular and enduring roles. To capitalise on the shady partnership he formed with co-star Peter Lorre★ in *The Maltese Falcon*, the two actors were cast together for a further eight films in the space of five years. The striking contrast in their outward appearance and demeanours saw the old Shakespearean trouper Greenstreet gain even wider exposure in wartime American culture via the pleasure cartoonists of all stripes took in drawing caricatures of the so-called 'Laurel and Hardy of crime'. JB

FILMS: *The Maltese Falcon, They Died with Their Boots On* (1941); *Across the Pacific, Casablanca* (1942); *Background to Danger* (1943); *Passage to Marseille, Between Two Worlds, The Mask of Dimitrios, The Conspirators, Hollywood Canteen* (1944); *Pillow to Post, Conflict, Christmas in Connecticut* (1945); *Three Strangers, Devotion, The Verdict* (1946); *That Way with Women, The Hucksters* (1947); *Ruthless, The Woman in White, The Velvet Touch* (1948); *Flamingo Road, It's a Great Feeling, Malaya* (1949).

status in American cinema of the 1940s certainly did much to cement and standardise this casting practice. Following his theatrical debut in Britain in 1902, Greenstreet first worked in the USA when accompanying the Ben Greet company on tour in 1904, and after returning for a series of provincial engagements with them over the next two years, he settled permanently in the USA in 1906. Shakespearean roles were a particular speciality, and the bulky weight Greenstreet carried all his adult life helped him earn particular fame as the definitive Sir Toby Belch for a generation of American theatregoers. In a Stateside stage career that spanned more than thirty-five years, Greenstreet received numerous overtures from film producers – and flatly turned them all down. It was only when he was left unexpectedly unengaged after the sudden closure of a politically contentious play he was appearing in that Greenstreet accepted an offer in 1941 from first-time director John Huston. Greenstreet's first film appearance thus came at the age of sixty as the unscrupulous art thief Kasper Gutman in Huston's proto-noir adaptation of Dashiell Hammett's *The Maltese Falcon*.

GRENFELL, Joyce (Joyce Irene Phipps) (1910–1979)
Much-loved English comedienne with an affinity for playing eccentric bluestocking characters. Grenfell appeared as 'Lovely Ducks' in Hitchcock's US-financed *Stage Fright*, but her only major Hollywood role (opposite Julie Andrews★) was the 'tweedy' Mrs Barnham in Arthur Hiller's wartime comedy, *The Americanization of Emily*. MW

FILMS: *Stage Fright* (1950); *The Old Dark House, The Americanization of Emily* (1964); *The Yellow Rolls-Royce* (1965).

GRETLER, Heinrich (1897–1977)

Gretler appeared in *Menschen am Sonntag* (1930), *M* (1931) and *Das Testament des Dr Mabuse* (1933) in Germany before becoming the biggest male movie star in his native Switzerland in the late 1930s, where he specialised in difficult, but lovable, patriarchs such as Heidi's grandfather Alp Öhi. Gretler's only US film was the European-shot Gene Kelly drama *The Devil Makes Three*. VH

FILM: *The Devil Makes Three* (1952).

GRIFFIES, Ethel (1878–1975)

The near-simultaneous release in 1963 of Hitchcock's *The Birds* and the British film *Billy Liar* highlighted the brilliance of this veteran, playing respectively an aggressive Californian ornithologist and a querulous North of England grandmother. She had migrated at age forty-six from the London stage to Broadway, and the numerous minor Hollywood roles that followed (many of them uncredited) were typified by her formidable academic in *A Yank at Oxford*. CB

FILMS: *Old English, Sweet Kitty Bellairs* (1930); *The Millionaire, Waterloo Bridge, The Road to Singapore, Once a Lady, Manhattan Parade, Chances* (1931); *Union Depot, Impatient Maiden, Devil's Lottery, Are You Listening?, Westward Passage, Love Me Tonight* (1932); *Tonight is Ours, A Lady's Profession, Looking Forward, Horseplay, Torch Singer, Doctor Bull, Bombshell, White Woman, Alice in Wonderland, The Midnight Club* (1933); *Four Frightened People, The House of Rothschild, Sadie McKee, Jane Eyre, Bulldog Drummond Strikes Back, We Live Again, The Painted Veil* (1934); *The Mystery of Edwin Drood, Vanessa: Her Love Story, Hold 'Em Yale, Werewolf of London, Anna Karenina, The Return of Peter Grimm* (1935); *Twice Branded, Not So Dusty, Guilty Melody* (1936); *A Yank at Oxford, Kathleen Mavourneen* (1937); *Crackerjack* (1938); *I'm from Missouri, We are Not Alone, The Star Maker* (1939); *Vigil in the Night, Irene, Waterloo Bridge, Stranger on the Third Floor, Anne of Windy Poplars* (1940); *Dead Men Tell, Billy the Kid, A Yank in the RAF, Man at Large, Great Guns, How Green Was My Valley, Remember the Day* (1941); *Son of Fury, Castle in the Desert, The Postman Didn't Ring, Between Us Girls, Time to Kill, Right to the Heart, Mrs Wiggs of the Cabbage Patch* (1942); *Forever and a Day, Holy Matrimony, First Comes Courage* (1943); *Jane Eyre, The White Cliffs of Dover, The Keys of the Kingdom, Pardon My Rhythm, Music for Millions* (1944); *Thrill of a Romance, The Strange Affair of Uncle Harry, Saratoga Trunk, Molly and Me, The Horn Blows at Midnight* (1945); *Devotion, Sing While You Dance* (1946); *Millie's Daughter, The Homestretch, The Brasher Doubloon* (1947); *The Birds* (1963); *Bus Riley's Back in Town* (1965)

GRÜNING, Ilka (1876–1964)

Austrian-born grande dame of the Berlin theatre and film scene. A Jew, she fled to the USA in 1933, but began cinema work only after the USA entered the war, taking on small roles in anti-Nazi films. A 1950 visit to Germany horrified Grüning, and she hurried back to California. RJK

FILMS: *Underground* (1941); *Dangerously They Live, Friendly Enemies, Casablanca, Kings Row, Iceland, Desperate Journey* (1942); *This is the Army, There's Something about a Soldier, The Strange Death of Adolf Hitler, Bomber's Moon, Madame Curie* (1943); *An American Romance* (1944); *Rendezvous 24, Temptation, Murder in the Music Hall* (1946); *Desperate, Repeat Performance* (1947); *Raw Deal, Words and Music, A Foreign Affair, Letters from an Unknown Woman* (1948); *Caught, The Great Sinner, Mr Soft Touch, Captain China* (1949); *Convicted* (1950); *Payment on Demand, Passage West* (1951).

GUARD, Kit (Kresten Klitgaard) (1894–1961)

Pug-nosed Danish actor who enjoyed some success in Hollywood comedies of the 1920s, usually in tandem with the plump and moustachioed Al Cooke. The partnership ended with the advent of sound and Guard spent the remainder of his incredibly prolific screen career playing either comic thugs or pugilists. HJW

FILMS: *The Face at Your Window* (1920); *The Telephone Girl* (1924); *The Go-Getters* (1925); *One Minute to Play, Bill Grimm's Progress* (1926); *The Beauty Parlor, The Fighting Blood, Her Father Said No, In a Moment of Temptation, Legionnaires in Paris, The Pacemakers* (1927); *Beau Broadway, Dead Man's Curve, Lingerie* (1928); *The Racketeer, Barney Google* (1929); *Big Money, Night Work* (1930); *Defenders of the Law, The Unholy Garden, Catch as Catch Can, Two-Fisted Justice, The Sky Raiders* (1931); *Flames, Racing Strain, Final Edition, Tom Brown of Culver, The County Fair, The Fighting Champ, They Never Come Back, The Thirteenth Guest, The Last Man, Madison Square Garden, A Strange Adventure* (1932); *Carnival Lady, Corruption, One Year Later, The Ship of Wanted Men,* 281

Terror Aboard, Sucker Money, The Phantom Broadcast, Police Call, Riot Squad, The Bowery, Her Forgotten Past, Before Midnight (1933); *The Cactus Kid, Broadway Bill, The Mighty Barnum, Palooka, It Happened One Night, Blind Date, Lady by Choice, Good Dame, I'll Fix It, Come on Marines, Murder in the Museum, Cockeyed Cavaliers, The Cat's Paw* (1934); *The Irish Gringo, The Whole Town's Talking, Kid Courageous, Rip Roaring Riley, Naughty Marietta, Stolen Harmony, Shadows of the Orient, Reckless Roads, Barbary Coast, The Case of the Lucky Legs, Dan Mathews,* (1935); *Murder at Glen Athol, The Fighting Coward, Missing Girls* (1936); *When's Your Birthday?, Dick Tracy* [serial], *Kid Galahad, Sweetheart of the Navy, Anything for a Thrill, A Fight to the Finish, The Hit Parade, SOS Coast Guard* [serial], *Headin' East* (1937); *Spirit of Youth, Where the West Begins, When G-Men Step In, Code of the Rangers, Gunsmoke Trail, You and Me, Professor Beware, Heroes of the Hills, You Can't Take it with You, Frontier Scout, The Spider's Web* [serial], *Prison Train, In Early Arizona* (1938); *Homicide Bureau, Frontiers of '49, Six-Gun Rhythm, Nancy Drew, Reporter, Let Us Live, Star Reporter, The Oklahoma Kid, Lone Star Pioneers, Mandrake the Magician* [serial], *Torchy Runs for Mayor, The Man from Sundown, Behind Prison Gates, Golden Boy, The Flying Deuces, El Diablo Rides* (1939); *The Shadow* [serial], *The Cheyenne Kid, The House across the Bay, Terry and the Pirates* [serial], *Nutty but Nice, Wagons Westward, The Carson City Kid, Deadwood Dick* [serial], *City for Conquest, The Green Archer* [serial], *Tin Pan Alley, Riders from Nowhere* (1940); *White Eagle* [serial], *So Long Mr Chumps, A Man Betrayed, Dutiful but Dumb, They Met in Argentina, Sergeant York, The Pittsburgh Kid, Doctors Don't Tell, Jesse James at Bay, Shadow of the Thin Man, Honolulu Lu, Among the Living* (1941); *Jailhouse Blues, Mr Wise Guy, Man with Two Lives, Alias Boston Blackie, My Favorite Spy, Parachute Nurse, The Secret Code, The Glass Key, The Devil with Hitler, Valley of Vanishing Men* [serial] (1942); *A Blitz on the Fritz, It Ain't Hay, Edge of Darkness, Lady of Burlesque, Alaska Highway, The Chance of a Lifetime, Is Everybody Happy?* (1943); *The Lodger, The Fighting Seabees, Meet the People, Haunted Habor* [serial], *Call of the Rockies, My Buddy, Here Come the Waves, Double Exposure, See Here, Private Hargrove, Barbary Coast Gent* (1944); *She Gets Her Man, Frisco Sal, Along the Navajo Trail, Frontier Gal* (1945); *Days of Buffalo Bill, A Night in Paradise, Nobody Lives Forever, The Fighting Frontiersman, Dick Tracy vs. Cueball* (1946); *Johnny O'Clock, South of the Chisholm Trail, Trail Street, The Perils of Pauline* (1947); *When My Baby*

Smiles at Me (1948); *Master Minds, Always Leave Them Laughing* (1949); *Hi-Jacked, Atom Man vs. Superman* [serial], *Copper Canyon, Experiment Alcatraz* (1950); *Abbott and Costello Meet the Invisible Man, Fort Defiance, Golden Girl* (1951); *The Bushwackers, Outlaw Women, Glory Alley, Carrie* (1952); *Crime Wave, It Should Happen to You, Riding with Buffalo Bill* (1954); *Fury at Gunsight Pass, Around the World in Eighty Days* (1956); *The Joker is Wild* (1957).

GUÉTARY, Georges (Lambros Worldou) (1915–1997)
One of France's most popular stage operetta actors and singers. Guétary's sole but striking Hollywood role was in Vincente Minnelli's landmark musical *An American in Paris*. As singer 'Henri Baurel', Guétary exuded elegance and traditional 'Frenchness' next to Gene Kelly and Leslie Caron★. TH
FILM: *An American in Paris* (1951).

GUINNESS, Alec (Alec Guinness de Cuffe) (1914–2000)
Unlike many of his generation, Alec Guinness was not tempted to exploit his popularity by forging a career in Hollywood. He gained a following in the USA instead for his work with Ealing Studios. In 1950, Guinness starred as Disraeli opposite Irene Dunne (as Queen Victoria) in Jean Negulesco's *The Mudlark*. In 1956, he was offered the role of the prince in MGM's *The Swan*, a comedy co-starring Grace Kelly and Louis Jourdan★, and a year later he enjoyed major success in the Anglo-American production *The Bridge on the River Kwai*, for which he won a Best Actor Academy Award. After that, he appeared in numerous Hollywood films and played a variety of character roles, including a Japanese diplomat in Mervyn Leroy's *A Majority of One*, Marcus Aurelius in *The Fall of the Roman Empire* and Zhivago's half-brother in *Doctor Zhivago*.

In the 1970s, Guinness appeared in as Obi-Wan Kenobi in George Lucas' box-office blockbuster *Star Wars*, a role that he disliked intensely, even though his involvement in the film was lucrative and won him an Academy Award for Best Actor in a Supporting Role. He nevertheless starred in the sequels, *The Empire Strikes Back* and *Return of the Jedi*. Although his performance style was understated, Guinness exuded a quiet authority, intelligence and laconic humour. He avoided publicity whenever possible and was not comfortable with Hollywood's general expectations of star behaviour. SS

FILMS: *The Mudlark* (1950); *Father Brown* (1954); *The Swan* (1956); *The Bridge on the River Kwai, The Barretts of Wimpole Street, Barnacle Bill* (1957); *Our Man in Havana, Shake Hands with the Devil* (1959); *A Majority of One* (1961); *H.M.S. Defiant, Lawrence of Arabia* (1962); *The Fall of the Roman Empire* (1964); *Situation Hopeless . . . but Not Serious, Doctor Zhivago* (1965); *Hotel Paradiso* (1966); *The Comedians* (1967); *Cromwell, Scrooge* (1970); *Murder by Death* (1976); *Star Wars* (1977); *The Empire Strikes Back* (1980); *Lovesick, Return of the Jedi* (1983); *A Passage to India* (1984); *Kafka* (1991).

GWENN, Edmund (1875–1959)

Edmund Gwenn came to prominence as an actor of considerable distinction on the West End stage in the 1910s and 1920s. Through the sponsorship of dramatists like Shaw and Galsworthy and parts in several British sound films, including *The Skin Game, Hindle Wakes* (both 1931) and *The Good Companions* (1933), he became a specialist in working-class characters protected by a core of dreamy idealism despite being battered by years of hard work and disillusionment. He also appeared in the US-financed crime drama, *Father and Son*. After permanently relocating to Hollywood in 1939, he became the character actor of choice for producers looking for short, round, soft-tempered old gentlemen to help unite stubborn young lovers. His biggest moment in the spotlight was his Academy Award-winning turn as the avuncular department store Santa Claus who claims to be the real thing in *Miracle on 34th Street*. A few directors remained aware of his steelier strengths, such as his regular employer Alfred Hitchcock, who cast him as a sly assassin in *Foreign Correspondent*, and George Cukor, who allowed Gwenn's trademark self-delusionism to tip into full-blown insanity in *Sylvia Scarlett*. JB

FILMS: *Father and Son* (1934); *The Bishop Misbehaves* (1935); *Sylvia Scarlett, The Walking Dead, Anthony Adverse, All American Chump, Mad Holiday* (1936); *Parnell* (1937); *The Earl of Chicago, Foreign Correspondent, Pride and Prejudice, The Doctor Takes a Wife* (1940); *The Devil and Miss Jones, Charley's Aunt, One Night in Lisbon, Scotland Yard, Cheers for Miss Bishop* (1941); *Random Harvest, A Yank at Eton* (1942); *Forever and a Day, Lassie Come Home, The Meanest Man in the World* (1943); *Between Two Worlds, The Keys of the Kingdom* (1944); *Dangerous Partners, She Went to the Races, Bewitched* (1945); *Undercurrent, Of Human Bondage* (1946); *Miracle on 34th Street, Life with Father, Green Dolphin Street, Thunder in the Valley* (1947); *Hills of Home, Apartment for Peggy* (1948); *Challenge to Lassie* (1949); *A Woman of Distinction, Louisa, Pretty Baby, Mister 880, For Heaven's Sake* (1950); *Peking Express* (1951); *Les Miserables, Something for the Birds, Sally and Saint Anne, Bonzo Goes to College* (1952); *Mr Scoutmaster, The Bigamist* (1953); *Them!, The Student Prince* (1954); *The Trouble with Harry, It's a Dog's Life* (1955).

HAAS, Hugo (1901–1968)

Czech cinema's first actor-director star who came to Hollywood following the Nazis' 1939 invasion. An unsettled outsider, Haas eventually found a niche playing guttural 'ethnic' heavies, before producing, directing and starring in a series of lurid, critically panned melodramas, beginning with *Pickup*. He died in Vienna while undertaking his return to his native country. RJK

FILMS: *Days of Glory, Mrs Parkington, The Princess and the Pirate, Summer Storm, Strange Affair* (1944); *Jealousy, Dakota, What Next, Corporal Hargrove?, A Bell for Adano* (1945); *Holiday in Mexico, Two Smart People* (1946); *The Private Affairs of Bel Ami, Fiesta, The Foxes of Harrow, Northwest Outpost, Merton of the Movies, Leben des Galilei* (1947); *My Girl Tisa, For the Love of Mary, Casbah* (1948); *The Flying Kentuckian* (1949); *King Solomon's Mines, Vendetta* (1950); *Pickup, The Girl on the Bridge* (1951); *Strange Fascination* (1952); *Thy Neighbor's Wife, One Girl's Confession* (1953); *The Other Woman, Bait* (1954); *The Tender Trap, Hold Back Tomorrow* (1955); *Edge of Hell* (1956); *Lizzie, Hit and Run* (1957); *Born to be Loved, Night of the Quarter Moon* (1959); *Paradise Alley* (1962).

HAIG, David (David Haig Collum Ward) (1955–)

A versatile actor who has appeared frequently on British television, mainly in comedy. His role as Bernard, one of the bridegrooms in *Four Weddings and a Funeral* (1994), led to occasional minor roles in American films, usually playing British characters. AS

FILMS: *The Four Corners of Nowhere* (1995); *Timequest, Rachel's Attic, Two Weeks Notice* (2002).

HALE, Creighton (Patrick Fitzgerald) (1882–1965)

The son of an Irish actor and singer, Hale travelled to the USA in 1909 with a theatre group and stayed there. He started as an extra with Pathé and continued to make a phenomenal number of films, notably in the silent era. He **283**

Creighton Hale: Irish character actor with phenomenal Hollywood filmography

did not play Irish roles and was typecast instead – often uncredited – as the dapper Englishman in parts such as the gambler enquiring about the casino's honesty in *Casablanca*.
RB

FILMS: *The Million Dollar Mystery, The Taint, The Three of Us, The Exploits of Elaine, The Warning, The Stain* (1914); *A Fool There Was, The New Exploits of Elaine, The Romance of Elaine, The Old Homestead* (1915); *Hazel Kirke, The Iron Claw, Snow White, Charity* (1916); *The Seven Pearls* (1917); *Mrs Slacker, For Sale, Waifs, His Bonded Wife, The Woman the Germans Shot, Annexing Bill* (1918); *The Great Victory, Wilson or the Kaiser?, The Fall of the Hohenzollerns, Oh Boy!, The Thirteenth Chair, The Love Cheat, A Damsel in Distress, The Black Circle* (1919); *The Idol Dancer, Way Down East, A Child for Sale* (1920); *Forbidden Love, Orphans of the Storm* (1921); *Fascination, Her Majesty* (1922); *Mary of the Movies, Broken Hearts of Broadway, Forbidden Lover, Trilby, Three Wise Fools, Tea: With a Kick!* (1923); *Name the Man, Marriage Circle, How to Educate a Wife, Riders Up, Wine of Youth, The Mine with the Iron Door, This Woman* (1924); *The Bridge of Sighs, Seven Days, The Circle, Exchange of Wives, Time, the Comedian, The Shadow on the Wall, Wages for Wives* (1925);

Beverly of Graustark, A Poor Girl's Romance, Oh, Baby!, The Midnight Message, Speeding Through, The Nickel-Hopper (1926); *Should Men Walk Home?, Why Girls Say No, One Hour Married, Annie Laurie, Thumbs Down, The Cat and the Canary* (1927); *Rose-Marie, Riley of the Rainbow Division, Sisters of Eve, The House of Shame* (1928); *Seven Footprints to Satan, The Great Divide* (1929); *Holiday, School's Out* (1930); *Big Ears, Grief Street* (1931); *Prestige, The Greeks Had a Word for Them, Shop Angel, Free Wheeling* (1932); *The Masquerader, Only Yesterday* (1933); *Sensation Hunters, George White's Scandals, The Thin Man, Bulldog Drummond Strikes Back* (1934); *One More Spring, Life Begins at Forty, Becky Sharp, Men without Names, Your Uncle Dudley* (1935); *The Millionaire Kid, Custer's Last Stand, Country Beyond, Princess Comes Across, Hollywood Boulevard, Under Your Spell, Music Goes 'Round, Death from a Distance* (1936); *Midnight Taxi, Charlie Chan on Broadway* (1937); *International Settlement* (1938); *Confessions of a Nazi Spy, Nancy Drew . . . Trouble Shooter, Torchy Plays with Dynamite, Cowboy Quarterback, Indianapolis Speedway, Everybody's Hobby, Nancy Drew and the Hidden Staircase, Dust Be My Destiny, On Your Toes, The Roaring Twenties, Kid Nightingale, On Dress Parade, The Return of Doctor X, Slapsie Maxie's* (1939); *A Child is Born, The Fighting 69th, Granny Get Your Gun, One Million B.C., Tear Gas Squad, Saturday's Children, Flight Angels, Brother Orchid, A Fugitive from Justice, All This, and Heaven Too, My Love Came Back, The Man Who Talked Too Much, Money and the Woman, Knute Rockne All American, Tugboat Annie Sails Again, East of the River, Always a Bride, Lady with Red Hair, She Couldn't Say No, Santa Fe Trail, Father is a Prince* (1940); *Honeymoon for Three, Footsteps in the Dark, Knockout, Affectionately Yours, Out of the Fog, Sergeant York, The Bride Came C.O.D., Bad Men of Missouri, Dive Bomber, The Smiling Ghost, Nine Lives are Not Enough, One Foot in Heaven, The Maltese Falcon, Law of the Tropics, Blues in the Night, The Body Disappears, Steel against the Sky, The Strawberry Blonde, Strange Alibi, Passage from Hong Kong, Here Comes Happiness, Bullets for O'Hara* (1941); *The Man Who Came to Dinner, Bullet Scars, Larceny, Inc., Wings for the Eagle, Spy Ship, Yankee Doodle Dandy, Escape from Crime, Busses Roar, The Hidden Hand, Casablanca, The Gorilla Man, Murder in the Big House, The Male Animal, The Gay Sisters* (1942); *The Mysterious Doctor, Action in the North Atlantic, Watch on the Rhine, Thank Your Lucky Stars, Old Acquaintance* (1943); *Meet the People, Uncertain Glory, Mr Skeffington, Adventures of Mark Twain, Crime by Night* (1944); *Three*

Strangers, A Stolen Life, Night and Day, Humoresque, Two Guys from Milwaukee (1946); *Nora Prentiss, The Two Mrs Carrolls, The Perils of Pauline, Possessed, Life with Father, That Way with Women, Stallion Road, Cry Wolf* (1947); *Always Together, The Woman in White, Johnny Belinda, Smart Girls Don't Talk, The Big Punch* (1948); *The Fountainhead, John Loves Mary, Beyond the Forest, Night unto Night, The Story of Seabiscuit, The Girl from Jones Beach, A Kiss in the Dark, Homicide* (1949); *Montana, Backfire, Perfect Strangers, The Great Jewel Robber, Sunset Boulevard* (1950); *Goodbye, My Fancy, The Enforcer, On Moonlight Bay* (1951); *Scarlet Angel, Because You're Mine* (1952); *Walking My Baby Back Home* (1953); *The Steel Jungle, Serenade* (1956); *Westbound* (1958).

HANIN, Roger (Roger Lévy) (1925–)

Respected French screen actor whose only American film was *The Revengers*, a Hollywood Western starring William Holden, in which he played a French prison inmate. VO

FILM: *The Revengers* (1972).

HANSON, Einar (1899–1927)

Swedish performer who made his acting debut in 1919. After work in Danish and German films (including *Die freudlose Gasse/Joyless Street* [1925]), Hanson followed his mentor Mauritz Stiller to Hollywood in 1926. Despite his Nordic looks, he soon achieved success as an exotic and charming lover in films with Clara Bow and Pola Negri★. His appearance as Negri's brother in *Barbed Wire* may well have led to greater roles, but he died in a car accident a few months later. MBj

FILMS: *Her Big Night, Into Her Kingdom* (1926); *The Lady in Ermine, The Masked Woman, Children of Divorce, Fashions for Women, Barbed Wire, The Woman on Trial* (1927).

HANSON, Lars (1886–1965)

One of Sweden's leading actors who worked at Stockholm's Intima Teatern, a small theatre founded by August Strindberg, before developing his film career from 1916 onwards in Swedish crime films and melodramas. In 1924, he achieved international recognition for the title role in *Gösta Berlings saga/The Legend of Gosta Berling*. Louis B. Mayer soon contracted Hanson as well as the film's female lead, Greta Garbo★, and its director Mauritz Stiller. Hanson arrived in Hollywood in 1926 and starred or co-starred in a number of films that, despite being high profile and

expensive, were never particularly lucrative for the major studios. Reviews, however, were often positive and always indicated the possibility of future stardom.

Hanson's background as a stage actor was often used as a quality marker for his acting skills. His Swedishness was likewise often emphasised: being blond, blue-eyed, silent, shy and hard working were the predominant characteristics of this national stereotype. Hanson was a discreet professional and at his best when working with female stars like Lillian Gish (twice) and Garbo (three times). In comparison to Jean Hersholt★, the other Scandinavian male character actor in Hollywood at the time, Hanson seems to have been rather more important as a Swedish expatriate than as a member of the broader international Hollywood community.

The majority of his American films were typical late silent era quality Hollywood productions. He was the deceived and tormented husband of Greta Garbo in *Flesh and the Devil* and the more virile husband of Lillian Gish in *The Wind*. Hanson's theatre background and appearances in Victor Sjöström's Swedish films of the late 1910s and early 1920s clearly made him fit for the visual and emotional excess of a cinema often more appreciated in Europe than in the USA. He made one sound film in the UK in 1930 and returned to European screens in 1935 to become one of the leading male Swedish film stars of the 1940s and 1950s. MBj

FILMS: *The Scarlet Letter, Flesh and the Devil* (1926); *Captain Salvation, Buttons* (1927); *The Divine Woman, The Wind* (1928).

HARDWICKE, Cedric (1893–1964)

Success on the London stage – particularly in the plays of his friend George Bernard Shaw – brought Hardwicke a modest amount of film work in Britain (including *The Lady is Willing* funded by Columbia) and a knighthood in 1934. The latter, however, attracted a lucrative courtship from Hollywood even before he had appeared on Broadway. In his own words, 'I regarded England as my wife and America as my mistress.' He succumbed to the latter on many occasions, usually for roles as stern patricians or masterly villains. Such categories adequately describe his appearances in various genres: literary costume dramas like *Becky Sharp*, historical biopics like *Stanley and Livingstone*, horror movies like *The Ghost of Frankenstein* and biblical epics like *The Ten Commandments*. JB

British stage and film actor Cedric Hardwicke specialised in stern patricians or masterly villains in his Hollywood films

FILMS: *The Lady is Willing* (1934); *Les Misérables, Becky Sharp* (1935); *The Green Light* (1937); *The Hunchback of Notre Dame, Stanley and Livingstone, On Borrowed Time* (1939); *The Invisible Man Returns, Victory, Tom Brown's School Days, The Howards of Virginia* (1940); *Sundown, Suspicion* (1941); *The Ghost of Frankenstein, Invisible Agent, Valley of the Sun, Commandos Strike at Dawn* (1942); *Forever and a Day, The Moon is Down, The Cross of Lorraine* (1943); *The Lodger, Wilson, The Keys of the Kingdom, Wing and a Prayer* (1944); *The Picture of Dorian Gray* (1945); *Sentimental Journey* (1946); *Tycoon, Song of My Heart, Lured, Ivy, The Imperfect Lady, Dark Delusion* (1947); *A Woman's Vengeance, I Remember Mama, Rope* (1948); *Now Barabbas, A Connecticut Yankee in King Arthur's Court* (1949); *The White Tower* (1950); *Mr Imperium, Desert Fox: The Story of Rommel* (1951); *The Green Glove, Caribbean* (1952); *Salome, Botany Bay, The War of the Worlds* [voice] (1953); *Bait* (1954); *Helen of Troy* (1955); *The Ten Commandments, Around the World in Eighty Days, The Vagabond King, The Power and the Prize, Gaby, Diane* (1956); *The Story of Mankind, Baby Face Nelson* (1957); *The Magic Fountain* (1961); *Five Weeks in a Balloon* (1962); *The Pumpkin Eater* (1964).

286

HARRIS, Richard (1930–2002)

Irish actor whose reputation for drink and hard living overshadowed his considerable acting talents. After a London stage debut, Harris' breakthrough screen appearance as the ambitious, self-destructive Frank Machlin in Lindsay Anderson's *This Sporting Life* (1963) gained him his first Academy Award nomination. Always in need of money, he took any number of Hollywood roles, notably in *A Man Called Horse* and notoriously as Bo Derek's father in *Tarzan, the Ape Man*. In the 1980s, Harris bought the rights to the stage production of *Camelot* and toured it for five years. He gained a second Academy Award nomination for Jim Sheridan's *The Field* (1989). This marked a late-life resurgence that included parts in the hugely successful Harry Potter series. RB

FILMS: *Shake Hands with the Devil, The Wreck of the Mary Deare* (1959); *A Terrible Beauty* (1960); *The Guns of Navarone* (1961); *Mutiny on the Bounty* (1962); *Major Dundee, The Heroes of Telemark* (1965); *The Bible – in the Beginning . . . , Hawaii* (1966); *Caprice, Camelot* (1967); *The Molly Maguires, A Man Called Horse, Cromwell* (1970); *Man in the Wilderness* (1971); *The Deadly Trackers* (1973); *Juggernaut, 99 and 44/100% Dead* (1974); *Echoes of a Summer, The Return of a Man Called Horse, Robin and Marian* (1976); *Orca* (1977); *Ravagers, The Last Word* (1979); *Tarzan, the Ape Man* (1981); *Triumphs of a Man Called Horse* (1982); *Mack the Knife* (1990); *Patriot Games* (1992); *Unforgiven* (1992); *Wrestling Ernest Hemingway, Silent Tongue* (1993); *Cry, the Beloved Country* (1995); *Savage Hearts, This is the Sea* (1997); *Gladiator* (2000); *Harry Potter and the Sorcerer's Stone, The Pearl* (2001); *The Count of Monte Cristo, Harry Potter and the Chamber of Secrets* (2002).

HARRISON, Kathleen (1892–1995)

Popular British character actress who frequently played cheery working-class cockneys such as Mrs Lightbody in the Fox-financed *They Came by Night* and the famous Mrs Huggett, who appeared in three UK films in the late 1940s. She was the cook in Richard Thorpe's *Night Must Fall*, made during a brief visit to Hollywood. MHu

FILMS: *Night Must Fall* (1937); *They Came by Night* (1940); *Girl in the News* (1941).

HARRISON, Rex (Reginald Carey Harrison) (1908–1990)

British actor Rex Harrison's first full American film role was an Asian monarch in *Anna and the King of Siam*. This was somewhat surprising given the image of a suave, urbane, upper-class English roguish charmer that he had established on the stage both in London and on Broadway, where he had first appeared in 1936, and in a number of British films of the 1930s and 1940s. Several of his 1930s films were low-budget quota pictures for US companies based in Britain, although he did sign for Alexander Korda's London Films, appearing with Hollywood star Miriam Hopkins in *Men are Not Gods* (1936) and with Merle Oberon★ in *Over the Moon* (1940). He also played a supporting role in the MGM-British 'prestige picture', *The Citadel*.

He made his mark with American audiences in 1940 with the US success of Carol Reed's Hitchcock-like *Night Train to Munich* and attracted the attention of Darryl F. Zanuck, head of Twentieth Century-Fox, with whom he subsequently signed a long-term contract in 1946. After *Anna and the King of Siam*, he appeared in a small number of films, including *Unfaithfully Yours*. However, a few months before the release of the Preston Sturges picture, his Hollywood career was somewhat blighted by scandal when the actress Carole Landis, with whom he was having an affair, committed suicide. Following this setback, Harrison concentrated on stage work for a time and indeed his career was given a substantial boost when he starred in the Broadway production of *My Fair Lady* (1956) opposite Julie Andrews★. However, he continued to intersperse theatre work with film appearances both in Britain and in Hollywood. *The Constant Husband* (1954), *The Reluctant Debutante* and *The Yellow Rolls-Royce* drew upon his established image as an upper-class Englishman, as did the screen version of *My Fair Lady*, in which he repeated his stage performance and won the Best Actor Academy Award for the year. Yet his range as a dramatic actor was also demonstrated during this period when he played alongside major stars such as Richard Burton★, Elizabeth Taylor and Charlton Heston in two American films made in Europe by directors important to his earlier film career. Harrison was an imposing Julius Caesar in Joseph Mankiewicz's *Cleopatra* (for which he earned a Best Actor Academy Award nomination) and he played Pope Julius II with considerable authority in Carol Reed's *The Agony and the Ecstasy*. TR

FILMS: *Leave it to Blanche* (1934); *All at Sea* (1935); *The Citadel* (1938); *Anna and the King of Siam* (1946); *The Ghost and Mrs Muir*, *The Foxes of Harrow* (1947); *Unfaithfully Yours*, *Escape* (1948); *The Four Poster* (1952); *Main Street to Broadway* (1953); *King Richard and the Crusaders* (1954); *The Reluctant Debutante* (1958); *Midnight Lace* (1960); *The Happy Thieves* (1961); *Cleopatra* (1963); *My Fair Lady* (1964); *The Yellow Rolls-Royce*, *The Agony and the Ecstasy* (1965); *Doctor Dolittle*, *The Honey Pot* (1967); *A Flea in Her Ear* (1968); *Staircase* (1969); *Crossed Swords* (1977); *Ashanti* (1979); *A Time to Die* (1983).

HART, Ian (1964–)

Liverpudlian actor who entered independent American cinema by mimicking the most influential Merseysider in American cultural history – John Lennon – in *The Hours and Times*. Hart played Lennon again in *Backbeat* (1993), a British film made carefully with one eye on the US market. Hart has often played Irishmen or Irish-Americans because of his Liverpool roots and ethnic ties to the Irish Sea. His supporting American screen roles are usually diffident and sometimes seedy misfits. JB

FILMS: *The Hours and Times* (1991); *Michael Collins*, *Still Waters Burn* (1996); *Snitch*, *Frogs for Snakes*, *Enemy of the State* (1998); *Spring Forward*, *The End of the Affair* (1999); *Harry Potter and the Sorcerer's Stone* (2001); *Killing Me Softly* (2002); *Den of Lions* (2003); *Mr Ripley's Return* (2004).

HARVEY, Laurence (Larushka Mischa Skikne) (1928–1973)

The likes of Michael Caine★ and Terence Stamp★ have argued that Laurence Harvey was the only home-grown leading man whom they looked to as a role model of comparable stature and dynamism to their favourite American stars during the 1950s. Certainly, Harvey stood apart from his peers through his distinctive looks – a slim athletic figure, pronounced cheekbones and a flamboyant quiff – and ethnic origins. He was born a Lithuanian Jew and arrived in England in 1946 to enrol at RADA, having lived as a refugee in South Africa for the previous decade. Visiting agents at RADA regularly mistook Harvey for an American actor. He swiftly aroused a lot of interest among British studios and signed his first film contract in 1947, **287** which initially led to a number of restrictive roles as flashy spivs and unstable Teddy boys.

The independent production team of John and James Woolf placed Harvey under exclusive contract when they saw him as an actor tailor-made to make a bigger impact in the American market. A round of Hollywood screen tests in 1952 bore little fruit, but the Woolfs' persistence won a Warner Bros. deal in 1954. Harvey's breakthrough came in the 1958 hit *Room at the Top*, a film that helped kick-start a vogue for sardonic, insolent anti-heroes and also demonstrated the international box-office potential of racy, adult subject matter. Harvey's star turn as Joe Lampton, a ruthlessly ambitious working-class careerist who calculatingly marries into money and status while satisfying his libidinal desires in a torrid extramarital affair, earned him a Best Actor Academy Award nomination and an instant entrée into front-rank Hollywood stardom. Harvey permanently relocated to California at the beginning of the 1960s and a swift integration into the upper echelons of Hollywood society was aided by his long relationship with Joan Cohn, the widow of Columbia mogul Harry Cohn, whom he eventually married in 1968.

Harvey's early big Hollywood roles in a number of sexually overheated melodramas such as *Walk on the Wild Side* and *Summer and Smoke* traded off the star persona forged by the success of *Room at the Top*. In MGM's *BUtterfield 8*, his philandering lawyer Weston Liggett is a distinctly Lampton-esque character who has married into wealth, but seeks emotional and sexual sustenance from his relationship with a call girl. Few of these movies were commercial hits. Their mixture of conventional studio production values and timid Production Code euphemisms sat ill at ease with their pretensions towards worldliness. Harvey – once a man ahead of his time in Britain – had also moved to Hollywood at an inopportune moment in its history when the existing studio system was breaking down and momentarily looking to its British affiliates and subsidiaries for new ideas and creative leadership. Harvey, therefore, belatedly returned to British films in the second half of the decade but had fallen behind the likes of Caine, Stamp and Sean Connery★ in the queue for the most desirable and iconic roles. His subsequent death at the age of forty-five was obviously untimely, but it nonetheless came some while after his star had waned. This is not to say that Harvey's years in Hollywood were exclusively spent working on stolidly old-fashioned

pictures. His curious star image as an ersatz American leading man (with unusually arrogant, aloof tendencies) was put to memorable use in the innovative and prescient political thriller *The Manchurian Candidate*, where the plot turns upon there being an intangible 'something' that is not completely convincing about the all-American hero Harvey plays. JB

FILMS: *The Black Rose* (1950); *Knights of the Round Table* (1953); *King Richard and the Crusaders* (1954); *Room at the Top* (1958); *The Alamo, Butterfield 8* (1960); *Two Loves, Summer and Smoke* (1961); *Walk on the Wild Side, The Wonderful World of the Brothers Grimm, The Manchurian Candidate, A Girl Named Tamiko* (1962); *The Running Man* (1963); *The Ceremony, The Outrage, Of Human Bondage* (1964); *A Dandy in Aspic, The Charge of the Light Brigade* [scenes deleted] (1968); *The Magic Christian* (1969); *WUSA, The Deep* [unreleased] (1970); *Night Watch* (1973); *Welcome to Arrow Beach* (1974).

HARVEY, Lillian (Lilian Helen Muriel Pape) (1906–1968)

For the trilingual Lillian Harvey, the course seemed set fair early on for a career in international entertainment. After ballet and revue performances in Czechoslovakia, Hungary and Austria, she was engaged for her first film role in *Der Fluch / The Curse* (1924). Under contract to Berlin producer Richard Eichberg, Harvey starred in several German silent comedies and melodramas, including opposite the 1920s heart-throb Harry Liedtke. But it was as romantic partner to Willy Fritsch in a series of romantic melodramas and musical comedies, including the hugely successful *Der Kongress tanzt / Congress Dances* (1931), that Harvey rose to European stardom. Like Hollywood actresses such as Ginger Rogers who were typecast as 'better halves' to leading men, Harvey excelled in established star partnerships or 'dream couples'. Unlike Rogers, however, Harvey's star persona embodied a cosmopolitan Europeanism that often demanded that she switch not only languages but also romantic partners, since many of her early 1930s films were shot in English and French versions.

Harvey's Hollywood partners never elicited the grace and sparkle of her European performances. Contracted to Fox in spring 1932, she failed to secure a Hollywood contract for her preferred director and real-life romantic partner, Paul Martin, playing instead in four lacklustre musical comedies, each under a different director, and opposite a different male lead. Harvey's Hollywood titles were never popular with US audiences; but they did advance Harvey's career when she returned to Germany in 1935. The Third Reich industry often favoured non-German stars who lent a cosmopolitan air to an increasingly provincial German cinema, hence her German success in two Hollywood-style screwball comedies, *Glückskinder/Lucky Kids* (1936) and *Sieben Ohrfeigen/Seven Slaps* (1937). These represented the high point of a career cut short when Harvey emigrated again following interrogation by the Gestapo because she had helped the cinematographer Jens Keith flee Germany. She returned to the USA in 1941, not as an actress this time, but as a Red Cross nurse tending the war-wounded. EC

FILMS: *My Lips Betray, My Weakness, I Am Suzanne* (1933); *Let's Live Tonight* (1935).

HASSO, Signe (1911–2002)

Swedish actress celebrated for her early maturity and presence. Signe Hasso made her Swedish stage breakthrough with the play *Flickor i uniform/Girls in Uniform* in 1934. Following the launch of her film career with *Karriär/Career* (1938) and *Vi två/You and Me* (1939), she went to Hollywood in 1940 on an MGM contract. Hasso acted in a number of films directed by Cecil B. DeMille and Ernst Lubitsch, and later became popular on Broadway and American television. YH

FILMS: *Journey for Margaret* (1942); *Assignment in Brittany, Heaven Can Wait* (1943); *The Story of Dr Wassel, The Seventh Cross* (1944); *Dangerous Partners, Johnny Angel, The House on 92nd Street* (1945); *Strange Triangle, A Scandal in Paris* (1946); *A Double Life, Where There's Life* (1947); *To the Ends of the Earth* (1948); *Outside the Wall, Crisis* (1950); *Picture Mommy Dead* (1966); *A Reflection of Fear* (1973); *The Black Bird* (1975); *I Never Promised You a Rose Garden* (1977).

HAUER, Rutger (1944–)

Dutch actor whose brooding Aryan looks and powerful, but also credible and vulnerable physique has determined the roles he has been asked to play by Hollywood. Hauer has become one of the most successfully integrated European actors working in the USA. Although he has kept his original Dutch citizenship, he has learned to speak American English without an accent, thus becoming one of the few originally non-English-speaking European actors also to play American characters. He mainly specialises in action and thriller genres, although he has also appeared in a number of comedies and romantic and historical dramas. His US breakthrough was as the android Roy Batty in Ridley Scott's influential science-fiction film *Blade Runner* in 1982. It was a role that personified the villainous and unnatural evil that has dominated his later screen persona.

After touring theatre work in the Netherlands, Hauer made his screen debut in Paul Verhoeven's *Turks Fruit/Turkish Delight* (1973). It made him a star in his native country, where he was nicknamed 'the Dutch Paul Newman' because of his steely-blue eyes, fair hair and charismatic performance style. The film received an Academy Award nomination for Best Foreign Film in 1974, but it was another Verhoeven film that finally introduced him to American audiences and critical press acclaim, when *Soldaat van Oranje/Soldier of Orange* (1977) was screened all over the USA (unusually with English subtitles). His Dutch manager, Paul Brandenburg, and his first American agent, Robert Lantz, subsequently helped Hauer to find successful follow-up starring roles. In 1981, he played the lead character in two films: *Nighthawks*, in which he starred opposite Sylvester Stallone as Europe's most feared international terrorist, and *Eureka*, in which he played an international playboy, Claude Maillot van Horn, who is accused of murder. His first specifically American character role was as a powerful television journalist who gets involved with the CIA in *The Osterman Week-End*. He followed the high-profile *Blade Runner* by playing an extreme sadist in *The Hitcher*, again directed by Ridley Scott.

Recently, Hauer has learned to use his voice more effectively. He is well aware of Hollywood's preference for type-casting according to the physical appearance of its stars. As he puts it: 'Hollywood's number one rule is: American actors play heroes, foreign actors play villains.' In the 1990s, Hauer tried to move beyond the stereotypical aspects of his persona underlined in the 'pure genius' character he played in the very successful series of Guinness beer adverts (1987–93, directed by Ridley Scott and others). He has continued to work in Europe, often starring in independent films such as Ermanno Olmi's *The Legend of the Holy Drinker* (1988), in which he played a homeless alcoholic.

Hauer's career in Hollywood, which also includes many television roles such as his Golden Globe Award-winning performance in *Escape from Sobibor* (1988), has been received in his home country with ambivalence. He is praised for realising his dream, but critics regularly demand his return 'home', pointing to the negative aspect of the characters he plays in Hollywood. Hauer himself feels that there is a great discrepancy between the nature of American culture and what he would like to do best: that is being, in his own words, 'a lyrical person [and] a romanticist'. SdL

FILMS: *Nighthawks, Eureka* (1981); *Blade Runner, The Osterman Week-End* (1982); *A Breed Apart* (1984); *Flesh & Blood, Ladyhawke* (1985); *The Hitcher, Wanted Dead or Alive* (1986); *Bloodhounds of Broadway, Blind Fury* (1989); *Wedlock* (1991); *Split Second, Buffy, the Vampire Slayer, Past Midnight* (1992); *Arctic Blue, Blind Side, Surviving the Game* (1993); *Nostradamus, The Beans of Egypt, Maine, Beyond Forgiveness* (1994); *Mariette in Ecstasy* (1995); *Omega Doom, Precious Find, Blast, Crossworlds* (1996); *Redline, Tactical Assault, Hemoglobin* (1997); *Bone Daddy* (1998); *New World Disorder, Partners in Crime* (1999); *Turbulence 3, Lying in Wait, Jungle Juice* (2000); *Flying Virus* (2001); *Warrior Angels, Scorcher, Confessions of a Dangerous Mind* (2002); *Dracula III: Legacy* (2003).

HAUFLER, Max (1910–1965)

Haufler directed two films (including *Farinet* [1938] with Jean-Louis Barrault) before starting an acting career in some of his native Switzerland's most popular films of the 1940s and 1950s. He was renowned for his complex character performances and was much revered by a later generation of Swiss film-makers and critics. He appeared in *White Cradle Inn* as well as several European-shot US or US co-produced films of the 1960s, most notably Orson Welles' *The Trial*. VH

FILMS: *White Cradle Inn* (1946); *Town without Pity* (1961); *Freud* (1962); *The Trial, The Miracle of the White Stallions* (1963); *Morituri* (1965).

HAWKINS, Jack (1910–1973)

Doughty major British film star of the 1950s whose earlier British screen career included a small number of US-financed productions. Hawkins typically played solid and dependable authority figures such as police inspectors and submarine commanders. These roles often showed him saddened and wearied by responsibility – something that his commanding, but slightly hoarse, voice was well suited to reinforce. Hawkins was similarly cast by Hollywood in roles such as the galley commander and adopted father of Charl-

ton Heston in *Ben-Hur*, but these were shorn of the trademark hints of equivocation seen in his British work. JB

FILMS: *The Frog* (1936); *Who Goes Next?* (1938); *Murder Will Out* (1940); *The Black Rose* (1950); *No Highway* (1951); *Land of the Pharaohs* (1955); *The Man in the Sky, The Bridge on the River Kwai* (1957); *Gideon's Day* (1958); *Ben-Hur* (1959); *Two Loves* (1961); *Five Finger Exercise, Lawrence of Arabia* (1962); *Rampage* (1963); *Guns at Batasi, Zulu* (1964); *Lord Jim* (1965); *Poppies are Also Flowers* (1966); *Great Catherine* (1968); *Monte Carlo or Bust!, Oh! What a Lovely War* (1969); *Young Winston* (1972).

HAWTHORNE, Nigel (1929–2001)

Distinguished British actor with an international profile on stage, film and television from the early 1980s. Hawthorne won a Best Actor Academy Award for *The Madness of King George* (1994) and subsequently successfully balanced theatrical work with varied Hollywood roles that exploited his prestige. These included the part of President Martin Van Buren in Spielberg's *Amistad* and the menacing foil to Sylvester Stallone in *Demolition Man*. MW

FILMS: *Young Winston* (1972); *S*P*Y*S* (1974); *The Hiding Place* (1975); *History of the World: Part I* (1981); *Firefox, The Plague Dogs* [voice] (1982); *The Black Cauldron* [voice], *Turtle Diary* (1985); *Demolition Man* (1993); *Richard III* (1995); *Twelfth Night: Or What You Will* (1996); *Amistad* (1997); *The Object of My Affection, Madeline, At Sachem Farm* (1998); *Tarzan* [voice], *The Big Brass Ring, The Winslow Boy* (1999).

HAYDN, Richard (1905–1985)

Actor-comedian (and occasional director) who made his way from the London stage to Hollywood via Broadway. Haydn's distinctive nasal tones were both his comic trademark and trump card, leading to a variety of supporting roles that invariably played upon his stereotypically 'English' combination of pomposity, neurosis and eccentricity. MF

FILMS: *Ball of Fire, Charley's Aunt* (1941); *Are Husbands Necessary?, Thunder Birds* (1942); *Forever and a Day, Super-Rabbit* [voice], *No Time for Love, Who Killed Who?* [voice] (1943); *Henry Aldrich, Boy Scout* (1944); *And Then There Were None, Tonight and Every Night, Adventure* (1945); *Cluny Brown, The Green Years* (1946); *The Beginning or the End, The Late George Apley, Singapore, The Foxes of Harrow, Forever Amber* (1947); *Sitting Pretty, The Emperor Waltz,*

Miss Tatlock's Millions (1948); *Dear Wife* (1949); *Mr Music* (1950); *Alice in Wonderland* [voice] (1951); *The Merry Widow* (1952); *Never Let Me Go, Money from Home* (1953); *Her Twelve Men* (1954); *Jupiter's Darling* (1955); *The Toy Tiger* (1956); *Twilight for the Gods* (1958); *Please Don't Eat the Daisies, The Lost World* (1960); *Mutiny on the Bounty, Five Weeks in a Balloon* (1962); *The Sound of Music, Clarence the Cross-Eyed Lion* (1965); *The Adventures of Bullwhip Griffin* (1967); *Young Frankenstein* (1974).

HELLSTRÖM, Gunnar (1928–)

Swedish actor who, apart from his minor role in *Return to Peyton Place* as a ski-instructor, has mainly achieved success in the USA directing prime-time television series such as *Gunsmoke, Bonanza* and *Dallas*. MJ

FILM: *Return to Peyton Place* (1961).

HEMMINGS, David (1941–2003)

Although the success of Antonioni's *Blow-Up* turned Hemmings into an icon of the 'Swinging London' scene obsessively chronicled by American journalists, his status as a leading man proved unsustainable in the USA. His short stature and extremely boyish looks may have counted against him in the 1960s and 1970s. With a startling transformation in his physical appearance and vocal timbre in his sixties – his eyebrows rivalled C. Aubrey Smith's★ in length – Hemmings ironically became increasingly prolific in imposing elder patriarch roles towards the end of his career. JB

FILMS: *Saint Joan* (1957); *Blow-Up* (1966); *Eye of the Devil, Camelot* (1967); *The Charge of the Light Brigade, The Long Day's Dying, Only When I Larf* (1968); *Alfred the Great, The Best House in London* (1969); *The Walking Stick, Fragment of Fear* (1970); *Unman, Wittering and Zigo, The Love Machine* (1971); *Juggernaut* (1974); *Mr Quilp* (1975); *The Squeeze, Islands in the Stream* (1977); *Crossed Swords* (1978); *Prisoners* (1981); *Swan Lake* [voice] (1982); *Man, Woman and Child* (1983); *Gladiator* (2000); *Spy Game, Mean Machine* (2001); *Equilibrium, Gangs of New York* (2002); *The Night We Call it a Day, The League of Extraordinary Gentlemen* (2003).

HENIE, Sonja (1912–1969)

Although she is now largely forgotten by modern film buffs, the Norwegian-born Sonja Henie was in the late 1930s one of Hollywood's greatest stars. In 1936, Henie won her third Olympic Gold Medal and her tenth World Championship in a row in figure-skating. She was twenty-four and had achieved worldwide fame. Henie decided it was time to give up her sports career and pursue a career as a film actress. The strategy for this career change was put together with the help of her father Wilhelm, who until his death in 1937 was his daughter's manager. After her success at the Olympics in Garmish Partenkirchen and the World Championships in Paris, Henie travelled to USA. There, she set out on a tour across the USA, giving figure-skating shows to packed audiences, leading her to believe she had a future in the country. She went to Los Angeles, where she arranged two performances at the Polar Palace ice rink. Henie and her father invited many prominent people from the Hollywood film community and obtained broad press coverage with support from the famous couple William Randolph Hearst and Marion Davies. The performances were a great success, with many famous names watching from the stands. Henie became the talk of the town almost overnight. Twentieth Century-Fox contacted her and after some tough negotiating with studio manager Darryl F. Zanuck, she signed a five-year contract. Through this contract, Henie was to be launched in a leading role, receive $70,000 per film and be allowed to continue her skating exhibitions between shooting periods.

Before her debut Hollywood film, *One in a Million*, Henie's only film experience was a small supporting role in the Norwegian film *Seven Days for Elisabeth* (1927). To compensate for her lack of experience as an actress, Fox gave her a simple role with easy lines and surrounded her with the studio's biggest stars, such as Adolphe Menjou and Don Ameche. The problem of her accent was solved by giving the films a European setting, usually in Switzerland or Norway, or by giving Henie the role of a refugee or immigrant from one of these countries. *One in a Million* was a light romantic farce and a musical. Jean Hersholt★ played her father, while Ameche played an admiring reporter. The success of the film stemmed from the extravagant figure-skating scenes, a form of entertainment that was relatively unknown in the USA. The film was semi-biographical, which helped transform Henie from sports star to film star. *Thin Ice* and *Happy Landing* were built on the same recipe and reinforced Henie's popularity. After *Thin Ice*, she renegotiated her contract to receive $110,000 per film. In the late 1930s, she was in Hollywood's top-ten **291**

Sonja Henie: Hollywood's ice-rink star

list of most popular stars and the USA had become 'ice-minded'.

The unique feature of Henie's stardom was her physical prowess, which made the romantic union of traditional Hollywood musicals difficult. Her films often ended on a scene with Henie alone on the ice, elevated and divine. One reason for this was, of course, that it was hard to find a male partner who could match her skating skills. Thus, she was made to appear childlike in order to tone down her 'potentially radical' physical superiority. This was helped by the fact that the blonde, fresh-faced Henie had a striking resemblance to Shirley Temple (also a Twentieth Century-Fox star); as a result, she often portrayed young girls who were referred to and talked to as if they were children. Henie's contradictory star image, both naive child and divine goddess, was accommodated through the tension between narrative and performance. In the narrative, her childlike, ordinary aspect was emphasised along with a romantic union, while in the numbers, she was trans-

formed into an extraordinary, super-talented solo performer.

Sun Valley Serenade was choreographed by Hermes Pan and Glenn Miller's Orchestra played the score, which included the hit song 'Chattanooga Choo Choo'. The success of *Sun Valley Serenade* led Twentieth Century-Fox to extend Henie's contract. She was now to receive $125,000 per film and her popularity was such that rival studio MGM countered with Esther Williams' synchronised swimming routines. However, it was to be Henie's last major success at Twentieth Century-Fox. Her relationship with the studio was stormy, because she wanted some degree of control over her films, and she did not hesitate to break with studio etiquette by going straight to studio boss Zanuck with her wishes and demands. Henie also wanted to break away from her stereotypical 'good girl' image, to try films that did not revolve around ice-skating and to make films in colour. In *Everything Happens at Night*, the studio tried to create a new formula for her, but this was an exception. *Iceland* and *Win-*

tertime, made in 1942 and 1943, mark the point when the market for ice-skating films became saturated and Henie left Twentieth Century-Fox. She made two films after the break: *It's a Pleasure* – her only colour film – for RKO, and *The Countess of Monte Cristo* for Universal International. However, neither of these films offered Henie the challenges she was looking for, and they received a lukewarm response from the public.

In parallel with her film career, Henie continued to tour with her ice shows, in which she repeated the skating routines from her movies. It was during this period that she created the highly popular 'Hollywood Ice Revue': in 1947, it was estimated that more than 15 million Americans had paid over $25 million to see her ice shows. At the time, she was believed to be the richest woman in the world.

Sonja Henie became an American citizen in 1941 through her marriage to Dan Topping on 4 July 1940. This did not go down well in Norway. The country had been invaded by Germany a few months earlier and her former compatriots believed she was turning her back on the country at a difficult time. This was one of the reasons why Henie's popularity waned in her homeland immediately after World War II. Another was that the repetitive formula of her films seemed out of touch with audiences' taste. She was married for the second time in 1949 (to Winthorp Gardner), but this was unsuccessful too. With her third husband, Niels Onstad, she tried to make a comeback with the British produced *Hello London* (1958), a low point in her film career.

Towards the end of her life, Henie and Onstad became keen collectors of modern art and the collection formed the basis for the Henie Onstad Art Centre outside Oslo, opened in 1968. Henie kept in touch with the Hollywood community right up until her death. MP

FILMS: *One in a Million* (1936); *Thin Ice, Happy Landing* (1937); *My Lucky Star* (1938); *Second Fiddle, Everything Happens at Night* (1939); *Sun Valley Serenade* (1941); *Iceland* (1942); *Wintertime* (1943); *It's a Pleasure* (1945); *The Countess of Monte Cristo* (1948).

HENREID, Paul (Paul Georg Julius Hernried Ritter von Wasel-Waldingau) (1908–1992)

Austrian aristocrat-turned-actor who gained minor acclaim in his homeland before his anti-Nazi sentiments prompted him to move to Britain in 1935. Here, he played support-

ing roles in major productions, including the US-financed *Goodbye, Mr Chips* and *Under Your Hat*, before being threatened with deportation as an Axis national. Henreid secured a Broadway contract (that subsequently fell through) and arrived in the USA in 1940. Near-destitute, he came to Hollywood and was signed by Warner Bros. He rose to meteoric fame as the suave Continental gentleman – first as Bette Davis' double-cigarette-lighting lover Jerry in *Now, Voyager*, then as Victor Laszlo in *Casablanca*. However, Henreid was considered difficult and the studio swiftly dispensed of his services. In 1945, he became an American citizen, but was blacklisted in 1947 for his opposition to McCarthy's House Un-American Activities Committee. Hereafter, he was limited to playing a succession of unlikely Spaniards and Arabs in garish swashbucklers, before starting a successful second career as a director. RJK

FILMS: *Goodbye, Mr Chips* (1939); *Under Your Hat* (1940); *Joan of Paris, Now, Voyager, Casablanca* (1942); *Between Two Worlds, In Our Time, The Conspirators, Hollywood Canteen* (1944); *The Spanish Main* (1945); *Devotion, Deception, Of Human Bondage* (1946); *Song of Love* (1947); *Hollow Triumph* (1948); *Rope of Sand* (1949); *So Young, So Bad* (1950); *Last of the Buccaneers, Pardon My French* (1951); *Thief of Damascus, For Men Only* (1952); *Siren of Bagdad* (1953); *Deep in My Heart* (1954); *Pirates of Tripoli* (1955); *A Woman's Devotion, Meet Me in Las Vegas* (1956); *Ten Thousand Bedrooms* (1957); *Holiday for Lovers, Never So Few* (1959); *Four Horsemen of the Apocalypse* (1961); *Operation Crossbow* (1965); *Peking Remembered* [voice] (1967); *The Madwoman of Chaillot* (1969); *Exorcist II: The Heretic* (1977).

HENRY, Lenny (Lenworth George Henry) (1958–)

British comedian and comic actor who signed a three-film contract with Disney after the success of the film of his stand-up comedy show *Lenny Live and Unleashed* (1989). *True Identity*, however, failed at the box office and led to the premature end of his Hollywood career. MHu

FILMS: *True Identity* (1991); *Harry Potter and the Prisoner of Azkaban* (2004).

HEPBURN, Audrey (Edda Kathleen van Heemstra Hepburn-Ruston) (1929–1993)

An enduring icon of feminine sophistication on the American screen beloved by generations, Audrey Hepburn was born in Belgium to a Dutch mother and Irish father and **293**

held a British passport. Such origins led to her being marked as securely European, and certainly 'different' in many of her American roles, but at the same time she was always difficult to locate precisely in terms of national identity. Educated in England and trained as a dancer with the Ballet Rambert, she had an early modelling career and a number of parts in London chorus lines. Hepburn had a brief European film career with parts in *Nederlands in zeven lessen/Dutch in Seven Lessons* (1948) and *Nous irons à Monte Carlo/We Will All Go to Monte Carlo* (1952). She signed with Associated British Pictures Corporation, with whom she made *Young Wives Tale* and *Laughter in Paradise* (both 1951). She also made two films for Ealing Studios, with a small part in *The Lavender Hill Mob* (1951) and a more substantial role in *The Secret People* (1952).

In 1951, she screen-tested for William Wyler to play Princess Ann opposite Gregory Peck in *Roman Holiday*. Wyler was won over by her natural charm and spontaneity when she thought the cameras had stopped rolling and cast her for the part. She was subsequently contracted to Paramount Pictures, initially on a two-picture deal that also allowed her to do television and stage work, namely the Broadway productions of *Gigi* and *Ondine* in which she starred in the 1950s. It was with *Roman Holiday*, in which she played a European princess who escapes her royal duties for a day to explore Rome, that Hepburn's career moved to Hollywood and into international stardom. She won an Academy Award for her part in the film and arrived breathlessly to collect her Oscar still in her heavy stage make-up as Giraudoux's water sprite *Ondine*.

The key Hollywood films of Hepburn's career were marked by the presence of father figures and relationships with older men (such as Gary Cooper and Maurice Chevalier★ in *Love in the Afternoon*), and were structured around a narrative of transformation. This 'Cinderella motif' marked her career, from her meeting with Hubert de Givenchy, the couturier who dressed her on screen and off, through her film roles to the broader trajectory of her professional life – the little girl who almost starved hiding from the Nazis in occupied Holland and who became one of Hollywood's most beloved stars. While *Roman Holiday* was a Cinderella story in reverse, in *Sabrina* she played a chauffeur's daughter who returns stylishly transformed from two years in Paris to enchant the master's sons. In *Funny Face*, she played a Greenwich Village bookstore assistant who is taken to

Paris and transformed into a couture model. Paris, or France, or 'Frenchness' thus played a significant part in many of Hepburn's films and cemented her European connections in narrative terms. *My Fair Lady* was perhaps her clearest Cinderella story. Based on George Bernard Shaw's *Pygmalion*, it saw Hepburn's Eliza Doolittle transformed from ragged flower girl to society lady. The changes undergone by Hepburn's Cinderellas also often involved a painful shift in social class. This is clearly evident in *Breakfast at Tiffany's*, despite the fact that the transformation of Hepburn's character from Lulamae Barnes to Holly Golightly took place before the film began.

Fashion was central to Hepburn's star image and her Hollywood films therefore often centred both narratively and aesthetically on dress. The *mise en scène* was frequently tied to the spectacular presentation of her Givenchy clothes as, for instance, in *Funny Face*, which self-consciously played on key aspects of Hepburn's star persona. Her performance style was a winning, complex mixture of poised precision and apparent naturalness; her demeanour and expression recalling quite clearly her earlier careers as model and dancer.

While the majority of Hepburn's films were romantic comedies, she also tackled other genres, including the Western in John Ford's *The Unforgiven* and fantasy in the strange *Green Mansions* (directed by her then husband Mel Ferrer). In the 1960s, she successfully took on some stronger and more difficult films such as *The Children's Hour*, in which she co-starred with Shirley MacLaine as a pair of teachers accused of a lesbian relationship. In *Wait Until Dark*, in many ways her most powerful role, she was a blind woman who managed to defeat a group of drug smugglers.

Hepburn's career changed pace in the 1970s and 1980s, with a few film roles, television work and documentaries, and a live concert stage performance in 1990 where she read extracts from *The Diary of Ann Frank* integrated into an original orchestral work by Michael Tilson Thomas. Her most significant role during this later period saw her star opposite Sean Connery★ in *Robin and Marian*.

Hepburn travelled constantly during her Hollywood career, carrying her belongings with her in trunks. She lived in Rome for some time during her second marriage to Andrea Dotti. She always considered Switzerland home, however, and she later settled there with her last partner Robert Wolders at the house they called 'La Paisible' in **295**

Tolochenaz. For the last five years of her life, Hepburn worked for UNICEF as a Special Ambassador, to whom she felt indebted for her own rescue as a child in occupied Holland.

Hepburn was the epitome of sophisticated European femininity, but she was also somehow wholly American in her democratic beauty and the narratives of success she played in. In many respects, it was her 'in-between-ness' that secured her enduring appeal and success. She was difficult to place in terms of age, class and national identity, but the impossibility of pinning her down has therefore also made her stardom timeless. RMO

FILMS: *Roman Holiday* (1953); *Sabrina* (1954); *Funny Face, War and Peace* (1956); *Love in the Afternoon* (1957); *The Nun's Story* (1958); *Green Mansions, The Unforgiven* (1959); *Breakfast at Tiffany's, The Children's Hour* (1961); *Charade* (1963); *My Fair Lady, Paris When it Sizzles* (1964); *How to Steal a Million* (1966); *Wait Until Dark, Two for the Road* (1967); *Robin and Marian* (1976); *Bloodline* (1979); *They All Laughed* (1981); *Always* (1989).

HERBERT, Holmes (Edward Sanger) (1882–1956)
Prolific British actor (also credited as H. E. Herbert and Holmes E. Herbert) who played leads in Hollywood until the sound era, when he then became a character actor in both the USA and UK. A Sherlock Holmes fan, Herbert adopted the detective's surname as his stage name and eventually played secondary parts in Universal's own cycle of Holmes films. He generally appeared in horror and suspense features. TJ

FILMS: *His Wife* (1915); *Her Life and His, The Man without a Country* (1917); *The Whirlpool, The Death Dance* (1918); *The Divorcee, The Rough Neck, The White Heather, Other Men's Wives, The ABC of Love, The Market of Souls* (1919); *His House in Order, Black is White, My Lady's Garter, The Right to Love, The Lady Rose's Daughter, The Truth about Husbands, Dead Men Tell No Tales* (1920); *Heedless Moths, The Wild Goose, The Inner Chamber, The Family Closet, Her Lord and Master* (1921); *A Stage Romance, Evidence, Divorce Coupons, Moonshine Valley, A Woman's Woman, Any Wife* (1922); *Toilers of the Sea* (1923); *The Enchanted Cottage, Her Own Free Will, Sinners in Heaven, Love's Wilderness, Another Scandal* (1924); *Daddy's Gone A-Hunting, Up the Ladder, Wildfire, Wreckage, A Woman of the World, The Wanderer* (1925); *The Passionate Quest, The Honeymoon Express, Josse-*

lyn's Wife, The Fire Brigade (1926); *One Increasing Purpose, When a Man Loves, Mr Wu, Lovers?, Heart of Salome, Slaves of Beauty, The Gay Retreat, East Side, West Side, The Silver Slave, The Nest* (1927); *Gentlemen Prefer Blondes, Their Hour, The Sporting Age, The Terror, Through the Breakers, On Trial* (1928); *The Charlatan, Careers, Madame X, Say it with Songs, The Careless Age, The Thirteenth Chair, The Kiss, Untamed, Her Private Life* (1929); *The Ship from Shanghai* (1930); *The Hot Heiress, Daughter of the Dragon, The Single Sin, Dr Jekyll and Mr Hyde, Chances, Broadminded* (1931); *Miss Pinkerton, Shop Angel* (1932); *Mystery of the Wax Museum, The Invisible Man, Sister to Judas* (1933); *Beloved, The Count of Monte Cristo, The House of Rothschild, The Pursuit of Happiness, The Curtain Falls* (1934); *Accent on Youth, Captain Blood, Sons of Steel, One in a Million, Mark of the Vampire, Cardinal Richelieu* (1935); *The Country Beyond, Gentleman from Louisiana, House of Secrets, Lloyds of London, Fifteen Maiden Lane, Brilliant Marriage* (1936); *The Prince and the Pauper, Slave Ship, The Girl Said No, The Thirteenth Chair, The Man without a Country, Love under Fire* (1937); *Here's Flash Casey, The Buccaneer, The Black Doll, Say it in French* (1938); *The Mystery of Mr Wong, The Little Princess, The Mystery of the White Room, Juarez, Bad Boy, The Adventures of Sherlock Holmes, Stanley and Livingstone, Wolf Call, We are Not Alone, Trapped in the Sky, Hidden Power, Everything Happens at Night* (1939); *Women in War, Foreign Correspondent, South of Suez, Phantom Raiders, British Intelligence, An Angel from Texas* (1940); *Man Hunt, International Squadron* (1941); *The Ghost of Frankenstein, Danger in the Pacific, Invisible Agent, The Undying Monster, This Above All, Strictly in the Groove* (1942); *Sherlock Holmes in Washington, Two Tickets to London, Calling Dr Death* (1943); *The Pearl of Death, The Mummy's Curse, Enter Arsene Lupin* (1944); *Jealousy, The House of Fear* (1945); *Dressed to Kill, The Verdict* (1946); *Over the Santa Fe Trail, The Ghost Goes Wild, Singapore, This Time for Keeps, Bulldog Drummond Strikes Back, Bulldog Drummond at Bay* (1947); *The Swordsman, Jungle Jim, The Wreck of the Hesperus, Command Decision, Sorry, Wrong Number* (1948); *Post Office Investigator, Barbary Pirate* (1949); *The Iroquois Trail* (1950); *David and Bathsheba, The Law and the Lady* (1951); *The Brigand* (1952).

HERSHOLT, Jean (1886–1956)
Danish actor who was regarded by his Hollywood peers as an actor's actor for his many character roles played with

great sensitivity, and for his long and very prolific career in the American film industry. Hersholt made his stage debut at the end of the 1890s and his first film in 1905. He initially came to the USA in 1913 on tour with a Danish theatre company and his Hollywood film debut was in the Thomas Ince film *Never Again*. From 1916, he was contracted by Universal and his first major studio role was in the adventure film *The Show Down*. Hersholt's debut was in the Thomas Ince Triangle film in 1918, after Ince had left the company. Following the company's demise, he became a co-owner of the American Lifeograph Company in Portland, Oregon.

Hersholt returned to Hollywood in 1921, in the role of a German officer in *The Four Horsemen of the Apocalypse*. He continued to work as a character actor and during the early 1920s he was also employed as a co-director. In 1924, Hersholt, Mary Pickford and Douglas Fairbanks founded the Motion Pictures Relief Fund (later renamed the Motion Picture and Television Fund), for which he would receive a special Academy Award in 1939 for his service to the community.

Hersholt's most successful Hollywood role was undoubtedly as Marcus Schouler in Erich von Stroheim's *Greed*, in which he played a character obsessed with money and desire. With the advent of sound, he had problems in getting good roles with Universal and he signed a contract with MGM instead in 1931. Here, he gave a memorable performance as the anxious hotel porter Senf in *Grand Hotel*. For Twentieth Century-Fox, where he moved in 1936, he played Sonja Henie's★ father in the romantic ice-skating musical *One in a Million*. During the late 1930s, apart from his work in charity, Hersholt also starred in the radio show *Dr Christian*. This series was soon adapted to film by RKO and the closure of the show signalled the end of his acting career. His last screen role was as Viveca Lindfors'★ father in *Run for Cover* in 1955.

Hersholt was elected president of the Motion Picture Academy in 1945, although he resigned from the position in the aftermath of the Paramount Case in 1948. The following year, Ronald Reagan, president of the Screen Actors Guild, presented him with an award for 'distinguished service to the motion picture industry'. His final recognition came in 1956, when the Academy of Motion Picture Arts and Sciences created the Jean Hersholt Humanitarian Award. MBj

FILMS: *Never Again, The Disciple* (1915); *The Apostle of Vengeance, The Aryan, As the Candle Burned, Hell's Hinges, It's All Wrong, Kinkaid, Gambler, Bullets and Brown Eyes, Some Medicine Man* (1916); *Black Orchids, The Clash of Steel, Fighting for Love, '49–'17, The Greater Law, The Gunman's Gospel, Her Primitive Man, Love Aflame, Princess Virtue, The Saintly Sinner, The Show Down, The Soul Herder, Southern Justice, A Stormy Night, The Terror, The Townsend Divorce Case* (1917); *The Answer, Little Read Decides, Madame Spy, Smashing Through, Who is to Blame?* (1918); *In the Land of the Setting Sun, Whom the Gods Would Destroy* (1919); *The Deceiver, The Golden Trail* [also director], *Merely Mary Ann, The Red Lane, The Servant in the House* (1920); *A Certain Rich Man* [also director], *The Four Horsemen of the Apocalypse* [also make-up], *The Man of the Forest* [also director] (1921); *Golden Dreams* [also director], *The Gray Dawn* [also director], *Hearts Haven* [also director], *The Stranger's Banquet, Tess of the Storm Country, When Romance Rides* [also director] (1922); *Jazzmania, Quicksands, Red Lights* (1923); *Cheap Kisses, The Gold Fish, Greed, Her Night of Romance, Sinners in Silk, So Big, Torment, The Woman on the Jury* (1924); *Dangerous Innocence, Don Q, Son of Zorro, Fifth Avenue Models, If Marriage Fails, Stella Dallas, A Woman's Faith* (1925); *The Greater Glory, Flames, It* **297**

Jean Hersholt: prolific Danish character actor

Must Be Love, My Old Dutch, The Old Soak (1926); *The Student Prince in Old Heidelberg, The Wrong Mr Wright* (1927); *Alias the Deacon, The Battle of the Sexes, Give and Take, Jazz Mad, The Secret Hour, 13 Washington Square* (1928); *Abie's Irish Rose, The Girl on the Barge, Modern Love, The Younger Generation* (1929); *The Case of Sergeant Grischa, The Cat Creeps, The Climax, Hell Harbor, Mamba, A Soldier's Plaything, The Third Alarm, Viennese Nights* (1930); *Daybreak, The Phantom of Paris, Private Lives, The Sin of Madelon Claudet, Susan Lenox (Her Fall and Rise), Transatlantic* (1931); *Are You Listening?, Beast of the City, Emma, Flesh, Grand Hotel, Hearts of Humanity, The Mask of Fu Manchu, New Morals for Old, Night Court, Skyscraper Souls, Unashamed* (1932); *Christopher Bean, The Crime of the Century, Song of the Eagle* (1933); *The Cat and the Fiddle, Dinner at Eight, The Fountain, Men in White, The Painted Veil* (1934); *Mark of the Vampire, Break of Hearts, Murder in the Fleet* (1935); *The Country Doctor, His Brother's Wife, Reunion, Sins of Man, Tough Guy, One in a Million* (1936); *Heidi, Seventh Heaven* (1937); *Alexander's Ragtime Band, Five of a Kind, I'll Give a Million, Happy Landing* (1938); *Meet Dr Christian, Mr Moto on Danger Island* (1939); *The Courageous Dr Christian, Remedy for Riches* (1940); *Dr Christian Meets the Women, Melody for Three, They Meet Again* (1941); *Stage Door Canteen* (1943); *Dancing in the Dark* (1950); *Run for Cover* (1955).

HEYWOOD, Anne (Violet Pretty) (1932–)

Former Miss Great Britain who had a chequered European screen career in various UK and Italian films. Her first Hollywood film, *The Fox*, courted controversy in the USA because of its prominent lesbian theme. JS
FILMS: *The Fox* (1968); *The Chairman, Midas Run* (1969); *Trader Horn* (1973); *Good Luck, Miss Wyckoff* (1979).

HILLER, Wendy (1912– 2003)

British stage actress who came to Hollywood's attention with her Academy Award-nominated performance as Eliza Doolittle in the first screen version of George Bernard Shaw's *Pygmalion* (1938). Hiller's West End and Broadway commitments deferred her Hollywood debut until 1957, though she had appeared in the Fox-funded *Single-Handed* shot in the UK in 1953. She generally appeared in prestige pictures that exploited her distinguished association with the theatre: *Toys in the Attic* was based on a Lillian Hellman play while *Separate Tables* (for which Hiller won a Best

Supporting Actress Academy Award) was written by the English playwright Terence Rattigan. JB
FILMS: *Single-Handed* (1953); *How to Murder a Rich Uncle, Something of Value* (1957); *Separate Tables* (1958); *Sons and Lovers* (1960); *Toys in the Attic* (1963); *A Man for All Seasons* (1966); *The Elephant Man* (1980); *Making Love* (1982).

HINDS, Ciarán (1953–)

Irish actor whose multiple commitments in UK and local film and theatre have predominated over work in Hollywood films such as *Road to Perdition*, in which he played an archetypal Irish mobster. RB
FILMS: *Excalibur* (1981); *Mary Reilly, Some Mother's Son* (1996); *Oscar and Lucinda* (1997); *The Sum of All Fears, Road to Perdition, The Weight of Water* (2002); *Veronica Guerin, Lara Croft Tomb Raider: The Cradle of Life* (2003).

HJEJLE, Iben (1971–)

A graduate of Copenhagen's state theatre school, Iben Hjejle displayed no discernible foreign accent in her American screen debut, Stephen Frears' comedy *High Fidelity*. Yet despite the inevitable Hollywood offers that followed, Hjejle publicly decided to return to the less frenetic atmosphere of Danish Dogme films. HJW
FILMS: *High Fidelity* (2000); *Dreaming of Julia* (2001).

HOBBES, Halliwell (Herbert Halliwell Hobbes) (1877–1962)

British actor who appeared in over a hundred US films from the 1920s. He often played butlers and other assorted English stiff-upper-lipped types in such films as *Mr Skeffington*, where he was Bette Davis' personal servant. MW
FILMS: *Lucky in Love, Jealousy* (1929); *Charley's Aunt, Grumpy, Scotland Yard* (1930); *The Woman Between, The Lady Refuses, The Right of Way, Five and Ten, Platinum Blonde, The Sin of Madelon Claudet, The Bachelor Father, Dr Jekyll and Mr Hyde* (1931); *Lovers Courageous, Six Hours to Live, Cynara, Forbidden, Payment Deferred, Man about Town, Love Affair, Weekends Only, The Menace, Devil's Lottery* (1932); *The Masquerader, Looking Forward, Should Ladies Behave, Midnight Mary, Captured!, I Am Suzanne, A Study in Scarlet, Lady for a Day, If I Were Free* (1933); *Menace, We Live Again, British Agent, Now I'll Tell, Mandalay, The Key, Double Door, Riptide, All Men are Enemies, Madame DuBarry, Bulldog Drummond Strikes Back* (1934); *Father Brown, Detective, Charlie Chan in Shanghai, The*

Story of Louis Pasteur, Millions in the Air, Cardinal Richelieu, Whipsaw, Jalna, Folies-Bergère, Captain Blood, The Right to Live, Vanessa: Her Love Story (1935); *Dracula's Daughter, Hearts Divided, Rose-Marie, Love Letters of a Star, Here Comes Trouble, Give Me Your Heart, The White Angel, Spendthrift* (1936); *Parnell, The Prince and the Pauper, Maid of Salem, Varsity Show, Fit for a King* (1937); *A Christmas Carol, Service de Luxe, Bulldog Drummond's Peril, You Can't Take it with You, Kidnapped, Storm over Bengal, The Jury's Secret* (1938); *Remember?, The Light that Failed, Naughty but Nice, Tell No Tales, The Hardys Ride High, Nurse Edith Cavell, Pacific Liner* (1939); *The Lady with Red Hair, The Sea Hawk, The Earl of Chicago, Third Finger, Left Hand, Waterloo Bridge* (1940); *Here Comes Mr Jordan, That Hamilton Woman, Sunny* (1941); *Journey for Margaret, The Undying Monster, The War against Mrs Hadley, Son of Fury, To Be or Not to Be* (1942); *Mr Muggs Steps Out, Sherlock Holmes Faces Death, Forever and a Day* (1943); *Gaslight, Mr Skeffington, The Invisible Man's Revenge, Casanova Brown* (1944); *Canyon Passage* (1946); *If Winter Comes* (1947); *The Black Arrow, You Gotta Stay Happy* (1948); *That Forsyte Woman* (1949); *Miracle in the Rain* (1956).

HOBSON, Valerie (1917–1998)

Irish-born actress who signed a contract with Universal and moved to the USA at the age of seventeen in 1935. After a handful of films – she was Elizabeth Frankenstein in *Bride of Frankenstein* – she returned to Britain in 1936, disillusioned with typecasting and the production-line approach of the Hollywood studio system. MHu

FILMS: *Strange Wives, The Mystery of Edwin Drood, Rendezvous at Midnight, Bride of Frankenstein, Werewolf of London, The Great Impersonation, Life Returns, Chinatown Squad* (1935); *August Weekend, Tugboat Princess* (1936); *Atlantic Ferry* (1941); *Sabotage Agent* (1943).

HOEY, Dennis (Samuel David Hyams) (1893–1960)

British actor who mainly worked on the London and New York stage. Hoey appeared in a number of British films (including the US-financed *A People Eternal*) up to his move to Hollywood in 1941. He is best remembered for his personification of dim-witted and inefficient English officialdom in the role of Inspector Lestrade, which he played in six *Sherlock Holmes* films during the 1940s. JB

FILMS: *A People Eternal* (1939); *A Yank in the RAF, Confirm or Deny, How Green Was My Valley* (1941); *Son of Fury, Cairo,*

We Were Dancing, This Above All, Sherlock Holmes and the Secret Weapon (1942); *Forever and a Day, Frankenstein Meets the Wolf Man, Sherlock Holmes Faces Death, They Came to Blow up America, Bomber's Moon* (1943); *Sherlock Holmes and the Spider Woman, The Pearl of Death, Uncertain Glory, National Velvet, The Keys of the Kingdom* (1944); *A Thousand and One Nights, The House of Fear* (1945); *Terror by Night, Kitty, Anna and the King of Siam, Roll on Texas Moon, Tarzan and the Leopard Woman, The Strange Woman, She Wolf of London* (1946); *The Crimson Key, Second Chance, Golden Earrings, The Foxes of Harrow, Where There's Life, Christmas Eve* (1947); *Joan of Arc, Wake of the Red Witch, Ruthless* (1948); *Bad Men of Tombstone, The Secret Garden* (1949); *The Kid from Texas* (1950); *David and Bathsheba* (1951); *Plymouth Adventure, Caribbean* (1952).

HOLDEN, Fay (Fay Hammerton) (1895–1973)

English actress whose stage career postponed any screen appearances until she was forty years old. Inevitably, Hollywood struggled to cast the middle-aged Holden as anything other than a devoted mother, hence her most famous (and frequently reprised) role as the hyper-maternal Mrs Emily Hardy in the popular *Andy Hardy* series (1937–58). MF

FILMS: *The Accusing Finger, The White Angel, Wives Never Know, Polo Joe, The Pace that Kills, I Married a Doctor* (1936); *Guns of the Pecos, Bulldog Drummond Escapes, Souls at Sea, Internes Can't Take Money, You're Only Young Once, King of Gamblers, Exclusive, Double or Nothing* (1937); *Love is a Headache, Judge Hardy's Children, Test Pilot, Hold that Kiss, Love Finds Andy Hardy, Out West with the Hardys, Sweethearts* (1938); *Sergeant Madden, Hardys Ride High, Judge Hardy and Son, Andy Hardy Gets Spring Fever* (1939); *Andy Hardy Meets Debutante, Bitter Sweet* (1940); *Andy Hardy's Private Secretary, Blossoms in the Dust, Life Begins for Andy Hardy, Ziegfeld Girl, Washington Melodrama, I'll Wait for You, H.M. Pulham, Esq., Dr Kildare's Wedding Day* (1941); *The Courtship of Andy Hardy, Andy Hardy's Double Life* (1942); *Andy Hardy's Blonde Trouble* (1944); *Canyon Passage, Little Miss Big* (1946); *Love Laughs at Andy Hardy* (1947); *Whispering Smith* (1948); *Samson and Delilah* (1949); *The Big Hangover* (1950); *Andy Hardy Comes Home* (1958).

HOLLOWAY, Stanley (1890–1982)

Genial star actor who became synonymous with British cinema and Ealing Studios in the 1940s by playing a series **299** of likeable down-to-earth roles exemplified by his Arthur Pemberton in *Passport to Pimlico* (1949). Holloway played a police sergeant in the US/UK noir, *Wanted for Murder*. He was nominated for an Academy Award for his role as Alfred Doolittle in *My Fair Lady*. MW

FILMS: *Wanted for Murder* (1946); *Midnight Episode* (1950); *Hello London* (1958); *My Fair Lady* (1964); *In Harm's Way* (1965); *Target: Harry* (1969); *The Private Life of Sherlock Holmes* (1970); *Flight of the Doves* (1971).

HOLM, Ian (Ian Holm Cuthbert) (1931–)

Accomplished British stage, screen and television actor who has made irregular appearances in Hollywood productions. He had a leading role alongside Gena Rowlands, for instance, in Woody Allen's *Another Woman*. MHu

FILMS: *The Fixer* (1968); *Oh! What a Lovely War* (1969); *Mary, Queen of Scots* (1971); *Young Winston* (1972); *Juggernaut* (1974); *Robin and Marian* (1976); *March or Die* (1977); *Greystoke: The Legend of Tarzan* (1984); *Another Woman* (1988); *Kafka* (1991); *Blue Ice* (1992); *Mary Shelley's Frankenstein* (1994); *Big Night* (1996); *Incognito, Night Falls on Manhattan* (1997); *Joe Gould's Secret, Beautiful Joe, Bless the Child* (2000); *From Hell* (2001); *Garden State* (2004).

HOLMQUIST, Sie (Sigrid Andrea Holmquist) (1899–1970)

Swedish actress who, thanks to her looks, charm and appearances in three light film comedies in 1920, became known as 'Sweden's Sweetheart'. Holmquist moved to the USA later that year and immediately starred in *Just around the Corner*. She replaced Marguerite Clarke at Paramount and was often compared to a young Anna Q. Nilsson★. She was generally cast in small roles, though, and made her last Hollywood film in 1925. In 1927, she modelled in a one-reel Technicolor fashion short. MBj

FILMS: *Just around the Corner* (1921); *The Prophet's Paradise, My Old Kentucky Home* (1922); *Hollywood, A Gentleman of Leisure, The Light that Failed* (1923); *Youth for Sale, The Age of Innocence, Two Shall Be Born, Meddling Women* (1924); *The Early Bird, School for Wives, The Crackerjack* (1925).

HOMOLKA, Oscar (Oskar Homolka) (1898–1978)

Viennese-born actor whose burly build, menacing scowl and celebrated bushy eyebrows established him as a heavy in German films after 1926. Homolka came to Britain to

Viennese-born Oskar Homolka played numberous Soviet and Nazi heavies in Hollywood films

escape the Nazis in 1935 and played the lead in Hitchcock's *Sabotage* (1936). His guttural gravely tones found him cast as a 'foreign' heavy par excellence. A single-picture deal with Paramount, for *Ebb Tide*, first brought Homolka to Hollywood. He returned there in 1939 when threatened, like Paul Henreid★ and Conrad Veidt★, with deportation from Britain as an Axis national. Forever playing Soviet heavies, initially in anti-Nazi movies, then in 'Iron Curtain thrillers', Homolka seldom received a chance to demonstrate his versatility. His Academy Award-nominated supporting role as kindly Uncle Chris in *I Remember Mama* in 1948 proved a memorable exception. Homolka resettled in England in the early 1950s and commuted between London and California to continue playing Soviet and Nazi heavies on stage, screen and television. RJK

FILMS: *Ebb Tide* (1937); *Seven Sinners, Comrade X, The Invisible Woman* (1940); *Rage in Heaven, Ball of Fire* (1941); *Mission to Moscow, Hostages* (1943); *I Remember Mama* (1948); *Anna Lucasta* (1949); *The White Tower* (1950); *Prisoner of War* (1954); *The Seven Year Itch* (1955); *War and Peace* (1956); *A Farewell to Arms* (1957); *The Key* (1958); *Mr Sardonicus* (1961); *Boys'*

Night Out, The Wonderful World of the Brothers Grimm (1962); *Joy in the Morning* (1965); *Funeral in Berlin* (1966); *Billion Dollar Brain, The Happening* (1967); *Assignment to Kill* (1968); *The Madwoman of Chaillot* (1969); *The Executioner, Song of Norway* (1970); *The Tamarind Seed* (1974).

HOPKINS, Anthony (1937–)

After a long and distinguished career on stage and screen, the renowned Welsh actor Anthony Hopkins became a surprise Hollywood superstar in the 1990s after appearing as Hannibal Lecter in Jonathan Demme's *The Silence of the Lambs*. It was a role for which he won a Best Actor Academy Award and he has subsequently reprised the part in *Hannibal* and *Red Dragon*. Hopkins' remarkable performance as the almost charming serial killer was distinguished by a calm, intense concentration. With the addition of his strong build, rugged looks and an ability to slip between a lilting voice and authoritative bellow, the actor has now adapted to a permanent Hollywood career with ease.

Hopkins grew up in Port Talbot, Wales, where Richard Burton★ was also educated. Burton became a hero of Hop-

Welsh-born Anthony Hopkins in his famous role as Hannibal Lecter in Jonathan Demme's *The Silence of the Lambs* (1991)

kins and both actors had similar career paths from early critical theatrical success to later fame in Hollywood. Hopkins' American career began rather slowly and he initially played a number of small parts in television movies. His first major role in a film shot in the USA was in *Audrey Rose* in 1977. The film was a spiritualist thriller in which Hopkins played a father convinced his deceased daughter has been reincarnated in another girl's body. He then had a more memorable part as a ventriloquist who becomes taken over and driven to murder by his dummy in Richard Attenborough's *Magic*. While this murderous, unhinged character foreshadowed the part of Lecter, Hopkins was also associated with gentle, diffident, English characters until this point. He played the kind doctor in David Lynch's *The Elephant Man* and the shy bookshop owner in *84 Charing Cross Road*.

Hopkins explored further creative eccentricities as Dr Kellogg in Alan Parker's *The Road to Wellville*, and the eponymous painter in the overly reverential *Surviving Picasso*. He won an Academy Award nomination for his admirable attempt to portray the tortured Richard Nixon in Oliver Stone's biopic of the American president. The actor continues to display a willingness to play a number of diverse British and American film roles in parts ranging from an East Coast Classics professor (*The Human Stain*) to Alexander the Great's trusted general, Ptolemy (*Alexander*). JS

FILMS: *The Lion in Winter* (1968); *Hamlet* (1969); *The Looking Glass War* (1970); *Young Winston* (1972); *Juggernaut; The Girl from Petrovka* (1974); *A Bridge Too Far, Audrey Rose* (1977); *Magic* (1978); *A Change of Seasons, The Elephant Man* (1980); *The Bounty* (1984); *84 Charing Cross Road* (1987); *Desperate Hours* (1990); *The Silence of the Lambs* (1991); *Freejack, Bram Stoker's Dracula, Chaplin* (1992); *Legends of the Fall, The Road to Wellville* (1994); *Nixon, Surviving Picasso* (1995); *The Edge, Amistad* (1997); *The Mask of Zorro, Meet Joe Black* (1998); *Instinct, Titus* (1999); *Mission: Impossible II, How the Grinch Stole Christmas* [voice] (2000); *Hannibal, Hearts in Atlantis, The Devil and Daniel Webster* [unreleased] (2001); *Bad Company, Red Dragon* (2002); *The Human Stain* (2003); *Alexander* (2004).

HORDERN, Michael (1911–1995)

Unassuming British film character actor who made his screen debut in an uncredited role in *The Adventures of Robin Hood*. Hordern's presence stood out because of his **301** marked hangdog features and unmistakable low, reverberating voice that, particularly in later years, had something of the quality of a pained groan. These qualities could project an image of authoritative bearing and dignity and Hollywood producers called upon Hordern to play weary Roman statesmen, military leaders and – in voiceover form – wise narrators. Regrettably, none of these mainly perfunctory parts explored the same studied repression and tortured loneliness behind such authority figures in British films like *The Spanish Gardner* (1956). JB

FILMS: *The Adventures of Robin Hood* (1938); *The Hour of 13, The Story of Robin Hood and His Merrie Men* (1952); *The Dark Avenger* (1955); *The Man Who Never Was, Alexander the Great* (1956); *I Accuse!* (1958); *Sink the Bismarck!* (1960); *El Cid* (1961); *Cleopatra, The V.I.P.s* (1963); *The Yellow Rolls-Royce* (1964); *Genghis Khan, The Spy Who Came in from the Cold* (1965); *Khartoum, Cast a Giant Shadow, A Funny Thing Happened on the Way to the Forum* (1966); *The Taming of the Shrew, How I Won the War, I'll Never Forget What's'isname* (1967); *Prudence and the Pill* (1968); *Where Eagles Dare, The Bed Sitting Room, Anne of the Thousand Days* (1969); *A Christmas Carol* [voice] (1971); *The Possession of Joel Delaney* (1972); *The MacKintosh Man* (1973); *Juggernaut* (1974); *Royal Flash, Barry Lyndon* [voice], *Mr Quilp, Lucky Lady* (1975); *Joseph Andrews* (1977); *Young Sherlock Holmes* [voice] (1985); *Lady Jane, Labyrinth* [voice] (1986); *The Trouble with Spies* (1987).

HORN, Camilla (1903–1996)

Horn was a German dancer 'discovered' by F. W. Murnau after a walk-on part alongside Lil Dagover★. She starred as Gretchen in Murnau's *Faust* (1926). Horn was contracted in 1927 to United Artists, where she appeared in a number of German-language films such as *Sonntag des Lebens* (1931). Her English-language roles included the romantic heroine in Ernst Lubitsch's Canadian Rockies variant on the German mountain film genre, *Eternal Love*. She was typecast as a blonde vamp after her return home in 1929 and slid into relative obscurity after 1945, despite a brief film career renaissance in 1980s' West Germany. EC

FILMS: *Tempest* (1928); *Eternal Love* (1929); *The Royal Box* (1929).

HOSKINS, Bob (1942–)

Stocky, English film and television actor whose ordinary blokeish appearance and distinctive cockney accent have often been used to portray engaging everyman characters such as his leading role in *Who Framed Roger Rabbit*. JS

FILMS: *Royal Flash* (1975); *Zulu Dawn* (1979); *The Cotton Club* (1984); *Sweet Liberty* (1986); *A Prayer for the Dying* (1987); *Who Framed Roger Rabbit* (1988); *Heart Condition, Mermaids* (1990); *Shattered, Hook* (1991); *Passed Away, Blue Ice* (1992); *Super Mario Bros.* (1993); *Balto* [voice]; *Nixon* (1995); *Michael* (1996); *Spice World* (1997); *The White River Kid* (1999); *Enemy at the Gates* (2001); *Maid in Manhattan* (2002); *The Sleeping Dictionary, Den of Lions* (2003); *Beyond the Sea, Vanity Fair* (2004).

HOVE, Anders (1956–)

A menacing presence in the American television soap opera *General Hospital* and as the vampire Radu in the *Subspecies* series of films, the classically trained Danish actor Anders Hove has also used his brooding features to great effect in such Dogme films as *Idioterne/The Idiots* (1998) and *Mifune's sidste sang/Mifune's Last Song* (1999). HJW

FILMS: *Subspecies, Critters 4* (1991); *The Silencer* (1992); *Bloodstone: Subspecies II* (1993); *Bloodlust: Subspecies III* (1994); *Subspecies 4: Bloodstorm* (1998).

HOWARD, Leslie (Leslie Howard Stainer) (1893–1943)

Leslie Howard's image is that of the 'ideal Englishman' yet his father, in fact, was Hungarian and a good part of his early childhood was spent in Vienna. He was, however, born in London to an English mother, from whom he took his professional surname. Though his name is associated predominantly with Hollywood in the 1930s and Britain during World War II, his film career began much earlier in his native country. In 1914, he acted in an early war short film, *The Heroine of Mons*, and between then and the early 1920s, he appeared in two feature films as a supporting actor, as well as acting in and producing comedy shorts for Minerva Films, a production company he had set up with Adrian Brunel. At this point, however, opportunities within the British cinema were deteriorating as the industry moved towards the severe crisis of the mid-1920s, and it was in the theatre that Howard established his career as an actor. He spent the 1920s partly on the London stage and partly on Broadway, where he acquired a considerable reputation in a number of plays, including highly successful and long-running titles such as *Outward Bound* and *Berkeley*

Leslie Howard: 'the ideal Englishman'

Square, both later adapted for the screen with him. Towards the end of the decade, like many of his contemporaries on the Broadway stage, he attracted the attention of a Hollywood industry coming to terms with the new demands of the dialogue film and was offered a contract by Warner Bros.

His American film career began with the screen adaptation of one of his Broadway successes – *Outward Bound* – and, by the middle of the decade, Howard was established as a major star earning a Best Actor Academy Award nomination for his role in *Berkeley Square*. Indeed, as early as 1932, *Variety* was describing him as having 'weight at the box-office' alongside co-stars such as Norma Shearer and Fredric March. Later in the decade, Howard was to appear with some of the biggest stars of the day, including Bette Davis and Clark Gable. Critics wrote about his star status in terms of a sophisticated image appealing to the intelligentsia rather than the ordinary moviegoer. Compared with, say, the more visceral appeal of a James Cagney or an Edward G. Robinson, Howard presented a somewhat otherworldly figure removed from the cut and thrust of the fast-talking action-oriented genres of Hollywood in the

early sound period. During his Hollywood career, he did appear in a variety of genres, including crime films, comedies and even a Western, playing a rancher in *Secrets*, Mary Pickford's last film. However, his image as a dreamy romantic intellectual, a thinker rather than a man of action, was better served in films with a mystical turn, such as *Outward Bound* and *Berkeley Square*, and *The Petrified Forest*, where he played a somewhat introverted and pessimistic writer-philosopher against Bette Davis' sparky waitress and Humphrey Bogart's menacing bank robber. His talents were also suited to the elegant and precise delivery of the English language and, despite being almost thirty years too old for the role, this characteristic skill was demonstrated most effectively in his performance as Romeo opposite Norma Shearer's Juliet in MGM's 1936 adaptation of the Shakespeare play.

If in the 1920s Howard had divided his time between the London and New York theatres, in the 1930s his time was divided between Hollywood and the reviving British film industry. He worked for Warner Bros., MGM and RKO in the USA and interspersed this with trips to Britain to work for Alexander Korda's internationally oriented London Films (*Service for Ladies* [1932], *The Scarlet Pimpernel* [1934]), Columbia's British production arm (a quota picture, *The Lady is Willing*) and Gabriel Pascal, for whom he acted in and co-directed (with Anthony Asquith) the part-MGM-funded adaptation of *Pygmalion* (1938).

After *Pygmalion*, a success both in Britain and the USA, where it was nominated for a Best Picture Academy Award, Howard returned to Hollywood. David O. Selznick chose him for *Gone with the Wind* in the part of Ashley Wilkes, Rhett Butler's competitor for Scarlet O'Hara's affections, and, in many respects, Howard's image was well suited to the role of a 'Southern gentleman'. However, he failed to find favour with Margaret Mitchell, who considered that his performance presented the character as somewhat weaker than the one defined in her novel. In fact, Howard himself was reluctant to take the part and only agreed after Selznick had offered him the opportunity to have associate producer status as well as the leading male acting role on *Intermezzo: A Love Story*, the American film debut of Ingrid Bergman★.

After *Intermezzo: A Love Story*, Howard returned to Britain and contributed both as actor and director during the wartime renaissance of British cinema, with films such as *49th Parallel* (1941). He died in 1943, a victim of the war, **303** when a plane carrying him back to Britain after a lecture tour of Spain was shot down by the Germans. TR

FILMS: *Outward Bound* (1930); *Never the Twain Shall Meet, Devotion, Five and Ten, A Free Soul* (1931); *Service for Ladies, The Animal Kingdom, Smilin' Through* (1932); *Berkeley Square, Captured!, Secrets* (1933); *The Lady is Willing, Of Human Bondage, British Agent* (1934); *The Petrified Forest, Romeo and Juliet* (1936); *It's Love I'm After, Stand-In* (1937); *Gone with the Wind, Intermezzo: A Love Story* (1939).

HOWARD, Ronald (1918–1996)

British character actor and son of Leslie Howard★ whose moderately successful UK film career often involved playing doctors, army officers and policemen (occasionally in US-financed productions). He made his film debut in George Cukor's *Romeo and Juliet* and played Clay Allen in the Hollywood Western *Drango*. MHu/AP

FILMS: *Romeo and Juliet* (1936); *Now Barabbas* (1949); *The Hideout* (1956); *Drango* (1957); *Gideon's Day* (1958); *Murder She Said, Come September* (1961); *Africa – Texas Style!* (1967).

HOWARD, Trevor (1913–1988)

Trevor Howard was the favourite leading man of David Lean and Carol Reed, Britain's most internationally respected and successful directors in the late 1940s and early 1950s, and he starred in several of their most memorable films, including *Brief Encounter* (1945) and *The Third Man* (1949). But despite also proving himself as one of the few British actors capable of expressing the requisite bitter cynicism of a film noir hero in *They Made Me a Fugitive* (1947) – a commendable early attempt to translate the genre to a London setting – Howard was given far less of a shot at leading-man status in Hollywood than a number of his less-celebrated British peers. This was not through any lack of American exposure or effort on Howard's part. He appeared in prestigious American television adaptations of famous plays throughout the 1950s and even reprised his *Brief Encounter* role opposite Ginger Rogers in a live broadcast of Noel Coward's original playlet *Still Life* (1953).

Howard's solitary leading role in a Hollywood film, *The Roots of Heaven*, was the result of a concerted personal campaign to persuade Darryl F. Zanuck to cast him after Zanuck's first choice, William Holden, dropped out at a late stage. The rest of his Hollywood career playing aristocratic

villains (*Run for the Sun*) and military martinets (*Mutiny on the Bounty*) falls into the similar pattern of supporting roles followed by many British actors. It is certainly possible that Howard's celebrated willingness to explore the more unsympathetic qualities of his heroes – as seen in the abject suicidal despair of the character he played in *The Heart of the Matter* (1953) – showcased too much off-putting weakness and passivity for the tastes of Hollywood casting directors. JB

FILMS: *The Cockleshell Heroes* (1955); *Run for the Sun, Around the World in Eighty Days* (1956); *Interpol* (1957); *The Key, The Roots of Heaven* (1958); *Sons and Lovers* (1960); *Mutiny on the Bounty* (1962); *Father Goose* (1964); *Operation Crossbow, The Liquidator, Von Ryan's Express, Morituri* (1965); *Poppies are Also Flowers* (1966); *Pretty Polly* (1967); *The Charge of the Light Brigade* (1968); *Battle of Britain, Monte Carlo or Bust* (1969); *Ryan's Daughter* (1970); *Mary, Queen of Scots* (1971); *The Offence, Who?* (1973); *The Last Remake of Beau Geste* (1977); *Superman* (1978); *Meteor, Hurricane* (1979); *The Sea Wolves, Windwalker* (1980); *The Unholy* (1988).

HUBSCHMID, Paul (1917–2001)

Labelled 'the most handsome man in German cinema' at the height of his fame in the 1950s and 1960s, Paul Hubschmid was actually born in Switzerland and made his screen debut in the Swiss army drama *Füsilier Wipf* (1938). He became the country's foremost young leading man throughout the war years. Between 1949 and 1953, Hubschmid appeared in three minor Hollywood films under the screen name of Paul Christian. He later had starring roles in major European productions such as Fritz Lang's 1959 epics *Das indische Grabmal/The Indian Tomb* and *Der Tiger von Eschnapur/The Tiger of Eschnapur*. He made three more Hollywood films under his real name between 1966 and 1970. VH

FILMS: *Bagdad* (1949); *No Time for Flowers* (1952); *The Beast from 20,000 Fathoms* (1953); *Funeral in Berlin* (1966); *In Enemy Country* (1968); *Skullduggery* (1970).

HUME, Benita (1906–1967)

Willowy stage-trained English actress who played a string of stylish modern flapper heroines in various late silents and early talkies in Britain, before exposure on Broadway in the early 1930s sealed a contract with MGM. Substantial fame in Hollywood, however, ultimately came more from her off-screen role as the wife of Ronald Colman★, whom she married in 1938. Although Hume promptly retired from acting, she remained an important figure in the West Coast film-making community as a legendary party hostess. JB

FILMS: *Clear All Wires, Looking Forward, Gambling Ship, Only Yesterday, The Worst Woman in Paris?* (1933); *The Gay Deception* (1935); *The Garden Murder Case, Moonlight Murder, Suzy, Tarzan Escapes, Rainbow on the River* (1936); *The Last of Mrs Cheyney* (1937); *Peck's Bad Boy with the Circus* (1938).

HUNGARY

Although Hungarian stars asserted their presence in classical Hollywood, their passage to the USA came almost without exception via the cinema of a third nation – most frequently Germany – that enjoyed a greater international reputation. The nation's first wave of emigration of cinema personnel followed the overthrow of Béla Kun's communistic Council of Republics, which held power from April to August 1919. Kun supported and nationalised the Hungarian cinema industry, already in a strong position following a ban on French and American imports throughout World War I. In turn, many leading talents, including directors Mihály Kertész and Sándor Korda (later Michael Curtiz and Alexander Korda) and actor Bela Lugosi★, lent Kun's regime vociferous support. During the right-wing reprisals that followed Kun's quashing, these luminaries fled to Berlin, Munich and Vienna, all hubs of European production at this time. Although 'the American dream' was a potent concept in Hungary – as depicted in Béla Balogh's film *A tizennegyedik/ The Fourteenth* (1920) – Hollywood, to whose influence Hungary had remained largely unexposed, was not part of this configuration. Thus, while Lugosi and Kertész/Curtiz did finally make their way to the USA, this was due to a desire to escape German hyperinflation rather than to reach California; indeed, Lugosi would not make a Hollywood movie for seven years after setting foot in the New World. In all cases, these artists' former Hungarian careers were paid scant attention in the USA – something that would also characterise the experience of later Hungarian émigrés – so that they had to rely on their reputation in more cosmopolitan German productions, or else relaunch their screen career from scratch.

In 1920, under the Trianon treaty, through which the Allies aimed to reduce Hungary's power in the wake of

World War I, the nation ceded 70 per cent of its territory. The ensuing national economic meltdown also left its mark on Hungarian cinema, which faded to a mere shadow during the 1920s and 1930s. Consequently, rising stars – including Vilma Bánky★, Mihály (later Victor) Varconi★, Lya de Putti★ and Franciska Gaal★ – now continued to head to Berlin to establish themselves internationally, and it was from there that most were signed for Hollywood. Hence there was also no great exodus of cinema émigrés following the imposition of anti-Jewish laws in Hungary on 1 January 1939, since most of those affected had already been working in Berlin and had left years earlier to escape equivalent Nazi legislation. In Hollywood, Hungarians were correspondingly often absorbed within the German and Austrian émigré communities, all of whom used Miklosz Dora's restaurant 'Little Hungary' on Sunset Boulevard as a meeting place.

Following World War II, Hollywood influence in Hungary again became negligible under Soviet control, so that there was no American appropriation of screen talent, a situation that has also remained largely unchanged since 1989.

Roles and opportunities for Hungarian actors in classical Hollywood differed somewhat between the silent and sound periods. In the silent era, 'Hungarian' seemed to connote a kind of Latinesque romanticism and exoticism, as evidenced by the careers of Vilma Bánky and Victor Varconi. Bela Lugosi also received Valentino-style roles at this time in pictures shot in New York. Following the introduction of sound, a few brief opportunities arose in Hungarian-language versions shot by Paramount and Universal, while several major stars, including Bánky and Lya de Putti, now fell from favour due to their 'unsympathetic' Magyar accents. This latter perceived 'shortcoming' in turn opened up the major sound era role for Hungarians in Hollywood – that of a grotesquely non-realist, over-the-top personality for whom pronounced Hungarian intonation was crucial, as with the horror star Bela Lugosi and, later, the larger-than-life 'dahlink' Zsa Zsa Gabor★. RJK

HUNTER, Ian (1900–1975)
British actor whose long screen career included three early English Hitchcock films. Hunter usually played sympathetic male characters and was the romantic foil of Kay Francis in seven of his Hollywood productions. TJ

FILMS: *The Girl from 10th Avenue, I Found Stella Parish, A Midsummer's Night's Dream, Jalna* (1935); *The White Angel, The Devil is a Sissy, Stolen Holiday* (1936); *Call it a Day, Another Dawn, Confession, That Certain Woman, 52nd Street* (1937); *The Adventures of Robin Hood, Secrets of an Actress, Always Goodbye, The Sisters, Comet over Broadway* (1938); *The Little Princess, Broadway Serenade, Tarzan Finds a Son!, Maisie, Yes, My Darling Daughter, Bad Little Angel, Tower of London* (1939); *Broadway Melody of 1940, Strange Cargo, The Long Voyage Home, Bitter Sweet, Gallant Sons, Dulcy, Come Live with Me* (1940); *Andy Hardy's Private Secretary, Billy the Kid, Dr Jekyll and Mr Hyde, Ziegfeld Girl, Smilin' Through* (1941); *A Yank at Eton* (1942); *Forever and a Day, It Comes up Love* (1943); *Edward, My Son* (1949).

HUPPERT, Isabelle (1953–)

Who would have thought that the unassuming, pale, almost drab French redhead of *La Dentellière / The Lacemaker* (1977) would blossom into such a brilliant actress who is masterly at portraying harshness, even cruelty? To achieve her goal, Huppert has refused to compromise: she has never been interested in being a popular actress. She is more interested in performances that ring true, as testified by her impressive portrayal of a sado-masochist in *La Pianiste / The Piano Teacher* (2001). Likewise, Huppert has never been drawn to Hollywood to further her career, but to seek out creative experiences similar to those she had accumulated with European auteurs (Claude Chabrol, Jean-Luc Godard, Raul Ruiz). It is therefore because of Michael Cimino, and on the back of the success of *The Deer Hunter*, that she accepted a role in the doomed but magnificent *Heaven's Gate*. Here, she was a fragile but also combative and tight-fisted prostitute involved in a triangular love story with Kris Kristofferson and Christopher Walken, before dying in an unforgettable way. It may be the former film critic Curtis Hanson's love of cinema that also persuaded Huppert to play an elegant and heartless middle-class lady, a dark version of the Hitchcockian heroine, in his amusing pastiche *The Bedroom Window*. Once again, Huppert's performance was faultless. CV

FILMS: *Heaven's Gate* (1980); *The Bedroom Window* (1987); *I Heart Huckabees* (2004).

HURST, Brandon (1866–1947)

English stage actor who appeared in his first film role at the age of fifty. Hurst played a number of screen villains during the silent era, but was reduced to numerous (often uncredited) minor supporting roles as butlers, legal officials, coachmen and the like with the coming of sound. JS/AP

FILMS: *Via Wireless* (1915); *Dr Jekyll and Mr Hyde, A Dark Lantern* (1920); *Legally Dead, The Hunchback of Notre Dame, The World's Applause* (1923); *Cytherea, The Silent Watcher, One Night in Rome, The Lover of Camille, He Who Gets Slapped, The Thief of Bagdad* (1924); *The Lady Lightnin'* (1925); *The Enchanted Hill, Made for Love, The Grand Duchess and the Waiter, Secret Orders, Paris at Midnight, The Shamrock Handicap, The Rainmaker, Volcano, The Amateur Gentleman, The Lady of the Harem* (1926); *Seventh Heaven, Annie Laurie, High School Hero, Love, The King of Kings* (1927); *The Man Who Laughs, News Parade, Interference* (1928); *The Voice of the Storm, The Wolf of Wall Street, The Greene Murder Case, Her Private Life* (1929); *High Society Blues, The Eyes of the World* (1930); *The Right of Way, A Connecticut Yankee, Young as You Feel, Murder at Midnight* (1931); *Murders in the Rue Morgue, Scarface, Midnight Lady, White Zombie, Down to Earth, Sherlock Holmes* (1932); *Rasputin and the Empress, Cavalcade* (1933); *Bombay Mail, The Lost Patrol, The House of Rothschild, House of Mystery, Viva Villa!, Have a Heart, Crimson Romance, Bright Eyes, The Little Minister, The Gay Divorcee* (1934); *The Woman in Red, While the Patient Slept, Red Morning, Bonnie Scotland, Annie Oakley, The Great Impersonation, A Tale of Two Cities* (1935); *Gasoloons, The Moon's Our Home, Mary of Scotland, The Plough and the Stars, The Charge of the Light Brigade* (1936); *Stolen Holiday, Maid of Salem, Maytime, Wee Willie Winkie, The Firefly* (1937); *Four Men and a Prayer, Kidnapped, Professor Beware, Suez, If I Were King* (1938); *East Side of Heaven, Tell No Tales, The Sun Never Sets, Stanley and Livingstone, The Adventures of Sherlock Holmes* (1939); *The Blue Bird, Rhythm on the River, The Howards of Virginia, If I Had My Way* (1940); *Sign of the Wolf, Charley's Aunt, Birth of the Blues, Road to Happiness, Dr Jeckyll and Mr Hyde* (1941); *The Remarkable Andrew, The Ghost of Frankenstein, The Mad Martindales, The Pied Piper, Road to Morocco, Tennessee Johnson* (1942); *Dixie, The Constant Nymph, The Man from Down Under, Thank Your Lucky Stars, The Leopard Man* (1943); *Radio Bugs, Shine on Harvest Moon, The Adventures of Mark Twain, Mrs Parkington, The Princess and the Pirate, House of Frankenstein, Jane Eyre, The Canterville Ghost* (1944); *The Man in Half Moon Street, The Corn is Green, The Spanish Main, Confidential Agent, San Antonio* (1945); *Road to Utopia, Devotion* [scenes deleted], *The Green Years, Monsieur Beau-*

caire, *Sister Kenny, Magnificent Doll, The Time, The Place and the Girl* (1946); *My Favorite Brunette, Welcome Stranger, Where There's Life, My Wild Irish Rose, Road to Rio* (1947); *Two Guys from Texas* (1948).

HURT, John (1940–)

With his pale, crumpled complexion, frail, consumptive physique and a once-mellifluous voice cracked by years of smoking, John Hurt carries a distinctive air of spiritual exhaustion that has found him fairly prolific work as a character actor specialising in passive figures wearied by years of victimisation and/or debauchery. His career, accordingly, has an Indian summer pattern to it. Hurt only really caught the eye of British casting directors some time after his 1961 film debut by showing his knack for portraying tortured camp and effete decadence in mid-1970s' television roles as Quentin Crisp and the Roman emperor Caligula. International attention followed his Academy Award-nominated supporting role as a seedy drug-addled English toff wasting away in a harsh Turkish prison regime in *Midnight Express* and Hurt gained another Academy nomination for his first major starring role in an American film as the much abused and exploited nineteenth-century 'freak' John Merrick in *The Elephant Man*. Since he was physically unrecognisable under his heavy latex make-up, it was far from a traditional star role and he has rarely been cast as a leading man in subsequent Hollywood pictures.

Although there are consistent traits running through his roll of largely eccentric screen characters, Hurt's American filmography has been increasingly dominated by comedies and cartoons rather than straight drama. He can, however, boast the relatively rare distinction for a contemporary British actor of having appeared in several major Westerns: *Heaven's Gate, Wild Bill* and *Dead Man*. Such unusual use of a theatrically trained British actor in Hollywood is definitely more of a testament to the desire of modern filmmakers to defamiliarise well-worn Western conventions with an injection of non-stereotypically sickly, lily-livered English (or New England) interlopers than to Hurt's conventional iconic affinity with this genre. JB
FILMS: *A Man for All Seasons* (1966); *Sinful Davey* (1969); *Midnight Express, Lord of the Rings* [voice] (1978); *Alien* (1979); *The Elephant Man, Heaven's Gate* (1980); *History of the World: Part I* (1981); *Partners* (1982); *The Osterman Weekend* (1983); *The Black Cauldron* [voice] (1985); *Jake Speed*

(1986); *From the Hip, Spaceballs* (1987); *Frankenstein Unbound* (1990); *King Ralph* (1991); *Even Cowgirls Get the Blues, Monolith* (1993); *Thumbelina* [voice] (1994); *Rob Roy, Dead Man, Wild Bill* (1995); *Contact* (1997); *Night Train* (1998); *If . . . Dog . . . Rabbit* (1999); *The Tigger Movie* [voice], *Lost Souls* (2000); *Harry Potter and the Sorcerer's Stone* (2001); *Crime and Punishment* (2002); *Owning Mahoney* (2003); *Hellboy* (2004).

HYDE-WHITE, Wilfrid (1903–1991)

Archetypal white-haired, mischievous English gent who lent bewildered charm and a distinguished, often whimsical, air to numerous US film and television productions. He played Colonel Pickering in *My Fair Lady*. MW
FILMS: *Josser on the Farm* (1934); *Smith's Wives* (1935); *Change for a Sovereign* (1937); *The Claydon Treasure Mystery, Keep Smiling* (1938); *Wanted for Murder* (1946); *Conspirator, Britannia Mews* (1949); *The Man on the Eiffel Tower, Midnight Episode, The Mudlark* (1950); *No Highway* (1951); *Betrayed* (1954); *The Adventures of Quentin Durwood* (1955); *Tarzan and the Lost Safari* (1957); *Libel* (1959); *Let's Make Love* (1960); *On the Double, Ada* (1961); *In Search of the Castaways, Aliki My Love* (1962); *My Fair Lady* (1964); *The Liquidator, You Must Be Joking!, John Goldfarb, Please Come Home* (1965); *Our Man in Marrakesh, Chamber of Horrors* (1966); *P.J.* (1968); *The Magic Christian, Gaily, Gaily* (1969); *Fragment of Fear, Skullduggery* (1970); *No Longer Alone, A Touch of the Sun* (1979); *Oh, God! Book II, Xanadu* [voice], *In God We Tru$t* (1980); *Tarzan, the Ape Man* (1981); *The Toy* (1982).

HYLAND, Peggy (Gladys Hutchinson) (1895–unknown)

Peggy Hyland was the very first British film actress to have been directly snatched from a British studio by Hollywood. She was signed by Famous Players principally for her looks and talent (her British screen career having been too short to build up a substantial fan base) and crossed the Atlantic in February 1916. For the remainder of the decade, Hyland was a prolific leading lady for Vitagraph and Fox. JB
FILMS: *Saints and Sinners, The Chattel, Rose of the South, The Enemy* (1916); *Her Right to Live, Intrigue, Babette, Womanhood, The Sixteenth Wife, Persuasive Peggy* (1917); *The Other Woman, The Debt of Honor, Peg of the Pirates, Other Men's Daughters, Bonnie Annie Laurie, Marriages are Made, Caught in the Act* (1918); *The Girl with No Regrets, The Rebellious Bride,* **307**

Miss Adventure, Cowardice Court, Cheating Herself, The Merry-Go-Round, A Girl in Bohemia, The Web of Chance (1919); *Faith, Black Shadows* (1920); *Shifting Sands* (1923).

HYTTEN, Olaf (1888–1955)

Hytten was a prolific Scottish character actor who transferred from the British stage to the British screen during the 1920s. By the beginning of the sound era, he was well established in Hollywood, where he appeared in a series of (usually uncredited) minor roles as butlers, valets, MPs, police officials, professors and other assorted Englishmen during the 1930s and 1940s. Hytten is best remembered for his various parts in Universal B-films made during World War II. AP

FILMS: *It is the Law* (1924); *The Salvation Hunters* (1925); *The Better 'Ole, Marriage License?* (1926); *Old Age Handicap, His Unlucky Night* (1928); *City of Play* (1929); *The Return of Dr Fu Manchu, Grumpy, Playboy of Paris* (1930); *Daughter of the Dragon, Peach-O-Reno, Platinum Blonde, Newly Rich, Born to Love, Unfaithful* (1931); *The Crooner, The Man Called Back, Beauty and the Boss, But the Flesh is Weak, The Wet Parade, Impatient Maiden, Lovers Courageous* (1932); *Berkeley Square, Lost in Limehouse, Design for Living, Lady Killer, He Couldn't Take It, Women in His Life, The House on 56th Street, Blind Adventure, A Study in Scarlet, The Eagle and the Hawk* (1933); *The Richest Girl in the World, Happiness Ahead, Mandalay, Journal of a Crime, Money Means Nothing, The Little Minister, Mystery Liner, Murder in the Private Car, Let's Talk it Over, British Agent, Girl O' My Dreams, Glamour, The Key, Whom the Gods Destroy, One Night of Love, Shock, Jane Eyre, The Moonstone, Jimmy the Gent, The Mystery of Mr X, What Every Woman Knows, The Painted Veil, Have a Heart* [scenes deleted], *Bulldog Drummond Strikes Back, Secret of the Chateau, Sisters under the Skin* (1934); *Strange Wives, After Office Hours, Red Morning, The Widow from Monte Carlo, The Last Outpost, Becky Sharp, Bonnie Scotland, The Florentine Dagger, Clive of India, The Dark Angel, Les Misérables, Traveling Saleslady, The Spanish Cape Mystery, Ship Café, Living on Velvet, Atlantic Adventure, I Found Stella Parish, A Feather in Her Hat, She Couldn't Take It, The Lone Wolf Returns, Thanks a Million, Metropolitan, The Perfect Gentleman, It's in the Air* [scenes deleted], *Going Highbrow, Anna Karenina, Kind Lady, The Gay Deception, His Night Out, Mister Dynamite, Two Sinners, Vanessa: Her Love Story* (1935); *The Garden Murder Case, House of Secrets, Sons O' Guns, Trouble for Two, Camille, The*

Last of the Mohicans, Sylvia Scarlet, Libeled Lady, The Charge of the Light Brigade, The White Angel, Doughnuts and Society, And So They were Married, Don't Get Personal, Shakedown, White Hunter, Love Letters of a Star, With Love and Kisses, The House of a Thousand Candles (1936); *The Grand Bounce, Double or Nothing, Souls at Sea, Ebb Tide, Dangerous Holiday, Lancer Spy, The Great Garrick, Lloyd's of London, Angel, Parnell, Easy Living, I Cover the War, First Lady, California Straight Ahead, We Have Our Moments, The Emperor's Candlesticks, Conquest, The Good Earth* (1937); *Marie Antoinette, The Adventures of Robin Hood, A Christmas Carol, Bluebeard's Eighth Wife, Arrest Bulldog Drummond, Secrets of an Actress, Blond Cheat, The Lone Wolf in Paris, Up the River, Lord Jeff, Youth Takes a Fling* (1938); *Allegheny Uprising, The Little Princess, The Sun Never Sets, The Lady and the Mob, The Flying Irishman, Mr Smith Goes to Washington, Broadway Serenade, Pride of the Bluegrass, Television Spy, Man of Conquest, Our Leading Citizen, Rulers of the Sea, Six Thousand Enemies, Little Accident, Our Neighbors – the Carters, Rio, Andy Hardy Gets Spring Fever, The Bill of Rights, We are Not Alone, The Great Commandment, Zaza* (1939); *Drums of Fu Manchu, Escape to Glory, Arise My Love, Captain Caution, The Howards of Virginia, No Time for Comedy, Parole Fixer, Gaucho Serenade, The Earl of Chicago, Calling Philo Vance* (1940); *Bedtime Story, The Blonde from Singapore, Blondie in Society* [scenes deleted], *The Bride Came C.O.D., Dr Jekyll and Mr Hyde, Footsteps in the Dark, For Beauty's Sake, Nine Lives are Not Enough, Passage from Hong Kong, Washington Melodrama, When Ladies Meet, Man Hunt, Rage in Heaven, The Wolf Man, That Hamilton Woman, All the World's a Stooge, The Great Commandment* (1941); *Lucky Jordan, Affairs of Jimmy Valentine, The Black Swan, Destination Unknown, Eagle Squadron, The Ghost of Frankenstein, The Great Impersonation, Journey for Margaret, Sherlock Holmes and the Voice of Terror, Son of Fury, Spy Ship, This Above All, To Be or Not to Be, You're Telling Me, Casablanca* (1942); *Drums of Fu Manchu, Flesh and Fantasy, The Gorilla Man, Happy Go Lucky, Hit Parade of 1943, Holy Matrimony, London Blackout Murders, Mission to Moscow, The Return of the Vampire, Sherlock Holmes Faces Death, Silent Witness, The Amazing Mrs Holliday* (1943); *Detective Kitty O'Day, Leave it to the Irish, The Lodger, Ministry of Fear, Oh, What a Night, Our Hearts were Young and Gay, Passport to Destiny, The Scarlet Claw, Babes on Swing Street* (1944); *National Velvet, The Suspect, The Brighton Strangler, Christmas in Connecticut, Confidential Agent, A Guy, A Gal, and a Pal,*

Hold that Blonde, House of Frankenstein, Pursuit to Algiers, My Name is Julia Ross, Scotland Yard Investigator, The Woman in Green (1945); *Black Beauty, Holiday in Mexico, Magnificent Doll, The Notorious Lone Wolf, She-Wolf of London, Three Strangers, The Verdict, Alias Mr Twilight* (1946); *Bells of San Angelo, The Ghost Goes Wild, The Imperfect Lady, The Private Affairs of Bel Ami, That Way with Women* (1947); *If Winter Comes, Unconquered, Kidnapped, Shanghai Chest* (1948); *Challenge to Lassie, A Connecticut in King Arthur's Court, The Secret of St Ives, That Forsythe Woman* (1949); *Fancy Pants, Rogues of Sherwood Forest* (1950); *Kim, Anne of the Indies, The Son of Dr Jekyll* (1951); *Against All Flags, Million Dollar Mermaid, Les Misérables* (1952); *Fort Ti, Perils of the Jungle* (1953); *The Scarlet Coat* (1955).

IRELAND

The Irish have constituted a formidable presence in American cinema since the days of silent film and before the dominance of Hollywood. As a model of ethnic assimilation and a vast potential audience complete with their own neighbourhood cinemas, Irish clubs and Irish networks, Irish-Americans were the subjects of endless short films, most of them comedies.[19] If these representations were initially drawn from the stereotypes of earlier stage entertainers and had little in common with the aspirations of the rapidly gentrifying immigrants, they served as reminders of what had been left behind in Europe. The parade of drunken fathers, hapless maids, pious mothers and luckless labourers that entertained early audiences evoked an era when to be Irish meant to be at the bottom of the social heap. Inter-titles conveyed heavily accented speech to comic effect and Irish parts were performed by actors from any available ethnic background; some of these included Irish-born and Irish-American performers such as Thomas Meighan, William Desmond and Creighton Hale★.

As pressure groups, including the Ancient Order of Hibernians, demanded more nuanced depictions of the Irish, a new generation of Irish-American actors rose to prominence in Hollywood. Although they are not the subject of this particular project, performers such as James Cagney, Pat O'Brien and Australian-born Errol Flynn came to symbolise a new type of Irishman on screen; with little trace of accent, they stood for the successfully assimilated immigrant.[20] Playing cops, priests, professional fighters and soldiers and identified by their Catholicism and their emo-

tional spontaneity, they gradually moved into roles as tough guys and honest heroes. There were more screen parts for Irish men but a few Irish and Irish-American women actors achieved some fame in this period, notably Greer Garson★, Ann Sheridan and Barbara Stanwyck. Their roles evolved little as time passed, being divided into one or other of two character types: feisty colleens or virginal sweethearts.

The growing influence of Irish directors and producers in Los Angeles from the 1920s onwards, notably John Ford but also Herbert Brenon, Raoul Walsh and the co-founder of Universal Studios, Patrick Powers from Waterford, ensured the prominence of Irish themes on the screen and hence the demand for actors to play those roles. First-generation emigrants boasted 'genuine' accents, even if this usually meant the kind of undifferentiated Irish inflection associated with the acting style of Dublin's Abbey Theatre. To progress beyond the often simplistic stereotypes Hollywood was reluctant to abandon, ambitious actors such as George Brent★, and later Gabriel Byrne★, Liam Neeson★, Pierce Brosnan★ and their contemporaries, had to abandon their native inflections and learn to speak 'American'.

The principal source of early actors was the Abbey Theatre. Founded by W. B. Yeats and Lady Gregory in 1903 as part of the project of the literary revival, the Abbey attracted the most ambitious performers of the day and, through its world tours, established itself internationally as the voice of Irish drama. From *The Informer* (1935) onwards, John Ford relied heavily on Abbey actors for his Irish character players, making many of them part of his stock company. For most of these, this was their introduction to Hollywood film-making and, in the absence of any indigenous industry worth speaking of, their only opportunity to make a living out of screen acting. Many such as Arthur Shields★, Una O'Connor★, Sara Allgood★ and her sister, Maire O'Neill, settled in the USA; others, like Denis O'Dea★, found it uncongenial. For a Hollywood producer, the inclusion of Abbey actors in a film was a guarantor of authenticity, a signal to the immigrant audience and a claim to the respectability that association with the theatre was assumed to hold. Films loudly proclaimed their participation, even if that was usually in minor parts with bigger-name American stars in the lead.[21]

In the postwar period, the demand diminished for actors to fill the countless minor roles that the Hollywood **309** studio system required. So, correspondingly, did the migration of Irish talent across the Atlantic. Now actors such as Richard Harris★ and Peter O'Toole★ had to rely on making a name for themselves on the British stage or screen before being spotted by Hollywood film-makers and, even then, they regarded Hollywood as little more than a cash cow to be milked to fund their flamboyant lifestyles.

The success of Irish actors, particularly stars such as Maureen O'Hara★ and Maureen O'Sullivan, was a source of infinite pride in a country that for many years suffered from a cultural inferiority complex born of its post-colonial condition and compounded by an inheritance of Catholic guilt. If the hierarchy viewed Hollywood as the ultimate expression of Mammon, going to 'the pictures' provided its constituency with a brief escape into a world of luxury and sin. As Diane Negra has noted, early 'Irish' stars such as Colleen Moore were markers of white racial purity in American culture.[22] But of late, Irish female stars have made poor headway in Hollywood, perhaps because purity of any kind is little called for in contemporary cinema.

A younger generation of male Irish actors, including Gabriel Byrne, Liam Neeson and most recently Colin Farrell★, has, however, laid claim to leading roles in big-budget Hollywood productions. Often cast as 'hard men', frequently in non-Irish parts, they represent Hollywood's ambiguity about European actors in general. Their off-screen identities as 'outsiders' feeds into their roles, which often situate them in opposition to their 'insider' American counterparts. What this success suggests is an overall shift in the screen image of the Irishman away from a comic stage persona towards a more threatening, sexualised characterisation. Furthermore, these contemporary actors have been able to maintain simultaneous careers in a now more buoyant Irish cinema, itself often funded by Hollywood money. In a nice twist in the history of migrant Irish screen actors, many now use their position in Los Angeles to secure financing for Irish productions back in Europe. RB

IRELAND, Jill (1936–1990)

Ireland was one of the few Rank Organisation 'Charm School' graduates to achieve a career of substance in the USA, although this may have also been partly due to her marriage to Charles Bronson, whose films she appeared in

on several occasions. Ireland became a well-known public figure in the USA on account of her long battle against cancer and role as a prominent spokesperson for the American Cancer Society. JB

FILMS: *The Karate Killers* (1967); *Villa Rides* (1968); *The Mechanic* (1972); *Breakout, Hard Times, Breakheart Pass* (1975); *From Noon Till Three* (1976); *Love and Bullets* (1979); *Death Wish II* (1982); *Assassination, Caught* (1987).

IRONS, Jeremy (Jeremy John Irons) (1948–)

'Tall, thin and rather British.' These adjectives, which form Irons' own description of himself, have pursued the actor from the beginning of his screen career in 1980 when he made his debut in *Nijinsky*. It was the success and promotion of prestige productions such as *The French Lieutenant's Woman* (1981) and the UK television series *Brideshead Revisited* (1981), however, that finally sealed the international screen image of a man once described as '6ft 2 of pencil-thin pure public schoolboy'.

Irons' attitude to Hollywood seems rather ambivalent. While he has demonstrated an inclination towards offbeat and eclectic parts – such as his dual role as the disturbed twin gynaecologists in David Cronenberg's *Dead Ringers*, which won him a Best Actor Award from the New York Film Critics Circle – he has also been willing to ham it up as an East German psychopath opposite Bruce Willis in *Die Hard: With a Vengeance*. Underlying such choices may be the fact that Irons is expedient in exploiting his public image. Under those charming good looks, immaculate manners and all-too-lean physique is a pronounced desire to avoid being pigeon-holed as the suave English gent. There is a recognition that, at least in Hollywood, such impossibly refined or controlled qualities can be readily twisted into something altogether more suspicious. As Irons has observed: 'smiling is bad for my image'. Thus, along with the psychopaths, has come further sexual obsession as the English Professor Humbert Humbert in Adrian Lyne's *Lolita*. The controversy surrounding the film saw Irons threatening to leave the UK permanently in 1997 if British distributors persisted with their refusal to handle it amid a flurry of tabloid outrage.

It was Irons' earlier Academy Award-winning role as Claus von Bülow, the European aristocrat accused of murder in *Reversal of Fortune*, that really established him as an actor capable of great nuance and ambiguity in the

USA. With fitting irony, the part brought him to the attention of the Disney executives, who used his voice in *The Lion King*. His seductive and disturbing performance as the villainous Scar, with his meticulously enunciated, purring vowels inflecting a blend of class, intellect and sadism, certainly presented the perfect distillation of Irons' persona to international audiences. MW

FILMS: *Nijinsky* (1980); *The French Lieutenant's Woman* (1981); *Betrayal* (1983); *The Statue of Liberty* (1986); *Dead Ringers* (1988); *Reversal of Fortune* (1990); *Kafka* (1991); *From Time to Time* (1992); *M. Butterfly, The House of the Spirits* (1993); *The Lion King* [voice] (1994); *Die Hard: With a Vengeance* (1995); *Chinese Box, Lolita* (1997); *The Man in the Iron Mask* (1998); *Dungeons & Dragons* (2000); *The Time Machine* (2002); *The Merchant of Venice, Being Julia* (2004).

ITALY

Italy may not have supplied American cinema with a large number of stars, but it nonetheless, throughout its history, provided a continuous flow of talented actors. Hollywood has always been well supplied with Italian character actors, from the silent era when Cesare Gravina★ was one of Eric von Stroheim's favourite performers, to Mimi Cecchini★, who played Angelina in Woody Allen's *Broadway Danny Rose* (1984). Only in the immediate post-World War II period, following the international success of neo-realism, were Italian stars such as Sophia Loren★ a major presence in Hollywood.

Paradoxically, industrial motivations do not seem to have been particularly relevant to the overall patterns of emigration of Italian actors to Hollywood. They did not travel to the USA when jobs were scarce in Italy but, rather, when the industry was doing well. During the silent era, for example, after a phase of worldwide popularity for Italian divas and spectacular historical films, the Italian film industry underwent a serious crisis. However, with the exception of people like Lido Manetti★, Tullio Carminati★ and Rina De Liguoro★, few stars moved to Hollywood. Maybe Italian actors were so gratified by the idea of belonging to a proven art that they distrusted the commercial aspects of Hollywood cinema and stayed in Europe, sometimes working on the stage when underemployed in the film studios. The opposite is true when the Italian film industry was very successful after World War II: Loren, Gina Lollobrigida★, Anna Magnani★ and Alida Valli★ indeed went

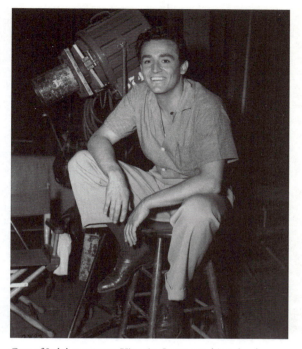

One of Italy's great stars, Vittorio Gassman achieved only modest success in Hollywood

to the USA, lending a touch of exotic glamour and quality at a time when American cinema was undergoing its own industrial and critical crisis. The tradition of Italian actors' poor adaptability to Hollywood endured, though, and these stars never became permanent Californian residents. People like Magnani were too closely associated with neo-realism or, in the case of Lollobrigida and Loren, its 'softer' commercial versions.

How can we further explain the relatively small numbers of Italian actors who went to Hollywood? Rather than political reasons such as the flight from Fascism, cultural resistances to the commercialism of Hollywood seem to have been at play, as well as the problem of language. Italian actors rarely spoke English well enough to say their lines without memorising them phonetically. Only in recent years have representatives of a younger generation, such as Valeria Golino★, been more fluent in English and moved more freely between the two industries. If, on the other hand, we look at Hollywood's own needs, it is clear that while the Italian market was always very profitable for Hollywood, American cinema did not have to address Italian audiences with a specifically targeted product. Apart from **311** the early 1930s phenomenon of the Italian multi-language films shot in Hollywood with Italian-speaking actors such as Luisa Caselotti, Hollywood had no need for recognisable Italian actors and stars to sell its films. And with the exception of gangster films and some prestige pictures, usually sophisticated comedies about high society in Venice, there were few American films on Italian subjects. Those that were made tended to use American stars and some European actors, including Italian character actors, and to be shot in the American studios. There were two exceptions to this rule. In the 1920s, some of these pictures were actually shot in Italy, using Italian actors as extras. This happened again for a while after World War II when, for different reasons, some American films were shot in Italy. The largest concentration of Italian names in American films, in terms of both stars and character actors, thus occurred as the result of a combination of Italian stars travelling to Hollywood and the filming of American feature films in Italy.

Paradoxically, music played an important role in the enrolment of Italian actors, especially *before* the 1930s – an oddity, given the potential benefits of sound. Even before the 1920s, important Italian opera singers such as Lina Cavalieri★ and Enrico Caruso★ appeared in Hollywood films. Many English-speaking Italian character actors such as Eduardo Ciannelli★, Paul Porcasi★ and Franco Corsaro★ in fact made their American debut as singers. The 1930s, when interest in American cinema started to grow in Italy, is actually the period in which almost no Italian actor moved to Hollywood even on a temporary basis. The international Italian star Isa Miranda★ went to Hollywood, but she only made two films there, while Vittorio De Sica★ did a screen test for Fox, singing 'Blue Moon', but was not offered a contract. The Italian versions of American films were entrusted to the representatives of the immigrant stage, and, rarely, to minor actors coming from Italy such as Agostino Borgato★, Sandro Salvini★ and Guido Trento★. In fact, the career of Italian actors in the 1920s and 1930s indicates a strong interaction between stage and screen. As well as finding Italian talent on Broadway, as in the case of Eduardo Ciannelli, or variety shows, in the case of Henry Armetta, who had emigrated to the USA as a child, Hollywood located most of its talent in the New York immigrant theatre. At times, American directors discovered Italian actors on the stage, as in the case of Herbert Brenon with Sandro Salvini, George Fitzmaurice with Gugliemo Ric-

ciardi★ and D. W. Griffith with Francesco (Frank) Puglia★. They often played European (or Latin) characters, and only at times specifically Italians. Maybe only Armetta, with his trademark moustache and mannerisms, was always recognisable as an Italian.

Hollywood hired Italian actors for two seemingly opposite reasons: for their association with high culture on the one hand, and spontaneity and naturalness on the other. There were thus often associations with music, art and a cultured sensibility and this is true also of Rudolph Valentino, John Travolta and Leonardo DiCaprio. But generally, the Italian stereotype on screen tended to emphasise his or her 'otherness'. The Italian was portrayed as racially different from the WASP, and right from the time of silent cinema, more primitive, fun-loving (always with a *fiasco* of wine and spaghetti, as in Billy Wilder's *Avanti!* [1972]), and more natural: he or she was passionate to the point of violence. There is even the suggestion of a stronger bodily presence, from Luciano Albertini★ to Sylvester Stallone. To be precise, 'Italian' usually implied Southern Italian in Hollywood. This was because North America mainly received Southern Italians as immigrants and because the majority of the performers available to Hollywood came from the Southern Italian immigrant theatre and variety shows. In this respect, it remains a poignant irony that the Austrian-born Paul Muni (*Scarface* [1932]) and the Romanian-born Edward G. Robinson with (*Little Caesar* [1931]) contributed more to the stereotype of the Southern Italian gangster than Italian actors such as Ciannelli, Porcasi and Puglia, who played numerous gangster roles during their careers.

In American cinema, Italy thus has always been the place to get in touch with human feelings and nature, as seen in the numerous war brides of the postwar rural idylls. The late 1940s and 1950s were indeed the moment for Italian actresses. While American cinema 'invaded' Italy in a conscious plan to divert audiences from leftist neo-realist films, Italian actresses were invited to Hollywood as the representatives of this new, powerful aesthetic. Anna Magnani went to the USA to play in a film scripted for her by Tennessee Williams and she was followed by Pier Angeli★, Lollobrigida, Loren, Elsa Martinelli★ and Marisa Pavan★. The lavish make-up and rigid hairdos these actresses were compelled to wear did not work well with their neo-realist performance style. The paradox was that while Hollywood wanted these actresses as representatives of neo-realism, it also tried to 'Hollywoodise' them, thus destroying the very naturalness that was their leading asset. Furthermore, American cinema was unable to find a balance between the Method acting that dominated Hollywood in those years and the more sober performance style characteristic of neo-realism.

Since this highpoint of exchange, the contribution of Italian actors has continued, though in a less marked fashion in the increasingly global Hollywood. In the 1960s and 1970s, Marcello Mastroianni★, Claudia Cardinale★, Valentina Cortese★, Franco Nero★, Fabio Testi★, Monica Vitti★, Luigi Proietti★, Rossana Podestà★ and Michele Placido★ all acted in American films, but they never made any real impact. More interesting has been the phenomenon of Roberto Benigni★, who went to work not in Hollywood, but in New York's independent cinema with Jim Jarmusch. This particular journey of desire signalled a renewed alliance between the American auteur and the eccentric European performer. GM

IURES, Marcel (1951–)

Internationally acclaimed Romanian classical actor who, during the post-Communist era, has deployed his swarthy features, broad frame and velvety tones to unsettling effect in a number of charming yet ruthless character roles – including terrorists, Nazis and vampires – in major Hollywood productions filmed partly on location in Europe. Iures has also gained American attention through his participation in Romanian films shot in English and aimed at international markets, such as *Hope . . .* (2001) and *Dracula the Impaler* (2002). RJK

FILMS: *Interview with the Vampire: The Vampire Chronicles* (1994); *Mission: Impossible* (1996); *The Peacemaker* (1997); *Elite* (2000); *Hart's War* (2002).

JACKSON, Glenda (1936–)

During her heyday as a heavyweight theatrical actress, before she retired to become a British Labour MP, Glenda Jackson was courted (somewhat incongruously) by American film producers to appear mainly in light comedies. It is possible that the harsh forbidding exterior seen in Jackson's iconic film and television performances as Elizabeth I seemed too severe for straight American female roles, though the virginal associations may account for the comedy nun she was cast as in *Nasty Habits*. It is certainly

significant that despite a respective Academy Award and Academy Award nominations for the feisty, uncompromising characters she played in *Women in Love* and *Sunday Bloody Sunday*, neither film resulted in a concrete Hollywood offer. This came instead after Jackson poked gentle fun at her own stern image in an Astaire–Rogers pastiche dance sequence on a 1971 edition of the BBC's *Morecambe and Wise Show*. The appearance prompted American scriptwriter Melvin Frank to switch the nationality of both the location and female lead of his modern screwball comedy *A Touch of Class* in order to accommodate Jackson. Her performance as an English divorcee embarking upon a tempestuous affair with visiting American George Segal won her another Academy Award and the same pairing and generic template was repeated in *Lost and Found*. The comic formula of Jackson's combative and acerbic English career woman finding her match in a strong-minded, unpretentious American male was revived in *House Calls* and *Hopscotch*, which both pitted her against Walter Matthau. JB

FILMS: *Marat/Sade* (1967); *Women in Love* (1969); *The Music Lovers, The Boy Friend, Sunday, Bloody Sunday, Mary, Queen of Scots* (1971); *A Touch of Class, A Bequest to the Nation* (1973); *The Incredible Sarah* (1976); *Nasty Habits* (1977); *House Calls* (1978); *Lost and Found* (1979); *Hopscotch* (1980); *Health* (1982); *Turtle Beach* (1985); *Beyond Therapy* (1987).

JACOBI, Derek (1938–)

Widely admired English actor who gained a formidable reputation on the British stage from the 1960s onwards. Regular roles in British films have been interspersed with sporadic American appearances, including Kenneth Branagh's★ neo-noir *Dead Again* and a reprisal of *I, Claudius'* cynical Roman senator for Ridley Scott's *Gladiator*. MF

FILMS: *The Secret of NIMH* [voice] (1982); *The Statue of Liberty* [voice] (1986); *Discovering Hamlet* (1990); *Dead Again* (1991); *Looking for Richard, Hamlet* (1996); *Gladiator, Up at the Villa, Joan of Arc: The Virgin Warrior* (2000); *The Body, Gosford Park* (2001).

JADE, Claude (Claude Marcelle Jorré) (1948–)

French actress who starred in François Truffaut's★ *Baisers volés/Stolen Kisses* (1968), where she played the prim and proper Christine Darbon who becomes Antoine Doinel's **313**

wife in the sequel, *Domicile conjugal/Bed and Board* (1970). Truffaut introduced her to Hitchcock, who cast her in *Topaz*, but her Hollywood career stopped there. VO
FILM: *Topaz* (1969).

JAGGER, Mick (1943–)

Lead singer of the Rolling Stones who has also enjoyed a sporadic film acting career. Jagger's debut role as the washed-up rock star in the US/UK-funded *Performance* remains his most notable screen appearance to date. JS
FILMS: *Performance* (1970); *Freejack* (1992); *The Man from Elysian Fields* (2001).

JANNINGS, Emil (Theodor Friedrich Emil Janenz) (1884–1950)

When Emil Jannings first arrived in the USA – as screen image, not yet in person – he travelled incognito. His first US success was Ernst Lubitsch's *Passion/Madame DuBarry* (1919); but the production company Ufa, fearing audience hostility to German titles, deleted from the credits both Jannings' name and that of director Ernst Lubitsch. By 1920, by contrast, Jannings' role in *Passion* had gained him US star status, and he featured prominently in credits for *Deception/Anna Boleyn* (1920). Subsequent US successes in the German films *Der letzte Mann/The Last Laugh* (1924) and *Varieté* (1925) secured a contract with Paramount (brokered by former Ufa producer Erich Pommer), and established the role type with which Jannings would remain associated throughout his Hollywood career. In *Der letzte Mann*, he had played a hotel porter humiliated by his demotion to toilet attendant. Here, as in subsequent Hollywood titles, Jannings compellingly enacted the pathos of class displacement, coupled in such films as *The Way of All Flesh* and *Sins of the Fathers* with sexual betrayal by low-life adventuresses. For *The Way of All Flesh* and Josef von Sternberg's *The Last Command*, he won the first ever Best Actor Academy Award (1928). The coming of sound precipitated his return to Germany, to play first opposite Marlene Dietrich★ in Sternberg's *The Blue Angel* (1930) and later in several genius-figure roles that would help earn him the title of State Actor – one of numerous accolades Jannings gained during a buoyant theatre and film career under Nazism. EC
FILMS: *The Way of All Flesh*, *The Street of Sin*, *The Last Command* (1927); *The Patriot*, *Sins of the Fathers* (1928); *Betrayal* (1929).

JAQUE-CATELAIN (Jacques Maxime Guérin-Catelain) (1897–1965)

French matinée idol and romantic lead of the 1920s, star of many films by Marcel L'Herbier. In the USA during World War II, he worked in radio, gave lectures and appeared (uncredited) in one film. MB/GV
FILM: *This Love of Ours* (1945).

JEANMAIRE, Zizi (Renée Jeanmaire) (1924–)

A stunning, sensual and witty dancer, French performer Zizi Jeanmaire burst onto Broadway with *La Croqueuse de diamants*, created by her husband, the choreographer Roland Petit, and later in *The Girl in Pink Tights*, the last stage musical by veteran composer Sigmund Romberg. It was impossible for Hollywood to ignore her and so it was through dance that she made her film debut. In *Hans Christian Andersen*, she was the flirtatious dancer who cruelly, though unintentionally, toyed with Danny Kaye's heart. She then played opposite Bing Crosby in *Anything Goes*, which gave her the opportunity of singing some Cole Porter, something she could do well. Unfortunately, these two engaging films were not sufficient to provide her with the status that she craved. Back in France, she made only a handful of films, including two humble attempts at an American-style musical directed by Henri Decoin and a working-class Parisian comedy by Jean Delannoy, where she reprised Arletty's celebrated cheeky humour. She then almost gave up dancing but pursued a successful career in music hall, remaining true to her love of Broadway and Hollywood musicals. CV
FILMS: *Hans Christian Andersen* (1952); *Anything Goes* (1956).

JEANS, Isabel (1891–1985)

Glamorous vamp of the UK screen and fashionable London stage in the 1920s who periodically continued to play sophisticated or aristocratic types in Hollywood and British films. She was Mrs Newsham in *Suspicion*, her third role with Alfred Hitchcock. MW
FILMS: *Rolling in Money* (1934); *Tovarich* (1937); *Hard to Get, Fools for Scandal, Garden of the Moon, Secrets of an Actress, Youth Takes a Fling* (1938); *Good Girls Go to Paris, Man about Town* (1939); *Suspicion* (1941); *Great Day* (1945); *Gigi* (1958); *A Breath of Scandal* (1960); *The Magic Christian* (1969).

JEANS, Ursula (Ursula McMinn) (1906–1973)

English stage actress (and younger sister of Isabel Jeans★) who appeared in such key British films as *The Life and Death of Colonel Blimp* (1943) and *The Dam Busters* (1954). Jeans was in the all-British cast of *Cavalcade* and a couple of US-funded productions shot in Europe. MW/AP

FILM: *Cavalcade* (1933); *The Green Helmet* (1961); *The Battle of the Villa Fiorita* (1965).

JOKOVIĆ, Mirjana (1967–)

Cold, but beautiful, Serbian actress who made her international acting debut in the leading role of the Yugoslav-Argentinian melodrama *Put na jug/El camino del sur/Southbound* (1988). She has continued to appear in lead roles in popular Yugoslav films on an almost annual basis despite being based in the USA since the early 1990s. Jokovi´c appeared in Tony Gerber's independently produced *Side Streets* and had a supporting role in the Hollywood action-adventure film *A Better Way to Die*. She has also appeared in *Yugodvias* (2001), an atmospheric New York documentary about diasporic female artists. DI

FILMS: *Liability Crisis* (1995); *Side Streets* (1998); *A Better Way to Die* (2000); *Maid in Manhattan, Private Property* (2002).

JONES, Freddie (1927–)

Diminutive character actor whose wild-eyed intensity and elongated, rasping diction have brought regular employment in British horror films and television Dickens adaptations. Jones' melodramatic performance style suited his role as a sadistic Victorian freak-show impresario in David Lynch's *The Elephant Man*. Lynch subsequently became a regular Hollywood patron and used the actor's more eccentric qualities in *Dune, Wild at Heart* and his short-lived 1993 television show *Hotel Room*. JB

FILMS: *Marat/Sade, Far from the Madding Crowd* (1967); *The Bliss of Mrs Blossom* (1968); *Sitting Target* (1972); *Juggernaut* (1974); *Zulu Dawn* (1979); *The Elephant Man* (1980); *Firefox* (1982); *Firestarter, Dune* (1984); *The Black Cauldron* [voice], *Young Sherlock Holmes* (1985); *Spies Inc.* (1988); *Wild at Heart* (1990); *The NeverEnding Story III* (1994); *The Count of Monte Cristo* (2002).

JONES, Vinnie (1965–)

Former English footballer whose acting debut in *Lock, Stock and Two Smoking Barrels* (1998) has led to a number of relatively minor appearances in US films. JS

FILMS: *Gone in Sixty Seconds* (2000); *Mean Machine, Swordfish* (2001); *Night at the Golden Eagle* (2002); *The Big Bounce, Euro Trip* (2004).

JOURDAN, Louis (Louis Gendre) (1919–)

Louis Jourdan is one of the very few French actors to have been more successful in the USA than his native country, though his American career trajectory was undoubtedly hampered by the limitations of the old-fashioned Continental lover persona created for him by the Hollywood studios. 'I'm French, and a Frenchman in American eyes is a certain stereotyped concept,' he argued. 'I've tried to fight it, but unsuccessfully. You just have to accept it and do the best you can.'

Jourdan's parents were hoteliers and he learned English as a child by chatting with tourists. He received an international education, then trained at the René Simon theatrical school. Jourdan made his screen debut alongside Charles Boyer★ in Marc Allégret's uncompleted *Le Corsaire* (1939), but after appearing in several other French romantic comedies and dramas, his developing European film career was temporarily halted when he refused to take part in German-supervised French films shot during World War II.

Jourdan's international break came in 1947 when he was invited to London for an interview with one of David O. Selznick's European talent scouts. He subsequently went to the USA to appear in Alfred Hitchcock's *The Paradine Case*. Selznick cast him as André Latour, the devoted stableman pursued by Mrs Paradine (played by fellow émigré Alida Valli★). The same year, Jourdan also played the romantic but duplicitous concert pianist Stefan in Max Ophuls' critically acclaimed *Letter from an Unknown Woman*. Jourdan's intense and concentrated performance style, dignified but vulnerable bearing, trademark black, polished hair and distinguished foreign accent helped define a screen persona that endured for the next decade, though it was not until his starring role as Gaston in Vincente Minnelli's musical *Gigi*, alongside Leslie Caron★ and Maurice Chevalier★, that he was fully able to repeat this artistic success. The film won nine Academy Awards, including that of Best Picture. Jourdan was reunited with Maurice Chevalier two years later in *Can-Can*.

Jourdan continued to work in European cinema during the 1950s – he had a leading role in Jacques Becker's *Rue de l'estrapade* (1953) – and this pattern became exacerbated as the studio system began to disintegrate and roles became fewer and less challenging in the 1960s and 1970s. By then, Jourdan had moved into character film parts and US television, and by the following decade, he was playing the part of the evil doctor in *Swamp Thing* and its disappointing sequel. His remaining part of note was the villain Kamal Khan in the James Bond film *Octopussy*.

Jourdan's elegance and charm undoubtedly endeared him to a generation of international audiences, but, as Robin Wood has observed, his talents as an émigré actor were generally wasted by Hollywood. In an era of more masculine and rugged leading men, his sophisticated and somewhat 'feminine' persona became a foreign element in its own right. Finding himself out of time with his suave, older European-style manner, expression and voice, there was ultimately nowhere left for Jourdan to journey to within American cinema's limited repertoire of male representation at the time. AP/OR

FILMS: *The Paradine Case* (1947); *No Minor Vices, Letter from an Unknown Woman* (1948); *Madame Bovary* (1949); *Bird of Paradise, Anne of the Indies* (1951); *The Happy Time* (1952); *Three Coins in the Fountain* (1954); *The Swan* (1956); *Julie* (1956); *Gigi* (1958); *The Best of Everything* (1959); *Can-Can* (1960); *Irma La Douce* [voice], *The V.I.P.s* (1963); *Made in Paris* (1966); *A Flea in Her Ear* (1968); *Gamble on Love, Bayou Romance, Swamp Thing* (1982); *Octopussy* (1983); *The Return of Swamp Thing* (1989); *Year of the Comet* (1992).

JÜRGENS, Curt (Curd Gustav Andreas Gottlieb Franz Jürgens) (1915–1982)

Curt Jürgens once remarked that it was his stereotypically austere German persona that motivated his casting in *The Inn of the Sixth Happiness* opposite Ingrid Bergman★, whom the film sought to rehabilitate after her very public adultery and divorce. Yet Jürgens was by this time neither typecast as respectable, nor was he simply an icon of Germanness. Certainly, his Hollywood career began with roles as World War II German officers more committed to military honour than to the Nazi cause (*Bitter Victory, The Enemy Below*). The

manly eroticism of Jürgens' war film persona resurfaced in numerous comedy, melodrama, action/adventure and horror roles, but his image here often invoked a more generalised Europeanism. A son of the mercantilist *haute bourgeoisie*, Jürgens regularly played figures from the European aristocracy and officer class (*Me and the Colonel, Hello-Goodbye*). His cosmopolitanism was underscored by his postwar prominence in international co-productions, as well as the ubiquity in Hollywood and European cinema both of his star image (he played in over a hundred films *in toto*) and of his voice (in his numerous multi-language titles, the polyglot Jürgens dubbed himself). EC

FILMS: *Bitter Victory, The Enemy Below* (1957); *The Inn of the Sixth Happiness, This Happy Feeling, Me and the Colonel* (1958); *The Blue Angel* (1959); *I Aim at the Stars* (1960); *The Longest Day* (1962); *Miracle of the White Stallions, Of Love and Desire* (1963); *Lord Jim* (1964); *The Karate Killers* (1967); *The Invincible Six* (1968); *Battle of Britain, The Assassination Bureau* (1969); *Hello-Goodbye, The Mephisto Waltz* (1970); *Nicholas and Alexandra* (1971); *Vault of Horror* (1973); *The Spy Who Loved Me* (1977); *Goldengirl* (1979).

JUSTIN, John (1917–2002)

Handsome British stage actor whose long career as a leading man led to occasional forays into British cinema such as his debut film, Alexander Korda's *The Thief of Bagdad* (1940). Justin's two principal Hollywood films – *King of the Khyber Rifles* and *Untamed* – both co-starred Tyrone Power. MHu

FILMS: *King of the Khyber Rifles* (1953); *Seagulls over Sorrento* (1954); *Untamed* (1955); *Safari* (1956); *Island in the Sun* (1957).

KAPRISKY, Valérie (Valérie Chérès) (1962–)

French sex symbol who made her American film debut opposite Richard Gere in *Breathless*, an intelligent remake of Jean-Luc Godard's *À Bout de Souffle/Breathless* (1960), set in Los Angeles. The film explicitly played with Kaprisky's soft-core erotic persona, best exemplified in the 1984 French hit *La Femme publique*. However, although it successfully showcased her sexual aura, the film failed to convince the American film industry of Kaprisky's acting skills. She resurfaced only in Josh Evans' *Glam* – a dark and, at times, brutal satire of Hollywood. TH

FILMS: *Breathless* (1983); *Glam* (1997).

KARLOFF, Boris (William Henry Pratt) (1887–1969)
Karloff's role as the Creature in *Frankenstein* in 1931 identified him permanently with the horror film; off screen, he
remained a Hitchcock-like icon of sedate Hollywood Englishness in dress, deportment and interests, which for him
centred on cricket. Breaking with the expectations created
by his public-school education and by a family tradition of
imperial service, he had left England in 1909 to work in
Canada and the USA as a labourer, and then in repertory
theatre and silent films. His gaunt appearance brought him
a profusion of exotic supporting roles as Orientals, Native
Americans and criminals, culminating in fourth billing for
a repeat of his stage role in *The Criminal Code* (Howard
Hawks). It is easy to see why this performance alerted Universal, and director James Whale, to his potential for
Frankenstein: his long-sentence prisoner exhibits a frightening combination of menacing stillness and sudden violence,
fuelled by an awareness of legitimate grievance that creates
strong sympathy for him, as it will for the Creature. The
celebrated make-up job for *Frankenstein* simply emphasises
the strong contours of his own face, with its deep-set eyes,
and the face and body-language carried him through a rich
variety of sinister roles in the following decades: sometimes
as 'monsters', as in the *Frankenstein* sequels, but more often
as 'mad scientists' closer to the Baron himself. Meanwhile –
again like Hitchcock – he exploited his fame in other
media, editing collections of horror stories and presenting
his own television series. In cinema, he survived some
indignities, such as involvement with Abbott and Costello
and with beach bikini films, to renew his career decisively
at certain points: with producer Val Lewton (*The Body
Snatcher* and its two successors), with producer/director
Roger Corman (*The Raven* and its two successors), and
with occasional work in Continental Europe and in
Britain, notably Michael Reeves' *The Sorcerers* in 1967. Like
that film, *Targets*, made by another bright young director in
Peter Bogdanovich, uses Karloff in a way that reflects upon
and exploits his iconic status within the horror genre, and
constitutes a peculiarly satisfying climax to an extraordinary
fifty-year career. Karloff had retained his British citizenship,
and he died in England, by now his main home. CB
FILMS: *His Majesty the American* (1919); *The Prince and
Betty, The Deadlier Sex, The Courage of Marge O'Doone, The
Last of the Mohicans* (1920); *The Hope Diamond Mystery*

Boris Karloff arrives in America

[serial], *Without Benefit of Clergy, The Cave Girl, Cheated
Hearts* (1921); *The Man from Downing Street, The Infidel,
Omar the Tentmaker, The Altar Stairs, The Woman Conquers*
(1922); *The Prisoner, The Gentleman from America* (1923);
Dynamite Dan, Parisian Nights, The Hellion (1924); *Forbidden
Cargo, The Prairie Wife, Lady Robinhood, Never the Twain Shall
Meet* (1925); *The Greater Glory, Flames, The Bells, The Nick-
elhopper, Valencia, The Golden Web, Her Honor the Governor,
The Eagle of the Sea, Old Ironsides, Flaming Fury* (1926);
*Tarzan and the Golden Lion, Let it Rain, The Meddlin'
Stranger, The Phantom Buster, Soft Cushions, Two Arabian
Nights, The Love Mart, The Princess from Hoboken* (1927); *Vul-
tures of the Sea* [serial] (1928); *The Fatal Warning* [serial],
*Burning the Wind, Little Wild Girl, Phantom of the North, The
Devil's Chaplain, Two Sisters, Behind that Curtain, The King of
the Kongo* [serial], *The Unholy Night* (1929); *The Bad One,
The Sea Bat, The Utah Kid, Mothers Cry* (1930); *The Crimi-
nal Code, King of the Wild* [serial], *Cracked Nuts, Young Dono-
van's Kid, Smart Money, The Public Defender, Graft, Five Star* **317**

Final, I Like Your Nerve, The Yellow Ticket, The Mad Genius, Frankenstein, The Guilty Generation, Tonight or Never (1931); *Business and Pleasure, Alias the Doctor, The Miracle Man, Behind the Mask, Night World, The Cohens and Kellys in Hollywood, Scarface, The Old Dark House, The Mask of Fu Manchu, The Mummy* (1932); *The Lost Patrol, The House of Rothschild, The Black Cat* (1934); *Bride of Frankenstein, The Raven, The Black Room* (1935); *The Invisible Ray, The Walking Dead, Charlie Chan at the Opera* (1936); *Night Key, West of Shanghai* (1937); *The Invisible Menace, Mr Wong Detective, Devil's Island, Son of Frankenstein, The Mystery of Mr Wong, Mr Wong in Chinatown, The Man They Could Not Hang* (1938); *Tower of London* (1939); *The Fatal Hour, British Intelligence, The Devil Commands, Black Friday, The Man with Nine Lives, Doomed to Die, Before I Hang, The Ape, You'll Find Out* (1940); *The Boogie Man Will Get You* (1942); *The Climax, House of Frankenstein* (1944); *The Body Snatcher, Isle of the Dead* (1945); *Bedlam* (1946); *The Secret Life of Walter Mitty, Unconquered, Lured, Dick Tracy Meets Gruesome* (1947); *Tap Roots* (1948); *Abbott and Costello Meet the Killer* (1949); *The Emperor's Nightingale, The Strange Door* (1951); *The Black Castle* (1952); *Abbott and Costello Meet Dr Jekyll and Mr Hyde* (1953); *The Hindu* (1955); *Voodoo Island, The Juggler of Our Lady* (1957); *Frankenstein 1970* (1958); *The Raven, The Terror, The Comedy of Terrors* (1963); *Bikini Beach* (1964); *Die Monster Die* (1965); *The Ghost in the Invisible Bikini, The Daydreamer, Mad Monster Party* (1966); *The Venetian Affair* (1967); *Targets* (1968).

KATCH, Kurt (Isser Kač) (1896–1958)

German character actor of Russian-Jewish extraction who fled to Poland in 1933, then to the USA, where he became an American citizen. His guttural accent, bald head and leering expression led to casting as Nazi and Arab villains for the rest of his career. RJK

FILMS: *Man at Large, The Wolf Man* (1941); *The Wife Takes a Flyer, Secret Agent of Japan, Counter-Espionage, Berlin Correspondent, Quiet Please – Murder, Don Winslow of the Navy* [serial], *Desperate Journey* (1942); *Edge of Darkness, Secret Service in Darkest Africa* [serial], *Watch on the Rhine, The Strange Death of Adolf Hitler, They Came to Blow up America, The Purple V, Mission to Moscow, Background to Danger* (1943); *Ali Baba and the Forty Thieves, The Mask of Dimitrios, The Seventh Cross, The Conspirators, The Mummy's Curse, The Purple Heart, Make Your Own Bed* (1944); *Salome, Where She Danced*

(1945); *Rendezvous 24, Angel on My Shoulder, Strange Journey* (1946); *Song of Love* (1947); *The Secret of the Incas, The Adventures of Hajji Baba* (1954); *Abbott and Costello Meet the Mummy* (1955); *Never Say Goodbye, Pharaoh's Curse, Hot Cars* (1956); *The Girl in the Kremlin* (1957); *The Gift of Love, The Beast of Budapest, The Young Lions, When Hell Broke Loose* (1958).

KAUFMANN, Christine (1945–)

A child actress in 1950s German films who emigrated to Hollywood in 1962 to join Tony Curtis, whom she then married. Kaufmann briefly developed into a leading lady and enjoyed the Hollywood highlife of the 1960s. She returned to Germany in 1967 to pursue a stage and screen career, later becoming known as Germany's most beautiful grandmother. FG

FILMS: *Town without Pity* (1961); *Taras Bulba, Escape from East Berlin* (1962); *Wild and Wonderful* (1964); *Murders in the Rue Morgue* (1971); *Willow Springs* (1973).

KELLER, Marthe (1945–)

Swiss-born Keller worked for German television before emerging as a successful screen actress in France in the late 1960s. After a brief appearance in Russ Meyer's *The Seven Minutes*, her Hollywood career started properly with a supporting role in *Marathon Man*. Despite work with Al Pacino (in *Bobby Deerfield*) and Billy Wilder (*Fedora*), her box-office appeal remained limited, and after being increasingly typecast as a chilly, exotic beauty, Keller returned to European film and television work in the early 1980s. VH

FILMS: *The Seven Minutes* (1971); *Marathon Man* (1976); *Black Sunday, Bobby Deerfield* (1977); *Fedora* (1978); *The Formula* (1980); *The Amateur* (1981).

KENDALL, Kay (Justine Kay Kendall McCarthy) (1926–1959)

From the earliest days of her film career, this tall, scatty British comedienne was compared to American screwball comedy specialists like Carole Lombard and Rosalind Russell. Stranded in an industry that typically came up with few parts that lent themselves to Kendall's vivacious and worldly screen persona, the actress first tried to get work in Hollywood on a speculative visit to California in the late 1940s. After her domestic breakthrough in the rare British screwball film *Genevieve* (1953), Kendall's seven-year contract with the Rank Organisation gave her few other appropriate showcase roles and she went on a well-publicised 'strike' in 1954. MGM, whose British subsidiary had loaned Kendall away from Rank to cast her in their historical swashbuckler *The Adventures of Quentin Durward*, tried and failed to buy out her contract in 1955. But when Kendall absconded from the UK to follow her lover and future husband Rex Harrison★ to New York, her employers were forced to agree to loan-out deals with MGM and Columbia, if only to make their investment pay. Kendall was hand picked to appear in musicals and high-society comedies by directors of the calibre of George Cukor, Stanley Donen and Vincente Minnelli. Having finally made it in the USA, her early death at the age of thirty-three was exceptionally cruel – though it has to be said that as an actress who specialised in a form of comedy rooted in the 1930s and 1940s, it is difficult to imagine how her career would have progressed in the 1960s. It is a measure of her instant acceptance by the US entertainment industry that although she never starred on Broadway and made only one film in Hollywood (her other American pictures being filmed in Paris), special memorial services were held in New York and Los Angeles and several big studios shut down filming for the day as a mark of respect. JB

FILMS: *Night and the City* (1950); *The Adventures of Quentin Durward* (1955); *Les Girls* (1957); *The Reluctant Debutante* (1958); *Once More with Feeling!* (1960).

KENDALL, Suzy (Frieda Harrison) (1944–)
After a promising British debut, Kendall appeared in several US-financed productions and is now more associated with her roles in cult European horror films. TJ

FILMS: *The Liquidator, Thunderball* (1965); *To Sir, with Love* (1967); *Up the Junction, 30 is a Dangerous Age, Cynthia* (1968); *Fraulein Doktor, The Gamblers* (1969); *Darker than Amber* (1970).

KENT, Arnold (Lido Manetti) (1899–1928)
Despite having a highly successful career in his homeland, Manetti left Italy for the USA in 1925 because of a slump in Italian film production. He changed his name to Arnold Kent and proceeded to make a brief name for himself as a handsome young Italian actor in Paramount's silent films. He starred in Stiller's *The Woman on Trial* with Pola Negri★ in 1927. Manetti died in a road accident in Hollywood just before a scheduled film with Mary Pickford. CS

FILMS: *Evening Clothes, The Woman on Trial, Hula, The World at Her Feet* (1927); *Beau Sabreur, The Woman Disputed, Easy Come, Easy Go, The Showdown* (1928).

KERR, Deborah (Deborah Jane Kerr-Trimmer) (1921–)
Deborah Kerr was a fine-featured, petite redhead British actress with a distinctive pale complexion. Her performance style was graceful, and marked by an assured physical stature that was 'ladylike' yet, at the same time, easily adaptable to playing assertive, distinctive characters. Her compelling eyes were capable of conveying deep emotional resonance and vulnerability. By 1947, Kerr was already an established star in Britain with leading roles in two US-backed films, among others. After winning the New York Critics' Award for *I See a Dark Stranger* (1946) and *Black Narcissus* (1947), she attracted offers from Hollywood studios, including Paramount and MGM. MGM bought her contract from Gabriel Pascal, her producer in Britain, for $200,000. Kerr's subsequent seven-year contract with the studio guaranteed her $3,000 a week (to advance on a gradual basis to $7,000 a week during the last two years), as well as star or co-star status.

Kerr sailed to New York on the *Queen Elizabeth* in November 1946 and on first arrival did a screen test for *The Hucksters*, a film set in the world of commercial broadcasting. Her reserved, dignified image in British films was maintained in her first Hollywood roles, particularly in this film. In Los Angeles, she was befriended by Douglas and Mary Lee Fairbanks and was welcomed by the British community, particularly David Niven★. Kerr was groomed to be a major star and she received the first of six Academy Award Best Actress nominations for *Edward, My Son*, an MGM film made in Britain and directed by George Cukor. Her performance as a married woman who descends into disillusionment and alcoholism clearly demonstrated her versatility (although she did not win the Award).

Kerr was disturbed by changes at MGM when Dore Schary replaced Louis B. Mayer as head of production. Schary was not concerned to develop her image beyond that of a genteel Englishwoman. Consequently, she then starred in several spectacular epics that presented her as a 'period lady': *The Prisoner of Zenda, King Solomon's Mines,* **319** filmed on location in Africa, and *Quo Vadis*, filmed at Cinecittà in Rome. She was also frequently cast alongside other British actors, including Stewart Granger★, Peter Ustinov★ and James Mason★. Kerr was anxious for a change of style and she persuaded Schary to allow her to star as a modern American career woman in the comedy *Dream Wife*, as well as appear in a classical role as Portia in *Julius Caesar*. Towards the end of her seven-year contract with MGM, Kerr asked for an amendment so that she could appear in films for other studios. A major artistic break came when MGM loaned her to Columbia to play Karen, a (supposedly) sexually rapacious American woman in *From Here to Eternity*, a part she was keen to win to break her image as the well-bred Englishwoman. The role was originally destined for Joan Crawford, but when conflict developed between her and Harry Cohn, the part of Karen was offered to Kerr on the suggestion of her new agent, Bert Allenberg. Despite critical acclaim and box-office success, an Academy Award eluded her yet again.

Kerr returned to stage acting in 1953 when she appeared in a New York production of *Tea and Sympathy*, directed by Elia Kazan, and went on tour when it proved a huge hit, winning numerous stage awards. A film version was produced in 1956 by MGM, but it was subject to the strictures of censorship because of the play's homosexual subtext. She did not renew her contract with the studio and starred in *The End of the Affair* for Columbia, filmed on location in Britain. Her next major screen success was with a role that reverted to her dominant persona of the ladylike Englishwoman: the governess in Twentieth Century-Fox's musical *The King and I*.

Kerr's subsequent roles were more varied, as she worked for several studios in various genres. These included a highly regarded performance as a nun stranded on an island with a sailor (Robert Mitchum) in *Heaven Knows, Mr Allison*. Then *The Sundowners*, filmed in Australia, revealed the full range of her acting abilities and earned her another Academy Award nomination. *The Innocents*, an adaptation of Henry James' *Turn of the Screw*, received high critical acclaim, although it did not do well at the box office. Despite never winning an award, the Academy honoured her in 1994 as 'an artist of impeccable grace and beauty, a dedicated actress whose motion picture career has always stood for perfection, discipline and elegance'. In 1969, Kerr announced her retirement from film acting, although she did some television

work in subsequent years and starred in the British 'Film on Four', *The Assam Garden* (1985). In 1958, Kerr was divorced from Anthony Bartley and in 1960 married writer Peter Viertel, with whom she lived in Switzerland when she no longer appeared regularly on the screen.

While her career in Hollywood was long and distinguished, Kerr was never comfortable with the press's unrelenting curiosity about the private lives of the stars. Once she had proved her box-office and critical success, she refused to be moulded into the image preferred by MGM. Her determination to demonstrate her versatility as an actress, as well as to pursue a stage career, allowed her a degree of freedom from studio strictures that was rare for British performers in Hollywood. On the other hand, despite her Scottish background and desire to avoid being typecast, the dominant image of her that persists is still as a refined and graceful Englishwoman. SS

FILMS: *Hatter's Castle* (1942); *Perfect Strangers* (1945); *The Hucksters, If Winter Comes* (1947); *Edward, My Son, Please Believe Me* (1949); *King Solomon's Mines* (1950); *Quo Vadis* (1951); *Thunder in the East, The Prisoner of Zenda* (1952); *Young Bess, Dream Wife, Julius Caesar, From Here to Eternity* (1953); *The End of the Affair* (1955); *The Proud and Profane, The King and I, Tea and Sympathy* (1956); *Heaven Knows, Mr Allison, An Affair to Remember* (1957); *Separate Tables, Bonjour Tristesse, The Journey* (1958); *Count Your Blessings, Beloved Infidel* (1959); *The Sundowners, The Grass is Greener* (1960); *The Naked Edge, The Innocents* (1961); *The Chalk Garden, The Night of the Iguana* (1964); *Marriage on the Rocks* (1965); *Casino Royale, Eye of the Devil* (1967); *Prudence and the Pill* (1968); *The Gypsy Moths, The Arrangement* (1969).

KERRIGAN, J. M. (1884–1964)

Kerrigan, one of the many Irish Abbey Theatre actors who moved to the USA, was typecast as the crafty Irishman in many Hollywood films such as *The Informer, The Luck of the Irish* and *Three Cheers for the Irish*. RB

FILMS: *Little Old New York* (1923); *Lucky in Love* (1929); *Song o' My Heart, Lightnin'* (1930); *Under Suspicion, Don't Bet on Women, The Black Camel, Merely Mary Ann* (1931); *The Rainbow Trail, Careless Lady, State's Attorney, Rockabye* (1932); *Air Hostess, A Study in Scarlet, The Monkey's Paw, Paddy the Next Best Thing* (1933); *Lone Cowboy, The Lost Patrol, A Modern Hero, The Key, Treasure Island, The Fountain, Happiness Ahead* (1934); *The Mystery of Edwin Drood, Vanessa: Her*

Love Story, The Informer, WereWolf of London, The Farmer Takes a Wife, Hot Tip, Barbary Coast, A Feather in Her Hat (1935); *The Prisoner of Shark Island, Laughing Irish Eyes, Colleen, Special Investigator, Hearts in Bondage, The General Died at Dawn, Lloyd's of London, The Plough and the Stars, Timothy's Quest, Spendthrift, Let's Make a Million* (1936); *Motor Madness, Shall We Dance, The Barrier, London by Night* (1937); *Vacation from Love, Spring Madness, Little Orphan Annie, Ride a Crooked Mile* (1938); *Boy Slaves, The Great Man Votes, Union Pacific, The Zero Hour, 6,000 Enemies, The Witness Vanishes, Sabotage, Gone with the Wind, Undercover Agent, Two Thoroughbreds, Two Bright Boys, Sorority House, The Kid from Texas, The Flying Irishman* (1939); *Congo Maisie, Young Tom Edison, Three Cheers for the Irish, The Sea Hawk, One Crowded Night, No Time for Comedy, The Long Voyage Home, Untamed, Curtain Call* (1940); *The Wolf Man, Appointment for Love, Adventure in Washington* (1941); *The Vanishing Virginian, Captains of the Clouds* (1942); *Action in the North Atlantic, Mr Lucky* (1943); *The Fighting Seabees, An American Romance, The Big Bonanza* (1944); *Wilson, Tarzan and the Amazons, The Spanish Main, She Went to the Races, The Great John L, Crime Doctor's Warning* (1945); *Black Beauty, Abie's Irish Rose* (1946); *Call Northside 777, The Luck of the Irish* (1948); *The Fighting O'Flynn, Mrs Mike* (1949); *Two of a Kind, Sealed Cargo* (1951); *Park Row, Wild North, My Cousin Rachel* (1952); *The Silver Whip* (1953); *20,000 Leagues under the Sea* (1954); *It's a Dog's Life* (1955); *The Fastest Gun Alive* (1956).

KIEPURA, Jan (1902–1966)

At the peak of his opera career, Kiepura, a famous Polish tenor, decided to turn to the cinema. He appeared successfully in musicals produced mostly in Germany and Austria. He also sang in one American film. During World War II, he spent several years in the USA, where he gave many concerts for the benefit of the Allied forces. EO

FILM: *Give Us this Night* (1936).

KIER, Udo (Udo Kierspe) (1944–)

With his distinctly non-naturalistic acting style and striking physical appearance that combines handsomeness with a slightly creepy edge, Kier blends the sexual decadence of the 1970s with the expressionist legacy of Conrad Veidt★ and later Klaus Kinski★. He began appearing in European B-movies in the late 1960s and was an occasional member

of Rainer Werner Fassbinder's entourage in the 1970s. He was also associated with Andy Warhol. Primarily known for his over-the-top, scene-stealing character parts, Kier has frequently portrayed vampires and other roles that demand demonic villainy, sleaziness or haughty European intensity. He became more bankable in Hollywood following his roles in two Gus van Sant films in the early 1990s and through his camp appearances in music videos by Madonna and Supertramp. Based in Los Angeles since 1991, Kier continues a transatlantic career. A regular collaborator of Lars von Trier, he remains a prolific performer in films by other European auteurs, including Wim Wenders, Werner Herzog and Monika Treut. His US productions, meanwhile, range from quirky independents (*There's No Fish Food in Heaven*) to big-budget blockbusters (*Armageddon* and *Blade*) via cult oddities such as *Barb Wire*. TB

FILMS: *The Salzburg Connection* (1972); *Flesh for Frankenstein, Andy Warhol's Dracula* (1974); *Moscow on the Hudson* (1984); *My Own Private Idaho* (1991); *Even Cowgirls Get the Blues, For Love or Money, Josh and S.A.M.* (1993), *Ace Ventura: Pet Detective* (1994); *Johnny Mnemonic* (1995); *Barb Wire* (1996); *Betty* (1997); *Armageddon, Blade, Modern Vampires, There's No Fish Food in Heaven, The Last Call, Simon Says* (1998); *The Debtors, The New Adventures of Pinocchio, End of Days* (1999); *Red Letters, Just One Night, Critical Mass* (2000); *The Last Minute, Invincible, Megiddo – The Omega Code 2, Double Deception* (2001); *Love Object* (2003).

KING, Dennis (Dennis Pratt) (1897–1971)

Versatile English matinée idol who appeared in a couple of early Hollywood musicals. He played parts in other comedies and melodramas including Casimir in Irving Rapper's *The Miracle*. King became a US citizen in 1953. JS

FILMS: *The Vagabond King, Paramount on Parade* (1930); *The Devil's Brother* (1933); *Between Two Worlds* (1944); *The Miracle* (1959); *Some Kind of a Nut* (1969).

KINGSLEY, Ben (Krishna Banji) (1943–)

Kingsley's part-Indian parentage helped him to land the eponymous title role in the British film *Gandhi* (1982) and his magisterial performance won him a Best Actor Academy Award. Despite additional intervening success on Broadway, it took nearly ten years before Kingsley first appeared in a Hollywood film. Since 1991, he has appeared in a modest number of American productions, none of 321 which have explicitly traded on the *Gandhi* association or his ethnic background. Kingsley has not overly discriminated between parts in run-of-the-mill Hollywood genre films and prestige productions and, like most British theatrical knights, he tends to play educated, eloquent characters. His proven ability to explore the flipside of this slick veneer – demonstrated in his extraordinary portrayal of a violent, inarticulate cockney gangster in the British film *Sexy Beast* (2000) – has remained underexploited by American casting directors, with the exception of his supporting role as Meyer Lansky in Warren Beatty's *Bugsy*. JB

FILMS: *Betrayal* (1983); *Bugsy* (1991); *Sneakers* (1992); *Dave, Searching for Bobby Fischer, Schindler's List* (1993); *Species* (1995); *What Planet are You From?, Rules of Engagement* (2000); *AI: Artificial Intelligence* [voice] (2001); *Tuck Everlasting* (2002); *House of Sand and Fog* (2003); *Thunderbirds, Suspect Zero* (2004).

KINGSTON, Alex (1963–)

Alex Kingston is best known as the beautiful and determined upper-middle-class English surgeon Elizabeth Corday in American television's long-running *E.R.*, but she has interspersed this with various parts in European and Hollywood films that usually profile similar elements of her forceful and charismatic screen persona. AP

FILM: *This Space Between Us* (2000).

KINSKEY, Leonid (1903–1998)

Lanky, hatchet-faced Russian actor best known for kissing Humphrey Bogart in *Casablanca*, shouting 'Phooey! Phooey! and PHOOEY!!' in Ernst Lubitsch's *Trouble in Paradise* and singing 'I'm an Old Cowhand' with a thick Russian accent in *Rhythm on the Range*. Kinskey was born of Austrian parents and started his theatrical career as a mime actor in the Imperial Russian Theatre. He left Russia with his mother in 1921, first for Poland and then for Germany, where he performed in the experimental Firebird Theatre troupe. He toured South America with Firebird and then switched to the commercial stage when he came to New York with Al Jolson's musical comedy *Wonder Bar* in 1931. Stranded in a Chicago restaurant theatre, he was lured to Hollywood by his friend Akim Tamiroff* and immediately landed a series of jobs at Paramount.

For the next thirty years, Kinskey played small character parts in many of Hollywood's best-known films. He was

invariably the comic foreigner. His shaggy, unruly hair, watery eyes, thick lips and demonic grin made him the perfect Hollywood Bolshevik. Kinskey began with Russian radicals and anarchists in *Trouble in Paradise* and *Duck Soup* but as he polished an assortment of foreign accents, he also played generic and multi-ethnic nationals in such films as *Algiers, The Great Waltz, Casablanca* and *The Talk of the Town*. Always freelance, he never received a studio contract, but he most frequently appeared in Paramount and Twentieth Century-Fox features.

From the 1950s, Kinskey also appeared on assorted television shows, usually playing eccentric Russian professors. This was the part he played opposite Jackie Cooper in *The People's Choice* between 1955 and 1956. RM

FILMS: *The Big Broadcast, Trouble in Paradise* (1932); *Duck Soup, The Storm at Daybreak* (1933); *Manhattan Melodrama, Marie Galante, Fugitive Road* (1934); *I Live My Life, Goin' to Town, Les Misérables, The Gilded Lily* (1935); *The Next Time We Love, A Son Comes Home, Rhythm on the Range, The Road to Glory* (1936); *Make a Wish, The Sheik Steps Out, Married before Breakfast, Maytime, Meet the Boyfriend, My Dear Miss Aldrich, Cafe Metropole* (1937); *The Great Waltz, Outside of Paradise, Three Blind Mice, A Trip to Paris, Flirting with Fate* (1938); *Everything Happens at Night, The Story of Vernon and Irene Castle, The Spellbinder, Day-Time Wife* (1939); *Down Argentine Way* (1940); *So Ends Our Night* (1941); *Broadway Limited, I Married an Angel, Lady for a Night, Brooklyn Orchid, Somewhere I'll Find You, The Talk of the Town, Ball of Fire, Casablanca* (1942); *Let's Have Fun, Cinderella Swings It, Gildersleeve on Broadway, Presenting Lily Mars* (1943); *The Fighting Seabees, That's My Baby, Can't Help Singing* (1944); *Monsieur Beaucaire* (1946); *The Great Sinner, Alimony* (1949); *Nancy Goes to Rio* (1950); *Honeychile* (1951); *That Night in Rio* (1952); *The Man with the Golden Arm* (1955); *Glory* (1956); *The Legend of Mandinga* [voice only] (1961).

KINSKI, Klaus (Claus Günther Nikolaus Nakszynski) (1926–1991)

Kinski's brief appearance in MGM's *Doctor Zhivago* as a ranting prisoner is emblematic of his international roles, where he frequently transformed minor parts through the intense physicality of his screen presence. For much of his career, Kinski was a wandering character player. He led an excessive and anarchic life that he combined with a shamelessly mercenary approach to his profession. During the

1950s, he appeared in many German B-thrillers; in the 1960s, in Italian Westerns – most notably as a twitching hunchback in *Per qualche dollari in più/For a Few Dollars More* (1965) – and from the mid-1970s, he acted mainly in French productions.

Although he had small roles in Hollywood movies in the 1950s and 1960s, including that of a Gestapo officer in Douglas Sirk's *A Time to Love and a Time to Die*, Kinski's lasting reputation derives from his mesmerising performances as the deranged protagonists in Werner Herzog's films. These brought him international critical acclaim and led to a return to Hollywood and more substantial roles. He appeared as the ruthless tycoon in James Toback's *Love and Money* and, against type, the unworldly Dr Daniel in *Android*. He also starred alongside Jack Lemmon and Walter Matthau as a criminal, sex-obsessed medical officer in Billy Wilder's *Buddy Buddy*. Off screen, during this time, Kinski remained obsessively egocentric, deluded and passionate. He could also be cold and rational. On screen, his villainous persona regularly involved the successful ability to parody existing German archetypes. His daughter is the fellow émigré actor Nastassja Kinski★. US

FILMS: *A Time to Love and a Time to Die* (1958); *The Counterfeit Traitor* (1962); *Doctor Zhivago* (1965); *Our Man in Marrakesh* (1966); *The Million Eyes of Sumuru* (1967); *Schizoid* (1980); *Buddy, Buddy*, *The Soldier* (1981); *Love and Money*, *Android* (1982); *The Secret Diary of Sigmund Freud*, *The Little Drummer Girl*, *Creature* (1984); *Crawlspace* (1986).

KINSKI, Nastassja (Nastassja Nakszynski) (1959–)
The estranged daughter of Klaus Kinski★ who first gained attention in West Germany playing Mignon, the sexually precocious Lolita figure in Wim Wenders' *Falsche Bewegung/One False Move* (1974). A number of similar roles followed, culminating in Roman Polanski's Franco-British production *Tess* (1979), which propelled the actress and her personal life into the international spotlight. Kinski had been romantically involved with Polanski – twenty-six years her senior – since 1976 and moved with him to New York in 1978, where she studied acting under Lee Strasberg and Stella Adler. Her performance as Tess revealed the ability of the multilingual actress to effectively mask her German accent, a talent that subsequently allowed her to play American-born characters in Hollywood alongside an array of cosmopolitan foreigners. *Tess* earned Kinski a

Golden Globe and led to her meeting Francis Ford Coppola at the 1979 Cannes film festival. She made her Hollywood debut, *One from the Heart*, with him. Leads in several A-movies followed, all of which showcased Kinski's vulnerable, sensual gamine features and seemingly instinctive depictions of sexuality. *Cat People*, her archetypal film from this period, in which she played the incestuous, innocent yet deadly Irena Gallier, failed at the box office but a contemporaneous poster by Richard Avedon, showing the naked actress entwined with a snake, remained a best-seller for years. Kinski disappeared from American productions in the mid-1980s after Hugh Hudson's ill-fated historical epic *Revolution*. She spent the next decade working in often relatively minor European and international co-productions. Following the end of her marriage to film producer Ibrahim Moussa, Kinski became a permanent US resident in 1992 and returned to Hollywood movies in 1994 in the hi-tech action film *Terminal Velocity*. Kinski has since been employed primarily in low-end A- and high-end B-productions in which she deploys sexy chic and a trained physique as part of a strong, new millennium female identity. RJK

FILMS: *One from the Heart*, *Cat People* (1982); *Exposed* (1983); *The Hotel New Hampshire*, *Unfaithfully Yours*, *Maria's Lovers* (1984); *Revolution* (1985); *Terminal Velocity*, *Crackerjack* (1994); *Somebody is Waiting* (1996); *Fathers' Day*, *One Night Stand*, *Little Boy Blue* (1997); *Savior*, *Your Friends & Neighbors*, *Susan's Plan*, *Playing by Heart*, *Off the Menu: The Last Days of Chasen's* (1998); *The Lost Son* (1999); *The Magic of Marciano*, *Red Letters*, *Time Share* (2000); *Cold Heart*, *Town & Country*, *An American Rhapsody*, *Diary of a Sex Addict*, *Beyond the City Limits*, *.com for Murder* (2001).

KNEF, Hildegard Frieda Albertine (1925–2002)
Knef became famous in the immediate aftermath of World War II with her roles in contemporary German social-realist 'rubble films' (*Trümmer Filme*) such as *Die Mörder sind unter uns/The Murderers are Among Us* (1946) and *Film ohne Titel/Film without a Title* (1947). With her tall, blonde and expressive fresh-faced features, she embodied the resilient survivor and became the most promising new German actress of the era. She was offered a contract with David O. Selznick in 1948, but despite being newly married to an American film representative she had met in Berlin, Knef's German identity and looks did not adapt well to Holly- **323**

wood. She returned to Germany in 1950 to star in *Die Süderin / The Sinner* (1951), whose brief nude scene caused a national scandal. During the shoot, Fox signed her for a major role in Anatole Litvak's war drama *Decision before Dawn*, which was filmed in West Germany. She briefly returned to the USA in 1952 and was groomed as a glamorous star, alongside Tyrone Power, in Hathaway's *Diplomatic Courier*. Her name was anglicised to Neff when she starred with Gregory Peck, Susan Hayward and Ava Gardner in *The Snows of Kilimanjaro*. After *Night without Sleep*, she left Hollywood and switched to an international art-film career that she combined with a role as an international cabaret chanteuse. Thanks to her adventurous life and diverse talents, she achieved a similar controversial iconic status to Marlene Dietrich★ in her home country. US

FILMS: *Decision before Dawn* (1951); *Diplomatic Courier, The Snows of Kilimanjaro, Night without Sleep* (1952).

KNOWLES, Patric (Reginald Lawrence Knowles)
(1911–1995)

British character actor who made his mark in Hollywood playing Errol Flynn's brother and romantic rival in *The Charge of the Light Brigade*. Knowles continued as a leading and then supporting player into the 1970s. MW

FILMS: *Irish Hearts* (1934); *Honours Easy* (1935); *Give Me Your Heart, The Charge of the Light Brigade, Wedding Group, Fair Exchange, Crown vs. Stevens, The Brown Wallet* (1936); *The Littlest Diplomat, Expensive Husbands, It's Love I'm After* (1937); *Storm over Bengal, The Patient in Room 18, The Sisters, The Adventures of Robin Hood, Heart of the North, Four's a Crowd* (1938); *Torchy Blane in Chinatown, Another Thin Man, Beauty for the Asking, The Spellbinder Five Came Back, The Honeymoon's Over* (1939); *Anne of Windy Poplars, Married and in Love, A Bill of Divorcement, Women in War* (1940); *How Green Was My Valley, The Wolf Man* (1941); *Who Done It?, Sin Town, The Strange Case of Doctor Rx, Lady in a Jam, Mystery of Marie Roget* (1942); *Forever and a Day, Crazy House, Always a Bridesmaid, Frankenstein Meets the Wolf Man, Hit the Ice, All by Myself* (1943); *This is the Life, Pardon My Rhythm, Chip Off the Old Block* (1944); *Masquerade in Mexico, Kitty* (1945); *Of Human Bondage, Monsieur Beaucaire, O.S.S., The Bride Wore Boots* (1946); *Ivy, Variety Girl* (1947); *Dream Girl, Isn't it Romantic?* (1948); *The Big Steal* (1949); *Three Came Home* (1950); *Quebec* (1951); *Tarzan's Savage Fury, Mutiny* (1952); *Flame of Calcutta, Jamaica Run* (1953);

Khyber Patrol, World for Ransom (1954); *No Man's Woman* (1955); *Band of Angels* (1957); *From the Earth to the Moon, Auntie Mame* (1958); *Elfego Baca: Six Gun Law* (1962); *The Wolfman, The Way West* (1967); *The Devil's Brigade, In Enemy Country* (1968); *Chisum* (1970); *The Man* (1972); *Arnold, Terror in the Wax Museum* (1973).

KOLKER, Henry (Joseph Henry Kolker)
(1870–1947)

Versatile German actor with heavy-set features who played a huge number of roles in a wide variety of Hollywood genre films from the teens onwards. He was, for example, the repressive and authoritarian patriarch in George Cukor's vivacious comedy *Holiday*. FG

FILMS: *The Bigger Man, How Molly Malone Made Good, The Warning* (1915); *Gloria's Romance* (1916); *The Shell Game, Social Hypocrites, The House of Mirth* (1918); *The Parisian Tigress, Blackie's Redemption, The Red Lantern, Tangled Threads, Her Purchase Price, The Brat, The Great Victory, Wilson or the Kaiser? The Fall of the Hohenzollerns* (1919); *A Man of Stone* (1921); *Any Woman, Sally, Irene and Mary* (1925); *The Palace of Pleasure, Hell's 400, Winning the Futurity, Wet Paint* (1926); *A Kiss in a Taxi, Annie Laurie, Rough House Rosie, West Point* (1927); *Soft Living, Midnight Rose, Don't Marry* (1928); *Coquette, The Valiant, Pleasure Crazed, Love, Live and Laugh* (1929); *The Bad One, Good Intentions, Abraham Lincoln, The Way of All Men, Du Barry, Woman of Passion, East is West* (1930); *One Heavenly Night, Don't Bet on Women, Doctors' Wives, Quick Millions, Indiscreet, I Like Your Nerve, The Unholy Garden, The Yellow Ticket, The Spy* (1931); *Washington Masquerade, Jewel Robbery, Faithless, The First Year, Down to Earth, Devil and the Deep, The Crash* (1932); *Rasputin and the Empress, The Keyhole, Gabriel over the White House, A Bedtime Story, Hell Below, Baby Face, The Narrow Corner, Notorious but Nice, Bureau of Missing Persons, I Loved a Woman, Golden Harvest, Love, Honor and Oh Baby!, The Power and the Glory, Meet the Baron, Blood Money, Hello, Sister, Gigolettes of Paris* (1933); *The Cat and the Fiddle, The Wonder Bar, Let's Talk it Over, Let's Try Again, Whom the Gods Destroy, Stamboul Quest, The Girl from Missouri, One Exciting Adventure, Million Dollar Ransom, Blind Date, She Loves Me Not, A Lost Lady; Lady by Choice, Madame DuBarry, Love Time, Kid Millions, Imitation of Life, Sing Sing Nights, The Band Plays On, Success at Any Price, Sisters under the Skin, Now and Forever, Name the Woman, Massacre, Journal of a*

Crime, I've Got Your Number, The Hell Cat, The Ghost Walks, Black Moon (1934); *Charlie Chan in Paris, Society Doctor, The Mystery Man, Times Square Lady, The Florentine Dagger, Reckless, Honeymoon Limited, Three Kids and a Queen, Shipmates Forever, The Last Days of Pompeii, Frisco Waterfront, Spring Tonic, Red Salute, Red Hot Tires, One New York Night, Mad Love, Ladies Love Danger, Here Comes the Band, Diamond Jim, The Case of the Curious Bride, The Black Room* (1935); *Collegiate, Bullets or Ballots, Sitting on the Moon, In His Steps, Theodora Goes Wild, My Marriage, The Man Who Lived Twice, Romeo and Juliet* (1936); *Great Guy, Green Light, Maid of Salem, The Devil is Driving, Conquest, Thoroughbreds Don't Cry, Under Cover of Night, They Wanted to Marry, Once a Doctor, Let Them Live* (1937); *Love is a Headache, The Invisible Menace, The Adventures of Marco Polo, Marie Antoinette, The Cowboy and the Lady, Too Hot to Handle, Safety in Numbers, Holiday* (1938); *Parents on Trial, Should Husbands Work?, These Glamour Girls, The Real Glory, Here I am a Stranger, Main Street Lawyer, Union Pacific, Let Us Live!, Hidden Power* (1939); *Grand Ole Opry, Money and the Woman* (1940); *The Man Who Lost Himself, A Woman's Face, The Parson of Panamint, Sing for Your Supper, Las Vegas Nights, The Great Swindle* (1941); *Reunion in France* (1942); *Sarong Girl* (1943); *Bluebeard* (1944); *The Secret Life of Walter Mitty* (1947).

KORFF, Arnold (Arnold Kirsch) (1870–1944)
Veteran Austrian-Jewish character player of aristocrats in German silents who was contracted by MGM in 1930 to play similar parts in Hollywood French- and German-language talkies. After the Nazis came to power, he remained in the USA. RJK
FILMS: *Doughboys, Men of the North, The Royal Family of Broadway* (1930); *An American Tragedy, The Unholy Garden, The Yellow Ticket, Ambassador Bill* (1931); *Scarlet Dawn, Secrets of the French Police, Evenings for Sale* (1932); *All the King's Horses, Black Moon, Behold My Wife* (1934); *Three Kids and a Queen, Wings in the Dark, Alias Mary Dow, Paris in Spring, Magnificent Obsession, Shanghai* (1935).

KORTNER, Fritz (Fritz Nathan Kohn) (1892–1970)
Sophisticated-looking Viennese-born luminary of 1920s Berlin theatre who starred in numerous German and Austrian silent and early sound features. The Jewish, vociferously anti-Fascist Kortner learned of the Nazis' rise to power while touring Scandinavia and immediately resettled in England. After two years studying English, he gained film roles playing Arabesque rulers and Slav ministers before moving to New York in 1937, then to Hollywood in 1938. Here, Kortner became an American citizen and worked primarily as a writer of political articles and film scripts, including *The Strange Death of Adolf Hitler* (1943), in which he took a supporting role. From 1943, Kortner played a number of decidedly minor, sometimes even unbilled, character parts as generally nefarious Middle Europeans in anti-Nazi pictures, film noirs and B-thrillers. In Nazi Germany, meanwhile, Kortner was defamed in the propaganda film *Der ewige Jude/ The Eternal Jew* (1940) and eleven members of his family were gassed. An anxious 1947 return to Berlin, where Kortner hoped to help define postwar German theatre, was fraught with difficulties, since offers of employment all came from the Soviet Zone in which Kortner, as a US citizen, was forbidden from working. Erich Pommer, now film officer for the American Zone, furnished him with film work instead. This included the US-financed *Der Ruf/The Last Illusion* (1949), which Kortner scripted and starred in. The film depicted an ageing émigré's return to postwar Germany, but it met with widespread rejection and anti-Semitic press coverage. Kortner was nevertheless able to re-establish himself in German theatre during the 1950s and received a lifetime achievement award in 1966. RJK
FILMS: *The Purple V, The Strange Death of Adolf Hitler* (1943); *The Hitler Gang* (1944); *The Wife of Monte Cristo, Somewhere in the Night, The Razor's Edge* (1946); *The Brasher Doubloon* (1947); *Berlin Express, The Vicious Circle* (1948).

KOSLECK, Martin (Nikolai Yoschkin) (1904–1994)
Up-and-coming supporting actor in German talkies who fled to the USA in 1933 after appearing on an SS 'death list' due to his vocal anti-Fascism. He became an American citizen, and when the war began, dedicated himself to anti-Nazi films. He played Goebbels five times. RJK
FILMS: *Fashions of 1934* (1934); *Confessions of a Nazi Spy, Nurse Edith Cavell, Espionage Agent, Nick Carter – Master Detective* (1939); *Calling Philo Vance, Foreign Correspondent* (1940); *The Devil Pays Off, Underground, The Mad Doctor, International Lady* (1941); *All through the Night, Nazi Agent, Berlin Correspondent, Manila Calling, Fly-by-Night* (1942); *Tarzan Triumphs, The North Star, Chetniks – The Fighting Guerrillas, Bomber's Moon* (1943); *The Hitler Gang, The* **325**

Mummy's Curse, Secrets of Scotland Yard, The Great Alaskan Mystery [serial] (1944); *The Frozen Ghost, Pursuit to Algiers, The Spider, Gangs of the Waterfront* (1945); *The Wife of Monte Cristo, Strange Holiday, She-Wolf of London, Just Before Dawn, House of Horrors, Crime of the Century* (1946); *The Beginning or the End* (1947); *Smugglers' Cove, Half Past Midnight, Assigned to Danger* (1948); *Something Wild* (1961); *Hitler* (1962); *The Flesh Eaters, 36 Hours* (1964); *Morituri* (1965); *Agent for H.A.R.M.* (1966); *Which Way to the Front?* (1970); *The Man with Bogart's Face* (1980).

KRABBÉ, Jeroen (1944–)

In 1979, Jeroen Krabbé, along with Rutger Hauer★, impressed American critics and audiences in Paul Verhoeven's film *Soldaat van Oranje/Soldiers of Orange*. But while Hauer received promising offers from Hollywood, Krabbé returned to his native Netherlands empty-handed. He openly stated that he was not after an American career and continued to be involved in Dutch film production and a second career as a painter. Success in Hollywood, however, was around the corner and Krabbé became an international actor who travels between Europe and the USA while simultaneously keeping a firm foothold in his home country.

Another Dutch film, again directed by Verhoeven, became his international passport. *De vierde man/The Fourth Man* (1982) did well in the Netherlands, Europe and the USA, and Krabbé won several European prizes for his psychologically convincing performance, allied to idiosyncratic dark looks. In his first two American films, *Jumpin' Jack Flash* (with Whoopi Goldberg) and *No Mercy* (with Kim Basinger), both 1986, he played stereotypically evil characters, but he managed to make both parts dramatically credible. He subsequently got a leading role next to Timothy Dalton★ in the James Bond film *The Living Daylights*. Since then, Krabbé has switched from action movies (*The Fugitive*) to romance (*Ever After*) to comedy (*An Ideal Husband*) to existential dramas such as *Kafka* and *King of the Hill*, both directed by Steven Soderbergh. His star image exudes a sense of sophisticated European-ness, in which a charismatic screen presence signifies a deeper inner persona striving for the meaning of life. SdL

FILMS: *Jumpin' Jack Flash, No Mercy* (1986); *The Living Daylights* (1987); *Crossing Delancey* (1988); *The Punisher* (1989); *Till There was You* (1990); *Kafka, The Prince of Tides*

(1991); *The Fugitive, King of the Hill* (1993); *Immortal Beloved* (1994); *Business for Pleasure* (1996); *Dangerous Beauty, Ever After* (1998); *An Ideal Husband* (1999); *Ocean's Twelve* (2004).

KREUGER, Kurt (1916–)

Handsome, blond supporting actor who played an assortment of Nazis in Hollywood films of the 1940s, as well as occasional romantic roles. Kreuger became an American citizen in 1944 but following an argument with his studio, he returned to Europe in 1949 to more prominent screen roles. He came back to the USA in 1955 and took up his Hollywood career where he had left off. FG

FILMS: *Arise, My Love* (1940); *A Yank in the RAF* (1941); *Tonight We Raid Calais, Edge of Darkness, The Purple V, The Moon is Down, Secret Service in Darkest Africa, The Strange Death of Adolf Hitler, Sahara, Background to Danger, Action in the North Atlantic* (1943); *Mademoiselle Fifi, The Hitler Gang, None Shall Escape* (1944); *Hotel Berlin, Christmas in Connecticut, The Spider, Paris Underground, Escape in the Desert* (1945); *Sentimental Journey, The Dark Corner* (1946); *Unfaithfully Yours* (1948); *Spy Hunt* (1950); *The Enemy Below* (1957); *Legion of the Doomed* (1959); *What Did You Do in the War, Daddy?* (1966); *The St Valentine's Day Massacre* (1967).

KRÜGER, HARDY (Franz Eberhard August Krüger) (1928–)

Krüger's blond and blue-eyed appearance helped make the actor appear a clichéd on-screen German, yet the success of the British *The One that Got Away* (1956) also established him as a new type of good and apolitical soldier. This sense of the good German in uniform has been taken up in the majority of his Hollywood productions. CF

FILMS: *Hatari!* (1960); *The Flight of the Phoenix* (1965); *The Secret of Santa Vittoria* (1969); *Barry Lyndon* (1975); *A Bridge Too Far* (1976); *The Wild Geese* (1977); *Wrong is Right* (1981).

LAAGE, Barbara (Claire Colombat) (1920–1988)

Her appearance on the cover of *Life* allowed this glamorous blonde to be noticed by Hollywood, and Orson Welles in particular. Welles wanted her to replace Rita Hayworth, who had initially turned down the lead role in *The Lady from Shanghai* (1947). After Hayworth came to her senses, Laage played opposite Welles on the stage in *Macbeth*. Her bilingualism and acting were well received in Hollywood, but she returned to France, while later she made the occasional American film. VO

FILMS: *B.F.'s Daughter* (1948); *An Act of Love* (1953); *The Happy Road* (1956); *Paris Blues* (1961); *Therese and Isabelle* (1968).

LA COUR, Else (1902–unknown)

Danish born ingénue who appeared in a series of Westerns filmed in New York between 1919 and 1920. She later billed herself as Elsie Fuller and relocated to Germany. HJW

FILMS: *His Pal's Gal, The Holdup Man, Tex of the Timberlands* (1920); *The Matrimonial Web* (1921).

LAFAYETTE, Andrée (Andrée de la Bigne) (1903–unknown)

Silent supporting actress who made a handful of French films and two American films in which she played the leading role. VO

FILMS: *Trilby* (1923); *Why Get Married?* (1924).

LAGRANGE, Louise (Louise Vinot) (1898–1979)

Lagrange was a French film extra at the age of thirteen. She then worked at the Comédie Française and received star billing in numerous silent movies. In 1919, she left for Hollywood, where she met and married her first husband, the actor Robert Elliott. Although she played opposite Rudolph Valentino in *A Sainted Devil*, her Hollywood career was brief and disappointing. After separating from Elliott, Lagrange returned to France, where she had more luck with her career, earning the title of 'Princess of the cinema'. VO

FILMS: *The Side Show of Life, A Sainted Devil* (1924).

LAMARR, Hedy (Hedwig Kiesler) (1913–2000)

Born in Vienna, the extremely beautiful Hedwig 'Hedy' Kiesler started her career on the German stage and in Austrian films of the early 1930s. Her breakthrough came in 1932 with the Czech film *Extase/Ecstasy*, a *succès de scandale*, which due to its representation of female orgasm and nudity caused outrage and boycotts across Europe and in the USA. It cemented Kiesler's notoriety for years to come, but also brought her to the attention of Louis B. Mayer, who offered her a ten-year contract with MGM. By the time of her Hollywood debut, *Algiers* (a remake of *Pépé le Moko*, co-star-

Hedy Lamarr was billed by MGM as 'the world's most beautiful woman'

ring Charles Boyer★), much of the sensual, childlike sexuality the actress displayed in *Extase* had been streamlined into a more conventionally glamorous, statuesque icon of femininity. MGM renamed her Lamarr (after the late silent vamp Barbara LaMarr), and billed her 'the world's most beautiful woman', explicitly eschewing any reference to her national background in favour of a more mythical ideal of the 'eternal female'. Although Hollywood often teamed Lamarr with major stars, her career was hampered by mediocre vehicles and the fact that MGM seemed unable to develop her image beyond the purely decorative. She was acutely aware of the screen persona she was trapped in and once quipped that 'any girl can be glamorous. All you have to do is stand still and look stupid.'

While not as limited an actress as some critics have claimed, Lamarr showed an occasional tendency to overact, gaining some of her films the retrospective appeal of high camp: for example, *White Cargo* (in which she played a sarong-clad native girl), *Samson and Delilah* (as the biblical temptress) and *The Story of Mankind* (as Joan of Arc). Lamarr's career petered out in the early 1950s, and an attempted comeback in European cinema (in the Franco- **327**

Italian *L'Amante di paride/Loves of Three Queens* [1953], in which she portrayed several mythical-historical characters, including Helen of Troy) failed. In later years, she made headlines primarily for her successive marriages, shoplifting charges and her surprisingly frank autobiography *Ecstasy and Me* (1966), which included an introduction by Lamarr's psychotherapist, attesting to the actress's uninhibited sexuality. She spent her last years as a recluse in Florida, declining invitations to return to her native Austria. The revelation, shortly before her death, that since the early 1940s she held the patent as the co-inventor of a radio-guiding system for torpedoes, was an apt coda to the contradictions of Lamarr's complex life and career. TB

FILMS: *Algiers* (1938); *I Take this Woman, Lady of the Tropics* (1939); *Boom Town, Comrade X* (1940); *Come Live with Me, Ziegfeld Girl, H.M. Pulham Esq.* (1941); *Tortilla Flat, White Cargo, Crossroads* (1942); *The Heavenly Body* (1943); *The Conspirators, Experiment Perilous* (1944); *Her Highness and the Bellboy* (1945); *The Strange Woman* (1946); *Dishonored Lady* (1947); *Let's Live a Little* (1948); *Samson and Delilah* (1949); *A Lady without Passport, Copper Canyon* (1950); *My Favorite Spy* (1951); *The Story of Mankind, The Female Animal* (1957); *Instant Karma* (1990).

LAMBERT, Christophe (1957–)

French actor who shot to international fame in the 1980s when his intense stare landed him the largely non-speaking title role in the British-made *Greystoke: The Legend of Tarzan, Lord of the Apes* (1984). Lambert has straddled the Atlantic for most of his life. Born in Long Island and educated in Geneva, he is bilingual, though he retains a gentle French accent. His stardom was confirmed in Luc Besson's *Subway* (1985), for which he won a César. Lambert's American films have subsequently tended to exploit his stubble-cheeked looks and athletic physique and he has been consistently cast in action films such as *Highlander* and its sequels, where he played Connor McLeod, an immortal who is fated to duel from sixteenth-century Scotland to modern-day Manhattan. Lambert's American career has been prolific though unremarkable and unchallenging. He has, however, succeeded in eschewing stereotypically French typecasting. VO

FILMS: *Greystoke: The Legend of Tarzan, Lord of the Apes* (1984); *Highlander* (1986); *The Sicilian* (1987); *To Kill a Priest* (1988); *Why Me?, Highlander 2: The Quickening* (1990);

Knight Moves (1992); *Loaded Weapon 1* (1993); *Gunmen, The Road Killers* (1994); *Mortal Kombat, The Hunted* (1995); *Adrenalin: Fear the Rush* (1996); *Mean Guns* (1997); *Beowulf, Resurrection, Operation Splitsville, Fortress 2, Gideon* (1999); *Highlander: Endgame* (2000).

LANCHESTER, Elsa (Elizabeth Sullivan) (1902–1986)

Lanchester was a highly versatile British character actress whose Hollywood career began in 1935, the year in which she made two films, *David Copperfield* and *Naughty Marietta*. Among other films, she had previously made *The Officer's Mess* for Paramount British. She had moved to the USA with her husband, Charles Laughton★, but on first arrival did not share his success at being cast in film roles. After playing Anne of Cleves in Korda's *The Private Life of Henry VIII* (1933), she returned to Hollywood in 1934 and had better luck. Her most highly regarded early film performances were as both Mary Shelley and the bride in *The Bride of Frankenstein*.

Laughton and Lanchester settled into life in Hollywood well, and Lanchester went on to appear regularly on screen. She had a quick-witted and vivacious persona and although she was small in stature, her commanding and distinctive performances were regularly marked by a compelling magnetism. She also presented a series of one-woman shows at the Turnabout Theatre in Los Angeles and later toured the USA in her show 'Elsa Lanchester Herself'. Like Laughton, Lanchester did not fit into the mould of the typical English émigré, preferring instead to live a more bohemian, cosmopolitan lifestyle. In 1950, she became an American citizen. She was nominated for an Academy Award as Best Supporting Actress when she appeared with Laughton in Billy Wilder's *Witness for the Prosecution*. In later years, she appeared in cameo and supporting roles in films such as *Bell, Book and Candle* and, in the 1970s, *Willard* and *Murder by Death*, which exploited her reputation as a gifted comedienne with the ability to play eccentric characters. SS

FILMS: *The Officer's Mess* (1931); *David Copperfield, Naughty Marietta, The Bride of Frankenstein* (1935); *Ladies in Retirement, Sullivan's Travels* (1941); *Son of Fury, Tales of Manhattan* (1942); *Forever and a Day, Lassie Come Home, Thumbs Up* (1943); *Passport to Destiny* (1944); *The Spiral Staircase* (1945); *The Razor's Edge* (1946); *The Bishop's Wife, Northwest Outpost, The Big Clock* (1947); *Come to the Stable,*

The Secret Garden, The Inspector General (1949); *Buccaneer's Girl, The Petty Girl, Mystery Street, Frenchie* (1950); *Dreamboat, Les Misérables, Androcles and the Lion* (1952); *The Girls of Pleasure Island* (1953); *Three Ring Circus, Hell's Half Acre, The Glass Slipper* (1954); *Witness for the Prosecution* (1957); *Bell, Book and Candle* (1958); *Mary Poppins, The Pajama Party* (1964); *That Darn Cat!* (1965); *Easy Come, Easy Go* (1966); *Blackbeard's Ghost* (1967); *Rascal* (1968); *Me, Natalie* (1969); *Willard* (1970); *Terror in the Wax Museum, Arnold* (1973); *Murder by Death* (1976); *Die Laughing* (1979).

LANE, Lupino (Henry Lane George Lupino) (1892–1959)

Music-hall and musical comedy star who is best remembered for 'Doin' the Lambeth Walk' on the British stage and screen in the 1930s. After an earlier career in British comedy shorts in the 1910s, Lane was signed by a Fox representative who saw him on Broadway in 1920. He became a popular Hollywood comedian over the next ten years and worked in both comic two-reelers and major features for directors such as D. W. Griffith (*Isn't Life Wonderful*) and Ernst Lubitsch (*The Love Parade*). JB

FILMS: *The Reporter, The Broker* (1922); *A Friendly Husband* (1923); *Isn't Life Wonderful* (1924); *Time Flies, Roaming Romeo, Maid in Morocco, Fighting Dude* (1925); *Fool's Luck, Naughty Boy, Movieland, Howdy Duke, His Private Life* (1926); *Ship Mates, Monty of the Mounted, Hello Sailor, Half-Pint Hero, Drama Deluxe* (1927); *His Private Life, Sword Points, Privates Beware, Listen Sister, Hectic Days, Fisticuffs, Fandango* (1928); *Only Me, The Love Parade, Show of Shows, Summer Saps, Purely Circumstantial, Joyland, Fire Proof, Evolution of the Dance, Crossed Swords, Buying a Gun, Be My King, Battling Sisters* (1929); *Bride of the Regiment, Golden Dawn* (1930).

LAUGHTON, Charles (1899–1962)

The British actor Charles Laughton considered his distinctively rotund physical appearance and pronounced features to be ugly. On screen, however, he was capable of conveying a wide range of gestures and emotions, including boisterousness, vulnerability, sadness and gentleness. Laughton was first invited to Hollywood in 1931 on the strength of his reputation as a stage actor, although he had by then appeared in a few British films. Jesse Lasky of Paramount offered him a role in *Devil and the Deep*, but the first film he

actually made in Hollywood was *The Old Dark House*, an adaptation of a J. B. Priestley story directed by James Whale, for which Paramount loaned Laughton to Universal. *The Old Dark House* was then released after *Devil and the Deep*, because Paramount was keen to publicise that they, rather than Universal, had 'discovered' Laughton, thus including on the credits: 'Introducing the eminent English character actor'. Cecil B. DeMille was similarly impressed by Laughton's theatrical credentials when he saw him on stage as a murderer in *Payment Deferred* and thought he would be an excellent choice for Nero in his forthcoming film *The Sign of the Cross*. By the end of 1932, Laughton had gained valuable film acting experience with starring roles in five major Hollywood films. He was able to combine a high salary of $2,500 a week with numerous critical accolades.

Alexander Korda persuaded him to return to Britain temporarily to star in *The Private Life of Henry VIII* (1933), an international success in which he co-starred with his wife Elsa Lanchester★. He returned to Britain to make the occasional film, but thereafter his main career was in the USA. Both he and Lanchester became US citizens in 1950. His most important film roles of the 1930s, and arguably of

Charles Laughton and his wife, Elsa Lanchester, in their Hollywood home: a frequent port of call for fellow émigré actors

his entire film career, were as Inspector Javert in *Les Misérables*, as Captain Bligh in *Mutiny on the Bounty* and as Quasimodo in *The Hunchback of Notre Dame*. These parts established Laughton's versatility and ability both to draw on his skills of improvisation and transform his appearance in different contexts. His recitation of Lincoln's Gettysberg address in *Ruggles of Red Gap* prefigured his later American reading tours and radio broadcasts that dominated the latter part of his career. When Mayflower Productions, a production company he established in Britain with Erich Pommer, failed, RKO offered to repay its debts as part of a five-film contract that began with *The Hunchback of Notre Dame*.

During World War II, Laughton and Lanchester stayed in the USA and, along with other British émigré actors, were criticised for not returning to Britain. Laughton participated in *Forever and a Day*, an episodic film whose proceeds were donated to wartime charities. The production featured several other British stars, including C. Aubrey Smith★, Claude Rains★, Merle Oberon★ and Anna Neagle★. While in Hollywood, Laughton was appreciated as English, but he was also seen to have an air of cosmopolitan intellectualism. The actor collaborated with another émigré, Bertholt Brecht, and his high salary facilitated a passion for art collecting.

Laughton's subsequent film roles were less well reviewed, and the highs he had reached in the 1930s were not repeated after the war, with the exception of a few distinguished performances, such as Sir Wilfrid Roberts in *Witness for the Prosecution* and Gracchus in *Spartacus*. His career consequently diversified: as well as continuing to appear in films, he embarked on reading tours, particularly of George Bernard Shaw's work and extracts from the Bible. He also appeared in various stage productions. While he was nominated for two Academy Awards for Best Actor (for *Witness for the Prosecution* and *Mutiny on the Bounty*) and starred mostly in American films, Laughton actually won, somewhat ironically, an Academy Award in 1933 for a British film, *The Private Life of Henry VIII*. Laughton directed only one film himself, *The Night of the Hunter* (1955). The film was not appreciated on first release but it has subsequently been regarded as a brilliant debut. SS

FILMS: *The Old Dark House, Devil and the Deep, Payment Deferred, The Sign of the Cross, If I Had a Million, Island of Lost Souls* (1932); *White Woman* (1933); *The Barretts of Wimpole Street* (1934); *Ruggles of Red Gap, Les Misérables, Mutiny*

on the Bounty (1935); *The Hunchback of Notre Dame* (1939); *They Knew What They Wanted* (1940); *It Started with Eve* (1941); *Tales of Manhattan, The Tuttles of Tahiti, Stand by for Action* (1942); *Forever and a Day, The Man from Down Under, This Land is Mine* (1943); *The Canterville Ghost, The Suspect* (1944); *Captain Kidd* (1945); *Because of Him* (1946); *The Big Clock, The Paradine Case* (1947); *Arch of Triumph, Girl from Manhattan, On Our Merry Way* (1948); *Man on the Eiffel Tower, The Bribe* (1949); *The Blue Veil, The Strange Door* (1951); *O. Henry's Full House, Abbott and Costello Meet Captain Kidd* (1952); *Young Bess, Salome* (1953); *Witness for the Prosecution* (1957); *Under Ten Flags, Spartacus* (1960); *Advise and Consent* (1962).

LAUREL, Stan (Arthur Stanley Jefferson) (1890–1965)

Stan Laurel's path to fame in films was neither short nor easy. Born Arthur Stanley Jefferson in Ulverston, England, both his parents were stage veterans, his actress mother Madge having hitched her career to Arthur Jefferson Senior, former actor, playwright and theatrical entrepeneur, who opened theatres throughout the north of England to cater for working people. Stan's early desire to forge a career as a stage comedian was not immediately pleasing to his father, and, indeed, Arthur Jefferson preserved an ambivalent attitude to his son's success in the laughter business, in a foreign land, practically until his death. Nevertheless, his contacts enabled young Stanley to appear in traditional musical shows like *The Sleeping Beauty*, in 1907. In 1909, Stan took the first step towards his future profession by enrolling with Fred Karno's troupe of Speechless Comedians, whose rising star was another young comic, Charlie Chaplin★. Chaplin and Laurel sailed together from Southampton, in September 1910, with the Karno group, en route for the USA.

The Karno troupers were veterans of a discipline that was not common to American stage comedians – the use of physical pantomime. When Karno presented his hit sketch starring Chaplin, *A Night at an English Music Hall*, a local Minneapolis paper commented that 'broad English humor is very broad indeed. It smacks even more of the slapstick than our old friend, the burlesque comedian. Yet there are always moments of unexpectedness. Where the American would do the obvious thing, the Englishman does the unusual . . .'. In other words, while American

Stan Laurel achieved lasting worldwide fame, opposite Oliver Hardy, as the fool who muddles through against all odds

comics mostly used familiar ethnic humour, the English were trained in a kind of shock tactics, an often aggressive mime that created moments that we would today call 'surreal'. Stanley Jefferson, who had at the time no fixed comic persona of his own, imbibed his art at first so slavishly from Chaplin that his first appearances on the American stage after leaving the Karno troupe were as a Chaplin imitator, with two other partners – 'The Keystone Trio'.

Chaplin had left the Karno group for Mack Sennett's movie studio late in 1913, and within a year was world famous, leaving Stanley scratching his head and wondering, why him and not me? Reluctant to return to an England that had, in the summer of 1914, been sucked into a European war, he remained behind, eking a living for three years at the lower end of vaudeville. This culminated in his teaming up with an Australian comedienne, Charlotte Mae Dahlberg. Touring with her as man and wife in practice but not in law (Mae had left a husband in Australia), the duo decided to adopt a new name, and thus were born Stan and Mae Laurel.

Stan had not given up the ambition to follow Chaplin into the movies, which, it was clear, were now eclipsing vaudeville. In 1917, he made his first reputed short, *Nuts in May*, which has since disappeared, though it was remade later as *Mixed Nuts*. This led nowhere, but in 1918 he found a new, enterprising producer who would give him a chance, the mercurial Hal Roach, who had already launched another future comic star, Harold Lloyd. Lloyd had just discovered his 'glasses character', but Stan still had no clear idea what kind of comic actor he might be. He experimented with an eccentric young man about town, in films that aped the frenetic style of Mack Sennett's Keystones. During the next seven years, Stan would move from company to company, trying to build a career as a solo star, which he finally achieved with a series of spoofs, commencing with *Mud and Sand*, a burlesque of Rudolph Valentino, in 1922. In 1921, a chance encounter linked him with another jobbing solo actor, Oliver Hardy, in *The Lucky Dog*. But this movie gave no hint of a joint future.

Stan's American stage career as a burlesquer of other styles was hampering his movie progress, however, and he would have remained a hazily remembered second-string silent comic were it not for his return to the Hal Roach studio, in 1925, where director Leo McCarey eventually teamed him up with Oliver Hardy, in *Duck Soup*, in 1927.

By this time, Laurel had gained experience both as an actor and as a comedy writer-director, and *Duck Soup* was his own script, based as a homage to one of his father's old stage sketches, a comedy of errors originally entitled 'Home from the Honeymoon'. Half a dozen short movies later, the comedy team of Laurel and Hardy was officially launched, together with their regular foil, Scotsman Jimmy Finlayson, in *The Second Hundred Years*.

Stan had made over eighty films as a solo performer, writer and director, and would make thirty-three silent and thirty-nine sound shorts with Oliver Hardy, between 1927 and 1935, and twenty-five features. His personal life was somewhat tumultuous. He had parted from Mae Dahlberg after a few early joint appearances in his spoofs, and married eight times, though only four wives, as two of the ladies enjoyed multiple nuptials with him. But his life mainly consisted, between 1918 and 1945 (with the last Laurel and Hardy film, *Atoll K*, in 1951), of non-stop work on films. He was the gag master par excellence of film comedy, honing the character that he had fixed as an inversion of his early manic eccentric. In essence, this was a version of an old *commedia dell'arte* clown, the rebellious servant, the fool who muddles through against all odds. His logic is not that of other humans, but it makes sense to him, despite being a constant bane to his partner, the long-suffering Ollie, from whom he cannot be parted. To the end, he never lost the tone of his Lancashire roots, and he never became a US citizen. He maintained to the last a modesty that could never quite fathom his universal fame and success. 'I mean, we were just two-reel comics,' he used to protest, 'that wasn't art.' Oh yes it was! SLO

FILMS: *Nuts in May* (1917); *Phoney Photos, Hickory Hiram, Whose Zoo, O It's Great to Be Crazy, Do You Love Your Wife?, Just Rambling Along, Hoots Mon, No Place Like Jail, Hustling for Health, Huns and Hyphens, Bears and Bad Men, Frauds and Frenzies* (1918); *The Lucky Dog* (1921); *A Weak-End Party, The Handy Man, The Egg, The Pest, Mixed Nuts, Mud and Sand* (1922); *When Knights were Cold, Under Two Jags, The Noon Whistle, White Wings, Pick and Shovel, Kill or Cure, Collars and Cuffs, Gas and Air, Oranges and Lemons, Short Orders, Save the Ship, A Man about Town, Roughest Africa, Scorching Sands, The Whole Truth, Frozen Hearts, The Soilers, Mother's Joy* (1923); *Smithy, Zeb vs. Paprika, Postage Due, Brothers under the Chin, Wide Open Spaces, Rupert of Hee Haw, Short Kilts, Detained, Mandarin Mix-Up, Monsieur Don't Care, West of Hot*

Dog (1924); *Somewhere in Wrong, Twins, Pie-Eyed, The Snow Hawk, Navy Blue Days, The Sleuth, Dr Pyckle and Mr Pride, Half a Man* (1925); *45 Minutes from Hollywood, Get 'Em Young, What's the World Coming To, On the Front Page* (1926); *Seeing the World, Eve's Love Letters, Duck Soup, Slipping Wives, Love 'Em and Weep, Why Girls Love Sailors, With Love and Hisses, Sailors Beware, Do Detectives Think?, Flying Elephants, Sugar Daddies, Call of the Cuckoos, The Second Hundred Years, Hats Off, Putting Pants on Philip, The Battle of the Century* (1927); *Leave 'Em Laughing, Should Tall Men Marry?, The Finishing Touch, From Soup to Nuts, You're Darn Tootin', Their Purple Moment, Should Married Men Go Home?, Early to Bed, Two Tars, Habeas Corpus, We Faw Down* (1928); *Liberty, Wrong Again, That's My Wife, Big Business, Double Whoopee, Bacon Grabbers, Angora Love, Unaccustomed As We Are, Berth Marks, Men O' War, Perfect Day, They Go Boom, The Hoose-Gow* (1929); *Night Owls, Blotto, Brats, Below Zero, Hog Wild, The Laurel-Hardy Murder Case, Another Fine Mess, The Rogue Song* (1930); *Pardon Us, Beau Hunks, Be Big, Chickens Come Home, The Stolen Jools, Laughing Gravy, Our Wife, Come Clean, One Good Turn* (1931); *Helpmates, Any Old Port, The Music Box, The Chimp, County Hospital, Pack up Your Troubles, Scram, Their First Mistake, Towed in a Hole* (1932); *Twice Two, Me and My Pal, The Midnight Patrol, Busy Bodies, Dirty Work, The Devil's Brother, Sons of the Desert* (1933); *Babes in Toyland, Oliver the Eighth, Going Bye Bye, Them Thar Hills, The Live Ghost* (1934); *Tit for Tat, The Fixer-Uppers, Thicker than Water, Bonnie Scotland* (1935); *The Bohemian Girl, Our Relations* (1936); *Way Out West* (1937); *Swiss Miss, Block-Heads* (1938); *The Flying Deuces* (1939); *A Chump at Oxford, Saps at Sea* (1940); *Great Guns* (1941); *A-Haunting We Will Go* (1942); *Air Raid Wardens, Jitterbugs, The Dancing Masters* (1943); *The Big Noise* (1944); *Nothing but Trouble, The Bull-fighters* (1945); *Atoll K* (1951)

LAURENT, Jacqueline (1920–)

Laurent was still in her teens when she was approached by an MGM talent scout after her successful performance in *Sarati le Terrible/Sarati the Terrible* (1937) and offered a contract of $300 a week. The young French actress met Louis B. Mayer in London and was promised a new career as one of the studio's leading stars. Laurent and her partner, the writer Jacques Prévert, were duly installed in a Beverly Hills villa and she began to receive daily English lessons. After a disappointingly girlish role as Mickey Rooney's brother in

Judge Hardy's Children, Laurent quickly tired of the studio scriptwriters' limited expectations and returned to France, where she was famously cast as Jean Gabin's★ florist girl-friend in Marcel Carné's *Le Jour se lève/Daybreak* (1939). AP

FILM: *Judge Hardy's Children* (1938).

LAW, Jude (David Jude Law) (1972–)

Talented and strikingly handsome actor at the forefront of the 1990s' generation of young British actors. Law's screen image manages to suggest regal intensity alongside a neurotic vulnerability that is often tempered with an ambivalent sexual energy. He boasts impressive theatrical credentials, including a Tony award for his 1995 Broadway debut in *Indiscretions* and an Olivier award for his performance as Euripedes' *Ion* with the RSC. His UK film debut came as a joy-riding car thief in *Shopping* (1994). After success as Lord Alfred Douglas in 1997's *Wilde*, Law played another gay role as Kevin Spacey's lover in Clint Eastwood's *Midnight in the Garden of Good and Evil*.

A series of upmarket US productions, including the stylish, image-obsessed *Gattaca*, led to the actor's breakthrough Academy Award-nominated role as the effortlessly attractive Dickie Greenleaf, whose chiselled good looks and conceited nouveau riche lifestyle beguiled Matt Damon's Tom in Anthony Minghella's *The Talented Mr Ripley*. Law's siren looks and arresting eyes also facilitated the airbrushed perfection of Gigolo Joe, the 'robo-rent-boy' of Spielberg's *A.I.*

With a now fully matured star profile, Law seems intent on combining high-profile US films such as Martin Scorsese's *The Aviator* with UK productions like *Marlowe* (made by his own production company). MW

FILMS: *I Love You, I Love You Not* (1996); *Midnight in the Garden of Good and Evil, Gattaca* (1997); *Music from Another Room* (1998); *The Talented Mr Ripley* (1999); *Artificial Intelligence: AI, Enemy at the Gates, Road to Perdition* (2001); *Cold Mountain* (2003); *I Heart Huckabees, Alfie, Closer, The Aviator, Lemony Snicket's a Series of Unfortunate Events* [voice] (2004).

LAWFORD, Peter (1923–1984)

British child actor who moved to the USA in 1938 and signed a long-term contract with MGM in 1942. Lawford's handsome features and debonair manner led to well-suited roles in light comedy and musicals. He became a member of Hollywood's 'Rat Pack', as well as the brother-in-law of President Kennedy. MHu

FILMS: *Lord Jeff* (1938); *Eagle Squadron, London Blackout Murders, Thunder Birds, A Yank at Eton, Random Harvest, Junior Army, Mrs Miniver* (1942); *Assignment in Brittany, The Man from Down Under, Pilot #5, Girl Crazy, Sahara, Flesh and Fantasy, Paris after Dark, Corvette K-225, Sherlock Holmes Faces Death, West Side Kid, Someone to Remember, Above Suspicion, The Sky's the Limit, The Purple V, Immortal Sergeant* (1943); *The Canterville Ghost, Mrs Parkington, The Adventures of Mark Twain, The White Cliffs of Dover* (1944); *Son of Lassie, The Picture of Dorian Gray* (1945); *My Brother Talks to Horses, Two Sisters from Boston, Cluny Brown* (1946); *It Happened in Brooklyn, Good News* (1947); *Julia Misbehaves, Easter Parade, On an Island with You* (1948); *The Red Danube, Little Women* (1949); *Please Believe Me* (1950); *Royal Wedding* (1951); *Just This Once, Rogue's March, You for Me, The Hour of 13, Kangaroo* (1952); *It Should Happen to You* (1954); *Never So Few* (1959); *Exodus, Pepe, Ocean's Eleven* (1960); *The Longest Day, Advise and Consent, Sergeants 3* (1962); *Dead Ringer* (1964); *Harlow, Sylvia* (1965); *A Man Called Adam, The Oscar* (1966); *Buona Sera, Mrs Campbell, Skidoo* (1968); *Hook, Line & Sinker, The April Fools* (1969); *One More Time, Togetherness* (1970); *Clay Pigeon* (1971); *They Only Kill Their Masters* (1972); *That's Entertainment!* (1974); *Rosebud* (1975); *Won Ton Ton, the Dog Who Saved Hollywood* (1976); *Angels' Brigade* (1979); *Gypsy Angels* (1980); *Body and Soul* (1981).

LAWSON, Wilfrid (Wilfrid Worsnop) (1900–1966)

Work on Broadway brought this versatile British character actor to the attention of Hollywood. His short career there became a subject of debate in Parliament in 1940 when the RAF – sensitive to the controversial presence of British 'deserters' in California – refused him an exit visa to join the cast of *How Green Was My Valley*. JB

FILMS: *White Hunter, Ladies in Love* (1936); *The Man Who Made Diamonds* (1937); *Allegheny Uprising* (1939); *The Long Voyage Home* (1940); *War and Peace* (1956); *The Naked Edge* (1961).

LAWTON, Frank (1904–1969)

Refined English stage and screen actor who moved to Broadway. He worked with luminaries such as James Whale, Tod Browning and John Ford for his occasional Hollywood screen appearances. MF

FILMS: *Cavalcade* (1933); *One More River* (1934); *David Copperfield* (1935); *The Invisible Ray, The Devil-Doll* (1936); *The Rising of the Moon* (1957); *Gideon's Day* (1958).

LEBEAU, Madeleine (Marie-Thérèse Lebeau) (1921–)

French actress who emigrated to the USA with her partner Marcel Dalio* because of the war. Lebeau's Hollywood career began under contract to Warner Bros., with parts ranging from extras to supporting roles. She is best remembered for her small part as one of the hostesses at Rick's Café in *Casablanca*: it is her tearful face that we see during the Marseillaise sequence. After returning to France, she starred in the historical drama, *Les Chouans* (1947). Her career then dwindled until Federico Fellini cast her as a beautiful evanescent apparition, a gentle caricature of a graceful and affected French star, in *Otto e mezzo/ 8½* (1963). CV

FILMS: *Hold Back the Dawn* (1941); *Gentleman Jim, Casablanca* (1942); *Paris after Dark* (1943); *Music for Millions* (1944).

LEBEDEFF, Ivan (1895–1953)

Lithuanian actor and officer of the White Russian army who was noted for his romantic roles such as Gloria Swanson's lover in *The Love of Sunya*. Lebedeff's screen persona was that of a typically crafty, but handsome, seducer of Russian or Latin origin. His unpublished novel, *The Legion of Dishonor*, was partly about Hollywood's Russian émigrés. RY

FILMS: *The Sorrows of Satan* (1926); *The Love of Sunya, The Angel of Broadway, The Forbidden Woman* (1927); *Let 'Er Go Gallegher, Walking Back* (1928); *Sin Town, The Veiled Woman, The One Woman Idea, Street Girl, They Had to See Paris* (1929); *Men Without Women, The Cuckoos, Midnight Mystery, Conspiracy* (1930); *The Lady Refuses, The Gay Diplomat, Laugh and Get Rich, Bachelor Apartment, Woman Pursued* (1931); *The Hollywood Handicap, Unholy Love* (1932); *Sweepings, Made on Broadway, Laughing at Life, Bombshell* (1933); *Moulin Rouge, The Merry Frinks, Kansas City Princess* (1934); *China Seas, Strange Wives, Sweepstake Annie, Goin' to Town, She Couldn't Take It* (1935); *The Golden Arrow, Pepper, Love on the Run* (1936); *Mama Steps Out, History Is Made at Night, Fair Warning, Maytime, Atlantic Flight, Conquest, Angel, Wise Girl* (1937); *Straight, Place and Show* (1938); *You Can't Cheat an Honest Man, The Mystery of Mr Wong, Trapped in the Sky, Hotel for Women* (1939); *Passport to Alcatraz, Public Deb No. 1* (1940);

The Shanghai Gesture (1941); *Blue, White and Perfect, Love of the Islands, Foreign Agent* (1942); *Journey into Fear, Mission to Moscow, Around the World* (1943); *Are These Our Parents?, Oh, What a Night* (1944); *Rhapsody in Blue* (1945); *Heartbeat* (1946); *California Conquest, The Snows of Kilimanjaro* (1952); *The War of the Worlds* (1953).

LEDERER, Francis (František Lederer) (1899–2000)
Prague-born German matinée idol who came to the USA in 1932, found success on Broadway and was signed to RKO. A series of unlikely romantic leading roles – beginning with a displaced Eskimo – failed to make him a major star. A US citizen, Lederer founded the Los Angeles-based American National Academy of Performing Arts in 1958. With a particular focus on Method acting, it swiftly became recognised as one of the USA's foremost preparatory schools for theatrical talent. Lederer continued to teach there until the age of one hundred. RJK
FILMS: *Man of Two Worlds, The Pursuit of Happiness* (1934); *Romance in Manhattan, The Gay Deception* (1935); *One Rainy Afternoon, My American Wife* (1936); *It's All Yours* (1937); *The Lone Wolf in Paris* (1938); *Confessions of a Nazi Spy, Midnight* (1939); *The Man I Married* (1940); *Puddin' Head* (1941); *A Voice in the Wind, The Bridge of San Luis Rey* (1944); *The Madonna's Secret, The Diary of a Chambermaid* (1946); *Million Dollar Weekend* (1948); *Captain Carey, USA, A Woman of Distinction, Surrender* (1950); *The Ambassador's Daughter, Lisbon* (1956); *The Return of Dracula, Maracaibo* (1958).

LEDOUX, Fernand (Jacques Joseph Félix Fernand Ledoux) (1897–1993)
Distinguished and versatile Belgian character actor who took French nationality in 1920 in order to become a full-time member of the Comédie Française. Ledoux combined stage work with a successful career in French cinema (e.g. *La Bête humaine* [1938]). He appeared in one French-language multi-language film shot in the USA, *Folies Bergère* (1935), as well as a number of American productions shot in Europe during the 1960s. AP/MB
FILMS: *The Big Gamble* (1961); *The Longest Day, Freud* (1962); *Up from the Beach* (1965).

LEDOYEN, Virginie (1976–)
Spirited and strikingly attractive modern French actress who came to international attention following her leading role in Benoît Jacquot's *La Fille seule/A Single Girl* (1995). Ledoyen was subsequently approached by Hollywood, but her first English-language role only came three years later in James Ivory's international co-production, *A Soldier's Daughter Never Cries* (1998). She followed this with the part of Guillaume Canet's★ French girlfriend, Françoise, in *The Beach*. Ledoyen did not go to the USA to publicise the film and has since refused offers of further American roles declaring, 'I didn't want to go to Hollywood in order to play the French girl who always wants to be nude.' AP
FILM: *The Beach* (2000).

LEE, Anna (Joan Boniface Winnifrith) (1913–2004)
Charming and energetic British actress who pursued a successful film career in Britain – including two US-financed productions – before leaving for Hollywood with then husband, director Robert Stevenson, in 1939. She made eight films with John Ford throughout her long career – she was Emily Collingwood in *Fort Apache* and Bronwyn Morgan in *How Green Was My Valley*. She also enjoyed great popularity as Lila Quartermaine in the ABC television soap opera *General Hospital*. MHu
FILMS: *Ebb Tide* (1932); *Chelsea Life* (1933); *Return to Yesterday, Seven Sinners* (1940); *My Life with Caroline, How Green Was My Valley* (1941); *Commandos Strike at Dawn, Flying Tigers* (1942); *Flesh and Fantasy, Hangmen Also Die, Forever and a Day* (1943); *Summer Storm* (1944); *Bedlam, G.I. War Brides* (1946); *The Ghost and Mrs Muir, High Conquest* (1947); *Best Man Wins, Fort Apache* (1948); *Prison Warden* (1949); *Gideon's Day, The Last Hurrah* (1958); *The Crimson Kimono, Jet over the Atlantic, This Earth is Mine, The Horse Soldiers* (1959); *The Big Night* (1960); *Two Rode Together* (1961); *Jack the Giant Killer, What Ever Happened to Baby Jane?, The Man Who Shot Liberty Valance* (1962); *The Prize* (1963); *For Those Who Think Young, The Unsinkable Molly Brown* (1964); *The Sound of Music* (1965); *Picture Mommy Dead, 7 Women* (1966); *In Like Flint* (1967); *Star!* (1968); *Beyond the Next Mountain* (1987); *Beverly Hills Brats, Listen to Me* (1989); *What Can I Do?* (1994).

LEE, Christopher (1922–)
Tall, gaunt and imposing British actor who won international celebrity as the principal representative of evil in Hammer's legendary cycle of British horror films. By bestowing an aristocratic bearing and polished charm upon **335**

the character of Dracula, Lee established, against stiff competition from Max Schreck and Bela Lugosi*, what many consider to be the definitive interpretation of the vampire. Lee's Hollywood excursions largely amount to an extension of his enormous European filmography. Many of his later American film appearances are simply knowing cameos respectfully inserted by blockbuster directors like Steven Spielberg and Tim Burton keen to acknowledge the formative influence of British exploitation cinema. Fittingly, the iconic shadow Lee still casts over fantasy cinema has provided an august twilight to his career, since having remained very lithe and fit for an octogenarian, he has taken substantial villainous roles in the *Star Wars* prequels and *The Lord of the Rings* trilogy. JB

FILMS: *Captain Horatio Hornblower, R.N.* (1951); *The Crimson Pirate, Babes in Bagdad, Moulin Rouge* (1952); *That Lady, The Warriors, The Cockleshell Heroes* (1955); *Port Afrique, Beyond Mombasa* (1956); *Bitter Victory* (1957); *The Battle of the V1* (1958); *The Longest Day* (1962); *The Magic Christian* (1969); *One More Time, The Private Life of Sherlock Holmes, Julius Caesar* (1970); *Hannie Caulder* (1971); *The Man with the Golden Gun* (1974); *Airport '77, End of the World, Meatcleaver Massacre* (1977); *Return from Witch Mountain, Caravans* (1978); *Circle of Iron, 1941, Jaguar Lives!* (1979); *Serial* (1980); *An Eye for an Eye, The Salamander* (1981); *Safari 3000, The Last Unicorn* [voice] (1982); *The Rosebud Beach Hotel* (1984); *The Howling II* (1985); *Jocks* (1987); *Honeymoon Academy, Gremlins 2: The New Batch* (1990); *Police Academy: Mission to Moscow* (1994); *The Stupids* (1996); *Tale of the Mummy* (1998); *Sleepy Hollow* (1999); *The Lord of the Rings: The Fellowship of the Ring* (2001); *Star Wars: Episode II – Attack of the Clones, The Lord of the Rings: The Two Towers* (2002); *The Lord of the Rings: The Return of the King* [voice] (2003).

LEIGH, Suzanna (Suzanna Smyth) (1945–)
Leigh featured in two UK films before being brought to the USA by Hal B. Wallis, producer of *Boeing Boeing*. After only two films, the second with Elvis Presley, she returned to British cinema. TJ

FILMS: *Boeing Boeing* (1965); *Paradise, Hawaiian Style* (1966).

LEIGH, Vivien (Vivian Mary Hartley) (1913–1967)
English actress whose two signature roles, for each of which she won the Academy Award for Best Actress, are both Southern belles, one in full bloom, the other sadly wilted. Almost all her later films present variations on one or other of these figures, sometimes both. They seem generations apart, yet they appeared within barely a decade of one another. Her slim filmography (only twenty films, including a mere five in her last two decades) makes Leigh's screen career appear oddly compressed. She seemed to age quickly, real-life illness doubtless hurrying the transition from romantic leading lady to worn character actress, while her turbulent private life mirrored the on-screen melodrama.

Leigh was born in India to British parents and after early stage experience made her first screen appearance in *Things are Looking Up* (1935). Eight more British films followed, including *Fire over England* (1936), in which she appeared for the first time opposite her future husband, Laurence Olivier*. These were mostly ingénue roles, generally uninteresting parts in some interesting pictures, until the MGM-British production *A Yank at Oxford* cast her as the bookshop coquette who stirs collegiate hearts. It now seems like a rehearsal for the coquette to end them all, Scarlett O'Hara.

After a much-publicised industry-wide search had failed to yield an appropriate star for his monumental prestige picture and box-office colossus *Gone with the Wind*, David O. Selznick was introduced to Leigh when she was brought, with Olivier, by his agent brother Myron on a set visit to watch the burning of Atlanta. She was, of course, awarded the plum part, to general surprise but instant popular acceptance. An Academy Award followed, along with two more 'Hollywood British' films. Both were tragic romances shot in American studios while the real Britain withstood the Blitz: MGM's *Waterloo Bridge*, in which she played opposite Robert Taylor; and Korda's *That Hamilton Woman*, in which she co-starred again with Olivier in the story of Lord Nelson's extramarital passion. In both, Leigh's character ends up an abandoned scarlet woman, throwing herself under a passing ambulance in one, and languishing in a French prison, contemplating her faded looks and lamenting her lost love, in the other.

There followed a return to the theatre and to Britain, including starring roles in ill-conceived, big-budget productions of *Caesar and Cleopatra* (1945) and *Anna Karenina* (1948), the latter title role being another period coquette and world literature's best-known adulteress.

After playing Blanche DuBois on the West End stage under Olivier's direction, in 1951 she was cast by Elia Kazan in the film version of *A Streetcar Named Desire* opposite Brando. The clash of acting styles works for or against the film according to taste, but the American Academy favoured Leigh for the second time. Mental instability had already revealed itself when the onset of tuberculosis forced her to withdraw from Paramount's Ceylonese melodrama *Elephant Walk* – she was replaced by Elizabeth Taylor – but Leigh can still be glimpsed in some location long shots, while Taylor invariably acts in front of back-projection plates.

While her marriage to Olivier collapsed and her sanity wavered, her last three American films returned to tragedy. In *The Deep Blue Sea* and *The Roman Spring of Mrs Stone*, filmed in Britain by Fox and Warner's from works by Tennessee Williams and Terence Rattigan respectively, she is first an adulteress (again), then a pitiful widow soliciting love and death from Italian hustlers. In *Ship of Fools*, she is a cynical divorcée, once more chasing young men, and beating up Lee Marvin's ill-mannered lecher when he withdraws his drunken advances. SH

FILMS: *A Yank at Oxford* (1938); *Gone with the Wind* (1939); *Waterloo Bridge* (1940); *That Hamilton Woman* (1941); *A Streetcar Named Desire* (1951); *Elephant Walk* [footage remaining] (1953); *The Deep Blue Sea* (1955); *The Roman Spring of Mrs Stone* (1961); *Ship of Fools* (1965).

LEIGHTON, Margaret (1922–1976)

Classically trained stage actress who rose to prominence in British cinema at the end of the 1940s, often playing neurotic women. Her Hollywood roles included the part of Caddy Compson (opposite Yul Brynner) in *The Sound and the Fury*. JS

FILMS: *The Sound and the Fury* (1959); *The Best Man* (1964); *The Loved One* (1965); *7 Women* (1966); *The Madwoman of Chaillot* (1969).

LEWIS, Fiona (1946–)

British film actress whose Hollywood work has mainly included horror and fantasy roles with a comic twist. She was the 'evil' scientist in Joe Dante's *Innerspace*. MW

FILMS: *The Fearless Vampire Killers* (1967); *Where's Jack?* (1969); *Dr Phibes Rises Again* (1972); *Drum* (1976); *Stunts* (1977); *The Fury* (1978); *Wanda Nevada, Double Take* (1979);

Strange Behavior (1981); *Strange Invaders* (1983); *Innerspace* (1987).

LEYSSAC, Paul (unknown–1946)

Highly regarded Danish stage actor of French descent who also became known for his translations of Hans Christian Andersen. He appeared in a number of Hollywood films shot during World War II such as *Paris Calling*, in which he played a Resistance leader. HJW

FILMS: *Arise My Love* (1940); *Two-Faced Woman, Paris Calling* (1941); *Assignment in Brittany* (1943).

LHERMITTE, Thierry (1952–)

French comedy actor who, like Christian Clavier*, hailed from the 'Splendid' theatre tradition. He was cast as a stereotypical 'French lover' in *Until September* thanks to his playboy good looks and piercing blue eyes. More recently, he has appeared as a middle-aged philanderer who initiates Kate Hudson to Parisian mores in Merchant-Ivory's *Le Divorce*. VO

FILMS: *Until September* (1984); *Le Divorce* (2003).

LINDER, Max (Gabriel Maximilien Leuvielle) (1883–1925)

Linder worked in the US film industry twice, once in 1916–17 and again in 1920–1. Given the enormous global reputation he had achieved as the first popular film comic in the USA by 1910, a popularity that held firm in his *Max* series of one-reelers through 1914, it seems at first surprising that most of the American films in which Linder starred were disappointing. By 1917, however, a host of American film comics – Chaplin, Arbuckle, Normand, Fairbanks, Lloyd – had matched or surpassed him and could cater more easily to American tastes.

World War I provided the impetus for Linder's initial visit to the USA. Wartime conditions curtailed film production in France and forced companies to work with fewer financial and material resources. This, in conjunction with ill health (a severe bout of pneumonia suffered in voluntary service during the war), limited Linder's options, and, in late 1916, he jumped at the opportunity that a generous contract with Essanay seemed to offer that would require him to make one two-reel comedy per month for the following year. Unfortunately, Linder agreed to make his first two films in and around Essanay's Chicago studio, **337** and an unusually harsh winter so threatened his health that he moved to Los Angeles to make what would turn out to be his third and last film of his first American stay. None of these films were as profitable as hoped, and when pneumonia caught up with him again, Linder and Essanay mutually agreed to dissolve their contract; he returned to Europe and a Swiss sanatorium, where he hoped to recover his health.

After the war, a starring role in *Le Petit café* (1919) suggested that Linder's French acting career was on the rebound, but that proved illusory. Desperate to resume film-making, he decided to travel once more to the USA. Soliciting the help of friends (probably including Charlie Chaplin★), Linder risked much of his own money to set up a company in Los Angeles through which he could produce, direct and star in a series of feature-length comedies to be distributed by United Artists. This time, Linder

adapted much better to the American production system, and his first two films were profitable enough that he could mount a relatively lavish project, a spoof of Douglas Fairbanks' *The Three Musketeers* (1921), using sets left over from that film. Linder's *The Three Must-Get-Theres* was a hit not only because it exploited the earlier film's popularity but also because it craftily 'burlesqued' Fairbanks' persona and surrounding spectacle much in the way that the American star himself had mocked genre heroes at the start of his film career. Flush with success, Linder returned to France, but again ran into personal and professional difficulties. In November 1925, he and his young wife committed suicide in mysterious circumstances in a Paris hotel.
RA

FILMS: *Max Comes Across, Max Wants a Divorce, Max in a Taxi* (1917); *Be My Wife, Seven Years Bad Luck* (1921); *The Three Must-Get-Theres* (1922).

338 Max Linder and Charlie Chaplin: émigré actors in arms

LINDFORS, Viveca (1920–1996)

Swedish actress with a passionate and expressive emotional register. Viveca Lindfors' talent and sensual beauty were noticed while she was a drama student. She received an offer from Ufa in 1939, but instead made her first Swedish film in 1941. After two Italian films (1941–2), she arrived in Hollywood on a seven-year contract in 1945. Despite her vibrant sex appeal, her American career was slow in gaining momentum. It became, however, a remarkably long and productive one. She is best remembered today for her roles opposite Jean Hersholt★ in Nicholas Ray's *Run for Cover* and Stewart Granger★ in Fritz Lang's *Moonfleet*. YH

FILMS: *To the Victor, Adventures of Don Juan* (1948); *Night unto Night, Backfire* (1949); *No Sad Songs for Me, This Side of the Law, Dark City, The Flying Missile* (1950); *Journey into Light* (1951); *No Time for Flowers, The Raiders* (1952); *Run for Cover, Moonfleet* (1955); *The Halliday Brand* (1957); *I Accuse!, Weddings and Babies* (1958); *The Story of Ruth* (1960); *King of Kings* (1961); *No Exit* (1962); *The Damned, An Affair of the Skin* (1963); *Sylvia, Brainstorm* (1965); *Coming Apart* (1969); *Puzzle of a Downfall Child* (1970); *The Way We Were* (1973);

Swedish Viveca Lindfors' talent and sensual beauty earned her a long and productive career in Hollywood

Welcome to L.A. (1977); *Girlfriends, A Wedding* (1978); *Natural Enemies, Voices* (1979); *The Hand* (1981); *Creepshow* (1982); *Silent Madness* (1984); *The Sure Thing* (1985); *Rachel River, Unfinished Business* (1987); *Yellow Pages* (1988); *Forced March, Misplaced* (1989); *Exiled in America, The Exorcist III* (1990); *Zandalee, The Linguini Incident, Goin' to Chicago* (1991); *North of Pittsburgh* (1992); *Backstreet Justice, Stargate* (1994); *Last Summer in the Hamptons* (1995).

LLOYD, Doris (1896–1968)

Broadway success, rather than a brief spell as an ingénue lead in British films, earned Doris Lloyd a prolific career – spanning five decades – in Hollywood as a character actress specialising in women domiciled in high-society settings, both below stairs (*The Great Lie*) and above stairs (*The Sound of Music*). JB

FILMS: *The Lady, The Man from Red Gulch* (1925); *The Blackbird, Black Paradise, The Midnight Kiss, Exit Smiling* (1926); *The Auctioneer, The Broncho Twister, Is Zat So?, Rich but Honest, Lonesome Ladies, Two Girls Wanted, Come to My House* (1927); *The Trail of '98* (1928); *The Drake Case, The Careless Age, Disraeli* (1929); *Sarah and Son, Old English, Reno, Way for a Sailor, Charley's Aunt* (1930); *The Bachelor Father, Transgression, Bought, Waterloo Bridge, Devotion, Once a Lady* (1931); *Tarzan the Ape Man, Washington Masquerade, Back Street, A Farewell to Arms* (1932); *Robbers' Roost, Oliver Twist, Secrets, Looking Forward, A Study in Scarlet, Peg o' My Heart, Voltaire* (1933); *Long Lost Father, Glamour, Tarzan and His Mate, Kiss and Make Up, One Exciting Adventure, British Agent, Madame DuBarry, The Man Who Reclaimed His Head, Sisters under the Skin, She was a Lady, Dangerous Corner* (1934); *Strange Wives, Clive of India, A Shot in the Dark, The Woman in Red, Motive for Revenge, Becky Sharp, Peter Ibbetson, Mutiny on the Bounty, Kind Lady, Two for Tonight, Straight from the Heart, The Perfect Gentleman, A Feather in Her Hat, Chasing Yesterday* (1935); *Follow the Fleet, Mary of Scotland, The Luckiest Girl in the World, Too Many Parents, The Plough and the Stars, Don't Get Personal, Brilliant Marriage* (1936); *The Soldier and the Lady, Bulldog Drummond Escapes, Alcatraz Island, Tovarich* (1937); *The Black Doll, Lord Jeff, Port of Seven Seas, Letter of Introduction* (1938); *They Made Me a Criminal, I'm from Missouri, Murder is News, The Spellbinder, The Old Maid, First Love, The Private Lives of Elizabeth and Essex, Barricade, We are Not Alone, The Under-Pup* (1939); *Vigil in the Night, 'Til We Meet Again, The Boys from Syracuse, The Letter, The Lady with Red Hair, The Great Plane Robbery* **339**

(1940); *The Great Lie, Dr Jekyll and Mr Hyde, The Wolf Man, Suspicion, Shining Victory, Scotland Yard, Life with Henry, Keep 'Em Flying, International Squadron* (1941); *The Ghost of Frankenstein, Night Monster, Journey for Margaret, This Above All* (1942); *Eyes of the Underworld, Forever and a Day, Frankenstein Meets the Wolf Man, Two Tickets to London, Flesh and Fantasy, What a Woman!, No Place for a Lady, Mission to Moscow, The Constant Nymph* (1943); *The Lodger, Phantom Lady, Follow the Boys, The White Cliffs of Dover, The Invisible Man's Revenge, Frenchman's Creek, The Conspirators* (1944); *The House of Fear, Incendiary Blonde, Scotland Yard Investigator, Allotment Wives, My Name is Julia Ross, Molly and Me* (1945); *Three Strangers, To Each His Own, Kitty, Devotion, G.I. War Brides, Holiday in Mexico, The Jolson Story, Tarzan and the Leopard Woman, Sister Kenny, Of Human Bondage* (1946); *The Secret Life of Walter Mitty, The Imperfect Lady, Escape Me Never* (1947); *The Sign of the Ram* (1948); *The Red Danube* (1949); *Tyrant of the Sea* (1950); *Alice in Wonderland* [voice], *The Son of Dr Jekyll, Kind Lady* (1951); *The Prisoner of Zenda* (1952); *Young Bess* (1953); *The Black Shield of Falworth* (1954); *Interrupted Melody, A Man Called Peter* (1955); *The Swan* (1956); *Jeanne Eagels* (1957); *Midnight Lace, The Time Machine* (1960); *The Notorious Land-lady* (1962); *Mary Poppins* (1964); *The Sound of Music* (1965); *Rosie!* (1968).

LLOYD, Emily (1970–)

Lloyd came to international attention with her striking portrayal of a rebellious, foul-mouthed teenager in *Wish You Were Here* (1987). She was deluged with offers from American agencies and was launched in the USA with the kind of publicity blitz not seen for a teenage actress since the heyday of Tatum O'Neal. Lloyd was remade as an ersatz native star and assigned a series of thick American accents ranging from Brooklyn to Kentucky. None of her Hollywood films were particularly successful and the size of the parts and budgets of her subsequent American work has been slimmed down considerably. JB
FILMS: *Cookie, In Country* (1989); *Chicago Joe and the Showgirl* (1990); *Scorchers* (1991); *A River Runs through It* (1992); *Under the Hula Moon* (1995); *Dead Girl* (1996); *Welcome to Sarajevo, Livers Ain't Cheap, Boogie Boy* (1997).

LOCKWOOD, Margaret (Margaret Day) (1911–1990)

British actress who appeared in two US-financed films, among others, before starring in two substantial box-office hits for Gainsborough Studios – *Bank Holiday* and *The Lady Vanishes* (both 1938) – when she then looked set to become a leading UK star. But before these successes were consolidated, Twentieth Century-Fox used its close ties with Lockwood's employers – Fox had a co-production arrangement with Gainsborough and were major stockholders in their parent company Gaumont-British – to negotiate a star-exchange deal that took her to Hollywood. The timing of this move may have had something to do with the sudden wave of interest in British actresses on the other side of the Atlantic after Vivien Leigh's★ casting in *Gone with the Wind* (1939). This concurrent headline-grabbing event certainly contributed to a flurry of press interest upon Lockwood's arrival. Lockwood's six-week stay at Fox was an unhappy one. She felt more at home with Paramount, who borrowed her for one film and took an option on her services for further pictures. Her return to Britain in the interim period turned out to be permanent and she subsequently became a major star there during the war years. Among other roles, she had the lead in Carol Reed's *Girl in the News* funded by Fox. Lockwood specialised for a time in feisty bad-girl parts in costume dramas after her notable success in Gainsborough's *The Wicked Lady* (1945). When this film was widely distributed in the USA, Fox's interest in Lockwood was rekindled and they offered her an ostensibly similar leading role in Otto Preminger's upcoming *Forever Amber* (1947), but once bitten, the actress had become twice shy. JB
FILMS: *Someday* (1935); *Irish for Luck* (1936); *Susannah of the Mounties, Rulers of the Sea* (1939); *Girl in the News* (1941).

LODER, John (John Muir Lowe) (1898-1988)

John Loder began his acting career in Germany in the 1920s as an extra in an Alexander Korda film alongside Marlene Dietrich★. He made one film at Elstree Studios, was signed by Paramount in the late 1920s and appeared in a number of Hollywood films in the early sound period. He then returned to his native Britain and carved out a solid career during the 1930s as a supporting actor in films that included the Fox British production *Rolling in Money* (1934) and key titles of the day, such as *The Private Life of Henry VIII* (1933) and Hitchcock's *Sabotage* (1936). He moved back to the USA in 1940 but despite appearances in major films such as *How Green Was My Valley* and *Now, Voy-*

ager failed to establish anything more than a supporting-role status in Hollywood. He became an American citizen in 1947 and concentrated thereafter on a Broadway career, before returning to films in Britain in the late 1950s. TR

FILMS: *The Racketeer, Rich People, Love, Live and Laugh, Her Private Affair, The Unholy Night, Sunset Pass, The Doctor's Secret, Black Waters* (1929); *One Night at Susie's, Sweethearts and Wives, The Man Hunter, The Second Floor Mystery, Lilies of the Field* (1930); *Seas Beneath, On the Loose* (1931); *Rolling in Money* (1934); *Meet Maxwell Archer, Murder Will Out, Tin Pan Alley, Diamond Frontier, Adventure in Diamonds* (1940); *Scotland Yard, How Green Was My Valley, One Night in Lisbon, Confirm or Deny* (1941); *Gentleman Jim, Now, Voyager, Eagle Squadron* (1942); *The Gorilla Man, Old Acquaintance, The Mysterious Doctor, Murder on the Waterfront, Adventure in Iraq* (1943); *Abroad with Two Yanks, Passage to Marseille, The Hairy Ape* (1944); *The Woman Who Came Back, Jealousy, A Game of Death, The Fighting Guardsman, The Brighton Strangler* (1945); *One More Tomorrow, Dishonored Lady, The Wife of Monte Cristo* (1946); *Gideon's Day* (1958).

LOLLOBRIGIDA, Gina (Luigiana Lollobrigida) (1927–)

Considered Italy's postwar embodiment of Mediterranean beauty, Gina Lollobrigida was offered a contract by Hollywood tycoon Howard Hughes three years after her first appearance on Italian screens as a belly dancer in *Aquila nera/Black Ostrich* (1946). However, no film roles were forthcoming and after a long legal dispute with Hughes, Lollobrigida's debut in an American film came in Carol Reed's Hollywood directing debut, *Trapeze*. She arrived in Hollywood as one of Europe's most popular sex goddesses and rapidly gained popularity among American audiences. Lollobrigida soon became one of the archetypes of late 1950s feminine glamour and beauty, perhaps at the cost of losing some of her original spontaneous charm. Together with Yul Brynner, she starred in King Vidor's Old Testament epic *Solomon and Sheba*, hoping that the portrayal of the exotic queen would gain her more prestige as an actress. Next, she appeared in *Never So Few*, a World War II drama set in Burma, but her performance as Carla, Frank Sinatra's lover, was not well received by either critics or audiences. During the 1960s, Lollobrigida's appearances in Hollywood films were mainly in romantic comedies such as *Come September* and *Strange Bedfellows*, both of which co-starred Rock

Hudson. After retiring from acting in the early 1970s, she returned to work in the USA in 1984, where she appeared in the television series *Falcon Crest*. CBu

FILMS: *Trapeze* (1956); *Solomon and Sheba, Never So Few* (1959); *Go Naked in the World, Come September* (1961); *Woman of Straw, Strange Bedfellows* (1964); *Hotel Paradiso* (1966); *The Private Navy of Sgt O'Farrell* (1968); *Buona Sera Mrs Campbell* (1969); *King, Queen, Knave* (1972).

LOM, Herbert (Herbert Charles Angelo Kuchacevich ze Schluderpacheru) (1917–)

Czech actor who has been based in Britain since the invasion of his homeland in 1939. Lom was promoted as 'Britain's Charles Boyer' for a while and thereafter became a scene-stealing character actor in international productions, most famously as Commissioner Dreyfus in the *Pink Panther* series. His stints in Hollywood cinema have seldom exceeded single-picture deals playing eccentric foreigners. RJK

FILMS: *The Young Mr Pitt* (1942); *The Dark Tower* (1943); *Hotel Reserve* (1944); *Night and the City, The Black Rose* (1950); *The Man Who Watched Trains Go By* (1953); *War and Peace* (1956); *Fire Down Below* (1957); *The Roots of Heaven, I Accuse!* (1958); *Third Man on the Mountain, I Aim at the Stars, The Big Fisherman* (1959); *Spartacus* (1960); *El Cid, Mysterious Island* (1961); *A Shot in the Dark* (1964); *Return from the Ashes* (1965); *Gambit, Our Man in Marrakesh* (1966); *The Karate Killers* (1967); *Assignment to Kill, Villa Rides!* (1968); *Murders in the Rue Morgue* (1971); *The Pink Panther Strikes Again* (1976); *Revenge of the Pink Panther* (1978); *Hopscotch, The Man with Bogart's Face* (1980); *Trail of the Pink Panther* (1982); *Curse of the Pink Panther, The Dead Zone* (1983); *King Solomon's Mines* (1985); *Skeleton Coast, Going Bananas* (1987); *River of Death, Master of Dragonard Hill* (1989); *Son of the Pink Panther* (1993).

LOREN, Sophia (Sofia Scicolone) (1934–)

Italy's biggest ever film star arrived in Hollywood preceded by a strong publicity campaign referring to her appearance in several American productions shot in Europe. Her acting talents and her good spoken English allowed her to transcend the label of the Italian sex goddess – something that Gina Lollobrigida*, her contemporary who also emigrated to the USA during the same period, never managed to overcome.

Sophia Loren: Italian 'sex goddess'

In her actual Hollywood film debut, the modern tragedy *Desire under the Elms*, she appeared as Anna Cabot, the young third wife of a farmer who engages in a semi-incestuous love affair with her husband's son (Anthony Perkins). Although some thought Loren seemed out of place within the American farming milieu, her work was also praised for the variety of credible emotions that she managed to expose. Throughout her Hollywood career, Loren co-starred with some of the most important male stars of the period. She worked twice with Anthony Quinn: first in *The Black Orchid*, in which she appeared as a pretty widow of Italian origin, and then later on in George Cukor's Western satire *Heller in Pink Tights*, in which Loren and Quinn battled side by side for the survival of a travelling theatre. She also performed twice alongside Cary Grant★: first in *The Pride and the Passion*, a film about the Spanish resistance to the invading French legions in 1810, and then again, one year later, in the romantic comedy *Houseboat*, where Loren played the part of the sexy Italian maid who conquers the hearts of both Grant's widower and his children.

After 1960, Loren returned to Italy, where she continued working in American-financed films, such as *It Started in*

Naples, another notable romantic comedy co-starring Clark Gable. She also appeared in the epic *El Cid* playing the part of Jimena, the wife of the eponymous legendary Spanish hero (Charlton Heston), and in the big-budget production *The Fall of the Roman Empire*, where she was Lucilla, Emperor Marcus Aurelius' unhappy daughter. In the musical *Man of La Mancha*, based on Cervantes' classic novel, she played the dual role of Dulcinea and Aldonza. While Peter O'Toole★ as Don Quixote had to be dubbed for the musical numbers, Loren sang hers. In 1961, she received the Academy Award for Best Actress for her performance in Vittorio De Sica's★ *La ciociara/Two Women* (1960), becoming the first actress to win this Academy Award for a role in a foreign-language film. In 1991, she received a second Academy Award for Lifetime Achievement. Latterday Hollywood appearances have been in the comedy *Grumpier Old Men* and Robert Altman's *Prêt-à-Porter/Ready to Wear*, where she played opposite Marcello Mastroianni★, her partner in several acclaimed Italian films. CBu

FILMS: *Boy on a Dolphin, Legend of the Lost, The Pride and the Passion* (1957); *Desire under the Elms, Houseboat, The Key, The Black Orchid* (1958); *That Kind of Woman* (1959); *The Millionairess, It Started in Naples, Heller in Pink Tights, A Breath of Scandal* (1960); *El Cid* (1961); *The Fall of the Roman Empire* (1964); *Operation Crossbow, Lady L* (1965); *Judith, Arabesque* (1966); *Man of La Mancha* (1972); *Brass Target* (1978); *Prêt-à-Porter/Ready to Wear* (1994); *Grumpier Old Men* (1995); *Between Strangers* (2002).

LORRE, Peter (László Löwenstein) (1904–1964)
Born in Rózsahegy, Austro-Hungary (now Ružomberok, Slovakia), the diminutive, baby-faced, bug-eyed Lorre performed Brecht in 1920s Berlin theatre, before gaining international attention playing the child killer in Fritz Lang's *M* (1931). The role brought offers from Hollywood, which Lorre declined due to fear of typecasting. When the Nazis came to power, however, the Jewish actor fled via Paris to London – where he starred as another murderer in Hitchcock's *The Man Who Knew Too Much* (1934) – and then, in 1935, to the USA. Columbia signed Lorre but was initially unable to identify a workable part for him. He was loaned to MGM for his American debut as the bald-headed Dr Gogol in Karl Freund's expressionistic horror *Mad Love*. After playing Raskolnikov in Columbia's *Crime and Punishment*, Lorre applied for American citizenship, before

undertaking a return trip to Britain to appear in Hitchcock's *Secret Agent* (1936). Four years at Twentieth Century-Fox followed, with Lorre squinting his way through eight popular Mr Moto mysteries. However, it was as Joel Cairo in *The Maltese Falcon* that Lorre first gained appreciation as a character actor of conspicuously strange roles in A-pictures. His pairing opposite hulking Sydney Greenstreet★ – frequently likened to a devilish Laurel and Hardy – proved box-office dynamite and eight further Warner Bros. pictures together followed, including *Casablanca*. In 1950, Lorre staged a fateful return to Germany, where his image had been vilified during the Third Reich in the propaganda film *Der ewige Jude/ The Eternal Jew* (1940). Lorre scripted, directed and starred in the vehemently anti-Fascist *Der Verlorene/ The Lost One* (1951), which went largely ignored, leaving the actor dejected, unemployed and suffering from a glandular condition that caused him to gain fifty kilograms. Returning to the USA, Lorre hereafter specialised in tragicomic clowns and rotund stooges, and earned the affection of a new generation through his scene-stealing performances in Roger Corman's Poe movies. An enduring cult favourite, Lorre's wheedling accent has been imitated endlessly. RJK

FILMS: *Mad Love, Crime and Punishment* (1935); *Crack-Up, Think Fast, Mr Moto, Thank You, Mr Moto, Nancy Steele is Missing, Lancer Spy* (1937); *Mr Moto's Gamble, I'll Give a Million, Mysterious Mr Moto, Mr Moto Takes a Chance* (1938); *Mr Moto's Last Warning, Danger Island, Mr Moto Takes a Vacation* (1939); *Strange Cargo, I Was an Adventuress, Stranger on the Third Floor, You'll Find Out, Island of Doomed Men* (1940); *They Met in Bombay, The Maltese Falcon, Mr District Attorney, The Face behind the Mask* (1941); *All through the Night, In this Our Life, Invisible Agent, The Boogie Man Will Get You, Casablanca* (1942); *The Cross of Lorraine, The Constant Nymph, Background to Danger* (1943); *The Mask of Dimitrios, The Conspirators, Arsenic and Old Lace* [produced and copywritten 1941], *Passage to Marseille, Hollywood Canteen* (1944); *Confidential Agent, Hotel Berlin* (1945); *Three Strangers, Black Angel, The Chase, The Verdict, The Beast with Five Fingers* (1946); *My Favorite Brunette* (1947); *Casbah* (1948); *Rope of Sand* (1949); *Quicksand* (1950); *Beat the Devil* (1953); *20,000 Leagues under the Sea* (1954); *Around the World in Eighty Days, Meet Me in Las Vegas, Congo Crossing* (1956); *Silk Stockings, The Story of Mankind, The Sad Sack, Hell Ship Mutiny, The Buster Keaton Story* (1957); *The Big Circus* (1959); *Scent of Mystery* (1960); *Voyage to the Bottom of the Sea* (1961); *Tales of Terror, Five Weeks in a Balloon* (1962); *The Raven, The Comedy of Terrors, Muscle Beach Party, The Patsy* (1964).

Peter Lorre's distinctive features led to renown as a character actor in numerous Hollywood features such as *The Maltese Falcon* (1941) and *Casablanca* (1942)

LORY, Jacques (1904–1947)

French journalist for popular film weekly *Cinémonde* and bit-part player – often uncredited – in Hollywood films of the 1930s and 1940s. Lory was usually employed as a French character or in productions with a French theme. CH

FILMS: *The Merry Widow* (1934); *The Road to Glory* (1936); *Maytime, The King and the Chorus Girl, I Met Him in Paris, Café Métropole, The Firefly* (1937); *Marie Antoinette, The Courtship of the Newt, Fools for Scandal, Dramatic School, Suez* (1938); *Mr Moto's Last Warning, The Story of Vernon and Irene Castle, Bulldog Drummond's Bride* (1939); *The Fighting 69th* (1940); *Dick Tracy vs. Crime Inc.* (1941); *Secret Service in Darkest Africa, Paris after Dark, The Leopard Man* (1943); *Action in Arabia, The Falcon in Hollywood* (1944); *Cornered* (1945).

LOVE, Montagu(e) (1877–1943)

This British stage actor made a solitary film appearance in his native country before relocating to the USA in 1913, where he became one of the most regular and memorable villains in silent and early sound cinema. JB

FILMS: *Hearts in Exile, The Face in the Moonlight, Sunday, A Royal Family, The Greater Will, The Antique Dealer* (1915); *The Devil's Toy, A Woman's Way, Husband and Wife, Friday the 13th, The Gilded Cage, The Hidden Scar, The Scarlet Oath, Bought and Paid For, The Men She Married, The Challenge* (1916); *The Dancer's Peril, Forget-Me-Not, Yankee Pluck, The Brand of Satan, The Guardian, Rasputin, the Black Monk, The Dormant Power, The Awakening, The Good for Nothing, The Volunteer* (1917); *Broken Ties, The Cross Bearer, Vengeance, Stolen Orders, The Cabaret, To Him that Hath, The Grouch* (1918); *The Rough Neck, The Hand Invisible, The Quickening Flame, Three Green Eyes, Through the Toils, A Broadway Saint, The Steel King, She's Everywhere* (1919); *The World and His Wife, The Riddle: Woman, The Wrong Woman, The Place of the Honeymoons, Man's Plaything* (1920); *Shams of Society, The Case of Becky, Forever, Love's Redemption* (1921); *The Beauty Shop, What's Wrong with Women?, Secrets of Paris, The Darling of the Rich* (1922); *The Leopardess, The Eternal City* (1923); *Restless Wives, Roulette, Week End Husbands, The Son of the Sahara, Love of Women, Sinners in Heaven, Who's Cheating?* (1924); *The Mad Marriage, The Ancient Highway, The Desert's Price* (1925); *Hands Up!, Brooding Eyes, Out of the Storm, The Social Highwayman, The Son of the Sheik, Don Juan, The Silent Lover* (1926); *One Hour of Love, The Night of Love, The King of Kings, The Tender Hour, Rose of the Golden West, Jesse James, Good Time Charley, The Haunted Ship* (1927); *The Noose, The Devil's Skipper, The Hawk's Nest, The Haunted House, The Wind* (1928); *Synthetic Sin, The Last Warning, Silks and Saddles, Bulldog Drummond, A Most Immoral Lady, The Voice Within, The Mysterious Island, Midstream, Her Private Life, The Divine Lady, Charming Sinners* (1929); *Love Comes Along, Double Cross Roads, A Notorious Affair, Inside the Lines, Reno, Kismet, The Cat Creeps, Outward Bound, Back Pay* (1930); *Alexander Hamilton, The Lion and the Lamb* (1931); *Stowaway, Love Bound, The Silver Lining, The Riding Tornado, The Midnight Lady, Out of Singapore, Vanity Fair, The Bride's Bereavement* (1932); *The Mystic Hour* (1933); *His Double Life, Menace, Limehouse Blues* (1934); *Clive of India, The Man Who Broke the Bank at Monte Carlo, The Crusades* (1935); *Sutter's Gold, The Country Doctor, Sing, Baby, Sing, The White Angel, Reunion, One in a Million, Lloyds of London, Hi Gaucho, Champagne Charlie* (1936); *Parnell, The Prince and the Pauper, The Prisoner of Zenda, The Life of Emile Zola, A Damsel in Distress, Adventure's End, Tovarich, London by Night* (1937); *The Buccaneer, The Adventures of Robin Hood, The Fighting Devil Dogs, Professor Beware, Kidnapped, If I Were King* (1938); *Gunga Din, Juarez, The Man in the Iron Mask, Rulers of the Sea, We are Not Alone, Sons of Liberty* (1939); *Northwest Passage, Private Affairs, All This, and Heaven Too, Dr Erlich's Magic Bullet, The Mark of Zorro, North West Mounted Police, The Lone Wolf Strikes, The Son of Monte Cristo, The Sea Hawk, Hudson's Bay, A Dispatch from Reuters* (1940); *The Devil and Miss Jones, Shining Victory, Lady for a Night* (1941); *Sherlock Holmes and the Voice of Terror, Tennessee Johnson, The Remarkable Andrew* (1942); *Forever and a Day, Fighting Devil Dogs, Wings over the Pacific, Holy Matrimony, The Constant Nymph* (1943); *Devotion, A Scandal in Paris* (1946).

LUGOSI, Bela (Béla Ferenc Dezsö Blaskó) (1882–1956)

Hungarian stage and screen actor forever associated with the role of Dracula. After supporting the failed Béla Kun socialist uprising, Lugosi fled to Germany in 1919, before becoming a ship's engineer and entering New Orleans as an illegal immigrant in 1920. Naturalised as an American in 1921, Lugosi at first worked in New York Hungarian-language theatre, and later appeared on Broadway and in silents shot on the East Coast. He starred (and toured) from 1927 in the Broadway version of *Dracula* and played over 1,000 performances before receiving attention from Hollywood. Following initial suave supporting roles, Lugosi gained international stardom in Universal's movie adaptation of *Dracula*. His faltering melodic accent, Old World sophistication and matinée-idol looks effectively redefined Hollywood horror in terms of an evil couched within sexual seduction, to the extent that in the mid-1930s, Lugosi's fan mail from women exceeded that of Clark Gable. However, the actor became immediately typecast and went jobbing from film to film without ever being able to secure a long-term contract. Paid just $500 per week on *Dracula* – one-third of third-billed David Manners' salary – Lugosi thereafter commanded $1,500 per week, although often on poverty-row productions offering less than two weeks' employment. After becoming an American citizen

Hungarian-born Bela Lugosi gained international stardom in Universal's adaptation of *Dracula* (1931)

in 1931, Lugosi helped found the Screen Actors Guild. In the lean years of the 1950s, he became the first Hollywood personality to 'go public' about his drug addiction and rehabilitation. Increasingly overlooked during his lifetime, Lugosi has subsequently earned a huge cult following fêting him as a Western cultural icon. In 1994, Martin Landau ironically received an Academy Award – an honour that Hollywood would never have dreamed of bestowing upon Lugosi – for his portrayal of the actor as a Hollywood has-been in Tim Burton's historically questionable *Ed Wood* (1993). RJK

FILMS: *The Silent Command* (1923); *The Rejected Woman* (1924); *The Midnight Girl, Daughters Who Pay* (1925); *Punchinello* (1926); *How to Handle Women* (1927); *The Veiled Woman, Prisoners, The Thirteenth Chair* (1929); *Such Men are Dangerous, Wild Company, Renegades, Viennese Nights, Oh, for a Man* (1930); *Dracula, Women of All Nations, Fifty Million Frenchmen, Broadminded, The Black Camel* (1931); *Intimate Interviews, Murders in the Rue Morgue, White Zombie, Chandu the Magician* (1932); *The Death Kiss, Night of Terror, International House, The Whispering Shadow* [serial], *Island of Lost Souls, Hollywood on Parade No. A8, The Devil's in Love* (1933); *The Black Cat, Gift of Gab, The Return of Chandu* [serial], *Screen Snapshots No. 11* (1934); *Best Man Wins, The Mysterious Mr Wong, The Raven, Murder by Television, Mark of the Vampire* (1935); *House of 1,000 Candles* [footage deleted], *The Invisible Ray, Revolt of the Zombies* [in footage from *White Zombie* (1932)], *Shadow of Chinatown* [serial], *Postal Inspector* (1936); *SOS Coastguard* [serial] (1937); *Son of Frankenstein, The Gorilla, Ninotchka, The Phantom Creeps* [serial] (1939); *The Saint's Double Trouble, Black Friday, You'll Find Out* (1940); *The Devil Bat, Spooks Run Wild, The Wolf Man, The Invisible Ghost, The Black Cat* (1941); *Black Dragons, The Ghost of Frankenstein, The Corpse Vanishes, Night Monster, Bowery at Midnight* (1942); *Frankenstein Meets the Wolf Man, The Ape Man, Dr Terror's House of Horrors* [in footage from *White Zombie* (1932)], *Ghosts on the Loose* (1943); *Return of the Vampire, Voodoo Man, Return of the Ape Man, One Body Too Many* (1944); *Zombies on Broadway, The Body Snatcher* (1945); *Genius at Work* (1946); *Scared to Death* (1947); *Abbott and Costello Meet Frankenstein* (1948); *Bela Lugosi Meets a Brooklyn Gorilla* (1952); *Glen or Glenda* (1953); *Bride of the Monster, The Black Sleep* (1956); *Lock Up Your Daughters* [released in UK only], *Plan 9 from Outer Space* (1959).

LUGUET, André (1892–1979)

Experienced French stage actor who specialised in suave, charming male leads. Due to the success of his role in Jacques Feyder's MGM French-language version *Le Spectre vert* (1930), but despite his bilingual status, Luguet was signed by Irving Thalberg to appear in other Hollywood French-language titles. Dissatisfied, he moved to a contract with Warner Bros. and appeared in a succession of English-language roles as elegant and charming noblemen. He returned briefly to Hollywood at the end of his career. AP

FILMS: *The Mad Genius* (1931); *The Man Who Played God, Jewell Robbery, Love is a Racket* (1932); *The Roots of Heaven* (1959); *Paris Blues* (1962); *Love is a Ball* (1963).

LUKAS, Paul (Pál Lukács) (1887–1971)

Lukas, whose soft voice always retained the accent of his native Hungary, epitomised Central European sophistication and sartorial elegance in Hollywood films from the 1920s to the late 1960s. He provided an authoritative presence both in benignly patriarchal roles (as in *Berlin Express*

Paul Lukas: the epitome of central European sophistication

and *20,000 Leagues under the Sea*) and as a suave villain (e.g. in Jacques Tourneur's *Experiment Perilous*, where he plays Hedy Lamarr's★ sadistic husband). Prior to his prolific Hollywood career, Lukas had been a prestigious stage actor and matinée idol in Europe, working with Max Reinhardt in Vienna and Berlin. Lukas also appeared in numerous Austrian, German and Hungarian films from 1915, frequently working with directors Alexander Korda and Márton Garas. The producer Adolph Zukor, of Hungarian origin himself, spotted Lukas while on business talent-hunting in Europe, and brought the actor to Hollywood in 1927 on a contract with Paramount. During the 1930s, Lukas filmed both in the USA and Britain, where he gave a memorable performance as a sinister doctor and spymaster in Alfred Hitchcock's *The Lady Vanishes* (1938). Lukas also pursued a stage career in the USA, which culminated in phenomenal success as an anti-Nazi leader in the film adaptation of Lillian Hellman's play *Watch on the Rhine*. Lukas' performance earned him an Academy Award for Best Actor, and the New York Film Critics Award. Lukas was a prominent member of Hollywood's Hungarian émigré community, which also included the director

Michael Curtiz and fellow actor Bela Lugosi★, and which organised cultural events and supported anti-Nazi causes during World War II. TB

FILMS: *Two Lovers, Three Sinners, Hot News, Loves of an Actress, Night Watch, The Woman from Moscow, Manhattan Cocktail, The Shopworn Angel* (1928); *The Wolf of Wall Street, Illusion, Halfway to Heaven* (1929); *Slightly Scarlet, Young Eagles, The Benson Murder Case, The Devil's Holiday, Grumpy, Anybody's Woman, The Right to Love, Behind the Make-Up* (1930); *Unfaithful, The Vice Squad, City Streets, Beloved Bachelor, Working Girls, Women Love Once, Tomorrow and Tomorrow, Strictly Dishonorable* (1931); *No One Man, Downstairs, A Passport to Hell, Thunder Below* (1932); *By Candlelight, Grand Slam, The Kiss before the Mirror, Secret of the Blue Room, Little Women, Sing, Sinner, Sing, Rockabye, Captured!* (1933); *The Countess of Monte Cristo, Glamour, Affairs of a Gentleman, The Fountain, Gift of Gab, I Give My Love* (1934); *The Casino Murder Case, Age of Indiscretion, Father Brown, Detective, The Three Musketeers, I Found Stella Parish* (1935); *Ladies in Love, Dodsworth* (1936); *Espionage* (1937); *Confessions of a Nazi Spy, Captain Fury* (1939); *Strange Cargo, The Ghost Breakers* (1940); *They Dare Not Love, The Monster and the Girl* (1941); *Watch on the Rhine, Hostages, Don't Be a Sucker* (1943); *Address Unknown, Experiment Perilous, Uncertain Glory* (1944); *Deadline at Dawn, Temptation* (1946); *Berlin Express* (1948); *Kim* (1950); *20,000 Leagues under the Sea* (1954); *The Roots of Heaven* (1958); *Scent of Mystery* (1960); *Four Horsemen of the Apocalypse, Tender is the Night* (1962); *Fun in Acapulco, 55 Days at Peking* (1963); *Lord Jim* (1965); *Sol Madrid* (1968).

LUNDGREN, Dolph (Hans Lundgren) (1959–)

With nearly thirty films to his credit, the six-foot-five, 230–40 pound Swedish actor Dolph Lundgren is popular worldwide for his film (and straight-to-video) action roles, though he has also starred in a number of thrillers and appeared (as himself) in the German romantic comedy *Sunny Side Up* (1994). Success has been primarily as a villain in parts opposite Sylvester Stallone in *Rocky IV*, and Jean-Claude van Damme★ in *Universal Soldier*.

Lundgren was a weak and skinny child and turned to martial arts during adolescence. He now holds several black belts in karate and has won the European heavyweight championship and the Australian heavyweight division titles. With no acting training and a previous career in modelling swimsuits and sportswear, Lundgren gained his first screen role in 1985, a bit part in the James Bond film *A View to a Kill*, thanks to co-star and former partner Grace Jones. After failing an audition for *Rambo III*, his big break came when he was chosen for the part of the evil Drago in *Rocky IV*.

Lundgren generally plays working class and/or military heroes. These are most often loners and some have African or African-American sidekicks. Other noteworthy screen partners or opponents include Brandon Lee in *Showdown in Little Tokyo* and Keanu Reeves in *Johnny Mnemonic*. The actor's enemies are cold-blooded Soviets, smelly East Germans and nasty South Africans. They are usually, but not always, white. In early films, there were no love interests. As Lundgren said in relation to *Universal Soldier*, 'my romance was with my machine gun'. In later films, characters do occasionally garner girlfriends. Lundgren is multilingual and usually plays Americans who speak perfect, accent-free English, although has also excelled as Soviets (*Red Scorpion* and *Rocky IV*) and East Germans (*Pentathlon*). Critics have commented on the association between the tanned and toned muscled stars of the 1980s and 1990s and a Californian identity that links crypto-fascism and Christianity. Clearly, the fact that Lundgren is blond, unlike his Hollywood counterparts Sylvester Stallone and Arnold Schwarzenegger★, only adds weight to this particular form of Aryan appeal.

In screen fights, Lundgren throws punches or shoots guns rather than employing martial-arts moves. As he puts it, 'if you're my size, it looks corny to throw all those high kicks'. His deep, deadpan delivery and the relative absence of dialogue generally make his intentions hard to distinguish. It is not surprising, therefore, that Lundgren is often cast as a robot or alien in films like *Universal Soldier*, *Johnny Mnemonic* and *I Come in Peace*. He has also played leading roles in films based on toy lines (*Masters of the Universe*) and comic books (*The Punisher*).

Screen framing often underlines Lundgren's size. In *Red Scorpion*, he dwarfs the mountains behind him. Occasionally, in films like *Showdown in Little Tokyo* and *The Punisher*, audiences are treated to rear nudity but, more frequently, spectacle is tied to torture. That Lundgren always bursts his bonds and frequently leads others to independence relates to Christian traditions of representation that offer the suffering white male body as spectacle. In *Johnny Mnemonic*, he

is even dressed and coiffed to look like a Sunday School Christ, a mode of representation that also evokes colonial traditions of the great white leader. Whether he is assigned Anglo-American, German or Russian passports or whether he is hero or villain, Lundgren is therefore clearly anchored in a persona that is stamped stolidly and solidly by Northern European cultural values. CHo

FILMS: *A View to a Kill*, *Rocky IV* (1985); *Masters of the Universe* (1987); *Red Scorpion*, *The Punisher* (1989); *I Come in Peace*, *Cover Up* (1990); *Showdown in Little Tokyo* (1991); *Universal Soldier* (1992); *Joshua Tree* (1993); *Pentathlon*, *Men of War* (1994); *Hidden Assassin*, *Johnny Mnemonic* (1995); *The Peacekeeper* (1997); *The Minion* (1998); *Sweepers*, *Bridge of Dragons*, *Storm Catcher* (1999); *Jill the Ripper*, *The Last Patrol*, *Captured* (2000); *Retrograde*, *The Defender* (2004).

LYS, Lya (Natalia Lyecht) (1907–1986)

French actress born in Berlin best known for her leading role in Buñuel's *L'Âge d'or* (1930). After a few French versions of multi-language films such as *Buster se marie* (1931) (USA: *Parlour, Bedroom and Bath*), she appeared in supporting roles in a variety of American films. MB/GV

FILMS: *Clear All Wires!*, *Jimmy and Sally*, *The Big Brain* (1933); *The Lives of a Bengal Lancer*, *The Vagabond Lady* (1935); *My Dear Miss Aldricht*, *The Great Gambini* (1937); *The Young in Heart*, *Confessions of a Nazi Spy*, *The Return of Doctor X* (1939); *Murder in the Air* (1940).

MACGINNIS, Niall (1913–1978)

Ruddy-faced Irish character actor who played a variety of supporting film roles in American-funded productions shot in Europe. He played the Satanic cult leader in Jacques Tourneur's *Night of the Demon*. RB

FILMS: *The Hundred Pound Window* (1944); *No Highway* (1951); *Knights of the Round Table*, *Martin Luther* (1953); *Hell below Zero*, *Betrayed* (1954); *Helen of Troy*, *Alexander the Great*, *Lust for Life* (1956); *Night of the Demon* (1957); *Tarzan's Greatest Adventure*, *Shake Hands with the Devil*, *The Nun's Story* (1959); *A Terrible Beauty*, *In the Nick*, *Kidnapped* (1960); *Face in the Rain* (1963); *Becket*, *The Truth about Spring* (1964); *The Spy Who Came in from the Cold*, *The War Lord* (1965); *A Man Could Get Killed* (1966); *The Shoes of the Fisherman* (1968); *Sinful Davey*, *Krakatoa, East of Java* (1969); *The Kremlin Letter*, *Darling Lili* (1970); *The Mackintosh Man* (1973).

MACGOWRAN, Jack (1918–1973)

Distinguished Irish actor best known for his stage performances in Samuel Beckett plays. He died making *The Exorcist*, his final Hollywood film. RB

FILMS: *The Quiet Man* (1952); *The Rising of the Moon* (1957); *Darby O'Gill and the Little People* (1959); *Tom Jones* (1963); *The Ceremony* (1964); *Young Cassidy, Lord Jim, Doctor Zhivago* (1965); *How I Won the War, The Fearless Vampire Killers* (1967); *Start the Revolution without Me* (1970); *The Exorcist* (1973).

MACKAILL, Dorothy (1903–1990)

Versatile, former English dancer who became a silent Hollywood star of the 1920s via Broadway. While the majority of her roles were in light comedies, Mackaill achieved her major breakthrough playing a drug addict in *The Man Who Came Back*. Although she made the transition to early talkies with some success, her contract with First National was not renewed in 1931. Mackaill subsequently flitted between the studios, but diminishing returns eventually led to her premature retirement. MF

FILMS: *Bits of Life, The Lotus Eater* (1921); *A Woman's Woman, The Streets of New York, The Inner Man* (1922); *Mighty Lak' a Rose, The Broken Violin, The Fighting Blade, The Fair Cheat, His Children's Children, Twenty-One, The Next Corner* (1923); *What Shall I Do?, The Man Who Came Back, The Painted Lady, The Mine with the Iron Door* (1924); *The Bridge of Sighs, Chickie, The Making of O'Malley, Shore Leave, One Year to Live, Joanna* (1925); *The Dancer of Paris, Ranson's Folly, Subway Sadie, Just Another Blonde* (1926); *The Lunatic at Large, Convoy, Smile, Brother, Smile, The Crystal Cup, Man Crazy* (1927); *Ladies' Night in a Turkish Bath, Lady Be Good, The Whip, The Waterfront, The Barker* (1928); *His Captive Woman, Children of the Ritz, Two Weeks Off, Hard to Get, The Great Divide, The Love Racket* (1929); *Strictly Modern, The Flirting Widow, The Office Wife, Man Trouble, Bright Lights, Once a Sinner* (1930); *Kept Husbands, Their Mad Moment, The Reckless Hour, Safe in Hell* (1931); *No Man of Her Own, Love Affair* (1932); *The Chief, Picture Brides, Neighbors' Wives* (1933); *Curtain at Eight, Cheaters* (1934).

MACNEE, Patrick (1922–)

While to most he will first and foremost always be the
348 dapper Mr Steed from British television's *The Avengers*,

Macnee has also appeared in numerous supporting roles and cameos on both sides of the Atlantic. MW

FILMS: *Until They Sail, Les Girls* (1957); *Mission of Danger* (1959); *Dead of Night* (1977); *Battlestar Galactica* (1978); *The Sea Wolves* (1980); *The Hot Touch, The Creature Wasn't Nice, The Howling, Sweet 16* (1981); *Young Doctors in Love* (1982); *This is Spinal Tap* (1984); *A View to a Kill* (1985); *Waxwork* (1988); *Eye of the Widow, Cult People, Lobster Man from Mars, Masque of the Red Death, Transformations* (1989); *Incident at Victoria Falls* (1991); *Waxwork II: Lost in Time* (1992); *The Avengers* (1998); *The Low Budget Time Machine* (2003).

MAGEE, Patrick (1924–1982)

Steely-eyed Northern Irish performer who considered cinema a necessary evil to augment his stage actor's salary. He was often typecast as a villain in horror or crime films. RB

FILMS: *The Young Racers, Dementia 13* (1963); *Die, Monster, Die!, Portrait in Terror* (1965); *Hard Contract* (1969); *A Clockwork Orange, The Trojan Women* (1971); *Tales from the Crypt, Young Winston* (1972); *Lady Ice* (1973); *Telefon* (1977); *Rough Cut* (1980).

MAGNANI, Anna (1908–1973)

Hollywood never offered Anna Magnani (affectionately known in Italy as Nannarella) the opportunity to match her extraordinary importance in her native cinema. She had been a well-known, popular star since the late 1930s, but she was propelled to international fame when she starred in Roberto Rossellini's *Roma città aperta/Rome, Open City* (1945), probably the best-known neo-realist film (she had a long relationship with Rossellini that came to an end when he began his infamous affair with Ingrid Bergman★). She was widely celebrated for her natural, earthy qualities that shone through in every performance she gave. According to Morando Morandini, she embodied 'the incarnation of popular passion'.

Magnani starred in four Hollywood films while continuing to work with the most prestigious directors in Italy. Her first role in Hollywood was as Serafina Delle Rose, opposite Burt Lancaster, in *The Rose Tattoo*. The part was originally written with her in mind by her close friend Tennessee Williams, for a Broadway production. She did not appear in the stage version, but as a result of taking on the film role offered to her by Paramount, she won various awards including a Best Actress Academy Award and a Golden Globe. Magnani's second American role – for which she received an Academy Award nomination – was as a mail-order bride who seeks satisfaction outside her marriage, opposite Anthony Quinn in the Paramount production *Wild is the Wind*. Directed by George Cukor, the film was a remake of the Italian film *Furia* (1946) that had been directed by Geoffredo Alessandrini, Magnani's ex-husband (though she did not appear in it). The American version did not prove as successful, and its strongest elements lay in the performances by Magnani and Quinn.

Three years later, in 1960 Magnani starred in another Tennessee Williams adaptation *The Fugitive Kind* based on the play *Orpheus Descending*. Again, it was written with her (and her co-star Marlon Brando) in mind, although neither had appeared in the short-lived Broadway run. Sidney Lumet directed the film for United Artists, but it did not deliver the anticipated spark between the two leads. Magnani's final appearance in Hollywood was the comedy *The Secret of Santa Vittoria*, in which she played the frustrated wife of a drunk and a failure (Anthony Quinn again). This was to be her final appearance there and Magnani returned to Italy to continue her career. When she died four years later, Nannarella's enduring popularity in her native country was underlined by the enormous crowds that attended her funeral in Rome. CS

FILMS: *The Rose Tattoo* (1955); *Wild is the Wind* (1957); *The Fugitive Kind* (1960); *The Secret of Santa Vittoria* (1969).

MALATESTA, Fred (Frederic M. Malatesta) (1889–1952)

Italian actor whose stage career took him to Broadway and then to Hollywood. He frequently played foreigners, and often villains. Although his best roles were in the silent era, he remained a prolific character actor until the 1940s and is remembered as a soldier in *A Farewell to Arms* and as a waiter in Chaplin's★ *Modern Times*. AM

FILMS: *Sherlock Holmes* (1916); *The Claim, The Demon, The Border Raiders, The Legion of Death* (1918); *Full of Pep, The Devil's Trail, The Four-Flusher, Terror of the Range* (1919); *Big Happiness, The Challenge of the Law, The Sins of Rosanne, The Valley of Tomorrow, Risky Business, The Best of Luck* (1920); *The Mask, Little Lord Fauntleroy, All Dolled Up* (1921); *The Woman He Loved, White Shoulders* (1922);

Refuge, The Man Between, The Girl Who Came Back (1923); *The Lullaby, The Night Hawk, Broadway or Bust, The Reckless Age, Honor among Men, Forbidden Paradise* (1924); *Without Mercy* (1925); *Madame Mystery, Don Key (A Son of Burro), Long Live the King, Bardelys the Magnificent, Get 'Em Young* (1926); *The Wagon Show, Galloping Ghosts, The Gate Crasher* (1928); *The Black Book, The Peacock Fan, Wings of Adventure* (1930); *Possessed, Caught Cheating* (1931); *Trouble in Paradise, Get that Girl, A Farewell to Arms, The Man from Yesterday* (1932); *Picture Brides, Beer and Pretzels, Flying Down to Rio, What's Your Racket* (1933); *Riptide, Call it Luck, Perfectly Mismatched, The Gay Bride, The Thin Man, Student Tour, Enter Madame* (1934); *Under the Pampas Moon, The Crusades, $1,000 a Minute, A Night at the Opera, Love Me Forever, Let's Live Tonight, Fighting Shadows, Dressed to Thrill, The Lone Wolf Returns* (1935); *Señor Jim, Modern Times, Under Two Flags, Anthony Adverse, Mary of Scotland, Lady of Secrets, Dodsworth, Love on the Run* (1936); *Mama Steps Out, The Gold Racket, The Bride Wore Red, Beg, Borrow or Steal, Espionage, Conquest* (1937); *The Black Doll, Four Men and a Prayer, Suez, Sharpshooters, International Settlement, Submarine Patrol, Artists and Models Abroad, I'll Give a Million, Port of Seven Seas* (1938); *Blackwell's Island, Bridal Suite, Juarez, The Arizona Wildcat* (1939); *Road to Singapore, Down Argentine Way, Argentine Nights, Arise My Love, North West Mounted Police, The Mark of Zorro, Rangers of Fortune* (1940); *That Night in Rio, Blood and Sand, Week-End in Havana* (1941); *Bill and Coo* (1948).

MANDER, Miles (Lionel Mander) (1888–1946)

Former English novelist, playwright and film exhibitor who also directed and wrote a number of screenplays. He appeared in two Paramount British films in 1932 and went to Hollywood in 1935, where his numerous character parts included Mr Lockwood in *Wuthering Heights*. JS

FILMS: *Lily Christine, That Night in London* (1932); *Here's to Romance, The Three Musketeers* (1935); *Lloyds of London* (1936); *Wake up and Live, Youth on Parole, Slave Ship* (1937); *Kidnapped, The Mad Miss Manton, Suez* (1938); *The Three Musketeers, The Little Princess, Daredevils of the Red Circle, The Man in the Iron Mask, Stanley and Livingstone, Tower of London, Wuthering Heights* (1939); *The Earl of Chicago, Laddie, The House of the Seven Gables, Road to Singapore, Primrose Path, Babies for Sale, Captain Caution, South of Suez* (1940); *Free and Easy* [scenes deleted], *Shadows on the Stairs,* **349**

That Hamilton Woman, They Met in Bombay, Dr Kildare's Wedding Day (1941); *Fly-by-Night, A Tragedy at Midnight, Captains of the Clouds, Fingers at the Window, This above All, Tarzan's New York Adventure, The War against Mrs Hadley, Somewhere I'll Find You, Apache Trail, Journey for Margaret, Lucky Jordan, Secrets of the Underground, To Be or Not to Be, Mrs Miniver* (1942); *Assignment in Brittany, The Fallen Sparrow, First Comes Courage, The Phantom of the Opera, Guadalcanal Diary, Madame Curie, Five Graves to Cairo* (1943); *The Return of the Vampire, Four Jills in a Jeep, The Story of Dr Wassell, The White Cliffs of Dover, The Scarlet Claw, The Pearl of Death, Enter Arsene Lupin, The Brighton Strangler, Crime Doctor's Warning, Week-End at the Waldorf, Confidential Agent, The Picture of Dorian Gray, Murder, My Sweet* (1945); *The Bandit of Sherwood Forest, The Walls Come Tumbling Down* (1946); *The Imperfect Lady* (1947).

MARCEAU, Sophie (Sophie Maupu) (1966–)

A hugely popular star in France (and in Asia) since she appeared as a perky adolescent in *La Boom* (1980), Marceau may become one of the few French actresses to 'make it' in Hollywood and English-speaking international productions.

After a Franco-American small venture, *Pacific Palisades* in 1990, she hit the big time with Mel Gibson's Scottish epic *Braveheart*, as Princess Isabelle. She then appeared in the title role in the USA–Russia co-production *Anna Karenina*, and as the female lead in both the comedy *Lost & Found* and the Bond movie *The World is Not Enough*. Her stunning beauty is clearly key to this success and indeed, like Emmanuelle Béart★, she does not entirely escape 'French babe' stereotyping. However, clever casting making her play 'foreign' parts – thus justifying a sometimes shaky accent – has meant leading parts of some substance. Marceau has an American agent and is on record as saying, 'French movies bore me, they are too slow and pretentious.' She claims to receive more American than French offers. So far, however, her most interesting roles have been in French cinema. As Michael Apted, director of *The World is Not Enough*, has put it: 'There is a risk that Hollywood will only be interested in her beauty. I strongly advise her to choose parts which allow her to exploit her talent as an actress.' GV
FILMS: *Pacific Palisades* (1990); *Braveheart* (1995); *Anna Karenina* (1997); *Lost & Found, The World is Not Enough* (1999); *Alex and Emma* (2003).

MARCHAL, Arlette (Lucienne Marie Marchal) (1902–1984)

Sophisticated French brunette who landed her first major role in Jacques Feyder's *L'Image* (1923) after winning a beauty contest. She appeared alongside Gloria Swanson in *Madame Sans-Gêne*, directed by Léonce Perret in Hollywood. She subsequently embarked on a minor Hollywood career that did not, however, survive the transition to sound. VO
FILMS: *Madame Sans-Gêne* (1925); *Born to the West, Forlorn River, The Cat's Pajamas, Diplomacy* (1926); *Blonde or Brunette, A Gentleman of Paris, Hula, The Spotlight, Wings* (1927).

MARCHAND, Colette (1925–)

Former dancer at the Moulin Rouge in Paris who exploited her skills in John Huston's 1952 *Moulin Rouge*, for which she was nominated for an Academy Award in her supporting role. VO
FILM: *Moulin Rouge* (1952).

MARGOLYES, Miriam (1941–)

Stout, diminutive British character actress who has been repeatedly cast in British film and television adaptations of classic nineteenth-century novels. She may be seen as the heir to a long line of British actresses such as Elsa Lanchester★ and Hermione Gingold★ who were famous for their eccentric spinsterish ladies. Margolyes has likewise been cast by Hollywood whenever batty dowagers are needed for period costume dramas (*The Age of Innocence*), while her high, crisp vocal register has brought her regular transatlantic work as a voice artist on cartoons. Margolyes' dark, slightly exotic features and ear for different accents have also led to credible 'ethnic' – particularly Latin American – roles; something unthinkable for her nominal forebears. JB
FILMS: *The Apple* (1980); *Yentl* (1983); *Electric Dreams* (1984); *Little Shop of Horrors* (1986); *I Love You to Death, Pacific Heights* (1990); *Dead Again, The Butcher's Wife* (1991); *The Age of Innocence, Ed and His Dead Mother* (1993); *Immortal Beloved* (1994); *Babe* [voice], *Balto* (1995); *James and the Giant Peach* [voice], *Romeo + Juliet* (1996); *Mulan* [voice], *Babe: Pig in the City* [voice] (1998); *End of Days, Magnolia* (1999); *Cats & Dogs* (2001); *Harry Potter and the Chamber of Secrets* (2002); *Chasing Liberty, The Life and Death of Peter Sellers, Modigliani* (2004).

MARIN, Jacques (1919–2001)

Prolific French character actor whose roles were often uncredited. He played a number of supporting roles in American films, including a police inspector in Stanley Donen's *Charade*. VO

FILMS: *The Vintage* (1957); *The Roots of Heaven* (1958); *Crack in the Mirror, The Enemy General* (1960); *The Big Gamble* (1961); *Gigot* (1962); *Charade* (1963); *The Train* (1964); *Lost Command, How to Steal a Million* (1966); *The Night of the Following Day* (1968); *Darling Lili* (1970); *Shaft in Africa, The Island at the Top of the World* (1973); *S*P*Y*S* (1974); *Marathon Man* (1976); *Herbie Goes to Monte Carlo, Who is Killing the Great Chefs of Europe?* (1977).

MARKOVIĆ, Rade (1921–)

Well-known Serbian film and theatre actor who started his acting career in 1948. A Marcello Mastroianni★ lookalike, he appeared in several classic Yugoslav films by Radoš Novaković and Mladomir 'Puriša' Djordjević, co-starring with Milena Dravić★ and Bekim Fehmiu★. His only appearance in an American film was in the farcical Sigmund Freud biopic *The Secret Diary of Sigmund Freud*. DI

FILM: *The Secret Diary of Sigmund Freud* (1984).

MARLY, Florence (Hana Smekalova) (1918–1978)

Czech-born, French actress and singer famed for her spectacular good looks and platinum-blonde hair. She was married to prominent French Jewish director Pierre Chenal, with whom she went to Argentina during World War II and made a number of films. Marly moved on to Hollywood in 1944, where she remarried and stayed until her death. CH

FILMS: *Sealed Verdict* (1948); *Tokyo Joe* (1949); *Tokyo File 212* (1951); *Gobs and Gals* (1952); *Undersea Girl* (1957); *Queen of Blood* (1966); *Games* (1967); *Space Boy, Dr Death: Seeker of Souls* (1973).

MARMONT, Percy (1883–1977)

British actor who progressed from romantic leads to aristocratic father types with the onset of the talkies and his return to the UK in 1928. There, among other films, he appeared in a number of US-financed productions. He had a street in Hollywood named after him: Marmont Lane, off Sunset Boulevard. TJ

FILMS: *Die Voortrekkers* (1916); *The Rose of the World, The Lie, The Turn of the Wheel, In the Hollow of Her Hand* (1918); *Three Men and a Girl, The Winchester Woman, The Climbers, The Vengeance of Durand, The Indestructible Wife* (1919); *Slaves of Pride, The Sporting Duchess, Away Goes Prudence, Dead Men Tell No Tales, The Branded Woman* (1920); *Without Benefit of Clergy, Love's Penalty, Wife against Wife, What's Your Reputation Worth?* (1921); *The First Woman, Married People* (1922); *The Midnight Alarm, The Light that Failed, Broadway Broke, You Can't Get Away with It, The Man Life Passed By, If Winter Comes* (1923); *The Shooting of Dan McGrew, The Marriage Cheat, When a Girl Loves, Legend of Hollywood, The Enemy Sex, The Clean Heart, Broken Laws, K – The Unknown, Idle Tongues* (1924); *Daddy's Gone A-Hunting, Just a Woman, The Street of Forgotten Men, A Woman's Faith, Fine Clothes, Infatuation, Lord Jim* (1925); *The Miracle of Life, Mantrap, Fascinating Youth, Aloma of the South Seas* (1926); *San Francisco Nights, The Stronger Will* (1928); *The Lady of the Lake* (1930); *The Silver Greyhound* (1932); *Her Imaginary Lover* (1933); *The White Lilac* (1935); *Swiss Honeymoon* (1947); *Footsteps in the Fog* (1955); *Lisbon* (1956).

MARQUAND, Christian (1927–2000)

French actor known principally for his romantic roles in films such as Alexandre Astruc's *Une Vie/One Life* (1958). By contrast, Marquand was often cast in war or action films during his minor Hollywood career. SL/AP

FILMS: *The Longest Day* (1962); *Dictionary of Sex, Behold a Pale Horse* (1964); *The Flight of the Phoenix* (1965); *Ciao! Manhattan* (1972); *The Other Side of Midnight* (1977); *Apocalypse Now* (1979; in redux version only, 2001).

MARSAC, Maurice (1920–)

The French actor Maurice Marsac arrived in Hollywood during the war, where he started appearing in small character roles as a token Frenchman. As his career developed, Marsac's parts extended slightly in range but not in importance; he was typically cast (uncredited) as a Gaullist in *To Have and Have Not*, and as Prince Berensky in *Gigi*. He became a well-known face on American film and television. CH

FILMS: *Paris after Dark* (1943); *This is the Life, To Have and Have Not, Our Hearts were Young and Gay* (1944); *The Searching Wind* (1946); *Crime Doctor's Gamble* (1947); *The Woman from Tangier, Rogues' Regiment* (1948); *Take One False Step, The* **351**

Secret of St Ives, Once More, My Darling (1949); *Tyrant of the Sea, Three Husbands* (1950); *Captain Pirate, One Minute to Zero, The Happy Time, Assignment: Paris, April in Paris, Against All Flags* (1952); *The Caddy, How to Marry a Millionaire* (1953); *The Black Shield of Falworth* (1954); *Jump into Hell* (1955); *Ride the High Iron, Four Girls in Town* (1956); *China Gate, Les Girls, Band of Angels* (1957); *Lafayette Escadrille, Gigi, Twilight of the Gods, Tarzan and the Trappers, Me and the Colonel* (1958); *It Started with a Kiss* (1959); *Can-Can, Scent of Mystery* (1960); *Armored Command, Kings of Kings, Perro Golfo, Lycanthropus* (1961); *Take Her, She's Mine, Come Fly with Me, Captain Sindbad* (1963); *What a Way to Go!, Wild and Wonderful, The Pleasure Seekers* (1964); *The Art of Love, Clarence, the Cross-Eyed Lion* (1965); *Gambit* (1966); *Monkeys, Go Home!, Double Trouble, Caprice* (1967); *How Do I Love Thee?* (1970); *Herbie Rides Again* (1974); *The Jerk* (1979); *The Big Red One* (1980); *Deal of the Century* (1983); *Dragnet* (1987).

MARSHALL, Herbert (1890–1966)

Although he is best remembered as one of Hollywood's most prolific and distinguished character actors, Marshall began his Hollywood career in 1929 in the same vein in which he had graced London's West End and various British films: as a romantic leading man. He permanently relocated to California in 1932 and remained in constant demand there for three-and-a-half decades.

Marshall was firmly established on Broadway before making the trip west. He first performed on stage in New York in 1915 and transplanted some of his biggest London successes there in the latter half of the 1920s. Marshall made his first screen appearance in British silent films in 1927, but in the next year he made his Hollywood debut in an adaptation of Somerset Maugham's *The Letter*. He continued to shuttle across the Atlantic between the West End and Broadway, and between British and American film studios, but in 1932, Marshall and his actress wife Edna Best★ settled in Hollywood for good and became pillars of the British émigré community in Los Angeles. 'Nanny Marshall', the family childminder they brought with them from London, is reputed to have been the most powerful and well-connected gossip in Hollywood over two decades! Despite the impeccably respectable façade, Marshall himself was a frequent subject of rumour in Hollywood for his affairs with the likes of Miriam Hopkins and Gloria Swanson, and his three subsequent marriages.

Herbert Marshall: prolific and distinguished British character actor

This is not entirely out of keeping with the caddish roles Marshall came to prominence with in Hollywood: the adulterous lover in *The Letter* and a predatory high-class conman in *Trouble in Paradise*. He was always, however, a less than commanding physical presence on screen, as a consequence of the need to disguise a marked limp caused by the wooden leg he acquired in World War I. His chief asset as a performer was undoubtedly his mellifluous voice. This combination of attributes marked Marshall out as a man of words rather than action – a failing, according to mainstream Hollywood values, which is at least partly responsible for his noticeable typecasting as a noble and dignified but essentially passive and ineffectual man, regularly betrayed and crushed by cleverer and worldlier women. The pattern begins with *Blonde Venus*, in which he is cuckolded by Marlene Dietrich's★ nightclub singer. In the 1940 remake of *The Letter*, he switched roles to play the fatuous trusting husband, cuckolded this time by Bette Davis. He was victimised by Davis in quick succession the following year in *The Little Foxes*, as the wheelchair-bound husband she withholds vital medicine from. And he is cuckolded once again by a red-blooded Native American wife he is unable to satisfy or control in *Duel in the Sun*.

The novelist Graham Greene had no doubt that such effeteness and emasculation represented particular tropes of Englishness to American eyes, and he memorably described Marshall as an amalgam of 'national characteristics one does not wish to see exported, characteristics which it is necessary to describe in terms of inanimate objects – a kind of tobacco, a kind of tweed, a kind of pipe – or in terms of dogs, something large, sentimental and moulting that confirms one's preference for cats.' JB

FILMS: *The Letter* (1929); *Secrets of a Secretary* (1931); *Trouble in Paradise, Blonde Venus, Evenings for Sale* (1932); *The Solitaire Man, I was a Spy, Clear All Wires* (1933); *Four Frightened People, Riptide, The Painted Veil, Outcast Lady* (1934); *The Good Fairy, The Flame Within, Accent on Youth, If You Could Only Cook, The Dark Angel* (1935); *Forgotten Faces, Make Way for a Lady, A Woman Rebels, Till We Meet Again, The Lady Consents, Girls' Dormitory* (1936); *Angel, Breakfast for Two* (1937); *Mad about Music, Always Goodbye, Woman against Woman* (1938); *Zaza* (1939); *A Bill of Divorcement, Foreign Correspondent, The Letter* (1940); *The Little Foxes, When Ladies Meet, Kathleen, Adventure in Washington* (1941); *The Moon and Sixpence* (1942); *Forever and a Day, Flight for Freedom, Young Ideas* (1943); *Andy Hardy's Blonde Trouble* (1944); *The Enchanted Cottage, The Unseen* (1945); *Crack-Up, The Razor's Edge, Duel in the Sun* (1946); *High Wall, Ivy* (1947); *The Secret Garden* (1949); *The Underworld Story* (1950); *Anne of the Indies* (1951); *Angel Face* (1952); *Riders to the Stars, Gog, The Black Shield of Falworth* (1954); *The Virgin Queen* (1955); *The Fly, Stage Struck* (1958); *Midnight Lace, College Confidential* (1960); *A Fever in the Blood* (1961); *Five Weeks in a Balloon* (1962); *The Caretakers, The List of Adrian Messenger* (1963); *The Third Day* (1965).

MARTINELLI, Elsa (Elsa Tia) (1935–)

Starting as a stunning Italian model in her teenage years, Martinelli moved to screen acting with small parts in Italian films of the early 1950s. Her American debut has been romanticised through the story that Kirk Douglas spotted her on the cover of *Life* magazine and subsequently offered her a part in *The Indian Fighter*. This was in fact the only film she appeared in while under contract with Douglas' Bryna Productions, but it still remains her most successful Hollywood role. Martinelli played Onahti, the beautiful daughter of the Sioux chief who becomes unwittingly

involved with Douglas' wagon-train scout. Differences of opinion forced Martinelli to leave the company and Douglas stated that if the Italian actress wanted to work for Bryna again she would have to pay him.

The following year, Martinelli won the Silver Berlin Bear Award for Best Actress in the Italian film *Donatella* (1956). She continued to work in international cinema, being given a few choice parts in Hollywood films, such as the sultry leading lady opposite John Wayne in Howard Hawks' *Hatari!* In 1962, she also played a minor role in Orson Welles' European production, *The Trial*. Martinelli retired in the mid-1980s, and made an unsuccessful comeback in the all-star comedy *Once upon a Crime*. CS

FILMS: *The Indian Fighter* (1955); *Four Girls in Town* (1956); *Hatari!, The Pigeon that Took Rome* (1962); *Rampage, The V.I.P.s* (1963); *Woman Times Seven* (1967); *Candy* (1968); *If It's Tuesday, This Must Be Belgium* (1969); *Once upon a Crime* (1992).

MASON, James (1909–1984)

James Mason, whose saturnine good looks were matched by a dark and brooding demeanour, was one of Britain's most popular film stars of the 1940s. His performance style was controlled, yet suggestive of emotional complexity and the actor exuded an aura of intelligence that could sometimes be aloof and sardonic. His voice was particularly distinctive, with its rich tones that could either be gentle or menacing. Mason had already appeared in several Hollywood-financed UK films, among others, before deciding that his career could only advance further in the USA. He argued that despite the success of melodramas such as *The Seventh Veil* (1945), and the popularity of his screen persona as a sadistic but attractive man, a Hollywood career would extend his range and choices. As he later wrote in his autobiography: 'I thought it more than likely that I might have to go on knocking myself out in an unbroken line of banalities, whereas the Hollywood people were liable to be much more impressed by my highly touted popularity.' His much-publicised criticism of the Rank Organisation and controversial remarks about British films lacking glamour provided another reason for Mason to sail on the *Queen Elizabeth* in November 1946.

He did not make a film in Hollywood for eighteen months, however, because of a legal dispute with David E. Rose, an American with connections in the film industry whom Mason had consulted about his chances of a contract **353**

James Mason relaxes on set in the American studio

with Paramount. While Mason and his wife were waiting the legal decision, they stayed in New York, where Mason appeared in a play and on radio. They moved to Los Angeles and laid low until news came through that Mason was free to work with whoever he chose.

The actor spent the rest of his career working mainly in Hollywood, although he made several films in Europe after he moved to Switzerland in 1962. His first American films were not major box-office successes, although he enjoyed working with fellow émigré Max Ophuls on the subsequently highly regarded *Caught* and *The Reckless Moment*. His dislike of the press gained him a reputation for being 'difficult', and in particular he made an enemy of gossip columnist Louella Parsons. Mason's first major Hollywood success was his portrayal of Rommel in *The Desert Fox*, followed by *5 Fingers*, an espionage thriller he considered to

be his best Hollywood film. He managed to obtain good parts in subsequent years, including Brutus in *Julius Caesar*, Captain Nemo in *20,000 Leagues under the Sea* and Norman Maine in *A Star is Born*, for which he was nominated for an Academy Award.

Mason had ambitions to direct and produce films, but the only film he is credited as directing is *The Child* (1954), a half-hour film featuring his daughter Portland. He produced several films, including *Lady Possessed*, based on a novel by his wife, and *Age of Consent* (1969), made in Australia. Many of his later roles were distinctive, particularly his portrayal of Humbert Humbert in *Lolita*, a British-registered film but made for MGM with a largely American cast and setting.

When he lived in Los Angeles, Mason was perceived as somewhat of an outsider, in part because of his aversion to the prevailing expectations of full co-operation from actors in Hollywood's intense publicity rounds. He was also seen as a touch eccentric, with his superior 'English' demeanour at times causing resentment. Mason's divorce settlement in 1965 from his first wife was very expensive. It was the reason given for the large number of somewhat indiscriminate supporting roles that he accepted thereafter. SS

FILMS: *Late Extra* (1935); *Blind Man's Bluff, Troubled Waters* (1936); *Catch as Catch Can* (1937); *Hatter's Castle* (1942); *Hotel Reserve* (1944); *Caught* (1948); *Madame Bovary, The Reckless Moment, East Side, West Side* (1949); *One Way Street, Pandora and the Flying Dutchman* (1950); *The Desert Fox* (1951); *Lady Possessed, Five Fingers, The Prisoner of Zenda, Face to Face, Charade* (1952); *The Story of Three Loves, The Desert Rats, Julius Caesar, Botany Bay, The Tell-Tale Heart* [voice] (1953); *Prince Valiant, A Star is Born, 20,000 Leagues under the Sea* (1954); *Forever Darling* (1955); *Bigger than Life* (1956); *Island in the Sun, Cry Terror* (1957); *The Decks Ran Red* (1958); *Journey to the Centre of the Earth, A Touch of Larceny, North by Northwest* (1959); *The Marriage-Go-Round* (1960); *Escape from Zahrain* (1961); *Lolita, Hero's Island* (1962); *The Fall of the Roman Empire, The Pumpkin Eater* (1964); *Lord Jim, Genghis Khan* (1965); *The Blue Max, Georgy Girl, The Deadly Affair* (1966); *The Sea Gull, Duffy* (1968); *Child's Play* (1972); *The Last of Sheila, The Mackintosh Man* (1973); *11 Harrowhouse* (1974); *Mandingo, Inside Out* (1975); *Heaven Can Wait, The Boys from Brazil, The Passage* (1978); *Bloodline* (1979); *The Verdict* (1982); *Yellowbeard* (1983).

MASSEN, Osa (Aase Madsen) (1915–)

Her accent was 'neither definite nor recognisable', according to one US critic in 1939. Along with her exotic, almost catlike allure, this feature allowed the Danish actress Osa Massen to play a variety of foreign types in Hollywood. She appeared as a Dutch-Polynesian in her American screen debut *Honeymoon in Bali*, for example, and later played such Continental characters as the vaguely Eastern European Ana Remzi in *Background to Danger*.

Massen had studied to become a film editor, but was awarded ingénue parts in a couple of minor Danish films instead. She caught Hollywood's attention and Edward H. Griffith cast her as the 'other woman' in *Honeymoon in Bali*, which several critics thought she stole outright from the film's leading lady, Madeleine Carroll★. Massen lacked the distinctive lilting Swedish accent so ingrained in the Amer-

ican consciousness by the likes of Greta Garbo★ and Ingrid Bergman★. This might have precluded her becoming a major star, since she was repeatedly cast in solely decorative parts. Tired of being confused with Ona Munson and the Hungarian émigré Ilona Massey★, she became Stephanie Paull for the low-budget *Million Dollar Weekend*, but returned as Osa Massen for a co-starring role opposite Lloyd Bridges in her best-remembered film, the minor science-fiction classic *Rocketship X-M*. Massen married one of Jean Hersholt's★ sons in 1938 and became a US citizen in 1941. HJW

FILMS: *Honeymoon in Bali* (1939); *Honeymoon for Three, A Woman's Face, Accent on Love, You'll Never Get Rich, The Devil Pays Off* (1941); *Iceland* (1942); *What We are Fighting For, Background to Danger, Jack London* (1943); *The Black Parachute, Cry of the Werewolf, The Master Race* (1944); *Tokyo Rose, The Gentleman Misbehaves, Deadline at Dawn, Strange Journey* (1946); *Million Dollar Weekend* (1948); *Night unto Night* (1949); *Rocketship X-M* (1950); *Outcasts of the City* (1958).

MASSEY, Ilona (Ilona Hajmássy) (1910–1974)

Hungarian-born opera singer and Austrian film musical star, who along with Hedy Lamarr★ was signed during Louis B. Mayer's 1937 European talent-seeking tour. She was promoted briefly as 'the singing Garbo', but her reluctance to pursue English and acting classes soon found her relegated to B-movies and nightclub appearances. RJK

FILMS: *Rosalie* (1937); *Balalaika* (1939); *New Wine, International Lady* (1941); *Invisible Agent* (1942); *Frankenstein Meets the Wolf Man* (1943); *Holiday in Mexico* (1946); *Northwest Output* (1947); *The Plunderers* (1948); *Love Happy* (1950); *Jet over the Atlantic* (1959).

MASTROIANNI, Marcello (1923–1996)

One of Italy's most famous actors who demonstrated his vast repertoire of acting skills in a prestigious career that spanned almost fifty years. Mastroianni first came to the attention of audiences in Fellini's *La dolce vita* (1960). He was nominated for a Best Actor Academy Award and won a BAFTA for Best Foreign Actor for his performance as a Sicilian count who tries to murder his wife in Pietro Germi's black comedy *Divorzio all'italiana/Divorce Italian Style* (1962). In 1963, the same year he played Guido, Fellini's alter-ego in *8½*, he embarked on a long-standing **355** screen partnership with Sophia Loren★ in *Ieri, oggi, domani / Yesterday, Today and Tomorrow*. By 1965, he had won a Golden Globe for World Favourite Male.

Although Mastroianni was among the most successful European male screen actors of his generation, his Hollywood career was limited. His English was far from fluent and the fact that he was not using his mother tongue and therefore had to recite his lines phonetically created a noticeable unease in his performance style. His first American role was as a police inspector in the drug-trafficking action-adventure *Poppies are Also Flowers*. It was originally made for television and co-starred such famous names as Grace Kelly (who introduced the film), Omar Sharif and Eli Wallach. In 1992, he appeared opposite Shirley MacLaine in the comedy *Used People*, portraying the Latin lover type he had been so commonly associated with. Two years later, he was cast in Robert Altman's *Prêt-à-Porter* looking 'weary and old but still handsome', as one critic put it. In a part for which he won a Golden Globe nomination for Best Actor, Mastroianni was finally reunited with Loren. They re-enacted the famous bedroom striptease of *Yesterday, Today and Tomorrow*, but this time Mastroianni had fallen fast asleep by the time Loren had removed her stockings. CS

FILMS: *Poppies are Also Flowers* (1966); *Used People* (1992); *Prêt-à-Porter* (1994).

MATIESEN, Otto (Otto Matthiessen) (1893–1932)

'Something has got to be done,' Otto Matiesen's Joel Cairo whispered conspiratorially in Danish in the first screen version of Dashiell Hammett's *The Maltese Falcon* (1931). Alas, this was the only time the actor spoke his native tongue on screen, and it also proved to be the émigré actor's penultimate screen role.

A pupil of the Danish stage star Gerda Christophersen, Matiesen appeared in Danish and British films of the early 1910s and later toured North America with Herbert Beerbohm Tree★. He made his American screen debut in *The Golden Trail* in 1920, a minor Western melodrama produced in Oregon by another Danish émigré, Jean Hersholt★. Dark and brooding, Matiesen went on to become one of Hollywood's few true intellectuals and a favourite of fellow malcontents such as Josef von Sternberg, who cast him in the experimental *The Salvation Hunters*, and Paul Féjos, for whom he played the suicidal protagonist in the equally innovative *The Last Moment*. Although never a major star,

Matiesen usually made his supporting presence felt, more often than not by playing exotic and slightly depraved characters. Short of stature, he portrayed Napoleon Bonaparte no fewer than three times, lastly in John Ford's early sound experiment *Napoleon's Barber*. He was well positioned to become one of the burgeoning sound era's more interesting character actors, but was killed in the same car accident that also severely injured the Romanian-born actor Duncan Renaldo. HJW

FILMS: *The Golden Trail* (1920); *Bells of San Juan, Money to Burn* (1922); *Alias the Night Wind, Vanity Fair, Boston Blackie, Scaramouche, The Dangerous Maid* (1923); *Revelation, Captain Blood, Folly of Vanity* (1924); *The Salvation Hunters, Sackcloth and Scarlet, The Happy Warrior, Parisian Love, Morals for Men* (1925); *Bride of the Storm, Yellow Fingers, The Silver Treasure, Christine of the Big Top, Whispering Wires, While London Sleeps* (1926); *The Beloved Rogue, Too Many Crooks, Old San Francisco, The Road to Romance, Surrender* (1927); *The Last Moment, The Desert Bride, The Scarlet Lady, The Woman from Moscow, Napoleon's Barber* (1928); *Behind Closed Doors, Strange Cargo, Prisoners, The Show of Shows* (1929); *General Crack, Golden Dawn, Conspiracy, The Last of the Lone Wolf, A Soldier's Plaything* (1930); *Beau Ideal, The Maltese Falcon, Men of the Sky* (1931).

MATTHEWS, Jessie (1907–1981)

Top box-office British star of film musicals in the 1930s who received several offers to star in Hollywood. Her commitments in Britain and ill health prevented her from taking them up, but she did have a part in *Forever and a Day*, the film made in the USA in aid of war charities and featuring British actors. SS

FILMS: *Forever and a Day* (1943); *tom thumb* (1958).

MATTHEWS, Lester (1900–1975)

After first appearing in early British sound films (including a few US-financed productions) on the back of a stage career, Matthews became a long-serving Hollywood supporting player thanks to the industry's regular need for sundry English brigadiers, archbishops and knights of the realm between the 1930s and 1960s. JB

FILMS: *The Stolen Necklace, Out of the Past, The Melody Maker* (1933); *The Raven, Werewolf of London* (1935); *Crack-Up, Tugboat Princess, Too Many Parents, Thank You, Jeeves!, The Song and Dance Man, Professional Soldier, Lloyds of*

London, *Fifteen Maiden Lane* (1936); *The Prince and the Pauper*, *Lancer Spy* (1937); *The Adventures of Robin Hood*, *There's Always a Woman*, *Three Loves Has Nancy*, *Time Out for Murder*, *If I were King*, *I am a Criminal*, *Think it Over*, *Mysterious Mr Moto* (1938); *The Three Musketeers*, *Conspiracy*, *Rulers of the Sea*, *Susannah of the Mounties*, *Should a Girl Marry?*, *Everything Happens at Night* (1939); *Northwest Passage*, *Gaucho Serenade*, *Women in War*, *Sing, Dance, Plenty Hot*, *The Sea Hawk*, *British Intelligence*, *The Biscuit Eater* (1940); *Man Hunt*, *Life Begins for Andy Hardy*, *A Yank in the RAF*, *Scotland Yard*, *The Lone Wolf Keeps a Date* (1941); *Son of Fury*, *Across the Pacific*, *Now, Voyager*, *Sunday Punch*, *The Pied Piper*, *Manila Calling*, *London Blackout Murders*, *Desperate Journey*, *Born to Sing* (1942); *Two Tickets to London*, *Tonight We Raid Calais*, *Northern Pursuit*, *The Mysterious Doctor*, *Corvette K-225* (1943); *Nine Girls*, *Four Jills in a Jeep*, *The Story of Dr Wassell*, *Between Two Worlds*, *The Invisible Man's Revenge*, *Ministry of Fear*, *Shadows of the Night* (1944); *Two O'Clock Courage*, *Son of Lassie*, *Salty O'Rourke*, *Objective, Burma!*, *Jungle Queen*, *I Love a Mystery* (1945); *The Beautiful Cheat* (1946); *The Exile*, *The Paradine Case*, *Dark Delusion*, *Addio Mimi!* (1947); *Fighting Father Dunne* (1948); *Malaya*, *I Married a Communist*, *Free for All* (1949); *Montana*, *Tyrant of the Sea*, *Rogues of Sherwood Forest* (1950); *Tales of Robin Hood*, *Lorna Doone*, *Anne of the Indies*, *The Son of Dr Jekyll*, *Desert Fox: The Story of Rommel*, *Corky of Gasoline Alley* (1951); *5 Fingers*, *Les Miserables*, *The Brigand*, *Captain Pirate*, *Stars and Stripes Forever*, *Rogue's March*, *Operation Secret*, *Lady in the Iron Mask*, *Jungle Jim in the Forbidden Land*, *Against All Flags* (1952); *Niagara*, *Trouble along the Way*, *Sangaree*, *Savage Mutiny*, *Bad for Each Other*, *Young Bess*, *Jamaica Run*, *Fort Ti* (1953); *Charge of the Lancers*, *King Richard and the Crusaders*, *Man in the Attic*, *Jungle Man-Eaters*, *Désiree* (1954); *Ten Wanted Men*, *The Seven Little Foys*, *Moonfleet*, *Flame of the Islands*, *The Far Horizons* (1955); *Something of Value* (1957); *The Miracle* (1959); *The Prize* (1963); *Mary Poppins* (1964); *Assault on a Queen* (1966); *Star!* (1968).

MAUDE, Cyril (1862–1951)

Maude was one of the leading West End actor-managers in the 1910s. His occasional British film CV was supplemented by a few American films, one an early Ibsen adaptation made during an American theatrical tour in 1915. *Winning His Wife* was one of several shorts made by the Stage Women's War Relief Fund. JB

FILMS: *Peer Gynt*, *The Greater Will* (1915); *Winning His Wife* (1919); *Grumpy* (1930); *These Charming People* (1931).

MAUREY, Nicole (1925–)

In 1955, Maurey featured on the cover of *Life* magazine and this subsequently led to a contract with RKO. Her roles tended to be stereotypical and she found it difficult to avoid French typecasting. Maurey never intended to settle in the USA, but fame in Europe was not forthcoming and the remainder of her career was mainly in French television. VO

FILMS: *Little Boy Lost* (1953); *Secret of the Incas* (1954); *The Bold and the Brave* (1956); *Me and the Colonel* (1958); *The Jayhawkers* (1959); *High Time* (1960).

McANALLY, Ray (1926–1989)

Although McAnally is now best known as Christy Brown's 'Da' in *My Left Foot* (1989), this Irish stage actor also made a number of occasional, but versatile, Hollywood appearances. RB

FILMS: *Shake Hands with the Devil* (1959); *The Naked Edge* (1961); *Billy Budd*, *Desert Patrol*, *Murder in Eden*, *She Didn't Say No!* (1962); *He Who Rides a Tiger* (1968); *The Looking Glass War* (1970); *The Sicilian* (1987); *We're No Angels* (1989).

McCALLUM, David (1933–)

Blond-haired, good-looking British actor with a strong and brooding screen presence. McCallum remains best known for his role as Illya Kuryakin in television's *The Man from U.N.C.L.E* (1964–8), which he reprised in several spin-off films such as *One of Our Spies is Missing*. He was also Lieutenant-Commander Eric 'Dispersal' Ashley-Pitt in *The Great Escape*. JS

FILMS: *Freud* (1962); *The Great Escape* (1963); *To Trap a Spy* (1964); *The Greatest Story Ever Told*; *The Spy with My Face* (1965), *Around the World under the Sea*, *One Spy Too Many*, *One of Our Spies is Missing*, *The Spy in the Green Hat* (1966); *Three Bites of the Apple*, *The Karate Killers* (1967); *Sol Madrid*, *How to Steal the World* (1968); *Dogs* (1976); *The Watcher in the Woods* (1980); *The Haunting of Morella* (1990); *Healer* (1994); *Cherry* (1999).

McCANN, Donal (1943–1999)

Talented Irish stage actor whose performance style was characterised by a combination of intensity and world- **357** weariness. Despite a number of minor Hollywood appearances, his film work was predominately restricted to independent Irish films. RB

FILMS: *The Fighting Prince of Donegal* (1966); *The Mackintosh Man* (1973); *Out of Africa* (1985); *Illuminata* (1998).

McCLORY, Sean (1924–)

McClory began acting with Dublin's Abbey Theatre before moving to the USA in 1949, where he was signed by Twentieth Century-Fox. His screen career was prolific, if undistinguished. His best roles were in films such as John Ford's *The Quiet Man* and Fritz Lang's *Moonfleet*. RB

FILMS: *Dick Tracy's Dilemma, Dick Tracy Meets Gruesome* (1947); *Beyond Glory* (1948); *Roughshod* (1949); *The Daughter of Rosie O'Grady, The Glass Menagerie* (1950); *Storm Warning, David and Bathsheba, Lorna Doone, Anne of the Indies, The Desert Fox: The Story of Rommel* (1951); *The Quiet Man, Les Miserables, What Price Glory, Rogue's March, Face to Face* (1952); *Niagara, Plunder of the Sun, Island in the Sky, Charade, The Child* (1953); *Ring of Fear, Man in the Attic, Them!* (1954); *The Long Gray Line, I Cover the Underworld, The King's Thief, Moonfleet* (1955); *Diane* (1956); *The Guns of Fort Petticoat* (1957); *Valley of the Dragons* (1961); *Cheyenne Autumn* (1964); *Follow Me, Boys!, Mara of the Wilderness* (1966); *The Happiest Millionaire, The Gnome-Mobile, The King's Pirate* (1967); *Roller Boogie* (1979); *My Chauffeur* (1986).

McCORMICK. F. J. (Peter Judge) (1890–1947)

Famous Irish Abbey Theatre actor associated with his roles in Sean O'Casey's plays. McCormick became disillusioned with Hollywood after appearing as Captain Brennan in John Ford's *The Plough and the Stars*. RB

FILM: *The Plough and the Stars* (1936).

McDOWALL, Roddy (Roderick Andrew Anthony Jude McDowall) (1928–1998)

English child actor who, unlike his near-contemporaries Shirley Temple and Freddie Bartholomew★, transcended the usual Hollywood cul-de-sac of youthful success and sustained an American screen career spanning some six decades. After appearing in more than a dozen British films since his debut in *Murder in the Family* in 1938 – some of which were US funded – McDowall was brought to Hollywood by his ambitious Irish mother in 1940. Rejected by MGM for being 'too English', McDowall was tested by

Twentieth Century-Fox and subsequently cast in his breakthrough role as Huw Morgan in John Ford's *How Green Was My Valley*. The twelve-year-old's charismatic and naturalistic performance complemented the film's overtly nostalgic allure and brought him almost immediate fame. McDowall appeared in numerous American films throughout the next decade, including leads in definitive boy-and-animal features such as *My Friend Flicka, Lassie Come Home* and their sequels. Despite his early success, after his third-billing in *Molly and Me*, McDowall was casually released from his contract with Twentieth Century-Fox. Aged just seventeen, he continued to squeeze the last out of his childhood popularity over seven pictures for Monogram as both star and co-producer.

He moved successfully into television and stage work for much of the 1950s and a matured McDowall returned to the big screen in the early 1960s in increasingly high-profile and versatile cross-genre features. His adult career is still best remembered for his latex-clad simian role in *Planet of the Apes* and three of its sequels. McDowall continued to work prolifically in various media over the next three decades as actor, producer and director. Although his projects varied wildly in terms of quality, his gentle charm was rarely absent. MF

FILMS: *Murder in the Family, John Halifax* (1938); *His Brother's Keeper, Murder Will Out* (1940); *Man Hunt, Confirm or Deny, How Green Was My Valley* (1941); *Son of Fury, On the Sunny Side, The Pied Piper* (1942); *Lassie Come Home, My Friend Flicka* (1943); *The White Cliffs of Dover, The Keys of the Kingdom* (1944); *Thunderhead – Son of Flicka, Molly and Me, Hangover Square* [voice] (1945); *Holiday in Mexico* (1946); *Macbeth, Kidnapped, Rocky* (1948); *Black Midnight, Tuna Clipper* (1949); *Killer Shark, Everybody's Dancin', Big Timber* (1950); *The Steel Fist* (1953); *The Subterraneans, Midnight Lace* (1960); *The Longest Day* (1962); *Cleopatra* (1963); *Shock Treatment* (1964); *The Greatest Story Ever Told, The Third Day, That Darn Cat!, The Loved One, Inside Daisy Clover* (1965); *Lord Love a Duck* (1966); *The Adventures of Bullwhip Griffin, The Cool Ones, It!* (1967); *Planet of the Apes, 5 Card Stud* (1968); *Midas Run, Hello Down There* (1969); *Angel, Angel, Down We Go* (1970); *Pretty Maids All in Row, Escape from the Planet of the Apes, Bedknobs and Broomsticks* (1971); *Corky, Conquest of the Planet of the Apes, The Poseidon Adventure, The Life and Times of Judge Roy Bean* (1972); *Battle for Planet of the Apes, Arnold* (1973); *Dirty Mary, Crazy Larry*

(1974); *Funny Lady* (1975); *Mean Johnny Barrows, Embryo* (1976); *Sixth and Main* (1977); *The Cat from Outer Space, Rabbit Test, Laserblast* (1978); *Circle of Iron, Scavenger Hunt, The Black Hole* [voice], *The Nutcracker Fantasy* [voice] (1979); *Charlie Chan and the Curse of the Dragon Queen* (1981); *Fright Night, Zoo Ship* [voice] (1985); *GoBots: War of the Rock Lords* [voice] (1986); *Dead of Winter, Overboard* (1987); *Doin' Time on Planet Earth* (1988); *Fright Night II, Cutting Class, The Big Picture, Heroes Stand Alone* (1989); *Shakma, Going Under, Carmilla* (1990); *Double Trouble* (1992); *Angel 4: Undercover* (1993); *Mirror Mirror 2: Angel Dance, The Color of Evening* (1994); *The Grass Harp, Last Summer in the Hamptons* (1995); *It's My Party* (1996); *The Second Jungle Book: Mowgli & Baloo* (1997); *Something to Believe In, A Bug's Life* [voice] (1998).

McDOWELL, Malcolm (Malcolm Taylor) (1943–)

Although Malcom McDowell made his name as a danger-ously seductive hoodlum in Lindsay Anderson's *if. . . .* and Stanley Kubrick's *A Clockwork Orange*, his early Hollywood career was marked by a range of diverse roles. He played the part of H. G. Wells in the fantasy *Time after Time* with characteristic innocence, but he was also mischievous and dastardly in the title role of the notorious *Caligula*. McDowell claims to be proud of this sensationalist and pornographic film written by Gore Vidal and financed by *Penthouse* magazine, though he has also admitted that it did his subsequent career no favours. The 1980s certainly seem to have born that out. McDowell appeared in Paul Schrader's colourful reworking of Tourneur's horror classic *Cat People* and the financially successful *Blue Thunder*, but it was downhill from then on in, with a period of drug addic-tion and walk-on parts in films or formulaic television series.

The roles began to return in the 1990s. McDowell appeared in big-budget spectaculars such as *Star Trek: Generations* and the unsuccessful *Tank Girl*. In the former, he played Dr Soran, a demented figure with a grudge against the universe. The older McDowell has now shed the sweet undertow that gave his earlier nasty character a more rounded and sympathetic feel. He tends to specialise in vil-lains by essentially riffing on his earlier persona as Alex in *A Clockwork Orange*. While he seems to be enjoying him-self, he has also become a virtual self-parody who effort-lessly exploits his own screen history. JS

FILMS: *if. . . .* (1968); *A Clockwork Orange* (1971); *O Lucky Man* (1973); *Royal Flash* (1975); *Caligula, Time after Time* (1979); *Cat People* (1982); *Get Crazy, Blue Thunder, Cross Creek* (1983); *The Caller* (1987); *Buy and Cell, Sunset* (1988); *Disturbed, Class of 1999, Jezebel's Kiss, Schweitzer* (1990); *The Player* (1992); *Chain of Desire, Bopha!, Happily Ever After* [voice] (1993); *Milk Money, Star Trek: Generations, Fatal Pur-suit, In the Eye of the Snake* (1994); *Dangerous Indiscretion, Tank Girl* (1995); *Exquisite Tenderness, Fist of the North Star, Cyborg 3, Kids of the Round Table* (1995); *Where Truth Lies, The Little Riders, Yesterday's Target, Ringer* (1996); *Hugo Pool, Mr Magoo, Asylum* (1997); *Beings, The First 9 ½ Weeks, The Gardener* (1998); *Love Lies Bleeding, My Life So Far, Y2K, Southern Cross* (1999); *Island of the Dead* (2000); *Just Visiting* (2001); *I Spy* (2002); *I'll Sleep When I'm Dead, The Company, Red Roses and Petrol* (2003); *Hidalgo, Bobby Jones – Stroke of Genius* (2004).

McGOOHAN, Patrick (1928–)

McGoohan was born in the USA of Irish immigrant par-ents, but moved at an early age to Ireland and then Eng-land. He is now most famous for his title role in the cult television series *The Prisoner*, but his American film career has been largely associated with playing villains. RB

FILMS: *The Dark Avenger* (1955); *Zarak* (1956); *The Quare Fellow* (1962); *The Three Lives of Thomasina, All Night Long* (1963); *Two Living, One Dead* (1964); *Walk in the Shadow* (1966); *Ice Station Zebra* (1968); *The Moonshine War* (1970); *Mary, Queen of Scots* (1971); *The Silver Streak* (1976); *Brass Target* (1978); *Escape from Alcatraz* (1979); *Baby . . . Secret of the Lost Legend* (1985); *Braveheart* (1995); *The Phantom, A Time to Kill* (1996); *Treasure Planet* [voice] (2002).

McGREGOR, Ewan (1971–)

British actor who established a witty, sardonic and intelli-gent screen image in films such as *Shallow Grave* (1994) and *Trainspotting* (1996). He became recognisable for his dis-tinctive Scottish accent, rugged appearance and compelling, direct address for the camera. Although his antipathy towards Hollywood has been a consistent feature in inter-views, he has starred in leading roles in the high-profile *Star Wars* prequels, in which he has a personal interest. Another three of his films have been part-financed by American money: *Nightwatch*, a thriller, *Eye of the Beholder*, a Canadian/UK/US co-production, and the highly success-

359

ful musical *Moulin Rouge!*, a co-production with Australia, distributed by Twentieth Century-Fox. A commitment to the British film industry, however, remains the focus of this versatile young actor. SS

FILMS: *Nightwatch* (1997); *Star Wars: Episode I: The Phantom Menace, Eye of the Beholder* (1999); *Black Hawk Down, Moulin Rouge!* (2001); *Star Wars: Episode II: The Attack of the Clones* (2002); *Big Fish, Down with Love* (2003).

McKELLEN, Ian (1939–)

Shakespearean actor who won acclaim in the UK and then on Broadway before achieving Hollywood success with characterisations that fell into a rather bizarre hinterland between the mystical Jew and Nazi-like villain. McKellen played a Jewish man attempting to uncover the nature of a mysterious force in Michael Mann's cult horror *The Keep*. His leading part opposite Meryl Streep in *Plenty* and his role as John Profumo in *Scandal* led up to his 1990 knighthood for his overall contribution to the performing arts. McKellen's award-winning revisionist adaptation (as co-writer, co-producer and actor) of *Richard III* further enhanced his international profile.

The actor publicly 'came out' in the early 1990s and became a leading spokesman for gay rights. This added resonance to his appearances in *Bent* (1997) and his highly touching Academy Award-nominated portrayal of the legendary gay director James Whale in *Gods and Monsters*.

McKellen's distinctive hollow features may explain Hollywood's keenness to associate him with hard, fascistic roles. Another such part came in *X-Men*, when the film's director, Bryan Singer, persuaded him to appear by pitching the story of a young Jew whose wartime experiences transformed him into the leather-clad arch-villain Magneto as an allegory of gay rights activism.

McKellen's highly successful leading role as Gandalf in Peter Jackson's *Lord of the Rings* trilogy has certainly softened his overall profile. It has also proved that, along with fellow British actors Anthony Hopkins★ and Ewan McGregor★, he has become a master of the contemporary Hollywood franchise. MW

FILMS: *A Touch of Love, Alfred the Great* (1969); *The Keep* (1983); *Plenty* (1985); *Scandal* (1989); *The Ballad of Little Jo, Six Degrees of Separation, Last Action Hero* (1993); *The Shadow, I'll Do Anything* (1994); *Restoration, Richard III* (1995); *Swept from the Sea* (1997); *Apt Pupil, Gods and Monsters* (1998); *X-Men* (2000); *The Lord of the Rings: The Fellowship of the Ring* (2001); *The Lord of the Rings: The Two Towers* (2002); *X2, The Lord of the Rings: The Return of the King* (2003).

McKENNA, Siobhan (1923–1986)

Irish actress, married to Denis O'Dea★, who began her career with the Abbey Theatre. Although she mainly worked in British cinema and on the Irish stage, she had a major Hollywood role as Mary in Nicholas Ray's religious epic *King of Kings*. RB

FILMS: *King of Kings* (1961); *Doctor Zhivago* (1965).

McKENNA, T. P. (1929–)

McKenna trained with Dublin's Abbey Theatre and has predominately worked in British film and television. His Hollywood work has been minimal and usually in European co-productions. RB

FILMS: *A Terrible Beauty* (1960); *The Quare Fellow* (1962); *Of Human Bondage* (1964); *Young Cassidy* (1965); *The Charge of the Light Brigade* (1968); *Anne of the Thousand Days* (1969); *Straw Dogs* (1971); *The Outsider* (1979); *The Doctor and the Devils* (1985); *Red Scorpion, Valmont* (1989).

McKENNA, Virginia (1931–)

Spirited British stage and screen actress who is still most closely associated with her role as the compassionate and determined naturalist and environmental activist, Joy Adamson, in *Born Free*. McKenna starred opposite Bill Travers★ in the film. AP

FILMS: *The Barretts of Wimpole Street* (1957); *The Wreck of the Mary Deare* (1959); *Born Free* (1966); *Sliding Doors* (1998).

McLAGLEN, Victor (1886–1959)

As a former world-class boxer and circus performer, Victor McLaglen was an unusually physically imposing presence in British cinema of the 1920s. Despite his coarse and battered features, he became a genuine leading man and often played the kind of parts more often found in Hollywood films such as a Native American chief in *Little Brother of God* (1922). A Hollywood contract, with Vitagraph, inevitably followed and McLaglen arrived in the USA in July 1924. His most prominent success there would be as Gypo Nolan in John Ford's remake of *The Informer*, which earned him a Best Actor Academy Award. This was not the first time that

Former British world-class boxer and circus performer Victor McLaglen became an imposing presence in Hollywood films, notably those of John Ford

he played an ethnically Irish character and it was certainly not the last. McLaglen was regularly described as Irish in many reviews and fan magazine profiles, but his steadfast affiliation to his country of birth was reflected in the fact that he founded the British United Services Club for actors in California who had served in the British military. *The Informer* was also neither the first nor last time he would work with Ford. McLaglen became an iconic presence in this legendary director's films for over twenty years as a character actor specialising in hard-drinking and gruff sentimentalists. JB

FILMS: *The Glorious Adventure* (1922); *The Beloved Brute* (1924); *The Hunted Woman, Percy, The Unholy Three, The Fighting Heart, Winds of Chance* (1925); *The Isle of Retribution, Men of Steel, Beau Geste, What Price Glory* (1926); *The Loves of Carmen* (1927); *Mother Machree, A Girl in Every Port, Hangman's House, The River Pirate* (1928); *Captain Lash, Strong Boy, Black Watch, Hot for Paris, The Cock-Eyed World* (1929); *On the Level, A Devil with Women, Happy Days* (1930); *Three Rogues, The Slippery Pearls, Annabelle's*

Affairs, Women of All Nations, Wicked, Dishonored (1931); *The Gay Cabellero, Devil's Lottery, While Paris Sleeps, Rackety Rax, Guilty as Hell* (1932); *Hot Pepper, Laughing at Life* (1933); *The Lost Patrol, Wharf Angel, Murder at the Vanities, No More Women, The Captain Hates the Sea* (1934); *The Great Hotel Murder, The Informer, Under Pressure* (1935); *Klondike Annie, Under Two Flags, Magnificent Brute, Professional Soldier* (1936); *Sea Devils, This is My Affair, Wee Willie Winkie, Nancy Steele is Missing!* (1937); *Battle of Broadway, The Devil's Party, We're Going to be Rich, Pacific Liner* (1938); *Gunga Din, Let Freedom Ring, Full Confession, The Big Guy, Rio, Ex-Champ, Captain Fury* (1939); *Diamond Frontier, South of Pago Pago* (1940); *Broadway Limited* (1941); *Call Out the Marines, Powder Town, China Girl* (1942); *Forever and a Day* (1943); *The Princess and the Pirate, Tampico, Roger Touhy, Gangster* (1944); *Rough, Tough and Ready, Love, Honor and Obey* (1945); *Whistle Stop* (1946); *Calendar Girl, The Foxes of Harrow, Michigan Kid* (1947); *Fort Apache* (1948); *She Wore a Yellow Ribbon* (1949); *Rio Grande* (1950); *The Quiet Man* (1952); *Fair Wind to Java* (1953); *Prince Valiant* (1954); *City of Shadows, Many Rivers to Cross, Lady Godiva, Bengazi* (1955); *Around the World in Eighty Days* (1956); *The Abductors* (1957).

McSHANE, Ian (1942–)

British actor best known for his eponymous leading role in the UK television series *Lovejoy* and his performance as Don Lockwood in *Dallas*. His occasional film appearances have included a handful of minor Hollywood films. MHu

FILMS: *If It's Tuesday, This Must Be Belgium, Battle of Britain* (1969); *Sitting Target* (1972); *The Last of Sheila* (1973); *Ransom* (1975); *Cheaper to Keep Her* (1980); *Exposed* (1983); *Torchlight* (1984); *Too Scared to Scream* (1985); *Agent Cody Banks* (2003).

MEANEY, Colm (1953–)

Versatile screen actor in both Hollywood and low-budget Irish cinema. Meaney is most famous for his long-running role as Chief O'Brien in the latter-day *Star Trek* series. RB

FILMS: *The Omega Syndrome* (1987); *Dick Tracy, Die Hard II, Come See the Paradise* (1990); *Far and Away, The Last of the Mohicans, Under Siege* (1992); *The Road to Wellville* (1994); *Ripple* (1995); *Con Air* (1997); *Snitch, Claire Dolan* (1998); *Mystery, Alaska, Chapter Zero* (1999).

MEDINA, Patricia (1919–)

Voluptuous dark-haired British film actress who went to Hollywood with her husband, Richard Greene★. Medina initially signed to MGM, but was frequently loaned out by the studio. She went on to become a lively heroine of numerous costume dramas. MW

FILMS: *Hotel Reserve* (1944); *The Secret Heart* (1946); *Moss Rose, The Beginning or the End, The Foxes of Harrow* (1947); *The Three Musketeers* (1948); *The Fighting O'Flynn* (1949); *Abbott and Costello in the Foreign Legion, Francis, Fortunes of Captain Blood, The Jackpot* (1950); *Valentino, The Lady and the Bandit, The Magic Carpet* (1951); *Captain Pirate, Lady in the Iron Mask, Desperate Search, Aladdin and His Lamp* (1952); *Botany Bay, Sangaree, Plunder of the Sun, Siren of Bagdad* (1953); *The Black Knight, Drums of Tahiti, Phantom of the Rue Morgue, Screen Snapshots: Hula from Hollywood* (1954); *Duel on the Mississippi, Pirates of Tripoli* (1955); *Miami Expose, The Beast of Hollow Mountain, Uranium Boom, Stranger at My Door* (1956); *The Buckskin Lady* (1957); *The Battle of the V.1* (1958); *Count Your Blessings* (1959); *Snow White and the Three Stooges* (1961); *The Killing of Sister George* (1968); *Timber Tramps* (1973).

MEEK, Donald (1880–1946)

Scottish character actor who moved to the USA in 1912. He appeared in over a hundred films after pursuing a successful stage career. Being a small, bald man, Meek often played nervous, timidly respectable American characters such as the whisky salesman in John Ford's 1939 *Stagecoach*. MHu

FILMS: *Six Cylinder Love* (1923); *The Hole in the Wall* (1929); *The Love Kiss* (1930); *The Babbling Book, The Clyde Mystery, The Cole Case, The Symphony Murder Mystery, Personal Maid, The Habit* (1931); *The Crane Poison Case, Murder in the Pullman, The Side Show Mystery, The Skull Murder Mystery, The Studio Murder Mystery, The Trans-Atlantic Murder Mystery, The Wall Street Mystery, The Week End Mystery, Wayward* (1932); *Ever in My Heart, College Coach, Love, Honor and Oh Baby!, China Seas* (1933); *Bedside, Hi, Nellie!, The Last Gentleman, The Captain Hates the Sea, Mrs Wiggs of the Cabbage Patch, The Merry Widow, The Defense Rests, Murder at the Vanities* (1934); *She Couldn't Take It, Village Tale, Captain Blood, Baby Face Harrington, The Bride Comes Home, Kind Lady, Peter Ibbetson, Happiness C.O.D., Barbary Coast, The*

Return of Peter Grimm, Top Hat, Accent on Youth, Old Man Rhythm, The Informer, Mark of the Vampire, The Whole Town's Talking, The Gilded Lily, Society Doctor, Romance in Manhattan, Biography of a Bachelor Girl (1935); *One Rainy Afternoon, Pennies from Heaven, Three Married Men, Three Wise Guys, And So They Were Married, Love on the Run, Two in a Crowd, Old Hutch, Everybody's Old Man* (1936); *Make a Wish, You're a Sweetheart, Breakfast for Two, Double Wedding, Artists & Models, The Toast of New York, Three Legionnaires, Parnell, Behind the Headlines, Maid of Salem* (1937); *Hold that Co-ed, Little Miss Broadway, You Can't Take it with You, Having Wonderful Time, Goodbye Broadway, The Adventures of Tom Sawyer, Double Danger* (1938); *Nick Carter – Master Detective, Hollywood Cavalcade, The Housekeeper's Daughter, Blondie Takes a Vacation, Young Mr Lincoln, Stagecoach, Jesse James* (1939); *The Ghost Comes Home, Hullabaloo, Sky Murder, Star Dust, Third Finger, Left Hand, Turnabout, Dr Ehrlich's Magic Bullet, The Return of Frank James, Phantom Raiders, My Little Chickadee, The Man from Dakota, Oh Johnny, How You Can Love* (1940); *Babes on Broadway, Blonde Inspiration, The Feminine Touch, Rise and Shine, A Woman's Face, Barnacle Bill, Come Live with Me, The Wild Man of Borneo* (1941); *Maisie Gets Her Man, Keeper of the Flame, The Omaha Trail, Seven Sweethearts, Tortilla Flat* (1942); *Lost Angel, Du Barry was a Lady, Air Raid Wardens, They Got Me Covered* (1943); *Barbary Coast Gent, Maisie Goes to Reno, The Thin Man Goes Home, Two Girls and a Sailor, Bathing Beauty, Rationing* (1944); *Colonel Effingham's Raid, State Fair* (1945); *Janie Gets Married, Affairs of Geraldine, Because of Him* (1946); *Magic Town, The Fabulous Joe* (1947).

MELCHIOR, Lauritz (1890–1973)

Lauritz Melchior, 'the finest Wagnerian tenor of his time', was one of the guilty pleasures of 1940s filmgoing. He added his own brand of blustering humour to such escapist films as *Thrill of a Romance* and *Two Sisters from Boston*, but in the end, this mass exposure cost him his career with the Metropolitan Opera.

Melchior was from a musical family and made his operatic debut in 1913. His Metropolitan debut came thirteen years later. He added radio commercials to his US repertoire and was awarded a contract by MGM's producer Joe Pasternak in 1945. The hefty singer seems to have had the time of his life spoofing his own image while performing snippets from *Aida*, Franz Schubert and Cole Porter – with a Danish folk song or two thrown in for good measure.

War-weary audiences enjoyed the spectacle of this imposing tenor playing a cuddly cupid to the likes of Esther
Williams and Kathryn Grayson. Unfortunately, The Metropolitan's new manager, Rudolf Bing, took a dim view of
Hollywood musicals and Melchior's contract was not
renewed. The stout opera star continued to record extensively, however, and a 1963 Carnegie Hall concert marking
his fiftieth anniversary proved a major event in his adopted
country. HJW

FILMS: *Thrill of a Romance* (1945); *Two Sisters from Boston*
(1946); *This Time for Keeps* (1947); *Luxury Liner* (1948); *The
Stars are Singing* (1953).

MERCIER, Louis (1901–1993)

French actor who started in Hollywood in the 1920s and
successfully made the transition to sound. He was almost
invariably cast as a Frenchman in – often uncredited – bit
parts in an impressive number of American films and television programmes, until he retired in the late 1970s. His
characters were often nameless, but Mercier may be
remembered as Mario in *An Affair to Remember* and as Jean
Leroux in *Sahara*. CH

FILMS: *Paris* (1926); *Seven Footprints to Satan, Tiger Rose*
(1929); *Quick Millions* (1930); *Careless Lady* (1932); *Riptide*
(1934); *Naughty Marietta* (1935); *Under Two Flags, The Road
to Glory, The Garden of Allah, That Girl from Paris* (1936);
*Café Métropole, I'll Take Romance, Charlie Chan at Monte
Carlo* (1937); *Jezebel, Adventure in Sahara, Artists and Models
Abroad* (1938); *The Story of Vernon and Irene Castle, Midnight,
Bulldog Drummond's Bride, Everything Happens at Night, Char-
lie Chan in City in Darkness* (1939); *Adventure in Diamonds,
Arise, My Love* (1940); *This Woman is Mine* (1941); *Dr
Renault's Secret, Casablanca, Reunion in France, The Lady has
Plans* (1942); *Sahara, The Song of Bernadette* (1943); *The Mask
of Dimitrios, To Have and Have Not, The Conspirators, Passage
to Marseille* (1944); *Johnny Angel, Saratoga Trunk, Prison Ship,
Cornered* (1945); *The Razor's Edge, My Darling Clementine,
Tarzan and the Leopard Woman, So Dark the Night, The Return
of Monte Cristo* (1946); *Jewels of Brandenburg, High Conquest*
(1947); *I, Jane Doe, To the Victor* (1948); *When Willie Comes
Marching Home* (1950); *Show Boat, Go for Broke!* (1951);
Lydia Bailey, What Price Glory? (1952); *The French Line*
(1954); *Pirates of Tripoli, Untamed, To Catch a Thief, Jump into
Hell, We're No Angels* (1955); *The Man Who Knew Too Much,
Attack* (1956); *An Affair to Remember, Will Success Spoil Rock

Hunter? (1957); *Lafayette Escadrille* (1958); *The Wreck of the
Mary Deare* (1959); *Seven Thieves* (1960); *The Devil at 4
O'Clock* (1961); *Tender is the Night* (1962); *Wild and Won-
derful* (1964); *The Art of Love* (1965); *Darling Lili* (1970); *The
Other Side of Midnight* (1977).

MERCIER, Michèle (Jocelyne Mercier) (1939–)

Mercier's relationship to Hollywood has been a long hit-
and-miss affair. As a beautiful young starlet, she was invited
in 1959 to do a screen test for producer Hal B. Wallis. This
led nowhere, and her first experience of American cinema
came with a small part in the Franco-American *Goodbye
Again* (1961), an adaptation of Françoise Sagan's best-selling
novel *Aimez-vous Brahms?* She then co-starred in a Bob
Hope comedy, *A Global Affair*, earning the label 'A touch of
Paris'. But her career took off in Italy and France, where she
briefly became top box office, thanks to the 'Angélique'
series of swashbucklers, starting with *Angélique Marquise des
Anges/Angélique* (1964). Wishing to break with Angélique
stereotyping in the early 1970s, Mercier tried to start a new
career in Hollywood, as actress and producer. She bought
the rights to Charles Williams' thriller *A Touch of Death*, hired
the Coppola studios and Rod Steiger as co-star. This
ambitious venture unfortunately collapsed and Mercier's
career never recovered either in the USA or Europe, where
she returned in 1976. She perceptively noted that 'A European actress cannot make it in Hollywood unless she stays
permanently. If you go and make just one film, it's a flash in
the pan and you are quickly forgotten.' GV

FILMS: *Goodbye Again* (1961); *A Global Affair* (1964).

MERCOURI, Melina (Maria-Amalia Mercouri) (1920–1994)

Greek stage star who won European recognition and a
nomination at Cannes for her role in Michael Cacoyannis'
drama *Stella* (1954). Her character's ardent sexuality, paired
with a uniquely strong personality, made her only 100 per
cent Greek film an instant domestic hit, as well as a runaway European success. Her performance in this role, and
in a number of subsequent films, saw Mercouri successfully
combine feminine strength, sexuality and integrity. Her rise
to international stardom came with her success in the
comedy *Never on Sunday* (1960), a Greek production
directed by American expatriate Jules Dassin, who became
Mercouri's second husband from 1966 to her death. Mer-

couri's Greek 'prostitute with a golden heart' Ilya won her the Best Actress award at Cannes in 1960 and an Academy Award nomination in 1961.

Though not typically Greek-looking, blonde-haired Mercouri nevertheless played characters of Greek, Mediterranean or Eastern European origin in a bid to justify her deep, husky, almost masculine voice that always kept its Greek accent. Her American films also emphasised her exotic sexuality and vibrant personality. In Dassin's *Topkapi*, she was the glamorous emerald thief Elizabeth Lipp, a role for which she was nominated for a Golden Globe in 1965. In the spy comedy *A Man Could Get Killed*, she played the seductive Aurora-Celeste da Costa who chases James Garner in the hope that she can get hold of more stolen diamonds. She was the glamorous Queen Lil, a wealthy brothel madam, in *Gaily, Gaily*, and in *Once is Not Enough* she was cast as the retired, but still glamorous, film star Carla who has a lesbian affair. Mercouri also appeared in a number of American co-productions, most of them filmed in Europe and many directed by Dassin, such as *Phaedra* (1961) *The Victors, 10:30 P.M. Summer, Promise at Dawn* (1970) and *A Dream of Passion* (1978). She also presented the one-hour documentary *Melina's Greece* (1966) for the American ABC network.

The collapse of Greek democracy in 1967 found Mercouri in New York, while she and Dassin were staging a musical version of *Never on Sunday* entitled *Ilya Darling* at the Mark Hellinger Theatre. She encouraged active resistance against the Junta in the USA and Europe, and her passionate involvement resulted in a temporary loss of Greek citizenship. After the restoration of democracy in 1974, Mercouri moved back to Greece. In 1981, she became Minister of Culture and campaigned until the end of her life for the return to Greece of the Elgin Marbles kept at the British Museum. TH

FILMS: *The Victors* (1963); *Topkapi* (1964); *10:30 P.M. Summer* (1966); *A Man Could Get Killed, Gaily, Gaily* (1969); *The Rehearsal* (1973); *Once is Not Enough* (1975).

MÉRIL, Macha (Marie-Madeleine Merilova) (1940–)
Moroccan-born French actress of Russian ancestry who made her film debut as the sexy Yvette in Gérard Oury's★ *La Main chaude/The Itchy Palm* (1959), and was cast next to Brigitte Bardot★ in Roger Vadim's *Le Repos du guerrier/Love on a Pillow* (1962). Méril then paralleled stardom in the

French New Wave with a sporadic English-language career, for example in supporting roles in *Who's Been Sleeping in My Bed?* and the French/British/American co-production *A Soldier's Daughter Never Cries* (1998). TH
FILMS: *Who's Been Sleeping in My Bed?* (1963); *Duet for One* (1986).

METAXA, Georges (1899–1950)
Elegant, olive-skinned Romanian baritone who came to Britain in 1926 and scored West End successes in Cole Porter's *Wake Up and Dream* and Noel Coward's *Bitter Sweet*. Metaxa transferred to Broadway with both productions in 1931. He became a permanent US resident and undertook his first work in musical films. Only one sizeable role in Hollywood followed, when he played the Latin bandleader Ricky Romero in the Fred Astaire and Ginger Rogers vehicle *Swing Time*. Metaxa's subsequent film work consisted of minor parts as Continental types and Nazi agents. RJK
FILMS: *Secrets of a Secretary* (1931); *Kissing Time* (1933); *Swing Time* (1936); *The Doctor Takes a Wife* (1940); *Paris Calling* (1941); *Submarine Base, Hi Diddle Diddle, West Side Kid* (1943); *The Mask of Dimitrios* (1944); *Scotland Yard Investigator* (1945).

MEYER, Greta (1883–1965)
Plump and broad-featured German character actress (sometimes credited as Mayer or Meyers) who played numerous (often uncredited) cooks, cleaners, nurses and Middle European hausfraus during her long Hollywood career. AP
FILMS: *The Royal Box* (1929); *Private Lives* [scenes deleted], *Tonight or Never* (1931); *Faithless, Flesh, Grand Hotel, The Man from Yesterday, The Match King* (1932); *Whistling in the Dark, The White Sister, Stage Mother, Bombshell, The Chief, Jennie Gerhardt, Let's Fall in Love, Meet the Baron, The Nuisance, Pilgrimage* (1933); *As Husbands Go, Elmer Steps Out, All Men are Enemies, Forsaking All Others, The Line Up, The Mighty Barnum, Most Precious Thing in Life, Private Scandal, Servants' Entrance, Strange Wives, Young and Beautiful* (1934); *Biography of a Bachelor Girl, Twin Triplets, Diamond Jim, Four Hours to Kill!, His Night Out, Laddie, Mister Dynamite, Naughty Marietta, Public Hero No. 1, The Return of Peter Grimm, Smart Girl* (1935); *Dimples* [scenes deleted], *These Three, The Gorgeous Hussy, Libeled Lady, Moonlight Murder, Spendthrift, Suzy, Wife vs. Secretary*

(1936); *Bill Cracks Down, Heidi, I'll Take Romance, Lancer Spy, Marriage Forbidden, Night of Mystery, Prescription for Romance, Fly Away Baby, Reported Missing, The Road Back, Thin Ice, Damaged Goods, When Love is Young* (1937); *The Great Waltz, Paradise for Three, The Patient in Room 18, Swiss Miss, Three Loves has Nancy, Torchy Gets Her Man* (1938); *No Place to Go, Paris Honeymoon, Twelve Crowded Hours, When Tomorrow Comes, The Women* (1939); *Bitter Sweet, Dr Ehrlich's Magic Bullet, Four Sons, The Man I Married* (1940); *Come Live with Me, Million Dollar Baby* (1941); *Friendly Enemies, Reunion in France* (1942); *They Got Me Covered* (1943); *An American Romance* (1944).

MEYER, Torben (1884–1975)

Supporting player who, after fifteen years in Danish silents, came to Hollywood under his own steam in 1927, in the hope of 'hitting the big time'. Although fame eluded him, the sour-looking, bald-headed actor remained a familiar face on American film (and television) screens, where he invariably played an urbane European waiter, maître d', valet or butler in numerous A- and B-productions over the next three decades, including *Letter from an Unknown Woman*. During the 1940s, Meyer was also part of producer-director Preston Sturges' regular entourage of stock players. He appeared in nine Sturges comedies, from *Christmas in July* through to *The Beautiful Blonde from Bashful Bend*. Meyer's role as guilt-ridden German judge Werner Lammpe in *Judgment at Nuremberg* was perhaps the actor's most striking and dramatic screen moment. An American citizen, Meyer remained in Hollywood, largely forgotten in his native Denmark, until his death. Despite recent research efforts, his American filmography is likely to remain incomplete. RJK

FILMS: *The Man Who Laughs, The Viking, Jazz Mad* (1928); *The Last Warning, Behind Closed Doors* (1929); *Lummox, Mamba, The Bad One, Just Like Heaven, A Soldier's Plaything, Behind the Make-Up* (1930); *Just a Gigolo* (1931); *Broken Lullaby, Murders in the Rue Morgue, What Price Hollywood?, Downstairs, Big City Blues, The Animal Kingdom, Six Hours to Live, The Match King* (1932); *The Crime of the Century, Reunion in Vienna* (1933); *Little Man, What Now?, Mandalay, All Men are Enemies, The World Moves On, Pursued, Music in the Air* (1934); *Mark of the Vampire* [scenes deleted], *If You Could Only Cook, Enter Madame, The Good Fairy, Roberta, Bride of Frankenstein, Break of Hearts, Front Page Woman, The Gay Deception, Special Agent, The Girl Who Came Back, The Man Who Broke the Bank at Monte Carlo, East of Java, Two for Tonight, To Beat the Band, Splendor, Mark of the Vampire, King of Burlesque, The Night is Young, Thunder in the Night, Charlie Chan in Shanghai, A Tale of Two Cities, The Black Room* (1935); *The Farmer in the Dell, Anything Goes, Piccadilly Jim, In His Steps, Wedding Present, The Accusing Finger, Preview Murder Mystery, Star for a Night, Champagne Charlie, Till We Meet Again, It Had to Happen* (1936); *The Good Old Soak, She's No Lady, Wife, Doctor and Nurse, The King and the Chorus Girl, Shall We Dance?, The Emperor's Candlesticks, The Prisoner of Zenda, Madame X, Fight for Your Lady, Thin Ice, Espionage, Tovarich, Prescription for Romance* (1937); *Romance in the Dark, Bulldog Drummond's Peril, The First Hundred Years, I'll Give a Million, The Great Waltz* (1938); *Topper Takes a Trip, Island of Lost Men, Everything Happens at Night* (1939); *Four Sons, Dr Ehrlich's Magic Bullet, The Great Dictator, The Way of All Flesh, No, No, Nanette, Christmas in July* (1940); *Bedtime Story, Sunny, The Lady Eve* (1941); *Crossroads, Berlin Correspondent, Casablanca, Sullivan's Travels, The Adventures of Martin Eden, Journey into Fear, The Palm Beach Story* (1942); *Frankenstein Meets the Wolf Man, Edge of Darkness, They Came to Blow Up America, Jack London* (1943); *Once upon a Time, Hail the Conquering Hero, The Purple Heart, The Miracle of Morgan's Creek, Greenwich Village, The Great Moment* (1944); *A Royal Scandal, Yolanda and the Thief, Hotel Berlin* (1945); *Heartbeat, The Kid from Brooklyn, Monsieur Beaucaire, Alias Mr Twilight* (1946); *The Sin of Harold Diddlebock, The Mighty McGurk, Variety Girl, The Beginning or the End, Millie's Daughter, Song of Love, The Exile* (1947); *Julia Misbehaves, To the Victor, Unfaithfully Yours, Sealed Verdict, Letter from an Unknown Woman* (1948); *The Great Lover, Hold that Baby!, And Baby Makes Three, The Beautiful Blonde from Bashful Bend* (1949); *The Great Rupert* (1950); *The Company She Keeps, Grounds for Marriage, Night into Morning, That's My Boy, My Favorite Spy, Come Fill the Cup, The Blue Veil* (1951); *The Merry Widow, What Price Glory* (1952); *Ma and Pa Kettle on Vacation, The Caddy, Call Me Madam, The Story of Three Loves, Houdini* (1953); *About Mrs Leslie, Casanova's Big Night, Deep in My Heart, Living it Up* (1954); *We're No Angels* (1955); *Hollywood or Bust, The Conqueror, Anything Goes* (1956); *The Helen Morgan Story, Public Pigeon No. 1, The Fly, The Matchmaker* (1958); *This Earth is Mine* (1959); *G. I. Blues* (1960); *Judgment at Nuremberg* (1961); *A New Kind of Love* (1963).

MIKAËL, Ludmila (Ludmilla Dmitrienko) (1947–)
An Anouk Aimée★ lookalike, Mikaël has made a large number of films in France, although her career has been more distinguished on stage than in the cinema. Her only Hollywood movie was *The Sergeant*, where she played the French love interest. VO
FILM: *The Sergeant* (1968).

MILES, Sarah (1941–)
RADA-trained actress who came to fame in a series of teen roles in British films such as *Term of Trial* (1962) and *The Servant* (1963), in which she was principally characterised by a sexual precociousness and manipulativeness. Her association with highly sexed and taboo-breaking roles continued into full adulthood and culminated in the adulterous heroines she played in the big-budget costume dramas *Ryan's Daughter* and *Lady Caroline Lamb* (1972). *The Man Who Loved Cat Dancing*, her one major appearance in a Hollywood film proper – the others were majority or solely US-funded productions shot overseas – saw her play a haughty genteel lady reluctantly forced to endure the close company of Burt Reynolds' coarse, rugged train robber. Such patent miscasting and mismatching of different conceptions of period English femininity helped to ensure that it remained her solitary transatlantic excursion. JB

FILMS: *The Ceremony* (1964); *Those Magnificent Men in Their Flying Machines, or How I Flew from London to Paris in 25 Hours, 11 Minutes* (1965); *Blow-Up* (1966); *Ryan's Daughter* (1970); *The Man Who Loved Cat Dancing, The Hireling* (1973); *The Sailor Who Fell from Grace with the Sea* (1976); *Hope and Glory, White Mischief* (1987).

MILLAND, Ray (Reginald Truscott-Jones) (1907–1986)
Ray Milland (aka Spike Milland, or Raymond Milland in some of his earliest films) is a notable rarity among the first wave of successful British actors in Hollywood: a leading man who crossed the Atlantic without any theatrical credentials to introduce himself with. The tale of his 'discovery' is itself more akin to a hyperbolic Hollywood publicity story than a typically British rise through the ranks. The Welsh-born Milland was on leave from the Royal Household Cavalry in 1928 when he met the visiting American actress Estelle Brody in a nightclub. Buoyed by her suggestion that his striking good looks would register well on screen, he went to call on her at Elstree after being demobbed and found himself hired on the spot as an extra in E. A. Dupont's *Piccadilly* (1929). Further minor roles followed but conscious that he had thus far pushed his luck to the limit, Milland decided to gain a proper theatrical training with a repertory company. He had, however, already been spotted by Robert Rubin, a scout for MGM. A contract swiftly followed and Milland embarked for Hollywood in August 1930.

Here the narrative becomes more untidy. MGM loaned Milland out to Warner Bros. for relatively small roles in relatively small pictures, and then declined to renew his option. Forced abruptly to abandon his new American life and his new American bride, Milland returned to London, where work on two further British films helped to pay for his return passage. A spell as the assistant manager of a Hollywood gas station preceded a contract with Paramount, who had been specifically looking for a British male lead. There can be little doubt that Paramount, in common with many other studios, were desperately hoping to find another Ronald Colman★ type. For several years, Milland dutifully presented himself as a cut-price Colman, following directly in the original's footsteps by appearing in *Bulldog Drummond Escapes* and the 1939 remake of *Beau Geste*.

Milland's association with Paramount extended throughout the 1940s. It is fair to say, though, that he was more adaptable and/or had a less rigidly predefined 'English' persona than many of his fellow countrymen. He went on to appear in a strikingly diverse number of genres, ranging from musicals, light comedies and female-centred melodramas to action-adventure films, hard-boiled film noirs and – most unusually for a British male lead in Hollywood – he played the hero in several Westerns. Perhaps his most surprising demonstration of versatility came in his Academy Award-winning and emotionally raw turn in Billy Wilder's *The Lost Weekend* as an alcoholic holed up for a four-day bender. In the latter stages of his career, his ability to retreat behind a stereotypically guarded and reserved English gentleman's demeanour and unruffled eloquence saw him follow a more typical career pattern for the Hollywood British émigré: he was a gentlemanly villain – to best effect in Alfred Hitchcock's *Dial M for Murder* – or an arrogant scientist in various horror and science-fiction films. JB

FILMS: *Way for a Sailor, Passion Flower* (1930); *The Bachelor Father, Strangers May Kiss, Just a Gigolo, Bought, Ambassador Bill, Blonde Crazy* (1931); *The Man Who Played God, Polly of the Circus, But the Flesh is Weak, Payment Deferred* (1932); *The Mystery of Mr X, We're Not Dressing, Bolero, Menace, Many Happy Returns, Charlie Chan in London* (1934); *The Gilded Lily, Four Hours to Kill!, Alias Mary Dow, One Hour Late, The Glass Key* (1935); *The Big Broadcast of 1937, The Jungle Princess, Three Smart Girls, The Return of Sophie Lang, Next Time We Love* (1936); *Bulldog Drummond Escapes, Ebb Tide, Wise Girl, Wings over Honolulu, Easy Living* (1937); *Her Jungle Love, Tropic Holiday, Say it in French, Men with Wings* (1938); *Hotel Imperial, Beau Geste, Everything Happens at Night* (1939); *Irene, Arise, My Love, Untamed, The Doctor Takes a Wife* (1940); *I Wanted Wings, Skylark* (1941); *Reap the Wild Wind, Are Husbands Necessary?, The Major and the Minor, Star Spangled Rhythm, The Lady has Plans* (1942); *Forever and a Day, The Crystal Ball* (1943); *Lady in the Dark, The Uninvited, Ministry of Fear, Till We Meet Again* (1944); *The Lost Weekend* (1945); *Kitty, The Well-Groomed Bride, California* (1946); *Golden Earrings, Variety Girl, The Trouble with Women, The Imperfect Lady* (1947); *Miss Tatlock's Millions, Sealed Verdict, The Big Clock* (1948); *Alias Nick Beal, It Happens Every Spring* (1949); *A Woman of Distinction, A Life of Her Own, Copper Canyon* (1950); *Close to My Heart, Rhubarb, Night into Morning, Circle of Danger* (1951); *Something to Live For, Bugles in the Afternoon, The Thief* (1952); *Let's Do it Again, Jamaica Run* (1953); *Dial M for Murder* (1954); *A Man Alone, The Girl in the Red Velvet Swing* (1955); *Lisbon* (1956); *Three Brave Men, The River's Edge* (1957); *The Premature Burial, Panic in Year Zero!* (1962); *X: The Man with the X-Ray Eyes* (1963); *The Confession* (1964); *Love Story* (1970); *Frogs, The Thing with Two Heads, Embassy* (1972); *Terror in the Wax Museum* (1973); *Escape to Witch Mountain* (1975); *The Last Tycoon* (1976); *Oliver's Story, Battlestar Galactica* (1978); *The Attic* (1979); *Survival Run* (1980).

MILLER, Bodil (1928–)

Stage-trained, exotic-looking Danish fashion model who earned a seven-year contract with Universal in 1951. The dark brunette played distinctly non-Scandinavian types – including a French girl – in a couple of B-movies, but returned to Denmark after the failure of her marriage to the veteran screenwriter Eugene Solow. HJW

FILMS: *Scarlet Angel, Because of You* (1952); *Ma and Pa Kettle on Vacation* (1953).

MILLER, Jonny Lee (1972–)

Miller was born into a theatrical family – his grandfather Bernard Lee played 'M' in the Bond films. His role as Sick Boy in *Trainspotting* (1996) led to some American film parts, but his persona hovers somewhat uneasily between edgy, quirky characters and conventional leading man, which makes him slightly difficult to cast. AS

FILMS: *Afterglow* (1997); *Dracula 2000* (2000); *Mindhunters, Melinda and Melinda* (2004).

MILLS, Hayley (1946–)

British actress, daughter of Sir John Mills★ and sister of Juliet Mills★, who made her British film debut, aged thirteen, in *Tiger Bay* (1959). Her outstanding performance led to a five-year contract with Disney, but after a successful career as a lively and impish child star, the transition to adult roles proved problematic. Since the 1970s, she has concentrated on stage and television work. MHu

FILMS: *Pollyanna* (1960); *The Parent Trap* (1961); *In Search of the Castaways* (1962); *Summer Magic* (1963); *The Chalk Garden, The Truth about Spring, The Moon Spinners* (1964); *That Darn Cat!* (1965); *The Trouble with Angels, The Daydreamer* [voice], *The Family Way* (1966); *Africa – Texas Style!, Pretty Polly* (1967); *Take a Girl Like You* (1970); *Appointment with Death* (1988); *A Troll in Central Park* [voice] (1993); *2B Perfectly Honest* (2004).

MILLS, John (Lewis Ernest Watts Mills) (1908–2005)

John Mills appeared mainly in British films and is identified with a quiet, reserved but strong portrayal of Britishness. Initially a stage actor, in 1931 Mills was offered the chance to recreate the part he had played on stage in *Cavalcade* in Fox's screen version. Mills turned the offer down because he did not want to be bound to the seven-year contract Fox was proposing. He appeared with Robert Donat★ in MGM's *Goodbye, Mr Chips*, and continued to star in British films during World War II. His roles in *In Which We Serve* (1942), *This Happy Breed* (1944) and, in particular, *Great Expectations* (1946), made him an international star. When he visited the USA in 1947, he was offered several parts in Hollywood films, including the role Bogart subsequently played in *The African Queen* **367**

(1951). The Rank Organisation was unwilling to loan him out and he stayed in Britain, where he starred in some of the most notable films of the 1950s. He had a brief cameo appearance in *Around the World in Eighty Days* and starred in *The Swiss Family Robinson*, a film registered as British but funded by Disney. In the 1960s, his film work was typified by character roles, and he also appeared on US television. One of his most challenging later parts was as a mute villager in *Ryan's Daughter*, directed by David Lean and registered as British, but part-funded by MGM. SS

FILMS: *Doctor's Orders* (1934); *Goodbye, Mr Chips* (1939); *The Young Mr Pitt* (1942); *The End of the Affair* (1955); *Around the World in Eighty Days, War and Peace* (1956); *Town on Trial* (1957); *The Swiss Family Robinson* (1960); *The Parent Trap* (1961); *The Truth About Spring, The Chalk Garden* (1964); *Operation Crossbow, King Rat* (1965); *The Wrong Box* (1966); *Chuka, Africa – Texas Style!* (1967); *Oh! What a Lovely War* (1969); *Ryan's Daughter* (1970); *Oklahoma Crude* (1973); *Zulu Dawn* (1979); *Sahara* (1983); *Who's That Girl?* (1987); *Hamlet* (1996).

MILLS, Juliet (1941–)

Though generally eclipsed by her sister Hayley Mills★, regular Broadway and American television appearances have brought Juliet occasional Hollywood parts, most memorably as a prematurely dowdy spinster wooed by Jack Lemmon in Billy Wilder's *Avanti!*. JB

FILMS: *The Rare Breed* (1966); *Oh! What a Lovely War* (1969); *Avanti!* (1972); *The Deadly Trackers, Jonathan Livingston Seagull* [voice] (1973); *Waxwork II: Lost in Time* (1992); *The Other Sister* (1999).

MILUSHEV, Boyan (1958–)

Bulgarian actor who emigrated to the USA in the early 1990s, where he claimed that his artistic career had been suppressed by the Communist authorities at home. Milushev set up a production company and obtained Hollywood financing for an unsuccessful post-Communist thriller that he co-wrote and produced. Milushev has since had a minor role in a Dolph Lundgren★ vehicle. DI

FILMS: *Bird of Prey* (1996); *Bridge of Dragons* (1999).

MINOTES, Alexis (1900–1990)

Greek actor and husband of Katina Paxinou★ who started his career in the theatre. In 1930, he appeared in Vasilis

Perides' drama *Gia tin agapi tis/For Her Love*, his only Greek film. He arrived in the USA in 1942, where he was mostly cast as a foreigner. His most memorable supporting roles are Joseph, butler to Nazi spy Alexander Sebastian (Claude Rains★) in Alfred Hitchcock's *Notorious*, and Hamar in Howard Hawks' epic drama *Land of the Pharaohs*. TH

FILMS: *Notorious, The Chase* (1946); *Siren of Atlantis* (1949); *Panic in the Streets* (1950); *Land of the Pharaohs* (1955); *Boy on a Dolphin* (1957).

MIRANDA, Isa (Inès Isabella Sampietro) (1909–1982)

Beautiful, blonde Italian actress with elegant looks and almond-shaped eyes whose strong dramatic temperament made her one of the most noted Italian stars of the 1930s and 1940s. Her first lead role came with Guido Brignone's *Tenebre* (1934). In the same year, she reached international stardom in Max Ophuls' *La signora di tutti* (1934). She then signed a contract with Paramount and made two American films. The first, *Hotel Imperial*, saw Miranda taking the lead role of Anna Warschawska, a vengeful woman who is searching for the man she blames for her sister's suicide. Miranda was replacing Marlene Dietrich★ and Margaret Sullavan in the part, even though her English was of such a poor standard she had to recite her lines phonetically. *Adventure in Diamonds*, in which she played opposite George Brent as a jewel thief, however, marked the end of Miranda's stay in Hollywood. Strong differences of opinion led to her being fired from George Cukor's 1939 *Zaza* (although Miranda later starred in the 1944 Italian version, *Zazà*). She occasionally returned to Hollywood. Perhaps her most memorable latter-day role was as Signora Fiorina, the owner of a Venetian *pensione* who encourages Katharine Hepburn's character to seek out male company in David Lean's *Summertime*. CS

FILMS: *Hotel Imperial* (1939); *Adventure in Diamonds* (1940); *Summertime* (1955); *Do You Know this Voice?* (1964); *The Yellow Rolls-Royce* (1965); *The Shoes of the Fisherman* (1968).

MIRREN, Helen (Ilyena Lydia Mironoff) (1945–)

Intelligent, versatile and widely respected English actress of theatre, film and television who transcended early sex-kittenish typecasting in sexploitation movies like *Caligula* by attracting Hollywood's attention with commanding performances in *The Long Good Friday* and *Excalibur* (both

1981). Mirren's Russian heritage – her father was an aristocratic émigré – led to more substantial American roles as stern Soviets in *2010* and *White Nights*. However, her high-profile role as Harrison Ford's beleaguered wife in Peter Weir's *The Mosquito Coast* failed to become her desired American breakthrough, and audiences' rejection of the film's dark themes led to a decade-long exile from Hollywood. She returned to the limelight with an Academy Award nomination for *The Madness of King George* (1994), and her stock was raised further after a searing performance in the American co-funded *Some Mother's Son*. Mirren's US career has since stabilised and she has worked with Sidney Lumet in *Critical Care* and taken the title role in *The Passion of Ayn Rand*. The respect with which she is now viewed by Hollywood is indicated by a key supporting role alongside Jack Nicholson in *The Pledge* and memorable parts in films directed by Robert Altman and Hal Hartley. MF

FILMS: *Caligula, The Fiendish Plot of Dr Fu Manchu* (1980); *2010* (1984); *White Nights* (1985); *The Mosquito Coast* (1986); *Some Mother's Son, Losing Chase* (1996); *Critical Care* (1997); *The Prince of Egypt* [voice] (1998); *The Passion of Ayn Rand, Teaching Mrs Tingle* (1999); *Greenfingers* (2000); *The Pledge, Gosford Park, No Such Thing* (2001); *The Clearing, Raising Helen* (2004).

MOFFAT, Donald (1930–)

Imposing English stage and screen actor whose versatility has earned the admiration of such influential Hollywood figures as Robert Altman and Brian De Palma. MF

FILMS: *Rachel, Rachel* (1968); *R.P.M.* (1970); *The Great Northfield Minnesota Raid* (1972); *Showdown* (1973); *Earthquake, Terminal Man* (1974); *Land of No Return* (1975); *Promises in the Dark, H.E.A.L.T.H.* (1979); *Popeye, On the Nickel* (1980); *White Lions* (1981); *The Thing* (1982); *The Right Stuff* (1983); *Alamo Bay* (1985); *The Best of Times, Monster in the Closet* (1986); *The Unbearable Lightness of Being, Far North* (1988); *The Bonfire of the Vanities, Music Box* (1990); *Class Action, Regarding Henry* (1991); *Housesitter* (1992); *Clear and Present Danger, Trapped in Paradise* (1994); *The Evening Star* (1996); *A Smile Like Yours* (1997); *Cookie's Fortune* (1999).

MOLINA, Alfred (1953–)

Latin-featured British actor who made his film debut in *Raiders of the Lost Ark*. Since then Molina has worked in British and American theatre, film and television. His US film appearances have included two films with Paul Thomas Anderson and a powerful performance as Diego Rivera in *Frida*. MHu

FILMS: *Raiders of the Lost Ark* (1981); *Ladyhawke* (1985); *Manifesto* (1988); *Not without My Daughter* (1991); *White Fang II: Myth of the White Wolf, Maverick* (1994); *Hideaway, The Perez Family, Species* (1995); *Before and After, Mojave Moon* (1996); *Anna Karenina, Scorpion Spring, Boogie Nights* (1997); *The Imposters, The Treat, Pete's Meteor* (1998); *Dudley Do-Right, Magnolia* (1999); *Texas Rangers* (2001); *Frida* (2002); *Identity, Coffee and Cigarettes* (2003); *Spider-Man 2* (2004).

MONTAND, Yves (1921–1991)

A hugely popular singer and actor in France for over four decades, Montand had a brief though high-profile brush with American cinema in the 1960s. Hollywood took note of tall, charismatic Montand after his international hit *Le Salaire de la peur/The Wages of Fear* (1953) and his triumphant 1959 Broadway one-man show. His first American role, as French billionaire Jean-Marc Clément in George Cukor's musical *Let's Make Love*, and especially his affair with co-star Marilyn Monroe propelled him further into the limelight. However, although he worked with major directors (Cukor, Minnelli, Litvak) and co-stars (Monroe, Ingrid Bergman★, Shirley MacLaine, Barbra Streisand) and was hailed 'The greatest gift since the French sent us the Statue of Liberty', Montand never found parts in Hollywood that remotely matched his French work.

After wavering between different genres in the 1950s, Montand's French star persona evolved a distinctive brand of strong, self-contained masculinity that he honed after *Le Salaire de la peur* in thrillers such as *Compartment tueurs/The Sleeping Car Murders* (1965) and *Le Cercle rouge/The Red Circle* (1970). By contrast, Hollywood went for the Gallic charmer and – up to a point – the singer, in romance (*Goodbye Again*, with Bergman, based on Françoise Sagan's novel *Aimez-vous Brahms?*), comedy (*My Geisha* with MacLaine) and musicals (*Let's Make Love* with Monroe; *On a Clear Day You Can See Forever* with Streisand). But despite his charm, *joli laid* good looks and the calibre of his co-stars, on-screen chemistry was lacking. His stilted delivery of English was partly to blame, as was the fact that musicals were on the wane. But the problem was also a set of perverse plot and casting decisions. *Let's Make Love* is a telling example. **369**

Having fallen in love with sexy singer Amanda (Monroe), Clément (Montand) pretends to be an actor impersonating the billionaire lampooned by the show, i.e. 'himself'. He therefore has to show he cannot act, sing or dance. As a result Montand the star, like Clément the character, is humiliatingly shown up by the teachers he hires (wicked cameos by Milton Berle, Bing Crosby and Gene Kelly) and by dynamic crooner Frankie Vaughan★. His only on-stage 'performance' is a grotesque 'cock-a-doodle-do!', hardly redeemed by a brief real song on the end credits.

Although Montand was given more leeway in his other Hollywood films, he tended to be dominated by his female partners: comic dynamo Streisand sadly shows up his gauche psychiatrist/hypnotist in On a Clear Day – explaining why some of his part allegedly ended up on the cutting-room floor. His Cajun bootlegger in Deep South drama Sanctuary (based on Faulkner) and racing driver in Grand Prix were closer to his French roles, but neither his parts nor the films were first-rate. Hollywood proved unwilling or unable to exploit Montand's singing talent (unlike Maurice Chevalier★), and his brand of laconic masculinity proved as inexportable as that of Jean Gabin★. Luckily his unfortunate Hollywood record did not damage his highly successful career in French cinema up to his death in 1991. GV

FILMS: Let's Make Love (1960); Sanctuary, Goodbye Again (1961); My Geisha (1962); Grand Prix (1966); On a Clear Day You Can See Forever (1970).

MONTÉNÉGRO, Conchita (Concepción Andrés Picado) (1911–)

Spanish silent film actress whose door to Hollywood was opened after her success as the lead protagonist in Jacques de Baroncelli's La Femme et le pantin/The Woman and the Puppet (1928). She signed a contract with MGM in 1930 and subsequently appeared in a number of Spanish multi-language films including Sevilla de mis amores (1930), the directorial debut of Ramón Novarro, and De frente marchen (1930) with Buster Keaton. At the end of 1931, she signed with Fox and starred in a number of modest English-language productions with strong Hispanic and Latino elements such as The Gay Caballero. She returned to Europe in the mid-1930s to work with the likes of Carmine Gallone and Robert Siodmak, before retiring from the film industry in the postwar period, after marrying an international diplomat. AQ

FILMS: Strangers May Kiss, Never the Twain Shall Meet, The Cisco Kid (1931); The Gay Caballero (1932); Laughing at Life (1933); Handy Andy, Hell in Heavens (1934).

MONTEVECCHI, Liliane (1932–)

A Broadway celebrity and an accomplished French ballerina, Montevecchi may have arrived too late in Hollywood. Ten years earlier, she could have embarked on a great career in her chosen genre, musicals, since her talent had already been confirmed by her Broadway hits. But in the 1950s, her uneven filmography was chiefly marked by her memorable dance routines, even if her acting was occasionally excellent (for instance, in The Young Lions or King Creole). Her greatest roles were as Cyd Charisse's rival in the 'Frankie and Johnny' number in Meet Me in Las Vegas, and particularly as the colourful gypsy whose tabletop flamenco number was a landmark moment in Fritz Lang's Moonfleet. CV

FILMS: The Glass Slipper, Daddy Long Legs, Moonfleet (1955); Meet Me in Las Vegas (1956); The Living Idol, The Sad Sack (1957); The Young Lions, King Creole, Me and the Colonel (1958); Wall Street (1987); How to Lose a Guy in 10 Days (2003).

MONTIEL, Sara (María Antonia Abad Fernández) (1928–)

Glamourous Spanish actress who became Spain's first female screen sex symbol following stints in Mexico and Hollywood. Montiel's film career began at the age of sixteen and she had minor roles in several films such as Juan de Orduña's Locura de amor/Love Crazy (1948). Frustrated by her lack of options, she moved to Mexico in 1950, and made fourteen films between 1951 and 1956, including three box-office successes with singing romantic lead Pedro Infante. Although Montiel played a Spanish character opposite Infante, she was often cast as Cuban in order to acknowledge her 'foreign' origins and accent.

Montiel first travelled to the USA in 1951 as the opening act of a musical review. Following the popularity of her second film with Infante among Hispanic audiences, she signed up for a Los Angeles singing engagement with Mexican composer and singer Agustín Lara in 1953. There, she was approached by Columbia's artistic director, Max Arnow, but when studio head Harry Cohn later offered her a seven-year contract, she promptly rejected it, complaining that the conditions it imposed were akin to slavery. Nevertheless, Arnow approached her again in 1954 for the role of Nina, the charming pickpocket-turned-patriotic supporter of Benito Juárez in Robert Aldrich's *Vera Cruz*.

Montiel was given the full star treatment for her Hollywood launch, although her role in the film was that of the conventional, fiery Latina stereotype. This reportedly facilitated Montiel's collaboration with co-star Gary Cooper, for whom she evoked memories of his longtime girlfriend, Lupe Vélez, the originator of the 'Mexican spitfire' image. Montiel credited Burt Lancaster (her other co-star and the film's co-producer) with valuable assistance in negotiating the hidden codes of ethnic identification in Hollywood. She recalled that he advised her to stay with the diminutive form of her name, 'Sarita', 'since Sarah with an "h" is Jewish and Sara without the "h" is the name of a Negro slave'.

Montiel signed a four-film contract with Warner Bros. In Anthony Mann's *Serenade*, she was cast as the spirited daughter of a famous dead Mexican bullfighter opposite the Italian-American tenor sensation Mario Lanza. Montiel married Mann in 1957 and continued to reside in Los Angeles for a number of years, even after resuming her Spanish film career. She was then loaned out to RKO to appear in Samuel Fuller's *Run of the Arrow*, in which she played Yellow Moccasin, Rod Steiger's Sioux wife. Her hair was dyed black and skin darkened with full body make-up for the part.

The actress became increasingly disillusioned with being confined to exotic Hollywood roles and sought a new outlet in her home country. She appeared in *El último cuplé/The Last Torch Song* (1957), a melodramatic anthology of popular cabaret-type songs from the 1910s and 1920s that catapulted her to fame and fortune throughout the Spanish-speaking world. With nine separate million-dollar film contracts in hand, Montiel broke her Warner Bros.' contract. Her dreams of Hollywood-style stardom were finally realised. KV

FILMS: *Vera Cruz* (1954); *Serenade* (1956); *Run of the Arrow* (1957).

MOODY, Ron (Ronald Moodnick) (1924–)

English character actor and singer who achieved lasting fame as Fagin in the stage and film versions of *Oliver!*. His American television roles have been more numerous than his appearances on American film. TJ

FILMS: *Murder Most Foul* (1964); *The Twelve Chairs* (1970); *Flight of the Doves* (1971); *The Spaceman and King Arthur* (1979); *Wrong is Right* (1982); *A Kid in King Arthur's Court* (1995).

MOORE, Dudley (1935–2002)

British comedian, actor and musician who because of his famously short stature became one of the more unlikely sex symbols in the history of Hollywood. Moore first achieved fame as a member of the influential comedy revue *Beyond the Fringe* that enjoyed considerable success in both Britain and the USA. After a series of relatively unsuccessful films shot in the UK (such as Stanley Donen's US-funded production *Bedazzled*), he moved to Hollywood in 1978 to appear in *Foul Play*, a screwball comedy-thriller that co-starred Goldie Hawn and Chevy Chase. On the back of his well-received performance, he was cast in the leading role in Blake Edwards' *10*, after George Segal had walked out on the film. Moore demonstrated an astute and appealing blend of charm and comedic virtuosity in the tale of the trials and tribulations of a composer undergoing a mid-life crisis. The film was an international hit and his status as a romantic-comic leading man seemed assured with the subsequent success of *Arthur* in 1981. He was nominated for a Best Actor Academy Award for his performance as Arthur Bach, the idle, wealthy, self-indulgent drunk who finds love and a sense of purpose with the working-class Linda (Liza Minnelli). The role was ideally suited to Moore's skills in verbal and physical comedy, and his impish charm and talent for the sentimental ensured audiences warmed to a potentially unlikeable character.

A flurry of films followed, but none were able to repeat the commercial and critical successes of *10* and *Arthur*. Most, such as *Lovesick* and *Micki + Maude*, were weak replays of his earlier roles, and even the attempt to recreate his partnership with Minnelli in *Arthur 2: On the Rocks* failed to restore his screen fortunes.

Moore was also an accomplished jazz pianist and composer and composed a number of film scores, including those for *Bedazzled* and *Six Weeks*. In 1999, he was diagnosed with an incurable condition that prevented him from working until his untimely death. His long career and the affection in which he was held in his native Britain was recognised by the award of a CBE in 2001. MHu

FILMS: *The Wrong Box* (1966); *Bedazzled* (1967); *30 is a Dangerous Age, Cynthia* (1968); *Monte Carlo or Bust!*, *The Bed Sitting Room* (1969); *Foul Play* (1978); *10* (1979); *Wholly Moses* (1980); *Arthur* (1981); *Six Weeks* (1982); *Lovesick, Romantic Comedy, Unfaithfully Yours* (1983); *Micki + Maude, Best Defense* (1984); *Santa Claus* (1985); *Like Father Like Son* (1987); *Arthur 2: On the Rocks* (1988); *Crazy People* (1990); *Blame it on the Bellboy* (1992); *The Pickle* (1993).

MOORE, Kieron (Kieran O'Hanrahan) (1925–)

Dark, good-looking Irish actor who played Vronsky, opposite Vivien Leigh★, in *Anna Karenina* (1948). In 1951, Moore briefly moved to Hollywood, where he played various stocky, masculine types in films such as *Ten Tall Men*. RB

FILMS: *David and Bathsheba, Ten Tall Men* (1951); *The Angry Hills, Darby O'Gill and the Little People* (1959); *The Day They Robbed the Bank of England* (1960); *The 300 Spartans* (1962); *The Thin Red Line* (1964); *Crack in the World, Son of a Gunfighter, Bikini Paradise* (1965); *Arabesque* (1966); *Custer of the West, Run Like a Thief* (1967).

MOORE, Roger (1927–)

Affable and easy-going British male lead actor who personified the suave English gentleman during the 1970s. Moore acquired the polish that became his trademark under the tutelage of director Brian Desmond Hurst, to whom he was introduced by his policeman father. Hurst also helped him secure a number of early minor parts in UK films. Moore spent much of the 1950s shuttling back and forth across the Atlantic, with various roles in British and American film and television, including the lead in the popular British television series *Ivanhoe*. In 1962, he came to even greater public attention as the suave Simon Templar in the long-running UK television series *The Saint*. He appeared in 114 episodes before the show's conclusion in 1968. Moore's performance tempered the ruthlessness of the character in the original novels by Leslie Charteris, just as he was later to soften the character of James Bond. Between 1973 and 1985, Moore starred in seven movies as 007. He brought the same urbanity as his predecessor Sean Connery★, but he also managed to inject more humour and less menace into the part. The 1970s were the period of Moore's greatest success. As well as the Bond films, he made a number of other successful British films. He also

had a starring role in television's *The Persuaders*, some episodes of which he directed.

Moore's association with the James Bond role has ensured that his star has shone more brightly in international terms than his actual work might otherwise merit. He has always been content to relax and enjoy the fruits of his success, and has not tried that hard to stretch a screen persona that still connotes a well-groomed and good-humoured gentlemanly modesty. He has said himself that 'my success has been 99% luck and 1% talent'. Occasional post-Bond Hollywood films have been accompanied by a willingness to host American television specials and to guy his established screen persona in such films as *Spice World* and *Boat Trip*. This ability to trade on his image has been given an altruistic spin by his work as Goodwill Ambassador for UNICEF, a charity that he was introduced to by Audrey Hepburn★. TJ

FILMS: *The Last Time I Saw Paris* (1954); *Interrupted Melody, The King's Thief* (1955); *Diane* (1956); *The Miracle* (1959); *The Sins of Rachel Cade, Gold of the Seven Saints* (1961); *Crossplot* (1969); *Live and Let Die* (1973); *The Man with the Golden Gun* (1974); *The Spy Who Loved Me* (1977); *Moonraker* (1979); *The Sea Wolves, Sunday Lovers* (1980); *The Cannonball Run, For Your Eyes Only* (1981); *Octopussy* (1983); *The Naked Face* (1984); *A View to a Kill* (1985); *Bullseye!* (1990); *Bed and Breakfast* (1992); *The Quest* (1996); *The Saint* [voice], *Spice World* (1997); *The Enemy* (2001); *Boat Trip* (2002).

MORE, Kenneth (1914–1982)

As the epitome of English unflappability, this British leading man was equally at home in dramatic and comedic roles. In a thirty-year screen career, he starred in many successful British films such as *Genevieve* (1953) and a number of Hollywood-funded productions such as *Never Let Me Go*, in which he appeared alongside Clark Gable and Gene Tierney. MHu

FILMS: *No Highway* (1951); *Never Let Me Go* (1953); *The Deep Blue Sea* (1955); *The Sheriff of Fractured Jaw* (1958); *Sink the Bismarck!* (1960); *The Greengage Summer* (1961); *The Longest Day* (1962); *The Collector* (1965); *The Mercenaries* (1968); *Fraulein Doktor, Oh! What a Lovely War, Battle of Britain* (1969); *Scrooge* (1970); *The Spaceman and King Arthur* (1979).

MOREAU, Jeanne (1928–)

Jeanne Moreau's brief engagement with Hollywood followed her international success in many of the leading

European auteur films of the 1960s. After appearances in a small number of American-funded productions shot in Europe, her first full Hollywood role was in *Monte Walsh* – a film that belonged to that characteristic Hollywood genre, the Western. Moreau played an ageing female prostitute – a type she would later reprise to the point of exaggeration in R. W. Fassbinder's *Querelle* (1982). The character dies in the film unable to make a living and unwilling to 'hang on', as she puts it. This question of 'hanging on' is interesting in relation to both genre and Moreau's career. While the Western was in decline, Moreau's career was, at this point, in transition. She was becoming 'the older woman' – a figure Hollywood, more so than European cinema, has had difficulty representing. Perhaps then it was no accident that Moreau's subsequent American roles just replayed, rather than reworked, her blend of mature experience and confident, lived-in sensuality developed during the period of the French New Wave. In *Alex in Wonderland*, she literally played herself in a film that also boasted a performance by its director, Paul Mazursky, as Federico Fellini. Later, in *The Last Tycoon*, she played the part of a disputatious screen goddess. Both parts seemed to indicate that, as far as Hollywood was concerned, her screen persona should remain embalmed, not enriched, by the encounter between European art cinema and mainstream American production. Jeanne Moreau was married to the American director William Friedkin during the 1970s and she had a part-time home in Los Angeles. AP

FILMS: *Five Branded Women* (1960); *The Victors* (1963); *The Yellow Rolls-Royce, The Train* (1965); *Great Catherine* (1968); *Monte Walsh, Alex in Wonderland* (1970); *The Last Tycoon* (1976).

MORENO, Antonio (Antonio Garrido Monteagudo Moreno) (1887–1967)

Dark, handsome and muscular Spanish actor with twinkling eyes and a gentle, soft voice whose career as Hollywood's first major Spanish-speaking star spanned five decades. In 1902, Moreno arrived in the USA where he played various small parts with Maude Adams' theatre company. He subsequently appeared in two productions with the great stage actor William Hawtrey. After his debut screen role in 1912 in *The Voice of the Millions*, Moreno went on to become one of Vitagraph's biggest stars during the 1910s. He appeared in numerous silent serials, as well as

a number of feature films, including several directed by D. W. Griffith. He was Hollywood's most eligible bachelor until he married the divorced socialite Daisy Canfield Danziger at the age of thirty-five in 1923. By now working for Paramount, he was also at the apex of his career as the studio released three of his most successful films the same year: *The Trail of the Lonesome Pine* with Mary Miles Minter, *My American Wife* with Gloria Swanson, and *The Spanish Dancer* with Pola Negri★. In the latter, he played a penniless nobleman who rescues his gypsy dancer lover, Maritana, from the arms of a despotic king.

With the coming of sound, Moreno turned to Hollywood's Spanish-language only productions, where he continued to play a number of leading or major roles. He also appeared in joint English and Spanish versions like *Veija Hildalguia/Romance of the Rio Grande* (1929) and *El precio de un beso/One Mad Kiss* (1930). His noticeable foreign accent limited his English-language film career, though, and he usually had to make do with minor supporting roles, often as kind and amiable sorts. During this time, he also worked temporarily in Mexico, where he directed the first two Mexican talkies.

Over the next two decades, Moreno became a busy character actor supporting leading men such as Tyrone Power in the costume drama *Captain from Castile* and Gary Cooper in *Dallas*. His last US screen appearance was in John Ford's epic Western *The Searchers* as Figueroa, a dignified Mexican who takes the leading men to Scar's camp. EU

FILMS: *The Voice of the Millions, Iola's Promise, His Own Fault, An Unseen Enemy, Two Daughters of Eve, So Near, Yet So Far, The Musketeers of Pig Alley* (1912); *Oil and Water, A Misunderstood Boy, No Place for Father, By Man's Law, The House of Discord* (1913); *Classmates, Strongheart, Judith of Bethulia, Men and Women, Too Many Husbands, The Accomplished Mrs Thompson, The Ladies' War, The Persistent Mr Prince, The Song of the Ghetto, John Rance, Gentleman, The Memories in Men's Souls, The Hidden Letters, Politics and the Press, The Lone Shark King, The Peacemaker, Under False Colours, Goodbye Summer, The Old Flute Player* (1914); *In the Latin Quarter, The Island of Regeneration, The Quality of Mercy, The Park Honeymooners, Love's Way, Youth, The Dust of Egypt, Anselo Lee, The Gypsy Trail, A 'Model' Wife, A Price for Folly, On Her Wedding Night* (1915); *Kennedy Square, The Supreme Temptation, Susie, the Sleuth, She Won the Prize, The Shop Girl, The Tarantula, The Devil's Prize, Rose of the South* **373**

(1916); *Her Right to Love, Money Magic, Aladdin from Broadway, The Captain of the Gray Horse Troop, The Magnificent Meddler, A Son of the Hills, By Right of Possession, The Angel Factory, The Mark of Cain* (1917); *The Naulahka, The House of Hate, The First Law, The Iron Test* (1918); *The Perils of Thunder Mountain* (1919); *The Invisible Hand, The Veiled Mystery* (1920); *Three Sevens, The Secret of the Hills* (1921); *A Guilty Conscience* (1922); *My American Wife, Look Your Best, Lost and Found, On a South Sea Island, The Trail of the Lonesome Pine, The Exciters, The Spanish Dancer* (1923); *Flaming Barriers, Bluff, Tiger Love, The Story without a Name, The Border Legion* (1924); *Learning to Love, One Year to Live, Her Husband's Secret* (1925); *Beverly of Graustark, Mare Nostrum, The Temptress, The Flaming Forest, Love's Blindness* (1926); *It, Venus of Venice, Madame Pompadour, Come to My House* (1927); *The Whip Woman, Nameless Men, The Midnight Taxi* (1928); *The Air Legion, Synthetic Sin, Careers, The Benson Murder Case, Romance of the Rio Grande, Romance of the Rio Grande* (1929); *One Mad Kiss, The Bad Man, Rough Romance, The Cat and the Canary* (1930); *Those Who Dance, The Wide Open Spaces* (1931); *Spring in Autumn, The Cardboard City* (1932); *Rose of France, A Married Woman Needs a Husband* (1933); *Storm over the Andes* (1935); *The Bohemian Girl* (1936); *Rose of the Rio Grande* (1938); *Ambush* (1939); *Seven Sinners* (1940); *They Met in Argentina, Two Latins from Manhattan, The Kid from Kansas, Fiesta* (1941); *The Valley of the Sun, Undercover Man* (1942); *Tampico* (1944); *The Spanish Main* (1945); *Notorious* (1946); *Captain from Castille* (1948); *Lust for Gold* (1949); *Crisis, Saddle Tramp, Dallas* (1950); *Mark of the Renegade* (1951); *Thunder Bay, Untamed Frontier, Wings of the Hawk* (1953); *The Creature from the Black Lagoon, Saskatchewan* (1954); *The Searchers* (1956).

MORENO, Rosita (Gabriela Carmen Victoria Viñolas) (1909–1993)

Born in Spain and educated in Cuba, Rosita Moreno worked for some time in vaudeville before her first Hollywood appearance in 1930. Her handsome face, soft voice and Latin ethnicity were her main assets, as she was often cast in specifically European roles. In 1934, she played Cary Grant's★ Parisian lover in the comedy *Ladies Should Listen*. As well as her American English-language film career, Moreno also had major roles in more than a dozen Spanish-language productions shot in Hollywood.

FILMS: *The Santa Fe Trial, Her Wedding Night* (1930); *Stamboul* (1931); *Walls of Gold* (1933); *Ladies Should Listen* (1934); *The Scoundrel* (1935); *The House of a Thousand Candles* (1936).

MORGAN, Michèle (1920–)

The beautiful Morgan, who had risen to fame in Marcel Carné's Poetic Realist film *Le Quai des brumes / Port of Shadows* (1938), had previously turned down several offers to work in Hollywood when she decided to sign a contract with RKO after the onset of World War II. She arrived in Los Angeles in 1940 and after an uncredited part in *My Life with Caroline*, she played the lead role in *Joan of Paris*, a French Resistance film typical of Hollywood's contribution to the war effort. Her character was a humble waitress who sacrifices herself by hiding an RAF pilot with whom she has fallen in love. The film was not a huge success. In September 1942, Morgan married the American actor Bill Marshall (who would later marry Micheline Presle★), with whom she had a son in 1944.

Morgan then starred in *Two Tickets to London*, another war drama, this time set in Britain. She played Jeanne, a

French star Michèle Morgan stars as Humphrey Bogart's wife in the war effort drama *Passage to Marseille* (1944)

widowed singer – she sang three songs in English – who falls in love with an American sailor suspected of treason. In the musical *Higher and Higher*, made in the summer of 1943, Morgan obtained official star billing: she played a kitchen maid who has to transform herself into a debutante so as to marry a wealthy man to save her boss from bankruptcy. Again, she had a singing part but the film became a vehicle for Frank Sinatra, who made it a hit. Released in 1947 in Paris and retitled *Amour et swing*, the film was poorly received by critics, who considered it debasing for this talented and serious actress. In the 1944 war drama *Passage to Marseille*, she had a minor role as Humphrey Bogart's wife, with Bogart playing a former anti-Nazi journalist. The film, which starred many other émigré actors – such as Peter Lorre★, Sydney Greenstreet★ and Victor Francen★ – was intended to give Americans a heroic image of the French Resistance before the Normandy landings. Morgan returned to France at the end of the war to star in *La Symphonie pastorale*, a film that relaunched her French career. Her last American film, *The Chase*, was a noir war drama starring Robert Cummings as a traumatised veteran. It was slated at the Cannes film festival.

Morgan was called 'the most charmingly Americanized damsel in Hollywood's foreign colony' by one New York journalist, but she humbly accepted the harsher judgment of the French press regarding her short-lived American career, as if it was the price she had to pay to regain her national audience's respect. Morgan's American roles between 1942 and 1946 progressively faded into oblivion, but she enjoyed prestige and status as one of the major stars of the late 1940s and 1950s French cinema, and she has remained one of its grandes dames. Clearly, her acting talent combined with her delicate features were difficult to slot into the limited and formulaic Hollywood roles offered to French actresses in general. GS

FILMS: *My Life with Caroline* (1941); *Joan of Paris* (1942); *Two Tickets to London* (1943); *Higher and Higher, Passage to Marseille* (1944); *The Chase* (1946).

MORGAN, Paul (Georg Paul Morgenstern) (1886–1938)

Austrian stage actor and cabaret artist with an active pre-World War II stage career in Vienna and Berlin. His brief American career involved appearances in the German-language film *Wir schalten um auf Hollywood/We Now Switch*

over to Hollywood* (1931) (with Joan Crawford, Ramon Novarro and John Gilbert) and the French-language film *Buster se marie* (with Buster Keaton). FG

FILM: *Sh! The Octopus* (1937).

MORLEY, Robert (1908–1992)

Ebullient Academy Award-nominated English actor and playwright whose distinctive portly frame and prodigious quizzical eyebrows were archly deployed in numerous larger-than-life roles – typically in comedies – as a blustering, but kind-hearted gent. MW

FILMS: *Marie Antoinette* (1938); *The Young Mr Pitt* (1942); *Edward, My Son* (1949); *The African Queen* (1951); *Beat the Devil* (1953); *Beau Brummell* (1954); *The Adventures of Quentin Durward* (1955); *Around the World in Eighty Days* (1956); *The Doctor's Dilemma, The Sheriff of Fractured Jaw* (1958); *The Journey, The Battle of the Sexes, Libel* (1959); *The Road to Hong Kong* (1962); *Take Her, She's Mine, Nine Hours to Rama, The Old Dark House, Murder at the Gallop* (1963); *Topkapi, Of Human Bondage* (1964); *Genghis Khan, Those Magnificent Men in Their Flying Machines, or How I Flew from London to Paris in 25 Hours, 11 Minutes, The Alphabet Murders, The Loved One, The Dot and the Line* [voice] (1965); *Way . . . Way Out, Hotel Paradiso* (1966); *Woman Times Seven* (1967); *Hot Millions* (1968); *Sinful Davey* (1969); *Cromwell, Song of Norway* (1970); *The Blue Bird* (1976); *Who is Killing the Great Chefs of Europe?* (1978); *Scavenger Hunt* (1979); *Oh, Heavenly Dog!* (1980); *The Great Muppet Caper* (1981); *High Road to China* (1983); *The Trouble with Spies* (1987).

MOSJOUKINE, Ivan (Ivan Ilyitch Mozzhukhin) (1889–1939)

The Russian Ivan Mosjoukine was one of Europe's greatest stars of the silent era, but his Hollywood career was extremely brief and disappointing. During his 1926 winter trip to Europe, Carl Laemmle saw Mosjoukine in the French-Russian film *Michel Strogoff*. He urged Universal's agent in Paris, Ivan Serzhinsky, to contact the star, who eventually signed a five-year contract with Universal on 26 March 1926. He arrived in Hollywood via New York in December of that year. The Franco-Russian émigré press commented, 'European film has lost its king'.

In Russia, Mosjoukine had specialised in tragic roles, but in other European films he demonstrated comic talent and acrobatic abilities. However, in his first (and only) American picture, *Surrender,* he played a 'Cossack' prince who forces a Jewish beauty to come to his room under the threat of exterminating her people. But Mosjoukine's playful ironic performance style did not fit the American stereotype of the Cossack as cruel oppressor of Jews. The planned filmed operetta, *Polish Blood,* to be directed by the German expressionist film-maker Paul Leni, was never made. Universal wanted the actor to change his nose through plastic surgery and his name to a more pronounceable 'John Moskin'. Though he was paid $750 a week, Mosjoukine spent six months without work and decided to leave. The Russian émigré press interpreted the whole episode in terms of the desecration of a great Russian artist who sacrificed wealth and global fame for the sake of art and the Russian soul. Back in Europe, he made two remarkable films in Germany, *Manolescu* (1929) and *Der Weiße Teufel/The White Devil* (1930), but the coming of sound ended his brilliant career and he died in poverty. OB

FILM: *Surrender* (1927).

MOWBRAY, Alan (1896–1969)

Versatile English actor who rose to prominence in the American film industry after starting his career late on the London stage and Broadway. Mowbray's numerous Hollywood parts often drew upon his stiff-upper-lipped, gentlemanly persona. He also played drunken, hammy British actors in two John Ford films: *My Darling Clementine* and *Wagon Master.* JS/AP

FILMS: *God's Gift to Women, The Man in Possession, Alexander Hamilton, Leftover Ladies, Horror of the Family, Guilty Hands, The Big Irons* (1931); *Lovers Courageous, Nice Women, Silent Witness, Hotel Continental, The World and the Flesh, Man about Town, The Man from Yesterday, Winner Takes All, The Man Called Back, Jewel Robbery, Two Against the World, The Phantom President, Sherlock Holmes, The Bride's Bereavement, Two Lips and Juleps* (1932); *Our Betters, A Study in Scarlet, A Peg o' My Heart, Voltaire, The Midnight Club, Berkeley Square, The World Changes, Her Secret, Roman Scandals* (1933); *Long Lost Father, Embarrassing Moments, One More River, Where Sinners Meet, The Girl from Missouri, Cheaters, Charlie Chan in London, Little Man, What Now?* (1934); *In Person, She Couldn't Take It, The Gay Deception, Lady Tubbs, Becky Sharp, The Night Life of the Gods* (1935); *Rose Marie, Muss 'Em Up, Give Us this Night, Desire, The Case against Mrs Ames, Fatal Lady, Mary of Scotland, Ladies in Love, Rainbow on the River,* **376** *My Man Godfrey* (1936); *Four Days' Wonder, On the Avenue, The King and the Chorus Girl, Marry the Girl, Vogues of 1938, On Such a Night, Music for Madame, Stand-In, Hollywood Hotel, As Good as Married, Topper* (1937); *Merrily We Live, There Goes My Heart* (1938); *Topper Takes a Trip, Never Say Die, Way Down South, The Llano Kid* (1939); *Music in My Heart, Curtain Call, Scatterbrain, The Boys from Syracuse, The Villain Still Pursued Her, The Quarterback* (1940); *That Hamilton Woman, That Uncertain Feeling, The Cowboy and the Blonde, French Fried Patootie, Ice-Capades, Moon over Her Shoulder, I Wake up Screaming, The Perfect Snob, Footlight Fever* (1941); *Three Blonde Mice, Yokel Boy, We Were Dancing, The Mad Martindales, The Isle of Missing Men, Panama Hattie, A Yank at Eton, The Devil with Hitler* (1942); *The Powers Girl, Slightly Dangerous, So this is Washington, Holy Matrimony, His Butler's Sister* (1943); *The Doughgirls, Ever Since Venus, My Gal Loves Music* (1944); *Bring on the Girls, Earl Carroll Vanities, The Phantom of 42nd Street, Where Do We Go from Here?, Tell it to a Star, Men in Her Diary, Sunbonnet Sue* (1945); *Terror by Night, Idea Girl, My Darling Clementine* (1946); *The Pilgrim Lady, Lured, Merton of the Movies, Captain from Castille* (1947); *The Main Street Kid, The Prince of Thieves, An Innocent Affair, My Dear Secretary, Every Girl Should Be Married* (1948); *The Lone Wolf and His Lady, The Loveable Cheat, You're My Everything, Abbott and Costello Meet the Killer, Boris Karloff* (1949); *The Jackpot, Wagon Master* (1950); *The Lady and the Bandit, Crosswinds* (1951); *Just across the Street, Blackbeard the Pirate, Androcles and the Lion* (1952); *Ma and Pa Kettle at Home* (1954); *The King's Thief* (1955); *Once upon a Honeymoon, Around the World in Eighty Days, The Man Who Knew Too Much, The King and I* (1956); *A Majority of One* (1962).

MUELLER-STAHL, Armin (1930–)

The breakthrough of this former East German film and theatre star and character actor of New German Cinema was based on the international attention caused by István Szabó's *Oberst Redl/Colonel Redl* (1984) and Agnieszka Holland's *Bittere Ernte/Angry Harvest* (1985) when they were both nominated for Academy Awards. Mueller-Stahl's first US lead performances were based on his strength in psychologically focused roles, most notably in *Music Box, Kafka* and later also in the highly successful Australian film *Shine* (1996). His 'exoticism' as a character actor has been further enhanced by the fact that he rarely portrays Germans. On the contrary, his Soviet, Hungarian, Polish and most importantly Jewish heroes convey a more general sense of Eastern European-ness. Many of his characters are defined by ambiguity, in that they seem to dissolve a clear distinction between victim and oppressor. This is true, in particular, with the former brutal Nazi supporter-turned-gentle grandfather Laszlo in *Music Box* and the once suppressed, but now turned oppressive, father in *Shine*. His helpless, yet courageous East German clown in Jim Jarmusch's *Night on Earth* is another example. Apart from these leading roles, Mueller-Stahl has regularly performed alongside established US stars in major productions such as David Fincher's *The Game*. Although he has returned to Germany for television work, he now works and lives in California. CF

FILMS: *Music Box* (1989); *Avalon* (1990); *Night on Earth, Kafka* (1991); *The House of Spirits* (1993); *The Last Good Time* (1994); *Theodore Rex* (1995); *The Peacemaker, The Game* (1997); *The X-Files* (1998); *The Third Miracle, The Thirteenth Floor, Jakob the Liar* (1999); *Mission to Mars* (2000); *The Dust Factory* (2004).

MUMBA, Samantha (1983–)

One of a number of formulaic Irish pop singers with ambitions to move into screen acting. She had a supporting role in Simon Wells' *The Time Machine*. RB

FILM: *The Time Machine* (2002).

MUNDIN, Herbert (1898–1939)

Stout British character actor whose prolific career in Hollywood from the early 1930s was cut short by his early death in a car crash. He was Much-the-Miller's-Son in *The Adventures of Robin Hood*. MW

FILMS: *Love Me Tonight, Life Begins, Almost Married, Devil's Lottery, Bachelor's Affairs, Sherlock Holmes, Chandu the Magician, One Way Passage, The Trial of Vivienne Ware, Silent Witness* (1932); *Hoopla, Arizona to Broadway, Dangerously Yours, It's Great to Be Alive, Shanghai Madness, The Devil's in Love, Adorable, Cavalcade, Hell Below, Pleasure Cruise* (1933); *Orient Express, Love Time, Springtime for Henry, All Men are Enemies, Call it Luck, Bottoms Up, Hell in the Heavens, Ever Since Eve, Such Women are Dangerous* (1934); *Spring Tonic, Mutiny on the Bounty, The Personal History, Adventures, Experience, and Observation of David Copperfield, the Younger, The Perfect Gentleman, Black Sheep, Ladies Love Danger, The Widow from*

Monte Carlo (1935); *A Message to Garcia, Tarzan Escapes, King of Burlesque, Champagne Charlie, Charlie Chan's Secret, Under Two Flags* (1936); *Another Dawn, You Can't Beat Love, Angel* (1937); *The Adventures of Robin Hood, Exposed, Lord Jeff, The Invisible Enemy* (1938); *Society Lawyer* (1939).

MURAT, Jean (1888–1968)

Prolific French screen actor of the 1930s who also made a number of Hollywood comedies and musicals in which he played aristocrats, lawyers or ageing womanisers. American films include the Jayne Mansfield vehicle *It Happened in Athens* and *Paris Holiday* with Bob Hope and Fernandel★. His first wife was Annabella★. VO

FILMS: *On the Riviera, Rich, Young and Pretty* (1951); *Paris Holiday* (1958); *It Happened in Athens* (1962).

MURATORE, Lucien (1878–1954)

French performer whose career in international lyric theatre included a long association with the Chicago Opera. Muratore was married to the opera tenor Lina Cavalieri★ and appeared with her in two American films shot during the 1910s. AP

FILMS: *Manon Lescaut* (1914); *A Woman of Impulse* (1918).

MUTI, Ornella (Francesca Rivelli) (1955–)

Powerfully beautiful Italian actress with dark hair and penetrating almond-shaped eyes who is often compared to Sophia Loren★ and Claudia Cardinale★. Muti's natural and instinctive sexual presence has been a prominent element in European films such as Marco Ferreri's *Storie di ordinaria follia / Tales of Ordinary Madness* (1981), though her Hollywood debut role as Princess Aura in *Flash Gordon* diluted her brand of strong and modern Continental femininity in favour of something more timeless and mythical. Muti's Swiss childhood has left her with a marked German accent and this, alongside a successful European film career, may account for her relatively minor American filmography. AP

FILMS: *Flash Gordon* (1980); *Love and Money* (1982); *Oscar* (1991); *Once upon a Crime* (1992); *Somewhere in the City* (1998).

MYRTIL, Odette (1898–1978)

Myrtil was a stage star in Paris and then New York. Her success on the American stage made her appealing to Hol- **377** lywood, where she was typecast as a Frenchwoman in a variety of productions in the 1930s and 1940s. CH

FILMS: *Dodsworth* (1936); *The Girl from Scotland Yard* (1937); *Suez* (1938); *Kitty Foyle* (1940); *Out of the Fog* (1941); *Yankee Doodle Dandee, I Married an Angel, Reunion in France, The Pied Piper* (1942); *Forever and a Day, Thousands Cheer, Assignment in Brittany* (1943); *Uncertain Glory, Dark Waters* (1944); *Devotion* (1946); *The Lucky Stiff* (1948); *The Fighting Kentuckian* (1949); *Strangers on a Train, Here Comes the Groom* (1951); *Lady Possessed* (1952).

NALDER, Reggie (Alfred Reginald Natzick) (1904–1991)

Scar-faced Austrian-born actor who entered films in 1948 but became internationally recognisable after Hitchcock brought him to Hollywood to play the assassin in the remake of *The Man Who Knew Too Much*. In the 1960s, he moved to California, where he played numerous film and television horror roles and appeared (clothed) in hard-core sex movies. RJK

FILMS: *Adventures of Captain Fabian* (1951); *Betrayed* (1954); *The Man Who Knew Too Much* (1956); *Convicts 4, The Manchurian Candidate, The Spiral Road* (1962); *Crash!* (1977); *Dracula's Dog* (1978); *Seven, Dracula Sucks* (1979); *The Devil and Max Devlin* (1981); *Blue Ice* (1985).

NANSEN, Betty (1873–1943)

Danish stage star Betty Nansen was brought to New York by the producer William Fox in the expectation that her aristocratic presence would balance the lurid, but hugely popular, Theda Bara. Nansen made five films for Fox in 1915, all directed by J. Gordon Edwards, all box-office failures and all presumed lost. HJW

FILMS: *The Celebrated Scandal, Anna Karenina, A Woman's Resurrection, Should a Mother Tell?, The Song of Hate* (1915).

NAPIER, Alan (Alan Napier-Clavering) (1903–1988)

Tall and dignified British actor, cousin of Prime Minister Neville Chamberlain, whose success as Alfred the Butler in the 1966 version of *Batman* has tended to obscure a long Hollywood career during which he played, for instance, Parson Glennie in Fritz Lang's *Moonfleet*. MW

FILMS: *Stamboul* (1931); *We are not Alone* (1939); *The House of the Seven Gables, The Invisible Man Returns* (1940); *Confirm or Deny, Eagle Squadron* (1941); *Cat People, Random*

Harvest, We were Dancing, A Yank at Eton (1942); *Madame Curie, Assignment in Brittany, Lost Angel, The Song of Bernadette, Appointment in Berlin, Lassie Come Home* (1943); *Dark Waters, The Uninvited, Ministry of Fear, Mademoiselle Fifi, Action in Arabia, The Hairy Ape, Thirty Seconds over Tokyo* (1944); *Hangover Square, Isle of the Dead* (1945); *The Strange Woman, A Scandal in Paris, House of Horrors, Three Strangers* (1946); *Driftwood, Sinbad the Sailor, High Conquest, Lured, Ivy, Forever Amber, Unconquered, Fiesta, The Lone Wolf in London, Adventure Island* (1947); *My Own True Love, Joan of Arc, Hills of Home, Macbeth, Johnny Belinda* (1948); *Master Minds, Tarzan's Magic Fountain, Criss Cross, A Connecticut Yankee in King Arthur's Court, Challenge to Lassie, The Red Danube, Manhandled* (1949); *Double Crossbones, Tripoli* (1950); *The Great Caruso, Tarzan's Peril, The Strange Door, The Blue Veil, Across the Wide Missouri, The Highwayman* (1951); *Big Jim McLain* (1952); *Julius Caesar, Young Bess* (1953); *Desirée* (1954); *Moonfleet* (1955); *Miami Exposé, The Court Jester, The Mole People* (1956); *Until They Sail* (1957); *Island of Lost Women, Journey to the Center of the Earth* (1959); *Wild in the Country* (1961); *Tender is the Night, The Premature Burial* (1962); *The Sword in the Stone* [voice] (1963); *Signpost to Murder, Marnie, My Fair Lady, 36 Hours* (1964); *The Loved One* (1965); *Batman* (1966).

NAZIMOVA, Alla (Adelaida Yakovlevna or Miriam Edez Adelaide Leventon) (1879–1945)

Magnetic Russian stage star (who studied with Stanislavsky at the Moscow Art Theatre) who, with her lithe, androgynous looks and eccentric personality, created a new type of Hollywood screen sexuality later explored by the likes of Marlene Dietrich★. Nazimova's American film career started after a successful tour of East Coast theatres. She had arrived in New York in 1905 with the troupe of her lover, the legendary Russian actor Pavel Orlenev [Paul Orleneff], and became a hugely famous diva, dubbed 'the new Duse'. Her first movies were made at the Fort Lee studios in New Jersey in 1915 (after she had turned down an offer from Chicago-based Essanay). *Revelation*, and three films directed by the French émigré director Albert Capellani – *Eye for Eye, Out of the Fog, The Red Lantern* – turned her into a film star. This led to Hollywood, where she signed a five-year contract with Maxwell Karger at Metro Pictures. Nazimova fitted the new type of exotic screen vamp typified by Theda Bara. Her contract offered $13,000 a week, along with approval rights over director, script and leading man, making her the highest-paid actress in American cinema at the time.

Nazimova's characters embodied or related to dangerous and exotic female myths, such as Cleopatra and Salome, carefully concealing her Jewish-Russian origins. Her exoticism was also sometimes channelled through dual roles such as the Chinese and Caucasian women in *The Red Lantern* and the Broadway star and daughter in *Madame Peacock*. She was 'married' for twelve years to the British-born gay actor Charles Bryant, her co-star on several early films, who also directed two of her films (*A Doll's House* and *Salome*). She also reputedly had numerous affairs with men and women, although she always denied the latter. The marriage to Bryant was a deal for tax purposes and to obtain American citizenship, which she did in 1927. In her villa at 8080 Sunset Boulevard, nicknamed 'The Garden of Allah', Nazimova created the first movie-colony salon – the 8080 Club – which hosted European and American celebrities like Eleonora Duse and Somerset Maugham. Her extravagant clothes and performance style contributed to the glamorous and idiosyncratic 'Nazimova look' – much imitated by other film stars.

Unable to find finance for some of her more ambitious projects for serious play adaptations, she formed her own production company in 1922, producing, for instance *A Doll's House*. The venture was not commercially successful, however, and soon she was superseded by Greta Garbo★. She went back to New York and reconquered the American stage. Nazimova returned to California in 1936 for health reasons and appeared in a number of small screen roles before her death. OB

FILMS: *War Brides* (1916); *Revelation, Eye for Eye, Toys of Fate* (1918); *The Brat, The Red Lantern, Out of the Fog* (1919); *Billions, Madame Peacock, The Heart of a Child, Stronger than Death, Madam Peacock* (1920); *Camille* (1921); *A Doll's House* (1922); *Salome* (1923); *Madonna of the Streets* (1924); *My Son, The Redeeming Sin* (1925); *Escape* (1940); *Blood and Sand* (1941); *The Bridge of San Luis Rey, In Our Time, Since You Went Away* (1944).

NEAGLE, Anna (Marjorie Robertson) (1904–1986)

Neagle was regularly voted Britain's favourite film star from the late 1930s to the early 1950s, and in roles such as Florence Nightingale and Queen Victoria (twice) she became, more than any other actress of the period, something of an over-determined signifier of English national identity. With one exception, her few starring roles in Hollywood films played down this talismanic status by placing her in generic musicals that drew upon her early experience as a West End singer and dancer. JB

FILMS: *Nurse Edith Cavell* (1939); *Irene, No, No, Nanette* (1940); *Sunny* (1941); *They Flew Alone* (1942); *Forever and a Day* (1943).

NEESON, Liam (1952–)

Much of the handsome physicality that Liam Neeson has displayed in his American film roles draws upon his early training in Northern Ireland as a boxer. His acting career started with the Lyric Players Theatre in Belfast. He then moved to Dublin's Abbey Theatre and became associated, along with Gabriel Byrne★, with the experimental Project Arts Theatre, where he was spotted by John Boorman who cast him in *Excalibur*. Neeson went on spec to Hollywood insisting that his agents should not 'say I was an Irish actor. They could say I was an actor from Ireland, which is different, or that I was European.' After a television role in *Miami Vice*, he played a menacing serial killer in Peter Yates' low-budget hit *Suspect*, where Neeson's character, given the actor's strong accent, was conveniently a deaf-mute. He had a similar part in Sam Raimi's *Darkman* and seemed to settle into being typecast as a lethal hulk. Neeson's acting range broadened with a memorable supporting role in Woody Allen's *Husbands and Wives* and his subsequent leading part as Oskar Schindler, the ambiguous hero of Spielberg's *Schindler's List*. He was nominated for a Best Actor Academy Award for this performance. He also gained a Tony nomination for his first Broadway appearance in *Anna Christie*, in which he co-starred with his future wife, Natasha Richardson★. Neeson received a second Academy Award nomination for the title role in Neil Jordan's *Michael Collins* – a part that clearly emphasised his physique over his statesmanship. In 1999, Neeson surprised the industry by announcing that he was retiring from film acting, as he was disgusted at being treated like a 'puppet'. He had just finished playing the singularly one-dimensional Jedi warrior Qui-Gon Jinn in the special-effects-laden *Star Wars: Episode I – The Phantom Menace*. He later announced that he had been joking and appeared in the leading role of Kathryn Bigelow's submarine blockbuster, *K-19: The Widowmaker*. Despite predominantly **379** working in big-budget American features, one of Neeson's finest screen parts was in the little-seen Irish film *Lamb* (1985), where he played a religious brother who runs away with a young boy. It may be that his talents are least on view in his most widely seen films. In 1999, Neeson was awarded an OBE. RB

FILMS: *Excalibur* (1981); *The Bounty* (1984); *A Prayer for the Dying, Suspect, Duet for One* (1987); *Satisfaction, The Good Mother, The Dead Pool* (1988); *Next of Kin* (1989); *Darkman* (1990); *Shining Through, Husbands and Wives* (1992); *Ethan Frome, Ruby Cairo, Schindler's List* (1993); *Nell* (1994); *Rob Roy* (1995); *Before and After, Michael Collins* (1996); *Les Misérables* (1998); *Star Wars: Episode I – The Phantom Menace, The Haunting* (1999); *Gun Shy* (2000); *K-19: The Widowmaker, Gangs of New York, Star Wars: Episode II – Attack of the Clones* [voice] (2002); *Love Actually* (2003); *Kinsey* (2004).

NEGRI, Pola (Apolonia Chałupiec) (1897–1987)

With eight films to her credit, Pola Negri already symbolised the figure of the femme fatale in her native Poland, where she was a leading star. In 1917, she moved to Germany, where, during a brief episode on Max Reinhardt's stage, she met Ernst Lubitsch who helped her get a five-year contract with Ufa. Lubitsch and Negri made several films together, including *Madame DuBarry* (1919), which met with unexpected success in the USA and led to Hollywood offers. When she arrived in New York in 1923, newspapers introduced Negri to American audiences as an exotic beauty with a fantastic biography. In Hollywood, she was able to build on this femme fatale image, partly through notorious liaisons with Charlie Chaplin★ and Rudolph Valentino.

With her expressive, sensual and shapely body, dark hair and large dark eyes, emphasised through heavy make-up to contrast with a snow-white complexion, Negri was presented as a sexual persona to be both desired and feared. In short, she was a perfect replacement for Theda Bara, the earlier personification of the Hollywood vamp. This contradictory femininity, openly played upon in her movies, was coupled with and enhanced by an exotic ethnicity attributed to an obscure blend of Polish, Slovak and gypsy 'otherness'. These features made Negri an attractive commodity, and the image of an exotic, sexy, passionate woman subsequently prevailed in her films, which were successful at the box office, turning her for a while into a Hollywood star.

Pola Negri en route to Hollywood

Unlike Greta Garbo★ and Marlene Dietrich★, Negri does not appear to have wanted to adapt her image to prevailing American standards. She slightly modified her hairstyle and sharp black-and-white make-up. But neither these changes nor the diffuse Hollywood style of photography of the period significantly altered her distinctiveness as a vamp icon. Negri neither fully retained her original screen image nor managed to acquire a new identity. The fact that her mode of feminine representation, in any case, was soon to be replaced by the 'all-American girl' type meant that her own 'American dream' was incompletely realised. Her various liaisons with non-American actors also placed her on the margins of the 'Hollywood dream factory'. Negri tried to rejuvenate her career by returning to Germany in the mid-1930s, but this did not yield the desired result. Increasingly terrified by Nazi terror, she returned to Hollywood in 1940 but she never recaptured her standing. EO

FILMS: *Bella Donna, The Cheat, The Spanish Dancer, Hollywood* (1923); *Shadows of Paris, Forbidden Paradise, Lily of the*

Dust, Men, East of Suez (1924); *Flower of Night, The Charmer, A Woman of the World* (1925); *The Crown of Lies, Good and Naughty, Hotel Imperial* (1926); *Barbed Wire, The Woman on Trial* (1927); *Three Sinners, The Secret Hour, The Woman from Moscow* (1928); *A Woman Commands* (1932); *Hi Diddle Diddle* (1943); *The Moon-Spinners* (1964).

NELL, Nathalie (Nathalie Palle) (1950–)

French actress whose career in the American film industry was short-lived. She appeared in the psychological horror movie *Echoes* and the melodramatic *Man, Woman and Child*, where she played an independent French doctor who has a brief romance with Martin Sheen somewhere in rural France. TH

FILMS: *Echoes, Man, Woman and Child* (1983).

NERO, Franco (Francesco Sparanero) (1941–)

Handsome Italian actor who came to fame as the star of the Italian spaghetti Western series *Django*. His first Hollywood appearance was as Abel in John Huston's *The Bible* in 1966. Despite his poor English, this probably remains his most famous American screen part, although he did win a Golden Globe nomination for his role as Lancelot, opposite Vanessa Redgrave★, in *Camelot*. Since then, Nero has spent a great deal of time working in Europe, but he has continued to make regular appearances in American film and television productions including *Die Hard 2: Die Harder*, in which he played the villain Esperanzo. Nero won a Lifetime Achievement Award at the Los Angeles Italian Film Awards. CS

FILMS: *The Bible, The Tramplers* (1966); *Camelot* (1967); *The Visitor* (1979); *The Man with Bogart's Face* (1980); *Enter the Ninja, The Salamander* (1981); *Die Hard 2: Die Harder* (1990); *Touch and Die* (1991); *From Time to Time* (1992); *The Versace Murder, Talk of Angels* (1998); *Uninvited, White Lies* (1999); *Megiddo: Omega Code 2* (2001).

NESBITT, Cathleen (1889–1982)

Prolific English stage, television and film performer – she appeared in Fox British's *Against the Tide* – who only made a handful of minor Hollywood appearances, perhaps most famously as Cary Grant's grandmother in *An Affair to Remember*. MF

FILMS: *Against the Tide* (1937); *Three Coins in the Fountain, Desirée, Black Widow* (1954); *An Affair to Remember* (1957);

Separate Tables (1958); *The Parent Trap* (1961); *Staircase* (1969); *French Connection II* (1975); *Family Plot* (1976); *Julia* (1977).

NETHERLANDS, THE

Until the 1970s, the emigration of actors from the Netherlands to the USA took place only incidentally. In most cases, such as Audrey Hepburn★ and Philip Dorn★, it was as a result of personal and historical circumstances. The 1970s marked a turning point. Hollywood doubled its market share in the Netherlands to 80 per cent, while Dutch films managed to regain a market share of 10 per cent, mainly as a consequence of a small number of domestic successes. Dutch film-makers were thus increasingly encouraged to choose commercially oriented productions aimed at a mainstream audience. Despite this, home production remained limited and subsidy was needed to keep the industry afloat. Within these limits, a few actors such as Monique van de Ven★ and Rutger Hauer★, both of whom played together in the hit *Turks Fruit/Turkish Delight* (1973), became visible as potential stars. A few Dutch films were subsequently released in the USA and American audiences, and more importantly American agents, came to know Dutch faces. A number of Dutch film-makers looking for commercial opportunities, such as the cinematographer Jan de Bont and his wife Monique van de Ven, director Paul Verhoeven and, importantly, two of his actors, Rutger Hauer and Jeroen Krabbé★, all tried their luck overseas with varying degrees of success. Dutch actors in the USA, however, have never been hired because of their Dutchness. Except for Hauer, who managed to play 'American' characters, they have mainly impersonated Europeans of various origins. Thus, while the Netherlands from the 1980s onwards supplied Hollywood with a number of successful émigrés, 'Dutchness' as such has not made a significant impact as a separate identity in terms of national representations. SdL

NEWLEY, Anthony (1931–1999)

Versatile British actor, singer and composer who came to prominence as the Artful Dodger in David Lean's *Oliver Twist* (1948). In addition to a successful songwriting partnership with Leslie Bricusse, Newley made a number of appearances in largely minor Hollywood films, including several US-financed productions shot in Europe. MHu

FILMS: *The Cockleshell Heroes* (1955); *Port Afrique, High Flight* (1956); *Fire Down Below, How to Murder a Rich Uncle* (1957); *No Time to Die, The Man Inside* (1958); *Idle on Parade, The Bandit of Zhobe, Killers of Kilimanjaro* (1959); *In the Nick, Jazz Boat* (1960); *Doctor Dolittle* (1967); *Sweet November* (1968); *Can Hieronymous Merkin Ever Forget Mercy Humppe and Find True Happiness?* (1969); *Mr Quilp* (1975) *The Garbage Pail Kids Movie* (1987); *Boris and Natasha* (1992).

NEWMAN, Nanette (1934–)

Brunette English actress with long UK screen career, mainly in films directed by her husband Bryan Forbes. Forbes also directed Newman as the leading housewife in her principal Hollywood success, *The Stepford Wives*. TJ
FILMS: *Of Human Bondage* (1964); *The Wrong Box* (1966); *The Whisperers* (1967); *Deadfall* (1968); *Oh! What a Lovely War, Captain Nemo and the Underwater City, The Madwoman of Chaillot* (1969); *The Stepford Wives* (1975); *International Velvet* (1978).

NEWTON, Robert (1905–1956)

British film and stage actor who appeared in a small number of US-financed UK films, among others, before enjoying a brief period of leading-man status in British cinema in the late 1940s. Despite this, the husky-voiced but somewhat pudgy-nosed and bug-eyed actor was often employed on screen in more malevolent character roles. His big introduction to American audiences came in the part of Long John Silver in Disney's British-shot *Treasure Island* in 1950. The enthusiastic transatlantic reception Newton received for this performance encouraged him to relocate permanently to California a year later. Although Hollywood casting directors did not altogether ignore his prior experience in playing both a more thoughtful, urbane style of villainy and, on occasion, proletarian cheeriness, his greatest popular successes outside Britain saw him return to the high seas and a broader vein of pantomime. RKO gave Newton the title role in *Blackbeard, the Pirate* and, two years later, he played Long John Silver again in an eponymously titled film that led to spin-off television series made in Australia. JB
FILMS: *Busman's Honeymoon* (1940); *Hatter's Castle, They Flew Alone* (1942); *Kiss the Blood off My Hands* (1948); *Treasure Island* (1950); *Soldiers Three* (1951); *Les Miserables, Blackbeard, the Pirate, Androcles and the Lion* (1952); *The Desert Rats* (1953); *The High and the Mighty* (1954); *Around the World in Eighty Days* (1956).

NIELSEN, Brigitte (1963–)

Best known for her ruthless ambition and powerful blonde physique, this Amazonian Danish model enjoyed some popularity in Hollywood films during her tumultuous marriage to action star Sylvester Stallone, but she has largely been relegated to the gossip columns since. HJW
FILMS: *Red Sonja, Rocky IV* (1985), *Cobra* (1986); *Beverly Hills Cop II* (1987); *Bye Bye Baby* (1988); *Domino* (1989); *976 EVIL 2: The Astral Factor* (1991); *Mission of Justice, Chained Heat II, The Double O Kid* (1992); *Codename Silencer, Galaxis, Compelling Evidence* (1995); *Snowboard Academy* (1996); *She's Too Tall, Hostile Environment* (1998); *Doomsdayer* (1999).

NIELSEN, Connie (1965–)

A cool beauty cast in the mould of Grace Kelly, Connie Nielsen has alternated between blockbusters such as *Gladiator* and smaller independent films in her American film career to date. HJW
FILMS: *The Devil's Advocate* (1997); *Permanent Midnight, Rushmore, Soldier* (1998); *Dark Summer* (1999); *Mission to Mars, Gladiator* (2000); *One Hour Photo* (2002); *The Hunted, Basic* (2003).

NIETO, José (José García Nieto) (1903–1982)

José Nieto appeared in several Spanish-language films such as *Cuerpo y alma/Body and Soul* (1931) and *Marido y mujer/Man and Wife* (1931) during his short Hollywood stay in the 1930s. He was also cast in numerous American-funded productions shot in Europe during the 1950s and 1960s. EU
FILMS: *That Lady* (1955); *Alexander the Great* (1956); *The Pride and the Passion, A Farewell to Arms* (1957), *Spanish Affair* (1958); *John Paul Jones, Soloman and Sheba* (1959); *King of Kings* (1961); *55 Days at Peking, The Ceremony* (1963); *Doctor Zhivago, Kid Rodelo* (1965); *Catlow* (1971).

NILSSON, Anna Q. (1888–1974)

The first Scandinavian star in American cinema, Nilsson came to New York as a housemaid in 1905 and soon began modelling for artists. She made her screen debut for Kalem in 1911 and stayed there for four years appearing in a huge number of war and frontier melodramas that were then this leading production company's speciality. She soon became famous for appearing in action scenes without using stand-ins, and went on to work for most of the major studios throughout the teens. She made her only Swedish film, *Värmlänningarna*, in 1921.

Back in Hollywood, Nilsson shifted to a vampier performance style observable in Cecil B. DeMille's *Adam's Rib* and in her role as the Blond Vamp promoted by columnist Adele St John in *Inez from Hollywood*, a film often regarded as Nilsson's last major release. Her last silent film was *Block-ade*, after which her career came to a halt due to a severe riding accident. When she returned to work, the coming of sound had changed the industry for ever, and Nilsson subsequently played minor parts for the rest of her career. One of her last roles was as herself in Billy Wilder's *Sunset Boulevard*. MBj

FILMS: *Mollie Pitcher* (1911); *Victim of Circumstances, Battle of Pottsburg Bridge, Tide of Battle, The Drummer Girl of Vicksburg, The Colonel's Escape, The Bugler of Battery C, War's Havoc, Fighting Dan McCool, Under a Flag of Truce, The Siege of Petersburg, The Prison Ship, Saved from Court Martial, The Darling of the C.S.A., A Railroad Lochinvar, A Girl in the Caboosa, The Pony Express Girl, Battle in the Virginia Hills, The Water Right War, The Battle of Wits, A Race with Tinc, The Grit of the Girl Telegrapher, The Confederate Ironclad, His Mother's Picture, The Fraud at the Hope Mine, The Farm Bully, The Grim Tale of War* (1912); *The Toll-Gate Raiders, Prisoners of War, A Sawmill Hazard, A Desperate Chance, The Turning Point, A Treacherous Shot, Infamous Don Miguel, Captured by Strategy, The Battle of Bloody Ford, A Mississippi Tragedy, John Burns of Gettysburg, Shenandoah, Shipwrecked, The Fatal Legacy, Retribution, The Breath of Scandal, The Counterfeit's Confederate, Uncle Tom's Cabin* (1913); *A Shot in the Night, Tell-Tale Stains, Perils of the White Light, The Secret of the Will, Regeneration, A Diamond in the Rough, The Man with the Glove, The Ex-Convict, The Man in the Vault, Wolfe or the Conquest of Quebec* (1914); *In the Hands of the Jury, Barriers Swept Aside, The Hazards of Helen: The Night Operator at Buxton, The Siren's Reign, The Second Commandment, The Haunted House of Wild Isle, The Destroyer, A Sister's Burden, Rivals, The Haunting Fear, Hiding from the Law, The Regeneration, Voices in the Dark, The Night of the Embassy Ball, Barbara Frietchie* (1915); *The Scarlet Road, The Supreme Sacrifice, Who's Guilty?* [serial], *Her Surrender* (1916); *Infidelity, The*

Moral Code, The Inevitable, The Silent Master, Seven Keys to Baldpate, Over There (1917); *Heart of the Sunset, The Trail to Yesterday, No Man's Land, In Judgement, The Vanity Pool* (1918); *Venus in the East, Cheating Cheaters, Auction of Souls, The Way of the Strong, The Love Burglar, Her Kingdom of Dreams, Soldiers of Fortune, A Very Good Young Man, A Sporting Chance* (1919); *The Thirteenth Commandment, The Luck of the Irish, The Toll Gate, The Figurehead, One Hour before Dawn, The Fighting Chance, The Brute Master, In the Heart of a Fool* (1920); *What Women Will Do, Without Limit, The Oath, Why Girls Leave Home, The Lotus Eater* (1921); *Three Live Ghosts, The Man from Home, Pink Gods* (1922); *Hearts Aflame, Adam's Rib, The Isle of Lost Ships, Souls for Sale, The Rustle of Silk, The Spoilers, Hollywood, Ponjola, Thundering Dawn, Innocence, Enemies of the Children* (1923); *Half-a-Dollar Bill, Painted People, Flowing Gold, Between Friends, Broadway after Dark, The Side Show of Life, The Fire Patrol, Vanity's Price, Inez from Hollywood* (1924); *The Top of the World, If I Marry Again, One Way Street, The Talker, Winds of Chance, The Splendid Road* (1925); *The Greater Glory, Too Much Money, Her Second Chance, Miss Nobody, Midnight Lovers* (1926); *The Masked Woman, Easy Pickings, Babe Comes Home, Lonesome Ladies, Sorell and Son, The Thirteenth Juror* (1927); *The Whip, Blockade* (1928); *The World Changes* (1933); *The Little Minister* (1934); *The Wanderer of the Wasteland, School for Girls* (1935); *Paradise for Three, Prison Farm* (1938); *Riders of the Timberline, The People vs. Dr Kildare, The Trial of Mary Dugan* (1941); *The Great Man's Lady, Crossroads, I Live on Danger, Girls' Town, They Died with Their Boots On* (1942); *Headin' for God's Country* (1943); *Cry Havoc* (1944); *The Valley of Decision* (1945); *The Sailor Takes a Wife, The Secret Heart* (1946); *The Farmer's Daughter, Cynthia, Magic Town, It Had to Be You* (1947); *Fighting Father Dunne, Every Girl Should Be Married, The Boy with Green Hair* (1948); *In the Good Old Summertime, Adam's Rib* (1949); *Malaya, The Big Hangover, Sunset Boulevard* (1950); *Showboat, The Law and the Lady, An American in Paris, The Unknown* (1951); *Seven Brides for Seven Brothers* (1954).

NISSEN, Greta (Grethe Rutz-Nissen) (1906–1988)
Norwegian performer who came to the USA in 1924 with a ballet troupe after training at the Royal Danish Theatre. Nissen made her American film debut in *In the Name of Love* in 1925 and subsequently made three films with Adolphe Menjou for which she was praised as a cool, ele- **383**

gant and charming femme fatale. Her Hollywood career ended when she was replaced by Jean Harlow in Howard Hughes' World War I drama *Hell's Angels*. MBj

FILMS: *In the Name of Love, The King of Main Street, Lost – a Wife* (1925); *The Lady of the Harem, The Love Thief, The Lucky Lady, The Popular Sin, The Wanderer* (1926); *Blind Alleys, Blonde or Brunette* (1927); *The Butter and Egg Man, Fazil* (1928); *The Tempest* (1929); *Ambassador Bill, Good Sport, Women of All Nations, Transatlantic* (1931); *Rackety Rax, The Silent Witness, The Unwritten Law* (1932); *Best of Enemies, The Circus Queen Murder, Life in the Raw, Melody Cruise* (1933); *Hired Wife* (1934).

NIVEN, David (James David Graham Niven) (1910–1983)

David Niven was an English gentleman hero comparable to actors such as Ronald Colman★ and Robert Donat★, though it is worth noting that he was also cast as an ageing Count Dracula late in his career in Clive Donner's *Vampira* (1974). Many of his films, however, tend to blend the 'gentleman' dimension with an armed services context creating an image that reflects Scottish-born Niven's back-

David Niven epitomised the suave English gentleman and/or military man in a long and distinguished career

ground of an English public school, the Royal Military College, Sandhurst and a commission in the Highland Light Infantry.

Early uncredited film roles include a galley slave in *Cleopatra* and bit parts in Hopalong Cassidy films, but after signing with Samuel Goldwyn, the leading independent producer of the day, he was soon cast in more substantial roles, including an army captain in *The Charge of the Light Brigade* and a World War I airman in *The Dawn Patrol*. The fighting-man aspect of his image was sustained throughout his career and one of his final screen appearances was as a retired army officer working undercover during World War II in *The Sea Wolves*. Indeed, Niven's one Best Actor Academy Award success was for a military role, a retired army major in *Separate Tables*. His career, however, even in its early years, ranged wider than the military/action roles and similarly exploited the debonair English gentleman dimensions of his persona. He played Bertie Wooster in *Thank You, Jeeves!*, the eponymous gentleman thief in *Raffles*, Edgar Linton in William Wyler's prestige adaptation of *Wuthering Heights* and a romantic foil to Ginger Rogers in the comedy, *Bachelor Mother*.

At the outbreak of World War II, Niven interrupted his Hollywood career and returned to Britain to re-enlist in the army. He rose to the rank of lieutenant colonel and received a number of decorations for his war service, including the American Legion of Merit. Niven's acting career took second place to his war work during this period, though he did appear in three of the most important British wartime films – *The First of the Few* (1942), *The Way Ahead* (1944) and *A Matter of Life and Death* (1946) – before returning to Hollywood. The high spots of the 1950s for Niven were his role as Phileas Fogg in *Around the World in Eighty Days* and his award-winning performance in *Separate Tables*. He moved to Europe in the 1960s and appeared in a number of international Hollywood films, including *The Guns of Navarone, 55 Days at Peking* and *The Pink Panther*. He also appeared as James Bond – the ultimate English gentleman hero – in the spoof *Casino Royale* and though this oddity of a film compared unfavourably with the successful Sean Connery★ films, author Ian Fleming did regard Niven as the ideal actor for the lead role. Niven became a best-selling author in the 1970s with his autobiographical works, *The Moon is a Balloon* and *Bring on the Empty Horses*. TR

FILMS: *Cleopatra* (1934); *Barbary Coast, A Feather in Her Hat, Splendor, Without Regret, Mutiny on the Bounty* (1935); *Palm Springs, Beloved Enemy, Dodsworth, Thank You, Jeeves!, The Charge of the Light Brigade, Rose Marie* (1936); *We have Our Moments, The Prisoner of Zenda* (1937); *The Dawn Patrol, Three Blind Mice, Four Men and a Prayer, Bluebeard's Eighth Wife* (1938); *Eternally Yours, The Real Glory, Bachelor Mother, Wuthering Heights* (1939); *Raffles* (1940); *The Perfect Marriage, Magnificent Doll* (1946); *The Other Love, The Bishop's Wife* (1947); *Enchantment* (1948); *A Kiss for Corliss, A Kiss in the Dark* (1949); *The Toast of New Orleans* (1950); *Soldiers Three* (1951); *The Lady Says No* (1952); *The Moon is Blue* (1953); *The King's Thief* (1955); *The Birds and the Bees, Around the World in Eighty Days* (1956); *My Man Godfrey, The Silken Affair, Oh, Men! Oh, Women!, The Little Hut* (1957); *Separate Tables, Bonjour Tristesse* (1958); *Ask Any Girl, Happy Anniversary* (1959); *Please Don't Eat the Daisies* (1960); *The Best of Enemies, The Guns of Navarone* (1961); *The Road to Hong Kong* (1962); *55 Days at Peking* (1963); *The Pink Panther, Bedtime Story* (1964); *Lady L, Where the Spies Are* (1965); *Casino Royale* (1967); *Eye of the Devil, Prudence and the Pill, The Impossible Years* (1968); *Before Winter Comes, The Extraordinary Seaman* (1969); *The Statue* (1971); *King, Queen, Knave* (1972); *No Deposit, No Return, Murder by Death* (1976); *Candleshoe* (1977); *A Nightingale Sang in Berkeley Square* (1979); *Rough Cut, The Sea Wolves: The Last Charge of the Calcutta Light Horse* (1980); *Better Late than Never, Trail of the Pink Panther* (1982); *Curse of the Pink Panther* (1983).

NOIRET, Philippe (1930–)

Distinguished French actor with a huge filmography. With his tall and portly physique and hangdog facial expressions, Noiret has long been one of the most highly acclaimed and prolific of contemporary French screen actors. He made his film debut in Agnès Varda's *La Pointe courte* (1956) and has worked with several celebrated international directors including Bertrand Tavernier. In his first English-speaking film *Lady L*, his voice was dubbed by Peter Ustinov★, but his real accent can be heard in subsequent features, in which he often played French state officials such as a diplomatic attaché (*Justine*) and a government administrator (*Murphy's War*). VO

FILMS: *Lady L* (1965); *Woman Times Seven, The Night of the Generals* (1967); *The Assassination Bureau, Justine, Topaz* (1969); *Murphy's War* (1971); *Who is Killing the Great Chefs of Europe?* (1978).

NORLUND, Evy (1938–)

The blonde and shapely Evy Norlund, Miss Denmark of 1958, arrived in Hollywood with some fanfare to star in the circus melodrama *The Flying Fontaines*. She married the actor-singer James Darren the following year and promptly retired. HJW

FILM: *The Flying Fontaines* (1959).

NOVELLO, Ivor (David Ivor Novello Davies) (1893–1951)

Novello was a well-known English popular songwriter before he became a film star. His first film roles were in French and British films. In particular, *Bohemian Girl* (1922) attracted attention in the USA, especially when Novello went there with his co-star Gladys Cooper★ in 1923 to publicise the film. D. W. Griffith thought that Novello looked like the actor Richard Barthelmess when he visited London for the opening of his film *Orphans of the Storm* and subsequently offered Novello a role in his forthcoming film melodrama *The White Rose*. Novello attracted widespread attention with his Latinate looks and resemblance to Valentino and the film performed reasonably well at the box office. Despite having optioned him for further roles, Griffith did not renew Novello's contract. He was disappointed with the actor's performance and described the film, rather dismissively, as a 'pot boiler'. Novello felt that an opportunity had been lost to carve out a career in Hollywood and returned to Britain. His only subsequent appearance in an American film was in *Once a Lady*. SS

FILMS: *The White Rose* (1923); *Once a Lady* (1931).

NUNGESSER, Charles (1892–1927)

French armed forces-based dare-devil aviator who appeared as himself in his only American feature film. VO

FILM: *The Sky Raider* (1925).

OBERON, Merle (Estelle Merle O'Brien Thompson) (1911–1979)

Merle Oberon's first film roles for Alexander Korda in Britain, particularly in *The Private Life of Henry VIII* (1933), drew her to the attention of Hollywood studios and in 1934 she sailed to the USA on the *SS Paris*. Once **385** in Hollywood, she made four films, *Folies Bergère de Paris*, *The Dark Angel*, *These Three* and *Beloved Enemy*. The latter three were made for producer Samuel Goldwyn, with whom Korda was connected because of his partnership in United Artists. Oberon starred in films in Britain and the USA throughout the 1930s. In Hollywood, she mixed with the expatriate community and in particular was befriended by David Niven★, Ronald Colman★ and Maurice Chevalier★.

After the success of *The Dark Angel*, for which she received an Academy Award nomination for Best Actress, she was much in demand, but she sued David O. Selznick for not casting her in *The Garden of Allah* (1936) when she understood she was under contract to his company. After a screen test in Technicolor, Selznick decided against casting her in favour of Marlene Dietrich★. The case was eventually settled, earning Oberon $80,000. An indication of her high status in Hollywood was her ability to win the role of Cathy in *Wuthering Heights*, co-starring with Laurence

Olivier★, even though he wanted Vivien Leigh★ to play the part. In later years, Oberon's films were usually unfavourably compared to *Wuthering Heights*, generally regarded as her best performance. A dark-haired beauty with a pale complexion, Oberon played her parts with a distant, 'regal' bearing that was emphasised by her clipped, rather stilted English accent.

For most of the war Oberon lived in the USA. She starred in *That Uncertain Feeling*, a comedy directed by Ernst Lubitsch, and participated in the fund-raising venture *Forever and a Day*. She did not sustain her early success, however, and she made several other films in subsequent years that were generally not received well by the critics. She also acquired a reputation for being difficult and insecure about her appearance and health. In 1957, Oberon married Bruno Pigliai, a rich industrialist, and settled in Mexico. She financed and starred in *Of Love and Desire*, a film that while not a critical success did reasonably well at the box office.

386 The beautiful Merle Oberon as Cathy in *Wuthering Heights* (1939), co-starring Laurence Olivier

After Oberon died in 1979 it was discovered that she, and the studios, had falsified her birth place. All her publicity claimed that she was born in Tasmania, the posthumous daughter of a British major who had been raised by aristocratic foster parents. In fact, she was a Eurasian, the daughter of an English engineer and an Indian mother, and brought up in Bombay. The studios clearly wanted to protect the image of her as the well-bred 'lady' that had been emphasised by her aristocratic accent and demeanour. SS

FILMS: *Service for Ladies* (1932); *Folies Bergère de Paris, The Dark Angel* (1935); *These Three, Beloved Enemy* (1936); *The Cowboy and the Lady* (1938); *Wuthering Heights* (1939); *'Til We Meet Again* (1940); *That Uncertain Feeling, Affectionately Yours, Lydia* (1941); *Forever and a Day, Stage Door Canteen, First Comes Courage* (1943); *The Lodger, Dark Waters, A Song to Remember* (1944); *This Love of Ours* (1945); *A Night in Paradise, Temptation* (1946); *Night Song* (1947); *Berlin Express* (1948); *Pardon My French* (1951); *Desirée, Deep in My Heart* (1954); *The Price of Fear* (1956); *Of Love and Desire* (1963); *The Oscar* (1965); *Hotel* (1967); *Interval* (1972).

O'CONNOR, Una (Agnes Teresa McGlade) (1893–1959)

Irish actress who played a succession of cockney domestic servants with the Abbey Theatre. In 1932, she went to Hollywood to recreate her stage role of the maid, Ellen Bridges, in *Cavalcade*. She stayed on to work in both American film and theatre. RB

FILMS: *Cavalcade, Pleasure Cruise, Horseplay, Mary Stevens, M.D., The Invisible Man* (1933); *The Poor Rich, Orient Express, All Men are Enemies, Stingaree, Chained* (1934); *The Barretts of Wimpole Street, The Personal History, Adventures, Experience, and Observation of David Copperfield, the Younger, Father Brown, Detective, Bride of Frankenstein, The Informer, Thunder in the Night, The Perfect Gentleman* (1935); *Rose-Marie, Little Lord Fauntleroy, Suzy, Lloyd's of London, The Plough and the Stars* (1936); *Personal Property, Call it a Day* (1937); *The Adventures of Robin Hood* (1938); *We are Not Alone, All Women Have Secrets* (1939); *It All Came True, Lillian Russell, The Sea Hawk, He Stayed for Breakfast* (1940); *Her First Beau, Three Girls about Town, How Green Was My Valley* [scenes deleted], *The Strawberry Blonde, Kisses for Breakfast* (1941); *Always in My Heart, My Favorite Spy, Random Harvest* (1942); *Forever and a Day, This Land is Mine,*

Holy Matrimony, Government Girl (1943); *The Canterville Ghost, My Pal Wolf* (1944); *Christmas in Connecticut, The Bells of St Mary's* (1945); *Cluny Brown, Child of Divorce, The Return of Monte Cristo, Of Human Bondage* (1946); *Unexpected Guest, Lost Honeymoon, Banjo, The Corpse Came C.O.D., Ivy* (1947); *Fighting Father Dunne, Adventures of Don Juan* (1948); *Witness for the Prosecution* (1957).

O'CONOR, Hugh (1975–)

As a child actor in Ireland, O'Conor played the young Christy Brown in *My Left Foot* (1989). He later starred as the lead in *The Young Poisoner's Handbook* (1995). So far, his Hollywood work has been less impressive. RB

FILMS: *Da* (1988); *Deathwatch* (2002).

O'DEA, Denis (1905–1978)

As a member of the Irish Abbey Players, O'Dea was offered a full-time contract in Hollywood, along with his wife Siobhan McKenna★. He turned it down in favour of occasional parts instead, often in John Ford's films. RB

FILMS: *The Informer* (1935); *The Plough and the Stars* (1936); *Treasure Island* (1950); *Captain Horatio Hornblower R.N.* (1951); *Sea Devils, Niagara, Mogambo* (1953); *Captain Lightfoot* (1955); *The Rising of the Moon* (1957); *Darby O'Gill and the Little People* (1959); *Esther and the King* (1960).

O'HARA, Maureen (Maureen FitzSimons) (1920–)

Maureen O'Hara, Hollywood's quintessential Irish colleen, was dubbed 'The Queen of Technicolor' in the 1940s in deference to the impact of her flaming red hair on screen. She was born to a middle-class Catholic family in Dublin, many of whom went on to become actors and producers. She started in the Abbey Theatre, where she was spotted and screen-tested for a role in *Kicking the Moon Around* (1939). Her break came when Charles Laughton★ took her on to play opposite him in *Jamaica Inn* (1939), produced by Germany's Erich Pommer. On the strength of this, Laughton, Pommer and O'Hara went to the USA to take up contracts with RKO, where Pommer produced Dorothy Arzner's *Dance, Girl, Dance* – later the subject of much feminist film criticism – with O'Hara playing the outspoken dancer alongside Lucille Ball.

O'Hara's screen career encompassed several roles as a swashbuckler (she played opposite Errol Flynn in *Against* **387**

Maureen O'Hara: Hollywood's quintessential Irish colleen

All Flags and Cornel Wilde in At Sword's Point), but her outstanding Hollywood performances were in John Ford's films, beginning with *How Green Was My Valley*. The director had bought part of her contract from RKO, who, in turn, had bought her from Laughton. He first teamed O'Hara up with John Wayne as the estranged Irish-American wife in *Rio Grande* and their partnership was reprised in *The Quiet Man* – the classic Irish-American fantasy of return. O'Hara's role as the wild Irish girl, determined that her new husband should claim her dowry, has been alternately considered the height of Hollywood typecasting and a stand for women's rights in a traditional society.

O'Hara was offered a contract with Columbia in 1953. She played with Wayne again in Ford's *Wings of Eagles* at MGM and in 1963 they teamed up for *McLintock!*, a film with many overtones of *The Quiet Man*. O'Hara remains best known for her on-screen fiery temperament but she also moved into playing maternal roles in the 1960s, notably in *The Parent Trap* and *Big Jake*, in which she made her final appearance with Wayne (as a grandmother). She briefly returned from retirement in 1991 for a much-praised performance as the daunting mother in Chris **388** Columbus' *Only the Lonely*. RB

FILMS: *The Hunchback of Notre Dame* (1939); *A Bill of Divorcement, Dance, Girl, Dance* (1940); *They Met in Argentina, How Green Was My Valley* (1941); *Ten Gentlemen from West Point, The Black Swan, To the Shores of Tripoli* (1942); *Immortal Sergeant, This Land is Mine, The Fallen Sparrow* (1943); *Buffalo Bill* (1944); *The Spanish Main* (1945); *Do You Love Me, Sentimental Journey* (1946); *Sinbad the Sailor, Miracle on 34th Street, The Foxes of Harrow, The Homestretch* (1947); *Sitting Pretty* (1948); *A Woman's Secret, Britannia Mews, Bagdad, Father was a Fullback* (1949); *Comanche Territory, Rio Grande, Tripoli* (1950); *Flame of Araby* (1951); *The Quiet Man, At Sword's Point, Kangaroo, Against All Flags* (1952); *The Redhead from Wyoming, War Arrow* (1953); *Malaga* (1954); *The Long Gray Line, The Magnificent Matador, Lady Godiva* (1955); *Lisbon, Everything but the Truth* (1956); *The Wings of Eagles* (1957); *Our Man in Havana, The Parent Trap, The Deadly Companions* (1961); *Mr Hobbs Takes a Vacation* (1962); *McLintock!, Spencer's Mountain* (1963); *The Battle of the Villa Fiorita* (1965); *The Rare Breed* (1966); *How Do I Love Thee?* (1970); *Big Jake* (1971); *Only the Lonely* (1991).

O'HERLIHY, Dan (1919–)

Irish actor who moved to the USA to join Orson Welles' Mercury Theatre. In 1952, he received an Academy Award nomination for his title role in Luis Buñuel's *Las adventuras de Robinson Crusoe*. Since then, he has continued to appear in American film and television. RB

FILMS: *Larceny* (1947); *Macbeth, Kidnapped* (1948); *The Iroquois Trail* (1950); *The Highwayman, Soldiers Three, The Blue Veil* (1951); *Actors and Sin, At Sword's Point, Operation Secret, Invasion USA* (1952); *Sword of Venus* (1953); *Bengal Brigade, The Black Shield of Falworth* (1954); *The Virgin Queen, The Purple Mask* (1955); *Home before Dark* (1958); *Imitation of Life, The Young Land* (1959); *A Terrible Beauty, One Foot in Hell* (1960); *King of the Roaring 20s – The Story of Arnold Rothstein* (1961); *The Cabinet of Dr Caligari* (1962); *Fail-Safe* (1964); *100 Rifles, The Big Cube* (1969); *The Carey Treatment* (1972); *The Tamarind Seed* (1974); *MacArthur* (1977); *Halloween III: Season of the Witch* (1982); *The Last Starfighter* (1984); *The Whoopee Boys* (1986); *RoboCop* (1987); *RoboCop 2* (1990).

OLDMAN, Gary (1958–)

The latter part of Gary Oldman's career provides remarkable testimony to the persistence of a long-running casting pattern that finds distinguished stage-trained British actors in Hollywood inexorably shoehorned into roles as overly articulate villains. This is surprising where Oldman is concerned, because he came to fame in Britain (and thence to American attention) in a series of raw portraits of disenfranchised youth, such as the dole-queue punk in Mike Leigh's *Meantime* (1983) and Sid Vicious in *Sid and Nancy* (1986). In the early phase of Oldman's career in Hollywood (where he is now permanently domiciled), he was handled as potential leading-man material, though his divergent roles, such as a mixed-up Lee Harvey Oswald or a perversely decadent Dracula, meant that a coherent star image was never likely. The latter performance can be seen retrospectively as the ur-template for Oldman's increasingly frequent turns as camp baddies in big-budget blockbuster films such as *Lost in Space*. He has also followed another less prominent émigré trend that sees British actors such as Herbert Marshall★, Vivien Leigh★, James Fox★ and Kenneth Branagh★ commonly employed to supply the haughty rhetorical fussiness of speech stereotypically associated with folks from the Deep South. JB

FILMS: *Track 29* (1988); *Criminal Law, Chattahoochee* (1989); *State of Grace, Henry and June* (1990); *JFK* (1991); *Bram Stoker's Dracula* (1992); *True Romance, Romeo is Bleeding* (1993); *Immortal Beloved* (1994); *Murder in the First, The Scarlet Letter* (1995); *Basquiat* (1996); *Air Force One* (1997); *Lost in Space* (1998); *The Contender* (2000); *Hannibal* (2001); *Interstate 60, The Hire: Beat the Devil* (2002); *Tiptoes, Sin* (2003).

OLIN, Lena (1956–)

Talented daughter of Swedish actor Stig Olin who became known to international audiences for her leading role in *The Unbearable Lightness of Being*. She had already achieved significant domestic success for her film work for the likes of Ingmar Bergman. Early on in her international career, Olin was nominated for an Academy Award for Best Supporting Actress for her performance as a passionate and independently minded lover in *Enemies: A Love Story*, but soon after, her American career seemed almost to come to a full stop. Her follow-up role in *Havana* failed to lead to bigger and better offers within Hollywood, but despite this significant drawback, Olin still managed to deliver some notable characterisations in films such as *Romeo is Bleeding*,

The Ninth Gate and *Chocolat*. The latter film was directed by her husband since 1994, Lasse Hallström. Olin's persona currently rests in the portrayal of highly emotional and sexually obsessed women whose memorable screen presence combines cunning deviousness with sexual attraction. MJ

FILMS: *The Unbearable Lightness of Being* (1988); *Enemies: A Love Story* (1989); *Havana* (1990); *Romeo is Bleeding, Mr Jones* (1993); *Night Falls on Manhattan* (1997); *Polish Wedding* (1998); *Mystery Men, The Ninth Gate* (1999); *Chocolat* (2000); *Ignition, Darkness* (2001); *Queen of the Damned* (2002); *The United States of Leland, Hollywood Homicide* (2003).

OLIVIER, Laurence (1907–1989)

'Hollywood? Yes. Bit of fame. Good' was the advice given by Ralph Richardson★ to Laurence Olivier when Samuel Goldwyn offered him the part of Heathcliff in *Wuthering Heights*. Olivier had been in Hollywood in the early 1930s, under contract to RKO for three films: *The Yellow Ticket*, *Friends and Lovers* and *Westward Passage*. His success on Broadway in Noel Coward's★ play *Private Lives* had made him an attractive prospect for RKO, and on his first visit to Hollywood he was accompanied by his first wife Jill Esmond★. Esmond was a popular actress and David O. Selznick offered her an excellent part in *A Bill of Divorcement* (1932), a role eventually played by Katharine Hepburn. She was prevented from taking up this offer because Olivier disliked Hollywood, and the couple returned to Britain so that he could appear in *Perfect Understanding* (1933), a film made by Gloria Swanson's independent production company in Britain. At that time, Olivier's reputation was not firmly established and he was happy for his film career to continue in Britain, particularly after the news that Greta Garbo★ had rejected him as her co-star in *Queen Christina* (1933) in favour of John Gilbert.

In 1937, Tyrone Guthrie invited Olivier to become leading man at the Old Vic, and he also acted on Broadway. As with many British actors, a good stage reputation on Broadway made him an increasingly attractive prospect for Hollywood. It was on the recommendation of playwright and screenwriter Ben Hecht that Goldwyn offered Olivier the lead role in *Wuthering Heights*, co-starring with Merle Oberon★ as Cathy. Olivier wanted the part of Cathy to go to Vivien Leigh★, but Goldwyn and the director, William Wyler, were unwilling to offer the part to an actress who **389**

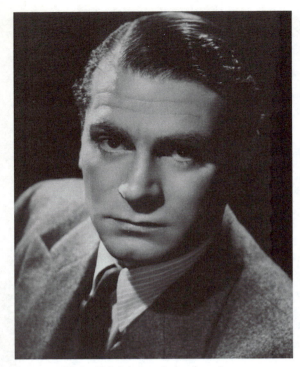

Laurence Olivier: Britain's theatrical ambassador

ganda films. During and after the war, he established a reputation as a film director and continued to pursue his theatrical career. His British films, *Henry V* (1944) and *Hamlet* (1948), were extremely successful in the USA, winning numerous awards and yielding good box-office returns. Wary of signing long-term contracts, Olivier proceeded to work on film on an intermittent basis, usually to accommodate periods when he was not totally committed to stage acting. His next Hollywood film was Paramount's *Carrie*, an adaptation of a novel by Theodore Dreiser and directed by William Wyler, a director he highly respected and with whom he worked very well. By the 1950s, he was able to negotiate excellent contracts. Olivier's contract for *Carrie* gave him first-star billing and generous payment of £55,000 for eleven weeks' work. In this role, he proved that he was able to command an American accent, breaking away from his reputation as the epitome of 'English' charm. His promotion of the film by giving numerous interviews to the American press further enhanced his reputation as a sought-after film star.

In a somewhat controversial project, he produced, directed and co-starred with Marilyn Monroe in *The Prince and the Showgirl* (1957), the first independent production by Monroe's film company that was filmed in Britain. The collaboration was not a happy one, however, as conflict developed between Monroe as actress and Olivier as director, particularly when Monroe was coached on the set by Paula Strasberg. Thereafter, Olivier directed most of his energies to the stage. He became director of the National Theatre in 1962. His subsequent Hollywood acting parts were mainly supporting roles, the most distinguished being his portrayal of Crassus in *Spartacus*, the sinister ex-Nazi in *Marathon Man* and the Jewish Nazi-hunter in *The Boys from Brazil*. Olivier was an astute businessman and his film deals were carefully arranged via his company Laurence Olivier Productions. Although the cameo and supporting roles of his later film career were very lucrative, he always privileged his theatre work. He remained Britain's representative of a theatrical tradition that was incorporated and adapted by Hollywood, although his film performances demonstrate very well the different craft and challenges of film acting. ss

FILMS: *Friends and Lovers, The Yellow Ticket* (1931); *Westward Passage* (1932); *As You Like It* (1936); *Wuthering Heights* (1939); *Rebecca, Pride and Prejudice* (1940); *That Hamilton Woman* (1941); *Carrie* (1952); *The Devil's Disciple* (1959);

was unknown in Hollywood. The shooting of the film was a humbling and educative experience for Olivier, who had previously not taken film acting very seriously. *Wuthering Heights* was a great success, and he was nominated for an Academy Award. The following year, Olivier was cast in two key roles, as Maxim de Winter in Hitchcock's *Rebecca* and as Darcy in MGM's *Pride and Prejudice*. All three films were British in setting and theme, and established Olivier's screen persona as an English romantic leading man with theatrical kudos. This continued when Alexander Korda, working in Hollywood, cast Olivier as Nelson in *That Hamilton Woman*, a key film that sought to counter isolationism in the USA during the early years of World War II. Contemporary parallels abounded in this historical film, in which as Lord Nelson, Oliver was the popular naval hero who defended Britain as a land of liberty and democracy against Continental invasion. Olivier co-starred with Vivien Leigh – now a popular star because of her successful leading role in *Gone with the Wind* (1939) – whom he had recently married after divorcing Jill Esmond.

During the war, Olivier joined the Fleet Air Arm of the **390** Royal Navy and secured release to make British propa-

Spartacus (1960); *Bunny Lake is Missing* (1965); *Khartoum* (1966); *The Shoes of the Fisherman, Romeo and Juliet* [voice] (1968); *Battle of Britain, Oh! What a Lovely War* (1969); *Sleuth* (1972); *The Rehearsal* (1974); *The Gentleman Tramp* [voice] (1975); *The Seven-Per-Cent Solution, Marathon Man* (1976); *A Bridge Too Far* (1977); *The Betsy, The Boys from Brazil* (1978); *A Little Romance, Dracula* (1979); *The Jazz Singer* (1980); *Inchon* (1981); *The Bounty* (1984).

ORLAMOND, William (William Andersen Orlamundt) (1867–1957)

Hailing from a famous Danish acting family, William Orlamond emigrated to the USA in the latter part of the nineteenth century. He started working in films in 1912 and soon exhibited a proclivity for playing comical old codgers, notably Sourdough in Victor Sjöström's *The Wind*. His brother, Fritz, also appeared in a smaller number of films made during the 1910s. HJW

FILMS: *Caught Bluffing, Taming Their Parents, The Stroke Oar, The Heavenly Voice, A Husband's Awakening* (1912); *Just out of College, Making a Baseball Bug, Jane's Waterloo* (1913); *The Pit* (1915); *The Half Back, The Boy Who Cried Wolf* (1917); *Elmo the Mighty* [serial], *A Rogue's Romance* (1919); *Stronger than Death, Vanishing Trails* [serial], *Madame Peacock* (1920); *Camille, Beating the Game, Doubling for Romeo* (1921); *Arabian Love, Golden Dreams, The Sin Flood, Broken Chains* (1922); *All the Brothers were Valiant, Look Your Best, Souls for Sale, Slander the Woman, The Eternal Three, Slave of Desire, The Eagle's Feather* (1923); *Name the Man, Nellie, the Beautiful Cloak Model, When a Girl Loves, True as Steel, Girl Shy, The White Moth, The Wife of the Centaur* (1924); *Smouldering Fires, The Great Divide, Boys Will Be Boys, Seven Keys to Baldpate, The Dixie Handicap* (1925); *Good Cheer, Kiki, That's My Baby, Baby Clothes, Up in Mabel's Room, Mantrap, Bromo and Juliet, Flesh and the Devil, Dog Shy* (1926); *The Red Mill, The Taxi Dancer, Getting Gertie's Garter, Fashions for Women, See You in Jail, A Texas Steer* (1927); *Rose Marie, Aching Youths, The Little Yellow House, Skinner's Big Idea, While the City Sleeps, The Awakening, The Wind, Give and Take* (1928); *Blue Skies, House of Horror, Words and Music, Her Private Affair, The Girl from Woolworth's* (1929); *The Way of All Men* (1930); *Cimarron, Are These Our Children?* (1931); *Roar of the Dragon* (1932); *Rafter Romance* (1933); *King Kelly of the U.S.A.* (1934); *Anna Karenina* (1935); *The Gorgeous Hussy, Sworn Enemy* (1936); *The Declaration of Independence* (1938).

ORMOND, Julia (1965–)

Dark-haired British actress who briefly came to Hollywood's attention in the mid-1990s following a successful trajectory in UK film, theatre and television. Ormond was Brad Pitt's soulful love-interest in *Legends of the Fall* and reprised Audrey Hepburn's★ leading role in the unsuccessful remake of *Sabrina*. JS

FILMS: *Legends of the Fall* (1994); *Sabrina, First Knight* (1995); *The Prime Gig* (2000); *Resistance* (2003).

O'SHEA, Milo (1926–)

Member of the Irish Abbey Players whose most famous film role has been as Leopold Bloom in *Ulysses* (1967). O'Shea also made an enduring impression as the paedophile priest in Neil Jordan's *The Butcher Boy*. RB

FILMS: *Romeo and Juliet* (1968); *The Adding Machine* (1969); *The Angel Levine* (1970); *The Pilot* (1979); *The Verdict* (1982); *The Purple Rose of Cairo* (1985); *The Dream Team* (1989); *Opportunity Knocks* (1990); *Only the Lonely* (1991); *The Butcher Boy, The Matchmaker* (1997); *Moonglow* (2000).

O'TOOLE, Peter (1932–)

O'Toole's career in American film reads much like that of his lifelong friend and erstwhile drinking companion, Richard Harris★. Both actors found themselves at odds with the system and railed about it off screen while simultaneously relying on Hollywood money to finance their flamboyant personal lives. O'Toole was born in Ireland and made his way to England with his father, an itinerant bookkeeper. After naval service, he attended the Royal Academy of Dramatic Arts (RADA) and by the time he joined the Shakespeare Memorial Theatre company in 1956, he was being heralded as the next Laurence Olivier★. O'Toole made his first film, *The Day They Robbed the Bank of England*, in 1960. On the strength of this, David Lean cast the Irish actor in his 1962 epic *Lawrence of Arabia*, where his blonde hair and blue eyes suggested an almost effeminate beauty. O'Toole's career-defining performance reflected the wild instability, monolithic egotism and insecure sexuality of the legendary Englishman who had gone native but who remained a figurehead of Empire. He was nominated for an Academy Award for this and his next film, *Becket*. Five other nominations followed: *The Lion in Winter, Goodbye, Mr Chips, The Ruling Class, The Stunt Man* and *My Favourite*

Year. In 2003, in recognition of his long film career, O'Toole was awarded a Lifetime Achievement Academy Award.

O'Toole has long been associated in both serious drama and comedy with representatives of an aristocracy in decline. He has twice been cast as Henry II and dutifully hammed it up as a down-at-heel lord of a haunted castle in Neil Jordan's supernatural comedy-thriller *High Spirits* (1988). In *The Ruling Class*, he played a demented earl who suffers from paranoid schizophrenia, believing one moment that he is Jesus Christ and the next that he is Jack the Ripper. It is this love of irony that has probably made O'Toole less successful in his Hollywood roles than his British and European parts. On the whole, American directors have seemed less able to play on his sense of madcap subversiveness. As a result, O'Toole has maintained a successful parallel stage career in parts such as the award-winning leading role in *Jeffrey Bernard is Unwell.* RB

FILMS: *The Savage Innocents, Kidnapped, The Day They Robbed the Bank of England* (1960); *Lawrence of Arabia* (1962); *Becket* (1964); *Lord Jim, What's New Pussycat, The Sandpiper* [voice] (1965); *How to Steal a Million, The Bible – in the Beginning . . .* (1966); *Casino Royale, The Night of the Generals* (1967); *Great Catherine, The Lion in Winter* (1968); *Goodbye, Mr Chips* (1969); *Country Dance* (1970); *Murphy's War* (1971); *Man of La Mancha, The Ruling Class* (1972); *Rosebud, Man Friday* (1975); *Zulu Dawn, Caligula, The Stunt Man* (1979); *The Antagonists* (1981); *My Favorite Year* (1982); *Supergirl* (1984); *Creator* (1985); *Club Paradise* (1986); *King Ralph* (1991); *The Seventh Coin* (1992); *FairyTale: A True Story* (1997); *Phantoms* (1998); *The Final Curtain* (2002); *Troy* (2004).

OTTIANO, Rafaela (1888–1942)

Italian-born actress educated in England. Her distinctive sharp, bird-like features and wide, bulging eyes invariably led her to play mean and spiteful characters. She is best remembered for her role as the cruel governess in *Bondage.* AM

FILMS: *The Law and the Lady* (1924); *Married?* (1926); *Grand Hotel, As You Desire Me, Night Court, The Washington Masquerade* (1932); *She Done Him Wrong, Her Man, Female, Bondage, Ann Vickers* (1933); *Mandalay, A Lost Lady, The Last Gentleman, Great Expectations, All Men are Enemies* (1934); *The Florentine Dagger, One Frightened Night, We're Only Human, Remember Last Night?, Lottery Lover, Enchanted April,*

Break of Hearts, Curly Top, Crime and Punishment, We're Only Human (1935); *Riffraff, The Devil Doll, Anthony Adverse, That Girl from Paris, Mad Holiday* (1936); *Seventh Heaven, Maytime, The League of Frightened Men* (1937); *The Toy Wife, Marie Antoinette, Suez, I'll Give a Million* (1938); *Paris Honeymoon* (1939); *Vigil in the Night, The Long Voyage Home, Victory, A Little Bit of Heaven* (1940); *Topper Returns* (1941); *I Married an Angel, The Adventures of Martin Eden* (1942).

OURY, Gérard (Max-Gérard Tannenbaum) (1919–)

Better known as a director of highly successful French comedies in the 1960s and 1970s, Oury also had a modest acting career in France and the UK. He appeared in Hollywood in a few archetypal French roles such as Napoleon in Raoul Walsh's *Sea Devils.* GV

FILMS: *Sea Devils, The Sword and the Rose* (1953); *Father Brown* (1954); *The Journey* (1959); *The Prize* (1963).

OUSPENSKAYA, Maria (1876–1949)

Diminutive grande dame of Russian theatre and 'quality' film who worked under Stanislavsky at his Moscow Art Theatre (MKHaT). When the Art Theatre toured the USA in 1922, Ouspenskaya – together with Richard Boleslawski – defected. The two chief promulgators of Method acting in the USA founded the influential American Laboratory Theatre and School of Dramatic Art in New York in 1929. It was to fund the school that Ouspenskaya turned to Hollywood acting in 1936 and she immediately gained an Academy Award nomination for her performance as Baroness von Obersdorf in William Wyler's *Dodsworth.* Some twenty lucrative roles as thickly accented, venerable matriarchs with Old World wisdom followed, with Ouspenskaya again being Academy Award-nominated for her role as Grandmother Janou in *Love Affair.* Ouspenskaya gained icon status as the gypsy Maleva in Universal's 'Wolf Man' horror series when she intoned Curt Siodmak's fatalistic verse 'Even a Man who is Pure of Heart . . .'. As with Bela Lugosi★, it was her performance style that became encoded as part of the iconography of Hollywood horror. Venerated by feminists in the 1970s as a powerful genre female, Ouspenskaya's Maleva was affectionately paid homage to by Anne Bancroft in Mel Brooks' *Dracula: Dead and Loving It* (1995). RJK

FILMS: *Dodsworth* (1936); *Conquest* (1937); *Love Affair, Judge Hardy and Son, The Rains Came* (1939); *Waterloo Bridge, The*

Maria Ouspenskaya: grande dame of Russian theatre on set in Hollywood

Mortal Storm, Dance, Girl, Dance, Beyond Tomorrow, Dr Ehrlich's Magic Bullet, The Man I Married (1940); *The Wolf Man, The Shanghai Gesture* (1941); *Mystery of Marie Rôget, Kings Row* (1942); *Frankenstein Meets the Wolf Man* (1943); *Tarzan and the Amazons* (1945); *I've Always Loved You* (1946); *Wyoming* (1947); *A Kiss in the Dark* (1949).

OWEN, Reginald (John Reginald Owen)
(1887–1972)

After appearing as a leading man on the London and Broadway stage until 1928, Owen worked in Hollywood alongside major stars throughout his life. He often had military or aristocratic roles such as the eccentric Admiral Boom in *Mary Poppins*. MW

FILMS: *The Letter, Pusher-in-the-Face* (1929); *Platinum Blonde, The Man in Possession* (1931); *A Woman Commands, Robbers' Roost, Downstairs, Lovers Courageous, The Man Called Back, Sherlock Holmes* (1932); *Voltaire, The Narrow Corner, A Study in Scarlet, The Big Brain, Queen Christina, Double Harness* (1933); *The Countess of Monte Cristo, The Human Side, The House of Rothschild, Music in the Air, Stingaree, Of Human Bondage, Mandalay, Madame DuBarry, Here Is My Heart, Nana, Fashions of 1934, Where Sinners Meet* (1934); *A Tale of Two Cities, The Bishop Misbehaves, The Call of the Wild, Escapade, The Good Fairy, Anna Karenina, Enchanted April* (1935); *Adventure in Manhattan, The Girl on the Front Page, The Great Ziegfeld, Yours for the Asking, Love on the Run, Rose-Marie, Trouble for Two, Petticoat Fever* (1936); *Rosalie, Dangerous Number, The Bride Wore Red, Personal Property, Madame X, Conquest* (1937); *Vacation from Love, Kidnapped, The Girl Downstairs, A Christmas Carol, Stablemates, Three Loves has Nancy, Paradise for Three, Everybody Sing* (1938); *Bad Little Angel, The Real Glory, Remember?, Hotel Imperial, Bridal Suite, Fast and Loose* (1939); *The Earl of* **393**

Chicago, The Ghost Comes Home, Hullabaloo, Florian (1940); *A Yank in the R.A.F., A Woman's Face, They Met in Bombay, Charley's Aunt, Lady Be Good, Tarzan's Secret Treasure, Blonde Inspiration, Free and Easy* (1941); *White Cargo, Reunion in France, Random Harvest, I Married an Angel, Woman of the Year, Crossroads, Somewhere I'll Find You, Cairo, Pierre of the Plains, Mrs Miniver, We were Dancing* (1942); *Assignment in Brittany, Forever and a Day, Salute to the Marines, Madame Curie, Three Hearts for Julia, Above Suspicion* (1943); *National Velvet, The Canterville Ghost* (1944); *Kitty, The Sailor Takes a Wife, The Valley of Decision, The Picture of Dorian Gray, She Went to the Races, Captain Kidd* (1945); *Monsieur Beaucaire, Cluny Brown, The Diary of a Chambermaid* (1946); *Thunder in the Valley, The Imperfect Lady, If Winter Comes, Green Dolphin Street* (1947); *Julia Misbehaves, Hills of Home, The Pirate, The Three Musketeers* (1948); *Challenge to Lassie, The Secret Garden* (1949); *Grounds for Marriage, Kim, The Miniver Story* (1950); *The Great Diamond Robbery* (1953); *Red Garters* (1954); *Darby's Rangers* (1958); *Five Weeks in a Balloon* (1962); *Tammy and the Doctor, The Thrill of it All* (1963); *Mary Poppins, Voice of the Hurricane* (1964); *Rosie!* (1968); *Bedknobs and Broomsticks* (1971).

PACULA, Joanna (Joanna Pacuła) (1957–)

When martial law was announced in Poland in 1981, Joanna Pacuła found herself in Paris. Her first significant role in a Hollywood movie was as a Russian woman in *Gorky Park*. Since then, she has appeared in numerous minor films. EO

FILMS: *Gorky Park* (1983); *Death before Dishonor* (1987); *The Kiss, Sweet Lies, Options* (1988); *Marked for Death* (1990); *The Good Policeman* (1991); *Eyes of the Beholder, Black Eyes* (1992); *Warlock: The Armageddon, Tombstone, Every Breath* (1993); *Deep Red* (1994); *Timemaster, Not Like Us, Last Gasp, Captain Nuke and the Bomber Boys* (1995); *Heaven Before I Die, Haunted Sea* (1997); *My Giant, The White Raven, Error in Judgment* (1998); *Virus, The Art of Murder* (1999); *No Place Like Home, The Hit* (2001); *Warrior Angels, Cupid's Prey* (2002); *El Padrino* (2003).

PAGE, Geneviève (Geneviève Bonjean) (1930–)

Elegant French actress, best remembered as Catherine Deneuve's★ madam in Buñuel's *Belle de jour* (1967). Page made her American debut opposite Ingrid Thulin★ and Robert Mitchum in the European-set thriller *Foreign*

Intrigue. She was Richard Widmark's wife in the comedy-Western *A Talent for Loving*. SL/AP

FILMS: *Foreign Intrigue* (1956); *Song without End* (1960); *El Cid* (1961); *Youngblood Hawke* (1964); *Grand Prix* (1966); *A Talent for Loving* (1969); *The Private Life of Sherlock Holmes* (1970); *Beyond Therapy* (1987).

PAILHAS, Géraldine (1971–)

Elegant, dark-haired French actress who by the time she was cast opposite Johnny Depp and Marlon Brando in her single American film to date was already an established figure in French cinema, with roles in films by Jean-Jacques Beineix and Jacques Demy among others. Pailhas claimed to enjoy the experience: '[a]cting in English, I feel very free. I don't have my usual references,' she commented. AP

FILM: *Don Juan DeMarco* (1995).

PALEY, Natalie (1908–1981)

Russian-born princess exiled in France. Paley was a fashion model in Paris before starring with Charles Boyer★ in L'Herbier's *L'Epervier/The Sparrowhawk* (1933). The beautiful blonde actress went to Hollywood in 1934 and worked mostly in French versions of multi-language films, except for an uncredited part alongside Katharine Hepburn in *Sylvia Scarlett*. CH

FILM: *Sylvia Scarlett* (1936).

PALFI, Lotte (Lotte Mosbacher) (1903–1991)

Minor German-Jewish stage actress (also credited as Lotte Palfi-Andor and Lotte Andor-Palfi) who arrived in Hollywood in 1937 with her film-editor husband Victor Palfi following an unsettling passage through France, Czechoslovakia and Spain. Palfi worked as a housekeeper to make ends meet and received occasional bit parts in anti-Nazi films – she notably played the woman desperate to sell her jewellery in *Casablanca*. She divorced her husband to marry Wolfgang Zilzer, known in the USA as Paul Andor★, in 1943. The couple settled in New York after the war and undertook further low-key stage and screen appearances. RJK

FILMS: *Confessions of a Nazi Spy* (1939); *Four Sons, Escape* (1940); *Underground, Blossoms in the Dust, Out of Darkness* (1941); *Casablanca, Reunion in France* (1942); *Above Suspicion* (1943); *In Our Time, The Hitler Gang, The Mask of Dimitrios, The Seventh Cross, Enemy of Women* (1944); *Son of Lassie*

(1945); *Walk East on Beacon* (1952); *Marathon Man* (1976); *All that Jazz* (1979); *Lovesick* (1983).

PALMER, Lilli (Lilli Peiser) (1914–1986)

Palmer's restless international career began early, and stands as a prime example of the diasporic lifestyle of many actors of her generation. Born into a Jewish-Austrian family in Silesia (now Poland), the young actress fled Nazi persecution in the early 1930s via Paris, where she was discovered by Alexander Korda, and then to London. Until the mid-1940s, Palmer had a prolific career in British films, often in parts that emphasised her Continental background. In 1945, she followed her then husband, actor Rex Harrison★, to Hollywood. A delicate, dark-haired beauty as well as a commanding tragedienne, she was publicised by Warner Bros. as a new Vivien Leigh★ (alongside Harrison as a new Laurence Olivier★). However, already on her first American film, *Cloak and Dagger*, Palmer acquired a reputation for being difficult and 'too intelligent', clashing with the film's director, Fritz Lang. When news broke in 1948 about Harrison's affair with the starlet Carole Landis (and Landis' subsequent suicide), public opinion turned against the couple, and Palmer returned to Europe, where she eventually remarried. In the early 1950s, Palmer established herself as a major star in German cinema, frequently in elegant, aristocratic roles. She also became a sought-after character actress in French, Italian and British productions, sporadically returned to Hollywood and gradually matured into a graceful and revered grande dame of European films. In her later years, she also wrote best-selling novels and autobiographical books. TB

FILMS: *Cloak and Dagger* (1946); *Body and Soul* (1947); *My Girl Tisa*, *No Minor Vices* (1948); *The Four Poster* (1952); *Main Street to Broadway* (1953); *But Not for Me* (1959); *The Pleasure of His Company*, *The Counterfeit Traitor* (1960); *The Miracle of the White Stallions* (1963); *Jack of Diamonds* (1967); *Hard Contract* (1969); *De Sade* (1970); *The Boys from Brazil* (1978).

PAPAS, Irene (Irini Lelekou) (1929–)

Austerely beautiful actress with dark, classical Greek features who, alongside Melina Mercouri★, is the Greek star best known to international audiences. Her engagement with the American film industry started improbably, opposite James Cagney, in the Western *Tribute to a Bad Man*, where

Irene Papas, renowned for her dark, classical Greek features

she was cast as a Greek emigrant. She was subsequently cast mostly in dramas and is best remembered today for her performance as the Greek Resistance member Maria Pappadimos in the American and British co-production *The Guns of Navarone*, and for her role next to Anthony Quinn in Michael Cacoyannis' film *Zorba the Greek*. Some years later, she appeared next to Quinn again as his Greek wife Calliope in *A Dream of Kings*.

Papas always felt more at ease in Europe. A great number of her American films were European co-productions and many were shot in Europe. *The Moon-Spinners*, a Walt Disney production, was filmed in Crete for example, with Papas playing the villager Sophia. Similar international productions include *The Assisi Underground* and *Lion of the Desert*. Papas also excelled in cinematic adaptations of theatrical tragedies such as *The Trojan Women*, for which she won the Best Actress Award from the National Board of Review in the USA. In 1993, she was given a Distinguished Achievement Award at the Hamptons International Film Festival. The veteran Papas also appeared in the British/French/American co-production of *Captain Corelli's Mandolin* (2001). TH

FILMS: *Tribute to a Bad Man* (1956); *The Guns of Navarone* (1961); *Zorba the Greek, The Moon-Spinners* (1964); *Anne of a Thousand Days, The Brotherhood, A Dream of Kings* (1969); *The Trojan Women* (1971); *Bloodline* (1979); *Lion of the Desert* (1980); *Into the Night, The Assisi Underground* (1985); *Sweet Country* (1986).

PARMA, Tula (Tuulikki Paananen) (1915–1974)
Successful Finnish actress, known for her leading role in *Jääkärin morsian/A Soldier's Bride* (1938), who spent part of her upbringing in Hollywood because of her American mother. Parma fled Europe at the onset of World War II and signed to Universal. She played one of the murder victims in Jacques Tourneur's RKO film, *The Leopard Man*. TS/AP
FILM: *The Leopard Man* (1943).

PATRICK, Nigel (Nigel Dennis Wemyss) (1913–1981)
Suave and charming British leading man who appeared in many outstanding British films of the 1950s, including *The Browning Version* (1951). Patrick briefly worked in Hollywood alongside Elizabeth Taylor and Montgomery Clift in *Raintree County*. MHu
FILM: *Raintree County* (1957).

PAVAN, Marisa (1932–)
Sardinian-born actress and twin sister of Pier Angeli★. Pavan won a Golden Globe and was nominated for an Academy Award for her role as the teenage daughter of Anna Magnani★ in *The Rose Tattoo*. Her Hollywood film career was limited to the 1950s. AM
FILMS: *What Price Glory* (1952); *Down Three Dark Streets, Drum Beat* (1954); *The Rose Tattoo* (1955); *The Man in the Gray Flannel Suit, Diane* (1956); *The Midnight Story* (1957); *John Paul Jones, Solomon and Sheba* (1959).

PAWLE, Lennox (1872–1936)
Stage-trained British film actor of the late 1910s and early 1920s whose regular Broadway excursions led to Hollywood engagements as gentlemen of high social standing in the lower reaches of the credits. JB
FILMS: *The Glorious Adventure* (1922); *Hot for Paris, Married in Hollywood* (1929); *The Sky Hawk* (1930); *The Sin of Madelon Claudet* (1931); *David Copperfield, The Gay Deception* (1935); *Sylvia Scarlett* (1936).

PAXINOU, Katina (Katina Konstantopoulou) (1900–1973)
Distinguished Greek stage actress who started her career with the Greek National Theatre. At the outset of World War II, Paxinou moved to London, where she acted at the Duchess Theatre. Unable to return to Greece, she left for the USA in 1942, where she was approached by Paramount and given a screen test. This led to a substantial role next to Gary Cooper and Ingrid Bergman★ in the Spanish Civil War drama *For Whom the Bell Tolls*. Her performance as the Spanish Republican Pilar won her both a Golden Globe and an Academy Award for Best Supporting Actress in 1944.

Paxinou was subsequently cast by Hollywood in dramas where she always appeared in powerful character roles. She played the Czechoslovakian Maria, for example, in the World War II drama *Hostages*. In the espionage thriller *Confidential Agent*, she was the brutal Spanish nationalist Mrs Melandez, and in the costume film *Prince of Foxes*, Paxinou played Tyrone Power's mother Mona Zeppo Constanza.

The distinguished Greek stage actress Katina Paxinou strongly supported the war effort on and off screen while in Hollywood

Her final US appearance was in the television show *The Name of the Game* in 1970.

During her time in the USA, Paxinou protested against the Nazi occupation in Europe and regularly visited military hospitals. She also staged theatrical productions, donating the proceeds to the Red Cross and other war charities. While expatriate Greeks in the USA were delighted with her actions, emotions were mixed at home. There was both pride for her success and anger that she had deserted her country at such a difficult time. However, soon after the liberation of Greece, she resumed a successful stage and screen career both at home and internationally. TH

FILMS: *For Whom the Bell Tolls, Hostages* (1943); *Confidential Agent* (1945); *Mourning Becomes Electra* (1947); *Prince of Foxes* (1949); *The Miracle* (1959).

PEÑA, Julio (1912–1972)

Spanish film actor who appeared in several Spanish-language Hollywood productions during the 1930s, first at Paramount's Joinville Studios in France, and then for Metro and Fox in the USA (e.g. *Una viuda romántica/The Romantic Widow* [1933]). He later worked on a number of Spanish-American co-productions. CBu

FILMS: *Alexander the Great* (1956); *Spanish Affair* (1958); *Solomon and Sheba* (1959); *Kid Rodelo* (1965).

PEREZ, Vincent (1962–)

Swiss-born French stage and screen actor whose remarkable chiselled good looks led to several romantic leads in French hits of the 1990s, in particular *Cyrano de Bergerac* (1990), *Indochine* (1992) – whose co-star Catherine Deneuve★ described Perez as 'irresistible' in her memoirs – and *La Reine Margot* (1994). Perez is on record, however, as saying that what attracted him to his breakthrough Hollywood part in the horror film *The Crow: City of Angels* is that 'The Crow is definitely not a pretty face'. The film took $11.3 million in its opening weekend, but critics were unimpressed, considering this 'Gothic mess' inferior to the film's cult prequel *The Crow* (1994), and Perez a paler version of the first film's star (Brandon Lee).

Perez's subsequent English-speaking parts have oscillated between erotico-romantic leads, for instance opposite Rachel Weisz★ in the British-American *Swept from the Sea* and Kim Basinger in *I Dreamed of Africa*, or in the bizarre *The Treat*, and more horror, as in *Queen of the Damned*.

None have exactly made a mark in the USA or elsewhere. The reason for this lacklustre international career may be due in equal part to Perez's imperfect accent, to a series of unremarkable films and to the unstable identity of his heroes – he has embodied characters of almost as many different nationalities as films, being in turn Spanish, Italian, Russian, Austrian, not to mention a crow and a vampire. Perez has had better luck at home, where he has continued to meet success in both popular and art films, and has embarked on a career as a film director. GV

FILMS: *The Crow: City of Angels* (1996); *Swept from the Sea* (1997); *The Treat, Talk of Angels* (1998); *I Dreamed of Africa* (2000); *Queen of the Damned* (2002).

PERTWEE, Sean (1964–)

The son of Jon Pertwee, a well-known comic actor, Sean Pertwee followed a traditional British path of drama-school training and seasons with the RSC before moving into television and film work. A versatile actor who can play in comedy or drama, he has yet to develop a distinctive persona that would secure star status. AS

FILMS: *Tale of the Mummy* (1998); *Equilibrium* (2002).

PICCOLI, Michel (Jean Daniel Michel Piccoli) (1925–)

Distinguished and unconventionally handsome French actor with a long-running career in international film and theatre. Piccoli played a villainous high-ranking French civil servant in Hitchcock's cold war thriller *Topaz* whose affair with the hero's wife leads to his exposure as the head of a ring of Soviet spies. SL

FILMS: *Lady L* (1965); *Topaz* (1969); *From Time to Time* (1992); *Passion in the Desert* (1997).

PIERLOT, Francis (1875–1955)

French actor who had a successful stage career on Broadway before engaging in a long Hollywood career, specialising in small roles as an elderly man from the 1940s onwards. CH

FILMS: *The Path Forbidden* (1914); *Night Angel* (1931); *The Captain is a Lady, Strike up the Band, Escape to Glory, Always a Bride* (1940); *Public Enemies, Rise and Shine, Remember the Day, The Trial of Mary Dugan, Know for Sure, International Lady, Cracked Nuts, Barnacle Bill* (1941); *My Heart Belongs to Daddy, Yankee Doodle Dandee, A-Hunting We will Go, Just off Broadway, Night Monster, Henry Aldrich, Editor, A Gentleman* **397** at Heart, Edge of Darkness (1942); Stage Door Canteen, Mystery Broadcast, Madame Curie, You're a Lucky Fellow, Mr Smith, Mission to Moscow (1943); Bathing Beauty, The Adventures of Mark Twain, Uncertain Glory, The Very Thought of You, The Doughgirls (1944); Grissly's Millions, Yolanda and the Thief, Life with Blondie, How Doooo You Do!!!, A Tree Grows in Brooklyn, Roughly Speaking, Our Vines have Tender Grapes, I Live in Grosvenor Square, The Horn Blows at Midnight, The Hidden Eye, Bewitched, The Affairs of Susan (1945); Fear, Dragonwyck, The Catman of Paris, G.I. War Brides, Two Guys from Milwaukee, The Show-Off, Hit the Hay, Crime Doctor's Manhunt (1946); Cigarette Girl, The Late George Apley, Philo Vance's Gamble, The Trespasser, Second Chance, Song of Love, The Senator was Indiscreet, Moss Rose (1947); State of the Union, I, Jane Doe, The Dude Goes West, A Date with Judy, The Babe Ruth Story, That Wonderful Urge, That Lady in Ermine, The Loves of Carmen, Chicken Every Sunday, The Accused (1948); Bad Boy, Take One False Step, My Friend Irma (1949); The Flame and the Arrow, Cyrano de Bergerac, Copper Canyon (1950); Anne of the Indies, That's My Boy, The Lemon Drop Kid, Savage Drums, The Man with a Cloak (1951); Hold that Line, Hoodlum Empire, The Prisoner of Zenda (1952); The Robe, It Happens Every Thursday (1953).

PILAR-MORIN (dates unknown)

Renowned French pantomime artist who occupies an important transitional place in the history of the emergence of the American star system. Following successful US engagements as a leading vaudeville attraction, Pilar-Morin was contracted to the Edison Company in September 1909. She was promoted in relation to both her previous accomplishments and expertise as a stage performer, and her potential to become a contemporary screen personality in her own right. Edison only ever used Pilar-Morin for special releases in their production schedule and, as a result, she never received the same overwhelming exposure given to newer and younger native talents such as Florence Lawrence. AP

FILMS: Comedy and Tragedy (1909); Carminella, The Cigarette Maker of Seville, From Tyranny to Liberty, The Greater Love, A Japanese Peach Boy, The Piece of Lace, The Key of Life (1910).

PINON, Dominique (1955–)

Although best known for his starring role in Marc Caro and Jean-Pierre Jeunet's Délicatessen (1991), Pinon usually plays marginal, sinister or comic secondary characters, where he puts to full use his odd, rubbery face. His American career includes 'the wino' in Polanski's Frantic and a paraplegic space pirate in Jeunet's Alien: Resurrection. Pinon lived in the USA as a child and speaks fluent English. VO

FILMS: Frantic (1988); Alien: Resurrection (1997).

PISIER, Marie-France (1944–)

Sophisticated French brunette actress who emerged in the early films of François Truffaut★ and came to international fame in a starring role in Jean-Charles Tacchella's comedy Cousin, Cousine (1975), for which she won a Best Actress César. Pisier's attempt to break into the American market with The Other Side of Midnight was successful, but she never wanted to remain in Hollywood and described her experience there as 'an odd dream [and] a challenge'. VO

FILMS: The Other Side of Midnight (1977); French Postcards (1979).

PLACIDO, Michele (1946–)

Discovered by Monica Vitti★ while acting on stage, Placido became a familiar face in Italian theatre, television and cinema. He broke into the American market playing alongside Bette Midler in Big Business, although most of his work has remained in Europe. CS

FILMS: Big Business (1988); Searching for Paradise (2002).

PLEASENCE, Donald (1919–1995)

Donald Pleasence made over 170 films in many different countries and in many different genres. He remains best known, however, for his performances in various horror films such as the highly successful Halloween series, in which he earned the nickname of 'the man with the hypnotic eye' for his part as Sam Loomis, the obsessed doctor on the trail of the mass murderer, Michael Myers.

Pleasence came to prominence in British film, theatre and television. He starred as Prince John in the television hit The Adventures of Robin Hood (1955–8) and received international acclaim for his role in the theatrical production of Harold Pinter's The Caretaker (1960). Pleasence's first Hollywood film was John Sturges' big-budget POW hit, The Great Escape. After playing the Bond villain Ernst Blofeld in You Only Live Twice, he went on to appear in numerous other US films including *The Last Tycoon* and George Lucas' first feature *THX 1138*. John Carpenter's low-budget *Halloween* may have proven a surprise hit, but it marked the beginning of Pleasence being typecast as the 'oddball' in horror cinema. With his trademark bald-headed appearance and intense, mobile eyes, he subsequently became the victim of both Hollywood's tendency to stereotype and his own inability to turn down undemanding screen roles. JS/AP

FILMS: *Barnacle Bill, The Man in the Sky* (1957); *The Two-Headed Spy* (1958); *Killers of Kilimanjaro* (1959) *Sons and Lovers* (1960); *What a Carve Up!, Lisa* (1962); *The Great Escape* (1963); *The Greatest Story Ever Told, The Hallelujah Trail* (1965); *Matchless, The Fantastic Voyage* (1966); *The Night of the Generals, Will Penny, Eye of the Devil, You Only Live Twice* (1967); *The Madwoman of Chaillot* (1969); *Soldier Blue* (1970); *THX 1138* (1971); *The Jerusalem File* (1972); *The Black Windmill* (1974); *Hearts of the West, Escape to Witch Mountain* (1975); *The Last Tycoon* (1976); *Telefon, Oh, God!* (1977); *Night Creature, Halloween, Sgt Pepper's Lonely Hearts Club Band* (1978); *Jaguar Lives!, Dracula, Good Luck, Miss Wyckoff* (1979); *Escape from New York, Halloween II* (1981); *Alone in the Dark* (1982); *The Devonsville Terror* (1983); *The Ambassador, A Breed Apart* (1984); *Reel Horror* (1985); *Prince of Darkness* (1987); *Hanna's War, The House of Usher, Halloween 4: The Return of Michael Myers* (1988); *Halloween 5: The Revenge of Michael Myers, River of Death* (1989); *Shadows and Fog* (1991); *Halloween: The Curse of Michael Myers* (1995).

PLOWRIGHT, Joan (1929–)

Established British stage actress who has mostly appeared before British cameras in adaptations of famous plays (*The Entertainer* [1960], *Uncle Vanya* [1963]). With her enhanced social gravitas as the third wife of Laurence Olivier★, she has more recently found a Hollywood niche in colourful matriarch roles. JB

FILMS: *Moby Dick* (1956); *Equus* (1977); *Avalon, I Love You to Death* (1990); *Last Action Hero, Dennis the Menace* (1993); *The Scarlet Letter* (1995); *Mr Wrong, Surviving Picasso, 101 Dalmations* (1996); *The Assistant* (1997); *Dance with Me* (1998); *Dinosaur* [voice], *Back to the Secret Garden* (2000); *Global Heresy* (2001); *Bringing Down the House, I am David* (2003).

PODESTÀ, Rossana (Carla Podestà) (1934–)

Italian actress who is best remembered in Hollywood for her lead role in *Helen of Troy*. She starred in further American-funded films, but never achieved the same popularity she had in Italy. CS

FILMS: *Helen of Troy, Santiago* (1956); *Raw Wind in Eden* (1958); *Sodom and Gomorrah* (1962); *Sunday Lovers* (1980).

POLAND

Although millions of Poles, drawn by the myth of the 'American dream', emigrated to the USA in the nineteenth and twentieth centuries, very few of them found their way, as actors, to the Hollywood dream factory. Among this small number, only Pola Negri★ acquired the status of a star. What made this career possible was her success in Germany, particularly in Ernst Lubitsch's films. Similarly, the famous Polish tenor, Jan Kiepura★, found work – though briefly – in Hollywood thanks to fame in German and Austrian opera and film. After World War II, the 'Polish route' to Hollywood was more likely to go through France, as was the case for Roman Polanski★ and Joanna Pacula★. In general, for Polish actors strongly attached to the tradition of art cinema, it was easier to find a space within European cinema than in mainstream Hollywood.

It was Polish actresses in the main who became successful in Hollywood. Kiepura's one film and Polański's episode in *Chinatown* (1974) are significantly outnumbered by the roles played by Negri and Pacuła, even if the latter only appeared in minor productions. Both of their screen personae exuded exoticism. Negri's half-gypsy, half-Slavic beauty allowed her to define the figure of the vamp in the silent era and her American screen persona built on her beauty and strong sexual appeal. Similarly, Pacuła's face, with its 'Slavic' high cheekbones, along with her distinctive accent made her a good choice to play 'other' women, whether from behind the Iron Curtain as in *Gorky Park* (1983), or in horror fantasy as with *The Kiss* (1988). EO

POLANSKI, Roman (Roman Polański) (1933–)

Before his directorial debut, *Knife in the Water* (1962), Roman Polanski had already performed in a number of episodic roles in Polish films. In *Chinatown*, he appeared as the sinister 'Man with a Knife'. EO

FILMS: *The Fearless Vampire Killers* (1967); *The Magic Christian* (1969); *Chinatown* (1974).

PONS, Lily (Alice Pons) (1898–1976)

Pons made her name as a coloratura soprano and stage actress in France. A relative unknown when she joined the Metropolitan Opera in New York, Pons became one of their most popular divas, attracting RKO's interest in a bid to rival Columbia's Grace Moore. CH

FILMS: *I Dream Too Much* (1935); *That Girl from Paris* (1936); *Hitting a New High* (1937); *Carnegie Hall* (1947).

PORCASI, Paul (1879–1946)

Italian singer and actor who moved to Hollywood after a successful career as a tenor in his native Italy. His long American film career only took off with the introduction of sound, after which he worked as a character actor, usually playing foreigners. Heavily set and usually moustachioed, he was frequently cast as a waiter or restaurant owner, but he also played men of authority, including Mussolini in *Star Spangled Rhythm*. AM

FILMS: *The Fall of the Romanoffs* (1917); *Say it Again* (1926); *Broadway* (1929); *Murder on the Roof, The Three Sisters, Born Reckless, A Lady's Morals, Morocco, Derelict* (1930); *The Criminal Code, Gentleman's Fate, Doctors' Wives, Svengali, Party Husband, Smart Money, Bought, I Like Your Nerve, The Good Bad Girl, Children of Dreams* (1931); *The Man Who Played God, Stowaway, While Paris Sleeps, Under Eighteen, The Painted Woman, A Parisian Romance, The Woman from Monte Carlo, The Kid from Spain, The Passionate Plumber, The Death Kiss, Cynara, A Woman Comands, Under-Cover Man, The Red-Haired Alibi, Men are Such Fools, A Farewell to Arms, Devil and the Deep* (1932); *Grand Slam, King Kong, Terror Aboard, Hell Below, Reunion in Vienna, No Marriage Ties, Devil's Mate, I Loved a Woman, Saturday's Millions, Footlight Parade, Big Time or Bust, Havana Widows, He Couldn't Take It, By Candlelight, Flying Down to Rio, Roman Scandals, When Strangers Marry, The Secret of Madame Blanche, Gigolettes of Paris* (1933); *The Cat and the Fiddle, Coming-Out Party, Looking for Trouble, Riptide, Tarzan and His Mate, Chained, British Agent, Wake Up and Dream, The Gay Divorcee, Imitation of Life, Million Dollar Baby, The Great Flirtation, Enter Madame!* (1934); *La Cucaracha, A Night at the Ritz, The Florentine Dagger, Under the Pampas Moon, Charlie Chan in Egypt, Waterfront Lady, The Pay Off, Coronado, I Dream Too Much, La fiesta*

di Santa Barbara, Baby Face Harrington, Stars over Broadway, Rumba, Broadway Gondolier, Hi, Gaucho! (1935); *Rose-Marie, Muss 'Em Up, The Leathernecks have Landed, Mr Deeds Goes to Town, Down to the Sea, Crash Donovan, Two in a Crowd, Trouble for Two, The Lady Consents* (1936); *Seventh Heaven, Maytime, That I May Live, Café Metropole, The Emperor's Candlesticks, The Bride Wore Red, Big Town Girl, Madame X* (1937); *Crime School, Bulldog Drummond in Africa, Vacation from Love, I'll Give a Million* (1938); *Topper Takes a Trip, Lady of the Tropics, Everything Happens at Night* (1939); *I Was an Adventuress, Brother Orchid, Argentine Nights, The Border Legion, Torrid Zone, Moon over Burma, Dr Kildare's Strange Case* (1940); *Road to Zanzibar, It Started with Eve, Rags to Riches, Doctors Don't Tell, Two in a Taxi, The Trial of Mary Dugan, Road to Happiness* (1941); *Casablanca, Star Spangled Rhythm, We Were Dancing* (1942); *Quiet Please: Murder, Melody Parade, Hi Diddle Diddle, Background to Danger* (1943); *Hot Rhythm, Hail the Conquering Hero, Swing Hostess, An American Romance* (1944); *Nothing but Trouble, I'll Remember April* (1945).

PORTMAN, Eric (1903–1969)

Distinguished British stage actor whose film work included two classics of wartime British cinema – *Millions Like Us* (1943) and *A Canterbury Tale* (1944) – and various Hollywood-funded productions shot in Europe. MHu

FILMS: *The Prince and the Pauper* (1937); *Wanted for Murder* (1946); *The Deep Blue Sea* (1955); *The Naked Edge* (1961); *Freud* (1962); *The Bedford Incident* (1965); *The Whisperers* (1967); *Deadfall, Assignment to Kill* (1968).

PORTUGAL

Portugal's relatively small film industry has often privileged an auteur-led rather than a star-led national cinema. Paradoxically, therefore, the only Hollywood film star who was of Portuguese origin was in fact not quite Portuguese. Carmen Miranda, the 'Brazilian bombshell', was born in Portugal to Portuguese parents who emigrated to Brazil when she was a child. The presence of Portuguese actors in American cinema is thus rare and always the result of individual circumstances. In the 1920s, Helena d'Algy★ worked with Sjöström in *Confessions of a Queen* (1925) and played a supporting role opposite Rudolph Valentino in *A Sainted Devil* (1924). Occasionally, actors who were stars in Portugal, such as Virgílio Teixeira★, became extras or had very minor roles in American films shot in Europe. More recently, Joaquim de Almeida★ and Maria de Medeiros★ – the latter having essentially built her career outside Portugal – have both worked on high-profile American productions. They do not, however, play Portuguese characters. Because the Portuguese are totally absent from the American imaginary – the only memorable 'Portuguese' character created in Hollywood was the fisherman played by Edward G. Robinson in Howard Hawks' *Tiger Shark* (1932) – mainstream American cinema has not created clichés to represent Portuguese characters, unlike the representational treatment of characters from France, Britain, Italy or Russia. AR

POSTLETHWAITE, Pete (1945–)

British film and television actor who specialises at home in playing downtrodden, provincial working-class characters. Postlethwaite was nominated for a Best Supporting Actor Academy Award for his impassioned portrayal of a wrongly imprisoned IRA suspect in *In the Name of the Father* (1993) and thanks to his lack of association with English behavioural characteristics typically represented by Hollywood, he has made various American film appearances under a wide range of ethnic guises, ranging from an Indian in *The Usual Suspects* to a South African in *The Lost World*. JB
FILMS: *Alien³*, *The Last of the Mohicans* (1992); *The Usual Suspects* (1995); *James and the Giant Peach*, *Dragonheart*, *Romeo + Juliet* (1996); *The Lost World: Jurassic Park*, *Amistad* (1997); *Wayward Son* (1999); *Cowboy Up*, *The Shipping News* (2001).

POTENTE, Franka (1974–)

Potente graduated from acting school in Houston, Texas, and Munich to begin a German film and television career in 1995. She achieved international success as a star actress and singer/lyricist in Germany's top-grossing film of 1998, *Lola rennt/Run Lola Run*. Potente continued Lola's preoccupation with memory and narrative in Hollywood roles, including being partner to an amnesiac in *The Bourne Identity*. EC
FILMS: *Blow*, *Storytelling* (2001); *The Bourne Identity* (2002); *I Love Your Work* (2003); *The Bourne Supremacy* (2004).

PRESLE, Micheline (1922–)

Micheline Presle started as a child actress in the 1930s and became famous thanks to her dual lead part in Abel Gance's romantic melodrama *Paradis perdu/Paradise Lost* (1940). The elegant and beautiful actress subsequently rose to stardom in wartime and postwar France, in particular in the World War I drama *Le Diable au corps/Devil in the Flesh* (1946). In 1948, she left for Hollywood, where she met Bill Marshall, who became her husband after his divorce from Michèle Morgan★. She was placed under contract with Twentieth Century-Fox for two films. *Under My Skin* was a Hemingway adaptation set in Paris in the horse-racing milieu. Presle played a French singer whose lover has been killed because of rigged bets, but the film really centred on co-star John Garfield. *American Guerrilla in the Philippines*, a war film reluctantly made by Fritz Lang, similarly focused on Tyrone Power. Presle played the wife of a rich Filipino who resists the Japanese occupation by hiding American soldiers. After her husband's death, she escapes with Tyrone Power, with whom she falls in love, and they are liberated thanks to the American landings.

Adventures of Captain Fabian was an independent production by Bill Marshall, part-funded by a French company and by Errol Flynn, who also wrote the script. The making of the film was disastrous because of Marshall's lack of experience and Flynn's alcoholism. In this costume drama, which also starred Victor Francen★, Presle played a deposed aristocrat who seeks revenge through murder and blackmail by spurning the only man who loves her (Flynn), whose death she provokes. The film was a resounding failure both in the USA and France. A pregnant Presle returned to France in 1951 to give birth (to her daughter, the director Tonie Marshall) and to divorce, but – unlike Morgan a few years earlier – after those three disastrous years spent in Hollywood, she never regained her former box-office glory. GS
FILMS: *Under My Skin*, *American Guerrilla in the Philippines* (1950); *Adventures of Captain Fabian* (1951).

PROCHNOW, Jürgen (1941–)

Prochnow's roles as a calm, withdrawn loner with sudden emotional outbreaks made him an acknowledged character actor of New German Cinema and television, but 'Alaaaaarm' is the word that marked his entry into Hollywood. The immense international success of Wolfgang Petersen's historic action drama *Das Boot/The Boat* (1981), with Prochnow as the submarine commander, set him up as a performer in action genres in many international produc- **401** tions that were to follow. His role in *Das Boot* diverged slightly from his established European persona, in that it also presented him as a father figure with a high sense of duty and discipline. To a certain degree, starting with David Lynch's *Dune* in 1983, this then became the type that was taken up by Hollywood. Lynch's honourable knight was for a while, however, replaced by more conventional typecasting as far as non-US actors are concerned, in that Prochnow went on to play a succession of villains and traitors. A combination of his German accent, his slightly scarred face and athletic figure led to the role of the manipulating author of horror novels in *In the Mouth of Madness* and diabolic figures in *The Seventh Sign* and *Interceptor*. Prochnow has now established himself in leading roles in numerous minor Hollywood films and has also appeared in supporting roles in major productions such as *The English Patient* (as Major Muller) and *Air Force One*. Although he is based in Los Angeles, he occasionally appears in television productions in Germany, Italy and Australia. CF

FILMS: *Dune, The Keep* (1983); *Forbidden* (1985); *Beverly Hills Cop II, The Seventh Sign* (1987); *A Dry White Season* (1988); *The Man Inside, The Fourth War* (1989); *Twin Peaks: Fire Walk with Me, Interceptor, Body of Evidence* (1992); *In the Mouth of Madness* (1993); *Trigger Fast* (1994); *Judge Dredd* (1995); *The English Patient* (1996); *Air Force One* (1997); *The Replacement Killers* (1998); *Wing Commander, Youri* (1999); *Jack the Dog, Elite,* (2000); *Dark Asylum, Last Run* (2001); *House of the Dead* (2003).

PROIETTI, Gigi (Luigi Proietti) (1940–)

Italian actor who took on supporting roles in Hollywood comedies that exploited his nationality. In Robert Altman's *A Wedding*, for instance, he played the part of Dino Corelli I. CS

FILMS: *The Appointment* (1969); *A Wedding, Who is Killing the Great Chefs of Europe?* (1978).

PRYCE, Jonathan (1947–)

Distinguished and versatile Welsh actor who has successfully balanced careers on both the stage and screen. His offbeat persona and nervous intensity have equipped him well for an eclectic range of roles, including Rivière in Martin Scorsese's period drama, *The Age of Innocence*, a James Bond villain in *Tomorrow Never Dies* and a singing Juan Perón in Alan Parker's *Evita*. MW

FILMS: *Something Wicked this Way Comes* (1983); *The Doctor and the Devils* (1985); *Haunted Honeymoon, Jumpin' Jack Flash* (1986); *The Heat is On* (1989); *A Child's Garden of Verses, Glengarry Glen Ross* (1992); *The Age of Innocence* (1993); *A Troll in Central Park* (1994); *Evita* (1996); *Tomorrow Never Dies* (1997); *Ronin* (1998); *Stigmata* (1999); *The Testimony of Taliesin Jones, The Suicide Club* (2000); *The Affair of the Necklace* (2001); *Unconditional Love* (2002); *What a Girl Wants, Pirates of the Caribbean: The Curse of the Black Pearl* (2003); *De-Lovely* (2004).

PUGLIA, Frank (Francesco Puglia) (1892–1975)

Italian actor discovered by D. W. Griffith on the New York stage. After a few films in the silent era and a stint of dubbing at Fox, he went on to become one of Hollywood's most prolific minor character actors. He often played priests, waiters or café owners; he was the orchestra conductor in the 1943 *The Phantom of the Opera* and the (uncredited) disastrous taxi driver in *Now, Voyager*. His severe, balding and angular features also led to many roles as a villain or foreigner, although he was not always cast as of Latin extraction. AM

FILMS: *Orphans of the Storm* (1921); *Fascination* (1922); *Romola, Isn't Life Wonderful* (1924); *The Beautiful City* (1925); *The Man Who Laughs* (1927); *The Solitaire Man, The White Sister* (1933); *Men in White, Viva Villa!, Stamboul Quest, Chained, One More River* (1934); *Bordertown, Captain Blood, Red Hot Tires, The Melody Lingers On* (1935); *Wife vs. Secretary, His Brother's Wife, Bulldog Edition, The Devil is a Sissy, The Gay Desperado, The Public Pays, The Garden of Allah, Love on the Run, Fatal Lady* (1936); *Mama Steps Out, Beg Borrow or Steal, When You're in Love, Seventh Heaven, Maytime, We Have Our Moments, Song of the City, King of Gamblers, A Doctor's Diary, You Can't Have Everything, She's No Lady, Thin Ice, The Bride Wore Red, The Firefly, Mannequin, Bulldog Drummond's Revenge, Lancer Spy, Exclusive, Bulldog Drummond Comes Back* (1937); *Invisible Enemy, Rascals, Barefoot Boy, Spawn of the North, The Sisters, Tropic Holiday, The Shining Hour, Sharpshooters, Change of Heart, Dramatic School, I'll Give a Million, Yellow Jack, A Trip to Paris* (1938); *Zaza, Mystery of the White Room, Society Lawyer, Forged Passport, In Old Caliente, Maisie, The Spellbinder, In Name Only, Mr Smith Goes to Washington, The Monroe Doctrine, Balalaika, Pirates of the Skies, Lady of the Tropics, The Girl and the Gambler, Code of the Secret Service* (1939); *The Fatal*

Frank Puglia: one of Hollywood's most prolific character actors

Hour, Charlie Chan in Panama, Castle on the Hudson, 'Til We Meet Again, Love, Honor and Oh Baby!, Down Argentine Way, Arise My Love, The Mark of Zorro, Behind the News, Torrid Zone, Rangers of Fortune, Argentine Nights, City of Darkness, No, No, Nanette, Meet the Wildcat (1940); *That Night in Rio, Billy the Kid, The Parson of Panamint, World Premiere, Law of the Tropics* (1941); *Always in My Heart, Secret Agent of Japan, Jungle Book, Who is Hope Schuyler?, Escape from Hong Kong, Now, Voyager, The Boogie Man Will Get You, Casablanca, In Old California, Flight Lieutenant* (1942); *For Whom the Bell Tolls, The Phantom of the Opera, Around the World, Tarzan's Desert Mystery, Princess O'Rourke, Pilot #5, Mission to Moscow, The Iron Major, Background to Danger, Action in the North Atlantic* (1943); *Ali Baba and the Forty Thieves, The Story of Dr Wassell, This is the Life, Tall in the Saddle, Passage to Marseille, Brazil, Together Again, Dragon Seed* (1944); *A Song to Remember, Blood on the Sun, Week-End at the Waldorf, Roughly Speaking* (1945); *Without Reservations* (1946); *My Favorite Brunette, Fiesta, Brute Force, Easy Come, Easy Go, Stallion Road, Road to Rio, The Lost Moment, Escape Me Never* (1947); *Dream Girl, Joan of Arc* (1948); *Bride of Vengeance, Special Agent, Colorado Territory, Bagdad* (1949); *Black Hand,*

Captain Carey, U.S.A., Federal Agent at Large, The Desert Hawk, Walk Softly, Stranger (1950); *The Bandits of Corsica, Son of Belle Starr, The Caddy, The Steel Lady* (1953); *Casanova's Big Night, Jubilee Trail, The Shanghai Story, A Star is Born* (1954); *Serenade, The First Texan, Accused of Murder, The Burning Hills* (1956); *Duel at Apache Wells, 20 Million Miles to Earth* (1957); *The Black Orchid* (1958); *Cry Tough* (1959); *Girls! Girls! Girls!* (1962); *The Sword of Ali Baba* (1965); *The Spy in the Green Hat* (1966); *Mr Ricco* (1975).

PULVER, Lilo (Liselotte Pulver) (1929–)

Spirited, popular leading actress in German cinema and various European co-productions of the 1950s and 1960s who appeared with Dorothea Wieck★ in her first Hollywood film: Douglas Sirk's *A Time to Love and a Time to Die*, based on the novel by Erich Maria Remarque. She also had a supporting role in Billy Wilder's Berlin comedy, *One, Two, Three*. AP

FILMS: *A Time to Love and a Time to Die* (1958); *One, Two, Three* (1961); *A Global Affair* (1964).

PURCELL, Noel (1900–1985)

Tall, bearded Irish character actor who mainly worked on the Irish stage and in British cinema during his long career. The bulk of Purcell's Hollywood appearances were in US-funded productions shot in Europe. He was a prominent member of the crew in John Huston's *Moby Dick*. AP

FILMS: *The Crimson Pirate* (1952); *Moby Dick, Lust for Life* (1956); *The Rising of the Moon* (1957); *Merry Andrew, The Key* (1958); *Shake Hands with the Devil* (1959); *The Millionairess* (1960); *Mutiny on the Bounty* (1962); *The Running Man, The List of Adrian Messenger, The Ceremony* (1963); *Lord Jim* (1965); *Drop Dead Darling* (1966); *The Violent Enemy* (1968); *Where's Jack?, Sinful Davey* (1969); *Flight of the Doves* (1971); *The Mackintosh Man* (1973).

PURDOM, Edmund (1924–)

Handsome English actor whose brief American career included prestigious title roles in MGM's *The Student Prince* and *The Prodigal*. Modest American box-office returns led to a permanent return to Europe. MF

FILMS: *Titanic, Julius Caesar* (1953); *Athena, The Egyptian, The Student Prince* (1954); *The Prodigal, The King's Thief* (1955); *Strange Intruder* (1956); *The Yellow Rolls-Royce* (1965).

403

QUAYLE, Anthony (1913–1989)

Classical British stage actor who because of his distinctive voice, physique and bearing was ideally suited to serious, authoritative roles in his occasional American film performances. Quayle first appeared on screen in Laurence Olivier's★ *Hamlet* (1948) and made his Hollywood debut in Hitchcock's *The Wrong Man* in 1957. His performance as Verulus in Anthony Mann's *The Fall of the Roman Empire* proved him to be adept at demonstrating a quiet command and sense of duty while hinting at passions and contradictions beneath the surface. Quayle's other American appearances included the curious Western melodrama *Mackenna's Gold* and (perhaps with a hint of self-parody) the King in Woody Allen's *Everything You Always Wanted to Know about Sex*. He received a Best Supporting Actor Academy Award nomination for his performance as Cardinal Wolsey in *Anne of the Thousand Days* and was knighted in 1985. MHu

FILMS: *The Wrong Man* (1957); *Tarzan's Greatest Adventure* (1959); *The Guns of Navarone* (1961); *H.M.S. Defiant, Lawrence of Arabia* (1962); *The Fall of the Roman Empire* (1964); *Operation Crossbow* (1965); *Anne of the Thousand Days, Mackenna's Gold* (1969); *Everything You Always Wanted to Know about Sex* (1972); *A Bequest to the Nation* (1973).

QUENNESSEN, Valérie (1957–1989)

Described as a 'French gamine', Quennessen played young, sexy French characters in *French Postcards* and *Summer Lovers* and a princess opposite Arnold Schwarzenegger★ in *Conan the Barbarian*. VO

FILMS: *French Postcards* (1979); *Conan the Barbarian* (1982); *Summer Lovers* (1982).

RABAGLIATI, Alberto (1906–1974)

Rabagliati arrived in Hollywood having won a 'successor to Rudolph Valentino' contest organised by Fox in Europe. After a brief appearance as a policeman in *Street Angel*, he set up an unsuccessful production company with fellow Italian immigrant Guido Trento★ and then returned to Italy as a singer in 1938. Rabagliati possessed good spoken English and later appeared in two European-shot American films during the 1950s. CBu

FILMS: *Street Angel* (1928); *The Barefoot Countess* (1954); *Monte Carlo Story* (1956).

RABAL, Francisco (Francisco Rabal Valera) (1926–2001)

Major Spanish film star who appeared in almost two hundred films throughout his career. Despite important contributions to Italian, French, Mexican and Argentinian productions, he worked in only one Hollywood film, portraying a Basque patriarch in the Mexican–Basque director Gregory Nava's *A Time of Destiny*. CBu

FILM: *A Time of Destiny* (1988).

RADFORD, Basil (1897–1952)

British light comic character actor who made two films in the USA before returning to Britain, where he established a much-loved film partnership with Naunton Wayne playing Charters and Caldicott, the two bemused Englishmen abroad in films like Hitchcock's *The Lady Vanishes* (1938). Radford also appeared in Walter Forde's *Flying Fortress*, financed by Warner Bros. MHu

FILMS: *Barnum was Right* (1929); *Seven Days' Leave* (1930); *Flying Fortress* (1942).

RAINER, Luise (1910–)

Trained under Max Reinhardt, Rainer appeared on the German and Austrian stage and screen before being contracted by MGM in 1935. A fey, fragile, brunette beauty, Rainer gave her American debut opposite William Powell in the comedy-drama *Escapade*, a remake of the Austrian film *Maskerade*. Rainer then appeared in two of Hollywood's most prestigious productions of the time: *The Great Ziegfeld*, the plush biopic starring William Powell, and the adaptation of Pearl S. Buck's best-seller about the lives of Chinese peasants, *The Good Earth*. These films won her the Academy Award for Best Actress in two consecutive years. Rainer's acting resembled the performance style of her contemporary Elisabeth Bergner★, in that it ranged from tearful, wide-eyed naiveté to playful capriciousness. This may appear slightly artificial to modern audiences, while her portrayal of submissive Chinese womanhood in *The Good Earth* now seems to border on racial stereotyping, but at the time Rainer represented the height of her profession. Following *The Good Earth*, Rainer found herself typecast as a sophisticated European, appearing as Russian, Austrian and French characters in increasingly mediocre productions, and her stardom waned as quickly as it had arisen. Although this dramatic decline has often been blamed on MGM's mismanagement of her career, and on her own unwillingness to conform to Hollywood lifestyle and studio pressures, it is equally likely that Rainer's specifically European appearance and sensibility, and her mannered performances, had fallen out of favour with American audiences. A brief, turbulent marriage to playwright Clifford Odets may have additionally accelerated her disenchantment with Hollywood. Only a year after her second Academy Award, Rainer's career in the USA was effectively over, although she starred once more in a World War II Resistance drama, *Hostages*, with several other émigré actors in the cast (Oscar Homolka★, Katina Paxinou★, Paul Lukas★). Rainer retired from filmmaking, remarried and moved to London, but re-emerged in the 1980s and 1990s, still a graceful and charming presence, on television programmes, as a witty raconteur of Hollywood and exile life, and finally, again, in acting roles on television, and in the Hungarian film *A Játékos/The Gambler* (1997). TB

FILMS: *Escapade* (1935); *The Great Ziegfeld* (1936); *The Good Earth, The Emperor's Candlesticks, Big City* (1937); *The Toy Wife, The Great Waltz, Dramatic School* (1938); *Hostages* (1943).

RAINS, Claude (1889–1967)

In the 1920s, Claude Rains was the tutor of both John Gielgud★ and Charles Laughton★ at the Royal Academy of Dramatic Art (RADA), but his own West End stage career had never begun to approach the heights they would soon attain. Despite his lower-class origins, Rains' theatrical apprenticeship was impeccable: he had been taken on as a boy by Herbert Beerbohm Tree★ in the 1900s, and served the influential dramatist and manager Harley Granville-Barker with distinction for many years. It is possible that Rains appeared on screen as early as 1910, since a play he was then appearing in was filmed in situ, but he did not set foot in a British film studio until 1920, and then only for a solitary engagement. Rains had first visited Broadway back in 1915, and increasingly disillusioned with his failure to match the achievements of his peers in London, he returned with his wife to New York in 1926 and accompanied her on stage for a minor role as a butler.

Rains would subsequently become a major figure in the American Theatre Guild, but his next window of opportunity in the cinema did not appear until 1933. In that year,

Academy Award nominated Claude Rains was famed for his measured vocal delivery as a Hollywood supporting actor

he unsuccessfully tested for a role that he had originally created on stage in 1921 in the screen version of *A Bill of Divorcement*. Another director, James Whale, saw the test and was convinced that Rains would nonetheless be perfect for his new film. One can safely assume that it was not Rains' five-foot-six frame that impressed Whale, nor even his somewhat cramped face and bulbous eyes (one of them blind). As with so many of the Hollywood British émigrés in the early 1930s, Rains' most distinctive attribute was his measured vocal delivery, enhanced by a seductive huskiness reputedly bestowed upon him by a gas attack in World War I. It made him an ideal choice for the title role in Whale's *The Invisible Man*, in which he remained mostly unseen and disembodied.

On the back of this film's enormous success, a number of attempts were made to launch Rains as a leading man, both in Britain and the USA, but he was to achieve lasting fame as Warners' pre-eminent character actor after signing a long-term contract with them in 1936. The silky voice and unflappably civil demeanour were regularly the duplicitous veneer for a career of power-hungry corruption and considerable sadism on the screen, with *The Adventures of Robin Hood, Mr Smith Goes to Washington, King's Row, The Phantom* of the *Opera* and *Notorious* making up a list of only the better-known examples. Alternatively, as in his much-loved performance as the French police captain in *Casablanca*, it was an effective technique for maintaining the sheer inscrutability of his character's motivations until the last possible moment. For that and three other performances between 1939 and 1946, he was nominated for Academy Awards. JB

FILMS: *The Invisible Man* (1933); *The Man Who Reclaimed His Head, Crime without Passion* (1934); *The Mystery of Edwin Drood, The Last Outpost* (1935); *Hearts Divided, Anthony Adverse, Stolen Holiday* (1936); *The Prince and the Pauper, They Won't Forget* (1937); *White Banners, The Adventures of Robin Hood, Gold is Where You Find It, Four Daughters* (1938); *They Made Me a Criminal, Juarez, Daughters Courageous, Mr Smith Goes to Washington, Four Wives, Sons of Liberty* (1939); *Saturday's Children, The Lady with Red Hair, The Sea Hawk* (1940); *Four Mothers, Here Comes Mr Jordan, The Wolf Man* (1941); *Now, Voyager, Casablanca, Moontide, Kings Row* (1942); *Forever and a Day, The Phantom of the Opera* (1943); *Mr Skeffington, Passage to Marseille* (1944); *This Love of Ours* (1945); *Notorious, Strange Holiday, Angel on My Shoulder, Deception* (1946); *The Unsuspected* (1947); *Rope of Sand, Song of Surrender* (1949); *Where Danger Lives, The White Tower* (1950); *Sealed Cargo* (1951); *The Man Who Watched Trains Go By* (1953); *Lisbon* (1956); *This Earth is Mine* (1959); *The Lost World* (1960); *Lawrence of Arabia* (1962); *Twilight of Honor* (1963); *The Greatest Story Ever Told* (1965).

RAMPLING, Charlotte (1946–)

Rampling's debut in the US-backed comedy *The Knack – and How to Get It . . .* (1965) and subsequent American trajectory seems to sum up a mixture of sexual charisma and idiosyncratic career choice. After featuring in Roger Corman's *Target: Harry*, she went on to star in several other inconsequential American movies before returning to Europe for her most powerful performance in *Il Portiere di notte/The Night Porter* (1974), where her relationship to an ex-Nazi officer (Dirk Bogarde*) gave her an enduring aura of perverse sexuality. Hollywood took note and she was subsequently cast as a striking femme fatale opposite Robert Mitchum's Phillip Marlowe in *Farewell My Lovely*. Excellent in Woody Allen's *Stardust Memories*, Rampling was equally impressive opposite Paul Newman in Sidney Lumet's courtroom thriller *The Verdict*. During the 1980s, Rampling relocated to France, where she has since carved

out a career in art films by the likes of François Ozon and Nagisa Oshima that have sometimes tended to reprise her *Night Porter* persona. She has continued to exude a power and subtlety beyond the relative brevity of her actual part in infrequent Hollywood appearances. MF

FILMS: *The Knack – and How to Get It . . .* (1965); *Georgy Girl* (1966); *Target: Harry* (1969); *Vanishing Point* [scenes deleted], *The Ski Bum* (1971); *Corky* (1972); *Zardoz* (1974); *Farewell My Lovely* (1975); *Orca* (1977); *Stardust Memories* (1980); *The Verdict* (1982); *Angel Heart* (1987); *D.O.A.* (1988); *Invasion of Privacy* (1996); *The Wings of the Dove* (1997); *Spy Game* (2001); *I'll Sleep When I'm Dead* (2003).

RATHBONE, Basil (Philip St John Basil Rathbone) (1892–1967)

Rathbone, though born in South Africa, was educated in England and established his acting reputation in the early 1920s first on the London stage and subsequently on Broadway, where he attracted the attention of Hollywood. His silent film career was limited to a handful of films in both countries, but during the 1930s he achieved prominence as a supporting actor rather than an A-list star. His appearances, which included prestige pictures at MGM such as *David Copperfield, Anna Karenina, A Tale of Two Cities* and *Romeo and Juliet*, established a somewhat unsympathetic villainous image for him, epitomised in the role of Sir Guy of Gisbourne in Warner Bros.' *The Adventures of Robin Hood*. Rathbone's villainous image was cemented in the late 1930s in the horror films *Son of Frankenstein* and *Tower of London* but then dramatically altered when he was cast as Sherlock Holmes in *The Hound of the Baskervilles*. The transformation was highly successful, however, and Rathbone's crisp and decisive clipped vocal delivery, English accent and tall and gaunt physical appearance that echoed Sidney Paget's original illustrations for Conan Doyle's stories in *The Strand Magazine*, gave an authority to his performance and established him as the definitive Sherlock Holmes. His postwar American career had few highlights, though in the late 1950s and early 1960s he appeared in films directed by John Ford and Roger Corman. TR

FILMS: *Trouping with Ellen* (1924); *The Masked Bride* (1925); *The Great Deception* (1926); *The Last of Mrs Cheyney* (1929); *Sin Takes a Holiday, The Bishop Murder Case, A Lady Surrenders, The Lady of Scandal, The Flirting Widow, A Notorious Affair, This Mad World* (1930); *A Woman Commands* (1932);

Basil Rathbone, the definitive Sherlock Holmes

David Copperfield, Anna Karenina, A Feather in Her Hat, Captain Blood, A Tale of Two Cities, Kind Lady, The Last Days of Pompeii (1935); *Private Number, The Garden of Allah* (1936); *Confession, Romeo and Juliet, Make a Wish, Tovarich* (1937); *The Dawn Patrol, If I were King, The Adventures of Marco Polo, The Adventures of Robin Hood* (1938); *Rio, The Sun Never Sets, Tower of London, The Adventures of Sherlock Holmes, The Hound of the Baskervilles, Son of Frankenstein* (1939); *Rhythm on the River, The Mark of Zorro* (1940); *The Black Cat, International Lady, The Mad Doctor* (1941); *Crossroads, Fingers at the Window, Sherlock Holmes and the Voice of Terror, Paris Calling* (1942); *Crazy House, Sherlock Holmes in Washington, Sherlock Holmes and the Secret Weapon, Sherlock Holmes Faces Death, Above Suspicion* (1943); *The Scarlet Claw, The Spider Woman, The Pearl of Death, Frenchman's Creek, Bathing Beauty* (1944); *The Woman in Green, Pursuit to Algiers, The House of Fear* (1945); *Dressed to Kill, Heartbeat, Terror by Night* (1946); *The Wind in the Willows* [voice] (1949); *Casanova's Big Night* (1953); *We're No Angels* (1954); *The Court Jester* (1955); *The Black Sleep* (1956); *The Last Hurrah* (1958); *Tales of Terror, The Magic Sword* (1962); *The Comedy of Terrors* (1963); *The Ghost in the Invisible Bikini, Pajama Party in the Haunted House, Queen of Blood* (1966); *Hillbillys in a Haunted House* (1967).

RATOFF, Gregory (Grigory Vasilyevich Ratov) (1897–1960)

Many Russian compatriots in Hollywood considered Ratoff to be a rude and untalented pretender who had only managed to achieve success through unrestrained self-advertising and impudence. To a great extent, this opinion was true. After the decline of the Russian émigré colony in the German film and theatre industries in the mid-1920s, Ratoff moved to New York to join the Yiddish stage despite introducing himself publicly as a Russian Catholic. He went to Hollywood in 1932, where, as well as working as a supporting actor, he eventually became a screenwriter and director of varying critical and commercial distinction. Ratoff often played Russian military officers, barons and villains, but is best remembered as the emotional theatre producer Max Fabian in *All about Eve*. He became an active and loyal supporter of the Soviet Union during World War II and was one of the key figures in Hollywood's Russian Club and Committee of Assistance to Struggling Russia. The HUAC took an interest in the latter, but Ratoff managed to prove his personal loyalty to the USA and escape professional unemployment. RY

FILMS: *Symphony of Six Million, Skyscraper Souls, Under-Cover Man, Secrets of the French Police, What Price Hollywood?, Once in a Lifetime* (1932); *Sweepings, Professional Sweetheart, I'm No Angel, Headline Shooter, Broadway through a Keyhole, Sitting Pretty, Girl without a Room, Let's Fall in Love* (1933); *George White's Scandals* (1934); *Hello, Sweetheart, 18 Minutes, Remember Last Night?, King of Burlesque* (1935); *Here Comes Trouble, Under Two Flags, The Road to Glory, Sing, Baby, Sing, Trouble Ahead, Under Your Spell* (1936); *Seventh Heaven, Top of the Town, Café Metropole* (1937); *Gateway, Sally, Irene and Mary* (1938); *The Great Profile* (1940); *Something to Shout About* (1943); *All about Eve, My Daughter Joy* (1950); *O. Henry's Full House* (1952); *The Moon is Blue* (1953); *Sabrina* (1954); *The Sun Also Rises* (1957); *Exodus, Once More, with Feeling* (1960); *The Big Gamble* (1961).

RAUCOURT, Jules (1890–1967)

Belgian stage actor who in physique and clothing displayed the same distinguished type of Continental elegance as Victor Francen★ and Fernand Gravey★. Raucourt first arrived in the USA in 1917 with a British theatrical company and was immediately spotted by Maurice **407**

Tourneur. He made his American screen debut for Mutual in 1917. He then returned to Europe, where he appeared in avant-garde films and worked as a film journalist. Back in the USA in 1926, he featured in Robert Florey's fascinating short film, *Life and Death of 9413: A Hollywood Extra* – a satirical pamphlet against the film industry's cynical treatment of actors. He went on to appear in French versions of multi-language films such as Ernst Lubitsch's *La Veuve joyeuse* (1934; USA: *The Merry Widow*), and mainly secondary roles in American films, before ending his Hollywood career to become a painter in California. He published a book of memoirs entitled *Hollywood Star, Hollywood Extra*. DN/MB

FILMS: *The Seven Swans, Somewhere in America, Please Help Emily, The Outsider, Outcast, At First Sight* (1917); *Prunella, La Tosca, My Wife* (1918); *Ranger of the North, The Life and Death of 9413: A Hollywood Extra* (1927); *His Tiger Wife* (1928); *The Kiss* (1929); *Marie Galante* (1934); *Folies Bergère de Paris* (1935); *Café Metropole* (1937); *I'll Give a Million, Artist and Model Abroad, Always Goodbye, Sharpshooters* (1938).

REA, Stephen (1949–)

After spending a brief period with the Abbey Theatre, Rea moved to London and was introduced to the London stage by Jack MacGowran★. In 1981, he appeared as Danny in *Angel*, the first of many performances in films directed by Neil Jordan that have included the Academy Award-nominated leading role in *The Crying Game* (1992). Rea's parts in these films enhanced an existing political reputation, though he has also appeared in a succession of non-political roles, including that of melancholy British civil servant Henry Miles in *The End of the Affair*, Santiago in *Interview with the Vampire: The Vampire Chronicles* and, recently, several doctor roles in genre films such as *The I Inside*. RB

FILMS: *The Company of Wolves* (1984); *The Doctor and the Devils* (1985); *Princess Caraboo, Angie, Interview with the Vampire: The Vampire Chronicles, Prêt-à-Porter* (1994); *Michael Collins* (1996); *The Butcher Boy, Double Tap, Hacks* (1997); *In Dreams, Guinevere, The End of the Affair* (1999); *The Musketeer* (2001); *FearDotCom* (2002); *Proud, The I Inside, Evelyn* (2003); *Control* (2004).

REDGRAVE, Corin (1939–)

Distinguished British supporting actor, son of Michael Redgrave★, who made his screen debut in Fred Zinne-

mann's *A Man for All Seasons*. While Redgrave has appeared in a number of US-funded productions over the years, his career profile retains a strong commitment to domestic film, theatre and television. AP

FILMS: *A Man for All Seasons, The Deadly Affair* (1966); *The Charge of the Light Brigade, The Magus* (1968); *Oh! What a Lovely War* (1969); *The Red Baron* (1971); *Excalibur* (1981); *Eureka* (1984); *In the Name of the Father* (1993).

REDGRAVE, Lynn (1943–)

The daughter of Michael Redgrave★, Lynn Redgrave came to international prominence with her Academy Award-nominated performance in the US/UK-financed *Georgy Girl*. Various leading roles followed, including several comic parts in Hollywood productions. Her career pattern since has largely favoured British and American theatre work interspersed with films such as *Gods and Monsters*, where she appeared opposite Ian McKellen★ as James Whale's housemaid. AP/TJ

FILMS: *Tom Jones* (1963); *The Deadly Affair, Georgy Girl* (1966); *Smashing Time* (1967); *The Virgin Soldiers* (1969); *Last of the Mobile Hot Shots* (1970); *Everything You Always Wanted to Know about Sex, Every Little Crook and Nanny* (1972); *The Happy Hooker* (1975); *The Big Bus* (1976); *Sunday Lovers* (1980); *Morgan Stewart's Coming Home* (1987); *Gods and Monsters* (1998); *The Annihilation of Fish* (1999); *The Simian Line, How to Kill Your Neighbor's Dog, The Next Best Thing* (2000); *The Wild Thornberrys Movie* [voice], *Unconditional Love, Hansel & Gretel* (2002); *Charlie's War, Peter Pan* (2003); *Kinsey* (2004).

REDGRAVE, Michael (1908–1985)

Michael Redgrave was a major British film actor before he went to the USA in 1947. His image in Britain was as a sensitive, idealistic, somewhat eccentric romantic hero who fought against social injustice, particularly in *The Stars Look Down* (1940) and *Fame is the Spur* (1947). He also appeared in two US-financed UK productions. His first role in Hollywood – for Universal – was Fritz Lang's *The Secret beyond the Door*. He also worked for RKO on an adaptation of Eugene O'Neill's play *Mourning Becomes Electra*. There was a conflict between the two studios regarding Redgrave's image. In his autobiography, Redgrave recalled that while Universal promoted him as a 'clean-limbed, all-weather type of Englishman', RKO preferred the image of the classical actor, 'reclusive and deeply philosophical'. Although *Mourning Becomes Electra* was not a box-office success, Redgrave was nominated for an Academy Award for Best Actor. He did not stay in the USA, because he was under contract to the Rank Organisation and disliked working in Hollywood. In subsequent years, he appeared in several American films and co-productions, but the bulk of his films were completed in Britain. SS

FILMS: *Kipps, Atlantic Ferry* (1941); *Mourning Becomes Electra* (1947); *The Secret beyond the Door* (1948); *The Happy Road* (1957); *The Quiet American* (1958); *Shake Hands with the Devil, The Wreck of the Mary Deare* (1959); *The Innocents* (1961); *The Heroes of Telemark, The Hill, Young Cassidy* (1965); *Battle of Britain, Oh! What a Lovely War* (1969); *A Christmas Carol* [voice] (1971).

REDGRAVE, Vanessa (1937–)

Tall, elegant classical actress who has largely divided her career between stage and screen, acting and politics and Britain and the USA. Vanessa Redgrave belongs to one of Britain's leading acting families. She is the daughter of Michael Redgrave★, sister to Lynn Redgrave★ and Corin Redgrave★ and mother of Joely Richardson★ and Natasha Richardson★. She made her British film debut in *Behind the Mask* (1958) and returned to the cinema in 1966, when she received the first of several Academy Award nominations for her performance in *Morgan: A Suitable Case for Treatment*. Her Hollywood film appearances shot in the USA have been occasional. However she won a Best Actress Academy Award for her eponymous performance alongside Jane Fonda (as Lillian Hellman) in Fred Zinnemann's 1977 *Julia*. Her trademark poise and quiet command of space was well suited to the role. Redgrave currently combines a highly successful British stage career with appearances in both mainstream American films (*Mission: Impossible* and *Deep Impact*) and independent American projects (*Cradle Will Rock*). MHu

FILMS: *Young Cassidy* (1965); *Blow-Up, A Man for All Seasons* (1966); *Camelot* (1967); *Isadora, The Charge of the Light Brigade* (1968); *Oh! What a Lovely War* (1969); *Mary, Queen of Scots, The Devils, The Trojan Women* (1971); *Out of Season* (1975); *The Seven Per Cent Solution* (1976); *Julia* (1977); *The Bostonians* (1984); *Little Odessa, Mother's Boys* (1994); *Mission: Impossible, Looking for Richard* (1996); *Déjà Vu* (1997); *Deep Impact, Lulu on the Bridge* (1998); *Cradle Will Rock, Girl, Interrupted* (1999); *A Rumor of Angels* (2000); *The Pledge* (2001); *Crime and Punishment* (2002); *Good Boy!* [voice] (2003); *The Fever, The Keeper: The Legend of Omar Khayyam* (2004).

REED, Oliver (1938–1999)

Despite a thick-set physique that initially typecast him in 'heavy' roles, Reed's sullen screen persona by the mid-1960s fitted a vogue for inscrutable anti-heroes, and the preference he showed for restricting his powerful deep voice to a sensuous whisper helped to mark him out as a man of hidden depths and genuine star charisma. He attracted international interest as a result of his appearance in the Academy Award-winning *Women in Love*, but Reed was fond of boasting about how he unreservedly turned down many Hollywood overtures, perhaps because Californian notions of fame and luxury sat uneasily with his self-image as a down-to-earth country-pub ruffian. A small flurry of appearances in American films and television programmes in the latter half of his career – predominantly in minor roles and/or low-budget productions, as in his earliest years as an actor – can be mostly attributed to a lack of work on the home front as the British film industry was drastically scaled down in the 1980s. He subsequently diminished his credibility in straight roles as the extreme toll of a lifetime's heavy drinking on his physique and public behaviour became increasingly apparent on various British television chat shows. JB

FILMS: *I'll Never Forget What's'isname* (1967); *Oliver!* (1968); *The Assassination Bureau, Hannibal Brooks, Women in Love* (1969); *The Devils, The Hunting Party* (1971); *Z.P.G., Sitting Target* (1972); *Tommy, Royal Flash, Lisztomania* (1975); *The Sell-Out, The Great Scout and Cathouse Thursday, Burnt Offerings* (1976); *The Ransom* (1977); *The Prince and the Pauper* (1978); *A Touch of the Sun* (1979); *Dr Heckyl and Mr Hype* (1980); *Condorman* (1981); *Two of a Kind, The Sting II* (1983); *The Misfit Brigade, Skeleton Coast, Rage to Kill* (1987); *The Adventures of Baron Munchausen, The House of Usher, Gor* (1988); *Hired to Kill* (1991); *Severed Ties* (1992); *Funny Bones* (1995); *The Incredible Adventures of Marco Polo* (1998); *Gladiator* (2000).

REICHOW, Otto (1904–2000)

German-Jewish bit-player who gained his first film experience in France after fleeing Nazi Germany. He **409** arrived in the USA in 1937, and became a US citizen. Although a recognisable face in his roles as Nazi hoodlums and Gestapo heavies, he received screen credit in just twenty of his, so far, identified Hollywood pictures. RJK

FILMS: *Confessions of a Nazi Spy* (1939); *Arizona Gangbusters, Mystery Sea Raider* (1940); *Man Hunt, A Yank in the R.A.F., King of the Texas Rangers* [serial], *Underground, Paris Calling, International Lady, Down in San Diego* (1941); *All through the Night, To Be or Not to Be, Joan of Ozark, Invisible Agent, Berlin Correspondent, Once upon a Honeymoon, Reunion in France, Lucky Jordan, Ship Ahoy, Seven Miles from Alcatraz, The Pied Piper, My Favorite Blonde, Desperate Journey, Joan of Paris* (1942); *Tarzan Triumphs, Action in the North Atlantic, The Moon is Down, Hangmen Also Die, Above Suspicion, Paris after Dark, Assignment in Brittany, The Strange Death of Adolf Hitler, They Came to Blow up America, Hitler's Madman, Tonight We Raid Calais, I Dood It, Five Graves to Cairo, First Comes Courage, Chetniks – The Fighting Guerrillas, Bomber's Moon, Sahara, The Cross of Lorraine, Background to Danger, Hostages, Crash Dive* (1943); *Tampico, And the Angels Sing, Resisting Enemy Interrogation, The Black Parachute, Wilson, The Hitler Gang, Passport to Destiny, The Seventh Cross, Address Unknown, The Conspirators, A Voice in the Wind, The Unwritten Code, The Hour Before the Dawn, Till We Meet Again, Two-Man Submarine* (1944); *Nob Hill, Within these Walls, Son of Lassie, Paris Underground, Counter-Attack* (1945); *Rendezvous 24, The Searching Wind, Cloak and Dagger, Dangerous Millions, 13 Rue Madeleine* (1946); *Jewels of Brandenburg, Golden Earrings, The Beginning or the End, Where There's Life, The Secret Life of Walter Mitty* (1947); *Silver River, Sealed Verdict, A Foreign Affair, Rogues' Regiment* (1948); *Alaska Patrol, I was a Male War Bride, Battleground* (1949); *When Willie Comes Marching Home* (1950); *Mara Maru* (1952); *The Desert Rats* (1953); *Night People, The Student Prince, King Richard and the Crusaders* (1954); *Love Me or Leave Me, To Hell and Back* (1955); *Never Say Goodbye, The Man in the Gray Flannel Suit, D-Day the Sixth of June* (1956); *Istanbul, Operation Mad Bull, Looking for Danger, Back from the Dead* (1957); *The Young Lions, Imitation General, Frankenstein 1970, Fräulein, Me and the Colonel* (1958); *Operation Eichmann* (1961); *Hitler, Four Horsemen of the Apocalypse, The Pigeon that Took Rome, Billy Rose's Jumbo* (1962); *The Prize* (1963); *36 Hours* (1964); *Ulzana's Raid* (1972).

RENAVENT, Georges (Georges de Cheux) (1894–1969)

French stage actor whose long-running American film career began in the mid-1910s. Renavent worked as a Hollywood character actor specialising in French waiters, hotel managers, police officials and embassy staff. He also managed his own Grand Guignol theatrical troupe that toured the USA during the 1930s and 1940s. AP

FILMS: *The Seven Sisters, Gussie, the Graceful Lifeguard* (1915); *American – That's All* (1917); *The Light, Erstwhile Susan* (1919); *Rio Rita* (1929); *Slightly Scarlet, Scotland Yard* (1930); *Once a Sinner, The Magnificent Lie, East of Borneo* (1931); *Arsène Lupin, Whistlin' Dan, Two Lips and Juleps, The Bride's Bereavement* (1932); *Private Detective 62, Ever in My Heart, Queen Christina* (1933); *Bombay Mail, Moulin Rouge, The House of Rothschild, Stingaree, Stamboul Quest* (1934); *The White Cockatoo, Folies Bergère de Paris, The Flame Within, Front Page Woman, Anna Karenina, The Last Outpost, Whipsaw, Captain Blood* (1935); *The Invisible Ray, Sky Parade, China Clipper, The Charge of the Light Brigade, Love Letters of a Star, Lloyd's of London* (1936); *She's Dangerous, History is Made at Night, Seventh Heaven, The King and the Chorus Girl, Café Metropole, Love under Fire, Thin Ice, The Sheik Steps Out, That Certain Woman, Wife, Doctor and Nurse, Fight for Your Lady, Charlie Chan at Monte Carlo, Love and Hisses* (1937); *Jezebel, Judge Hardy's Children, A Trip to Paris, Gold Diggers in Paris, I'll Give a Million, Four's a Crowd, Suez, The Young in Heart, Sharpshooters, Artists and Models Abroad* (1938); *Mr Moto's Last Warning, Topper Takes a Trip, The Three Musketeers, The Adventures of Jane Arden* [scenes deleted], *Chasing Danger, Indianapolis Speedway, Lady of the Tropics, Pack up Your Troubles, Everything Happens at Night, Old Hickory* (1939); *The House across the Bay, Turnabout, Brother Orchid, Christmas in July, A Dispatch from Reuters, The Son of Monte Cristo, Comrade X* (1940); *Back Street, That Hamilton Woman, The Great Lie, That Night in Rio, Road to Zanzibar, They Dare Not Love, Night of January 16th, Paris Calling, Sullivan's Travels* (1941); *Spy Smasher, Perils of Nyoka, I Married an Angel, Now, Voyager, Silver Queen, Casablanca* (1942); *The Hard Way, Mission to Moscow, Background to Danger, Secret Service in Darkest Africa, Wintertime, Around the World, The Desert Song* (1943); *Action in Arabia, The Tiger Woman, The Mask of Dimitrios, The Desert Hawk, Till We Meet Again, Our Hearts were Young and Gay, Storm over Lisbon, Experiment Perilous* (1944);

Cornered, Saratoga Trunk, Yolanda and the Thief, This Love of Ours, Scotland Yard Investigator, Rhapsody in Blue, You Came Along, Captain Eddie, Those Endearing Charms (1945); *Tarzan and the Leopard Woman, The Return of Monte Cristo, The Catman of Paris, The Hoodlum Saint* (1946); *The Foxes of Harrow, Ladies' Man, The Perils of Pauline, The Trespasser, Tarzan and the Huntress, The Perfect Marriage* (1947); *Rope of Sand, It's a Great Feeling* (1949); *Fortunes of Captain Blood* (1950); *Secrets of Monte Carlo, Strangers on a Train* (1951); *Because You're Mine, Son of Ali Baba, Mara Maru* (1952).

RENNIE, Michael (1909–1971)

After playing a number of small roles in postwar British films, Rennie secured a contract with Twentieth Century-Fox and went on to appear in Hollywood films shot in the USA and Europe. He was the robot Klaatu in the science-fiction classic *The Day the Earth Stood Still*. JS

FILMS: *The Black Rose* (1950); *Desert Fox: The Story of Rommel, The House in the Square, The Day the Earth Stood Still, The 13th Letter* (1951); *Phone Call from a Stranger, Les Misérables, Pony Soldier, 5 Fingers* (1952); *Titanic, Dangerous Crossing, King of the Khyber Rifles, The Desert Rats, Single-Handed, The Robe* (1953); *Prince Valiant, Princess of the Nile, Mambo, Desirée, Demetrius and the Gladiators* (1954); *Soldier of Fortune, Seven Cities of Gold, The Rains of Ranchipur* (1955); *Teenage Rebel* (1956); *Island in the Sun, Omar Khayyam* (1957); *The Battle of the V1* (1958); *Third Man on the Mountain* (1959); *The Lost World* (1960); *Mary, Mary* (1963); *Cyborg 2087* (1966); *Hotel* (1967); *The Nude, The Devil's Brigade* (1968); *The Last Generation* (1971).

RENO, Jean (Juan Moreno) (1948–)

Born the same year as Gérard Depardieu★, though in Casablanca and to Andalusian parents, Reno shares some similarities with his French compatriot. For a decade, Reno was known abroad for his association with Luc Besson, which in itself heralds an attraction to American cinema. Although he does not favour the Hollywood ethos, he has adapted well to the American blockbuster system.

His English-language debut was in a French film, as the eponymous contract killer in *Léon/The Professional* (1994), an international hit that gave him a head start in Hollywood. Reno subsequently took supporting roles in Lawrence Kasdan's *French Kiss*, Brian De Palma's *Mission: Impossible* and the lead role (as an Italian) in a low-key black

comedy by Paul Weiland, *Roseanna's Grave*. He turned down the role of Agent Smith in the Wachowski brothers' *The Matrix* because of family comitments, and, instead, accepted the part of a 'French good guy' in Roland Emmerich's *Godzilla*, as well as that of a tough guy, opposite Robert De Niro, in John Frankenheimer's *Ronin*. Like Depardieu in the remake *My Father the Hero* (1994), Reno starred alongside Christian Clavier★ in both the original French hit – *Les Visiteurs* (1993) – and its American remake: the commercially unsuccessful *Just Visiting*. In this and other films, his acting style has been consistently, calmly menacing, with a hint of humour. VO

FILMS: *French Kiss* (1995); *Mission: Impossible* (1996); *Roseanna's Grave* (1997); *Godzilla, Ronin* (1998); *Just Visiting* (2001); *Rollerball* (2002).

REY, Fernando (Fernando Casado d'Arambillet) (1917–1994)

Despite being one of Spain's most prolific and important screen actors, and receiving international acclaim after his collaboration with Luis Buñuel in *Viridiana* (1961), Fernando Rey began work in American cinema through minor roles in Spanish-American co-productions filmed in Spain during the 1960s. His strong accent when speaking English meant that Rey was always cast as the foreigner in Hollywood. In Westerns, for example, such as *Return of the Seven* and *Guns of the Magnificent Seven*, he always played the part of a Mexican. It was only after his role in *The French Connection* as Alain Charnier, an unscrupulous French heroin dealer, that Rey became popular with American audiences. His final Hollywood appearance was in Ridley Scott's *1492: Conquest of Paradise*. CBu

FILMS: *The Ceremony* (1963); *Son of a Gunfighter* (1965); *Return of the Seven* (1966); *Run Like a Thief* (1967); *The Desperate Ones* (1968); *Guns of the Magnificent Seven, Land Raiders* (1969); *The Adventurers* (1970); *The French Connection* (1971); *French Connection II* (1975); *A Matter of Time* (1976); *Quintet* (1979); *Caboblanco* (1980); *Monsignor* (1982); *Saving Grace, Rustler's Rhapsody* (1985); *Moon over Parador* (1988); *1492: Conquest of Paradise* (1992).

RHYS-DAVIES, John (1944–)

Rhys-Davies' rotund frame has been ubiquitous on UK, but mainly US, television since the 1970s. The RADA-trained Welsh actor is probably most associated with the **411** fantasy genre through his role as Sallah in the Indiana Jones films, and more recently – and unrecognisably – as Gimli in Peter Jackson's *Lord of the Rings* trilogy. MW

FILMS: *A Nightingale Sang in Berkeley Square* (1979); *Raiders of the Lost Ark, Sphinx* (1981); *Victor/Victoria, Best Revenge* (1982); *Sahara* (1983); *King Solomon's Mines* (1985); *Firewalker* (1986); *The Living Daylights* (1987); *Waxwork* (1988); *Indiana Jones and the Last Crusade* (1989); *Rebel Storm, Tusks* (1990); *South Beach, The Seventh Coin* (1992); *The Double 0 Kid, Sunset Grill, Cyborg Cop* (1993); *Blood of the Innocent, Stargate* (1994); *Marquis de Sade, Bloodsport 3, The Great White Hype, Glory Daze* (1996); *The Protector, Cats Don't Dance* [voice] (1997); *Delta Force One: The Lost Patrol* (1999); *Sinbad: Beyond the Veil of Mists* [voice] (2000); *Lord of the Rings: The Fellowship of the Ring* (2001); *Endangered Species, Scorcher, Sabretooth, The Lord of the Rings: The Two Towers* (2002); *Vlad, The Lord of the Rings: The Return of the King, Highbinders, The Jungle Book 2* [voice] (2003); *The Princess Diaries 2: Royal Engagement, Catching Kringle* [voice] (2004).

RICCIARDI, William (Guglielmo Ricciardi) (1871–unknown)

Italian actor who emigrated to New York in 1891 and made his American stage debut in a musical in 1907. He worked extensively in New York immigrant theatre and on Broadway. His cinema career was mainly restricted to supporting roles playing Italians such as the owner of a speakeasy with opera connections in John Stahl's *Strictly Dishonorable*. AM

FILMS: *That Woman* (1922); *The Humming Bird, The Side Show of Life, Greater than Marriage* (1924); *A Man Must Live, Heart of a Siren* (1925); *Say it Again, Puppets* (1926); *Strictly Dishonorable* (1931); *As You Desire Me, Crooner, Tiger Shark, Scarlet Dawn* (1932); *Stars over Broadway, The Scoundrel* (1935); *Under Two Flags, San Francisco, Anthony Adverse* (1936); *Man of the People* (1937).

RICHARDSON, Joely (1965–)

Richardson's distinctively English willowy features have appeared in a number of independent and mainstream films over the years. She is the daughter of Vanessa Redgrave★ and Tony Richardson and made her screen debut as an extra in her father's extravagant production, *The Charge of the Light Brigade*. Her limited American filmography reflects a deliberate decision not to pursue a permanent acting career in Los Angeles. AP

FILMS: *The Charge of the Light Brigade* (1968); *The Hotel New Hampshire* (1984); *King Ralph* (1991); *Shining Through* (1992); *I'll Do Anything* (1994); *101 Dalmations* (1996); *Wrestling with Alligators, Under Heaven* (1998); *Return to Me, The Patriot* (2000); *The Affair of the Necklace* (2001); *Shoreditch* (2003).

RICHARDSON, Miranda (1958–)

Richardson made a powerful British screen debut with her startling performance as the porcelain-blonde Ruth Ellis in Mike Newell's tragic *Dance with a Stranger* (1985). She has been careful in her choice of work ever since and has often stated that she prefers quality over more commercial choices. While understandably resistant to the 'woman on the brink' pigeon-hole, she excels at slightly edgy characters whose sharp, distinctive features can command an authority sometimes underscored by a note of pathos.

Richardson's first US film was Spielberg's *Empire of the Sun*, but she resisted beckoning Hollywood opportunity and turned down the part that eventually went to Glenn Close in *Fatal Attraction* (1987). She continued to build her profile in independent UK productions such as Neil Jordan's *The Crying Game* (1992). The film crossed over to become a mainstream hit on both sides of the Atlantic and brought her a BAFTA nomination and a Best Supporting Actress award from the New York Film Critics Circle. Her most prominent Hollywood roles in recent years have been as a witch in Tim Burton's fog-enshrouded comic-horror film, *Sleepy Hollow*, and the voice of the despicable plasticine chicken hater, Mrs Tweedy, in Nick Park and Peter Lord's *Chicken Run*. MW

FILMS: *Empire of the Sun* (1987); *Tom & Viv* (1994); *Kansas City, The Evening Star* (1996); *The Apostle* (1997); *The Big Brass Ring, The King and I* [voice], *Sleepy Hollow* (1999); *Chicken Run* [voice], *Get Carter* (2000); *The Hours* (2002); *The Prince & Me* (2004).

RICHARDSON, Natasha (1963–)

The elder daughter of Vanessa Redgrave★, Richardson enjoyed a rapid graduation from British theatre and cinema to Hollywood in the late 1980s. A career on Broadway has largely predominated since. JB

FILMS: *The Charge of the Light Brigade* (1968); *Gothic* (1986); *Patty Hearst* (1988); *The Handmaid's Tale* (1990); *Nell* (1994); *The Parent Trap* (1998); *Chelsea Walls* (2001); *Waking up in Reno, Maid in Manhattan* (2002).

RICHARDSON, Ralph (1902–1983)

Commanding figurehead of the British stage and screen from the 1930s until the 1980s. Richardson also possessed a soft touch that raised the quality of many epic Hollywood productions through his presence. Two years after he received his knighthood in 1947, Richardson won an Academy Award nomination for his role as Olivia de Havilland's cruel father in *The Heiress*. This success led to an irregular but long-term association with Hollywood, especially in international productions such as *Long Day's Journey into Night* (with Katharine Hepburn) and *Doctor Zhivago*. MW

FILMS: *Thunder in the City* (1937); *The Citadel* (1938); *The Heiress* (1949); *Our Man in Havana* (1959); *Exodus* (1960); *Long Day's Journey into Night, The 300 Spartans* (1962); *Woman of Straw* (1964); *Doctor Zhivago, Moscow in Madrid* (1965); *Khartoum, The Wrong Box* (1966); *Oh! What a Lovely War, Midas Run, The Looking Glass War, The Bed Sitting Room* (1969); *Who Slew Auntie Roo?, Eagle in a Cage, Tales from the Crypt* (1972); *O Lucky Man!* (1973); *Rollerball* (1975); *Dragonslayer* (1981); *Greystoke: The Legend of Tarzan, Lord of the Apes* (1984).

RICKMAN, Alan (1946–)

Even though this highly respected British stage actor was a relatively late starter, Rickman's film and television career conspicuously lagged behind glittering theatrical success for many years. Film producers became nervous about hiring him, even in tailor-made roles such as Valmont in the American film adaptation of Christopher Hampton's play *Dangerous Liaisons* (1988). Rickman had played the part to huge acclaim on stage but lost out to John Malkovich, an actor of broader multimedia celebrity and experience. He nonetheless appeared in the play's Broadway transfer and attracted sufficient interest among casting agents to enable him to follow a route trodden by many émigré British stage actors in Hollywood: hamming it up as the baddie. Following his film debut as a German terrorist in *Die Hard*, Rickman's nasal, supercilious voice and heavy-lidded sneering eyes have been put to use in similar roles in subsequent

blockbuster productions such as *Robin Hood – Prince of Thieves* and the *Harry Potter* films. His wide exposure has also opened doors to rich supporting roles and indulgent cameos in a number of more prestigious as well as offbeat projects. JB

FILMS: *Die Hard* (1988); *Robin Hood – Prince of Thieves* (1991); *Bob Roberts* (1992); *Sense and Sensibility* (1995); *Michael Collins* (1996); *Dogma, Galaxy Quest* (1999); *Harry Potter and the Sorcerer's Stone* (2001); *Harry Potter and the Chamber of Secrets* (2002); *Harry Potter and the Prisoner of Azkaban* (2004).

RIGAUD, Georges (Pedro Jorge Rigato Delissetche) (1905–1984)

Argentinian-born French actor (sometimes credited as Jorge Rigaud) who started his screen career in European films directed by René Clair, Robert Siodmak and Max Ophuls. He made his American debut in the musical comedy *Masquerade in Mexico* and appeared in the crime thriller *I Walk Alone* next to Burt Lancaster and Kirk Douglas. Rigaud, however, is best remembered for his roles in a few Westerns, some co-produced with Spain such as *Finger on the Trigger* (1965). TH

FILMS: *Masquerade in Mexico, Paris Underground* (1945); *I Walk Alone* (1948); *Native Son* (1951); *John Paul Jones* (1959); *The Happy Thieves* (1962); *Lost Command* (1966); *Guns of the Magnificent Seven* (1969).

RIGG, Diana (1938–)

Diana Rigg built her formidable acting reputation as a RADA-trained Shakespearean actress and won a 1994 Tony award for her typically powerful stage performance in *Medea*. In the minds of the US and UK public alike, however, Rigg will always be Emma Peel – the leather catsuited secret agent of the 1960s British television series, *The Avengers*. It was a role that brought her two Emmy Award nominations. In 1971, the actress played opposite George C. Scott in Arthur Hiller's comedy *The Hospital*. She subsequently appeared as an Englishwoman in New York in her own US television comedy series, *Diana*. Rigg has shown little interest in pursuing a Hollywood career and prefers occasional roles in UK film and television alongside regular theatrical work. MW

FILMS: *The Assassination Bureau, On Her Majesty's Secret Service* (1969); *Julius Caesar* (1970); *The Hospital* (1971); *The*   413

Great Muppet Caper (1981); *Snow White* (1988); *A Good Man in Africa* (1994); *Cinderella* (2002).

RISDON, Elisabeth (1887–1958)

English stage and screen actress who earned fame at home in early silent cinema. Risdon moved to New York in 1917 and featured in a couple of films before opting to concentrate on her stage career. She migrated to Hollywood in the mid-1930s and carved out a niche as a stern matriarch in numerous minor and supporting roles in such films as *The Roaring Twenties* and *High Sierra*. MF

FILMS: *Hypocrites, Home* (1915); *Mother* (1917); *A Star Overnight* (1919); *Guard that Girl, Crime and Punishment* (1935); *The King Steps Out, Craig's Wife, Theodora Goes Wild, Lady of Secrets, The Final Hour, Don't Gamble with Love* (1936); *The Woman I Love, Dead End, They Won't Forget, Mountain Justice, Make Way for Tomorrow* (1937); *Mannequin, Mad about Music, The Cowboy from Brooklyn, The Affairs of Annabel, My Bill, Tom Sawyer, Detective, Girls on Probation* (1938); *The Great Man Votes, The Adventures of Huckleberry Finn, The Girl from Mexico, The Man Who Dared, Five Came Back, Full Confession, The Roaring Twenties, Sorority House, The Forgotten Woman, Disputed Passage* (1939); *Mexican Spitfire, Abe Lincoln in Illinois, Ma, He's Making Eyes at Me, Saturday's Children, Slightly Tempted, The Man Who Wouldn't Talk, Mexican Spitfire Out West, Sing, Dance, Plenty Hot, Let's Make Music, The Howards of Virginia, Honeymoon Deferred* (1940); *High Sierra, Mr Dynamite, Nice Girl?, At the Stroke of Twelve, Paris Calling, Mexican Spitfire's Baby, Footlight Fever* (1941); *Jail House Blues, The Man Who Returned to Life, The Lady is Willing, Reap the Wild Wind, Are Husbands Necessary?, Mexican Spitfire Sees a Ghost, Mexican Spitfire's Elephant, Random Harvest, Journey for Margaret, Mexican Spitfire at Sea, I Live on Danger* (1942); *The Amazing Mrs Holliday, Never a Dull Moment, Mexican Spitfire's Blessed Event, Lost Angel* (1943); *Weird Woman, Cobra Woman, Tall in the Saddle, Higher and Higher, Blonde Fever, In the Meantime, Darling, The Canterville Ghost* (1944); *The Unseen, A Song for Miss Julie, Mama Loves Papa, Grissly's Millions, The Fighting Guardsman* (1945); *The Walls Came Tumbling Down, They Made Me a Killer, Roll on Texas Moon, Lover Come Back* (1946); *The Egg and I, Life with Father, The Shocking Miss Pilgrim, The Romance of Rosy Ridge, Mourning Becomes Electra, High Wall* (1947); *The Bride Goes Wild, Sealed Verdict, Every Girl Should Be Married, Bodyguard* (1948); *Down Dakota Way, Guilty of Treason* (1949); *The Secret*

Fury, Hills of Oklahoma, Sierra, The Milkman, Bunco Squad (1950); *Bannerline, It's a Big Country, My True Story, In Old Amarillo* (1951); *Scaramouche* (1952).

RITZAU, Erik von (1877–1936)

Danish actor who played one of the Pharisees in D. W. Griffith's *Intolerance*. Another Pharisee, and another bogus 'von', Erich von Stroheim, cast von Ritzau in his remaining memorable role: Dr Painless Potter, the travelling dentist in *Greed*. HJW

FILMS: *Eleven-Thirty P.M., A Bold Impersonation, Old Heidelberg, A Wayward Son* (1915); *Intolerance* (1916); *The Master Spy* (1917); *The Border Wireless* (1918); *Greed, The Prairie Wife* (1925).

ROBERTS, Rachel (1927–1980)

Just like Kay Kendall★, Welsh actress Rachel Roberts went to the USA as a direct consequence of her marriage to Rex Harrison★, but the resemblances emphatically end there. Roberts had come to prominence playing the older woman romantically entangled in a complicated relationship with the hero in *Saturday Night and Sunday Morning* (1960) and *This Sporting Life* (1963). She won a Best Supporting Actress Academy Award nomination for the latter and elements of the blowsy sensuality shown in these British 'New Wave' films were sometimes exploited in her American work – she played a brothel madam in the Western *Wild Rovers*. For the most part, however, her unconventional buxom glamour was downplayed for American audiences and her most substantial success in the USA was as a no-nonsense housekeeper in television's *The Tony Randall Show* (1976–8). JB

FILMS: *Our Man in Havana* (1959); *A Flea in Her Ear* (1968); *The Reckoning* (1969); *Doctors' Wives, Wild Rovers* (1971); *O Lucky Man!* (1973); *Foul Play* (1978); *Yanks, When a Stranger Calls* (1979); *Charlie Chan and the Curse of the Dragon Queen* (1981).

ROBIN, Dany (1927–1995)

One of France's popular young female stars of the late 1940s and 1950s who was often cast as a naive young woman in love due to her childlike voice and youthful appearance. This trend continued in the Franco-American co-production *Act of Love*, in which Robin played a Parisian in love with an American soldier (Kirk Douglas).

Robin's final American film role was as the cool, but sensual, traitorous wife in Hitchcock's *Topaz*. SL/AP

FILMS: *Act of Love* (1953); *Follow the Boys* (1963); *The Best House in London, Topaz* (1969).

ROBSON, Flora (1902–1984)

Distinguished and formidable British stage and screen actress who made a handful of films in Hollywood between 1939 and 1945. Robson was nominated for a Best Supporting Actress Academy Award for her performance as Angelique Buiton in *Saratoga Trunk*. She also appeared in several postwar US-financed films shot in Europe. MHu

FILMS: *Wuthering Heights, Invisible Stripes, We are Not Alone* (1939); *The Sea Hawk* (1940); *Bahama Passage* (1941); *Great Day, Saratoga Trunk* (1945); *55 Days at Peking, Murder at the Gallop* (1963); *Guns at Batasi* (1964); *Young Cassidy, Those Magnificent Men in Their Flying Machines, or How I Flew from London to Paris in 25 Hours, 11 Minutes* (1965); *Eye of the Devil* (1967); *Fragment of Fear* (1970).

ROC, Patricia (Felicia Riese) (1918–2003)

Pat Roc – as she was affectionately known to her British fans – had a career pattern strikingly similar to that of James Mason★, Margaret Lockwood★ and Phyllis Calvert★. Like them she came to prominence in the hugely successful costume melodramas and tales of everyday wartime life produced by Gainsborough Studios in the 1940s and was at one point ranked as the third most popular star among British audiences. This led to a postwar loan-out contract with Universal (one of several such arrangements that Roc's employers hoped would help prepare the way for more reciprocal 'star trading' between Britain and the USA). As an actress who had predominantly specialised in playing exceptionally innocent, artless, uncompromisingly virtuous and somewhat passive heroines, Roc was perhaps the most out of place of the former Gainsborough stars in Hollywood and her Californian stay was restricted to one supporting role in a Technicolor Western. She also appeared in an American–French co-production part shot in Paris and an American–British co-production directed by Jacques Tourneur. Her earlier British screen career included a couple of US-financed films. JB

FILMS: *The Mind of Mr Reeder* (1939); *We'll Meet Again* (1943); *Canyon Passage* (1946); *The Man on the Eiffel Tower* (1950); *Circle of Danger* (1951).

ROCHEFORT, Charles de (Charles d'Authier de Rochefort) (1887–1952)

Handsome French stage and screen actor as well as filmmaker. Success in the British film *The Spanish Jade* (1922) led to a contract from Jesse Lasky and a brief career in 1920s Hollywood, where he was dubbed 'the French Adonis'. Rochefort – usually credited as Charles (or Chas) de Roche – was modestly successful in roles that ranged from Rameses in Cecil B. DeMille's *The Ten Commandments* to 'Fernand the Apache' in *Shadows of Paris*. He lived in high Hollywood style, however, the target, among other things, of court cases, a threat by the Ku Klux Klan and gunshots – at least, as recounted in his memoirs *Le Film de mes souvenirs* (1943). Safely back in Paris, he directed French versions of multi-language films for Paramount and resumed his stage career. GV

FILMS: *Law of the Lawless, The Cheat, The Marriage Maker, The Ten Commandments* (1923); *Shadows of Paris, The White Moth* (1924); *Madame Sans-Gêne* (1925).

ROLF, Tutta (Jenny Berntzen) (1907–1994)

Norwegian revue stage performer who became one of the most popular female stars in Swedish cinema of the 1930s in films such as *Kära släkten* (1933) and *En stilla flirt* (1934). Although her Hollywood films made with Twentieth Century-Fox were unsuccessful, she continued to live in the USA with her husband, choreographer Jack Donahue, until 1950. YH

FILMS: *Dressed to Thrill* (1935); *Rhythm in the Air* (1936).

ROLFE, Guy (1915–2003)

Former English boxer who played minor and supporting American film roles from the early 1950s. His gaunt and haunting features lent themselves to a number of horror movies in the 1990s. MF

FILMS: *Ivanhoe* (1952); *The Veils of Baghdad, Young Bess, King of the Khyber Rifles* (1953); *The Barbarians* (1960); *King of Kings, Snow White and the Three Stooges, Mr Sardonicus* (1961); *Taras Bulba* (1962); *The Fall of the Roman Empire* (1964); *The Alphabet Murders* (1965); *Land Raiders* (1969); *Nicholas and Alexandra* (1971); *The Bride* (1985); *Dolls* (1986); *Puppet Master III: Toulon's Revenge* (1991); *Puppet Master IV* (1993); *Puppet Master V: The Final Chapter* (1994); *Retro Puppetmaster* (1999).

ROMAIN, Yvonne (1938–)

Curvaceous and dramatic-looking Franco-British brunette who was a leading lady in many British horror B-movies, but made few American films. In the musical *Double Trouble*, she acted opposite Elvis Presley. VO

FILMS: *The Swinger* (1966); *Double Trouble* (1967); *The Last of Sheila* (1973).

ROMANIA

It is almost impossible to define a clearly expressed national Romanian contribution to the American film industry. On the whole, the phenomenon of Hollywood actors with origins in the Romanian region – that is ethnic Romanians, Hungarians, Germans and Jews born in Romania before World War I or in the historical provinces such as Transylvania that were then integrated into the Romanian state after 1918 – is dominated by the fact that the majority of these people were very young emigrants who were only professionally trained *after* contact with the American film industry. Prestigious stars such as Edward G. Robinson (Emanuel Goldenberg) or Johnny Weissmuller (Johann Weissmüller), actors with rich filmographies in B-features such as Bob Curwood (Ioan Balas), Nick Stuart (Nicolae Pratza), Ferike Boros (Ferike Weinstock) and Elinor Carlid and actors with minor but still noteworthy filmographies such as John Housemann (Jacques Haussmann) and Nadia Gray (Nadia Herescu-Cantacuzino) did not have any significant pre-existing film or stage career in their native country. Exceptions such as the actress Lisette Verea★, the Marx Brothers' brilliant partner in *A Night in Casablanca* (1946) who made only one Romanian film, Jean Mihail's *Trenul fantomă/The Ghost Train* (1934), tend only to confirm the rule. BR

ROME, Stewart (Septimus Wernham Ryott) (1886–1965)

In 1915, readers of a British fan magazine voted Rome their favourite native male star. He belatedly attempted to try his luck in Hollywood in the mid-1920s, with little success. His subsequent filmography contained a few American-funded UK productions. JB

FILMS: *The Desert Sheik* (1924); *The Silver Treasure* (1926); *The Ware Case* (1928); *Confidential Lady, Shadowed Eyes* (1940).

RONET, Maurice (1927–1983)

Ronet made his name in France playing the suicidal alcoholic in Louis Malle's *Le Feu follet* (1966). His US films were thrillers, with the exception of a 1968 musical with James Garner and Debbie Reynolds. SL

FILMS: *The Victors* (1963); *Lost Command* (1966); *How Sweet it Is!* (1968); *Bloodline* (1979); *Sphinx* (1980).

ROOS, Camilla Overbye (1969–)

Despite having most of her role as a Scandinavian immigrant in *Titanic* end up on the cutting-room floor, the blonde Danish ingénue Camilla Overbye Roos has embarked on a Hollywood career. She hails from a prominent Danish family of documentary film-makers. HJW

FILMS: *White Squall* (1996); *Titanic, Vicious Circles* (1997); *On the Border* (1998); *Facade, The Contract* (1999); *The Guilty* (2000); *Under the Influence, Infested* (2002); *Intoxicating* (2003).

ROSAY, Françoise (Françoise Bandy de Nalèche) (1891–1974)

Arguably one of the greatest female stars, if not the only one, of 1930s French cinema, Françoise Rosay, wife of the Belgian director Jacques Feyder, was a key member of the French community in Hollywood at the end of the 1920s during the time of the multi-language versions. Having returned to France, Feyder, who had already employed her during the silent era, offered her some magnificent roles in films such as *Pension Mimosas* (1934) and *La Kermesse héroïque/Carnival in Flanders* (1935). For Feyder, Duvivier (*Carnet de bal/Dance of Life* [1937]) and Carné (*Drôle de drame/Bizarre, Bizarre* [1937]), she played varied and original versions of mature and bossy women. During the war, she was an active Resistant based in London and she built up an international reputation by acting in Britain, Italy and the USA. Her Hollywood roles are admittedly a pale imitation of her French talent: she was an avenging mother in *The 13th Letter* (a remake of *Le Corbeau/The Raven* [1943]), devoted in *Interlude* and a Normandy villager in *The Longest Day*, but Françoise Rosay always retained her natural authority compounded by her 'masculine' voice, her white hair and her half-closed eye (she had only one valid eye) and a very distinctive strangeness. These roles were sometimes successful, but a far cry from her greatness in her 1930s French films. CV

Françoise Rosay: key member of Hollywood's French community during the early sound era

FILMS: *The One Woman Idea* (1929); *The Playboy of Paris* (1930); *The Magnificent Lie* (1931); *September Affair* (1950); *The 13th Letter* (1951); *That Lady* (1955); *The Seventh Sin, Interlude* (1957); *Me and the Colonel* (1958); *The Sound and the Fury* (1959); *The Longest Day* (1962); *Up from the Beach* (1965).

ROSING, Bodil (Bodil Hammerich) (1878–1942)

Born into a well-known Danish acting family, Rosing had officially retired from performing when she was lured back into the limelight by her son-in-law, the veteran actor Monte Blue. Along with Germany's Greta Meyer★, she cornered the market in Hollywood for Middle European hausfraus during the 1930s. HJW

FILMS: *Pretty Ladies, The Tower of Lies, Lights of Old Broadway* (1925); *The Sporting Lover, It Must Be Love, The Midnight Kiss, The Return of Peter Grimm, The City* (1926); *Stage Madness, Sunrise, Blondes by Choice, Wild Geese* (1927); *The Law of the Range, The Big Noise, The Port of Missing Girls, Wheel of Chance, Ladies of the Mob, Out of the Ruins, The Fleet's In, The Woman from Moscow* (1928); *King of the Rodeo,*

Why Be Good?, Eternal Love, Betrayal, Broadway Babies (1929); *The Bishop Murder Case, Hello Sister, All Quiet on the Western Front, A Lady's Morals, Oh, for a Man, Part Time Wife* (1930); *Three Who Loved, Surrender* (1931); *Downstairs, The Match King* (1932); *Hallelujah I'm a Bum, The Crime of the Century, Reunion in Vienna, Ex-Lady* (1933); *Mandalay, All Men Are Enemies, Little Man, What Now?, Such Women are Dangerous, King Kelly of the U.S.A., Crimson Romance, The Painted Veil* (1934); *A Night at the Ritz, Roberta, Four Hours to Kill, Let 'Em Have It, Thunder in the Night* (1935); *Hearts in Bondage, Libeled Lady, Rose Bowl, The Plot Thickens* (1936); *Michael O'Halloran, Little Pioneer, Thin Ice, Conquest* (1937); *The First Hundred Years, You Can't Take it with You, The Great Waltz* (1938); *Confessions of a Nazi Spy, Hotel Imperial, The Star Maker, Nurse Edith Cavell, Hitler – Beast of Berlin* (1939); *Four Sons, The Mortal Storm* (1940); *Reaching for the Sun, They Dare Not Love, No Greater Sin, Man at Large, Marry the Bo$$'s Daughter* (1941).

ROTH, Tim (1961–)

Hollywood has tended to limit Roth to the more menacing side of his screen persona that featured in his forceful leading debut role in Alan Clarke's British television film *Made in Britain* (1982). In Quentin Tarantino's controversial *Reservoir Dogs* – the film that really established the actor's name outside the UK – the actor spent most of his time soaked in blood as the undercover cop Mr Orange. Roth continued to play gritty characters involved in violent situations in *Pulp Fiction* and James Gray's bleak gangster film, *Little Odessa*.

Having said this, Roth has not entirely been typecast by the American film industry. He played the feckless television salesman in *Bodies, Rest and Motion* and Woody Allen perceptively combined Roth's more romantic side with his established criminal persona in the surprise musical *Everyone Says I Love You*. Roth's roles in a number of big-budget Hollywood features – he won a Best Supporting Actor Academy Award nomination for his role as the foppish and mean Archibald Cunningham in *Rob Roy* – are now combined with more demanding appearances in various European co-productions. JS

FILMS: *Jumpin' at the Boneyard, Reservoir Dogs* (1992); *Bodies, Rest and Motion* (1993); *Pulp Fiction, Little Odessa* (1994); *Rob Roy, Four Rooms* (1995); *No Way Home, Mocking the Cosmos, Everyone Says I Love You* (1996); *Gridlock'd,* **417**

Hoodlum, Deceiver (1997); *Animals and the Tollkeeper* (1998); *The Million Dollar Hotel, Lucky Numbers* (2000); *Planet of the Apes* (2001); *Emmett's Mark* (2002); *Whatever We Do* (2003); *With It, Silver City* (2004).

RUMAN, Sig (Siegfried Albon Rumann) (1884–1967)

Originally a serious actor in German provincial theatre, Ruman came to New York to appear in German-language plays in 1924, but soon found acclaim on Broadway playing blustering comic embodiments of Prussian pomposity. Transferring this persona to Hollywood talkies, he became a favourite of Ernst Lubitsch and Billy Wilder, and is best remembered as one of the three Soviet envoys (alongside Felix Bressart★ and Alexander Granach★) in *Ninotchka* and as Sergeant Schulz in *Stalag 17*. From 1941, he spelled his surname 'Ruman'. RJK

FILMS: *Lucky Boy* (1929); *The World Moves On, Servants' Entrance, Marie Galante* (1934); *Under Pressure, The Wedding Night, The Farmer Takes a Wife, Spring Tonic, A Night at the Opera, East of Java* (1935); *The Princess Comes Across, The Bold Caballero* (1936); *On the Avenue, Seventh Heaven, Maytime, Midnight Taxi, The Great Hospital Mystery, This is My Affair, A Day at the Races, Think Fast, Mr Moto, Love Under Fire, Thin Ice, Lancer Spy, Heidi, Nothing Sacred, Thank You, Mr Moto* (1937); *The Saint in New York, Paradise for Three, I'll Give a Million, Suez, Girls on Probation, The Great Waltz* (1938); *Honolulu, Never Say Die, Confessions of a Nazi Spy, Only Angels Have Wings, Ninotchka, Remember?* (1939); *Dr Ehrlich's Magic Bullet, Outside the 3-Mile Limit, I Was an Adventuress, Four Sons, Bitter Sweet, Comrade X, Victory* (1940); *So Ends Our Night, This Woman is Mine, The Man Who Lost Himself, That Uncertain Feeling, The Wagons Roll at Night, Love Crazy, Shining Victory, World Premiere* (1941); *To Be or Not to Be, Remember Pearl Harbor, Crossroads, Enemy Agents Meet Ellery Queen, Berlin Correspondent, Desperate Journey, China Girl* (1942); *Tarzan Triumphs, They Came to Blow up America, Sweet Rosie O'Grady, Government Girl, The Song of Bernadette* (1943); *The Hitler Gang, It Happened Tomorrow, Summer Storm, House of Frankenstein* (1944); *A Royal Scandal, Men in Her Diary, She Went to the Races, The Dolly Sisters* (1945); *A Night in Casablanca, Night and Day, Faithful in My Fashion* (1946); *Mother Wore Tights* (1947); *If You Knew Susie, The Emperor Waltz, Give My Regards to Broadway* (1948); *Border Incident* (1949); *Father is a Bachelor* (1950); *On the Riv-*

iera (1951); *O. Henry's Full House, The World in His Arms* (1952); *Ma and Pa Kettle on Vacation, Stalag 17, Houdini, The Glenn Miller Story* (1953); *Living it Up, White Christmas, 3 Ring Circus* (1954); *Carolina Cannonball, Many Rivers to Cross, Spy Chasers* (1955); *The Wings of Eagles* (1957); *The Errand Boy, One, Two, Three* [voice] (1961); *Robin and the 7 Hoods, Kisses for My President* (1964); *36 Hours* (1965); *The Last of the Secret Agents?, The Fortune Cookie, Way . . . Way Out* (1966).

RUSSIA (former Soviet Union)

The American studio system was run by Jewish émigrés born in the Polish, Ukrainian or Lithuanian provinces of the Russian Empire, but when these figures gained success and power in Hollywood, they deliberately chose not to consider themselves 'Russian'. Instead, they preferred to create a global Americanised film culture that erased their original European ethnicities. In many cases, it was ironically left to non-Russian European émigré actors such as Greta Garbo★ and Marlene Dietrich★ to portray Russians on screen. While he was writing scripts at United Artists in 1925–6, Vladimir Nemirovich-Danchenko, the Russian director and co-founder of the Moscow Art Theatre, suggested building a Russian film studio in Hollywood. The idea failed to find support and only a small number of Russian film professionals were ever personally invited to Hollywood. The actress Alla Nazimova★ and the director Rouben Mamoulian, both discovered on the New York stage, were rare exceptions. The most famous Russian actor in French exile, Ivan Mosjoukine★, and the most famous Soviet film director, Sergei Eisenstein (who signed a contract with Paramount in 1930), were both resounding failures in Hollywood.

The majority of Russian actors, directors, set designers, cinematographers, technical advisers and producers who went to Hollywood did so not at the invitation of studio agents, but as a result of political exile following the 1917 Revolution. They came to a foreign film industry in order to change their professions and identities. Generals of the White Army such as Alexander Ikonnikov, Fyodor (Theodore) Lodyzhensky and Vyacheslav Savitsky worked for the studios as technical advisers or extras. Russian Cossacks even created a special team of Hollywood stunt riders, performing in a number of Westerns. Most Russian film figures came via Germany or

France, as was the case with the actor and then director Richard Boleslawski and the actress Anna Sten★. Many were already established figures in Russia, but they rarely managed to make a career in the USA. Only a few actors such as Akim Tamiroff★, Leonid Kinskey★, Mischa Auer★ and Vladimir Sokoloff★ were able to make a success of ethnic, though not necessarily Russian, character parts and supporting roles.

In its portrayal of Russian identity, Hollywood relied on cultural stereotypes previously established in literature, theatre and popular entertainment. The decorative style of Diaghilev's Ballets Russes in Paris, for example, not only influenced stage design and fashion, it also created an accepted pattern for the 'Russian style'. The novels of Dostoevsky and Tolstoy also helped construct the image of a national character full of dark passions and male neuroses. The psychological acting method of the Moscow Art Theatre contributed further to this powerful image of Slavic emotionalism and the mysterious 'Russian soul'. But the truth was that the tragic endings of Russian novels were often transformed into Hollywood happy ends. In *Love* (1927), for instance, Anna Karenina does not commit suicide, but instead marries her lover after the death of her husband.

At the beginning of the 1920s, Russians were depicted as wild children of nature and in *Cossacks* (1928), for example, they were thrown together with gypsies, Tartars and 'oriental Barbarians'. In films like *The Volga Boatman* (1926) and *The Tempest* (1928), the Russian Revolution was presented in somewhat idealised romantic stories that depicted the transformation of a hierarchical society into a 'democratic' one. By contrast, in the 1930s, *Ninotchka* (1939), with Vladimir Sokoloff★ in the cast, and *Comrade X* (1940), with Alexander Granach★, portrayed the Soviet Union more harshly as a state of terror.

During World War II, the military alliance with the Soviet Union gave rise to the production of pro-Russian propaganda films such as *Mission to Moscow* (1943), *Song of Russia* (1943) and *The North Star* (1943), in which Russian émigré actors participated. After the war, films such as *The Brothers Karamazov* (1958) and *War and Peace* (1956), among others, evoked a fascination with imperial splendour in a nostalgic vision of Old Russia. Much more common, however, were the cold war movies. Here, in order to embody the emerging political scenario of a dangerous nuclear

super-power, the former 'children of nature' were transformed into emotionless killing machines. *Red Dawn* (1984) presented the invasion of the USA in a highly dramatic way, while earlier *The Russians are Coming, the Russians are Coming* (1966) treated the same plot as comedy. Hollywood resorted to portraying Soviet Russia as a drab and gloomy world full of rigid and taciturn people, the actors' immobility contributing to the sense of traumatised repression.

The collapse of the Soviet Union has produced yet another kind of representation. The new Russians (often former Party officials or KGB officers) are often linked to international terrorism, or in different ways perverted through involvement with cocaine, child sex and sadism. In films like *Air Force One* (1997), the Bond movie *GoldenEye* (1995) and *The Saint* (1996), Russians are seen dealing with uranium, drugs or under-age prostitutes. These negative images are a final twist on the altogether modest success of Russians in Hollywood. OB

RYEN, Richard (Richard Anton Robert Felix) (1885–1965)

Respected modernist stage director Richard Révy appeared in several sound films before departing Nazi Germany for Switzerland in 1934. He emigrated to the USA in 1938, changed his surname to Ryen, and took low-paid bit parts as senior (due to his age) Axis officials in anti-Nazi films. His role as Major Strasser's aide in *Casablanca* exceptionally earned him $1,600, since the character was present alongside Conrad Veidt★ throughout. Ryen remained in Hollywood as a freelance writer after the war, but also undertook occasional stage work in Europe. RJK

FILMS: *Berlin Correspondent, Desperate Journey, Casablanca* (1942); *Chetniks – The Fighting Guerrillas, Mission to Moscow, Hitler's Madman, The Constant Nymph, First Comes Courage, Hostages, The Strange Death of Adolf Hitler, Gangway for Tomorrow, The Cross of Lorraine* (1943); *The Hitler Gang, Secrets of Scotland Yard, An American Romance* (1944); *A Royal Scandal, Salome, Where She Danced, Paris Underground, This Love of Ours* (1945); *Crack-Up* (1946); *A Foreign Affair* (1948).

SAGNIER, Ludivine (1979–)

Young French blonde beauty who first attracted attention in the all-star cast of François Ozon's *8 femmes* (2002). Her **419** semi-naked cavorting in Ozon's Provence-set *Swimming Pool* (2003), where she displayed voluptuous curves and a mischievous character, generated much international magazine coverage and prompted comparisons to the young Brigitte Bardot★. Her first foray into Hollywood was non-speaking, but high profile. She played Tinker Bell in the live-action *Peter Pan* as, in her own words, a 'funny, nutty fairy'. GV

FILM: *Peter Pan* (2003).

SAKALL, S. Z. 'Cuddles' (Jenö ['Eugene'] Gerö Szakall) (1882–1955)

Rotund Hungarian character actor who, following a lengthy screen career in Germany, fled Europe in 1939. Despite learning his first English-speaking roles phonetically, he went on to become an American citizen and audience favourite, playing a succession of lovable uncles and jolly immigrant shopkeepers. RJK

FILMS: *My Love Came Back, It's a Date, Florian, Spring Parade* (1940); *The Man Who Lost Himself, That Night in Rio, The Devil and Miss Jones, Ball of Fire* (1941); *Yankee Doodle Dandy, Broadway, Gentleman Jim, Casablanca, Seven Sweethearts* (1942); *Thank Your Lucky Stars, Wintertime, The Human Comedy* (1943); *Hollywood Canteen, Shine On, Harvest Moon* (1944); *Christmas in Connecticut, San Antonio, Wonder Man, The Dolly Sisters* (1945); *The Time, the Place, and the Girl, Two Guys from Milwaukee, Never Say Goodbye, Cinderella Jones* (1946); *Cynthia* (1947); *Romance on the High Seas, Whiplash, Embraceable You, April Showers* (1948); *My Dream is Yours, Oh, You Beautiful Doll, Look for the Silver Lining, In the Good Old Summertime, It's a Great Feeling* (1949); *The Daughter of Rosie O'Grady, Montana, Tea for Two* (1950); *Sugarfoot, Painting the Clouds with Sunshine, It's a Big Country, Lullaby of Broadway* (1951); *Small Town Girl* (1953); *The Student Prince* (1954).

SALVINI, Sandro (Alessandro Salvini) (1890–1955)

Italian theatre actor with important stage experience who performed in Italian silent films before emigrating to the USA, where he initially contributed to the script of *Monte Cristo* (1922). After one American film, he then acted in Italian-language Hollywood films such as *Il richiamo del cuore/ The Calling from the Heart* (1931) in the early 1930s before working as a dubbing director. CBu

FILM: *The Shepherd King* (1925).

SÁNCHEZ-GIJÓN, Aitana (Victoria Aragón) (1968–)

One of Spain's most respected actresses and former president of the Spanish Film Academy. Sánchez-Gijón made her American debut starring opposite Keanu Reeves in the romantic drama *A Walk in the Clouds*. In her second US film appearance, she played a sensual torch singer in the thriller *Love Walked In*. EU

FILMS: *A Walk in the Clouds* (1995); *Love Walked In* (1998).

SANDA, Dominique (Dominique Varaigne) (1948–)

Former French model, famous for her first role in Robert Bresson's *Une Femme douce/A Gentle Creature* (1969). She became an actress of note and appeared in films by leading European auteurs, including Visconti and Bertolucci. Her American debut was in John Huston's *The MacKintosh Man*. She went on to make several American films, but George C. Scott turned her down as his co-star in *The Formula* (1980), allegedly because of her 'unsatisfactory' English. VO

FILMS: *The MacKintosh Man* (1973); *Steppenwolf* (1974); *Damnation Alley* (1977); *Caboblanco* (1980).

SANDERS, George (1906–1972)

George Sanders described himself in the title of his 1960 memoirs as a 'professional cad' and the suggestion that he pragmatically accepted his perpetual typecasting as Hollywood's premier English debonair rake seems hard to dispute. The vague facts of Sanders' early life, as disclosed by their subject, only confirm the dominant public image of fecklessness and bored impatience. He was born in Russia but returned with his parents to Britain during the 1917 Revolution and ended up drifting through jobs in a Manchester textile mill and an Argentinian tobacco factory before a secretary at an advertising agency – the as-yet-undiscovered Greer Garson★ – suggested he try his hand at acting. After appearing in musical revues and radio, he made his debut on the legitimate stage in the early 1930s. The combination of his height, imposing forehead and a voice with the sensuous haughtiness of a cat's purr (an affinity later recognised by Disney in 1967 when they cast him as the voice of the tiger Sher Khan in their animated *The Jungle Book*) saw him quickly progress to become Noel Coward's★ understudy. He had briefly appeared in four British films by 1936 – most memorably as a bare-chested

George Sanders: Hollywood's 'professional cad'

god in *The Man Who Could Work Miracles* – before Twentieth Century-Fox bought out his contract and transported him directly to California in the same year.

From 1939 to 1942, Sanders was tried out as a leading man in the mould of Ronald Colman★ (whose widow he married in 1958) playing gentleman-sleuths in two B-picture series from RKO: first *The Saint*, from the popular books by Leslie Charteris, and then *The Falcon*. The air of ironic detachment and supercilious intelligence created by his studied diction saw him largely marked out for villainy in A-list pictures, however, and, especially with the onset of war, he was regularly seen as devious spies and arrogant Nazis.

Sanders' Hollywood career was not quite as one-dimensional as he resignedly liked to suggest. The director Albert Lewin approvingly perceived in his playfully sardonic composure the idealist hauteur of a nineteenth-century aesthete and cast him as such in three period-set adaptations: Somerset Maugham's Gaugin-inspired *The Moon and Sixpence*, Wilde's *The Picture of Dorian Gray* and Maupassant's *The Private Affairs of Bel Ami*. In each case, Sanders' facility for epigrammatic wit is mirrored by the tastes and fashions of the society around him. The same was also occasionally true in

certain modern-day settings, as with his uncompromisingly cynical theatre critic Addison DeWitt in *All about Eve* – for which he won an Academy Award – and his ruthless newspaper columnist in Fritz Lang's *While the City Sleeps*. JB

FILMS: *Lloyds of London* (1936); *Love is News, Slave Ship, Lancer Spy, The Lady Escapes* (1937); *International Settlement, Four Men and a Prayer* (1938); *Mr Moto's Last Warning, The Saint Strikes Back, Confessions of a Nazi Spy, The Saint in London, Nurse Edith Cavell, Allegheny Uprising* (1939); *The Saint's Double Trouble, The House of the Seven Gables, Rebecca, Green Hell, Foreign Correspondent, Bitter Sweet, The Son of Monte Cristo, So this is London, The Saint Takes Over* (1940); *The Saint in Palm Springs, Rage in Heaven, Man Hunt, The Gay Falcon, Sundown, A Date with the Falcon* (1941); *The Falcon Takes Over, Son of Fury, Tales of Manhattan, Quiet Please, Murder, The Moon and Sixpence, Her Cardboard Lover, The Falcon's Brother, The Black Swan* (1942); *This Land is Mine, Paris after Dark, They Came to Blow up America, Appointment in Berlin* (1943); *The Lodger, Action in Arabia, Summer Storm* (1944); *The Picture of Dorian Gray, The Strange Affair of Uncle Harry, Hangover Square* (1945); *A Scandal in Paris, The Strange Woman* (1946); *The Private Affairs of Bel Ami, The Ghost and Mrs Muir, Lured, Forever Amber* (1947); *Samson and Delilah, The Fan* (1949); *Treasure Island, All about Eve* (1950); *I Can Get it for You Wholesale, The Light Touch* (1951); *Ivanhoe, Assignment Paris* (1952); *Call Me Madam* (1953); *Witness to Murder, King Richard and the Crusaders* (1954); *Jupiter's Darling, The Big Tip-Off, Night Freight, The Scarlet Coat, Moonfleet, The King's Thief* (1955); *Never Say Goodbye, While the City Sleeps, Death of a Scoundrel, That Certain Feeling* (1956); *The Seventh Sin* (1957); *From the Earth to the Moon* (1958); *Solomon and Sheba, That Kind of Woman* (1959); *The Last Voyage* (1960); *In Search of the Castaways* (1962); *Cairo* (1963); *A Shot in the Dark* (1964); *Warning Shot, Good Times, The Jungle Book* [voice] (1967); *Thin Air, The Best House in London, The Candy Man* (1969); *The Kremlin Letter* (1970).

SANDS, Julian (1957–)

Appealing, blond English actor whose career was given a significant boost by his performance in Merchant-Ivory's *A Room with a View* (1986). Sands moved to Hollywood the following year and has subsequently appeared in both mainstream parts such as the title role in *Warlock* and independent productions like Wim Wenders' *The Million Dollar Hotel*. MW

FILMS: *The Doctor and the Devils* (1985); *Gothic* (1986); *Siesta* (1987); *Vibes* (1988); *Tennessee Nights, Warlock* (1989); *Impromptu, Arachnophobia* (1990); *Grand Isle* (1991); *Boxing Helena, Warlock: The Armageddon* (1993); *The Browning Version* (1994); *Leaving Las Vegas* (1995); *Never Ever* (1996); *One Night Stand, Long Time Since* (1997); *The Loss of Sexual Innocence* (1999); *Mercy, The Million Dollar Hotel, Timecode* (2000); *The Scoundrel's Wife* (2002); *Easy Six* (2003).

SAVAL, Dany (Danielle Nadine Suzanne Savalle) (1942–)

Blonde French comedy actress whose appearance as a French air hostess alongside Tony Curtis and Jerry Lewis in the vaudevillesque *Boeing Boeing* was typical of her comic style. VO

FILMS: *Moon Pilot* (1962); *Boeing Boeing* (1965).

SCACCHI, Greta (Greta Gracco) (1960–)

Anglo-Italian actress who despite being a versatile and subtle performer in various European productions remains typecast in a series of overtly sexualised roles by Hollywood. 'It seems', she rues, 'that I'm damned to be an adulteress.' Scacchi made her international breakthrough alongside Julie Christie★ in the Merchant-Ivory production *Heat and Dust* (1982). Her femme fatale roles in her American debut *Presumed Innocent* and in *Shattered* served to fix a limited conception of her image in the minds of both American producers and audiences – she was originally offered the Sharon Stone role in *Basic Instinct*. Scacchi's notorious willingness to undertake nude scenes was gently mocked in Robert Altman's industry satire *The Player*, where, against all expectations, she remained fully clothed throughout. Supporting roles in period costume dramas such as *Jefferson in Paris* and *Emma* have helped steer her in a new direction, but her profile has waned as a result. MF

FILMS: *Presumed Innocent* (1990); *Shattered, Fires Within* (1991); *The Player* (1992); *The Browning Version* (1994); *Jefferson in Paris* (1995); *Emma* (1996); *Bravo Randy* (1997); *Tom's Midnight Garden, Cotton Mary* (1999); *Festival in Cannes* (2001); *Beyond the Sea* (2004).

SCANDINAVIA

Hollywood actors with a Scandinavian background may be loosely divided into three categories: those who have been highly successful such as Greta Garbo★ and Ingrid Bergman★; those who have been relatively successful such as Nils Asther★ and Jean Hersholt★; and those who did not really make it at all such as Mai Zetterling★ and Tula Parma★ (Tuulikki Paananen). The impact of Garbo's and others' success has had a profound effect. On the one hand, it has signalled to aspiring European actors that Hollywood success is possible. On the other hand, it has also suggested to the American film industry that investing in Scandinavian 'quality' may be worthwhile.

For Hollywood, 'Scandinavian-ness' has consistently meant an identity based on a blond(e) and blue-eyed beauty with a touch of mystery and exoticism attached. Another potential component has been the alluring myth of Scandinavian femininity, with its candid attitude towards sexuality. From very early on, Scandinavian films depicted pretty, naked girls bathing in the sea and this contributed to an internationally held image of Scandinavian sinfulness. However, as the Swedish film historian Bengt Forslund has argued, mythology and appearance are not enough. Three further elements have also been necessary to attain success in the USA. First, a prospective Scandinavian Hollywood actor needs confidence and ambition – she or he needs to be a 'go-getter'. Second, they have to be a gifted and well-trained performer. Finally, it is also important for any actor to be seen – they have to have had at least one part in an internationally acknowledged film before any Hollywood appearance.

Scandinavian actors with a Hollywood career have either been noticed through their performances in prominent films – e.g. Garbo in Mauritz Stiller's *Gösta Berlings saga/The Legend of Gosta Berling* (1924) and Ingrid Bergman in *Intermezzo* (1936) – or they have been introduced to American studios by a well-known director, as in the cases of Lars Hanson★, who followed Victor Sjöström to Hollywood, and the many distinguished actors such as Max von Sydow★, Liv Ullman★ and Ingrid Thulin★ who have been introduced to international audiences by the films of Ingmar Bergman. In this context, it is worth noticing that among the Scandinavian performers in Hollywood, roughly two-thirds have been Swedish, with almost half of them affiliated to Bergman. Finnish, Danish and Norwegian actors such as Torben Meyer★, Taina Elg★ and Greta Nissen★ have made up a minority of the émigrés, as have internationally famed film directors native to these countries.

Signe Hasso★ and Viveca Lindfors★ are examples of talented and professional Scandinavian actors who, while never becoming huge stars, have nonetheless made a decent career in Hollywood. They both worked with established directors such as Cecil B. DeMille and Ernst Lubitsch (Signe Hasso) and Don Siegel and Sidney Pollack (Viveca Lindfors). But still, their personae were mainly created on the stage. Today, the era of glamorous screen goddesses is over. Among the younger generation of Scandinavian actors, perhaps only Lena Olin★ could still be categorised as a star. She and Stellan Skarsgård★ are the only contemporary Scandinavian actors continually offered leading character roles in international cinema.

During the heyday of the studio period, Hollywood also used a number of specially skilled Scandinavian actors such as the Finnish dancer Taina Elg or the Norwegian ice-skater Sonja Henie★, who made eight winter sports films after winning skating gold medals in three Olympic Games. Many other experienced performers did not make it to a successful career in Hollywood. Tula Parma was a popular star in Finland, as was Tutta Rolf★ in Sweden. Both made only one or two films in Hollywood – all failures. Nevertheless, these two actors are examples of individuals who stayed in the USA and made a good living either through marriage or a successful business career. One should also note the many Scandanvian émigrés such as the Finnish Carl von Haartman and the Danish Anders Randolf who arrived in Hollywood without any prior career in the performing arts. Von Haartman and Randolf were both soldiers; the former played a German officer in William Wellman's *Wings* (1927) and also supervised the film's flying sequences, while Randolf became one of the great villains of the silent era.

It is difficult to discern the underlying reason for the number of aborted Scandinavian careers in Hollywood, since most Scandinavian actors had a prominent career in their home countries before leaving for the USA. In rare cases, it is clear that a star like Mai Zetterling simply hated the place and its lifestyle and refused to work there. The English language may have also been an additional, invincible obstacle. Language is an actor's foremost instrument and the profession demands perfect mastering of idioms, nuances and intonation. Improvisation is out of question without any real linguistic proficiency and, as the quest for realism has constantly increased, the demand for the skilled use of spoken English has similarly risen.

Hollywood has sometimes used the foreignness of the Scandinavian accent as an asset in its own right, since it can fit into a gallery of pre-existing cultural stereotypes. Many Scandinavian actors, such as Max von Sydow, have played sinister characters such as spies, criminals or Nazi officers. Among younger actors, Peter Stormare★ is also a typical example of such typecasting. After appearing as a psychologically disturbed gangster in the Coen brothers' *Fargo* (1996), he briefly became Hollywood's pet psychopath. Lately though, he has moved away from the thriller towards comedy. This points to the interesting fact that the majority of films starring Scandinavian actors in Hollywood may be classified as either dramas or comedies, with the occasional action or spy film in between. Even if Garbo failed in her career as a comedienne, Ingrid Bergman and numerous others excelled in the genre. As many have observed, depicting the foreign as a threat, or as something merely humourous, has been a common strategy on the part of Hollywood film-makers when dealing with the representation of ethnic otherness. TS

SCHELL, Maria (Margarethe Schell) (1926–2005)
Born in Vienna, but brought up in Switzerland, to where her family fled after the Nazi annexation of Austria, Schell started out in Swiss films in the 1940s, but quickly established herself as one of the most popular female stars of 1950s German cinema. Most of her vehicles were lachrymose melodramas, in which the blonde, blue-eyed Schell portrayed tearful, long-suffering ingénues and housewives with great emotional pathos. Film offers from Britain (*The Magic Box* [1951], *The Heart of the Matter* [1954]), France (*Napoléon* [1955], *Gervaise* [1956]) and Italy (*Le notti bianche/White Nights* [1957]) gave her the opportunity to widen her range, and by the mid-1950s she had a busy and high-profile pan-European career that brought her to Hollywood's attention. Although essentially miscast, Schell convinced critics as an exceptionally sensual and non-sentimental Grushenka in Richard Brooks' adaptation of Dostoevsky's *The Brothers Karamazov*. She fared equally well as a blind woman in the prestige Western *The Hanging Tree* (co-starring Gary Cooper) and in the adaptation of Edna Ferber's epic *Cimarron*, where she played a frontier matriarch. Thereafter, Schell continued her career in Europe, only sporadically appearing in cameo parts in American films and television series such as *Kojak*. Schell's brother is the actor Maximilian Schell★. TB

FILMS: *The Brothers Karamazov* (1958); *The Hanging Tree* (1959); *Cimarron* (1960).

SCHELL, Maximilian (1930–)

The younger brother of Maria Schell★, Maximilian established himself as a stage (and to a lesser extent film) actor in the 1950s; he was praised as the best German Hamlet of his generation. Success on Broadway in the late 1950s brought him to Hollywood. Good-looking, but with an intensely intellectual, physically awkward demeanour, Schell initially portrayed highly strung, often stereotypically 'German' characters, veering between fanatical determination and nervous insecurity. His role as a manipulative German defence attorney in *Judgment at Nuremberg* won him an Academy Award for Best Supporting Actor. He was nominated again in the same category for *The Man in the Glass Booth* and *Julia*. Despite these early successes, Schell's Hollywood acting career has been erratic, though he has managed to balance stage and film work in the USA and in Europe. He successfully branched out into directing from the late 1960s (his most acclaimed film being the documentary *Marlene* [1984]). The older Schell displayed a more subdued, melancholy style, and found a niche in Hollywood as a benign, eccentric or sinister, but decidedly 'European', character. TB

FILMS: *The Young Lions* (1958); *Judgment at Nuremberg* (1961); *Five Finger Exercise, The Reluctant Saint* (1962); *Topkapi* (1964); *Return from the Ashes* (1965); *The Deadly Affair* (1966); *Counterpoint* (1968); *Krakatoa, East of Java* (1969); *The Man in the Glass Booth* (1975); *St Ives* (1976); *Julia, A Bridge Too Far* (1977); *Avalanche Express, The Black Hole, Players* (1979); *The Chosen* (1981); *The Assisi Underground* (1985); *The Rose Garden* (1989); *The Freshman* (1990); *A Far Off Place* (1993); *Little Odessa* (1994); *Telling Lies in America, The Eighteenth Angel* (1997); *Vampires, Left Luggage, Deep Impact* (1998); *Festival in Cannes* (2001).

SCHILDKRAUT, Joseph (1896–1964)

The son of eminent stage and screen actor Rudolph Schildkraut★, Joseph, born in Vienna, gave his theatre debut in 1913 under Max Reinhardt in Berlin, and appeared in numerous German and Austrian films from 1915. On the New York stage from 1920, Schildkraut moved to Hollywood in 1924. In the following decades, he conducted successful careers on both stage and screen. A strikingly beautiful, almost androgynous, actor in his youth, Schildkraut became a matinée idol in the 1920s, playing romantic leads for directors such as D. W. Griffith and Cecil B. DeMille. His star appeal faded by the end of the decade, and for the next thirty years he settled into supporting roles, frequently portraying dandy-like villains and charming rogues, often of French origin. In 1937, he won an Academy Award for Best Supporting Actor as Dreyfus in *The Life of Emile Zola*, and he proved a veritable scene-stealer as a foppish gigolo in Ernst Lubitsch's *The Shop around the Corner*. Schildkraut's popularity peaked once again in the 1950s, when he hosted his own show on American television, and when he gave the definitive portrayal of Otto Frank in the stage and screen versions of *The Diary of Anne Frank*. TB

FILMS: *Orphans of the Storm* (1921); *The Song of Love* (1923); *The Road to Yesterday* (1925); *Shipwrecked, Meet the Prince, Young April* (1926); *The King of Kings, The Heart Thief, His Dog, The Forbidden Woman* (1927); *The Blue Danube, Tenth Avenue* (1928); *Show Boat, Mississippi Gambler* (1929); *Night Ride, Cock o' the Walk* (1930); *Viva Villa!, Cleopatra, Sisters under the Skin* (1934); *Hollywood Extra Girl, The Crusades* (1935); *The Garden of Allah* (1936); *Souls at Sea, The Life of Emile Zola, Slave Ship, Lancer Spy, Lady Behave* (1937); *The Baroness and the Butler, Marie Antoinette, Suez* (1938); *Idiot's Delight, The Three Musketeers, The Man in the Iron Mask, The Rains Came, Mr Moto Takes a Vacation, Pack up Your Troubles, Lady of the Tropics* (1939); *The Shop around the Corner, Rangers of Fortune, Phantom Raiders, Meet the Wildcat* (1940); *The Parson of Panamint* (1941); *The Tell-Tale Heart* (1942); *Flame of Barbary Coast, The Cheaters* (1945); *Monsieur Beaucaire, The Plainsman and the Lady* (1946); *Northwest Outpost* (1947); *The Gallant Legion, Old Los Angeles* (1948); *The Diary of Anne Frank* (1959); *The King of the Roaring 20's – The Story of Arnold Rothstein* (1961); *The Greatest Story Ever Told* (1965).

SCHILDKRAUT, Rudolph (Rudolf Schildkraut) (1862–1930)

Stage actor who first emigrated to the USA in 1911 after the Deutsches Nationaltheater demanded he convert from Judaism to Christianity. Schildkraut subsequently returned to Europe and starred with his son Joseph Schildkraut★ in several prestigious German and Austrian films during the mid-1910s. He resettled permanently in New York, where he headed the Yiddish Art Theatre. Schildkraut also played a number of sympathetic leads in films about Jewish and other recent immigrants to the USA. He was a Dutch patriarch in his lone sound feature, *Christina*. RJK

FILMS: *His People* (1925); *Young April, Pals in Paradise* (1926); *The King of Kings, The Country Doctor, A Harp in Hock, Turkish Delight, The Main Event* (1927); *A Ship Comes In* (1928); *Christina* (1929).

SCHNEIDER, Romy (Rosemarie Magdalena Albach-Retty) (1938–1982)

Romy Schneider first attracted US attention with a composite version of her *Sissi* trilogy (1955–7), launched in the USA as *Forever My Love* (1962). Part *Heimatfilm*, part costume drama, the trilogy featured Schneider as Princess Elisabeth of Bavaria ('Sissi'), later Empress of Austria. 'Sissi' captured audiences across Europe; but in 1958, Schneider (the daughter of well-known star Magda Schneider) fled German-language cinema to relaunch herself as a 'serious' actress. Theatre and film work with Luchino Visconti brought acclaim, as did Schneider's role in Orson Welles' *The Trial/Le Procès* (1962). Subsequent European roles emphasised Schneider's break with 'Sissi''s saccharine image, especially in France, where she began a long and successful second career. Increasingly, her characters were dramatically mature and sexually free-wheeling in films such as *La Piscine/The Swimming Pool* (1969) and *Max et les ferrailleurs/Max and the Scrapmongers* (1971). To many German fans' dismay, Schneider also countered *Sissi*'s celebration of an imperial past with films exploring the darker aspects of German history, including her first Hollywood film shot in the USA, *The Cardinal* – a tale of Catholic intrigue and political reaction in the USA and Nazi Austria. Hollywood also attempted to develop a new comedy persona for Schneider, alongside Jack Lemmon in the bedroom farce *Good Neighbour Sam*, and Peter Sellers in *What's New, Pussycat*. None of Schneider's American work, however, matched the star status she had attained in France, where she was posthumously voted 'most popular actress' in 2000, in equal parts for her beauty, her tragic private life and her powerful performances in films such as the war drama *La Passante du Sans-Souci/The Passerby* (1982), her final appearance before her untimely death. EC

FILMS: *The Victors, The Cardinal, Good Neighbour Sam* (1963); *What's New, Pussycat* (1964); *10:30 P.M. Summer* (1966); *My Lover, My Son* (1970); *Bloodline* (1979).

SCHUMM, Hans (Hans Josef Schumm) (1896–1990)

Commanding, gravelly voiced actor who journeyed to the USA in 1928 to work in German-language theatre. Schumm played bit parts as sneering German officers after Hitler came to power and especially stood out as the Axis villain 'The Mask' in the hit Republic serial *Spy Smasher*. Hoping for more sympathetic casting, he renamed himself Andre Pola from 1948, but only received light-hearted roles in a couple of 'Three Stooges' shorts. In 1955, Schumm returned to Germany, where he portrayed authority figures in films, including several American co-productions, before retiring to California in the 1970s. RJK

FILMS: *The Song of Songs* (1933); *One Night of Love* (1934); *Folies Bergère de Paris* (1935); *The Invisible Ray, Revolt of the Zombies* (1936); *The Baroness and the Plumber* (1938); *Confessions of a Nazi Spy, Thunder Afloat, Espionage Agent, Hitler – Beast of Berlin, The Amazing Mr Williams* (1939); *Scandal Sheet, Calling Philo Vance, British Intelligence, Escape to Glory, Four Sons, Mystery Sea Raider, The Man I Married, Escape, Moon over Burma* (1940); *So Ends Our Night, They Dare Not Love, Underground, A Yank in the R.A.F., Sea Raiders* [serial], *Down in San Diego* (1941); *All through the Night, The Lady has Plans, To Be or Not to Be, Spy Smasher* [serial], *Atlantic Convoy, Invisible Agent, Pardon My Sarong, Berlin Correspondent, Desperate Journey, Foreign Agent, Destination Unknown, The Devil with Hitler, The Navy Comes Through, Once upon a Honeymoon, Underground Agent* (1942); *Margin for Error, Chetniks – The Fighting Guerrillas, They Got Me Covered, Assignment in Brittany, The Moon is Down, This Land is Mine, Mission to Moscow, Hitler's Madman, Action in the North Atlantic, Bomber's Moon, Above Suspicion, The Strange Death of Adolf Hitler, Sahara* (1943); *Passport to Destiny, Up in Arms, A Voice in the Wind, Uncertain Glory, Resisting Enemy Interrogation* (1944); *Son of Lassie, Escape in the Desert* (1945); *Cloak and Dagger* (1946); *The Beginning or the End, Golden Earrings, Desire Me* [voice] (1947); *Casbah, Billie Gets Her Man, Smugglers' Cove, Act of Violence* [voice] (1948); *The Lovable Cheat, Fuelin' Around, Waiting in the Lurch* (1949); *Target Unknown, I was a Communist for the FBI* (1951); *The Stars are Singing, No Escape* (1953); *The Fire Chaser* (1954); *Hot Stuff* (1956); *I Aim at the Stars* (1960); *Question 7* (1961); *The Bashful Elephant* (1962); *Captain Sindbad* (1963).

SCHÜNZEL, Reinhold (1886–1954)

German actor-turned-director who received perhaps the chilliest welcome of any émigré upon arriving in Hollywood in September 1937. The half-Jewish Schünzel had remained in Germany after 1933 and with the aid of a special work permit achieved his greatest successes: *Viktor und Viktoria/ Viktor and Viktoria* (1933) and *Amphitryon* (1935). He left Germany with an MGM contract, after rejecting a Universal contract in 1935 as 'insubstantial', when his 1937 Ruritanian comedy *Land der Liebe/ Land of Love* met with Goebbels' disapproval. Instead of being seen as a genuine refugee, he was harangued for months in the émigré press as a dismissed collaborator. The anti-Schünzel campaign dissipated only after his efforts to aid colleagues while in Germany became known. He was dumped by MGM after directing three pictures (*Rich Man, Poor Girl, Ice Follies of 1939* [both 1938] and *Balalaika* [1939]), because Louis B. Mayer considered his demands for artistic freedom incompatible with the studio production system. Schünzel secured just one more directing job, *New Wine* (1941). In 1943, in order to generate income, Schünzel returned to acting after a gap of twelve years. He played Gestapo officers in films like *Notorious*, but never became a bankable name. Schünzel returned to Germany in 1949 hoping to resume his directing career, but instead ended up commuting between acting jobs in the USA and Germany until his death. RJK

FILMS: *Hangmen Also Die, Hostages, First Comes Courage* (1943); *The Hitler Gang* (1944); *The Man in Half Moon Street, Dragonwyck, Notorious, The Plainsman and the Lady* (1946); *Golden Earrings* (1947); *Berlin Express, The Vicious Circle* (1948); *Washington Story* (1952).

SCHWARZENEGGER, Arnold (1947–)

How does a muscle-bound Austrian with a thick accent, an unpronounceable name and an acting style that might generously be described as wooden become one of the biggest movie stars in Hollywood and, perhaps stranger still, one of Hollywood's chief ambassadors to the world? It seems, in fact, that much of Arnold Schwarzenegger's career trajectory has been accidental. While he did come to the USA in search of fame and fortune after establishing himself as the leading European bodybuilder, the avenue through which he pursued this dream was bodybuilding, not acting. Despite an early misadventure in cinema in the form of the unintentionally hilarious *Hercules in New York*, in which his voice was deemed unusable and re-dubbed, Schwarzenegger's acting career got off to a surprisingly good start when he was awarded a Golden Globe for Best Newcomer for his dramatic performance in *Stay Hungry*. Schwarzenegger's real breakthrough, however, came a year later when he played himself in the bodybuilding documentary *Pumping Iron*. He shone as the wide-grinning prankster who played head games with the dumb but lovable Lou Ferrigno (later television's *Incredible Hulk*, a role for which Schwarzenegger reportedly considered himself 'too pretty' and for which the show's producers reputedly considered him 'too short' at six-foot-two). Schwarzenegger, already the consummate self-promoter, had actually delayed his departure from bodybuilding – where he had already won every significant title multiple times – in order to shoot *Pumping Iron*. His retirement at the end of the shoot forced him to find a new livelihood and his now proven screen charisma therefore made the transition to cinema a logical choice.

Despite the kudos he received for his performance in *Stay Hungry*, his celebrity in narrative films came only after he turned away from the more emotionally subtle performance style that had won him such early attention. His fame spread in the early 1980s, first as a sword-wielding hero in the two *Conan* films, and then as the eponymous antagonist of *The Terminator*. While his subsequent film, *Red Sonja*, returned him to *Conan* territory, the rest of his output in the 1980s spanned the fairly tiny gap between straight action-hero roles (*Commando, Red Heat*) and science-fiction action-hero roles (*Predator, The Running Man, Total Recall*). By the end of the decade, Arnold Schwarzenegger was one of the top box-office draws in the world.

Unlike the case with the more typically American Sylvester Stallone and Bruce Willis, the two other pre-eminent 1980s action heroes with whom he launched the Planet Hollywood restaurant chain in 1991, Schwarzenegger's status as an all-American hero seemed far from natural. The transformation of his on-screen persona between the two *Terminator* films is telling of the general pattern of his career. In the first installation, his foreignness was so alienating that he had to be cast as a killer robot from the future (a role that he cannily chose when director James Cameron gave him the choice between the evil Terminator or the hero, Kyle Reese), while in his reincarnation as the T-101 in *Terminator 2: Judgment Day*, he became a loving, if somewhat awkward, father figure to the young John Conner. Schwarzenegger had himself become a father between the two films and had made attempts, sometimes more successful than others, at softening his star persona with paternal comedies like *Twins* and *Kindergarten Cop*. Throughout the 1990s, he continued to alternate between reprises of his now classic action hero (*Eraser*, *End of Days*) and goofy comedy roles that played off that persona (*Junior*, *Jingle All the Way*). Few of these films were highly successful – the remarkable exception was *True Lies*, again directed by Cameron – and a number were substantial failures. Despite this, his earnings remained considerable. He earned $25 million for a brief appearance as Mr Freeze in the commercially disappointing *Batman & Robin*.

Despite the vagaries of Schwarzenegger's performance at the box office, he does remain a genuine cultural phenomenon that has inspired endless critical commentary and comic parody. Furthermore, Schwarzenegger has proved a canny businessman from the start, being able to turn his early career earnings into a small fortune through investments in real estate and a mail-order fitness business. He has also shown a fondness for Republican politics in his adoptive homeland, where he became a citizen in 1983. He served as the Chairman of the President's Council of Physical Fitness and Sport under George Bush senior and flirted with a gubernatorial bid in California on more than one occasion before finally running successfully in the 2003 recall election. While certainly high profile, his political career has also been marked by a number of ambivalences and contradictions. These include his entry, through marriage to Maria Shriver, into the left-leaning Kennedy clan. Perhaps, then, it is precisely these contradictions that have afforded Schwarzenegger his seemingly inexplicable success. Markedly foreign and at the same time a classic American rags-to-riches success, fiscally conservative but a social liberal, Arnold Schwarzenegger has become one of the more privileged signifiers of Hollywood-style free-market capitalism in an era of cultural and commercial globalisation. RBe

FILMS: *Hercules in New York* (1970); *The Long Goodbye* (1973); *Stay Hungry* (1976); *Pumping Iron* (1977); *The Villain, Scavenger Hunt* (1979); *Conan the Barbarian* (1982); *Conan the Destroyer, The Terminator* (1984); *Red Sonja, Commando* (1985); *Raw Deal* (1986); *Predator, The Running Man* (1987); *Red Heat, Twins* (1988); *Total Recall, Kindergarten Cop* (1990); *Terminator 2: Judgment Day* (1991); *Last Action Hero* (1993); *True Lies, Junior* (1994); *Eraser, Jingle All the Way, T2 3-D: Battle across Time* (1996); *Batman & Robin* (1997); *End of Days* (1999); *The 6th Day* (2000); *Dr Doolittle 2* [voice] (2001); *Collateral Damage* (2002); *The Rundown, Terminator 3: Rise of the Machines* (2003); *Around the World in 80 Days* (2004).

SCHWEIGER, Til (Tilman Valentin Schweiger) (1963–)

German, blue-eyed, mousy-haired and chisel-featured former soap opera heart-throb whose leading roles in *Der bewegte Mann/ The Most Desired Man* (1994) and *Der grosse Bagarozy/ The Devil and Ms D* (1999) have helped secure his place as the leading male star of post-Berlin Wall German cinema. Frequently dubbed 'the German Tom Cruise', Schweiger employs a primarily physical mode of acting that breaks with German theatrical traditions and clearly draws on Hollywood performance styles. Like Cruise, he has a screen persona that combines machismo with sensitivity. Working in Hollywood always seems to have featured high on Schweiger's agenda and following his 1995 celebrity marriage to American model Dana Carlsen, the actor relocated to Malibu and began to take supporting roles in Hollywood action pictures and sex comedies. He has simultaneously maintained his German career and has now branched out into directing and producing in his native country. Anxious to avoid Hollywood typecasting as a 'German bad guy', Schweiger famously turned down playing the soldier who shoots Tom Hanks in *Saving Private Ryan* (1998), but he clearly remains determined to develop a career from a transcontinental platform. RJK

FILMS: *The Replacement Killers, Judas Kiss* (1998); *SLC Punk!* (1999); *Magicians* (2000); *Driven, Investigating Sex* (2001); *Sea Devils* (2002); *Lara Croft Tomb Raider: Cradle of Life, In Enemy Hands* (2003); *King Arthur* (2004).

SCHYGULLA, Hanna (1943–)

Hanna Schygulla's work for the American film industry in the mid-1980s constitutes a brief interlude in a career notable for her collaboration with numerous European auteurs, including Wenders, Schlöndorff, von Trotta, Scola, Godard, Saura and Wajda. The one real star to emerge from the New German Cinema of the 1970s and 1980s, Schygulla garnered international acclaim, particularly in the USA, for two of the last films she made with Rainer **427**

Werner Fassbinder, *Die Ehe der Maria Braun/The Marriage of Maria Braun* (1978) – for which she received an Oscar nomination – and *Lili Marleen* (1980). By 1985, her star status was such that Schygulla could appear on the front cover of *Time*, but while the magazine's critic Richard Corliss celebrated her iconic potential – 'fiery and icy, solid and sexy, Schygulla embodies the new European woman' – this was scarcely the image sustained by her subsequent American work. Whether marooned in the hijacked TWA plane in the action thriller *The Delta Force* or submerged in the star-studded casts of the television biopics of *Peter the Great* (1985) and *Barnum* (1986), Schygulla had little opportunity to substantiate *Time*'s description of her as 'Europe's most exciting actress'. Her one starring role was in *Forever, Lulu*, a quirky black comedy about a suicidal would-be novelist who accidentally gets involved in a mystery that changes her life. After the television film *Casanova* (1987), where, along with Faye Dunaway, Sylvia Kristel, Ornella Muti★ and Sophie Ward★, she features as one of the eponymous hero's many conquests, Schygulla went back to Europe, returning to the USA only once more for a supporting role in Kenneth Branagh's★ attempted recreation of the film noir, *Dead Again*. RBu

FILMS: *The Delta Force* (1986); *Forever, Lulu* (1987); *Dead Again* (1991).

SCOFIELD, Paul (David Paul Scofield) (1922–)
Widely regarded as the greatest British stage actor of his generation, Paul Scofield has made relatively few American films despite being fêted by American studios after his Academy Award for his portrayal of Thomas More in the US-funded *A Man for All Seasons*. There is a predictable consistency to the projects he has been offered: prestigious theatrical source material (*The Crucible*) and/or New England patrician characters (*Quiz Show*). JB

FILMS: *That Lady* (1955); *The Train* (1965); *A Man for All Seasons* (1966); *Scorpio, A Delicate Balance* (1973); *Quiz Show* (1994); *The Crucible* (1996).

SCOTT, Janette (1938–)
Daughter of fellow British actress Thora Hird who pursued a moderately successful UK film career that included a small number of US-funded productions. Scott shot two films in Hollywood, including *Crack in the World*, in which she had a leading role opposite Dana Andrews. MHu

FILMS: *No Highway* (1951); *Helen of Troy* (1955); *The Devil's Disciple* (1959); *Siege of the Saxons, The Old Dark House* (1963); *Crack in the World, Bikini Paradise* (1965).

SCOTT THOMAS, Kristin (1960–)
Kristin Scott Thomas has built up a reputation for playing aristocratic 'English roses' who reveal a suppressed passionate side to their somewhat chilly personalities. With her chiselled cheekbones, refined looks and cut-glass accent, she has played a number of upper-class and reserved characters such as Fiona in *Four Weddings and a Funeral* (1994) – for which she won a BAFTA as Best Supporting Actress – and Fiona in Roman Polanski's *Bitter Moon*. Yet she is far from being stereotypically 'British' in real life: she lives in France, has a French husband and has starred in a number of French films such as *Petites coupures* (2003).

Scott Thomas' first major film role was as a spoilt French girl opposite Prince in his financially and critically disastrous folly, *Under the Cherry Moon*. It was not until 1988 that she featured in a British film as the privileged and learned Brenda Last in an adaptation of Evelyn Waugh's *A Handful of Dust*. She briefly appeared as an espionage agent in the Tom Cruise/Brian De Palma blockbuster *Mission: Impossible*, but it was in Anthony Minghella's lavish, award-winning *The English Patient* that she really caught the public's eye. Here, she played another decorous, very English role as the married lover of the Hungarian spy Count Laszlo de Almásy (Ralph Fiennes★). The film brought Scott Thomas considerable acclaim, but she has remained wary of Hollywood's obsession with glamour and fashion. In her subsequent American films – opposite Robert Redford in *The Horse Whisperer* and opposite Harrison Ford in *Random Hearts* – she has continued to mix aloofness with more romantic undertones. She was cast as an upper-class Englishwoman yet again in *Gosford Park*. JS

FILMS: *Under the Cherry Moon* (1986); *Bitter Moon* (1992); *Richard III, Angels & Insects, The Pompatus of Love* (1995); *Mission: Impossible, The English Patient* (1996); *Souvenir, The Horse Whisperer* (1998); *Random Hearts* (1999); *Up at the Villa* (2000); *Life as a House, Gosford Park* (2001).

SELLARS, Elizabeth (1923–)
British film actress who was frequently cast as an aristocrat before and after her major Hollywood appearances in the mid-1950s. Sellars' feline, triangular face radiated intelli-

gence and she continued to appear in a number of US-financed films and co-productions shot in Europe. TJ

FILMS: *The Barefoot Contessa, Desirée* (1954); *Prince of Players* (1955); *The Man in the Sky* (1957); *The Day They Robbed the Bank of England* (1960); *55 Days at Peking* (1963); *The Chalk Garden* (1964); *The Hireling* (1973).

SELLERS, Peter (Richard Henry Sellers) (1925–1980)
Sellers made his name in British radio's satirical *The Goon Show*, in which he played an assortment of crazy characters. This penchant for multiple characterisation fed directly into his film career and subsequent perceptions of it.

After a number of small film roles, Sellers attracted widespread critical acclaim for his performances in *The Mouse that Roared* and *I'm Alright Jack* (both 1959). His first major Hollywood part was the role for which he would become most remembered: the incompetent Inspector Clouseau in the *Pink Panther* series. While Sellers was not supposed to be the main attraction of the original film, he stole the show and went on to play the character in four more *Panther* films. This included a posthumous appearance in *The Trail of the Pink Panther* that controversially pasted together earlier out-takes with a simulacra of the actor.

Sellers suffered from health problems and had to pull out of Billy Wilder's *Kiss Me, Stupid* (1964) due to a heart attack. There was also much publicised friction between director and star. Despite this setback, he went on to enjoy a successful career in the 1960s, with appearances in such comedies as *What's New, Pussycat, The Party* and *I Love You, Alice B. Toklas!*. Sellers had an undeniable talent for playing straight-faced, clumsy characters whose blend of irreverence and slapstick was perfectly suited to the times. His popularity began to wane in the 1970s, however, perhaps due to a certain amount of overfamiliarity. Regrettably, a man with the ability to play multiple characters had seemingly become reduced to one formulaic type.

Clouseau certainly proved to be a safe haven for Sellers. It enabled him to remain in the public eye long enough to star in Hal Ashby's poignant comedy *Being There*. It was one of the best roles of his career, and a part he was desperate to secure. By playing a simple gardener who is mistaken for a guru, Sellers took his expressionless mien to new extremes. His character became a virtual cipher only 'constructed' through the projections of others. Though he was ill when he played the role, Sellers managed to combine pathos with comedy in his performance, reminding viewers that he was a virtuoso performer who could portray nothingness, as well as lunacy. JS

FILMS: *The Black Rose* [voice] (1950); *The Man Who Never Was* [voice] (1956); *tom thumb* (1958); *The Mouse that Roared* (1959); *The Millionairess* (1960); *Lolita, The Road to Hong Kong, The Dock Brief* (1962); *Dr Strangelove or: How I Learned to Stop Worrying and Love the Bomb, The Pink Panther, The World of Henry Orient, A Shot in the Dark* (1964); *What's New, Pussycat* (1965); *The Wrong Box, After the Fox* (1966); *Casino Royale, Woman Times Seven, The Bobo* (1967); *The Party, I Love You, Alice B. Toklas!* (1968); *The Magic Christian* (1969); *There's a Girl in My Soup* (1970); *Where Does it Hurt?* (1972); *Murder by Death, The Pink Panther Strikes Again* (1976); *Revenge of the Pink Panther* (1978); *The Prisoner of Zenda, Being There* (1979); *The Fiendish Plot of Dr Fu Manchu* (1980); *Trail of the Pink Panther* (1982).

SELWART, Tonio (Antonio Franz Theus Selmair-Selwart) (1896–2002)
Bavarian theatre actor and director who became a permanent New York resident and US citizen after Broadway success in Lawrence Langner and Armina Marshall's *The Pursuit of Happiness* in 1930. Selwart played villainous roles in anti-Nazi films after the USA entered World War II such as the part of the Gestapo chief in Fritz Lang's *Hangmen Also Die*. A regular in CBS and NBC television plays from the late 1940s until the 1960s, he also appeared in several American-Italian co-productions shot in Europe. RJK

FILMS: *Hangmen Also Die, Edge of Darkness, The North Star, The Cross of Lorraine* (1943); *Tampico, The Hitler Gang, Wilson, Strange Affair* (1944); *Unconquered* (1947); *My Favorite Spy* (1951); *The Barefoot Contessa* (1954); *Helen of Troy, Congo Crossing* (1956); *The Naked Maja* (1959); *5 Branded Women* (1960); *Romanoff and Juliet* (1961); *The Reluctant Saint* (1962); *Anzio* (1968).

ŠERBEDŽIJA, Rade (1946–)
Šerbedžija is a Yugoslav diasporic actor whose increasingly high-profile career is split between Hollywood, Europe and the cinema of the Yugoslav successor states. He was born to an ethnically mixed family in the Croatian part of Yugoslavia and from the early 1970s onwards, in conjunction with a high-profile theatre career, he established him- **429**

self as a leading Yugoslav film actor. He has appeared in over fifty feature films by directors such as Vatroslav Mimica and Dušan Makavejev and now enjoys the reputation of being a versatile and handsome performer who, depending on the role, can come across as intelligent, shrewd or macho.

Šerbedžija disapproved of the growing nationalism in Yugoslavia and emigrated in 1992. His early years in exile were spent in London, where he enjoyed the support of Vanessa Redgrave★ and appeared on stage in Corin Redgrave's★ 1994 staging of *Brecht in Hollywood*. Gradually learning English, he was cast in roles of heavily accented East Europeans in films made in the UK (Nicolas Roeg's *Two Deaths* [1995]) and New Zealand (Gregor Nicholas' *Broken English* [1997]). He also had a number of other important supporting roles in European cinema.

Šerbedžija's Hollywood career started in the mid-1990s. He had leads in low-profile films, where he played a Czech intellectual in love with Gina Gershon in Prague (*Prague Duet*) and a Polish husband to Lena Olin★ in a small Midwest town (*Polish Wedding*). His real Hollywood breakthrough, however, has been as a character actor. He soon became a favourite for all sorts of variations on the villainous crook with an articulate accent, drunkard's voice and oily grey hair. Despite his 'unpronounceable' name – he has also been credited as Sherbedgia and Serbegia – he has become a favourite for criminal roles such as the suspicious former Eastern bloc entrepreneur Ivan Tretiak in Phillip Noyce's *The Saint* and Boris The Blade in Guy Ritchie's *Snatch*. DI

FILMS: *Prague Duet, The Saint* (1997); *Mighty Joe Young, Polish Wedding* (1998); *Stigmata, Eyes Wide Shut* (1999); *Mission: Impossible II, Space Cowboys, Snatch* (2000); *The Quiet American* (2002); *The Keeper: The Legend of Omar Khayyam* (2004).

SERNA, Assumpta (1957–)

Through her work with leading contemporary Spanish directors such as Bigas Luna and Pedro Almodóvar – she played the murderous seductress in *Matador* (1986) – Serna's screen image has combined an alluring sexuality with assertive self-expression. The dark-haired Spaniard is multilingual and has combined relatively undistinguished American screen work with various appearances in European film and television. AP

FILMS: *Wild Orchid* (1990); *Chain of Desire* (1992); *Hidden Assassin* (1994); *The Craft* (1996); *Bullfighter* (2000); *The Journeyman* (2001).

SERNAS, Jacques (1925–)

Lithuanian-born Jacques Sernas (sometimes credited as Jack Sernas) came to Paris at a young age, but mostly lived and worked in Italy. His sporadic Hollywood roles include Paris in the American-Italian historical epic *Helen of Troy* and Captain Guy Bertrand in the Vietnam war film *Jump into Hell*. TH

FILMS: *Jump into Hell* (1955); *Helen of Troy* (1956); *55 Days at Peking* (1963); *Midas Run* (1969); *Superfly T.N.T.* (1973).

SEYMOUR, Jane (Joyce Penelope Wilhelmina Frankenberg) (1951–)

Despite being adored by international television audiences for her middle-aged domestic beauty in *Dr Quinn, Medicine Woman*, the beautiful Seymour has largely failed to translate this fame into success on the big screen. She initially came to Hollywood's attention after scantily clad British screen appearances in *Live and Let Die* and *Sinbad and the Eye of the Tiger* (1977). Following parts in American television's *Battlestar Galactica* and its 1978 theatrical version, Seymour was cast alongside Christopher Reeve in the bizarre romance-fantasy *Somewhere in Time*. The film was a modest success, but it was four years before American cinema audiences saw her again as Tom Selleck's love interest in *Lassiter*. Seymour's tenuous status as a box-office property waned following its failure. She has since carved out a significant niche in numerous American television films and big-budget mini-series, where she often takes additional high-profile production credits. MF

FILMS: *Live and Let Die* (1973); *Battlestar Galactica* (1978); *Somewhere in Time, Oh, Heavenly Dog* (1980); *Lassiter* (1984); *Head Office* (1986); *Keys to Freedom* (1988); *Quest for Camelot* [voice], *New Swiss Family Robinson* (1998).

SEYRIG, Delphine (Delphine Claire Beltiane Seyrig) (1932–1990)

Quintessential European art-cinema star who spent seven years in New York and studied acting under Lee Strasberg. Among her many English-language films, only one was actually American: her very first film, *Pull My Daisy*, an independent black-and-white short written by Jack Kerouac and co-directed by photographer Robert Frank. VO

FILM: *Pull My Daisy* (1958).

SHAW, Fiona (1958–)

Although she is best known for her collaborative theatrical work with the stage director Deborah Warner, this Irish-born actress has also made a screen livelihood largely out of playing repressed spinsters. RB

FILMS: *Mountains of the Moon, 3 Men and a Little Lady* (1990); *Super Mario Bros, Undercover Blues* (1993); *Anna Karenina, The Butcher Boy* (1997); *The Avengers* (1998); *Harry Potter and the Philosopher's Stone* (2001); *Harry Potter and the Chamber of Secrets* (2002); *Harry Potter and the Prisoner of Azkaban* (2004).

SHAW, Robert (1927–1978)

Swarthy and athletic British stage actor who like his misfit RADA classmate Laurence Harvey★ took many years to break away from lowly spear-carrier roles. Following the short-lived television series *The Buccaneer* (1956), modelled on Burt Lancaster's contemporaneous swashbuckling pirate films, Shaw was launched by the émigré American producer Phillip Yordan as a viable leading man for American audiences in two European-shot productions: the war picture *Battle of the Bulge* and the Western *Custer of the West*. The films were out of step with current box-office tastes and despite earning a Best Supporting Actor Academy Award nomination as Henry VIII in *A Man for All Seasons*, Shaw became more successful as a respected novelist and playwright. He was forced to find overseas film work after leaving England for Ireland in 1970 for tax reasons. His role as a steely-eyed villain in *The Sting* attracted the attention of producers Richard Zanuck and David Brown, who cast Shaw as the irascible shark-hunter Quint in *Jaws*. This throwback to an older brand of less equivocal masculine confidence and strength – undiluted and unsentimentalised by any of the nostalgic connotations an American star of the same vintage might have brought to the role – led to major Hollywood star status and a multi-picture contract with Universal. With a leading role in *Swashbuckler*, Shaw finally seemed poised to become a natural successor to Burt Lancaster, but most of his post-*Jaws* films actually flopped. His sudden death at the age of fifty-one provided the final untimely twist to a strangely lopsided career. JB

FILMS: *Libel* (1959); *From Russia with Love* (1963); *Battle of the Bulge* (1965); *A Man for All Seasons* (1966); *Custer of the West* (1967); *Young Winston* (1972); *The Sting* (1973); *The Taking of Pelham 1 2 3* (1974); *Jaws* (1975); *Swashbuckler* (1976); *Black Sunday* (1977); *The Deep* (1978); *Avalanche Express* (1979).

SHEARER, Moira (Moira King) (1926–2006)

British professional ballet dancer who starred in three Michael Powell films, including *The Red Shoes* (1948). In her single Hollywood appearance, she was again cast as a ballerina. JS

FILM: *The Story of Three Loves* (1953).

SHIELDS, Arthur (1896–1970)

Shields was a member of Dublin's Abbey Players and fought in the 1916 Easter Rising. He went to the USA in 1939 to take part in *Drums along the Mohawk* – one of his many Hollywood film roles as a priest. His brother is Barry Fitzgerald★. RB

FILMS: *The Sign of the Cross* (1932); *The Plough and the Stars* (1936); *Drums along the Mohawk* (1939); *The Long Voyage Home, Little Nellie Kelly* (1940); *Lady Scarface, The Gay Falcon, How Green Was My Valley, Confirm or Deny* (1941); *This above All, The Loves of Edgar Allan Poe, Dr Renault's Secret, Nightmare, Broadway, Gentleman Jim, Random Harvest, The Black Swan, Pacific Rendezvous, Dr Gillespie's New Assistant* (1942); *Above Suspicion, Lassie Come Home, Madame Curie, The Man from Down Under* (1943); *The White Cliffs of Dover, National Velvet, The Keys of the Kingdom, Youth Runs Wild* (1944); *The Corn is Green, The Valley of Decision, Phantoms, Inc., Too Young to Know, Roughly Speaking, The Picture of Dorian Gray* (1945); *Three Strangers, Gallant Journey, The Verdict, Never Say Goodbye* (1946); *Seven Keys to Baldpate, The Shocking Miss Pilgrim, The Fabulous Dorseys, Easy Come, Easy Go* (1947); *Fighting Father Dunne, Tap Roots* (1948); *My Own True Love the Fighting O'Flynn, She Wore a Yellow Ribbon, Red Light, Challenge to Lassie* (1949); *Tarzan and the Slave Girl* (1950); *Blue Blood, The People Against O'Hara, The Barefoot Mailman, Apache Drums, The River, Sealed Cargo* (1951); *The Quiet Man, Scandal at Scourie* (1952); *South Sea Woman, Main Street to Broadway* (1953); *World for Ransom, Pride of the Blue Grass, River of No Return* (1954); *Lady Godiva* (1955); *The King and Four Queens* (1956); *Daughter of Dr Jekyll* (1957); *Enchanted Island* (1958); *Night of the Quarter Moon* (1959); *For the Love of Mike* (1960); *The Pigeon that Took Rome* (1962).

SIGNORET, Simone (Simone Henriette Charlotte Kaminker) (1921–1985)

The international success of Signoret's second major film, *Dédée d'Anvers* (1947), brought her to the attention of Hollywood, in particular Howard Hughes, with whom she signed a four-year non-exclusive contract to make four films. It was never fulfilled. She was due to leave for the USA in 1949, but having met and fallen in love with Yves Montand★, she postponed the trip. The cold war prevented her from going until 1959, when she went to Los Angeles to receive her Academy Award for Jack Clayton's British film *Room at the Top* (1958). She had been banned entry as a Communist sympathiser.

Along with Stanley Kramer's *Ship of Fools* and Curtis Harrington's *Games*, Signoret made two US-financed British productions directed by Sidney Lumet (*The Deadly Affair* and *The Seagull*). All three American directors were very precise in wanting to work with Signoret. They highly valued her minimalist style, her ability to embody any number of roles and her extraordinary sensuality, which, in her now mature body, could still range (as in her early years) from a rich, deeply knowing and moving sexuality to a masquerade disguising a monstrous drive to get her own way. Signoret was nominated for an Academy Award for her performance as the unhappy and drug-addicted Contessa in *Ship of Fools*. While in the USA in the1960s, she also made a television programme – *A Small Rebellion* (1965) – for which she won an Emmy Award. She also had a minor uncredited role in the Columbia-funded Roman epic, *Barabbas*. SHa

FILMS: *Barabbas* (1962); *Ship of Fools* (1965); *The Deadly Affair* (1966); *Games* (1967); *The Seagull* (1968).

SIMMONS, Jean (Jean Merilyn Simmons) (1929–)

Simmons made her British screen debut as Margaret Lockwood's★ daughter in *Give Us the Moon* (1944) while attending the Aida Foster School of Dance at the age of fourteen. Although Foster is said to have prevented her from signing an ensuing contract with Gainsborough, stardom soon beckoned through her performance as Estella in David Lean's *Great Expectations* (1946). Simmons later reflected her greatest regret was to turn down Lawrence Olivier's★ offer of theatrical training at the Old Vic after her Academy Award-nominated performance as Ophelia in his 1948 screen adaptation of *Hamlet*.

This transatlantic success goes some way towards answering the question 'what next for Jean Simmons?' that C. A. Lejeune posed in a 1950 article describing the young actress as 'the nearest thing to a great potential film star in this country'. Though Simmons' move to Hollywood might have already seemed inevitable, it actually came about through the combination of her marriage to Stewart Granger★ and a clandestine business deal involving the sale of her contract with Rank to the Hollywood tycoon Howard Hughes. Although she felt that she had been 'sold like a packet of tea', Simmons soon found herself a star in the USA, particularly after Twentieth Century-Fox bought her out. Her subtle glamour and respectable background brought a sense of prestige to Hollywood productions at a time when they were becoming larger and more colourful. She was cast in ostentatious Technicolor epics such as the first CinemaScope production, *The Robe*, William Wyler's Technirama *The Big Country* and Stanley Kubrick's Super Technirama 70 *Spartacus*. She also proved her versatility with roles such as Diane Tremayne, the alluring femme fatale of Otto Preminger's *Angel Face*.

Despite her Hollywood status, Simmons always seemed to maintain a down-to-earth 'girl next door' quality in interviews, particularly when she returned to Britain. Thus, upon her first trip back to the UK in 1954, her mother proudly informed her fans that Simmons had sent a telegram in advance requesting 'fish and chips for supper'. She divorced Granger in 1960 to marry Richard Brooks, who directed her in *Elmer Gantry*, and returned temporarily to England, where she made fewer films and expressed an apparent affinity for domestic life. Since then, her film roles have declined and she largely works for US television, where she usually maintains her English accent in productions such as Disney's *Great Expectations* (1989). This time, however, Simmons played the role of Miss Haversham. MW

FILMS: *Androcles and the Lion, Angel Face* (1952); *Affair with a Stranger, The Robe, Young Bess, The Actress* (1953); *A Bullet is Waiting, Desirée, Demetrius and the Gladiators, She Couldn't Say No, The Egyptian* (1954); *Footsteps in the Fog, Guys and Dolls* (1955); *Hilda Crane* (1956); *Until They Sail, This Could Be the Night* (1957); *Home before Dark, The Big Country* (1958); *This Earth is Mine* (1959); *The Grass is Greener, Elmer Gantry, Spartacus* (1960); *All the Way Home* (1963); *Mister Buddwing* (1966); *Divorce American Style, Rough Night in Jericho* (1967); *The Happy Ending* (1969); *Say Hello to Yesterday*

(1971); *Mr Sycamore* (1974); *Yellow Pages* (1988); *How to Make an American Quilt* (1995); *Final Fantasy: The Spirits Within* [voice] (2001).

SIMON, Simone (1911–2005)

Simone Simon's career started early. As a sharp and feline actress in *Lac aux dames/Ladies Lake* (1934), she delighted French and European audiences, as well as Colette, who had adapted Vicki Baum's novel to the screen. Like Danielle Darrieux★, that other childlike star, she left for Hollywood at the height of her French career and was put under contract by Twentieth Century-Fox as one of Darryl F. Zanuck's favourite French imports. However, like the other French actresses that Zanuck was periodically interested in, her career was disappointing. She was often cast as an affected but bland ingénue in musicals such as *Josette* or *Love and Hisses*, where she neither danced nor sang. In the remake of *Seventh Heaven*, Simon – bravely replacing Janet Gaynor – and James Stewart played the ideal, chocolate-box couple, but it was nevertheless obvious that she was not Hollywood material. The only high point of that period in her career was in a French film, Jean Renoir's *La Bête humaine* (1938), where she was magnificent in the role of Séverine, a dark-haired femme fatale-cum-nymphet, whom she portrayed with perverse and voluptuous seductiveness. Having returned to Hollywood because of the war, she had to be content with a series of potboilers for RKO, who only wanted her for low-budget films. Paradoxically, it is thanks to one of these films that she left her mark in the Hollywood imaginary. She played Irena in *Cat People*, the logical culmination of her role in *La Bête humaine*, an innocent but dangerous cat-woman who clawed velvet armchairs with her painted nails when in the throes of jealousy. In the sequel to this masterpiece, *The Curse of the Cat People*, she returned as Irena's frail and dreamy ghost. The co-director, Robert Wise, cast her in a little-known film, *Mademoiselle Fifi*, an adaptation of a Maupassant story, where she played a laundress (a prostitute in Maupassant) who behaves heroically to save the lives of middle-class people who despise her. She then returned to France, where, despite a couple of memorable films by Max Ophuls, her career never regained its prewar greatness. CV

FILMS: *Girls' Dormitory, Ladies in Love* (1936); *Seventh Heaven, Love and Hisses* (1937); *Josette* (1938); *The Devil and Daniel Webster* (1941); *Cat People* (1942); *Tahiti Honey* (1943); *Mademoiselle Fifi, The Curse of the Cat People, Johnny Doesn't Live Here Anymore* (1944).

SKARSGÅRD, Stellan (1951–)

Skarsgård achieved domestic fame at an early age when he excelled in the title role in *Bombi Bitt och jag* (1968), one of the largest television productions ever made in Sweden. The series made him an overnight sensation, and ever since then he has been regarded as one of the country's most renowned and respected actors. His European film career received a significant boost when he was awarded a Silver Bear at the Berlin film festival in 1982 for his portrayal of an *idiot savant* in the Swedish historical melodrama *The Simple-Minded Murder*. Since his real international breakthrough in Lars von Trier's *Breaking the Waves* (1996), in which he played the oilrig worker who falls in love with Emily Watson★, Skarsgård has mainly concentrated on making films abroad, particularly in Hollywood. He has been given demanding supporting roles in films such as *Good Will Hunting* and *Amistad*, and in the likes of *Ronin, Deep Blue Sea* and *Timecode*, he has portrayed a variety of complex characters often speaking in various Northern or Eastern European accents in order to exaggerate their otherness. MJ

FILMS: *The Unbearable Lightness of Being* (1988); *The Hunt for Red October* (1990); *Wind* (1992); *Amistad, Good Will Hunting* (1997); *Savior, Ronin* (1998); *Deep Blue Sea* (1999); *Passion of Mind, Signs & Wonders, Timecode* (2000); *The Hire: Powder Keg, The Glass House* (2001); *No Good Deed, City of Ghosts* (2002); *Dogville* (2003); *King Arthur, Exorcist: The Beginning* (2004).

SKIPWORTH, Alison (Alison Groom) (1863–1952)

British actress best remembered for her haughty screen characterisations of the 1930s, and for her verbal sparring with W. C. Fields in films such as *If I Had a Million* and *Tillie and Gus*. MW

FILMS: *39 East* (1920); *Handcuffs or Kisses* (1921); *Oh, for a Man, Strictly Unconventional, Outward Bound, Raffles, Du Barry, Woman of Passion* (1930); *The Virtuous Husband, Tonight or Never, Night Angel, The Road to Singapore, Devotion* (1931); *Madame Racketeer, High Pressure, Night after Night, The Unexpected Father, Sinners in the Sun, If I Had a Million* (1932); *Alice in Wonderland, The Song of Songs, A Lady's Profession, He Learned about Women, Tonight is Ours, Tillie and Gus, The Midnight Club* (1933); *Coming-Out Party, Wharf Angel, Here* **433** *is My Heart, Shoot the Works, Six of a Kind, Notorious Sophie Lang, The Captain Hates the Sea* (1934); *Hitch Hike Lady, Dangerous, Doubting Thomas, The Girl from 10th Avenue, Shanghai, Becky Sharp, The Casino Murder Case, The Devil is a Woman* (1935); *White Hunter, The Princess Comes Across, Two in a Crowd, The Gorgeous Hussy, Satan Met a Lady* (1936); *Stolen Holiday, Two Wise Maids* (1937); *Ladies in Distress, Wide Open Faces, King of the Newsboys* (1938).

SLEZAK, Walter (1902–1983)

Austrian actor who worked on the Broadway stage from 1930, but did not make his Hollywood debut until 1942. Slezak was generally typecast on screen as either a menacing heavy or a bumbling idiot. He continued to pursue an American screen career, but largely remained known for his theatre work. In 1955, he won both a Tony and New York Critics award for his role in the stage version of *Fanny*. FG

FILMS: *Once upon a Honeymoon* (1942); *This Land is Mine, The Fallen Sparrow* (1943); *Step Lively, Lifeboat, Till We Meet Again, The Princess and the Pirate, The Spanish Main* (1944); *Salome, Where She Danced, Cornered* (1945); *Born to Kill, Riffraff, Sinbad the Sailor* (1947); *The Pirate* (1948); *The Inspector General* (1949); *Abbott and Costello in the Foreign Legion, The Yellow Cab Man, Spy Hunt* (1950); *People Will Talk, Bedtime for Bonzo, The Name's the Same* (1951); *Call Me Madam, White Witch Doctor, Confidentially Connie* (1953); *The Steel Cage* (1954); *This is Show Business* (1956); *Pinocchio, Ten Thousand Bedrooms, High Low Quiz* (1957); *The Miracle* (1959); *Come September* (1961); *The Wonderful World of the Brothers Grimm* (1962); *Emil and the Detectives, Wonderful Life* (1964); *The Man Who Bought Paradise, A Very Special Favor* (1965); *Twenty-Four Hours to Kill* (1966); *The Caper of the Golden Bulls* (1967); *Dr Copelius* (1968).

SMITH, C. Aubrey (1863–1948)

In Britain, C. Aubrey Smith made his name as much on the cricket field, where he captained Sussex and, briefly, England, as on the legitimate stage, where he specialised in supporting roles as noblemen from the 1890s onwards. Beginning in 1907, he made regular (and lengthy) appearances in American theatres, and on one visit stayed long enough to be invited to California to make four films for Charles Frohman in 1915 and 1916. Though somewhat too old and craggy to maintain his leading-man status in the cinema, on his return to Britain he made further prominent

C. Aubrey Smith: off the cricket field in Hollywood

appearances in native films in the first half of the 1920s. In 1930, at the age of sixty-seven, his career pattern changed more dramatically when he transferred from Broadway to become MGM's favourite patrician aristocrat and/or retired colonel for the next twenty years or so. Off screen, he was the public figurehead of the émigré British community in Hollywood, marshalling willing recruits into his cricket team and flying the Union Flag on his lawn. On screen, he became the shorthand symbol of an age of Empire and conquest in British history. As Bosley Crowther wrote in *The New York Times* in 1937: 'he is Great Britain personified in the eyes of millions of people. Whenever he appears on the screen – his elderly figure erect, his chin up and his eyes flashing out from under those beetling brows – it is as though an invisible band were playing *Rule Britannia*.' It was for precisely this kind of sterling ambassadorial service, rather than any notable achievements back home, that Smith was knighted in June 1944. JB

FILMS: *The Builder of Bridges, John Glayde's Honor* (1915); *Jaffery, The Witching Hour* (1916); *The Bachelor Father, Daybreak, Trader Horn, Just a Gigolo, Guilty Hands, The Squaw Man, Surrender, Son of India, The Phantom of Paris, Never the*

Twain Shall Meet, The Man in Possession, Contraband Love (1931); *Polly of the Circus, Tarzan the Ape Man, But the Flesh is Weak, Love Me Tonight, Trouble in Paradise, No More Orchids, The Monkey's Paw* (1932); *Luxury Liner, The Barbarian, Adorable, Morning Glory, Bombshell, They Just Had to Get Married, Secrets, Queen Christina* (1933); *Bulldog Drummond Strikes Back, Cleopatra, The Scarlet Empress, The House of Rothschild, We Live Again, One More River, Gambling Lady, The Firebird, Curtain at Eight, Caravan* (1934); *Clive of India, The Lives of a Bengal Lancer, The Gilded Lily, The Florentine Dagger, China Seas, The Right to Live, Jalna, The Crusades* (1935); *Little Lord Fauntleroy, Romeo and Juliet, The Garden of Allah, Lloyds of London* (1936); *Wee Willie Winkie, The Prisoner of Zenda, The Hurricane, Thoroughbreds Don't Cry* (1937); *Four Men and a Prayer, Kidnapped* (1938); *East Side of Heaven, Five Came Back, Another Thin Man, Balalaika, The Under-Pup, The Sun Never Sets, Eternally Yours* (1939); *Rebecca, Waterloo Bridge, A Bill of Divorcement, Beyond Tomorrow, A Little Bit of Heaven, City of Chance* (1940); *Free and Easy, Dr Jekyll and Mr Hyde, Maisie was a Lady* (1941); *Forever and a Day, Two Tickets to London, Madame Curie, Flesh and Fantasy* (1943); *The White Cliffs of Dover, Sensations of 1945, The Adventures of Mark Twain, Secrets of Scotland Yard* (1944); *Forever Yours, Scotland Yard Investigator, And Then There Were None* (1945); *Terror by Night, Cluny Brown, Rendezvous with Annie, High Conquest, Unconquered* (1947); *Little Women* (1949).

SMITH, Constance (1928–2003)

Irish actress who entered film by winning a Hedy Lamarr★ lookalike competition. After several small roles, she failed to break through and her career languished. She was imprisoned for attempting to kill her lover, the writer and documentarist Paul Rotha, and later vanished after a mental breakdown. RB

FILMS: *The Mudlark* (1950); *The 13th Letter* (1951); *Red Skies of Montana, Lure of the Wilderness* (1952); *Treasure of the Golden Condor, Taxi, Man in the Attic* (1953); *The Big Tip Off* (1955).

SMITH, Maggie (Margaret Natalie Smith) (1934–)

Highly talented British stage and screen actress who has appeared in innumerable award-winning roles on both sides of the Atlantic such as the deliciously formidable Countess of Trentham in Robert Altman's *Gosford Park*.

Smith's cutting, often improvised, remarks in the film – which come at the expense of all around her – served to underscore the actress's charismatic upper-class persona.

Smith won a 1958 BAFTA award for Most Promising Newcomer. Her role as Miss Mead in *The V.I.P.s*, opposite Elizabeth Taylor and Richard Burton★, and her Academy Award-nominated performance as Lawrence Olivier's★ Desdemona in *Othello* (1965) further consolidated her profile as a distinguished and versatile actress. Her most famous role to date came in 1969 when she played the inspirational and mildly eccentric Edinburgh schoolteacher in *The Prime of Miss Jean Brodie*.

Smith has continued to turn out a series of deft character studies that often come with a comic or whimsical edge. She won an Academy Award for her role in *California Suite* and a nomination for *Travels with My Aunt*. More recently, she has personified the wizened old lady and stern schoolmistress in Anglo-American productions such as *Hook, The Secret Garden* and the *Harry Potter* films. MW

FILMS: *The V.I.P.s* (1963); *The Pumpkin Eater* (1964); *Young Cassidy* (1965); *The Honey Pot* (1967); *Hot Millions* (1968); *The Prime of Miss Jean Brodie, Oh! What a Lovely War* (1969); *Travels with My Aunt* (1972); *Love and Pain and the Whole Damn Thing* (1973); *Murder by Death* (1976); *California Suite* (1978); *Hook* (1991); *Sister Act* (1992); *The Secret Garden, Sister Act 2: Back in the Habit* (1993); *Richard III* (1995); *The First Wives Club* (1996); *Washington Square* (1997); *Curtain Call* (1999); *Gosford Park, Harry Potter and the Philosopher's Stone* (2001); *Harry Potter and the Chamber of Secrets, Divine Secrets of the Ya-Ya Sisterhood* (2002); *Harry Potter and the Prisoner of Azkaban* (2004).

SØEBERG, Camilla (1966–)

Danish actress whose performance as the betrayed teenager in Bille August's *Tro, håb og kærlighed / Twist and Shout* (1994) opened doors in Hollywood. *The Empty Mirror*, in which she played Eva Braun, of all people, seems to have closed them again. HJW

FILMS: *Yellow Pages, Manifesto* (1988); *Erotique* (1994); *The Empty Mirror* (1996); *Mouse Hunt* (1997).

SOKOLOFF, Vladimir (1889–1962)

Russian-born alumnus of Stanislavsky's Moscow Art Theatre (MKHaT) who defected to Berlin in 1923 and established himself as a highly successful character actor. He **435**

Russian-born Vladimir Sokoloff played many 'ethnic' types –
Russians, Arabs, Mexicans and East Asians – in Hollywood
movies from the 1930s to the 1960s

first journeyed to Hollywood in 1930 to appear in Warner
Bros.' German-language versions such as *Kismet* (1931),
directed by recent émigré William Dieterle. Back in
Europe, Sokoloff moved to Paris after the Nazis came to
power before returning to Hollywood in 1937 and taking
American citizenship. Playing ethnic 'types' – including
Russians, but also Arabs, Italians, Mexicans and East Asians
– he remained a familiar face in popular movies. Sokoloff
specialised in kindly father figures and occasionally surprised when cast as a villain. RJK

FILMS: *The Life of Emile Zola, Conquest, West of Shanghai,
Alcatraz Island, Expensive Husbands, Tovarich* [scenes deleted],
Beg, Borrow or Steal (1937); *Blockade, Arsène Lupin Returns,
The Amazing Dr Clitterhouse, Spawn of the North, Ride a
Crooked Mile* (1938); *Juarez, Sons of Liberty, The Real Glory*
(1939); *Comrade X* (1940); *Love Crazy* (1941); *Road to
Morocco, Crossroads* (1942); *For Whom the Bell Tolls, Song of
Russia, Mr Lucky, Mission to Moscow* (1943); *The Conspirators,
Passage to Marseille, Till We Meet Again* (1944); *A Royal Scan-
dal, Back to Bataan, The Blonde from Brooklyn, Scarlet Street,
Paris Underground* (1945); *A Scandal in Paris, Cloak and
Dagger, Two Smart People* (1946); *To the Ends of the Earth*
(1948); *The Baron of Arizona* (1950); *Macao* (1952); *While the
City Sleeps* (1956); *Istanbul, I Was a Teenage Werewolf, Sabu and
the Magic Ring* (1957); *Twilight for the Gods, Monster from
Green Hell* (1958); *Man on a String* (1959); *The Magnificent
Seven, Cimarron, Beyond the Time Barrier* (1960); *Mr Sardonicus*
(1961); *Escape from Zahrain, Taras Bulba* (1962).

SOMMER, Elke (Elke Schletz) (1940–)

One of the archetypal blonde bombshells of 1960s cinema,
Berlin-born Sommer was discovered in the late 1950s by
director Vittorio de Sica★ after she won a beauty pageant
in Italy. She subsequently appeared in a number of Italian,
German, French and British films, before being recognised
by Hollywood talent spotters in the Anglo-American war
drama *The Victors*. In the 1960s, Sommer moved to LA and
starred in mainstream Hollywood productions, often spy
thrillers that imitated the contemporaneous Bond films.
Her parts were primarily designed to show off her busty
physique, although, given the opportunity, she could be a
very able comedienne, as in the Peter Sellers★ *Pink Panther*
film *A Shot in the Dark*. Her career took a downward turn
in the 1970s, and had largely ebbed out with European B-
movies and cameo appearances on television by the mid-
1980s. She resurfaced in the 1990s, however, through her
art exhibitions, and as the author of a book on painting.
TB

FILMS: *The Prize* (1963); *A Shot in the Dark* (1964); *The Art
of Love, The Money Trap* (1965); *Boy, Did I Get a Wrong
Number!, The Oscar* (1966); *The Venetian Affair* (1967); *The
Wicked Dreams of Paula Schultz, The Invincible Six* (1968);
The Wrecking Crew (1969); *Zeppelin* (1971); *The Swiss Con-
spiracy* (1975); *One Away, Invisible Strangler* (1976); *The
Double McGuffin, A Nightingale Sang in Berkeley Square, The
Prisoner of Zenda* (1979); *Hollywood Ghost Stories, Severed Ties*
(1992).

SOREL, Jean (Jean de Combaud-Roquebrune) (1934–)

With his dark good looks and athletic, though delicate,
physique, Sorel played romantic leads in many Italian and
French films. He was Catherine Deneuve's husband in
Buñuel's *Belle de jour* (1967). In the USA, he was relegated
to insubstantial 'Frenchman' roles. VO

FILMS: *Model Shop* (1969); *Trader Horn* (1973).

SOUSSANIN, Nicholas (Simkov Nikolai Ilyich) (1889–1975)

Russian stage actor who began his US film career in the early 1920s as a humble Hollywood extra. He went on to specialise in playing noblemen of various nationalities such as the Adjutant of the Grand Duke in Sternberg's *The Last Command*. Soussanin's 1929 marriage to Olga Baclanova★ enhanced his public profile and the couple launched a brief and unsuccessful joint film venture. After the collapse of Baclanova's film career, they moved to New York in 1933 to work on the stage but divorced two years later. Soussanin went back to Los Angeles, where he returned to performing in largely uncredited roles. RY

FILMS: *The Swan* (1925); *The Midnight Sun* (1926); *A Gentleman of Paris, Hotel Imperial, One Increasing Purpose, The Yankee Clipper, The Spotlight* (1927); *Night Watch, Yellow Lily, The Woman Disputed, Adoration, The Last Command* (1928); *Trent's Last Case, The Squall* (1929); *Are You There?* (1930); *The Criminal Code, White Shoulders, Daughter of the Dragon* (1931); *Arsène Lupin, A Parisian Romance* (1932); *The Man Who Broke the Bank at Monte Carlo* (1935); *Muss 'Em Up, Under Two Flags, Champagne Charlie* (1936); *Artists and Models Abroad* (1938); *Captain Fury, Those High Grey Walls* (1939); *My Life with Caroline* (1941); *Black Magic* (1949).

SOUTENDIJK, Renée (1957–)

Renée Soutendijk's acting style can be characterised as simultaneously pure and mysterious. She built a successful career in the Netherlands and in Europe, playing a range of deeply psychological characters. During her short and disappointing stay in the USA in the early 1990s, she claimed her artistic strengths were not sufficiently tested. SdL

FILMS: *Grave Secrets, Forced March* (1989); *Eve of Destruction* (1991); *Dial 9 for Love* (2001).

SPAAK, Catherine (1945–)

Daughter of celebrated Belgian screenwriter Charles Spaak whose first role was as an extra in Jacques Becker's *Le Trou* (1960). She made a few relatively unknown American films and her career has remained predominantly based in Italy. VO

FILMS: *Hotel* (1967); *If It's Tuesday, This Must Be Belgium* (1969); *Take a Hard Ride* (1975).

SPAIN

The migration of Spanish actors to Hollywood over the last hundred years might best be characterised as an intermittent trickle marked by one major and then one minor wave of arrivals. While the Spanish presence was minimal during the silent era, the coming of sound cinema provided a new and somewhat paradoxical impetus to the journeys of Iberian actors to the USA. Sound certainly put an end to many Spanish-speaking performers' careers, since their heavily accented English pronunciation suddenly made them unacceptable for most Hollywood roles. But it was this very issue of accent and language that simultaneously enabled a new migration of actors, writers and directors from Spain to Hollywood in what Alvaro Armero has termed 'the second landing of Spaniards in California' (after the Spanish conquest of the sixteenth century).[23]

Between the first implementation of sound in 1930 and the perfecting of dubbing technologies in 1935, Paramount, MGM and Fox turned out more than 170 Spanish-language films destined for the sizeable Spanish-language market in Europe and the Americas. The great majority of these were near exact Spanish-language versions of original English-language productions, but they were often shot more quickly, with lower budgets and at the hands of lesser-known directors. Although some were shot at Paramount's Joinville studio outside Paris, the majority were filmed in Los Angeles. According to the actress Ana María Custodio (who like many performers never appeared in an English-language Hollywood film), studio gossip held that directors were punished for going over budget on a picture by being assigned to direct Spanish-language versions.[24]

Most Spanish actors were recruited from Madrid's better-known theatre companies and lured to California by lucrative contracts and the promise of a luxurious Hollywood lifestyle. Once there, they joined a handful of fellow Spaniards already working in the industry as well as numerous other performers and extras from Mexico and South America. The frequently indiscriminate pairing of actors and accents from different countries in a single film gave way to a conflict between Castilian and Spanish-American pronunciation that became known as 'the Battle of the Z'. There were similar debates over who actually spoke 'real' Spanish. These battles shed light on the prob- **437** lematic intersections between language, culture and narrative coherence within Spanish-language versions that clearly limited their success in their target markets.

By 1932, Paramount and MGM began shutting down their Spanish-language operations and the majority of actors returned to Spain. However, because Fox had made a major investment in the project, the studio shifted tactics and began to employ writers and actors on films directly created for Spanish audiences. These were generally regarded as artistically superior to those made under the previous model and include *La ciudad de cartón/The Cardboard City* (1933), described as an early precursor of *A Star is Born* (1937), and *Angelina o el honor de un brigadier/Angelina or the Honor of a Brigadier* (1935), a verse adaptation of the play by Enrique Jardiel Poncela.

The list of actors who returned from Hollywood to successful careers in Spain includes romantic leading men such as Jose Nieto★ and Julio Peña★; character actors such as Manuel Arbó (who played Charlie Chan in the Spanish versions) and Juan de Landa (who appeared in Edgar Neville's adaptation of Vidor's *The Big House*, *El presidio* [1930]); the Argentinian comic actor Miguel Ligero and the Chilean actor and singer Roberto Rey (known as the 'Spanish Chevalier'). It also consists of female performers such as Luana Alcañiz★, Catalina Bárcena, María Fernanda Ladrón de Guevara and Rosita Díaz Gimeno.

Antonio Moreno★ was the exception since he was the best-known Spanish actor working in Hollywood during the 1930s. He had arrived in the USA nearly twenty years earlier and had quickly established star status as the original 'Latin Lover' by sharing the screen with leading ladies like Lillian Gish, Mary Pickford, Pearl White, Colleen Moore, Pola Negri★ and Greta Garbo★. Though he would never return to the level of success he enjoyed during the silent era, Moreno was given a boost by appearances in Hollywood's Spanish-language versions. He continued to work as a supporting actor well into the 1950s in films such as John Ford's *The Searchers* (1956) and the 3-D classic, *The Creature from the Black Lagoon* (1954). His sole remaining appearance in a film actually made in Spain was in the role of a mysterious Spaniard who returns from American exile in *María de la O* (1936).

An interval of nearly fifty years separates the first wave of Hollywood's Spanish actors from the next significant incursion by a much smaller group of high-profile per-

formers. The exception lies in the brief US career of Sara Montiel★, who made three films in Hollywood between 1954 and 1957 following a successful career in Mexico. It is tempting to speculate on the reasons behind the disappearance of Spanish performers from US screens in an era when actors from the rest of Europe and Spanish-speaking America continued to make their way to Hollywood. Although Francoist cultural policies sought to impose the virtues of isolationist self-sufficiency on nearly every aspect of national life, the Spanish cinema industry actively sought alliances with its European and Latin American counterparts, and actors and directors regularly pursued career opportunities across national boundaries. It seems more likely that, as far as Hollywood was concerned, Spain simply had nothing to offer, since Spanish cinema and Spanish actors were unknown commodities to US audiences. Montiel only attracted the attention of Californian studio executives thanks to her work in Mexico across the border. Indeed, Mexico and the rest of Spanish-speaking America (or Brazil, in the case of Carmen Miranda) could supply Hollywood's undiscriminating appetite for exotic Latins more conveniently.

Why then have the major Spanish stars Antonio Banderas★, Penélope Cruz★ and Javier Bardem★ appeared in a range of American films over the last decade? It is clearly no coincidence that each has featured in one or more films directed by Pedro Almodóvar, prior to being sought out by American producers. The Almodóvar 'brand' with its image of artful, Mediterranean passion expressed through fluid sexual and gender identities has certainly given Spanish culture a new legibility for international audiences. Nevertheless, if the association with Almodóvar facilitated Banderas, Cruz and Bardem's respective entries into the American market, each has embarked on a quite different career path. These have been conditioned by a number of variable personal circumstances and industrial paradigms. And with the possible exception of Bardem, none has yet been offered roles that match the complexity of his or her best Spanish work. KV

STAMP, Terence (1939–)

Compared with other 'new wave' stars from working-class backgrounds who came to prominence in British cinema of the 1960s, Terence Stamp made relatively little impact in the USA at the height of his fame. After winning an Academy

Award nomination for his performance in the title role of his debut British film *Billy Budd* (1962), Stamp was fêted for a number of major international roles. His almost androgynous pretty-boy looks seem to have discomfited many producers, however, and though Stamp shot his third film – William Wyler's *The Collector* – in Hollywood in 1965, it was in a part that equated his unusual male beauty with an immature sexuality and sinister malevolence. After a self-imposed career sabbatical spent on a spiritual odyssey in India, Stamp began to gain regular Hollywood work in the 1980s, generally playing slick, sophisticated corporate villains in supporting roles. One notable exception to this trend is his casting as the main protagonist of Stephen Soderbergh's *The Limey*. The film is constructed as a general homage to the screen image of the cockney gangster, but it also offers a knowing tribute to Stamp's residual glamour, since extracts from his 1967 British film *Poor Cow* function as flashbacks for his character. JB

FILMS: *The Collector* (1965); *Modesty Blaise* (1966); *Far from the Madding Crowd* (1967); *Blue* (1968); *Superman* (1978); *Superman II* (1980); *Monster Island* (1981); *The Company of Wolves* (1984); *Legal Eagles*, *Link* (1986); *Wall Street*, *The Sicilian* (1987); *Young Guns*, *Alien Nation* (1988); *Genuine Risk* (1990); *The Real McCoy* (1993); *Mindbender* (1996); *Bliss* (1997); *Love Walked In*, *Kiss the Sky* (1998); *The Limey*, *Star Wars: Episode I – The Phantom Menace*, *Bowfinger* (1999); *Red Planet* (2000); *Full Frontal* (2002); *The Haunted Mansion*, *The Kiss*, *My Boss's Daughter* (2003).

STEELE, Barbara (1937–)

English actress who earned a considerable cult reputation thanks to the combination of photogenic looks and psycho-sexual typecasting in a series of outrageously lurid Italian Gothic films of the 1960s. Her iconic performance as a vengeful, recently resurrected witch in *La maschera del demonio/Black Sunday* (1960) attracted Roger Corman's attention and the following year she crossed the Atlantic to appear in *The Pit and the Pendulum*. Despite tiring of horror movies, Steele found it increasingly difficult to escape the genre and the erotic-sadistic persona it had created for her. She returned to the USA in 1974 to find that little had altered and starred as a viciously repressed prison warden in Jonathan Demme's *Caged Heat*, before giving a memorable performance as a vampish bisexual seductress in David Cronenberg's Canadian debut film *Shivers*. Pointlessly cast in small roles in several American films of the late 1970s,

Steele successfully turned her hand to production work and the occasional acting part for American television throughout the 1980s and 1990s. MF

FILMS: *The Pit and the Pendulum* (1961); *Caged Heat* (1974); *Shivers* (1975); *I Never Promised You a Rose Garden* (1977); *Pretty Baby*, *Piranha* (1978); *Silent Scream* (1980); *The Prophet* (1999).

STEN, Anna (Annel Stenskaya Sudakevich) (1908–1993)

Blonde, half-Swedish, half-Ukrainian actress who entered Soviet films in 1927 and gained local celebrity through libidinous roles in works directed by Boris Barnet and Yevgeni Chervyakov. In 1930, Sten defected to Berlin, where she starred in five major productions embodying a kind of subdued yet smouldering Slavic sexuality. Samuel Goldwyn, who had just lost the services of former European protégée Vilma Bánky★ and was searching for a box-office competitor to Marlene Dietrich★ and Greta Garbo★, offered Sten a contract. Despite not speaking a single word of English, she was imported to Hollywood in 1933 on the strength of the opening reel of her performance in *Der Mörder Dimitri Kara-*

Anna Sten: 'The Passionate Peasant'

masoff/ The Brothers Karamazov (1931). While Sten received daily language, deportment and acting lessons throughout the next year, studio publicists launched an unprecedented campaign to market the unknown actress to American audiences. Dubbed 'The Passionate Peasant', the former waitress was provided with a largely fictitious biography that asserted that she had been a childhood ballet and circus star before training at the Moscow Art Theatre (MKHaT) and Film Academy, where she was ostensibly 'discovered' by Sergei Eisenstein. At the same time, Goldwyn's publicists ensured that Sten's picture appeared in the national press on a daily basis. Her 1932 movie *Stürme der Leidenschaft/ Tempest* also enjoyed a larger-than-usual Stateside release before her first Hollywood film, *Nana*. Based on Émile Zola's novel, this $2 million production proved a monumental flop, with Sten's unlikely accented Parisian *demi-mondaine* receiving particular criticism. Although the script had been substantially reworked in order to accommodate only dialogue that the actress could enunciate comprehensibly, her English delivery remained, as John Kobal later remarked, 'a series of semi-colons and dashes'. Furthermore, Sten's linguistic uncertainty seemed to have translated to her acting style. Goldwyn's employment of the Academy Award-winning team of Rouben Mamoulian and Fredric March did little to aid her follow-up picture, *We Live Again*, a Ruritanian retelling of Tolstoy's *Resurrection*. Likewise, *The Wedding Night*, which paired Sten with former Dietrich leading-man Gary Cooper, proved box-office poison and became known in Hollywood as 'Goldwyn's Last Sten'. Cole Porter quipped in the original draft of *Anything Goes*: 'If Sam Goldwyn can with great conviction/Instruct Anna Sten in diction/Then Anna shows/Anything Goes'. Sten's fame was so ephemeral, however, that this verse was swiftly dropped. The actress's contract with Goldwyn was dissolved, and although she remained in Hollywood and became an American citizen, her subsequent acting work was restricted to a few wartime anti-Nazi pictures and a brief comeback attempt in the mid-1950s, whereafter Sten pursued a career as an artist. RJK

FILMS: *Nana, We Live Again* (1934); *The Wedding Night* (1935); *Exile Express* (1939); *The Man I Married* (1940); *So Ends Our Night* (1941); *They Came to Blow up America, Chetniks – The Fighting Guerrillas* (1943); *Three Russian Girls* (1944); *Let's Live a Little* (1948); *Soldier of Fortune* (1955); **440** *Runaway Daughters* (1956); *The Nun and the Sergeant* (1962).

STEPHENSON, Henry (Henry S. Garroway) (1871–1956)

Stephenson was born in the West Indies and returned to Britain to take up acting in the mid-1920s. After a successful London and New York stage career, he appeared in a number of silent productions, before beginning a prolific career as a character actor in Hollywood talkies following his supporting role in *The Animal Kingdom*. Stephenson was invariably cast as an aristocrat or well-bred professional and his English identity led to a roll-call of genial patricians, doctors and high-ranking military types. Stephenson often acted in literary adaptations and historical melodramas, and in the 1930s made notable appearances in the likes of *Little Women, Mutiny on the Bounty* and *The Prince and the Pauper.* MF

FILMS: *The Spreading Dawn* (1917); *A Society Exile* (1919); *The Tower of Jewels* (1920); *The Black Panther's Club* (1921); *Men and Women, Wild, Wild Susan* (1925); *Red Headed Woman, A Bill of Divorcement, Cynara, The Animal Kingdom, Guilty as Hell* (1932); *Double Harness, Blind Adventure, Little Women, If I Were Free, Tomorrow at Seven, My Lips Betray* (1933); *The Mystery of Mr X, Stingaree, The Richest Girl in the World, She Loves Me Not, What Every Woman Knows, Thirty Day Princess, Outcast Lady, One More River, Man of Two Worlds, All Men are Enemies* (1934); *Vanessa: Her Love Story, Reckless, The Flame Within, Rendezvous, Mutiny on the Bounty, Captain Blood, The Perfect Gentleman, O'Shaughnessy's Boy, The Night is Young* (1935); *Little Lord Fauntleroy, Half Angel, Hearts Divided, Walking on Air, Give Me Your Heart, The Charge of the Light Brigade, Beloved Enemy* (1936); *When You're in Love, The Emperor's Candlesticks, The Prince and the Pauper, Conquest, Wise Girl* (1937); *The Baroness and the Butler, Marie Antoinette, The Young in Heart, Dramatic School, Suez* (1938); *Tarzan Finds a Son!, The Adventures of Sherlock Holmes, The Private Lives of Elizabeth and Essex* (1939); *Little Old New York, It's a Date, Down Argentine Way, Spring Parade* (1940); *The Man Who Lost Himself, Lady from Louisiana* (1941); *Half Way to Shanghai, This Above All, Rings on Her Fingers* (1942); *Mr Lucky, The Mantrap* (1943); *Two Girls and a Sailor, Secrets of Scotland Yard, Reckless Age, The Hour before Dawn* (1944); *Tarzan and the Amazons* (1945); *The Green Years, Night and Day, Her Sister's Secret, The Return of Monte Cristo, Of Human Bondage, The Locket, Heartbeat* (1946); *Time Out of Mind, Song of Love, Ivy, The Homestretch, Dark Delusion* (1947); *Julia Misbehaves* (1948); *Challenge to Lassie* (1949).

STÉVENIN, Jean-François (1944–)

Prolific French supporting actor as well as director. He played a French Resistance fighter in John Huston's war comedy *Victory*. VO

FILMS: *Victory* (1981); *Treasure Island* (1985).

STEWART, Patrick (1940–)

Highly respected British stage actor who achieved international stardom relatively late in his career through playing Captain Picard in the *Star Trek* television series and four film spin-offs. With his resonant, patrician voice, Stewart projects authority and compassion, as in his role as the good mutant, Professor Charles Xavier, in the *X-Men* films. AS

FILMS: *Dune* (1984); *Code Name: Emerald* (1985); *L.A. Story* (1991); *Robin Hood: Men in Tights* (1993); *Gunmen, Star Trek: Generations* (1994); *Jeffrey* (1995); *Star Trek: First Contact* (1996); *Conspiracy Theory, Masterminds* (1997); *Star Trek: Insurrection* (1998); *X-Men* (2000); *Star Trek: Nemesis* (2002); *X2* (2003); *The Game of Their Lives* (2004).

STORMARE, Peter (1953–)

Early on in his career, Stormare became famous for his stunning performances at the Royal Dramatic Theatre in Stockholm, where he quickly emerged as one of Ingmar Bergman's favourite actors during the 1980s. Stormare continued to develop his dramatic skills both on and behind the stage by respectively performing and/or directing a number of plays in Sweden as well as abroad. His first role in a major Hollywood production was in *Awakenings*, but it was not until his performance as one of the kidnappers in Joel and Ethan Coen's *Fargo* that his American career really took off. (He had previously been offered a role in the Coens' *Miller's Crossing* [1990], but due to circumstances beyond his control was unable to take it.) Stormare has now established himself as a highly sought-after supporting actor renowned for the extraordinary and surreal caricatures he manages to deliver. The personae he creates often act in a peculiar and violent manner and they usually talk with strange European or 'foreign' accents. It thus seems, as is the case with so many of his European colleagues working in Hollywood, that Stormare has been forced, for now, to take roles that fail to move beyond caricature. MJ

FILMS: *Awakenings* (1990); *Fargo* (1996); *The Lost World: Jurassic Park, Playing God* (1997); *The Big Lebowski, Mercury Rising, Somewhere in the City, Armageddon* (1998); *8MM* (1999); *The Million Dollar Hotel, Circus, Chocolat* (2000); *Happy Campers* (2001); *Windtalkers, 13 Moons, Minority Report, Spun, The Tuxedo* (2002); *The Movie Hero, Bad Boys II* (2003); *Birth* (2004).

STÖSSEL, Ludwig (1883–1973)

Officious-looking Austrian-Jewish character actor who fled Nazi Germany in 1933 and emigrated via Austria and Britain to Hollywood. Stössel specialised in playing Middle European doctors and bureaucrats, especially in anti-Nazi films. He became an American citizen and a 1950s and 1960s television regular. RJK

FILMS: *Four Sons, Dance, Girl, Dance, The Man I Married, Jennie* (1940); *Man Hunt, Back Street, Great Guns, Underground, Marry the Boss's Daughter, Down in San Diego* (1941); *All through the Night, Woman of the Year, I Married an Angel, The Pride of the Yankees, Who Done It?, Casablanca, Pittsburgh, Kings Row, Iceland, The Great Impersonation* (1942); *What We are Fighting For, Above Suspicion, The Strange Death of Adolf Hitler, Hers to Hold, Tennessee Johnson, They Came to Blow up America, Hitler's Madman, Action in the North Atlantic* (1943); *Bluebeard, Lake Placid Serenade, The Climax* (1944); *Dillinger, Her Highness and the Bellboy, Yolanda and the Thief, House of Dracula* (1945); *Girl on the Spot, Miss Susie Slagle's, Cloak and Dagger, Temptation* (1946); *The Beginning or the End, This Time for Keeps, Song of Love, Escape Me Never* (1947); *A Song is Born* (1948); *The Great Sinner* (1949); *As Young as You Feel, Too Young to Kiss, Corky of Gasoline Alley* (1951); *Somebody Loves Me, The Merry Widow, No Time for Flowers, Diplomatic Courier* (1952); *White Goddess, The Sun Shines Bright, Call Me Madam* (1953); *Deep in My Heart, Geraldine* (1954); *Me and the Colonel, From the Earth to the Moon* (1958); *The Blue Angel* (1959); *G.I. Blues* (1960).

STRADNER, Rose (1913-1958)

Famed Austrian actress who starred in many of Max Reinhardt's stage comedies in Vienna. She began working in cinema in 1933 and moved to the USA in 1937. In her short Hollywood career, she played opposite actors of the stature of Edward G. Robinson and Gregory Peck. She was married to the director Joseph Mankiewicz. FG

FILMS: *The Last Gangster* (1937); *Blind Alley* (1939); *The Keys of the Kingdom* (1944).

SULLIVAN, Francis L. (1903–1956)

This corpulent British character actor had two spells in Hollywood. His striking resemblance to a Cruikshank novel illustration placed him in particular demand for Dickens adaptations. JB

FILMS: *Cheating Cheaters, Great Expectations, Strange Wives* (1934); *The Mystery of Edwin Drood* (1935); *The Red Danube* (1949); *Night and the City* (1950); *My Favorite Spy, Behave Yourself!* (1951); *Caribbean* (1952); *Sangaree, Plunder of the Sun* (1953); *Drums of Tahiti* (1954); *Hell's Island, The Prodigal* (1955).

SWINBURNE, Nora (Elinore Johnson) (1902–2000)

English actress and star of numerous British silent movies who supplemented her prolific domestic career (which included several US-funded productions) with occasional Hollywood appearances, perhaps most famously as the mother in Jean Renoir's *The River*. MF

FILMS: *These Charming People, A Man of Mayfair* (1931); *A Voice Said Goodnight* (1932); *Too Many Wives* (1933); *The Office Wife* (1934); *Dante's Inferno* (1935); *The Citadel* (1938); *They Flew Alone* (1942); *Quo Vadis, The River* (1951); *Betrayed* (1954); *The End of the Affair* (1955); *Helen of Troy* (1956); *Third Man on the Mountain* (1959); *A Man Could Get Killed* (1966); *Anne of the Thousand Days* (1969).

SWINTON, Tilda (1960–)

Swinton's intense and androgynous features have largely been linked to roles in the films of such leading independent British film-makers as Derek Jarman and Sally Potter. Her American work is similarly distinguished by a commitment to strong, individually talented directors, regardless of the size of the part. She had a powerful leading role in Scott McGehee and David Siegel's knowing remake of Max Ophuls' *The Reckless Moment, The Deep End*. AP

FILMS: *Conceiving Aida* (1997); *The Beach* (2000); *The Deep End, Vanilla Sky* (2001); *Adaptation* (2002).

SWITZERLAND

With a relatively small domestic film industry for most of the first century of film history, Switzerland has not been a particularly fertile seedbed for screen actors who would then go on to have substantial careers in Hollywood. Only four names fit the profile: Maria Schell★, Maximilian

Schell★, Ursula Andress★ and, to a lesser degree, Marthe Keller★. The Schell siblings were Austrian-born Swiss expatriates who grew up in Vienna and Zurich. They were part of the 'Golden Age' of popular Swiss cinema in the 1940s and 1950s, with Maria debuting at the age of sixteen in *Steibruch/The Quarry* in 1942 and Maximilian playing the romantic lead in *Taxifahrer Bänz/Taxidriver Bänz* in 1957, the year before his Hollywood breakthrough in *The Young Lions*. Andress and Keller, on the other hand, never even played in a Swiss film but made their way to Hollywood stardom via the Italian and French film industries respectively. Andress' only domestic acting credit dates from 1988 in *Klassezämekunft/Class Reunion*, a nostalgic Swiss all-star vehicle. Although Keller has only been marginally claimed as a Swiss star by the country's media, both Schells have fully enjoyed this status and Andress has been a staple of tabloid journalism ever since 1962 and her starring role in *Dr No*.

In its only period of sustained feature-film production from the late 1930s through to the late 1950s, the Swiss film industry produced a number of box-office draws, most notably Anne-Marie Blanc★ and Heinrich Gretler★ and the soccer star-cum-actor Hannes Schmidhauser, who played the farmhand-turned-farmer in Switzerland's most popular film of the 1950s, *Uli, der Knecht* (1954). Most of these domestic stars were stage actors who came to represent various facets of Switzerland's war and postwar identity through their film work. Blanc, for instance, was bilingual and in juggling rural and city life in both her roles and off-screen persona, she represented an ideal of cultural unity and innocence (read as neutrality) that became specifically adapted to the values of the wartime period. In a similar vein, the independently minded heroism of Gretler's wary patriarchs made an important contribution to the construction of a national myth of resistance. This went over particularly well with wartime and postwar audiences in search of an explanation for why Switzerland had been spared by World War II.

These symbolic meanings, as well as the commercial appeal of the stars, remained strictly limited to the Swiss scene, however, as Blanc was to learn in 1946 when she got a shot at Hollywood stardom with *White Cradle Inn*, a British-Swiss-US co-production initiated by Blanc's husband, the producer Heinrich Fueter. Slightly more successful was the US career of the young Swiss leading man Paul

Hubschmid★. He was a staple of wartime Swiss and postwar German cinema and starred in six, mostly minor, Hollywood films from the late 1940s through to the early 1970s.

With the possible exception of Jean-Luc Bideau and cult actor François Simon (son of Michel Simon), the New Swiss Cinema of the 1970s and 1980s produced no stars of its own, but relied instead on established actors like Bruno Ganz★ or French actors like Isabelle Huppert★ and Jean-Louis Trintignant★ for its star power and national, as well as international, appeal. VH

SYDNEY, Basil (Basil Nugent) (1894–1968)

Imposing British stage actor who often played stern authority figures during an occasional film career that included parts in various US-funded 'runaway productions' and 'quota films'. He played Pontius Pilate in William Dieterle's *Salome*. MHu

FILM: *The Third Clue* (1934); *The White Lilac, The Riverside Murder* (1935); *Blind Man's Bluff* (1936); *Shadowed Eyes* (1940); *Treasure Island* (1950); *Hell Below Zero, Salome* (1953); *Around the World in Eighty Days* (1956); *The Devil's Disciple* (1959).

SYDOW, Max von (1929–)

Max von Sydow, one of Sweden's most admired actors at home and abroad, made his screen debut in 1949 while still a student at the Royal Dramatic Theatre's acting school. In the 1950s, he joined Ingmar Bergman at the Malmö municipal theatre and soon became a leading man in Bergman's films such as *Det sjunde inseglet/ The Seventh Seal* (1957) and *Såsom i en spegel/ Through a Glass Darkly* (1961). By the 1960s, his authoritative voice and tall, blond, attractively angular physiognomy were well known to filmgoers the world over. This undoubtedly helped him to get the role of Jesus in George Stevens' *The Greatest Story Ever Told*. Von Sydow's later career has continued to be split between extremes. On the one hand, he has continued to play complex character roles in European films such as Bille August's *Pelle erobreren/ Pelle the Conqueror* (1987), for which he received a Best Actor Academy Award nomination in 1988. On the other hand, in Hollywood, von Sydow has continually been typecast, regardless of genre, as either a brooding, vaguely spiritual Scandinavian like the priest in *The Exorcist*, or as an ominously European or demonic, otherworldly villain in films such as *Flash Gordon*. Von Sydow

does, however, often add an unexpected touch to the most hackneyed of roles. In Sydney Pollack's *Three Days of the Condor*, for example, he gave his mercenary character a strangely charismatic and unassuming savoir-faire. MK

FILMS: *The Greatest Story Ever Told, The Reward* (1965); *The Quiller Memorandum, Hawaii* (1966); *The Kremlin Letter* (1970); *The Night Visitor* (1971); *The Exorcist* (1973); *Steppenwolf* (1974); *The Ultimate Warrior, Three Days of the Condor* (1975); *Exorcist 2 – The Heretic* (1977); *Hurricane, Brass Target* (1979); *Flash Gordon* (1980); *Victory, She Dances Alone* (1981); *Conan the Barbarian* (1982); *Strange Brew, Never Say Never Again* (1983); *Dreamscape, Dune, A Soldier's Tale* [voice] (1984); *Codename: Emerald* (1985); *Hannah and Her Sisters, Duet for One* (1986); *Awakenings* (1990); *A Kiss before Dying* (1991); *Needful Things* (1993); *Judge Dredd* (1995); *What Dreams May Come* (1998); *Snow Falling on Cedars* (1999); *Minority Report* (2002).

TAMIROFF, Akim (Akim Mikhailovich Tamirov or Tamiryan) (1899–1972)

Talented Armenian performer who became a popular supporting actor in Hollywood, playing timid villains or comic heroes of various ethnicities. Tamiroff joined New York's Guild Theatre in 1923 while touring with Nikita Balieff's Chauve Souris revue. He moved to Los Angeles in 1932 and was immediately recruited by his former Moscow Art Theatre schoolmates, directors Richard Boleslawski and Rouben Mamoulian. By the middle of the decade, he was earning $500 a week on a seven-year contract with MGM. Tamiroff received Best Supporting Actor Academy Award nominations for roles in *The General Died at Dawn* and *For Whom the Bell Tolls*. In the postwar period, he combined Hollywood work with roles in American television and European cinema. RY

FILMS: *Okay, America!* (1932); *The Barbarian, Storm at Daybreak, The Devil's in Love, Murder in the Private Car, Professional Sweetheart, Gabriel over the White House, Clear All Wires!, Queen Christina* (1933); *The Murder in the Private Car, Straight is the Way, The Scarlet Empress, The Merry Widow, The Captain Hates the Sea, The Great Flirtation, Now and Forever, Here is My Heart, The Scarlet Empress, Chained, Whom the Gods Destroy, Sadie McKee, Fugitive Lovers* (1934); *The Winning Ticket, The Story of Louis Pasteur, The Big Broadcast of 1936, Reckless, Chasing Yesterday, Paris in Spring, Ladies Love Danger, Rumba, Two-Fisted, Black Fury, The Last Outpost, Go into Your* **443**

Akim Tamiroff became a popular supporting player in numerous Hollywood films – here he is 'Tony the window washer' (right) opposite Madeleine Carroll and Fred McMurray in *Honeymoon in Bali* (1939)

Dance, The Gay Deception, China Seas, Naughty Marietta, The Lives of a Bengal Lancer (1935); *Desire, I Loved a Soldier, Woman Trap, The Jungle Princess, The General Died at Dawn, Anthony Adverse* (1936); *This Way Please, High, Wide, and Handsome, Her Husband Lies, King of Gamblers, The Soldier and the Lady, The Great Gambini* (1937); *The Buccaneer, Dangerous to Know, Ride a Crooked Mile, Spawn of the North* (1938); *King of Chinatown, The Magnificent Fraud, Honeymoon in Bali, Paris Honeymoon, Union Pacific, Disputed Passage* (1939); *The Way of All Flesh, The Texas Rangers Ride Again, Untamed, North West Mounted Police, The Great McGinty, North West Mounted Police* (1940); *The Corsican Brothers, New York Town* (1941); *Tortilla Flat, Reap the Wild Wind* [voice] (1942); *For Whom the Bell Tolls, His Butler's Sister, Five Graves to Cairo* (1943); *The Miracle of Morgan's Creek, The Bridge of San Luis Rey, Dragon Seed, Can't Help Singing* (1944); *Pardon*

My Past (1945); *A Scandal in Paris* (1946); *The Gangster, Fiesta* (1947); *Relentless, My Girl Tisa* (1948); *Outpost in Morocco, Black Magic* (1949); *Desert Legion, They Who Dare* (1953); *You Know What Sailors Are* (1954); *Mr Arkadin* (1955); *The Black Sleep, Anastasia* (1956); *Me and the Colonel, Touch of Evil* (1958); *Ocean's Eleven* (1960); *Romanoff and Juliet* (1961); *The Reluctant Saint* (1962); *Topkapi, Panic Button* (1964); *The Liquidator, Lord Jim* (1965); *After the Fox, Lt. Robin Crusoe, U.S.N.* (1966); *Great Catherine* (1968); *The Great Bank Robbery* (1969).

TANDY, Jessica (1909–1994)

Talented and versatile English stage and screen actress whose Hollywood fame peaked unusually in her autumnal years. Tandy gained an impressive reputation on the London stage playing opposite the likes of Laurence Olivier* and John

Gielgud★ and appeared in a few British films (including *Murder in the Family* funded by Fox) before making her American movie debut in 1944. Tandy felt undervalued by Twentieth Century-Fox and commuted between Los Angeles and New York forging a formidable reputation as one of *the* leading ladies on Broadway after appearing as Blanche DuBois in the original production of *A Streetcar Named Desire*. After appearing as Rod Taylor's domineering mother in Hitchcock's *The Birds*, she did not work in Hollywood for almost three decades. During the 1980s, Tandy was cast in increasingly high-profile parts before she finally attracted the plaudits she deserved with a Best Actress Academy Award for *Driving Miss Daisy* and a Best Supporting Actress nomination for *Fried Green Tomatoes*. MF

FILMS: *Murder in the Family* (1938); *Blonde Fever, The Seventh Cross* (1944); *The Valley of Decision* (1945); *Dragonwyck, The Green Years* (1946); *Forever Amber* (1947); *A Woman's Vengeance* (1948); *September Affair* (1950); *The Desert Fox* (1951); *Light in the Forest* (1958); *Hemingway's Adventures of a Young Man* (1962); *The Birds* (1963); *Honky Tonk Freeway* (1981); *The World According to Garp, Still of the Night, Best Friends* (1982); *The Bostonians* (1984); *Cocoon* (1985); *★batteries not included* (1987); *Cocoon: The Return, The House on Carroll Street* (1988); *Driving Miss Daisy* (1989); *Fried Green Tomatoes* (1991); *Used People* (1992); *Nobody's Fool* (1994).

TAUTOU, Audrey (1978–)

The petite, dark-haired gamine-looking Tautou became an instant national and international sensation as the sweet eponymous heroine of the global hit *Le Fabuleux destin d'Amélie Poulain / Amélie* (2001). Hollywood offers followed, but her 'American' debut, *Nowhere to Go but Up*, was a modest American-Franco-German co-production shot in New York, which tries to suggest some resemblance to the other Audrey (Hepburn★), after whom Tautou was apparently named. GV

FILM: *Nowhere to Go but Up* (2003).

TCHÉRINA, Ludmilla (Monique Tchemerzine) (1924–2004)

Franco-Russian former prima ballerina of the Monte Carlo ballet who was much favoured by Powell and Pressburger and played feminine leads in French and international films from the mid-1940s. She was a princess in Douglas Sirk's *Sign of the Pagan*. VO

FILM: *Sign of the Pagan* (1954).

TEIXEIRA, Virgílio (1917–)

Romantic lead and star of Portuguese cinema in the 1940s and 1950s, also known as Virgil Texera, who appeared in American productions shot in Europe such as *El Cid*, in which he was a mere extra. His most successful Hollywood role was in *The Return of the Seven*. AR

FILMS: *Alexander the Great* (1956); *The 7th Voyage of Sinbad* (1958); *El Cid* (1961); *The Happy Thieves* (1962); *The Fall of the Roman Empire* (1964); *Doctor Zhivago* [uncredited] (1965); *A Man Who Could Get Killed* (1966); *The Return of the Seven* (1967).

TELLEGEN, Lou (Isadore Louis Bernard van Dommelem) (1881–1934)

The handsome Lou Tellegen, born in the Netherlands of Greek and Dutch descent, had already had a colourful career driving taxis in Brussels, working on a French cargo ship, selling birth-control pamphlets in Russia and starring as a trapeze artist in Berlin before he accompanied Sarah Bernhardt★ on a North American tour in 1910. He had been introduced to the great French actress after being rescued from a Parisian prison by his actor friend, Edouard de Max. Tellegen starred opposite Bernhardt in films such as *La Dame aux camélias* (1910) and *Les Amours de la reine Elisabeth* (1912), and following the great American success of the latter, he appeared on Broadway the following year. Hollywood success as a sophisticated matinée idol soon ensued, but by the early years of the sound era, he was beset by financial and medical problems. He committed suicide in 1934. AP

FILMS: *The Explorer, The Unknown* (1915); *The Victory of Conscience, The Victoria Cross* (1916); *The Long Trail, The Black Wolf* (1917); *The World and its Women, Flame of the Desert* (1919); *The Woman and the Puppet* (1920); *Between Friends, The Breath of Scandal, Greater than Marriage, Let Not Man Put Asunder, Single Wives, Those Who Judge* (1924); *After Business Hours, Borrowed Finery, East Lynne, Fair Play, Parisian Love, Parisian Nights, The Redeeming Sin, The Sporting Chance, The Verdict, With this Ring* (1925); *The Outsider, Siberia, The Silver Treasure, Three Bad Men, Womanpower* (1926); *The Princess from Hoboken, The Little Firebrand, Married Alive, Stage Madness* (1927); *Enemies of the Law* (1931); *Together We Live* (1935).

445

TENNANT, Victoria (1950–)

Engaging blonde British actress who appeared in several UK and European films before various roles in American television. Tennant played a typically charming scatterbrained character in *L.A. Story* alongside her then husband Steve Martin. TJ

FILMS: *Strangers Kiss* (1983); *All of Me* (1984); *Flowers in the Attic, Best Seller* (1987); *The Handmaid's Tale* (1990); *L.A. Story* (1991); *Legend of the Mummy, Edie & Pen* (1997).

TESTI, Fabio (1941–)

Italian actor who began his film career as a stuntman. He was spotted by Vittorio De Sica★ and went on to appear in various Italian action films. His powerful physical presence and famously dreamy and expressive eyes led to a leading role in *The Ambassador*, but since then, alongside his European film work, he has mainly appeared on American television. CS

FILMS: *The Ambassador* (1984); *Iguana* (1988).

THATCHER, Torin (1905–1981)

Born in India to British parents, this former schoolteacher had a muscular presence and menacing stare that he utilised to play a number of villainous screen roles. Although he appeared uncredited in Hitchcock's *Saboteur*, he did not actually move to Hollywood until 1952, where he initially played a troublemaking pirate in Robert Siodmak's *The Crimson Pirate*. JS/AP

FILMS: *Saboteur* (1942); *The Crimson Pirate, Affair in Trinidad, The Snows of Kilimanjaro, Blackbeard the Pirate* (1952); *The Desert Rats, Houdini, The Robe* (1953); *Knock on Wood, The Black Shield of Falworth, Bengal Brigade* (1954); *Love is a Many-Splendored Thing, Lady Godiva* (1955); *Diane, Helen of Troy* (1956); *Istanbul, Band of Angels, Witness for the Prosecution* (1957); *Darby's Rangers, The 7th Voyage of Sinbad* (1958); *The Miracle* (1959); *The Canadians* (1961); *Jack the Giant Killer, Mutiny on the Bounty* (1962); *Drums of Africa* (1963); *The Sandpiper* (1965); *Hawaii, Hell of Borneo* (1966); *The King's Pirate* (1967).

THESIGER, Ernest (1879–1961)

Skeletal embroidery fanatic with a highly successful career on the English stage and in British silent cinema.

Thesiger achieved lasting fame through his association with James Whale, playing delightfully mad and effeminate eccentrics such as the mad scientist Dr Praetorious in *Bride of Frankenstein*. He also appeared in a number of US-funded films shot in Europe at the end of his career. MW

FILMS: *The Old Dark House* (1932); *The Only Girl* (1933); *Bride of Frankenstein* (1935); *The Robe* (1953); *Father Brown* (1954); *The Adventures of Quentin Durwood* (1955); *The Battle of the Sexes* (1959); *Sons and Lovers* (1960); *The Roman Spring of Mrs Stone* (1961).

THEWLIS, David (1963–)

After widespread critical acclaim for his seething performance in Mike Leigh's *Naked* (1993), Thewlis has gone on to appear in a number of eclectic, but occasional, supporting Hollywood roles. JS

FILMS: *Black Beauty* (1994); *Restoration* (1995); *Dragonheart, The Island of Dr Moreau* (1996); *American Perfekt, Seven Years in Tibet* (1997); *The Big Lebowski* (1998); *Timeline* (2003); *Harry Potter and the Prisoner of Azkaban* (2004).

THOMAS, Jameson (1888–1939)

British stage and screen actor who appeared in nearly fifty Hollywood films from 1930 until his death. Thomas chiefly played bit parts and supporting roles such as Claudette Colbert's aviator husband in Frank Capra's *It Happened One Night*. MW

FILMS: *Extravagance* (1930); *Lover Come Back, The Devil Plays, Chances, Night Life in Reno, Convicted* (1931); *The Phantom President, No More Orchids, The Trial of Vivienne Ware, Self Defense, Three Wise Girls, Escapade* (1932); *Brief Moment, The Invisible Man, The Secret of Madame Blanche, The Solitaire Man* (1933); *It Happened One Night, A Woman's Man, Jane Eyre, Happiness Ahead, The Man Who Reclaimed His Head, Bombay Mail, A Lost Lady, Sing Sing Nights, The Moonstone, Stolen Sweets, The World Accuses, A Successful Failure, Beggars in Ermine, Now and Forever, The Scarlet Empress, The Curtain Falls* (1934); *Coronado, Charlie Chan in Egypt, Rumba, Mister Dynamite, The Last Outpost, The Lives of a Bengal Lancer, The Lady in Scarlet* (1935); *Lady Luck, Mr Deeds Goes to Town, House of Secrets* (1936); *The League of Frightened Men, Girl Loves Boy, One Hundred Men and a Girl, Parnell, The Man Who Cried Wolf* (1937); *Death Goes North* (1938).

THOMAS, Terry (Thomas Terry Hoar Stevens) (1911–1990)

Much-loved British comic actor who became an icon of the international screen for his caricatural Englishness in the form of a devious upper-class cad with a gap-toothed grin. MW

FILMS: *tom thumb* (1958); *A Matter of WHO, Bachelor Flat* (1961); *The Wonderful World of the Brothers Grimm* (1962); *It's a Mad Mad Mad Mad World, The Mouse on the Moon* (1963); *Strange Bedfellows, How to Murder Your Wife, Those Magnificent Men in Their Flying Machines, or How I Flew from London to Paris in 25 Hours 11 Minutes, You Must Be Joking!* (1965); *Our Man in Marrakesh, Munster, Go Home, The Daydreamer* (1966); *A Guide for the Married Man, The Perils of Pauline, The Karate Killers, Don't Raise the Bridge, Lower the River* (1967); *Where Were You When the Lights Went Out?, How Sweet it Is!, Monte Carlo: C'est La Rose* (1968); *Monte Carlo or Bust!, 2000 Years Later* (1969); *Robin Hood* [voice], *The Vault of Horror* (1973); *The Last Remake of Beau Geste* (1977).

THOMPSON, Emma (1959–)

Initially part of the British comedy scene in the early 1980s, the youthful Emma Thompson appeared in such television successes as *The Young Ones* and *The Comic Strip Presents*. Later, however, her name became virtually synonymous with heritage cinema and it was therefore restrained period drama, rather than bawdy irreverence, that brought Thompson to Hollywood's attention when she won an Academy Award for her role in Merchant-Ivory's visually lush adaptation of E. M. Forster's *Howards End* (1992). She had actually made her American debut the previous year with *Dead Again*, an enjoyable (if slight) neo-noir thriller that co-starred her director, and then husband, Kenneth Branagh★. If the film was in retrospect mainly a showcase for the couple's respective talents, it nevertheless pointed to a playful impiousness that would reappear only fleetingly in Thompson's later vehicles.

Thompson followed her triumph by signing up for further American-funded literary adaptations such as Merchant-Ivory's production of Kazuo Ishiguro's *The Remains of the Day* and Branagh's playful version of *Much Ado about Nothing*. She delicately matched the pathos that emanated from co-star Anthony Hopkins's★ irredeemably repressed butler in the former, while in the latter, she was a lively, sharp-tongued Beatrice opposite Branagh's posturing

Benedick. Her performance in *The Remains of the Day* earned her a second Best Actress Academy Award nomination, a feat she repeated for her part as a liberal English lawyer in the political melodrama *In the Name of the Father*. Thompson was subsequently cast opposite Arnold Schwarzenegger★ in *Junior*, a bizarre double-act that worked well against all the odds. After this return to her comic roots, the actress-screenwriter maintained her critical and commercial popularity with a long-cherished adaptation of Jane Austen's *Sense and Sensibility*. Her screenplay won an Academy Award.

Thompson withdrew to hone her undoubted talents as a screenwriter after these high-profile successes, though she was an excellent 'Hilary' to John Travolta's 'Bill' in the Clinton era satire *Primary Colors*. *Judas Kiss*, featuring Thompson as an FBI agent, failed to gain an American cinema release the same year, though, perhaps indicating the restrictive cul-de-sac of genteel politeness that epitomises her popular star persona. On the other hand, a made-for-television adaptation of Margaret Edson's Pulitzer Prize-winning play *Wit*, in which Thompson played a doctor who bravely fights cancer, earned her prestigious Emmy nominations for both her lead performance and screenplay. They also prompted a belated, if limited, theatrical release. MF

FILMS: *Dead Again* (1991); *Much Ado about Nothing, The Remains of the Day, In the Name of the Father* (1993); *Junior, My Father the Hero* (1994); *Sense and Sensibility* (1995); *The Winter Guest* (1997); *Primary Colors, Judas Kiss* (1998); *Treasure Planet* [voice] (2002); *Love Actually, Imagining Argentina* (2003); *Harry Potter and the Prisoner of Azkaban* (2004).

THORSEN, Sven-Ole (1944–)

Former Danish bodybuilding champion-turned-stuntman who moved to Hollywood in 1985 as part of the Arnold Schwarzenegger★ coterie. He has since contributed stunt work and played numerous, mostly villainous, supporting roles in a number of action films. HJW

FILMS: *Conan the Barbarian* (1982); *Conan the Destroyer* (1984); *Raw Deal* (1986); *Lethal Weapon, Predator, The Running Man* (1987); *Red Heat, Twins* (1988); *Pink Cadillac* (1989); *The Hunt for Red October* (1990); *Harley Davidson and the Marlboro Man, Dead On: Relentless II, Abraxas, Guardian of the Universe* (1991); *Lethal Weapon 3* (1992); *Dragon: The Bruce Lee Story, Nowhere to Run, Last Action Hero, Hard Target, Cyborg 2* (1993); *On Deadly Ground, A* **447**

Low Down Dirty Shame, The Dangerous (1994); *The Quick and the Dead, Mallrats, The Viking Sagas, No Exit* (1995); *Eraser, Fox Hunt* (1996); *George of the Jungle, Kull the Conqueror* (1997); *The Bad Pack* (1998); *Foolish, The 13th Warrior, Best of the Best: Without Warning, End of Days* (1999); *Facade, Gladiator* (2000); *Bandits, Route 666, Extreme Honor* (2001); *Collateral Damage, The Sums of All Fears* (2002); *Hidalgo, Charlie's Angels: Full Throttle, The Rundown, Timecop: The Berlin Decision* (2003); *In Enemy Hands* (2004).

THULIN, Ingrid (1929–2004)

Ingrid Thulin could be dubbed the female counterpart to her compatriot Max von Sydow★. Both began their careers in Swedish films in the 1940s while students at the Royal Dramatic Theatre's acting school, and both acted with Ingmar Bergman at the Malmö municipal theatre in the 1950s while also being cast in Bergman films such as *Smultronstället/Wild Strawberries* (1957) and *Nära livet/Brink of Life/So Close to Life* (1958). The pair have also worked internationally thanks to their blond hair and strikingly good looks. However, in contrast to von Sydow, Thulin's non-Swedish roles have only rarely made the most of her cool and meditative acting style. After the forgettable *Foreign Intrigue*, co-starring Robert Mitchum, her voice was even dubbed by Angela Lansbury in Vincente Minnelli's *The Four Horsemen of the Apocalypse*, most probably because of her then still heavy Swedish accent. MK

FILMS: *Foreign Intrigue* (1956); *The Four Horsemen of the Apocalypse* (1962); *Return from the Ashes* (1965); *The Damned* (1969).

THYSSEN, Greta (Grethe Thygesen) (unknown)

Miss Denmark of 1952 who appeared in various Hollywood drive-in movies, played a foil for The Three Stooges and had a minor role in John Cassavetes' *Shadows*. HJW

FILMS: *Bus Stop* [scenes deleted], *Accused of Murder* (1956); *Quizz Whizz, Pies and Guys, The Beast of Budapest* (1958); *Sappy Bullfighters, Shadows, Terror is a Man, Catch Me If You Can* (1959); *Three Blondes in His Life* (1961); *Journey to the Seventh Planet* (1962); *The Double-Barrelled Detective Story* (1965); *Cottonpickin' Chickenpickers* (1966).

TODD, Ann (1909–1993)

Beautiful British actress who became a UK star following her leading role opposite James Mason★ in *The Seventh Veil*

(1945). She had a leading role as Gay Keane opposite Gregory Peck in Hitchcock's *The Paradine Case*. MHu

FILMS: *These Charming People* (1931); *Tower of London* (1939); *How Green Was My Valley* (1941); *Perfect Strangers* (1945); *The Paradine Case* (1947); *So Evil My Love* (1948).

TODD, Richard (Richard Palethorpe-Todd) (1919–)

Handsome Irish leading man who often made use of his military upbringing to play stereotypical British officer and gentleman characters. Todd's first major stage role was as the terminally ill Scottish soldier Lachie in the Broadway production of *The Hasty Heart*. He received an Academy Award nomination for his repeat performance in the Warner Bros.-funded British production. The first of two brief spells in Hollywood followed and while he appreciated the professionalism of the American studios, Todd preferred to combine stage and screen work in Britain, where he was one of the best-known faces of the immediate postwar period. RB

FILMS: *The Hasty Heart* (1949); *Stage Fright* (1950); *Lightning Strikes Twice* (1951); *The Story of Robin Hood and His Merrie Men* (1952); *The Sword and the Rose* (1953); *Rob Roy, the Highland Rogue* (1954); *The Virgin Queen, A Man Called Peter* (1955); *D-Day the Sixth of June* (1956); *Saint Joan* (1957); *The Naked Earth* (1958); *The Longest Day* (1962); *The Battle of the Villa Fiorita* (1965); *Blood Bath* (1966); *The Love-Ins* (1967).

TOMLINSON, David (1917–2000)

British character actor who established his reputation in British cinema playing genial, silly-ass roles, typified by his performance as 'Prune' Parsons in *The Way to the Stars* (1945). He is best remembered for his role as George Banks opposite Julie Andrews★ in *Mary Poppins* and subsequently made two other successful films for Disney: *The Love Bug* and *Bedknobs and Broomsticks*. MHu

FILMS: *Tom Jones* (1963); *The Truth about Spring, Mary Poppins* (1964); *The Liquidator* (1965); *The Love Bug* (1969); *Bedknobs and Broomsticks* (1971); *The Fiendish Plot of Dr Fu Manchu* (1980).

TORRENCE, David (1864–1951)

David Torrence (the brother of Ernest Torrence★) appeared in two minor American film roles after performing on Broadway. Following a failed venture as a Mexican cattle rancher, the Englishman moved to Hollywood to become a successful character actor. He had a tall and imposing physical presence and therefore initially appeared in outdoors roles in various Westerns and sports films. He later specialised in domineering lawyers, merchants or bankers such as the anti-Semitic head of the Bank of England in *Disraeli*. AP

FILMS: *The Prisoner of Zenda, Tess of the D'Urbervilles* (1913); *The Inside of the Cup* (1921); *Forsaking All Others, The Power of a Lie, Received Payment, Sherlock Holmes, Tess of the Storm Country, A Virgin's Sacrifice* (1922); *Abysmal Brute, The Drums of Jeopardy, The Light that Failed, The Man Next Door, Railroaded, Trimmed in Scarlet* (1923); *The Dawn of a Tomorrow, Idle Tongues, Love's Wilderness, Sawdust Trail, Surging Seas, Tiger Love, Which Shall it Be?* (1924); *Fighting the Flames, He Who Laughs Last, Her Husband's Secret, The Mystic, The Other Woman's Story, The Reckless Sex, The Tower of Lies, What Fools Men, The Wheel* (1925); *The Auction Block, Brown of Harvard, Forever After, The Isle of Retribution, The King of the Turf, Laddie, The Man in the Shadow, Oh, What a Nurse!, Race Wild, Sandy, The Third Degree, The Unknown Cavalier, The Wolf Hunters* (1926); *Annie Laurie, Hazardous Valley, The Midnight Watch, The Mysterious Rider, On the Stroke of Twelve, Rolled Stockings, The World at Her Feet* (1927); *The Big Noise, The Cavalier, City of Purple Dreams, The Little Shepherd of Kingdom Come, Undressed* (1928); *The Black Watch, Disraeli, Hearts in Exile, Silks and Saddles, Strong Boy, Untamed Justice* (1929); *City Girl, Raffles, River's End, Scotland Yard, The Devil to Pay* (1930); *The Bachelor Father, East Lynne, Five Star Friend* (1931); *Smilin' Through, A Successful Calamity, The Mask of Fu Manchu* (1932); *Berkeley Square, Cavalcade, Horseplay, The Masquerader, Queen Christina, Voltaire* (1933); *All Men are Enemies, Charlie Chan in London, The House of Rothschild, Jane Eyre, Madame Spy, Mandalay, What Every Woman Knows* (1934); *Black Sheep, Bonnie Scotland, Captain Blood, Charlie Chan in Shanghai, The Dark Angel, Harmony Lane, Mutiny on the Bounty* (1935); *Annie Laurie, Beloved Enemy, The Country Doctor, Mary of Scotland* (1936); *Ebb Tide, Lost Horizon* (1937); *Five of a Kind* (1938); *Bulldog Drummond's Bride, Rulers of the Sea, Stanley and Livingstone* (1939); *Botany Bay* (1953).

TORRENCE, Ernest (1878–1933)

Imposingly built Scottish actor who arrived in the USA in 1911 to perform in stage musicals. He began playing a variety of often villainous Hollywood roles in the 1920s and appeared in a number of now classic silent Westerns. MF

FILMS: *A Dangerous Affair* (1919); *Tol'able David* (1921); *Prodigal Judge, Singed Wings, Broken Chains, The Kingdom Within* (1922); *The Brass Bottle, The Covered Wagon, Ruggles of Red Gap, The Trail of the Lonesome Pine, The Hunchback of Notre Dame* (1923); *West of the Water Tower, The Fighting Coward, The Side Show of Life, North of 36, Peter Pan, Heritage of the Desert* (1924); *The Dressmaker from Paris, Night Life of New York, The Pony Express, The Wanderer* (1925); *The American Venus, The Blind Goddess, The Rainmaker, Mantrap, The Lady of the Harem* (1926); *The King of Kings, Captain Salvation, Twelve Miles Out* (1927); *Across to Singapore, Steamboat Bill, Jr, The Cossacks* (1928); *Desert Nights, The Bridge of San Luis Rey, Speedway, The Unholy Night, Untamed* (1929); *Officer O'Brien, Strictly Unconventional, Call of the Flesh, Sweet Kitty Bellairs* (1930); *Fighting Caravans, Sporting Blood, New Adventures of Get Rich Quick Wallingford, Shipmates, The Great Lover, The Cuban Love Song* (1931); *Sherlock Holmes, Hypnotized* (1932); *I Cover the Waterfront* (1933).

TOWNSEND, Stuart (1972–)

Good-looking Irish actor who came to attention through his roles as the demented Loyalist killer in *Resurrection Man* (1998) and the romantic lead in *About Adam* (2000). His Hollywood supporting roles include the part of Dorian Gray in *The League of Extraordinary Gentlemen*. RB

FILMS: *Queen of the Damned, Trapped, Shade* (2002); *The League of Extraordinary Gentlemen* (2003).

TRAVERS, Bill (1922–1994)

Travers enjoyed a relatively low-key career in British movies of the 1950s as a cut-price Kenneth More★, offering a similar brand of solid heartiness framed by a well-fed physique. Some of these films shot in Europe were largely financed by Hollywood. Proper international success came as a Kenyan game warden opposite his wife Virginia McKenna★ in the US-funded wildlife drama *Born Free*. It presumably led United Artists to cast him in another outdoors setting – the American West – in *Duel at Diablo*. JB

FILMS: *The Story of Robin Hood and His Merrie Men* (1952); *Footsteps in the Fog* (1955); *Bhowani Junction* (1956); *The Barretts of Wimpole St, The Seventh Sin* (1957); *The Green Helmut* (1961); *Born Free, Duel at Diablo* (1966).

449

TRAVERS, Henry (Travers Heagerty) (1874–1965)

British supporting actor who began his stage career in 1894 and moved to the USA in 1901. Travers made his screen debut in 1932 and worked constantly until his retirement in 1949. He generally played elderly, genial characters and is most fondly remembered as Clarence, James Stewart's guardian angel in *It's a Wonderful Life*. MHu

FILMS: *The Invisible Man, My Weakness, Another Language, Reunion in Vienna* (1933); *The Party's Over, Ready for Love, Born to Be Bad, Death Takes a Holiday* (1934); *Captain Hurricane, Escapade, Seven Keys to Baldpate, Pursuit, Four Hours to Kill!, After Office Hours, Maybe It's Love* (1935); *Too Many Parents* (1936); *The Sisters* (1938); *On Borrowed Time, Remember?, The Rains Came, Stanley and Livingstone, You Can't Get Away with Murder, Dark Victory, Dodge City* (1939); *Anne of Windy Poplars, Wyoming, Edison, the Man, The Primrose Path* (1940); *The Bad Man, I'll Wait for You, Ball of Fire, A Girl, a Guy, and a Gob, High Sierra* (1941); *Pierre of the Plains, Random Harvest, Mrs Miniver* (1942); *Madame Curie, Shadow of a Doubt, The Moon is Down* (1943); *Dragon Seed, None Shall Escape, The Very Thought of You* (1944); *The Bells of St Mary's, The Naughty Nineties, Thrill of a Romance* (1945); *It's a Wonderful Life, The Yearling, Gallant Journey* (1946); *The Flame* (1947); *The Accused, Beyond Glory* (1948); *The Girl from Jones Beach* (1949).

TREACHER, Arthur (Arthur Veary Treacher) (1894–1975)

Tall and spindly British actor with a disdainful mien who appeared as a manservant in numerous Hollywood productions, including four Shirley Temple vehicles. Treacher was usually cast as a supporting player, but he achieved greater prominence as Jeeves in two films in 1936 and 1937. TJ

FILMS: *The Battle of Paris* (1929); *California Weather* (1933); *Fashions of 1934, Gambling Lady, Madame DuBarry, The Captain Hates the Sea, Here Comes the Groom, The Key, Hollywood Party, When Do We Eat?, School for Romance* (1934); *No More Ladies, I Live My Life, A Midsummer Night's Dream, Personal Maid's Secret, Magnificent Obsession, Splendor, Remember Last Night?, Orchids to You, Let's Live Tonight, Going Highbrow, The Daring Young Man, Curly Top, Cardinal Richelieu, Bright Lights* (1935); *Hitch Hike Lady, Anything Goes, Hearts Divided, Satan Met a Lady, Mister Cinderella, The Case Against Mrs Ames, Stowaway, Under Your Spell, Thank You, Jeeves!* (1936); *She Had to Eat, You Can't Have Everything, Thin Ice, Step Lively, Jeeves!, Heidi* (1937); *Mad about Music, My Lucky Star, Up the River, Always in Trouble* (1938); *The Little Princess, Barricade, Bridal Suite* (1939); *Brother Rat and a Baby, Irene* (1940); *Star Spangled Rhythm* (1942); *Forever and a Day, The Amazing Mrs Holliday* (1943); *Chip Off the Old Block, National Velvet, In Society* (1944); *That's the Spirit, Swing Out, Sister, Delightfully Dangerous* (1945); *Fun on a Weekend, Slave Girl* (1947); *The Countess of Monte Cristo* (1948); *That Midnight Kiss* (1949); *Love that Brute* (1950); *Mary Poppins* (1964).

TREE, Herbert Beerbohm (1853–1917)

Herbert Tree had been the unofficial leader of the British theatrical profession following the death of Henry Irving in 1904. Unusually for a theatrical knight in the vanguard of his profession, he had acted upon his fascination with the cinema as a medium for actors as early as 1899 and had appeared in two further British films by 1914, even as his immediate peers looked on with disdain. In 1915, at the instigation of its head of production D.W. Griffith, the Fine Arts Film Company invited Tree – then in the middle of an American theatrical tour – to make a series of Shakespeare films. He arrived in California in late December of that year to sign a contract worth an extravagant $100,000 for thirty-one weeks' work. Tree is claimed to have played a walk-on part in *Intolerance*, but Griffith otherwise opted to produce rather than personally direct his star signing in an ambitiously mounted production of *Macbeth*. This first significant association between Hollywood money and a British high-culture icon was not a happy one. Tree's private correspondence reveals his delight with the finished film, but the financially troubled Fine Arts lost all faith in the scheme somewhere along the way and pressed Tree into humiliating supporting roles to get him to break his costly contract. He called their bluff for one such picture and then resentfully departed $76,000 richer, if little wiser about Hollywood business methods and casting practices. JB

FILMS: *Intolerance, Macbeth, The Old Folks at Home* (1916)

TRENTO, Guido (1882–1957)

Italian stage and screen actor who left for the USA in the early 1920s and worked in Hollywood until 1932. After appearances in films such as *Street Angel*, Trento participated in Italian- and Spanish-language productions such as *Una nueva y gloriosa nación/ The Charge of the Gauchos* (1928). He also worked in dubbing at Fox. In the late 1920s, he founded Italtone Film Production, without great success, with fellow Italian émigré Alberto Rabagliati★. CBu

FILMS: *It is the Law* (1924); *The Shepherd King* (1925); *Street Angel* (1928); *Secrets of the French Police* (1932).

TRIESAULT, Ivan (1902–1980)

Triesault emigrated from Germany to the USA at the age of eighteen and after a period of training in New York and London, appeared as a pantomime artist and dancer on the stage of Radio City Music Hall. He went to Hollywood following a brief stint on Broadway, where he played character roles as a Nazi, Communist agent or other such 'undesirable' foreigner. FG

FILMS: *The Strange Death of Adolf Hitler, Hostages, Mission to Moscow* (1943); *Days of Glory, The Hitler Gang, The Story of Dr Wassall, Song of Russia, The Black Parachute, The Mummy's Ghost, In Our Time, Uncertain Glory, Strange Affair, Cry of the Werewolf* (1944); *A Song to Remember, Escape in the Fog, Counter Attack* (1945); *Notorious, The Return of Monte Cristo, Crime Doctor's Man Hunt* (1946); *The Crimson Key, Golden Earrings, Escape Me Never* (1947); *To the Ends of the Earth, The Woman from Tangier* (1948); *Home in San Antone, The Sickle or the Cross, Johnny Allegro, Battleground* (1949); *Captain Carey USA, D.O.A., Spy Hunt* (1950); *Kim, Target Unknown, The Lady and the Bandit, My Favorite Spy, My True Story, The Desert Fox: The Story of Rommel* (1951); *5 Fingers* (1952); *The Bad and the Beautiful, Ma and Pa Kettle on Vacation, Desert Legion, Scandal at Scourie, How to Marry a Millionaire, Young Bess, Back to God's Country* (1953); *Charge of the Lancers, Her Twelve Men, Border River, The Student Prince, The Gambler from Natchez* (1954); *The Girl in the Red Velvet Swing* (1955); *Operation Cicero, I'll Give My Life* (1956); *Silk Stockings, Top Secret Affair, Jet Pilot, The Buster Keaton Story* (1957); *The Young Lions* (1958); *Journey to the Center of the Earth* (1959); *Cimarron, The Amazing Transparent Man* (1960); *Barabbas, It Happened in Athens, The 300 Spartans* (1962); *The Prize* (1963); *Viva Las Vegas* (1964); *Von Ryan's Express, Morituri* (1965); *Batman* (1966).

TRIFUNOVIĆ, Sergej (1972–)

Bosnian actor who is one of the leading Yugoslav theatre and film performers of his generation. Due to the rebellious energy of his performance style, Trifunović is often com-

pared in his home country to James Dean. In *Savior*, the Hollywood take on the Bosnian war produced by Oliver Stone, he had a memorable supporting role as the bloody Serbian villain Goran. DI

FILMS: *Savior* (1998); *3 A.M.* (2001).

TRINTIGNANT, Jean–Louis (1930–)

Emerging at the time of the New Wave, Trintignant came to international fame in Claude Lelouch's *Un homme et une femme/A Man and a Woman* (1966). His small but well-built physique and rich, authoritative and seductive voice have led to a richly diverse and distinguished long European film career. He has reputedly refused numerous roles in US films, including *Apocalypse Now* (1979) and *Close Encounters of the Third Kind* (1977). He played a French CIA agent in his one Hollywood production. SL

FILM: *Under Fire* (1983).

TRUFFAUT, François (1932–1984)

The celebrated New Wave critic and director (and occasional actor in his own films such as the Warners-funded *La Nuit américaine*) appeared in only one Hollywood fiction film shot in the USA. Steven Spielberg invited Truffaut to play a French scientist in his sci-fi movie *Close Encounters of the Third Kind* out of admiration for his work. GV

FILMS: *La Nuit américaine* (1973); *Close Encounters of the Third Kind* (1977).

ULLMAN, Tracey (1959–)

Versatile British actress, comedienne and singer who came to prominence in the British television comedy series *Three of a Kind*. She moved to the USA in the mid-1980s and has had great success with her own shows on American television. Her screen profile has grown with a series of successful appearances such as 'Frenchy' Winkler in Woody Allen's *Small Time Crooks*. MHu

FILMS: *Jumpin' Jack Flash* (1986); *I Love You to Death* (1990); *Happily Ever After* [voice], *Household Saints* (1993); *I'll Do Anything, Bullets over Broadway, Prêt-à-Porter* (1994); *Panic, Small Time Crooks, C-Scam* (2000); *A Dirty Shame* (2004).

ULLMANN, Liv (1939–)

Norwegian stage and film actress who won international fame in the late 1960s and 1970s for her roles in films **451** directed by Ingmar Bergman such as *Persona* (1966) and *Viskningar och rop/Cries and Whispers* (1972). Ullmann enjoyed great popularity in the USA, where she was lauded for her radiant beauty and her intimate, subtle and expressive performance style. She won the New York Film Critics award for Best Actress in *Scener ur ett äktenskap/Scenes from a Marriage* in 1974 and *Ansikte mot ansikte/Face to Face* in 1976. It is ironical, therefore, that a character actress of such range would allow herself to be so miscast when offered work in Hollywood. This was certainly the case with the musical *Lost Horizon* that followed the Scandanavian and American co-production *The Night Visitor*. She did not fare much better in the comedy *40 Carats*, although she was relatively more successful on Broadway when she starred in *Anna Christie* (1977) and a musical adaptation of *I Remember Mama* (1979). Ullmann was more in her element in *Zandy's Bride*. Here, she played a Scandinavian mail-order bride in the American West who is maltreated by a bully of a husband and is forced to tap into her particular brand of seemingly brittle beauty and sturdy, strong-willed down-to-earthness. That combination is also evident in the US/German co-production *The Serpent's Egg/Das Schlangenei*, where she was a cabaret singer in prewar Germany who combines wide-eyed naivety with indomitable will to survive. Ullmann's noticeable, vaguely European accent served her well once more, in two productions made by Swedish directors she had previously worked with: Jan Troell (director of *The Emigrants* [1971], for which Ullmann had won the New York Film Critics award for Best Actress) and Ingmar Bergman. Ullmann has subsequently made a successful transition to wise and maternal middle-aged roles such as the public defender in the US/German-funded *The Rose Garden* and the reclusive scientist in *Mindwalk*. She has also started a career as the director of films scripted by Bergman such as *Trolösa/Faithless* (2000). MK

FILMS: *The Night Visitor* (1971); *Lost Horizon, 40 Carats* (1973); *The Abdication, Zandy's Bride* (1974); *A Bridge Too Far, The Serpent's Egg, A Bridge Too Far* (1977); *Players* (1979); *Gaby: A True Story* (1987); *The Rose Garden* (1989); *Mindwalk* (1990); *The Long Shadow* (1992).

UNITED KINGDOM

There is no doubt that the single largest source of émigré European actors and actresses in Hollywood for most of the last century has been Britain. This notable 'export' trend was of a sufficient scale before the end of World War II to have inspired both popular and scholarly book-length studies in the recent past.[25] Sheridan Morley has characterised the British presence in Hollywood in the 1930s and 1940s — the boom years for this phenomenon — as 'an extraordinary feat of colonization . . . It was India all over again and a century later: the British arrived as an army of expert settlers.'[26] These words were printed in 1983, at a point when the notorious contemporary declaration by Colin Welland that 'The British are coming' at the 1982 Academy Awards ceremony was beginning to look like foolhardy hot air. The years when British (and predominantly English) performers most conspicuously populated Hollywood films have thus become the focus of considerable nostalgia and national pride, concomitant with the increasing weakness and instability of the domestic film industry.[27]

The fact that British audiences and commentators should choose to treat patriotically the overseas success of British actors as significant local achievements has tended to obscure the reasons why Hollywood has been so receptive to British talent. Metaphors of conquest can certainly be found in the publicity discourse that articulated the success stories of particular British stars. And it does appear to be true that many British settlers in California *behaved* like members of a colonial outpost, transplanting various English customs and rituals intact and fashioning their own exclusive social scene. Tea was always served at four, both at home and on the studio backlot, for many of the Hollywood British; an article published in 1935 in the *Christian Science Monitor* documented a sizeable increase in the number of Californian 'equestrian events and dog shows, which . . . attract a generous sprinkling of titled British names to give Hollywood affairs a distinction which Hollywood people like to think can only be matched in Europe'. These were not the only conspicuous signs of a community determined to preserve a distinct sense of national identity:

> Several English cake shops now exist, catering almost exclusively to the English, who maintain a stricter aloofness than do most other resident aliens; steak and kidney pies have miraculously made their appearance all over town and are sometimes even eaten by the natives; Devonshire cream is also manufactured, but in very small

quantities. The Americans prefer it whipped. Once a year, on New Year's Eve, the principal members of the British colony gather in a Hollywood café to hear the bells of Big Ben ring out over the radio, bearing out the British reputation for loving whatever is British. Billiards are now played regularly at the homes of most British stars, and officers of British warships visiting in California harbours entertain and are entertained by a group founded by Victor McLaglen[*] and known as the British United Services Club, comprised in large part of actors who have served in one of the branches of the British military.[28]

The focal point, and certainly the most visible symbol, of this British émigré network was the Hollywood Cricket Club founded and captained by C. Aubrey Smith*. Not only did the team regularly field British actors like David Niven*, Nigel Bruce* and Basil Rathbone*, but its matches on the grounds of the UCLA campus and its annual dance at the Roosevelt Hotel were defining social events for the British settlers' sense of community and status.

But it still ultimately makes more sense to talk about the arrival of the British en masse as a considered Anglophile recruitment drive on the part of Hollywood producers rather than an act of invasion. We can clearly identify a number of economic and cultural factors that motivated such headhunting efforts in the interwar period. It is commonly known, of course, that in the latter half of the 1910s the American film industry had become extremely successful at penetrating overseas markets. By the end of the World War I, foreign earnings regularly accounted for 20 to 40 per cent of an American film's overall revenues, and much of this 'extra' income made the difference between breaking even and securing a significant profit.[29] Breaking down the figures even further, Britain was far and away the single most lucrative territory for Hollywood exporters. By 1927, remittances from Britain constituted 30.5 per cent of all Hollywood's foreign income. Comparably sized territories like France and Germany provided, respectively, only 8.5 and 5.25 per cent of overseas earnings. Australasia, however, contributed 15.2 per cent.[30] So, thanks to a combination of comparatively weak indigenous film industries, well-developed exhibition sectors, generous trading legislation and, of course, the con-

Teatime with Deborah Kerr in Hollywood

venience of a common language, nearly half of Hollywood's non-domestic income came from Britain and British dominions. By 1940, as various European markets were closed to the USA with the onset of war, 70 per cent of its net overseas earnings came from Britain alone.[31]

Hollywood's economic dependence upon the British market thus explains why between 1930 and 1950 its studios produced at least 172 films that constitute what H. Mark Glancy has called Hollywood's 'British' output.[32] All of these films are either derived from British works of literature and/or feature predominantly British characters and settings. And, crucially, they are all extensively populated with authentically British actors. The commercial merit of this production policy can be seen in the earnings of a representative 'British' film made by MGM in 1935, David Copperfield. The cast features no fewer than fifteen British-born players, with a further three from current or former British dependent territories. It was a substantial hit at the American box office, earning $1,621,000. Factoring in the extremely lavish $1,073,000 budget for this production ultimately leaves a relatively modest domestic profit. But its overseas run brought in a further $1,348,000. **453**

$700,000 of this international income came from Britain and British Empire markets, and this represents a gross over 10 per cent higher than the average earnings of non-'British' Hollywood product in UK-affiliated territories.[33]

The proliferation of British actors in Hollywood cannot be entirely reducible to blunt commercial imperatives, however. The American film industry first began actively 'poaching' stars of the British stage and screen back in 1916. One of its earliest recruits was Ivy Close*, who signed with Kalem in May of that year. The terms in which Kalem publicised its 'capture' are quite revealing. She is described as 'the English stage star, recently announced as a recruit to moving pictures', and no time was lost in suggesting that 'Critics in England and on the continent have been lavish in their praise of Miss Close for her work in both drama and comedy on the stage.'[34] In reality, nothing could have been further from the truth. Ivy Close had entered moving pictures in Britain as the winner of a 1911 beauty contest organised by the *Daily Mirror*. She came fifth in a 1915 fan magazine poll of the most popular native-born film stars in Britain, but the theatrical training and distinguished West End reputation that Kalem heralded simply did not exist. What this incident clearly indicates is how Hollywood publicists identified and exploited an effective marketing angle in the perceived association between British actors and the august traditions of the English stage. Theatricality and Britishness went hand in hand from the very beginning – even in the case of an actress like Ivy Close, whose links to this internationally famous sector of the British heritage industry were non-existent.

In one sense, the recruitment of British performers was simply part of a broader trend in Hollywood's talent scouting. It has been frequently suggested by film historians that a major difference between British and American cinema lies in their respective geographical proximity to and distance from their national theatrical heartlands.[35] But this overly neat distinction underestimates the substantial cultural and economic ties between Hollywood and Broadway in the first half of the twentieth century. It is common knowledge that Hollywood producers looked to Broadway for creative direction in the early days of the conversion to sound, but the ties between the two entertainment industries substantially pre- and post-dated this relatively short period of panic and confusion. The direct financing of stage productions by Hollywood studios looking for complete

and pre-established dramatic packages to adapt for the screen was such a widespread practice in the 1920s that a regulatory code of practice had to be drafted in 1926. Throughout the 1930s, up to fifty of the orchestra seats on a Broadway opening night would be filled with Hollywood scouts. In 1934, Frank Gilmore, the head of the Actors' Equity Association, suggested that around 70 per cent of the creative talent in Hollywood came from the stage.[36] Since there was always plenty of space reserved on Broadway for successful West End plays and casts, it is hardly surprising that so many British actors ended up in Hollywood. Before 1945, an overwhelming majority of them only arrived on the West Coast after a successful stage engagement on the East Coast. Relatively few were plucked directly from London, and even fewer made any headway without some kind of theatrical CV.

This situation changed somewhat after World War II. As previously inaccessible overseas markets were opened up, British cinemas remained extremely lucrative outlets for Hollywood product, but became proportionally less important. On a different front, mainstream Broadway acting began to borrow on a significantly reduced scale from the British stage with the popularisation of the Method. Hollywood's transatlantic recruitment tactics were modified in response to these and other altered conditions. British film production had become significantly stronger during the war, and something more akin to a Hollywood star system had emerged. Consequently, it was increasingly more common for British players to be poached directly from British studios, bypassing the Broadway–West End connection. And performers like Jean Simmons*, Deborah Kerr*, Stewart Granger* and James Mason* became far less narrowly identified on screen with their national origins than their predecessors. This trend has intensified dramatically in recent years. The USA's major talent agencies are now capitalised as global corporations, which undoubtedly further encourages the elision of Anglo-American national differences. A British actress like Minnie Driver* has secured prominent roles in Hollywood films in which she almost exclusively speaks with an American accent.

The one conspicuous exception to this rule remains the casting of villains in Hollywood films. Numerous British cultural commentators in the late 1980s and early 1990s identified a high incidence of relatively distinguished male British actors, including Jeremy Irons*, Malcom

McDowell★, Ian McKellen★, Alan Rickman★, Joss Ackland★, Michael Gambon★ and Nigel Hawthorne★, being cast as villains in Hollywood action films. Suggestions were even made that the apparent trend reflected a broader thawing of Anglo-American relations in the political sphere. It is probably more sensible, however, to see this as a casting tradition with a much longer lineage. Richard Maltby has commented on the significance of the performance style of a British stage actor of a much older vintage, Montagu Love★, cast as the villain to Rudolph Valentino's hero in *The Son of the Sheik* (1926). As Maltby points out, Love's excessive gestural theatricality, his patent dissimulation and artifice, serves the crucial narrative function of emphasising by contrast the sincerity and, above all, the authenticity of the star.[37]

Within the sound era, it has frequently been the case that the distinctively mellifluous voices of many British actors (aided by years of specialised vocal training at theatre schools like RADA), along with their immaculate diction, have been both major attractions for Hollywood casting agents while proving difficult to square with conventional star discourse. The silky voice and distinguished accent of Ronald Colman★ functioned as signifiers of class and breeding that undoubtedly served to enhance his appeal, particularly in heroic roles drawn from reputable British literary sources. But it has been more common to find the British acting voice implicitly stigmatised for the way that it creates an impression of privilege and an overly polished façade. The studied eloquence and aristocratic hauteur of such figures as Claude Rains★, George Sanders★ and Herbert Marshall★ has in the long run proved incompatible with a Hollywood star system that promotes itself as a democratic meritocracy based upon values like hard work and truthful sincerity. Legions of British 'stars' have therefore ended up following a career path in Hollywood as character actors with a perceived fitness for villainy. The list would include the likes of Rains, Marshall, Sanders, Ray Milland★ and James Mason, and has been augmented in recent years by the likes of Anthony Hopkins★, Gary Oldman★ and Tim Roth★. In these latter cases, the cut-glass elocution of an earlier generation of actors has been replaced by a pronounced facility for varied and 'exotic' accents, which has similarly militated against the fostering of stable star personae. There is still a common perception in both popular and scholarly writing on acting that a

British theatrical training places greater emphasis upon the 'external' facets of performance than the values of spontaneity and personal experience that are ubiquitous in post-Strasberg drama teaching in the USA.[38] Pantomime villainy has thus proved to be the most enduringly useful outlet for the fruits of an apprenticeship on the British stage when in California. JB

USTINOV, Peter (1921–2004)

Throughout a career which lasted over sixty years, Peter Ustinov achieved success and recognition not only as an actor on both stage and screen but also as a writer, director, producer and presenter. His cosmopolitan ancestry, wide-ranging cultural interests and humorous and sophisticated persona made him the epitome of a now almost vanished form of European identity. After making his debut in 1940, Ustinov's first major success as a film actor was in Carol Reed's *The Way Ahead* (1944). His performance as Rispoli, the owner of a North African café caught up in the conflict between the British and Germans in World War II, demonstrated an abiding capacity for playing characters of different nationalities. It also revealed an affinity for roles involving a certain deviousness and capacity for survival.

Ustinov's first American film role was as Nero, the vain and petulant Roman Emperor in Mervyn LeRoy's *Quo Vadis*. He was nominated for a Best Supporting Actor Academy Award and the part established him as an actor well suited to the historical epic genre then in fashion in Hollywood. After playing the Prince of Wales in *Beau Brummell*, he was a conniving one-eyed servant in *The Egyptian*, a part that was something of a dress rehearsal for his Best Supporting Actor Academy Award-winning role as the gladiator trainer in Stanley Kubrick's *Spartacus*. Along with an often-insinuating tone of voice, Ustinov used his bulky physical appearance to personify the ambiguities of these characters. He won a second Academy Award for his performance in Jules Dassin's 1964 jewel robbery caper *Topkapi*.

Ustinov's prominent international career included four films for Disney made between 1968 and 1976: *Blackbeard's Ghost*, *Robin Hood*, *One of Our Dinosaurs is Missing* and *Treasure of Matecumbe*. In 1976, he gave a touching and revealing performance as an elderly man long alone in the ruins of the world in the science-fiction adventure *Logan's Run*. Following considerable success and acclaim as Hercule Poirot in five Agatha Christie adaptations during the 1980s, **455** his film appearances grew less frequent. He was, however, a notable and sympathetic medical professor in *Lorenzo's Oil*. Ustinov maintained a presence in the public's eye with his work as a Goodwill Ambassador for UNICEF. He was knighted in 1990. MHu

FILMS: *Quo Vadis* (1951); *Beau Brummell, The Egyptian* (1954); *We're No Angels* (1955); *Spartacus, The Sundowners* (1960); *Romanoff and Juliet* (1961); *Topkapi* (1964); *John Goldfarb, Please Come Home, Lady L* (1965); *The Comedians* (1967); *Blackbeard's Ghost, Hot Millions* (1968); *Viva Max!* (1969); *Hammersmith is Out* (1972); *Robin Hood* [voice] (1973); *One of Our Dinosaurs is Missing* (1975); *Logan's Run, Treasure of Matecumbe* (1976); *The Last Remake of Beau Geste, The Mouse and His Child* [voice] (1977); *Ashanti* (1979); *Charlie Chan and the Curse of the Dragon Queen* (1980); *The Great Muppet Caper* (1981); *Appointment with Death* (1988); *Lorenzo's Oil* (1992); *The Bachelor* (1999).

VALKYRIEN, Valda (Adele von Friesenfeldt) (1895–1956)

Danish baroness and, so she claimed, former prima ballerina who starred in various melodramas of the late 1910s shot in Florida. A breach of contract suit against producer William Fox ended her acting career and she thereafter became an extra. HJW

FILMS: *Youth, The Valkyrie* (1915); *The Unwelcome Mother, Diana, Silas Marner, The Cruise of Fate, Hidden Valley* (1916); *The Image Maker, Magda, The Crusher* (1917); *T'Other Dear Charmer, The Huns within Our Gates* (1918); *Bolshevism on Trial* (1919).

VALLI, Alida (Alida Maria Laura von Altenberger) (1921–)

With her sultry dark looks and striking green eyes, Valli had become one of the most famous and highest-paid

The beguiling Italian star Alida Valli in her most famous Hollywood film, Alfred Hitchccok's *The Paradine Case* (1947)

actresses in Italy by the age of twenty-one. Her move to Hollywood was provoked in part by the fact that after the war she was unable to develop as a screen diva in Italy due to neo-realist cinema's apparent preference for non-professional actors. She accepted an offer from David O. Selznick and beguiled audiences with her unusual beauty and natural charm under the name of 'Valli'. The Italian actress made two of her most famous films with Selznick. In Hitchcock's *The Paradine Case*, she played the mysterious figure of Maddalena Anna Paradine who is accused of poisoning her husband, a respected hero blinded in the war. Her character goes on to bewitch her defence lawyer, played by Gregory Peck, and she almost ruins his marriage. Valli went on to even greater success in *The Third Man* (1949), Carol Reed's British film for Selznick. After her contract with the producer expired, Valli returned to Italy to star in films by Antonioni, Bertolucci and Visconti, with whom she made her most famous film, *Senso* (1954). Although her career was violently disrupted at the time by a sex, drugs and murder scandal, she was able to continue a prolific career in European cinema, as well as reappear sporadically on American screens in various international co-productions. CS

FILMS: *The Paradine Case* (1947); *The Miracle of the Bells* (1948); *The White Tower, Walk Softly, Stranger* (1950); *The Cry* (1957); *This Angry Age* (1958); *The Naked Maja* (1959); *The Happy Thieves, The Castilian* (1962); *A Month by the Lake* (1995).

VALLONE, Raf (Raffaele Vallone) (1916–2002)

Dark and athletic star of 1940s and 1950s Italian cinema whose powerful physical presence lit up the screen even when silent. He started his acting career in neo-realist cinema and eventually broke into the American market in the 1960s in the historical epic *El Cid*, where he starred alongside Sophia Loren★ and Charlton Heston. In 1964, he co-starred with Stewart Granger and Mickey Rooney in the precursor to *The Dirty Dozen, The Secret Invasion*. Its director Roger Corman described Vallone as one of the most talented actors he had ever worked with. Although he was frequently typecast as either a jet-setting playboy (Constantin Demeris in *The Other Side of Midnight*) or an unsavoury character (Mario Belli in *Harlow*), Vallone most frequently played members of the clergy in his American films – from Cardinal Quarenghi in Otto Preminger's *The*

Cardinal to Cardinal Lamberto in Francis Ford Coppola's *The Godfather: Part III*. CS

FILMS: *El Cid* (1961); *The Cardinal* (1963); *The Secret Invasion* (1964); *Harlow* (1965); *Nevada Smith, Kiss the Girls and Make Them Die* (1966); *The Desperate Ones* (1968); *The Italian Job* (1969); *The Kremlin Letter, Cannon for Cordoba* (1970); *A Gunfight* (1971); *Rosebud* (1975); *The Other Side of Midnight* (1977); *The Greek Tycoon* (1978); *An Almost Perfect Affair* (1979); *Lion of the Desert* (1980); *A Time to Die* (1982); *The Godfather: Part III* (1990).

VAN DAMME, Jean-Claude (Jean-Claude Van Varenberg) (1960–)

Muscular Belgian actor with a large worldwide following for his roles in spectacular and violent action films. The vitality of this success belies the fact that Van Damme's distinctive physical appeal is largely self-made. He was a skinny, working-class boy who wore thick unappealing glasses during childhood. At his father's urging, he started studying karate and ballet and eventually won a black belt and the 'Mr Belgium' bodybuilding title. In a sign of his long-term ambition, he ran 'The California Gym' fitness centre in his native Brussels before leaving for Hollywood.

It took five years for Van Damme to land his first small American film role as a 'Gay Karate Man' in *Monaco Forever*. A year later in 1985, Chuck Norris took Van Damme under his wing and cast him as a Russian villain in *No Retreat, No Surrender*. The actor's breakthrough came when he met action impresario Menahem Golan of Cannon Films outside a restaurant and directed a well-placed roundhouse kick above Golem's head. In an interview the next day, Van Damme performed another trademark move: a split, perched between two chairs. Impressed, Golem gave him the starring role in the martial-arts biopic *Bloodsport*. This film, and two subsequent late 1980s Cannon action features, *Cyborg* and *Death Warrant*, cost roughly $5 million to make and together they earned more than $150 million. This success attracted studio attention. By 1993, Van Damme was earning $3 million a picture. Several of these early to mid-1990s films netted strong domestic box-office profits, with *Timecop*, for example, earning $45 million for Universal. Today, Van Damme has nearly thirty action films to his credit and is as renowned as Arnold Schwarzenegger★ in Europe and Asia.

At five-foot-nine and 185 pounds, the tautly muscled star appeals to both male and female and gay and straight audiences, but young people – especially teenage boys – are his core fans. Smaller than his opponents, Van Damme is set apart by both looking vulnerable and proving invincible. Studio publicity suggests he is a combination of Baryshnikov and Jean-Paul Belmondo and popular nicknames include 'The Muscles from Brussels' and 'The Van Damminator'. Film after film features his bulging biceps in tight clothing, straining against ropes and chains. They also showcase his firm bottom, whose buttocks he describes as being so tight he could 'crack walnuts with them'.

Van Damme's life off and on screen is known for its violence. He has choreographed his fight scenes for a number of years. In *Lionheart*, which he co-wrote, he carefully timed them to occur every five minutes. *Cyborg* and *The Quest* even had to be shot outside the USA to avoid censorship for their action sequences. This has also meant that the casts of his films are more multi-ethnic than in most similar vehicles and that the scripts display a wider range of martial-arts styles. Over the years, Van Damme has thus worked with several key Hong Kong action directors: with John Woo on *Hard Target*, Ringo Lam on *Double Impact* and *Replicant* and Tsui Hark on *Knock Off* and *Double Team*. Though not always hits, all five films skilfully utilise multiple camera set-ups, intricate camera movements and rapid editing to enhance Van Damme's own grace and speed. The actor also has a notorious temper. A suit for wilfully gouging the eyeball of an extra during the filming of *Cyborg* was settled out of court, and another fight with a stunt man resulted in $500,000 being paid in damages.

Typically, Van Damme plays the hero (*Black Eagle* is another early exception). In three films (*Double Impact*, *Maximum Risk* and *Replicant*), he also played his own twins or doubles. Often he fights on behalf of a family and/or to rescue a female love interest. Most characters benefit from a soupçon of romance thanks to his thick Belgian accent and carefully groomed good looks. Although Van Damme tends to play Anglo-Saxon roles, his Continental accent is sometimes matched to characters identified as French, French Canadian or Cajun. Usually, he is involved with a white woman, though he was matched with an Asian girl in *Bloodsport*. An attempt in *Nowhere to Run* to move from action to romance proved a dismal failure largely because, as a *Variety* critic put it, his 'inexpressiveness is embarrass-

ing'. Van Damme has often been pilloried for his acting qualities, but in the words of Tom Tunney, in relation to *Sudden Death*, it may be that it is his 'very lack of range as an actor' and 'sheer blank simplicity of personality' that 'makes him so indispensable as an action hero'.

In 1997, Van Damme formed Long Road, his own production company. To date, he has directed and co-authored one film: *The Quest*, an homage to the action-adventure movies he loved as a boy. It features the semi-autobiographical life of a French New York émigré in the 1930s. CHO/DN

FILMS: *Monaco Forever* (1984); *No Retreat, No Surrender* (1985); *Bloodsport, Black Eagle* (1988); *Kickboxer, Cyborg* (1989); *Lionheart, Death Warrant* (1990); *Double Impact* (1991); *Universal Soldier* (1992); *Nowhere to Run, Last Action Hero, Hard Target* (1993); *Timecop, Street Fighter* (1994); *Sudden Death* (1995); *The Quest, Maximum Risk* (1996); *Double Team* (1997); *Knock Off, Legionnaire* (1998); *Universal Soldier: The Return* (1999); *Replicant, The Order* (2001); *Abominable, Derailed* (2002); *The Savage* (2003); *Wake of Death* (2004).

VAN DE VEN, Monique (1952–)
Highly popular Dutch film actress who made her debut with Rutger Hauer★ in Paul Verhoeven's 1973 hit *Turks Fruit/Turkish Delight*. She spent twelve years in the USA from 1978 with her then husband, the cinematographer Jan de Bont. Her stereotypical blonde, pure and 'natural' Dutch presence failed to generate much success in the USA and she claimed she felt uncomfortable within the Hollywood production system. SdL

FILMS: *Stunt Rock* (1978); *Breach of Contract* (1982); *Paint it Black* (1989); *The Man Inside* (1990).

VANEL, Charles (1892–1989)
A distinguished French actor of over 140 films from the 1920s to the 1980s, including *Le Salaire de la peur/The Wages of Fear* (1953), Vanel appeared in Hitchcock's *To Catch a Thief*, where he plays Bertani, a restaurateur friend of the hero (Cary Grant★). GV

FILM: *To Catch a Thief* (1955).

VAN EYCK, Peter (Götz von Eick) (1911–1969)
Fair-haired, cold-eyed German-born actor who was a regular in West German and French films after 1949. Postwar

Hollywood cinema utilised him as the epitome of the 'Teutonic-terror' type, although Van Eyck had ironically been a US citizen since 1943. He spent the war in the USA playing minor roles. His final three films were entirely Hollywood-financed productions shot in Europe. RJK

FILMS: *The Wife Takes a Flyer, Once upon a Honeymoon, Hitler's Children, Edge of Darkness* (1942); *The Moon is Down, Action in the North Atlantic, Five Graves to Cairo, Hitler's Madman* (1943); *Address Unknown, The Hitler Gang, The Impostor, Resisting Enemy Interrogation* (1944); *The Desert Fox: The Story of Rommel* (1951); *Single-Handed* (1953); *Night People* (1954); *Jump into Hell, Tarzan's Hidden Jungle, A Bullet for Joey* (1955); *The Rawhide Years, Run for the Sun, Attack* (1956); *The Longest Day* (1962); *The Spy Who Came in from the Cold* (1965); *Assignment to Kill* (1968); *The Bridge at Remagen* (1969).

VAN VOOREN, Monique (1933–)

After winning a free ticket to Hollywood in a beauty contest for film magazine *Ciné-Revue*, this Belgian starlet briefly found fame when she was chosen for the part of the sexy, exotic, devilish Lyra in *Tarzan and the She-Devil*. Her other minor Hollywood credits include brief appearances in eclectic genre films. DN

FILMS: *Tarzan and the She-Devil* (1953); *Ten Thousand Bedrooms* (1957); *Happy Anniversary* (1959); *Fearless Frank* (1967); *Ash Wednesday* (1973); *Andy Warhol's Frankenstein* (1974); *Sugar Cookies* (1977); *Wall Street* (1987).

VARCONI, Victor (Mihály Várkonyi) (1891–1976)

Regal-looking actor who, like Michael Curtiz, Alexander Korda and Bela Lugosi★, fled Hungary following the 1919 Béla Kun uprising. Arriving in the USA in 1924, he found great fame in Cecil B. DeMille epics and the Academy Award-winning *The Divine Lady*. A move back to Europe in 1932 was cut short when the Nazis came to power. Varconi returned to Hollywood, but never regained his celebrity. RJK

FILMS: *Poisoned Paradise, Triumph, Changing Husbands, Feet of Clay, Worldly Goods* (1924); *Silken Shackles, The Volga Boatman, For Wives Only* (1926); *Fighting Love, The Little Adventuress, The King of Kings, The Angel of Broadway, The Forbidden Woman, Chicago* (1927); *Tenth Avenue, Sinner's Parade* (1928); *Eternal Love, The Divine Lady* (1929); *Captain Thunder* (1930); *Doctors' Wives, The Men in Her Life, Safe in*

Hell, The Black Camel (1931); *Roberta, Mister Dynamite, A Feather in Her Hat* (1935); *The Plainsman, Dancing Pirate* (1936); *Men in Exile, Big City, Trouble in Morocco* (1937); *King of the Newsboys, Suez, Submarine Patrol* (1938); *The Story of Vernon and Irene Castle, Mr Moto Takes a Vacation, Everything Happens at Night, Disrupted Passage* (1939); *The Man from Dakota, Strange Cargo, The Sea Hawk, Pound Foolish* (1940); *Federal Fugitives, Forced Landing* (1941); *Reap the Wild Wind, They Raid by Night, My Favorite Blonde* (1942); *For Whom the Bell Tolls* (1943); *The Story of Dr Wassell, The Hitler Gang* (1944); *Dakota, Scotland Yard Investigator* (1945); *Unconquered, Where There's Life, Pirates of Monterey* (1947); *Samson and Delilah* (1949); *The Man Who Turned to Stone* (1957); *The Atomic Submarine* (1959).

VARDEN, Norma (1898–1989)

Varden was a prolific British character actress who began her performing career as a piano prodigy. She made a name for herself in marital comedies and farces on the London stage and started working in British cinema with the arrival of sound. She was tall with doughty, but not unkindly, features, and these lent themselves to a succession of dowagers, aristocratic ladies and intimidating well-to-do mothers when she moved permanently to Hollywood with the onset of World War II. Varden played Mrs Cunningham, the society mistress who is almost strangled by Robert Walker in Hitchcock's *Strangers on a Train*. She became a prominent voice of the Screen Actors Guild after her retirement. AP

FILMS: *Get Off My Foot* (1935); *Fools for Scandal* (1938); *Shipyard Sally* (1939); *The Earl of Chicago, Waterloo Bridge, Hit Parade of 1941* (1940); *The Mad Doctor, Road to Zanzibar, Glamour Boy, Scotland Yard* (1941); *We Were Dancing, Flying with Music, The Major and the Minor, The Glass Key, Casablanca, Random Harvest, Johnny Doughboy* (1942); *Slightly Dangerous, Dixie, The Good Fellows, Sherlock Holmes Faces Death, My Kingdom for a Cook, What a Woman!* (1943); *The White Cliffs of Dover, Mademoiselle Fifi, National Velvet* (1944); *Bring on the Girls, Those Endearing Young Charms, The Cheaters, Girls of the Big House, Hold that Blonde* (1945); *The Searching Wind, The Green Years* (1946); *Millie's Daughter, The Trouble with Women, Ivy, Thunder in the Valley, Where There's Life, The Senator was Indiscreet* (1947); *The Amazing Mr X, Hollow Triumph, Let's Live a Little* (1948); *My Own True Love, Adventure in Baltimore, The Secret Garden* (1949); *Fancy Pants* (1950); *Strangers on a Train, Thunder on the Hill* (1951); *Wash-* **459**

ington Story, Les Misérables, Something for the Birds (1952); Young Bess, Loose in London, Gentlemen Prefer Blondes (1953); Elephant Walk, Three Coins in the Fountain, Superman in Scotland Yard, The Silver Chalice (1954); Jupiter's Darling (1955); The Birds and the Bees (1956); Witness for the Prosecution (1957); In the Money, The Buccaneer (1958); Moochie of Pop Warner Football (1960); Door-to-Door Maniac (1961); Rome Adventure (1962); Island of Love, 13 Frightened Girls (1963); Kisses for My President (1964); The Sound of Music (1965); A Very Special Favor, Doctor Dolittle (1967); The Impossible Years (1968).

VAUGHAN, Frankie (1928–1999)

Frankie Vaughan was one of Britain's leading popular singers during the 1950s. In addition to a number of youth-oriented UK films, he was chosen by Marilyn Monroe to appear opposite her and Yves Montand★ as 'the new Sinatra' in MGM's Let's Make Love. AP

FILM: Let's Make Love (1960).

VAVITCH, Michael (Mikhailo Ivanovich Vavich) (1885–1930)

Russian supporting actor who in addition to a successful early US film career was recognised as an informal leader of Hollywood's Russian colony. By his 1914 film debut in Alexander Khanzhonkov's musical drama Tsyganskie romansy/Gypsy Romances, Vavitch's gramophone recordings of operetta and romantic gypsy melodies were known throughout Russia. He emigrated to France via Turkey and Italy and during an American tour of Nikita Balieff's Chauve Souris revue in 1923, he decided to stay in the USA. Vavitch moved to Hollywood in 1925 and by 1928, he was earning $700 a week on a ten-week contract. Vavitch primarily played crooks, of Iberian or Arabian origins, though his Russian background was also highlighted in films such as The Midnight Sun. His career fell into decline with the introduction of sound, though he appeared in early sound movies. As well as being the founder of the Russian-American Arts Club and being the host of its Saturday concerts, Vavitch was the chairman of the Russian Orthodox Society in Los Angeles. RY

FILMS: The Swan, Graustark (1925); The Crown of Lies, Her Man of War, The Midnight Sun, The Third Degree, Valencia (1926); Hotel Imperial, Venus of Venice, The Devil Dancer, The Gaucho, Two Arabian Knights, The Dove (1927); Glorious Betsy, Thief in the Dark, The Woman Disputed (1928); The Wolf Song, The Bridge of San Luis Rey, The Divine Lady (1929); A Devil with Women, War Nurse, The Big House (1930).

VEIDT, Conrad (Hans Walter Conrad Weidt) (1893–1943)

Lean, chiaroscuro-featured German actor with piercing eyes and an air of sinister sophistication, whose multifaceted career included two hugely successful stints in Hollywood. Veidt entered German films in 1916 and swiftly became established as a player par excellence of uncanny and historical roles, including Cesare in Das Cabinet des Dr Caligari (1920). By the mid-1920s, he was the nation's second-highest-earning screen actor after Emil Jannings★ and his lead performance in Der Student von Prag/The Student of Prague (1926) prompted John Barrymore to invite Veidt to Hollywood to play Louis XI alongside his François Villon in The Beloved Rogue. A contract at Universal followed that brought Veidt starring roles in Ufa-influenced extravaganzas by émigré directors, including Paul Leni's The Man Who Laughs and Pál Fejös' part-talkie The Last Performance. American distributors also released hitherto unseen European titles such as Orlacs Hände/The Hands of Orlac (1924) to cash in on Veidt's popularity.

The star's return to Germany in 1929 seems unlikely to have been due to worries about his English for the talkies, as has generally been suggested, but rather prompted by his desire to maintain an international profile, since he now started appearing in English- and French-language versions of his latest German hits. The Nazis' rise to power caused Veidt and his Jewish wife Ilona (known as Lily) to move to England in 1933, where he continued to star in historical fantasies, including the paeans to racial equality The Wandering Jew (1933) and Jew Suss (1934). A 1935 sojourn to Berlin almost became an international incident when Nazi 'medics' refused to allow the 'ill' actor to leave the country until British-Gaumont sent over its own team of doctors to ensure his safe return. Although he and Lily became British citizens in 1939, they still faced official problems when war broke out as former Axis nationals. A mainstay of Alexander Korda's primarily Hungarian émigré community in London, Veidt vowed to continue working for and promoting British cinema. However, the war soon interrupted production of Korda's Technicolor fantasy The Thief of

Bagdad (1940) and the cast – including Veidt in one of his best-remembered roles as the evil Jaffar – was shipped over to Hollywood to complete shooting.

MGM immediately signed Veidt and he again gained iconic status playing a series of show-stealing villains and thoroughly unsympathetic Nazis, which he viewed as his contribution to the war effort. As the unrelenting Major Strasser in *Casablanca*, he received the highest fee of any actor on the film. Veidt's continued success seemed assured when he suddenly died of a heart attack. Lily remained in Hollywood, working as an agent. In 1993, on the centenary of his birth, Veidt's ashes were returned to Berlin during the *Internationale Filmfestspiele* held in his honour that year. RJK

FILMS: *The Beloved Rogue, A Man's Past* (1927); *The Man Who Laughs* (1928); *The Last Performance* (1929); *Escape* (1940); *A Woman's Face, Whistling in the Dark, The Men in Her Life* (1941); *All through the Night, Nazi Agent, Casablanca* (1942); *Above Suspicion* (1943).

VEREA, Lisette (1914–)

Wasp-waisted Romanian-born chanteuse, raised in Hungary, who starred in the Romanian comedy classic *Trenul fantoma/ The Ghost Train* (1933). Verea left war-torn Europe for New York in 1940 and found success on Broadway. She made a single Hollywood film appearance, playing a Teutonic femme fatale opposite the Marx brothers, before retiring from public life. RJK

FILM: *A Night in Casablanca* (1946).

VERNAC, Denise (Denise Eveillard) (1918–1984)

French actress who had only one supporting role in Hollywood, next to her long-time companion Erich von Stroheim in the horror film *The Mask of Diijon*. TH

FILM: *The Mask of Diijon* (1946).

VERNON, Suzy (Appolinie Paris) (1901–1997)

Pretty French actress, popular in French and German silent films. She left briefly for the USA in 1930, was put under contract by Warner Bros. and paid $500 per week to make French versions of multi-language films, and made one English-language film. Back in France, she worked in Paramount's French versions and resumed her French career. MB/GV

FILM: *Girls for Sale!* (1930).

VIBART, Henry (1863–1939)

Vibart was the pre-eminent player of patrician supporting roles in British cinema in the 1910s and briefly fulfilled a similar function in Hollywood in the late 1920s. JB

FILMS: *A Kiss for Cinderella* (1925); *Just Suppose, The Dancer of Paris, The Wilderness Woman, Prince of Tempters* (1926); *The Poor Nut* (1927); *Stranglehold* (1930).

VICTOR, Henry (1892–1945)

British actor, raised in Germany, who divided his screen acting career between Europe and the USA until the onset of World War II, when, because of his distinctive Teutonic accent, he had a run of playing minor Hollywood Nazi villains. JS

FILMS: *The Picture of Dorian Gray* (1916); *The White Monkey, Braveheart* (1925); *Fourth Commandment, Mulhall's Greatest Catch, Crossed Signals* (1926); *The Beloved Rogue, Topsy and Eva* (1927); *Are You There?* (1930); *World and the Flesh, The Mummy* [scenes deleted], *Freaks* (1932); *Luxury Liner* (1933); *The Great Barrier* (1937); *Confessions of a Nazi Spy, Hotel Imperial, Nurse Edith Cavell, Thunder Afloat, Espionage Agent, Pack up Your Troubles, Nick Carter, Master Detective* (1939); *Zanzibar, Enemy Agent, Mystery Sea Raider, Escape, Charter Pilot, The Mortal Storm, Seven Sinners* (1940); *The Mad Doctor, Underground, King of the Zombies* (1941); *Blue, White and Perfect, All through the Night, Dangerously They Live, The Wife Takes a Flyer, Desperate Journey, Underground Agent, Sherlock Holmes and the Secret Weapon, To Be or Not to Be, Once upon a Honeymoon* (1942); *They Got Me Covered, Mission to Moscow, Nasty Nuisance, Above Suspicion, Don Winslow of the Coast Guard* (1943); *Betrayal from the East, A Royal Scandal* (1945).

VIGNON, Jean-Paul (1935–)

Former star of French *chanson* who has made frequent television and cabaret appearances in the USA. He has generally played ancillary Frenchmen in his American films. VO

FILMS: *The Devil's Brigade* (1968); *Lucky Stiff* (1988); *Perfect Alibi* (1995); *Shrek* [voice] (2001).

VILLARIAS, Carlos (1892–1976)

Dark-haired Spanish actor with a prominent square jaw and intense dark eyes who is best known for his starring role in *Drácula* (1931), the Spanish-language version of Universal's **461**

Dracula. Villarias had major or supporting roles as military officers, doctors, judges and authority figures in at least thirty-four other Hollywood Spanish-language films, but his strong foreign accent limited his English-language film career, where he played mainly minor roles. EU

FILMS: *The California Trail* (1933); *An Old Spanish Onion* (1935); *Starlight over Texas, Tropic Holiday, Flirting with Fate* (1938); *Frontiers of '49, Tropic Fury* (1939); *Meet the Wildcat* (1940); *Hold Back the Dawn* (1941).

VISAROFF, Michael (Mikhail Semyonovich Vizarov) (1892–1951)

Russian theatre actor who specialised in playing minor (often uncredited) supporting ethnic roles, frequently of Russian origin. Visaroff went to New York in 1922 as the legal manager of the American tour of Alexander Tairov's theatre company and continued to work on the stage throughout his long-running American film career. During Sergei Eisenstein's 1930 Hollywood visit, Visaroff failed in his request for assistance regarding repatriation to the Soviet Union. RY

FILMS: *The Swan, Lullaby* (1925); *Paris, The Nickel-Hopper, Valencia, Camille* (1926); *The Sunset Derby, Two Arabian Knights* (1927); *We Americans, Ramona, Tempest, The Adventurer, The Night Bird, Plastered in Paris, Four Devils, The Last Command* (1928); *Marquis Preferred, House of Horror, The Exalted Flapper, Illusion, Disraeli* (1929); *Morocco* (1930); *Night Class, Dracula, Sweepstakes, Arizona Terror, Chinatown after Dark, Mata Hari* (1931); *The Man Who Played God, Freaks, Murder in the Rue Morgue, Devil's Lottery, Downstairs* (1932); *Diplomaniacs, King of the Arena, Strange People, Let's Fall in Love* (1933); *Viva Villa!* [scenes deleted], *Picture Brides, The Merry Frinks, Fugitive Road, The Cat's-Paw, Wagon Wheels, Marines are Coming, We Live Again* (1934); *One More Spring, Roberta, Mark of the Vampire, Break of Hearts, Escapade, Man on the Flying Trapeze, Paddy O'Day, Sylvia Scarlett* (1935); *The Gay Desperado, Magnificent Brute, The Charge of the Light Brigade, Ellis Island* (1936); *Champagne Waltz, Espionage, The Soldier and the Lady, Lancer Spy, Angel* (1937); *Air Devils, Tropic Holiday, I'll Give a Million, Suez, Sharpshooters* (1938); *Chasing Danger, Paris Honeymoon, Midnight, Juarez, The Flying Deuces, Everything Happens at Night, Sergeant Madden* (1939); *The Mad Empress, Four Sons, Charlie Chan at the Wax Museum, Second Chorus, The Son of Monte Cristo* (1940); *Never Give a Sucker an Even Break, Blood and Sand* (1941); *Woman*

of the Year, Pacific Rendezvous, Invisible Agent, Reunion in France (1942); *For Whom the Bell Tolls, Mission to Moscow, Hostages, Du Barry was a Lady, Paris after Dark, Madame Curie, Song of Russia* (1943); *In Our Time, The Mask of Dimitrios, An American Romance, Experiment Perilous* (1944); *A Song to Remember, A Royal Scandal, Out of this World, Yolanda and the Thief, Dakota* (1945); *Flight to Nowhere, Don Ricardo Returns* (1946); *Desperate, Northwest Outpost, Intrigue* (1947); *Macao* (1952).

VIŠNJIĆ, Goran (1972–)

Handsome Croatian actor who is best known as Luka Kovac, the doctor who took over from George Clooney in the hit American TV series *E.R.* Višnjić arrived in the European spotlight in 1996 as the driver Risto in *Welcome to Sarajevo*. He subsequently worked hard on removing his accent and, despite a rather bland and forgettable presence, was cast in supporting American roles of increasing importance opposite actresses such as Sandra Bullock and Nicole Kidman. His performance alongside Tilda Swinton★ as the charming blackmailer Alek Spera in *The Deep End* was received coldly by critics and audiences alike, but it granted him the benefit of further significant media exposure. DI

FILMS: *The Peacemaker* (1997); *Rounders, Practical Magic* (1998); *Committed* (2000); *The Deep End* (2001); *Ice Age* [voice] (2002).

VITALE, Milly (1932–)

Italian actress who starred alongside Bob Hope as the wife of the legendary vaudeville performer Eddie Foy in *The Seven Little Foys*. Vitale's career was predominantly based in Italy, although she also worked on several co-productions between the USA and Europe. CS

FILMS: *Black Magic* (1949); *The Juggler* (1953); *The Seven Little Foys* (1955); *War and Peace* (1956); *The Battle of the V.1* (1958); *A Breath of Scandal, The Barbarians* (1960).

VITTI, Monica (Maria Luisa Ceciarelli) (1931–)

Michelangelo Antonioni's muse and later female figurehead of *commedia all'italiana*, Vitti had the leading role in Joseph Losey's Twentieth Century-Fox-funded *Modesty Blaise*. In *An Almost Perfect Affair*, she portrayed the wife of an Italian producer who helps a young film-maker (Keith Carradine) while having a romantic affair with him during the Cannes film festival. CBu

FILMS: *Modesty Blaise* (1966); *An Almost Perfect Affair* (1979).

VON MORHART, Hans (ca.1890–ca.1960)

Former German army officer who was one of three World War I military veterans-cum-actors (together with Wilhelm von Brincken and Otto Bibber) whom Universal employed as technical advisers on *All Quiet on the Western Front* (1930). Von Morhart returned to Hollywood after Hitler seized power in 1933, and had bit parts and walk-on roles as German soldiers in over fifty anti-Nazi films before resettling in West Germany in 1951. RJK

FILMS: *Hell Below* (1933); *Eight Girls in a Boat, No More Women, One Night of Love, The Pursuit of Happiness, The Painted Veil* (1934); *The Black Room* (1935); *Under Two Flags, The General Died at Dawn* (1936); *It Could Happen to You, Lancer Spy* (1937); *Thunder Afloat, Hitler – Beast of Berlin* (1939); *Escape to Glory, Four Sons, Safari, The Man I Married, Foreign Correspondent* (1940); *Shining Victory, Underground, The Deadly Game, A Yank in the R.A.F., Paris Calling, Down in San Diego* (1941); *Blue, White and Perfect, The Lady has Plans, Dangerously They Live, The Dawn Express, Spy Smasher* [serial], *Pacific Rendezvous, Submarine Raider, The Pied Piper, Berlin Correspondent, Desperate Journey, Miss V from Moscow, The Great Impersonation, Reunion in France* (1942); *Immortal Sergeant, Chetniks – The Fighting Guerrillas, Assignment in Brittany, This Land is Mine, Tonight We Raid Calais, Crash Dive, Three Hearts for Julia, Action in the North Atlantic, Hitler's Madman, Bomber's Moon, Secret Service in Darkest Africa* [serial], *Above Suspicion, Hostages, Watch on the Rhine, The Strange Death of Adolf Hitler, I Dood It* (1943); *Tampico, The Seventh Cross, Resisting Enemy Interrogation* (1944); *Hotel Berlin, Where Do We Go from Here?* (1945); *The Searching Wind, Cloak and Dagger* (1946); *The Beginning or the End, Golden Earrings, Where There's Life* (1947); *Decision Before Dawn* (1951).

VON TWARDOWSKI, Hans Heinrich (1898–1958)

Thin, raven-haired, openly gay German actor with haunted eyes who was hired in 1930 to appear in German-language versions of Warner Bros. films such as *The Sacred Flame* (1931). After the Nazis came to power in Germany, he remained in Hollywood and became a US citizen. Because he mainly received uncredited roles as an extra, often playing Nazis, his filmography is likely to remain incomplete. RJK

FILMS: *Scandal for Sale, Six Hours to Live* (1932); *Adorable, Private Jones, The Devil's in Love* (1933); *The Scarlet Empress* (1934); *The Crusades* (1935); *Thin Ice* (1937); *Confessions of a Nazi Spy, Espionage Agent, Hitler – Beast of Berlin* (1939); *The Dawn Express, Once upon a Honeymoon, Casablanca, The Pied Piper, The Navy Comes Through, Joan of Ozark, Desperate Journey* (1942); *Hangmen Also Die, The Strange Death of Adolf Hitler, Margin for Error, The Cross of Lorraine, First Comes Courage, Hitler's Madman, Background to Danger* (1943); *The Hitler Gang, Resisting Enemy Interrogation* (1944).

VOYA, Georges (1895–1951)

Serbian actor who had the leading role, alongside Jules Raucourt★, in Robert Florey's satirical experimental short film *The Life and Death of 9413: A Hollywood Extra*, which told the story of an actor who comes to Hollywood in search of stardom and fails. The character becomes dehumanised and is only identified by a serial number marked on his forehead. He then dies and goes to heaven, where the offending number is finally removed. AP

FILMS: *The Life and Death of 9413: A Hollywood Extra* (1927); *The Legion of the Condemned* (1928).

WALBROOK, Anton (Adolf Anton Wilhelm Wohlbrück) (1896–1967)

Suave, yet stern-looking, dark-haired Austrian-born star of 1930s German cinema, including the lavish German-French co-production *Der Kurier des Zaren/Michel Strogoff* (1936). RKO bought the rights, and reshot dialogue scenes in English with Walbrook and new cast members in Hollywood. Thereafter, Walbrook turned to a career in mainly British films. RJK

FILM: *The Soldier and the Lady* (1937); *Saint Joan* (1957); *I Accuse!* (1958).

WALTERS, Julie (1950–)

Walters successfully converted her success as a television comedienne into a career as a viable leading lady in British films of the 1980s and 1990s. Her most typical screen roles (*Educating Rita* [1983] and *Intimate Relations* [1996]) have presented a highly sexed version of provincial mature working-class femininity that has no obvious prominent equivalent in American cinema. This may help to account for the reason that her nominally 'American' films use her principally to provide local colour in British settings. JB

FILMS: *Mack the Knife* (1990); *Stepping Out* (1991); *All Forgotten* (2000); *Harry Potter and the Sorcerer's Stone* (2001); **463**

Harry Potter and the Chamber of Secrets (2002); *Harry Potter and the Prisoner of Azkaban* (2004).

WARD, Sophie (1965–)

Talented British actress who began her performing career as a child. Ward combines a strong presence in British cinema with occasional work in US-funded films such as *Wuthering Heights*, where she had a starring role as Isabella Linton opposite Juliette Binoche★ and Ralph Fiennes★. AP

FILMS: *The Hunger, The Lords of Discipline* (1983); *Young Sherlock Holmes* (1985); *Waxworks II: Lost in Time, Wuthering Heights* (1992); *Taking Liberty* (1993); *The Big Fall* (1996); *Crime and Punishment* (2002); *Nobody Knows Anything!* (2003).

WARNER, David (1941–)

Wiry British actor – acclaimed as the definitive Hamlet of his generation – who has become one of Hollywood's most prolific villains since permanently moving to California. Overexposure has progressively led to a descent into lower and lower-budget horror (and more and more voiceover work in television cartoons), but Warner's distinctive skills still occasionally surface in such high-concept blockbusters as *Titanic* and *Planet of the Apes.* JB

FILMS: *Tom Jones* (1963); *The Deadly Affair* (1966); *The Sea Gull, The Fixer* (1968); *The Ballad of Cable Hogue* (1970); *Straw Dogs* (1971); *Mr Quilp* (1975); *The Omen* (1976); *Nightwing, The Concorde: Airport '79, Time after Time* (1979); *The Island* (1980); *The French Lieutenant's Woman* (1981); *Tron, The First Time* (1982); *The Man with Two Brains* (1983); *The Company of Wolves* (1984); *Waxwork, Mr North, Spies Inc., My Best Friend is a Vampire, Keys to Freedom* (1988); *Star Trek V: The Final Frontier, Grave Secrets* (1989); *Mortal Passions, Tripwire* (1990); *Teenage Mutant Ninja Turtles II: The Secret of the Ooze, Star Trek VI: The Undiscovered Country* (1991); *Drive* (1992); *The Unnamable II: The Statement of Randolph Carter, Taking Liberty, Quest of the Delta Knights* (1993); *Inner Sanctum II, Tryst, Necronomicon, Loving Deadly* (1994); *Naked Souls, In the Mouth of Madness, Ice Cream Man, Final Equinox, Felony* (1995); *Money Talks, Titanic, Scream 2* (1997); *The Little Unicorn* (1998); *Wing Commander, Shergar* (1999); *Back to the Secret Garden, The Code Conspiracy, Planet of the Apes* (2001); *Straight into Darkness* (2003).

WARNER, H. B. (Henry Byron Warner-Lickford) (1876–1958)

Tall and distinguished British character actor who moved to the USA, where he had a long and successful career in the American film industry. His greatest success during the silent era was as Jesus in Cecil B. DeMille's 1927 *King of Kings*. Warner made six films with Frank Capra and received a Best Supporting Actor Academy Award nomination for his performance as Chang in *Lost Horizon*. He worked with DeMille again on *The Ten Commandments* in 1956. MHu

FILMS: *Your Ghost and Mine, The Ghost Breaker, The Lost Paradise* (1914); *The Vagabond Prince, Shell 43, The Market of Vain Desire, The Beggar of Cawnpore, A Wife's Sacrifice, The Raiders* (1916); *God's Man, The Seven Deadly Sins, Danger Trail, The Seventh Sin, Wrath* (1917); *A Fugitive from Matrimony, Haunting Shadows, The Gray Wolf's Ghost, For a Woman's Honor, The Pagan God, The Man Who Turned White* (1919); *Uncharted Channels, Dice of Destiny, Felix O'Day, One Hour before Dawn, The White Dove* (1920); *When We Were 21* (1921); *Zaza* (1923); *Is Love Everything?* (1924); *Silence, Whispering Smith* (1926); *French Dressing, Sorrell and Son, King of Kings* (1927); *Conquest, The Naughty Duchess, Romance of a Rogue, Man-Made Woman* (1928); *The Divine Lady, Wedding Rings, Tiger Rose, The Show of Shows, The Argyle Case, The Gamblers, The Trial of Mary Dugan, Stark Mad, The Doctor's Secret* (1929); *Princess and the Plumber, Liliom, On Your Back, Wild Company, The Second Floor Mystery, The Furies, The Green Goddess* (1930); *Expensive Women, Five Star Final, The Reckless Hour, A Woman of Experience* (1931); *Cross Examination, The Crusader, A Woman Commands, The Son-Daughter, The Phantom of Crestwood, Tom Brown of Culver, Unholy Love, The Menace, Charlie Chan's Chance* (1932); *Jennie Gerhardt, Supernatural, Christopher Bean, Justice Takes a Holiday* (1933); *Grand Canary, Sorrell and Son, Night Alarm, In Old Santa Fe* (1934); *A Tale of Two Cities, Born to Gamble, Behold My Wife* (1935); *Along Came Love, Blackmailer, Rose of the Rancho, The Garden Murder Case, Mr Deeds Goes to Town, Moonlight Murder* (1936); *Lost Horizon* (1937); *Kidnapped, Bulldog Drummond in Africa, You Can't Take it with You, Army Girl, The Toy Wife, The Adventures of Marco Polo, The Girl of the Golden West* (1938); *The Gracie Allen Murder Case, Mr Smith Goes to Washington, The Rains Came, Nurse Edith Cavell, Bulldog Drummond's Bride, Bulldog

Drummond's Secret Police, Let Freedom Ring, Arrest Bulldog Drummond (1939); *New Moon* (1940); *The Corsican Brothers, The Devil and Daniel Webster, South of Tahiti, Ellery Queen and the Perfect Crime, City of Missing Girls, Topper Returns* (1941); *Crossroads, Hitler's Children, Boss of Big Town, A Yank in Libya* (1942); *Women in Bondage* (1943); *Faces in the Fog, Enemy of Women, Action in Arabia* (1944); *Rogues' Gallery, Captain Tugboat Annie* (1945); *It's a Wonderful Life, Gentleman Joe Palooka, Strange Impersonation* (1946); *High Wall, Driftwood* (1947); *The Prince of Thieves* (1948); *The Judge Steps Out, El Paso, Hellfire* (1949); *Sunset Blvd.* (1950); *The First Legion, Journey into Light, Here Comes the Groom, Savage Drums* (1951); *The Ten Commandments* (1956).

WATSON, Emily (1967–)

Emily Watson's debut film performance as Bess in Lars Von Trier's *Breaking the Waves* (1996) received widespread critical acclaim and made her an overnight star. She received an Academy Award nomination for her complex and moving portrait of an inarticulate young woman who descends into madness. Watson's brief Hollywood career to date highlights how difficult it is for a sensitive and talented performer like her to find a niche there. After a minor supporting role in Tim Robbins' *Cradle Will Rock*, she was given the leading role in the screen adaptation of *Angela's Ashes*. She has continued to impress critics with distinctive appearances in films by the likes of Paul Thomas Anderson, but she generally remains constrained by typecasting in intense, but vulnerable parts. JS/AP

FILMS: *Cradle Will Rock, Angela's Ashes* (1999); *Trixie,* (2000); *Gosford Park* (2001); *Punch-Drunk Love, Red Dragon, Equilibrium* (2002); *The Life and Death of Peter Sellers* (2004).

WEISZ, Rachel (1970–)

Award-winning British film, theatre and television actress whose screen persona combines striking physical looks with a sharp emotional intelligence. As well as appearing in a number of largely European-funded productions such as Michael Winterbottom's *I Want You* (1998), Weisz has also played the female lead opposite Brendan Fraser in the successful series of *Mummy* films. AP

FILMS: *Chain Reaction* (1996); *Going All the Way, Swept from the Sea* (1997); *The Mummy* (1999); *Enemy at the Gates, The Mummy Returns* (2001); *About a Boy* (2002); *The Shape of Things, Runaway Jury* (2003); *Envy* (2004).

WERNER, Oskar (Oskar Josef Bschließmayer) (1922–1984)

Blond, blue-eyed, youthful-looking Austrian who, although primarily a stage actor, secured a prominent position in international cinema through a handful of memorable, award-winning performances. Werner's first film was the Austrian anti-Nazi picture *Der Engel mit der Posaune / The Angel with the Trumpet* (1948), substantial footage from which was used in British Lion's *The Angel with the Trumpet* (1950). His Hollywood debut followed in another anti-Nazi film, *Decision before Dawn*, shot on location in Europe. Werner's performance as a German prisoner-of-war earned him a trip to Hollywood and a seven-year contract at Twentieth Century-Fox. However, the studio felt unable to identify any 'positive' German-accented roles for the actor and dissolved the contract in 1953. Werner did not return to Hollywood for a decade, by which time he had gained international celebrity playing Jules, the sensitive, self-sacrificing intellectual in Truffaut's *Jules et Jim* (1962). He won the New York critics' prize and was nominated for an Academy Award and a Golden Globe for his performance as the melancholy Dr Schumann headed for 1933 Germany aboard Stanley Kramer's *Ship of Fools*. Despite little subsequent American screen work, Werner remained known in the country for his numerous recital tours. RJK

FILMS: *Decision before Dawn* (1951); *The Spy Who Came in from the Cold, Ship of Fools* (1965); *Fahrenheit 451* (1966); *The Shoes of the Fisherman, On Location: The Shoes of the Fisherman* (1968).

WHALLEY-KILMER, Joanne (Joanne Whalley) (1964–)

English actress who attracted Hollywood's attention with her role in BBC television's *The Singing Detective* (1986). After marrying Val Kilmer, her co-star in *Willow*, Whalley-Kilmer's profile inevitably rose, but several miscast films and a string of routinely sexualised femme fatale roles have so far led to a disappointing American screen career. MF

FILMS: *Willow, To Kill a Priest* (1988); *Kill Me Again* (1989); *Navy SEALS* (1990); *Shattered* (1991); *Storyville* (1992); *Mother's Boys* (1993); *A Good Man in Africa, Trial by Jury* (1994); *The Man Who Knew Too Little* (1997); *A Texas Funeral, The Guilty* (1999); *Run the Wild Fields* (2000); *Virginia's Run* (2002); *The Californians* (2004).

465

WHITE, Carol (1941–1991)

This earthy British actress found few appropriate outlets for her peculiarly cockney glamour when she moved to Hollywood and quickly drifted into fringe roles. JB

FILMS: *Moby Dick* (1956); *Surprise Package* (1960); *A Matter of Who* (1961); *Bon Voyage!* (1962); *I'll Never Forget What's-'is-name* (1967); *The Fixer* (1968); *Daddy's Gone A-Hunting* (1969); *Something Big* (1971); *Up the Sandbox* (1972); *Some Call it Loving* (1973); *Chained Heat* (1983); *Body Rock* (1984); *The Naked Cage* (1986); *Talking Walls* (1987); *The Wrong Guys* (1988); *Eating* (1990); *Grand Canyon* (1991).

WHITTY, May (1865–1948)

Redoubtable English actress who was made Dame Commander of the British Empire in 1918 after a successful stage career. She appeared in a number of British films from 1914 onwards, and made her Hollywood debut in 1937, after which she began playing a series of irrepressible old ladies such as Lady Beldon in *Mrs Miniver*. TJ

FILMS: *Night Must Fall, The Thirteenth Chair* (1937); *I Met My Love Again* (1938); *Raffles, A Bill of Divorcement* (1940); *One Night in Lisbon, Suspicion* (1941); *Mrs Miniver, Thunder Birds* (1942); *Forever and a Day, Crash Dive, The Constant Nymph, Stage Door Canteen, Lassie Come Home, Flesh and Fantasy, Madame Curie, Slightly Dangerous* (1943); *The White Cliffs of Dover, Gaslight* (1944); *My Name is Julia Ross* (1945); *Devotion* (1946); *This Time for Keeps, Green Dolphin Street, If Winter Comes* (1947); *The Sign of the Ram, The Return of October* (1948).

WIECK, Dorothea (1908–1986)

Swiss-born theatre actress who entered German-language cinema in 1936. Best known for role as adored teacher in the lesbian-identified *Mädchen in Uniform / Girls in Uniform* (1931). She starred in two unsuccessful Hollywood melodramas before returning to supporting roles in German-language cinema. EC

FILMS: *Miss Fane's Baby is Stolen, Cradle Song* (1933); *Man on a Tightrope* (1953); *A Time to Love and a Time to Die* (1958).

WIETH, Mogens (1919–1962)

A highly regarded stage star, both in his native Copenhagen and in London's West End, Wieth's only memorable screen appearance came as the Ambassador in Alfred Hitchcock's second version of *The Man Who Knew Too Much*. HJW

FILMS: *Tales of Hoffman* (1951); *The Man Who Knew Too Much* (1956); *Private Potter* (1962).

WILCOXON, Henry (Harry Wilcoxon) (1905–1984)

After winning two leading roles for Cecil B. DeMille (for whom he would later act as associate producer), this Dominican-born British actor continued in both leading and supporting roles until the 1980s, such as the vicar in *Mrs Miniver* and *The Miniver Story*. MW

FILMS: *Cleopatra* (1934); *The Crusades* (1935); *The President's Mystery, The Last of the Mohicans* (1936); *Souls at Sea* (1937); *Five of a Kind, Keep Smiling, Mysterious Mr Moto, Prison Nurse, If I Were King* (1938); *The Arizona Wildcat, Woman Doctor, Tarzan Finds a Son!, Chasing Danger* (1939); *Earthbound, Free, Blonde and 21, Mystery Sea Raider, The Crooked Road* (1940); *South of Tahiti, The Corsican Brothers, That Hamilton Woman, Scotland Yard, The Lone Wolf Takes a Chance* (1941); *Mrs Miniver, Johnny Doughboy, The Man Who Wouldn't Die* (1942); *Unconquered, Dragnet* (1947); *Samson and Delilah, A Connecticut Yankee in King Arthur's Court* (1949); *The Miniver Story* (1950); *Scaramouche, The Greatest Show on Earth* (1952); *The Ten Commandments* (1956); *The Buccaneer* (1958); *The War Lord* (1965); *The Doomsday Machine* (1967); *The Private Navy of Sgt O'Farrell* (1968); *Man in the Wilderness* (1971); *The Doomsday Machine* (1972); *Against a Crooked Sky* (1975); *Pony Express Rider, Won Ton Ton, the Dog Who Saved Hollywood* (1976); *F.I.S.T.* (1978); *The Man with Bogart's Face, Caddyshack* (1980); *Sweet 16* (1981).

WILDING, Michael (1912–1979)

Aristocratic-looking lead actor who had an established career in British films before moving to Hollywood. He made his American screen debut as the Detective Inspector in Alfred Hitchcock's *Stage Fright*. TJ

FILMS: *Stage Fright* (1950); *The Law and the Lady* (1951); *Torch Song* (1953); *The Egyptian* (1954); *The Glass Slipper, The Scarlet Coat* (1955); *Zarak* (1956); *The World of Suzie Wong* (1960); *The Best of Enemies, The Naked Edge* (1961); *A Girl Named Tamiko* (1962); *The Sweet Ride* (1968).

WILLIAMS, Hugh (Brian Williams) (1904–1969)

Williams made his way from Broadway to Hollywood in the early 1930s as studios voraciously signed up English actors blessed with crisp diction and any faint behavioural resemblances to Ronald Colman★. He specialised in debonair and well-mannered light comedy character parts, though he was also cast as Hindley in *Wuthering Heights*. Williams interspersed his US career with appearances in UK films, including a number of US-funded productions. JB

FILMS: *Charley's Aunt* (1930); *All Men are Enemies, Elinor Norton, Outcast Lady* (1934); *David Copperfield, Let's Live Tonight* (1935); *Side Street Angel, The Windmill* (1937); *The Dark Stairway* (1938); *Inspector Hornleigh, Wuthering Heights* (1939); *Khartoum* (1966).

WILLIAMS, John (1903–1983)

English actor who generally moved between the British stage and screen and Broadway before relocating to the USA in the late 1940s, where he had a long-running career in American film and television. Williams is perhaps best known as Audrey Hepburn's★ father in *Sabrina* and the canny Chief Inspector Hubbard in Hitchcock's *Dial M for Murder*. MF

FILMS: *The Chumps* (1930); *Mr Deeds Goes to Town* (1936); *The Paradine Case* (1947); *A Woman's Vengeance* (1948); *Kind Lady* (1951); *Thunder in the East* (1953); *Dial M for Murder, Sabrina, The Student Prince* (1954); *To Catch a Thief* (1955); *D-Day the Sixth of June, Solid Gold Cadillac* (1956); *Island in the Sun, Witness for the Prosecution, Will Success Spoil Rock Hunter?* (1957); *The Young Philadelphians* (1959); *Visit to a Small Planet, Midnight Lace* (1960); *Harlow, Dear Brigitte* (1965); *The Last of the Secret Agents?* (1966); *Double Trouble* (1967); *The Secret War of Harry Frigg, A Flea in Her Ear* (1968); *No Deposit, No Return* (1976); *Hot Lead and Cold Feet* (1978).

WILLIAMS, Olivia (1969–)

Classically trained English actress who made her Hollywood debut after being cast by Kevin Costner as a lead character in *The Postman*. Williams has subsequently combined appearances in big-budget Hollywood films with roles in British and American independent projects. MHu

FILMS: *The Postman* (1997); *Rushmore* (1998); *The Sixth Sense, Four Dogs Playing Poker* (1999); *The Man from Elysian Fields* (2001); *Below* (2002); *Peter Pan* (2003).

WILLIAMSON, Nicol (1938–)

English actor who has played such memorable US roles as Merlin in *Excalibur*. Williamson simultaneously maintains a

presence in British television and theatre, most notably in Shakespeare productions. TJ

FILMS: *The Reckoning, Hamlet* (1969); *The Jerusalem File* (1972); *The Seven-Per-Cent Solution, Robin and Marian* (1976); *The Goodbye Girl* (1977); *The Cheap Detective* (1978); *Excalibur* (1981); *I'm Dancing As Fast As I Can* (1982); *Black Widow* (1986); *The Exorcist III* (1990); *Spawn* (1997).

WILSON, Lambert (1958–)

The son of respected French stage actor Georges Wilson, the handsome Lambert Wilson has maintained a solid reputation in French theatre and auteur cinema since his debut at the tender age of eleven. His first significant American screen role was in the romantic drama *Five Days One Summer* alongside Sean Connery★. His role as Merovingian in *The Matrix Reloaded* and its sequel may yet trigger more Hollywood offers. TH

FILMS: *Julia* (1977); *Five Days One Summer* (1982); *Sahara* (1983); *Strangers* (1991); *Jefferson in Paris* (1995); *The Matrix Reloaded, The Matrix Revolutions, Timeline* (2003); *Catwoman* (2004).

WINSLET, Kate (1975–)

For many, the scale and extraordinary commercial longevity of *Titanic* has led to justifiable comparisons with *Gone with the Wind* (1939). This might suggest that its English female lead Kate Winslet would be well positioned to emulate the impact her compatriot Vivien Leigh★ made on American audiences nearly sixty years earlier (and many such direct comparisons were made at the time), but Winslet's relationship with Hollywood has subsequently turned a little tepid.

Winslet's screen image in *Titanic* was certainly congruous with her previous roles. She first came to prominence in Peter Jackson's *Heavenly Creatures* (1994), in which she played a teenage schoolgirl fantasist in 1950s New Zealand. This set the template for a film career than has been spent almost exclusively in historical dramas playing characters chafing and rebelling against the restraints of their corsetry. The makers of *Titanic* – her first starring-role film actually made in the USA – clearly saw Winslet as an actress accustomed to period costume, but one who could also inspire emotional identification from modern audiences. Her role as the freethinking Rose DeWitt Bukater who escapes the starchiness of New England high society to drink, smoke and dance a jig with the liner's Irish steerage passengers is a **467**

Kate Winslet in *Titanic* (1997)

clear transplantation of the liberated nineteenth-century provincial heroine she played in *Jude* (1996).

Why has Winslet's subsequent career largely failed to capitalise upon the success of *Titanic*? In part, this relates to her preference for working on more independent projects with strong-minded (usually European or Australasian) directors in control, but there is also the fact that Winslet is slightly fuller of figure than most American actresses. Her role as an investigative journalist in the legal thriller *The Life of David Gale* has been frequently played by more conventional American female stars like Sandra Bullock. It may not be entirely coincidental, therefore, that early publicity interviews for the film were accompanied by controversial magazine cover pictures in which Winslet's body was digitally 'thinned'. This clearly suggests the strain still required to fit the British actress into a mainstream Hollywood star image. JB

FILMS: *A Kid in King Arthur's Court, Sense and Sensibility* (1995); *Hamlet* (1996); *Titanic* (1997); *Holy Smoke* (1999);

Quills (2000); *Iris* (2001); *The Life of David Gale* (2003); *Eternal Sunshine of the Spotless Mind* (2004).

WINWOOD, Estelle (Estelle Goodwin) (1883–1984)
British actress who enjoyed a lengthy Hollywood acting career. Although known for her wide-eyed naivety in early British roles, Winwood was often cast as an eccentric old woman in later years. JS
FILMS: *Night Angel* (1931); *Quality Street* (1937); *The Glass Slipper* (1955); *23 Paces to Baker Street, The Swan* (1956); *This Happy Feeling* (1958); *Darby O' Gill and the Little People* (1959); *Sergeant Rutledge* (1960); *The Misfits* (1961); *The Cabinet of Dr Caligari, The Magic Sword, The Notorious Landlady* (1962); *Dead Ringer* (1964); *Games, Camelot* (1967); *The Producers* (1968); *Jenny* (1970); *Murder by Death* (1976).

WISDOM, Norman (1920–)
Enormously successful British cockney slapstick comedian whose lopsided grin and speciality in pratfalls led to numerous appearances in British films of the 1950s and 1960s as the cheeky underdog who triumphs in the end. Wisdom also enjoyed Tony-nominated success on Broadway and a solitary role in Hollywood. MW
FILM: *The Night They Raided Minsky's* (1968).

YORK, Michael (Michael Hugh Johnson) (1942–)
The son of an army officer, York grew up in privileged surroundings and had a long stage career before he became involved in films in 1967, with breakthrough roles in Joseph Losey's *Accident* and Franco Zeffirelli's *The Taming of the Shrew*. Although he is best known for his performance as the inexperienced and naive Brian in Bob Fosse's *Cabaret*, based on the Berlin writings of Christopher Isherwood, his fine-boned looks, impeccable Oxbridge accent and upper-class pedigree have led him to play other decorous, reserved English parts such as his character in the musical fantasy *Lost Horizon*, based on the original Frank Capra film. York's career suffered a slump in the 1980s despite appearances in a number of films made in Britain and other countries. His restrained performance style may have been a hindrance with the rise of big-budget spectaculars in Hollywood. The 1990s saw a comeback, though, but not in roles that stretched his abilities. His most notable screen persona has been as Austin Powers' Secret Service contact, Basil Exposition. JS

FILMS: *The Taming of the Shrew, Smashing Time* (1967); *The Strange Affair, Romeo and Juliet* (1968); *Alfred the Great, The Guru, Justine* (1969); *Something for Everyone* (1970); *Zeppelin* (1971); *Cabaret* (1972); *Lost Horizon* (1973); *Seven Nights in Japan, Logan's Run* (1976); *The Island of Dr Moreau, The Last Remake of Beau Geste* (1977); *The White Lions* (1979); *Come See the Paradise* (1990); *The Long Shadow* (1992); *Discretion Assured* (1993); *Not of this Earth* (1995); *Austin Powers: International Man of Mystery, Dark Planet, A Christmas Carol* [voice] (1997); *Wrongfully Accused, 54, Merchants of Venus, The Treat, Lovers and Liars* (1998); *Austin Powers: The Spy Who Shagged Me, The Omega Code, The Haunting of Hell House, Puss in Boots* (1999); *Megiddo: Omega Code 2* (2001); *Austin Powers in Goldmember* (2002).

YORK, Susannah (Susannah Yolande Fletcher) (1941–)
Like Michael Caine★, Julie Christie★ and others, York was a beneficiary of the Hollywood companies' extensive investment in British production in the 1960s. After playing Cicely Koertner to Montgomery Clift's *Freud* for John Huston, her breakthrough to stardom came as Sophie Western, the spirited heroine of Tony Richardson's hugely popular, Academy Award-winning *Tom Jones*. But few of her subsequent films delivered on this early promise. Most distinctive were her roles as Lady Margaret, Sir Thomas More's loyal daughter, in Fred Zinnemann's *A Man for All Seasons* and Childie, the feminine half of the central lesbian relationship of Robert Aldrich's *The Killing of Sister George*, in which she was memorably partnered by Beryl Reid and seduced by Coral Browne. She also received an Academy Award nomination as Best Supporting Actress for *They Shoot Horses, Don't They?*, contributed the original story of Robert Altman's *Images* (filmed in Ireland) and co-wrote the screenplay of *Falling in Love Again*. Thereafter, her American roles were few and far between, and rarely in distinguished films, though she did make several appearances as Superman's mother, opposite Marlon Brando in *Superman* and without him in two of its sequels, all of which were shot in British studios. SH
FILMS: *Tunes of Glory* (1960); *The Greengage Summer* (1961); *Freud* (1962); *Tom Jones* (1963); *The 7th Dawn* (1964); *Sands of the Kalahari* (1965); *Kaleidoscope, A Man for All Seasons* (1966); *Sebastian* (1967); *Duffy, The Killing of Sister George* (1968); *Lock up Your Daughters!, Oh! What a Lovely War, Battle of Britain, They Shoot Horses, Don't They?*, *Country Dance* (1969); *Happy Birthday, Wanda June, Zee & Co.* (1971); *Images* (1972); *Sky Riders* (1976); *Superman* (1978); *Falling in Love Again, The Awakening, Superman II* (1980); *Alicja* (1982); *Yellowbeard* (1983); *Prettykill, Superman IV: The Quest for Peace* (1987); *Fate* (1990).

YOUNG, Roland (1887–1953)
Young began his career on the stage in Britain in 1908, but from 1914 onwards he was a Broadway regular and became a naturalised American citizen in 1918. He made occasional films in Britain in the 1930s and 1940s, but his film career began in the the USA in the 1920s. He only became a recognisable fixture among Hollywood supporting players in the sound era, when his screen image was definitively fixed as a comically vague, perpetually bemused and befuddled gentleman. He defined its chief characteristics most famously in the Academy Award-nominated role of the strait-laced, henpecked banker 'Topper' who is taken for a ride by thrill-seeking ghosts in the 1937 film of that name and its two sequels. JB
FILMS: *Sherlock Holmes* (1922); *Grit* (1924); *The Unholy Night, Wise Girls, Her Private Life* (1929); *The Bishop Murder Case, Madam Satan, New Moon* (1930); *Don't Bet on Women, Annabelle's Affairs, The Squaw Man, Pagan Lady, The Guardsman, The Prodigal* (1931); *Lovers Courageous, One Hour with You, This is the Night, Street of Women, A Woman Commands* (1932); *Blind Adventure, They Just Had to Get Married, Pleasure Cruise, A Lady's Profession* (1933); *His Double Life, Here is My Heart, David Copperfield, Ruggles of Red Gap* (1935); *The Unguarded Hour, Give Me Your Heart, One Rainy Afternoon* (1936); *Call it a Day, Topper, Ali Baba Goes to Town* (1937); *The Young in Heart* (1938); *Topper Takes a Trip, Yes, My Darling Daughter, The Night of Nights* (1939); *Irene, Private Affairs, The Philadelphia Story, Star Dust, No, No, Nanette, He Married His Wife, Dulcy* (1940); *Topper Returns, The Flame of New Orleans, Two-Faced Woman* (1941); *They All Kissed the Bride, Tales of Manhattan, The Lady has Plans* (1942); *Forever and a Day* (1943); *Standing Room Only* (1944); *And Then There Were None* (1945); *You Gotta Stay Happy* (1948); *The Great Lover* (1949); *Let's Dance* (1950); *St Benny the Dip* (1951).

(FORMER) YUGOSLAVIA
During the Communist period, Yugoslavia's attitudes toward the West were softer than those of other Eastern **469**

bloc countries. This resulted in a number of American-funded productions being shot in the country. Films financed by the likes of Universal and United Artists subsequently employed local Yugoslav actors in supporting roles and as extras. Examples of these films include Orson Welles' *The Trial* (1963), Norman Jewison's *Fiddler on the Roof* (1973), Sam Pekinpah's *Cross of Iron* (1977) and Alan Pakula's *Sophie's Choice* (1982). Yugoslav actors were free to be employed abroad and this was an opportunity taken by actors such as Gojko Mitić, who became a leading figure in DEFA's films. While the majority of high-profile Yugoslav actors appeared in various European productions – Miki Manojlović and Dragan Nikolić in France, and Bata Zivojnović in Germany – they were not generally engaged by Hollywood. Only occasionally did Yugoslav actors like Bekim Fehmiu★, Milena Dravić★ and Rade Marković★ make appearances in American cinema.

As a result of the break-up of Yugoslavia in the1990s, many actors either emigrated or started taking international cinematic roles. People like Sergej Trifunović★ can be seen appearing simultaneously in both Hollywood and independent American cinema and European productions and domestic Yugoslav features. Rade Šerbedžija★ and Goran Višnjić★ now work both in Hollywood and the former Yugoslavia and they have been the most successful émigré Yugoslav actors to date. Each has filled a specific stereotypical void: Šerbedžija has been typecast as a sleazy villain of unspecified East European/Russian origins, and Višnjić as an attractive lover prone to suspicious affairs. Trifunović and Šerbedžija have also been used in caricatural roles that depict Balkan men as wild and uncontrollable bullies. Female émigré actresses have not been as successful as their male counterparts. Mirjana Joković★, the best-known face of Yugoslav cinema in the 1990s, has mainly lived in New York since 1991 and has struggled to launch herself in American cinema. She made a Hollywood appearance in Scott Wiper's action-adventure film *A Better Way to Die* (2000). Mira Furlan, a high-profile Croatian actress with a cult following in Yugoslavia, was forced to emigrate in 1991 and has since lived in the USA, where she works mostly for television in roles like Ambassador Delenn in the science-fiction series *Babylon 5*. The Serbian actor Branka Katić and the Australian-based Aleksandra Vujcić have also worked internationally and they may well appear in Hollywood at some point. DI

470

YVES, Christiane (1905–)

French silent actress whose brief filmography was almost entirely American. Despite speaking English, she had to content herself with secondary roles in Hollywood. In 1930, she decided to return to Europe. VO

FILMS: *Confession, They Had to See Paris, Slightly Scarlet, The Man Hunter, What a Man, Sweet Kitty Bellairs* (1930).

ZETA-JONES, Catherine (1969–)

It is a long way from West Glamorgan in Wales to the Californian West Coast glamour but this Swansea-born actress has managed to bridge that gulf with apparent effortlessness. Her role as the pastoral ingénue in British television's *The Darling Buds of May* brought her to Hollywood's attention in 1991 and the following year she was given the role of the eponymous explorer's lover in *Christopher Columbus: The Discovery*. Her major breakthrough, however, only came some years later when she epitomised Hollywood's conception of the sexy, feisty heroine as Anthony Hopkins'★ Hispanic daughter in the action-adventure blockbuster *The Mask of Zorro* in 1998. With her Welshness remaining firmly closeted, Zeta-Jones' pouting sexuality was used to similar effect with supporting roles in *The Phantom*, as an implicitly bisexual villain, and in the CGI-extravaganza *The Haunting* as an explicitly bisexual New York socialite.

Marriage to Michael Douglas consolidated Zeta-Jones' position as a photogenic celebrity. She carried a $3 million fee and received a Best Supporting Actress Academy Award nomination for her impressive role in Steven Soderbergh's *Traffic*. Confirmation of a place on Hollywood's A-list came with her turn as a bitchy Hollywood starlet opposite Julia Roberts in the self-reflexive romantic comedy *America's Sweethearts*, and a second Best Supporting Academy Award nomination for a typically vampish role in *Chicago*. MF

FILMS: *Christopher Columbus: The Discovery* (1992); *The Phantom* (1996); *The Mask of Zorro* (1998); *Entrapment, The Haunting* (1999); *Traffic, High Fidelity* (2000); *America's Sweethearts* (2001); *Chicago* (2002); *Sinbad: Legend of the Seven Seas* [voice], *Intolerable Cruelty* (2003); *The Terminal, Ocean's Twelve* (2004).

ZETTERLING, Mai (1925–1994)

Working-class Swedish actress who began her career in films such as *Hets/Frenzy* (1942) and *Driver dagg faller regn/Rain Follows the Dew* (1948). Zetterling's acting style was low key and sensitive and many cinematographers focused on her seductive large eyes. Her intellectual and professional roots lay in the thoughts of theorists such as Stanislavsky and Pudovkin, and her time in Hollywood therefore proved to be a disappointment. She hated the atmosphere, which she perceived as corrupt, and she wrote with resentment in her memoirs about Danny Kaye, her partner in *Knock on Wood*. Her remaining Hollywood films were American-funded European productions. TS

FILMS: *Knock on Wood* (1954); *A Prize of Gold* (1955); *Seven Waves Away* (1957); *The Witches* (1990).

Notes

1. For full details, see Helmut G. Asper, '*Etwas Besseres als den Tod . . .*'. *Filmexil in Hollywood, Porträts, Filme, Dokumente* (Marburg: Schüren, 2002), pp. 15ff., and Jan-Christopher Horak, *Fluchtpunkt Hollywood. Eine Dokumentation zur Filmemigration nach 1933* (Munich: MAkS, 1986), pp. 6ff.
2. Asper, '*Etwas Besseres als den Tod . . .*'.
3. Hans Kafka, 'What Our Immigration Did for Hollywood and Vice Versa', in Asper, '*Etwas Besseres als den Tod . . .*', p. 33.
4. Mike Budd (ed.), *The Cabinet of Dr Caligari. Texts, Contexts, Histories* (New Brunswick, NJ: Rutgers University Press, 1990), p. 81.
5. Thomas Saunders, *Hollywood in Berlin. American Cinema and Weimar Germany* (Berkeley, Los Angeles and London: University of California Press, 1994), pp. 63–4.
6. For a detailed study of star/audience relations in Weimar Germany, see Joseph Garncarz, 'Warum kennen Filmhistoriker viele Weimarer Topstars nicht mehr', *montage/av* vol. 6 no. 2. (1997), p. 67.
7. A banner unfurled for Jannings on his 1926 arrival in Pasadena greeted him as 'the screen's foremost dramatic artist'. John Baxter, *The Hollywood Exiles* (London: Macdonald and Jane's, 1976), p. 37.
8. Emil Jannings, *Theater, Film – Das Leben und Ich* (Berchtesgaden: Zimmer und Herzog, 1951), p. 193.
9. See Ruth Vasey, *The World According to Hollywood, 1918 – 1939* (Madison: University of Wisconsin Press, 1997), p. 26.
10. See Peter Baxter, *Just Watch! Sternberg, Paramount and America* (London: BFI, 1993), p. 33.
11. Markus Spieker, *Hollywood unterm Hakenkreuz. Der amerikanische Spielfilm im Dritten Reich* (Trier: Wissenschaftlicher Verlag, 1999), p. 115.
12. Kortner in a 1937 letter to his wife, the actress Hanna Hofer, cited in Heiko R. Blum, *Meine zweite Heimat Hollywood: Deutschsprachige Filmkünstler ind den USA* (Berlin: Henschel, 2001), p. 28.
13. Horak, *Fluchtpunkt Hollywood*, pp. 24–28.
14. 'FBI files reveal attempt to prove Dietrich was a spy', *Guardian*, 4 May 2002.
15. Letter of 8 June, 1939, cited in Asper '*Etwas Besseres als den Tod . . .*', p. 302.
16. Cited in Hildegard Knef, *The Gift Horse* (London: Andre Deutsch, 1971), p. 299.
17. Cited in Claudia Fellmer, 'Armin Mueller-Stahl – From East Germany to the West Coast', in Tim Bergfelder, Erica Carter and Deniz Göktürk (eds), *The German Cinema Book* (London: BFI, 2002), p. 94.
18. Cited in Blum, *Meine zweite Heimat Hollywood*, p. 158.
19. Charles Musser, 'Ethnicity, Role-Playing, and American Film Comedy: From *Chinese Laundry Scene* to *Whoopee* (1894–1930)', in Lester D. Friedman (ed.), *Unspeakable Images* (Urbana and Chicago: University of Illinois Press, 1991), pp. 43–60.
20. For thumbnail sketches of these actors and their roles, see the early chapters of Joseph M. Curran, *Hibernian Green on the Silver Screen* (New York, Westport, CT, and London: Greenwood Press, 1989), and Anthony Slide, *The Cinema and Ireland* (Jefferson, NC, and London: McFarland, 1989).
21. The 1926 Paramount production, *Irish Luck*, starring Thomas Meighan, advertised the participation of the Abbey Players but, as Roger Dooley notes, no recognisable names appear in the cast. Roger Dooley, 'The Irish on the Screen: 1', *Films in Review* vol. 3 no. 5 (1957), pp. 211–17, p. 214.
22. Diane Negra, *Off-White Hollywood* (London and New York: Routledge, 2001).
23. Alvaro Armero, *Una aventura americana. Españoles en Hollywood* (Madrid: Compañía Literaria, 1995), p. 20.
24. Florencio Hernández Girbal, *Los que pasaron por Hollywood*, ed. by J. B. Heinink (Madrid: Verdoux, 1992), pp. 24–5.
25. Sheridan Morley, *Tales from the Hollywood Raj: The*

British Film Colony On Screen and Off (London: Weidenfeld & Nicolson, 1983), counts as an example of the former, while H. Mark Glancy, *When Hollywood Loved Britain: The Hollywood 'British' Film 1939–45* (Manchester: Manchester University Press, 1999), stands as the definitively illuminating and useful academic account.

26. Morley, *Tales from the Hollywood Raj*, p. 1.

27. British newspapers regularly run extended features in their glossy supplements at 'Oscar' time, celebrating the number of past British actors who have been Academy Award winners: see, for example, *The Express*, 25 March 2000, Saturday supplement, pp. 14–22.

28. Quoted in Morley, *Tales from the Hollywood Raj*, pp. 139–40.

29. Kristin Thompson, *Exporting Entertainment: America in the World Film Market 1907–1934* (London: BFI, 1985),
p. 103.

30. Vasey, *The World According to Hollywood*, p. 85.

31. Glancy, *When Hollywood Loved Britain*, p. 213.

32. Ibid., pp. 238–66.

33. These financial statistics come from Glancy, ibid., p. 77.

34. *Moving Picture World*, 20 May 1916, p. 1338; 27 May 1916, p. 1522.

35. See, for example, Richard Dyer, *Brief Encounter* (London: BFI, 1993), p. 43.

36. These dates and figures come from Robert McLaughlin, *Broadway and Hollywood: A History of Economic Interaction* (New York: Arno Press, 1974), pp. 63–7, 108, 116.

37. Richard Maltby, *Hollywood Cinema: An Introduction* (Oxford: Blackwell, 1995), p. 274.

38. Witness, for example, the inexhaustible delight that is still taken in retelling an anecdote about Laurence Olivier's and Dustin Hoffman's difference of opinion on the set of *Marathon Man* (1976) over the desirability of 'acting' tired rather than actually 'being' tired (caricatured as a typical Method approach), a fuller account of which is given in Maltby, *Hollywood Cinema: An Introduction*, pp. 246–7. The same distinction between apparently fundamentally different national acting traditions is maintained by various Hollywood actors and directors interviewed in Carole Zucker, *Figures of Light: Actors and Directors Illuminate the Art of Film Acting* (New York: Plenum, 1995), where it is suggested that there is 'a dominant British [acting] tradition, in which more externalized manifestations of emotion, or theatricalized behavior, are valorized, rather than the more internalized, anguished, poetic naturalism that prevails among American actors. The British are often admired for a combination of theatrical imagination and technical brilliance instead of for performances that plumb the depths of internal states' (p. 83). John Lithgow makes essentially this same point (pp. 87–8), as does Sydney Pollack (p. 229).

Select Bibliography

Hollywood and European Film Emigration

Abel, Richard, *The Red Rooster Scare: Making Cinema American, 1900–1910* (Berkeley: University of California Press, 1999).

Aleandri, Emelise, *The Italian-American Immigrant Theatre in New York City* (Charleston, SC: Arcadia, 1999).

Angst-Nowik, Doris and Jane Sloan (eds), *One-Way Ticket to Hollywood: Film Artists of Austrian and German Origin in Los Angeles. Emigration, 1884–1945* (Los Angeles: Max Kade Institute, 1987).

Armero, Alvaro, *Una aventura americana. Españoles en Hollywood* (Madrid: Compañía Literaria, 1995).

Arnold, Frank and Michael Esser, 'Ich hatte keinen Paß: Deutsche Schauspielerinnen und Schauspieler im Exil', *Zitty* no. 5 (1983), pp. 73–7.

Asper, Helmut G., *'Etwas Besseres als den Tod . . .'. Filmexil in Hollywood, Porträts, Filme, Dokumente* (Marburg: Schüren, 2002).

Balio, Tino, *United Artists. The Company that Changed the Film Industry* (Madison: University of Wisconsin Press, 1987).

Balio, Tino, *Grand Design: Hollywood as a Modern Business Enterprise, 1930–39* (New York: Scribner's Sons, 1993).

Barnier, Martin, *Des films français made in Hollywood. Les Versions multiples* (Paris: L'Harmattan, 2004).

Barnier, Martin and Raphaëlle Moine (eds), *France/Hollywood. Échanges cinématographiques et identités nationales* (Paris: L'Harmattan, 2002).

Baxter, John, *The Hollywood Exiles* (London: Macdonald and Jane's, 1976).

Belach, Helga and Hans Helmut Prinzler (eds), *Exil. Sechs Schauspieler aus Deutschland: Elisabeth Bergner – Dolly Haas – Hertha Thiele – Curt Bois – Francis Lederer – Wolfgang Zilzer* (Berlin: Stiftung Deutsche Kinemathek, 1983).

Birdwell, Michael E., *Celluloid Soldiers – Warner Bros.'s Campaign against Nazism* (New York: New York University Press, 1999).

Blum, Heiko R., *Meine zweite Heimat Hollywood: Deutschsprachige Filmkünstler in den USA* (Berlin: Henschel, 2001).

Boujut, Michel and Jules Chancel, *Europe-Hollywood et retour: cinémas sous influences* (Paris: Autrement, 1986).

Bruno, Michael, *The Continental Enchantress from Garbo to Loren* (New York: Lyle Stuart, 1970).

Cargnelli, Christian and Michael Omasta (eds), *Aufbruch ins Ungewisse: Österreichische Filmschaffende in der Emigration vor 1945, Volume One* (Vienna: Wespennest, 1993).

Cecchittini, Philip Alan and Don Whittemore, *Passport to Hollywood: Film Immigrants Anthology* (New York: McGraw-Hill, 1976).

Day, George Martin, *The Russians in Hollywood: A Study in Cultural Conflict* (Los Angeles: University of Southern California Press, 1934).

Deutsches Filmmuseum (ed.), *Von Babelsberg nach Hollywood: Filmemigranten aus Nazideutschland* (Frankfurt am Main: Deutsches Filmmuseum, 1987).

Dittrich, Kathinka, 'Spielfilme: Die Niederlande und die deutsche Emigration', in Kathinka Dittrich and Hans Würzner (eds), *Die Niederlande und das deutsche Exil* (Amsterdam/Königstein: Athenäum, 1982), pp. 186–214.

Durovicova, Natasa, 'Translating America: The Hollywood Multilinguals 1929–1933', in Rick Altman (ed.), *Sound Theory, Sound Practice* (New York: Routledge, 1992), pp. 138–53.

Elsaesser, Thomas, 'European Cinema: Germany and Hollywood 1927–1934' in Giuliana Muscio (ed.), *Before the Hays Code* (Venice: Marsilio, 1991), pp. 201–12.

Ezra, Elizabeth and Rourden, Terry (eds), *Transnational Cinema: The Film Reader* (London and New York: Routledge, 2006).

Filmexil (Berlin: Stiftung Deutsche Kinemathek, 1995–).

Florey, Robert, *Hollywood d'hier* (Paris: Prisma, 1948).

Gabler, Neal, *An Empire of Their Own. How the Jews Invented Hollywood* (New York and London: Anchor Books, 1989).

García de Dueñas, J., *Nos vamos a Hollywood* (Madrid: Nikel Odeon, 1993).

Ghezzi, Enrico (ed.), *Vienna-Berlino-Hollywood: Il cinema della grande emigrazione* (Venice: Bienniale, 1981).

Giovacchini, Saverio, *Hollywood Modernism. Film and Politics in the Age of the New Deal* (Philadelphia: Temple University Press, 2001).

Glancy, H. Mark, *When Hollywood Loved Britain: The Hollywood 'British' Film, 1939–45* (Manchester: Manchester University Press, 1999).

Goethe Institute of North America, *German Film Directors in Hollywood: Film Emigration from Germany and Austria* (San Francisco: Goethe Institute, 1978).

Guback, Thomas, 'Hollywood's International Market', in Tino Balio (ed.), *The American Film Industry* (Madison: University of Wisconsin Press, 1976), pp. 387–409.

Hagwood, John A., *The Tragedy of German-America. The Germans in the United States of America During the Nineteenth Century and After* (New York and London: G. P. Putnam's & Sons, 1940).

Hardt, Ursula, *From Caligari to California: Erich Pommer's Life in the International Film Wars* (Providence, RI, and Oxford: Berghahn, 1996).

Heilbut, Anthony, *Exiled in Paradise* (Berkeley: University of California Press, 1993).

Helbich, Wolfgang, Walter D. Kamphoefner and Ulrike Sommer (eds), *Briefe aus Amerika. Deutsche Auswanderer schreiben aus der Neuen Welt, 1830–1930* (Munich: C. H. Beck, 1988).

Hernández Girbal, F., *Los que pasaron por Hollywood* (Madrid: Verdoux, 1992).

Higson, Andrew and Richard Maltby (eds), *'Film Europe' and 'Film America': Cinema, Commerce and Cultural Exchange 1920–1939* (Exeter: University of Exeter Press, 1999).

Hilchenbach, Maria, *Kino im Exil* (Munich: K. G. Saur, 1982).

Holmlund, Chris, 'Europeans in Action', in Yvonne Tasker (ed.), *Action and Adventure Cinema* (London and New York: Routledge, 2004), pp. 284–96.

Horak, Jan-Christopher, *Middle European Emigrés in Hollywood: An American Film Institute Oral History* (Beverly Hill, CA: Louis B. Mayer Foundation, 1977).

Horak, Jan-Christopher, 'The Palm Trees were Gently Swaying: German Refugees from Hitler in Hollywood', *Image* vol. 23 no. 1 (June 1980), pp. 21–32.

Horak, Jan-Christopher, *Fluchtpunkt Hollywood: Eine Dokumentation zur Filmemigration nach 1933* (Münster: MAkS, 1984).

Horak, Jan-Christopher, *Anti-Nazi-Filme der deutschsprachigen Emigration von Hollywood 1939–1945* (Münster: MAkS, 1985).

Horak, Jan-Christopher, 'Rin-Tin-Tin in Berlin or American Cinema in Weimar', *Film History* no. 5 (1993), pp. 49–62.

Horak, Jan-Christopher, 'German Exile Cinema, 1933–1950', *Film History* no. 8 (1996), pp. 373–89.

Hudson, Alice C. and Barbara Cohen-Stratyner, *Heading West / Touring West: Mapmakers, Performing Artists, and the American Frontier* (New York: New York Public Library, 2001).

Kohner, Frederick, *The Magician of Sunset Boulevard: The Improbable Life of Paul Kohner, Hollywood Agent* (Palos Verdes, CA: Morgan Press, 1977).

Kracauer, Siegfried, 'National Types as Hollywood Presents Them', in Roger Manvell (ed.), *The Cinema 1950* (Harmnondsworth: Penguin Books, 1950), pp. 140–69.

Langman, Larry, *Destination Hollywood: The Influence of Europeans on American Filmmaking* (London: McFarland, 2000).

Lebrun, Dominique, *Paris-Hollywood: les français dans le cinéma américain* (Paris: Hazan, 1987).

Lebrun, Dominique, *Trans Europe Hollywood: les européens du cinéma américain* (Paris: Bordas, 1992).

Leyens, Erich and Lotte Palfi-Andor, *Die fremden Jahre: Erinnerungen an Deutschland* (Frankfurt am Main: Fischer, 1994).

Liebe, Ulrich, *Verehrt, verfolgt, vergessen: Schauspieler als Naziopfer* (Weinheim and Berlin: Quadriga, 1995).

Loacker, Armin and Martin Prucha (eds), *Unerwünschtes Kino: Der deutschsprachige Emigrantenfilm 1934–1937* (Vienna: Filmarchiv Austria, 2000).

Loewy, Ronny, *Von Babelsberg nach Hollywood: Filmemigranten aus Nazideutschland* (Frankfurt am Main: Deutsches Filmmuseum, 1987).

Miller, Randall M. (ed.), *The Kaleidoscopic Lens: How Hollywood Views Ethnic Groups* (Englewood, NJ: Jerome S. Ozer, 1980).

Moltmann, Günter, 'The Pattern of German Emigration to the United States in the Nineteenth Century', in Frank Trommler and Joseph McVeigh, *America and the Germans. An Assessment of a Three-Hundred-Year History, Volume One* (Philadelphia: University of Pennsylvania Press, 1985), pp. 15–24.

Morley, Sheridan, *Tales from the Hollywood Raj: The British Film Colony On Screen and Off* (London: Weidenfeld & Nicolson, 1983).

Morrison, James, *Passport to Hollywood: Hollywood Films, European Directors* (Albany, NY: SUNY Press, 1998).

Naficy, Hamid (ed.), *Home, Exile, Homeland. Film, Media, and the Politics of Place* (London and New York: Routledge, 1999).

Negra, Diane, *Off-White Hollywood: American Culture and Ethnic Female Stardom* (London and New York: Routledge, 2001).

Noussinova, Natalia, 'Russkie v Amerike', *Kinoverdcheskie zapiski* no. 43 (1999), pp. 174–88.

Nowell-Smith, Geoffrey and Steven Ricci (eds), *Hollywood and Europe: Economics, Culture, National Identity 1945–95* (London: BFI, 1998).

Petrie, Graham, *Hollywood Destinies: European Directors in America, 1922–31* (London: Routledge & Kegan Paul, 1985).

Phillips, Alastair (ed.), 'Screen Dossier: European Actors in Hollywood', *Screen* vol. 43 no. 2 (Summer 2002), pp. 174–218.

Phillips, Alastair, 'Changing Bodies/Changing Voices. Success and Failure in Hollywood in the Early Sound Era', *Screen* vol. 43 no. 2 (Summer 2002), pp. 187–200

Phillips, Gene D., *Exiles in Hollywood: Major European Film Directors in America* (London: Associated University Presses, 1998).

Polan, Dana, 'Methodological Reflections on the Study of the Émigré Actor', *Screen* vol. 43 no. 2 (Summer 2002), pp. 178–86.

Raeff, Marc, *Russia Abroad: A Cultural History of the Russian Emigration, 1919–1939* (New York: Oxford University Press, 1990).

Reyes, Luis and Peter Rubie, *Hispanics in Hollywood: A Celebration of 100 Years in Film and Television* (Los Angeles: Lone Eagle Publishing Co., 2000).

Rodeck, Hans Georg, 'Europaische Filmemigration in die USA vor 1920', *KINtop* no. 10 (2001).

Russell-Taylor, John, *Strangers in Paradise: The Hollywood Émigrés 1933–1950* (London: Faber and Faber, 1983).

Saunders, Thomas J., *Hollywood in Berlin: American Cinema and Weimar Germany* (Berkeley, Los Angeles and London: University of California Press, 1994).

Schnauber, Cornelius and Barbara Zeisl Schoenberg, *Hollywood Haven: Homes and Haunts of the European émigrés and Exiles in Hollywood* (Riverside, CA: Ariadne Press, 1997).

Sellier, Geneviève, 'Danielle Darrieux, Michèle Morgan and Micheline Presle in Hollywood: The Threat to French Identity', *Screen* vol. 43 no. 2 (Summer 2002), pp. 201–14.

Servel, Alain, *Frenchie Goes to Hollywood: la France et les Français dans le cinéma américain de 1929 à nos jours* (Paris: Éditions Henri Veyrier, 1987).

Street, Sarah, *Transatlantic Crossings: British Feature Films in the USA* (London and New York: Continuum, 2002).

Suleiman, Susan Rubin (ed.), *Exile and Creativity. Signposts, Travelers, Outsiders, Backwards Glances* (Durham and London: Duke University Press, 1996).

Thomas, Victoria, *Hollywood's Latin Lovers: Latino, Italian and French Men Who Make the Screen Smolder* (Santa Monica, CA: Angel City Press, 1998).

Thompson, Kristin, *Exporting Entertainment: America in the World Film Market 1907–1934* (London: BFI, 1985).

Ulrich, Rudolf, *Österreicher in Hollywood* (Vienna: Verlag Filmarchiv Austria, 2004).

Vasey, Ruth, *The World According to Hollywood, 1918–1939* (Madison: University of Wisconsin Press, 1997).

Waldman, Harry, *Hollywood and the Foreign Touch. A Dictionary of Foreign Filmmakers and Their Films from America 1910–1995* (Metuchen, NJ: Scarecrow Press, 1996).

Whitteman, Don and Philip Alan Cecchettini, *Passport to Hollywood* (New York: McGraw Hill, 1976).

Wicclair, Walter, *Von Kreuzberg bis Hollywood* (Berlin (GDR): Henschelverlag, 1975).

Wollstein, Hans J., *Strangers in Hollywood: The History of Scandinavian Actors in America* (Metuchen, NJ: Scarecrow Press, 1994).

Further Reading on Film Acting, Stardom, European Cinema and Hollywood

Abel, Richard, *French Cinema: The First Wave, 1915–1929* (Princeton, NJ: Princeton University Press, 1984).

Abel, Richard, *The Ciné Goes to Town: French Cinema, 1896–1914* (Berkeley: University of California Press, 1994).

Aeppli, Felix, *Der Schweizer Film 1929–1964. Die Schweiz als Ritual. Band 2: Materialien* (Zurich: Limmat, 1981).

Affron, Charles, *Star Acting: Gish, Garbo, Davies* (New York: Dutton, 1977).

Åhlander, Lars (ed.), *Svensk Filmografi, Part 4* (1980); *Svensk Filmografi, Part 5* (1984); *Svensk Filmografi, Part 7* (1989) (Stockholm: Svenska filminstitutet).

Åhlander, Lars and Qvist, Per Olov (eds), *Svenska skådespelare i film och tv (a-k)* and *Svenska skådespelare i film och tv (l-ö)* (Stockholm: Svenska filminstitutet, 2002).

Albera, François, *Albatros: des Russes à Paris, 1919–1929* (Paris: La Cinémathèque française/Mazzoti, 1995).

Albera, François and Maria Tortajada (eds), *Cinéma suisse: nouvelles approches* (Lausanne: Payot, 2000).

Arenskii, K., *Pisma v Khollivud* (Monterey/Munich: K. Arensburger, 1968).

Athanasatou, G., *Greek Cinema (1950–1967): Popular Memory and Ideology* (Athens: Finatec A. E., 2001).

Babington, Bruce (ed.), *British Stars and Stardom* (Manchester: Manchester University Press, 2001).

Baron, Cynthia, Diane Carson and Frank Tomasulo (eds) *More than a Method: Essays on Film Acting* (Detroit, MI: Wayne State University Press, 2003).

Barrios, Richard, *A Song in the Dark: The Birth of the Musical Film* (Oxford: Oxford University Press, 1995).

Barrot, Olivier and Raymond Chirat, *Inoubliables: Visages du cinéma français 1930–1950* (Paris: Calmann-Lévy, 1986).

Barrot, Olivier and Raymond Chirat, *Noir & blanc, 250 acteurs du cinéma français 1930–1960* (Paris: Flammarion, 2000).

Barton, Ruth, *Irish National Cinema* (London and New York: Routledge, 2004).

Basinger, Jeanine, *Silent Stars* (New York: Alfred A. Knopf, 1999).

Bergfelder, Tim, 'The Nation Vanishes: European Co-Productions and Popular Genre Formulae in the 1950s and 1960s', in Mette Hjort and Scott Mackenzie (eds), *Cinema & Nation* (London and New York: Routledge, 2000).

Bergfelder, Tim, Erica Carter and Deniz Göktürk (eds), *The German Cinema Book* (London: BFI, 2002).

Berghaus, Günter (ed.), *Theatre and Film in Exile: German Artists in Britain, 1933–1945* (Oxford, New York and Munich: Berg, 1989).

Bermingham, Cedric Osmond (ed.), *Stars of the Screen 1931* (London: Herbert Joseph, 1931).

Berry, David, *Wales and the Cinema: The First Hundred Years* (Cardiff: University of Wales Press, 1994).

Berry, Sarah, *Screen Style. Fashion and Femininity in 1930s Hollywood* (Minneapolis: University of Minnesota Press, 2000).

Bertellini, Giorgio, *Southern Crossings: Italians, Cinema and Modernity (Italy, 1861–New York, 1920)*, PhD dissertation (New York University, 2001).

Beyer, Friedemann, *Die Gesichter der UFA: Starportraits einer Epoche* (Munich: Heyne, 1992).

Bock, Hans-Michael (ed.), *Cine-Graph: Lexikon zum deutschsprachigen Film* (Munich: edition text+kritik, 1984).

Bowers, Ronald, *The Selznick Players* (South Brunswick, NJ, and London: A. S. Barnes, 1976).

Brownlow, Kevin, *The Parade's Gone By* (New York: Knopf, 1968).

Brownlow, Kevin, *Behind the Mask of Innocence. Sex, Violence, Prejudice, Crime: Films of Social Conscience in the Silent Era* (New York: Alfred A. Knopf, 1990).

Brunetta, Gian-Piero, *Storia del cinema Italiano* (Rome: Editori Reuniti, 1993).

Brunetta, Gian-Piero (ed.), *Storia del cinema mondiale II, Gli Stati Uniti* (Turin: Einaudi, 1999).

Bruno, Giuliana, *Streetwalking on a Ruined Map: Cultural Theory and the City Films of Elvira Notari* (Princeton, NJ: Princeton University Press, 1993).

Buache, Freddy, *Le Cinéma suisse 1898–1998* (Lausanne: L'Âge d'homme, 1998).

Burton, Hal (ed.), *Acting in the Sixties* (London: BBC, 1970).

Butler, Jeremy G. (ed.), *Star Texts: Image and Performance in Film and Television* (Detroit, MI: Wayne State University Press, 1991).

Cantacuzino, I. I. and B. T. Rîpeanu, *Productia cinematografica din Romania, 1897–1970* (Bucharest: Arhiva Nationala de Filme, 1970, 1998).

Catalogus Nederlandse Filmdagen 1991 (Utrecht: Stichting Nederlandse Filmdagen, 1991).

Catalogus Nederlandse Filmdagen 1994 (Utrecht: Stichting Nederlandse Filmdagen, 1994).

Caughie, John with Kevin Rockett, *The Companion to British and Irish Cinema* (London: Cassell/BFI, 1996).

Chiti, Roberto, Enrico Lancia and Roberto Poppi, *Dizionario del Cinema Italiano: Le Attrici* (Rome: Gremese, 1999).

Clark, Danae, *Negotiating Hollywood: The Cultural Politics of Actors' Labor* (Minneapolis: University of Minnesota Press, 1995).

Crowl, Samuel, *Shakespeare at the Cineplex* (Athens: Ohio University Press, 2003).

Curran, Joseph M., *Hibernian Green on the Silver Screen* (New York, Westport, CT, and London: Greenwood Press, 1989).

DeCordova, Richard, *Picture Personalities: The Emergence of the Star System in Hollywood* (Urbana: University of Illinois Press, 1990).

D'Lugo, Marvin, *Guide to the Cinema of Spain* (Westport, CT: Greenwood Press, 1997).

Demopoulos, M. (ed.), *Le Cinéma Grec* (Paris: Éditions du Centre Pompidou, 1995).

Donnelly, Paul, *Fade to Black: A Book of Movie Obituaries* (London, New York and Sydney: Omnibus, 2000).

Donner, Jörn (ed.), *Svensk Filmografi, Part 6* (Stockholm: Svenska filminstitutet, 1977).

Dumont, Hervé, *Histoire du cinéma Suisse. Films de fiction 1896–1965* (Lausanne: Cinémathèque Suisse, 1987).

Dyer, Richard, *Heavenly Bodies: Film Stars and Society* (London: BFI/Macmillan, 1987).

Dyer, Richard, *Stars*, 2nd edn (London: BFI, 1997).

Ellwood, David W. and Rob Kroes (eds), *Hollywood in Europe: Experiences of a Cultural Hegemony* (Amsterdam: VU University Press, 1994).

Elsaesser, Thomas and Michael Wedel (eds), *The BFI Companion to German Cinema* (London: Cassell/BFI, 1999).

Elsaesser, Thomas, *Weimar Cinema and After: Germany's Historical Imaginary* (London: Routledge, 2000).

Elsaesser, Thomas, *European Cinema: Face to Face with Hollywood* (Amsterdam: Amsterdam University Press, 2005).

Exarchos, T., *Greek Actors: Looking for Their Roots* (Athens: Dodoni, 1996).

Faller, Greg, *The Function of Star-Image and Performance in the Hollywood Musical: Sonja Henie, Esther Williams, and Eleanor Powell*, PhD dissertation (Evanston, IL: North Western University, 1987).

Faulstich, Werner and Helmut Korte (eds), *Fischer Filmgeschichte Band 2: Der Film als gesellschaftliche Kraft 1925–1944* (Frankfurt am Main: Fischer, 1991).

Feuer, Jane, *The Hollywood Musical*, 2nd edn (Bloomington: Indiana University Press, 1993).

Forslund, Bengt, *Bengt Forslund presenterar filmstjärnor: En bok om svenska skådespelerskor i världen* (Stockholm: Alfabeta, 1995).

Foucart, Yvan, *Dictionnaire des comédiens français disparus* (Mariembourg: Éditions Grand Angle, 2000).

Fulgheri, Ennio, *Manuale del cinema Italiano* (Milan: Nuove Edizioni Swan, 1998).

Garncarz, Joseph, *Populäres Kino in Deutschland: Internationalisierung einer Filmkultur 1925–1990* (unpublished *Habilitationsschrift*, University of Cologne, 1996).

Gilbert, Douglas, *American Vaudeville: Its Life and Times* (New York: Dover, 1963).

Gilles, Christian (ed.), *Le Cinéma des années trente par ceux qui l'ont fait. Tome I* (Paris: L'Harmattan, 2000).

Gledhill, Christine (ed.), *Stardom: Industry of Desire* (London and New York: Routledge, 1991).

Gomery, Douglas, *The Hollywood Studio System* (New York: St Martin's Press, 1986).

Hake, Sabine, *German National Cinema* (London and New York: Routledge, 2002).

Hansen, Miriam, *Babel and Babylon: Spectatorship in American Silent Film* (Cambridge, MA: Harvard University Press, 1991).

Harmetz, Aljean, *Round up the Usual Suspects: The Making of 'Casablanca' – Bogart, Bergman, and World War II* (London: Weidenfeld & Nicolson, 1993).

Hayward, Susan, *French National Cinema* (London and New York: Routledge, 1993).

Hediger, Vinzenz, Jan Sahli, Alexandra Schneider and
  Margrit Tröhler (eds), *Home Stories. Neue Studien zu Film
  und Kino in der Schweiz* (Marburg: Schüren, 2001).

Hibbin, Nina, *Screen Series: Eastern Europe* (London and
  New York: Zwemmer & Barnes, 1969).

Hirsch, Foster, *Acting Hollywood Style* (New York: Harry
  N. Adams, 1991).

Hofstede, B., *Nederlandse cinema wereldwijd. De internationale
  positie van de Nederlandse film* (Amsterdam:
  Boekmanstudies, 2000).

Hogan, David J., *Who's Who of the Horrors and Other
  Fantasy Films* (London: Tantivy Press, 1981).

Holmlund, Chris, *Impossible Bodies: Femininity and
  Masculinity at the Movies* (London and New York:
  Routledge, 2002).

Hoopes, Roy, *When the Stars Went to War* (New York:
  Random House, 1994).

Iordanova, Dina, *Cinema of Flames: Balkan Film, Culture
  and the Media* (London: BFI, 2001).

Izod, John, *Hollywood and the Box-Office 1895–1986* (New
  York: Columbia University Press, 1988).

Jacobs, Lea, *The Wages of Sin: Censorship and the Fallen
  Woman Film, 1928–1942* (Madison: University of
  Wisconsin Press, 1991).

Jarvis, Everett G., *Final Curtain: Deaths of Noted Movie and
  TV Personalities, 1915–1994* (Secaucus, NJ: Citadel,
  1995).

Jeanne, René and Charles Ford, *Histoire encyclopédique du
  cinéma 1: le cinéma français, 1895–1929* (Paris: Robert
  Laffont, 1947).

Jungstedt, Torsten (ed.), *Svensk Filmografi, Part 3*
  (Stockholm: Svenska filminstitutet, 1979).

Juran, Robert A., *Old Familiar Faces: The Great Character
  Actors and Actresses of Hollywood's Golden Era* (Sarasota,
  FL: Movie Memories Publishing, 1995).

Katchmer, George A., *Eighty Silent Film Stars* (Jefferson:
  NC: McFarland, 1991).

Katz, Ephraim, *The Macmillan International Film
  Encyclopedia*, 4th edn. (London: Macmillan, 2001).

Keller, D. Gary, *A Biographical Handbook of Hispanics and
  United States Film* (Tempe, AZ: Bilingual Press, 1997).

Kobal, John, *People Will Talk: Personal Conversations with the
  Legends of Hollywood* (London: Aurum, 1991).

Kohl, Leonard J., 'How Can a Hungarian Be a Nice
  Guy?', *Cult Movies* no. 33 (2001), pp. 38–54.

Krämer, Peter and Alan Lovell (eds), *Screen Acting*
  (London: Routledge, 1999).

Lacalmita, Michele *et al.* (eds), *Film Lexicon degli autori
  e delle opere* (Rome: Edizioni di Bianco e Nero,
  1958).

Lancia, Enrico, *Italian Movie Goddesses* (Rome: Gremese
  International, 1996).

Lauritzen, Einar and Gunnar Lundquist, *American Film-
  Index 1916–1920* (Stockholm: Film-Index, 1984).

Leyda, Jay, *Kino. A History of the Russian and Soviet Film*
  (London, Boston and Sydney: Collier Books, 1973).

Liebman, Roy, *From Silent to Sound. A Biographical
  Encyclopedia of Performers Who Made the Transition to
  Talking Pictures* (Jefferson, NC: McFarland, 1998).

Liehm, Mira and Antonin J. Liehm, *The Most Important
  Art: Soviet and Eastern European Film after 1945*
  (Berkeley: University of California Press, 1977).

Low, Rachel, *The History of the British Film* (seven vols.):
  Vol. 1 *1896–1906* (1948); Vol. 2 *1906–1914* (1949);
  Vol. 3 *1914–1918* (1950); Vol. 4 *1918–1929*; Vol. 5
  Documentary and Educational Films of the 1930s (1979);
  Vol. 6 *Films of Comment and Persuasion* (1979); Vol. 7
  Filmmaking in 1930s Britain (1985) (London: Allen &
  Unwin).

Mack Truitt, Evelyn, *Who Was Who on Screen* (New York:
  R. R. Co., 1983).

Maltin, Leonard, *Leonard Maltin's Movie Encyclopedia* (New
  York: Penguin Putnam, 1994).

Matei, J. P., *La Corse et le cinéma* (Ajaccio: Editions Alain
  Piazzolla, 1996).

McClelland, Doug, *The Golden Age of B-Movies* (New
  York: Bonanza, 1981).

McDonald, Paul, *The Star System: Hollywood and the
  Production of Popular Identities* (London: Wallflower Press,
  2000).

McFarlane, Brian (ed.), *Sixty Voices: Celebrities Recall the
  Golden Age of British Cinema* (London: BFI, 1992).

McFarlane, Brian (ed.), *The Encyclopedia of British Film*
  (London: BFI and Methuen, 2003).

McLaughlin, Robert, *Broadway and Hollywood: A History of
  Economic Interaction* (New York: Arno Press, 1974).

Miller, Toby, Nitin Govil, John McMurria and Richard
  Maxwell, *Global Hollywood* (London: BFI, 2001).

Mitropoulou, A., *History of the Greek Cinema* (Athens:
  Media, 1980).

Mitry, Jean, *Anthologie du cinéma II* (Paris: L'Avant-Scène/CIB, 1967).

Monush, Barry, *The Encyclopedia of Hollywood Film Actors from the Silent Period to 1965* (New York: Applause Theatre and Cinema Books, 2003).

Morin, Edgar, *The Stars* (New York: Grove, 1960).

Moseley, Leonard, *Zanuck. The Rise and Fall of Hollywood's Last Tycoon* (Boston, MA: Little, Brown and Co., 1984).

Murphy, Robert (ed.), *The British Cinema Book*, 2nd edn (London: BFI, 2002).

Muscio, Giuliana, *Hollywood's New Deal* (Philadelphia: Temple University Press, 1996).

Musser, Charles, 'Ethnicity, Role-Playing, and American Film Comedy: From *Chinese Laundry Scene* to *Whoopee* (1894–1930)', in Lester D. Friedman (ed.), *Unspeakable Images* (Urbana and Chicago: University of Illinois Press, 1991), pp. 43–60.

Naremore, James, *Acting in the Cinema* (Berkeley: University of California Press, 1988).

Noose, Theodore, *Hollywood Film Acting* (South Brunswick, NJ: A. S. Barnes, 1979).

Nowell-Smith, Geoffrey, James Hay and Gianni Volpi, *The Companion to Italian Cinema* (London: Cassell and BFI, 1996).

O'Connor, Áine, *Leading Hollywood* (Dublin: Wolfhound Press, 1996).

Parish, James Robert, *The Fox Girls* (New York: Arlington House, 1971).

Parish, James Robert (ed.), *Film Actors Guide: Western Europe* (Metuchen, NJ, and London: Scarecrow Press, 1977).

Parish, James Robert (ed.), *Hollywood Character Actors* (New York: Arlington House Publishers, 1978).

Parish, James Robert, *The Hollywood Celebrity Death Book* (Las Vegas, NV: Pioneer, 1993).

Parish, James Robert, *The Encyclopedia of Ethnic Groups in Hollywood* (New York: Facts on File Inc., 2003).

Parish, James Robert and William T. Leonard, *Hollywood Players: The Thirties* (New Rochelle, NY: Arlington House, 1976).

Pearson, Roberta, *Eloquent Gestures: The Transformation of Performance Style in the Griffith Biograph Film* (Berkeley: University of California Press, 1992).

Peary, Danny, *Cult Movie Stars* (London, Sydney and New York: Simon & Schuster, 1991).

Pendergast, Sara and Tom (eds), *International Dictionary of Films and Filmmakers*. Volume 3: *Actors and Actresses*, 4th edn (Farmington Hills, MI: St James Press, 2000).

Phillips, Alastair, *City of Darkness, City of Light. Émigré Filmmakers in Paris 1929–1939* (Amsterdam: Amsterdam University Press, 2004).

Picture Show Annual 1928–1958.

The Picturegoer's Who's Who and Encyclopaedia of the Screen To-Day (London: Odhams, 1933).

Pitts, Michael R., *Horror Film Stars* (Jefferson, NC, and London: McFarland, 1991).

Quinlan, David, *Quinlan's Illustrated Directory of Film Character Actors* (London: Batsford, 1997).

Quinlan, David, *Quinlan's Film Stars* (Dulles, VA: Brassey's, 2001).

Ramsaye, Terry, *A Million and One Nights: A History of the Motion Picture through 1925* (New York: Simon & Schuster, 1926).

Richards, Jeffrey, *Swordsmen of the Screen: From Douglas Fairbanks to Michael York* (London: Routledge & Kegan Paul, 1977).

Robertson Wojcik, Pamela (ed.), *Movie Acting, The Film Reader* (London: Routledge, 2004).

Robinson, David, *Hollywood in the Twenties* (New York: Paperback Library, 1970).

Romani, Cinzia, *Tainted Goddesses. Female Film Stars of the Third Reich* (New York: Sarpedon, 1992).

Ryall, Tom, *Britain and the American Cinema* (London: Sage, 2001).

Schaub, Martin, *The Swiss Cinema* (Zurich: Pro Helvetia, 1998).

Schlappner, Martin and Martin Schaub, *Cinéma suisse: regards critiques 1896–1987* (Zurich: Schweizerisches Filmzentrum, and Basel: Stroemfeld/Roter Stern, 1987).

Schöning, Jörg, *London Calling: Deutsche im britischen Film der dreißiger Jahre* (Munich: edition text+kritik, 1993).

Senelick, Laurence (ed.), *Wandering Stars: Russian Émigré Theatre, 1905–1940* (Iowa City: University of Iowa Press, 1992).

Shipman, David, *The Great Movie Stars. The Golden Years* (London: Hamlyn, 1970).

Shipman, David, *The Great Movie Stars 2: The International Years* (London: MacDonald, 1989).

Shipman, David, *The Great Movie Stars 3: The Independent Years* (London: MacDonald, 1991).

Sieglohr, Ulrike (ed.), *Heroines without Heroes: Reconstructing Female and National Identities in European Cinema, 1941–51* (London: Cassell, 2000).

Siscot, André, *Les Gens du cinéma: encyclopédie* (Brussels: Memor/Cinéma, 1998).

Slide, Anthony, *The Cinema and Ireland* (Jefferson, NC, and London: McFarland, 1989).

Slide, Anthony, *Silent Players. A Biographical and Autobiographical Study of 100 Silent Film Actors and Actresses* (Lexington: University of Kentucky Press, 2002).

Soila, Tytti, Astrid Soderbergh Widding and Gunnar Iversen (eds), *Nordic National Cinemas* (London and New York: Routledge, 1998).

Soldatos, Y., *History of Greek Cinema, 1900–1967, Vol. 1* (Athens: Aigokeros, 1999).

Soldatos, Y., *History of Greek Cinema, 1900–1967, Vol. 2* (Athens: Aigokeros, 1999).

Spicer, Andrew, *Typical Men: The Representation of Masculinity in Popular British Cinema* (London: I. B. Tauris, 2001).

Spieker, Markus, *Hollywood unterm Hakenkreuz: Der amerikanische Spielfilm im Dritten Reich* (Trier: Wissenschaftlicher Verlag, 1999).

Stewart, J., *Italian Film: A Who's Who* (Jefferson, NC: McFarland, 1994).

Studlar, Gaylyn, *This Mad Masquerade: Stardom and Masculinity in the Jazz Age* (New York: Columbia University Press, 1996).

Sturm, Sibylle and Arthur Wohlgemuth (eds), *Hallo? Berlin? Ici Paris! Deutsche-französische Filmbeziehungen 1918–1939* (Munich: edition text+kritik, 1996).

Taylor, Richard, Nancy Wood, Julian Graffy and Dina Iordanova (eds), *The BFI Companion to Eastern European and Russian Cinema* (London: BFI, 2000).

Temple, Michael and Michael Witt (eds), *The French Cinema Book* (London: BFI, 2004).

Thompson, David, *A Biographical Dictionary of Film* (London: Deutsch, 1994).

Triana-Toribio, Nuria, *Spanish National Cinema* (London and New York: Routledge, 2002).

Uricchio, William and Roberta Pearson, *Reframing Culture: The Case of Vitagraph Quality Films* (Princeton, NJ: Princeton University Press, 1993).

Uusitalo, Kari, *Ruutia, riitoja rakkautta: Suomalaisen elokuvan sotavuoden 1940–1948* (Helsinki: Suomen elokuvasäätiö, 1977).

Uusitalo, Kari, *Hei rillumarei, Suomalaisen elokuvan mimmiteollisuusvuodet 1949–1955* (Helsinki: Suomen elokuvasäätiö, 1978).

Uusitalo, Kari (ed.), *Suomen Kansallisfilmografia, Part 3* (Helsinki: Edita, 1992).

Uusitalo, Kari (ed.), *Suomen Kansallisfilmografia, Part 4* (Helsinki: Edita, 1993).

Vazzana, Eugene Michael, *Silent Film Necrology* (Jefferson, NC, and London: McFarland, 2001).

Villiers, Mara and Gilles Gressard, *Stars d'aujourd'hui* (Paris: Ramsay, 1985).

Vincendeau, Ginette (ed.), *The Encyclopedia of European Cinema* (London: Cassell/BFI 1995).

Vincendeau, Ginette, *The Companion to French Cinema* (London: Cassell/BFI, 1996).

Vincendeau, Ginette, *Stars and Stardom in French Cinema* (London and New York: Continuum, 2000).

Vizcaino Casas, Fernando, *Diccionario del cine español (1896–166)*, 2nd edn (Madrid: Editora Nacional, 1968).

Wagnleitner, Reinhold and Elaine Tyler May (eds), *'Here, There and Everywhere': The Foreign Politics of American Popular Culture* (Hanover: University Press of New England, 2000).

Walker, Alexander, *The Shattered Silents: How the Talkies Came to Stay* (New York: William Morrow, 1979).

Walker, John (ed.), *Halliwell's Film Guide*, 10th edn (London: HarperCollins 1994).

Wathelet, Gérard, *L'Histoire du cinéma français de 1950 à 1960* (Paris: Éditions Pygmalion, 1994).

Wexman, Virginia Wright, *Creating the Couple: Love, Marriage and Hollywood Performance* (Princeton, NJ: Princeton University Press, 1993).

Wottrich, Erika (ed.), *Deutsche Universal: Transatlantische Verleih- und Produktionsstrategien eines Hollywood-Studios in den 20er und 30er Jahren* (Munich: edition text+kritik, 2001).

Wright, Gene, *Horrorshows: Horror in Film, Television, Radio and Theatre* (Newton Abbot, Devon: David & Charles, 1986).

Yangirov, Rashif, 'Pod razvesistoi kliukvoi russkoj kinoekzotiki', *Iskusstvo kino* no. 12 (1993), pp. 100–8.

Zucker, Carole (ed.), *Making Visible the Invisible: An Anthology of Original Essays on Film Acting* (Metuchen, NJ: Scarecrow Press, 1990).

Zucker, Carole, *Figures of Light: Actors and Directors Illuminate the Art of Film Acting* (New York: Plenum, 1995).

Selected Internet Resources

Academy of Motion Picture Arts and Sciences: Margaret Herrick Library
<www.oscars.org/mhl/index.html>

All Movie Guide

American Film Institute
<www.afi.com>

Ancestry.com

Bifi

British Film Institute

CineGraph
<www.cinegraph.de>

The German Hollywood Connection

Immigration Research History Center, University of Minnesota
<www.ihrc.umn.edu/collage/index.htm>

Internet Movie Database

Library of Congress: National Film Preservation Board
<www.loc.gov/film/>

Picture History

Screenonline
<www.screenonline.org.uk/index.html/>

List of Illustrations

Whilst considerable effort has been made to correctly identify the copyright holders, this has not been possible in all cases. We apologise for any apparent negligence and any omissions or corrections brought to our attention will be remedied in any future editions.

Casablanca, Warner Bros.; *Conquest*, Metro-Goldwyn-Mayer Corporation; *Titanic*, Twentieth Century Fox Film Corporation/Paramount Pictures Corporation/Lightstorm Entertainment; *Gigi*, Loew's Incorporated/Arthur Freed Productions; *Vanilla Sky*, © Paramount Pictures Corporation; *Cat People*, RKO Pictures/Universal Pictures; *The Last Command*, Paramount Famous Lasky Corporation; *The Beach*, © Twentieth Century-Fox Film Corporation; *Notorious*, RKO Radio Pictures; *Desperado*, Columbia Pictures Corporation/Hooligans Productions; *Mickey Blue Eyes*, © CR Films; *Thieves' Highway*, Twentieth Century-Fox Film Corporation; *The Age of Innocence*, Cappa Productions; *Shanghai Express*, Paramount Publix Corporation; *Green Card*, Green Card Production Company/U.G.C./Rio/SEDIF; *Sense and Sensibility*, Columbia Pictures Corporation/Mirage Enterprises; *Hudson Hawk*, Silver Pictures/Ace Bone/TriStar Pictures/Flying Heart Films; *The Silence of the Lambs*, Orion Pictures Corporation/Strong Heart/Demme; *Dracula*, Universal Pictures Corporation; *Passage to Marseilles*, Warner Bros.; *Wuthering Heights*, Samuel Goldwyn Inc.; *The Adventures of Sherlock Holmes*, © Twentieth Century-Fox Film Corporation; *Honeymoon in Bali*, Paramount Pictures; *The Paradine Case*, Vanguard Films.

Index

À bout de souffle/Breathless 316
A moi le jour, à toi la nuit/Early to Bed 278
A-Haunting We Will Go 226
Abbadie d'Arrast, Henri d' 199
Abbey Films 224
Abbey Players 220, 391, 431
Abbey Theatre, Dublin 157, 190, 248, 309, 320, 358, 360, 379, 387, 408
Abbott and Costello 241, 317
ABC network 364
Abie's Irish Rose 190
About Adam 449
About a Boy 144, 277
Abrahams, Jim 100
Abre los ojos/Open Your Eyes 133, 220, 221
Abril, Victoria 133, 153
Academy of Motion Picture Arts and Sciences 244, 297
Accident 170, 468
Ackland, Joss 153, 455
Act of Love 414
Actors' Equity Association 454
Actor's Studio 176, 250
Adams, Maude 373
Adam's Rib 383
Adamson, Joy 360
Address Unknown 208
Adjani, Isabelle 153–4
Adler, Jacob 51*n*
Adler, Stella 323
Adorable 259
Adorée, Renée 10, 24, 154, *154*, 252
Las adventuras de Robinson Crusoe 388
Adventure 262
Adventure in Diamonds 49, 368
The Adventures of Baron Munchausen 218
Adventures of Captain Fabian 401
The Adventures of Quentin Durward 319
The Adventures of Robin Hood 34, 203, 216, 279, 301, 377, 398, 405, 406
An Affair to Remember 363, 381
The African Queen 367–8
Against All Flags 387–8
Against the Tide 381
Age of Consent 354

L'Âge d'or 347
The Age of Innocence 42, 229, 350, 402
Agel, Henri 96, 100–101*n*
The Agony and the Ecstasy 287
Aguglia, Mimi 46, 48, 154
Agutter, Jenny 155
Aherne, Brian 155
Aho, Betty 155
A.I. 333
Aida Foster School of Dance 432
Aimée, Anouk 155, 366
Aimez-vous Brahms? 363, 369
Air Force One 41, 402, 419
Airborne 144
Airport 182
Aitken, Harry 204
Akerman, Chantal 181
Alba, Maria 155–6
Alberghetti, Anna Maria 156
Alberni, Luis 156
Albertini, Luciano 48, 156, 312
Alcañiz, Luana 156, 438
Aldrich, Robert 158, 232, 371, 469
Aleandri, Emelise 46
Alessandrini, Goffredo 349
Alex in Wonderland 373
Alexander 244, 301
Alexander the Great 170, 194, 227
Alfie 196
Algiers 87, 322, 327
Alien: Resurrection 398
All About Eve 270, 407, 421
All the King's Horses 191
All the Pretty Horses 220
All Quiet on the Western Front 463
All Through the Night 110
Allan, Elizabeth 156–7
Allégret, Marc 167, 315
Allégret, Yves 230
Allen, Woody 48, 51*n*, 173, 175, 183, 187, 196, 277, 300, 311, 379, 404, 406, 417, 451
Allenberg, Bert 320
Allgood, Sara 157, 309
Allied Artists 56

Almeida, Joaquim de 401
Almodóvar, Pedro 133, 138, 153, 171, 430, 438
An Almost Perfect Affair 462
Altman, Rick 90
Altman, Robert 51*n*, 100, 155, 187, 262, 314, 342, 356, 402, 422, 435, 469
Amadeus 223
Amalric, Mathieu 71
L'Amante di paride/Loves of Three Queens 328
Les Amants du Pont-Neuf/The Lovers on the Bridge 181
Les Amants de Vérone/The Lovers of Verona 155
The Amazing Quest of Ernest Bliss 275
The Ambassador 446
Ameche, Don 291
Amenábar, Alejandro 133
American Cancer Society 310
American Film Institute 143
American Guerrilla in the Philippines 401
American Laboratory Theatre and School of Dramatic Art 392
American Lifeograph Company 297
American National Academy of Performing Arts 335
An American in Paris 201, 282
American Psycho 142
American Theatre Guild 405
The Americanization of Emily 161, 280
America's Sweethearts 470
Amistad 145, 290, 433
Amore e morte 47
Les Amours de la reine Elisabeth/Queen Elizabeth 22, 445
Amphitryon 426
Anastasia 170, 180
Ancient Order of Hibernians 309
Anders, Rudolph 104, 105, 108, 157
Andersen, Hans Christian 337
Anderson, Lindsay 286, 359
Anderson, Paul Thomas 356, 465
Anderson, Robert 157
Andersson, Bibi 157–8, 263

Andor, Paul (Wolfgang Zilzer) 104, 105, 107, 108, 109, 110, 158, 394
Andre, Gwili 158
André, Marcel 17*n*, 253
Andress, Ursula 158, 442
Andreu, Gaby 159
Andrews, Dana 428
Andrews, Deborah 14
Andrews, Harry 9, 159
Andrews, Julie 159, 250, 280, 287, 448
Andrews, Ted 159
Andriot, Lucien 22
Android 323
Andy Hardy films 245
Angel 97, 98, 408
Angel Face 432
Angel, Heather 161
The Angel with the Trumpet 465
The Angel Wore Red 234
Angela's Ashes 465
Angeli, Pier 95, 100, *160*, 161–2, 169
Angelina o el honor de un brigadier/ Angelina or the Honour of a Brigadier 229, 438
Angélique films 363
Angélique Marquise des Anges/Angélique 363
Anglo–American Film Agreement 9
The Animal Kingdom 440
Anna Boleyn/Deception 265
Anna Christie 96, 260, 261, 379, 452
Anna Karenina (1935) 95, 97, 188, 261, 406
Anna Karenina (1948, stage version) 336, 372
Anna Karenina (1997) 72, 251, 350
Anna and the King of Siam 287
Annabella 11, 85–7, 89–90, 92, 115, 118, 162, *162*, 253, 377
Anne of the Indies 125, 127
Anne of the Thousand Days 404
Annie 247
Annis, Francesca 163, 245
Another Country 242, 243
Another Time, Another Place 214
Another Woman 300
Ansikte mot ansikte/Face to Face 452
Anthony Adverse 47, 64–65
anti-Nazi films 107–9, 267–8
Anti-Nazi League 267
Antoine, André 25
Antonioni, Michelangelo 207, 218, 290, 457, 462
Anwar, Gabrielle 163
Anys, Georgette 163
Anything Goes 314, 440
Apocalypse Now 210, 451
Apocalypse Now Redux 210
The Appointment 155

Appointment with Danger 198
The April Fools 232
Apted, Michael 72, 350
Aquila nera/Black Ostrich 341
Aranda, Vicente 153
Arau, Alfonso 100
Arbó, Manuel 438
Arbuckle, Roscoe 'Fatty' 23, 49, 234, 337
Archansky, Michael 80
Arco, Louis V. 163
Ardmore Studios 224
The Aristocats 258
Arlen, Richard 64
L'Arlésienne 25
Arletty 121, 123*n*, 314
Arliss, George 163–4
Armageddon 321
Armero, Alvaro 437
Armetta, Henry 49–50, 312
Arna, Lissy 164, 266
Arnaud, Etienne 22
Arno, Sig 16, 40, 103, 108, 164, 267
Arnow, Max 370–1
Around the World in Eighty Days 237, 244, 368, 384
Around the World in 80 Days 20, 25, 22, 427
Arquette, Rosanna 233
Arroy, Juan 25
Arthur 269, 371
Arthur 2: On the Rocks 371
Arthur, George K. 164–5, *164*, 225
Arthur, Jean 90–1
Arzner, Dorothy 98, 387
As You Desire Me 47, 95
Ashby, Hal 429
Asher, Irving 64–5
Aslan, Grégoire 165
Asquith, Anthony 303
The Assam Garden 320
Assante, Armand 138, 171
Assassins 171
Assignment in Brittany 167, 253
The Assisi Underground 395
Associated British Picture Corporation 64, 295
Astaire, Fred 101*n*, 183, 193, 209, 256, 258, 313, 364
Asther, Nils 165, 422
Astor, Mary 202
Astruc, Alexandre 351
At Sword's Point 388
Átame!/Tie Me Up! Tie Me Down! 138, 171
Atoll K 332
Attack of the Clones 146
Attenborough, Richard 165–6, 301
Atwill, Lionel 166

Au Secours! 28*n*
L'Auberge espagnole/Pot Luck 229
Aubry, Cécile 166, 253–4
Audran, Stéphane 166
Audrey Rose 301
Auer, Leopold 167
Auer, Mischa 77, 166–7, 419
Aufbau 265
Auger, Claudine 167
August, Bille 435, 443
Aumont, Jean-Pierre 115, 167–8, *168*, 227, 253
Aumont, Tina 169
Aunt Sally 66
Austen, Jane 447
Austria 169–70
Autant-Lara, Claude 263
The Auto Bandits of Paris 22
Autour d'une enquête 92
Avalanche 80
Avanti! 312, 368
Avec le sourire/With a Smile 207
Avedon, Richard 323
The Avengers 145, 246, 348, 413
The Aviator 333
The Awakening 96
Awakenings 441
The Awful Truth 226, 274
An Awfully Big Adventure 277
Aylmer, Felix 5, 170
Aznavour, Charles 170

Babbit, Jamie 72
Babes in Baghdad/Muchachas de Bagdad 136
Babylon 5 470
Bachelor Mother 384
Backbeat 287
Background to Danger 355
Baclanova, Olga 77, 78, 79, 80–1, 169–70, 437
Bad Company 145
Baddeley, Hermione 170
Baisers volés/Stolen Kisses 313
Baker, Stanley 170, 196
Le Bal 227
Balalaika 49, 426
Balcon, Michael 62, 64, 66, 228
Bale, Christian 142
Balfour, Eve 171
Balibar, Jeanne 71
Balieff, Nikita 443, 460
Balin, Mireille 253
Balio, Tino 87
Ball, Lucille 387
Ballet des Champs-Élysées 201
Ballet Rambert 295
Ballets Russes 78, 419
Ballhaus, Michael 42

Ballykissangel 243
La Bamba 139n
Bancroft, Anne 392
The Band Wagon 193
La Bandera/Escape from Yesterday 116, 118, 257
Banderas, Antonio 16, 17, 100, 133, *134*, 135, 137–9, 171–2, *171*, 229, 438
Bank Holiday 340
Banks, Leslie 172
Banks, Monty 49
Bánky, Vilma 10, 12, 96, 172–3, *173*, 212, 266, 305, 439
Bara, Theda 96, 139, 171, 378, 380
Barabbas 432
Barb Wire 321
Barbato, Attilio 48
Barbato, Olga 48, 173
Barbed Wire 285
La Barcarolle d'amour 92n
Bárcena, Catalina 17n, 438
Bardem, Javier 133, 173–4, 438
Bardem, Juan Antonio 173
Bardem, Pilar 173
Bardem, Rafael 173
Bardot, Brigitte 74, 125, 129, 174, 186, 208, 254, 364, 420
The Barefoot Contessa 189, 218
The Barkleys of Broadway 256
Barnes, Binnie 174
Barnet, Boris 81, 439
Barnum 428
Baron, Cynthia 90
Baroncelli, Jacques de 28n, 370
The Baroness and the Butler 87, 89, 162
Barrault, Jean-Louis 290
Barrault, Marie-Christine 174–5
The Barretts of Wimpole Street 155
Barrie, Wendy 175
Barrymore, John 50n, 156, 460
Barrymore, Lionel 50n
Barthelmess, Richard 385
Bartholomew, Freddie 175, 358
Bartley, Anthony 320
Bary, Léon 23–4, 25, 175, 252
Baryshnikov, Mikhail 458
Basch, Felix 103, 175
Basch, Peter 175
Basehart, Richard 218
Basic Instinct 422
Basinger, Kim 72, 326, 397
Bassermann, Albert 40, 106, 107, 112n, 169, 175–6, 265, 267
La Bataille 86, 186
Bates, Alan 147n, 176
Batman 378
Batman & Robin 427
Batman films 272

Battle of the Bulge 431
Battleground 226
Battlestar Galactica 430
Bauchau, Patrick 176, 177
Baum, Vicki 433
Baxter, Anne 225
Baxter, John 61
Be My Wife 24
The Beach 70n, 73, 74, 199, 200, 335
Bean, Sean 143–4, 176–7
Béart, Emmanuelle 14, 16, 71, 72–3, 74, 95, 177, 181, 350
The Beast with Five Fingers 255
The Beatles 196
Beatrice 45, 50n
Beatty, Warren 153, 208, 322
Beau Brummell 455
Beau Geste 213, 250, 366
The Beautiful Blonde from Bashful Bend 365
Becherer, Richard 28n
Becker, Jacques 199, 263, 316, 437
Becket 269, 391
Beckett, Samuel 348
Becky Sharp 285
Bedazzled 371
Bedknobs and Broomsticks 448
The Bedroom Window 306
A Bedtime Story 55
Beery, Noah 64
Before Night Falls 174
Before Sunrise 72, 230
Before Sunset 72
Behind the Mask 409
Behold My Wife 229
Beineix, Jean-Jacques 394
Being There 429
Belgium 177
Bell, Book and Candle 328
Bell, Monta 95
Bell, Tom 178
Bella Donna 50n
Belle de jour 232, 394, 436
Belle époque 133, 220
La belle équipe/They Were Five 205
The Bells of St Mary's 99
Bellucci, Monica 178
Belmondo, Jean-Paul 71, 244, 458
The Beloved 207
Beloved Enemy 386
The Beloved Rogue 460
The Beloved Vagabond 207
Bemberg, Maria Luisa 208
Ben Greet company 280
Ben-Hur 45, 185
Benchley, Peter 182
Benelli, Sam, *La cena delle beffe* 50n
Benigni, Roberto 178, 194, 200, 313
Bennett, Constance 64, 245

Bennett, Tony, and Woollacott, Janet 129
Benoit, Georges 22
Bent 360
Berbérova, Nina 77
Berger, Helmut 178
Berger, Ludwig 207
Berger, Senta 14, 178–9, 268
Bergfelder, Tim 10
Bergin, Patrick 179
Bergman, Ingmar 158, 180, 223, 389, 391, 422, 441, 448, 452
Bergman, Ingrid *4*, 14, 15, 16, *95*, 98–100, 127, 179–80, *179*, 185, 275, 285, 303, 316, 348, 369, 396, 422, 423, 448
Bergner, Elisabeth 180, 267, 404
Berkeley Square 302–3
Berkoff, Steven 180
Berle, Milton 370
Berley, André 17n, 92n, 253
Berlin Correspondent 103
Berlin Document Center 104
Berlin Express 345
Berlin Film Museum 103–4, 235
Bern, Paul 86, 186
Bernard, Tristan 21, 24
Bernhardt, Kurt 207
Bernhardt, Sarah 6, 21–2, 23–4, 25, 180–1, 231, 252, 270, 445
Bernstein, Matthew 86
Beröringen/The Touch 158
Bertellini, Giorgio 47
Berti, Marina 181
Bertini, Francesca 45
Bertolucci, Bernardo 233, 420, 457
Besson, Luc 328, 411
Best, Edna 181, 352
La Bête humaine/The Human Beast 258, 335, 433
A Better Way to Die 315, 470
Der bewegte Mann/The Most Desired Man 427
Bewitched 243
Beyond the Fringe 371
Bibber, Otto 463
The Bible 381
Bideau, Jean-Luc 443
Big Business 398
The Big Country 432
Big Fish 218
The Big House 92n, 438
Big Jake 388
The Big Lift 100, 185
The Big Parade 24, 154, 225
The Big Pond 55, 207
Bigas Luna 133, 430
Bigelow, Kathryn 246, 379
The Biggest Bundle of Them All 234
A Bill of Divorcement 389, 405

Index

Billy Budd 439
Billy Liar 208, 281
Bing, Rudolf 363
Binoche, Juliette 15, 71, 72, 74, 181, 201, 254, 464
Biograph 219, 246
Bird, Antonia 200
The Birds 281, 445
Birell, Tala 181–2
Birth of a Nation 219
Birthday Girl 202
Bisset, Jacqueline 182
The Bitch 212
Bitter Moon 277, 428
Bitter Sweet 278, 364
The Bitter Tea of General Yen 165
Bitter Victory 316
Bizet, Georges 139*n*
Björk, Anita 100, 182
Blaché, Alice Guy 22
Blaché, Herbert 232
The Black Bird 166
Black Eagle 458
The Black Hand 50
Black Hawk Down 42, 218
Black Magic 218
Black Narcissus 67, 319
The Black Orchid 342
The Black Shield of Falworth 243
Black Widow 256
Blackbeard, the Pirate 382
Blackbeard's Ghost 455
Blade 321
Blade Runner 14, 288
Blades, Rubén 135
Blah, Blah, Blah 230
Blain, Gérard 182, 254, 270
Blanc, Anne-Marie 182, 442
Le Blanc et le noir 244
Blasco Ibañez, Vicente 95
Der blaue Engel/The Blue Angel 98, 236, 266, 267, 314
Blazhevich, Olga 33
Blessed, Brian 182–3
Blier, Bertrand 233
Blind Date 170
Blindfold 200
Blockade 202, 267, 383
Blonde Venus 97, 98, 205, 236, 267, 274, 352
Blondell, Joan 278
Bloodsport 457, 458
Bloom, Claire 183
Blore, Eric 16, 183
Blossoms in the Dust 262
Blow 221
Blow-Up 291
Blue, Monte 417

Blue Thunder 359
Bluebeard's Eighth Wife 158
Boat Trip 372
Bobby Deerfield 240, 318
Bodies, Rest and Motion 417
The Body Snatcher 317
Boehm, Karl 183
Boeing Boeing 336
Bogarde, Dirk 5, 183–4, 199, 406
Bogart, Humphrey 99, 118, 127, 194, 303, 322, 367, *374*, 375
Bogdanovich, Peter 317
Bogus 233
La Bohème 24
Bohemian Girl 385
Bois, Curt 40, 103, 108, 169, 184
Boleslawski, Richard 96, 97, 392, 419, 443
Bombi Bitt och jag 433
Bonanova, Fortunio 184
Bonanza 291
Bond films 9, 72, 128–30, 144, 158, 185, 188, 192, 210, 214–15, 225, 257, 316, 326, 347, 350, 367, 372, 384, 398, 402, 436
Bondage 392
Bongini, Raffaelle 47
Bonham Carter, Helena 184–5, 228
Bonjour New York! 55, 206
Bonjour Tristesse 231, 278
The Bonnie Brier Bush 219
La Boom 350
Boorman, John 195, 379
Das Boot/The Boat 268, 401–2
Booth, Edwin 194
Borau, José-Luis 153
Borchers, Cornell 100, 185
Bordoni, Irène 185
Borgato, Agostino 48, 185, 312
Born Free 360, 449
Bornedal, Ole 218
Boros, Ferike 416
Borzage, Frank 97, 205
La Boum 71
The Bounty 228
The Bourne Identity 41, 401
Bow, Clara 47, 285
Bowie, David 130, 185, 232, 236
Box, Betty 241
The Boy Friend 159
Boyd, Stephen 185–6
Boyer, Charles *4*, 7, 10, 11, 13, 15, 17, 56, 85–92, *85*, 115, 117, 119, 120, 125, 126, 127, 162, 167, 169, 186–8, *186*, 193, 206, 230, 251, 253, 254, 255, 258, 315, 327, 341, 394
Boyle, Danny 73, 200
The Boys from Brazil 259, 390
Bozzuffi, Marcel 187

Bracken 195
Bradna, Olympe 187
Brady, Alice 23, 199
Braggiotti, Francesca 48, 187
Brainville, Yves 187
Bram Stoker's Dracula 42, 143
Branagh, Kenneth 143, 146*n*, 187, 313, 389, 428, 447
Brandauer, Klaus-Maria 170, 187–8
Brandenburg, Paul 288
Brando, Marlon 73, 174, 256, 337, 349, 394, 469
Brandt, Willy 236
Brasseur, Pierre 92*n*, 188
The Bravados 185
Braveheart 72, 350
Brazzi, Rossano 13, 16, 189–90, *189*
Break of Hearts 187
Break the News 207
Breakfast at Tiffany's 295
Breaking the News 193
Breaking the Waves 433, 465
A Breath of Scandal 58
Breathless 316
Brecht, Bertolt 3, 330, 342
Brecht in Hollywood 430
Breen Office 97
Brenon, Herbert 6, 45, 309, 312
Brent, George 190–1, *190*, 309, 368
Bressart, Felix 40, 108, 191, 273, 418
Bresson, Robert, *Une Femme douce/A Gentle Creature* 420
Briac, Jean de 93*n*
Bridal Suite 87, 90, 162
Bride of Frankenstein 211, 299, 328, 446
Brideshead Revisited 310
The Bridge on the River Kwai 282
Bridges, Lloyd 355
Bridget Jones: the Edge of Reason 144, 248
Bridget Jones's Diary 144, 248, 277
Brief Encounter 304
Brighton Rock 165
Brignone, Guido 368
Brincken, Wilhelm von 463
Bring On the Empty Horses 384
Bringing Up Baby 275
Brisson, Carl 191
Brisson, Frederick 191
British male actors 141–6
British United Services Club 361, 453
Broadway Danny Rose 48, 173, 311
Broccoli, Albert R. 'Cubby' 9, 214
Brody, Estelle 366
Broken Blossoms 219
Broken English 430
Bromfield, John 198
Bronson, Charles 200, 310
Brook, Clive 64, 97, 191–2, *235*

Brooks, Louise 176
Brooks, Mel 392
Brooks, Richard 423, 432
Brosnan, Pierce 144, 192, 243, 309
The Brothers Karamazov 419, 423
The Brothers Rico 154
Brower, Otto 80
Brown, Clarence 34, 88, 95, 96, 259
Brown, David 431
Brown, Divine 144, 277
Browne, Coral 469
Browning, Tod 81, 170, 237, 334
The Browning Version 396
Brownlow, Kevin 31
Bruce, Nigel 192–3, 453
Brunel, Adrian 302
Bryant, Charles 379
Bryant, Damon 148*n*
Bryna Productions 353
Brynner, Yul 128, 193, 206, 245, 263, 337, 341
The Buccaneer 257, 431
Buchanan, Jack 193, 274
La Bûche 71
Buchholz, Horst 42, 193–4
Buchman, Sidney 107
Buck, Pearl S. 404
Budd, Mike 265
Buddy Buddy 323
La Buenaventura 156
Bugsy 322
Bulldog Drummond 213
Bulldog Drummond Escapes 366
Bulldog Drummond films 211, 232
Bullitt 182
Bullock, Sandra 37, 144, 462, 468
Bülow, Claus von 310
Bunny, John 246
Buñuel, Luis 232, 347, 388, 394, 411, 436
Burgère, André 253
Burns, Lilian 90
Burrows, Jon 7
Burton, Richard 129, 130, 186, 194–5, 248, 287, 301, 435
Burton, Tim 185, 218, 336, 345, 412
Bush, George, Sr 427
Bushell, Anthony 195
Bussières, Raymond 195
Buster se marie/Parlour, Bedroom and Bath 347, 375
But I'm a Cheerleader 72
The Butcher Boy 391
Butterfield 8 288
Byrne, Gabriel 195–6, 243, 309, 310, 379

Cabaret 468
Das Cabinet des Dr Caligari/The Cabinet of Dr Caligari 223, 265, 460

Cabot, Sebastian 196
Cacoyannis, Michael 363, 395
Cadillac Man 48
La caduta degli dei/The Damned 178
Caesar and Cleopatra 336
Cage, Nicholas 221
Caged Heat 439
Cagney, James 65, 303, 309, 395
Caine, Michael 10, 145, 196–8, *197*, 215, 279, 287, 288, 469
The Caine Mutiny 196
California Suite 196, 435
Caligula 359, 368
Callow, Simon 198
Calvert, Phyllis 198, 415
Calvet, Corinne 198–9, 254
Cambio de sexo/Change of sex 153
Camelot 159, 286, 381
Cameron, James 73, 426, 427
Camille 21, 23, 95, 97, 261
Camille Claudel 153
Cammi, Orazio 47
Campbell, Eric 199, 204
Campbell, Martin 100
Campbell, Mrs Patrick 66, 199
Can-Can 58, 224
Canale, Gianna-Maria 199
Candy 170
Canet, Guillaume 71, 73, 199, 335
Cannon, Maurice 199, 251
Cannon Films 457
A Canterbury Tale 400
Capelier, Margot 231
Capellani, Albert 21, 23, 199, 378
Capellani, Paul 23, 199
Capra, Frank 446, 464, 468
Captain Blood 65
Captain Corelli's Mandolin 221, 395
Captain from Castile 373
Capucine 183, 199–200
Caramitru, Ion 200
Caravan/Caravane 86, 87, 90, 162, 186
Carax, Leos 181
Carco, Francis 86
The Cardinal 250, 425, 457
Cardinale, Claudia 200, 313, 377
Carère, Christine 200
The Caretaker 398
Carlid, Elinor 416
Carlsen, Dana 427
Carlyle, Robert 200
Carmen 265
Carmen (as role) 138–9
Carminati, Luciano 48
Carminati, Tullio 200–1, 311
Le Carnaval des vérités 23
Carné, Marcel 120, 167, 333, 374, 416
Carne tremula/Live Flesh 133, 174, 220

Carnet de bal/Dance of Life 416
Caro, Marc 398
Carol, Martine 201
Caron, Leslie *11*, 95, 129, 201–2, *201*, 227, 282, 315
Carpenter, John 399
Carpentier, Georges 202
Carradine, Keith 462
Carré, Ben 22
Carrie 390
La Carrière de Suzanne/Suzanne's Career 176
Carroll, Madeleine 64, 67, 202, 281, *444*
Caruso, Enrico 46, 202, 312
Casablanca 3, *4*, 12, *37*, 40, 49, 99, 108, 116, 118, 163, 179, 217, 224, 231, 267, 284, 293, 322, 334, 343, 394, 406, 419, 461
Casanova 428
The Case against Mrs Ames 202
The Case of Lena Smith 155
Caselotti, Adriana 51*n*
Caselotti, Luisa 17*n*, 47, 311
Casino Royale 384
Cassavetes, John 233, 362
Cassavetes, Nick 233
Cassel, Vincent 202
Casualty 257
Cat People 13, 14, 99, 126, 323, 359, 433
Catch as Catch Can 222
Catherine the Great 180
Caught 354
Cavalcade 182, 315, 367, 387
Cavalieri, Lina 202–3, 312, 377
Cavanagh, Paul 203
Cavens, Fred 177, 203
Cazenove, Christopher 203
CBS 56, 57, 429
Ceausescu, Nicolae 200
Cecchini, Mimi 48, 203–4, 311
Celebrity 187
Céline, Louis-Ferdinand 121
Central School of Speech and Drama 243
Le Cercle rouge/The Red Circle 369
Cervantes, Miguel 342
Chabrol, Claude 166, 306
Chaliapin, Feodor, Jr 77, 80
Chamberlain, Neville 378
Champagne 226
Chanel 232
Chaplin, Charlie 5, 6, 10, 16, 23, 24, 80, 81, 164, 183, 199, 204–5, 223, 252, 274, 330, 330–2, 337, 338, 349, 380
Charade 275, 351
Charell, Erik 86, 105, 162, 186
The Charge of the Light Brigade 324, 384, 412
Charisse, Cyd 201, 370

Charlie Bubbles 247
Charteris, Leslie 372, 421
The Chase 250, 375
Chase, Chevy 371
'Chattanooga Choo Choo' 292
Chautard, Emile 16, 22, 23, 25, 205
Chauve Souris revue 443, 460
Chayanne 135, 139*n*
The Cheat 24
Cheirel, Micheline 205–6
Chekhov, Anton 80, 206
Chekhov, Michael (Mikhail) 77, 82, 206
Chenal, Pierre 351
Chéreau, Patrice 71
Cherniovsky Institute, Moscow 169
Chervyakov, Yevgeni 439
Chevalier, Maurice 8, 10, *11*, 12, 13, 16,
    17, 53–60, *53*, 86, 92*n*, 115, 117, 119,
    120, 125, 126, 129, 138, 177, 191, 193,
    201, 206–7, *206*, 225, 236, 253, 254,
    255, 258, 259, 295, 315–16, 370, 386
Chicago 470
Chicken Run 412
The Child 354
Child in the House 170
The Children's Hour 295
Chinatown 399
Chocolat 72, 181, 201, 389
The Chocolate Soldier 56
Choose Me 176
Les Chouans 334
Choureau, Etchika 207
Christa: Swedish Fly Girls 264
Christensen, Hayden 146
Christian Science Monitor 452
Christians, Mady 38, 207–8
Christians, Rudolph 207, 208
Christie, Julie 10, 15, 100, 176, 208, 422,
    469
Christina 425
Christmas in July 365
Christopher Columbus: The Discovery 470
Christophersen, Gerda 356
Christy, Ivan 208–9
A Chump at Oxford 222
Churchill, Sarah 209
Churchill, Sir Winston 209
Ciannelli, Eduardo 16, 45, *45*, 49, 50, 51*n*,
    209, *209*, 312
Foolscap 51*n*
The Cider House Rules 145, 196
Cimarron 423
Cimino, Michael 100, 306
Ciné-Revue 459
Cinémagazine 28*n*
Cinémonde 343
La ciociara / Two Women 342
Circle of Friends 240

The Citadel 5, 238, 287
Citizen Kane 184, 218
City Lights 205
La ciudad de cartón / The Cardboard City 438
The Claim 100
Clair, René 86, 162, 207, 413
Clark, Petula 210
Clarke, Alan 417
Clarke, Charles G. 116
Clarke, Marguerite 300
Clavell, James 198
Clavier, Christian 210, 337, 411
Clayton, Jack 432
Cleese, John 210
Clément, Aurore 210
Clément, René 230, 250
Cleopatra 185–6, 194, 287, 384
Clift, Montgomery 185, 396, 469
Clive, Colin 90, 91, 195, 210–11
Clive, E. E. 211
Clive of India 213
Cloak and Dagger 395
A Clockwork Orange 359
Clooney, George 462
Close Encounters of the Third Kind 451
Close, Glenn 412
Close, Ivy 211, 454
Clouzot, Henri-Georges 153, 166, 219
The Cobweb 187
'Cocktails for Two' 191
Cocteau, Jean 279
Coen, Ethan and Joel 247, 423, 441
Cohan, Steven 128
Cohl, Emile 22
Cohn, Harry 40, 107, 288, 320, 370
Cohn, Joan 288
Colbert, Claudette 49, 86, 88, 186, 192,
    206, 446
Il colchico e la rosa / Sisters 50*n*
Colette 57, 433
La Collectionneuse / The Collector (1967) 176
The Collector (1965) 241, 439
Collier, Constance 89, 211
Collier's 57
Collins, Jackie 212
Collins, Joan 211–12
Collins, Michael 190
Colman, Ronald 13, 17, 45, 50*n*, 61, 62,
    96, 173, 202, 212–13, *213*, 275, 305,
    366, 384, 386, 421, 455, 467
Columbia 54, 103, 107, 199, 202, 274,
    285, 303, 319, 320, 342, 370, 388
Columbus, Chris 388
Come September 341
Comédie Française 327, 335
Comedy and Tragedy 22
The Comic Strip Presents 447
The Coming of Amos 272

Commando 426
The Commitments 258
Committee of Assistance to Struggling
    Russia 407
Comont, Mathilde 213–14
Compagnia Comico-Drammatica Italiana,
    New York 46
Compagnia Drammatica Siciliana 47
*Compartiment tueurs / The Sleeping Car
    Murders* 369
Compton, Fay 214
Comrade X 419
Conan the Barbarian 404
Conan films 426
Confessions of a Nazi Spy 108, 110, 157,
    267
Confessions of a Queen 224, 400
Confidential Agent 396
Conlon, Gerry 229
Connelly, Jennifer 171
Conner, John 427
Connery, Sean 10, 128–30, 145, 179, 186,
    196, 214–15, 288, 295, 372, 384, 467
Conquest 4, 34, 88, 95, 187
The Constant Husband 287
Conti, Tom 215
Continental Films 115
Coogan, Steve 215, 229
Cooke, Al 281
Cooper, Gary 136, 174, 202, 230, 274,
    295, 371, 373, 396, 423, 440
Cooper, Gladys 215–16, *216*, 242, 385
Cooper, Jackie 322
Cooper, Melville 216
Coote, Robert 216, 222
Coppola, Francis Ford 51*n*, 187, 210, 268,
    323, 363, 457
Coppola family 46, 48
Le Corbeau / The Raven 416
Corday, Marcelle 93*n*
Corliss, Richard 428
Corman, Roger 317, 343, 406, 439, 457
Cornell, Katherine 184
Cornered 206
Coronet Magazine 126, 128
Corri, Adrienne 216–17
Le Corsaire (project) 315
Corsaro, Franco 49, 217, 312
Cortese, Valentina 217–18, *217*, 313
Cortez, Ricardo 95, 259
Così è la vita 51*n*
Coslow, Sam 191
Cossacks 419
Coster-Waldau, Nikolaj 218
Costner, Kevin 467
Cotillard, Marion 218
Coulouris, George 218
Count Dracula 128

The Count of Monte Cristo 237, 238
Count Your Blessings 58
Counter-Espionage 103
The Countess of Monte Cristo 293
Cours Simon 263
Courtneidge, Cicely 66, 218
Cousin, Cousine 175, 398
Coward, Noel 165, 215, 218–19, 274, 304, 364, 389, 420
Cox, Brian 147n, 219
Crack in the World 428
Cradle Will Rock 409, 465
Crawford, Joan 95, 99, 101n, 169, 320, 375
Crawford, Michael 219, 269
The Creature from the Black Lagoon 438
Cremer, Bruno 219
Crespo, José 133, 219
Crime and Punishment 199, 342
The Criminal 170
The Criminal Code 317
The Crimson Pirate 446
Crisp, Donald 219–20
Crispin, Jeanine 169, 220
Critical Care 369
Cronenberg, David 246, 310, 439
La Croqueuse de diamants 314
Crosby, Bing 314, 370
Crosland, Alan 33
Cross of Iron 470
The Cross of Lorraine 116, 167, 253
The Crow 72, 397
The Crow: City of Angels 72, 397
Crowe, Cameron 133
Crowe, Eileen 220
Crowther, Bosley 116, 122n, 125, 128, 129, 434
The Crucible 229, 428
Cruise, Tom 13, 16, 72, 133, 142, 172, 177, 221, 271, 427, 428
Cruz, Celia 138
Cruz, Penélope 13, 15, 95, 100, 133, 438
Cry of the City 154
Cry of the Hunted 262
The Crying Game 408, 412
Csibi der Fratz / Csibi the Brat 257
Cuba 215
Cuerpo y alma / Body and Soul 382
Cugat, Xavier 138, 221
Cukor, George 49, 95, 96, 179, 199, 201, 232, 275, 283, 304, 319, 324, 342, 349, 368, 369
Culver, Roland 221
Cummings, Robert 375
Cummins, Peggy 221–22
Currie, Finlay 222
Curry, Tim 222
The Curse of the Cat People 433
The Curse of Frankenstein 223

Curtis, Michael 34
Curtis, Richard 277
Curtis, Tony 318, 422
Curtiz, Michael 101n, 219, 223, 305, 346, 459
Curwood, Bob 416
Cusack, Cyril 222
Cusack, John 240
Cushing, Peter 222–3
Custer of the West 431
Custodio, Ana María 17n, 437
Cyborg 457, 458
Cyrano de Bergerac 233, 397
Czechoslovakia (former) 223

Daddy Long Legs 201
Dagerman, Stig 182
Dagover, Lil 39, 223, 266, 302
Dahlbeck, Eva 223–4
Dahlberg, Charlotte Mae 332
Daily Mirror 454
d'Algy, Helena 224, 400
d'Algy, Tony 224
Dali, Salvador 116
Dalio, Marcel 16, 92n, 115, 224, 253, 334
Dallas 291, 361, 373
Dalton, Audrey 224–5
Dalton, Emmet 224
Dalton, Timothy 142, 225, 326
The Dam Busters 315
Damage 181
Damaged Goods 212
damaged men 143–4
La dame aux camélias 180, 445
Damita, Lili 225
The Damned / La caduta degli dei 5
Damon, Matt 220, 333
Damone, Vic 162
Dance with the Devil 174
Dance, Girl, Dance 387
Dance with Me 139n
Dance with a Stranger 243, 412
The Dancer Upstairs 174
Dane, Karl 225
Dangerous Liaisons 413
Dangerous When Wet 226
Dann, Roger 225
Danning, Sybil 170, 225–6
Danova, Cesare 226
Dante, Joe 337
Dante the Magician 226
Dante's Peak 192
Dantine, Helmut 14, 40, 42n
Danziger, Daisy Canfield 373
Darcel, Denise 137, 226
D'Arcy, Alexander 226
The Dark Angel 173, 213, 386
Dark Victory 190, 249

Darkman 379
Darling 208
The Darling Buds of May 470
Darò un milione 49
Darren, James 385
Darrieux, Danielle 99, 226–7, 433
Darvi, Bella 99, 227, 231
Dassin, Jules 217, 218, 363–4, 455
Date with an Angel 72, 177
Dauphin, Claude 227
Daven, André 227, 253
David Copperfield 175, 328, 406, 453–4
Davies, Marion 291
Davis, Bette 65, 95, 99, 155, 187, 190, 249, 255, 293, 298, 303, 352
D'Avril, Yola 227–8, 228
The Dawn Patrol 384
Day, Doris 37, 263
Day, George Martin 33–4
Day Dreams 24
The Day the Earth Stood Still 411
The Day the Ponies Come Back 73
The Day They Robbed the Bank of England 391
Day-Lewis, Cecil 228
Day-Lewis, Daniel 181, 228–9, 228, 257
de Acosta, Mercedes 236, 260
De Almeida, Joaquim 229
de Bont, Jan 381, 458
de Carlo, Yvonne 169
De France, Cécile 229
De frente marchen 370
de Havilland, Olivia 64, 221, 413
de la Iglesia, Alex 173
De Lacey, Robert 32
De Liguoro, Rina 48, 229, 311
De Liguoro, Wladimiro 229
de Lint, Derek 230
de Mornay, Rebecca 172
De Niro, Robert 100, 144, 233, 411
De Palma, Brian 48, 72, 177, 356, 411, 428
de Putti, Lya 12, 96, 233–4, 305
de Segurola, Andrés 234
De Sica, Vittorio 49, 234, 312, 342, 436, 446
Dead Again 187, 313, 428, 447
Dead Man 307
The Deadly Affair 432
Dean, James 162, 193, 230, 243, 254, 451
Dear Brigitte 174
Death Warrant 457
Deathtrap 196
Deception / Anna Boleyn 314
Decision before Dawn 324, 465
Decla-Bioscop 265
Decoin, Henri 226, 314
deCordova, Richard 22

Dédée d'Anvers 432
The Deep 182
The Deep Blue Sea (1955) 337
Deep Blue Sea (1999) 433
The Deep End 442, 462
Deep Impact 409
The Deer Hunter 306
DEFA 470
Defence of the Realm 195
del Río, Dolores 136, 139
Del Val, Jean 230–2
Delac, Charles 24
Delannoy, Jean 314
Delgado, Miguel M. 136
Délicatessen 398
Delon, Alain 11, 14, 16, 71, 230, 254
Delpy, Julie 12, 71, 72, 74, 230, 254
The Delta Force 428
Demick, Irina 99, 231
DeMille, Cecil B. 24, 25, 68, 78, 229, 272,
    288, 329, 383, 415, 423, 424, 459, 464,
    466
Demme, Jonathan 143, 301, 439
Demolition Man 290
Demongeot, Mylène 231
Demy, Jacques 232, 394
Deneubourg, Georges 231–2
Deneuve, Catherine 71, 232, 394, 436
Denicourt, Marianne 71
Denny, Reginald 232
La Dentellière/The Lacemaker 306
Depardieu, Gérard 71, 122n, 129, 173,
    233, *252*, 254, 411
Depp, Johnny 73, 181, 220, 394
Le dernier combat 71
The Desert Fox 354
Desfontaines, Henri 22
Desire 97, 236, 267
Desire under the Elms 342
Desmond, William 309
Desny, Ivan 234
Desperado *134*, 138, 171, 229
Desplechin, Arnaud 71
Desrichard, Yves 118
Destry Rides Again 98, 236
The Detective (1968) 182
Détective (1985) 71, 230
Detmers, Maruschka 138
Deutsch, Ernst 40, 108, 110, 234
Deutsches Nationaltheater 424
Les Deux Fragonard 229
*Deux ou trois choses que je sais d'elle/Two or
    Three Things I Know about Her* 240
The Devil Dances 32
Devil and the Deep 329
The Devil is a Woman 97, 98, 236
The Devil Makes Three 100, 281
A Devil with Women 156

The Devil's Brother 50
Devotion 255
Devushka s korobkoj/Girl with the Hat Box
    81
Le Diable au corps/Devil in the Flesh 401
Diabolique 153
Les Diaboliques 153
Diaghilev, Serge 419
Dial M for Murder 366, 467
Diamant-Berger, Henri 24
Diamonds are Forever 214
Diana 413
The Diary of Anne Frank 295, 424
Díaz Gimeno, Rosita 17n, 438
DiCaprio, Leonardo 37, 50, 70n, 73, 147n,
    199, 312
Die Hard 413
Die Hard: With a Vengeance 310
Die Hard 2: Die Harder 381
Dieterle, Charlotte 267
Dieterle, William (Wilhelm) 98, 164, 198,
    267, 436, 443
Dietrich: Shadow and Light 235
Dietrich, Marlene 7, 8, 10, 12, 14, 15, 16,
    17, 37, 39, 40–1, 49, 55, 95, 97–8, 99,
    106, 116, 120, 125, 127, 155, 158, 178,
    192, 207, 235–7, *235*, 242, 261, 266–7,
    268, 274, 314, 324, 340, 352, 368, 378,
    380, 386, 418, 439, 440
Diffring, Anton 237
*Les Dimanches de Ville d'Avray/
    Sundays and Cybele* 272
Dione, Rose 237
Diplomatic Courier 100, 324
The Dirty Dozen 457
The Dirty Game 270
Dishonored 97
Disney, Walt 159
Disney 367, 368, 382, 395, 420, 432, 448,
    455
Disraeli 163, 449
The Divine Lady 459
The Divine Woman 24, 95
Le Divorce 337
Divorzio all'italiana/Divorce Italian Style
    355
Dix, Richard 64
Django 381
Djordević, Mladomir 'Puriša' 351
Dmytryk, Edward 206
Döblin, Alfred 106
The Docks of New York 80, 169
Doctor Jekyll and Mr Hyde 179
Doctor Zhivago 208, 282, 322, 413
Dodsworth 392
Dogme 302
La dolce vita 241
Dolenz, George 237

Doll, Dora 237
A Doll's House 379
Dom na Trubnoj/The House on Trubnaya 81
Domicile conjugal/Bed and Board 314
Dominguin, Luis Miguel 237
Dominick and Eugene 48
Don Juan (project) 65
Don Juan DeMarco 73–4
Don Juan Tenorio 184
Don Q 219
Don Quixote (project) 245
Donahue, Jack 415
Donaldsson, Arthur 238
Donat, Robert 5, 61, 62, *63*, 64–6, 67,
    202, 238, 262, 367, 384
Donatella 353
Donath, Ludwig 104, 105, 107, 108–9,
    239
Donen, Stanley 319, 351, 371
Donmar Warehouse, London 243
La donna più bella del mondo 203
Donnelly, Donal 239
Donner, Clive 200, 384
Donohoe, Amanda 239
Don't Look Now 208
Don't Say A Word 144
Doody, Alison 239
Dora, Miklosz 7, 305
Dorn, Philip 239, 381
Dors, Diana 67, 68, 239
Dostoevsky, Vladimir 419, 423
Dotti, Andrea 295
Double Impact 458
A Double Life 213
Double Team 458
Double Trouble 416
Douglas, Kirk 162, 353, 413, 414
Douglas, Michael 144, 470
Douglas, Robert 239–40
Down by Law 178
Down, Lesley-Anne 240
Doyle, Arthur Conan 406
Doyle, Roddy, *The Commitments* 258
Dr Christian 297
Dr Ehrlich's Magic Bullet 106
Dr Jekyll and Mr Hyde 99
Dr No 158, 185, 214, 442
Dr O'Dowd 221
Dr Quinn, Medicine Woman 430
Dr X 166
Dracula 142, 344, 462
Drácula 461–2
Dracula: Dead and Loving It 392
Dracula the Impaler 313
Drango 304
Drankov, Aleksandr O. 81
Dravić, Milena 16, 240, 351, 470
A Dream of Kings 395

A Dream of Passion 364
Dream Wife 320
Dreiser, Theodore 390
Dressed to Kill 196
Drew, Ellen 118
Dreyer, Carl T. 207
Drimmer, Dr Erik 258
Driven 41
The Driver 153
Driver dagg faller regn/Rain Follows the Dew 470–1
Driver, Minnie 240, 454
Driving Miss Daisy 445
Drôle de drame/Bizarre, Bizarre 416
Drums along the Mohawk 431
Duchess Theatre, London 396
Duck Soup (1927) 332
Duck Soup (1933) 322
Duel at Diablo 158, 449
Duel in the Sun 353
Duflos, Huguette 253
Duigan, John 277
Dukhonin, Nikolai 33
Dulac, Germaine 28*n*
Duna, Steffi 240
Dunajev, Nickolai 34*n*
Dunaway, Faye 73, 428
Dune 315, 402
Dungeons & Dragons 142
Dunne, Irene 187, 282
Dunst, Kirsten 37
Duperey, Anny 240
Dupont, E. A. 234, 266, 366
Duprez, June 241
Durbin, Deanna 191, 234, 257
Duse, Eleonora 46, 48, 378, 379
Duval, Paulette 24, 241, 252
Duvivier, Christian 121*n*
Duvivier, Julien 87, 88, 116, 118–19, 120, 167, 170, 205, 207, 224, 255, 257, 278, 416
Dynasty 178, 203, 212

Eady Levy production fund 9
The Eagle 173
Ealing Studios 62, 228, 282, 295, 299
East of Eden 162
Eastwood, Clint 51*n*, 333
Ebb Tide 300
Echoes 381
Éclair 205, 252
Ed Sullivan Show 57
Ed Wood 345
Las edades de Lulu/The Ages of Lulu 174
Eddy, Nelson 60*n*, 191
Edge of Darkness 116
Edison, Thomas 22
Edison Company 398

Edson, Margaret 447
Educating Archie 159
Educating Rita 196, 463
Edward, My Son 319
Edwards, Blake 161, 178, 371
Edwards, J. Gordon 378
Eggar, Samantha 241
The Egyptian 455
Die Ehe der Maria Braun/The Marriage of Maria Braun 428
Eichberg, Richard 288
Eichinger, Bernd 42
84 Charing Cross Road 301
Eisenstein, Sergei 418, 440, 462
Ekberg, Anita 241
Ekran 31
El Cid 342, 445, 457
The Elephant Man 143, 301, 307, 315
Elephant Walk 337
Elg, Taina 241, 422, 423
Elizabeth 202
Elliott, Denholm 241–2
Elliott, Robert 327
Elliott, William 28*n*
Ellis, Mary 191
Elmer Gantry 432
Elsaesser, Thomas 40
Elsom, Isobel 242
Elstree Studios 340, 366
Elwes, Cary 242
The Emigrants 452
Emma 422
Emmerich, Roland 41, 411
The Emperor Waltz 217
Empire magazine 172
The Empire Strikes Back 282
Empire of the Sun 412
The Empress and I 92*n*
The Empty Mirror 435
En plein coeur 71
En stilla flirt 415
The End of the Affair 246, 320, 408
End of Days 195, 427
Endfield, Cy 170
Enemies: A Love Story 389
The Enemy Below 268, 316
Enemy of Women 109, 110
Der Engel mit der Posaune/The Angel with the Trumpet 465
Engels, Wera 242
The English Patient 72, 143, 181, 246, 402, 428
Enright, Ray 98
ENSA 245
The Entertainer 399
Entrapment 215
Entrée des artistes/The Curtain Rises 159
Eon 214

L'Epervier/The Sparrowhawk 394
Equus 248
E.R. 322, 462
Eraser 427
Erin Brockovich 247
Ermolieff, Joseph 79
Es liegt in der Luft/It's in the Air 236
Escapade 404
Escape 109, 110
Esmond, Carl 14, 40, 104, 105, 108, 109, 110, 242, 268
Esmond, Jill 243, 389, 390
Essanay 204, 337–8, 378
Et Dieu … créa la femme/And God Created Woman 174
Etchepare, Pierre 17*n*, 253
Eternal City 50*n*
Eternal Love 302
Etlinger, Karl 17*n*
Eureka 288
Europa, Europa 230
European Film Fund 7, 106, 267
Eva 170
Evans, Josh 316
Evans, Maurice 243
Evelyn 192
Ever After 326
Everett, Rupert 145, 242, 243
Everyone Says I Love You 417
Everything Happens at Night 292
Everything You Always Wanted to Know about Sex 404
Evita 172, 402
Der ewige Jude/The Eternal Jew 184, 325, 343
Excalibur 195, 368, 379, 467
The Exorcist 348, 443
Experiment Perilous 346
Extase/Ecstasy 327
extras 31–5
Extreme Measures 277
Eye of the Beholder 359
Eye for Eye 378

Le fabuleux destin d'Amélie Poulain/Amélie 445
Fahrenheit 451 208
Fairbanks, Douglas 10, 23, 24, 33, 35*n*, 80, 175, 202, 204, 206, 273, 274, 297, 319, 337, 338
Fairbanks, Douglas, Jr 226
Fairbanks, Mary Lee 319
Falaise, Henri de la 199
The Falcon 421
Falcon Crest 341
The Fall of the Roman Empire 222, 282, 342, 404
The Fall of the Romanoffs 231

Falling in Love Again 469
Falsche Bewegung/One False Move 323
Fame is the Spur 408
Famous Players 181, 265, 307
Famous Players-Lasky 202, 234
Fanny 58, 193, 255, 434
Fantômas 22
The Far Country 198
Far from the Madding Crowd 176, 208
Farewell My Lovely 406
A Farewell to Arms 234, 349
Farfariello 47
Fargo 423, 441
Farinet 290
Farrar, David 243
Farrell, Colin 243–4, 310
Fassbinder, Rainer Werner 321, 373, 427–8
Fatal Attraction 412
Father and Son 283
Faulkner, William 370
Faust 302
Fawlty Towers 210
Faye, Julia 78
FBI 205, 267–8
Fedora 235, 268, 318
Fehmiu, Bekim 244, 351, 470
Fejös, Pál (Féjos, Paul) 92n, 356, 460
Feld, Fritz 244
Feldman, Charles 87, 186, 199, 224
Fellini, Federico 200, 218, 241, 334, 355, 373
The Fellowship of the Ring 144
La Femme et le pantin/The Woman and the Puppet 370
La Femme publique 316
femmes fatales, European women as 14–15, 96
Ferber, Edna 423
Fernandel 244–5, 377
Fernández, Emilio 'Indio' 136
Ferrando's Hall, New York 46
Ferrar, Geraldine 28n
Ferrer, Mel 278, 295
Ferreri, Marco 232, 377
Ferrigno, Lou 426
Le Feu follet 416
Feuer, Howard 142
Feuillade, Louis 28n
Feyder, Jacques 7, 28n, 86, 95, 177, 226, 253, 345, 350, 416
Fiddler on the Roof 470
The Field 257, 286
Field, Shirley Anne 245
Fields, Grace 245
Fields, W. C. 433
Fiennes, Joseph 245
Fiennes, Ralph 141, 143, 145, 146, 181,

245–6, 428, 464
55 Days at Peking 9, 384
Fight Club 184–5
The Fighting 69th 190
La Fille seule/A Single Girl 335
Film Foundation 47
Film ohne Titel/Film without a Title 323
La Fin du jour/The End of a Day 255
Finch, Flora 246–7, *246*
Fincher, David 184–5, 377
Finding Forrester 145
Fine Arts Film Company 450
A Fine Madness 215
Finger on the Trigger 413
Finlay, Frank 247
Finlayson, Jimmy 332
Finney, Albert 147n, 155, 176, 218, 245, 247–8
Fire over England 336
Firebird Theatre 322
First Comes Courage 109, 116
The First of the Few 384
First National 193, 221, 250, 265, 348
First National Exhibitor's Circuit 204
Firth, Colin 144, 248
Firth, Peter 248
Fischer, Terence 142
A Fish Called Wanda 210
Fitzgerald, Barry 248–9, *248*, 431
Fitzgerald, Geraldine 249
Fitzmaurice, George 47, 50n, 95, 96, 312
Five Days One Summer 467
5 Fingers 227, 354
The Fixer 176
Flash Gordon 377, 443
Fleming, Ian 214, 384
Fleming, Victor 96, 99, 179
Flesh and the Devil 95, 96, 260, 285
Fletcher, Bramwell 249
Fleur de Paris 25
Flickor i uniform/Girls in Uniform 288
Flight from Ashiya 263
Flood, James 32
Florelle 259
Floren, Latty 32
Florey, Robert 28n, 33, 98, 206, 244, 251, 263, 408, 463
Der Fluch/The Curse 288
Flügel und Fesseln/The Future of Emily 268
The Flying Fontaines 385
Flying Fortress 404
Flynn, Errol 65, 225, 273, 309, 324, 387, 401
Folies Bergère 335
Folies Bergère de Paris 56, 386
Fonda, Henry 126, 162, 200
Fonda, Jane 409
Fontaine, Joan 126, 208, 275

Foolish Wives 208
fools 144–5
Fools for Scandal 278
For Whom the Bell Tolls 99, 179, 279, 396, 443
Forbes, Bryan 249, 382
Forbes, Mary 249–50
Forbes, Ralph 250
Forbes-Robertson, Johnston 250
Ford, Gypo 360
Ford, Harrison 144, 369, 428
Ford, John 5, 6, 202, 219, 220, 239, 248, 273, 279, 295, 309, 316, 334, 335, 356, 358, 360, 362, 373, 376, 386, 388, 406, 438
Forde, Walter 404
foreign accents 10–12
A Foreign Affair 98, 236
Foreign Correspondent 176, 267, 283
Foreign Intrigue 394, 448
Forever Amber 221, 340
Forever and a Day 330, 356, 386
Forever, Lulu 428
Forever My Love 425
Forman, Milo 223
The Formula 420
Forquet, Philippe 250
Forslund, Bengt 422
Forster, E. M. 447
Forster, Rudolf 169, 250, 265
Fort Apache 335
Fort Lee Studios 378
49th Parallel 303
40 Carats 452
Fosse, Bob 468
Fossey, Brigitte 250
Foster, Aida 432
Foul Play 371
The Four Horsemen of the Apocalypse 297, 448
Four Men and a Prayer 279
Four Star Television 187
Four Weddings and a Funeral 144, 276–7, 283, 428
1492: Conquest of Paradise 122n, 233, 411
The Fourth Protocol 192
The Fox 298
Fox *see* Twentieth Century-Fox
Fox British 157, 222, 261, 340, 381
Fox, James 250–1, 389
Fox, William 39, 378, 456
France 251–4
Francen, Victor 177, 227, 255, *255*, 375, 401, 407
Francis, Kay 305
François, Jacques 255–6
Frank, Melvin 313
Frank, Robert 430

Frankenheimer, John 411
Frankenstein 210, 317
Franklin, Pamela 163, 256
Franklin, Sidney 96
Frantic 398
Fraser, Brendan 145, 465
Fraser, Richard 256
Freaks 81, 170, 237
Frears, Stephen 100, 298
Freda, Riccardo 199
Free French army 116, 120, 258
French actors 85–93
The French Connection 187, 411
French Kiss 411
The French Lieutenant's Woman 310
French Postcards 404
French Research Foundation 88, 187, 253
French War Relief Commission 187
Freud 469
Freud, Sigmund 351
Die Freudlose Gasse/Joyless Street 259, 285
Freund, Karl 342
Frey, Arno 8, 104, 105, 109, 256
Frey, Sami 256
Fricker, Brenda 257
Frida 356
Fried Green Tomatoes 445
Friedkin, William 373
Friend, Philip 257
Friends and Lovers 389
Fritsch, Willy 288
Fröbe, Gert 257
Fröhlich, Gustav 17n, 266
Frohman, Charles 434
From Here to Eternity 67, 274, 320
From Russia with Love 214
The Front Page 51n
Frost, Sadie 148n
Frühjahrsparade/Spring Parade 257
Fueter, Heinrich 442
The Fugitive 326
The Fugitive Kind 349
The Full Monty 200
Fuller, Mary 26n
Fuller, Samuel 371
Fun in Acapulco 158
Funny Face 295
Furia 349
Furlan, Mira 470
Füsilier Wipf 304

Gaal, Franciska 40, 257, 305
Gabin, Jean 11, 12, 14, 16, 87, 115–21,
    115, 129, 173, 187, 233, 236, 253, 254,
    257–8, 333, 370
Gable, Clark 67, 187, 262, 278, 303, 342,
    344, 372
Gabler, Neal 38–9

Gabor, Eva 258
Gabor, Magda 258
Gabor, Zsa Zsa 258, 305
Gaby 201
Gaiety School of Drama 243
Gaily, Gaily 364
Gainsborough 67, 163, 191, 340, 415, 432
Gallagher, Bronagh 258
Galli, Rosina 46
Gallian, Ketti 258
Gallone, Carmine 48, 370
Galsworthy, John 211, 283
Gambon, Michael 14, 146n, 259, 455
The Game 377
Games 432
Gance, Abel 28n, 162, 255, 401
Gandert, Gero 103
Gandhi 165, 228, 321–2
Gangs of New York 229, 271
Ganschaft, Matilda 32
Ganz, Bruno 259, 443
Garas, Márton 346
Garat, Henri 259
Garbo, Greta *4*, 7, 8, 10, 14, 15, 16, 17,
    28n, 33, 40, 47, 49, 54, 86, 88, 95–9,
    100, 125, 127, 138, 165, 177, 181, 186,
    187, 199, 229, 258, 259–61, *260*,
    266–7, 268, 281, 285, 379, 380, 389,
    418, 422, 423, 438, 439
García, Andy 100, 138
Gardel, Carlos 224
The Garden of Allah 97, 386
Gardiner, Reginald 261
Gardner, Ava 200, 237, 324
Gardner, Gail 269
Gardner, Winthorp 293
Garfield, John 255, 401
Garland, Alex 73
Garner, James 364, 416
Garnett, Tay 98
Garson, Greer 62, 99, 216, 261–2, *261*,
    309, 420
Gaslight 15, 179, 187
Gasnier, Louis 22
Gassman, Vittorio 262–3, *262*, *311*
Gattaca 333
Gaubert, Danièle 263
The Gaucho 35n
Gaumont-British 62, 64, 66, 202, 340
Gaumont/Solax 252
The Gay Caballero 370
The Gay Desperado 167
Gaye, Gregory 263
Gaynor, Janet 95, 433
Gélin, Daniel 187, 199, 263–4
The General Died at Dawn 202, 443
General Hospital 302, 335
Genevieve 318, 372

Genn, Leo 264
Gentlemen Prefer Blondes 202
George of the Jungle 210
George, Susan 264
Georgy Girl 408
Geray, Steven 264
Gerber, Tony 315
Gere, Richard 316
German Universal 103
Germany 264–8
Germi, Pietro 355
Gerron, Kurt 105, 267
Gershon, Gina 430
Gervaise 423
Get Carter 196
The Ghost of Frankenstein 285
Gia tin agapi tis/For Her Love 368
Giannini, Giancarlo 268
Gibbons, Cedric 28n
Gibson, Mel 72, 178, 271, 350
Gide, André, *L'Immoraliste/The Immoralist*
    128
Gielgud, John 61, 194, 268–9, 405, 444–5
Giermann, Frederick 104, 109, 269
Gigi 11, 57, 125, 128, 129, 201, 207, 269,
    295, 315, 351
Gilbert, John 33, 154, 252, 260, 375, 389
Gilberte de Courgenay 182
Gilda 50, 264
Gilles, Geneviève 99, 269
Gilliam, Terry 218
Gilmore, Frank 454
The Gingerbread Man 187
Gingold, Hermione 269, 350
Girardon, Michèle 269–70
Girardot, Annie 270
Girardot, Etienne 270
Girl in the News 340
The Girl in Pink Tights 314
Les Girls 201, 241
A Girl's Folly 205
Gish, Lillian 10, 45, 50n, 212, 285, 438
Give Us the Moon 432
Givenchy, Hubert de 295
Gladiator 42, 313, 382
Glam 316
Glancy, Mark 61, 453
Glass, Gaston 24, 25, 154, 252, 270–1,
    270
The Glass Mountain 217–18
The Glass Slipper 201
The Glass Wall 262
Gleeson, Brendan 271
Glimcher, Arne 138
A Global Affair 363
Glory Alley 201
Glückskinder/Lucky Kids 288
The Go-Between 208

Godard, Jean-Luc 230, 240, 254, 306, 316, 427
Goddard, Paulette 169
The Godfather Part III 178, 457
Gods and Monsters 360, 408
Godzilla 41, 411
Goebbels, Joseph 109, 110, 175, 264, 325, 426
Goin' to Town 49
Going My Way 248
Golan, Menahem 457
The Gold Diggers 208
Goldberg, Whoopi 233, 326
Golden Earrings 41, 98
The Golden Trail 356
GoldenEye 144, 419
Goldfinger 214, 257
Goldmeyer, Kurt 223
Goldstein, Bob 214
Goldwyn, Sam 81–2, 98, 172, 212, 225, 384, 386, 389, 439, 440
Golejzovsky, Kasyan 78
Golino, Valeria 12, 100, 271, 311
Gone with the Wind 303, 336, 340, 390, 467
The Good Companions 283
The Good Earth 267, 404
Good Morning Babylon 229
Good Neighbour Sam 425
Good Will Hunting 240, 433
Goodbye Again 363, 369
Goodbye, Mr Chips 238, 262, 293, 367, 391
The Goon Show 429
Gordon, Mary 271–2
Gorky Park 394, 399
Gosford Park 278, 428, 435
Gösta Berlings saga/The Legend of Gösta Berling 101n, 259, 285, 422
Gottschalk, Joachim 267
Goudal, Jetta 10, 14, 24–5, 252, 272
Gough, Michael 272
Gould, Elliot 158
Goulding, Edmund 95
Gowland, Gibson 272
Goya, Mona 253
Gozzi, Patricia 272–3
Grahame, Margot 273
Granach, Alexander 103, 108, 273, 418, 419
Grand Eden Theatre, New York 51n
Grand Hotel 95
Grand Prix 370
La Grande illusion/The Grand Illusion 115, 118, 120
Granger, Stewart 12, 61, 64, 65, 66, 273–4, 320, 339, 432, 454, 457
Grant, Cary ii, 16, 17, 100, 216, 230, 241, 273, 274–6, *275*, 342, 374, 381, 458

Grant, Hugh 13, 141, *141*, 142, 144–5, 248, 276–7, *276*
Grant, Julian 144
Grant, Richard E. 141, 142, 277–8, *277*
Granville-Barker, Harley 405
Grasso, Giovanni 46, 48, 154, 173
Gravey, Fernand 177, 278, 407
Gravina, Cesare 45, 47, 278, 311
Gray, James 417
Gray, Nadia 416
Grayson, Kathryn 363
The Great Dictator 204
The Great Escape 357, 398
Great Expectations 367, 432
The Great Lie 339
The Great Waltz 170, 278, 322
The Great Ziegfeld 267, 404
The Greatest Story Ever Told 443
Gréco, Juliette 99, 278–9
Greece 279
Greed 272, 297, 414
Greek National Theatre 396
Green Card 3, 122n, 233, 254
Green Mansions 295
Green, Nigel 279
Greene, Graham 353
    The Quiet American 145
Greene, Richard 279, 362
The Greengage Summer 227
Greenstreet, Sydney 16, 279–80, *280*, 343, 375
Gregory, Lady 309
Grémillon, Jean 115
Grenfell, Joyce 161, 280–1
Gretler, Heinrich 281, 442
Greyfriars Bobby 219
Greystoke: The Legend of Tarzan, Lord of the Apes 328
Griffies, Ethel 281
Griffith, D. W. 49, 157, 169, 204, 211, 219, 246, 265, 272, 312, 329, 373, 385, 402, 414, 424, 450
Griffith, Edward H. 281
Griffith, Melanie 133, 172
Der grosse Bagarozy/The Devil and Ms D 427
Grosse Pointe Blank 240
Grot, André 88
Grumpier Old Men 342
Grüning, Ilka 281
Guard, Kit 281–2
Guazzoni, Enrico 229
Guback, Thomas 9
La Guerre des valses 278
Guétary, Georges 282
Guevara, Che 172
Guilbert, Yvette 21
Guild Theatre, New York 443
Guinness, Alec 69n, 146, 187, 282–3

Guissart, René 22
Gun Crazy 221
Gunga Din 275
Guns of the Magnificent Seven 411
The Guns of Navarone 170, 384, 395
Gunsmoke 291
Guthrie, Tyrone 389
Guttenberg, Steve 144
Guy, Alice 232
Gwenn, Edmund 283

Haartman, Carl von 423
Haas, Hugo 223, 283
Hackman, Gene 187
Haig, David 144, 283
La Haine/Hate 202
Hale, Creighton 283–5, *284*, 309
Hale, Sonnie 64
Hall, Gladys 85, 89
Hall, Mordaunt 25
Hall, Peter 201
Hallmark Hall of Fame 209
Halloween 399
Halloween series 398–9
Hallström, Lasse 389
Hamlet (1948) 390, 404, 432
Hamlet (1964, stage) 194
Hamlet (1990) 184
Hamlet (1996) 208
Hammer 222, 335
Hammett, Dashiell 280, 356
Hampton, Christopher 413
A Handful of Dust 428
The Hanging Tree 423
Hangmen Also Die 108, 116, 273, 429
Hanin, Roger 285
Hanks, Tom 16, 171, 427
Hannah and Her Sisters 196
Hannibal 143, 268, 301
Hans Christian Andersen 314
Hansen, Miriam 5, 128
Hanson, Curtis 306
Hanson, Einar 285
Hanson, Lars 10, 15, 285, 422
Happy Landing 291
The Happy Road 250
Hard Target 458
Hardwicke, Cedric 61, 285–6, *286*
Hardy, Oliver 50, 222, 225, 332, 343
Hark, Tsui 177, 458
Harlow 457
Harlow, Jean 186, 258, 273, 384
Harrington, Curtis 432
Harris, Laura 138
Harris, Richard 176, 286, 310, 391
Harrison, Kathleen 286
Harrison, Rex 5, 194, 274, 287, 319, 395, 414

Harron, Mary 142
Harry Potter films 286, 413, 435
Hart, Ian 287
Hartley, Hal 356
Hart's War 244
Harvey, Laurence 287–8, 431
Harvey, Lillian 4, 39, 259, 265, 288–9
Hasso, Signe 288, 422–3
The Hasty Heart 448
Hatari! 182, 270, 353
Hathaway, Henry 100, 324
Hauer, Rutger 14, 17, 230, 288–9, 326, 381, 458
Haufler, Max 290
The Haunting 470
Haute tension/High Tension 229
Havana 389
Hawke, Ethan 230
Hawkins, Jack 166, 290
Hawks, Howard 182, 219, 270, 275, 317, 353, 368, 401
Hawn, Goldie 371
Hawthorne, Nigel 290, 455
Hawtrey, William 373
Haydn, Richard 290–1
Hayek, Salma 135
Hayes, Helen 166
Hayward, Susan 324
Hayworth, Rita 198, 326
He Who Gets Slapped 24
Hearst, William Randolph 291
The Heart of the Matter 304, 423
Heartbreak House 65
Hearts in Atlantis 145
Hearts of Fire 243
Hearts of the World 157, 219
Heat and Dust 422
Heaven Can Wait 208
Heaven Knows, Mr Allison 320
Heavenly Creatures 466
Heaven's Gate 100, 306, 307
Hecht, Ben 136, 389
Heflin, Van 127
Heilbut, Anthony, *Exiled in Paradise* 3
The Heiress 413
Helbling, Jeanne 17n, 253
Helen of Troy 170, 174, 399, 430
Hell Drivers 170
Hell and High Water 227
Heller in Pink Tights 342
Hellinger, Mark 116
Hellman, Lillian 298, 346, 409
Hello Dolly! 219
Hello London 293
Hello-Goodbye 269, 316
Hell's Angel 384
Hellström, Gunnar 291
Hemingway, Ernest 99, 179

Hemmings, David 291
Henie Onstad Art Centre 293
Henie, Sonja 15, 16, 291–3, *292*, 297, 423
Henie, Wilhelm 291
Henreid, Paul *4*, 12, 14, 40, 99, 106, 108, 169, 265, 267, 268, 293, 300
Henry and June 231
Henry, Lenny 293
Henry V 187, 390
Hepburn, Audrey 12, 125, 177, 201, 215, 293–6, *294*, 372, 381, 391, 445, 467
Hepburn, Katharine 101n, 189, 368, 389, 394, 413
Herbert, Holmes 296
Hercules in New York 426
The Heroine of Mons 302
Hersholt, Jean 285, 291, 296–8, *297*, 339, 355, 356, 422
Herzog, Werner 321, 323
Heston, Charlton 127, 185, 287, 290, 342, 457
Hets/Frenzy 470
Heydrich, Reinhard 108
Heymann, Werner Richard 105
Heywood, Anne 298
The Hi-Lo Country 100, 220
High Fidelity 298
High Sierra 414
High Spirits 392
Higher and Higher/Amour et swing 375
Highlander 328
Highsmith, Patricia, *The Talented Mr Ripley* 230
Hijuelos, Oscar, *Los reyes del mambo tocan canciones de amor* 138
A Hill in Korea 196
Hill, Walter 153
Hiller, Arthur 280, 413
Hiller, Wendy 298
Hilton, Conrad 258
Hilton, Francesca 258
Hilton, James 213
Der Himmel über Berlin/Wings of Desire 40
Himmler, Heinrich 109
Hindle Wakes 283
Hinds, Ciarán 298
Hird, Thora 428
His Girl Friday 275
Hispanic Organisation of Latino Actors 139n
History is Made at Night 87, 90–1
Hitchcock, Alfred 98, 99, 100, 161, 176, 179, 182, 187, 191, 202, 206, 211, 214, 225, 226, 232, 263, 267, 275, 280, 281, 283, 287, 300, 305, 306, 314, 315, 340, 342, 343, 346, 366, 368, 378, 390, 397, 404, 415, 445, 446, 448, *456*, 457, 458, 459, 466, 467

The Hitcher 288
Hitler – Beast of Berlin 269
Hitler, Adolf 40, 109
The Hitler Gang 109
Hitler's Madman 109
Hjejle, Iben 298
Hobbes, Halliwell 298–9
Hobson, Valerie 299
Hoey, Dennis 299
Hoffman, Dustin 100, 153, 472n
Hold Back the Dawn 255
Holden, Fay 245
Holden, William 127, 285, 304
Holiday 275, 324
Holland, Agnieszka 230, 376
Holloway, Stanley 299–300
Hollywood Anti-Nazi League 7, 110
Hollywood Boulevard 263
Hollywood Canteen 255
Hollywood Cricket Club 453
Hollywood Ice Revue 293
Hollywood Now 267
Hollywood Reporter 116, 118
Hollywood Star, Hollywood Extra 408
Holm, Ian 147n, 300
Holmquist, Sie 300
L'Homme du jour/The Man of the Hour 207
Un Homme et une femme/A Man and a Woman 155, 232, 451
Homolka, Oscar 104, 105, 109, 300–1, *300*, 405
Honey Pot 200
Honeymoon in Bali 355, *444*
Hook 435
Hopalong Cassidy films 384
Hope ... 313
Hope, Bob 57, 231, 245, 363, 377, 462
Hope Springs 144
Hopkins, Anthony 141, 142, 143, 145, 146, 172, 301, *301*, 360, 447, 455, 470
Hopkins, Miriam 99, 287, 352
Hopscotch 313
Horak, Jan-Christopher 77, 80, 108
Hordern, Michael 301–2
Horn, Camilla 39, 266, 302
Hornby, Nick, *About a Boy* 277
The Horse Whisperer 428
Hoskins, Bob 147n, 302
The Hospital 413
Hostages 109, 396, 405
Höstsonaten/Autumn Sonata 180
Hot Shots! 100
Hotel Imperial 49, 96, 98, 368
Hotel Room 315
Houdini, Harry 226
The Hound of the Baskervilles 250, 406
The Hours and Times 287
House Calls 313

The House of the Spirits 171
The House on Telegraph Hill 218
Houseboat 342
Housemann, John 416
Hove, Anders 302
How Green Was My Valley 219, 256, 334, 335, 340, 358, 388
How to Marry a Millionaire 226
Howard, Leslie 61, 99, 302–4, *303*
Howard, Ronald 304
Howard, Trevor 304
Howards End 184, 447
HUAC (House Un-American Activities Committee) 170, 187, 208, 293, 407
Hubschmid, Paul 304, 442–3
The Hucksters 67, 319
Hudson Hawk 142, 277
Hudson, Hugh 323
Hudson, Kate 337
Hudson, Rock 128, 341
Hughes, Howard 237, 341, 384, 432
8 femmes 227, 420
Hulbert, Jack 66, 218
The Human Stain 301
Hume, Benita 304–5
The Humming Bird 47
The Hunchback of Notre Dame 330
Hungary 305
The Hunger 232
Hunter, Ian 305–6
Huppert, Isabelle 15, 100, 254, 306, 443
Hurley, Elizabeth 276, 277
Hurst, Brandon 306–7
Hurst, Brian Desmond 372
Hurt, John 147*n*, 307
Hustle 232
Huston, John 158, 182, 215, 227, 247, 278, 280, 350, 381, 403, 420, 441, 469
Hyde-White, Wilfrid 307
Hyland, Peggy 307–8
Hytner, Nicholas 229
Hytten, Olaf 8, 308–9

I, Claudius 313
I Come in Peace 347
I Confess 182, 225
I Dreamed of Africa 72, 397
The I Inside 408
I Love You, Alice B. Toklas! 429
I Married a Woman 239
I Never Promised You a Rose Garden 158
I Remember Mama 207, 300, 452
I See a Dark Stranger 319
I Walk Alone 413
I Want You 465
Ice Follies of 1939 426
Iceland 292
An Ideal Husband 145, 243, 326

Idioterne/The Idiots 302
if 359
If I Had a Million 433
I.F. 1 ne répond plus 92*n*
Ikonnikov, Alexander 32, 418
I'll Give a Million 49
Ilya Darling 364
I'm Alright Jack 429
I'm No Angel 274
L'Image 350
Images 469
The Immigrant 204
Imperial Russian Theatre 322
The Importance of Being Earnest 145, 243
The Impostor 115, 116–20, 257
In Again, Out Again 27*n*
In the Mouth of Madness 402
In the Name of the Father 229, 401, 447
In the Name of Love 383
In Which We Serve 165, 367
Ince, Thomas 191, 297
The Incredible Hulk 426
Independence Day 41
The Indian Fighter 353
The Indian Runner 100
Indiana Jones and the Last Crusade 215
Indiana Jones films 241
Das indische Grabmal/The Indian Tomb 304
Indiscretions 333
Indochine 397
Inez from Hollywood 383
Infante, Pedro 136, 370
The Informer 234, 273, 309, 320, 360–1
The Inn of the Sixth Happiness 238, 316
Innerspace 337
An Innocent Affair 202
Innocents of Paris 54, 57, 206
The Insider 259
Inspiration 95
The Insult 269
Interceptor 402
Interlude 416
Intermezzo 99, 179, 422
Intermezzo: A Love Story 179, 303
International Kinema Research 251
Internationale Festspiele, Berlin 461
Interview with the Vampire: The Vampire Chronicles 171, 408
Intima Teatern, Stockholm 285
Intimate Relations 463
Intolerance 211, 414, 450
L'Intrigo/Dark Purpose 190
Introducing Dorothy Dandridge 188
Investigating Sex 41
Invisible Agent 109
The Invisible Man 405
Ion 333
The Ipcress File 196, 279

Iran: Days of Crisis 264
Ireland 309–10
Ireland, Jill 310
Irish Dreamtime 192
Irish Times 73
Irma La Douce 254
The Iron Man 47, 156
The Iron Mask 24, 175
Irons, Jeremy 14, 142, 181, 310–11, 454
Irving, Henry 450
Irving Place Theater, New York 38, 208
Isherwood, Christopher 468
Ishiguro, Kazuo 447
Ishtar 153
Island Wives 208
Isn't Life Wonderful 329
Isn't She Great 210
It Happened in Athens 377
It Happened One Night 446
It Started in Naples 234, 342
Italian Actors Union 173
The Italian Job 170, 190, 196
'Italianicity' 47, 49, 50
Italtone Film Production 451
Italy 311–13
It's Love Again 64
It's a Pleasure 293
It's Simple, Darling! 258
It's a Wonderful Life 450
Iures, Marcel 313
Ivanhoe 372
Ivory, James 73, 335

Jääkärin morsian/A Soldier's Bride 396
J'accuse/That They May Live 255
Jackson, Glenda 313
Jackson, Peter 316, 360, 412
Jacobi, Derek 313
Jacquot, Benoît 71, 335
Jade, Claude 313–14
Jagger, Mick 314
Jaglom, Henry 223
Jaguar Lives! 200
Jakob the Liar 268
Jamaica Inn 387
James, C. L. R. 274
James, Henry 320
Jamón, Jamón 133, 174, 220
Janni, Joseph 208
Jannings, Emil 39, 169, 234, 236, 266, 314, 460
Jaque-Catelain 314
Jardiel Poncela, Enrique 408
Jarman, Derek 442
Jarmusch, Jim 178, 377
A Játékos 405
Jaws 431
Jeanmaire, Zizi 314

Jeanne Doré 21
Jeans, Isabel 314
Jeans, Ursula 315
Jefferson, Arthur and Madge 330
Jefferson in Paris 422
Jeffrey Bernard is Unwell 392
Jerome, Jerome K., *The Passing of the Third Floor Back* 250
Jet Storm 170
Jeunet, Jean-Pierre 5, 398
Jeux interdits/Forbidden Games 250
Jew Suss 460
Jewish actors 16, 104–5
Jewish Art Theatre, New York 38
Jewison, Norman 470
Jezebel 49, 190
Jimmy Hollywood 153
Jingle All the Way 427
Joachimson, Felix 257
Joan of Paris 253, 273, 374
Johnny Mnemonic 347
Johns, Glynis 274
Johnson, Claire 127
Johnson, Lyndon B. 146*n*
Johnson, Nunnally 100
Joinville Studios 397, 437
Joković, Mirjana 315, 470
Jolivet, Pierre 199
Jolson, Al 322
Jolson Sings Again 239
The Jolson Story 239
Jones, Freddie 315
Jones, Grace 347
Jones, Vinnie 315
Jordan, Neil 195, 379, 391, 392, 408, 412
Josette 433
Le Jour se lève/Daybreak 115, 333
Jourdan, Louis *11*, 13, 15, 16, 125–30, *125*, 201, 254, 263, 282, 315–16
Le Journal des Voyages 86
Le Journal du dimanche 72
The Journey 155
Journey's End 195
Jovovich, Milla 15, 100
Juarez 155, 267
Juarez, Benito 136
Judas Kiss 447
Jude 468
Judge Hardy's Children 333
Judgment at Nuremberg 236, 365, 424
Jules et Jim 465
Julia 237, 409, 424
Julia, Raul 229
Julius Caesar 269, 320, 354
Jump into Hell 430
Jumpin' Jack Flash 326
The Jungle Book 420
Junior 427, 447

Jurassic Park 166
Jürgens, Curt 10, 42, 268, 269, 316
Just around the Corner 300
Just a Gigolo 236
Just Visiting 210, 411
Justin, John 316
Justine 155, 385

K-19: The Widowmaker 379
Kael, Pauline 12, 196, 275
Kafka 326, 376
Kafka, Hans, 'What Our Immigration Did for Hollywood' 265
Kalem 211, 238, 382, 454
Kane, Robert 87, 162
Kaprisky, Valérie 316
Kära släkten 415
Karabanova, Zoia 77
Karger, Maxwell 378
Karloff, Boris 16, 155, 211, 317–18
Karlson, Phil 154
Karno, Fred 6, 199, 204
troupe 330–2
Karriär/Career 288
Kasdan, Lawrence 411
Kassovitz, Maurice 202
Katch, Kurt 103, *103*, 318
Katić, Branka 470
Kaufman, Philip 231
Kaufmann, Christine 318
Kaye, Danny 314, 471
Kazan, Elia 320, 337
Keaton, Buster 23, 24, 219, 370, 375
The Keep 360
Keighley, William 34
Keith, Jens 288
Keller, Fritz 106
Keller, Marthe 318, 442
Kelly, Gene 162, 167, 201, 216, 250, 281, 282, 370
Kelly, Grace 169, 282, 356, 382
Kendall, Kay 318–19, 414
Kendall, Suzy 319
Kennedy, J. F. 333
Kent, Arnold (Lido Manetti) 46, 48, 311, 319
La Kermesse héroïque/Carnival in Flanders 226, 416
Kerouac, Jack 430
Kerr, Deborah 14, 61, 66–7, 68, 273, 319–20, *453*, 454
Kerrigan, J. M. 320–1
Kessel, Georges 220
Kessel, Joseph 220
Keystone 204
Keystone Trio 332
Khanzhonkov, Alexander 460
Kicking the Moon Around 387

The Kid 204
Kid Auto Races at Venice 204
Kidman, Nicole 462
Kiepura, Jan 321, 399
Kier, Udo 42, 321
Kieślowski, Krzysztof 72, 181
The Killing of Sister George 469
Killing Zoe 230
Kilmer, Val 465
Kindergarten Cop 427
The King and the Chorus Girl 278
King Creole 370
King, Dennis 321
King, Henry 50*n*, 96, 212
King of the Hill 326
The King and I 320
King of the Khyber Rifles 316
King of Kings 136, 360, 464
King Rat 250
King Solomon's Mines 273, 319
King's Row 405
Kings of the Sun 245
Kingsley, Ben 321–2
Kingston, Alex 245, 322
Kinskey, Leonid 77, 82, 322, 418
Kinski, Klaus 321, 322–3
Kinski, Nastassja *13*, 323
Kipps 164
Kismet 41, 98, 436
The Kiss 28*n*, 86, 95, 97, 177, 399
Kiss Me Deadly 184
Kiss Me, Stupid 429
Kitty Foyle 209
Klassezämekunft/Class Reunion 442
Klein, Bertha 208
Kleine, George 27*n*
The Knack – and How to Get It ... 182, 406
Knef, Hildegard 14, 16, 41, 95, 100, 268, 323–4
Knife in the Water 399
Knights of the Round Table 170
Knock Off 458
Knock on Wood 471
Knocknagow 222
Knowles, Patric 324
Kobal, John 440
Kohner, Frederick 107–8
Kohner, Paul 7, 103–4, 105, 107–8, 109, 111, 267
Kojak 423
Kolker, Henry 324–5
Der Kongress tanzt/Congress Dances 86, 170, 288
Konovaloff, Nickolas 32
Korda, Alexander 61, 62, 64, 65, 169, 194, 216, 246, 287, 303, 305, 316, 328, 329, 336, 340, 385, 390, 395, 459, 460
Korda, Maria 169

Index

Korff, Arnold 325
Kortner, Fritz 14, 40, 103, 107, 267, 325
Kosleck, Martin 14, 325–6
Kosloff, Theodore 34n, 77, 78
Koster, Henry 98, 99, 174, 226, 250, 257
Krabbé, Jeroen 230, 326, 381
Kracauer, Siegfried 141
Krämer, Peter 40
Kramer, Stanley 432, 465
Krauss, Henry 23
The Kremlin Letter 158, 279
Kreuger, Kurt 326
Kreutzer, Elisabeth 255
Kristel, Sylvie 428
Kristofferson, Kris 306
Krüger, Hardy 42, 326
Kubrick, Stanley 51n, 359, 432, 455
Kun, Béla 169, 305, 344, 459
Der Kurier des Zaren/Michel Strogoff 463
Kurtz, St 31
Kurys, Diane 181

The L-Shaped Room 201
La Cava, Gregory 245
La Cour, Else 327
L.A. Law 239
La Rocque, Rod 173
L.A. Story 446
Laage, Barbara 326–7
Laberinto de pasiones/Labyrinth of Passion 171
Lac aux dames/Ladies Lake 167, 433
Lacombe Lucien 210
Ladies Should Listen 374
Ladrón de Guevara, María Fernanda 438
Lady Caroline Lamb 366
The Lady Eve 216
The Lady from Shanghai 326
The Lady is Willing 285, 303
Lady L 385
Lady of the Pavements 49, 272
Lady Possessed 354
A Lady to Love 173
The Lady Vanishes 340, 346, 404
Laemmle, Carl 39, 103, 105, 375
Lafayette, Andrée 327
Lagrange, Louise 24, 252, 327
The Lair of the White Worm 276
Lam, Ringo 458
Lamarr, Hedy 8, 14, 16, 40, 41, 95, 98, 169, 265, 267, 327–8, 346, 355, 435
   Ecstasy and Me 328
Lamb 380
Lambert, Christophe 328
Lambert, Gavin 127
Lancaster, Burt 136, 170, 198, 274, 348, 371, 413, 431
Lanchester, Elsa 238, 328–9, *329*, 330, 350

Land der Liebe/Land of Love 426
Land of the Pharaohs 212, 368
Landa, Juan de 438
Landau, Martin 345
Landi, Elissa 46
Landis, Carole 287, 395
Lane, Lupino 329
Lang, Fritz 86, 98, 116, 117, 223, 257, 268, 304, 339, 342, 358, 370, 378, 395, 401, 408, 421, 429
Lang, Walter 49
Langner, Lawrence 429
language problems 10–12
Lansbury, Angela 448
Lantz, Robert 288
Lanza, Mario 136, 164, 371
Lara, Agustín 370
Lara Croft Tomb Raider: The Cradle of Life 17n
Lasky, Jesse 8, 54, 206, 329, 415
Lassie Come Home 358
Lassiter 430
The Last Command 30, 33, 266, 314, 437
The Last of the Mohicans 229
The Last Moment 356
Last Orders 196
The Last Performance 460
The Last Tycoon 373, 399
The Last Valley 198
The Late George Apley 213
Latino image 135–9, 172
Laughter in Paradise 295
Laughton, Charles 7, 8, 12, 39, 61, 62, 66, 67–8, 238, 328, 329–30, *329*, 387, 388, 405
Laurel, Stan 10, 50, 222, 226, 330–3, *331*, 343
Lauren, Ralph 221
Laurence Olivier Productions 390
Laurent, Jacqueline 333
The Lavender Hill Mob 295
Law, Jude 142, 148n, 333
Lawford, Peter 209, 333–4
The Lawnmower Man 192
Lawrence, Florence 26n, 398
Lawrence of Arabia 247, 391
Lawson, Wilfrid 334
Lawton, Frank 334
Lea Lyon 25
The League of Extraordinary Gentlemen 449
Lean, David 165, 189, 208, 247, 304, 368, 432
Leather Pushers 232
LeBeau, Madeleine 224, 334
Lebedeff, Ivan 79, 80, 334–5
   The Legion of Dishonor 334
Lebrun, Dominique, *Paris-Hollywood: les Français dans le cinéma américain* 3

Leclerc, General 116
L'Écran français 119
Lederer, Francis 7, 223, 268, 335
Ledoux, Fernand 335
Ledoyen, Virginie 70n, 71, 73, 74, 199, 335
Lee, Anna 335
Lee, Bernard 367
Lee, Brandon 347, 397
Lee, Christopher 141, 142, 223, 335–6
The Legend of the Holy Drinker 288
Legend of the Lost 189
Legends of the Fall 391
Leigh, Mike 389, 446
Leigh, Suzanna 336
Leigh, Vivien 9, 62, 169, 273, 336–7, 340, 372, 389, 390, 395, 467
Leighton, Margaret 337
Leisen, Mitchell 98
Lejeune, C. A. 432
Lelouch, Claude 451
Lemmon, Jack 232, 323, 368, 425
Leni, Paul 28n, 169, 376, 460
Lennon, John 287
Lenny Live and Unleashed 293
Léon/The Professional 72, 411
Leonard, Robert Z. 96
Leone, Sergio 200
Leontovich, Eugenie 77
The Leopard Man 396
Lerner, Alan Jay, and Loewe, Frederick 58, 159
Leroy, Mervyn 282, 455
Lesseps, Ferdinand de 87
Lester, Richard 208
Let's Go to Paris 89
Let's Make Love 369, 460
Letscher, Matt 172
The Letter 352
Letter from an Unknown Woman 125, 126–7, 208, 315, 365
Der letzte Mann/The Last Laugh 266, 314
Leven, Jeremy 73
Levine, Joseph E. 170, 196
Levinson, Barry 153
Lewin, Albert 421
Lewis, Fiona 337
Lewis, Jerry 422
Lewton, Val 317
La ley del deseo/Law of Desire 171
Leyssac, Paul 337
Leza, Ana 172
L'Herbier, Marcel 23, 255, 314, 394
Lhermitte, Thierry 337
L'Histoire d'Adèle H./The Story of Adele H. 153
Liedtke, Harry 288
Life magazine 244, 326, 353, 357
Life of Brian 210

497

The Life of David Gale 468
Life and Death of 9413: A Hollywood Extra 33, 408, 463
The Life and Death of Colonel Blimp 315
The Life of Émile Zola 267, 424
'Life without Zoe' 268
Lifeboat 109, 161
Ligero, Miguel 438
The Light that Failed 213
Lili 201
Lili Marleen 428
Liliom 86
Limelight 183
The Limey 439
Limur, Jean de 199
Linder, Max 21, 21, 23, 24, 206, 252, 337–8
Lindfors, Viveca 297, 339, 339, 422–3
Linklater, Richard 72, 230
Linow, Ivan 77
Lion of the Desert 395
The Lion King 311
Lion, Margo 236
The Lion in Winter 391
Lionheart 458
Little Brother of God 360
Little Caesar 312
The Little Drummer Girl 256
The Little Foxes 352
'Little Hungary' restaurant 7, 305
The Little Minister 219
Little Odessa 417
Little Voice 196
Little Women 189, 440
Litvak, Anatole 155, 170, 324, 369
Live and Let Die 430
The Living Daylights 192, 326
Lloyd, Doris 339–40
Lloyd, Emily 340
Lloyd, Harold 23, 173, 332
Lock, Stock and Two Smoking Barrels 315
Lockwood, Margaret 66, 198, 340, 415, 432
Locura de amor/Love Crazy 370
Loder, John 206, 340–1
Lodge, John 48
Lodygevsky's (restaurant) 81
Lodyzhensky, Fyodor 32, 418
Logan, Joshua 193
Logan's Run 455
Lola 155
Lola Montès 242
Lola rennt/Run Lola Run 41, 401
Lolita 310, 354
Lollobrigida, Gina 95, 200, 203, 231, 311, 312, 341
Lom, Herbert 223, 240, 341
Lombard, Carole 278, 318

London Film Productions 62
London Films 287
The Londonderry Air 157
Long Day's Journey into Night 413
Un long dimanche de fiançailles/A Very Long Engagement 5
The Long Good Friday 192, 368
Long Road 458
The Longest Day 214, 231, 264, 416
Looking for Jimmy 72
López, Ana 139n
Lopez, Jennifer 135, 144, 246
Lord, Peter 412
The Lord of the Rings 141, 142, 146, 336
Lord of the Rings trilogy 360, 412
Loren, Sophia 95, 189, 200, 311, 312, 341–2, 342, 356, 377, 457
Lorenzo's Oil 456
Lorre, Peter 4, 16, 184, 223, 255, 265, 266, 267, 268, 280, 342–3, 343, 375
Lory, Jacques 93n, 251, 343
Los Lobos 139n
Los que danzan/Those Who Dance 155
Losey, Joseph 170, 250, 462, 468
Lost & Found 350
Lost Command 200, 230
Lost and Found 313
Lost Horizon 213, 452, 464, 468
Lost in Space 389
The Lost Weekend 366
The Lost World 401
'Louise' 55, 56, 57
Love 33, 96, 97, 260, 419
Love Affair 187, 392
Love in the Afternoon 56, 57, 207, 295
The Love Bug 448
Love and Hisses 433
Love is a Many-Splendored Thing 242
Love Me Tonight 119, 206
Love and Money 323
Love, Montagu(e) 344, 455
Love On the Dole 67
The Love Parade 54, 55, 56, 206, 207, 329
The Love of Sunya 234, 334
Love Walked In 420
Lovejoy 361
Loverol, Henri 202
Lovesick 371
Lowe, Edmund 64
Lowry, Malcolm, Under the Volcano 247
Lubin company 238
Lubitsch, Ernst 28n, 33, 34n, 39, 40, 54, 95, 97, 105, 158, 193, 206, 207, 236, 261, 265, 266, 267, 288, 302, 314, 322, 329, 380, 386, 399, 408, 418, 423, 424
Lucas, George 51n, 146, 282, 399
The Luck of the Irish 320
The Lucky Dog 332

Lugosi, Bela 16, 305, 336, 344–5, 345, 346, 392, 450
Luguet, André 92n, 345
Lukas, Paul 9, 208, 345–6, 346, 405
Lumet, Sidney 349, 369, 406, 432
Lundgren, Dolph 15, 17, 346–7, 368
Lupino, Ida 116, 117, 120, 257
Lupu, David 301, 315, 402
Lyne, Adrian 310
Lyric Players Theatre, Belfast 379
Lys, Lya 347

M 342
McAnally, Ray 357
Macbeth 326, 450
McCabe and Mrs Miller 100, 208
McCallum, David 357
McCann, Donal 357–8
McCarey, Leo 99, 332
McCarthy, Joseph 205, 208, 268, 293
McClory, Sean 358
McCormick, F. J. 220, 358
MacDonald, Jeanette 191, 193, 206
McDowall, Roddy 219, 358–9
MacDowell, Andie 233, 252
McDowell, Malcolm 14, 147n, 359, 454–5
McGehee, Scott 442
McGilligan, Patrick 116
MacGinnis, Niall 347
McGoohan, Patrick 359
MacGowran, Jack 348, 408
McGregor, Ewan 146, 148n, 187, 359–60
Mackaill, Dorothy 348
McKellen, Ian 14, 141, 142, 146, 360, 408, 455
McKenna, Siobhan 360, 387
McKenna, T. P. 360
McKenna, Virginia 360, 449
Mackenna's Gold 404
The MacKintosh Man 420
McLaglen, Victor 156, 273, 360–1, 361, 453
MacLaine, Shirley 190, 295, 356, 369
McLintock! 388
McLoughlin, Tom 72
McMurray, Fred 444
Macnee, Patrick 348
McQueen, Steve 174, 182
McShane, Ian 361
McTiernan, John 192
The Mad Empress 229
The Mad Genius 156
Mad Love 342
Madam Satan 229
Madame Bovary 125, 127
Madame Curie 262
Madame DuBarry/Passion 265, 314, 380
Madame Peacock 379

Madame Sans-Gêne 21, 28n, 180–1, 350
Mädchen in Uniform/Girls in Uniform 466
Made in Britain 417
Mademoiselle Fifi 433
The Madness of King George 290, 369
Madonna 145, 171, 172, 321
Madonna: Truth or Dare 171
Magee, Patrick 348
Magic 301
The Magic Box 423
The Magic Flame 96
Magnane, Georges 119
Magnani, Anna 14, 95, 311, 312, 348–9, 396
The Magnificent Lie 86, 186
The Magnificent Seven 193
Maguire, Tobey 145
Mai lányok/Yesterday's Girls 258
Maid in Manhattan 144–5, 246
Maiden Voyage 90
La Main chaude/The Itchy Palm 364
Maiori, Antonio 51n
Le Maître de Musique/The Music Teacher 176
A Majority of One 282
Makarenko, Daniil 34n
Makavejev, Dušan 240, 430
Make Me a Star 55
Malatesta, Fred 49, 93n, 349
Malaya 218
Malkovich, John 174, 413
Malle, Louis 181, 210, 416
Mallet-Stevens, Robert 28n
Malmö municipal theatre 448
Maltby, Richard 455
The Maltese Falcon 166, 280, 343, 356
Mambo 262
The Mambo Kings 138, 171
Mamoulian, Rouben 32, 96, 97, 98, 99, 206, 207, 418, 440, 443
A Man for All Seasons 408, 428, 431, 469
A Man Called Horse 286
A Man Could Get Killed 364
The Man from Home 50n
The Man from Laramie 219
The Man from U.N.C.L.E. 357
The Man from Yesterday 86, 186
The Man in the Glass Booth 424
Man Hunt 108
The Man I Married 109
The Man in the Iron Mask 222, 233
Man of La Mancha 342
The Man Who Came Back 348
The Man Who Could Work Miracles 421
The Man Who Fell to Earth 185
The Man Who Knew Too Much 187, 263, 342, 378, 466
The Man Who Laughs 169, 460

The Man Who Loved Cat Dancing 366
The Man Who Never Was 185
The Man Who Would Be King 196, 215
Man, Woman and Child 381
The Manchurian Candidate 288
Mandelstamm, Valentin 251
Mander, Miles 349
Manetti, Lido *see* Kent, Arnold
Mangano, Silvana 262
Manhunter 219
Mankiewicz, Joseph L. 200, 270, 287, 441
Mann, Anthony 136, 219, 222, 371, 404
Mann, Heinrich 106
Mann, Michael 229, 360
Manners, David 344
The Mannions of America 192
Manojlović, Miki 470
Manolescu 376
Manon 166
Manon des Sources 71
Mansfield, Jayne 377
The Manxman 191
Marathon Man 318, 390, 472n
Marceau, Sophie 71, 72, 74, 95, 350
March, Fredric 64, 303, 440
Marchal, Arlette 28n, 92n, 350
Marchand, Colette 350
Mare Nostrum 45
Margolyes, Miriam 350
María de la O 438
El Mariachi 138, 171
Marido y mujer/Man and Wife 382
Marie Walewska 97
La Mariée est trop belle 129
Marin, Jacques 351
Mark Hellinger Theatre, New York 364
The Mark of Zorro 49
Marked Woman 49, 209
Marković, Rade 351, 470
Marlene 235, 424
Marly, Florence 351
Marmont, Percy 351
Marnie 214–15
Marquand, Christian 210, 351
Marsac, Maurice 251, 351–2
Marshall, Armina 429
Marshall, Bill 374, 401
Marshall, George 98
Marshall, Herbert 16, 61, 62, 181, 352–3, *352*, 389, 455
Marshall, Tonie 401
Martell, Alphonse 251
Martin, Dean 158, 182
Martin, Paul 288
Martin Roumagnac 120
Martin, Steve 185, 446
Martinelli, Elsa 312, 353
Marton, Andrew 100

Marvin, Lee 337
Marx Brothers 416, 461
Mary Poppins 159–60, 393, 448
Mary of Scotland 219
Mary Shelley's Frankenstein 143, 187
La maschera del demonio/Black Sunday 439
The Mask of Diijon 461
The Mask of Dimitrios 255
The Mask of Zorro 100, 145, 172, 470
Maskerade 404
Mason, James 61, 66, 67, *154*, 198, 273, 274, 320, 353–5, 415, 448, 454, 455
Mason, Portland 354
Masquerade in Mexico 413
The Masquerader 212
Massen, Osa 355
Massey, Ilona 8, 11, 355
Masters of the Universe 347
Mastroianni, Marcello 11, 12, 16, 313, 342, 351, 355
Mata Hari 95, 97
Matador 430
Matiesen, Otto 356
The Matrix 178, 411
The Matrix Reloaded 467
A Matter of Life and Death 384
Matthau, Walter 313, 323
Matthews, Jessie 64, 356
Matthews, Lester 356–7
Maude, Cyril 357
Maugham, Somerset 352, 379, 421
 The Circle 274
Mauloy, Georges 17n, 253
Maupassant, Guy de 421, 433
Maurey, Nicole 357
Maurice 251
The Maurice Chevalier Show 57
Mauvais sang/Bad Blood 71, 181
Max, Edouard de 445
Max Comes Across 23
Max et les ferrailleurs/Max and the Scrapmongers 425
Max in a Taxi 23
Max Wants a Divorce 23
Max films 337
Maximilian, Emperor 136
Maximum Risk 458
May, Joe 105
Mayer, Louis B. 39, 154, 259, 260, 262, 273, 285, 319, 327, 333, 355, 426
Mayflower Productions 330
Mayo, Archie 116, 257
Maytime 49
Mazursky, Paul 176, 373
Me and the Colonel 316
Meaney, Colm 361
Meantime 389
Medea 413

Medeiros, Maria de 231, 401
Medicine Man 215
Medina, Patricia 362
Meek, Donald 362
Meet Me in Las Vegas 370
Meighan, Thomas 309
Melchior, Lauritz 362–3
Melesh, Alex 77, 80
Melina's Greece 364
Melodía de Arrabal 224
Melville, Jean-Pierre 153, 278
Memorial Enterprises 247
Men are not Gods 287
Menaul, Christopher 72
Ménessier, Henri 22, 23
Menjou, Adolphe 33, 97, 291, 383
Menschen am Sonntag 281
Mephisto 188
Le Mépris 254
Mercanton, Louis 21, 22, 23
Merchant–Ivory 184, 276, 337, 421, 422, 447
Mercier, Louis 251, 363
Mercier, Michèle 363
Mercouri, Melina 14, 279, 363–4, 395
Mercury Theatre 388
Méril, Macha 364
Mérimée, Prosper, *Carmen* 135
The Merry Widow 49, 56, 120, 191, 206, 224
Messalina 229
Metaxa, Georges 364
Metro 266, 397
Metro Pictures 378
Metropolitan Opera 362–3, 400
Meyer, Greta 364–5, 417
Meyer, Russ 226, 318
Meyer, Torben 365, 422
MGM 53, 54, 56, 57, 58, 65, 66, 86, 90, 95, 97, 103, 108, 154, 159, 161, 162, 167, 175, 176, 177, 191, 201, 206, 225, 230, 238, 253, 255, 259, 260, 262, 266, 273, 292, 297, 303, 304, 319, 320, 322, 325, 327, 333, 336, 342, 358, 362, 366, 367, 370, 388, 390, 403, 404, 405, 426, 434, 437, 438, 443, 453, 460, 461
Miami Rhapsody 171–2
Miami Vice 379
Michael Collins 379
Michel Strogoff 25, 375
Mickey Blue Eyes 141, 144, 277
Micki + Maude 371
Midler, Bette 210, 398
Midnight Express 307
Midnight in the Garden of Good and Evil 333
The Midnight Sun 460
Mifune's sidste sang/Mifune's Last Song 302

Mihail, Jean 416
Mikaël, Ludmila 366
Mildred Pierce 101n
Miles, Sarah 366
Milland, Ray 366–7, 455
Miller, Arthur 229
Miller, Bodil 367
Miller, Glenn 292
Miller, Jonny Lee 148n, 367
Miller's Crossing 195, 247, 441
Le Million 86
The Million Dollar Hotel 421
Millions Like Us 400
Mills, Hayley 367, 368
Mills, John 367–8
Mills, Juliet 367, 368
Milushev, Boyan 368
'Mimi' 55
Mimica, Vatroslav 430
Mindwalk 452
Minerva Films 302
Minghella, Anthony 245, 333, 428
Ministry of Fear 268
The Miniver Story 262, 466
Minnelli, Liza 371
Minnelli, Vincente 129, 201, 207, 232, 269, 282, 315, 319, 369, 448
Minority Report 244
Minotes, Alexis 368
Minter, Mary Miles 373
Il mio viaggio in Italia 51n
The Miracle 169, 321
Miracle on 34th Street 283
The Miracle of the Bells 100
Miranda, Carmen 133, 136, 400, 438
Miranda, Isa 11, 14, 16, 49, 98, 312, 368
Mirren, Helen 368–9
Les Misérables 23
Miss Mary 208
Mission: Impossible 72–3, 177, 181, 409, 411, 428
Mission to Moscow 419
Mister Malatesta 47
Mistinguett 25, 55, 259
Mitchell, Margaret 303
Mitchell, Thomas 117
Mitchum, Robert 320, 394, 406, 448
Mitić, Gojko 470
Mitry, Jean 23
Mix, Tom 35n
Mixed Nuts 332
Moby Dick 403
Model Shop 155
Modern Times 205, 349
Modesty Blaise 462
Modleski, Tania 127
Moffat, Donald 356
Moi et l'impératrice 92n

Molander, Gustav 99, 179
Molina, Alfred 356
Moll Flanders 257
The Molly Maguires 247
Molly and Me 245, 358
Mon père ce héros/My Father the Hero 233, 411
Mona Lisa 196
Monaco Forever 457
Monday Night at Eight 159
The Money Moon 199
Monkey Business 275
Monogram 221, 358
Monroe, Marilyn 206, 369–70, 390, 460
Monsieur Beaucaire 24
Monsieur Verdoux 205
Montand, Yves 356–7, 432, 460
Monte Carlo 193
Monte Cristo 24, 420
Monte Walsh 373
Montecarlo Story 234
Monteiro, João César 231
Monténégro, Conchita 92n, 370
Montevecchi, Liliane 370
Montez, Maria 169
Montgomery, Robert 156
Montiel, Sara 12, 135–7, 139, 370–1, 438
Monty Python and the Holy Grail 210
Monty Python's Flying Circus 210
Moody, Ron 371
The Moon is a Balloon 384
The Moon and Sixpence 421
The Moon-Spinners 395
Moonfleet 339, 358, 370, 378
Moontide 115–20, 257
Moore, Colleen 310, 438
Moore, Dudley 371–2
Moore, Grace 48, 56, 400
Moore, Kieron 372
Moore, Roger 13, 128, 372
Morandini, Morando 348
Der Mörder Dimitri Karamasoff/The Brothers Karamazov 439–40
Die Mörder sind unter uns/The Murderers are Among Us 323
Mordkine, Mikhail 78
More, Kenneth 227, 372, 449
Moreau, Jeanne 174, 254, 372–3
Morecambe and Wise Show 313
Moreno, Antonio 9, 10, 95, 133, 171, 373–4, 438
Moreno, Rosita 374
Morgan: A Suitable Case for Treatment 409
Morgan, Michèle 99, 115, 116, 125, 187, 253, 374–5, 374, 401
Morgan, Paul 375
Morhart, Hans von 104, 109, 111
Morley, Robert 375

Morley, Sheridan 452
Morocco 97, 236, 267
The Mortal Storm 108
Moscow Art Theatre 12, 80, 169, 206, 392, 418, 419, 435, 440, 444
Mosjoukine, Ivan 10, 16, 21, 25, 31, 32–3, 77, 78–80, 81, 82, 375–6, 418
The Mosquito Coast 369
Mostovoy, Leonid 77
Motion Picture Academy 274, 297
Motion Picture Production Code (Hays Code) 56, 95, 97, 99, 207, 234
Motion Pictures Relief Fund (Motion Picture and Television Fund) 297
Moulin Rouge (1952) 350
Moulin Rouge! (2001) 360
Mourning Becomes Electra 408–9
The Mouse that Roared 429
Moussa, Ibrahim 323
The Movie Actor 47
Moving Picture World 21, 22
Mowbray, Alan 376
MPPDA (Motion Picture Producers and Distributors of America) 252–3
Mr Moto films 343
Mr Skeffington 298
Mr Smith Goes to Washington 405
Mr Wroe's Virgins 240
Mr Wu 24
Mrs Miniver 262, 466
Mrs Parkington 262
Much Ado About Nothing 187, 447
Mud and Sand 332
Der müde Tod/Destiny 223
The Mudlark 282
Mueller-Stahl, Armin 42, 268, 376–7
Mujeres al bordo de un ataque de nervios/Women on the Verge of a Nervous Breakdown 171
Mumba, Samantha 377
Mumming Birds 204
Mummy films 465
Mundin, Herbert 377
Muni, Paul 16, 38, 39, 155, 312
Muñoz Sampedro, Matilde 173
Munson, Ona 348
Murat, Jean 93n, 162, 377
Muratore, Lucien 203, 377
Murder at the Vanities 191
Murder by Death 328
Murder in the Family 358, 445
Murder on the Orient Express 180
Murnau, F. W. 28n, 207, 266, 302
Murphy's Stroke 192
Murphy's War 385
Musco, Angelo 46
Music Box 376, 377
Mussolini, Benito 40, 48–9, 400

Mussolini, Vittorio 48–9
Muti, Ornella 377, 428
Mutiny on the Bounty 304, 330, 440
Mutual 204, 408
My American Wife 373
My Beautiful Laundrette 228
My Best Friend's Wedding 145, 243
My Darling Clementine 376
My Fair Lady 58, 159, 215, 242, 287, 295, 300, 307
My Favourite Year 391–2
My Friend Flicka 358
My Friend Irma Goes West 198
My Geisha 369
My Left Foot 228, 257, 357, 387
My Life with Caroline 374
My Love Came Back 170
My Man Godfrey 245
My Official Wife 31
Myers, Mike 257
Myrtil, Odette 93n, 377–8
Les Mystères de Paris/The Mysteries of Paris 23
The Mysterious Lady 95

Naked 446
Nalder, Reggie 378
Naldi, Nita 46, 47
The Name of the Game 397
The Name of the Rose 215
Nana 82, 98, 440
Nansen, Betty 378
Napier, Alan 378
Napoléon 423
Napoleon's Barber 356
Nära livet/Brink of Life/So Close to Life 158, 448
Nasty Habits 313
National Theatre, London 245, 390
National Velvet 219
Nattevagten/Nightwatch 218
Natural Nylon 146
Naughty Marietta 328
Nava, Gregory 404
The Navigator 219
Nazimova, Alla 10, 14, 16, 23, 31, 77, 77, 78, 166, 378–9, 418
Nazis
  played by European actors 14
  played by Jews 103–11
  regime 264–5
NBC 56, 429
Neagle, Anna 330, 379
Neame, Ronald 62
Nederlands in zeven lessen/Dutch in seven lessons 295
Neeson, Liam 195, 309, 310, 379–80
Negra, Diane 3, 15, 310

Negri, Pola 14, 16, 40, 46, 47, 79, 96, 98, 265–6, 266, 285, 319, 373, 380–1, *380*, 399, 438
Negulesco, Jean 128, 255, 282
Nell, Nathalie 381
Nemirovich-Danchenko, Vladimir 80, 418
Nero 45
Nero, Franco 313, 381
Nesbitt, Cathleen 381
Netherlands, the 381
Neue Illustrierte Filmwoche 234
Never Again 297
Never Let Me Go 372
Never Say Never Again 188, 214
Never So Few 341
Never on Sunday 279, 363–4
Neville, Edgar 438
New Wine 426
New Year's Day 223
New York Critics Circle 310
New York Dramatic Mirror 22
New York Film Company 204
The New York Herald Tribune 116, 230
New York Morning Telegraph 23
New York Stories 268
The New York Times 25, 73, 116, 117, 125, 129, 207, 434
New Yorker 116
Newell, Mike *276*, 412
Newley, Anthony 381–2
Newman, Nanette 382
Newman, Paul 162, 288, 406
Newton, Robert 382
The Next Best Thing 145
Niblo, Fred 32, 95, 96
Nicholas, Gregor 430
Nicholson, Jack 369
Nielsen, Asta 259
Nielsen, Brigitte 382
Nielsen, Connie 12, 382
Nieto, José 9, 133, 382, 438
A Night at an English Music Hall 330
A Night in Casablanca 416
Night of the Demon 347
Night on Earth 178, 377
The Night of the Hunter 330
The Night of the Iguana 195
The Night of Love 96
Night Must Fall 286
Night People 100
Night Train to Munich 287
The Night Visitor 452
Nighthawks 288
Nightwatch 359
Nijinsky 310
Nijinsky, Vaclav 78
Nikolić, Dragan 470
Nil by Mouth 146

Nilsson, Anna Q. 300, 382–3
Nin, Anaïs 231
La niña de tus ojos/The Girl of Your Dreams
    220
Nine Hours to Rama 193
Nine Months 144, 277
1900/Novecento 233
Ninotchka 3, 12, 95, 106, 191, 261, 273,
    418, 419
The Ninth Gate 389
Nissen, Greta 383–4, 422
Niven, David 9, 13, 212, 216, 244, 319,
    384–5, 386, 453
Nixon 141, 301
No Highway 98
No Mercy 326
No Retreat, No Surrender 457
Nobody's Baby 142
Nocturnes 276
Noiret, Philippe 385
Nomads 192
None but the Lonely Heart 241, 275
Nora 146
Norlund, Evy 385
Normand, Mabel 23, 337
Norris, Chuck 457
North by Northwest 275
The North Star 419
Northcliffe, Lord 204
Notorious 95, 99–100, 179, 275, 368, 406,
    426
Le notti bianche/White Nights 423
Notting Hill 144, 277
Nous irons à Monte Carlo/We Will All Go to
    Monte Carlo 295
Novaković, Rado 351
Novarro, Ramón 135, 154, 252, 370, 375
Novello, Ivor 164, 385
Novocaine 185
Now Barabbas 194
Now, Voyager 40, 215, 267, 293, 340–1, 402
Nowhere to Go but Up 445
Nowhere to Run 458
Noyce, Phillip 430
Una nueva y gloriosa nación/The Charge of
    the Gauchos 451
Nugent, Frank 49
La Nuit américaine/Day for Night 182, 451
The Nun and the Sergeant 82
Nurse Edith Cavell 110
Nuts in May 332

Oakhurst 170
Oberon, Merle 62, 64, 202, 287, 330,
    385–6, 386, 389
Oberst Redl/Colonel Redl 376
O'Brien, Pat 309
O'Casey, Sean 157

O'Connell, Jack 264
O'Connor, Una 309, 387
O'Conor, Hugh 387
Octopussy 125, 128–9, 130, 316
O'Dea, Denis 309, 360, 387
Odets, Clifford 405
L'Odissea 244
Of Love and Desire 386
Of Love and Shadows 171
The Officer's Mess 328
Oh! What a Lovely War 165
O'Hara, Maureen 310, 387–8, *388*
O'Herlihy, Dan 388
O'Keefe, Dennis 240
Oland, Warner 165
Olcott, Sidney 24
The Old Dark House 329
Old Vic theatre, London 194, 389, 432
Oldman, Gary 14, 142, 143, 146, 388–9,
    455
Olin, Lena 389, 423, 430
Oliveira, Manoel de 232
Oliver! 371
Olivier, Laurence 9, 10, 12, 17, 39, 61,
    178, 187, 194, 196, 259, 273, 336, 337,
    386, *386*, 389–91, *390*, 395, 399, 404,
    432, 435, 444, 472n
Olmi, Ermanno 288
Omen III: The Final Conflict 190
On a Clear Day You Can See Forever 369,
    370
On the Line 153
Once is Not Enough 364
Once a Lady 385
Once a Thief 230
Once Upon a Crime 353
Once Upon a Time in the West 200
Ondine 295
One Flew Over the Cuckoo's Nest 223
One from the Heart 323
One Hour with You 55, 206
One in a Million 291, 297
One More River 210–11
One Night of Love 48, 234
One of Our Dinosaurs is Missing 455
One of Our Spies is Missing 357
The One that Got Away 326
One, Two, Three 193
102 Dalmatians 233
O'Neal, Tatum 340
Onegin 246
O'Neill, Eugene 408
O'Neill, Maire 309
Only the Lonely 388
Onstad, Niels 293
Ophuls, Max 7, 127, 242, 263, 315, 354,
    368, 413, 433, 442
Ordinary Decent Criminal 243

Orduña, Juan de 370
Orlacs Hände/The Hands of Orlac 460
Orlamond, Fritz 391
Orlamond, William 391
Orleneff, Pavel 78, 378
Ormond, Julia 391
Orphans of the Storm 49, 385
Orpheus Descending 349
Ortega, Juan José 136
O'Shea, Milo 391
Oshima, Nagisa 406
The Osterman Week-End 288
O'Sullivan, Maureen 310
O'Sullivan, Thaddeus 243
Oswald, Lee Harvey 389
Othello 213, 214, 435
The Other Side of Midnight 398, 457
O'Toole, Peter 310, 342, 391–2
Otsep, Fyodor 81
Ottiano, Rafaela 392
Otto e mezzo/8 ½ 334, 355
Oury, Gérard 364, 392
Ouspenskaya, Maria 77, 80, 392–3, *393*
Out of Africa 188
Out of the Fog 23, 378
Outward Bound 302, 303
Over the Moon 287
Owen, Reginald 393–4
Ozon, François 227, 406, 419–20

Pabst, G. W. 259
Pacific Palisades 72, 350
Pacino, Al 100, 240, 318
Le Pacte des loups/The Brotherhood of the
    Wolves 178
Pacula, Joanna 394, 399
Page, Geneviève 394
Paget, Sidney 406
Pagnol, Marcel 58, 193, 255
Pailhas, Géraldine 71, 73–4, 394
The Painted Veil 96
Pakula, Alan 470
Palance, Jack 214
Paley, Natalie 394
Palfi (Palfi-Andor), Lotte 12, 106, 108,
    158, 394–5
Palfi, Victor 394
Palmer, Lilli 16, 41, 395
Pan, Hermes 292
Panama Hattie 107
Paname 86
Papas, Irene 14, 279, 395–6, *395*
The Paradine Case 100, 125, 126, 127, 315,
    448, *456*, 457
Paradis perdu/Paradise Lost 401
Paramount 53–6, 58, 64, 67, 86, 97, 107,
    108, 163, 170, 191, 192, 198, 202, 207,
    208, 211, 225, 259, 267, 274, 297, 300,

314, 319, 322, 329, 340, 346, 349, 354, 366, 373, 390, 396, 397, 437, 438
Paramount British 238, 328
The Parent Trap 388
Parera, Valentín 133
Paris 193
Paris – Underground 245
Paris Calling 116, 180, 337
Paris Holiday 245, 377
Paris-Precinct 227
Park, Nick 412
Parker, Alan 247, 258, 301, 402
Parker, Sarah Jessica 171
Parma, Tula 396, 422, 423
Parola, Danièle 17n
Parsons, Louella 154, 173, 354
The Party 429
Pascal, Gabriel 303, 319
Passage to Marseille 116, 121n, *374*, 375
La Passante du Sans-Souci/The Passerby 425
The Passing of the Third Floor Back 250
The Passion of Ayn Rand 72, 369
La Passion Béatrice 72
The Passion of the Christ 178
Passport to Pimlico 300
Pasternak, Joe 257, 362
The Path to War 146n
Pathé 185, 252, 283
Pathé-Exchange 252
Patrick, Nigel 396
Patriot Games 144, 251
Pavan, Marisa 169, 312, 396
Pavlova, Anna 78
Pawle, Lennox 396
Paxinou, Katina 279, 368, 396–7, *396*, 405
Payment Deferred 329
Pearl Harbor 248
Peck, Gregory 99, 182, 206, 295, 324, 441, 448, 457
Peckinpah, Sam 230, 470
Peeping Tom 183
Pelle erobreren/Pelle the Conqueror 443
Peña, Julio 133, 397, 438
Pender troupe 274
Penn, Arthur 250
Penn, Sean 100
Pennino, Francesco 51n
Pension Mimosas 416
Pentathlon 347
Penthouse magazine 359
A People Eternal 299
People magazine 153, 172
The People vs. Zsa Zsa Gabor 258
The People's Choice 322
Pépé le Moko 87, 115, 118, 224, 253, 327
Per qualche dollari in più/For a Few Dollars More 323
Perdita Durango 173–4

Perez, Rosie 174
Perez, Vincent 71, 72, 74, 397
The Perfect Gentleman 66
The Perfect Storm 41
Perfect Strangers 238
Perfect Understanding 389
Performance 250, 314
Perides, Vasilis 368
Perkins, Anthony 342
Perola, Danièle 253
Perón, Juan 402
Perret, Léonce 21, 24, 189, 229
Persona 158, 452
The Persuaders 372
Pertwee, Sean 148n, 397
Pesci, Joe 153
Pétain, Philippe 119
Peter the Great 428
Peter Pan 420
Peters, Hélène 28n
Petersen, Wolfgang 41, 401
Le petit café 24, 338
Petit, Roland 314
Petites coupures 428
The Petrified Forest 303
Petrović, Aleksandar 244
Petulia 208
Phaedra 364
The Phantom 470
The Phantom Menace 146
The Phantom of the Opera 49, 402, 405–6
Philadelphia 171
The Philadelphia Story 275
Phillips, Alastair 125
Phroso 23
La Pianiste/The Piano Teacher 306
The Picasso Summer 237
Piccadilly 366
Piccoli, Michel 397
Pichel, Irving 100
Pickford, Mary 10, 26n, 204, 297, 303, 438
Pickup 283
The Picture of Dorian Gray 256, 421
The Piece of Lace 22
Pièges/Personal Column 207
Piel, Harry 266
Piel Canela 136
Pierlot, Francis 397
Pigliai, Bruno 386
Pilar-Morin 22, 23, 252, 398
Pin-Up Girl 224
The Pink Panther 200, 384
The Pink Panther Strikes Again 240
The Pink Panther series 200, 341, 429, 436
Pinon, Dominique 398
Pinter, Harold 398
Pintoff, Ernest 200
Pipe Dream 159

Pirandello, Luigi 100n
  As You Desire Me 47
La Piscine/The Swimming Pool 425
Pisier, Marie-France 398
La Piste des Géants 270
The Pit and the Pendulum 439
Pitt, Brad 171, 391
Pittsburgh 98
Placido, Michele 313, 398
Planet of the Apes 142, 358, 464
Play Dirty 196
The Playboy of Paris 55
The Player 422
Pleasence, Donald 398–9
The Pledge 369
Plein soleil/Purple Noon 230
Plenty 360
Pleshkoff, Michael 32
The Plough and the Stars 358
Plowright, Joan 399
Podestà, Rossana 313, 399
Poe, Edgar Allan 86, 162
La Pointe courte 385
Poiré, Jean-Marie 210
Poirot films 455–6
Poland 399
Polanski, Roman 182, 232, 277, 323, 398, 399–400, 428
Polgar, Alfred 103, 106
Polish Blood 376
Polish Wedding 430
The Politician's Wife 240
Politiquerías 229
Pollack, Sydney 51n, 240, 423, 443
Polonskii, Iosif 33
Poltergeist: The Legacy 230
Pommer, Erich 28n, 105, 314, 325, 330, 387
Pons, Lily 400
Poor Cow 439
Pope, Tim 72
Poppies Are Also Flowers 356
Porcasi, Paul 16, 49, 312, 400
Porten, Henny 266
Porter, Cole 314, 364
Les Portes de la nuit/Gates of the Night 120
Il Portiere di notte/The Night Porter 406
Portman, Eric 400
Portugal 400–1
Postlethwaite, Pete 401
The Postman 467
Potente, Franka 41, 268, 401
Potter, Sally 208, 442
Powell, Jane 209
Powell, Michael 176, 183, 431, 445
Powell, William 85, 162, 404
The Power of Darkness 273
Power, Tyrone 87, 89, 162, 166, 324, 373, 396, 401

Powers, Patrick 309
Prague Duet 430
El precio de un beso/One Mad Kiss 373
Predator 426
Preminger, Otto 106, 188, 231, 250, 340, 432, 457
Préparer vos mouchoirs/Get Out Your Handkerchiefs 233
El presidio 438
Presle, Micheline 129, 254, 374, 401
Presley, Elvis 158, 336, 416
Pressburger, Emeric 176, 445
Presumed Innocent 422
Prêt-à-Porter/Ready to Wear 155, 342, 356
Prévert, Jacques 120, 279, 333
The Pride and the Passion 342
Pride and Prejudice 216, 248, 390
Priestley, J. B. 329
Primary Colors 447
The Prime Minister 269
The Prime of Miss Jean Brodie 435
Prince 428
Prince of Foxes 181, 396
The Prince and the Pauper 440
Prince of Players 194
The Prince and the Showgirl 390
The Princess Bride 242
The Princess Diaries 161
La principessa misteriosa 50n
The Prisoner 359
The Prisoner of Zenda 67, 191, 202, 273, 319
The Private Affairs of Bel Ami 421
The Private Life of Don Juan 216
The Private Life of Henry VIII 62–4, 175, 238, 328, 329, 330, 340, 385
Private Lives 389
The Private Lives of Elizabeth and Essex 54
The Private Navy of Sgt O'Farrell 231
Private Worlds 86, 87, 186
Privileged 276
Le Procès de Mary Dugan 86, 186
Prochnow, Jürgen 42, 268, 401–2
The Prodigal 403
The Professionals 200
Profumo, John 360
Proietti, Gigi (Luigi) 312, 402
Project Arts Theatre 379
Promise at Dawn 364
The Proposition 187
Proyas, Alex 72
Pryce, Jonathan 402
Pterodactyl Woman from Beverly Hills 258
Publix theatres 54
Pudovkin, V. 471
Puente, Tito 138
Puglia, Frank 16, 49, 312, 402–3, *403*
Pull My Daisy 430

Pulp Fiction 231, 417
Pulver, Lilo 403
Pumping Iron 426
The Punisher 347
Puppets 47
Purcell, Noel 403
Purdom, Edmund 403
The Pursuit of Happiness 429
Purviance, Edna 139, 204
Put na jug/El camino del sur/Southbound 315
Pygmalion 298, 303

Le Quai des brumes/Port of Shadows 117, 118, 374
Quand la femme s'en mêle/When a Woman Meddles 230
Quatorze juillet 86
Quayle, Anthony 404
Queen Christina 96, 97, 260, 389
Queen of the Damned 397
Queen Elizabeth 28n, 181
Queen of Outer Space 258
Quennessen, Valérie 404
Querelle 373
The Quest 458
Question 7 163
The Quiet American 145
The Quiet Man 248, 358, 388
Quinn, Anthony 206, 342, 349, 395
La quinta marcha 133
Quintet 263
Quiz Show 143, 246, 428
Quo Vadis (1951) 264, 320, 455
Quo Vadis? (1913) 27n

Rabagliati, Alberto 47, 404, 451
Rabal, Francisco 404
Radford, Basil 404
Radio City Music Hall 451
Raffles 213, 384
Rage in Heaven 99
The Rage of Paris 99, 226
Raiders of the Lost Ark 356
The Railway Children 155
Raimi, Sam 379
Rain Man 271
Rainer, Luise 12, 40, 95, 98, 106, 265, 267, 404–5
Rains, Claude *4*, 16, 100, 116, 117, 330, 368, 405–6, *405*, 455
The Rains of Ranchipur 194
Raintree County 396
Ralston, Vera 64, 223
Rambo III 347
Rampling, Charlotte 182, 406
Ramsaye, Terry 23
Rancho Notorious 98

Randolf, Anders 423
Randolph, Jane 99
Random Harvest 213, 262
Random Hearts 428
Rank Organisation 61, 64, 67, 319, 353, 368, 409, 432
  'Charm School' 310
Rapf, Harry 225
Rapper, Irving 321
Rapture 273
Rasputin and the Empress 48
Rathbone, Basil 186–7, 271, 406, *407*, 453
Ratoff, Gregory 99, 179, 199, 407
Rattigan, Terence 129, 298, 337
Raucourt, Jules 177, 407, 463
The Raven 317
Ravenous 200
Ray, Nicholas 9, 339, 360
RCA 56
Rea, Stephen 408
Reagan, Ronald 297
Rebecca 390
Der Rebell/The Rebel 173, 266
The Reckless Moment 354, 442
The Recruit 244
Red Dawn 419
Red Dragon 143, 246, 301
Red Heat 426
The Red Lantern 23, 378, 379
Red Scorpion 347
The Red Shoes 176, 431
Red Sonja 426
Red-Headed Woman 186
Redford, Robert 51n, 143, 246, 428
Redgrave, Corin 408, 409, 430
Redgrave, Lynn 408, 409
Redgrave, Michael 62, 66, 408–9
Redgrave, Vanessa 55, 381, 409, 412
Reed, Carol 287, 304, 340, 341, 455, 457
Reed, Oliver 409
Reeve, Christopher 430
Reeves, Keanu 347, 420
Reeves, Michael 317
Les Régates de San Francisco 263
La Règle du Jeu 224
Reich Film Chamber 265
Reichow, Otto 104, 105, 109, 409–10
Reichskristallnacht 108
Reid, Beryl 469
La Reine Margot/Queen Margot 153, 397
Reinhardt, Luise 404
Reinhardt, Max 80, 207, 235–6, 237, 346, 380, 424, 441
Reisz, Karel 127
Réjane, Gabrielle 21, 181
Reliance 238
The Reluctant Debutante 144, 287
The Remains of the Day 276, 447

Remarque, Erich Maria 236, 403
Remington Steele 192
Remorques 115
Renaldo, Duncan 356
Renavent, Georges 251, 410–11
Rendez-vous 71
Rendez-vous de juillet/Rendezvous in July 199, 263
Rennie, Michael 411
Reno, Jean 71, 72, 74, 210, 411
Renoir, Jean 116, 118, 121, 187, 196, 224, 227, 253, 258, 278, 433, 442
Renouart, Jeanne 278
The Replacement Killers 41
Replicant 458
Le Repos du guerrier/Love on a Pillow 364
Republic Studios 223
Requiem for a Heavyweight 214
The Rescuers 258
Reservoir Dogs 417
Resident Evil 42
Restoration 277
Resurrection 440
Resurrection Man 449
Le Retour de Martin Guerre 233
Retribution 238
The Return of Chandu 155
Return of the Jedi 282
Return of the Seven 411
The Return of the Seven 445
The Return of Sherlock Holmes 192
Return to Peyton Place 291
Reuben, Reuben 215
Reunion in Vienna 51n
Revelation 378
The Revengers 285
Reversal of Fortune 310
Révolte dans la prison 86, 186
Revolution 323
Rey, Fernando 263, 411
Rey, Roberto 438
Reynolds, Burt 232, 366
Reynolds, Debbie 416
Reynolds, Lynn 154
Rhapsody 262
Rhys-Davies, John 411–12
Rhythm on the Range 322
Ricciardi, William (Guglielmo) 46–7, 312, 412
Rich Man, Poor Girl 426
Rich, Young and Pretty 226–7
Richard III 360
Richards, Denise 72
Richardson, Joely 409, 412
Richardson, Miranda 412
Richardson, Natasha 379, 409, 412–13
Richardson, Ralph 5, 389, 413
Richardson, Tony 412, 469

Il richiamo del cuore/The Calling from the Heart 420
Rickman, Alan 14, 141, 142, 413, 455
Rigaud, Georges 413
Rigg, Diana 413–14
The Right to Lie 231
The Ring 191
Rio Grande 388
Risdon, Elizabeth 414
The Rising of the Moon 239
Ritchie, Guy 430
Ritzau, Erik von 414
Riva, David 235
Riva, Maria 120, 121n, 236
  Marlene Dietrich by Her Daughter 235
Rive Gauche 259
The River 216, 442
Rivette, Jacques 71
RKO 56, 62, 206, 237, 242, 255, 293, 297, 303, 330, 357, 371, 374, 382, 388, 389, 396, 400, 408, 433, 463
Roach, Hal 222, 332
Road to Perdition 298
The Road to Wellville 301
The Road to Yesterday 25
The Roaring Twenties 414
Rob Roy 417
Robbery 170
Robbins, Tim 465
The Robe 194, 432
Roberts, Julia 145, 179, 243, 247, 277, 470
Roberts, Rachel 414
Robertson, John Stuart 96
Robertson, Pat 85, 88
Robeson, Paul 64
Robin, Dany 414–15
Robin Hood 455
Robin Hood: Prince of Thieves 141, 182, 413
Robin and Marian 215, 295
Robinson, Edward G. 16, 39, 42n, 173, 303, 312, 401, 416, 441
Robson, Flora 9, 415
Roc, Patricia 198, 415
Rocco e i suoi fratelli/Rocco and His Brothers 230, 270
Rochefort, Charles de 10, 25, 199, 415
  Le Film de mes Souvenirs 415
The Rock 215
The Rocketeer 142
Rocketship X-M 355
The Rocky Horror Picture Show 222
Rocky IV 346, 347
Rodgers and Hammerstein 159
Rodriguez, Robert 138, 171
Roeg, Nicolas 185, 208, 250, 430
Rogers, Ginger 116, 169, 183, 256, 258, 288, 304, 313, 364, 384
Rohmer, Eric 176, 269

Le Roi du cirque 28n
Rolf, Tutta 415, 423
Rolfe, Guy 415
Rollerball 72
Rolling in Money 340
Rolling Stone 171
Rolling Stones 314
Roma città aperta/Rome, Open City 348
Romain, Yvonne 416
Roman Holiday 48, 201, 295
The Roman Spring of Mrs Stone 337
Romance 95, 229
Romania 416
Romberg, Sigmund 314
Rome, Stewart 416
Romeo is Bleeding 389
Romeo and Juliet 238, 303, 304, 406
Romeo, Rosario 47
Romola 50n
La Ronde 263
Ronet, Maurice 416
Ronin 72, 144, 411, 433
Room at the Top 288, 432
A Room with a View 184, 198, 228, 421
Rooney, Mickey 333, 457
Roos, Camilla 416
Roosevelt, Franklin D. 116
Roosevelt Hotel, Hollywood 453
The Roots of Heaven 278, 304
Rope 211
Rope of Sand 198
Rosay, Françoise 7, 86, 251, 253, 416–17, 417
The Rose 176
Rose, David E. 353
The Rose Garden 452
The Rose Tattoo 348, 396
Roseanna's Grave 411
Rosing, Bodil 417
Rossellini, Isabella 180
Rossellini, Roberto 99, 180, 348
Rossen, Robert 227
Roth, Tim 14, 142, 146, 417–18, 455
Rotha, Paul 435
Rowing in the Wind 276
Rowlands, Gena 300
Royal Academy of Dramatic Art (RADA) 391
Royal Danish Theatre 383
Royal Dramatic Theatre, Stockholm 179, 259, 441, 443, 448
Royal Shakespeare Company 245
Royal Wedding 209
Rubens, Peter Paul 177
Rubin, Robert 366
Rudolph, Alan 176
Rue de l'estrapade 316
Der Ruf/The Last Illusion 325

Ruggles of Red Gap 330
Ruiz, Raul 232, 306
The Ruling Class 391, 392
Ruman, Sig 104, 105, 107, 109, 273, 418
Run of the Arrow 136, 371
Run for Cover 297, 339
Run for the Sun 304
The Runaway Bride 219
The Running Man 426
Russell, Ken 276
Russell, Rosalind 191, 318
Russell-Taylor, John 61, 67
Russia (former Soviet Union) 418–19
Russian actors 77–83
Russian Club, Hollywood 407
Russian Orthodox Society, Los Angeles 460
Russian–American Arts Club 7, 33, 81, 460
The Russians are Coming, the Russians are Coming 419
Ryan's Daughter 366, 368
Rydell, Mark 176
Ryder, Winona 171
Ryen, Richard 419

Sabotage 300, 340
Saboteur 446
Sabrina 295, 391, 467
Sachs, Gunther 174
The Sacred Flame 463
Sagan, Françoise 231, 278, 363, 369
Sagnier, Ludivine 419–20
Sahara 363
The Saint 372, 419, 421, 430
Saint Francis of Assisi 96
Saint Laurent, Yves 232, 269
A Sainted Devil 47, 224, 327, 400
Sakall, S. Z. 16, 420
Le salaire de la peur/The Wages of Fear 219, 369, 458
Salome 379, 443
Salome of the Tenements 25
Saltzman, Harry 9, 196, 214
Salute to France 227
The Salvation Hunters 356
Salvini, Sandro 32, 45, 312, 420
Salvini, Tommaso 45, 46
The Salzburg Connection 188
Samson and Delilah 327
San Francisco 47
Sánchez-Gijón, Aitana 100, 420
Sanctuary 370
Sanda, Dominique 420
Sanders, George 258, 273, 420–1, *421*, 455
Sandoval, Antonio 138
Sands, Julian 421–2

Sands of the Kalahari 170
Sano, Marcel de 28n
Santa Lucia Luntana 47
Santell, Alfred 96
The Sarah Churchill Show 209
Sarandon, Susan 232
Sarati le Terrible/Sarati the Terrible 333
Saratoga Trunk 415
Sardou, Victorien
  Cleopatra 21
  Theodora 21
  La Tosca 21, 22
Sartre, Jean-Paul 279
Såsom i en spegel/Through a Glass Darkly 443
Saturday Night and Sunday Morning 245, 247, 414
Saura, Carlos 427
Sautet, Claude 71
Saval, Dany 422
Saving Private Ryan 268, 427
Savior 451
Savitsky, Vyacheslav 32, 418
Scacchi, Greta 422
Scandal 360
Scandinavia 422–3
Scaramouche 273
Scarface 49, 312
The Scarlet Empress 97, 98, 236
The Scarlet Pimpernel 303
Scener ur ett äktenskap/Scenes from a Marriage 452
Scent of a Woman 163
Schary, Dore 319, 320
Schatzberg, Jerry 73
Schell, Maria 41, 423–4, 442
Schell, Maximilian 42, 235, 423, 424, 442
Schiff-Bassermann, Else 176
Schildkraut, Joseph 38, 424
Schildkraut, Rudolph 38, 424–5
Schindler's List 141, 143, 246, 379
Schlesinger, John 208
Schlöndorff, Volker 427
Schmidhauser, Hannes 442
Schneider, Magda 425
Schneider, Romy 14, 41, 268, 425
Schnitzler, Arthur 38
Schrader, Paul *13*, 359
Schreck, Max 336
Schumacher, Joel 243
Schumm, Hans 104, 105, 109, 425
Schünzel, Reinhold 14, 104, 105, 109, 426
Schwarzenegger, Arnold 15, 16, 42, 170, 225, 347, 404, 426–7, 447, 457
Schweiger, Til 17n, 41, 42, 268, 427
Schygulla, Hanna 41, 427–8
Scipione l'africano 48
Scofield, Paul 143, 428

Scola, Ettore 427
Scorsese, Martin 47, 48, 229, 333, 402
Scott, George C. 413, 420
Scott, Janette 428
Scott, Ridley 218, 233, 288, 313, 411
Scott Thomas, Kristin 143, 428
Screen Actors Guild 297, 345, 459
Screen International 229
Sea Devils 392
Sea Fury 170
The Sea Wolves 384
The Seagull 432
The Searchers 373, 438
Seaton, George 100
The Second Hundred Years 332
Secret Agent 343
The Secret beyond the Door 408
The Secret Diary of Sigmund Freud 351
The Secret Garden 435
The Secret Invasion 457
The Secret People 295
The Secret of Santa Vittoria 349
Secrets 303
Séeburger brothers 251
Segal, George 313, 371
Sei tu l'amore 47
Seiler, Lewis 98
Seldes, Gilbert 204
Sellars, Elizabeth 9, 428–9
Selleck, Tom 430
Sellers, Peter 240, 425, 429, 436
Selwart, Tonio 104, 105, 109, 429
Selznick, David O. 99, 120, 125, 126, 128, 158, 179, 189, 202, 230, 254, 273, 303, 315, 323, 336, 386, 389, 457
Selznick, Irene 273
Selznick, Myron 336
Semon, Larry 25
Sennett, Mack 204, 332
Sense and Sensibility 276, *276*, 447
Senso 457
Separate Tables 298, 384
Sequence 127
Šerbedžija, Rade 14, 429–30, 470
Serda, Julia 17n
Serenade 136, 371
The Sergeant 366
Serna, Assumpta 133, 430
Sernas, Jacques 9, 430
The Serpent's Egg/Das Schlangenei 452
The Servant 250, 366
Service for Ladies 303
Serzhinsky, Ivan 375
Seven Days for Elisabeth 291
The Seven Little Foys 462
The Seven Minutes 226, 318
Seven Sinners 98
Seven Years Bad Luck 24

Seventh Heaven 205, 433
The Seventh Sign 402
The Seventh Veil 67, 353, 448
Séverin 22, 252
Sevilla, Carmen 136
Sevilla de mis amores 370
Sexy Beast 322
Seymour, Jane 430
Seyrig, Delphine 430–1
Shadows 362
Shadows of Paris 415
Shakespeare in Love 245
Shakespeare Memorial Theatre 391
Shalako 186
Shall, Theo 266
Shall We Dance? 258
Shallow Grave 359
Shampoo 208
Shanghai 32, 87, 186
Shanghai Express 97, 182, *235*, 236, 267
Sharif, Omar 356
Sharpe 143, 177
Shatner, William 145
Shattered 422
Shaw, Fiona 431
Shaw, George Bernard 65, 66, 199, 204, 283, 285, 330
  Pygmalion 199, 295, 298
Shaw, Robert 431
She Done Him Wrong 274
Shearer, Moira 431
Shearer, Norma 92*n*, 95, 206, 303
Sheen, Martin 381
Shelley, Mary 210
The Shepherd King 45
Sheridan, Ann 309
Sheridan, Jim 195, 257, 286
Sheridan, Peter 195
Sherlock Holmes films 271, 296, 299, 406
Sherriff, R. C., *Journey's End* 210–11
The Shielding Shadow 24
Shields, Arthur 247, 309, 431
Shine 376, 377
Ship Café 191
Ship of Fools 337, 432, 465
Shipman, David 159
Shivers 439
The Shoes of the Fisherman 49, 247
Shoot the Moon 247
Shooting Stars 155
The Shop Around the Corner 40, 424
Shopping 333
A Shot in the Dark 436
Shoulder Arms 204
The Show Down 297
The Show of Shows 193, 202
Showdown in Little Tokyo 347
Shrek 202

Shriver, Maria 427
Shubert brothers (Lee, Samuel S. and Jacob J.) 78
Shubert, J. J. 104
Sid and Nancy 389
Side Streets 315
Sidney, Sylvia 64
Sieben Ohrfeigen/Seven Slaps 288
Sieber, Rudolph 236
Siegel, David 442
Siegel, Don 423
The Sign of the Cross 68, 329
Sign of the Pagan 445
Le Signe du lion/The Sign of the Lion 269
La signora di tutti 368
Signoret, Simone 125, 432
Le Silence est d'or/Man about Town 207
The Silence of the Lambs 141, 143, 301
The Silent Command 49
Silent Witness 166
Silverado 210
Silvestre 231
Simian Films 277
Simmons, Jean 273, 432–3, 454
Simon, François 443
Simon, Michel 443
Simon, René, school 315
Simon, Simone 14, 89, 99, 125, 126, 167, 187, 433
The Simple-Minded Murder 433
Simpson, Philip 142
Sinatra, Frank 158, 174, 182, 341, 375, 460
Sinbad and the Eye of the Tiger 430
Singer, Bryan 360
The Singing Detective 259, 465
The Single Standard 96, 97
Single-Handed 298
Sins of the Fathers 314
Siodmak, Robert 154, 157, 190, 198, 207, 370, 413, 446
Siren of Atlantis 169
Sirens 277
Sirk, Douglas 128, 323, 403, 445
Sissi trilogy 425
Six Weeks 371
Sjöström, Victor 24, 28*n*, 95, 224, 285, 391, 400, 422
Det sjunde inseglet/The Seventh Seal 158, 441
Skarsgård, Stellan 423, 433
The Skin Game 283
Skipworth, Alison 433–4
Skupljaci perja/I Even Met Happy Gypsies 244
Sky Riders 170
Slater, Christian 153
The Sleeping Beauty 330
Sleeping with the Enemy 179

Sleepy Hollow 412
Sleuth 196
Slezak, Walter 104, 105, 107, 109, 434
Sloman, Edward 25
A Small Rebellion 432
Small Time Crooks 277, 451
The Smiling Lieutenant 54, 55, 206
Smith, C. Aubrey 61, 62, 222, 291, 330, 434–5, *434*, 453
Smith, Constance 435
Smith, Maggie 435
Smultronstallet/Wild Strawberries 448
Snatch 430
Snegoff, Leonid 77
Snow White and the Seven Dwarfs 51*n*
The Snows of Kilimanjaro 324
So Dark the Night 264
So I Married an Axe Murderer 257
So This Is Paris 198
S.O.B. 161
A Society Exile 50*n*
Soderbergh, Steven 100, 247, 326, 439, 470
Sodom and Gomorrah 170
Søeberg, Camilla 435
Sokoloff, Vladimir 77, 80, 418, 435–6, *436*
Soldaat van Oranje/Soldier of Orange 288, 326
A Soldier's Daughter Never Cries 73, 335, 364
Solodukhin, Gavrila 35*n*
Solomon and Sheba 341
Solondz, Todd 41
Solow, Eugene 367
Sombrero 262
Some Mother's Son 369
Sommer, Elke 42, 436
Son altesse d'amour 92
Son of Frankenstein 406
Son of the Pink Panther 178, 200
The Son of the Sheik 32, 173, 455
Son of Zorro 219
The Song of Bernadette 215
The Song of the Flame 33
Song of Russia 419
The Song of Songs 97, 155
Song without End 183, 199
Sonnenstrahl/Gardez le sourire 92
Sonntag des Lebens 302
Sophie's Choice 470
The Sopranos 50
The Sorcerers 317
Sorel, Jean 436
The Sound and the Fury 337
The Sound of Music 161, 170, 339
Soussanin, Nicholas 77, 80, 437
Soutendijk, Renée 437
South Pacific 190

Spaak, Catherine 437
Spacey, Kevin 243, 333
Spain 437–8
Spanish actors 133–9
Spanish Affair/Aventura para dos 136
The Spanish Dancer 373
Spanish Film Academy 420
The Spanish Gardener 302
The Spanish Jade 415
Spanish Theatre, New York 219
Sparkuhl, Theodor 105
Spartacus 330, 390, 432, 455
Le Spectre vert/The Unholy Night 177, 272, 345
Spellbound 99, 179, 206
Spice World 372
Spider 246
Spielberg, Steven 51*n*, 143, 244, 245–6, 290, 333, 336, 379, 412, 451
The Spiral Staircase 157, 190
The Spoilers 98
Spoor, George 27*n*
Spy Kids 172
Spy Smasher 425
The Spy Who Came In from the Cold 222
Stage Fright 98, 280, 466
Stage Women's War Relief Fund 357
Stagecoach 362
Stahl, John 412
Staiger, Janet 40
Stalag 17 418
Stalin, Josef 273
Stallone, Sylvester 171, 288, 290, 312, 346, 347, 382, 426
Stamp, Terence 176, 241, 287, 288, 438–9
Stanislavsky, Konstantin 12, 80, 392, 435, 471
Stanley and Livingstone 285
Stanwyck, Barbara 95, 99, 190, 309
A Star is Born 274, 354, 438
Star Spangled Rhythm 400
star trading 62–4
Star Trek 145
Star Trek: Generations 145, 359
Star Trek: Nemesis 145
Star Trek films 141, 361, 441
Star Wars 142, 187, 223, 282, 336, 359
Star Wars: Episode 1 – The Phantom Menace 379
Star Wars films 146
Stardust Memories 175, 406
Starlight Roof 159
Stars and Bars 228
The Stars Look Down 408
State of Grace 142
Stay Hungry 426
Steele, Barbara 439
Steibruch/The Quarry 442

Steiger, Rod 363, 371
Stella 363
Sten, Anna 10, 14, 40, 77, 81–2, 98, 419, 439–40, *439*
The Stepford Wives 249, 382
Stephenson, Henry 440
Sternberg, Josef von *30*, 33, 80–1, 97, 155, 169, 192, 236, 266, 314, 356, 437
Stévenin, Jean-François 441
Stevens, George 443
Stevens, Risë 60*n*
Stevenson, Robert 335
Stewart, James 98, 174, 218, 263, 433, 450
Stewart, Patrick *141*, 145, 146, 441
Stigmata 195
Stiles-Allen, Lillian 159
Still Life 304
Stiller, Mauritz 28*n*, 95, 96, 97, 259, 285, 319, 422
The Sting 431
Stone, Oliver 141, 244, 301, 451
Stone, Sharon 154, 422
Storia d'amore 271
Storia di ordinaria follia/Tales of Ordinary Madness 377
Stormare, Max von 423
Stormare, Peter 441
The Story of Mankind 327
Storytelling 41
Stössel, Ludwig 14, 104, 105, 106, 108, 109, 441
Stracheck, Günther Peter 104
Stradner, Rose 441
The Strand Magazine 406
Strange Bedfellows 341
Strange Days 246
The Strange Death of Adolf Hitler 103, 109, 325
Strangers on a Train 459
Strasberg, Lee 323, 430, 455
Strasberg, Paula 390
Straw Dogs 264
Streep, Meryl 188, 360
Street Angel 49, 404, 450
Street of Sin 169
A Streetcar Named Desire (film) 337, 445
A Streetcar Named Desire (stage version) 273
Streisand, Barbra 369, 370
Strictly Dishonorable 412
Stroheim, Erich von 40, 47, 48, 208, 272, 297, 311, 414, 461
Stromboli 180
Stuart, Nick 416
The Stud 212
The Student Prince 403
Der Student von Prag/The Student of Prague 460

Studlar, Gaylyn 127
The Stunt Man 391
Sturges, John 193, 398
Sturges, Preston 253, 287, 365
Stürme der Leidenschaft/Tempest 440
Submarine Patrol 279
Subspecies films 302
Subway 328
Sudden Death 458
Suez 87, 89, 91, 162
Sullavan, Margaret 187, 368
Sullivan, Francis L. 442
Summer 364
Summer Lovers 404
Summer and Smoke 288
Summertime 49, 189, 368
The Sun Also Rises 278
Sun Valley Serenade 292
Sunday Bloody Sunday 313
Die Sünderin/The Sinner 324
The Sundowners 320
Sunny Side Up 346
Sunrise at Campobello 262
Sunset Boulevard 383
Sunshine 246
Superman 469
Superscope process 136
Supertramp 321
Surrender 25, 80, 376
Surviving Picasso 301
Susan Lenox, Her Fall and Rise 96
Suspect 379
Suspicion 275, 314
Sutherland, Donald 233
Svengali 156
Svensk Filmindustri 179
Swamp Thing 125, 128, 316
The Swan 282
Swanson, Gloria 28*n*, 96, 234, 334, 350, 352, 373, 389
Swashbuckler 431
Sweeney, Gael 144
Sweet Liberty 196
Swept from the Sea 397
Swimming Pool 420
Swinburne, Nora 5, 442
Swing Time 364
Swinton, Tilda 442, 462
Swiss Family Robinson (1940) 181
The Swiss Family Robinson (1960) 368
Switzerland 442–3
Sydney, Basil 443
Sydow, Max von 15, 157, 422, 423, 443, 448
Sylvia Scarlett 283, 394
La Symphonie pastorale 375
Synge, J. M. 157
Szabó, István 188, 376

Tacchella, Jean-Charles 174–5, 398
Tacones lejanos/High Heels 153
Taffin 192
Tairov, Alexander 462
Take Her, She's Mine 250
A Tale of Two Cities 406
A Talent for Loving 394
The Talented Mr Ripley 333
Tales of Manhattan 255
Talk of Angels 220
The Talk of the Town 322
The Taming of the Shrew 468
Tamiroff, Akim 77, 82, 322, 419, 443–4,
    444
Tandy, Jessica 444–5
Tank Girl 359
Tarantino, Quentin 231, 417
Target: Harry 406
Targets 317
Tarnished Reputations 231–2
Tarzan, the Ape Man 286
Tarzan and the She-Devil 459
Tautou, Audrey 445
Tavaszi zapor 92
Tavernier, Bertrand 72, 385
Taviani brothers 229
Taxi 218
Taxi 2 218
Taxifahrer Bänz/Taxidriver Bänz 442
Taylor, Elizabeth 129, 185, 194–5, 262,
    287, 337, 396, 435
Taylor, John Russell, Strangers in Paradise 3
Taylor, Robert 336
Taylor, Rod 445
Tchérina, Ludmilla 445
Tea and Sympathy 320
Teatro Costanzi, Rome 45
Teatro Italiano, Los Angeles 154
Teixeira, Virgilio 400, 445
Tell Me 72
Tellegen, Lou 28n, 445
Temoff, Serge 32
The Tempest 419
Temple, Shirley 16, 292, 358, 450
The Temptress 95, 96
10 371
The Ten Commandments 25, 285, 415, 464
Ten Tall Men 372
10.30 P.M. Summer 364
Tenebre 368
Tennant, Victoria 446
Teresa 162
Term of Trial 366
Terminal Velocity 323
The Terminator 426
Terminator 2: Judgment Day 426
Terminator films 426
Terry-Thomas 183

Tess 323
Das Testament des Dr Mabuse 281
Testi, Fabio 313, 446
Tetzlaff, Ted 100
Texas across the River 230
Thalberg, Irving 7, 8, 54, 56, 87, 186, 206,
    345
Thank You, Jeeves! 384
That Forsyte Woman (The Forsyte Saga) 262
That Hamilton Woman 336, 390
That Night in London 238
That Uncertain Feeling 386
Thatcher, Torin 446
That's Entertainment 193
Théâtre des Variétés, Paris 270
There's No Fish Food in Heaven 321
These Three 386
Thesiger, Ernest 446
Thewlis, David 446
They Came by Night 286
They Made Me a Fugitive 304
They Shoot Horses, Don't They? 469
The Thief of Bagdad 316, 460–1
Thieves' Highway 218
Thin Ice 291
Things are Looking Up 336
The Third Man 304, 457
13 Rue Madeleine 162
The 13th Letter 416
The 13th Warrior 172
The Thirty-Nine Steps 64, 202
This Happy Breed 367
This is Heaven 96, 173
This Land is Mine 116, 118, 121
This Other Eden 224
This Sporting Life 286, 414
Thoeren, Robert 103
The Thomas Crown Affair 192
Thomas, Jameson 446
Thomas, Terry 447
Thompson, Emma 276, 447
Thoroughly Modern Millie 161, 250
Thorpe, Richard 286
Thorsen, Sven-Ole 447–8
Those Magnificent Men 218
Three Cheers for the Irish 320
Three Coins in the Fountain 125, 189
Three Colours: White 72
Three Days of the Condor 443
The 300 Spartans 243
The Three Musketeers 24, 230, 338
The Three Must-Get-Theres 24, 338
Three Russian Girls 82
Three Smart Girls Grow Up 191
Three Stooges 425, 448
Thrill of a Romance 362
Thulin, Ingrid 5, 157, 394, 422, 448
Thunder in the East 186

Thunderball 167, 214
Thurman, Uma 231
Thyssen, Greta 448
Tierney, Gene 181, 227, 372
Tiger Bay 367
Tiger Fangs 256
Tiger Shark 401
Der Tiger von Eschnapur/The Tiger of
    Eschnapur 304
Tigerland 243
Tillie and Gus 433
Tilson Thomas, Michael 295
Time magazine 233, 428
Time after Time 359
A Time of Destiny 404
The Time Machine 377
Time Out of Mind 198
A Time to Love and a Time to Die 323, 403
Timecode 433
Timecop 457
Tiomkine, Dimitri 81
Titanic 6, 73, 416, 464, 468–9, 469
A tizennegyedik/The Fourteenth 305
To Be or Not to Be 40, 108, 109, 157
To Catch a Thief 458
To Each His Own 221
To Have and Have Not 224, 351
To Hell with the Kaiser 225
To the Victor 255
The Toast of New Orleans 164
Toback, James 323
Todd, Ann 67, 448
Todd, Mike 244–5
Todd, Richard 448
Todo sobre mi madre/All about My Mother
    133, 220
Tolstoy, Leo 419, 440
    Anna Karenina 33, 260
    The Power of Darkness 273
Tom Jones 469
Tomlinson, David 448
Tomorrow Never Dies 192, 402
Tonight We Raid Calais 253
The Tony Randall Show 414
Too Late the Hero 196
Topaz 314, 397, 415
Topkapi 364, 455
Topping, Dan 293
Tormento 51n
Torn Curtain 161
Torrence, David 448–9
Torrence, Ernest 448, 449
Torrent 95, 96, 259
Toscanini, Arturo 255
Total Recall 426
Totò 47
A Touch of Class 313
A Touch of Death 363

Touch of Evil 236
Toumanova, Tamara 77
Tourneur, Jacques 99, 346, 347, 396, 415
Tourneur, Maurice 21, 23, 167, 205, 207, 407–8
Tovarich 88, 186
Tower of London 250, 406
Townsend, Stuart 449
The Toymaker 269
Toys 259
Toys in the Attic 298
Tozzi, Giorgio 190
Tracy, Spencer 117, 119, 179, 218
Traffic 100, 470
The Trail of the Lonesome Pine 373
The Trail of the Pink Panther 429
Trainspotting 146, 359, 367
Trapeze 341
Travels with My Aunt 435
Travers, Bill 360, 449
Travers, Henry 450
La Traversée de Paris/Four Bags Full 163
Travolta, John 312, 447
Treacher, Arthur 450
Treasure Island 382
Treasure of Matecumbe 455
The Treat 397
Tree, Herbert Beerbohm 356, 405, 450
Trenker, Luis 266
Trento, Guido 45, 47, 312, 404, 450–1
Trenul fantomă/The Ghost Train 416, 461
Treut, Monika 321
The Trial 290, 353, 470
The Trial of Mary Dugan 92n
The Trial/Le Procès 425
Triangle 297
tribal elders 145–6
Tribute to a Bad Man 395
Trier, Lars von 232, 321, 433, 465
Triesault, Ivan 451
Trifunović, Sergej 14, 451, 470
Trintignant, Jean-Louis 443, 451
Tro, håb og kaerlighed/Twist and Shout 435
Troell, Jan 452
The Trojan Women 395
Trölosa/Faithless 452
Trotsky, Leon 31
Trotta, Margarethe von 427
Le Trou 437
Trouble in Paradise 322, 352
True Identity 293
True Lies 427
Truffaut, François 182, 208, 313–14, 398, 451, 465
Truman, Michael 62
Tsivian, Yuri 80
Tsyganskie romansy/Gypsy Romances 460
Tumultes 92n

Tunney, Tom 458
Turks Fruit/Turkish Delight 288, 381, 458
The Turn of the Screw 320
Turnabout Theatre, Los Angeles 328
Turner, Florence 26n
Turner, Lana 214
Twentieth Century-Fox 56, 58, 87, 89, 108, 115, 116, 117, 119, 154, 161, 166, 171, 174, 182, 185, 190, 194, 198, 202, 212, 214, 217, 221, 226, 245, 254, 255, 263, 265, 278, 286, 287, 288, 291, 292, 293, 297, 298, 307, 312, 322, 324, 337, 340, 358, 367, 370, 397, 401, 402, 404, 411, 415, 421, 432, 433, 437, 445, 451, 462, 465
20,000 Leagues under the Sea 346, 354
Twins 427
Two Deaths 430
Two Lovers 96
Two Much 172
Two Sisters from Boston 362
2010 369
Two Tickets to London 374
Two Weeks Notice 144
Two-Faced Woman 96, 97, 261
Tyrant of Red Gulch 32

UCLA 453
Ufa 86, 92n, 105, 314, 339, 380, 460
Uli, der Knecht 442
Ullman, Liv 422
Ullman, Tracey 451
Ullmann, Liv 451–2
El último cuplé/The Last Torch Song 136, 371
Ulysses 391
The Unbearable Lightness of Being 181, 228, 389
Uncle Vanya 399
Under Capricorn 100, 179
Under the Cherry Moon 428
Under My Skin 401
Under the Volcano 182, 247
Under Your Hat 218, 293
Underground 108, 155
Unfaithfully Yours 287
The Unforgiven 295
The Unholy Wife 239
Unhook the Stars 233
UNICEF 177, 295, 372, 456
United Artists 62, 64, 136, 146, 214, 302, 338, 349, 449
United Kingdom 452–5
United Services Organisation 236
Universal 7, 62, 64, 67, 79, 103, 116, 117, 156, 208, 226, 232, 237, 277, 297, 308, 309, 329, 375, 392, 408, 415, 431, 460, 461, 463

Universal Soldier 346, 347
An Unmarried Woman 176
Untamed 316
Until September 337
The Untouchables 145, 214, 215
Upstairs Downstairs 240
Uricchio, William, and Pearson, Roberta 46
Used People 356
Ustinov, Peter 16, 320, 385, 455–6
The Usual Suspects 195, 401

Vadim, Roger 364
Valée, Yvonne 253
'Valentine' 55
Valentino, Rudolph 24, 25, 32, 47, 48, 50, 88, 91, 126, 128, 135, 173, 212, 224, 227, 305, 312, 327, 332, 380, 385, 400, 404, 455
Valkyrien, Valda 456
Vallée, Marcel 92n
Vallée, Yvonne 17n, 206, 206
Valletti, Bruno 51n
The Valley of Decision 262
Valli, Alida 14, 100, 127, 311, 315, 456–7, 456
Valli, Virginia 46
Vallone, Raf 457
Vampira 384
Van Damme, Jean-Claude 15, 16–17, 177, 346, 457–8
van de Ven, Monique 381, 458
Van Dyke, W. S. 157
Van Eyck, Peter 458–9
Van Rooten, Luis 109
Van Sant, Gus 321
van Vooren, Monique 177, 459
Vanaire, Jacques 93n
Vandal, Marcel 24
Vanel, Charles 458
Vanilla Sky 13, 133, 221
Varconi, Victor 305, 459
Varda, Agnès 385
Varden, Norma 459–60
Variété (1925) 24, 266, 314
Varieté/Variétés (1935) 92
Variety magazine 54, 55, 56, 58, 67, 89, 116, 126, 141, 236, 303, 458
Variety Show 245
Värmländningarna 383
Vasey, Ruth 3, 7, 40, 85, 120
Vassiliev, Aleksandre 81
Vaughan, Frankie 370, 460
Vavitch, Michael 33, 77, 79, 81, 460
Veidt, Conrad 14, 37, 37, 39, 266, 300, 321, 460–1
Veidt, Ilona (Lily) 460–1
Veille d'armes 86

Vélez, Lupe 35*n*, 371
Vera Cruz 136, 371
'Veracruz' 137
The Verdict 406
Verea, Lisette 416, 461
Verhoeven, Paul 288, 326, 381, 458
Der Verlorene/The Lost One 343
Vernac, Denise 461
Verne, Jules 229
Vernon, Suzy 461
Vertinsky, Alexandre 78–9
La Veuve joyeuse/The Merry Widow 408
Vi tvä/You and Me 288
Vibart, Henry 461
Vicious, Sid 389
Victor, Henry 461
Victor/Victoria 161
The Victors 364, 436
Victory 441
Victory at Entebbe 178
Vidal, Gore 359
Vidocq 71
Vidor, Charles 199
Vidor, King 24, 99, 225, 241, 262, 341, 438
La Vie de Bohème 23
La Vie Parisienne 225
Une Vie/One Life 351
Vieja Hidalguia/Romance of the Rio Grande 373
De vierde man/The Fourth Man 326
Viertel, Peter 320
A View to a Kill 347
Vigil in the Night 222
Vignola, Robert G. 46, 49
Vignon, Jean-Paul 461
Viktor und Viktoria/Viktor and Viktoria 426
villains
    British actors as 141, 142–3
    European actors as 14, 15
Villarias, Carlos 461–2
Villiers, François 167
Vincendeau, Ginette 125, 130
I vinti/The Vanquished 207
The V.I.P.s 129, 435
The Virginian 274
Viridiana 411
Visaroff, Michael 77, 81, 462
Visconti, Luchino 5, 178, 200, 230, 270, 420, 425, 457
Les Visiteurs 71, 210, 411
Viskningar och rop/Cries and Whispers 452
Višnjić, Goran 12, 462, 470
La vita é bella/Life is Beautiful 178, 194
Vitagraph 307, 360, 373
Vital, Geymond 17*n*, 253
Vitale, Milly 51*n*, 462
Vitti, Monica 313, 398, 462

Una viuda romántica/The Romantic Widow 397
Viva Maria! 174
Viviani, Raffaelle 47
Voice of America 187
The Voice of the Millions 373
Le Voleur d'enfants 71
The Volga Boatman 78, 419
Volkoff, Alexandre 80
Voloshin, Alex 77
Von Morhart, Hans 463
Von Twardowski, Hans Heinrich 108, 110, 463
Voya, Georges 463
Vujčić, Aleksandra 470

Wachowski brothers 411
Wagon Master 376
Wait Until Dark 295
Wajda, Andrzej 427
Wake Up and Dream 364
Waking Life 230
Walbrook, Anton 463
A Walk in the Clouds 100, 268
Walk on the Wild Side 288
Walkabout 155
Walken, Christopher 306
Walker, Robert 459
Wallace, Edgar 62
Wallach, Eli 356
Wallburg, Otto 105
Wallis, Hal B. 198, 254, 336, 363
Walsh, Raoul 6, 309, 392
Walters, Julie 463–4
Walton, Tony 161
The Wandering Jew 460
Wangenheim, Gustav von 273
Wanger, Walter 87–8, 91, 115, 186, 202
Wanted for Murder 300
War Ministry (US) 187
War and Peace 241, 262, 419
The War Zone 146
Ward, Fannie 24
Ward, Sophie 428, 464
Warhol, Andy 321
Warlock 421
Warner, David 464
Warner, Deborah 431
Warner, H. B. 464–5
Warner, Jack 65
Warner Bros. 58, 64–5, 85, 88, 108, 110, 159, 163, 177, 182, 187, 190, 194, 202, 207, 212, 238, 243, 255, 266, 267, 280, 288, 293, 303, 334, 337, 343, 345, 366, 371, 395, 404, 405, 406, 436, 448, 451, 461, 463
Watch on the Rhine 207, 346
Waterloo Bridge 336

Watson, Emily 433, 465
Waugh, Evelyn 428
The Way Ahead 384, 455
The Way of All Flesh 314
Way Down West 265
The Way to Love 55
The Way to the Stars 448
Wayne, John 98, 269, 353, 388
Wayne, Naunton 404
We Live Again 32, 98–9, 440
Webb, Clifton 243
A Wedding 263, 402
The Wedding Night 99, 440
Wedekind, Frank 38
Weiland, Paul 411
Weill, Kurt 170
Weir, Peter 233, 369
Der weisse Teufel/The White Devil 376
Weissall, Jiří 223
Weissmuller, Johnny 416
Weisz, Rachel 397, 465
Welcome to Sarajevo 462
Welland, Colin 452
Welles, Orson 166, 181, 214, 218, 236, 256, 290, 326, 353, 388, 425, 470
Wellman, William 207, 423
Wells, Simon 377
Wenders, Wim 40, 321, 323, 421, 427
We're Going to Be Rich 245
Werner, Oskar 170, 188, 465
West, Mae 274
Wester, Emil 31
Westward Passage 389
Westward the Women 226
Whale, James 195, 210–11, 222, 317, 329, 334, 360, 405, 408, 446
Whalley-Kilmer, Joanne 465
Wharton, Edith 229
What a Girl Wants 144
What's New, Pussycat 200, 425, 429
Whelan, Tim 66
When Time Ran Out 218
Where's Jack? 170
While the City Sleeps 421
White, Carol 466
White, Pearl 24, 438
White, Susan 126, 127
White Cargo 327
White Cradle Inn 182, 290, 442
White Face 62
White Gold 272
White Nights 369
The White Rose 385
White Shadows in the South Seas 157
The White Sister 45, 212
The White Tower 100
Whitty, May 466
Who Framed Roger Rabbit 302

Who is Killing the Great Chefs of Europe? 182

Who's Afraid of Virginia Woolf? 195

Who's Been Sleeping in My Bed? 364

The Wicked Lady 221, 340

Widmark, Richard 227, 394

Wieck, Dorothea 403, 466

Wienfilme 170

Wieth, Mogens 466

Wilby, James 276

Wilcox, Herbert 193

Wilcoxon, Henry 466

Wild at Heart 315

Wild Bill 307

Wild is the Wind 349

Wild Orchids 96, 97, 165

Wild Rovers 414

Wild Wild West 187

Wilde 333

Wilde, Cornel 388

Wilde, Oscar 96, 421

Wilder, Billy 57, 98, 193, 207, 217, 235, 267, 312, 318, 323, 328, 366, 368, 383, 418, 429

Wilding, Michael 466

Willard 328

Williams, Charles 363

Williams, Esther 221, 292, 363

Williams, Hugh 466–7

Williams, John 467

Williams, Kathlyn 26*n*

Williams, Olivia 467

Williams, Robin 218

Williams, Tennessee 312, 337, 348, 349

Williamson, Nicol 467

Willis, Bruce 244, 310, 426

Wilson 224

Wilson, Georges 467

Wilson, Harold 170

Wilson, Lambert 467

Wilson, Sandy 159

Wilson, Woodrow 88

The Wind 285, 391

The Wind and the Lion 215

Wings 423

Wings of Eagles 388

Wings of the Morning 87, 162

Winning His Wife 357

Winslet, Kate 6, 467–8, *468*

Winterbottom, Michael 100, 465

Winters, Shelley 262, *262*

Winterset 51*n*

Wintertime 292–3

Winwood, Estelle 468

Wiper, Scott 470

Wir schalten um auf Hollywood/We Now Switch over to Hollywood 375

Wisdom, Norman 468

Wise Guys 48, 203

Wise, Robert 218, 433

Wish You Were Here 340

Wit 447

Withnail and I 277

Witness for the Prosecution 328, 330

Wolders, Robert 295

'Wolf Man' series 392

Wollstein, Hans, *Strangers in Hollywood: the History of Scandinavian Actors in America* 3

A Woman of Affairs 96, 97

A Woman Called Golda 180

A Woman of Paris 204

Woman Times Seven 190

Woman on Top 133, 221

The Woman on Trial 319

The Woman in White 280

Women in Love 313, 409

Wonder Bar 322

The Wonder Man 202

Wong, Anna May 97

Woo, John 177, 458

Wood, Robin 126, 127, 128, 316

Wood, Sam 99

Woolf, John and James 288

Working Title 277

The World of Fashion 269

The World in his Arms 249

The World is Not Enough 72, 350

The World Moves On 202

WR - misterije organizma/WR: Mysteries of the Organism 240

Wrangel, Maria 79

Wrangel, Piotr Nikolaievitch 79

The Wrecking Crew 279

The Wrong Man 404

Wuthering Heights 181, 245, 249, 349, 384, 386, *386*, 389–90, 464, 467

Wyler, William 185, 241, 261, 295, 384, 389, 390, 392, 432, 439

X-Men 141, 142, 145, 360, 441

A Yank at Oxford 281, 336

Yates, Herbert J. 223

Yates, Peter 379

Year of the Comet 125

Yeats, W. B. 309

The Yellow Rolls-Royce 287

The Yellow Ticket 389

Yesterday, Today and Tomorrow 356

Yiddish theatre 46

Yordan, Phillip 431

York, Michael 468–9

York, Susannah 469

You Can't Take it with You 167

You Only Live Twice 214, 398

Young, Clara Kimball 23, 199

Young, Loretta 86, 91

Young, Robert 64

Young, Roland 469

The Young Lions 370, 442

Young Man with Ideas 226

The Young Ones 447

The Young Poisoner's Handbook 387

Young Wives Tale 295

Younger and Younger 230

Yugodvias 315

Yugoslavia (former) 469–70

Yurenev Varginsky club 81

Yves, Christiane 470

Z Cars 182

Zandy's Bride 452

Zanuck, Darryl F. 7, 89–90, 99, 128, 162, 198, 212, 218, 227, 231, 245, 254, 269, 278, 279, 287, 291, 292, 304, 433

Zanuck, Richard 431

Zaza 49, 368

Zazà 49, 368

Zeffirelli, Franco 184, 218, 468

Zemlya v plenu/The Yellow Ticket 81

Zeta-Jones, Catherine 100, 172, 470

Zetterling, Mai 422, 423, 470–1

Zilzer, Wolfgang *see* Andor, Paul

Zimmer, Hans 42

Zinnemann, Fred 408, 409, 469

Zivojnović, Bata 470

Zola, Emile 440

Zorba the Greek 279

Zukor, Adolph 6, 39, 181, 234, 346

Zulu 170, 196

Zulu Dawn 170

Zwei Krawatten/Two Neckties 236